D1757900

LABOR ECONOMICS

LABOR ECONOMICS

PIERRE CAHUC
AND
ANDRÉ ZYLBERBERG

THE MIT PRESS

CAMBRIDGE, MASSACHUSETTS · LONDON, ENGLAND

This work has been published with support from the Ministère française chargé de la culture—Centre national du livre.

Translator: William McCuaig

Pierre Cahuc et André Zylberberg
Le marché du travail
© De Boeck & Larcier, 2001, 1ᵉ édition
Éditions De Boeck Université
Rue des Minimes 39, B 1000 Bruxelles

This book was set in Melior and MetaPlus by Asco Typesetters and was printed and bound in the United States of America.

Library of Congress Cataloging-in-Publication Data

Cahuc, Pierre.
    [Marché du travail. English]
    Labor economics / Pierre Cahuc and André Zylberberg.
       p. cm.
    Includes bibliographical references and index.
    ISBN 0-262-03316-X (hc. : alk. paper)
    ISBN-13 978-0-262-03316-9 (hc. : alk. paper)
    1. Labor economics.   I. Zylberberg, André.   II. Title.

HD4901.C24 2004
331—dc22   2003067181

10 9 8 7 6 5 4

To Manon and Marie-Christine,
Arthur, Jeanne, and Paul.

Contents

INTRODUCTION

Merchandise in the form of goods and services is exchanged in markets, and each of these markets possesses its own organization and functions by its own rules. Labor economics is the study of the markets in which labor services are exchanged for wages. The existence of labor economics is justified by the fact that, in the industrialized countries, income earned by working represents the largest component—around two-thirds—of total income. The remaining third is made up of income from invested capital. In addition, a large part of the population is made up of wage-earners, or those aspiring to become wage-earners if they have not yet left the educational system or are looking for work. Figure 1 traces the evolution of wage-earners as a proportion of the working-age population (those aged from 16 to 64) in six OECD countries between 1970 and 2001. The proportion of wage-earners is clearly significant. It is also heterogeneous: in these six OECD countries, the proportion of wage-earners in 2001 varied from 39% in Italy to 66% in the United States. This proportion may change over the course of time. It grew by 10% in the United States between 1970 and 2001, and shrank slightly in the United Kingdom over the same period. We shall see that labor economics helps to explain variations of this kind.

More generally, labor economics covers a very large field, and sheds light on economic and social problems of the greatest importance. It embraces topics as varied as wages, employment, unemployment, the cost of labor, the number of hours worked per week, how hard the work is, employees being fired, employees resigning, workplace injuries, decisions by individuals to participate in the labor market, unions, strikes, the impact of mandatory contributions, and many other subjects on which public debate frequently turns in modern society.

Labor markets evolve in the course of time. The abstract representations we use to understand how they function also change, although the competition model as an operational approximation of the actual functioning of markets has been at the center of economic analysis ever since it began. Indeed, economic knowledge has often made progress by striving to transcend the limitations of this model. The brief historical summary which follows will show that labor economics obeys this general rule.

Some History

Adam Smith, in *An Inquiry Into the Nature and Causes of the Wealth of Nations*, published in 1776, sets forth a theory of trade based on a perfectly competitive labor market. He assumes that the level of wages makes it possible to equalize supply and demand for every kind of job. This leads him to explain that wage differentials among jobs "compensate" for differences in the ability of workers and the difficulty of the tasks. Employers are indeed prepared to give higher pay to more efficient workers, and when a job is particularly difficult, it is necessary to offer a wage high enough to get workers to perform it. Thus, according to Smith, wage differentials are explained by

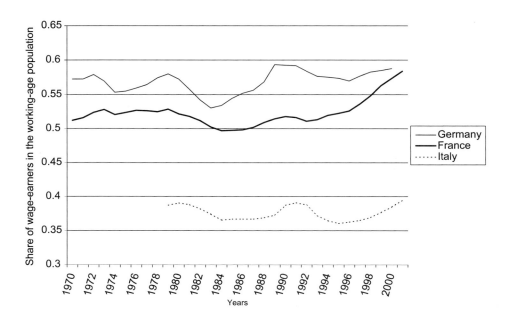

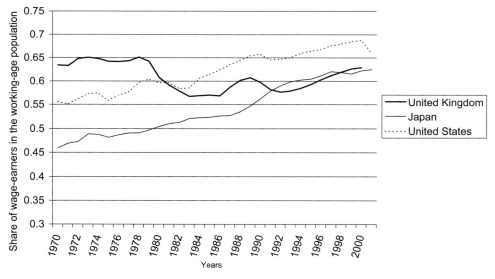

FIGURE 1

Wage-earners' share of the working-age population in six OECD countries over the period 1970–2001.

Source: OECD data.

the relative difficulty of jobs, the cost of acquiring the skills necessary to do them, whether they are permanent or short-lived, and the amount of responsibility they demand. This approach, developed in book 1, chapter 10 of the *Inquiry*, attributes a primordial role to the competition mechanism. Yet Smith also recognizes, in book 1, chapter 8, that "The workmen desire to get as much, the masters to give as little as possible. The former are disposed to combine in order to raise, the latter in order to lower the wages of labour." The existence of coalitions of "workmen" and "masters" affects the way perfect competition unfolds. Even its principal creator judged the theory of "compensating differentials" to be incomplete. It leaves out many characteristics of the labor market, such as the existence of united groups of employers and employees, the presence of information asymmetries, and the mobility costs of manpower. Nevertheless, this theory has left its mark on all subsequent thinking about wage setting and the functioning of the labor market, and is still an essential point of reference today. It has also provoked opposition, leading to attempts to elaborate alternative theories.

The marginalist revolution, which laid the groundwork for modern economic theory at the end of the nineteenth century, made the competition model systematic. In the beginning, at least, this new systematicity tended to conceal features that are specific to the labor market. Thus, the *Principles of Economics*, published by Alfred Marshall in 1890, retains the "incoherence" found in Smith (Reynolds, 1988, p. 134). In theory, wages equalize supply and demand for labor, but Marshall was driven by realism to recognize the role played by coalitions of employers and workers. He pointed out in particular that the least skilled workers, those with low incomes and few savings, have to sell their labor quickly, and thus are at a disadvantage in wage bargaining.

The crisis of 1929 threw fresh doubt on the representation of the market in terms of instantaneous equilibria of supply and demand. In the 1930s, many economists were alert to developments in the analysis of imperfect competition; notable contributions were Edward Chamberlin's *The Theory of Monopolistic Competition* and Joan Robinson's *The Economics of Imperfect Competition* (both 1933). Hicks, in his *Theory of Wages*, published in 1932, sought to adapt economic theory to the analysis of an imperfectly competitive labor market, and worked out a model of wage bargaining (see chapter 7 below) in which the power of workers increases the longer they are able to stay out on strike.

Labor economics emerged as an autonomous discipline in the United States in the 1940s, at the hands of John Dunlop, Clark Kerr, Richard Lester, and Lloyd Reynolds. Their approach, which was primarily descriptive, was to take the institutional specifics of the labor market into account in order to better understand wage formation, the level of employment, and in general all the elements that go to make up the wage relationship (see Kaufman, 1988). The textbook by Lloyd Reynolds entitled *Labor Economics and Labor Relations*, published in 1949, was the reference text in labor economics for almost twenty years. Right down to its last edition, in 1970, it contained no analysis of labor supply and demand, and wage setting was described in terms of the "practice" of firms or industries. The first textbooks of labor economics to be built on a theoretical foundation, neoclassical in inspiration, saw the light in the 1970s. The authors were Belton Fleisher (1970), Richard Freeman (1972), and Albert Rees (1973). In their books the descriptive aspect was considerably reduced, and the chapters were organized around topics that claimed to apply general principles of economic theory. Since then labor economics has undergone the same evolution as many other fields. Economic theory has made strides in the analysis of strategic relations, information asymmetries, and dynamic behavior; data of the most various kinds are now accessible, and statistical technique has been improved, along with the calculational capacities of modern computers; all these factors led to a profound restructuring of labor economics in the last three decades of the twentieth century. This discipline for the most part no longer concentrates on descriptive or institutional approaches. Today an article on labor economics is no different from an article on the economics of the firm, or macroeconomics or international economics: it begins by laying out the facts that require explanation, then proceeds to construct a theoretical model that in principle will allow these facts to be reproduced, and generally concludes with a comparison of the model to the facts using empirical tests (see Boyer and Smith, 2001, for a survey of the history of labor economics in the United States in the twentieth century).

Orthodox and Alternative Approaches
As in other areas of economics, developments in the analysis of different forms of imperfect competition have altered, indeed overturned, the traditional framework of labor economics. This book bears witness to the advances made by labor economics through the use of so-called "orthodox" methods of analysis, inasmuch as they represent the dominant current of thought, the one adhered to by most economists. Fundamentally, this approach postulates that individuals have rational behaviors and exercise their choices as a function of their preferences in an environment in which resources are scarce; it has also been termed "neoclassical," in recognition of a certain continuity between it and the founding fathers of the Lausanne school, Léon Walras and Vilfredo Pareto. But it has aroused, and continues to arouse, a strong reaction that condemns any sort of "economic" approach to the wage relationship. Neoclassical economists are indeed often suspected of supporting economic liberalism, of preaching the efficiency of the free market at every turn, and of trying to reduce to a minimum the role of the public authorities and unions. The critique put forward by the "alternative" approach focuses on what it takes to be the excessive reductionism of neoclassical theory: blind belief in the rationality of agents and neglect of the social dimensions of the wage relationship are the charges most often brought (the critique of neoclassical labor economics is set out in Kaufman, 1999, and Rutherford, 2001).

The alternative approaches rely on two important currents of economic thought, Marxism and institutionalism. In the contemporary period, "radical political economy" takes its inspiration from the works of Karl Marx and emphasizes the role of relations of domination, the need to change existing institutions, and the importance of the weight of history (for a critical presentation of this current, see Rebitzer, 1993). The institutionalist approach, developed between 1900 and 1930 by Thorstein Veblen, John Commons, and Wesley Mitchell, highlights collective action, working conditions, legal constraints, and in general all the social phenomena—such as customs and beliefs—that may influence the wage relationship. Hence it favors an interdisciplinary perspective that brings together concepts from sociology, economics, social psychology, and ergonomics. The history and methodological principles of institutionalism are well documented by Hodgson (1998), Williamson (2000), and Rutherford (2001).

The alternative approaches are of undeniable interest and often throw into relief problems or facts neglected by mainstream economics. Their method of investigation, which frequently takes the form of surveys, monographic studies, and historical research, constitutes an important source of information that enables us to know the practices of actors better. Despite that, the opposition between the ''alternative'' (or ''heterodox'') approaches and the ''neoclassical'' (or ''orthodox'') approach needs to be qualified. It is more a question of assigning roles than an opposition of method. A historical study, for example, is not opposed to analytical investigation; the two methods are complementary when it comes to assessing possible actions, especially in questions of economic policy. There are cases in which challenge has been fruitful, too. For example, radical and institutionalist economics have strongly criticized the theory of compensating differentials advanced by Smith, maintaining that the labor market is divided into two sectors. The primary sector, composed mainly of large firms, offers steady jobs with high wages, while the secondary one offers unsteady and poorly paid ones (Doeringer and Piore, 1971). The consequence, according to this thesis, is that the ''law of one price'' no longer applies. Wage differentials do not reflect differences in individual ability and the hardness of tasks alone, since the same wage-earner might receive different pay for performing an identical task. In this book we shall see (particularly in chapters 5, 6, and 7) that by now the orthodox approach has the means to shed light on this question and to supply empirically testable answers to it. As Rebitzer (1993, p. 1397) states, there is more mutual influence than there is deep division between the different approaches. As we shall see, moreover, the economic policy recommendations at which neoclassical labor economists arrive are not systematically more biased in favor of the free market than those put forward by the alternative approaches.

On Formalization

Today, labor economics, like many other areas of economic analysis, gives pride of place to teaching methods based on mathematical models. This textbook conforms to that rule. At least three reasons may be cited in justification. The first, and by no means the least compelling, lies precisely in the quasi-monopoly held by this approach. The student owes it to himself or herself to become familiar with it, if he or she wants to be able to read specialized journals in the field. But the domination of formalized economics is not the outcome of a random draw from among several possible equilibria. For one thing, economic science lends itself to formalization, since it deals with quantified magnitudes. The questions put to economists generally demand answers with empirical content: Is wage inequality rising? Is competition from low-wage countries destroying jobs? Are mandatory contributions favorable to employment? In order to be precise and operational, the answers to questions like these have to be given in numbers, justified by a coherent chain of reasoning, with the underlying hypotheses made clear. These requirements constitute another justification of formalization. A mathematical model allows us to clearly establish a linkage between hypotheses and results. It proves particularly effective, indeed indispensable, when the mechanisms studied are complex and involve the relations among a number of variables. Formal models of economic activity are entirely unavoidable if we want to understand strategic interactions, decisions taken in uncertainty, situations of asymmetric information, and the dynamic choices of agents, for example.

We have nevertheless taken great care to make our models as simple as possible. A mathematical appendix at the end of the book supplies the toolkit needed to understand all the models utilized in the text. Finally, we have tried to articulate our theoretical and empirical lines of reasoning. Readers should be aware that, beginning in the 1970s, labor economics has become the preferred arena in which to apply the most advanced econometric methods (microeconometrics in particular). The articles by Angrist and Krueger (1999), Moffit (1999), and Hamermesh (2000) trace the development of empirical research in this field.

The procedure adopted in this book is to move back and forth between factual data and theoretical reasoning. For each problem studied we present the facts, a theoretical model, ways of assessing this model empirically, and the results obtained with these methods. For example, the study of the labor supply includes descriptive material on the evolution of participation rates and the number of hours worked, as well as a model that explains individual choices on the basis of traditional hypotheses about individual rationality and scarcity of resources. Methods of assessing this model empirically, and the main empirical results, are laid out. In this way we are able, for example, to understand and assess quantitatively the impact of changes in wages, the fiscal system, or social assistance on the labor supply.

This book does devote more space to setting out theory than to empirical methods and results—a feature which may cause surprise, in view of what we said a moment ago regarding the high empirical content of labor economics. Two considerations justify our choice.

First, as mentioned above, labor economics and all of economics have undergone profound theoretical restructuring in recent decades, benefiting especially from advances made in the study of dynamics, strategic behavior, and decisions in uncertain environments. The analysis of labor supply, labor demand, wage formation, and the determinants of employment and unemployment have been deeply influenced by these advances. Our aim is to set out all these developments within a unified didactic framework, and to show that they have measurably improved our understanding of the functioning of the labor market.

Second, most published work in labor economics emphasizes empirical content, because most of it bears on a particular topic, such as (for example) the influence of the earned income tax credit on the supply of labor by single women with at least one child in the 1990s in the United States. But all the studies that attempt to assess the effect of fiscal policies on labor supply decisions make use of more or less the *same* theoretical models and the *same* methods of assessment, whatever the particular topic they are investigating. That is why this book privileges the exposition of theory and empirical method. As for results in the strict sense, we generally limit ourselves to presenting the most significant ones, for any attempt to list them all would be burdensome and would quickly become obsolete in a perpetually changing environment. Readers who do wish to learn more about empirical results will find guidance in the bibliographies at the end of each chapter.

Plan of the Book
This book is composed of four parts. The first part covers the determinants of labor supply and demand.

Chapter 1 presents consumption–leisure trade-off models and the theory of labor supply. Scrutiny of the trade-off between consumption and leisure is especially important for understanding fluctuations in the participation rates of different categories of the population and the choices people make about how much to work and when to retire. It includes a guide to the econometrics of labor supply. Chapter 2 presents decisions about education and their impact on individual performances in the labor market. This chapter specifies the determinants of individual choice about education, and also the role played by education, which serves not just to transmit knowledge that improves productivity and socialization, but also to select individuals within different productive sectors. The job search model is the topic of chapter 3. This model explores the costs arising from searching for a job when workers do not have cost-free access to perfect information about all the jobs available in the economy, and is very useful for explaining the duration of unemployment as a function of the characteristics of the labor market and the characteristics of the individuals who are looking for work. This model also allows us to illustrate problems arising from unemployment insurance. Chapter 4 is dedicated to labor demand, first from a static perspective, then a dynamic one. In it we look at important questions such as the impact of the costs of the factors of production on labor demand, or the effect on unemployment of a reduction in hours worked or an increase in firing costs.

The second part of the book presents the determinants of wages, including the influence of the wage policies of firms and collective bargaining.

Chapter 5 sets out the competitive theory of wages and some of its limitations. It is shown that competitive forces imply that wage differentials depend on productivity differences only. Thus, wage differentials are explained in theory by differences in ability, but also by differences in how hard tasks are. The obstacles to perfect competition, arising in particular from hindrances to free entry and imperfect information, imply that wages do not always reflect productivity differences alone. From this point of view, chapter 5 highlights how phenomena of discrimination can arise when the labor market is not perfectly competitive. Chapter 6 goes more deeply into wage policies in situations of uncertainty and imperfect information, using agency and implicit contract models. These models throw light on the logic of certain aspects of human resources management, such as advancement by seniority or systems of promotion. Chapter 7 introduces collective bargaining, focusing on the behavior of unions and the manner in which we formalize the bargaining process. It analyzes the impact of the bargaining power of workers on employment, profits, and productivity at the firm level. It also looks at the opposition between employees with a steady job, the insiders, and workers who do not have this security, the outsiders, and shows that this opposition may be detrimental to employment and favor the segmentation of the labor market.

The third part is more specifically dedicated to the explanations for unemployment and inequality. This problem is dealt with in a macroeconomic setting that takes account of interdependencies among labor markets, product markets, and the markets for other inputs.

Chapter 8 reviews the main facts regarding unemployment in the OECD countries and what traditional macroeconomic analysis has to tell us about this topic. It gives a central place to the Phillips curve (and more generally to wage equations), and clarifies the notion of a "natural rate" of unemployment. It also treats problems such as the sources of persistent unemployment and the efficiency of macroeconomic policies to stimulate aggregate demand. The following chapters show how recent developments in labor economics fill certain gaps in traditional macroeconomic analysis. Chapter 9 uses matching models to study the determinants of employment and wages in a labor market in which jobs are ceaselessly destroyed and created, and in which the reallocation of manpower is costly and takes time. In this chapter we make a diagnosis of the importance of frictional unemployment arising from the process of job destruction and creation.

Chapter 10 studies the effects of technological progress and the globalization of trade on income inequality and unemployment. It recognizes the heterogeneity of manpower by distinguishing between workers according to their skill level. This distinction is important, inasmuch as technological progress and globalization do not affect all wage-earners in the same way.

The fourth part of the book is dedicated to labor market policies and the impact of institutions on labor market performance.

Chapter 11 is dedicated to active and passive labor market policy. It sets out the macroeconomic effects of unemployment insurance and supplies a theoretical grid with which to analyze the efficiency of active policies. The empirical assessment of labor market policies, in regard to both methodology and results, is given detailed treatment. Finally, chapter 12 focuses on labor market institutions. Making use mostly of the matching model from chapter 9, it examines the principal implications of the minimum wage, employment protection, taxation, and the level at which wage bargaining takes place.

A mathematical appendix, as noted above, is placed at the end of the book.

How This Book May Be Used

A large number of topics are dealt with in this book, and not all of them present the same degree of formal and conceptual difficulty. They may be taught at different stages of the university curriculum, from undergraduate to graduate level and beyond. Moreover, the book's length dictates that instructors using it to prepare courses in labor economics will assign selected readings. Here we offer examples of what we think are practical sequences.

• A course in basic labor economics, foregrounding competitive structures and behaviors in an essentially static environment.

   1. The model of labor supply and its various extensions (chapter 1, sections 1.1 and 1.2), with an econometrics component (sections 2.1.1 and 2.1.2) followed by the empirical results (section 2.2).

   2. Problems connected to education (chapter 2), including the factual elements (section 1), the theory of human capital (section 2.1), and the empirical assessment of the returns to education (sections 4.2 to 4.4).

   3. The static theory of labor demand (chapter 4, section 1), as well as empirical estimates of the elasticities of labor demand (section 2).

   4. Wage formation, first within a framework of perfect competition (chapter 5, section 1), then with the introduction of obstacles to competition, leading to a discussion of monopsony and discrimination (section 2.1), statistical discrimination (section 3), and empirical work on compensating differentials (section 4.1), on discrimination (section 4.2), and on interindustry wage differentials (section 4.3).

   5. The evolution of wage inequalities (chapter 10, section 2.1), taking into consideration the role of technological progress (section 2.2), international competition (section 2.3), migratory flows (section 2.4) and institutional change (section 2.5).

   6. The assessment of policies on employment (chapter 11), including elements of methodology (section 3.1) and the main empirical results (section 3.2).

• An in-depth course oriented toward microeconomics and dealing with dynamic and informational problems.

   1. The intertemporal labor supply (chapter 1, section 1.3), with an econometrics component (sections 2.1.1 and 2.1.2) followed by the empirical results (section 2.2).

2. Problems connected to education (chapter 2), bringing in the determinants of the duration of studies (sections 2.2 and 2.3), the signaling model (section 3), and the shift from the model of human capital to Mincer's empirical equation, with the main results (sections 4.1 to 4.4).

3. The job search model and how it applies to wage formation and the efficiency of unemployment insurance systems (chapter 3).

4. The dynamic theory of labor demand (chapter 4, section 3).

5. The labor contract in the presence of uncertainty and problems of incentive (chapter 6).

6. Collective bargaining (chapter 7).

• A course in labor economics more focused on problems of unemployment and inequality.

1. Unemployment and inflation as seen in traditional macroeconomics, grounded in the concept of the natural rate of unemployment (chapter 8).

2. Reallocation of jobs and the matching model (chapter 9).

3. Technological progress and globalization (chapter 10).

4. Labor market policies (chapter 11).

5. Institutions and labor market performance (chapter 12).

REFERENCES

Angrist, J., and Krueger, A. (1999), "Empirical strategies in labor economics," in Ashenfelter, O., and Card, D. (eds), *Handbook of Labor Economics*, vol. 3, chap. 23, pp. 1277–1366, Amsterdam: Elsevier Science/North-Holland.

Boyer, G., and Smith, R. (2001), "The development of the neoclassical tradition in labor economics," *Industrial and Labor Relations Review*, 54(2), pp. 199–223.

Doeringer, P., and Piore, M. (1971), *Internal Labor Market and Manpower Analysis*, Lexington, Mass.: Heath.

Fleisher, B. (1970), *Labor Economics: Theory and Evidence*, Englewood Cliffs, N.J.: Prentice-Hall.

Freeman, R. (1972), *Labor Economics*, Englewood Cliffs, N.J.: Prentice-Hall.

Hamermesh, D. (2000), "The craft of labormetrics," *Industrial and Labor Relations Review*, 53, pp. 363–380.

Hodgson, G. (1998), "The approach of institutional economics," *Journal of Economic Literature*, 36, pp. 166–192.

Kaufman, B. (ed.) (1988), *How Labor Markets Work: Reflections on Theory and Practice by John Dunlop, Clark Kerr, Richard Lester and Lloyd Reynolds*, Lexington, Mass.: Heath.

Kaufman, B. (1999), "Expanding the behavioral foundations of labor economics," *Industrial and Labor Relations Review*, 52, pp. 361–392.

Moffit, R. (1999), "New developments in econometric methods for labor market analysis," in Ashenfelter, O., and Card, D. (eds.), *Handbook of Labor Economics*, vol. 3, ch. 24, pp. 1367–1397, Amsterdam: Elsevier Science/North-Holland.

Rebitzer, J. (1993), "Radical political economy and the economics of labor market," *Journal of Economic Literature*, 31, pp. 1393–1434.

Rees, A. (1973), *The Economics of Work and Pay*, New York: Harper & Row.

Reynolds, L. (1988), "Labor economics, then and now," in Kaufman, E. (ed.), *How Labor Markets Work*, pp. 117–145, Lexington, Mass.: Heath.

Rutherford, M. (2001), "Institutional economics: Then and now," *Journal of Economic Perspectives*, 15 (Summer), pp. 173–194.

Williamson, O. (2000), "The new institutional economics: Taking stock, looking ahead," *Journal of Economic Literature*, 38, pp. 595–613.

ACKNOWLEDGMENTS

This work took shape in courses given at the Université Paris 1 Panthéon-Sorbonne, at the Université des Antilles et de la Guyane, at the Ecole Nationale de la Statistique et de l'Administration Economique (ENSAE) at the Ecole Polytechnique (Paris), and at the High School of Economics (Moscow). We thank our students, whose curiosity and questions have been a constant source of inspiration to us.

We also thank all the individuals, teachers, and researchers who have helped us with their observations, encouragement, assistance, and advice during the writing of the book, in particular Yann Algan, Dominique Anxo, Antoine d'Autume, Georges Bresson, Jean-Louis Cayatte, Bart Cockx, Jacques Cremer, Huw Dixon, Manon Domingues Dos Santos, Christine Erhel, Patrick Fève, Gary Fields, Christian Gianella, Pierre Granier, Pierre Hallier, Michel Juillard, Hubert Kempf, Francis Kramarz, François Langot, Olivier L'Haridon, Thierry Laurent, Etienne Lehmann, Thierry Magnac, Marie-Laure Michaud, Pierre Morin, Yann Nicolas, Xavier Pautrel, Corinne Perraudin, Alain Pirotte, Fabien Postel-Vinay, Ana Prieto, Corinne Prost, Muriel Pucci, Jean-Marc Robin, Muriel Roger, Bernard Salanié, Jean-Marc Tallon, Emmanuelle Taugourdeau, Bruno van der Linden, and Yves Zenou.

We are also indebted to John Covell, economics editor at MIT Press; William McCuaig, translator; Joyce Cooper; and the production team at P. M. Gordon Associates for their outstanding cooperation, effectiveness, and professionalism.

SUPPLY AND DEMAND BEHAVIORS

LABOR SUPPLY

CONTENTS

In this chapter we will see:

- How people make choices between consumption, leisure, and household production

- What the reservation wage is

- How the shape of the labor supply curve results from the combination of substitution effects and income

- When and why people decide to retire

- The principles guiding the econometrics of labor supply and the main empirical results

- Examples of natural experiments

INTRODUCTION

To hold a paid job, you must first have decided to do so. This is the starting point of the so-called "neoclassical" theory of the labor supply. It posits that each individual disposes of a limited amount of time, which he or she chooses to allocate between paid work and leisure. Evidently the wage an individual can demand constitutes an important factor in the choice of the quantity of labor supplied. But it is not the only factor taken into account. Personal wealth, income derived from sources outside the labor market, and even the familial environment also play a decisive role.

In reality the allocation of one's time depends on trade-offs more complex than a simple choice between work and leisure. In the first place, the counterpart of paid work is not simply leisure in the usual sense, for much of it consists of time devoted to "household production" (the preparation of meals, housekeeping, minor repairs and upkeep, the raising of children, etc.), the result of which substitutes for products available in the consumer goods market. This implies that the supply of wage labor takes into account the costs and benefits of this household production, and that most often it is the result of planning, and even actual negotiation, within the family. The family situation, the number of children, the income a person enjoys apart from any wage labor (personal wealth, illegal work, spousal income, etc.), all weigh heavily in this choice. Decisions concerning labor supply also depend on trade-offs over the course of time that make the analysis of the decisions of agents richer and more complex.

Empirical studies on labor supply have also multiplied in the course of the last twenty years. The development of these studies—exhaustively reviewed in Blundell and MaCurdy (1999)—has profited from advances made in the application of econometric methods to individual data, and from a desire to evaluate public policies that attempt to influence labor supply directly. A number of countries have set up programs explicitly aimed at increasing labor supply among the most disadvantaged, rather than park them on the welfare rolls. These "welfare to work" programs, sometimes abbreviated as *workfare*, so as to contrast them with more traditional programs called simply *welfare*, have given a powerful incentive to empirical research on labor supply in the United States and Great Britain, as well as in certain continental countries like Sweden and France.

The first section of this chapter lays out the principal elements of the neoclassical theory of labor supply. This approach is based on the traditional microeconomic model of consumer choice. The basic model explains the choice between the consumption of products available in the marketplace and leisure. This simple model is then extended in such a way as to take into account household production and intrafamilial decisions. The basic model is also enhanced into a "life-cycle" model integrating the decisions taken by agents over the course of time. This enhancement is particularly important from the point of view of economic policy, for most employment policy measures aim to modify the behavior of agents permanently. It also furnishes an adequate framework for analyzing decisions taken from the onset of a career to retirement. The second section of this chapter is devoted to empirical matters. It begins by laying out the main lines of the econometrics of labor supply, elucidates the principles that guide empirical studies in this area, and concludes with a review of the principal quantitative results arrived at by studies of labor supply.

1 THE NEOCLASSICAL THEORY OF LABOR SUPPLY

The theory of labor supply is based on the model of a consumer making a choice between consuming more goods and consuming more leisure. With it, we can elucidate the properties of labor supply and begin to understand the conditions of participation in the labor market. The model has been variously enhanced to make the theory of labor supply more precise, and sometimes to modify it profoundly, principally by taking into account household production, the collective dimension of decisions about labor supply (most often within the family), and the life-cycle aspect of these decisions.

1.1 THE CHOICE BETWEEN CONSUMPTION AND LEISURE

The basic model of a trade-off between consumption and leisure gives us the principal properties of the supply of labor. In particular, it shows that labor supply is not necessarily a monotonic function of wages. It suggests that labor supply grows when the wage is low, and subsequently diminishes with the wage when the latter is sufficiently high. Further, the study of the trade-off between consumption and leisure makes it possible to grasp the factors that determine participation in the labor market.

1.1.1 The Basic Model

We indicated, in the general introduction to this chapter, that the traditional approach to labor supply arises, fundamentally, out of the idea that each of us has the possibility to make trade-offs between the consumption of goods and the consumption of leisure, this last being defined as time not spent at work. The analysis of this choice makes it possible to pinpoint the factors that determine labor supply, first at the individual, then at the aggregate, levels.

Preferences

The trade-off between consumption and leisure is shown with the help of a utility function proper to each individual, that is, $U(C,L)$, where C and L designate respectively the consumption of goods and the consumption of leisure. Given that an individual disposes of a total amount of time, L_0, the length of time worked, expressed, for example, in hours, is then given by $h = L_0 - L$. It is generally supposed that an individual desires to consume the greatest possible quantity of goods and leisure; his or her utility function therefore increases with each argument. Moreover, the same individual is capable of attaining the same level of satisfaction with much leisure and few goods, or little leisure and many goods. The set of pairs (C,L) by which the consumer obtains the same level of utility $\bar{U}$, i.e., such that $U(C,L) = \bar{U}$, is called an *indifference curve*. A curve of this type is shown in figure 1.1. Its properties follow directly from those of the utility function (for more detail, consult Varian, 1992, and Mas-Colell et al., 1995). In particular, the properties listed below will be useful for what follows:

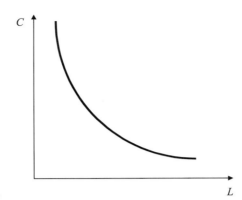

FIGURE 1.1
An indifference curve.

(i) Each indifference curve corresponds to a higher level of utility, the farther out the curve is from the origin. Hence the consumer will prefer indifference curves situated farther out from the origin.

(ii) Indifference curves do not intersect. If they did, the point of intersection would correspond to a combination of leisure and consumption through which the individual would have two different levels of satisfaction. Incoherence in preferences of this kind is excluded.

(iii) The increase in the utility function in relation to each of its components implies that the indifference curves are negatively sloped (see appendix 1 at the end of this chapter). The slope of an indifference curve at a given point defines *the marginal rate of substitution between consumption and leisure*. It represents the quantity of goods which a consumer must renounce in exchange for an hour of supplementary leisure, for his or her level of satisfaction to remain unchanged.

(iv) It is assumed that the individual is ready to sacrifice less and less consumption for an extra hour of leisure when the amount of time dedicated to leisure rises. This property signifies that the marginal rate of substitution between consumption and leisure diminishes with leisure time, or again that the indifference curves are convex, which is equivalent to the hypothesis of the quasi-concavity of the utility function (the relation between the shape of the indifference curves and the utility function is studied in appendix 1 at the end of this chapter).

Choices
An individual's income derives from his or her activity as wage-earner and from his or her activity (or inactivity) outside the labor market. If we designate the real hourly wage by w, the income from wages totals wh. Investment income, transfer income, even gains deriving from undeclared or illegal activities are examples of what an individual may acquire outside the labor market. We will designate the set of these resources expressed in real terms by the single scalar R.

Note that for a married or cohabiting person, a part of the income of his or her partner is capable of being integrated into this set. Thus the budget constraint of the agent takes the form:

$$C \leq wh + R$$

This constraint is also expressed in the following manner:

$$C + wL \leq R_0 \equiv wL_0 + R \tag{1}$$

In this way we arrive at the standard concepts of the theory of the consumer. The fiction is that the agent disposes of a potential income R_0 obtained by dedicating his entire endowment of time to working, and that he or she buys leisure and consumer goods using this income. From this point of view, the wage appears to correspond equally to the *price* and the *opportunity cost* of leisure. The solution of the consumer's problem then follows the path of utility optimization subject to the budget constraint. We thus derive the functions of demand for consumer goods and leisure (for more details, see the microeconomics textbooks by, for example, Varian, 1992; Mas-Colell et al., 1995). The decision of the consumer is expressed:

$$\underset{\{C,L\}}{\text{Max}} \quad U(C, L) \quad \text{subject to the budget constraint} \quad C + wL \leq R_0$$

We begin by studying the so-called "interior" solutions, such as $0 < L < L_0$ and $C > 0$.

The Interior Solutions

For an interior solution, the consumer puts forth a strictly positive supply of labor. Using $\mu \geq 0$ to denote the Lagrange (or Kuhn and Tucker) multiplier associated with the budget constraint, the Lagrangian of this program is[1]:

$$\mathscr{L}(C, L, \mu) = U(C, L) + \mu(R_0 - C - wL)$$

Designating the partial derivatives of the function U by U_L and U_C, the first-order conditions are expressed as:

$$U_C(C, L) - \mu = 0 \quad \text{and} \quad U_L(C, L) - \mu w = 0$$

On the other hand, the complementary-slackness condition is expressed as:

$$\mu(R_0 - C - wL) = 0 \quad \text{with} \quad \mu \geq 0$$

This relation, and the hypothesis that the utility function increases with each of its components, imply that the budget constraint is binding, since the first first-order condition is equivalent to $\mu = U_C(C, L) > 0$. Thus, the solution is situated on the budget line of equation $C + wL = R_0$. We obtain the optimal solution (C^*, L^*) by using this last equality and eliminating the Kuhn and Tucker multiplier μ of the first-order conditions, so that:

$$\frac{U_L(C^*, L^*)}{U_C(C^*, L^*)} = w \quad \text{and} \quad C^* + wL^* = R_0 \tag{2}$$

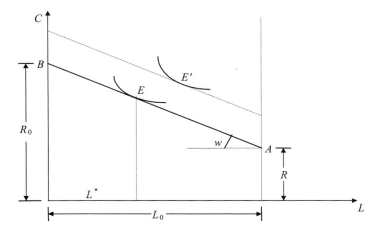

FIGURE 1.2
The trade-off between consumption and leisure.

Figure 1.2 proposes a graphic representation of this solution. It shows that the optimal solution is situated at a tangency point between the budget line AB, whose slope is w, and the indifference curve corresponding to the level of utility obtained by the consumer. For the comparative statics of the model, it is worth noting that any increase in w results in a clockwise rotation of the line AB around point A, of abscissa L_0, and of ordinate R, and that a rise in non-wage income corresponds to an upward shift of this budget line.

The Reservation Wage
For relation (2) actually to describe the optimal solution of the consumer's problem, point E has to lie to the left of point A, otherwise labor supply is null ($L = L_0$). Now, the convexity of indifference curves implies that the marginal rate of substitution between consumption and leisure, U_L/U_C, decreases as one moves to the southeast along an indifference curve (see appendix 1 at the end of this chapter).

Since this marginal rate of substitution also represents the slope of the tangent to an indifference curve, an agent offers a strictly positive quantity of hours of work if and only if the following condition is met:

$$\left(\frac{U_L}{U_C}\right)_A < w$$

The marginal rate of substitution at point A is called the *reservation wage*. It is thus defined by:

$$w_A = \frac{U_L(R, L_0)}{U_C(R, L_0)} \tag{3}$$

According to this model, assuming that the allocation of time L_0 designates a fixed quantity, the reservation wage depends only on the form of the function U at point A and on the value R of non-wage income. It determines the conditions of *participation* in the labor market. If the current wage falls below it, the agent does not supply any hours of work; we then say that he or she is not participating in the labor market. The decision to participate in the labor market thus depends on the reservation wage. Hence its determinants deserve special attention. In this model, setting aside any change in the consumer's tastes, the only parameter capable of modifying the reservation wage is non-wage income R. If, with respect to this last variable, we derive the relation (3) that defines the reservation wage, we can easily verify that the latter rises with R if, and only if, leisure is a *normal*[2] good (one, that is, the consumption of which increases with a rise in income). Under these conditions, an increase in non-wage income increases the reservation wage, and thus has a *disincentive* effect on entry into the labor market.

1.1.2   The Properties of Labor Supply

The properties of the supply of individual labor result from the combination of a substitution effect and income effect. The combination of these effects seemingly leads to a nonmonotonic relation between wages and the individual supply of labor. We shall see as well that, by starting with individual decisions and taking into account the heterogeneity of individuals, we will be able to grasp the factors that determine the aggregate supply of labor.

Substitution Effect and Income Effect

For an interior solution, the demand for leisure L^* is implicitly defined by relations (2). It is a function of the parameters of the model, which can conveniently be written in the form $L^* = \Lambda(w, R_0)$. The corresponding labor supply, i.e., $h^* = L_0 - L^*$, is often called the "Marshallian" or "uncompensated" labor supply. The impact of an increase in non-wage income R on time given over to leisure is indicated by the partial derivative of the function $\Lambda(w, R_0)$ with respect to its second argument, i.e., $\Lambda_2(w, R_0)$. It may be positive or negative. By definition, leisure is a *normal good* if its demand rises with R_0 (see appendix 2 to this chapter). In the opposite case, in which the time dedicated to leisure decreases with non-wage income, leisure is an *inferior good*. The consequences of an increase in non-wage income are represented in figure 1.2 by the shift from point E to point E'.

The impact of a variation in wages is obtained by differentiating function $\Lambda(w, R_0)$ with respect to w. Taking account of the fact that $R_0 = wL_0 + R$, we arrive at:

$$\frac{dL^*}{dw} = \Lambda_1 + \Lambda_2 \frac{\partial R_0}{\partial w} \qquad \text{with} \qquad \frac{\partial R_0}{\partial w} = L_0 > 0 \tag{4}$$

Figure 1.3 traces the movement of the consumer's equilibrium when wages go from a value of w to a value of $w_1 > w$. The partial derivative of the function Λ with respect to w, denoted Λ_1, corresponds to the usual compound of substitution and income effects in the theory of the consumer (the calculations are presented in appendix 2). To learn the sign of this derivative, it is best to reason in two stages. In the first stage, we suppose that the potential income R_0 does not change: the

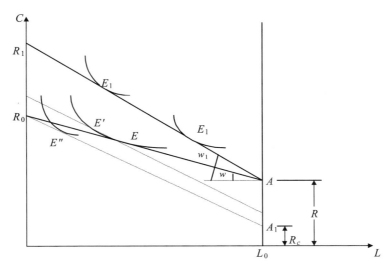

FIGURE 1.3
The effects of a wage increase.

consumer then faces a new budget line $A_1 R_0$. For him or her, it is as though his or her non-wage income had decreased from R to $R_c = R - (w_1 - w)L_0$. Income R_c is described as *compensated* income and the line $A_1 R_0$ is called the *compensated* budget constraint. In the second stage, we assume that the potential income grows from R_0 to $R_1 = R + w_1 L_0$.

Reckoning first with R_0 as a given, we discover the usual compound of substitution and income effects of the theory of the consumer. When the initial equilibrium lies at point E, the substitution effect moves it to point E' offering the same degree of utility as at E, but with the wage now worth w_1 (at point E' the tangent to the indifference curve is parallel to the budget line $A_1 R_0$). The shift from point E to point E' corresponds to a "Hicksian" or "compensated" modification of the labor supply, obtained by minimizing the outlay of the consumer under the constraint of reaching a given level of utility. The substitution effect thus implies a reduction of leisure. Starting from point E', and assuming that the wage keeps the value w_1, the income effect shifts the equilibrium of the consumer to point E''. If leisure is a normal good, the shift from E' to E'' being the consequence of a fall in income, the demand for leisure must diminish. Thus, the substitution effect and the (indirect) income effect work to produce the same result: an increase in wage leads to a diminution of the time allotted to leisure, or in other words, to an increase in labor supply. Consequently, in relation (4), we will have $\Lambda_1 < 0$ if leisure is a normal good. Finally, the increase in potential income from R_0 to R_1 causes the equilibrium to shift from point E'' to point E_1. What we have is a *direct* income effect identified by the partial derivative Λ_2 of the demand for leisure with respect to R_0 in relation (4). If leisure is a normal good, then by definition Λ_2 is positive and any rise in wage leads to a rise in the consumption of leisure, and thus to a fall in labor supply. This direct income effect runs counter to the usual substitution and "indirect" income effects of the theory of the consumer. In sum, a wage increase has an ambivalent effect on labor supply. In figure 1.3 the abscissa of point E_1 can as easily lie to the left as to the right of that of E.

For convenience, we can aggregate the two income effects by retaining only the shift from E' to E, in which case we refer to the global income effect. This allows us to analyze a rise in the hourly wage with the help of only two effects. In the first place, there is an incentive to increase labor supply, since this factor is better remunerated (the substitution effect). But equally there is an opportunity to consume the same quantity of goods while working less, which motivates a diminution of labor supply (the global income effect) if leisure is a normal good.

Compensated and Noncompensated Elasticity of Labor Supply
Along with the Marshallian supply of labor h^* considered to this point, we can also make use of the Hicksian supply of labor; it is arrived at by minimizing the consumer's expenditure, given an exogenous minimal level of utility $\bar{U}$. The Hicksian supply of labor, denoted $\hat{h}$, is then the solution of the problem:

$$\underset{(L,C)}{\text{Min}}\ C + wL \quad \text{subject to constraint} \quad U(C, L) \geq \bar{U}$$

The Marshallian supply depends on the wage and on non-wage income, whereas the Hicksian supply of labor depends on the wage and on the level of utility $\bar{U}$. The Hicksian elasticity of the labor supply, defined by $\eta_w^{\hat{h}} = (w/\hat{h})(d\hat{h}/dw)$, represents the percentage of variation of the Hicksian supply of labor that follows from a 1% rise in wage. It corresponds to the variation in labor supply for a shift from point E to point E' in figure 1.3. Hicksian elasticity is called "compensated" elasticity because it posits that the income of the consumer varies in order for him to stay on the same indifference curve. The Marshallian elasticity of labor supply, defined by $\eta_w^{h^*} = (w/h^*)(dh^*/dw)$, represents the percentage of variation of the Marshallian supply of labor that follows from a 1% rise in wage. It corresponds to the variation in the labor supply for a shift from point E to point E_1 in figure 1.3. Marshallian elasticity is also called noncompensated elasticity because it takes into account the real variation in income resulting from the variation in wages.

Marshallian and Hicksian elasticities are linked by the Slutsky equation, which is written thus:

$$\eta_w^{h^*} = \eta_w^{\hat{h}} + \frac{wh^*}{R_0}\eta_{R_0}^{h^*}$$

A demonstration of this equality is presented in appendix 3 at the end of this chapter. The Slutsky equation shows that Marshallian elasticity is to be interpreted as the sum of two effects. The substitution effect, represented by the Hicksian elasticity $\eta_w^{\hat{h}}$, is necessarily negative. The (global) income effect, represented by the term $(wh^*/R_0)\eta_{R_0}^{h^*}$, is positive if leisure is a normal good.

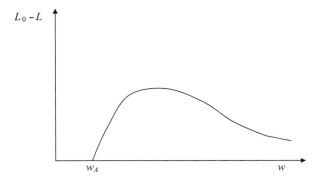

FIGURE 1.4
The individual labor supply.

The Shape of the Labor Supply Curve

We can now offer a plausible graph of labor supply. It is shown in figure 1.4. When the hourly wage rises just above the reservation wage, the substitution effect prevails over income effects, and labor supply grows. But the global income effect swells with the wage, and it is reasonable to believe that when the latter reaches a certain level, it will dominate the substitution effect. The supply of labor then begins to shrink. This is the reason why it is generally thought to turn down, as shown in figure 1.4.

Supplementary Constraints

The preceding analysis leaves out many elements that may play a part in the trade-off between work and leisure. For example, the budget constraint is actually piecewise linear, since on the one hand, overtime hours are not remunerated at the same rate as normal ones, and on the other hand income tax is progressive. This constraint may even present nonconvexities related to the ceilings on various social security contributions. Neither does the model hitherto presented take into account the fact that most often the decision to take a job entails a fixed cost independent of the number of hours worked, such as, for example, the purchase of a second vehicle, or the cost of child care. All these elements pose serious problems for empirical assessment (see below, section 2.1.3).

Another element that may alter the foregoing analysis comes from the relative absence of freedom of choice in the number of hours worked. The majority of wage-earners hold full-time employment, other workers hold part-time jobs, but the reality is always a far cry from a hypothetical complete flexibility in hours worked. To illustrate the effects of a rigidity constraint on hours worked, we present a situation in figure 1.5 in which the agent has a choice between working during a set period, represented by the abscissa point L_f, or not working at all.

Let us designate by E the nonconstrained optimum of the problem of the agent. If this point is situated to the left of E_f, the agent agrees to furnish $(L_0 - L_f)$ hours of

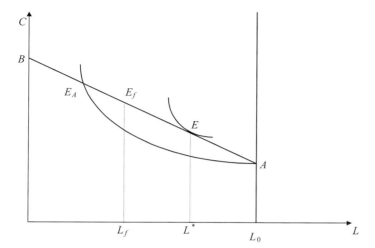

FIGURE 1.5
Constraint on hours of work.

work; in this situation, he or she would simply have liked to work more. Vice versa, when the point E lies to the right of E_f, he or she agrees to work the quantity of fixed hours offered if, and only if, the point E_A—corresponding to the intersection of the indifference curve passing through A with the budget line—lies to the left of E_f. In this case, he or she obtains a level of utility superior to what he or she would have attained by not participating at all in the labor market. The agent then works more than he or she would have wished to (since $L^* > L_f$). On the other hand, if the point E_A were to lie to the right of E_f, he or she would choose not to participate, since he or she would have preferred to supply $(L_0 - L^*) > 0$ hours of work. This individual is in a situation that we can call "involuntary nonparticipation," since he or she does wish to supply a certain quantity of work at the current wage and faces constraints that keep him or her from supplying them. The abscissa and the ordinate of point E_f being equal respectively to L_f and $w(L_0 - L_f) + R$, the reservation wage—which we will still denote by w_A—is defined by the equality:

$$U[R + w_A(L_0 - L_f), L_f] = U(R, L_0)$$

Aggregate Labor Supply and the Labor Force Participaton Rate
We arrive at the aggregate labor supply, for a wage level of w, by adding up the total number of hours supplied by each individual. The existence of indivisibilities in the amounts of working hours offered to agents implies that the elasticity of the aggregate supply differs from that of the individual supply. To show this result, let us take the case envisaged previously, in which each agent has the choice between working for a fixed length of time $\bar{h} = L_0 - L_f$ and not working at all. In a population of large size, the reservation wages differ from one individual to another, for preferences and

non-wage incomes are not identical. Let us imagine that this diversity of reservation wages $w_A \in [0, +\infty)$ may be represented by a cumulative distribution function $\Phi(\cdot)$. By definition, the quantity $\Phi(w)$ represents the *participation rate*, that is, the proportion of individuals in the population of working age whose reservation wage is below the current wage w. Since the function Φ is increasing, the participation rate climbs as the wage increases. If the total size of the population is N, the quantity $N\Phi(w)$ represents the aggregate labor supply. Supposing that the size of the population N does not vary, the wage elasticity of the aggregate supply of labor is identical to that of the participation rate. This elasticity is positive, since a rise in wages draws workers into the labor market.

This result extends far beyond the example given; it is confirmed whenever the hours offered to workers are not entirely flexible. From an empirical point of view this result has a certain importance, since it implies that the aggregate supply of labor or the global supply of labor of a subpopulation may be sensitive to changes in the wage, even if the labor supplied by most of the individual agents is not. We shall discover below that the elasticity of the individual's supply of labor is indeed slight, but that decisions to participate in the labor market turn out to be extremely sensitive to the various incentives, particularly fiscal ones, that suppliers of labor are faced with. In this case the total aggregate supply, or the supply of a given subpopulation, ought to follow the fluctuations in the participation rate (a point emphasized particularly by Heckman, 1993).

1.2 LABOR SUPPLY WITH HOUSEHOLD PRODUCTION AND WITHIN THE FAMILY

The basic model of a trade-off between consumption and leisure neglects numerous elements that may influence labor supply. In this subsection we extend the model in two important directions. By allocating time not dedicated to wage labor to leisure, the basic model fails to take account of production within households—production that represents a substitute for wage income from work. Furthermore, decisions about labor supply frequently result from bargaining involving several members of the household.

1.2.1 Household Production

The dichotomy between leisure and wage labor masks an important part of the complexity of individual decisions concerning the allocation of time. In reality, leisure is not the sole alternative to wage labor. Time devoted to household tasks is (generally) distinguished from leisure. Now, these tasks are not always unavoidable. The bulk of the goods and services produced domestically can be purchased. It is possible, for example, to eat a meal that one has prepared oneself, or go to a restaurant, or telephone a caterer, or hire a cook. Clearly each alternative entails a different expense, and an individual's choice depends on his or her preferences, effectiveness at performing household chores versus doing paid work, income, and prices. We can analyze the consequences of time devoted to household production by modifying our basic model of labor supply at the margin.

The Consumer's Program

Individual preferences are always represented by the utility function $U(C, L)$. Goods consumed may be purchased, in quantity C_M, or produced domestically, in quantity C_D, with $C = C_D + C_M$. The total endowment of time available L_0 breaks down into paid working time h_M, household working time h_D, and leisure L, hence $L_0 = h_M + h_D + L$. The efficiency of household tasks is represented by a "production function," $C_D = f(h_D)$, linking the amount of the good produced to the time spent on household work. This production function is increasing and concave; thus we will have $f' > 0$ and $f'' < 0$. Income is made up of wage earnings, wh_M, and non-wage ones, R. The consumer must choose the quantities C_M, C_D, h_D, h_M, and L that maximize his or her utility under the budget constraint $C_M \leq wh_M + R$. Let us further designate potential income as $R_0 = wL_0 + R$; since $h_M = L_0 - h_D - L$, the budget constraint is again written $C_M + wL \leq wh_D + R_0$. Taking into account the identity $C_M = C - f(h_D)$, the consumer's program then takes the following form:

$$\underset{\{C, L, h_D\}}{\text{Max}} \quad U(C, L) \quad \text{subject to the budget constraint} \quad C + wL \leq [f(h_D) - wh_D] + R_0$$

In this program the choice variables of the consumer are *total* consumption C, leisure L, and the time h_D given over to household production. Additionally, the budget constraint shows that the total income of the consumer is equal to the sum of the potential income R_0 and the "profit" derived from household activities. Since household production only comes into the consumer's program through the expression of this profit, its optimal value h_D^* is that which maximizes the value of this profit; hence it is defined by $f'(h_D^*) = w$. Given time h_D^* dedicated to household activities, the consumer's program becomes formally equivalent to that of the basic model, as long as we replace potential income R_0 by $\tilde{R}_0 \equiv R_0 + f(h_D^*) - wh_D^*$. The optimal solutions $C^* = C_M^* + f(h_D^*)$ and L^* are then defined by the equalities:

$$\frac{U_L(C^*, L^*)}{U_C(C^*, L^*)} = w = f'(h_D^*) \qquad \text{and} \qquad C^* + wL^* = \tilde{R}_0 \tag{5}$$

This result is close to the one described by equation (2) in the basic model. At the optimum, the marginal rate of substitution between consumption and leisure is equal to the wage. As previously, this condition describes the division between the consumption of goods and that of leisure. The equality $f'(h_D^*) = w$ shows that the allocation of working time between household and waged activities is determined by the relative productivities of the two types of activity. Consequently the wage reflects the individual productivity of wage labor. The agent thus has an interest in devoting his or her working time to household activities to the extent that the marginal productivity $f'(h_D)$ of an hour of this type of work is superior to an hour's wage. Therefore he or she augments the length of time given to household work to the point where $f'(h_D^*) = w$.

Elasticity of the Labor Supply

The possibility of making trade-offs between household and waged activities alters the elasticity of the labor supply curve. The system of equations (5) allows us to write the optimal demand for leisure in the form $L^* = \Lambda(w, \tilde{R}_0)$. Differentiating this equality with respect to w, we get:

$$\frac{dL^*}{dw} = \Lambda_1 + \Lambda_2 \frac{d\tilde{R}_0}{dw} \quad \text{with} \quad \frac{d\tilde{R}_0}{dw} = L_0 - h_D^*$$

Because $f'(h_D^*) = w$ implies that $dh_D^*/dw = 1/f''(h_D^*)$, the identity $h_M^* \equiv L_0 - h_D^* - L^*$ entails:

$$\frac{dh_M^*}{dw} = -(\Lambda_1 + \Lambda_2 L_0) + \left[\Lambda_2 h_D^* - \frac{1}{f''(h_D^*)}\right] \tag{6}$$

The term $-(\Lambda_1 + \Lambda_2 L_0)$ represents the impact of a variation in the wage on the supply of wage labor for a given amount of household activity. It corresponds to the set of effects discussed in the basic model—see equation (2) above and the accompanying remarks. We have seen, in particular, that a change in the wage has an ambivalent impact on labor supply. The second term of the right-hand side of equation (6) is positive if leisure is a normal good (that is, if $\Lambda_2 > 0$). Consequently the possibility of making trade-offs against household activity ought to increase the wage elasticity of the labor supply. This result might explain why empirical studies show that the wage elasticity of the supply of female labor is generally higher than that of the supply of male labor (see section 1.4.1 below). For men, the trade-off between household and waged activity is often marginal. An instructive limit case is that of an optimal "corner solution," with a null supply of domestic labor $h_D^* = 0$. This might be the case if the productivity of household work were far below the current wage. A high proportion of men would then trade leisure off against wage labor only, whereas many women, whose household productivity is high in relation to the wage that they could get, would trade off among leisure, household activity, and wage labor.

Taking household activity into consideration allows us to make the predictions of the basic model richer. It should be emphasized, however, that the model presented here remains very rudimentary. For one thing, it rests on the hypothesis of an identical disutility of work for waged and household activities. In reality, the inconvenience arising from these activities is different. A more general approach, proposed by Becker (1965) consists of taking into account the disutility (or the utility) associated with each activity by distinguishing the diverse kinds of work done in the home. Such an approach has the merit of analyzing the choices underlying the allocation of time among different activities with great precision (on this subject, see the syntheses of Gronau, 1986 and 1997).

1.2.2 Intrafamilial Decisions

The family has considerable influence on the behavior of its members. The supply of labor is not exempt from this rule, and the basic model has to be adapted so as to take into account the influence of family structures. The question bears an important empirical aspect, for numerous data (in particular those on consumption) only describe the behavior of the household, so we require a theory that goes beyond the basic individual frame of reference and gets us to a point where our estimates make some sense. The analysis of family choices has developed along two different lines. The first, known as the "unitary" model, starts from the principle that the family can be likened to a sole agent having its own utility function. The second, known generically as the "collective" approach, postulates that making choices is fundamentally something individuals do, and that the family is no more than a particular framework that enlarges (or constrains) the range of choices of each individual member of it.

The Unitary Model

This approach extends, as simply as possible, the basic model proposed hitherto. Let us imagine a family composed of two persons: we then postulate that the preferences of this entity are representable by a utility function $U(C, L_1, L_2)$, where C represents the *total* consumption of goods by the household and L_i ($i = 1, 2$) designates the leisure of individual i.[3] This formalization assumes that the satisfaction attained through the consumption of a good depends solely on its total amount, and not on the manner in which it is shared among the individual members. For agent i, let us denote his or her wage and non-wage income respectively as w_i and R_i; the optimal choices are then determined by maximizing utility under a single budget constraint. The program of the household is written as:

$$\underset{\{C, L_1, L_2\}}{\text{Max}} \ U(C, L_1, L_2) \quad \text{s.c.} \quad C + w_1 L_1 + w_2 L_2 \leq R_1 + R_2 + (w_1 + w_2)L_0$$

Scrutiny of this program reveals that the unitary representation of the household implies that the *distribution* of non-wage incomes has no importance; the only thing that counts is their *sum* $R_1 + R_2$. This hypothesis, known in the literature as "income pooling," signifies, for example, that it is not necessary to know which member of the couple is the beneficiary of transfer income. Now, the fact is that empirical studies refute this hypothesis for large segments of the population. For example, Fortin and Lacroix (1997) find that the unitary model only fits couples with pre-school-age children (see Blundell and MaCurdy, 1999, for a general overview). This invalidation is one of the reasons why the unitary model of the household is not completely satisfactory and is giving way to the collective model for the purpose of describing decisions made within a family.

The Collective Model

The most highly elaborated form of the collective model is due to Chiappori (1988, 1992). This model starts from the principle that household choices must arise out of individual preferences. In making the household the sole locus of decisions, the unitary model arbitrarily aggregates the preferences of its members, and hence does not respect the basic principle of "methodological individualism." Conversely, if one does adhere to this principle, it appears natural to assume that decisions made within a household are efficient in the Pareto sense, meaning that the possibility of mutually advantageous allocation does not occur. If we use $U_i(C_i, L_i)$, $i = 1, 2$, to designate the individual preferences of the persons composing the household, the efficient allocations will be the solutions of the following program:

$$\underset{\{C_1, C_2, L_1, L_2\}}{\text{Max}} \quad U_1(C_1, L_1)$$

Subject to constraints:

$$U_2(C_2, L_2) \geq \bar{U}_2$$

$$C_1 + C_2 + w_1 L_1 + w_2 L_2 \leq R_1 + R_2 + (w_1 + w_2) L_0$$

In this program the parameter $\bar{U}_2$ represents a given level of utility, and we may suppose that it depends on the parameters w_i and R_i. Chiappori (1992, proposition 1) then shows that the efficient allocations are also the solutions of *individual* programs in which each person would be endowed with a specific non-wage income and which would depend on the overall income of the household. More precisely, the program of agent i takes the following form:

$$\underset{\{C_i, L_i\}}{\text{Max}} \quad U_i(C_i, L_i) \quad \text{subject to constraint} \quad C_i + w_i L_i \leq w_i L_0 + \Phi_i$$

where Φ_i is a "sharing rule," depending on the parameters w_i and R_i, and such that $\Phi_1 + \Phi_2 = R_1 + R_2$. In other words, it is as if each member of the household received a fraction of the total non-wage income of the household. In a way this approach reinforces the basic model of choice between the consumption of goods and leisure by specifying, for the budget constraint of the individual, the composition of his or her non-wage income. It is possible to expand the collective model by taking into account the "public" goods pertaining to the household and the household production of its members.

From the empirical point of view, the collective model has the advantage of not adopting the hypothesis of "income pooling" a priori; the latter is no more than a particular case of this model. Moreover, Chiappori (1992) shows that this formulation of the decision-making process within a household allows us to deduct individual consumption—which is not, for the most part, observable—using the individual supplies of labor and the total consumption of the household, which are observable entities. Hence, the simple observation of the supplies of labor and individual incomes allows us to determine the sharing rules within households. Knowing these rules, it becomes possible to assess the consequences of public policies for each member of the household using available data. In this context, Browning et al. (1994) have shown, on the basis of Canadian data, that differences of age and income among the members of households, as well as the wealth of households, appear to be the sole elements that affect the sharing rules Φ_i.

The Additional Worker Effect

Models of intrafamilial choice throw a revealing light on decisions to participate in the labor market. Taking into account the familial dimension does indeed allow us to explain why certain members of the household specialize in household production, while others offer their services on the market for wage labor. From whatever angle the household is viewed, the choices of different members are interdependent, and an individual's fluctuations in income will have an impact on his or her own supply of labor, but also on that of the spouse or other members of the household, for example working-age children. This interdependence of choices may lead an individual to increase his or her supply of labor when the household income declines. It might even motivate him or her to participate in the labor market if he or she was not already doing so before the income fell. In principle, a fall in wages may thus entail an increase in the labor force, by spurring additional workers to enter the market for the precise purpose of making up for the loss of income in their household. From the empirical point of view, this *additional worker effect* seems to have little weight (see, for example, Lundberg, 1985). It is interesting to note that the additional worker effect implies a negative relationship between the participation rate and the average wage. When we constructed the aggregate supply of labor out of individuals making decisions in isolation, we obtained a positive relationship between the average wage and the participation rate (see above, section 1.2.2). In practice, this second relationship turns out to be dominant, and we do indeed observe a positive correlation between wages and the participation rate.

1.3   LIFE CYCLE AND RETIREMENT

The static models utilized to this point obviously do not allow us to understand how agents substitute for their consumption of leisure over time when their flow of income undergoes transitory or permanent shocks. Taking into explicit account a succession of periods does not markedly alter the conclusions of the static model, but it does provide an adequate framework within which to scrutinize certain theories about the business cycle. The decision to go into retirement—in other words, the definitive end of participation in the labor market—can also be analyzed suitably using a dynamic model of labor supply within which we have redefined the flow of income and legal constraints.

1.3.1   Intertemporal Labor Supply

The dynamic theory of labor supply gives a central role to the possibility of substituting for the consumption of physical goods and leisure over time. We highlight this possibility using a dynamic model in discrete time. This model likewise allows us to grasp the contrasting effects caused by a transitory change in wages or a permanent modification of the wage profile, and thus to examine critically certain aspects of the theory of "real business cycles."

A Dynamic Model of Labor Supply

In a dynamic perspective, a consumer must make his or her choices over a "life cycle" represented by a succession of periods that start with an initial date, conventionally taken as equal to 0, and end with an independent terminal date, annotated *T*. Assuming that the period t unfolds between the dates $(t-1)$ and t, the succession of periods is then given by the index $t = 1, 2, \ldots, T$. The date t is also used as an indicator of the age, professional experience, or seniority of an individual, according to the subjects under study. In a very general way, the preferences of the consumer must be represented by a utility function of the form $\mathscr{U}(C_1, \ldots, C_t, \ldots, C_T; L_1, \ldots, L_t, \ldots, L_T)$, where C_t and L_t designate respectively the consumption of physical goods and the consumption of leisure for the period t. But this very general form does not permit us to obtain analytically simple and easily interpretable results. That is why it is often assumed that the utility function of the consumer is temporally separable, in which case it is written $\sum_{t=1}^{t=T} U(C_t, L_t, t)$. Under this hypothesis, the term $U(C_t, L_t, t)$ represents simply the utility obtained by the consumer in the course of period t. It is sometimes called the "instantaneous" utility of the period t. We must bear in mind, however, that this representation of preferences is very restrictive: in particular, it does not allow us to take into account the inertia of habits of consumption, or "habit persistence," that empirical studies reveal (see Hotz et al., 1988). To bring out this phenomenon, the influence of past consumption on the utility of the current period would have to be incorporated. Another important limitation of the model presented here has to do with the absence of decisions about training. Training increases the human capital of an individual and raises his or her wage-earning prospects, so trading off must take place between leisure, working time, and time dedicated to training (we examine this question in detail in chapter 2, section 1).

In this dynamic model, we will assume that individuals have the opportunity to save, and we will use r_t to denote the real rate of interest between the dates $t-1$ and t. For each period, the endowment of time is an independent constant to which we shall give the value 1 in order to simplify the notation. On this basis, the hours worked during a period t are equal to $(1 - L_t)$. If we use A_t to designate the consumer's assets on date t, and B_t to designate his or her income apart from wages and the yield on savings on the same date, for a given initial value A_0 for the assets, the evolution of the wealth of the consumer is described by:

$$A_t = (1 + r_t)A_{t-1} + B_t + w_t(1 - L_t) - C_t, \qquad \forall t \geq 1 \tag{7}$$

This equation can easily be understood as follows: on date t, the increase in wealth $A_t - A_{t-1}$ is due to income $w_t(1 - L_t)$ from wage labor, to income $r_t A_{t-1}$ from savings, and to other income B_t. Consumption C_t for the period has to be deducted from these gains. The *non-wage* income R_t for the period t is thus equal to $B_t + r_t A_{t-1}$.

Optimal Solutions and Demands in Frisch's Sense
The consumer attempts to maximize his or her intertemporal utility subject to the budget constraint described, on each date, by equation (7). If we use v_t to denote the multiplier associated with this equation, the Lagrangian of the consumer's problem takes the form:

$$\mathscr{L} = \sum_{t=1}^{t=T} U(C_t, L_t, t) - \sum_{t=1}^{t=T} v_t[A_t - (1 + r_t)A_{t-1} - B_t - w_t(1 - L_t) + C_t]$$

The first-order conditions are obtained by equating the derivatives of this Langrangian to zero with respect to variables C_t, L_t, and A_t. After a few simple calculation, we arrive at:

$$U_C(C_t, L_t, t) = v_t \qquad \text{and} \qquad U_L(C_t, L_t, t) = v_t w_t \tag{8}$$

$$v_t = (1 + r_{t+1}) v_{t+1} \tag{9}$$

Relations (8) imply $U_L/U_C = w_t$. The equality between the marginal rate of substitution and the current wage is thus maintained at every date, but this result is not general, it is a direct consequence of the hypothesis of the separability of the utility function. Limiting ourselves to interior solutions, the optimal consumptions of physical goods and leisure are implicitly written in the following manner:

$$C_t = C(w_t, v_t, t) \qquad \text{and} \qquad L_t = L(w_t, v_t, t) \tag{10}$$

For a given level of marginal utility of wealth, in other words, for a given v_t,[4] these equations define the "Frischian" demands for period t. The elasticity of labor supply in Frisch's sense is then equal to the current wage elasticity of function $h(w_t, v_t, t) = 1 - L(w_t, v_t, t)$, assuming that v_t remains constant. This elasticity is often called "intertemporal substitution elasticity." If we take into account the fact that v_t is really an endogenous variable depending on, among other things, the current wage, by analogy with the static case we may define the "Marshallian" elasticity of labor supply as being the current wage elasticity of function $h(w_t, v_t, t)$, taking into account the dependence between v_t and w_t. In order to define this elasticity, it is necessary to specify this dependence.

Equation (9), which is known as the Euler equation, shows that the multipliers v_t depend solely on the interest rate. More precisely, successive iterations of the logarithms of equation (9) entail:

$$\ln v_t = -\sum_{\tau=1}^{\tau=t} \ln(1 + r_\tau) + \ln v_0 \tag{11}$$

This way of writing the law of motion of v_t proves extremely interesting from the empirical point of view, since it shows that v_t can be broken down into a fixed individual effect v_0 and an age effect $-\sum_{\tau=1}^{\tau=t} \ln(1 + r_\tau)$ common to all agents (see subsection 2.1 below on the econometrics of the labor supply). Introducing uncertainty into this model, for example concerning wages, does not change the essential results notably. We can verify that the first-order conditions (8) remain true, whereas the marginal utility of wealth v_t becomes a random variable, following a stochastic process described by equation (11), with an error term with zero average appearing on the right-hand side of this equation (see Blundell and MaCurdy, 1999).

A priori, the value of v_0 depends on all the wages received by an individual during his or her lifetime. If we want to estimate the effects of a modification of the wage profile, and not just those due to a change in the current wage, then we have to take account of the dependence of v_0 on all wages. On the other hand, variation in a single wage, for example w_t, ought to have little influence on v_0 and elasticity in

Frisch's sense will certainly measure the effect of a change in a single wage w_t on labor supply $h(w_t, v_t, t)$. This difference, fundamental on the level of economic policy, between a modification of the wage profile and a change in a particular wage, emerges clearly with the help of the following example, taken from Blanchard and Fischer (1989, chapter 7, section 7.2).

Transitory Shock Versus Permanent Shock
Let us suppose that the real interest rate is constant ($r_t = r, \forall t \geq 0$), that the consumer is receiving no exogenous income ($B_t = 0, \forall t \geq 0$), and that his or her instantaneous utility takes the explicit form:

$$U(C_t, L_t, t) = (1 + \rho)^{-t}\left(\ln C_t + \frac{\sigma}{\sigma - 1} L_t^{(\sigma-1)/\sigma}\right), \qquad \sigma > 1, \rho \geq 0$$

The constant factor ρ represents the psychological discount rate. The Frischian demand functions are then written:

$$C_t = \frac{1}{(1 + \rho)^t v_t} \qquad \text{and} \qquad L_t = \left[\frac{1}{(1 + \rho)^t v_t w_t}\right]^{\sigma}$$

We may note that the intertemporal elasticity of substitution of leisure—in other words, elasticity in Frisch's sense—is equal, in absolute value, to the constant coefficient σ. With a constant interest rate, the Euler equation (9) then gives $v_t = v_0/(1 + r)^t$, and the demand functions are expressed, as a function of v_0, in the form:

$$C_t = \frac{1}{v_0}\left(\frac{1 + r}{1 + \rho}\right)^t \qquad \text{and} \qquad L_t = \left[\frac{1}{v_0 w_t}\left(\frac{1 + r}{1 + \rho}\right)^t\right]^{\sigma} \tag{12}$$

In order to obtain an implicit equation giving the value of v_0, we have to write the intertemporal budget constraint of the consumer. This constraint is arrived at by eliminating assets A_t through successive iterations of the accumulation equation (7). With $r_t = r$ and $B_t = 0$ for all $t \geq 0$, we arrive at:

$$\sum_{t=1}^{T}(1 + r)^{-t}(C_t + w_t L_t) = \sum_{t=1}^{T}(1 + r)^{-t} w_t \tag{13}$$

This expression generalizes the budget constraint (1) of the static model: it states that the discounted present value of expenditure for the purchase of consumer goods and leisure cannot exceed the discounted present value of global income.

The value of v_0 is obtained by bringing the expressions of C_t and L_t given by (12) into the intertemporal budget constraint (13). It is implicitly defined by the following equation:

$$\sum_{t=1}^{T}(1 + \rho)^{-t}\left\{1 + \left[\left(\frac{1 + r}{1 + \rho}\right)^{-t} v_0 w_t\right]^{1-\sigma} - \left(\frac{1 + r}{1 + \rho}\right)^{-t} v_0 w_t\right\} = 0 \tag{14}$$

It emerges clearly that the multiplier v_0 depends on all wages over the life cycle of the individual. For sufficiently large T, this multiplier is affected very little by changes in a particular wage: what we have in that case is a transitory shock. On the other hand, it is affected by a change affecting all wages: what we have then is a modification of the wage profile, or a permanent shock. To grasp clearly the difference between these two types of shock, let us imagine that a permanent shock corresponds to a multiplication of all wages by a single positive quantity; relation (14) shows that v_0 will be divided by this quantity. But relation (12) then indicates that the optimal level of leisure—and therefore that of hours worked—remains unchanged. In this model, a permanent shock has no influence on labor supply, since the income effect and the substitution effect cancel each other out exactly. Let us now consider a transitory shock that causes only the wage w_t to change. This shock has only slight influence on the value of v_0, and relation (12) shows that leisure at date t diminishes, while leisure at all other dates remains unchanged. This particular model thus succeeds in conveying the notion that the permanent component of the evolution of real wages has no effect on labor supply, whereas the transitory component affects the level of supply immediately through the optimal response of agents who adjust their supply of labor in response to *temporary* changes in the wage.

Labor Supply and Real Business Cycles
Since the first publications of Lucas and Rapping (1969), a number of authors have studied changes in the labor supply as a function of movements in the real wage. The goal of these studies is to explain a striking fact of major importance, which is that aggregate employment fluctuates a great deal in the course of a cycle, whereas the transitory component of changes in the real wage proves limited in scope. At the outset, the theory referred to as that of "real business cycles" saw the mechanism of intertemporal substitution of leisure as the principal cause of fluctuations in the level of employment. Following this line of thought, the economy is always the object of multiple shocks (on technology, or on preferences) that have repercussions on the remuneration of labor and capital; to these agents respond in an optimal manner by instantaneously adjusting their supply of labor. More precisely, a favorable shock, one perceived as transitory, would motivate agents to increase their supply of labor today and to reduce it tomorrow when the shock has passed (for a comprehensive evaluation of the implications of the theory of real business cycles for the labor market, see Hall, 1999). This theory is simple, even seductive, but it runs up against a sizable obstacle. If it is to agree with empirical findings, it must explain how *small* movements in the real wage could entail *large* variations in the level of employment.

Hence in its original version, the theory of real business cycles requires employment to be very sensitive to small changes in the wage. Relation (12) shows that this will be the case if the absolute value of the intertemporal elasticity of substitution of leisure σ is large. Now, the majority of empirical studies arrive instead at small values (Hall, 1980, estimates that a value of 0.4 might apply at the macroeconomic level; Pencavel, 1986, suggests values even lower than that for men, while Blundell et al., 1993, find levels ranging from 0.5 to 1 for married women in the United Kingdom). In these circumstances, variations in the labor supply in response to transitory changes in the wage cannot serve as a sufficient basis for a theory of the business cycle. Relation (12) does indicate, however, that transitory shocks might influence the level of employment via interest rates. Since these variables are noticeably more volatile than wages, there would thus be another way to reproduce the stylized facts in question. This trail, however, also comes to a dead end. To demonstrate this, let us suppose that the intertemporal utility function of the consumer is temporally separable; the first-order conditions (8) then imply:

$$\frac{u_L(C_t, L_t, t)}{u_C(C_t, L_t, t)} = w_t \qquad \forall t = 1, \ldots, T$$

If the wage does not change, it can easily be verified that this expression defines an increasing relation between consumption and leisure if these are normal goods. In this case, movements in labor supply supposedly due to the variability of interest rates alone would be accompanied by an *inverse* movement of consumption. Here too we run up against contradictory empirical observations, which show a positive correlation between levels of employment and consumption. Faced with this fresh setback, one might try out other modifications of the formulation of the problem of the trade-off over time between consumption and leisure, such as, for example, giving up the hypothesis of separability, or introducing fixed costs into the decision to participate. To this day, no way has really been found to escape the substantially negative verdict that hangs over explanations of variability in employment based on the sole mechanism of intertemporal substitution of leisure (see the discussion and proposals of Hall, 1999).

1.3.2 Economic Analysis of the Decision to Retire

Economic analysis of the process by which a person ends his or her labor market participation fits well into the life-cycle model offered above, provided that legal constraints and the flow of income specific to retirement are brought into clear focus. In an uncertain environment, the process of making this decision can be analyzed with the help of the "option value" associated with the choice not to go into retirement today. Empirical studies show that workers generally react in a significant fashion to the financial incentives that accompany either early retirement or continued wage-earning.

Social Security and Private Pensions

Most countries in the OECD zone have put in place pension systems, public and private, enabling workers to receive income when they retire from the labor market. For example, in the United States there exists a public system (Social Security) funded by mandatory contributions coming from employers, which gives around 41% of his or her last wage to the median worker retiring at age 62. This ratio increases by 6.67% each year between 62 and 65. Every individual has the opportunity to supplement this public retirement payout with private pensions, contributions to which are negotiated between employer and employee at the moment the labor contract is signed. Taken as a whole, these contributions represent considerable financial accumulations—the celebrated pension funds—managed by specialized insurance companies that pay out retirement pensions to their members that vary according to the return their investments have made. In other countries like the Netherlands and France, the private system is practically nonexistent, and the replacement rate offered by the public pensions is, in these two countries, on the order of 91% for a person who ends his or her wage-earning activity at age 60 (for a comparative international perspective, see Gruber and Wise, 1999 and 2001, from which these isolated figures are taken).

The system of public and private pensions, to which we must add the tax system, creates incentives for workers to take their retirement earlier or later. Most retirement systems specify a legal age, sometimes called the "normal" age, past which a worker is obliged to end his or her wage-earning activity (for example, normal retirement falls at 65 in the United States and Japan, and 70 in the United Kingdom). But every individual obviously has the right to retire before this legal age. As a general rule, he or she receives a smaller pension the farther the age at which he or she ceases to work is from the legal age. Hence the decision to retire brings into play a number of elements that emerge very clearly with the help of the life-cycle model, significantly modified.

Option Value in the Life-Cycle Model

Let us consider a person employed on date τ—this date represents, if you like, the age of this person—and let us suppose that this person decides to retire on date $s \geq \tau$. The evolution of his or her wealth starting from date τ is always given by equation (7), provided that we redefine certain variables of this equation. So, to simplify, we will suppose that the agent does not work at all after date s; we will then have $L_t = 1$ for $t \geq s$. In practice, the process of ceasing to work can be gradual, and for that matter the legislation sometimes permits work to continue while the agent is receiving a retirement pension. We will use $B_t(s)$ to denote the income expected in the period $t \geq s$, composed of pension payments over the period t and other income which the agent may happen to have. Most often, this income is an increasing function of age s from career onset to retirement. To avoid any confusion, we will use $B_t(0)$ to designate the non-wage income of the agent while he or she is still working, hence for $t < s$, and we will use C_{et} and C_{rt} respectively to designate his or her consumption of physical goods before and after retirement. For given s, the agent solves the following problem:

$$\underset{C_{et}, C_{rt}, L_t}{\text{Max}} \left[\sum_{t=\tau}^{s-1} U(C_{et}, L_t, t) + \sum_{t=s}^{T} U(C_{rt}, 1, t) \right]$$

Subject to constraints:

$$A_t = \begin{cases} (1 + r_t)A_{t-1} + B_t(0) + w_t(1 - L_t) - C_{et} & \text{if } \tau \leq t \leq s - 1 \\ (1 + r_t)A_{t-1} + B_t(s) - C_{rt} & \text{if } s \leq t \leq T \end{cases}$$

Let us designate the value of the welfare of the consumer at the optimum of this problem by $V_\tau(s)$, and finally let us denote the legal age of retirement by T_m, after which it is not possible to work any more. An agent age τ chooses the date s on which to end his or her working life by solving the following problem[5]:

$$\underset{s}{\text{Max}} \ V_\tau(s) \quad \text{subject to constraint} \quad T_m \geq s \geq \tau \tag{15}$$

These problems never lend themselves to an explicit resolution and are generally solved numerically. In practice, we have to specify the utility function and the manner in which the replacement income is assembled to arrive at a model capable of being simulated or estimated empirically (one of the first attempts is found in Gustman and Steinmeier, 1986). Moreover, the decision to retire is made in an environment marked by numerous uncertainties (changes in one's professional and married life starting from date t, the chances of illness, changes in taste, retirement systems, etc.) that steadily subside as the legal age approaches. In order to simplify the explanation, we have written the agent's program without taking these uncertainties into account, but it is easy formally to introduce random factors into the utility function and into the equation for the evolution of wealth so as to obtain a stochastic model that fits reality more closely. In this case, $V_\tau(s)$ represents the intertemporal utility *expected* by an agent of age τ. Supplementary information may be acquired that will cause the decision taken at age $(\tau + 1)$ to be different from the decision taken at age τ. Let us denote by s^* the optimal solution of problem (15); for every period, the program (15) allows the agent to choose between two possibilities: retire today—the optimal solution of the problem of the agent is a corner solution such as $s^* = \tau$—or continue to work until age $(\tau + 1)$ and reconsider his or her decision then, in which case the optimal solution is of the kind $s^* > \tau$.

This way of envisaging the process of ending one's working life leads us to examine the *option value* attached to the decision not to take retirement right now (Stock and Wise, 1990). Supposing that the decision to retire is irreversible, we have just shown that if $s^* = \tau$, the agent stops working immediately, and on the other hand if $s^* > \tau$, the agent continues to work and reconsiders his or her decision at age $(\tau + 1)$ in light of the new situation that he or she will be in when that date comes. The option value of not retiring today is thus equal to $V_\tau(s^*) - V_\tau(\tau)$. If it is positive, the agent continues to work. If it is not, he or she goes into retirement. At the empirical level, this approach suggests that we estimate the probability of retirement at a given age by taking the option value as our principal explanatory variable. In order to obtain an indicator of this variable, we have to choose an explicit utility function, then estimate the option value tied to this utility function on the basis of a set of relevant variables, among which are income from public and private pensions and the wage outlook (readers may consult the survey of Lumsdaine and Mitchell, 1999, for more details). In general, the indicator of the option value strongly influences decisions about retiring.

Some Facts About the Impact of Eligibility Rules
Empirical studies carried out in the United States have shown that changes made to the eligibility rules regarding Social Security pensions (the elimination of means test-

ing, extension of the normal age for stopping work) have had little effect. The reason perhaps lies in the fact that private pension plans encourage workers to take their retirement starting at age 55, whereas Social Security only pays retirement pension starting at age 62. If one looks only at private pensions, Gustman et al. (1994) have shown that individuals with the highest pensions are those who retire soonest. But this income effect is relatively feeble, since at age 60, a 10% increase in expected income over the entire (expected) duration of retirement reduces the length of working life by less than two months. Conversely, workers under financial pressure to postpone their retirement do in fact extend their working lives. Here, too, the quantitative effects are faint: a 10% rise in expected income over the entire (expected) duration of retirement prolongs working life by less than six months.

These results reveal the effects of retirement plans entered into at the time the worker was hired. But it is possible that, for reasons of productive efficiency, firms may offer pension plans that make it advantageous to take retirement sooner. Such firms will therefore attract workers who have a stronger inclination to retire sooner. In this case, the observed correlation between the financial incentives and the age at which retirement is taken do not reveal a causality; they simply show a property of an optimal contract between particular types of firms and particular workers. In order to eliminate this endogenous bias, numerous studies analyze the behavior of workers in the face of *unanticipated* changes in their retirement conditions. For example, Lumsdaine et al. (1990) studied a large American firm that, in 1982, offered a "window" to its employees over 55 and enrolled in the pension plan, through which they could retire early; the financial bonus offered exceeded a year's worth of wages for certain categories of worker. By definition, this window of opportunity was of limited duration and had not been anticipated by the employees. Clearly, it therefore counts as an exogenous shock. Lumsdaine et al. (1990) found that, in the case of the workers most advantaged by the new arrangement, the rate of leaving more than tripled. For the overall workforce, this study estimates that, for a worker aged 50 employed in the firm, the likelihood of his or her retiring at age 60 was 0.77 under the new arrangement, whereas it was only 0.37 before it was put in place. These results are confirmed by Brown (1999), who systematically examined the effect of "windows" utilizing data on the entire American population provided by the Health and Retirement Study (HRS).

The effects of this type of financial incentive can also be studied through international comparisons. The studies of Gruber and Wise (1999, 2001) on a number of OECD countries show that financial incentives have, as a general rule, important impacts on the decision to retire.

2   EMPIRICAL ASPECTS OF LABOR SUPPLY

The supply of labor is probably the area of labor economics in which the greatest number of empirical studies have been carried out over the last twenty years.

Advances in econometric methods have accompanied and made possible this increase. The reason for this trend is that, for those whose job it is to plan employment policies or reforms of the fiscal system, the response of labor supply is a primary consideration. The econometrics of labor supply today rests on a solid foundation, of which we shall give the essential aspects. A retrospective of the principal results will complete this empirical tableau.

2.1 INTRODUCTION TO THE ECONOMETRICS OF LABOR SUPPLY

The econometrics of labor supply is today a domain of study in its own right, and we shall merely sketch the problems that arise within it and the principles that govern their resolution. For a comprehensive account, the reader will profit from consulting the survey of Blundell and MaCurdy (1999).

2.1.1 The Principal Ingredients of a Labor Supply Equation

The principal goal of empirical models of the individual labor supply is to furnish an estimate of the wage elasticity of this supply. But the preceding theoretical analyses have taught us that there are several possible definitions of this elasticity, according to whether or not we integrate a temporal dimension into the choices of consumers. On the empirical level, it is primarily the way an indicator of income from sources other than the current wage is constructed that permits us to discriminate between the different definitions of elasticity. Based on the preceding theoretical analyses, in what follows wages will be treated as exogenous or independent variables. This hypothesis is not entirely satisfactory. From the dynamic point of view in particular, an individual's wage must depend on, among other things, the training he or she has decided to acquire and his or her seniority. Because these considerations belong more properly to the theory of human capital than to that of labor supply, we shall return to them later in chapter 2.

The Basic Equation and the Specification of Control Variables
As a general rule, estimates of labor supply are made on the basis of cross-sectional data (perhaps with temporal elements as well) produced by investigating a population of large size, out of which a number of individuals or households are sampled. The empirical models which the econometrician tries to estimate always rest on a basic equation relating hours h worked by a given individual at hourly wage w at each date. The following log-linear relation is a typical form of this basic equation:

$$\ln h = \alpha_w \ln w + \alpha_R \ln \mathscr{R} + x\theta + \varepsilon \tag{16}$$

In this expression, $\mathscr{R}$ is a measure of income other than the current wage, x is a vector of dimension $(1, n)$—one row and n columns—describing the n individual charateristics or control variables used, and θ is a vector of dimension $(n, 1)$ comprising n parameters to be estimated. The coefficients α_w and α_R are also parameters to be estimated, and finally, ε designates a random term reflecting individual heterogeneity that is not observed. Certain studies take h as a dependent variable rather than $\ln h$ and/or income w and $\mathscr{R}$ rather than $\ln w$ or $\ln \mathscr{R}$. These different specifications correspond to different restrictions on preferences (see Blundell and MaCurdy, 1999) that do not alter the principles guiding the estimation of equation (16). In order to fit theoretical models, such as, for example, the one in section 1.1.1, it is also possible to introduce a polynomial form of wage into the right-hand side of equation (16) so as to avoid postulating a priori that hours worked are a monotonic function of the hourly wage.

Parameter α_w measures the wage elasticity of labor supply. This elasticity can be interpreted in several different ways according to the hypotheses made and the model utilized: a diversity of interpretation present here in the manner in which $\mathscr{R}$, indicating income apart from the current wage, is specified. The theoretical models taught us that individual labor supply at a given period was a function of the hourly wage for that period and other elements forming the expected wealth of an agent, such as, for example, his or her anticipated income from savings or work. If we limit ourselves to an equation of type (16), these elements have to be incorporated into variable $\mathscr{R}$. The important thing is to know how to carry out this incorporation.

One solution might be to consider only non-wage income for the period under investigation. During our study of the life-cycle model in section 1.3.1, we made it clear that this income, denoted by R_t, is composed of income from savings, which, for date t, are denoted by $r_t A_{t-1}$ (denoting by r_t the rate of interest between periods $t-1$ and t, and by A_{t-1} the assets of the agent in period $t-1$), and exogenous income B_t. To set $\mathscr{R}_t = R_t = r_t A_{t-1} + B_t$ amounts to supposing that agents make their choices in a myopic fashion, with no opportunity to save today for consumption tomorrow. But this hypothesis of total myopia is not in the least realistic, for agents largely make choices with an eye to the future, so that to estimate coefficient α_w while taking $\mathscr{R}$ to be only non-wage income at the date of the investigation does not give pertinent information about the real reactions of labor supply. It is possible to make up for this drawback by defining indicator $\mathscr{R}$ differently. To that end, it will help to return to what we learned from the life-cycle model laid out in section 1.3.1.

A Reexamination of the Life-Cycle Model
If, in the life-cycle model in section 1.3.1, the utility function is temporally separable, we have seen that the first-order condition (8) always implies equality between the marginal rate of substitution between consumption and leisure and the current wage *at each date*. This property suggests a two-stage resolution of this model, known in the literature as "two-stage budgeting." In the first stage, analogous to the basic static model, we define a potential income Ω_t for each period t in such a way that the consumer's program consists of maximizing his or her instantaneous utility for the period t under a budget constraint, of which the non-wage income would be exactly Ω_t. In the second stage, the consumer optimizes the series of Ω_t, given the resources, present or anticipated, at his or her disposal. To arrive at such a program, we must first point out that the intertemporal budget constraint (7) of the life-cycle model can be rewritten in the following way:

$$C_t + w_t h_t = (1 + r_t)A_{t-1} + B_t - A_t$$

Let us set $\Omega_t = (1 + r_t)A_{t-1} + B_t - A_t$; the two-stage procedure by which the consumer resolves the program then emerges quite naturally. In the first stage, the consumer makes his or her choices for period t while maximizing instantaneous utility $U(C_t, 1 - h_t, t)$ subject to the "static" budget constraint $C_t + w_t h_t = \Omega_t$. At the conclusion of this first stage, the consumer thus attains a level of indirect utility $V(\Omega_t, t)$. In the second stage, he or she selects the optimal path for his or her assets A_t by solving the program:

$$\underset{\{A_t\}}{\text{Max}} \sum_{t=0}^{t=T} V(\Omega_t, t) \quad \text{s.c.} \quad \Omega_t = (1 + r_t)A_{t-1} + B_t - A_t, \forall t$$

This two-stage procedure evidently gives the same solutions as the solution (in one stage) employed in section 1.3.1.

Changes in a Wage

On the empirical level, we should first note that the econometrician can know the values of Ω_t when he or she can observe the value of the consumption of physical goods C_t and the hours worked h_t, since $\Omega_t = C_t + w_t h_t$. If that is not the case, or if they cannot be known precisely enough, it is possible to estimate Ω_t by taking as explanatory variables the value A_{t-1} of assets at the outset of period t, the interest rate r_t, exogenous income B_t, all or part of the control variables of vector x, and the expectation of all these independent variables (inasmuch as the value A_t of the assets at the end of the period t is not necessarily known, and depends on expectations of future resources). Hence, if we wish to make a relevant assessment (that is, one that avoids the supposition that individuals are completely myopic) of the reactions of labor supply to changes in a given wage, it is best to take $\mathscr{R}$ as an estimator of potential income Ω. In other words, if t designates the date of the survey, the income indicator $\mathscr{R}_t$ to be taken into account in the basic equation (16) must then be estimated by a relation of the type:

$$\mathscr{R}_t = \mathscr{R}(A_{t-1}, r_t, B_t, x_t, Z_t)$$

Here, Z_t represents the vector of the anticipated values of r, w, B and x. Note that, according to the procedure of "two-stage budgeting," potential income is an *endogenous* variable, since its value depends on choices made by the consumer during the allocation through time of his or her wealth. Hence it is best to apply methods based on instrumental variables in order to estimate equation (16). The "two-stage budgeting" procedure allows us to estimate, in a pertinent manner, the elasticity of labor supply with respect to *one* particular wage (or *one* expected wage), but does not allow us to know the effects of a change in the *overall* wage profile, since under this hypothesis, potential income Ω_t changes as well. Now, it is indispensable to study the overall wage profile if one wants to know, for example, the impact of a reform of the tax system, or more generally any measure of economic policy likely to become permanent. Before answering this question, we will show how to measure elasticity in Frisch's sense.

Estimating Elasticity in Frisch's Sense

The dynamic model of section 1.3.1 has much to teach us. In particular, relations (10) and (11), defining its solutions, reveal that labor supply h_t depends on the current wage w_t and the marginal utility of wealth v_t, so that $h_t = h(w_t, v_t, t)$. According to relation (11) of this model, the logarithm of v_t breaks down into an individual fixed effect equal to $\ln v_0$ and an age effect $\sum_{\tau=1}^{\tau=t} \ln(1 + r_\tau)$, common to all agents and which may be written in the form ρt, supposing that r_τ is constant. To obtain the elasticity of the labor supply in Frisch's sense, also called the intertemporal elasticity of substitution, we view the marginal utility of wealth v_t as exogenously given, independent of the current wage. Following relation (11), we see that that amounts to supposing that $\ln v_0$ is also independent of the current wage, but evidently does depend on individual characteristics. This property suggests substituting $\ln v_0 + \rho t$ for $\ln \mathscr{R}$ in equation (16) to estimate Frischian elasticity. If we have longitudinal data available, we can eliminate individual fixed effects by taking the basic relation (16) in first-differences, which is written:

$$\Delta \ln h_t = \rho + \Delta x_t \theta + \alpha_w \Delta \ln w_t + \Delta \varepsilon_t$$

This equation allows us to estimate the elasticity of labor supply in Frisch's sense in a coherent manner, that is, the impact of a transitory change in the wage. It does not, however, allow us to evaluate the impact of a change in the overall wage profile, for a change of this type causes the marginal utility of wealth to vary a priori.

Changes in the Wage Profile

In order to evaluate the consequences of a change in the overall wage profile, we have to take into consideration variations in the marginal utility of wealth. The initial value of the marginal utility of wealth v_0 depends on individual preferences and all anticipated income; it may be approximated by the equation:

$$\ln v_0 = y\alpha_y + \sum_{i=0}^{T} \gamma_i E_0 \ln w_i + \phi A_0$$

In this expression, y, α_y and T $(T \geq \tau)$ designate respectively a vector of individual characteristics relating to the onset of working life, a vector of parameters to be estimated, and the duration of working life (putatively known). The term A_0 designates the initial value of the stock of wealth, ϕ is a parameter, and E represents the expectation operator. Replacing $\ln \mathscr{R}$ by $\ln v_0 + \rho t$ in the basic equation (16), this equation becomes:

$$\ln h_t = \alpha_w \ln w_t + x\theta + y\alpha_y + \sum_{\substack{i=0 \\ i \neq t}}^{T} \gamma_i E_0 \ln w_i + \phi A_0 + \rho t + \varepsilon_t \tag{17}$$

Expected wages, which are evidently not observed, can themselves be approximated by an equation of the form:

$$E_0 \ln w_t = a_0 + a_1 t + a_2 t^2 + u_t \tag{18}$$

In this equality we have set $a_j = z\alpha_j$, $j = 0, 1, 2$, where z is a vector of observable characteristics unchanging over time, α_j is a vector of parameters, and u_t is a random element. The term t^2 is introduced to account for a possible nonlinearity in the relation between wages and experience, which is generally confirmed by empirical work on this subject (see below, chapter 6, section 4.3). The simultaneous estimation of equations (17) and (18) allows us to obtain the parameters needed to assess the impact of an overall change in wages on labor supply. Parameter α_w measures the impact of a change in the current wage w_t, while parameters γ_i measure the consequences of changes in the overall wage profile (see Blundell and MaCurdy, 1999, pp. 1600–1603, for more details).

To sum up, it is necessary to define precisely the set of variables that explain labor supply—in particular, the indicators of non-wage income—in order to see what type of elasticity the model utilized allows us to estimate. Having thus set out the ingredients that go to make up an empirical labor supply equation of type (16), we can now present the principles that guide this estimation.

2.1.2 A Short Guide to Estimating Labor Supply

Estimating the basic equation by ordinary least squares leads to biased results, since it neglects to take into account participation decisions. If we want to obtain unbiased estimators of the elasticity of labor supply, we have to estimate jointly decisions to participate and decisions about the number of hours worked. These estimates oblige us to attribute a fictitious wage to those who do not participate in the labor market.

What We Must Not Do

The first idea that comes to mind is to apply the method of ordinary least squares to equation (16) alone. Until the 1970s most studies proceeded in this way. But it is not a correct method, for it fails to distinguish decisions about *participation* in the labor market from those about the number of hours an agent is prepared to offer. The question that faces the econometrician is, given a sample of individuals, how to take into account persons who do not work (or episodes during which an agent has not worked if the data are equally temporal)? Certain studies subsequent to the 1970s simply set $h_i = 0$ for these persons. In other words, these studies took the view that certain workers choose exactly $h_i = 0$, just like any other value of h_i, which entails that equation (16) holds for any wage value of h_i and w_i. It is precisely this last hypothesis that is false. Equation (16) is only valid for wages *above* the reservation wage, and for *all other* wages, labor supply is null. Making do with equation (16) and setting $h_i = 0$ for episodes of nonwork thus leads to specification errors. An alternative solution was simply to exclude the unemployed, and nonparticipants in the labor market, from the sample. But in this case the econometrician commits a selection bias, forgetting that not to supply any hours of work is a decision in the same way that supplying them is. The fact that this type of decision is not described by equation (16) does not authorize us to set it aside purely and simply. The solution is to employ an empirical model that, like the basic model of 1.1.1, describes participation and hours decisions *jointly*.

What We Must Do

The approach most often utilized today is "structural." It combines an explicit functional form for the direct utility function of consumers, dependent in parametric fashion on the different observable characteristics of an individual, and a random term representing the nonobserved heterogeneity among individuals. We then write the budget constraint, from which we deduce, by the usual maximization procedure, labor supply and the reservation wage. The participation condition is then arrived at using the probability distribution of the random term, by positing that the wage offered must be superior to the reservation wage. We estimate the model at which we arrive using cross-sectional data that specify, for each individual, the values of every variable we are interested in, and his or her decisions to participate or not in the labor market. Let us illustrate this approach using an example, for purely pedagogic purposes, based on the static model of section 1.1.1, with a utility function of the Cobb-Douglas type.

The utility of a consumer will then take the form $C^{1-\beta}L^{\beta}$, $1 > \beta > 0$, and the budget constraint continues to be written $C + wL = wL_0 + R$. We assume that the explanatory variables and the random term intervene via the coefficient β according to the linear form $\beta = x\theta + \varepsilon$. Following the static model of section 1.1.1, we know that the reservation wage w_A is equal to the marginal rate of substitution U_L/U_C taken at point (R, L_0) and that the maximization of utility subject to the budget constraint gives the optimal value of leisure. After several simple calculations, we find that:

$$w_A = \frac{\beta}{1-\beta}\frac{R}{L_0} \quad \text{and} \quad L = \begin{cases} \beta\left(L_0 + \dfrac{R}{w}\right) & \text{if } w \geq w_A \\ L_0 & \text{if } w \leq w_A \end{cases}$$

Since the coefficient β is a function of the random term ε, the inequality $w \geq w_A$ is equivalent to an inequality on the values of ε, which is written:

$$w \geq w_A \Leftrightarrow \varepsilon \leq \frac{wL_0}{R + wL_0} - x\theta$$

In conclusion, the decisions concerning labor supply $h = L_0 - L$ and participation may be summed up in this fashion:

$$h = \begin{cases} L_0 - (x\theta + \varepsilon)\left(L_0 + \dfrac{R}{w}\right) & \text{if } \varepsilon \leq \dfrac{wL_0}{R + wL_0} - x\theta \\ 0 & \text{if } \varepsilon \geq \dfrac{wL_0}{R + wL_0} - x\theta \end{cases} \tag{19}$$

This expression of labor supply is related, as regards the interior solution, to the basic equation (16). But we see that taking account of participation decisions constrains the variations of the random term, making them depend on explanatory variables. In these circumstances, the use of ordinary least squares is seen to be inadequate.

Joint Estimations of Hours Worked and Participation Decisions

Let us suppose that the econometrician has at his or her disposal a sample of individuals, N in size, specifying that individuals $i = 1, \ldots, J$ have worked h_i hours and that individuals $i = J + 1, \ldots, N$ have not worked. Let us denote by $F(.)$ and $f(.)$ respectively the cumulative distribution function and the probability density of the random term ε (the random term is most often assumed to follow a normal distribution). It is then possible to write the likelihood of the sample. Following rule (19) giving the optimal decisions of an agent, when an individual i has worked h_i hours, that means that the random term has taken the value $\varepsilon_i = w_i(L_0 - h_i)/(R_i + w_iL_0) - x_i\theta$. In this case its contribution to the likelihood of the sample is equal to $f(\varepsilon_i)$. If agent i has not worked, that means that the random term is bounded above by the value $\tilde{\varepsilon}_i = [w_iL_0/(R_i + w_iL_0)] - x_i\theta$. In this case, its contribution to the likelihood of the sample is given by $\Pr\{h_i = 0\} = 1 - F(\tilde{\varepsilon}_i)$. Setting $\bar{F} = 1 - F$, the likelihood function of the sample is written in logarithmic form:

$$\mathscr{L} = \sum_{i=1}^{i=J} \ln f \left[\frac{w_i(L_0 - h_i)}{R_i + w_iL_0} - x_i\theta \right] + \sum_{i=J+1}^{i=N} \ln \bar{F} \left[\frac{w_iL_0}{R_i + w_iL_0} - x_i\theta \right] \tag{20}$$

The maximization of the likelihood function by appropriate techniques (in this case of the *probit* type, since there is a mixture of continuous and discrete variables) furnishes estimates of the parameters in which we are interested. The expression of the likelihood function also permits us to understand clearly the mistakes made in failing to formalize participation decisions completely. If we set $h_i = 0$ for persons who do not work, that amounts to believing that their contribution to the likelihood is equal to $f[(w_iL_0/(R_i + w_iL_0)) - x_i\theta]$, which comes down to substituting function f for function $\bar{F}$ in the second term of the right-hand side of relation (20). If we exclude persons who do not work from the sample, then we are neglecting to take account of the second term on the right-hand side of relation (20). These two solutions result in biased estimators.

A Nonparticipant's Wage

The expression (20) of the likelihood function also highlights a delicate problem. By definition, the econometrician does not observe the wages of individuals $i = J + 1, \ldots, N$ who do not work. However, relation (20) shows that it is necessary to attribute a fictitious *wage* to these individuals if we want to maximize the likelihood function. We thus have to be able to assign a quantity to the (unobserved) wage notionally offered to an individual, which he or she has refused. The most common solution at present consists of deducing the wage of a nonparticipant using the wage received by participants with similar characteristics in terms of educational qualification, experience, age, and so on. In practice we can explain the wages of individuals participating in the labor market by a regression of the type $w_i = y_i\theta_p + u_i$ in which the vector y_i represents the characteristics of an individual i participating in the labor market, and θ_p designates the vector of the parameters to be estimated. Let us use $\hat{\theta}_p$ to denote the vector of the estimates of θ; we can then use this vector $\hat{\theta}_p$ to calculate the wage w_k of a nonparticipant k, using the vector y_k of his or her characteristics and setting $w_k = y_k\hat{\theta}_p$. This simple technique unfortunately presents a *selection bias*, since it assumes that the regression equation $w_i = y_i\theta_p + u_i$ also applies to the notional wages of nonparticipants. This hypothesis is highly likely to be mistaken, inasmuch as participants in the labor market must on average have nonobserved characteristics that allow them to demand wages higher than those that nonparticipants can demand. Formally this means that the distribution of the random disturbance u_i should not be the same for participants and nonparticipants. The distribution that applies to participants ought to weight the high values of the random factor more strongly than the one that applies to nonparticipants, and consequently the estimation procedure described previously will *overestimate* the notional wage attributable to a nonparticipant. One way to correct this bias consists of making simultaneous estimations of equations explaining wages and decisions to supply labor (see Heckman, 1974, for an application).

2.1.3 Nonlinear Budget Constraint

In practice, the budget constraint of an agent does not come down to a simple segment of a line, as in the basic model of section 1.1.1. Mandatory contributions and transfers make this constraint (at best) piecewise linear. The estimation of labor supply then runs into a new problem, that of the endogeneity of the choice of the "piece" on which an agent will settle. The method of virtual incomes and the construction of a differentiable approximation of the budget constraint make such an estimation possible, however.

The Method of Virtual Incomes

In all countries, the systems of tax and subsidy that agents come under present important differences according to income, so that, from the point of view of empirical estimations, it is not possible to assume that the budget constraint of an agent is represented by a single segment of a line, as in the basic model of section 1.1.1. In practice, the different schedules of marginal rates according to income brackets, and the different deductions to which certain contributors are entitled, imply that the budget constraint of an agent is piecewise linear. By way of illustration, let us consider the example of a tax system in which an agent whose income does not exceed an exogenous threshold R_{max} is not taxed, whereas if his or her income crosses this threshold, his or her wage will be taxed at rate τ. Let us use w and R to denote respectively the wage and the non-wage income of this agent. Our example of a fiscal system starts to tax the consumer from the point at which his or her working time surpasses the value h_{max} defined by $wh_{max} + R = R_{max}$. To this maximal value of working time there corresponds a value for leisure of $L_{min} = L_0 - h_{max}$. Figure 1.6 represents the budget constraint associated with this rudimentary fiscal system in the plane (L, C). In reality, the

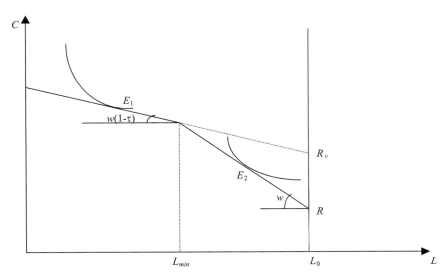

FIGURE 1.6
Piecewise linear budget constraint.

budget constraint is made up of more than two segments, and the set situated under the budget constraint can even present nonconvexities, due, for example, to the rate applied to overtime hours. The coherence of the tax system dictates, however, that the budget constraint should be continuous. Under this hypothesis, this constraint is characterized in the following manner:

$$C = \begin{cases} wh + R & \text{if } h \leq h_{\max} \\ wh(1 - \tau) + R + w\tau h_{\max} & \text{if } h \geq h_{\max} \end{cases}$$

When the consumer chooses what he or she will consume in such a way as to maximize his or her utility $U(C, L)$ subject to his or her budget constraint, figure 1.6 shows that an interior solution may be situated at points E_1 or E_2, according to whether or not labor supply is such that the consumer is taxed. This figure also indicates that point E_1 corresponds to the optimum of the consumer whose hourly wage would be equal to $w(1 - \tau)$ and who would receive a *virtual* non-wage income R_v equal to $R + w\tau h_{\max} = R + \tau(R_{\max} - R)$. It should be noted that this virtual income is perfectly well known, so it forms part of the "observations" available to the econometrician. Let us denote by $\varphi(w, R)$ the expression of labor supply if there were no taxes, that is to say, its value at point E_2. Let us again denote by w_A the reservation wage, which is once more equal to the marginal rate of substitution between leisure and consumption evaluated at the point of nonemployment. Since $h_{\max} = (R_{\max} - R)/w$, labor supply in the presence of our rudimentary fiscal system is then written:

$$h = \begin{cases} 0 & \text{if } w \leq w_A \\ \varphi[w(1 - \tau), R_v] & \text{if } \varphi(w, R) \geq (R_{\max} - R)/w \\ \varphi(w, R) & \text{if } \varphi(w, R) \leq (R_{\max} - R)/w \end{cases}$$

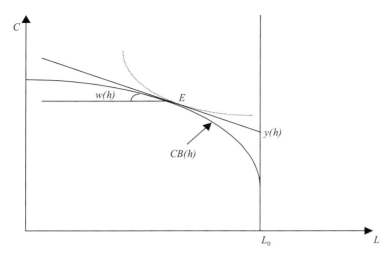

FIGURE 1.7
Differentiable budgetary constraint.

If we add other explanatory variables and a random term, which we have not done here so as not to burden the presentation, we arrive at an empirical model formally rather close to that described by equation (19). Here again, labor supply takes different values according to the values of the random term, and so can be estimated by the same methods as those envisaged above.

Approximation of the Budget Constraint by a Derivable Function
Another, more recent, method, relies on an approximation of the budget constraint by a derivable function (see, for example, MaCurdy et al., 1990, to see how such an approximation is constructed). The curve denoted $CB(h)$ in figure 1.7 represents a function of this type. Point E of this curve, where hours worked are equal to h, can be linked to a *virtual* wage, denoted $\omega(h)$, equal to the slope of the curve at this point, and a *virtual* non-wage income, denoted $y(h)$, corresponding to the intersection of the tangent of this curve with the vertical line with abscissa L_0. Note that this virtual wage and virtual income are "observable" by the econometrician from the moment he or she has been able to construct the curve $CB(h)$. All the optima of the consumer's program are then obtained by maximizing his or her utility under a (virtual) budget constraint written $C = \omega(h)h + y(h)$. For the interior solutions, the hours worked are then given by the implicit equation:

$$h = \varphi[\omega(h), y(h)]$$

This equation suggests a procedure for estimating labor supply: after having approximated the budget constraint by a derivable function, one "observes" the virtual wages and incomes and regresses the actual hours of work onto these virtual wages and incomes. Because these explanatory variables are manifestly not independent of hours worked, one has to resort to procedures utilizing instrumental variables.

This strategy, though simple in principle, poses problems owing to measurement errors that are almost always present in data relating to hours worked and wages. Thus, the dependent variable represents a priori the number of hours worked during the year—a piece of information that is rarely available. If, for example, we know the number of hours worked every week, then we multiply this figure by the number of weeks worked during the year. But this procedure is very arbitrary: in particular, it takes no account of voluntary or involuntary absences. As regards wages, the available data most often yield no more than a gross annual or monthly wage, when the explanatory variable that really counts ought to be the net hourly wage. Here again, the passage from the available data to the explanatory variable is a potential source of measurement errors (it should be noted that these problems of measurement errors extend to all the procedures by which labor supply is estimated, and not solely the one under study here). The upshot is that virtual wages and incomes are themselves the object of measurement errors. In these conditions, one solution lies in estimating a system of equations that takes the following form (see, for example, Bourguignon and Magnac, 1990):

$$h = \varphi(\omega, R, x_h, \varepsilon_h), \qquad \omega = \zeta(h, x_\omega, \varepsilon_\omega) \quad \text{and} \quad y = \xi(h, x_y, \varepsilon_y)$$

In this system, x_ω and x_y are two vectors of control variables that do not necessarily coincide with vector x_h of the control variables that appear in the equation defining labor supply. The random terms $(\varepsilon_h, \varepsilon_\omega, \varepsilon_y)$ capture the measurement errors and the nonobserved heterogeneity among individuals.

Having presented the problems encountered in the estimation of labor supply and the methods by which they can be solved, it is now time to examine the main results to which these estimates lead.

2.2 MAIN RESULTS

The econometric methods laid out above have made it possible to know better the value of the elasticity of labor supply. At the present time, the results obtained have converged toward a relative consensus. "Natural experiments" are another source of knowledge of the properties of the labor supply. The evolution of the amount of time worked and the participation rates fill out this factual panorama.

2.2.1 Form and Elasticity of Labor Supply

A consensus is emerging around the idea that movements in labor supply are principally owing to variations in the participation rate, and that the elasticity of the supply of female labor, especially that of married women, is greater than that of men.

The Hump-Shaped Curve

Does an individual's supply of labor take the form of a hump-shaped curve, as depicted in figure 1.4? The study of Blundell et al. (1992) suggests that it does. Using data from research on the expenditures of British families, these authors focus on a sample of single mothers, whose weekly supply of labor they estimate, distinguishing

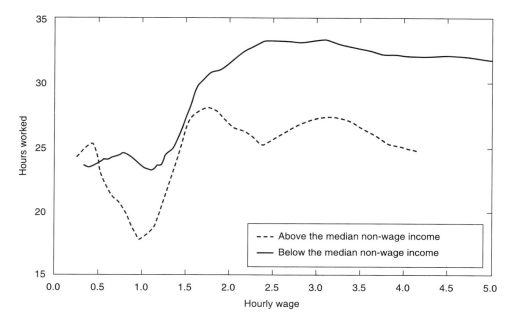

FIGURE 1.8

The labor supply of single mothers.

Source: Blundell et al. (1992).

between those who have non-wage income R greater than the median of the sample and those whose non-wage income is less than the median. The results of this study are represented in figure 1.8.

Scrutiny of this graph confirms, in the first place, that the hypothesis that leisure is a normal good is well-founded. We see that for practically all values of hourly wage, individuals in the sample who dispose of a non-wage income exceeding the median work less than the others. This graph also shows that the labor supply curve can indeed present a maximum (and even local maxima). Excluding wage values that are too low, we see that the labor supply curve for individuals whose non-wage income is less than the median strongly resembles the theoretical form of figure 1.4. For other individuals in the sample the resemblance is less marked, but the essential point remains: for low hourly wages (on the order of £1 to £1.5), there is little supply, and the substitution effect prevails, whereas for higher wages (from around £3 on up), the global income effect overrides the substitution effect.

The Elasticity of Labor Supply

The distinctive features and adaptations of the different fiscal systems found in different countries are often used to estimate the elasticity of labor supply of certain groups belonging to the population of working age (see Heckman, 1993, and Blundell and MaCurdy, 1999). These estimates run up against numerous difficulties. We have

Table 1.1

The elasticity of the labor supply of married women.

Authors	Sample	Uncompensated wage elasticity	Income elasticity
Hausman (1981)	U.S.	0.995	−0.121
Arrufat and Zabalza (1986)	U.K.	2.03	−0.2
Blundell et al. (1988)	U.K.	0.09	−0.26
Arellano and Meghir (1992)	U.K. (young children)	0.29	−0.40
Triest (1990)	U.S.	0.97	−0.33
Bourguignon and Magnac (1990)	France	[0.05; 1]	[−0.2; −0.3]

Source: Blundell and MaCurdy (1999, table 2, pp. 1649–1651).

already noted, for example, the need to distinguish clearly between decisions to participate, and decisions by people who already have a job about how many hours to work, and between hours freely supplied and ones that workers are forced to supply; and further, the complexity of budget constraints arising from different fiscal systems, the presence of fixed costs, the need to attribute a fictitious wage to nonparticipants, and so on.

Although the range of estimated elasticities is very broad, there is a relative consensus stressing the preponderance of variations in the participation rate over variations in hours. More precisely it is the variations in the rate of participation of a given group that explain the core of the elasticity of this group's labor supply. Another consensus emerges regarding the elasticity of labor supply by married women, which is demonstrably positive and greater than that of their spouses.

Table 1.1 furnishes some estimates obtained from empirical models utilizing methods set forth in sections 2.1.2 and 2.1.3. In this table, uncompensated elasticity designates the global effect of a wage change highlighted in equation (4) in section 1.2.2, that is, $(w/h^*)/(dh^*/dw)$. Income elasticity measures the impact of a change in income on labor supply, that is, with the notations in 1.2.2, $(R_0/h^*)(\partial h^*/\partial R_0) = (R_0/h^*)\Lambda_2$. Table 1.1 shows that the income elasticity of labor supply is negative, which means that leisure is a normal good (its consumption rises with income). Vice versa, wage elasticity is positive, so substitution effects prevail over income effects. Attention must be drawn to the large range of the estimates, however.

Table 1.2 shows that the wage elasticity of the labor supply is much weaker for married men, while income effects are, in general, more significant. If we turn to theoretical models, these results indicate that within the household, fiscal reforms affect principally the participation decisions of women, since on average they have access to lower wages than those of men and in all likelihood possess a comparative advantage when it comes to household production.

Table 1.2
The elasticity of the labor supply of married men.

Authors	Sample	Uncompensated wage elasticity	Income elasticity
Hausman (1981)	U.S.	[0; 0.03]	[−0.95; −1.03]
Blomquist (1983)	Sweden	0.08	[−0.03; −0.04]
Blundell and Walker (1986)	U.K.	0.024	−0.287
Triest (1990)	U.S.	0.05	0
Van Soest et al. (1990)	Netherlands	0.12	−0.01

Source: Blundell and MaCurdy (1999, table 1, pp. 1646–1648).

2.2.2 Natural Experiments

When a change is made to some aspect of economic policy, the econometrician has a chance to perform a "natural experiment." The basic idea is to compare the reactions of a group affected by the change with those of another group having similar characteristics but that is untouched by the change. The second group is the "control group." Changes in the fiscal system often provide a chance to apply this methodology to the study of labor supply behavior in a well-defined subpopulation (chapter 11, section 3, probes the question of the evaluation of economic policies in detail and problems arising from the utilization of the results of natural experiments; see also the surveys of Heckman et al., 1999, and Rosenzweig and Wolpin, 2000). Within the framework of a natural experiment, the effect of a change in economic policy is most often assessed with the help of an estimator called a "difference-in-differences estimator." Blundell and MaCurdy (1999, section 5) have shown that this estimator corresponds, under certain conditions, to the estimator of ordinary least squares of a standard model with fixed individual effect. What follows derives from their work.

The Methodology of Natural Experiments
Let us take a population of individuals of size N, out of which a group of size N_M has been affected by a change in economic policy, while the control group of size N_C has not been so affected. Suppose that we want to find out the effects of this change on a variable y (for example, hours worked or participation in the labor market). Let us denote by y_{it} the observed value of this variable on an individual i at date t, and let us use δ_{it} to designate the dummy variable, which equals 1 if the policy change applies to individual i at date t, and 0 if it does not. We can then try to evaluate the impact of the policy by estimating the following equation:

$$y_{it} = \alpha\delta_{it} + x_{it}\theta + \gamma_i + \zeta_t + \varepsilon_{it} \tag{21}$$

Parameter α is an indicator of the impact of the change, γ_i is a fixed effect proper to individual i, ζ_t is a temporal effect proper to all agents, x_{it} is the vector of the observable characteristics of individual i at date t, θ is a vector of parameters to be estimated, and ε_{it} designates an error term distributed independently among the individuals and also independent of γ_i and ζ_t.

Let us denote by Δ the difference operator; by definition $\Delta \kappa_t = \kappa_t - \kappa_{t-1}$ for any variable κ. When confronted with an equation like (21), the usual method consists of applying this operator to both sides of the equation in order to eliminate fixed individual effects γ_i. We thus obtain:

$$\Delta y_{it} = \alpha \Delta \delta_{it} + (\Delta x_{it})\theta + \Delta \zeta_t + \Delta \varepsilon_{it} \tag{22}$$

The general principles of econometrics with longitudinal data could be applied to equation (22), but the dummy variables δ_{it} have an interesting peculiarity that in certain cases lets us uncover simple expressions of the estimators. Let us therefore suppose that the observations concern only two periods. In period $(t-1)$ the same economic policy applies to all individuals, while in period t, economic policy is altered for individuals $i \in M$. For individuals $i \in C$ of the control group, there is no alteration. Since the model has only two periods, we can leave the time indexes out of equation (22). Let us suppose for simplicity's sake that individual characteristics do not vary ($\Delta x_i = 0$), and let us posit $\beta = \Delta \zeta_t$, $u_i = \Delta \varepsilon_{it}$. Equation (22) is now written:

$$\Delta y_i = \beta + \alpha \Delta \delta_i + u_i$$

By definition, the estimator of ordinary least squares of coefficient α is then given by:

$$\hat{\alpha} = \frac{cov(\Delta \delta, \Delta y)}{var(\Delta \delta)} = \frac{\sum\limits_{i \in M}(\Delta \delta_i - \overline{\Delta \delta})(\Delta y_i - \overline{\Delta y}) + \sum\limits_{i \in C}(\Delta \delta_i - \overline{\Delta \delta})(\Delta y_i - \overline{\Delta y})}{\sum\limits_{i \in M}(\Delta \delta_i - \overline{\Delta \delta})^2 + \sum\limits_{i \in C}(\Delta \delta_i - \overline{\Delta \delta})^2}$$

where $\overline{\Delta \delta}$ and $\overline{\Delta y}$ designate respectively the average values of $\Delta \delta$ and Δy. Since $\Delta \delta_i = 1$ for $i \in M$ and $\Delta \delta_i = 0$ for $i \in C$, after several simple calculations we get:

$$\hat{\alpha} = \frac{\sum\limits_{i \in M} \Delta y_i}{N_M} - \frac{\sum\limits_{i \in C} \Delta y_i}{N_C} \tag{23}$$

Estimator $\hat{\alpha}$ is called a "difference-in-differences" estimator. To construct it, we first calculate the average within each group of the differences between the dates $(t-1)$ and t of the dependent variable y, then we calculate the difference between these two averages. Its interpretation is very intuitive: if $\hat{\alpha}$ is equal to 0, that is because on average, the dependent variable y has undergone the same variations in the treated group (M) and in the control group (C). We may then conclude that the change of economic policy has had no effect. It is necessary, however, to look at the order of magnitude of $\hat{\alpha}$ carefully, for a change of economic policy often affects certain components of vector x_{it} of observed explanatory variables (for example, wages). It is also possible that the nonobserved heterogeneity included in the disturbance ε_{it} depends on variations in economic policy (for example, the entry into the labor market of less motivated persons may be favored by an increase in unemployment benefit). It is best,

Table 1.3

Participation rates of single women.

	Pre-TRA86	Post-TRA86	Difference	$\hat{a}$
Treated group	0.729 (0.004)	0.753 (0.004)	0.024 (0.006)	
Control group	0.952 (0.001)	0.952 (0.001)	0.000 (0.002)	0.024 (0.006)

Standard errors in parentheses.

Source: Eissa and Liebman (1996, table 2).

therefore, to specify carefully the content of exogenous variables in the estimation of equations grounded on natural experiments (the survey of Blundell and MaCurdy, 1999, clarifies in detail many points concerning the application of this methodology to labor supply; see also chapter 11, section 3, of the present work, which is dedicated to the problem of evaluating labor market policies and discusses the conditions under which the difference-in-differences estimator is valid).

Examples of Natural Experiments

Eissa and Liebman (1996) have studied the effects of the fiscal reform carried out in the United States in 1986 on labor force participation rates and hours worked.

The Tax Reform Act (TRA) of 1986 profoundly altered the system of earned income tax credits (EITC) by giving greater financial encouragement to take a low-wage job, but only to those with children in their care. To avoid difficulties arising from intrafamilial decisions (see section 1.2.2), Eissa and Liebman studied only single women. The control group therefore consisted of single childless women, while the treated group comprised single women with at least one child to care for. Eissa and Liebman (1996) then estimated the changes in the participation rate of each of these two groups. The data utilized were those of the March Current Population Survey for the years 1985–1991 (excluding 1987, which was considered the year of the change-over). The treated and control groups comprised respectively 20,810 and 46,287 individuals. The stages by which the difference-in-differences estimator $\hat{a}$ was calculated are summarized in table 1.3.

The first two columns of table 1.3 represent the average of the participation rates for the periods 1984–1986 and 1988–1990, respectively. The third column shows, for each group, the difference between these averages after and before the reform. In this column, the figures 0.024 and 0.000 thus respectively represent the terms $(\sum_{i \in M} \Delta y_i)/N_M$ and $(\sum_{i \in C} \Delta y_i)/N_C$ of relation (23). The difference-in-differences estimator is then deduced and reported in column 4. In order to guarantee the robustness of their results, Eissa and Liebman then estimated an equation of the probit type analogous to (21). In their study, y_{it} is a dummy variable equal to 1 if person i has worked (for at least one hour) during period t, and equal to 0 if he or she has not. The dummy variable δ_{it} is equal to 1 if person i is eligible for EITC during period t, and equal to 0 in all other cases; the term ζ_t is captured by the indicator variables relative to the years covered in the study; and vector x_{it} of observable characteristics contains indications of the number of children in school and not, the size of the family, level of education, age, and race. The estimation of this equation leads to the conclusion that single women caring for at least one child saw their probability of participating in the labor market grow, on average, by 1.9 percentage points (which is of the same order of magnitude as the 2.4 percentage points appearing in the third column of table 1.3). The further studies of Meyer and Rosenbaum (2000, 2001) on the same subject confirm the results of Eissa and Liebman (1996) and underline even more the importance of financial incentives in decisions to return to employment.

For France, an example of this approach grounded in a comparison between a treated group and a control group is the study of Piketty (1998) of the consequences of the extension of the parental education allowance (Allocation Parentale d'Education, or APE) starting in 1994. The APE is a monthly allowance of 3000 French francs (about 40% of the median wage) paid to a spouse who accepts leaving the workforce. Beginning in 1994, this measure was applied to families with two children (one of them under 3), whereas before that date a family had to have at least three children in order to be eligible. This "natural experiment" permits a precise analysis of the labor supply behavior of the subpopulation of mothers of two children (one of them under 3), taking as a control group the subpopulation of mothers with at least three children. Piketty (1998) shows that the fall in the participation rate, which was around 16% between 1994 and 1997 for the treated group, is entirely explained by the extension of the APE. He estimates that at least 35% of the mothers of young children would not have stopped working without this measure. The wage elasticity of the participation rate thus turns out to be particularly high for this category of women.

We may note that experiments can be carried out on purpose by the authorities, in which case we refer to "social" or "controlled" experiments. The Self-Sufficiency Project launched in the Canadian provinces of New Brunswick and British Columbia falls into this class. First, 6000 single parents who had been receiving only minimal social assistance for at least a year were selected at random. Then, from among these 6000, 3000 were picked at random and offered a bonus (amounting to around C$500 per month) which doubled the difference in disposable income between inactivity and employment if they found a full-time job. A year later more than 25% of the treated group were in full-time employment, as opposed to less than 11% of the control group (all the other results of the Self-Sufficiency Project can be found in Card and Robbins, 1996; see also Blundell et al., 1995, for studies of natural experiments in the United States and Great Britain).

To complete this rapid survey, we must note that natural experiments are not confined to the evaluation of public policies; they may also be applied to spontaneous events such as climate change. In this case economists sometimes speak of "natural" natural experiments (see Rosenzweig and Wolpin, 2000). In the domain of labor supply, studies have evaluated the consequences of meteorological change on the behavior of farm families, while others have focused on the impact of children on the working lives of women: the treated group consisted of women who had had twins at their first childbirth, and the control group consisted of women who had had a single child at first childbirth. These studies generally bring out a negative effect of parenthood on labor supply by women.

Value and Limits of the Methodology of Natural Experiments
At first sight the methodology of natural experiments constrasts, by its simplicity, with the structural or econometric approach presented above, which consists of specifying a model and deriving from it equations that are estimated by an appropriate statistical method. The methodological simplicity of natural experiments is an undeniable advantage. Furthermore, this approach makes it possible rigorously to identify the consequences of a particular event, if it is properly conducted. But it has its limitations. For one thing, situations capable of giving rise to natural or controlled experiments are few. For another, each natural experiment constitutes, by definition, a very particular event, the consequences of which cannot be generalized into other contexts in the absence of theory. From this perspective, the structural approach and the methodology of natural experiments are complementary. The structural approach, starting from an explicit model and relying by definition on particular hypotheses, leads to the estimation of elasticities that allow us to evaluate the effects of numerous changes in the economic environment, the fiscal system for example, on behaviors and welfare. The structural approach is thus a valuable aid to decision-making in matters of public policy, since it has the power to *predict*, given well-defined hypotheses, the consequences of different public initiatives. The methodology of natural experiments assists in testing, a posteriori and in a particular context, the success of the predictions of the theoretical models and to some extent the impact of public policies.

2.2.3 Amount of Time Worked and Labor Force Participation Rate

The neoclassical model of labor supply discussed thus far throws light on significant shifts in participation rates, the amount of time worked, and the part-time work of women.

The Evolution of Participation Rates
Figure 1.9 traces the evolution of male and female participation rates in the United States labor market since 1947. The participation rate is equal to the ratio between the labor force (composed of employed workers and the unemployed) and the total population for the category concerned. This figure brings out an important characteristic of the industrialized countries as a group, which is the continuing rise in the participation rate of women for the last several decades. This rise is surely explained by the profound changes in our way of life, but it also corresponds to a steep rise in the wages available to women, accompanied by a fall in the relative price of goods that can replace household work (washing machines, child care, etc.). In these conditions we have seen that, in the model with household production, the substitution effect

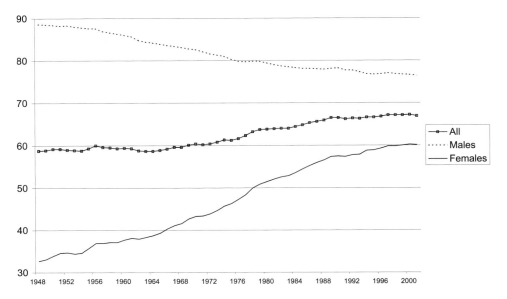

FIGURE 1.9

The evolution in participation rates in the United States for persons 16 years of age and older, 1948–2001.

Source: Bureau of Labor Statistics.

near the borderline of nonparticipation is very important, and induces a rise in participation in the labor market.

Figure 1.10 presents the evolution of participation rates for the whole of the population aged 15 to 64 in the United States, continental Europe (Germany, France, Italy), and Japan since the beginning of the 1960s. It is apparent that the participation rate of men has clearly diminished since the beginning of the 1960s in continental Europe and the United States. For example, it fell 17 points between 1960 and 2000 in the European countries and around seven points in the United States. On the other hand, the participation rate for women did not stop growing over the same period, having gained around seven points in the whole of the European Union and growing by more than 29% in North America. It should be noted that Japan forms an exception to the rule, inasmuch as its participation rates, both male and female, do not show a regular trend over this period. The male participation rate rose by 1.5 points, while for women it rose by five points. We also observe that, for the European countries, the contrary movements of the male and female participation rates approximately cancel each other out, and the total participation rate fell only slightly, by about two points. This observation does not apply to North America, where the very strong rise in the female participation rate has regularly caused the overall rate of participation to advance.

The data on labor force participation also confirm certain predictions of the model of the trade-off between consumption and leisure. Under the hypothesis that leisure is a normal good, we have seen that this model forecasts an increase in the

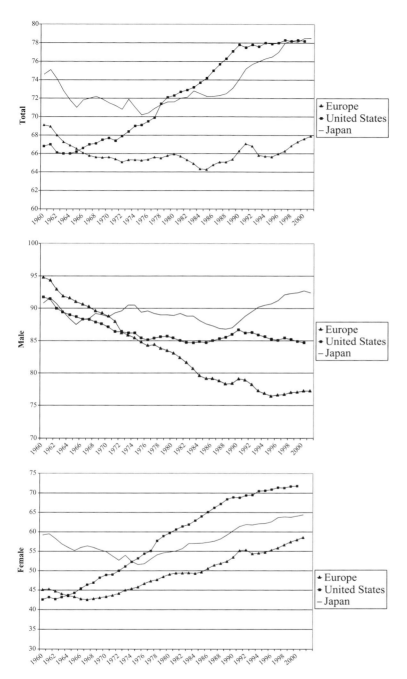

FIGURE 1.10
Participation rates in the United States, Europe (Germany, France, Italy), and Japan.

Source: OECD data.

Table 1.4

Participation rates of women classified by their marital status in the United States.

	Single	Married
1900	45.9	5.6
1950	53.6	21.6
1988	67.7	56.7
2001	78.7	69.6

Source: Ehrenberg and Smith (1994, table 6.1, p. 165) for 1900, 1950, and 1988, and Bureau of Labor Statistics for 2001.

reservation wage when the non-wage income of an individual climbs. Considering that within a couple, the non-wage income of one partner is often linked to the income of the other, the participation rate of married women ought to fall below that of single women. Table 1.4 shows that married North American women do in fact have a weaker rate of participation in the labor market than single women, even if the difference between these rates has a tendency to diminish over the long term. Additionally, empirical studies generally find that if a husband's income rises, his wife's labor supply falls off.

The Trend in the Amount of Time Worked

The long-term trend in the amount of time worked illustrates certain important characteristics of labor supply. Table 1.5 shows that labor productivity, which over the long term shapes the trend of real wages, has not stopped growing since the 1870s, though at a pace that varies at different times and in different countries. Production per hour worked was around 15 times greater in 1997 than in 1870 in Germany, France, and Sweden. It has multiplied by (only) six in the United States, and seven in the United Kingdom over the same period, since these two countries had much higher levels of productivity than the others at the end of the nineteenth century. In fact, before the agricultural and industrial revolutions, productivity had varied very little for several centuries. Likewise, until the industrial revolution, the amount of time worked probably remained stable, coinciding more or less with the hours of daylight. Subsequently, the onset of the industrial revolution saw longer hours: in the factories, we sometimes find that people were present at work for up to 17 hours per day. To work for 14 hours was normal, and a working day of 13 hours was considered short (Marchand and Thélot, 1997).

The historical movement in the amount of time worked can be grasped by using the same elements that allowed us to specify the form of the labor supply curve presented in figure 1.4. The substitution effect was probably prevalent for a few years during the economic take-off, as rural workers abandoned the countryside and went into the factories. But the number of hours worked rose so quickly, along with some growth in labor productivity, that the global income effect came to prevail. Hence the

Table 1.5

Hours worked annually per person and real hourly wages in the manufacturing sector.

	Amount of time worked				
	1870	1913	1938	1997	2000
Germany	2941	2584	2316	1507	1467
United States	2964	2605	2062	1850	1821
France	2945	2588	1848	1603	1532
United Kingdom	2984	2624	2267	1731	1711
Sweden	2945	2588	2204	1629	1603
	Wages				
Germany	100	185	285	1505	1569
United States	100	189	325	586	605
France	100	205	335	1579	1785
United Kingdom	100	157	256	708	819
Sweden	100	270	521	1601	1839

Source: Maddison (1995) for 1870, 1913, and 1938, and OECD data for 1997 and 2000.

diminution in hours of work after the industrial revolution can be interpreted as the consequence of an income effect due to a strong increase in the real wage.

Nevertheless, hours worked have undergone shifts less marked, and differing from one country to another, since the 1970s. In some countries the amount of time worked fluctuates, while it continues to shrink overall in others. Figure 1.11 shows that the annual amount of time worked has slightly increased in the United States and Sweden over this period, while it has diminished in Germany, France, and the United Kingdom. These aggregate figures, which portray the global trend in the amount of time worked, are, however, difficult to interpret without further ado using the labor supply model, inasmuch as they result from different composition effects owing to important changes in the structure of the labor force by age and sex that vary from country to country.

Part-Time Work by Women

For the same amount of work, women's wages are generally noticeably lower than men's (see chapter 5). We have observed that when an individual decides to participate in the labor market, the number of hours that he or she wants to provide decreases with his or her non-wage income. Supposing that for a married woman, non-wage income often corresponds to her husband's income, the model immediately implies that women ought more frequently to be found in jobs with reduced hours than men. Table 1.6 indicates that this is indeed the case, for in the majority of the industrialized countries, women's share of part-time work often exceeds 70%. Of

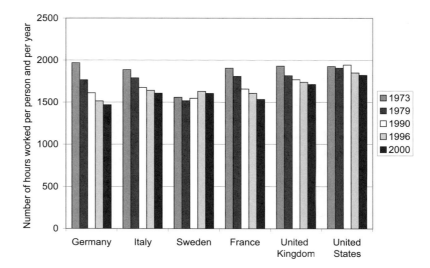

FIGURE 1.11

Amount of time worked annually in six OECD countries over the period 1973–2000 (total number of hours worked during the year divided by the average number of persons holding a job).

Source: OECD data.

Table 1.6

Women's share of part-time labor (in percentage terms).

	1979	1990	2000
Belgium	88.9	89.6	81.1
Canada	72.1	71.0	69.1
France	82.2	83.1	80.4
Germany	91.6	90.5	84.5*
Japan	70.1	73.0	67.5
Sweden	87.5	83.7	79.2
United Kingdom	92.8	87.0	79.9*
United States	68.0	67.6	67.5

Source: OECD data.

*1999.

course, other factors come into play to explain this state of affairs—in our day, household chores and the raising of children are still most frequently the tasks of women—but the value of women's relative wage must not be left out of account.

3   SUMMARY AND CONCLUSION

- According to the neoclassical theory of labor supply, every individual trades off between consuming a good and consuming leisure. The supply of individual labor is positive if the current wage exceeds the *reservation wage*, which depends on preferences and non-wage income. If labor supply is positive, the marginal rate of substitution between consumption and leisure is equal to the hourly wage.

- The relation between the individual supply of labor and the hourly wage is the result of combined substitution and income effects. The substitution effect implies an increasing relation between the wage and labor supply, while the income effect works in the opposite direction if leisure is a normal good. The supply of labor generally rises with the wage at low wage levels (the substitution effect prevails) and falls off when the wage reaches higher levels (the income effect prevails).

- In the neoclassical theory of labor supply, the labor force participation rate corresponds to the proportion of individuals whose reservation wage is less than the current wage. The fact that hours of work are offered to agents in indivisible blocks implies that the elasticity of the aggregate supply of labor may be very different from that of the individual supply of the majority of workers.

- When an individual has the opportunity to devote a part of his or her endowment of time to household production, at the optimum, the hourly wage is equal to the marginal productivity of household work. Household production increases the elasticity of the individual supply of wage work.

- As a general rule, the mechanism of substitution of leisure over time implies that the permanent component of the evolution of real wages has a feeble effect on labor supply, whereas the transitory component affects this variable more strongly.

- The elasticity of labor supply by women is, in general, greater than that of men, which is small. Moreover, variations in the total number of hours worked in an economy flow principally from variations in participation rather than from variations in hours worked by individuals.

- The methodology of natural experiments confirms the results of more traditional econometric studies, showing that financial incentives significantly influence labor supply by women.

- Finally, the neoclassical theory of labor supply permits the explanation of certain characteristics of long-term tendencies in amount of time worked and male and female participation rates.

Overall, the theory of labor supply sheds much light, often in agreement with empirical observations, on the manner in which agents decide how long to be active as wage-earners. It does not, however, allow us to understand why there should be unemployed people looking for work, since this category of the population has no reason to exist in a universe where information is perfect. The theory of the job search abandons the hypothesis of such a universe and succeeds in explaining the simultaneous presence of unemployed people and nonparticipants. It marks an important advance in the analysis of the functioning of the labor market, and forms the subject of the chapter 3.

4   RELATED TOPICS IN THE BOOK

- Chapter 2, section 2: Human capital and wage-earnings prospects

- Chapter 3, section 1: The choice between nonparticipation, job-search and employment

- Chapter 3, section 2.2: Optimal unemployment insurance

- Chapter 6, section 4: The relation between experience and wage

- Chapter 10, section 2.4: Migrations

- Chapter 11, section 3: The evaluation of active labor market policies

5   FURTHER READINGS

Blundell, R., and MaCurdy, T. (1999), "Labor supply: A review of alternative approaches," in Ashenfelter, O., and Card, D. (eds.), *Handbook of Labor Economics*, vol. 3A, chap. 27, Amsterdam: Elsevier Science/North-Holland.

Heckman, J. (1974), "Shadow prices, market wages and labor supply," *Econometrica*, 42(4), pp. 679–694.

Heckman, J. (1993), "What has been learned about labor supply in the past twenty years?" *American Economic Review, Papers and Proceedings*, 83(2), pp. 116–121.

Lumsdaine, R., and Mitchell, O. (1999), "New developments in the economic analysis of retirement," in Ashenfelter, O., and Card, D. (eds.), *Handbook of Labor Economics*, vol. 3, chap. 49, pp. 3261–3307, Amsterdam: Elsevier Science/North-Holland.

6 APPENDICES

6.1 APPENDIX 1: PROPERTIES OF INDIFFERENCE CURVES

If we suppose that the satisfaction of an agent increases with leisure and consumption, so that $U_C(C,L) > 0$, and $U_L(C,L) > 0$, the indifference curves are then negatively sloped. Consequently, the indifference curve associated with level of utility $\bar{U}$ is composed of the set of couples (C,L) satisfying $U(C,L) = \bar{U}$. This equality implicitly defines a function $C(L)$, which satisfies $U[C(L),L] = \bar{U}$. Differentiating this last expression with respect to L, we get:

$$C'(L) = -\frac{U_L(C,L)}{U_C(C,L)} < 0 \tag{24}$$

The indifference curves are indeed negatively sloped. We observe that the absolute value of the slope $C'(L)$ of an indifference curve is equal to the marginal rate of substitution U_L/U_C between consumption and leisure.

The hypothesis of the convexity of indifference curves is equivalent to the property of quasi-concavity of the utility function. Indifference curves are convex if and only if $C''(L)$ is positive. This second derivative is calculated using the equality $U(C,L) = \bar{U}$ and equation (24). We thus get:

$$C''(L) = \frac{U_L\left[2U_{CL} - U_{LL}\left(\frac{U_C}{U_L}\right) - U_{CC}\left(\frac{U_L}{U_C}\right)\right]}{(U_C)^2} \tag{25}$$

Since $C''(L)$ is of the sign of the term between square brackets of the numerator of the right-hand side of equation (25), the quasi-concavity of the utility function corresponds to the condition:

$$U(C,L) \text{ quasi-concave} \Leftrightarrow 2U_{CL} - U_{LL}\left(\frac{U_C}{U_L}\right) - U_{CC}\left(\frac{U_L}{U_C}\right) > 0 \tag{26}$$

6.2 APPENDIX 2: PROPERTIES OF THE LABOR SUPPLY FUNCTION

For an interior solution, relations (2) allow us to obtain the demand for leisure L^*. We thus have:

$$wU_C(R_0 - wL^*, L^*) - U_L(R_0 - wL^*, L^*) = 0 \tag{27}$$

This equation implicitly defines L^* as a function of $R_0 = wL_0 + R$ and of w. We denote this function $\Lambda(w, R_0) = L^*$. Its partial derivatives are obtained by differentiating equation (27), which implies:

$$dL^*(-w^2 U_{CC} + 2wU_{CL} - U_{LL}) + dw[U_C - L(wU_{CC} - U_{CL})] + dR_0(wU_{CC} - U_{CL}) = 0 \tag{28}$$

By replacing the value w defined by (27), so that $w = U_L/U_C$ in (28), we get the expressions of the partial derivatives of function Λ:

$$\Lambda_1 = \frac{\partial L^*}{\partial w} = \frac{-L\left(\dfrac{U_{CL}U_C - U_{CC}U_L}{U_L}\right) - U_C\left(\dfrac{U_C}{U_L}\right)}{\left[2U_{CL} - U_{LL}\left(\dfrac{U_C}{U_L}\right) - U_{CC}\left(\dfrac{U_L}{U_C}\right)\right]} \tag{29}$$

$$\Lambda_2 = \frac{\partial L^*}{\partial R_0} = \frac{\dfrac{U_{CL}U_C - U_{CC}U_L}{U_L}}{\left(2U_{CL} - U_{LL}\left(\dfrac{U_C}{U_L}\right) - U_{CC}\left(\dfrac{U_L}{U_C}\right)\right)} \tag{30}$$

According to relation (26), the quasi-concavity of the utility function implies that the denominator of the right-hand side of equations (29) and (30) is positive. Λ_2 then has the sign of $U_{CL}U_C - U_{CC}U_L$. It is positive if and only if leisure is a normal good (L^* then grows with R_0). If Λ_2 is negative, leisure is an inferior good. Scrutiny of equation (29) shows that an increase in the wage entails an income effect (which we have described as indirect) and a substitution effect corresponding to the first and second terms in square brackets of the numerator of the right-hand side. If leisure is a normal good, $U_{CL}U_C - U_{CC}U_L > 0$, the two effects work in the same way and Λ_1 is negative. If leisure is an inferior good, Λ_1 has an ambiguous sign.

6.3 APPENDIX 3: COMPENSATED AND NONCOMPENSATED ELASTICITY

The Hicksian demand functions of leisure and of consumption good are obtained by minimizing the expenditures of the consumer under the constraint of a minimal exogenous level of utility, denoted $\bar{U}$. They are thus solutions of the problem:

$$\underset{(L,C)}{\text{Min}}\ C + wL \quad \text{subject to constraint} \quad U(C,L) \geq \bar{U} \tag{31}$$

Let us use $\hat{L}(w,\bar{U})$ and $\hat{C}(w,\bar{U})$ to designate the solutions of this problem; the expenditure function, denoted $e(w,\bar{U})$, is defined by the identity $e(w,\bar{U}) = \hat{C}(w,\bar{U}) + w\hat{L}(w,\bar{U})$. By construction, the Hicksian and Marshallian demand functions, respectively $\hat{L}(w,\bar{U})$ and $L^* = \Lambda(w,R_0)$, given by the equation (2), satisfy the identity $\Lambda[w,e(w,\bar{U})] = \hat{L}(w,\bar{U})$. If we derive this identity with respect to w, we get:

$$\Lambda_1[w,e(w,\bar{U})] + e_1(w,\bar{U})\Lambda_2[w,e(w,\bar{U})] = \hat{L}_1(w,\bar{U}) \tag{32}$$

We may point out that function $d(w) \equiv \hat{C}(x,\bar{U}) + w\hat{L}(x,\bar{U}) - e(w,\bar{U})$ reaches a minimum for $w = x$, which implies $d'(w) = 0$ for $w = x$, and thus $e_1(w,\bar{U}) = \hat{L}(w,\bar{U})$. In order to simplify these notations, let us simply use L and $h = L_0 - L$ to designate the solutions of problem (31). Multiplying both sides of relation (32) by w/h, we get:

$$\frac{w}{h}\Lambda_1 + \frac{wL}{h}\Lambda_2 = \frac{w}{h}\hat{L}_1 \tag{33}$$

Moreover, since $L^* = \Lambda(w, R + wL_0)$ and $\hat{L} = \hat{L}(w,\bar{U})$, the Marshallian and Hicksian elasticities of labor supply are respectively defined by:

$$\eta_w^{h^*} = -\frac{w}{h}\frac{\partial L^*}{\partial w} = -\frac{w}{h}(\Lambda_1 + L_0\Lambda_2) \quad \text{and} \quad \eta_w^{\hat{h}} = -\frac{w\hat{L}_1}{h} \tag{34}$$

Comparing (33) and (34), we finally arrive at the equality:

$$\eta_w^{h^*} = \eta_w^{\hat{h}} + \frac{wh}{R_0}\eta_{R_0}^{h^*} \tag{35}$$

In this expression $\eta_w^{h^*} = -R_0\Lambda_2/h$ represents the Marshallian elasticity of the labor supply with respect to potential income. Identity (35) is the Slutsky equation. It links the Hicksian elasticity $\eta_w^{h^*}$ (also called compensated elasticity) to the Marshallian elasticity $\eta_w^{\hat{h}}$ (also called noncompensated elasticity).

REFERENCES

Arellano, M., and Meghir, C. (1992), "Female labour supply and on-the-job search: An empirical model using complementary data sets," *Review of Economic Studies*, 59, pp. 537–559.

Arrufat, J., and Zabalza, A. (1986), "Female labour supply with taxation, random preferences, and optimization errors," *Econometrica*, 54, pp. 47–63.

Becker, G. (1965), "A theory of the allocation of time," *Economic Journal*, 75, pp. 493–517.

Blanchard, O., and Fischer, S. (1989), *Lectures on Macroeconomics*, Cambridge, Mass.: MIT Press.

Blomquist, N. (1983), "The effect of income taxation on the labour supply of married men in Sweden," *Journal of Public Economics*, 22, pp. 169–197.

Blundell, R., and MaCurdy, T. (1999), "Labor supply: A review of alternative approaches," in Ashenfelter, O., and Card, D. (eds.), *Handbook of Labor Economics*, vol. 3A, chap. 27, Amsterdam: Elsevier Science.

Blundell, R., and Walker, I. (1986), "A life cycle consistent empirical model of labour supply using cross section data," *Review of Economic Studies*, 53, pp. 539–558.

Blundell, R., Duncan, A., and Meghir, C. (1992), "Taxation and empirical labour supply models: Lone parents in the UK," *Economic Journal*, 102, pp. 265–278.

Blundell, R., Duncan, A., and Meghir, C. (1995), "Estimation of labour supply responses using tax policy reforms," IFS Working Paper 95/17.

Blundell, R., Meghir, C., and Neves, P. (1993), "Labor supply: An intertemporal substitution," *Journal of Econometrics*, 59, pp. 137–160.

Blundell, R., Meghir, C., Symons, E., and Walker, I. (1988), "Labour supply specification and the evaluation of tax reforms," *Journal of Public Economics*, 36, pp. 23–52.

Bourguignon, F., and Magnac, T. (1990), "Labour supply and taxation in France," *Journal of Human Resources*, 25, pp. 358–389.

Brown, C. (1999), "Early retirement windows," in Mitchell, O., Hammond, B., and Rappaport, A. (eds.), *Forecasting Retirement Needs and Retirement Wealth*, Philadelphia: University of Pennsylvania Press.

Browning, M., Bourguignon, F., Chiappori, P.-A., and Lechène, V. (1994), "Income and outcomes: A structural model of intrahousehold allocation," *Journal of Political Economy*, 102, pp. 1067–1096.

Card, D., and Robbins, P. (1996), "Do financial incentives encourage welfare participants to work? Initial 18 months findings from the Self-Sufficiency Project," Vancouver, B.C., Canada: Social Research Corporation.

Chiappori, P.-A. (1988), "Rational household labor supply," *Econometrica*, 56(1), pp. 63–89.

Chiappori, P.-A. (1992), "Collective labor supply and welfare," *Journal of Political Economy*, 100, pp. 437–467.

Ehrenberg, R., and Smith, R. (1994), *Modern Labor Economics*, 5th ed., New York: HarperCollins.

Eissa, N., and Liebman, J. (1996), "Labour supply responses to the earned income tax credit," *Quarterly Journal of Economics*, 112(2), pp. 605–607.

Fortin, B., and Lacroix, G. (1997), "A test of neoclassical and collective models of household labor supply," *Economic Journal*, 107, pp. 933–955.

Gronau, R. (1986), "Home production," in Ashenfelter, O., and Layard, R. (eds.), *Handbook of Labor Economics*, vol. 1, chap. 4, Amsterdam: Elsevier Science/North-Holland.

Gronau, R. (1997), "The theory of home production: The past ten years," *Journal of Labor Economics*, 15(2), pp. 197–205.

Gruber, J., and Wise, D. (eds.) (1999), *Social Security and Retirement Around the World*, Chicago: University of Chicago Press.

Gruber, J., and Wise, D. (2001), "An international perspective on policies for an aging society," NBER Working Paper 8103.

Gustman, A., and Steinmeier, T. (1986), "A structural retirement model," *Econometrica*, 54(3), pp. 555–584.

Gustman, A., Mitchell, O., and Steinmeir, T. (1994), "The role of pensions in the labor market," *Industrial and Labor Relations Review*, 47(3), pp. 417–438.

Hall, R. (1980), "Labor supply and aggregate fluctuations," in Brunner, K., and Meltzer, A. (eds.), *On the State of Macroeconomics*, Carnegie-Rochester Conference Series on Public Policy, Amsterdam/North-Holland.

Hall, R. (1999), "Labor market frictions and employment fluctuations," *Handbook of Macroeconomics*, vol. IB, chap. 17, Amsterdam: Elsevier Science/North-Holland.

Hausman, J. (1981), "Labour supply," in Aaron, H., and Pechman, J. (eds.), *How Taxes Affect Economic Behaviour*, Washington, D.C.: Brookings Institution.

Heckman, J. (1974), "Shadow prices, market wages and labor supply," *Econometrica*, 42(4), pp. 679–694.

Heckman, J. (1993), "What has been learned about labor supply in the past twenty years?" *American Economic Review, Papers and Proceedings*, 83(2), pp. 116–121.

Heckman, J., Lalonde, R., and Smith, J. (1999), "The economics and econometrics of active labor market programs," in Ashenfelter, A., and Card, D. (eds.), *Handbook of Labor Economics*, vol. 3, chap. 31, pp. 1865–2097, Amsterdam: Elsevier Science/North-Holland.

Hotz, V., Kydland, F., and Sedlacek, G. (1988), "Intertemporal substitution and labor supply," *Econometrica*, 56, pp. 335–360.

Lucas, R., and Rapping, L. (1969), "Real wages, employment and inflation," *Journal of Political Economy*, 77, pp. 721–754.

Lumsdaine, R., and Mitchell, O. (1999), "New developments in the economic analysis of retirement," in Ashenfelter, O., and Card, D. (eds.), *Handbook of Labor Economics*, vol. 3, chap. 49, pp. 3261–3307, Amsterdam: Elsevier Science/North-Holland.

Lumsdaine, R., Stock, J., and Wise, D. (1990), "Efficient windows and labor force reduction," *Journal of Public Economics*, 43, pp. 131–159.

Lundberg, S. (1985), "The added worker effect," *Journal of Labor Economics*, 3, pp. 11–37.

MaCurdy, T., Green, D., and Paarsch, H. (1990), "Assessing empirical approaches for analyzing taxes and labour supply," *Journal of Human Resources*, 25, pp. 415–490.

Maddison, A. (1995), *The World Economy, 1820–1992*, Paris: OECD.

Marchand, O., and Thélot, C. (1997), *Le travail en France (1800–2000)*, Paris: Nathan.

Mas-Colell, A., Whinston, M., and Green, J. (1995), *Microeconomic Theory*, Oxford, U.K.: Oxford University Press.

Meyer, B., and Rosenbaum, D. (2000), "Making single mothers work: Recent tax and welfare policy and its effects," *National Tax Journal*, 53, pp. 1027–1162.

Meyer, B., and Rosenbaum, D. (2001), "Welfare, the earned income tax credit, and the labor supply of single mothers," *Quarterly Journal of Economics*, 116, pp. 1063–1114.

OECD (1991), *Employment Outlook*, Paris.

OECD (1995), *Employment Outlook*, Paris.

OECD (1999), *Employment Outlook*, Paris.

Pencavel, J. (1986), "Labor supply of men: A survey," in Ashenfelter, O., and Layard, R. (eds.), *Handbook of Labor Economics*, vol. 1, pp. 3–102, Amsterdam: Elsevier Science/North-Holland.

Piketty, T. (1998), "L'impact des incitations financières au travail sur les comportements individuels: Une estimation pour le cas français," *Economie et Prévision*, 132–133, pp. 1–36.

Rosenzweig, M., and Wolpin, K. (2000), "Natural 'natural experiments' in economics," *Journal of Economic Literature*, 38, pp. 827–874.

Stock, J., and Wise, D. (1990), "Pension, the option value of work and retirement," *Econometrica*, 58(5), pp. 1151–1180.

Triest, R. (1990), "The effect of income taxation on labor supply in the US," *Journal of Human Resources*, 25, pp. 491–516.

Van Soest, A., Woittiez, I., and Kapteyn, A. (1990), "Labor supply, income taxes and hours restrictions in the Netherlands," *Journal of Human Resources*, 25, pp. 517–558.

Varian, H. (1992), *Microeconomic Analysis*, 3rd ed., New York: W.W. Norton.

EDUCATION AND HUMAN CAPITAL

CONTENTS

In this chapter, we will:

- See that education represents a significant and rising investment in the OECD countries

- See how the theory of human capital explains the choice of how much education to get

- Understand why time spent on acquiring education can also serve to signal individual abilities to future employers

- Grasp how the returns, individual and social, to education are estimated, and gain an overview of the principal results

INTRODUCTION

A decent amount of education, certified by a recognized diploma, is often seen as a basic necessity for winning a well-paid job. There may be several reasons for this. According to the theory of human capital that became popular following Becker (1964), education is an investment that produces knowledge acquisition and increased productivity, which in turn lead to higher income. Some economists, though, see this concept of education as very reductive. Much of what is taught in primary, secondary, and postsecondary institutions brings no immediate payoff in the labor market (and seems not to have the virtue of promoting socialization, either). Studying mathematical functions, for example, is of practical value in only a handful of professions, so why inflict it on vast numbers of students who will never need it? Some justify this kind of study by arguing that it develops a capacity for abstract thought, and therefore promotes higher productivity. Others, however, take the view that the essential virtue of this type of learning is to select individual students. From this perspective, first formulated by Spence (1973), the educational system plays the role of a filter: it selects individuals on the basis of their intrinsic ability, allowing them to signal their abilities to potential employers. If education serves both to acquire knowledge and to select individuals, then we must try to determine the respective weight of each of these dimensions, not only in order to understand the impact of education on income and growth, but also in order to assess the effectiveness of expenditure on education, a large portion of which is paid by the state in all OECD countries. To enable us to grasp the exact role of education, and then if possible to quantify it, we will need a precise conceptual structure capable of representing the consequences of both knowledge acquisition and selection. This is what the economic analysis of education aims at.

Following a review of the main features of the educational systems in the OECD countries, we will see how the theory of human capital accounts not just for the relationship between education and income, but also for the choice of how much education to get. Individual choices will be seen to be socially efficient if the labor market is competitive and if education produces no externalities. We will then see how, when information asymmetries on the labor market were taken into account, Spence was led to emphasize the role played by the educational system as a selection mechanism. In this context, individual choices about education are generally socially inefficient and may lead, in certain circumstances, to overeducation—something that may appear paradoxical, given the degree to which the state strives to favor access to education. The final section of this chapter is devoted to empirical studies that attempt to estimate the returns to education and assess the causal linkage between education and income. These studies suggest that the educational system does make a significant contribution to improving the efficiency of individuals in the labor market by imparting knowledge to them. Thus they highlight the relevance of the model of human capital as a tool for analyzing problems arising from education and the labor market. They also show that education gives rise to externalities that justify, to a certain extent, state intervention in this area.

1   SOME FACTS

This section brings together the principal descriptive data regarding the extent of spending on education in the seventeen OECD countries, and the impact of the educational system on wages and employment for those who pass through it.

1.1   SPENDING ON EDUCATION

On average, the seventeen OECD countries shown in figure 2.1 spend 5.7% of their GDP on educational institutions. According to the OECD definition (OECD, 2002, p. 366), spending on educational institutions includes expenditure on instructional educational institutions as well as expenditure on noninstructional educational institutions. Noninstructional educational institutions are educational institutions that provide administrative, advisory, or professional services to other educational institutions, although they do not enroll students themselves. Examples include national, state, and provincial ministries or departments of education; other bodies that administer education at various levels of government or analogous bodies in the private sector; and organizations that provide such education-related services as vocational or psychological counseling, placement, testing, financial aid to students, curriculum development, educational research, building operations and maintenance services, transportation of students, and student meals and housing. Expenditure on educational institutions as a percentage of GDP runs from 4.5% in Ireland to 6.7% in Denmark and Sweden.

In all countries, education is financed primarily from the public purse, with the consequence that expenditure on education today constitutes a significant budget item. In the United States, where the portion of private expenditure directed to education is higher than anywhere else, the latter still came to only 32% of public expenditure in 1999. In Finland, where the portion of private expenditure directed to education is the lowest, it comes to only 1.8% of public expenditure. For all seventeen countries included in figure 2.1, this ratio averages 13.5%.

1.2   GRADUATION RATES

At the dawn of the twenty-first century, a majority of the population in the majority of OECD countries have obtained a diploma signifying the completion of upper secondary education. According to the definition of the OECD, upper secondary education corresponds to the final stage of secondary education in most OECD countries. The entrance age to this level is typically 15 or 16 years. There are substantial differences in the typical duration of programs both across and between countries, typically ranging from two to five years of schooling. Upper secondary education may either be "terminal" (i.e., preparing the students for entry directly into working life) or "preparatory" (i.e., preparing students for postsecondary education). Figure 2.2 shows that the average percentage of the working-age population that has completed secondary schooling is 65% for the seventeen OECD countries considered here. Educational levels are advancing, for in all countries the proportion of the population with at least

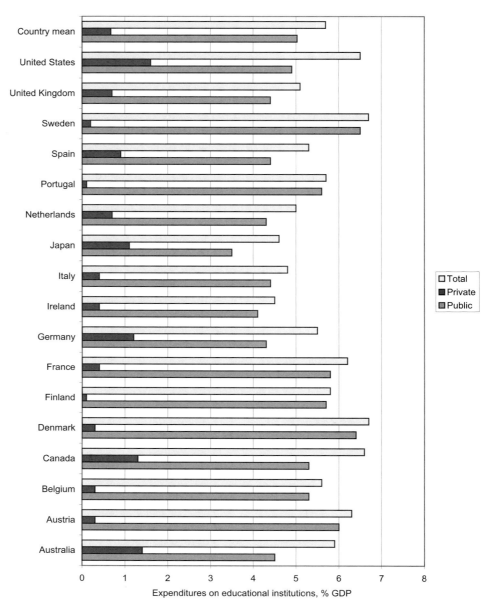

FIGURE 2.1

Expenditure on educational institutions as a percentage of GDP, 1999.

Source: OECD (2002, table B2.1a, p. 170).

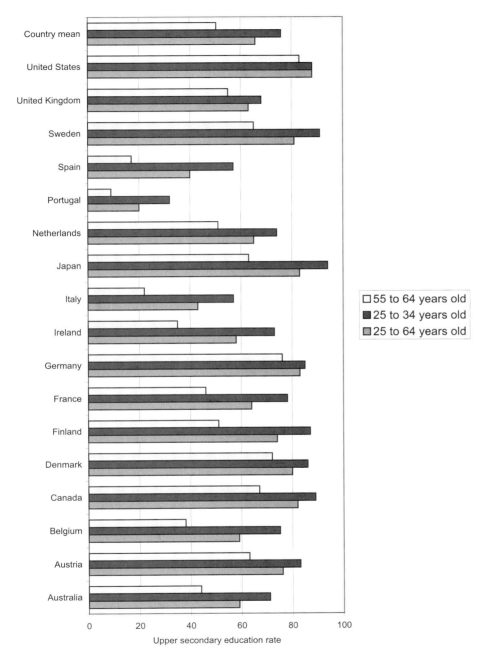

FIGURE 2.2
Percentage of the population that has attained at least upper secondary education, by age group, 2001.

Source: OECD (2002, table A1.2, p. 37).

secondary schooling is higher in the age range of 25 to 35 years than it is in the age range of 55 to 64 years. In this area a convergence phenomenon is observable, inasmuch as countries where the rates of secondary schooling were lower to start with have advanced more rapidly than the others.

Figure 2.3 shows that the percentage of those with a diploma signifying the completion of tertiary (or, in common parlance, postsecondary) education is, on average, 27% for the seventeen OECD countries under consideration. This figure is approximately two-thirds smaller than that for those with upper secondary diplomas. The proportion of individuals with tertiary education is almost twice as high in the age range from 25 to 35 as it is in the age range from 55 to 64. Tertiary education, like secondary education, is thus clearly on the rise, but between these two age ranges secondary education has been advancing more rapidly than tertiary education, since the difference in educational level is 25% for secondary education and 15% for tertiary education. Here again convergence is observable, for the countries where the rates of tertiary education have advanced most rapidly are the ones where these rates were lower to start with.

There is thus a significant increase in the duration of schooling in the OECD countries as a whole. Figure 2.4 shows that for persons aged 25 and over, the average duration of schooling went from 6.5 to 9.5 years in the seventeen OECD countries reported in figure 2.4. Moreover, the duration of schooling is increasing in all these countries without exception. Yet in 2000, average durations of schooling were still widely dispersed: the United States had the highest figure, 12.5 years, and Portugal had the lowest, 4.9 years. It is interesting to note that since the beginning of the 1960s, the United States has held a significant lead in this area. Conversely, some countries are lagging considerably: in 2000, Spain, France, Italy, and Portugal had not yet reached the average duration of schooling that the United States had in 1960.

1.3   Education and Performance on the Labor Market

Higher levels of education are positively correlated with greater labor market participation and with better performance in this market. Figure 2.5 shows that wages rise with educational level in all the countries considered. On average, a worker with less than upper secondary level receives a wage equal to 80% of the wage of a worker who has reached this level. Wage-earners with a tertiary-level diploma receive wages 44% higher than those with an upper secondary diploma. This suggests that acquiring an education is a way to strongly increase one's wages. As well, figure 2.6 shows that, on average, rates of unemployment fall as educational level rises. In 2001 the average rate of unemployment for those with a tertiary diploma was 2.9% in the seventeen countries reviewed in figure 2.6. Persons with an educational attainment below upper secondary level have a more than twice as great probability of experiencing unemployment, since their unemployment rate is 7.5%.

The factual elements just reviewed lead us to three essential conclusions. First, every country dedicates an important share of its total expenditures to education. Second, the majority of persons in the OECD countries that we reviewed stay in

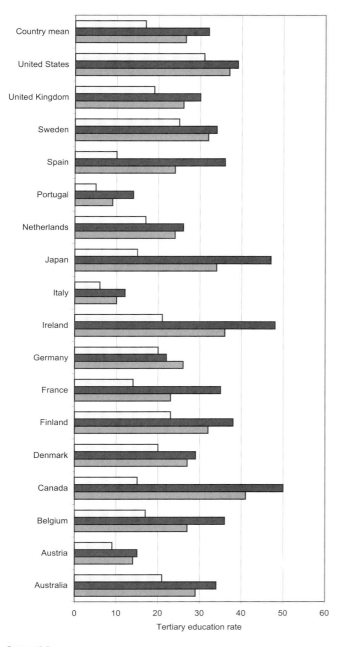

FIGURE 2.3
Percentage of the population that has attained at least tertiary education or advanced research programs, by age group, 2001.

Source: OECD (2002, table A2.3, p. 48).

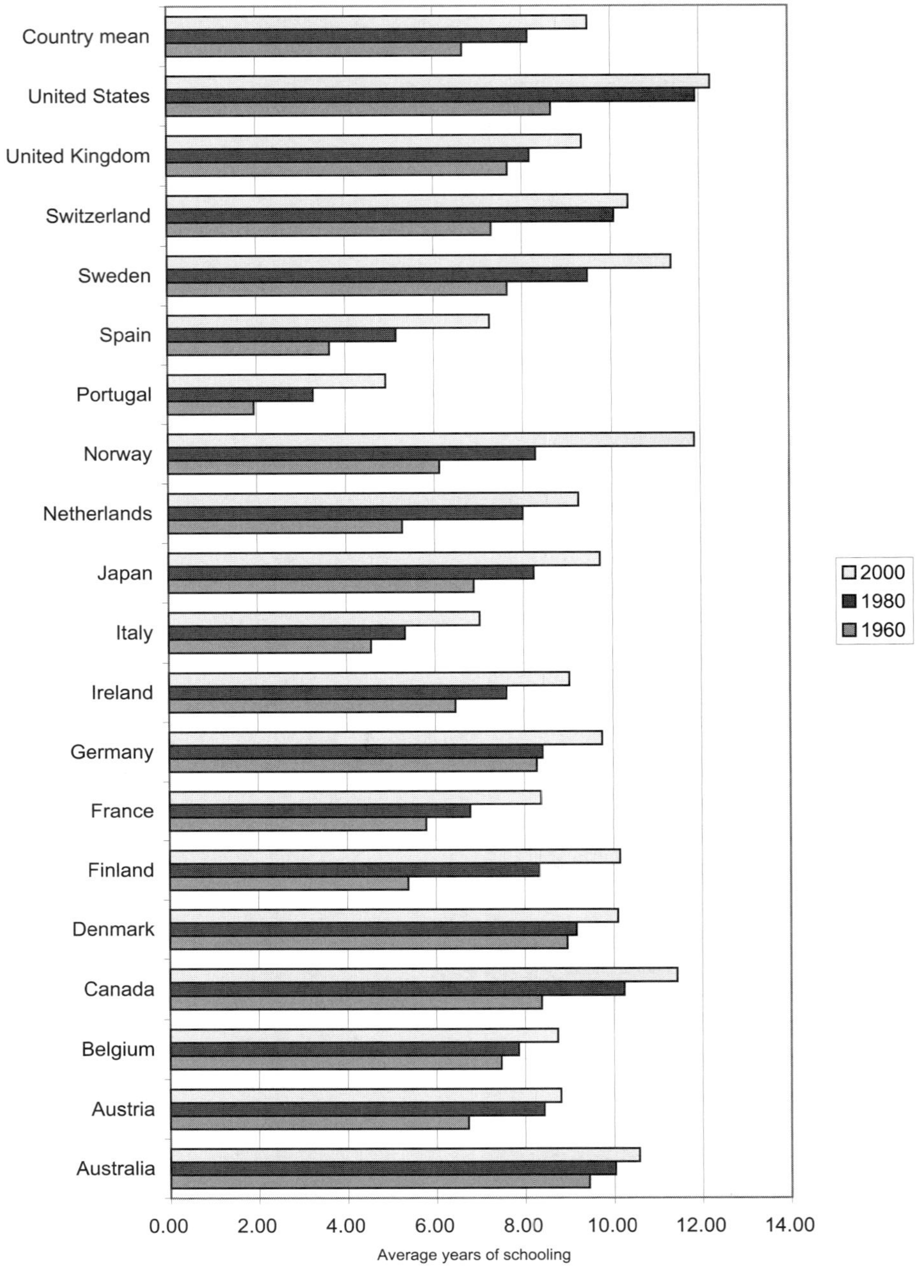

FIGURE 2.4

Years of schooling of the total population aged 25 and over.

Source: Barro and Lee (2000, education data set, available at www.nuff.ox.ac.uk/Economics/Growth/barlee.htm).

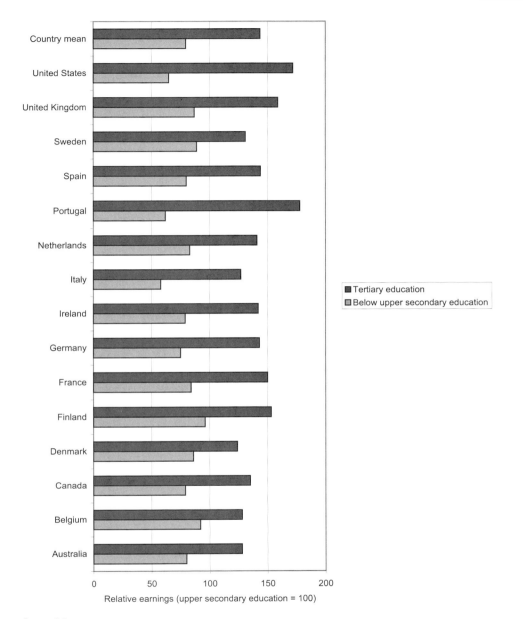

FIGURE 2.5

Relative earnings of the population with income from unemployment, by level of educational attainment, for 25- to 64-year-olds, 1999 and 2000.

Source: OECD (2002, table A13.1, p. 132).

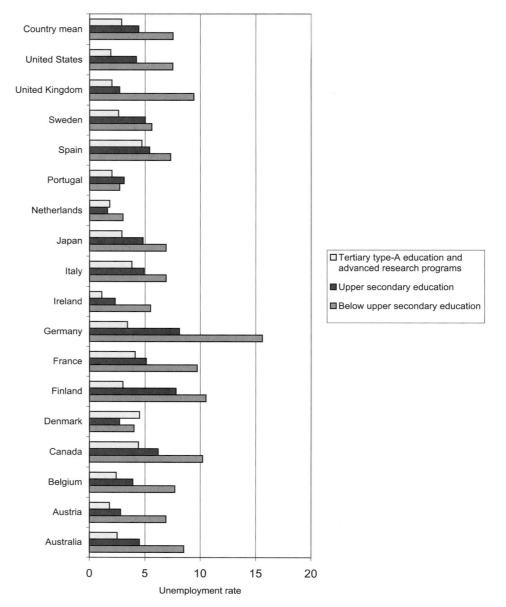

FIGURE 2.6

Unemployment rates by level of educational attainment for 25- to 64-year-old males, 2001. Tertiary type A programs are largely theory-based and are designed to provide sufficient qualifications for entry into advanced research programs and professions with high skill requirements, such as medicine, dentistry, or architecture. Tertiary type A programs have a minimum cumulative theoretical duration (at the tertiary level) of three years.

Source: OECD (2002, table A11.2, p. 118).

school long enough to reach the upper secondary level. Finally, it appears that higher levels of education are linked to better labor market performance. The rest of this chapter will be devoted to exploring and explaining this state of affairs. More precisely, we will see how economic analysis can clarify not only the linkage between education and labor market performance, but also the factors that determine individual decisions about education.

2   THE THEORY OF HUMAN CAPITAL

The theory of human capital, inaugurated by Becker (1964), starts with the hypothesis that education is an investment producing income in the future. In this context, wage differentials are influenced by differences in individual productivity, which are themselves influenced by investments in education or training (the two terms are used indifferently here) made by individuals throughout their lives. To acquire competencies that the labor market will reward brings "training costs" comparable to investments that will be sources of future income. These costs include the expenses of study (fees to enroll in specialized establishments, costs of lodging and travel, purchase of materials, etc.), potential loss of income because the time spent on study is not devoted to remunerated activity, and the psychological costs arising from stress and possibly the sheer difficulty of studying. Investments in education may pay off when they produce an accumulation of competencies—"human capital," as it is called—which brings returns in the form of higher remuneration.

We begin by showing how the mechanisms of competition allow individuals to make their investments in training pay off. We will prove that individual choices about training are socially efficient if markets are perfectly competitive. Next, we analyze the dynamic dimension of educational choices using a simple model in which individuals receive education only at the outset of their active lives—in other words, education is taken as equivalent to schooling (primary, secondary, and postsecondary). In this setting, the number of years spent on schooling is conditioned by individual characteristics and influences future income. We then extend this model by assuming that agents have the opportunity to add to their education over the course of their entire professional lives. We shall see that a simulation of this model conforms very closely to the path of income over the life cycle observed in the real world.

2.1   INVESTMENT IN HUMAN CAPITAL

From Becker's perspective, education can only be a source of future income if wages reflect differences in productivity. Now, it is not at all self-evident that improved productivity on the part of a wage-earner does lead systematically to an increase in his or her wage, even in a perfectly competitive labor market in which firms have perfect knowledge of workers' characteristics, and workers and jobs are both perfectly mobile.[1] In reality, a worker who has acquired competencies and expertise that improve his or her productivity can only make them pay off if he or she is able to play off two or more employers against one another. A single employer would indeed have no reason to raise the wage of a worker whose productivity had improved if that worker could not credibly threaten to take a better paid job elsewhere. This observation led Becker to adopt the distinction between *general training*, which enhances the productivity of the individual concerned for all types of job, and *specific training*, which only enhances his or her productivity for one particular type of job. This distinction is clearly theoretical, to the extent that all training has a certain degree of specificity, but it is analytically useful. General training is fundamentally associated with the worker, who can make it profitable in different types of job and so bring employers to compete for his or her services. Specific training is associated with a particular type of job.

The link between wages and human capital can be highlighted in a very simple model in which the labor force is made up of a continuum of identical workers, the size of which is normalized to 1. Each worker has a lifetime of infinite duration and discounts the future at the rate $r > 0$. If he or she has had the advantage of *general* training equal to i, he or she is capable of producing *over the whole course of his or her lifetime* a quantity of goods $y(i)$ at every instant at which he or she occupies any job whatever. On the other hand, if he or she has had the advantage of *specific* training equal to i for a particular job, he or she is capable of producing *over the whole course of his or her lifetime* a quantity of goods $y(i)$ at every instant at which he or she occupies that particular job. Whenever he or she is not holding a job, each worker obtains z units of goods at every instant. The production function $y(i)$ is assumed to be increasing, concave, and such that $y(0) \geq z$. For simplicity's sake, the amount of time needed to make an investment in training is assumed to be zero.

Competitive Equilibrium with General Training
In a situation of perfect competition, all suppliers of labor who have made an investment i in general training are instantaneously employed if they want to be. The condition of free entry into the market ensures that the profits of the entrepreneurs who employ trained individuals are zero, i.e., $y(i) = w(i)$, where $w(i)$ designates the wage received by a worker who has level i of general training.

In such a case, a worker cannot make a credible promise to share the fruits of an investment in general training with the first employer he or she encounters (the wage-earner receiving less than $y(i)$ if the entrepreneur participates in the investment in training), for once the investment has been made, the worker has an interest in quitting that employer, knowing that he or she will immediately find another firm to offer him or her wage $y(i)$. The upshot is that suppliers of labor are the only real beneficiaries of investments in general training, and so must bear the entire cost of it themselves. Since there is no unemployment, the discounted present value of earnings of a person who has invested an amount i at the time of his or her entry (which date is taken equal to zero) into the labor market comes to $\int_0^\infty y(i)e^{-rt}\,dt = y(i)/r$. Optimal investment maximizes $[y(i)/r] - i$, and is thus defined by relation:

$$y'(i) = r \tag{1}$$

This result signifies that each individual has an interest in investing to enhance his or her general training as long as the marginal discounted return $y'(i)/r$ of this investment is greater than its marginal cost, here equal to 1. Employers for their part have no incentive to finance this type of training, for every worker can obtain a wage increase by offering his or her services to competing bidders as soon as his or her productivity increases.

Competitive Equilibrium with Specific Training

By definition, when training is specific, workers can only make their training pay off in a particular job. Once trained, they are unable to demand wage increases from their employer by making him or her bid against other employers. Hence employers may have an incentive to invest in this type of training. This conclusion will emerge more clearly if we represent the decisions as a two-stage game. In the first stage, employers freely enter the market and compete through the wages they offer to workers. In the second stage, each employer chooses the level of investment in specific training that maximizes his or her profit. Given wage w offered in the first stage, this profit is written $\int_0^\infty [y(i) - w]e^{-rt}\, dt - i = \{[y(i) - w]/r\} - i$. Profit maximization then gives an investment i^* satisfying $y'(i^*) = r$. Free entry in the first stage of the game entails zero profit, and thus wage $w = y(i^*) - ri^*$. As in the case of general training, workers obtain an income equal to their productivity minus the cost of investment in training.

The Social Optimum

Choices made by individuals within the framework of perfect competition lead to social efficiency. This can be verified by writing the problem of a planner seeking to determine optimal investment in training, whether general or specific. Let us simplify matters by assuming that all individuals are born at date $t = 0$. Since $y(0) \geq z$, the planner decides to assign all of them to the technology $y(\cdot)$ in use in the market rather than let them produce z domestically at every moment. If the planner dedicates an amount i of resources to the training of an individual, his problem is written as follows:

$$\underset{i}{\text{Max}} - i + \int_0^\infty y(i)e^{-rt}\, dt \Leftrightarrow \underset{i}{\text{Max}} - i + \frac{y(i)}{r}$$

The solution to this problem is again given by the equality (1). Thus, in a perfectly competitive economy, individual choices regarding training are socially efficient.

The theory of human capital suggests that the mechanisms of competition give individuals an incentive to become educated for the purpose of acquiring knowledge or skills on which the market sets a premium. Moreover, it shows that individual educational choices are socially efficient if the labor market is perfectly competitive.

2.2 SCHOOLING AND WAGE EARNINGS

The theory of human capital throws light on the choice of the duration of studies. It shows that the length of time spent in school is influenced by individual characteristics such as aptitude and inherited human capital, by the discount rate, and by the productivity achieved thanks to the accumulation of human capital.

The Choice Between Getting Educated and Getting Paid

In order to illustrate these propositions, we will examine the choices of an individual who can get educated starting at date $t = 0$ and whose life in the labor force ends at date $T > 0$. The retirement period is set aside for the sake of simplification. We will work with a continuous time model in which the preferences of an agent are represented by an instantaneous utility function equal to his or her current income and by a discount factor $r > 0$. At every moment it is possible to study or work, but not to do both at the same time. Education allows the accumulation of "human capital," i.e., it allows the agent to increase his or her stock of knowledge. We assume that the law of motion of human capital, denoted by $h(t)$, is defined by the differential equation[2]:

$$\dot{h}(t) = \theta h(t)s(t) \tag{2}$$

In this equation, $s(t)$ is an indicator function with a value of 1 if the individual studies at date t and zero if not. The parameter θ represents the efficiency of the effort made by the agent to become educated, so it reflects his or her aptitude. Relation (2) simply means that if an individual decides to become educated, the relative increase $\dot{h}/h$ in his or her human capital is proportional to his or her individual efficiency θ. Assuming that an individual endowed with a stock of human capital h produces a quantity of good Ah, $A > 0$, per unit of time, and that there is free entry into any type of job, profits are zero and the wage received at date t by a person whose human capital is worth $h(t)$ will simply equal $Ah(t)$ when that person works.

In this simple model, we can show first of all that an individual has an interest in accumulating knowledge at the outset of his or her working life and then working without ever undertaking any fresh training (the following subsection, which is dedicated to income over the life cycle, looks at a more general situation). To establish this result, let $\tau > 0$ be the date at which the agent decides to undertake training for the *last* time before retirement, and let $x > 0$ be the duration of his or her training starting on that date (with $\tau + x \leq T$). Before this spell of training the agent possesses a stock of knowledge $h(\tau)$. Given the law of motion (2), his or her stock of human capital will rise to $h(\tau + x) = h(\tau)e^{\theta x}$ at the end of this training period. If we assume, in order to simplify, that the direct cost of education is zero (there is an indirect cost equal to the loss of earnings while not working) and that income is zero during periods devoted to education, the discounted present value of the gain of this agent over the course of his or her life before retirement is written:

$$\Omega = \int_0^\tau A[1 - s(t)]h(t)e^{-rt}\, dt + \int_{\tau+x}^T Ah(\tau)e^{\theta x}e^{-rt}\, dt \tag{3}$$

We can now calculate[3] the marginal return of education at date τ:

$$\frac{\partial \Omega}{\partial x} = \frac{Ah(\tau)}{r}e^{\theta x}[(\theta - r)e^{-r(\tau+x)} - \theta e^{-rT}] \tag{4}$$

For all τ, the optimal length of time spent on training ought to be such that $(\partial\Omega/\partial x) = 0$, with $(\partial^2\Omega/\partial x^2) < 0$. It can easily be verified that these conditions entail $\theta > r$. This signifies that expenses linked to education have to be at least as profitable as financial investments for an agent to have an interest in undertaking training. Taking the first-order condition, i.e., $(\partial\Omega/\partial x) = 0$, into account, we can also verify, by taking the derivative of (4) with respect to τ, that the marginal return to education decreases with the date at which study is begun, or $\partial^2\Omega/\partial x\partial\tau < 0$ when $\theta > r$. In consequence, if the rate θ at which the stock of human capital accumulates is higher than the discount rate r, the marginal return to an investment in training made at any date $\tau > 0$ is inferior to the marginal return to the same investment made at the initial date $\tau = 0$. Under these circumstances, an agent always has an interest in concentrating his or her whole period of training at the outset of his or her life.

The Optimal Duration of Schooling

In order to find the optimal amount of time an agent who decides to acquire education at the outset of his or her life during an interval of time $[0, x]$ should devote to schooling, it suffices to find the value of x, denoted by $x(\theta)$, which sets the marginal return (4) on education to zero for $\tau = 0$. We thus find:

$$x(\theta) = \begin{cases} T + \dfrac{1}{r}\ln\left(\dfrac{\theta - r}{\theta}\right) & \text{if } \theta \geq \dfrac{r}{1 - e^{-rT}} \\ 0 & \text{otherwise} \end{cases}$$

This equation shows that the duration of schooling increases with the duration of life T and with the efficiency parameter θ. Hence the most efficient individuals spend the longest amount of time on education. We also note that $x(\theta)$ is positive only if $r < \theta(1 - e^{-rT})$, in other words, if the efficiency of education and the age of retirement are sufficiently large with respect to the discount rate. Hence it might be optimal not to get any training when the efficiency parameter is too small, in which case the agent preserves the same stock of knowledge h_0 throughout his or her life, which procures for him or her a discounted gain equal to $Ah_0(1 - e^{-rT})$.

The law of motion of the stock of knowledge (2) entails that human capital acccumulated at the end of the training period is equal to $h_0 e^{\theta x(\theta)}$, and thus that the wage of an individual of type θ is worth $w(\theta) = Ah_0 e^{\theta x(\theta)}$ at all dates $t \geq x(\theta)$. Wage $w(\theta)$ increases with the efficiency θ of the educational investment for two reasons. For one thing, each period of education augments the stock of human capital to a greater degree the more efficient the individual is, and for another, more efficient individuals study longer. We also see that the wage depends on the initial stock of knowledge h_0. In this sense, "inherited" human capital influences income from work.

2.3 EDUCATION, TRAINING, AND LIFE-CYCLE EARNINGS

In all developed countries, for all professions, the relationship between age and annual income from employment over the life cycle presents the same characteristics (Psacharopoulos, 1985). After an initial period of education during which no wage

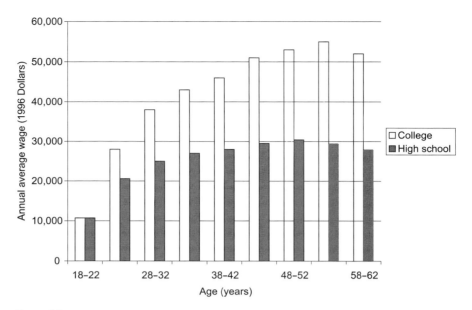

FIGURE 2.7
Average wage gains for college and high school graduates in the United States in 1996.

Source: Ashenfelter and Rouse (1999).

income is received, this curve is concave and reaches a maximum between the ages of 50 and 60 before gradually tailing off. Figure 2.7 portrays this relationship for holders of high school diplomas (12 years of schooling) and college degrees (16 years of study) in the United States.

Ben-Porath (1967), Heckman (1976), and Weiss (1986) have shown that the theory of human capital explains the relationship between age and labor income very naturally. These authors have enriched the basic model just laid out in various ways. For example, Heckman (1976) introduced a trade-off between consumption and leisure. In what follows, we shall limit ourselves to expounding the seminal model of Ben-Porath (1967), which focuses solely on the possibility of continuing to educate oneself throughout one's life. This model in fact arrives at an income profile analogous to the one represented in Figure 2.7.

A Model with Training over the Life Cycle
We shall assume from this point forward that over every interval of time $[t, t + dt]$, it is possible for an individual to dedicate a fraction $s(t)$ of this interval to training. In contradistinction to the basic model laid out above, $s(t)$ is no longer an indicator taking the value 0 or 1, but a *continuous* variable over $[0, 1]$. More precisely, if an individual dedicates a fraction $s(t)$ of period $[t, t + dt]$ to education, he or she works during a fraction $1 - s(t)$ of this period, and so receives income $A[1 - s(t)]h(t)\, dt$.

Thus, his or her gain discounted over the whole of his or her life cycle is henceforth defined by:

$$\Omega = \int_0^T A[1 - s(t)]h(t)e^{-rt} \, dt \tag{5}$$

In order to describe the evolution of the stock of human capital, we adopt a more general representation than the law of motion (2) from the previous basic model. Let $\delta \geq 0$ be the rate of depreciation of knowledge; this law of motion is now defined by:

$$\dot{h}(t) = \theta g[s(t)h(t)] - \delta h(t), \qquad g' > 0, \, g'' < 0 \tag{6}$$

The term $s(t)h(t)$ represents the effort made by an agent at date t to get training. For the same length of training time, this effort is more efficient the greater the stock $h(t)$ of knowledge this agent has. It has been assumed that the accumulation of human capital is a concave function of effort; the purpose of this hypothesis is to obtain solutions for which $s(t)$ is *strictly* comprised between 0 and 1, which signifies that at each period of his or her life, an individual may spend part of his or her time receiving training and part of it working. When $\delta > 0$, an individual's human capital depreciates as his or her knowledge and skills become obsolete.

In this environment, a supplier of labor must choose for each date t the fraction $s(t) \in [0, 1]$ of his or her time to be dedicated to training. His or her problem thus consists of maximizing his or her expected gains (5) subject to the law of motion of human capital given by equation (6). Let $\lambda(t)$ be the multiplier associated with this last equation. The Hamiltonian[4] of this problem is written:

$$H = A[1 - s(t)]h(t)e^{-rt} + \lambda(t)\{\theta g[s(t)h(t)] - \delta h(t)\}$$

If we limit ourselves to interior solutions for which $s(t) \in (0, 1)$, the first-order conditions take the form:

$$\frac{\partial H}{\partial s(t)} = 0 \Leftrightarrow -Ae^{-rt} + \lambda(t)\theta g'[s(t)h(t)] = 0 \tag{7}$$

$$\frac{\partial H}{\partial h(t)} = -\dot{\lambda}(t) \Leftrightarrow A[1 - s(t)]e^{-rt} + \lambda(t)\{s(t)\theta g'[s(t)h(t)] - \delta\} = -\dot{\lambda}(t) \tag{8}$$

Optimal solutions must also satisfy the transversality condition, which, in this problem with a finite horizon, comes down to:

$$\lambda(T) = 0 \tag{9}$$

If we substitute the expression of $\lambda(t)$ defined by (7) in (8), we arrive at the linear differential equation $\delta\lambda(t) - \dot{\lambda}(t) = Ae^{-rt}$. It appears that $\lambda(t) = Ae^{-rt}/(r + \delta)$ is a particular solution of this equation. $\lambda(t) = ce^{\delta t}$, where c is any constant, is a solution of the homogeneous equation $\delta\lambda(t) - \dot{\lambda}(t) = 0$. The general solution is obtained by adding the particular solution to the solution of the homogeneous equation, which gives us $\lambda(t) = ce^{\delta t} + Ae^{-rt}/(r + \delta)$. Finally, the transversality condition (9) yields the value of the constant c. After some calculations we find $c = -Ae^{-(r+\delta)T}/(r+\delta)$, and the multiplier $\lambda(t)$ is thus expressed:

$$\lambda(t) = \frac{Ae^{-rt}}{r+\delta}[1 - e^{-(r+\delta)(T-t)}] \tag{10}$$

The multiplier $\lambda(t)$ represents the marginal value of human capital at date t. Relation (10) indicates that this value decreases with age to reach zero value at date T, symbolizing the end of working life. At final date T, the time spent on education shows only loss of income without any future gains, which entails that $s(T) = 0$. This terminal condition and the expression (10) of the marginal value of capital allow us to determine the values of $s(t)$ and of the stock of human capital $h(t)$, thanks to the first-order condition (7) and the law of motion of human capital (6). Wage income $w(t) = A[1 - s(t)]h(t)$ is immediately deducible.

Calibration Exercises

It is not possible to arrive at completely explicit analytical expressions for functions $h(t)$ and $s(t)$. Still, by taking simple functional forms and reasonable values for the parameters, this model enables us to reproduce wage incomes over the life cycle similar to those generally observed in reality. By way of illustration, figure 2.8 represents the evolution of $s(t)$, $w(t)$, and $h(t)$, assuming $g(x) = x^{0.71}$, $A = 0.75$, $\delta = 0.06$, $r = 0.05$, $h_0 = 5$, $T = 60$, and $\theta = 0.5$. The model is thus calibrated on annual data with a discount factor r worth 5%. The 60-year horizon of working life is justified by the age of retirement, which is 65 in many countries, and the onset of schooling, which normally occurs at around age 5. Figure 2.8 reproduces very accurately the duration of schooling and the evolution of wage earnings for holders of a degree from a college in the United States. It shows that individuals follow a full-time course of studies—$s(t) = 1$—for 16 years, but after that invest less and less in training. The profile of wage earnings is increasing and concave, and reaches a maximum of $60,000 at around 10 years before retirement.

Interestingly, it is possible to represent the difference between the behaviors and the earnings of college and high school graduates by modifying only the value of the efficiency parameter θ. Figure 2.9 does indeed show that when θ has the value 0.4 (the values of all the other parameters remaining unchanged), we obtain a wage profile and a duration of full-time study corresponding to those of a high school graduate: schooling lasts only 12 years, and the wage reaches a maximum of a little under $30,000 at around 10 years before retirement.

These results show that in this model of human capital, the heterogeneity in abilities reflected by parameter θ explains to a large extent both educational behavior and the labor income that flows from it.

Extensions of the Human Capital Model

The model of human capital in which individuals choose the time they wish to dedicate to training reproduces very well the time path of income over the life cycle. Var-

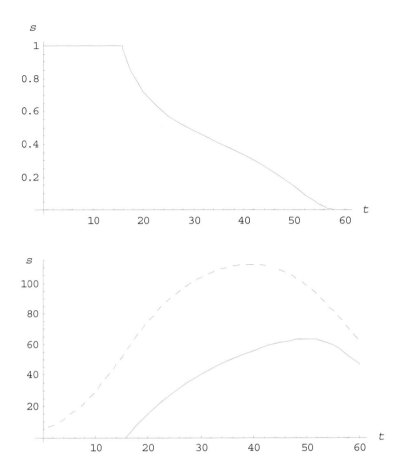

FIGURE 2.8
The law of motion of time dedicated to education (figure at the top), stock of human capital (dashed line in the figure at the bottom), and wage gains (solid line in the figure at the bottom) in the human capital model for an efficiency coefficient $\theta = 0.5$.

ious extensions of this model have been proposed for the purpose of explaining other characteristics of the professional life of an individual.

For example, the amount of hours worked and hourly earnings vary over the course of the life cycle. In a typical profile, the hourly wage begins by increasing and reaches a maximum before retirement. The amount of hours worked also increases at the outset, but peaks earlier than the hourly wage. By introducing hours worked into the human capital model, we are able to take these characteristics into account. To that end, we must assume, as in chapter 1, that the preferences are represented by a utility function $U(C, L)$ increasing with consumption C and leisure L. It is then possible to show that choices among consumption, leisure, and investment in human capital lead to profiles of hourly wages and length of time worked similar to those

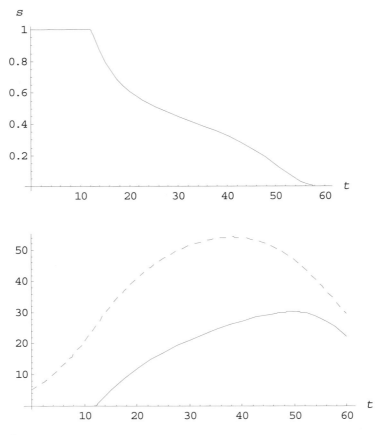

FIGURE 2.9
The law of motion of time dedicated to education (figure at the top), stock of human capital (dashed line in the figure at the bottom), and wage gains (solid line in the figure at the bottom) in the human capital model for an efficiency coefficient $\theta = 0.4$.

observed in reality (see Weiss, 1986, for a synthesis). If we take "learning by doing" into account, these effects are reinforced. Under these conditions, hours spent working are also a method of learning, and thus of improving productivity. There is therefore an incentive to work a great deal at the outset of the life cycle so as to build up experience, then reduce one's working schedule at the end of it.

In practice, choices about education and training are made in an uncertain environment. Intuition suggests that these choices are going to depend on the manner in which uncertainty affects the returns to education in relation to other possible sources of income. If the returns to education are little affected by uncertainty compared to other incomes, a supplementary investment in human capital becomes a way of hedging against risk. Rising uncertainty can thus augment the accumulation of human capital in certain cases (see Weiss, 1986).

As we pointed out at the beginning of this section, the theory of human capital rests on the hypothesis that wage differences reflect productivity differences, which are themselves influenced by the acquisition of competences by workers. The theory of human capital should thus allow us to gain insight into numerous aspects of individual decisions about education. But this conception of education is not uncontested: another theory assigns it the mere function of sending a "signal."

3   EDUCATION AS A SIGNALING DEVICE

The positive correlation, highlighted in figure 2.5, between duration of studies and income does not prove the existence of a causal relationship between these two variables. It is not, in fact, beyond dispute that education permits the accumulation of directly productive knowledge. The ability to resolve differential equations or to understand all the subtleties of Keynesian macroeconomics does not necessarily increase the productivity of a person working in a firm or an agency. On this basis, Spence (1973) put forward the idea that education also—and perhaps even primarily—serves to select individuals, without really influencing the productive efficiency that they will display in their future professional lives. The productive efficiency of a person is seen as a sort of intrinsic quality, which may certainly depend on a wide range of factors (family milieu, personal history, innate qualities or talents, etc.), but over which education exerts little influence.

The premise of Spence's theory is that those persons who perform most effectively in active life are also the ones who perform best while studying. If productive efficiency is not observable by potential employers, then success as a student simply serves to signal the presence of such productive characteristics—hence the term *theory of signaling* given to this view of education. From this standpoint, a person pursues education in order to signal his or her ability, without his or her studies really modifying this ability. If education serves only to signal intrinsic individual qualities, then the real significance of the positive correlation between duration of studies and income is just that more efficient individuals have higher incomes. The standpoint of the theory of human capital is completely at odds with that of signaling theory, because for the latter a prolongation of one's studies does nothing to increase one's productive capacity; all it does is send a signal to employers. Signaling theory also arrives at very different conclusions concerning the efficiency of investments in education. Whereas the theory of human capital indicates that individual decisions with regard to education are socially efficient under perfect competition, Spence (1973) shows that workers have a tendency to overeducate themselves with respect to the standard of social efficiency, if education does serve to signal their productive capacities to employers.

In this section, we present a model in which employers observe the productivity of workers imperfectly, but view a degree, or the length of time spent in schooling, as an indicator of potential productivity. In this context, workers may have an interest in investing in education in order to "signal" their abilities to employers. This aspect of education may lead, under certain circumstances that we will highlight, to over-investment in training.

3.1 A MODEL WITH SIGNALING

We here consider a labor market made up of a continuum of individuals whose productive abilities are different. The size of the continuum is normalized to 1. A worker with ability h can produce h units of a good. For simplicity, we will now assume that there are only two levels of personal ability, h^+ and h^-, with $0 < h^- < h^+$.

Workers do have the possibility to achieve a level of education $s \geq 0$ that is observed by employers. A level of education s bears a cost equal to s/h. Thus, the weaker the productive abilities of workers are, the more it costs. It should be noted that in this model, education does not improve individual productivity; it can serve only to signal ability when it is not observed by employers. At a later stage we shall examine the consequences of education when it fulfills more than one function. The preferences of workers are represented by a utility function $u(R, s, h) = R - (s/h)$, where R designates income, equal to wage w if the individual is employed and to zero otherwise.

We assume that decisions unfold in the following sequence:

1. Workers, knowing which of the two types they belong to, choose their level of education s.

2. Firms enter the labor market freely, observe the signals s, and make simultaneous wage offers to workers.

3. Workers accept or refuse the offers made to them.

Let us first consider a situation of perfect competition in which individual characteristics are perfectly observed. The hypothesis of free entry entails $w(h) = h$, for $h = h^-, h^+$. Since we have assumed that workers get zero income when they do not work and that the disutility of working is zero, hypothesis $h^- > 0$ entails that all workers are employed independently of the signal s which they may send. In consequence, in the first stage of the sequence of decisions, no one has any interest in utilizing resources to send a signal $s > 0$ and so they all choose a zero level of education.

Equilibrium When Ability Is Unobservable
When abilities are unobservable, on the other hand, the signal becomes a way for the high-ability workers to bring themselves to the attention of firms. To that end, it is sufficient for them to choose a level of education that is too costly for the low-ability workers, given the wage differential $w(h^+) - w(h^-)$. In that case, firms are capable of distinguishing between the two types of workers according to their respective signals,

and the equilibrium is called *separating equilibrium*. In this situation, the condition of free entry entails $w(h) = h$, for $h = h^-, h^+$, and workers with low ability send the signal $s = 0$, since a positive signal brings them no gain. For equilibrium actually to be separating, it must be verified that no person of type h^- has an interest in deviating by choosing a signal identical to that sent by higher-ability workers. By sending a zero signal, a worker of low ability obtains a utility $u[w(h^-), 0, h^-] = h^-$, while by sending a signal s^+ identical to that of high-ability workers, he or she obtains $u[w(h^+), s^+, h^-] = h^+ - (s^+/h^-)$. Hence a worker of low ability has no interest in sending a signal identical to that of higher-ability workers if $h^+ - (s^+/h^-) \leq h^-$, which is equivalent to $s^+ \geq h^-(h^+ - h^-)$. Knowing that, workers of type h^+ have an interest in sending the weakest signal possible, which workers of type h^- have no interest in imitating. This signal thus has the value $s^* = h^-(h^+ - h^-)$. Evidently, high-ability workers prefer $s = s^*$ to $s = 0$, since workers of type h^-, whose signaling costs are greater, are indifferent between these two values of s. So in this economy there does exist a separating equilibrium in which low-ability workers do not seek education and obtain a wage $w(h^-) = h^-$, and in which high-ability workers become educated to a level $s^* > 0$ and obtain a wage $w(h^+) = h^+$.

It is important to emphasize that, even in this simple model, the separating equilibrium just described is not the sole equilibrium possible. In fact, the definition of equilibria in signaling games raises difficulties having to do with the beliefs of agents (for an accessible and very thorough discussion of this subject, see Mas-Colell et al., 1995, chapter 13). In general, it is necessary to choose a very restrictive concept of equilibrium in order to eliminate outcomes that appear to have no relevance. It is also necessary to know that Cho and Kreps (1987) have proposed a criterion to be applied in situations of this type and known as the *intuitive criterion*, which results in only the separating equilibrium described here being maintained. In our elementary model, we implicitly selected the most efficient separating equilibrium, i.e., the one that corresponds to the smallest value of the signal that still makes it possible to distinguish between the two types of worker. Other separating equilibria exist in which the values of the signal are greater than s^*. Equilibria of this kind are eliminated if the intuitive criterion is used.

The Inefficiency of Education as a Signaling Device
In the example we gave, it is easy to show that education is a waste of resources that has no social utility. To reach that conclusion, it is enough to compare the allocations obtained with and without the opportunity to become educated when individual abilities are not observable.

Let λ be the proportion of high-ability workers, and let us begin by analyzing the situation in which education is absent and workers are indistinguishable. Since the opportunity cost of labor is assumed to be zero, and since $h^+ > h^- > 0$, everyone participates in the labor market and obtains an identical wage w given by $w = E(h) = \lambda h^+ + (1 - \lambda)h^-$. Normalizing the number of workers to 1, total output is then equal to $E(h)$.

Now let us introduce the opportunity to get an education. At the separating equilibrium, in which the high-ability workers get educated, overall production *net* of the costs of education is equal to the difference between gross production $E(h)$ and the costs of education, equal to $\lambda s^*/h^+ = \lambda h^-(h^+ - h^-)/h^+$. In this case, education is clearly a waste of resources, one moreover that has detrimental redistributive effects for the low-ability workers. These obtain a utility equal to $u(w, 0, h^-) = E(h)$ or $u[w(h^-), 0, h^-] = h^-$, in the absence and presence, respectively, of education. Workers with low ability are thus systematically disadvantaged by education. On the other hand, education has an ambiguous effect on the welfare of the most high-ability workers, who obtain a utility equal to $u(w, 0, h^-) = E(h)$ or $u[w(h^+), s^*, h^+] = [(h^+)^2 - h^+h^- + (h^-)^2]/h^+$ in the absence and presence, respectively, of education. What this means is that education improves the situation of high-ability workers if and only if $u[w(h^+), s^*, h^+] > u(w, 0, h^-)$, which is equivalent to $\lambda < (h^+ - h^-)/h^+$. High-ability workers thus benefit from education if their proportion is sufficiently small with respect to the ability gap between them and the low-ability workers.

So the model of Spence (1973) portrays the role played by education in a very negative light: all it does is select workers according to their ability, without improving the allocation of resources. This result is not a general one, however, and the model that follows offers a case in which signaling activity makes it possible, under certain circumstances, to improve the allocation of resources.

The Efficiency of Education as a Signaling Device
For education to become an efficient signaling device, all we have to do is adjust the preceding model at the margin by assuming that the opportunity cost of labor is something other than zero. The preferences of workers are now represented by the utility function $u(R, s, d, h) = R + d - (s/h)$, where R designates income, equal to wage w if the individual is employed and zero otherwise, d is an indicator function amounting to zero if the individual is employed and 1 if not, and the signal s still stands for the level of education. Let us further assume that the individual characteristic h takes only two values, h^- and h^+, such that $0 < h^- < 1 < h^+$, with $E(h) < 1$. Under these hypotheses, when abilities are not observable and there is no signaling activity, nobody enters the labor market, since the wage compatible with free entry, $w = E(h)$, is less than the opportunity cost of labor. Such a situation arises when the proportion of workers whose productivity is less than the opportunity cost of labor is large. The opportunity of using a costly signaling device may then allow the high-ability workers to enter the market, and so improve the allocation of labor. Let us take a closer look at this situation.

When the equilibrium is separating, workers with low ability stay out of the market, for their productive ability h^- does not permit them to obtain a wage greater than the opportunity cost of labor (free entry dictates $w(h^-) = h^- < 1$). These workers therefore send a zero signal s, since a positive signal brings them no gain. For equilibrium actually to be separating, it must be verified that individuals of low ability have no interest in choosing a signal identical to that of workers with high ability.

By sending a zero signal, a low-efficiency worker attains utility $u(0, 0, 1, h^-) = 1$. By sending a signal s^+ identical to that of high-ability workers, he or she obtains $u[w(h^+), s^+, 0, h^-] = h^+ - (s^+/h^-)$. Consequently a low-ability worker has no interest in sending a signal identical to the one sent by a high-ability worker if $h^+ - (s^+/h^-) \leq 1$, which is equivalent to $s^+ \geq h^-(h^+ - 1)$. Knowing that, workers of type h^+ have an interest in sending the smallest signal that workers of type h^- have no interest in imitating. This signal is given by $s^* = h^-(h^+ - 1)$. As in the preceding model, it is clear that high-ability workers prefer $s = s^*$ to $s = 0$, since individuals of type h^-, for whom signaling is more costly, are indifferent between these two values of s. This separating equilibrium dominates, according to the Pareto criterion, the equilibrium without signaling, since the low-ability workers obtain the same level of gain in the two equilibria—equal to $u(0, 0, 1, h^-) = 1$—while the high-ability workers obtain $u[w(h^+), s^*, 0, h^+] = [(h^+)^2 - h^+h^- + h^-]/h^+$ in separating equilibrium, which procures them a gain exceeding the opportunity cost of labor when $h^+ > 1 > h^-$.

3.2 OVEREDUCATION OR UNDEREDUCATION?

The previous example has shown that education might, through its role as a signal, improve the allocation of resources in certain circumstances. But this signaling role may also lead to "too much" education in relation to what the collective optimum requires. In this case, it is generally desirable to reduce signaling through cross-subsidization, financed by lump sum taxes. This policy consists of reducing the income differential between workers with different signals so as to reduce the incentive to acquire education while preserving positive levels of education.

A Model with Cross-Subsidies

To grasp the effect of cross-subsidies, it will be helpful to utilize a graphic representation of the model just laid out. In the plane (w, s), the indifference curves identified by u^+ and u^- in figure 2.10 apply respectively to workers of type h^+ and type h^-. As the slopes of the indifference curves, dw/ds, are equal to $(1/h)$, low-ability workers have more steeply sloped indifference curves. Moreover, the upward shift of an indifference curve corresponds to an improvement in satisfaction. In the absence of cross-subsidization, the separative equilibrium of the previous subsection corresponds to situation A, in which the high-ability workers obtain a wage h^+ and choose a level of education s^*, and low-ability individuals stay out of the labor market and obtain a gain of $d = 1$.

It is possible to improve this situation by declaring that workers whose level of education is at least equal to s^1 receive wage w^1 and that workers whose level of education is less than s^1 receive a subsidy of amount x if they do not work. This situation, labeled B in figure 2.10, is preferred by both types of workers to situation A. What is more, it limits the expenditures arising from signaling while allowing firms to make the distinction between the two types of wage-earners, since the low-ability workers have no interest in imitating the high-ability workers by getting an education. Cross-subsidies are thus a means of limiting the incentives to overeducation. In our model, it

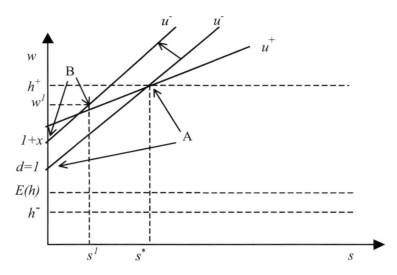

FIGURE 2.10
Overeducation in the model of Spence (1973).

is even possible to curb these incentives very drastically by causing outlays on education to remain positive but tend to zero.

To be compatible with a separating equilibrium that allows employers to distinguish between different types of workers, the wage $w(s)$ linked to a level of education s and the subsidy x accorded to individuals having a level of education inferior to s and not participating in the labor market, must satisfy the conditions $w(s) - (s/h^-) \leq 1 + x$ for low-ability workers not to seek education, and $w(s) - (s/h^+) \geq 1 + x$ for high-ability workers to do so. In consequence, a separating equilibrium is compatible with a value of x lying in the interval $[w(s) - (s/h^+) - 1, w(s) - (s/h^-) - 1]$, and it proves possible to define a value of s arbitrarily close to zero such that there exists a value of x falling within this interval. When $s \to 0$, we get $x = w(s) - 1$, which means that the choice of any wage $w(s) \in [1, h^+]$ and a subsidy $x = w(s) - 1$ leads to a separating equilibrium with a signal the cost of which is arbitrarily low. Such cross-subsidies, tied to an infinitesimal signal cost, allow us to obtain, at the limit, an efficient equilibrium similar to the one that arises in the absence of the problem of adverse selection.

Is There Really Overeducation?
In practice, limiting investment in education through cross-subsidies is only desirable if education is doing nothing but offering a signaling service and if the most productive workers are getting overeducated. Two sorts of reasons make it doubtful that this is a valid representation of education.

For one thing, it is evident that the signaling services supplied by education do not necessarily lead to overeducation of the high-ability workers. The result that there is overeducation rests on the hypothesis that employers do not hire individuals while they are still in school. The model of Spence (1973) does indeed assume that individuals must necessarily finish their schooling before presenting themselves in the labor market. This hypothesis has been criticized on the grounds that employers may have an interest in "intercepting" good students and hiring them before the completion of their schooling (Weiss, 1983). Intuition then suggests that if all employers offer to hire students enrolled in long and difficult courses of study on the same day they enroll, education can no longer play any signaling role. Swinkels (1999) has shown that there are probably good grounds for this intuition: introducing into Spence's model an opportunity for employers to make confidential hiring offers to students before they have completed their course of study entails a *pooling equilibrium* characterized by an absence of outlay on education and workers obtaining a remuneration equal to their expected productivity. Nonetheless, when education increases individual productivity (as above, unobservable by employers), individuals may have an interest in acquiring education. Swinkels (1999) shows that it is persons endowed with low ability who have a tendency to overeducate themselves, in order to mimic workers with high ability. The latter never overeducate themselves, and may even choose a level of education inferior to the one they would opt for in a situation of perfect information if they cannot be distinguished from workers of low ability. These results, which are at variance with those originally obtained by Spence (1973), show that the education system does not lead to a systematically excessive use of resources, even when it is simply acting as a signaling device. They also bring out the fragility of the predictions of models with asymmetric information, the properties of which appear highly sensitive to the manner in which the strategies of agents are represented.

In light of the theory of human capital, there is reason to doubt that public interventions to limit outlays on education are required, for according to this theory, education makes it possible to accumulate knowledge, and thus supplies other services besides that of sending a signal. These two dimensions of education are in fact difficult to separate from one another, but the numerous empirical studies dedicated to the problem suggest that education does help to improve individual productivity (see section 4.3 below).

4 EVALUATIONS OF THE RETURNS TO EDUCATION

The estimation of earnings functions, the goal of which is to evaluate the returns to education, constitutes the basis of empirical work dedicated to education. This type of estimate, which brings out a *correlation* between education and income earned through work, has stimulated a large quantity of research aimed at finding out whether or not this correlation betrays a *causal link* between education and income. This research tries to determine if education serves to accumulate knowledge that has value in the labor market, as in the theory of human capital, or if its main function is to select the most efficient individuals, without teaching them a great deal.

4.1 THE THEORY OF HUMAN CAPITAL: FROM THE MODEL TO ESTIMATES

The main prediction of the theory of human capital is that education is the source of an accumulation of competencies that make it possible to increase income. The assessment of this result is done by estimating earnings functions, which relate income to investment in education. Mincer (1974) proposed a form of earnings function deduced from the theoretical model presented in section 2.2 which arrives at an estimate of the internal rate of return to educational investment. The precision of these estimates is noticeably increased by taking experience into account.

The Internal Rate of Return to Education

Let us first put ourselves in the position of a person who acquires education at the outset of his or her life, but ceases to do so for good once he or she starts to work. By definition, the *internal rate of return to education*, denoted by ρ, represents the discount rate that equalizes the cost and the expected gain of investing in education. Let $y(t)$ be the potential income associated with an amount of time t spent in school. If we assume for the sake of simplicity that the cost of education is identical to the loss of potential income undergone during the time t spent in school, the cost of education at date t is simply equal to $y(t)$. This cost makes it possible to increase income by an amount $\dot{y}(t)$ at every future date. Let T be the date at which working life comes to an end; the present value at date t of the incremental gain $\dot{y}(t)$ discounted at rate ρ is given by $\dot{y}(t) \int_t^T e^{-\rho(\tau-t)} d\tau = \dot{y}(t)[1 - e^{-\rho(T-t)}]/\rho$. The internal rate of return to education equalizes the gain and the cost, and is thus defined by the equation:

$$\frac{\dot{y}(t)}{y(t)} = \rho \frac{1}{1 - e^{-\rho(T-t)}}$$

If we assume that T is much greater than t, the right-hand side of this equation is approximately equal to ρ, and it appears that income satisfies the differential equation $\rho = \dot{y}(t)/y(t)$. Integrating this last equation, we finally get:

$$\ln y(t) = \ln y(0) + \rho t \tag{11}$$

Knowing income $y(t)$ and the associated length of time spent in school, it is possible to estimate equation (11) by the method of ordinary least squares. If t is expressed in years, the internal rate of return ρ can be interpreted as the relative increase in income flowing from an extra year of schooling. The first line of table 2.1 presents the estimate of equation (11) obtained by Mincer (1974) using data concerning white men in the United States in 1959. It is clear that the length of time spent in school has a significant positive effect on income. The rate of return of an extra year of schooling is 7%. Still, the coefficient of determination, R^2, indicates that this equation explains less than 7% of the variation of the logarithm of income. Mincer suggests that this poor performance is caused by leaving out professional experience and the accumulation of human capital that takes place after leaving formal schooling behind.

Table 2.1

Estimates of wage equations: t designates the duration of schooling, x experience (measured by age minus the duration of schooling minus 6 years), and y the annual earnings of white men working in the nonagricultural sector in the United States in 1959 (t-statistics in parentheses).

$\ln y = 7.58 + \underset{(43.8)}{0.070t}$	$R^2 = 0.067$
$\ln y = 6.20 + \underset{(72.3)}{0.107t} + \underset{(75.5)}{0.081x} - \underset{(-55.8)}{0.0012x^2}$	$R^2 = 0.285$
$\ln y = 4.87 + \underset{(23.4)}{0.255t} - \underset{(-7.1)}{0.0029t^2} + \underset{(63.7)}{0.148x} - \underset{(-66.2)}{0.0018x^2} - \underset{(-31.8)}{0.0043xt}$	$R^2 = 0.309$

Source: Mincer (1974, table 5.1).

The Importance of Experience

To improve his estimates, Mincer makes the assumption that it is possible to acquire education while employed. The life-cycle model of human capital accumulation set out in section 2.3 does in fact suggest that it is optimal to begin with full-time schooling, then gradually diminish the proportion of one's time dedicated to schooling from the time one enters the labor force. Let $s(\tau) \in [0, 1]$ be the portion of time dedicated to further training by a person with τ years of experience who has already spent t years in school. As in the theoretical model of section 2.3, we assume that the law of motion of the human capital $h(t + \tau)$ of this person is described by the differential equation:

$$\dot{h}(t + \tau) = \rho_x s(\tau) h(t + \tau), \qquad \forall \tau \in [0, T - t]$$

In this expression, the constant coefficient ρ_x is interpretable as the rate of return to training after leaving school. The integration of this differential equation between dates $\tau = 0$ and $\tau = x$ then gives $h(t + x) = h(t)e^{\rho_x \int_0^x s(\tau)\,d\tau}$. Assuming again that income $y(t + \tau)$ is equal to $A[1 - s(\tau)]h(t + \tau)$, the income $y(t + x)$ of a person with x years of experience depends on his or her income $y(t)$ upon leaving school and on his or her time devoted to further training, according to the formula:

$$y(t + x) = [1 - s(x)]y(t)e^{\rho_x \int_0^x s(\tau)\,d\tau} \tag{12}$$

In order to arrive at an explicit wage equation, Mincer assumes $s(x) = s_0 - s_0(x/T)$. Under this hypothesis, the fraction of time dedicated to the accumulation of human capital decreases in linear fashion with the amount of time passed since leaving school. We then have $\int_0^x s(\tau)\,d\tau = s_0x - (s_0/2T)x^2$. Taking the logarithms of the two sides of relation (12), and bearing in mind that income $y(t)$ after t years of schooling satisfies the law of motion (11), we arrive at the wage equation:

$$\ln y(t + x) = \ln y(0) + \rho t + \rho_x s_0 x - \rho_x(s_0/2T)x^2 + \ln[1 - s(x)] \tag{13}$$

It should be noted that the variable x representing experience has an ambiguous status, for experience can result not only from—as we assume here—an investment that eats into efficient working time (*learning or doing*), but also from an accumulation of know-how that the worker builds up during his or her efficient working time (*learning by doing*). In the latter case, we can make the assumption that a worker acquires a significant amount of supplementary knowledge on the job at the beginning of his or her career, and that such supplements in knowledge then tail off over time. That being so, it is sufficient to assume $s(x) = 0$ in (13).

The second line of table 2.1 presents the results of the estimation of an earnings function deduced from equation (13) leaving out the term $\ln[1 - s(x)]$. It indicates that bringing experience into the mix considerably improves the explanatory power of the earnings function. This function now explains around 30% of the variation of the logarithms of income, as opposed to 7% earlier. Further, comparison of the first two lines of table 2.1 shows that the rate of return to formal schooling is greater than that obtained by leaving out experience. Leaving out experience biases the estimate of the returns to formal schooling downward, because schooling and experience are *negatively* correlated (those with the most experience are also those who leave school earliest). Hence, to estimate the return to education while leaving out the return to experience amounts to neglecting the fact that at a certain age, an extra year of schooling means one less year of experience. This omission leads to an estimate of the return to education from which the return to experience is *subtracted*, since the fact that persons who dedicate an extra year to schooling necessarily have one less year of experience is not taken into acccount.

The Importance of the Duration of Schooling

The earnings function defined by equation (13) is grounded in the hypothesis of a constant rate of return to formal schooling, equal to ρ. This hypothesis is debatable, for the impact of education very likely varies with the duration of schooling. The third line of table 2.1 takes this possibility into account by introducing a quadratic term t^2 and a term of interaction tx between experience and the duration of schooling. We see that the rate of return to education decreases with the duration of schooling. We also see that there is a negative interaction between the duration of schooling and experience, which would tend to prove that the return to experience decreases with the duration of schooling. Mincer (1974) shows, however, that this result is not significant when income is measured in weekly earnings.

This presentation of a procedure for estimating the returns to education gives us an overview of the method followed in the seminal work of Mincer. This method has been refined in several respects, in particular in order to analyze in more depth the causal relation between education and income.

4.2   IDENTIFYING THE CAUSAL RELATION BETWEEN EDUCATION AND INCOME

The correlation between duration of schooling, or more generally investments in training, on the one hand, and income on the other, of the kind revealed in table 2.1, does not signify that there exists a *causal* relation between these two variables. Indeed, the model of human capital presented in section 2.2 shows that individual capacities (measured by the parameter θ in this model) influence both wages and the duration of studies. In addition, according to the theory of *signaling* (see section 3.2 above), education plays a filtering role, serving to select those workers who are innately efficient and to signal productive characteristics of workers that employers cannot directly observe. That being so, the correlation between duration of schooling and income would stem from the fact that the high-ability individuals have higher incomes and stay in school longer.

Ability Bias and Selection Bias

The theories of signaling and human capital both predict that the high-ability persons study for longer durations and obtain, for a given level of education, higher incomes. Thus, duration of education and income are codetermined by individual capacities: the correlation between the duration of studies and income simultaneously reflects the fact that the high-ability persons study longer and the fact that education increases income by improving an individual's stock of knowledge. Hence, if the returns to education are estimated by the ordinary least squares method, the result will be biased. Following the simplest model, represented by equation (11), the returns to education can be estimated using the relation:

$$\ln y_i = a + \rho t_i + \varepsilon_i, \tag{14}$$

In this expression, y_i, t_i and ε_i designate respectively the income of individual i, his or her duration of studies, and an error term of zero mean reflecting the heterogeneity of individuals. The coefficients a and ρ are parameters to be estimated. The ordinary least squares estimator of the returns to education, ρ, is unbiased if t_i and the error term ε_i are independent. But as we have just seen, the theoretical models suggest that individual capacities (measured by the term ε_i) influence the duration of studies, so the two terms t_i and ε_i are not independent. Therefore the estimator of the returns to education by ordinary least squares is biased. More precisely, two types of bias may be distinguished.

Ability bias inheres in the relation between individual abilities and duration of schooling and leads to an overestimate of the returns to education. The theory of human capital and signaling theory both do predict that the most productive individuals have an interest in studying for the longest period. In these conditions, part of the return attributed to education comes, in fact, from individual capacities, and so the returns to education are overestimated.

The second type of bias is *selection bias*. It results from the fact that individuals likely choose the kinds of study at which they are most efficient and motivated. Let us assume that a lawyer who has engaged in the study of the law for many years is potentially a bad garage owner. Let us also assume that a garage owner—who has generally spent less time in school, and studied things that require different aptitudes—is potentially a mediocre lawyer. This being so, the estimation of an earnings function carried out by the ordinary least squares method leads to an underestimate of the return to education for those who study for long periods and an overestimate for those who study less or not at all. Hence the return to study of the law is underestimated for the lawyer and overestimated for the garage owner, and conversely the return to mechanical studies is overestimated for the lawyer and underestimated for the garage owner.

How to Correct for Biases?

Ideally we could correct the biases just mentioned using a "natural" experiment, which would consist of randomly imposing different durations of schooling on a sufficiently large number of individuals. On average, then, the only difference between two individuals would be the duration of their schooling. In this type of experiment, the estimation of earnings functions by ordinary least squares is unbiased, and the correlation does effectively correspond to a causal relation between duration of schooling and income. In practice there are obviously no such experiments, and the estimation of earnings functions made on the basis of available data is potentially biased. Two types of method have been adopted in order to escape ability bias and selection bias.

(i) The instrumental variable method consists of estimating the returns to education using a variable that influences the duration of studies while remaining independent of individual capacities. To be precise, this instrumental variable must be independent of the error term ε_i in equation (14) and correlated as closely as possible with duration of studies. We then regress the duration of studies t_i onto the instrumental variable, and so obtain the predicted values $\hat{t}_i$. In the next stage, we regress income y_i onto the predicted values $\hat{t}_i$ of the duration of studies, and thus arrive at the intrumental variable estimator. It must be emphasized that this method is valid only if the instrumental variable is indeed independent of the error term, yet correlated with the duration of studies. The difficulty of this approach thus lies in finding such variables. In this respect, Angrist and Krueger (1991) have made an interesting contribution: it consists of exploiting the existence of events that are much like natural experiments. Angrist and Krueger (1991) noted that individuals born early in the calendar year have shorter durations of schooling than those born later. This effect is due to the compulsory duration of schooling. Two persons born in the same year begin school on the same date, but the one born earlier is authorized to quit school earlier than the other. If we assume that the date of one's birth is independent of factors influencing abilities and preferences, this phenomenon entails an exogenous variation in the duration of schooling that may be utilized as an instrumental variable. The estimation of the impact of this exogenous component of variation in the duration of schooling in an earnings function leads to results close to those obtained by the ordinary least squares method. Angrist and Krueger generally obtain slightly higher coefficients, but not significantly different at the threshold of 5%. These results point to the conclusion that ability and selection biases do not have huge quantitative effects, a conclusion on which the numerous debates provoked by their study have failed to cast serious doubt (see Card, 1999).

(ii) The second method consists of using the ordinary least squares method with data about individuals whose abilities are as alike as possible. From this perspective, numerous contributions estimate the returns to education for siblings, and some studies have even used populations made up of homozygotic twins (Ashenfelter and Rouse, 1998). They find that the differences in the returns to education between such twins are slightly weaker (on the order of 10%) than those obtained by comparing the duration of schooling and incomes of any two individuals at random. If we accept the premise that homozygotic twins have identical abilities (a hypothesis documented by Ashenfelter and Rouse, 1998), these results also show that ability and selection biases have little weight. Estimations carried out by the ordinary least squares method on the whole of the population only overestimate the returns to education very slightly. This suggests that ability bias and selection bias, without being negligible, are not dominant in the educational process.

4.3 THE THEORY OF HUMAN CAPITAL: MEASURING THE BENEFITS AND COSTS OF EDUCATION

The evaluation of the returns to education proposed by Mincer relies on measuring the cost of education by years of schooling and measuring the benefits by annual income. In this area problems of measurement error, arising from the fact that persons state the duration of their studies inaccurately, bias the estimator by ordinary least squares systematically downward (see, for example, Kennedy, 2003, and Card, 1999). Card (1999) suggests that numerous studies are subject to this type of error and therefore significantly underestimate the returns to education (to a degree varying between 10% and 30%). In addition to measurement errors, the assessment of the returns to education proposed by Mincer takes into account only part of the costs and benefits of education. It is important to point out that, in reality, the costs and benefits of education have multiple components, most of which are not adequately taken into account in many empirical studies.

Better Measurement of the Gains of Education
Equating the benefits of education with annual income may lead to underestimating the return to education, for better trained workers generally work a longer amount of time over the course of a year. They enjoy higher incomes, which yield incentive to work more in order to fully exploit their investment in education. Table 2.2 shows that the duration of schooling does in fact have a positive impact on the length of time worked. It is also evident that the coefficient of annual earnings is equal to the sum of the coefficients of hourly income and hours worked. This result is verified by construction, for the logarithm of annual earnings is equal to the sum of the logarithms of hours worked and hourly earnings. Table 2.2 indicates that better educated individuals enjoy higher incomes for two reasons: their hourly incomes are higher, and their work schedules are heavier.

Taking exclusively the monetary and individual benefits of education into account also introduces biases that probably lead to underestimates of the individual

Table 2.2

Estimates of the return to education, based on an earnings equation in the United States in 1994–1996.

	Hourly income	Log hours per year	Log annual earnings
Men			
Coefficient linked to education	0.100 (0.001)	0.042 (0.001)	0.142 (0.001)
R^2	0.328	0.222	0.403
Women			
Coefficient linked to education	0.109 (0.001)	0.056 (0.001)	0.165 (0.001)
R^2	0.247	0.105	0.247

Standard errors in parentheses.

Source: Card (1999, p. 1809).

and social returns to education. Better educated workers generally enjoy better working conditions and greater social status. Schooling also equips individuals to grasp concepts that facilitate the comprehension of various political, psychological, and philosophical problems. These concepts do not necessarily have any direct impact on earnings won in the market, but they may contribute to an improvement in welfare. This dimension is important, inasmuch as it suggests that monetary returns capture only a part of all the benefits from education. It also suggests that individual returns are different from social returns. So, for example, education reduces criminality, favors voter participation, and appears to exert a positive influence on the performances of an individual's direct descendants (this last effect is a subject of controversy; see Solon, 1999, and Maurin, 2002). We shall come back to this issue in section 4.4 below.

Better Measurement of the Costs and the Quality of Education

Equating the cost of education with the loss of income arising from the time dedicated to schooling also amounts to a reductive hypothesis. In reality, this cost has multiple components. In particular, an investment in education requires effort to acquire knowledge. This acquisition, when successful, is generally rewarded with a degree capable of influencing the benefits derived from an extra year of study. Jaeger and Page (1996) estimate that the acquisition of a degree has a significant impact on hourly wages in the United States. Comparing the performances of individuals who obtained a degree with those of individuals who failed, these authors find that the degree contributes to around one-quarter of the return to education of 16 years of study, and to more than half of the return to the four years from the 12th (the last year of high school) to the 16th (the last year of undergraduate study in college). In France, the work of Goux and Maurin (1994) shows that years of study not recognized by a degree entail significant variations in remuneration (+3.2% per year), but nevertheless have an impact two to three times weaker than years that are so recognized. Goux and Maurin (1994) also estimate that the type of degree significantly influences earnings in France, where, as in Germany, different educational systems coexist and compete. An engineering degree from a *grande école* (an elite postsecondary institution) leads to wages 25% higher than the degree awarded upon completion of the *deuxième cycle* in university (the equivalent of a master's degree), though the periods of study are of comparable length. More generally, empirical studies generally find that persons who achieve the highest scores on tests measuring knowledge obtain higher incomes in the labor market (Murnane et al., 1995, 2001; Currie and Thomas, 2000).

It is possible that the quality of each year of education, which influences what students learn, is linked to the amount invested by society in this area. Indeed, in the OECD countries a significant part of the differences in students' performance on knowledge tests is explained by their attendance at different educational institutions. This fact is illustrated by figure 2.11, which breaks down the variation in reading literacy performance of 15-year-old students in OECD countries between schools and within schools. For the average of these countries, 33% of the variation in students' performance is explained by their attendance at different schools. A phenomenon of this kind may arise both from heterogeneity in the quality of schools and from a concentration of the best students in certain schools. The quality of schools is itself potentially linked to the financial resources at their disposal.

From this perspective, some studies find that the teacher/pupil ratio, the expenditure per pupil, and the wages of teachers appear to have a positive impact on income obtained by students when they leave school (Card and Krueger, 1992; Altonji and Dunn, 1996). For example, Card and Krueger (1992), using data for the United States, estimate that bringing the pupil/teacher ratio down by ten increases the rate of return to education by around nine percentage points. Hanushek et al. (1996) conclude, however, that these results stem from an aggregation bias due to the fact that Card and Krueger (1992) consider only the average characteristics of schools by state, and not the characteristics of the school of each individual. Moreover, numerous studies show there is no robust statistical relation between the quality of education and the performance of pupils on knowledge tests. Hanushek (2002) reviewed the results of 376 published studies focusing on the impact of expenditure on education on the performance of students; the results are summarized in table 2.3. Although the studies reviewed cannot all be regarded as identical in quality (a problem that Hanushek discusses), we see clearly that it is difficult to detect a systematic influence of expenditure on education on the performance of students.

These results suggest that the heterogeneity in the average performance of schools comes partly from the fact that some schools attract the best pupils while others attract the worst ones. If there does exist a positive interaction between the performances of pupils, and if these performances are themselves positively influenced by parental income, this selection may result in a phenomenon of segregation, in which the wealthiest persons mostly send their children to the same schools

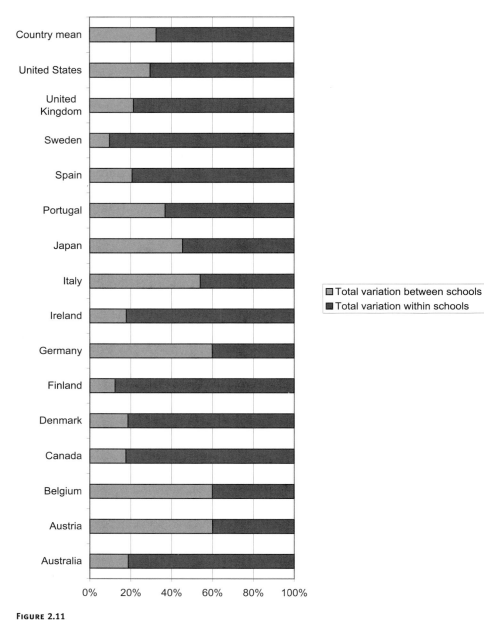

FIGURE 2.11

Variation in student performance between schools and within schools on the Programme for International Student Assessment (PISA) reading literacy scale, year 2000. Information on the PISA scale is available at http://www.pisa.oecd.org.

Source: OECD (2002, table A7.1, p. 90).

Table 2.3

Percentage distribution of estimated effect of key resources on student performance, based on 376 studies.

Resources	Number of estimates	Statistically significant		Statistically insignificant (%)
		Positive (%)	Negative (%)	
Classroom resources				
Teacher-pupil ratio	276	14	14	72
Teacher education	170	9	5	86
Teacher experience	206	29	5	66
Financial aggregates				
Teacher salary	118	20	7	73
Expenditure per pupil	163	27	7	66
Other				
Facilities	91	9	5	86
Administration	75	12	5	83
Teacher test scores	41	37	10	53

Source: Hanushek (2002, table 6).

(Benabou, 1993, 1996). The empirical identification of social interactions is nevertheless difficult to achieve, inasmuch as it is difficult to distinguish the influence of the unobserved characteristics of individuals from that of social interactions (Manski, 2000; Brock and Durlauf, 2001). In this context, there is a danger of explaining individual performances through the influence of peers, when they might actually be arising from personal characteristics not observed by the econometrician. Still, it should be noted that empirical studies focusing on the influence of peers on individual performance in educational settings do generally detect positive interactions (Hanushek et al., 2003; Zimmer and Toma, 2000).

4.4 SOME EMPIRICAL RESULTS

In recent decades, empirical work has essentially been dedicated to the estimation of the private returns to education, following the lead of Mincer. Although problems of interpretation continue to be raised, this work gives a fairly precise idea of the individual returns to education. More recently, empirical work has tried to go beyond the assessment of private returns to education in an attempt to estimate its returns to society as a whole.

Private Returns to Education

Numerous studies have focused on estimating the private returns to education. They use very diverse methods, such as ordinary least squares, instrumental variables, and comparison of the performance of twins or members of the same family (see section 4.2). With such a variety of methods, there was a risk of reducing the transparency of the results, and making consensus on the order of magnitude of the returns to education hard to achieve. Despite this, it turns out that the differences in the results obtained using ordinary least squares, instrumental variables, and the comparison of persons with similar family backgrounds are very slight. Ashenfelter et al. (2000) analyzed 27 studies that produced 96 estimations for nine countries. Their conclusion was that the average rate of return to education estimated according to the method of ordinary least squares is equal to 6.4% (with a standard error equal to 0.4%). This differs little from the rate obtained with the method of instrumental variables: 8.1% (with a standard error amounting to 0.9%).

Figure 2.12 presents estimates of the returns to education for 15 European countries in 1994 and 1995. These returns are calculated by estimating a Mincer equation close to equation (13) by ordinary least squares. On average, an extra year of schooling increases wages for women by 7.9% and increases wages for men by 7.2%. The returns estimated are very heterogeneous. They range from 11.8% for women in the United Kingdom to 3.8% in Sweden. We may note that the returns are relatively weak in the Scandinavian countries like Sweden, Denmark, and Norway, where centralized collective bargaining tends to reduce the spread of wages between different levels of qualification.[5] We see as well that returns to education are higher for women than for men on average, although this is not the case in all the countries considered. This should not make us forget that wages for women are still lower than those for men with the same educational level, as we shall see in chapter 5. Figure 2.12 shows clearly that, although they are less well paid than men for a given educational level, women nonetheless capture an average marginal gain from education exceeding that for men.

The results presented in figure 2.12 have the drawback, in common with many estimates of the returns to education, of not taking precise account of the costs of schooling. These costs are simply assimilated to the loss of earnings resulting from being enrolled in the education system. On that basis, the internal returns to education measure the returns to an extra year of schooling, or to a dollar invested in education, without distinction. Work carried out by the OECD (2002) and presented in figure 2.13 makes available estimates of the returns to education in a number of countries that take the costs of schooling into account in a more exact manner. As in Mincer's approach, the rates of return to education are calculated on the assumption that the student has no earnings while studying. The costs equal forgone earnings net of taxes adjusted for the probability of being in employment less the resources made available to students in the form of grants and loans, plus tuition fees. The benefits are the gains in post-tax earnings adjusted for higher employment probability less the repayment, if any, of public support during the period of study. Unemployment benefits and retirement pensions are left out of the reckoning.

Figure 2.13 shows that for these ten countries, the rates of return estimated are on average of the same order of magnitude, 11%, for men and women, as well as for

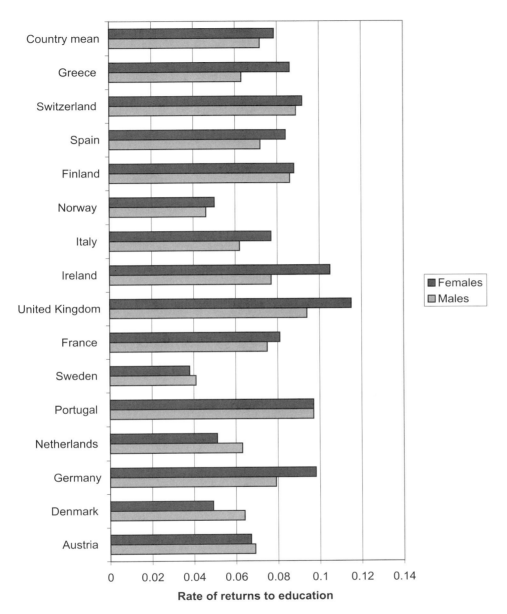

FIGURE 2.12

The returns to education for men and women in 1994 and 1995 in fifteen European countries.

Source: Brunello and Comi (2001, table 4).

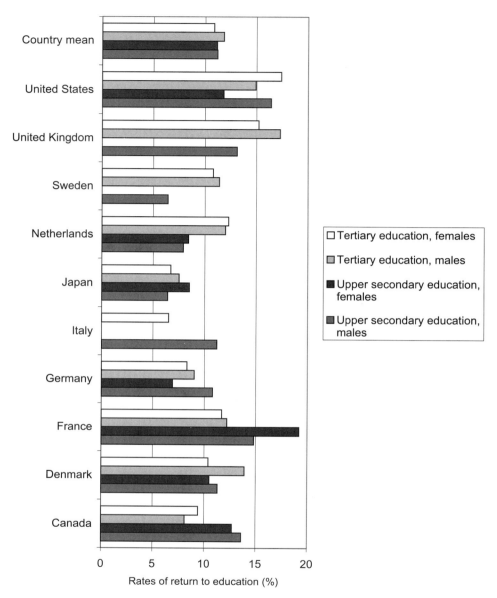

FIGURE 2.13

Internal rates of return to education for ten OECD countries, 1999–2000.

Source: OECD (2002, table A13.3, p. 134).

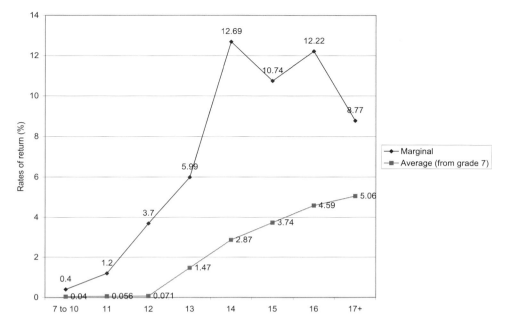

FIGURE 2.14
The return to schooling by grade.

Source: Belzil and Hansen (2002, table 4).

secondary and postsecondary education. These rates are higher than the ones in figure 2.12 because the omission of unemployment benefits tends to bias the estimates upward; the reason is that the risk of unemployment is highest among the least educated persons, as shown in figure 2.6. It is also worth pointing out that the returns to secondary and postsecondary education, while similar on average, differ from one country to another. It is not possible to set out the relative returns of these two types of education systematically on this graph.

The contribution of Belzil and Hansen (2002) sheds light on this point. These two authors estimated the returns to education for each year of study, using a structural model in which the choice of duration of studies is endogenous; the data came from the National Longitudinal Survey of Youth (NLSY) for the years 1979–1990. The results, presented in figure 2.14, show that the marginal returns to education are highly dependent on the duration of studies. The marginal returns to years spent in college are clearly greater than those to years spent in high school. The marginal returns to the early years of schooling are extremely feeble, 0.4% for grades seven to ten. Subsequently the marginal return rises sharply up to grade 14, then falls off. We may note that the average return is less than those estimated in figure 2.12, which are on the order of 7%. This is because the hypothesis of the constancy of the marginal returns to education, sometimes adopted by those who follow Mincer's

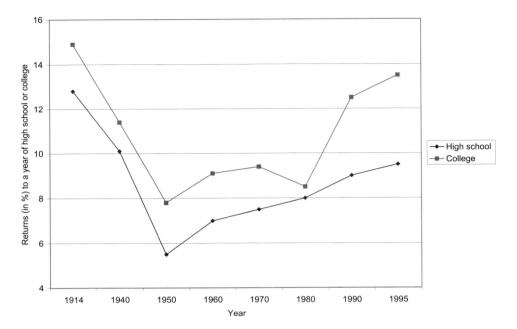

FIGURE 2.15

Returns to a year of schooling for men 18–34 years old in the United States from 1914 to 1995.

Source: Goldin and Katz (2001, table 4, figures 1 and 6).

method, amounts to making the estimate of the average return to education conditional on the duration of studies chosen by individuals. For example, in this context, the rate of return to secondary schooling is the average rate of return for those persons who have chosen to acquire secondary education. Belzil and Hansen show that this rate is very different from the "true" average rate corresponding to the average of the marginal rates of each year of schooling completed.

We have just seen that the returns to education vary according to country and duration of studies. It should also be noted that they vary over the course of time. This type of phenomenon has been much pondered, in light of the fact that certain countries have faced increasing wage inequality over the last four decades of the twentieth century (a problem to which we shall return in chapter 10). This increase in wage inequality, which is particularly sharp in the United States, goes in tandem with a rise in the returns to education, a phenomenon illustrated in figure 2.15. It shows that the returns to education for men fluctuated widely during the twentieth century in the United States, decreasing between 1914 and 1940, and then increasing between 1950 and 1995. Goldin (2001) and Goldin and Katz (2001) maintain that the phase of decrease resulted from a considerable expansion of secondary schooling at the end of the 1910s and in the 1940s. From this point of view, the slowdown in the expansion of schooling in the United States after the Second World War helps to explain the increase in the returns to education between 1950 and 1995.[6]

The Social Returns to Education

Estimates of the private returns to education no doubt fail to render a full account of the benefits that flow from investments in schooling to society as a whole. It is possible that education exerts positive externalities and that the social returns to education are superior to the private ones. Nevertheless, it is also possible that the social returns to education are inferior to the private ones, if the role of the educational system essentially consists of selecting individuals as a function of personal characteristics that employers cannot observe, as pointed out in section 3.

Empirical studies dedicated to the social returns to education are as yet scarce. They do tend to show, however, that education does indeed exert positive externalities, and that the social returns to education are superior to the private ones. Thus, Currie and Moretti (2002) estimate, while controlling for selection biases, that better education of mothers has a positive impact on the health of their offspring. Lochner and Moretti (2001), likewise controlling for selection biases and using data on men in the United States for the period 1960–1980, estimate that education to high school level reduces criminality. They find that the externality connected to the reduction of criminality represents between 14% and 26% of the private returns to education. More advanced education can also favor the discovery and adoption of new technologies (Foster and Rosenzweig, 1996), which themselves exert macroeconomic externalities that are a source of growth (Nelson and Phelps, 1966; Aghion and Howitt, 1998). Research on growth places a great deal of emphasis on the central role of education in this domain. Empirical work on international macroeconomic data generally highlights a positive impact of education on growth (see Topel, 1999; Hanushek and Kimko, 2000; and Krueger and Lindahl, 2003). Nonetheless, as Krueger and Lindahl (2003) point out, it is not possible on the basis of this work to make a robust claim for the existence of knowledge externalities linked to education and favoring growth. Work carried out on individual data supplies valuable information about this problem. Rauch (1993), Acemoglu and Angrist (2000), and Moretti (2002) have attempted to assess the difference between the private returns to education and the social ones arising from externalities by comparing the returns to education of individuals situated in environments in which the level of general education differs. Rauch (1993) estimates, through a comparison of the incomes of individuals situated in different cities, that knowledge externalities increase the returns to education by three to five percentage points. The studies of Acemoglu and Angrist (2000) and Moretti (2002) focus especially on the problem of the endogeneity of educational choices, which may bias estimates. Acemoglu and Angrist (2000) exploit the heterogeneity of compulsory attendance laws and child labor laws in U.S. states between 1920 and 1960 to pinpoint exogenous variations in the environment that may influence educational choices. In this context, they do find positive, though slight, knowledge externalities that improve the returns to education on the order of one percentage point and do not differ significantly from zero. Moretti (2002), using a different methodology, also finds positive externalities corresponding to an improvement of the returns to education lying between 0.6 and 1.2 percentage points.

On the whole, this empirical work does suggest that the social returns to education do exceed the private ones. This observation, which still requires some shoring up, justifies to some extent the preponderant role of the state in expenditure on education—a problem that is investigated more fully in chapter 11.

5   SUMMARY AND CONCLUSION

- Expenditure on education represents an important and growing percentage of GDP in the OECD countries. For example, in 1999 the United States and Sweden devoted 6.5% and 6.7% of GDP respectively to spending on education.

- The theory of human capital justifies educational choices by assuming that education favors the accumulation of competencies and increases wage earnings. It predicts that individuals have an interest, after completing their schooling, in gradually trimming back the amount of time they devote to training over the course of the life cycle. The profile of wages thus should be concave with respect to age, something solidly verified in practice.

- If the productive characteristics of individuals are unobservable, education may be regarded as a signaling activity, allowing the most productive workers to bring themselves to the notice of firms. Signaling activity may lead to "overeducation," which can be reduced by cross-subsidies aimed at limiting spending on education. In practice, the significance of overeducation remains to be proved. Empirical studies suggest that signaling activity, although not negligible, does not play an overwhelming role in the educational process.

- Estimation of the returns to education must deal with the existence of selection bias and ability bias. The techniques employed to control for these biases suggest that their quantitative importance is limited.

- Empirical studies have a great deal of difficulty in detecting any systematic influence of expenditure on education on the performance of students.

- The estimation of earnings functions linking earnings to, among other things, the duration of schooling and professional experience allows us to assess the return to a year of extra education. Overall, research in this field finds that this return lies on average in the 6%–15% range. On this point, it should also be noted that the marginal returns to education are very likely not constant.

- The few empirical studies available suggest that education does entail positive, but small, externalities.

6   RELATED TOPICS IN THE BOOK

- Chapter 1, section 1.3: Labor supply over the life cycle

- Chapter 5, section 4.2: Wage discrimination between men and women

- Chapter 6, section 4.3: Experience, seniority, and wage

- Chapter 10, section 2: Wage inequalities

- Chapter 11, section 2.3: General training, specific training, and labor market equilibrium

- Chapter 11, section 3.2: Evaluation of training policies

7   FURTHER READINGS

Becker, G. (1964), *Human Capital*, New York: National Bureau of Economic Research.

Card, D. (1999), ''The causal effect of education on earnings,'' in Ashenfelter, O., and Card, D. (eds.), *Handbook of Labor Economics*, vol. 3A, chap. 30, Amsterdam: Elsevier Science/North-Holland.

Hanushek, E. (2002), ''Public provided education,'' in Auerbach, A., and Feldstein, M. (eds.), *Handbook of Public Economics*, vol. 4, chap. 30, pp. 2045–2141, Amsterdam: Elsevier Science/North-Holland.

Manski, C. (2000), ''Economic analysis of social interactions,'' *Journal of Economic Perspectives*, 14(3), pp. 115–136.

Spence, M. (1974), *Market Signaling*, Cambridge, Mass: Harvard University Press.

REFERENCES

Acemoglu, D., and Angrist, J. (2000), ''How large are human capital externalities? Evidence from compulsory schooling laws,'' NBER Macroannual, pp. 9–59.

Aghion, P., and Howitt, P. (1998), *Endogenous Growth Theory*, Cambridge, Mass.: MIT Press.

Altonji, J., and Dunn, T. (1996), ''Using siblings to estimate the effect of school quality on wages,'' *Review of Economics and Statistics*, 78, pp. 665–671.

Angrist, J., and Krueger, D. (1991), ''Does compulsory school attendance affect schooling and earnings?'' *Quarterly Journal of Economics*, 106, pp. 976–1014.

Ashenfelter, O., Harmon, C., and Oosterbeek, H. (2000), ''A review of the schooling/earnings relationship, with tests for publication bias,'' NBER Working Paper 7457.

Ashenfelter, O., and Rouse, A. (1998), ''Income, schooling and ability: Evidence from a new sample of identical twins,'' *Quarterly Journal of Economics*, 113, pp. 253–284.

Ashenfelter, O., and Rouse, A. (1999), "The payoff to education," mimeo, Princeton University.

Becker, G. (1957), *The Economics of Discrimination*, Chicago: University of Chicago Press.

Becker, G. (1964), *Human Capital*, New York: National Bureau of Economic Research.

Belzil, C., and Hansen, J. (2002), "Unobserved ability and the return to schooling," *Econometrica*, 70, pp. 575–591.

Benabou, R. (1993), "Workings of a city: Location, education, and production," *Quarterly Journal of Economics*, 434(3), pp. 619–652.

Benabou, R. (1996), "Heterogeneity, stratification, and growth: Macroeconomic implications of community structure and school finance," *American Economic Review*, 86(3), pp. 584–609.

Ben-Porath, Y. (1967), "The production of human capital and the life cycle of earnings," *Journal of Political Economy*, 75, pp. 352–365.

Brock, W., and Durlauf, S. (2001), "Interactions-based models," in Heckman, J., and Leamer, E. (eds.), *Handbook of Econometrics*, vol. 5, pp. 3297–3380, Amsterdam: Elsevier Science.

Brunello, G., and Comi, S. (2000), "Education and earnings growth: Evidence from 11 European countries," IZA Working Paper No. 140: www.iza.org, forthcoming in *The Economics of Education Review*.

Brunello, G., and Comi, S. (2001), "The returns to education in Italy: A new look at the evidence," IZA Working Paper No. 130, http://www.iza.org, in Harmon, C., Walker, I., and Westergard-Nielsen, N. (eds.), *The Returns to Education in Europe*, Edward Elgar.

Card, D. (1999), "The causal effect of education on earnings," in Ashenfelter, O., and Card, D. (eds.), *Handbook of Labor Economics*, vol. 3A, chap. 30, Amsterdam: Elsevier Science/North-Holland.

Card, D., and Krueger, A. (1992), "Does school quality matter? Returns to education and the characteristics of public schools in the United States," *Journal of Political Economy*, 100, pp. 1–40.

Cho, K., and Kreps, K. (1987), "Signaling games and stable equilibria," *Quarterly Journal of Economics*, 102, pp. 179–221.

Currie, J., and Moretti, E. (2002), "Mother's education and the intergenerational transmission of human capital: Evidence from college openings and longitudinal data," NBER Working Paper No. 9360, forthcoming in *Quarterly Journal of Economics*.

Currie, J., and Thomas, D. (2000), "Early test scores, socioeconomic status, school quality, and future outcomes," mimeo, Department of Economics, University of California, Los Angeles.

Foster, A., and Rosenzweig, M. (1996), "Technical change in human capital return and investments: Evidence from the Green Revolution," *American Economic Review*, 86, pp. 931–953.

Goldin, C. (2001), "The human capital century and American leadership: Virtues of the past," *Journal of Economic History*, 61, pp. 263–292.

Goldin, C., and Katz, L. (2001), "Decreasing (and then increasing) inequality in America: A tale of two half centuries," in Welch, F. (ed.), *The Causes and Consequences of Increasing Income Inequality*, Chicago: University of Chicago Press.

Goux, D., and Maurin, E. (1994), "Education, expérience et salaires," *Economie et Prévision*, 116, pp. 155–179.

Hanushek, E. (1986), "The economics of schooling: Production and efficiency in public schools," *Journal of Economic Literature*, 24, pp. 1141–1177.

Hanushek, E. (2002), "Public provided education," in Auerbach, A., and Feldstein, M. (eds.), *Handbook of Public Economics*, vol. 4, chap. 30, pp. 2045–2141, Amsterdam: Elsevier Science/North-Holland.

Hanushek, E., Kain, J., Markman, J., and Rivkin, S. (2003), "Does peer ability affect student achievement?" *Journal of Applied Econometrics*, forthcoming.

Hanushek, E., and Kimko, D. (2000), "Schooling, labor force quality, and the growth of nations," *American Economic Review*, 90, pp. 1184–1208.

Hanushek, E., Rivkin, S., and Taylor, L. (1996), "Aggregation and the estimated effects of school resources," *Review of Economics and Statistics*, 78, pp. 611–627.

Heckman, J. (1976), "A life cycle model of earnings, learning and consumption," *Journal of Political Economy*, 84, pp. 11–44.

Jaeger, D., and Page, M. (1996), "Degrees matter: New evidence on sheepskin effects in the returns to education," *Review of Economics and Statistics*, 78, pp. 733–740.

Juhn, C., Murphy, K., and Pierce, B. (1993), "Wage inequality and the rise in returns to skill," *Journal of Political Economy*, 101, pp. 410–442.

Kennedy, P. (2003), *A Guide to Econometrics*, 5th ed., Cambridge, Mass.: MIT Press.

Krueger, A., and Lindahl, M. (2003), "Education for growth: Why and for whom?" *Journal of Economic Literature*, forthcoming.

Lochner, L., and Moretti, E. (2001), "The effect of education on criminal activity: Evidence from prison inmates, arrests and self-reports," NBER Working Paper 8606.

Manski, C. (2000), "Economic analysis of social interactions," *Journal of Economic Perspectives*, 14(3), pp. 115–136.

Mas-Colell, A., Whinston, M., and Green, J. (1995), *Microeconomic Theory*, New York: Oxford University Press.

Maurin, E. (2002), "The impact of parental income on early schooling transitions: A re-examination using data over three generations," *Journal of Public Economics*, 85(3), pp. 301–332.

Mincer, J. (1974), *Schooling, Experience and Earnings*, New York: National Bureau of Economic Research.

Moretti, E. (2002), "Estimating the social return to higher education: Evidence from longitudinal and repeated cross-sectional data," NBER Working Paper 9108, *Journal of Econometrics*, forthcoming.

Murnane, R., Willett, J., Braatz, M., and Duhaldeborde, Y. (2001), "Do different dimensions of male high school students skills predict labor market success a decade later? Evidence from the NLSY," *Economics of Education Review*, 20, pp. 311–320.

Murnane, R., Willett, J., and Levy, F. (1995), "The growing importance of cognitive skills in wage determination," *Review of Economics and Statistics*, 77(2), pp. 251–266.

Nelson, R., and Phelps, E. (1966), "Investment in humans, technological diffusion, and economic growth," *American Economic Review*, 56, pp. 69–75.

OECD (2002), *Education at a Glance*, Paris: OECD.

Psacharopoulos, G. (1985), "Returns to education: A further international update and implications," *Journal of Human Resources*, 20, pp. 583–604.

Rauch, J. (1993), "Productivity gains from geographic concentration of human capital: Evidence from the cities," *Journal of Urban Economics*, 34, pp. 380–400.

Solon, G. (1999), "Intergenerational mobility in the labor market," in Ashenfelter, O., and Card, D. (eds.), *Handbook of Labor Economics*, vol. 3A, chap. 29, Amsterdam: Elsevier Science/North-Holland.

Spence, M. (1973), "Job market signaling," *Quarterly Journal of Economics*, 87, pp. 355–374.

Spence, M. (1974), *Market Signaling*, Cambridge, Mass: Harvard University Press.

Swinkels, J. (1999), "Education signaling with preemptive offers," *Review of Economic Studies*, 66, pp. 949–970.

Topel, R. (1999), "Labor markets and economic growth," in Ashenfelter, O., and Card, D. (eds.), *Handbook of Labor Economics*, vol. 3C, chap. 30, Amsterdam: Elsevier Science/North-Holland.

Weiss, A. (1983), "A sorting-cum-learning model of education," *Journal of Political Economy*, 91, pp. 420–442.

Weiss, Y. (1986), "The determination of life-cycle earnings: A survey," in Ashenfelter, O., and Layard, R. (eds.), *Handbook of Labor Economics*, vol. 1, chap. 11, pp. 603–640, Amsterdam: Elsevier Science/North-Holland.

Zimmer, R. W., and Toma, E. (2000), "Peer effects in private and public schools across countries," *Journal of Policy Analysis and Management*, 19(1), pp. 75–92.

JOB SEARCH

CONTENTS

In this chapter, we will see:

- What the behavior of a person looking for work is

- How the duration of unemployment depends on the reservation wage

- The trade-off between insurance and incentive in designing an unemployment benefits schedule

- The principles of the econometrics of duration models

- How unemployment benefits influence the duration of unemployment

- What the effects are of job search help and checking on job search effort

INTRODUCTION

The neoclassical theory of labor supply pays no attention to the time and cost of looking for work. The consumption of "leisure"—even when this term is extended to cover home production—remains the sole alternative to waged work, and by definition an agent who utilizes the total amount of time at his disposal in the form of leisure is described as a *nonparticipant*. From this perspective, then, there is no place for the unemployed person, even though his or her principal activity amounts to looking for work. Such a description of the labor market implicitly assumes a structure of *perfect information*. It supposes that each agent knows all the particulars about all the jobs on offer, and that he or she merely has to decide the number of hours—potentially as low as zero—that he or she wants to devote to work, given the (supposedly) single and universally known wage prevailing in the labor market. There is no need to *look* for a job that would suit him or her. Such a hypothesis is no doubt too simplistic, so we must examine the consequences of *imperfect information*. This is precisely the purpose of job search theory: to study the behavior of an individual who has imperfect information about jobs and wages.

In the job market, the imperfection of the available information occurs in the form of a number of different possible wages that an agent might be able to command. Hence the job-seeker surveys the labor market so as to find the highest wage being paid for the services he or she can supply. This procedure is no different from that adopted by a person looking for an apartment (at the best possible rent) or a loan (at the best possible rate of interest). It was Stigler (1961, 1962) who first highlighted this common process in all markets where information is imperfect. The modern theory of the job search arose in the 1970s with the formalizations of McCall (1970) and Mortensen (1970). Section 1 of this chapter lays out the basic job search model, in which an agent keeps looking as long as he or she entertains the hope of improving his or her welfare by continuing to search. The duration of the search depends on his or her preferences and the overall characteristics of the environment in which the search takes place. The theory of job search is not in conflict with the theory of labor supply. By giving a prominent role to imperfect information, this theory adds the category "unemployed" to those of "employed" and "nonparticipant." In this way it sheds supplementary light on the decision to participate in the labor market, which no longer takes the form of a choice between work and nonparticipation; rather, it now lies in knowing whether it is *worthwhile* to *look* for work. In other words, to hold a paid job you must first have decided to look for one. A good synthesis of this theory can be found in Mortensen (1986) and Mortensen and Pissarides (1999).

Section 2 of this chapter extends the basic model in two different ways. The first analyzes the behavior of employers in the context of the job search, while the second looks at the behavior of the authorities in charge of the system of unemployment insurance. For a long time the theory of the job search developed within the framework of partial equilibrium, inasmuch as it did not explain the formation of the wage distribution that confronted job-seekers. To make it complete, the behavior of employers has been introduced so as to arrive at a description of labor market equilibrium. By attributing well-defined strategic behavior to firms, these models are able to portray the process of wage formation as endogenous (good examples are the works of Burdett and Mortensen, 1989 and 1998). On the other hand, the basic job search model takes the value of unemployment insurance benefits as given. But in reality, this value is determined by the authorities in charge of the system set up to compensate workers during unemployment. The theory of optimal unemployment benefits, initiated by the work of Shavell and Weiss (1979) and Hopenhayn and Nicolini (1997), takes the view that the organizations that manage unemployment insurance ought to give workers an incentive to actively look for work. The optimal level of compensation paid out is the result of a compromise between this requirement to provide incentive and the need to insure the unemployed against fluctuations in the income to which participants in the labor market aspire. From this perspective, the job search model constitutes a particularly useful tool for identifying the characteristics of efficient unemployment insurance systems.

Job search models arrive at relatively precise conclusions about the factors that determine the duration of unemployment. Surveys that monitor the work experience of a large number of individuals over time supply the data necessary to derive estimates from these models. Section 3 of this chapter gives an account of the econometric methods specific to "duration models," and lays out the principal results obtained in this domain.

1 BASIC JOB SEARCH THEORY

Job search theory arises initially out of a basic model, called today the partial model, that describes the behavior of a person looking for work in a situation of imperfect information. This model furnishes precise conclusions about the effects of a change in the environment or in economic policy. The basic model is grounded, however, on overly simple hypotheses, which we must abandon in order to describe the reality of the search process better. For one thing, in this model all the unemployed have access, in exogenous fashion, to unemployment insurance benefits, they are not allowed to select the intensity of their search, and they cannot look for (another) job once they are employed. Finally, the basic model is situated in a stationary environment. We will first lay out the basic model, then analyze the changes that emerge as we abandon these four hypotheses.

1.1 THE BASIC MODEL

In the job search model, the optimal strategy of a person looking for work consists simply of choosing a *reservation wage* that represents the lowest remuneration he or she will accept. The amount chosen depends on all the parameters that go to make up the economic environment, in particular the benefits paid to those who are unemployed and the arrival rate of job offers. Hence, most often it is enough to know how the reservation wage varies in order to discern the effects of economic policy on the duration of unemployment. As well, when it is linked to the labor supply model presented in the previous chapter, the job search model sheds light on the choice among nonparticipation, unemployment, and work.

1.1.1   The Search Process and the Reservation Wage

The basic job search model aims to describe the behavior of an unemployed person who dedicates all of his or her efforts to looking for a job, when the conditions in which this search takes place do not vary over time. The model is thus explicitly dynamic, but it is situated in a stationary environment. The unfolding of time may be described in continuous or discrete manner; we have chosen the former, since it is analytically simpler and has been adopted almost universally in all published work in this field.

The Discounted Expected Utility of an Employee

The main hypothesis of the job search model is that the job-seeker does not know exactly what wage each job pays. So, by looking, he or she can expect to improve his or her prospects of income. We epitomize these imperfections in the available information by postulating that the job-seeker knows only the cumulative distribution of the possible wages. We further assume that this distribution is the same at each date, and that successive wage offers are independent draws from this distribution. This stationarity assumption means that, at any time, a person looking for work faces the same structure of information. We shall use $H(.)$ to denote the cumulative distribution function of all possible wages.

A job offer comes down to the proposal of a constant real wage w that the worker will receive on each date as long as he or she remains with the firm that makes the offer. If we assume that the agent is risk-neutral, and if for the sake of simplicity we leave out of account the disutility of work, his or her *instantaneous* utility then simply equals w. This means that over a short interval of time, dt in length, the agent attains a level of instantaneous satisfaction equal to $w\,dt$. Let us further assume that over each short interval of time dt, any job whatsoever can disappear at the rate $q\,dt$, where $q > 0$ is a constant exogenous parameter. Over each short interval of time dt, a waged worker thus loses his or her job at the rate $q\,dt$. Let us assume that the real instantaneous rate of interest r is constant and exogenous. A single dollar invested in the financial market on date t brings in $1 + r\,dt$ dollars in $t + dt$. The discounted value of a dollar at date t that will be available at date $t + dt$ is thus equal to $1/(1 + r\,dt)$. The term $1/(1 + r\,dt)$ thus represents the discount factor over each short interval of time dt. In a stationary state, the discounted expected utility V_e of an employed person receiving wage w satisfies the following relation:

$$V_e = \frac{1}{1 + r\,dt}[w\,dt + (1 - q\,dt)V_e + q\,dt V_u] \tag{1}$$

This relation indicates that the discounted expected utility stemming from being hired is equal to the discounted sum of the flow of income $w\,dt$ over the interval of time dt, and the discounted expected future income. With probability $(1 - q\,dt)$ this future income does coincide with the expected utility V_e associated with continued employment, and with complementary probability $q\,dt$ it conforms instead to V_u, the discounted expected utility of an unemployed person. Multiplying the two sides of relation (1) by $1 + r\,dt$ and rearranging the terms of this expression, we arrive at:

$$rV_e = w + q(V_u - V_e) \tag{2}$$

This equation is easy to interpret.[1] It shows that, at every moment, a job entails discounted expected flow of income rV_e equal to wage w, to which is added average income $q(V_u - V_e)$ deriving from a possible change in the employee's status. This average income is in fact a loss resulting from the wage worker quitting his job.

Equality (2) allows us to express the discounted expected utility of an employee receiving wage w—which we shall henceforth denote $V_e(w)$—in the following manner:

$$V_e(w) - V_u = \frac{w - rV_u}{r + q} \tag{3}$$

It is thus apparent that the difference between the expected utility of an employee and that of an unemployed person rises with the wage accepted and falls with the discounted expected utility of the unemployed person.

The Optimal Search Strategy

In order to simplify the exposition, we will assume that a job-seeker can only meet a single employer on any date (see Mortensen, 1986, for the possibility of multiple offers). The employer offers the job-seeker the constant wage w over the duration of his or her employment, which he or she is free to accept or refuse. The optimal job search strategy is then as follows:

1. If the job-seeker receives no offer on date t, he or she continues looking. This behavior results from the stationarity of intertemporal utility V_u.

2. If the job-seeker receives a wage offer w, he or she accepts if $V_e(w) > V_u$. If not, he or she continues looking.

Since a job-seeker's expected utility V_u does not depend on a particular wage offer w, relation (3) shows that $V_e(w)$ is an increasing linear function of the wage offered. This relation also shows that phase 2 of the search strategy amounts to the adoption of a "stopping rule" that dictates accepting wage w if and only if it is superior to a threshold value x defined by:

$$x = rV_u \tag{4}$$

The acceptance of an offer equal to x procures for the job-seeker the same level of utility that he or she gets by remaining unemployed; in other words, $V_e(x) = V_u$. As in the theory of labor supply laid out in chapter 1, wage x continues to be called the *reservation wage*, but we will see in section 1.1.3 that it means something tangibly different.

The Discounted Expected Utility of a Job-Seeker

The existence of the stopping rule makes it possible to deduce numerous characteristics of the search process from those of the reservation wage. In order to make the factors that determine the reservation wage explicit, we need to specify more precisely the discounted expected utility V_u of a job-seeker. Accordingly, we shall designate by λ the arrival rate of job offers. This rate encapsulates the difficulties encountered while one looks for a job. It reflects the general state of the labor market, but it also depends on the personal characteristics of the job-seeker—age and educational qualifications, for example—and the effort he or she puts into the search. In the basic model, we will assume that this rate λ is a constant exogenous quantity. Moreover, the search for a job entails costs at every turn. Some are financial in nature, like the cost of getting about, for example, or buying specialized magazines, or sending out applications. But it is equally necessary to include the opportunity cost of the search, in other words the value of a period of time that could have been devoted to other activities. All these costs will be summed up, at each date, by a single scalar $c > 0$. There are also gains associated with periods of looking for work. These comprise unemployment benefits, and also perhaps the consumption of domestic production and leisure. If, for each date, we express the sum of these gains by the scalar $b > 0$, the *net* instantaneous income from looking for work, denoted by z, is then equal to $(b - c)$.

At any moment the status of a job-seeker may change with rate λ. If he or she does actually receive an offer, he or she will not accept unless the wage that goes with it is more than his or her reservation wage x. The discounted utility V_λ expected upon receiving an offer of employment is thus equal to

$$V_\lambda = \int_0^x V_u \, dH(w) + \int_x^{+\infty} V_e(w) \, dH(w)$$

Conversely, if the job-seeker receives no offers, he or she keeps looking, which procures for him or her a discounted expected utility equal to V_u. Now, during a short interval of time dt in length, a job-seeker gains $z \, dt$ and has a probability $\lambda \, dt$ of receiving a job offer. In the stationary state, his or her expected utility thus satisfies

$$V_u = \frac{1}{1 + r \, dt} [z \, dt + \lambda \, dt V_\lambda + (1 - \lambda \, dt) V_u]$$

If we multiply the two sides of this equality by $1 + r \, dt$ and rearrange terms, we find that a job-seeker's discounted expected utility is defined by the following trade-off equation:

$$rV_u = z + \lambda \int_x^{+\infty} [V_e(w) - V_u] \, dH(w) \tag{5}$$

Like relation (2), defining an employee's discounted expected utility, this equation also has to be interpreted by examining the various ways the assets V_u of an unemployed person may be invested. In the "financial" market these assets will bring in rV_u at any moment, while if "invested" in the labor market they will procure income z augmented by the value $\lambda(V_\lambda - V_u)$ of the average gain linked to the change of status of a person who is looking for work.

Reservation Wage, Hazard Rate, and Average Duration of Unemployment
With the help of relations (3) and (4), which define respectively the intertemporal utility $V_e(w)$ of an employee and the reservation wage x as a function of the discounted expected gain V_u of an unemployed person, we easily arrive at the following

equation, which implicitly characterizes the reservation wage as a function of the parameters of the model:

$$x = z + \frac{\lambda}{r+q} \int_x^{+\infty} (w - x)\, dH(w) \tag{6}$$

We can show a) that there is only one optimal value for this reservation wage, and b) that it maximizes the intertemporal utility of a job-seeker. For that, we need merely observe that relation (5) defines V_u as a function of x, and verify that the derivative of this function is null for the value of x given by (6). This way of characterizing the reservation wage is instructive, for it brings out clearly the optimality of the search strategy adopted by the job-seeker.

The values of two other important variables flow from knowing the reservation wage. These are the "hazard rate," or the exit rate from unemployment, and the averate duration of unemployment. Since a job-seeker becomes employed when a) he or she receives a wage offer—which occurs at rate λ—and b) the offer is at least equal to his or her reservation wage—which occurs with probability $[1 - H(x)]$—the exit rate from unemployment takes the value $\lambda[1 - H(x)]$ at any moment. When the number of job-seekers is large, this rate approaches the hazard rate. The average duration of unemployment, denoted T_u, is then given by:

$$T_u = \frac{1}{\lambda[1 - H(x)]} \tag{7}$$

The interpretation of this last relation is very intuitive: it means that if a job-seeker has one chance in ten of becoming employed in any week, he or she will on average remain unemployed for ten weeks.[2] Relation (7) also shows that the average duration of unemployment is an increasing function of the reservation wage: when a person who is looking for work raises the level of the wage he or she is demanding, on average it prolongs the duration of the search.

1.1.2 Comparative Statics of the Basic Model

The comparative statics properties of the job search model are very easily obtained if we write the relation (6) defining the reservation wage in the following form:

$$\Phi(x, z, r, \lambda, q) = 0 \qquad \text{with} \qquad \Phi(x, z, r, \lambda, q) \equiv x - z - \frac{\lambda}{r+q} \int_x^{+\infty} (w - x)\, dH(w) \tag{8}$$

We can easily verify that the partial derivatives of the function Φ possess the following properties:

$$\Phi_x > 0, \ \Phi_z < 0, \ \Phi_r > 0, \ \Phi_\lambda < 0, \ \text{and} \ \Phi_q > 0$$

As relation (8) implies $\partial x / \partial i = -\Phi_i / \Phi_x$, $i = z, r, \lambda, q$, we immediately obtain the direction of the variations in the reservation wage as a function of the parameters of the model, or:

$$\frac{\partial x}{\partial z} > 0, \ \frac{\partial x}{\partial \lambda} > 0, \ \frac{\partial x}{\partial r} < 0, \ \text{and} \ \frac{\partial x}{\partial q} < 0 \tag{9}$$

With the help of relation (7), we deduce from this the main comparative statics properties of the average duration of unemployment. The result is:

$$\frac{\partial T_u}{\partial z} > 0, \quad \frac{\partial T_u}{\partial r} < 0, \text{ and } \frac{\partial T_u}{\partial q} < 0$$

The rise in the reservation wage and the average duration of unemployment that follow from a rise in the net income z from looking for work constitute an important result of this theory. This means, all other things being equal, that an increase in unemployment benefits should have the effect of lengthening the duration of unemployment. This result is highly intuitive: it simply makes sense that a job-seeker receiving higher compensation will be more demanding in terms of the wage he or she hopes to get, and that on average will lengthen the amount of time he or she spends looking. This strong prediction of the theory of job search has often been contested (see Atkinson and Micklewright, 1991, for a detailed critical analysis of it). On the theoretical level, however, it is unassailable, since the person looking for work does in fact receive benefit payments from the unemployment insurance system (which is the case in the basic model just presented). Let us suppose, for example, that unemployment benefits rise from 0% to 100% of the current average wage. It is hard to believe that a change of that magnitude in the size of the payments will have no positive influence on the average duration of unemployment. But leaving aside this exaggerated example, the extent of the influence is a priori unknown. Moreover, a very large percentage of those looking for work receive no unemployment benefits. We will see that, for them, an increase in unemployment benefits is highly likely to have an inverse effect on their reservation wage (a point rigorously established in section 1.2.1 of this chapter, which deals with the eligibility effect). Given these circumstances, we have to turn to empirical studies to get an idea of the sign and the order of magnitude of the unemployment benefits elasticity of the average duration of unemployment. We will see later that in general this elasticity is slight when the amount of unemployment benefits falls in a "reasonable" magnitude.

The other implications of the model are also easy to grasp. A rise in r is characteristic of a job-seeker who places less value on the future than another. A person of this type has a lower reservation wage and on average spends less time looking for work. When the job loss rate q increases, the current demands of job-seekers diminish, since the gap between the expected utility of an employee and that of a job-seeker shrinks, which reduces the average duration of unemployment. On the other hand, relation (7) shows that an increase in λ, the arrival rate of wage offers, has an ambiguous effect on the amount of time devoted to looking for a job. In this case, job-seekers revise their reservation wage upward, which entails a lowering of the term $[1 - H(x)]$ representing the probability of accepting an offer. The direction of consequent change in the rate of exit from unemployment $\lambda[(1 - H(x)]$ and the average duration of unemployment $T_u = 1/\lambda[(1 - H(x)]$ is then unknown. It should be noted, however, that if the frequency with which job offers arrive has little effect on the reservation wage, the average duration of unemployment decreases with this frequency. Empirical studies do seem to indicate this (see section 3.2.2 below)

1.1.3 The Choice Among Nonparticipation, Job-Seeking, and Employment

Decisions to participate in the labor market are envisaged one way under the theory of labor supply and another way under the theory of job search. The theory of labor supply comprises only two possible states: either one is a participant or one is not. The theory of job search just outlined assumes that workers do participate in the labor market, and thus are faced only with the choice between unemployment and employment. It is possible, though, to contemplate a hybrid model that takes into account three possible states: nonparticipation, job-seeking, and employment.

The Reservation Wage and Alternative Income

In the theory of labor supply, participation in the labor market depends on a comparison between the current wage w and the reservation wage w_A defined by relation (3) in chapter 1. In this theory, decisions to participate can be summarized in the following manner:

$$\begin{cases} w > w_A \Longrightarrow \text{employee} \\ w \le w_A \Longrightarrow \text{nonparticipant} \end{cases} \tag{10}$$

The theory of job search defines the reservation wage x as the wage at which the job-seeker is indifferent between accepting a job and continuing to look. It depends on the overall characteristics of the labor market, which we will designate by Ω. According to equation (6) defining x, these characteristics include the distribution $H(.)$ of possible wages, the net income z associated with the job search, the job offers arrival rate λ, the interest rate r, and the job destruction rate q. Thus, in symbolic terms we may write $\Omega = \Omega(H, z, q, \lambda, r)$ and $x = x(\Omega)$. The choice between participation and nonparticipation is based on a comparison between the expected utility of a job-seeker V_u and that of a nonparticipant V_I. If the latter receives a constant income R_I at each date, his or her expected utility is defined by the equality $rV_I = R_I$. This can easily be compared to that of a job-seeker, which is such that $rV_u = x$. An agent decides to participate in the labor market if and only if $V_I \le V_u$, which translates into the inequality $x(\Omega) \ge R_I$. It is apparent that the decision to participate in the labor market is made by comparing the reservation wage to the "alternative income" R_I that a nonparticipant is capable of obtaining at any moment. Individual decisions hence take the following form:

$$\begin{cases} x(\Omega) \ge R_I \Longrightarrow \text{participant} \\ x(\Omega) \le R_I \Longrightarrow \text{nonparticipant} \end{cases} \tag{11}$$

Moreover, when a participant receives a wage offer w, he or she accepts if it exceeds his or her reservation wage. In other words, the decisions of a participant come down to:

$$\begin{cases} w > x(\Omega) \Longrightarrow \text{employed} \\ x(\Omega) \ge w \Longrightarrow \text{unemployed} \end{cases} \tag{12}$$

The theory of job search suggests that the rate of participation depends on the set Ω of all the factors affecting the labor market. For example, some studies reveal that a rise in unemployment insurance benefits (an increase of z) is often accompanied by a rise in the participation rate, which itself takes the form of a rise in the unemployment rate (see Moorthy, 1989). In the same way, an increase in the unemployment rate, by lessening the probability of exiting from unemployment, tends to diminish the reservation wage and thus the participation rate. This relationship augments the procyclical character of the participation rates deduced from the labor supply model, in which the lowering of wages in bad economic times gives individuals incentive to withdraw from the labor market.

Discouraged Workers

The theory of job search takes into account only the wage prevailing in the marketplace, through the distribution of its possible values. Hence, among nonparticipants, it is difficult to distinguish those who don't want to work at the "current" wage from those who would accept a job for that amount of remuneration but who give up looking because of the costs incurred by doing so and the time they would have to wait before being hired. These nonparticipants are called *discouraged workers*. If we assimilate the average of possible wages $Ew = \int_0^{+\infty} w \, dH(w)$ to the "current" wage, we can conclude that individuals for whom $x(\Omega) \leq R_I \leq Ew$ form the category of discouraged workers. More generally, the "discouraged worker effect" is cited whenever a change in certain characteristics of the economic environment implies a lowered participation rate. For example, if job offers arrive with reduced frequency, the reservation wage $x(\Omega)$ falls, and consequently the participation rate falls too (since the latter is by definition the percentage of the population for whom the relation $x(\Omega) \geq R_I$ is satisfied).

Numerous studies allow us to obtain an estimate of the number of discouraged workers. It suffices to identify, among the individuals who claim to be looking for work, those who have not made efforts that count as really "significant" (see OECD, 1994, volume 1, for a precise definition of this adjective). Table 3.1 shows that their

Table 3.1

Discouraged workers and job-seekers in 2000 (as a percentage of the labor force).

Country	Discouraged workers	Job-seekers
Denmark	0.2	4.5
Spain	0.8	13.9
France	0.1	10.1
Sweden	1.7	5.9
United States	0.4	4.0
Japan	3.1	5.0

Source: OECD data.

number is not negligible, and is in general relatively greater in countries with a low rate of unemployment.

The Frontier Between Nonparticipation and Job-Seeking

The existence of discouraged workers suggests that the frontier between nonparticipation and participation in the labor force is difficult to draw. When does the intensity of the effort made by an individual to find a job qualify him or her as an active job-seeker? The varying definitions of unemployment supply different and perforce arbitrary answers to this question. Measurements of unemployment derive from investigations in which, to be considered unemployed, you have to have been without work (during the period in question), have taken steps to look for work, and be ready to start work (in principle) immediately. But these three conditions, in particular the second, pertaining to the process of looking, can have different meanings. Thus, in the United States, individuals who employ passive methods (such as looking in the want ads) are classified as nonparticipants, while numerous OECD countries consider job-seekers employing both passive and active methods as unemployed (see OECD, 1995, chapter 2).

A number of factors point to the conclusion that the distinction between nonparticipation and unemployment often turns out to be arbitrary. Reinterview programs carried out in the United States with individuals already interviewed the week before reveal that, especially for individuals situated close to the frontier of nonparticipation, the answers given (regarding the same period of reference) can be quite different (Abowd and Zellner, 1985). Some people are hard to classify, and their answers are highly sensitive to the way the interviews are conducted. Jones and Riddell (1999) show that individuals classed as nonparticipants by surveys of the labor force in Canada are anything but uniform in their behavior. These authors distinguish four categories of individuals: the employed, the unemployed, individuals marginally attached to labor market participation, and nonparticipants. Individuals marginally attached to labor market participation, traditionally considered nonparticipants, say that they are not looking for a job but would like to work. They represent 25% to 30% of the volume of unemployment over the period studied by Jones and Riddell. The matrix of transition between different states is presented in table 3.2. It is apparent that individuals marginally attached to labor market participation behave differently on average than nonparticipants, because they have a much higher probability of returning to full participation. The rates at which individuals on the margin of participation do return to employment are closer to those of the unemployed than to those of genuine nonparticipants. Jones and Riddell also emphasize that the category of individuals marginally attached to participation is extremely heterogeneous. Consequently, within the overall group of those who say they would like to work but are not looking for a job, Jones and Riddell distinguish persons who are "waiting" for a job—because they are "waiting to be recalled by their former employer," or "have found a job but haven't been hired yet," or "are waiting for an answer from an employer"—and discouraged persons who "believe there are no jobs matching their qualifications

Table 3.2

The transition matrix between different states in the labor market. Monthly rates for the year 1992 in Canada.

From To → ↓	Employed	Unemployed	Nonparticipant + Marginally attached
Unemployed	0.112 (0.004)	0.708 (0.005)	0.180 (0.005)
Marginally attached	0.098 (0.005)	0.171 (0.007)	0.731 (0.008)
Nonparticipant	0.026 (0.001)	0.030 (0.001)	0.944 (0.002)

Standard errors are in parentheses.

Source: Jones and Riddell (1999).

available in their region." It is apparent that those who are waiting for a job have a rate of return to employment higher than that of the unemployed (equal to 0.200), whereas discouraged workers show behavior closer to that of genuine nonparticipants (their rate of return equals 0.044).

These examples show that taking job-search behavior into consideration renders the distinction between labor market participation and nonparticipation ambiguous. In consequence, assessments of unemployment and of the labor force are necessarily arbitrary, and it is generally useful to supplement them with other indicators in order to get a clear picture of the state of the labor markets. In this regard, the employment rate—equal to the ratio between the number of jobs and the population of working age, generally taken to be all those between 15 and 64 years of age—is a supplementary indicator frequently used in order to better gauge what is happening in the labor markets.

1.2   EXTENSIONS OF THE BASIC MODEL

The results obtained using the basic model are numerous and relatively precise. They have, however, been obtained using hypotheses that are sometimes very restrictive. In order to expand on what the basic model has to tell us, we will first examine the consequences of the conditions of eligibility for unemployment insurance benefits. We will then look at the changes we must make when an individual is able to look for a job while he or she is already working. After that we will make the assumption that agents can decide how much effort to put into their job search. And finally, we will study the consequences of the fact that unemployment insurance benefits are not stationary.

1.2.1   Eligibility and Unemployment

In most countries, those who work in exchange for wages have to pay premiums into an unemployment insurance system that allows a wage-earner to receive compensation if he or she loses his or her job. When these conditions are met, we say that the worker is *eligible* for unemployment insurance benefits. But many people, in particular new entrants into the labor market and those who have been unemployed for a long time, are not eligible for such benefits. For them, finding a job also means becoming eligible, or becoming eligible again. As a result, the reservation wage of those who are not eligible *falls* when the benefits paid to the unemployed *who do meet the eligibility requirements* rise.

Two Types of Job-Seeker

To make this intuition perfectly explicit, we will assume in what follows that there are two types of job-seekers: those who are eligible for unemployment insurance benefits and those who are not. This circumstance can be formalized quite simply by assuming on the one hand that the instantaneous income of the former always amounts to z while that of the latter has the value $z_n < z$, and on the other hand that an individual becomes and remains eligible if he or she has been employed at least once. In this context, z represents the benefits paid by the unemployment insurance system, while z_n is determined by the welfare system, which generally pays out smaller amounts.

The situation of the eligible job-seeker is identical to that of the basic model, and his or her reservation wage, always denoted by x, continues to be defined by equation (6). But the behavior of a noneligible job-seeker is not so simple, for his or her expected utility, denoted by V_{un}, depends on that of an eligible job-seeker, which continues to be denoted by V_u. When a noneligible job-seeker accepts a job offering an instantaneous wage w, his or her expected utility $V_e(w)$ satisfies the following equation:

$$rV_e(w) = w + q[V_u - V_e(w)] \tag{13}$$

It should be noted that it is the expected utility V_u of an *eligible* job-seeker that appears in this expression, for it is assumed, for the sake of simplicity, that unemployment insurance benefits are paid whenever an agent has been employed at least once. For given V_u, relation (13) indicates that $V_e(w)$ increases with w, and that the reservation wage of a noneligible job-seeker, denoted by x_n, satisfies the equality $V_e(x_n) = V_{un}$. Since we always have $x = rV_u$, equation (13) allows us to express the expected utility of a noneligible job-seeker as a function of the two reservation wages, x and x_n. The result is:

$$rV_{un} = \frac{rx_n + qx}{r + q} \tag{14}$$

Assuming that the frequency with which a noneligible job-seeker receives job offers is always equal to λ, his or her expected utility is defined by the following equation, which is analogous to relation (5) in the basic model:

$$rV_{un} = z_n + \lambda \int_{x_n}^{+\infty} [V_e(w) - V_{un}] \, dH(w) \tag{15}$$

The Reservation Wage of Noneligible Job-Seekers

Observing from (13) that $rV_e(w) = (rw + qx)/(r + q)$, and utilizing expression (14) of V_{un}, we arrive, thanks to (15) and after several simple calculations, at a relation that implicitly defines the reservation wage x_n of a noneligible person as a function of that of an eligible person. It is written:

$$rx_n = (r + q)z_n - qx + \lambda \int_{x_n}^{+\infty} (w - x_n)\, dH(w)$$

It is easy to verify that this relation implies a negative linkage between x_n and x. Since x increases with the instantaneous income z of eligible job-seekers, the reservation wage x_n of *noneligible* job-seekers is a *decreasing* function of z. This outcome is explainable as follows: a noneligible job-seeker knows that by accepting an offer of work, he or she risks becoming unemployed again in the future at rate q. But in that case, he or she also knows that he or she will henceforth be eligible for unemployment benefits $z > z_n$. A rise in z therefore increases the loss occasioned by refusing a job offer, which gives him or her incentive to lower his or her reservation wage. On the other hand, we may note that an increase in welfare payments z_n exerts upward pressure on the reservation wage of noneligible job-seekers. We shall see in section 2.4 that empirical studies have a hard time establishing any significant linkage between the amount of unemployment insurance benefit and the average duration of a spell of unemployment. The eligibility effect helps to explain this phenomenon (see also chapter 11, section 3.2, which looks at the consequences of the eligibility effect on wage bargaining).

1.2.2 On-the-Job Search

As a general rule, an individual who has a job is still able to carry out a search in order to find another one. For the sake of simplicity, we will assume that the costs of job search are negligible for a worker who is employed. The advantage of this hypothesis is that we do not have to make a distinction between employees who have a low wage and are looking for another job and those who are receiving a high wage and therefore are not looking, since the cost of doing so would be too high compared to their earnings prospects. If the costs of searching for a job are null for an employed worker, he or she always has an interest in looking for another job, and accepts the first offer that exceeds his or her present wage.

The Behavior of Agents

Let us assume that an employed person receives job offers with a frequency of λ_e, and that he or she risks losing his or her job, at any time, with an exogenous constant probability of q. The discounted utility $V_e(w)$ expected by a wage-earner whose current remuneration comes to w then has three components. The first corresponds to the instantaneous income w deriving from his or her waged labor, the second is the average discounted expected gain $q[V_u - V_e(w)]$ due to job loss, and the third is the discounted expected earnings $\lambda_e \int_w^{+\infty} [V_e(\xi) - V_e(w)]\, dH(\xi)$ consequent upon a change of employer (which occurs for every wage offer that exceeds the present wage w). Finally, $V_e(w)$ is defined by the following equation[3]:

$$rV_e(w) = w + q[V_u - V_e(w)] + \lambda_e \int_w^{+\infty} [V_e(\xi) - V_e(w)]\, dH(\xi) \qquad (16)$$

Deriving this relation with respect to w, we get:

$$V_e'(w) = \frac{1}{r + q + \lambda_e[1 - H(w)]} \qquad (17)$$

In this way we easily verify that the discounted expected utility $V_e(w)$ of an employee increases with wage w; hence the optimal search strategy for a job-seeker is characterized by a reservation wage x such that $V_e(x) = V_u$. Assuming that the arrival rate of job offers is equal to λ_u for a job-seeker, and again designating his or her instantaneous gain by z, his or her discounted expected utility V_u continues to be defined by equation (5), so that:

$$rV_u = z + \lambda_u \int_x^{+\infty} [V_e(\xi) - V_u]\, dH(\xi) \qquad (18)$$

Making $w = x$ in (16) and comparing (18), we immediately get:

$$x = z + (\lambda_u - \lambda_e) \int_x^{+\infty} [V_e(\xi) - V_u]\, dH(\xi) \qquad (19)$$

Compared to the basic model, this equation indicates that a job-seeker must henceforth weight the discounted expected utility of the job search $\int_x^{+\infty}[V_e(\xi) - V_u]\, dH(\xi)$ by the *difference* $\lambda_u - \lambda_e$ of the rates with which job offers arrive.

Properties of the Reservation Wage
We will see below in section 2.3 that the possibility of moving from one job to another plays an essential role in the elaboration of *equilibrium* search models—that is, models in which the cumulative distribution function $H(.)$ is endogenous. In this regard, it is useful to determine precisely the expression of $V_e(\xi) - V_u$ appearing in (19) so as to bring out the dependence between the reservation wage x and the function $H(.)$. By applying the formula of integration by parts[4] to the right-hand side of (19), we arrive at:

$$x = z + (\lambda_u - \lambda_e) \left[[-\bar{H}(\xi)[V_e(\xi) - V_u]]_x^\infty + \int_x^\infty \bar{H}(\xi) V_e'(\xi)\, d\xi \right]$$

As we still have $V_e(\bar{w}) - V_u = \int_x^{\bar{w}} V_e'(\xi)\, d\xi$, utilizing (17) and assuming that $\lim_{\xi \to \infty} \bar{H}(\xi)[V_e(\xi) - V_u] = 0$, we finally have:

$$x = z + (\lambda_u - \lambda_e) \int_x^\infty \frac{\bar{H}(\xi)}{r + q + \lambda_e \bar{H}(\xi)}\, d\xi \qquad \text{with} \qquad \bar{H}(\xi) \equiv 1 - H(\xi) \qquad (20)$$

This equation implicitly defines the reservation wage as a function of the parameters λ_u, λ_e and the cumulative distribution function $H(.)$. When $\lambda_e = 0$, that is, when there is no on-the-job search, we come back to the reservation wage of the basic model. Conversely, if $\lambda_e > 0$, the job-seeker takes account of the possibilities of future income associated with continuing to look for a job while employed. Adopting this stance has the effect of lowering the reservation wage. If $\lambda_e = \lambda_u$, the reservation wage is equal to the net income z of the job-seeker, for a worker then has as many chances of receiving an acceptable offer while employed as he or she does while unemployed. It is also interesting to note that if $\lambda_e > \lambda_u$, the reservation wage falls *below* z. In this configuration of the parameters, an employee has more chances of obtaining an acceptable offer than a job-seeker. The latter thus has an incentive to accept "bad" jobs which nevertheless afford him or her better prospects than his or her present situation of being unemployed. The bulk of the estimations show, however, that the inequality $\lambda_u \geq \lambda_e$ is the most probable. For example, using data from the Netherlands, van den Berg and Ridder (1998) find that λ_u differs very little from λ_e, while Bontemps (1998) and Kiefer and Neumann (1993) estimate, using French and American data, that λ_u is respectively ten times and five times higher than λ_e. This likely occurs because unemployed job-seekers devote more effort to looking for work than employed job-seekers do. Be that as it may, taking into account on-the-job search ($\lambda_e > 0$) has the effect of diminishing the size of the reservation wage in comparison to the one that emerges from the basic model ($\lambda_e = 0$).

1.2.3   Choosing How Hard to Look

The hypothesis that both the arrival rate of job offers and the costs of the job search do not vary is unsatisfactory, because it does not allow us to take into account the fact that a job-seeker may make sedulous efforts that increase the costs of the job search but at the same time increase his or her chances of receiving job offers.

Optimal Effort

If we designate the intensity of the job search by the scalar e, the notion that more job offers should result from greater effort devoted to search amounts to postulating that the rate at which offers arrive is an increasing function of e; it is natural to assume as well that the marginal returns of search are decreasing. So we postulate $\lambda = \alpha\lambda(e)$ with $\lambda' > 0$ and $\lambda'' < 0$. The parameter $\alpha > 0$ we interpret as an indicator of the state of the labor market, independent of individual efforts. This parameter is a function of, among other things, the number of vacant jobs, the number of job-seekers, and objective characteristics such as age, sex, and educational level. We will denote by $c(e)$ the cost arising from the search effort e, with $c' > 0$ and $c'' > 0$. Thus, henceforth the instantaneous utility of a job-seeker will be written $[b - c(e)]$. For ease of exposition, we will also assume that there is no on-the-job search—although the opposite assumption would change the outcome very little (see Mortensen, 1986). Thus we can follow exactly the line of reasoning worked out in the basic model in section 2.1, positing in the first stage that the amount of effort e is given. The reservation wage x is always implicitly defined by the equation (6), which will henceforth be written:

$$x = b - c(e) + \frac{\alpha\lambda(e)}{r + q}\int_x^{+\infty}(w - x)\,dH(w) \tag{21}$$

This relation gives the value of the reservation wage associated with a given amount of effort e. Now the optimal value of effort ought, by definition, to maximize the intertemporal utility V_u of a job-seeker. Since $V_u = x/r$, this value is reached by differentiating relation (21) with respect to e and looking for the value of e for which $\partial x/\partial e = 0$. The result is:

$$c'(e) = \frac{\alpha \lambda'(e)}{r + q} \int_x^{+\infty} (w - x)\, dH(w) \tag{22}$$

The reader can verify that the hypotheses made about the functions $\lambda(.)$ and $c(.)$ guarantee that the amount of effort defined by this relation is indeed a maximum. With the help of (21), we further obtain:

$$x = b + \frac{\lambda(e)}{\lambda'(e)} c'(e) - c(e) \tag{23}$$

The Properties of Optimal Effort
In what follows, it will be helpful to view equations (22) and (23) as forming a system determining in an implicit manner the reservation wage and the optimal effort, respectively written as $x(\alpha, b)$ and $e(\alpha, b)$. By differentiating relation (23) with respect to α, it is easy to show that $\partial x(\alpha, b)/\partial \alpha$ and $\partial e(\alpha, b)/\partial \alpha$ are of the same sign. With the help of this property, differentiating equation (22) with respect to α implies:

$$\frac{\partial x(\alpha, b)}{\partial \alpha} > 0 \qquad \text{and} \qquad \frac{\partial e(\alpha, b)}{\partial \alpha} > 0$$

We knew already that an improvement in the state of the labor market causes the reservation wage to rise—see (9)—and it is apparent that it also increases the intensity of the job search. In other words, when the economy is going well, it pays a job-seeker to look harder, which also allows him or her to raise his or her wage demands. Conversely when the economy slows, a job-seeker both lowers his or her reservation wage and reduces his or her search efforts (see also van den Berg and van Ours, 1994).

Differentiating relation (22) with respect to b, we deduce that $\partial x(\alpha, b)/\partial b$ and $\partial e(\alpha, b)/\partial b$ are of opposite signs. Using this result, differentiating relation (23) with respect to b further implies:

$$\frac{\partial x(\alpha, b)}{\partial b} > 0 \qquad \text{and} \qquad \frac{\partial e(\alpha, b)}{\partial b} < 0$$

Thus, as in the basic model, a rise in the income of a job-seeker raises the reservation wage—see further (9)—but we also observe that such a rise tends to reduce the search effort. This results from the fact that an increase in b increases the intertemporal utility of the job-seeker. He or she can thus reduce the amount of effort he or she puts into searching, for the marginal gain from intensified effort sinks below the level of marginal disutility that it provokes. Finally, it should be noted that a *simultaneous* lowering of α and b has an ambiguous effect on optimal effort. It can indeed happen that certain categories of persons (the long-term unemployed in particular) find themselves facing a reduced number of job offers and a reduction in their unemployment benefits. Observation shows, however, that they do not noticeably reduce their search effort (see below, section 3.2.2).

1.2.4 Nonstationary Environment

The hypothesis that a job-seeker's environment is stationary does not apply in a number of cases. Financial constraints increase the longer unemployment lasts, job offers most often grow scarcer, and net income from the search falls off, since as a general rule unemployment insurance systems mandate a reduction in, or even a termination of, the payment of benefits at the end of a certain period. In what follows we will focus only on this last cause of nonstationarity (van den Berg, 1990, presents a model that takes into account a number of causes of nonstationarity). More precisely, we will assume that the net instantaneous income of a job-seeker diminishes (in the broad sense) over time. We will thus have $z(t) \leq z(t')$ for all $t \geq t'$.

In this nonstationary environment, the discounted expected utility of a person entering unemployment, or $V_u(0)$, is no longer necessarily equal to the discounted expected utility $V_u(t)$ of a person who has already been unemployed for a period $t > 0$. We do, however, continue to assume that a job offer is a proposal of a constant wage that an employee will receive as long as he or she remains with the firm that makes the proposal. Thus, the discounted expected utility $V_e(w)$ of a person paid a constant wage w is stationary. Assuming for simplicity that there is no on-the-job search, it is defined by the following equation:

$$rV_e(w) = w + q[V_u(0) - V_e(w)] \tag{24}$$

The optimal job search strategy still consists of refusing all proposals that offer an expected utility less than that of an unemployed person and accepting all others. Since, following relation (24), $V_e(w)$ is an increasing function of w, the optimal strategy comes down to choosing, at every moment, a reservation wage such that only offers that exceed it will be accepted. Let us denote by $x(t)$ the reservation wage of a person whose duration of unemployment is equal to t; this wage is then characterized by the equality $V_e[x(t)] = V_u(t)$. Since the function $V_e(.)$ is increasing, the reservation wage $x(t)$ varies in the same direction as the discounted expected utility $V_u(t)$. Now, intuition suggests that $V_u(t)$ ought to decrease with the duration t of unemployment, inasmuch as the resources $z(t)$ of a job-seeker diminish with this duration. In order to see this clearly, we may focus on a short interval of time $[t, t + dt]$ and make explicit the trade-off equation giving the value of $V_u(t)$. If λ continues to designate the rate at which job offers arrive, we then have:

$$V_u(t) = \underset{s}{\text{Max}} \frac{z(t)\,dt + \lambda\,dt\left[\int_s^{+\infty} V_e(w)\,dH(w) + V_u(t+dt)H(s)\right] + (1 - \lambda\,dt)V_u(t+dt)}{1 + r\,dt} \tag{25}$$

In the maximization problem appearing in this equation, the discounted expected utility $V_u(t + dt)$ at date $(t + dt)$ has to be considered as given, for on that date the job-seeker decides on a *new* reservation wage independently of the choice made at date t. The optimal reservation wage is then obtained by setting to zero the derivative with respect to s of the term between brackets in expression (25) of $V_u(t)$. After several simple calculations we arrive at $V_e[x(t)] = V_u(t + dt)$, which corresponds exactly to the characterization $V_e[x(t)] = V_u(t)$ of the reservation wage $x(t)$ when $dt \to 0$.[5]

Since the net income $z(t)$ of an unemployed person decreases over time, equation (25) shows that $V_u(t) \leq V_u(t')$ necessarily obtains for every $t \geq t'$. Since his or her reservation wage and discounted expected utility vary in the same direction, we can deduce that $x(t) \leq x(t')$ for every $t \geq t'$. Hence reservation wages fall with time spent searching for a job when unemployment insurance benefits are regressive. This result implies that the rate of leaving unemployment, or $\lambda[1 - H(x(t))]$, increases with the duration t of the unemployment spell—a conclusion confirmed by a number of observations, in particular concerning the behavior of certain categories of job-seekers as the period of their entitlement to unemployment insurance benefits draws to a close (see section 3.2.2 below). On the other hand, the long-term unemployed have, in general, a smaller probability of exiting from unemployment than do the short-term unemployed. This phenomenon can be explained by the fact that job offers arrive less frequently the longer one is unemployed, either because the productive abilities of the individual decline or simply because employers take the view that too long a period of unemployment sends a bad ''signal.'' In these circumstances, the fact that one's reservation wage has fallen may be offset, or more than offset, by the declining arrival rate of job offers. The rate of exiting from unemployment is then no longer obliged to decrease with the duration of the job search.

The foregoing analysis can easily be applied to the case of a change in the length of time unemployment insurance benefits are paid.[6] For example, if this period is shortened, that means that the intertemporal resources of the job-seeker shrink, and that diminishes both his or her discounted expected utility and reservation wage. Thus, for a period of unemployment of the *same length*, and for the *same amount* of benefits, a shortened period of entitlement to benefits leads to a lowering of the reservation wage, and consequently a reduction in the average duration of unemployment.

2 THE EQUILIBRIUM SEARCH MODEL AND THE THEORY OF OPTIMAL UNEMPLOYMENT INSURANCE

In this section we extend the basic job search model in two ways. The aim of the first of these extensions is to render *endogenous* the dispersion of wages for individuals endowed with identical productive abilities and preferences. This perspective is important, inasmuch as the theory of perfect competition, which will be presented in greater detail in chapter 4, predicts that identical individuals with identical jobs should receive the same wage. We shall see that this conclusion no longer necessarily holds in a universe where information about the characteristics of jobs is costly and where employers set wages. The second extension exploits the job search model in order to define the optimal properties of unemployment insurance systems when the effort that job-seekers put into their search is imperfectly verifiable. It will be shown that unemployment benefits ought to decrease with the length of a spell of unemployment, and more generally ought to depend on the past history (episodes of unemployment, types of job held) of individuals in the labor market.

2.1 JOB SEARCH AND LABOR MARKET EQUILIBRIUM

The basic job search model focuses solely on the behavior of job-seekers and takes the distribution of wages as given. This approach leaves the setting of wages unexplained, and thus makes it difficult to analyze policies that might affect it. For example, we have seen that a rise in unemployment insurance benefits increases the reservation wage. Such a rise ought to influence the wage policies of firms, and consequently alter the distribution of existing wages in the economy. Equilibrium search models have as their goal the explanation of how wages are set through the attribution of well-defined strategic behavior to firms. Labor market equilibrium is therefore characterized by an *endogenous* distribution of wages.

2.1.1 The Inadequacies of the Basic Model

In the job search models that we have employed to this point, the cumulative distribution function $H(.)$ of wage offers is exogenous. This hypothesis must be abandoned if we wish to understand how wages are determined.

Diamond's Critique

Diamond (1971) was the first to emphasize that if the reactions of employers are introduced into the basic job search model, the outcome is necessarily a labor market equilibrium in which the distribution of wages is concentrated at a single point. To better understand this result, let us assume that the economy is composed of a large number of identical suppliers of labor and a large number of firms, likewise identical, and let us suppose that equation (6) defining the reservation wage represents the response of workers to the wage policies put in place by the firms. Since the workers accept *without distinction* all proposals that equal or exceed the reservation wage, the firms gain no advantage by offering wages that exceed it (because as a general rule, the profit per capita diminishes with the cost of labor). At equilibrium, the distribution of wages is thus concentrated at value x of the reservation wage, and relation (6) indicates that the latter is then equal to the instantaneous gain z of the workers. This result arises essentially out of the hypothesis that workers never (voluntarily) leave their employers. Hence, firms have no incentive to set wages superior to the minimum acceptable z. At first sight, Diamond's critique appears to deprive the basic job search model of all its relevance, since within this model we cannot explain why the distribution of wages does not degenerate to a single point.

Empirical Difficulties

Job search models with an exogenous distribution of wage offers are no more satisfactory at the empirical level. The estimation of these models is generally effected thanks to individual-temporal data that, for the most part, describe only the wages *accepted* by those who are looking for a job. Thus the econometrician has at his or her disposal only a distribution of wages truncated at the left by the (unobservable) reservation wage, and can identify the truncated part only through an a priori approach. In particular, he or she can cannot identify, without some a priori procedure, one of the essential parameters of these models: the probability of accepting or rejecting a job offer. To remedy this drawback, the econometrician may limit himself or herself to a given family of probability densities (so-called "parametric" estimations). The identification of the truncated part then becomes feasible, but there is nothing to guarantee the relevance of the parametrization utilized (van den Berg, 1999).

From the Partial Model to the Equilibrium Model

In reaction to the critiques aimed at the basic job search model, *equilibrium* search models have been elaborated in which the distribution of wages becomes an endogenous variable dependent on, among other things, the wage strategies of employers. An initial approach consists of extending the basic model—often termed the partial model, for clarity—by introducing heterogeneity among the workers (Albrecht and Axell, 1984). Under certain conditions, labor market equilibrium is compatible with a nondegenerated distribution of wages that coincides with that of the reservation wages of different categories. But this solution, which relies *solely* on the heterogeneity of agents, is not totally satisfactory, inasmuch as numerous studies reveal that part of the variance in wages always remains unexplained even when individual heterogeneity is taken into account (see, for example, Krueger and Summers, 1988, and Abowd et al., 1999).

Another approach, the one that currently prevails, takes as its point of departure the model (laid out in section 1.2.2 of this chapter) in which the job search takes place while the seeker is employed. In this model, it should be noted that a firm might have an incentive to offer relatively high wages so as to achieve a low quit rate and attract large numbers of workers. It is thus conceivable that, for a given firm, profit maximization might be attained indifferently through high wages and many employees, or conversely through low wages and few employees. In this case, labor market equilibrium is well characterized by an endogenous nondegenerated distribution of wages, yet with homogeneous workers. The model we now present, inspired by Burdett and Mortensen (1998), develops precisely these ideas.

2.1.2   An Equilibrium Search Model

In the stationary state, the equilibrium of flows in the labor market makes the distribution of wages depend on the volume of employment in each firm.

Flows on the Labor Market

The economy is composed of a continuum of firms and a continuum of workers. For simplicity, these two continua are assumed to be of unitary mass. This hypothesis allows us to account simply for the fact that there exists a large given number of firms and workers. The job search behavior of suppliers of labor is identical to that in the model with on-the-job searching studied in section 1.2.2. In particular, q always designates the instantaneous job destruction rate, and the parameters λ_u and λ_e represent respectively the arrival rate of job offers for an unemployed job-seeker and for one who has a job. The reservation wage of the former, always denoted by x, is then given by relation (20), in which the cumulative distribution function $H(.)$ is henceforth an endogenous variable.

Let us designate by $\ell(w)$ the employment level in a firm that pays wage w to its employees. Let us also designate by $L(w)$ the employment level in firms paying a wage that is less than a given value of w. This quantity satisfies the equality $L(w) = \int_0^w \ell(\xi)\, dH(\xi)$. Let us denote by u the unemployment rate; we may now consider entries in the set of firms that are paying a wage *superior* to w. These entries are composed, on the one hand, of unemployed job-seekers who have received a wage offer superior to w, and on the other of employees being paid a wage smaller than w who have received an offer above w. Now, at each date, an unemployed job-seeker receives offers at rate λ_u, and these offers are higher than w with a probability $[1 - H(w)]$. Entries of unemployed job-seekers into firms offering a wage higher than w then amount to $\lambda_u u[1 - H(w)]$. Similarly, for workers employed at a wage below w, the number of these entries amounts to $\lambda_e L(w)[1 - H(w)]$. In total, entries into firms paying a wage higher than w are equal to $[\lambda_u u + \lambda_e L(w)]\bar{H}(w)$, where we have posited $\bar{H}(w) = 1 - H(w)$. As regards exits, it suffices to remark that employment in the firms paying more than w is equal to $1 - u - L(w)$. Since the only source of exits from this set of firms is the destruction of jobs—which occurs at the exogenous rate q—the number of exits reaches the value $q[1 - u - L(w)]$. At stationary equilibrium, the equality of the flows of entries and exits is thus given by the following equation:

$$[\lambda_u u + \lambda_e L(w)]\bar{H}(w) = q[1 - u - L(w)]$$

Employment and the Distribution of Wages
The preceding equality being true for any wage level w, we get another equality by differentiating this relation with respect to w. Noting that the derivative of the function $L(w) = \int_0^w \ell(\xi)\, dH(\xi)$ satisfies $L'(w) = H'(w)\ell(w)$, we then get:

$$[q + \lambda_e \bar{H}(w)]l(w) = \lambda_u u + \lambda_e \int_0^w \ell(\xi)\, dH(\xi) \qquad \text{with} \qquad \bar{H}(w) \equiv 1 - H(w) \tag{26}$$

The equality of the flows of entries into and exits from employment thus furnishes a link between the employment function $\ell(.)$ and the cumulative distribution function $H(.)$. This link becomes even more apparent if we point out once again that equation (26) is true for any wage w. Since the rate of unemployment u does not depend on any particular wage, the derivation of this relation with respect to w leads to the following differential equation:

$$\frac{\ell'(w)}{\ell(w)} = \frac{2\lambda_e H'(w)}{q + \lambda_e \bar{H}(w)} \tag{27}$$

This differential equation implicitly defines all the functions $\ell(.)$ and $H(.)$ compatible with equilibrium of flows on the labor market. Examining the behavior of firms allows us to specify the properties of $\ell(.)$ and finally to make explicit the cumulative distribution function of wages.

2.1.3 Labor Market Equilibrium

The distribution of wages results from compatibility between the equilibrium of flows on the labor market and the strategic behavior of agents.

The Behavior of Firms

We will assume that firms compete using wages to attract workers. More precisely, each firm decides unilaterally on the *constant* wage that will be paid to its employees. It is thus assumed that the workers of the same firm all receive the same wage. We will also assume that at each moment a worker is capable of producing, if he or she is employed, a constant exogenous quantity y of goods. If there are $\ell(w)$ workers in a firm that pays wage w, the instantaneous profit of this firm works out to $(y - w)\ell(w)$. For simplicity we shall assume that the real rate of interest r is close to zero (an approximation we can justify by noting that in practice r is clearly smaller than the rates λ_u, λ_e and q). Under this hypothesis, each firm sets its wage in such a way as to maximize its stationary instantaneous profit $(y - w)\ell(w)$, with the wages being paid in the other firms being taken as given (so what we have is a noncooperative equilibrium of the Cournot-Nash type). Let us first note that each firm must necessarily propose a wage w higher than the reservation wage x, or $w \geq x$, so as to be able to attract the unemployed at least. The optimal wage is then defined by the equality:

$$\frac{\ell'(w)}{\ell(w)} = \frac{1}{y - w}, \qquad w \geq x \tag{28}$$

It is worth noting that this relation is true for all the values of $w \geq x$ and thus can be interpreted as a differential equation in which the unknown is the function $\ell(w)$.

The Relation Between Employment and Wages

At stationary equilibrium, the value of the unemployment rate results directly from the equality between the flows of workers entering and exiting from unemployment. The former amounts to $q(1 - u)$ and the latter is equal to $\lambda_u[1 - H(x)]u = \lambda_u u$. The stationary unemployment rate is then given by:

$$u = \frac{q}{\lambda_u + q} \tag{29}$$

This value for the unemployment rate has the feature of not depending on the income of the unemployed. In other words, a rise in unemployment insurance benefits has no influence on the unemployment rate, nor for that matter on the average length of a period of unemployment, which in this model equals $1/\lambda_u$. These results are the simple consequence of the coincidence between the reservation wage and the lower bound of the distribution of wages. In these conditions, all offers are accepted, and only the frequency λ_u with which offers arrive affects the duration and magnitude of unemployment.

The employment function $\ell(w)$ is obtained using relation (28), which characterizes the optimal behavior of a firm. Because this relation is true for all wages belonging to the support of H, it can be considered a first-order differential equation in $\ell(w)$. Quantity $\ell'(w)/\ell(w)$ representing the derivative of $\ln \ell(w)$, and the integral of $(y - w)^{-1}$ being equal to $-\ln(y - w)$, this equation is written $\int \ln \ell(w)\, dw = -\int \ln(y - w)\, dw$, or $\ln \ell(w) = -\ln(y - w) + a$, where a is a constant. Taking the exponential of the two sides of this equation, we get $\ell(w) = A/(y - w)$, with $A = \exp(a)$. The value of the constant A is deduced from that of $\ell(x)$. Making $w = x$ in equation (26), we find that $\ell(x) = \lambda_u u/(q + \lambda_e)$, and in consequence A is equal to $\lambda_u u(y - x)/(q + \lambda_e)$. Taking account of the value (29) of the stationary unemployment rate, the end result is:

$$\ell(w) = \frac{\lambda_u q}{(\lambda_e + q)(\lambda_u + q)} \frac{(y - x)}{(y - w)} \tag{30}$$

The intuitive view proves correct: employment does indeed increase with wages. Moreover, we note that the profits $(y - w)\ell(w)$ of the different firms are all equal at equilibrium. In other words, there exists a distribution of wages such that at equilibrium, firms can realize the same level of profit with low wages and a small workforce or with high wages and a large workforce. Consequently, firms that pay low wages face a relatively low hiring rate and a relatively high quit rate, which results, at stationary equilibrium, in a small workforce.

The Equilibrium Wage Distribution

Comparison of equations (28) and (27) reveals that distributions of wage offers compatible with both equilibrium of flows on the labor market and strategic behavior by firms in setting wages necessarily satisfy, for any value of w, relation:

$$2(y - w)H'(w) + H(w) = \frac{q + \lambda_e}{\lambda_e} \tag{31}$$

This equality, which holds for all w, is interpretable as a first-order differential equation in $H(w)$. If A designates any constant, then the general solution of this differential equation is written[7]:

$$H(w) = A\sqrt{y - w} + \frac{q + \lambda_e}{\lambda_e}$$

The constant A is obtained using the fact that firms have no interest in offering a wage smaller than the reservation wage x of unemployed job-seekers. Thus it is certain that $H(x) = 0$. Utilizing this property, we find that the *sole* possible equilibrium wage distribution is expressed by[8]:

$$H(w) = \frac{q + \lambda_e}{\lambda_e}\left[1 - \sqrt{\frac{y - w}{y - x}}\right] \tag{32}$$

The upper bound of the distribution of wages, denoted by $\bar{w}$, satisfies $H(\bar{w}) = 1$. It is defined as a function of the reservation wage by the formula:

$$\bar{w} = y - (y - x)\left(\frac{q}{q + \lambda_e}\right)^2 \tag{33}$$

If the reservation wage is less than the instantaneous production of a worker y (which is a necessary condition of the existence of equilibrium), we can verify that the upper bound $\bar{w}$ of wages is likewise smaller than individual production y. Taking into account (32), the equilibrium wage distribution takes the form:

$$H'(w) = \frac{q + \lambda_e}{2\lambda_e} \frac{1}{\sqrt{(y - x)(y - w)}} \tag{34}$$

The equilibrium distribution $H'(.)$ of this model turns out to *increase* as the level of wages rises. This result is a consequence both of the property that all agents are homogeneous and of the firms' strategy of simply proposing an invariable wage. Under these conditions, a firm that raises its wage w increases its volume of employment, to the detriment of employment in the other firms. This movement leads to an increasing relation between the wage and the size of the firms.

All the relations giving the equilibrium values of the endogenous variables of the model depend on the reservation wage x, which is itself an endogenous variable. Now, the reservation wage is always defined by equation (20) of the partial model, on condition of positing $r = 0$. Taking account of expression (32) of the equilibrium wage distribution, it is possible to obtain an explicit analytic form of this wage. After several calculations we arrive at:

$$x = \frac{z(q + \lambda_e)^2 + (\lambda_u - \lambda_e)\lambda_e y}{(q + \lambda_e)^2 + (\lambda_u - \lambda_e)\lambda_e} \tag{35}$$

If there is no possibility of on-the-job search, or $\lambda_e = 0$, we have $x = z$, and, following (33), $\bar{w} = z$. We thus come back to the paradox pointed out by Diamond (1971), namely, that the only possible equilibrium in the partial job search model occurs when the distribution of wages is entirely concentrated at the level of instantaneous gain z of an unemployed job-seeker. When $\lambda_u \to +\infty$, there is no friction in the labor market, and the workers obtain the totality of product. The wage is thus uniform and equal to the value of production ($x = \bar{w} = y$). Searching while working is thus pointless ($\lambda_1 = 0$). These characteristics describe a perfectly competitive equilibrium where there is no unemployment ($u = 0$) and where the wage equals the marginal productivity of labor.

2.1.4 Final Remarks on Equilibrium Search Models

Compared to the partial model, the equilibrium search model presents a number of advantages:

1. In the equilibrium search model, the wage of an individual employee rises only when he or she moves from one job to another. Although in practice, that is not

the only reason for individual pay to rise, this phenomenon is in fact observed in the majority of transitions of this type (see, for example, Topel and Ward, 1992). Moreover, in this model the wage is positively correlated with the size of the firm, which fits well with observations that tell us that, even after having controlled for the heterogeneity of workers and firms, bigger firms pay higher wages than smaller ones (Abowd et al., 1999).

2. Wages rise, on average, as workers gain seniority. Assuming that new entrants begin as job-seekers, the wage at which they are hired is a minimum corresponding to the reservation wage x. After that, their wage rises every time they change firms. More senior employees, who have on average had the most job offers, thus enjoy the highest wages. This prediction of the equilibrium search model agrees with the observation that a worker's wage increases with the time he or she has spent in the labor market (Abowd et al., 1999).

3. The lower bound of the equilibrium wage distribution being equal to the reservation wage, an unemployed job-seeker accepts all the offers he or she receives. This conclusion fits very well with that of empirical studies, which do in fact find that the probability of accepting an offer is close to 1 (see section 3.2.2 below for more details).

4. Unlike the partial model, which only looks at the behavior of unemployed job-seekers, the equilibrium search model integrates the reactions of all agents. When it has been estimated or calibrated, it thus allows us to quantify the effects of a change of parameters or economic policy while taking account of the interdependence of agents' decisions. For example, relations (33) and (34) reveal that a rise in the minimum wage—which in this model comes to the same thing as a rise in the lower bound x of the wage distribution considered as exogenous—shifts the *whole* distribution of wages to the right. An increase in the amount of unemployment insurance benefit has an analogous effect.

5. The wage offer distribution $H(.)$ is entirely determined—see relations (32) and (35)—by knowledge of the structural parameters of the model λ_u, λ_e, q, y, and z. Data obtained by following up a sample of individuals over a sufficient period allow us to estimate these parameters. Unlike the partial model, it is not necessary to specify a priori a form for the cumulative distribution function of wages in order to estimate the consequences of policies that change the reservation wage.

The search equilibrium model does, however, present one major flaw: the density of wage distribution—see (34)—is an *increasing* function of the wage. This prediction turns out to conflict with all observations, which reveal that this density is increasing at first, then decreasing, with a maximum generally not too far from the lower bound. To remedy this flaw, one solution lies in introducing heterogeneity among agents (a good illustration of this approach can be found in van den Berg and

Ridder, 1998, and Bontemps et al., 2000). The model, however, clearly becomes less workable, and most often it is impossible to obtain explicit solutions. What is more, even using this procedure, the fit with empirical wage distributions is still far from satisfactory. Another approach is to modify the equilibrium search model by assuming that wages are not necessarily equal within a firm, and that each firm can make counterproposals to workers who may be thinking of quitting because they have made contact with another employer (Postel-Vinay and Robin, 2002a, 2002b). These hypotheses no doubt fit reality more closely than those adopted in the equilibrium search model initially developed by Burdett and Mortensen (1998) and presented in this chapter. Postel-Vinay and Robin show that the mode of wage setting that they envisage, coupled with heterogeneity of firms, leads to a wage distribution endowed with empirically relevant properties.

An operational description of the labor market would also require that parameters λ_u, λ_e, and q describing a worker's transitions between different possible states be made endogenous. In particular, the job offers arrival rates depend on the number of vacant jobs and the number of job-seekers—quantities that derive from the behavior of firms and the way in which wages are set. The job destruction rate q is in all likelihood influenced by variations in productivity and by the way wages are set. The matching models that we develop in chapter 9 partly fill these gaps.

2.2 The Trade-off Between Insurance and Incentive in Compensating for Unemployment

Most often the agency managing the unemployment insurance system does not check thoroughly on whether its clients are making suitable efforts to find a job. In this textbook case, the agency is faced with a "moral hazard" problem, and perfect insurance, i.e., complete replacement of the unemployed person's lost wages, might also take away his or her incentive to actively look for a job. This moral hazard problem causes the authorities to set up relatively sophisticated incentive schemes in which benefit payments are dependent on the duration of unemployment and which provide for sanctions when it can be shown that a client's job search has been inadequate. At the theoretical level, the job search models with moral hazard whose guiding principles we will proceed to lay out do in fact show that unemployment insurance is necessarily imperfect. The models of Baily (1978) and Flemming (1978) already came to this conclusion, and went on to point out that the optimal replacement rate ought to be low because the exit rate from unemployment is highly sensitive to the income of the unemployed person, and because workers have low risk aversion.

A relevant analysis of unemployment insurance should also focus on the time profile of the benefit payments, which can provide at least as much incentive as their amount. This is the reason most unemployment insurance systems limit the period during which the unemployed can receive benefits, and provide for such benefits to tail off the longer that period lasts. The dynamic models with moral hazard of Shavell and Weiss (1979), Hopenhayn and Nicolini (1997), and Wang and Williamson (1996) do in fact prove that optimal unemployment benefits must necessarily decrease with the length of the unemployment spell. Using a model inspired by Hopenhayn and Nicolini (1997), we will attempt to grasp the workings of unemployment insurance in the absence and then in the presence of moral hazard.

In order to study the properties of unemployment insurance systems, we have chosen the framework of the "principal–agent" model, in which the principal proposes a contract to an agent that the latter can only accept or refuse (see chapter 6, section 3.1). Assuming that a contract should offer each person who enters into unemployment an expected exogenous utility, denoted by $\bar{V}$ and known as "promise value," the optimal contract should simply minimize the average cost of an unemployed person while at the same time offering him or her this utility $\bar{V}$. We will first lay out the model and the optimal contract when the effort made is verifiable. This benchmark model will subsequently allow us to analyze the optimal contract when the effort made cannot be verified.

2.2.1 An Agency Model for the Study of Unemployment Insurance

The effort an agent makes to find a job can take no more than two values at any moment: either the constant value $a > 0$, in which case the agent finds employment at rate $p\,dt$ over each short interval of time $[t, t + dt]$, where $p > 0$ is an exogenous constant, or the value 0, in which case the agent gets no job offers and remains unemployed. Our supposition is that the "principal"—in other words, the agency charged with managing unemployment insurance—proposes a *contract* to every person entering unemployment (by convention, unemployment begins on date $t = 0$) specifying the values $b(t)$ of the unemployment benefit received if the person is still looking for a job on date $t > 0$, and the values $g(t)$ of the transfers to be received if employment resumes on date t. It should be noted that the benefit payments $b(t)$ and the transfers $g(t)$ should employment resume are both conditional on the length t of the unemployment spell. We must also point out that if $g(t) < 0$ what we have is a tax, and if $g(t) > 0$, a subsidy.

The behavior of the principal and the agent differ according to whether the search effort is *verifiable* or not. The concept of verifiability will be explained in detail in chapter 6, section 1.1. In the situation that interests us here, the search effort will be called verifiable if there is irrefutable proof allowing a third party (that is, a person or organization different from the agency and the unemployed person) to conclude impartially that the client has really carried out search effort a. In that situation, the agency can check on the efforts made by agents and make the payment of unemployment insurance benefits conditional upon those efforts. In other words, when the effort is verifiable, the agency has no need to give the agent *incentive* to look for a job. The situation is completely different if the effort is not verifiable. There is then no impartial instance that can assess the effort actually made by the agent, who might be receiving benefit payments without really looking for a job. In practice, the checks carried out on the efforts of agents are imperfect, which leads us to privilege this second hypothesis. Thus the agency has to propose a system of benefit payments such that the client has a real interest in looking for work rather than receiving the payments and not searching at all, in which case he or she has no chance of finding a job. In other words, the agency has to design an incentive contract.

Workers' Behavior

It is assumed that suppliers of labor do not have access to financial markets, and therefore that they do not save or invest. Assuming access to financial markets and taking savings and investment into account do not qualitatively change the results as long as there do not exist complete insurance markets for unemployment risk (see Flemming, 1978, and Hansen and Imrohoroglu, 1992). Let us designate by z the exogenous constant income that a person obtains on each date while remaining outside the labor market; z then represents here the instantaneous income of a nonparticipant. If we confine our analysis to a small interval of time $[t, t + dt]$, it is possible to write the equation giving the discounted expected utility of a job-seeker, $V_u(t)$, in the following manner:

$$V_u(t) = \frac{1}{1 + r\,dt}\{[v(z + b(t)) - a]\,dt + p\,dt\,V_e(t + dt) + (1 - p\,dt)V_u(t + dt)\} \tag{36}$$

In this expression, r designates the discount rate and function $v(.)$ represents the instantaneous utility of the agent when at date t he or she receives wage z and unemployment insurance benefit $b(t)$. If the agent is risk-averse, function $v(.)$ is such that $v' > 0$ and $v'' < 0$. Equation (36) indicates that a job-seeker producing effort a during an interval of time $[t, t + dt]$ attains, over that period, the utility level $[v(z + b(t)) - a]\,dt$. With probability $p\,dt$, he or she can then find at date $t + dt$ waged employment that procures an expected utility equal to $V_e(t + dt)$. With the complementary probability $(1 - p\,dt)$, he or she remains unemployed, and his or her discounted expected utility then amounts to $V_u(t + dt)$. Making $dt \to 0$ in (36), we thus find that $V_u(t)$ is given by the equation (we omit the index t and in what follows, a dotted variable represents the time derivative of this variable):

$$rV_u = v(z + b) - a + p(V_e - V_u) + \dot{V}_u \tag{37}$$

We will assume that all jobs offer the same exogenous constant wage w, that there is no job-seeking by persons already on the job, and that jobs are never destroyed. If a job-seeker finds employment after an unemployment spell of duration t, he or she receives a net wage of $[w + g(t)]$ and keeps his or her new job indefinitely. The discounted expected utility of a person finding a job after an unemployment spell of duration t is thus given by:

$$V_e(t) = \int_t^\infty v[w + g(t)]e^{-r(\tau - t)}\,d\tau = v[w + g(t)]/r \tag{38}$$

The Cost of an Unemployed Person

In order to define the average cost of an unemployed person, we have to rely on the properties of the stochastic process governing the length of a period of unemployment. More precisely, in our model the exit from unemployment follows a Poisson process whose constant parameter p is identical to the exit rate from unemployment. In appendix D at the end of the book, we point out that that signifies that the probability of still being unemployed at date t is equal to e^{-pt}. We then show that the expectation of the discounted present value of the cost of an unemployed person on the date he or she enters unemployment is defined by (see the appendix at the end of this chapter):

$$C(0) = \int_0^{+\infty} \left[\frac{g(t)}{r} p + b(t) \right] e^{-(r+p)t} \, dt$$

This formula is intuitively clear: the probability of still being unemployed on date t being equal to e^{-pt}, a person in this situation costs the principal $b(t)$, and if this person finds a job on that date, which occurs with probability pe^{-pt}, he or she then costs the principal $g(t)/r$, since the latter has to pay (or receive) $g(t)$ on every date after t during which the worker remains employed. The discount factor being equal to e^{-rt}, we get the formula giving $C(0)$.

2.2.2 The Optimal Contract When the Search Effort Is Verifiable

When the effort made by the agent is a verifiable quantity, the principal has no need to give him or her incentive to look for work. In that situation, we can show that the optimal contract insures the agent completely against fluctuations in his or her income.

The Principal's Problem

Under the hypothesis of verifiability of effort, the principal minimizes the discounted expected cost of an unemployed agent, given the constraint linked to the promise value, or $V_u(0) \geq \bar{V}$. Formally the principal's problem is written (omitting the variable t so as to lighten the notation):

$$\underset{(b,g)}{\text{Max}} \ -C(0) = -\int_0^{+\infty} \left(\frac{g}{r} p + b \right) e^{-(r+p)t} \, dt$$

Subject to constraints:

$$\dot{V}_u = (r+p)V_u - v(z+b) + a - p\frac{v(w+g)}{r} \tag{39}$$

$$V_u(0) \geq \bar{V} \tag{40}$$

Relation (39) is a rewriting of equation (37) taking into account the value of V_e given by (38). The inequality (40) expresses the fact that the unemployment insurance system has to offer every individual beginning a period of unemployment a discounted expected utility $V_u(0)$ at least equal to $\bar{V}$. This way of writing the principal's problem shows that it is identical to a dynamic problem in which the expected utility V_u at date t plays the role of state variable. The differential equation (39) is the so-called transition equation, and the constraint (40) represents the initial conditions of this dynamic problem.

Mathematical appendix B at the end of the book explains the steps to follow in order to solve this type of dynamic optimization problem. Here we may first of all remark that the principal has nothing to gain from proposing a contract offering more than $\bar{V}$, since increasing the expected utility of an unemployed person requires increasing his or her expected cost. The constraint (40) is thus always binding. Let us denote by μ the multiplier associated with the transition equation (39). The Hamiltonian of the principal's problem is thus given by:

$$H = -\left(\frac{g}{r}p + b\right)e^{-(r+p)t} + \mu\left[(r+p)V_u - v(z+b) + a - p\frac{v(w+g)}{r}\right]$$

The first-order conditions are written:

$$\frac{\partial H}{\partial b} = \frac{\partial H}{\partial g} = 0 \quad \text{and} \quad \frac{\partial H}{\partial V_u} = -\dot{\mu}$$

These first-order conditions allow us to show that the unemployed are perfectly insured and that the optimal contract is stationary.

Perfectly Insured Unemployed Persons

Setting the derivatives of the Hamiltonian to zero with respect to b and g, we arrive at:

$$e^{-(r+p)t} + \mu v'(z+b) = 0$$

$$e^{-(r+p)t} + \mu v'(w+g) = 0$$

(41)

Comparison of these last two equalities immediately implies:

$$v'(z+b) = v'(w+g) \iff z+b = w+g$$

It is thus apparent that if the search effort is verifiable, the optimal contract completely insures the agent against fluctuations in his or her income. With it, he or she obtains the same income independently of his or her situation. It is worth noting that full insurance, which certainly implies equality of the marginal utility of consumption for an unemployed person and for one who is employed, does not necessarily take the form of an equalization of income. Hence, if preferences are represented by a utility function $v(c, \ell)$, where c and ℓ designate respectively the consumption of physical goods and time devoted to leisure, the equalization of the marginal utility of consumption is written $v_c(b+z, \ell_u) = v_c(w+g, \ell_e)$, where ℓ_u and ℓ_e represent the duration of leisure for an unemployed and an employed person, with $\ell_e < \ell_u$. It is then apparent that the equalization of marginal utilities does not entail identical incomes unless $v_{c\ell} = 0$. More generally the equalization of marginal utilities implies that the incomes of unemployed persons are higher than those of employed ones if consumption is a substitute for leisure in Edgeworth's sense ($v_{c\ell} < 0$) and lower if it is not. The representation of preferences adopted in our model, which is standard in the job search literature, corresponds to the case where $v_{c\ell} = 0$.

The Euler equation of the principal's problem is obtained by differentiating the Hamiltonian with respect to V_u, which produces:

$$\mu(r+p) = -\dot{\mu}$$

(42)

In order to characterize the time path of unemployment insurance benefits, it is sufficient to derive the first-order condition (41) with respect to time, then to take into account the Euler equation (42). After several simple calculations, we arrive at:

$$\mu v''(z+b)\dot{b} = [\mu(r+p) + \dot{\mu}]v'(z+b) = 0$$

The optimal contract thus proposes constant benefit payments, and in consequence constant transfers, since $z + b = w + g$. The result is evidently that the utility V_u expected by an unemployed person is stationary and equal to $\bar{V}$ at each date t. The optimal value of unemployment insurance benefits is then found by making $\dot{V}_u = 0$ and $V_u = \bar{V}$ in the transition equation (39). We thus find:

$$v(z+b) = v(w+g) = r\bar{V} + \frac{ra}{r+p}$$

These results are easily grasped. If there is no need to give the agent incentive to make effort a, the optimal contract must solve a pure insurance problem between a risk-neutral principal and a risk-averse agent. The latter can then be perfectly insured against variations in his or her consumption (see, for example, Varian, 1992, chapter 11, for a simple presentation of the main results of microeconomic theory in the presence of uncertainty). The stationarity of the optimal solution is likewise to be explained by pointing out that the principal has to solve the same insurance problem at every date.

It is important to note that this full insurance contract is no longer optimal if the effort made cannot be verified. Faced with a contract offering utility $\bar{V}$ at every date, and specifying the payment of the same benefits b and the same transfer g whatever the duration of unemployment, the agent evidently has an interest in not searching for a job at all and receiving unemployment insurance benefits. In this way he or she does not have to bear the cost a of looking for a job and obtains, at every moment, an intertemporal utility superior to $\bar{V}$. This consideration suggests that the optimal contract cannot be stationary in a context where the search effort is not verifiable.

2.2.3 The Optimal Contract When the Search Effort Is Unverifiable

When the search effort is no longer a verifiable quantity, the principal must give the agent an incentive to make this effort. The optimal contract no longer insures the agent perfectly, and it provides for benefit payments and transfers that decrease the longer the spell of unemployment lasts.

The Incentive Constraint

When the search effort is not directly checked on by the agency, the unemployed person has the opportunity to "cheat" by making no effort while continuing to receive unemployment insurance benefits. At each date, an unemployed person chooses to make search effort a only if he or she thus obtains an expected utility $V_u(t)$ superior to the utility denoted $V_s(t)$ that he or she obtains by "cheating." These discounted expected utilities are defined by the two following equations:

$$V_s(t) = \frac{1}{1 + r\,dt}\left[v(z + b(t))\,dt + \text{Max}[V_u(t + dt), V_s(t + dt)]\right] \tag{43}$$

$$V_u(t) = \frac{1}{1 + r\,dt}\left\{[v(z + b(t)) - a]\,dt + p\,dt V_e(t + dt) + (1 - p\,dt)\text{Max}[V_u(t + dt), V_s(t + dt)]\right\} \tag{44}$$

Under the hypothesis of unverifiable effort, equation (43) indicates that an unemployed person who does not make search effort a during interval of time $[t, t + dt]$ receives unemployment benefit payments during this period—precisely because his or her effort is not verifiable—and attains a utility level equal to $v(z + b(t))\,dt$. He or she therefore has no chance of finding a job at date $t + dt$ and so obtains, on that date, the discounted utility expected by an unemployed person, or $\text{Max}[V_u(t + dt), V_s(t + dt)]$.

To provide incentive to the unemployed person to make effort a at any date $t \geq 0$, the agency must offer him or her unemployment benefits and a transfer giving him or her an intertemporal utility $V_u(t)$ superior to intertemporal utility $V_s(t)$. Making the difference between equations (44) and (43), we get:

$$V_u(t) - V_s(t) = \frac{1}{1 + r\,dt}\left\{-a\,dt + p\,dt[V_e(t + dt) - \text{Max}(V_u(t + dt), V_s(t + dt))]\right\}$$

If we make $dt \to 0$, the incentive constraint, $V_u(t) - V_s(t) \geq 0$, $\forall t$, is finally written (omitting the index t for the sake of simplicity from now on):

$$V_e - V_u \geq \frac{a}{p} \tag{45}$$

This inequality shows that the need to give the unemployed an incentive to look for work obliges the principal to pay a "rent" at least equal to a/p when they do find work. Since we have seen that the contract proposed by the agency when the effort made can be verified leads to full insurance, such that $w + g = b + z$, we deduce on the basis of definitions (37) and (38) of V_u and V_e that we then get $V_e - V_u = a/(r + p)$. It is apparent that the full insurance contract gives no incentive, since the difference $V_e - V_u$ does not satisfy the inequality (45). The agency must thus offer the unemployed person a contract different from the one that applies when effort can be verified. Moreover, condition (45) is necessarily binding, for the agency has an interest in having the value of V_u as low as possible while remaining compatible with the constraint $V_u(0) \geq \bar{V}$ linked to the promise value $\bar{V}$. Consequently, with the help of (38), the incentive constraint (45) takes the form:

$$V_e - V_u = \frac{v(w + g)}{r} - V_u = \frac{a}{p} \tag{46}$$

The terms w and a/p being constants, equality (46) implicitly defines g as a function of V_u, which we shall denote by $g(V_u)$, with:

$$g'(V_u) = \frac{r}{v'(w + g)} > 0 \tag{47}$$

Moreover, the incentive constraint (46) allows us to write the equation (37) in the simple form:

$$rV_u = v(z + b) + \dot{V}_u \qquad (48)$$

This relation shows that the intertemporal utility of an unemployed person depends only on unemployment benefit b, when the incentive constraint (46) is satisfied.

The Principal's Problem and First-Order Conditions

From this point on, the principal has to take into account the incentive constraint (46). In this case, the discounted expected utility of an unemployed person is given by equation (48). We shall assume as well that at every date, the discounted expected utility of an unemployed person cannot be less than a constant exogenous value denoted by $V_{\min}$. This lower bound might correspond to a situation of *autarky*, in which the unemployed person would look for employment without any benefits and transfers (see Hopenhayn and Nicolini, 1997, and Ljungqvist and Sargent, 2000). The lower bound $V_{\min}$ must therefore be at least equal to the discounted expected utility of a nonparticipant, i.e., $v(z)/r$. The contract proposed by the principal must thus take into account a so-called "participation constraint," which at each date is written $V_u \geq V_{\min}$. It is necessary to take this participation constraint into account in order to avoid considering contracts in which the agency proposes a very small discounted expected utility (perhaps even with negative expected incomes) to the long-term unemployed. Such contracts, which give powerful incentive, are optimal in the absence of participation constraint but have limited relevance, since they assume that workers are obligated to remain within the system that pays them unemployment insurance benefits, whatever these payments may actually amount to.

For the same reasons previously cited, it is in the principal's interest that the constraint (40) linked to the promise value be binding, so that again we have $V_u(0) = \bar{V} > V_{\min}$. Consequently the principal's problem is now written in the following manner:

$$\underset{b}{\text{Max}} \; -C(0) = -\int_0^{+\infty} \left[\frac{g(V_u)}{r} p + b \right] e^{-(r+p)t} \, dt$$

subject to:

$$\dot{V}_u = rV_u - v(z + b) \qquad (49)$$

$$V_u \geq V_{\min} \qquad (50)$$

Let us again denote by μ the multiplier associated with transition equation (49) and let us designate by $v e^{-(r+p)t}$ the multiplier associated with the participation constraint (50). The Hamiltonian can now be written:

$$H = -\left[\frac{g(V_u)}{r} p + b \right] e^{-(r+p)t} + \mu[rV_u - v(z + b)] + v e^{-(r+p)t}(V_u - V_{\min})$$

The first-order conditions are therefore:

$$\frac{\partial H}{\partial b} = 0 \qquad \text{and} \qquad \frac{\partial H}{\partial V_u} = -\dot{\mu}$$

To which must be added the complementary-slackness conditions:

$$v(V_u - V_{\min}) = 0 \qquad \text{with} \qquad v \geq 0 \tag{51}$$

Bearing in mind that g is a function of V_u satisfying (47), the first-order conditions come to:

$$e^{-(r+p)t} + \mu v'(z+b) = 0 \tag{52}$$

$$\left[-\frac{p}{v'(w+g)} + v \right] e^{-(r+p)t} + \mu r = -\dot{\mu} \tag{53}$$

Differentiating (52) with respect to t we find:

$$(r+p)\mu + \dot{\mu} = -\mu \frac{v''(z+b)}{v'(z+b)} \dot{b}$$

And (53) then implies:

$$\left[-\frac{1}{v'(w+g)} + v \right] e^{-(r+p)t} - \mu p = -\mu(r+p) - \dot{\mu} = \mu \frac{v''(z+b)}{v'(z+b)} \dot{b}$$

Since according to (52) we have $\mu = -e^{-(r+p)t}/v'(z+b)$, the definitive result is:

$$-\frac{v''(z+b)}{v'^2(z+b)} \dot{b} = v + p \frac{v'(w+g) - v'(z+b)}{v'(w+g)v'(z+b)} \tag{54}$$

Bearing in mind that g is in reality a function $g(V_u)$ defined by equation (47), the dynamics of optimal unemployment benefits systems are completely described by equations (49) and (54), and by the complementary-slackness conditions (51). In the first place it can be shown that the participation constraint (50) is necessarily binding in a stationary state (where by definition, $\dot{b} = \dot{g} = 0$). Consequently, when $\dot{b} = 0$ and $v = 0$, (54) implies that $w + g = z + b$, which is incompatible with the incentive constraint (45), as we have previously emphasized. In consequence, v is strictly positive when $\dot{b} = 0$, and the participation constraint (50) is binding in the stationary state.

The Dynamics of the Unemployment Insurance Schedule

Let us designate by V_u^*, v^*, b^*, and g^* the stationary values of the variables in which we are interested. We have just seen that the participation constraint (50) is binding in the stationary state, or $V_u^* = V_{\min}$. In making $\dot{V}_u = 0$ in (49), we get $v(z + b^*) = r V_{\min}$. The incentive constraint (46) then gives the stationary value $w + g^*$ of the net wage, or:

$$v(w + g^*) = r \left(V_{\min} + \frac{a}{p} \right) \tag{55}$$

The stationary value v^* is obtained by making $\dot{b} = 0$ in (54). Note finally that, whatever the stationary state, we always have $v(z + b^*) = r V_u^* = r V_{\min} \geq v(z)$. In

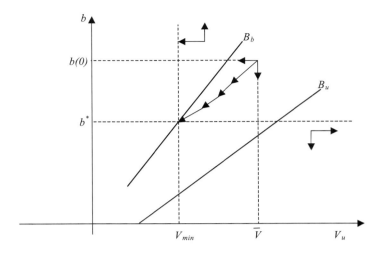

FIGURE 3.1
The dynamics of optimal unemployment insurance in the presence of unverifiable search effort.

consequence, b^* is positive. Conversely, the sign of the stationary value g^* of the transfer is undetermined. Equation (55) shows that g^* may be positive or negative according to the relative importance of wage w and the reservation utility $V_{\min}$.

Having defined the stationary values of the variables in which we are interested, we can then study the dynamics of V_u and of b, represented in figure 3.1. It is apparent that the dynamics[9] of the unemployment insurance schedule is saddle-path stable. There is thus no more than one trajectory converging toward the stationary state. On this trajectory the initial value $b(0)$ of unemployment insurance benefit is fixed by the (exogenous) value of utility $\bar{V}$. Confining ourselves to the only admissible points for which $V_u \geq V_{\min}$, we can then construct the phase diagram[10] of figure 3.1 using the dynamic equations (49) and (54). Making $\dot{V}_u = 0$ in (49) we obtain the stationarity locus of V_u, denoted B_u, defined by $rV_u = v(z + b)$; it is an increasing curve in the (V_u, b) plane. As well, (49) implies that $\dot{V}_u > 0$ (or < 0) for all points situated below (or above) B_u. Making $\dot{b} = 0$ in (54) and noting that $v = 0$ for the points of the trajectory where $V_u > V_{\min}$, we obtain the stationarity locus of b, denoted by B_b, defined by $v'(z + b) = v'[w + g(V_u)]$. Relation (49) implies as well that $\dot{b} > 0$ (respectively < 0) for all points situated above (respectively below) B_b. Utilizing condition (46) defining $g(V_u)$, we can easily show that B_u is situated below B_b in the (V_u, b) plane. We can thus establish, referring to figure 3.1, that there exists a sole trajectory passing through the point with abscissa $V_{\min}$ and ordinate b^*.

Figure 3.1 shows that unemployment insurance benefits are decreasing ($\dot{b} < 0$ on the stable arm) and converge toward a necessarily positive value b^*. Conversely, as the sign of the stationary value g^* of the transfer is not determined, the series of transfers $g(V_u)$ being decreasing—see (47)—it results that the transfers can be positive for short-term unemployment and become negative if the spell of unemployment persists. Simulations carried out by Hopenhayn and Nicolini (1997) and reported below exhibit a property of this kind.

In concluding this theoretical analysis, we may note that the optimal contract of unemployment insurance is similar to a relatively sophisticated system of the experience rating type. The unemployment insurance contracts of the real world share some of the characteristics highlighted in our model. The reduction of benefit payments with increasing duration of unemployment is a measure widely adopted, even though payments usually fall by just one level, from full to partial (France and Greece have put into place more sophisticated systems in which the benefit payments tail off through multiple levels). On the other hand, systems in which subsidies are received or taxes collected after a return to work, both of them varying with the length of the unemployment spell, are less common but do exist. Certain countries have put in place "return to work premiums" aimed precisely at encouraging the unemployed to find a job quickly. Premiums of this type exist in Japan, where the premium declines as the spell of unemployment persists (with a maximum benefit period of four months). In Australia and New Zealand there exist special premiums reserved for the long-term unemployed who find a job (OECD, 1996, chapter 2). Finally, the United States has tried out similar systems locally, and it has been found that they do in fact encourage the unemployed to find work more rapidly (a detailed study of these experiments can be found in Meyer, 1995).

A Calibrated Model for Optimal Unemployment Insurance

The model utilized to this point shows that unemployment benefits ought to diminish as the term of unemployment persists so as to manage the insurance system optimally, while offering the unemployed a predetermined level of utility. This model is a variant in continuous time of the model developed in discrete time by Hopenhayn and Nicolini (1997). These authors take the view, moreover, that job search effort is a variable that can be assigned any positive value, a hypothesis that adds considerable complication to the analytic results without, however, changing their qualitative prediction. Hopenhayn and Nicolini have also calibrated their model by taking as their benchmark the unemployment insurance system in place in the United States over the period 1978–1983. In this system, the replacement rate is 66% and benefits are paid for a maximum period of twenty-six weeks. In their basic calibration, Hopenhayn and Nicolini posit a utility function $v(c) = c^{1-\sigma}/(1-\sigma)$, with $\sigma = 1/2$. They assume that the exit rate from unemployment depends on job search effort a, according to the formula $p(a) = 1 - e^{-\rho a}$, where ρ is selected in such a way as to reproduce the estimated unemployment benefit elasticity of the probability of exiting from unemployment. It thus becomes possible to calculate the value $\bar{V}$ promised at the moment of entering unemployment by the system in place. Hopenhayn and Nicolini then compare two unemployment insurance systems that offer the same discounted expected utility $\bar{V}$. In the

Table 3.3

The optimal profile of the replacement rate in presence of moral hazard.

Weeks of unemployment	System with tax on wages		System without tax
	Replacement rate (%)	Tax on wages (%)	Replacement rate without tax on wages (%)
1	99.0	−0.5	85.8
2	98.9	−0.4	80.8
3	98.8	−0.3	76.3
4	98.7	−0.2	72.1
5	98.6	−0.1	68.2
6	98.5	0.0	64.7
7	98.4	0.1	61.4
8	98.3	0.2	58.4
12	97.9	0.6	48.2
16	97.5	1.0	40.5
26	96.5	2.0	27.7
52	94.0	4.5	13.4

Source: Hopenhayn and Nicolini (1997, p. 426).

first system, which approximates reality more closely, the agency cannot make transfers (this hypothesis amounts to positing $g = 0$ at every date in the theoretical model). The second system reproduces the optimal solution of the theoretical model, in which the agency is able to give subsidies to or levy taxes on those who find a job.

Table 3.3 presents the results obtained by Hopenhayn and Nicolini. The last column of this table shows that unemployment insurance benefits tail off sharply as unemployment persists when the insuring body cannot tax, or subsidize, wages. Conversely, if transfers to those who become employed are allowed, the rate at which benefit payments tail off becomes very weak, and the replacement rate is very high: 94% after a period of unemployment lasting 52 weeks (at that time horizon, the probability of being unemployed is close to zero, according to the calibrations used in this model). The third column of table 3.3 also shows that the transfers are subsidies when the period of unemployment does not exceed six weeks (the taxes appearing in this column are negative), and that they become deductions after six weeks of unemployment. Hopenhayn and Nicolini underline as well that the optimization of the unemployment insurance system would make it possible to reduce overall costs substantially compared to the system in place. According to their estimates, for the same promise value at entry into unemployment, costs are reduced 7% when transfers to wage-earners are not authorized, and 28% when they are.

The contribution of Hopenhayn and Nicolini (1997) underlines the potential importance of the ways in which unemployment insurance systems are structured when moral hazard is present. Wang and Williamson (1996) have extended their model by assuming that the probability of employment loss depends on the effort made by employees. In this hypothesis, moral hazard extends not just to the search efforts of the unemployed, but also to the assiduousness at work of those who are employed, for they may be tempted to shirk in order to lose their jobs if unemployment insurance benefits are too high. It is therefore desirable to adopt an experience rating scheme in which wages can be taxed and the income received depends on the duration not just of episodes of unemployment but also of employment.

The Profile of Unemployment Insurance Benefits and Wage Setting

It should be noted that all these results were obtained within a partial equilibrium framework, in which the impact of unemployment insurance on wage setting is ignored. We will see, especially in chapter 9, that the income of the unemployed exerts upward pressure on wages when the latter are being bargained over by the employee and the firm. From this perspective, shortening the period during which benefits are paid reduces the discounted expected utility of the unemployed and exerts downward pressure on the wage being bargained over, and this in turn reinforces the incentive effects of regressive unemployment insurance benefits on the search effort. The same thing does not necessarily apply, however, if we look at the effect of a different profile of benefit payments, with a *given budget* or *given tax rate*, which consists of paying more to the short-term unemployed and less to the long-term unemployed. Such a change of profile leads to an increase in the discounted expected gains of the short-term unemployed who have just lost their jobs, at the expense of the long-term unemployed. For the same discount rate, intertemporal utility at the onset of a spell of unemployment rises, which increases the bargaining power of employees and thus promotes a rise in wages. Regressive benefits thus exert upward pressure on the rate of unemployment. For a given budget, the total effect of regressive benefits on unemployment is thus ambiguous: it tends to increase wages fixed through bargaining, which is unfavorable to employment, but it also intensifies the search effort of job-seekers and lowers their reservation wage, which on the contrary promotes employment (Cahuc and Lehmann, 2000; Fredriksson and Holmlund, 2001). Changes in the rules regarding unemployment insurance thus have important consequences, and it is apparent that stricter rules may in certain cases have unfavorable effects in terms of employment. The reality is that the impact of the profile of benefit payments depends on the relative importance of the two effects just mentioned. When calibrated equilibrium models with an endogenous search effort, analogous to the matching model presented in chapter 9, are run, they suggest that rules providing for a rapid tailing off of unemployment insurance benefits produce a positive but small effect on employment (Cahuc and Lehmann, 2000; Fredriksson and Holmlund, 2001).

3   EMPIRICAL ASPECTS OF JOB SEARCH

In estimating job search models, the econometrician has at his or her disposal data on wages and/or the duration of unemployment spells. The sample of observed wages deals with wages that are *accepted*, and therefore does not represent the overall distribution of wages offered. Moreover, the econometrician does not directly observe the reservation wage. Certain surveys contain questions about the lowest acceptable wage, and the responses to these surveys do perhaps furnish an approximation of the reservation wage, but it is difficult to know how much confidence to have in this type of answer. Data on the length of unemployment spells, on the other hand, are more reliable and more directly manageable. This is why many empirical studies privilege the "reduced form approach," which utilizes only data bearing on the duration of the job search. In general, this approach is limited to estimating an equation that gives the job finding rate, without this equation really being deduced from any theoretical job search model. The "structural approach," on the contrary, aims to estimate the structural equations of the theoretical model using all the data available on search duration and wages. In the theoretical sections of this chapter we have seen that structural equations take into account the distribution of all possible wages, so the econometrician must be able to estimate this distribution. Because he or she only knows what wages were *accepted*, and perhaps also the reservation wages (as conveyed by the surveys just mentioned) he or she cannot, on the basis of these incomplete data alone, "recover" the true distribution of wages offered. The econometrician faces an identification problem known as the "nonrecoverability problem," which is usually solved by postulating a priori a parametric form for the distribution of wages offered and estimating the parameter or parameters of this form with the help of the available data. This approach thus has the defect of being based on nontestable restrictions on the form of wage distribution—restrictions that can have considerable influence on the results.

The reduced form approach relies on several basic models that give it a relatively unified character. The same does not hold true for the structural approach, in which each study is grounded on a specific model. In the first part of this section, we simply present the main lines of the reduced form approach (for a good example of the structural model, the reader may consult Wolpin, 1987, and Devine and Kiefer, 1991, chapter 5). In the second part, we summarize the principal results of empirical studies bearing on job search.

3.1   THE ECONOMETRICS OF DURATION MODELS

As their name indicates, "duration models" try to explain the time passed in a certain state—for example, the length of unemployment spells—with the help of administrative data and the characteristics of a sample of individuals followed over a certain period.[11] It will be instructive, however, to set these data and explanatory variables aside for the time being and concentrate instead on the probability distribution governing the duration of the phenomenon under study. Then the explanatory variables can be brought in with the help of particular specifications, the prevalent ones being the proportional hazard model and the accelerated lifetime model.

3.1.1 The Hazard Function

The basic concept of duration models is the "hazard function." Using this function it is possible to define the notion of "duration dependence."

Hazard and Duration Dependence

In what follows, we will denote the continuous random variable representing the duration of the phenomenon under study by T, and we will assume, for illustrative purposes, that this phenomenon is the duration of unemployment. As for every random variable, the duration of an individual's unemployment spell is characterized by knowledge of its cumulative distribution function denoted by $F(t)$, or its probability density $f(t) = F'(t)$. Readers will recall that the cumulative distribution function is defined by $F(t) = \Pr\{T < t\}$, and so represents the probability that the unemployment spell lasts less than t units of time. Theoretical job search models are capable of producing a certain number of predictions about this function, but they most naturally lead to characterizations of the "hazard function." The latter represents, for an individual, the instantaneous conditional probability of exiting from unemployment when he or she has been unemployed for at least a period of length t. For example, in the model in section 1.2.4, in which unemployment insurance benefits are not stationary, the hazard function is equal to $\lambda[1 - H(x(t))]$, where $x(t)$ designates the reservation wage after an unemployment spell equal in length to t. More generally, designating the hazard function by $\varphi(.)$ and knowing that the individual has been unemployed for at least a period of length t, the conditional probability $\varphi(t)\,dt$ that the duration of unemployment is located within the small interval of time $[t, t + dt]$ is defined by $\varphi(t)\,dt = \Pr\{t \leq T < t + dt | T \geq t\}$. Applying the definition of conditional probabilities[12] gives us:

$$\varphi(t)\,dt = \frac{\Pr\{t \leq T < t + dt\}}{\Pr\{T \geq t\}} = \frac{f(t)\,dt}{1 - F(t)}$$

The hazard function is thus characterized by the equality:

$$\varphi(t) = \frac{f(t)}{\bar{F}(t)}, \qquad \text{with} \qquad \bar{F}(t) \equiv 1 - F(t) \tag{56}$$

In this expression there appears the *survival function* $\bar{F}(t)$, representing the probability that the unemployment spell lasts at least a period of length t. We will see below that it is useful to link the survival function to the integral $\Phi(t)$ of the hazard function. This integral, also called the "integrated hazard," is defined by $\Phi(t) = \int_0^t \varphi(\xi)\,d\xi$. Relation (56) can also be written $\varphi(t) = -\partial[\ln \bar{F}(t)]/\partial t$. Integrating this equality, we find:

$$\Phi(t) = -\ln \bar{F}(t) \tag{57}$$

The integrated hazard is thus equal to the opposite of the logarithm of the survival function.

In practice, it is important to know if the duration of the phenomenon under study, in this case the duration of an unemployment spell, increases, diminishes, or remains constant with time already spent unemployed. The hazard function allows us to characterize this notion of "duration dependence" very easily. If $\varphi'(t) > 0$, the probability of exiting from unemployment increases with the amount of time t already spent unemployed, and we refer to "positive duration dependence." Conversely, if $\varphi'(t) < 0$, the probability of exiting from unemployment diminishes with the amount of time t already passed in this state, and we then refer to "negative duration dependence." The model presented in section 1.2.4, for example, in which unemployment benefits tail off as the time spent looking for a job lengthens, exhibits positive duration dependence. It should be noted that the hazard function is not necessarily monotonic: it may increase for certain values of t and diminish for others. The hazard function may equally be independent of the length of an unemployment spell, as is the case in the basic job search model in section 1.1, where the exit rate from unemployment $\lambda[1 - H(x)]$ is a constant.

Some Probability Distributions Currently in Use

Table 3.4 gives the properties of some probability distributions currently in use in the econometrics of duration models. The exponential distribution depends only on a single parameter $\gamma > 0$, its hazard function is a constant equal to this parameter, and it therefore presents no duration dependence. For that matter, it is easy to verify that it is the only law with this property by integrating equation (56) with φ constant. But since it depends only on a single parameter, it allows only limited flexibility in econometric applications. For example, the mean and the standard error of this probability distribution are both equal to $1/\gamma$. One cannot therefore estimate the mean and the standard error separately—but there is no practical reason why the standard error of the duration of unemployment spells should be equal to the average duration of unemployment.

The Weibull distribution offers more flexibility than the exponential distribution. We say that a random variable T follows a Weibull distribution of parameters

Table 3.4

Commonly used distributions in duration models.

Distribution	$f(t)$	$\bar{F}(t)$	$\varphi(t)$	$\Phi(t)$
Exponential	$\gamma e^{-\gamma t}$	$e^{-\gamma t}$	γ	γt
Weibull	$\gamma a t^{a-1} e^{-\gamma t^a}$	$e^{-\gamma t^a}$	$\gamma a t^{a-1}$	γt^a
Log-logistic	$\dfrac{\gamma a t^{a-1}}{(1 + \gamma t^a)^2}$	$\dfrac{1}{1 + \gamma t^a}$	$\dfrac{\gamma a t^{a-1}}{1 + \gamma t^a}$	$\ln(1 + \gamma t^a)$

γ and α $(\gamma > 0, \alpha > 0)$ if the random variable T^{α} follows an exponential distribution of parameter γ. Since the Weibull distribution depends on two parameters, it is more supple than the exponential distribution (to which we revert for $\alpha = 1$). The hazard is increasing for $\alpha > 1$ and it is decreasing for $\alpha < 1$. The Weibull distribution thus allows us to take duration dependence into account, but only in monotonic fashion. The log-logistic distribution (which also depends on two parameters) permits a non-monotonic hazard function. For $\alpha > 1$, the hazard is increasing then decreasing, whereas for $\alpha < 1$ it is always decreasing.

3.1.2 Parametric Estimation

The econometrics of duration models are applied most often to estimating the hazard function. Current practice consists of postulating an a priori form for this function, dependent on one or more parameters that one is trying to estimate. We then speak of *parametric* estimation. This estimation concludes with tests that try to assess the relevance of the form adopted. However, in the preliminary phase, it is now common to proceed to a direct *nonparametric* estimation of the hazard function. For this, the empirical distribution of the duration of unemployment spells in the sample is taken into account (see Kiefer, 1988, for a complete description of this technique, and Lancaster, 1990, for an application). One of the difficulties of estimation procedures derives from the fact that a number of observations are frequently incomplete in the surveys. This is the problem of "censored" observations, which we will now examine.

The Likelihood Function with Censored Observations

Let us assume that we know the durations of unemployment spells for n individuals between two dates τ_0 and τ_1, on the basis of, for example, a survey completely covering the history of these individuals in the labor market in the course of interval of time $[\tau_0, \tau_1]$. The principle of so-called parametric estimation consists of specifying a priori a probability density $f(t, \theta)$ for the duration of unemployment dependent on a vector θ of parameters that has to be estimated. Let us denote by t_i the duration of unemployment of individual i as it is reported in the survey. If the unemployment spell for all individuals in the sample lies strictly between the dates τ_0 and τ_1, the likelihood function of the sample is then written $\prod_{i=1}^{n} f(t_i, \theta)$. But in reality some individuals are already unemployed at the commencement of the survey, and others are still unemployed at its conclusion. In these conditions, the unemployment durations reported by the survey are *censored* data. We speak of "left censoring" when the (unknown) date of the start of the unemployment spell falls prior to the date τ_0 on which the survey commences, and "right censoring" when an individual is still looking for work on date τ_1, when the survey stops. If observation t_i is censored, the survey simply reveals that the duration of unemployment T_i of agent i is *at least* equal to t_i. The contribution of this observation to the likelihood of the sample is then equal to $\Pr\{T_i \geq t_i\} \equiv \bar{F}(t_i, \theta)$. Let us define the dummy variable c_i by $c_i = 1$ if the observation is not censored, and by $c_i = 0$ if it is. In logarithmic form, the likelihood function of the sample is then written[13]:

$$L(\theta) = \sum_{i=1}^{n} c_i \ln f(t_i, \theta) + \sum_{i=1}^{n} (1 - c_i) \ln \bar{F}(t_i, \theta)$$

It is possible to express this likelihood function solely with the help of the hazard function $\varphi(t, \theta)$ and its integral, the integrated hazard $\Phi(t, \theta)$. Relations (56) and (57) thus give $\ln f(t_i, \theta) = \ln \varphi(t_i, \theta) - \ln \bar{F}(t_i, \theta)$ with $\Phi(t_i, \theta) = -\ln \bar{F}(t_i, \theta)$, and the likelihood of the sample becomes:

$$L(\theta) = \sum_{i=1}^{n} c_i \ln \varphi(t_i, \theta) - \sum_{i=1}^{n} \Phi(t_i, \theta) \tag{58}$$

In practice, the estimator $\hat{\theta}$ of vector θ of the parameters corresponds to the value of θ that maximizes this likelihood function. This maximization most often gives no analytical solution, and it is necessary to fall back on numerical methods (the exponential distribution is a notable exception). It is possible to show, under a set of standard hypotheses, that the estimator $\hat{\theta}$ of the maximum likelihood is consistent and that the random variable $\sqrt{n}(\hat{\theta} - \theta)$ asymptotically follows a normal distribution with zero mean, the variance of which can be estimated by $-[n^{-1}\partial^2 L(\hat{\theta})/\partial\hat{\theta}\partial\hat{\theta}']^{-1}$.

An Example: The Exponential Distribution
By way of illustration, let us consider the simple case of an exponential distribution of parameter γ. Table 3.4 indicates that the hazard function and the integrated hazard are defined by $\varphi(t_i, \gamma) = \gamma$ and $\Phi(t_i, \gamma) = \gamma t_i$, for all i. Bringing these equalities into expression (58) of the likelihood of the sample, the latter is written:

$$L(\gamma) = \sum_{i=1}^{n} c_i \ln \gamma - \gamma \sum_{i=1}^{n} t_i$$

Setting to zero the derivative of function $L(\gamma)$ with respect to γ we find the value of the estimator $\hat{\gamma}$ of the parameter γ, or:

$$\hat{\gamma} = \sum_{i=1}^{n} c_i \Big/ \sum_{i=1}^{n} t_i$$

If we had not taken the censored observations into account (which would have meant assuming that $c_i = 1$ for all i), the estimator would then have been equal to $(n/\sum_{i=1}^{n} t_i) \geq \hat{\gamma}$. Thus, to neglect the fact that some observations have been censored biases the estimate of the exit rate from unemployment *upward*. In this case, the estimated variance is also too high.[14]

Different Properties According to Specifications
Table 3.5 presents estimations according to three different specifications of a duration model produced on the basis of French data for the period 1990–1993 by Bonnal et al. (1999).[15] The first thing to note is that if only the exponential specification had been

Table 3.5

An example of the estimation of a duration model.

	Exp.	Weibull	Log-L
γ	0.0629	0.0105	0.0120
α	1	1.6818	2.1163

Source: Bonnal et al. (1999, table 4).

used, the fact that the model exhibits duration dependence would not have emerged, since the estimation of parameter α is always strictly greater than 1 with the Weibull and log-logistic distributions. What is more, if only the Weibull distribution had been used, the conclusion would have been that duration dependence was positive, whereas the log-logistic distribution makes it clear that in reality this dependence is not monotonic. In their study, Bonnal et al. calculate that the hazard increases for a duration of unemployment of less than 12.33 months, then subsequently decreases (in this sample, the average duration of unemployment is 10.22 months). The exponential distribution is rejected by the statistical tests; the same tests lead us to prefer the Weibull distribution to the log-logistic distribution, which reinforces a conclusion in favor of a monotonic positive duration dependence.

3.1.3 Introducing Explanatory Variables

In duration models, the explanatory variables have a bearing on both the characteristics of the labor market (such as, for example, the value of unemployment insurance benefits, or the level of the unemployment rate) and the characteristics of individuals, such as sex, educational level, and professional experience. Explanatory variables are assumed to be exogenous, but are not necessarily independent of time. If the observations cover a sufficiently long period, characteristics such as age, number of offspring, marital status, or unemployment insurance benefits can evolve. Conversely, characteristics like sex, educational level, or past experience are generally constants independent of time for unemployed persons. For clarity of exposition, we first assume that all the explanatory variables do not depend on time. If we denote by x the vector of explanatory variables, the probability density of the random variable under study (here, the duration of unemployment) will then have as its argument the triplet (t, x, θ), where t and θ always designate the duration of unemployment and the vector of the parameters to be estimated. Thus, the hazard function is henceforth written $\varphi(t, x, \theta)$. Formally, what we have done to this point remains true on condition that we replace the pair (t, θ) by the triplet (t, x, θ). But remaining at this level of generality hides the difficulties linked to the estimation of parameters in the presence of explanatory variables. In practice it is necessary to state exactly how the explanatory variables and the parameters combine if we really want to estimate the latter and interpret them from an economic point of view. Two classes of models allow us to meet these objectives.

The Proportional Hazard Model

In the proportional hazard model, we assume that the vector θ of the parameters is composed of two subsets, θ_0 and θ_x, and that the hazard function takes the following form[16]:

$$\varphi(t, x, \theta) = \rho(x, \theta_x)\varphi_0(t, \theta_0) \tag{59}$$

Function φ_0 is called the "baseline hazard" because it is identical for all individuals. Most often we utilize a well-specified function, such as the Weibull distribution (see table 3.4). In that case the vector θ_0 is identical to the pair of parameters α and γ. Relation (59) shows that, in the proportional hazard model, the effect of the explanatory variables is to multiply the baseline hazard by the scale factor $\rho(x, \theta_x)$, independent of the duration t of unemployment. A specification frequently used for the scale factor is $\rho(x, \theta_x) = \exp(x\theta_x)$, which has the advantage of being positive and supplying a simple interpretation of the components of the vector θ_x. If we denote by x_k the kth component of vector x, relation (59) defining the hazard function shows that $(\partial \ln \varphi / \partial x_k) = \theta_{xk}$, where θ_{xk} designates the kth component of vector θ_x. If we have been careful to specify the explanatory variables in terms of logarithms, vector θ_x then represents the vector of the elasticities of the hazard function, that is, the elasticities of the conditional probability of exiting unemployment with respect to the explanatory variables.[17]

The estimators of vectors θ_x and θ_0 are obtained by maximizing the likelihood function of the sample with respect to the components of vectors θ_x and θ_0. If we denote by x_i the vector of the explanatory variables relative to individual i and if we assume that the scale factor takes the form $\exp(x_i\theta_x)$, in logarithmic terms the likelihood function is then written:

$$L(\theta_x, \theta_0) = \sum_{i=1}^{n} c_i[(x_i\theta_x) + \ln \varphi_0(t_i, \theta_0)] - \sum_{i=1}^{n} \Phi_0(t_i, \theta_0) \exp(x_i\theta_x)$$

In this expression, function Φ_0 represents the integrated hazard of the baseline hazard φ_0. The reader will be able to verify that, even with a constant baseline hazard, there is no analytical solution for the estimators of the parameters and consequently it is necessary to fall back on numerical methods. We must note finally that for proportional hazard models, it is possible to proceed to a semi-parametric estimation by specifying the scale factor a priori while not imposing any particular form for the baseline hazard (in that case, we must utilize the empirical distribution of the unemployment durations). This so-called "partial-likelihood approach" was suggested by Cox (1975), and one may consult Kiefer (1988, IV-C) for a good introduction to it.

The Accelerated Lifetime Model

In the accelerated lifetime model the explanatory variables have a multiplier effect on duration, that is, they change the scale of the time axis. The cumulative distribution function of the random variable T, or $F(t, x, \theta)$ thus takes the form $F_0[t\rho(x, \theta)]$. It is then easy to verify, using relation (56), that the hazard function is writtten:

$$\varphi(t, x, \theta) = \rho(x, \theta)\varphi_0[t\rho(x, \theta)] \tag{60}$$

In the frequently utilized case where $\rho(x, \theta) = \exp(x\theta)$, it is possible to find a linear version of the accelerated lifetime model. For that, we must first point out that $\Pr\{T < t\} = F_0[t \exp(x\theta)]$. Using the change of scale $\tau = t \exp(x\theta)$, we then have $\Pr\{T \exp(x\theta) < \tau\} = F_0(\tau)$. It thus is apparent that the distribution of the random variable $T \exp(x\theta)$ is independent of the explanatory variables. If we set $\exp \varepsilon = T \exp(x\theta)$, the lifetime accelerated model (60) is equivalent to the linear model:

$$\ln T = -x\theta + \varepsilon \qquad \text{with} \qquad \exp \varepsilon \rightsquigarrow F_0(.) \tag{61}$$

In this form, we note that if the variables linked to individual characteristics are written in logarithmic terms, the usual specification $\rho(x\theta) = \exp(x\theta)$ allows us to interpret each component of vector θ as the opposite of the elasticities of the unemployment duration with respect to the exogenous variables. Relation (61) also shows that the lifetime accelerated model is equivalent to a linear model, but one in which the error term ε does not follow a normal distribution. More precisely, the cumulative distribution function of the random variable ε satisfies $\Pr\{\varepsilon < v\} = \Pr\{\exp \varepsilon < \exp v\} = F_0(\exp v)$. This linear form of the lifetime accelerated model opens up the possibility of applying regression methods of the least ordinary squares type, but we then have to evaluate the results with care, given that the hypothesis that the error term is normally distributed has not been verified. A more serious difficulty in the application of regressions of the ordinary least squares type is caused by the presence of censored observations. The error term ε_i corresponding to a censored observation t_i has a probabiliy density different from that of an error term ε_j linked to a noncensored observation t_j. In other words, if one applies the linear relation (61) for observations i and j, cumulative distribution function F_{0i} is different from F_{0j}. These difficulties make it preferable to utilize the method of maximum likelihood in the presence of censored variables. We can apply this method when making the likelihood of the sample explicit, using either the linear model (61) or the more general relations (58) and (60). In the latter case, if we use Φ_0 to designate the integrated hazard of the hazard function φ_0, the reader can verify that the likelihood function is written:

$$L(\theta) = \sum_{i=1}^{n} c_i\{\ln \rho(x_i, \theta) + \ln \varphi_0[t_i\rho(x_i, \theta)]\} - \sum_{i=1}^{n} \rho(x_i, \theta)\Phi_0[t_i\rho(x_i, \theta)]$$

We pursue the estimation of the lifetime accelerated model by choosing functional forms for ρ et φ_0. For example, φ_0 may be deduced from a Weibull distribution or a log-logistic distribution, and as we have already pointed out, the usual choice for ρ is $\exp(x\theta)$.

Time-Dependent Explanatory Variables

Some explanatory variables may vary with time. To simplify, let us assume that they depend only on the duration of the phenomenon under study (for example, unemployment insurance benefits are most often regressive the longer the recipient remains unemployed). Formally, it is enough to replace the vector x in the preceding paragraphs by a vector denoted by $x(t)$. Thus the hazard function is written $\varphi[t, x(t), \theta]$ and the integrated hazard $\Phi[t, x(t), \theta]$ is then equal to $\int_0^t \varphi[\xi, x(\xi), \theta] \, d\xi$. However, the lifetime accelerated model is no longer equivalent to a linear model, and consequently vector θ of the parameters can no longer be interpreted in terms of elasticity. The likelihood of the sample takes the general form:

$$L(\theta) = \sum_{i=1}^{n} c_i \ln \varphi[t_i, x_i(t_i), \theta] - \sum_{i=1}^{n} \Phi[t_i, x_i(t_i), \theta]$$

When the explanatory variables are time-dependent, the maximum likelihood method most often creates difficulties in distinguishing that which belongs to duration dependence from that which belongs to the temporal trends of the regressors.

Heterogeneity

Explanatory variables, such as sex, educational attainment, or past experience, allow us to control the heterogeneity among individuals to a degree. But unobserved heterogeneity always remains: for example, job search effort is very imperfectly observed. The omission of some variables, or specification errors in the impact of the exogenous ones, are formally much like unobserved heterogeneity. Failure to take this type of heterogeneity into account leads to bias in the estimation of time dependency.[18] To get around these difficulties we may assume that the probability density of the dependent variable is written (leaving out vectors x and θ for the sake of simplicity) $f(t|v)$, where v is a random variable of density $p(.)$ marking the unobserved heterogeneity among agents. For example, in the proportional hazard model, it is possible to introduce this form of heterogeneity by assuming that the hazard function takes the form $\varphi(t, x, \theta) = \rho(x, \theta_x)\varphi_0(t, \theta_0)v$. We thus obtain the mixed proportional hazard model studied in detail by Lancaster (1979) and van den Berg (2001). The probability density function $p(.)$ of the random variable v is unknown and must therefore be estimated. In practice a discrete form (v_k, p_k) is often used, with $p_k = \Pr\{v = v_k\}$ for $k = 1, \ldots, K$, and we estimate the vector $(v_1, \ldots, v_K; p_1, \ldots, p_K)$ along with all the other parameters of the model.

Competing Risks

To this point we have paid no attention to the exact destination of an individual following an unemployment spell. In the foregoing models there was no difference between an exit from unemployment into nonparticipation and an exit from unemployment into employment. Some surveys do in practice give both an individual's duration of unemployment and his or her destination (regular employment, temporary employment, enrolment in a training course, nonparticipation, etc.). Competing risks models take this factor into account. The idea is to link each destination d to a duration T_d of unemployment, the exit from which would be d. To be sure, only one spell of unemployment and only one destination at exit from unemployment are observed for each individual. If we use S to designate the set of possible destinations, we do in fact observe the outcomes of the random variables $T = \min(T_d | d \in S)$ and $D = \{d | T_d \leq T_k, k \in S\}$. Assuming that the random variables T_j are independent of the regressors and the nonobserved heterogeneity, then it is possible to find the joint probability distribution of the pair (T, D). If we have at our disposal a sample of size n of independent observations (t_i, d_i), it becomes possible to write the likelihood function and thus to proceed to make estimations (see Florens et al., 1996).

3.2 MAIN RESULTS

The numerous econometric studies carried out within the framework of job search models have made it possible to clarify the determinants of the exit rates from unemployment. We have seen that these models give the income of unemployed persons an important role. But in practice it is a delicate matter to evaluate this income. We will begin by presenting problems linked to the evaluation of unemployment insurance benefits, and then set out the results of empirical work on the determinants of the reservation wage and the duration of unemployment.

3.2.1 Measuring Unemployment Insurance Benefit

In the basic job search model the average duration of unemployment is influenced by the amount of compensation paid to those who are looking for work. Empirically, comparison between the income of the unemployed and that of waged workers is a complex problem that requires richly detailed information.

Insurance and Social Assistance

When we attempt to assess the relevance of the job search model, the first thing to do is to measure the distance separating z in the theoretical model (analogous to the "wage" of an unemployed person) from the very different reality of the benefits actually paid out. Contrary to the elementary formalism of the models we have presented hitherto, these benefits are linked in particular to the career history of an individual, his or her job search efforts, and the reasons why he or she is currently unemployed. This diversity derives in part from the fact that systems set up to compensate for unemployment belong to the domains of both *insurance* and *social assistance*. Unemployment insurance depends on the contributions previously paid in, and it creates entitlement to compensation when a person loses his or her job, making up in a sense for the "accident" that has happened to him or her. That is why unemployment insurance benefits are not generally paid out to persons who have deliberately chosen to quit their jobs. Benefits are generally stopped, moreover, when a job offer is refused without good reason, and recipients have to furnish *proof* that they are really looking for work. Finally, the period of entitlement is limited (on all these points, see chapter 11; Grubb, 2000; and OECD, 2000). Social assistance, on the other hand, generally does not depend either on past contributions paid in or on the career history of the individual. It is paid over relatively long periods to persons whose income is judged inadequate.

Factual Elements

In applied work, the considerations just adduced lead to serious difficulties in working out the *replacement rate*, which is supposed to provide a significant measure of

Table 3.6

Net replacement rate in 1994–1995. (All figures in the table are percentages.)

Country	Average	Year 1	Years 2 and 3	Years 4 and 5
Belgium	51	65	55	40
France	55	73	50	40
Germany	54	71	45	45
Japan	45	68	33	33
Netherlands	69	81	74	53
Spain	49	70	52	24
Sweden	67	81	62	59
United Kingdom	51	61	46	46
United States	16	35	8	8

Source: OECD (1999), Martin (1996).

the relationship between the benefits paid out to an unemployed person and the wage of an employed one (see OECD, 1994, chapter 8, and Martin, 1996). Table 3.6 gives a glimpse of how diverse the situation can be from one OECD country to another. In this table, the average represents a "synthetic" replacement rate, established in 1991, that notionally assesses the overall generosity of the benefits offered to the unemployed. This indicator equals the average, expressed as a percentage of the average wage *net* of taxes, of the *net* benefits paid out to unemployed persons, both single and married, with either a dependent or working spouse, for a length of time in unemployment varying from zero to five years.[19] We should keep in mind the limitations of such a global indicator, which provides no more than a partial and necessarily arbitrary view of the replacement rate, given the strong heterogeneity of individual situations. The other columns present the values of the replacement rate for different durations of unemployment, thus giving a more precise indication of the lengths of time over which these benefits are paid. Clearly the replacement ratios diminish as unemployment persists. The coexistence of unemployment insurance benefits, which generally provide coverage for a limited time, and social assistance programs, which often have no time limit, explains this tendency to diminish.

3.2.2 The Determinants of Unemployment Duration

Numerous empirical studies have been carried out for the purpose of estimating the elasticity of reservation wages and/or the average duration of unemployment with respect to the income of unemployed persons. This income appears to have little influence, and in consequence the probability of accepting a job offer proves in the majority of cases to be close to unity. Empirical studies also throw light on the efficiency of certain measures designed to help job-seekers find work, and on the sanctions applied to job-seekers who do not respect the rules laid down by the bodies in charge of administering unemployment insurance.

Table 3.7

Elasticities of the reservation wages with respect to the income of unemployed persons.

Authors	Data	Elasticities
Lynch (1983)	U.K. (youth)	0.08–0.11
Holzer (1986)	U.S. (youth)	0.018–0.049
van den Berg (1990)	Netherlands (30–55 yr)	0.04–0.09

Source: Devine and Kiefer (1991, table 4.2, p. 75).

Table 3.8

Estimation of the relation between the reservation wage and the instantaneous income of unemployed persons, using an equilibrium search model.

	Age (yr)				
	16–22	23–29	30–38	39–70	Average
x/z	0.92	0.91	1.08	1.06	1.02

Source: van den Berg and Ridder (1998, table X, p. 1211).

The Elasticity of the Reservation Wage

An initial series of studies attempted to make direct estimates of relations like equation (6) giving the value of the reservation wage in the basic model. To that end, they relied on data from surveys in which unemployed persons were asked to answer more or less directly the question, "What for you is the lowest acceptable wage?" Table 3.7 gives the magnitudes of the elasticity of the reservation wage with respect to the income of an unemployed person for three studies that use this type of data.[20] It shows that, as the basic model predicts, this elasticity is positive. Its magnitude is, however, very slight.

More recent studies estimate the reservation wage using the equilibrium search model laid out in section 2.1 above. Table 3.8 shows the value of ratio x/z between the reservation wage and the net income of an unemployed person by age bracket using a study conducted by van den Berg and Ridder (1998) on Dutch data. We observe that this ratio is very close to one, which means that the job offer arrival rates, λ_u and λ_e, differ little between the unemployed and those who have a job. In this case, the elasticity of the reservation wage with respect to income z of an unemployed person would be practically equal to 1 (but we must bear in mind that in the equilibrium search model, z has no influence on the average duration of unemployment). Using French data, Bontemps (1998) finds on the contrary that λ_u is almost ten times larger than λ_e, and Kiefer and Neumann (1993), using American data, find that λ_u is approximately equal to $5\lambda_e$. In this configuration of the parameters, reservation wage elasticity

Table 3.9

Some empirical studies using duration models.

Authors	Data	Elasticity of unemployment benefits	Elasticity of duration of benefits
Lancaster (1979)	U.K. (not specified)	0.43–0.6	
Narendranathan et al. (1985)	U.K. (men)	0.08–0.65	
Moffit (1985)	U.S. (men)		0.16–0.36
Meyer (1990)	U.S. (men)		0.60–0.88
Katz and Meyer (1990)	U.S. (men)	0.8–0.9 (youth)	0.36–0.48

Source: Devine and Kiefer (1991, table 5.2).

with respect to the income of an unemployed person would clearly be smaller than unity.

Elasticity of the Duration of Unemployment

Survey data giving "direct" access to reservation wages are rare and their reliability is, to say the least, doubtful. This is why the econometrician turns more readily to longitudinal data describing the complete histories of a large number of individuals in the labor market (duration of periods of unemployment and employment, wages accepted, wages of previous jobs, etc.). These studies indicate for the most part that the elasticity of the *average duration* of unemployment with respect to unemployment benefit is positive, but at the same time modest in magnitude.

Table 3.9 gives an overview of results regarding the elasticities of the average duration of unemployment with respect to unemployment insurance benefits and the duration of such benefits. The results show large variations, among other reasons because of differences in the populations studied and measurement differences in the way the unemployed were counted or the calculation of unemployment benefit. The group of studies included in the very comprehensive overview of Devine and Kiefer (1991), however, point to the conclusion that unemployment insurance benefits exercise a (slight) positive influence on the duration of unemployment. In general, the exit rate from unemployment decreases with the duration of unemployment (the duration dependence is negative), but its order of magnitude is limited, especially if one controls for all types of heterogeneity. Other studies also show that the sensitivity of the average duration of unemployment to unemployment insurance benefits itself depends on the duration of unemployment. Van den Berg (1990) estimates that a rise of 10% in benefits at the end of two years would increase the average duration of unemployment by something on the order of five weeks (as opposed to one week for benefits paid in the first year of unemployment). Nickell (1979), however, reaches an opposite result, since he finds that the amount of unemployment insurance benefits has no significant effect on the exit rate from unemployment (after a period of 20 weeks in that state).

In general, unemployment insurance pays benefits for a limited period. Numerous empirical studies have looked at the consequences of the (generally large) diminution of income of individuals who lose their unemployment insurance benefits. The studies of Moffitt (1985) and Katz and Meyer (1990), using American data, indicate that a prolongation of ten weeks in the potential entitlement period would increase the average duration of unemployment by one to two weeks. This result conforms to the theoretical model of 1.2.4 and probably means that job-seekers lower their reservation wage (and/or augment their search effort) as the end of their period of entitlement approaches. The importance of the duration of this period is confirmed by the study of Meyer (1990) using American data. This author highlights a significant discontinuity in the exit rate from unemployment in the period immediately preceding the exhaustion of entitlement to unemployment insurance benefits. The studies of Dormont et al. (2001) on French data arrive at an analogous result. They show as well that the exit rate from unemployment to employment rises more at the end of the entitlement period for better qualified job-seekers. Figure 3.2 clearly illustrates this phenomenon. It traces the exit rate from unemployment for individuals whose benefits fall significantly in the 14th month of unemployment. At that time, benefits pass from a magnitude of 57% to 75% of the *previous* wage to a fixed sum corresponding to roughly 60% of the *minimum* monthly wage. Figure 3.2 shows that the probability of exit rises significantly as the 14th month approaches. Further, this effect is much more marked for job-seekers who previously earned high wages. Two causes contribute to this phenomenon. First, better-qualified workers, those earning higher wages, are also those who can find jobs more easily and behave in a more opportunistic manner. Second, the fall in income in the 14th month is weaker to the extent that the reference wage was low to begin with. The question of the relative importance of these two causes remains open.

Overall, these empirical results suggest that the effects of unemployment insurance benefits on the average duration of unemployment do indeed follow the predictions of theory: a reduction in benefit shortens the duration of the job search for eligible job-seekers, but this effect is modest in size.

The Probability of Accepting an Offer
Studies grounded in the labor market experience of large numbers of persons also permit us to estimate the probability that a job offer will be accepted; readers will recall that this probability is equal to $1 - H(x)$ in the partial model and is always equal to unity in the equilibrium search model. Table 3.10 summarizes the results of three different studies. We see that the probability of accepting an offer is close to 1, which means that the *first* employment offer is practically always accepted, a result that confirms results obtained by observing the attitude of employers. In general, the rate at which applications to fill vacant jobs are rejected is very high. For example, Stern (1989), in a study of a sample of young Americans in 1980, found a rate of

Reference wage in the bottom quartile

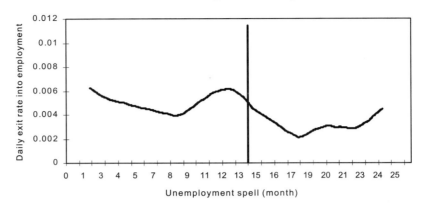

Reference wage in the top quartile

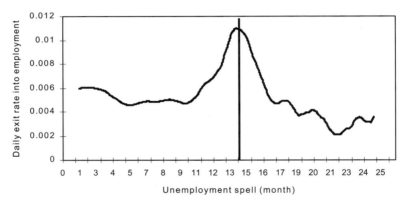

FIGURE 3.2

Exit rate from unemployment and the end of entitlement to benefits for the period 1986–1992, for individuals aged 25 and over. The reference wage corresponds to the average wage for the twelve months immediately preceding job loss.

Source: Dormont et al. (2001).

Table 3.10

The probability of accepting an offer.

Authors	Data	Probability
Devine (1988)	U.S.	0.91–1.0
Wolpin (1987)	U.S.	0.88
van den Berg (1990)	Netherlands	0.89–1.0

Source: Devine and Kiefer (1991, table 5.3, p. 138, and table 6.4, p. 174).

rejection between 0.78 and 0.958. That signifies that, on average, more than eight times out of ten, applications to fill vacant jobs will be turned down.

Overall, these results suggest that the reservation wage x lies very close to the lower bound of the distribution of wages existing in the economy. It thus confirms the relevance of the equilibrium search model, in which, as the reader will recall, the reservation wage aligns with the lower bound of the wage distribution. From this it results that the hazard rate, $\lambda[1 - H(x)]$ in the partial model, and thus the average duration of unemployment $T_u = 1/\lambda[1 - H(x)]$, depend above all on the frequency λ with which offers are received by a job-seeker, since $H(x)$ is close to zero. Hence differences between durations of unemployment will most often be a reflection of differences between the arrival rate of job offers, which themselves depend on the search effort of job-seekers, as we have emphasized in sections 1.2.3 and 2.2. From this point of view, help in looking for a job and checking on the search effort being made can significantly influence the rates of return to employment.

In light of this, the majority of OECD countries have adopted measures aimed at increasing the efficiency of the job search by those receiving unemployment insurance benefits. In the United States, Denmark, the Netherlands, and the United Kingdom, starting in the 1980s, these measures have combined help in looking for a job with sanctions, generally consisting of a reduction in benefit, when the rules imposed by the body administering unemployment insurance are not adhered to (Grubb, 2000). More precisely, we can distinguish three types of instruments that are generally used in combination: programs giving individual counseling to job seekers, stronger measures to check that eligibility conditions have been met and that suitable efforts to find a job are being made, and the payment of a premium upon return to work.

Individual Counseling for the Unemployed

Individual counseling programs generally consist of interviews with job-seekers to guide their efforts to find work. Starting in the 1980s, these programs have been evaluated on the basis of social experiments in the United States. Readers will recall that in social experiments there is a treatment group, which follows the program, and a control group, which does not. The two groups are selected in random fashion (see chapter 11, section 3, for a presentation of the methodology of social experiments). The help given to the job-seekers in the treatment groups is briefly summarized in table 3.11. Its impact on the average duration of unemployment is presented in table 3.12. It is apparent that this help significantly reduces the duration of unemployment. Further, Meyer (1995) underlines that it generally leads to a reduction in the total expenditure of the bodies administering unemployment insurance, inasmuch as the benefits that flow from this help outweigh its costs. It should nevertheless be noted that these experimental situations mingle help for the unemployed with surveillance of the search effort they are making. The contribution of each of these components is generally difficult to isolate. The same problem arises in evaluating the Restart program set up to help the long-term unemployed in the United Kingdom in 1987. The main component of this program is a compulsory 25-minute interview between the

Table 3.11

Experiments with help in job searching carried out in the US in the 1980s.

Place	Type of help
Nevada (1977–78)	Weekly interviews, checks on eligibility
Charleston (1983)	Two in-depth interviews and a 3-hour session on job searching
New Jersey (1986–87)	Obligation to contact the employment agency regularly, offer of training
Nevada (1988–89)	Improved counseling by permanent personnel
Minnesota (1988–90)	Intensive help from permanent personnel

Source: Meyer (1995, tables 4a, 4b, pp. 111–112).

Table 3.12

Effects of job search experiments on weeks of benefits; measured as treatments minus control. (Standard error in parentheses.)

Place	Weeks of benefits
Nevada (1977–78)	−3.90 (0.41)
Charleston (1983)	−0.70 (0.39)
New Jersey (1986–87)	−0.50 (0.22)
Nevada (1988–89)	−1.60 (0.30)
Minnesota (1988–90)	−4.32 (0.16)

Source: Meyer (1995, tables 5a, 5b, pp. 115–116).

job-seeker and a counselor from the local employment agency after six months of unemployment. Job-seekers receiving benefits for six months are summoned to take part in this interview. Refusal to do so, or inability to prove that efforts to find a job are being made, can lead to the suspension of benefits. This interview is omitted for the control group. Dolton and O'Neill (1996) have estimated that the exit rate from unemployment of the control group is 20% to 30% lower than that of the treatment group during the six months subsequent to the omitted interview. Nonetheless, it is difficult to identify the respective roles of counseling and surveillance.

The study of Black et al. (2002) on the program of job search help which the state of Kentucky set up in 1993 confirms the results of Meyer (1995) and Dolton and O'Neill (1996). This program lends itself to a natural experiment, since participation is in principle compulsory for all unemployed persons, but because of the limited capacities of the employment agencies only a portion of the unemployed are actually enrolled: the treatment group is selected from them, and the control group consists of unemployed persons excluded from the program. Black et al. find that on average, the treatment group receives unemployment benefits for a period 2.2 weeks shorter than the control group does. This study also shows that the rate at which the treatment group returns to work rises sharply during the interval between notification of (compulsory) participation in the program and the date on which participation actually begins. In other words, the disagreeable prospect of having to have regular contact (two to three hours per week) with the employment agencies, and of having them check on one's job search effort, is enough to quickly force those who are not experiencing any real difficulty in finding work out of the unemployment insurance system.

Checking on Efforts to Find Work
It is not clearly established that strengthened checks on eligibility for unemployment benefits and on job search effort significantly increase the exit rates from unemployment, since job search effort is a variable difficult to verify. Job-seekers may follow the rules in appearance but do things that prevent them from being hired, such as applying for jobs for which they are unsuited, or behaving in such a way at their job interviews that the result is failure. How effectively job search effort can be checked on is thus essentially an empirical question.

Studies focused specifically on the impact on exit rates from unemployment of strengthened checks on eligibility for unemployment benefits and job search effort come to qualified conclusions. Some find substantial effects. Van den Berg et al. (2001) have studied the impact of sanctions using Dutch data for the 1990s. They estimate a duration model, and find that a 20% reduction for two weeks in benefits paid to job-seekers sanctioned for not adhering to job search rules doubles the exit rates from unemployment of the individuals thus sanctioned. Further, they find that these effects last beyond the two-week period. Still, these studies encounter the same difficulties mentioned above, in that they do not succeed in distinguishing the impact of sanctions from that of measures that help job-seekers look for work (see Meyer, 1995). The contribution of Ashenfelter et al. (2000) eliminates these obstacles with the help of a social experiment carried out in the states of Connecticut, Massachusetts, Tennessee, and Virginia. Ashenfelter et al. compare the rates at which three different groups of job-seekers exited from unemployment. Through a random draw, they formed two treatment groups and a control group. The control group met the usual conditions of eligibility for unemployment insurance benefit. But the job-seekers from the two treatment groups, during the course of their first visit at the onset of their unemployment spell, were notified of the rules regarding job search effort in connection with eligibility for benefits. At their second visit, the two treatment groups were treated differently. For one, contacts with employers reported by the job-seekers were verified by a telephone call, while this was not done for those in the other treatment group. The job-seekers who could not prove that they had contacted an employer lost their benefits temporarily or permanently. Ashenfelter et al. found that the rates of exit from unemployment for the individuals in the two treatment groups were not statistically different. Further, the savings generated by excluding individuals at their second visit did not cover the extra costs of more rigorous checking.

Premiums upon Return to Work

The mechanism of premiums upon return to work consists of giving money to job-seekers eligible for unemployment insurance benefit when they are actually hired. Social experiments have been conducted in the states of Illinois (1984), New Jersey (1986–1987), Washington (1988–1989), and Pennsylvania (1988–1989) to evaluate the impact of such measures. These experiments, presented in detail by Meyer (1995), conclude by estimating that the premiums have a significant negative effect on the duration of unemployment. Nevertheless, this effect is small in extent and generally leads to financial losses, likewise small, for the bodies administering unemployment insurance. Meyer (1995) thus concludes that these measures have very limited effectiveness.

4   SUMMARY AND CONCLUSION

- Job search theory assumes that individuals know only the distribution of wages existing in the economy, and that they must search in order to encounter employers who will make them definite wage offers. The optimal strategy for a job seeker consists of accepting any wage offer higher than his or her *reservation wage*. The latter depends on the set of parameters affecting the labor market, in particular the job destruction rate, the arrival rate of job offers, and unemployment insurance benefits.

- In order to get unemployment insurance benefits, one must in general have worked previously and contributed to an unemployment insurance fund for a specified period. One is then eligible for unemployment insurance benefits. A rise in the level of benefits increases the duration of unemployment for eligible job-seekers but diminishes that of ineligible job-seekers.

- Because it integrates the strategic behavior of firms, the equilibrium search model is characterized by an endogenous distribution of wages. It offers the advantage of explaining the wage-setting process and thus making possible the analysis of the overall effects of economic policy. It affords a better fit than the partial model with empirical observations, according to which, on the one hand, the probability of accepting an offer is always close to unity for an unemployed worker, and on the other, the unemployment rate is not significantly correlated with the level of unemployment insurance benefits. On the empirical level, this model also has the advantage of permitting a nonparametric estimation of the distribution of wages.

- Most often the body that administers unemployment insurance can only do very partial checks on their clients' efforts to find a job. This means that the body in question is faced with a "moral hazard" problem. It can be shown that an efficient unemployment insurance system is characterized by a decreasing relation between the level of benefit payments and the duration of unemployment. More generally, unemployment insurance benefits ought to depend on all the periods of unemployment and employment taken together.

- Empirical studies of the determinants of the exit rates from unemployment generally utilize duration models, which explain the amount of time passed in a certain state—for example, the length of unemployment spells—as a function of institutional data and the characteristics of a sample of individuals followed over a certain period. The estimation of these models poses problems linked in particular to the specification of the functions defining the exit rates from unemployment and the existence of censored data.

- Empirical studies show that the reservation wage and the average length of an unemployment spell are (moderately) sensitive to the amount of unemployment insurance benefits. On the other hand, the impact of the duration of benefit payments proves to be more important. It is also apparent that the first job offer received is almost always accepted. Given that, the average length of an unemployment spell depends principally on the arrival rate of job offers.

- Unemployment insurance influences the arrival rates of job offers by its effect on the intensity and efficiency of the job search carried out by job-seekers receiving benefits. Empirical studies suggest that premiums paid on return to work, checking up on the job search effort, and help with the job search all have a positive impact on exit rates from unemployment. Nevertheless, cost-benefit analysis shows that the benefit of paying premiums on return to work only slightly outweighs the cost, while the benefit of measures combining counsel and verification of search effort, weighed against the cost, is somewhat greater.

5 RELATED TOPICS IN THE BOOK

- Chapter 1, section1: The reservation wage and the choice between consumption and leisure

- Chapter 6, section 2: The agency model and the trade-off between insurance and incentive

- Chapter 9, section 3: The matching model

- Chapter 11, section 3: The methodology of natural experiments

- Chapter 11, section 4: The macroeconomic effects of unemployment benefits

- Chapter 12, section 1: Minimum wage, labor market participation, and job search effort

6 FURTHER READINGS

Atkinson, A., and Mickelwright, J. (1991), "Unemployment compensation and labor market transitions: A critical review," *Journal of Economic Literature*, 29, pp. 1679–1727.

Devine, T., and Kiefer, N. (1991), *Empirical Labor Economics: The Search Approach*, Oxford, U.K.: Oxford University Press.

Meyer, B. (1995), "Lessons from the US unemployment insurance experiments," *Journal of Economic Literature*, 33, pp. 91–131.

Mortensen, D., and Pissarides, C. (1999), "New developments in models of search in the labor market," in Ashenfelter, O., and Card, D. (eds.), *Handbook of Labor Economics*, vol. 3B, chap. 39, Amsterdam: Elsevier Science/North-Holland.

Van den Berg, G. (2001), "Duration models: Specification, identification and multiple durations," in Heckman, J., and Leamer, E. (eds.), *Handbook of Econometrics*, vol. 5, chap. 55, Amsterdam: Elsevier Science/North-Holland.

7 APPENDIX: THE DISCOUNTED COST OF AN UNEMPLOYED PERSON

The exit from unemployment of a person who exerts search effort a follows a Poisson process of parameter p. Following appendix D at the end of this book, that signifies that the duration T of unemployment is a random variable having a probability density of pe^{-pt}. When an individual exits from unemployment at date t, the principal must pay him or her a discounted present value of transfers, which, at that date, comes to $\int_t^\infty g(t)e^{-r(\tau-t)}\,d\tau = g(t)/r$. Let us assume that a person entering unemployment on date $t = 0$ receives an unemployment insurance benefit payment $b(\tau)$ on each date τ for which he or she is looking for work. The discounted present value of the cost of an unemployed person on date $t = 0$ is then written:

$$C(0) = \int_0^\infty \left[\int_0^t b(\tau)e^{-r\tau}\,d\tau\right]pe^{-pt}\,dt + \int_0^\infty e^{-rt}\frac{g(t)}{r}pe^{-pt}\,dt \tag{62}$$

This expression can be simplified using the integration-by-parts formula, i.e., $\int u\,dv = uv - \int v\,du$. Let us posit $u = \int_0^t b(\tau)e^{-r\tau}\,d\tau$ and $dv = pe^{-pt}\,dt$; we then have $du = b(t)e^{-rt}\,dt$ and $v = -e^{-pt}$. The first term of the right-hand side of equation (62) thus becomes:

$$\int_0^\infty \left[\int_0^t b(\tau)e^{-r\tau}\,d\tau\right]pe^{-pt}\,dt = \left[-e^{-pt}\int_0^t b(\tau)e^{-r\tau}\,d\tau\right]_0^\infty + \int_0^\infty b(t)e^{-(r+p)t}\,dt \tag{63}$$

Assuming that the transversality condition $\lim_{t\to\infty} b(t)e^{-rt} = 0$, is satisfied, the first integral of the right-hand side is equal to zero, and bringing (63) into (62), we get:

$$C(0) = \left[\int_0^\infty b(t) + \frac{g(t)}{r}p\right]e^{-(r+p)t}\,dt$$

REFERENCES

Abowd, J., Kramarz, F., and Margolis, D. (1999), "High wage workers and high wage firms," *Econometrica*, 67, pp. 251–334.

Abowd, J., and Zellner, A. (1985), "Estimating gross labor force flows," *Journal of Business and Economic Statistics*, 3, pp. 254–283.

Albrecht, J., and Axell, B. (1984), "An equilibrium model of search employment," *Journal of Political Economy*, 92, pp. 824–840.

Ashenfelter, O., Ashmore, D., and Deschênes, O. (2000), "Do unemployment insurance recipient actively seek work? Evidence from randomized trial in four U.S. states," IZA Discussion Paper No. 128, www.iza.org.

Atkinson, A., and Mickelwright, J. (1991), "Unemployment compensation and labor market transitions: A critical review," *Journal of Economic Literature*, 29, pp. 1679–1727.

Baily, M. (1978), "Some aspects of optimal unemployment insurance," *Journal of Public Economics*, 10, pp. 379–402.

Black, D., Smith, J., Berger, M., and Noel, B. (2002), "Is the threat of reemployment services more effective than the services themselves? Experimental evidence from the UI system," NBER Working Paper 8825.

Bonnal, L., Cazals, C., Favard, P., and Kamionka, T. (1999), "Unemployment duration econometrics," Working Paper, University of Toulouse.

Bontemps, C. (1998), "Modèles de recherche d'emploi d'équilibre," thèse pour le doctorat en sciences économiques, Université de Paris I.

Bontemps, C., Robin, J.-M., and van den Berg, G. (2000), "An empirical job search model with search on the job and heterogeneous workers and firms," *International Economic Review*, 41(2), pp. 305–358.

Boone, J., and van Ours, J. (2000), "Modeling financial incentives to get unemployment back to work," IZA Working Paper No. 108.

Burdett, K., and Mortensen, D. (1989), "Equilibrium wage differentials and employer size," research memorandum, Northwestern University, Evanston, Ill.

Burdett, K., and Mortensen, D. (1998), "Wage differentials, employer size, and unemployment," *International Economic Review*, 39, pp. 257–273.

Cahuc, P., and Lehmann, E. (2000), "Should unemployment benefits decrease with unemployment spell?" *Journal of Public Economics*, 77, pp. 135–153.

Cox, D. (1975), "Partial likelihood," *Biometrika*, 62(2), pp. 269–276.

Devine, T. (1988), "Arrival versus acceptance: The source of variation in reemployment rates across demographic groups," working paper, Pensylvania State University.

Devine, T., and Kiefer, N. (1991), *Empirical Labor Economics: The Search Approach*, Oxford, U.K.: Oxford University Press.

Diamond, P. (1971), "A model of price adjustment," *Journal of Economic Theory*, 3, pp. 156–168.

Dolton, P., and O'Neill, D. (1996), "Unemployment duration and the restart effect: Some experimental evidence," *Economic Journal*, 106, pp. 387–400.

Dormont, B., Fougère, D., and Prieto, A. (2001), "The effect of the time profile of unemployment insurance benefits on exit from unemployment," Paris: CREST working paper, www.crest.fr.

Flemming, J. (1978), "Aspects of optimal unemployment insurance: Search, leisure, savings and capital market imperfections," *Journal of Public Economics*, 10, pp. 403–425.

Florens, J.-P., Fougère, D., and Mouchart, M. (1996), "Duration models," in Matyas, L., Sevestre, P., and Kluwer, D. (eds.), *The Econometrics of Panel Data*, 2nd ed., pp. 491–536, San Diego, Calif.: Academic Press.

Fredriksson, P., and Holmlund, B. (2001), "Optimal unemployment insurance in search equilibrium," *Journal of Labor Economics*, 19, pp. 370–399.

Gandolfo, G. (1997), *Economic Dynamics*, New York: Springer-Verlag.

Grubb, D. (2000), "Eligibility criteria for unemployment benefits," *OECD Economic Studies*, 31, pp. 171–211.

Hansen, G., and Imrohoroglu, A. (1992), "The role of unemployment insurance in an economy with liquidity constraint and moral hazard," *Journal of Political Economy*, 100, pp. 118–142.

Holzer, H. (1986), "Reservation wages and their labor market effects for black and white male youth," *Journal of Human Resources*, 21, pp. 157–177.

Hopenhayn, H., and Nicolini, J. (1997), "Optimal unemployment insurance," *Journal of Political Economy*, 105, pp. 412–438.

Jones, S., and Riddell, C. (1999), "The measurement of unemployment: An empirical approach," *Econometrica*, 67, pp. 142–167.

Katz, L., and Meyer, B. (1990), "The impact of potential duration of unemployment benefits on the duration of unemployment," *Journal of Public Economics*, 41(1), pp. 45–72.

Kiefer, N. (1988), "Economic duration data and hazard functions," *Journal of Economic Literature*, 26, pp. 646–679.

Kiefer, N., and Neumann, G. (1993), "Wage dispersion with homogeneity: The empirical equilibrium search model," in Bunzel et al. (eds.), *Panel Data and Labour Market Analysis*, Amsterdam: North-Holland.

Krueger, A., and Summers, L. (1988), "Efficiency wages and the inter-industry wage structure," *Econometrica*, 56, pp. 259–293.

Lancaster, T. (1979), "Econometric methods for the duration of unemployment," *Econometrica*, 47(4), pp. 939–956.

Lancaster, T. (1990), *The Econometric Analysis of Transition Data*, Cambridge, U.K.: Cambridge University Press.

Ljungqvist, L., and Sargent, T. (2000), *Recursive Macroeconomic Theory*, Cambridge, Mass.: MIT Press.

Lynch, L. (1983), "Job search and youth unemployment," *Oxford Economic Papers*, 35, pp. 271–282.

Martin, A. (1996), "Indicateurs de taux de remplacement aux fins de comparaisons internationales," *Revue Economique de l'OCDE*, 26, pp. 115–132.

McCall, J. (1970), ''Economics of information and job search,'' *Quarterly Journal of Economics*, 84, pp. 113–126.

Meyer, B. (1990), ''Unemployment insurance and unemployment spells,'' *Econometrica*, 58(4), pp. 757–782.

Meyer, B. (1995), ''Lessons from the US unemployment insurance experiments,'' *Journal of Economic Literature*, 33, pp. 91–131.

Moffitt, R. (1985), ''Unemployment insurance and the distribution of unemployment spells,'' *Journal of Econometrics*, 28, pp. 85–101.

Moorthy, V. (1989), ''Unemployment in Canada and the United States: The role of unemployment insurance benefits,'' *Federal Reserve Bank of New York Quarterly Review*, Winter, pp. 48–60.

Mortensen, D. (1970), ''Job search, the duration of unemployment, and the Phillips curve,'' *American Economic Review*, 60, pp. 505–517.

Mortensen, D. (1986), ''Job search and labor market analysis,'' in Ashenfelter, O., and Layard, R. (eds.), *Handbook of Labor Economics*, vol. 2, pp. 849–919, Amsterdam: Elsevier Science/North-Holland.

Mortensen, D., and Pissarides, C. (1999), ''New developments in models of search in the labor market,'' in Ashenfelter, O., and Card, D. (eds.), *Handbook of Labor Economics*, vol. 3B, chap. 39, Amsterdam: Elsevier Science/North-Holland.

Narendranathan, W., Nickell, S., and Stern, J. (1985), ''Unemployment benefit revisited,'' *Economic Journal*, 95, pp. 307–329.

Nickell, S. (1979), ''Estimating the probability of leaving unemployment,'' *Econometrica*, 47, pp. 1249–1266.

OECD (1991), *Employment Outlook*, Paris: OECD.

OECD (1994), *The OECD Jobs Study*, 2 vols., Paris: OECD.

OECD (1995), *Employment Outlook*, Paris: OECD.

OECD (1996), *Employment Outlook*, Paris: OECD.

OECD (1999), *Employment Outlook*, Paris: OECD.

OECD (2000), *Employment Outlook*, Paris: OECD.

Postel-Vinay, F., and Robin, J.-M. (2002a), ''The distribution of earnings in an equilibrium search model with state-dependent offers and counter-offers,'' *International Economic Review*, 43(4), pp. 989–1016.

Postel-Vinay, F., and Robin, J.-M. (2002b), ''Wage dispersion with worker and employer heterogeneity,'' *Econometrica*, 70(6), pp. 295–350.

Shavell, S., and Weiss, L. (1979), ''The optimal payment of unemployment benefits over time,'' *Journal of Political Economy*, 87, pp. 1347–1362.

Stern, S. (1989), ''Search, applications, and vacancies,'' in Weiss, Y., and Fishelson, G. (eds.), *Advances in the Theory and Measurement of Unemployment*, London: Macmillan.

Stigler, G. (1961), ''The economics of information,'' *Journal of Political Economy*, 69, pp. 213–225.

Stigler, G. (1962), ''Information in the labor market,'' *Journal of Political Economy*, 70, pp. 94–105.

Topel, R., and Ward, M. (1992), "Job mobility and the careers of young men," *Quarterly Journal of Economics*, 107, pp. 439–479.

van den Berg, G. (1990), "Nonstationarity in job search theory," *Review of Economic Studies*, 57, pp. 255–277.

van den Berg, G. (1999), "Empirical inference with equilibrium search models of the labour market," *Economic Journal*, 109, pp. 283–306.

van den Berg, G. (2001), "Duration models: Specification, identification and multiple durations," in Heckman, J., and Leamer, E. (eds.), *Handbook of Econometrics*, vol. 5, chap. 55, Amsterdam: Elsevier Science/North-Holland.

van den Berg, G., van der Klaauw, B., and van Ours, J. (2001), "Punitive sanctions and the transition from welfare to work," working paper, Tinbergen Institute.

van den Berg, G., and van Ours, J. (1994), "Unemployment dynamics and duration dependence in France, the Netherlands and the UK," *Economic Journal*, 104, pp. 432–443.

van den Berg, G., and Ridder, G. (1998), "An empirical equilibrium search model of the labor market," *Econometrica*, 66, pp. 1183–1221.

Varian, H. (1992), *Microeconomic Analysis*, 3rd ed., New York: W.W. Norton.

Wang, C., and Williamson, S. (1996), "Unemployment insurance with moral hazard in a dynamic economy," *Carnegie-Rochester Conference Series on Public Economics*, 44, pp. 1–41.

Wolpin, K. (1987), "Estimating a structural job search model: The transition from school to work," *Econometrica*, 55, pp. 801–818.

C H A P T E R **4**

LABOR DEMAND

CONTENTS

In this chapter, we will see:

- How firms choose their factors of production

- Substitution between capital and labor

- Substitution between different types of labor

- The trade-off between workers and hours

- What the estimates of the elasticities of labor demands with respect to the costs of the inputs are

- What the effects of the adjustment costs of labor are

INTRODUCTION

The theory of labor demand is part of a wider context, that of the demand for the factors of production. The basic assumption is that firms utilize the services of labor by combining them with other inputs, such as capital, for example, in order to maximize the profits they derive from the sale of their products. Labor demand theory thus sets out to explain the demand for manpower, as well as the amount of time worked by each employee. An entrepreneur has an interest in hiring a worker whenever the income that worker generates is greater than his or her cost. The demand for labor must therefore depend on the cost of labor, but also on the cost of the other factors, and on elements that determine what the firm can earn, such as how efficiently its labor force performs and the price at which it can sell its goods. The cost of labor is composed of wages and the social security contributions (also known as payroll taxes) borne by the employer. The efficiency of labor depends on the technology available and the quantities of the other factors of production, such as capital or energy, utilized by firms. It also depends on the qualities of each worker, which in turn depend on individual characteristics such as motivation, dexterity, and alertness, and on objective factors such as educational level and professional experience. The price of the good produced depends on the quality of the product, the preferences of purchasers, and the characteristics of competitors.

In order to study labor demand, it is helpful to make a distinction between short-run decisions and long-run ones. We assume that in the short run, the firm adjusts its quantity of labor; its stock of capital we take as a given. In the long run, however, it is possible for firms to substitute capital for certain categories of employees. Most works in the field (see, for example, Hamermesh, 1993) also distinguish the "static" theory of labor demand from the "dynamic" theory. The static theory sets aside the *adjustment costs* of labor, i.e., the costs connected solely to *changes* in the volume of this factor. If such costs do not exist, there are really no dynamics, since nothing prevents labor demand from reaching its desired level immediately.

By not taking adjustment delays into account, static theory throws the basic properties of labor demand—the "laws," as they are sometimes called—into relief in a simplified manner. It comes to precise qualitative conclusions about the directions in which the quantity of labor demanded varies as a function of the costs of all the factors, and at a deeper level, it also succeeds in characterizing the elements that determine the *extent* of the elasticities of labor demand. Knowing the orders of magnitude of these elasticities is essential when it comes to assessing the effects of economic policy, because they make it possible to quantify the response of firms when a change of policy goes into effect. For example, knowledge of the elasticity of unskilled labor with respect to its cost allows us to set out in approximate figures the changes in the demand for this category of wage-earners in the wake of a reduction in social security contributions or a rise in the minimum wage.

Dynamic labor demand theory puts flesh on the bones of this knowledge by adding the effects of adjustment costs. Among other things, it furnishes indications concerning the form and speed of labor adjustments (which have also been the object of numerous empirical studies). Taking adjustment costs into account proves especially valuable for random environments in which firms face shocks, sometimes negative and sometimes positive, for it throws light on hiring and firing strategies.

In this chapter, section 1 sets out the static theory of labor demand. The separation of substitution effects from scale effects supplies an operational grid within which to interpret the long-run determinants of this demand. Section 1 also looks at the case of multiple (more than two) factors of production, and analyzes the trade-off between manpower and hours in this context. Section 2 shows how, by specifying the production function or the cost function explicitly, we can more easily make the transition from theoretical models to estimates. It concludes with a review of the main empirical results. Section 3 integrates adjustment costs into labor demand theory in order to bring out the dynamics of employment more clearly. It shows that these dynamics, and the properties of the stationary state, depend heavily on the functional form chosen to describe the costs linked to changes in employment. It also highlights the role of forecasts in adjustments of employment. Like section 2, it concludes with a summary of the main results arrived at by empirical studies.

1   THE STATIC THEORY OF LABOR DEMAND

In the short run, we can make the assumption that only the volume of labor services is variable. But in the long term, there exist possibilities of substituting capital for labor that substantially change the determinants of labor demand. When we do set the time horizon farther out, we can no longer study labor demand by narrowly focusing on just two aggregate factors, capital and labor, for the firm can also, for example, change the composition of its workforce by changing the structure of skills it uses. Hence we are led to study the behavior of firms when there are more than two factors of production. The heterogeneity of labor shows up as well in the imperfect substitutability between manpower and number of hours worked. Hence every firm has to make trade-offs between the number of its employees and the length of time each employee works as a function of the costs incurred when each of these two dimensions of labor demand is utilized with greater or less intensity.

1.1   LABOR DEMAND IN THE SHORT RUN

In the short run, the volume of work within a firm is more easily adaptable than the stock of capital, so labor demand depends on the real wage and the market power of the firm.

Market Power

The demand $Y(P)$ for a particular good depends on, among other things, the price P at which a firm sells its product. To make the explanation easier, it is preferable to work with the inverse relationship $P = P(Y)$, called *the inverse demand function*. It is assumed to be decreasing, and we shall denote its elasticity by $\eta_Y^P \equiv YP'(Y)/P(Y)$. A further hypothesis will be made, though it is not necessary in order to establish most of the results in this chapter: we will assume, for simplicity's sake, that function $P(Y)$ is isoelastic, meaning that the elasticity η_Y^P is a constant independent of Y.

When $\eta_Y^P = 0$, the price of the good does not depend on the quantity produced by the firm. This situation characterizes perfect competition, and the firm is then described as a "price taker." Conversely, if $\eta_Y^P < 0$, the firm finds itself in a situation of imperfect competition, and we then say that it is a "price maker." In a general way, the absolute value $|\eta_Y^P|$ of this elasticity constitutes an indicator of the market power of the firm, inasmuch as the effects of a change in its level of production on the market price are greater the larger $|\eta_Y^P|$ is. We may also point out that the notation $P(Y)$ does not mean that the price P depends only on the quantity Y produced by the firm. For example, P may vary with decisions taken by competing firms. It is also influenced by the tastes and the incomes of consumers. At partial equilibrium, which is the situation assumed throughout this chapter, it is not useful to bring in all the parameters that have an influence on P explicitly, since it is only the decisions of a particular firm that interest us.

Fixed and Flexible Factors

The factors of production comprise different types of manpower (for example, skilled and unskilled personnel) and different types of plant (machinery and factories). For simplicity, the latter will be represented by a single factor bearing the generic name *capital*. For reasons having to do principally with the time necessary to put them in place and their cost of installation or replacement, certain factors of production cannot be adjusted in the short run. Factors of this kind are called *fixed* or *rigid* factors, and we will assume that capital belongs to this category. Conversely, factors whose level can be altered in the short run are called *flexible* or *variable*. By definition, the levels of all the factors of production can be altered in the long run; hence all factors of production are flexible in the long run. With regard to manpower, certain categories of personnel have to be placed among the fixed factors (choices regarding highly skilled personnel have much in common with decisions about investment), while others (temporary workers, for example) are similar to flexible factors. At the most aggregate level possible, that is, when the ensemble of the services performed by the workforce is represented by a single variable, measured in hours, for example, it is natural to take the view that labor is more flexible than capital.

Cost of Labor and Marginal Productivity

We will begin our study of labor demand by assuming that all the services performed by this factor can be represented by a single aggregate L that is flexible in the short run, the other inputs being taken to be rigid at that horizon. Their levels can therefore be considered as given, and we may, without risk of confusion, represent the production process by a function with a single variable, or $Y = F(L)$. We will assume that this function is strictly increasing and strictly concave, i.e., that the marginal productivity is positive ($F' > 0$) and decreasing with the level of employment ($F'' < 0$).

If we designate the price of a unit of labor by W, and set aside the costs tied to the utilization of fixed factors, the firm's profit is written this way:

$$\Pi(L) = P(Y)Y - WL \qquad \text{with} \qquad Y = F(L)$$

The entrepreneur's only decision is to choose his or her level of employment so as to maximize his or her profit. The first-order condition is obtained simply, by setting the derivative of the profit to zero with respect to L, so that:

$$\Pi'(L) = F'(L)[P(Y) + P'(Y)Y] - W = F'(L)P(Y)(1 + \eta_Y^P) - W = 0$$

When $(1 + \eta_Y^P) > 0$, the labor demand is defined by[1]:

$$F'(L) = v\frac{W}{P} \qquad \text{with} \qquad v \equiv \frac{1}{1 + \eta_Y^P} \tag{1}$$

This relation signifies that the profit of the firm attains its maximum when the marginal productivity of labor is equal to real wage W/P multiplied by a *markup* $v \geq 1$. The latter is an increasing function of the absolute value $|\eta_Y^P|$ of price elasticity with respect to production. The markup constitutes a measure of the firm's market power. In a situation of perfect competition, the firm has no market power ($\eta_Y^P = 0$), and marginal productivity is equal to the real wage.

The concept of cost function allows us to interpret the optimality condition (1) differently. In this model, with just one factor of production, this function simply corresponds to the cost of labor linked to the production of a quantity Y of a good, or $C(Y) = WL = WF^{-1}(Y)$, where F^{-1} designates the inverse function of F. Since the derivative of F^{-1} is equal to $1/F'$, the marginal cost is defined by $C'(Y) = W/F'(L)$, and relation (1) is written:

$$P = v\frac{W}{F'(L)} = vC'(L) \tag{2}$$

In other words, the firm sets its price by applying the markup v to its marginal cost $C'(Y)$. In the situation of perfect competition ($v = 1$), the price of a good exactly equals the marginal cost.

The expression of labor demand allows us to study the impact of a variation in the cost of labor on the volume of labor. Differentiating relation (1) with respect to W, we find again that:

$$\frac{\partial L}{\partial W} = v/(F'^2 P' + PF'') < 0$$

Hence short-run labor demand and thus the level of supply of the good are *decreasing* functions of labor cost. On the other hand, the selling price of the good produced by the firm rises with W. It could be shown in the same manner that labor demand and the level of production diminish, while price rises, when the markup v grows larger.

Thus, in the short run, the cost of labor, the determinants of demand for the good produced by the firm, the firm's technology, and the structure of the market for goods—represented by the markup v or the elasticity η_Y^P—all influence labor demand. In the longer run, the firm may contemplate replacing part of its workforce with machines, or conversely increasing the numbers of its personnel and reducing its stock of capital. Labor demand will then depend on the technical feasibility of these operations and the price of the other inputs.

1.2   THE SUBSTITUTION OF CAPITAL FOR LABOR

We will now shift to a long-run perspective, in which capital K also becomes a flexible factor. To better appreciate the different elements that bear on demands for the factors of production, it will be helpful to conduct the analysis in two stages. In the first stage, the level of production is taken as given, and we will look for the optimal combinations of capital and labor by which that level can be reached. In the second stage, we look for the volume of output that will maximize the firm's profit. This approach makes it possible to distinguish *substitution effects*, which occur in the first stage, where the volume of production is fixed, from *scale effects*, which are confined to the second stage, in which the optimal level of production is set. More precisely, substitution effects relate to the choice of one factor over another in order to attain a given level of production. Scale effects (also called quantity effects, or supply effects) have to do with the capacity to alter the level of production while retaining the same proportions among the various inputs. We begin by analyzing the first stage of the producer's problem; scale effects will be studied in section 1.3. The first stage makes it possible to define and characterize the cost function of the firm. We can then deduce the properties of the so-called *conditional factors demands*.

1.2.1   Minimization of Total Cost

Assuming a technology with just two inputs, capital and labor, the conditional demands for these inputs depend only on the relative price of each. The properties of these conditional demands can be deduced if we know the cost function of the firm.

A Technology with Two Inputs

Assuming once more that labor can be represented by a single aggregate L, the production function of the firm will now be written $F(K, L)$. If production of level Y requires that capital and labor always be combined in the same proportion—that is, that the ratio K/L remain a constant independent of Y—capital and labor are said to be *complementary*. In this case, it is enough to know the level of production in order to obtain the quantity of each factor utilized. Formally, we have reverted to the preceding analytical framework, where the production function had only one argument. But we will assume from now on that to attain a given level of production, capital and labor can always combine in different proportions. Factors possessing this property are said to be *substitutable*.

   More precisely, we will posit that the production function is strictly increasing with each of its arguments, so that its partial derivatives will be strictly positive, or, with the obvious notations, $F_K > 0$ and $F_L > 0$. We will also assume that this function is strictly concave, which signifies in particular that the marginal productivities of each factor diminish with the quantity of the corresponding factor. We will thus have $F_{KK} < 0$ and $F_{LL} < 0$. In order to make certain results clearer, it will sometimes be useful to assume that the production function is homogeneous. We may note that if $\theta > 0$ designates the degree of homogeneity, this property is characterized by the following equality:

$$F(\mu K, \mu L) = \mu^{\theta} F(K, L) \qquad \forall \mu > 0, \quad \forall (K, L) \tag{3}$$

Parameter θ represents the level of *returns to scale*. The homogeneity of the production function implies that this parameter is independent of the level of production. We say that returns to scale are decreasing if $0 < \theta < 1$, constant if $\theta = 1$, and increasing if $\theta > 1$.

Cost Function and Factor Demand

The optimal combination of inputs is obtained by minimizing the cost linked to the production level Y. Let us designate by R and W respectively the price of a unit of capital and a unit of labor; the quantities of inputs corresponding to this choice are given by the solution of the following problem:

$$\underset{\{K, L\}}{\mathrm{Min}}(WL + RK) \quad \text{subject to constraint} \quad F(K, L) \geq Y \tag{4}$$

The solutions, denoted $\bar{L}$ and $\bar{K}$, are called respectively the *conditional demand* for labor and the *conditional demand* for capital. The minimal value of the total cost, or $(W\bar{L} + R\bar{K})$, is then a function of the unit cost of each factor and the level of production. This minimal value is called the cost function of the firm, and we will denote it $C(W, R, Y)$.

A figure will help us to understand the solution of problem (4). In figure 4.1, we show, in the plane (K, L), an *isoquant* labeled (Y). By definition, this curve designates the set of values of K and L allowing a given level of production to be attained, in

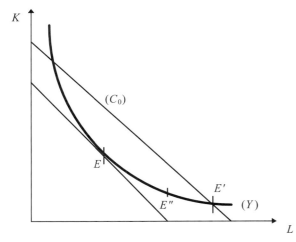

FIGURE 4.1
The minimization of total cost.

other words satisfying $F(K, L) = Y$. In the plane (K, L), an isoquant is thus a curve of equation $K(L)$ such that $F[K(L), L] = Y$. Its slope is negative, and the absolute value of its derivative is, by definition, equal to the *technical rate of substitution* between capital and labor, or $|K'(L)| = F_L/F_K$. The technical rate of substitution defines the quantity of capital that can be saved when the quantity of labor is augmented by one unit. In appendix 1 to this chapter it is shown as well that the isoquants are strictly convex ($K'' > 0$) when the production function is strictly concave. This means that the technical rate of substitution, equal to the absolute value of $K'(L)$, is decreasing: the larger the volume of labor, the less capital can be saved by augmenting the quantity of labor by one unit. In figure 4.1 we have also represented an *isocost* curve (C_0). This corresponds to the values of K and L such that $WL + RK = C_0$, where C_0 is a positive given constant. An isocost curve is thus a straight line with a slope $-(W/R)$ moving out toward the northeast when C_0 increases. It is evident, then, that if the isocost line is not tangent to the isoquant—at point E', for example—it is always possible to find a combination of factors K and L satisfying the constraint $F(K, L) \geq Y$ and leading to a cost lower than that of the combination represented by point E'. For that, we need only cause line (C_0) to shift in toward the origin (for example, at point E'' the total cost of production is lower than its value at point E'). To sum up, the producer's optimum lies at point E, where the isocost line is tangent to the isoquant. The reader will see that the property of strict convexity of the isoquant guarantees that point E represents a unique minimum for the cost of production. At this point, the technical rate of substitution is equal to the ratio of the costs of inputs. The conditional demands for capital and labor are thus defined by the following equations:

$$\frac{F_L(\bar{K}, \bar{L})}{F_K(\bar{K}, \bar{L})} = \frac{W}{R} \qquad \text{and} \qquad F(\bar{K}, \bar{L}) = Y \tag{5}$$

The Properties of the Cost Function
Relation (5) shows that $\bar{K}$ and $\bar{L}$ depend only on the level of production Y and the relative price W/R of labor. Evidently we could deduce the properties of the conditional demands using the two equations of relation (5). In fact, though, it proves simpler to proceed indirectly by relying on the cost function $C(W, R, Y)$. Thus, in appendix 2 of this chapter it is shown that the latter possesses the following properties:

(i) It is *increasing* with respect to each of its arguments and *homogeneous of degree 1* in (W, R).

(ii) It is *concave* in (W, R), which signifies in particular that the second derivatives C_{WW} and C_{RR} are negative.

(iii) It satisfies *Shephard's lemma*:

$$\bar{L} = C_W(W, R, Y) \qquad \text{and} \qquad \bar{K} = C_R(W, R, Y) \tag{6}$$

where C_W and C_R designate respectively the partial derivatives of the cost function with respect to W and R.

(iv) It is homogeneous of degree $1/\theta$ with respect to Y when the production function is homogeneous of degree θ. Under this hypothesis, the conditional demands for factors are also homogeneous of degree $1/\theta$ in relation to Y. Formally, we thus have:

$$C(W, R, Y) = C(W, R, 1)Y^{1/\theta}, \qquad \bar{L}\left(\frac{W}{R}, Y\right) = \bar{L}\left(\frac{W}{R}, 1\right)Y^{1/\theta} \qquad \text{and}$$

$$\bar{K}\left(\frac{W}{R}, Y\right) = \bar{K}\left(\frac{W}{R}, 1\right)Y^{1/\theta} \tag{7}$$

These properties of the cost function allow us to derive the properties of the conditional factor demands very easily.

1.2.2   The Properties of the Conditional Factor Demands

The most important properties of the conditional demands for labor and capital have to do with the way they vary in the wake of a rise or a fall in the prices of these factors. The extent of these variations depends on the elasticity of substitution between capital and labor, on the one hand, and the share of each factor in the total cost on the other hand.

Variations in Factor Prices

The differentiation of the first relation of Shephard's lemma (6) with respect to W entails:

$$\frac{\partial \bar{L}}{\partial W} = C_{WW} \leq 0$$

The conditional labor demand is thus *decreasing* with the price of this factor. Since the first-order conditions (5) show that conditional demand in reality depends only on the relative price of labor, i.e., on W/R, we can state that it increases with the price of capital. Symmetrically, we could show that the conditional demand for capital diminishes with R and increases with W.

Shephard's lemma allows us to characterize more precisely the cross effects of a change in the price of a factor on the demand for the other factor. Thus relation (6) immediately entails:

$$\frac{\partial \bar{L}}{\partial R} = \frac{\partial \bar{K}}{\partial W} = C_{WR} \tag{8}$$

Since it was shown above that the conditional demand for a factor is increasing with the price of the other factor, we can deduce that the cross derivative C_{WR} is necessarily positive.[2] The equality (8) portrays the symmetry condition of cross-price effects. It means that at the producer's optimum, the effect of a rise of one dollar in the price of labor on the volume of capital is equal to the effect of a rise of one dollar in the price of capital on the volume of labor. This (astonishing) equality is no longer verified in terms of elasticities.

Cross Elasticities and the Elasticity of Substitution Between Capital and Labor
Let us recall first that the *cross* elasticities $\bar{\eta}_R^L$ and $\bar{\eta}_W^K$ of the conditional demand for a factor with respect to the price of the other factor are defined by:

$$\bar{\eta}_R^L = \frac{R}{\bar{L}} \frac{\partial \bar{L}}{\partial R} \qquad \text{and} \qquad \bar{\eta}_W^K = \frac{W}{\bar{K}} \frac{\partial \bar{K}}{\partial W} \tag{9}$$

At the producer's optimum, relation (8) then entails $\bar{\eta}_R^L = (R\bar{K}/W\bar{L})\bar{\eta}_W^K$. Consequently, leaving aside the exceptional case where the cost $W\bar{L}$ of manpower would equal the cost $R\bar{K}$ of capital, the cross elasticities will always be different. They do not, therefore, constitute a significant indicator of the possibilities of substitution between these two factors. To get around this problem, it is preferable to resort to the notion of *elasticity of substitution*, which is the elasticity of the variable $\bar{K}/\bar{L}$ with respect to relative price W/R. The elasticity of substitution between capital and labor, denoted by σ, is defined by:

$$\sigma = \frac{W/R}{\bar{K}/\bar{L}} \frac{\partial(\bar{K}/\bar{L})}{\partial(W/R)} \tag{10}$$

This formula indicates that the capital–labor ratio increases by $\sigma\%$ when the ratio between the price of labor and the price of capital increases by 1%. Figure 4.1 shows that a rise (or a fall) of the relative price W/R increases (or diminishes) the slope of the straight lines of isocost and therefore shifts point E to the left (or the right) along the isoquant. In other words, the ratio $\bar{K}/\bar{L}$ varies in the same direction as the relative price W/R. The elasticity of substitution between capital and labor is thus always *positive* (though it should be noted that this result is no longer automatically verified when the production function has more than two factors of production; see section 1.4.1 below).

It is possible to obtain a simple expression of this elasticity of substitution by exploiting the homogeneity of the cost function. In appendix 2, it is established that the elasticity of substitution is written in the following manner[3]:

$$\sigma = \frac{C C_{WR}}{C_W C_R} \tag{11}$$

The reader can verify that σ is *symmetric* in W and R; therefore this variable also represents the elasticity of the ratio $\bar{L}/\bar{K}$ in relation to the relative cost R/W. It should also be noted that it does not depend on the level Y of production when the hypothesis (3) of the homogeneity of the production function is satisfied. Consequently, property (iv) of the cost function set out in the preceding section stipulates that the conditional demands $\bar{K}$ and $\bar{L}$ are homogeneous of degree $1/\theta$ in Y when the production function is homogeneous of degree θ. In this case, the ratio $\bar{K}/\bar{L}$ does not depend on Y, and consequently the elasticity of substitution σ depends only on the relative price W/R.

Conditional Demands and the Factor Shares in the Total Cost
It is instructive to express the cross elasticities defined by (9) as a function of σ. With the help of relation (8), we note that $\bar{\eta}_R^L$ is equal to $(R/\bar{L})C_{WR}$. The expression (11)

of the elasticity of substitution then leads to $\bar{\eta}_R^L = (RC_W C_R / \bar{L}C)\sigma$. Let us designate by $s \equiv W\bar{L}/C$ the labor share in the total cost. Since, following Shephard's lemma—see (6)—we have $\bar{L} = C_W$ and $\bar{K} = C_R$, we immediately arrive at $\bar{\eta}_R^L = (1-s)\sigma$. Thus, the elasticity of the conditional labor demand with respect to the cost of capital is equal to the elasticity of substitution multiplied by the share of capital in the total cost. It could be shown in the same way that the elasticity of the conditional capital demand with respect to the cost of labor is equal to the elasticity of substitution multiplied by the share of labor in the total cost. There exists as well a link between the *direct* elasticity $\bar{\eta}_W^L$ and the elasticity of substitution σ. The conditional demand for labor depending only on Y and on the ratio W/R, we have $\partial \bar{L} / \partial W = -(R/W)(\partial \bar{L}/\partial R)$, and consequently:

$$\bar{\eta}_W^L = -\bar{\eta}_R^L = -(1-s)\sigma \tag{12}$$

Relation (12) proves particularly interesting from an empirical point of view, for it supplies a simple linkage between estimates of the elasticity of substitution σ and those of $\bar{\eta}_W^L$ or $\bar{\eta}_R^L$ (see section 2.2.1). What is more, it offers very useful indications of the effect of a variation in the price of the factors on conditional labor demand. In the first place, it is apparent that this effect bulks larger (in absolute value) the greater the possibilities of substitution between capital and labor are. When the value of the elasticity of substitution is high, that means that to obtain a given level of production, the entrepreneur has the possibility of diminishing "greatly" the utilization of one factor and "greatly" increasing that of the other, in the wake of a change in the relative price of the factors. Thus, when W rises or R falls, the firm's interest in diminishing the utilization of labor so as to minimize the total cost is all the greater, the higher the value of σ is. This explains why the elasticities of conditional labor demand are increasing, in absolute value, with the elasticity of substitution σ.

Symmetrically, the influence of the relative share of the cost of a factor can easily be grasped by assuming that σ remains constant. For a given value of the relative price W/R, the fact that the share $(1-s)$ of capital is "small" reveals that the firm utilizes relatively little of this factor and a great deal of labor. Now, the larger the quantity of labor is, the smaller the variations in the quantity of labor expressed in percentage terms are. The logic goes the other way, of course, if the share of capital is large. Accordingly, the direct and cross elasticities of the conditional labor demand increase in absolute value with the share of capital in the total cost. In an equivalent fashion, these elasticities diminish in absolute value with the share of labor in the total cost.

Variation in the Level of Output

The effects of an exogenous change in the level of output Y on the total cost are easily characterized if total cost is defined by $C = W\bar{L} + R\bar{K}$ with $F(\bar{K}, \bar{L}) = Y$. It suffices to differentiate these last two equalities with respect to Y and to take account of the optimality condition (5) to get the following expression of the *marginal cost* (equal by definition to the partial derivative C_Y of the cost function with respect to the output level Y):

$$C_Y(W, R, Y) = \frac{W}{F_L} = \frac{R}{F_K} \tag{13}$$

In the first place, it is apparent that the marginal cost is always positive. This means that the total cost rises with the level of output. Conversely, it is not possible to know the direction of variations in factor demands without supplementary hypotheses. Clearly, factor demands do not diminish simultaneously when production increases. Thus a rise in production simply requires that the volume of one of the factors increase, but the volume of the other factor is not obliged to do so; it can even decrease. However, when the production function satisfies the homogeneity hypothesis (3), a more precise conclusion emerges. The factor demands are then homogeneous of degree $1/\theta$ with respect to Y—see property (iv) of the cost function set out in section 1.2.1—and relation (7) clearly shows that the conditional demands for labor and capital then rise simultaneously with the level of output.

Minimization of cost for a given level of output constitutes the first stage of the problem of the firm; we must now examine how the optimal volume of output is determined.

1.3   SCALE EFFECTS

The entrepreneur is generally in a position to choose his or her level of production. The desired quantities of the factors are then distinguishable from their conditional demands. The analysis of substitution and scale effects yields highly general properties for labor demand; among other things, it brings into play the elasticity of substitution between capital and labor, the share of each factor in the total cost, and the market power of the firm.

1.3.1   Unconditional Factor Demands

The entrepreneur chooses a level of output that maximizes his or her profit. Let us again designate by $P(Y)$ the inverse demand function. Then, profit $\Pi(W, R, Y)$ linked to a level of production Y when the unit costs of labor and capital are respectively W and R takes the following form:

$$\Pi(W, R, Y) = P(Y)Y - C(W, R, Y) \tag{14}$$

The first-order condition is obtained by setting the derivative of this expression to zero with respect to Y. Rearranging terms, we find that the optimal level of production is characterized by the equality:

$$P(Y) = vC_Y(W, R, Y) \qquad \text{with} \qquad v \equiv 1/(1 + \eta_Y^P) \tag{15}$$

In the case of a production function homogeneous of degree θ, the reader can verify[4] that it is indeed a maximum if and only if $v > \theta$. We confirm the result we obtained when we studied short-run labor demand (see (2)): the firm sets its price by applying the markup v to its marginal cost C_Y. Taking into account expression (13) of marginal cost, the optimality condition (15) takes the following form:

$$F_L(K, L) = v\frac{W}{P} \qquad \text{and} \qquad F_K(K, L) = v\frac{R}{P} \tag{16}$$

In other words, at the firm's optimum the marginal productivity of each factor is equal to its real cost multiplied by the markup. When the competition in the market for the good produced by the firm is perfect ($v = 1$), we confirm the usual equalities between the marginal productivity of a factor and its real cost. The values of K and of L, defined by equations (15) and (16), are called the *long-run* or *unconditional* demands for capital and for labor.

1.3.2   The "Laws" of Demand

The laws of demand refer to the manner in which *unconditional* demands for the factors of production vary with the unit costs of these same factors. They combine substitution and scale effects.

The Decreasing Relation Between the Demand for a Factor and Its Cost
We shall first demonstrate that the unconditional demand for a factor decreases with the cost of this factor. This property possesses a very general character; in particular, it does not depend on the production function of the firm being homogeneous. To establish this result, let us first consider the *profit function*, denoted by $\Pi(W, R)$, equal to the maximal value of profit for given values of the costs of the inputs. It is defined by:

$$\Pi(W, R) \equiv \underset{Y}{\text{Max}}\ \Pi(W, R, Y)$$

The cost function $C(W, R, Y)$ being concave in (W, R) for all Y, relation (14) signifies that function $\Pi(W, R, Y)$ is convex in (W, R), whatever the value of Y may be. Let us denote by Y^* the optimal level of production given by (15); since, by definition, we have $\Pi(W, R) = \Pi(W, R, Y^*)$, the profit function $\Pi(W, R)$ is thus equally convex in (W, R). Differentiating relation (14) with respect to W, we have:

$$\Pi_W(W, R) = [P(Y^*)(1 + \eta_Y^P) - C_Y(W, R, Y^*)]\frac{\partial Y^*}{\partial W} - C_W(W, R, Y^*)$$

According to optimality condition (15), the term in brackets is null. Moreover, Shephard's lemma (6) states that the partial derivative $C_W(W, R, Y^*)$ is equal to unconditional labor demand L^*. An analogous rationale evidently applies to the unconditional capital demand K^*. We thus arrive at the following relations, known as *Hotelling's lemma*:

$$\Pi_W(W, R) = -L^* \qquad \text{and} \qquad \Pi_R(W, R) = -K^* \tag{17}$$

The profit function $\Pi(W, R)$ being convex, we then have $\Pi_{WW} \geq 0$ and $\Pi_{RR} \geq 0$, and relation (17) immediately entails:

$$\frac{\partial L^*}{\partial W} = -\Pi_{WW} \leq 0 \qquad \text{and} \qquad \frac{\partial K^*}{\partial R} = -\Pi_{RR} \leq 0 \tag{18}$$

Thus, under very general conditions, unconditional demand for a factor is a decreasing function of the cost of this factor. It must also be noted that the direction in which this demand varies with the cost of the other factor is not determined a priori—a consequence of the fact that the scale effect may now be opposed to the substitution effect. More generally, it is important to know the determinants of the relative extent of these two effects.

Labor Demand Elasticities

It is possible to be more exact about unconditional labor demand L^* by noting that it always satisfies Shephard's lemma (6). Thus we have $L^* = C_W(W, R, Y^*)$. Differentiating this equality with respect to W, we get:

$$\frac{\partial L^*}{\partial W} = C_{WW} + C_{WY} \frac{\partial Y^*}{\partial W}$$

When we multiply the two members of this relation by W/L^*, we bring to light the elasticities η_W^L and η_W^Y of unconditional labor demand and of the level of output with respect to the wage. The result is:

$$\eta_W^L = \frac{W}{L^*} C_{WW} + \left(\frac{Y^* C_{WY}}{L^*} \right) \eta_W^Y$$

Since $L^* = C_W(W, R, Y^*)$, the terms $(W/L^*)C_{WW}$ and $(Y^*/L^*)C_{WY}$ designate respectively the elasticity $\bar{\eta}_W^L$ of the *conditional* labor demand and the elasticity of this demand with respect to the level of output taken at point $Y = Y^*$. This last elasticity can be denoted by $\bar{\eta}_Y^L$. We thus finally obtain:

$$\eta_W^L = \bar{\eta}_W^L + \bar{\eta}_Y^L \eta_W^Y \tag{19}$$

This relation clearly reveals the different effects of a rise in wage on the demand for labor. We may start by isolating a *substitution effect* represented by the elasticity $\bar{\eta}_W^L$ of conditional labor demand. We have seen in section 1.2.2 that this term is always negative, since for a given level of production, a rise in the cost of labor always leads to reduced utilization of this factor (and increased utilization of capital). Relation (19) likewise brings out a *scale effect* represented by the product $\bar{\eta}_Y^L \eta_W^Y$. The direction of this scale effect is obtained by first noting that the second-order conditions of profit maximization for the firm dictate that η_W^Y should be of opposite sign to C_{WY}.[5] Since, following Shephard's lemma (6), $\bar{\eta}_Y^L$ is of the same sign as C_{WY}, the scale effect is always *negative* and therefore accentuates the substitution effect.

It should be emphasized that formula (19) measures the wage elasticity of employment of a given firm, the wages of other firms remaining constant. If the wage rises simultaneously in several competing firms producing substitutable goods, we should expect that the elasticity of employment will be weaker than that defined by relation (19), because the prices of competitors must also rise, and for the same reason that the prices of the firm we are considering do. The demand for the goods of this firm thus diminishes less than in the case where competitors' wages remain constant. Consequently the scale effect is weaker. Formally, if $\eta_{\tilde{W}}^Y$ and $\eta_{\tilde{W}}^L$ denote respectively the sum of the elasticities of production and employment of the firm we are considering with respect to its own wage and with respect to all its competitors' wages (and bearing in mind that conditional elasticity $\bar{\eta}_W^L$ depends only on the wage of the firm we are considering), we get:

$$\eta_W^L = \bar{\eta}_W^L + \bar{\eta}_Y^L \eta_W^Y \qquad (20)$$

Since $|\eta_W^Y| > |\eta_{\overline{W}}^Y|$ when firms produce substitutable goods, $\eta_{\overline{W}}^L$ is smaller in absolute value to η_W^L in the most probable case, where $\bar{\eta}_Y^L$ is positive. It is important to keep this result in mind when we come to interpret empirical studies, inasmuch as the latter frequently evaluate the impact of variations in the cost of labor that affect several firms, or even several sectors, simultaneously.

Gross Substitutes and Gross Complements

Using the same procedure, it is possible to calculate the cross elasticity η_R^L of the unconditional labor demand with respect to the cost of capital. This comes to:

$$\eta_R^L = \bar{\eta}_R^L + \bar{\eta}_Y^L \eta_R^Y$$

In the case of two inputs, we have shown in section 1.2.2 that the conditional demand for a factor rises when the price of the other factor rises. The substitution effect, marked by the term $\bar{\eta}_R^L$, is thus positive. Conversely, the scale effect, represented by the term $\bar{\eta}_Y^L \eta_R^Y$, is a priori ambiguous, except in the case of a homogeneous production function, where it is necessarily positive.[6] The sign of cross elasticity η_R^L is thus undetermined.

By definition, if $\eta_R^L > 0$, labor and capital are qualified as *gross substitutes*: a rise in the price of capital causes demand for this factor to fall and that of labor to rise: the substitution effect dominates the scale effect. If $\eta_R^L < 0$, labor and capital are qualified as *gross complements*: a hike in the price of one of these factors signifies that demand for both of them falls off, with the scale effect now dominating the substitution effect.

The "Laws" of Demand with a Homogeneous Production Function

When the production function is homogeneous, it is possible to express scale effects as a function of the labor share s in the total cost, of the markup v, and of the degree of homogeneity θ. To achieve this, we must first note that relation (7) immediately implies that the output elasticity of conditional labor demand $\bar{\eta}_Y^L$ is equal to $1/\theta$. Then, replacing C_Y by $C/\theta Y$ in the optimality condition (15) and taking the logarithmic derivatives with respect to W of this relation, we arrive at:

$$\frac{1}{Y} \left[\frac{YP'(Y)}{P(Y)} - \frac{YC_Y}{C} \right] \frac{\partial Y}{\partial W} = \frac{C_W}{C}$$

Since $L = C_W$, and following (7), $YC_Y/C = 1/\theta$, we find after several calculations:

$$\eta_W^Y = \frac{\theta s}{\theta(\eta_Y^P + 1) - 1} = \frac{\theta v}{\theta - v} s \qquad (21)$$

The second-order conditions imposing $v > \theta$, we do indeed verify that $\eta_W^Y < 0$. Symmetrically, the value of η_R^Y is obtained by replacing s by $(1 - s)$ in relation (21). The scale effect of a rise in price of a factor is proportional to the share of the remuneration of this factor in the total cost. Taking account of relation (12), which gives the values of the *conditional* demand elasticities, it becomes possible to express, with the help of (21), the direct and cross elasticities of *unconditional* labor demand as a function of the share s of this factor in the total cost, as a function of the elasticity of substitution σ between capital and labor, as a function of the margin rate v, and as a function of the scale θ of overall returns. This is expressed as:

$$\eta_W^L = -(1-s)\sigma - \frac{v}{v-\theta}s \quad \text{and} \quad \eta_R^L = (1-s)\left(\sigma - \frac{v}{v-\theta}\right) \tag{22}$$

Knowledge of the order of magnitude of these elasticities becomes very important when the impact of economic policies must be assessed. That is why we need to understand clearly how they evolve when certain parameters change. Relations (22) yield relatively precise predictions concerning labor demand that in large measure confirm the "laws of demand" put forward by Marshall (1920) and Hicks (1932) in their time. They are best understood by combining the substitution effect, the absolute value of which is measured by the term $(1-s)\sigma$, with the scale effect measured by the other terms of these relations.

Market Power
The elasticity of the inverse demand function, η_Y^P, and so of market power v, do not play a role in the substitution effect. Conversely, it is evident that the scale effect *diminishes* in absolute terms when v rises. Faced with a rise in the cost of labor, a firm with weak market power (v approaching unity) cannot change its selling price very much—it cannot change it at all when competition in the market is perfect ($v = 1$)—and so the repercussion of the cost increase will essentially be felt in the output. If, on the other hand, the firm is highly monopolistic, or in other words if the elasticity of the inverse demand function, η_Y^P, is high, the firm is able to alter its price to a considerable degree without losing too much market share, i.e., without changing its output level very much. In sum, the elasticity of output and so that of labor demand with respect to factor costs will diminish in absolute value, the higher the degree of monopoly.

Substitution of Capital for Labor
We see that the elasticity of substitution σ appears only in the substitution effect, with no influence on the scale effect, and since we have already looked at the consequences of a rise in σ for a given level of production, readers may refer back to the comments following relation (12). The general conclusion to which we came was that the easier it is to substitute capital for labor, the greater the direct and cross elasticities of labor demand are in absolute value.

The Share of Labor in the Cost of Production
In section 1.2.2 we studied the reasons why the substitution effect, equal in absolute value to $(1-s)\sigma$, decreases as the share s of labor in the total cost decreases. Formulas (22) make it evident that the scale effect is indeed negative, but also that it increases

(or diminishes) in absolute value with *s* if the rise in the cost of production is caused by an increase in *W* (or *R*). These movements are to be explained in the following manner: if *s* is large, then the firm utilizes "a lot" of labor and "little" capital, and in consequence production and employment will be very sensitive to a variation in labor cost, but much less influenced by a change in the cost of capital. Hence the share *s* of labor in the total cost acts in opposite ways on the substitution effect and the scale effect. It is therefore the relative importance of an effect with respect to the other that will determine variations in the elasticities of labor demand. To be more precise, formulas (22) show that if capital and labor are gross substitutes—$\sigma > v/(v - \theta)$—then $|\eta_W^L|$ and η_R^L are decreasing functions of *s*. Under this hypothesis, the substitution effect dominates the scale effect and so it is normal that the behavior of unconditional demand should follow that of conditional demand. This result will obviously be inverted when the two factors of production are gross complements.

Adopting a production function limited to two factors thus allows us to assess the determinants of the level of capital and that of aggregate employment. But in many circumstances—for example, if we want to know the impact of an economic policy measure on the employment of unskilled persons—the labor factor can no longer be viewed as a single aggregate, and it becomes necessary to work with a production function comprising more than two inputs.

1.4   BEYOND TWO INPUTS

Here again it will be best to proceed in two stages. In the first, we seek to identify the optimal combinations of factors that enable a given level of production to be reached, and in the second, we determine the value of this level that maximizes the firm's profit. The first stage yields conditional demands, which are no longer necessarily characterized by a negative substitution effect. The second allows us to obtain unconditional demands.

1.4.1   Conditional Demands

Conditional factor demands result from the minimization of the total cost for a given level of production. But unlike the case in which there were only two inputs, the cross elasticities and thus the elasticities of substitution are no longer necessarily positive.

The Minimization of Total Cost
The production function of the firm is now written $Y = F(X^1, \ldots, X^n)$, where X^i is the quantity of factor *i* utilized in the production of a quantity *Y* of output. This function is assumed to be strictly increasing with each of its arguments and also strictly concave. If we designate by $W^i > 0$ the price of factor *i*, the *conditional* demands are obtained by minimizing the total cost linked to the production of a given quantity *Y* of output. They are thus solutions to the following problem:

$$\underset{(X^1, \ldots, X^n)}{\text{Min}} \sum_{i=1}^n W^i X^i \quad \text{subject to} \quad F(X^1, \ldots, X^n) \geq Y$$

When there are more than two inputs, this problem cannot be solved graphically, and it is therefore necessary to turn to conventional methods of optimization. Let $\lambda \leq 0$ be the multiplier linked to the production constraint. The Lagrangian of this problem is written:

$$\mathcal{L} = \sum_{i=1}^{n} W^i X^i + \lambda[F(X^1, \ldots, X^n) - Y]$$

Let F_i designate the partial derivative of function F with respect to its ith argument. Differentiating this Langrangian with respect to X^i gives the first-order conditions. We thus have $(\partial \mathcal{L}/\partial X^i) = W^i + \lambda F_i = 0$, for all $i = 1, \ldots, n$. Since W^i and F_i are strictly positive, the multiplier λ is strictly negative and the production constraint is always binding. In sum, the conditional factor demands, denoted $\bar{X}^i$ for $i = 1, \ldots, n$, are defined by the following equations:

$$F(\bar{X}^1, \ldots, \bar{X}^n) = Y \quad \text{and} \quad \frac{F_i(\bar{X}^1, \ldots, \bar{X}^n)}{F_j(\bar{X}^1, \ldots, \bar{X}^n)} = \frac{W^i}{W^j} \qquad \forall i, j = 1, \ldots, n \tag{23}$$

The strict concavity of function F guarantees that the necessary conditions for the minimization of total cost are also sufficient conditions. We note that the result described by relation (23) generalizes that obtained with two factors of production, i.e., that the technical rate of substitution (F_i/F_j) between factors i and j, is equal to the relative cost (W^i/W^j) of factor i with respect to factor j.

The Cost Function

The minimum value of the total cost, or $\sum W^i \bar{X}^i$, is also called the *cost function* of the firm. It depends on the price of inputs and the output level Y, so it can be denoted by $C(W^1, \ldots, W^n, Y)$. As in the case with two inputs, this function proves very useful for the study of the factor demands. In appendix 2 of this chapter, we show that it satisfies the following properties:

(i) It is *increasing* with each of its arguments and it is *homogeneous of degree 1* with respect to $(W^1, \ldots, W^n)$.

(ii) It is *concave* in $(W^1, \ldots, W^n)$, which signifies in particular that the partial second derivative C_{ii} is *negative* for all $i = 1, \ldots, n$.

(iii) It satisfies *Shephard's lemma*:

$$\bar{X}^i = C_i(W^1, \ldots, W^n, Y) \tag{24}$$

where C_i designates the partial derivative of function C with respect to its ith argument.

(iv) It is homogeneous of degree $1/\theta$ in Y when the production function is homogeneous of degree θ. Under this hypothesis, the conditional factor demands are also homogeneous of degree $1/\theta$ in relation to Y.

P-Substitute and P-Complement

Shephard's lemma allows us to obtain a very important property of the demand function of a production factor. Differentiating (24) with respect to W^i, we get:

$$\frac{\partial \bar{X}^i}{\partial W^i} = C_{ii} \le 0 \qquad \forall i = 1, \dots, n \tag{25}$$

In other words, the conditional demand for input is always *decreasing* with the price of this input. This is a property of a very general kind, and so does not depend on the *number* of inputs. However, contrary to the results obtained in the preceding paragraph with a production function having only two arguments, the variation in the conditional demand for a factor resulting from a change in the cost of another factor does not always have the same sign. In consequence, when W^i rises, the entrepreneur reduces his or her demand for factor i—this is the meaning of relation (25)—and he or she must perforce increase that of at least one other factor so as to achieve output level Y. But in the absence of further details about the firm's technology, it is not possible to know either which factor or factors will be utilized more, or which ones will be utilized at the same or a lower level. Nonetheless, the symmetry condition of cross-price effects remains satisfied with any number n of inputs, since relation (24) entails:

$$\frac{\partial \bar{X}^i}{\partial W^j} = \frac{\partial \bar{X}^j}{\partial W^i} = C_{ij} \qquad \forall i, j = 1, \dots, n \tag{26}$$

The symmetry condition of cross-price effects is a very general result. It indicates that the effect of a variation in the price of factor j on conditional demand for factor i is the same as that of a variation in the price of factor i on the conditional demand for factor j. As the direction of this effect turns out to be undetermined a priori, however, it will be convenient to make use of the following definitions: when $\partial \bar{X}^i / \partial W^j > 0$—or, in equivalent fashion $\partial \bar{X}^j / \partial W^i > 0$—goods i and j are called *substitutes in the Hicks-Allen sense*, or *p-substitutes* for short. In the opposite case, goods i and j are called *complements in the Hicks-Allen sense*, or simply *p-complements*. To put it another way, factors i and j are p-substitutes (or p-complements) if, to attain a given level of production, the demand for one of the factors increases (or diminishes) when the price of the other factor rises. It should be noted that if there are only two inputs, both are necessarily p-substitutes (see section 1.3.2 above).

Elasticity of Substitution

Taking into account relation (26), the *cross* elasticity of the conditional demand for factor i with respect to the price of factor j, or $\bar{\eta}_j^i$, takes the following form:

$$\bar{\eta}_j^i = \frac{W^j}{\bar{X}^i} \frac{\partial \bar{X}^i}{\partial W^j} = \frac{W^j}{\bar{X}^i} C_{ij} \tag{27}$$

As in the case with two inputs, it is apparent that cross elasticity is not a symmetrical notion—as a general rule, $\bar{\eta}_j^i \ne \bar{\eta}_i^j$—and that is why we resort to the notion of *elasticity of substitution* when it comes to assessing the extent to which utilization of one factor may replace utilization of another. But here a difficulty arises having to do with the number of factors. If we define the elasticity of substitution by a formula analogous to the one employed in the case of two inputs—see (10)—we would then, for a given level of production, have to assume that the prices of the other factors do not vary, and posit that the elasticity d_j^i of substitution between factors i and j represents the elasticity of ratio $\bar{X}^i/\bar{X}^j$ with respect to the relative cost W^j/W, or:

$$d_j^i = \frac{W^j/W^i}{\bar{X}^i/\bar{X}^j} \frac{\partial(\bar{X}^i/\bar{X}^j)}{\partial(W^j/W^i)}$$

The problem with this definition is that a variation in relative price W^j/W^i will not simply alter the ratio $\bar{X}^i/\bar{X}^j$ of the demands for inputs i and j but can set off a "domino effect" of substitutions in all the other inputs. In this case, the interpretation of d_j^i in terms of substitution between factors i and j alone becomes obscure, to say the least. A simple alternative, the one most frequently adopted, is to bring in the notion of *partial* elasticity of substitution in Allen's sense (as opposed to *direct* elasticity of substitution d_j^i). It is obtained by weighting the cross elasticity $\bar{\eta}_j^i$ by the inverse of the share of factor j in the total cost. By definition, we will thus have $\sigma_j^i = \bar{\eta}_j^i(C/W^j\bar{X}^j)$. With the help of relation (27) characterizing $\bar{\eta}_j^i$ and Shephard's lemma (24), we find that the partial elasticity of substitution is expressed by a formula analogous to equation (10) obtained with inputs, i.e.:

$$\sigma_j^i = \frac{CC_{ij}}{C_iC_j} \tag{28}$$

The elasticity of substitution thus defined is quite symmetrical, since $\sigma_j^i = \sigma_i^j$, but is not necessarily positive when there are more than two inputs.

Conditional Demands and Factor Shares
Let $s^j \equiv W^j\bar{X}^j/C$ be the share of factor j in the total cost. Since according to Shephard's lemma (24), $\bar{X}^i = C_i$ and $\bar{X}^j = C_j$, relations (27) and (28) lead us to:

$$\bar{\eta}_j^i = s^j\sigma_j^i \qquad \forall(i,j) \tag{29}$$

This relation is analogous to equality (12) from section 1.2.2. It is formally true for every couple (i,j), even when $i=j$, and is illuminating when it comes to interpreting the effect of variation in the price of a factor on conditional demand for the other factor. When the possibilities of substitution between two factors i and j are substantial—i.e., when σ_j^i is a fairly large positive number—it is possible to attain an identical level of production by reducing the utilization of one of the factors "a lot." Thus, when W^j rises (or W^i falls), the firm has all the more incentive to replace factor j by factor i, the greater σ_j^i is. As in the case of a production function with two factors, this logic allows us to understand why the elasticity of conditional demand for factor i with respect to the price of factor j rises with the elasticity of substitution σ_j^i when these two factors are p-substitutes. But here factors i and j can also be p-complements $(\sigma_j^i < 0)$. Let us suppose that this is in fact the case, and that σ_j^i is a relatively large number in absolute value. Faced with a hike in the price of factor j, the producer reduces jointly the quantity of factor j and factor i for reasons having to do with the technology of the firm.

The influence of the share s^j of factor j in the total cost is analyzed in the same way as in the case of a production function with two inputs: the elasticity of conditional demand for factor i with respect to the price of factor j rises in absolute value with the share s^j of factor j in the total cost.

1.4.2   Unconditional Demands

When overall cost has been minimized, the next stage is to maximize profit. Profit maximization allows us to characterize the unconditional factor demands. As in the case of two inputs, we are able to specify the sign of the cross elasticities by using the concepts of gross complementarity and gross substitutability.

Profit Maximization

Formally, the problem of the firm is analogous to the one dealt with in section 1.3.1, with a production technology comprising just two inputs, on condition that we replace the cost function $C(W, R, Y)$ by function $C(W^1, \dots, W^n, Y)$. In particular, equation (15) giving the optimal level of output is now written:

$$P(Y) = vC_Y(W^1, \dots, W^n, Y) \tag{30}$$

Consequently, the rule that the firm sets its price by applying the markup v to the marginal cost C_Y continues to hold with any number of inputs. Moreover, calculations identical to those laid out in section 1.3.1 would show that if the production function is homogeneous of degree θ, the second-order condition always requires that we have $v > \theta$.

The procedure adopted to define the profit function in the case of two inputs also applies here. This function, denoted $\Pi(W^1, \dots, W^n)$, corresponds to the maximal value of the firm's profit for given factor costs $(W^1, \dots, W^n)$. The logic developed in section 1.3.1 shows that the profit function is *convex* and that it always satisfies *Hotelling's lemma*. Using Π_i to designate the partial derivative of the profit function with respect to W^i, and X_i to designate the unconditional demand for factor i, this lemma now takes the following form:

$$X_i = -\Pi_i(W^1, \dots, W^n) \qquad \forall i = 1, \dots, n$$

The profit function being convex, we then have $\Pi_{ii} \geq 0$, and Hotelling's lemma immediately leads to:

$$\frac{\partial X_i}{\partial W^i} = -\Pi_{ii} \leq 0 \qquad \forall i = 1, \dots, n$$

The property that the (unconditional) demand for a factor diminishes with the price of this factor thus has a very general character, since it is satisfied whatever the number of inputs is. In fact, it is sometimes referred to as the "law" of demand.

Gross Substitutes and Gross Complements

The respective importance of substitution and scale effects emerges naturally when we note that unconditional factor demands satisfy Shephard's lemma (24) *and* that the optimal level of production satisfies relation (30). If we simply use X^i and Y to denote the optimal values of demand for factor i and production, and differentiate (24) with respect to W^j, we get:

$$\frac{\partial X^i}{\partial W^j} = C_{ij} + C_{iY}\frac{\partial Y}{\partial W^j} \qquad \forall i, j = 1, \ldots, n$$

Multiplying the two members of this equality by W^j/X^i, we find the expression of the elasticity η_j^i of the demand for factor i with respect to the price W^j of factor j. It is:

$$\eta_j^i = \frac{W^j}{X^i}C_{ij} + \left(\frac{YC_{iY}}{X^i}\right)\frac{W^j}{Y}\frac{\partial Y}{\partial W^j}$$

According to (27), the term $(W^j/X^i)C_{ij}$ represents the elasticity $\bar{\eta}_j^i$ of conditional demand taken at the profit optimum. Since, following Shephard's lemma, $X^i = C_i$, the term (YC_{iY}/X^i) designates the output elasticity of the conditional demand for input i, we will denote it by $\bar{\eta}_Y^i$. Let η_j^Y again designate the elasticity of production with respect to W^j; the end result is:

$$\eta_j^i = \bar{\eta}_j^i + \bar{\eta}_Y^i\eta_j^Y \qquad \forall i, j = 1, \ldots, n \tag{31}$$

This relation reveals the effects of a rise in price W^j of factor j on the demand for factor i. When $i = j$, relation (31) supplies the expression of the direct elasticity of factor i with respect to its price. The substitution effect represented by the direct conditional elasticity $\bar{\eta}_i^i$ is negative. Reasoning analogous to that followed in the case of inputs will show that the scale effect $\bar{\eta}_Y^i\eta_i^Y$ is also negative. Conversely, when $i \neq j$, the term $\bar{\eta}_j^i$ no longer has a determinate sign. We have seen above that it is positive (or negative) if the factors i and j, $i \neq j$, are p-substitutes (or p-complements). The second term on the right-hand side of relation (31), or $\bar{\eta}_Y^i\eta_j^Y$, reveals a scale effect which, as in the case of two inputs, has an indeterminate sign, except when the production function is homogeneous (in which case it is negative). In sum, it is not possible to state truly general rules regarding the sign of cross elasticity η_j^i for $i \neq j$. That is why it is best to continue with the definitions already given in the case of two inputs. Thus, factors i and j form *gross substitutes* if $\eta_j^i > 0$. They are described as *gross complements* when $\eta_j^i < 0$.

The Case of a Homogeneous Production Function

Proceeding in the same fashion as in section 1.3.2, it is easy to show that if the production function is homogeneous of degree θ, the output elasticity $\bar{\eta}_j^i$ of the conditional demand for factor j is equal to $1/\theta$, for all $j = 1, \ldots, n$. Since, in this case, $C_Y = C/\theta Y$, taking the logarithmic derivatives of the optimality condition (30) with respect to W^j, we find after several calculations:

$$\eta_j^Y = \frac{\theta v}{\theta - v}s^j$$

Since the second-order conditions dictate $v > \theta$, we verify that η_j^Y is negative. A rise in W^j thus entails a negative scale effect measured by the ratio $vs^j/(\theta - v)$. Finally, if we bring the value of $\bar{\eta}_j^i$ elicited from (29) into relation (31), we arrive at a formula giving the expression of the cross elasticity η_j^i of the unconditional demand for factor i with respect to the cost of factor j when the production function is homogeneous of degree θ. It is written:

$$\eta_j^i = s^j \left(\sigma_j^i - \frac{v}{v - \theta} \right) \qquad \forall (i, j) \tag{32}$$

This formula generalizes relations (22), which applied to the case with two inputs. The observations made there about the respective importance of market power v, the possibilities of substitution between two factors (represented now by the variable σ_j^i), and the share s^j of the cost of a factor in the total cost still hold true here and need not be repeated. But formula (32) now allows us to take into account the heterogeneity of the labor factor. If we consider two categories of manpower—skilled and unskilled workers, for example—we see that the elasticity of demand for skilled (or unskilled) workers with respect to the cost of unskilled (or skilled) workers is proportional to the share of unskilled (or skilled) manpower in the total cost. These conclusions have to be kept in mind when we want to analyze the effects of a change in minimum wage or a reduction in social security contributions as they apply to unskilled labor. Relation (32) shows that, if skilled and unskilled workers are gross substitutes—which is the case when $\sigma_j^i > v/(v - \theta)$—a rise in the cost of unskilled labor provokes a reduction in the demand for unskilled workers and an increase in the demand for skilled ones. Conversely, if $\sigma_j^i < v/(v - \theta)$, the two categories of workers are gross complements, and the rise in the cost of unskilled labor has the effect of reducing the utilization of the two categories of manpower at the same time.

Assuming that workers and hours worked can be considered different inputs, relations (29) and (32) then allow us to study the determinants of substitution between workers and hours. To that end, we have to define the relative costs of each of these factors and the technical possibilities of substituting one for the other.

1.5 THE TRADE-OFF BETWEEN WORKERS AND HOURS

It becomes necessary to distinguish the number of workers from the number of hours worked whenever, on the one hand, workers and hours are not perfectly substitutable, and, on the other, the costs attached to using these two dimensions of the workforce are not identical. The solution to the problem of the firm makes it clear that demands for workers and hours depend on the relative importance of these two costs.

1.5.1 The Distinction Between Workers and Hours

In order to grasp the determinants of the trade-off between workers and hours, it is necessary to distinguish the contributions of these two elements to the production process, and to differentiate between the costs arising from an increase in the number of employees and those that arise from a change in the number of hours worked by each employee.

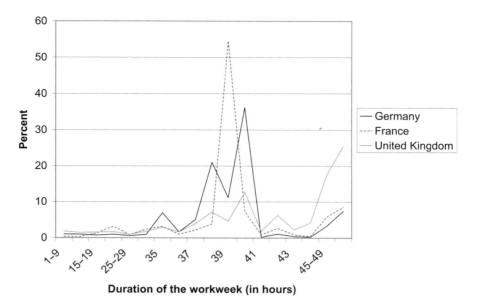

FIGURE 4.2

Distribution of the length of the work week in 1998 in Germany, France, and the United Kingdom.

Source: Anxo and O'Reilly (2000).

Heterogeneity in the Number of Hours Worked

It is especially important to distinguish between workers and hours because labor markets show strong heterogeneity when it comes to the number of hours in the workweek. Figure 4.2 shows the distribution of time worked by men in Germany, France, and the United Kingdom. It will be seen that the distribution of hours has two spikes in Germany; this arises from the joint influence of standard hours and wage negotiations in various sectors. In France, standard hours play a very important role for men, since about 55% of them work 39 hours per week. It is striking that the absence of standard hours in the United Kingdom leads to a very marked scatter in the length of the workweek there.

The scatter in the length of the workweek is generally greater for women, who more frequently hold part-time jobs (see Anxo and O'Reilly, 2000). These facts clearly show that firms make use of a large range of options in timetabling work, which makes it important to understand the causes and consequences of these choices.

The Imperfect Substitutability of Workers and Hours

To this point we have not made a distinction between the number of employees present in a firm and the overall amount of time that they devote to production. In the case of a production function $F(K, L)$ having only two factors, we thus implicitly assumed that labor services L were simply equal to the product NH, where N designates the number of persons employed and H represents the average individual length of time worked, expressed, for example, in hours. But that is a very special perspective, since it assumes that workers and hours are perfectly substitutable: the firm would then choose its amount of hours without any thought for the manner in which that amount was divided up among its workforce. This kind of choice is conceivable only if the productivity of an hour of work and the rate of utilization of capital do not depend on the average individual length H of time worked—in other words, if the production of two individuals each working four hours a day is identical to that of a single individual working eight hours a day. There are many reasons to think that this is not the case. Setup costs entail that the relationship between the productivity of an hour of work and the length of working time exhibits increasing returns for small values of the latter. Beyond a certain threshold, fatigue will set in, and this relation will exhibit decreasing returns. Moreover, when the duration of individual work changes, the duration of capital utilization, and thus its cost, likewise change if the firm undertakes no reorganization.

Accordingly, the production process should be represented by a function $F(K, N, H)$ having three arguments, which does effectively allow us to distinguish the marginal productivity of workers from that of hours. However, the properties of demand functions when there are more than two inputs, set out in section 1.4, do not directly apply here, since there is no simple way to separate the cost of labor into a cost assignable to workers and a cost assignable to hours. For that reason we choose a less general representation of technology, but one with the advantage of allowing us to characterize the main elements in the workers/hours trade-off. We will often use the notion of *efficiency* in connection with number of hours worked. It is represented by an increasing function denoted $e(H)$. This function can reveal effects that run counter to each other. Setup costs should cause the marginal efficiency $e'(H)$ of the number of hours worked to increase for small values of H, the effects of fatigue as the hours pass should cause marginal efficiency to decrease for larger values of H, and in consequence the function ought to be concave past a certain threshold. In sum, if N designates the number of persons employed in the firm, then labor services are expressed by the product $Ne(H)$, assuming, for the sake of simplicity, that all employees work the same number of hours.

Likewise, the duration of capital utilization depends on H. Denoting this duration by $d(H)$, capital services are expressed by the product $Kd(H)$, where K designates the stock of capital. The production function is then written $Y = F[Kd(H), Ne(H)]$. In what follows we will assume, for the sake of simplicity, that the duration of capital utilization is a constant normalized to 1. In other words, the duration of capital utilization is independent of the individual duration H of work. In that case, any change in the latter necessitates a reorganization of the production process, since the employees are working different hours, but the duration of capital utilization has not changed. This might lead to new work schedules, and eventually to a complete rearrangement of shifts in the plant.

The Cost of Labor

The distinction between workers and hours assumes greater importance in light of the fact that the cost of labor is not a linear function of its duration, for at least two reasons (Rosen, 1968; Hart, 1987). In the first place, certain costs do not depend on duration, principally the costs of hiring and firing, training costs, and certain social security contributions. We shall assume that they can be represented by a single positive scalar, equal to Z for each person employed. These costs can be defined on the basis of different periods, such as the day, the week, the month, or the year. For the sake of clarity, we will take the week as the period of reference. In the second place, in many countries there exists a *legal* or *standard* work duration, and every *overtime* hour worked beyond that limit is remunerated at a higher rate than regular or *standard* hours. For example, in the United States the Fair Labor Standards Act, signed in 1938, defines the standard workweek as 40 hours and establishes an overtime rate 50% higher for hours worked beyond that limit. We will use T to designate the standard workweek, Ω to designate the wage for a normal hour, and x to designate the overtime premium. There is generally an absolute limit, legal or physical, to how long anyone can work, but for simplicity we will leave it out of account. If R continues to represent the utilization cost of a unit of capital, then the total cost of production is written:

$$C = \begin{cases} [\Omega T + (1+x)\Omega(H-T) + Z]N + RK & \text{if } H > T \\ (\Omega H + Z)N + RK & \text{if } H \leq T \end{cases} \tag{33}$$

This expression of the total cost shows that labor demand, here the number of persons employed and hours worked, depends on the comparison between the value of the *variable costs*, represented by Ω and x, and that of the *fixed costs*, represented by Z. Intuition suggests that a reduction in fixed costs gives firms an incentive to substitute workers for hours, and thus ought to favor employment. Conversely, a reduction in variable costs ought to increase the number of hours worked, to the detriment of employment. The demand for workers and the demand for hours may thus vary in inverse directions. This logic does not, though, take into account the fact that the firm can also substitute labor services as a whole for those of capital. In order to assess the importance of these different effects, it is therefore necessary to know more precisely the expressions of the demand for workers and for hours.

1.5.2 The Optimal Number of Hours

Drawing on the notion of *efficient* labor, the demand functions result from an optimization problem with just two inputs. On this basis, it is easy to show that the optimal number of hours worked depends mainly on how high fixed costs are with respect to variable costs.

Efficient Labor and Minimization of Total Cost

Taking into account cost C defined by equation (33), for a given output level Y, the conditional factor demands correspond to the solutions of the following problem:

$$\underset{\{H,N,K\}}{\text{Min}} \quad C \quad \text{subject to} \quad F[K, Ne(H)] \geq Y$$

If we proceed directly to consider the quantity L of *effective* labor defined by $L \equiv Ne(H)$, this problem takes the form:

$$\min_{\{H, L, K\}} (WL + RK) \quad \text{subject to} \quad F(K, L) \geq Y$$

where the unit cost W of efficient labor is given by:

$$W = \begin{cases} [\Omega T + (1 + x)\Omega(H - T) + Z]/e(H) & \text{if } H \geq T \\ (\Omega H + Z)/e(H) & \text{if } H \leq T \end{cases} \tag{34}$$

Thus we see that the minimization of the cost of production can be carried out in two stages. In the first stage, we look for the *optimal* number of hours corresponding to the value of H that minimizes the unit cost W. In the second stage, we calculate the values of L and K that minimize the total cost of production, given this optimal value of W. This last problem involves only two inputs (K and L), with costs (W and R) that are given. The properties of the solutions follow directly from the results we already reached in section 1.2.2.

Relation (34) shows that the unit cost W is a function of H which is not differentiable at point $H = T$. To find the value of H minimizing this function, we thus have to compare its local minima over intervals $H > T$ and $H \leq T$. These calculations are presented in appendix 3, assuming for the sake of simplicity that the elasticity of function $e(H)$ is a positive constant η_H^e belonging to the interval $[0, 1]$. This hypothesis may seem restrictive, but is nevertheless corroborated by empirical studies (see below, section 2.2.2). The optimal value H^* of the number of hours is defined by:

$$H^* = \begin{cases} \eta_H^e Z/(1 - \eta_H^e)\Omega \leq T & \text{if } Z/\Omega T \leq (1 - \eta_H^e)/\eta_H^e \\ T & \text{if } (1 - \eta_H^e)/\eta_H^e \leq Z/\Omega T \leq (1 + x - \eta_H^e)/\eta_H^e \\ \eta_H^e(Z - x\Omega T)/(1 + x)(1 - \eta_H^e)\Omega \geq T & \text{if } Z/\Omega T \geq (1 + x - \eta_H^e)/\eta_H^e \end{cases} \tag{35}$$

We should first note that the optimal number of hours depends neither on quantity K of capital nor on level Y of output. This is a consequence of the particular form of the production function and would no longer hold if the technology were described by any function $F(K, N, H)$. It does, however, fit well with observation, for there is little difference in the actual numbers of hours worked between firms that are large or small, capital intensive or not.

We also see that the optimal value of H depends on the elasticity η_H^e of the function $e(H)$ measuring the efficiency of the number of hours worked by individuals. In this respect, it is illuminating to consider first the case where $\eta_H^e < 1$, and then the case where $\eta_H^e = 1$. When the elasticity of the efficiency of an employee with respect to hours is small (η_H^e is close to zero), the firm does not utilize overtime hours, for to do so would increase efficiency by only a small amount. On the other hand, the more the efficiency of labor depends on its duration—i.e., the more η_H^e approaches 1—the more the firm will tend to resort to overtime hours. When $\eta_H^e = 1$, workers and hours are perfectly substitutable. The interior solutions, described by equation (35), are no longer defined.

It should also be noted that the number of hours is low ($H \leq T$) when the fixed cost Z is small in comparison with variable cost ΩT corresponding to standard hours. Conversely, the firm uses overtime hours ($H \geq T$) when the ratio $Z/\Omega T$ grows larger, i.e., when the level of variable cost ΩT sinks relative to that of fixed cost Z. The optimal number of hours coincides with standard hours ($H = T$) for the intermediate values of ratio $Z/\Omega T$. In this situation the firm desires to set its number of hours beyond that of the legal limit T, but the rate x of extra pay for overtime hours proves too high for it to do so. The optimal solution is then $H = T$.

Fixed Costs, Variable Costs, and the Number of Hours Actually Worked
Relations (35) show precisely how the optimal number of individual hours of work varies when the exogenous parameters change. We have:

$$\frac{\partial H^*}{\partial Z} \geq 0, \qquad \frac{\partial H^*}{\partial \Omega} \leq 0 \quad \text{and} \quad \frac{\partial H^*}{\partial x} \leq 0,$$

$$\frac{\partial H^*}{\partial T} = 0 \text{ if } H^* < T, \qquad \frac{\partial H^*}{\partial T} = 1 \text{ if } H^* = T \quad \text{and} \quad \frac{\partial H^*}{\partial T} < 0 \text{ if } H^* > T$$

(36)

As intuition would suggest, a rise in fixed costs Z tends to increase the number of hours, while an increase in variable costs Ω or x tends to reduce it.

A change in standard hours has contrasting effects according to whether or not the firm makes use of overtime. In particular, when the optimal number of hours exceeds the legal limit ($H > T$), a reduction in the latter raises the number of hours worked by all employees. In other words, a *reduction* in standard hours has the effect of *increasing* the actual workweek by causing the number of overtime hours to rise. This result seems counterintuitive at first sight, and it runs counter to the overt purpose of a reduction in standard hours, which is precisely to bring down the actual number of hours worked by every individual so as to increase the number of jobs. But if we look closely at relation (35), which defines the optimal number of hours, we find that it arises because the propensity to make use of overtime, i.e., the ratio H/T, does not depend on Z but on the *ratio* $Z/\Omega T$. A lowering of standard hours is thus like a relative *rise* in fixed costs (see Calmfors and Hoel, 1988). The variable costs have sunk in relative importance, and thus we can see why the firm would increase the number of hours actually worked (in the following paragraph, we will demonstrate that this increase ought, as a general rule, to occur at the expense of the number of jobs). On the other hand, a reduction in standard hours evidently leads to a reduction in the actual workweek when these two variables are equal ($H = T$). It should be noted, however, that in this situation a drastic reduction in standard hours might cause firms to start making use of overtime, and we would no longer have the equality $H = T$.

1.5.3 Cost of Labor and Demand for Workers
The demand for workers is deducible from the optimal amount of efficient labor. When there are opportunities to trade off between workers and hours, analysis of the impact on employment of variations in the elements that influence the cost of labor

requires very lengthy calculations. We begin by presenting these calculations, before summarizing them and giving quantitative results in tables 4.1 and 4.2. Readers pressed for time may refer directly to these tables in order to get an idea of the underlying economic mechanisms and the relevant orders of magnitude.

A Synthetic Formula

Given the optimal values of H and of W, we have seen that total cost minimization took the form studied in section 1.2.1. The solutions of this minimization correspond to the conditional demands for capital and efficient labor, and we will continue to denote them by $\bar{K}$ and $\bar{L}$. They are functions of W^*, R, and Y, where W^* designates the optimal value of the unit cost of efficient labor. It is given by relation (34) when we replace H by its optimal value H^* defined by (35). We thus arrive at:

$$W^* = \begin{cases} (\Omega H^* + Z)/e(H^*) & \text{if } Z/\Omega T \leq (1 + x - \eta_H^e)/\eta_H^e \\ (1+x)\Omega H^*/\eta_H^e e(H^*) & \text{if } Z/\Omega T \geq (1 + x - \eta_H^e)/\eta_H^e \end{cases} \tag{37}$$

It should be remembered as well that in reality, $\bar{L}$ is only an auxiliary variable linked to the conditional demand for workers $\bar{N}$ by relation $\bar{L} \equiv \bar{N}e(H)$. If v represents one of the parameters Ω, x, Z, or T, differentiating this identity then implies:

$$\bar{\eta}_v^N = \bar{\eta}_v^L - \eta_H^e \eta_v^H \qquad \forall v = (\Omega, x, Z, T)$$

In this expression, $\bar{\eta}_v^N$ and $\bar{\eta}_v^L$ designate respectively the elasticities of $\bar{N}$ and of $\bar{L}$ with respect to v, and η_v^H represents the elasticity of the optimal number of hours with respect to this parameter. Since $\bar{L}$ depends only on W^*, R and Y, $\bar{\eta}_v^L$ will always equal $\bar{\eta}_W^L \eta_v^W$, where $\bar{\eta}_W^L$ and η_v^W are respectively the elasticity of $\bar{L}$ with respect to cost W of efficient labor taken at W^*, and the elasticity of W^* with respect to parameter v. We thus finally get:

$$\bar{\eta}_v^N = \bar{\eta}_W^L \eta_v^W - \eta_H^e \eta_v^H \qquad \forall v = (\Omega, x, Z, T) \tag{38}$$

This relation allows us to deduce the properties of conditional demand $\bar{N}$ from those of $\bar{L}$, W, and H. It shows that, in order to attain a given output level, it is possible for the firm to substitute men for hours, in which case $\bar{N}$ and H vary in opposite directions. This eventuality is represented by the term $-\eta_H^e \eta_v^H$. But the firm can also substitute labor services as a whole (men and/or hours) with capital services. The term $\bar{\eta}_W^L \eta_v^W$ conveys this possibility. Thus $\bar{N}$ and H do not necessarily vary in opposite directions, and the comparative statics of the demand for workers is not directly deducible from that of hours worked. We must also take into account capital/labor substitution, encapsulated in the extent of elasticity $\bar{\eta}_W^L$. According to the "laws" of demand, we know only that $\bar{\eta}_W^L < 0$, but all the estimates carried out in this domain indicate that the latter is, in absolute value, clearly inferior to unity (see section 2.2.1 below).[7] We may thus assume, without gravely compromising what follows, that the absolute value of $\bar{\eta}_W^L$ belongs to the interval $[0, 1]$. This spread of variation also applies, for that matter, to unconditional elasticity η_W^L. We begin by discussing the general results, insisting on their economic interpretation, then go on to give orders of magnitude for a particular form of the production function and probable values for the parameters.

Variations in Fixed Costs

The first-order condition of the minimization of the unit cost of efficient labor dictates that the optimal value of the number of hours worked should be such that $\partial W^*/\partial H = 0$ for $H^* \neq T$. At the optimum, we thus have:

$$\frac{dW}{dZ} = \frac{\partial W^*}{\partial H}\frac{\partial H^*}{\partial Z} + \frac{\partial W^*}{\partial Z} = \frac{\partial W^*}{\partial Z}$$

Definition (37) of W^* shows that $\partial W^*/\partial Z$ is always positive for all H^*. Consequently η_Z^W is positive, and as we know that $\bar{\eta}_W^L \leq 0$ and $\eta_Z^H \geq 0$, relation (38) entails $\bar{\eta}_Z^N \leq 0$. As intuition suggests, a rise in the fixed costs of labor tends to increase utilization of hours to the detriment of the number of workers, and to favor the utilization of capital as compared to labor. These two effects combine to reduce the number of workers.

The study of variations in the demand for workers as a function of other parameters proves a more delicate business. It is best to pursue it by distinguishing situations in which the firm utilizes overtime from those in which it does not.

Variations in the Hourly Wage

- When $H^* < T$, relation (35) shows that, setting fixed costs aside, the number of hours worked depends only on the hourly wage Ω. More precisely, we see that the elasticity of an individual's hours of work with respect to the hourly wage, or η_Ω^H, is equal to -1. It is possible to save several calculations by noting, with the help of equations (37) and (35), that the optimal values of W and H satisfy $W^* = \Omega H^*/\eta_H^e e(H^*)$. Differentiating this equality with respect to Ω, we get:

$$\eta_\Omega^W = 1 + (1 - \eta_H^e)\eta_\Omega^H = \eta_H^e$$

Bringing this value of η_Ω^W into (38), we finally arrive at:

$$\bar{\eta}_\Omega^N = \eta_H^e(1 + \bar{\eta}_W^L) = \eta_H^e[1 - (1 - s)\sigma]$$

As we adopt the hypothesis that $(1 - s)\sigma$ is less than unity, we have $\bar{\eta}_\Omega^N \geq 0$, which signifies that an increase in the hourly wage entails an increase in employment at the expense of hours. In other words, it would be necessary for the elasticity of capital/labor substitution to be very great, which is unlikely, for a rise in the hourly wage to be accompanied both by a reduction in the number of hours of work and by a reduction in employment. To attain a given output level, firms prefer to substitute workers for hours rather than to substitute capital for workers.

- If $H^* = T$, the optimal value of W is given by:

$$W^* = \frac{\Omega T + Z}{e(T)}$$

It is evident immediately that W^* rises with Ω (thus $\eta_\Omega^W \geq 0$) and, as η_Ω^H is null, (38) then implies $\bar{\eta}_\Omega^N \leq 0$. Unlike in the previous case, the level of employment falls when the level of the hourly wage rises. This result is not hard to understand: a rise in the cost of labor means that the firm utilizes less of this factor and more capital to attain the same output level. Since hours worked do not vary ($H = T$), the adjustment necessarily takes place through a reduction in employment.

- If $H^* > T$, equation (37) defining W^* gives $\eta_\Omega^W = 1 + (1 - \eta_H^e)\eta_\Omega^H$. Bringing this value of elasticity η_Ω^W into (38) with $v = \Omega$, we get:

$$\bar{\eta}_\Omega^N = \bar{\eta}_W^L \eta_\Omega^W - \eta_H^e \eta_\Omega^H = \bar{\eta}_W^L + \eta_\Omega^H[(1 - \eta_H^e)\bar{\eta}_W^L - \eta_H^e] \tag{39}$$

The expression (35) of the optimal number of hours of work implies, after several calculations, $\eta_\Omega^H = -Z/(Z - x\Omega T) < -1$. Taking this inequality into account, relation (39) entails $\bar{\eta}_\Omega^N > \eta_H^e(1 + \bar{\eta}_W^L)$. Because we may consider that elasticity $\bar{\eta}_W^L$ is smaller in absolute value than unity, a rise in the hourly wage will lead to an increase in the number of workers. Consequently, when the hourly wage rises, firms reduce the individual hours of work, and in order to attain a given output level, the elasticity of substitution between capital and labor would have to reach unimaginable values for firms to reduce their demand for workers as well.

Variations in the Overtime Premium

A variation in the overtime premium x influences the optimal level of hours worked only when the latter exceeds standard hours T. Differentiating equation (37) with respect to x, for $(Z/\Omega T) > (1 + x - \eta_H^e)/\eta_H^e$, after several rearrangements we find $\eta_x^W = -x\Omega T/(Z - x\Omega T) - \eta_H^e \eta_x^H$. The sign of η_x^W is thus ambiguous, since η_x^H is a negative quantity. In bringing this value of η_x^W into (38) with $v = x$, however, we arrive at:

$$\bar{\eta}_x^N = \bar{\eta}_W^L \eta_x^W - \eta_H^e \eta_x^H = -\eta_H^e \eta_x^H(1 + \bar{\eta}_W^L) - \bar{\eta}_W^L \frac{x\Omega T}{Z - x\Omega T}$$

It is evident that an increase in x *increases* the conditional demand for workers once we assume that $\bar{\eta}_W^L$ is, in absolute value, smaller than 1. The explanation is the same as that for a rise in hourly wage: any increase in the variable cost leads to a reduction in individual hours worked, and the possibilities of capital/labor substitution would have to extend farther than any empirical study warrants in order for firms to have an interest in reducing their level of employment as well.

The Reduction in Standard Hours

A change in standard hours T acts on the actual workweek H whenever H is not inferior to T. It is evident that the impact of such a change is not the same when $H > T$ and when $H = T$.

- If $H > T$, the derivative with respect to T of equation (37) defining W^* yields the equality $\eta_T^W = (1 - \eta_H^e)\eta_T^H$. Since, following (36), η_T^H is negative, it is certain that

η_T^W is also negative. In these conditions, relation (38) with $v = T$ indicates that the effect of substituting hours for workers $(-\eta_H^e \eta_T^H)$ is positive, and that the effect of substituting labor for capital $(\bar{\eta}_W^L \eta_T^W)$ is equally positive. In consequence, we may conclude unambiguously that $\bar{\eta}_T^N > 0$. In other words, a reduction in standard hours has the effect of *diminishing* the demand for workers, which probably runs directly counter to the objective aimed at with such a measure. This result, which may cause surprise, springs from the fact that a reduction in standard hours is the exact equivalent of a reduction in variable costs as compared to fixed costs, which, as we saw earlier, will provoke an *increase* in the actual number of hours worked (and a more intensive use of capital), to the detriment of the number of persons employed.

- If $H = T$, the impact of a rise in T is a priori ambiguous. On the one hand, this rise amounts to a reduction in fixed costs, which tends to reduce employment, but on the other, it also signifies that the efficiency of labor, $e(T)$, is raised, which may give the firm an incentive to raise its employment level. To escape this ambiguity, we have to be able to assign an order of magnitude to the different elasticities that occur in formula (38). Noting that $\eta_T^W = [\Omega T/(\Omega T + Z)]$ and $\eta_T^H = 1$, relation (38) gives:

$$\bar{\eta}_T^N = \bar{\eta}_W^L \eta_T^W - \eta_H^e \eta_T^H = \bar{\eta}_W^L \left[\frac{\Omega T}{\Omega T + Z} - \eta_H^e \right] - \eta_H^e$$

Utilizing the existence conditions (35) for the solution $H^* = T$, it is evident that $\bar{\eta}_T^N$ is negative, given that the absolute value of $\bar{\eta}_W^L$ is inferior to $(1 + x)/x$. Since the hypothesis of an absolute value of $\bar{\eta}_W^L$ less than unity is the most probable one, we can then conclude that $\bar{\eta}_T^N \leq 0$. Thus, a reduction in standard hours leads to a *rise* in employment when the actual workweek coincides with the standard one. In this case, a reduction in standard hours is equivalent to a reduction in fixed costs, which has the effect of increasing employment. It is evident that this last effect outweighs the countervailing effect on productivity (a reduction in hours worked reduces average production per employee, which may give the firm an incentive to restrain its demand for workers).

Synthesis of Results

The signs of the elasticities of the conditional demands for workers and hours with respect to the various parameters are summarized in table 4.1. The reader will see that the behavior of firms is very different, according to whether they utilize overtime hours or not. When the optimal number of hours H^* differs from standard hours T, a rise in the hourly wage induces an extension of working time, and in general, an increase in employment. Conversely, when the workweek chosen by the firm is equivalent to standard hours, a rise in the hourly wage reduces employment.

Reducing standard hours probably leads to increased employment in firms where the optimal workweek is equivalent to the standard one. Actually, for a given

Table 4.1

The signs of the elasticities of hours worked and the conditional demand for workers.

	η_z^H	η_Ω^H	η_x^H	η_T^H	$\bar{\eta}_z^N$	$\bar{\eta}_\Omega^N$	$\bar{\eta}_x^N$	$\bar{\eta}_T^N$
$H^* < T$	+	−	0	0	−	+(a)	0	0
$H^* = T$	0	0	0	+	−	−	0	−(a)
$H^* > T$	+	−	−	−	−	+(a)	+	+

(a) if $\bar{\eta}_W^L$ is less than 1 in absolute value.

Table 4.2

Values of elasticities of hours and conditional demand for workers.

	η_Ω^H	η_x^H	η_T^H	$\bar{\eta}_\Omega^N$	$\bar{\eta}_x^N$	$\bar{\eta}_T^N$
$H^* = 0.9 \times T$	−1	0	0	0.63	0	0
$H^* = T$	0	0	1	−0.21	0	−0.96
$H^* = 1.04 \times T$	−3	−2.23	−2	2.49	2.00	1.86

level of production, the reduction of hours has two opposing effects on employment. It gives the firm an incentive to hire more workers in order to meet its orders. But it also causes a rise in the fixed costs of labor, which pushes firms to substitute capital for labor. The first effect dominates for reasonable values of the elasticity of substitution between capital and labor. Reducing standard hours has a different impact on employment for firms that resort to overtime hours. A reduction in standard hours pushes these firms to *increase* hours worked by using more overtime hours. This increase in the actual workweek, combined with the rise in the cost of labor flowing from the remuneration of overtime hours, leads to a reduction in employment.

Finally, table 4.1 shows that an increase in the overtime premium pushes firms to reduce hours worked. The impact on employment is positive for probable values of the elasticity of substitution between capital and labor. The empirical study conducted by Hamermesh and Trejo (2000) using data from California confirms the result, according to which an increase in the overtime premium reduces the hours worked. Hamermesh and Trejo found an elasticity η_x^H of −0.5.

Some Quantitative Results

Table 4.2 gives the values for the elasticities of optimal hours and employment, assuming that the share s of the cost of labor in the total cost is equal to 0.7 and that the elasticity of substitution between capital and labor is equal to 1. As we shall see, empirical studies suggest that such values are relevant for an ''aggregate'' production function that represents the technology of the economy as a whole. This implies that

$\bar{\eta}_W^L = -(1-s)\sigma = -0.3$. We assume further that the elasticity of labor efficiency η_H^e is equal to 0.9. Relation (35) shows that firms in which the ratio of the fixed cost of labor to the variable cost corresponding to standard hours, or $(Z/\Omega T)$, is less than 0.11 choose a workweek shorter than the standard one. The optimal number of hours is equal to the standard number of hours if $(Z/\Omega T)$ lies somewhere between 0.11 and 0.44. The firm resorts to overtime when $(Z/\Omega T)$ is greater than 0.44. Thus we distinguish three types of firm according to the level of their fixed cost: 1) those with a share of fixed cost $(Z/\Omega T)$ equal to 10% and whose workweek is equal to 90% of standard hours, following relation (35); 2) firms for which $(Z/\Omega T) = 0.3$ and whose workweek is the same as the standard one; and finally 3) firms for which $(Z/\Omega T) = 0.45$ and whose optimal workweek is 4% longer than the standard one, assuming that the overtime premium x is equal to 30%.

Table 4.2 shows that variations in hourly wage have very different effects on employment, since elasticity $\bar{\eta}_\Omega^N$ runs from -0.21 to 2.49, when the only source of heterogeneity in firms is the extent of the fixed costs of labor. The same observation can be made about a reduction in the number of hours worked, which allows employment to be significantly increased (at a given hourly wage) when the actual number of hours is the same as the standard one, but has a very strong negative effect on employment in firms that make use of overtime. From this point of view, it is interesting to note that a reduction in standard hours has often been proposed in the United States (see Hamermesh, 2001) and was adopted in certain European countries such as France and Germany in the 1980s in order to increase employment in periods of recession. Models of labor demand suggest, however, that the effects of this measure on employment are ambiguous, which Hunt's (1999) emprirical study in the case of Germany confirms.

Taking Scale Effects into Account

To this point we have assumed that output level Y was given. But when the firm maximizes its profit, this level becomes a choice variable, and so-called "scale" effects—see sections 1.3.2 and 1.4.2—have to be added to the results obtained when Y was fixed. Since we are interested in the impact of changes in standard hours, the hourly wage, or overtime premium on labor demand at the macroeconomic level, scale effects have to be gauged by taking into account variation in the cost of labor across the whole economy, and not in one firm alone. These scale effects must therefore be calculated using relation (20). Formally, it suffices to replace conditional elasticity $\bar{\eta}_W^L$ by unconditional elasticity $\eta_{\overline{W}}^L$ in all the equations in this section. We will see below that empirical studies show that the term $\eta_{\overline{W}}^L$ is certainly negative, and that in absolute value it is greater than $\bar{\eta}_W^L$, since it is derived from it by adding scale effects, which are negative—see relations (19), (20), and (22) in section 1.3.2. Empirical studies suggest that -0.5 is a probable order of magnitude for $\eta_{\overline{W}}^L$ at the macroeconomic level, whereas the value of conditional elasticity $\bar{\eta}_W^L$ which we have used for an individual firm is -0.3. The difference between these two elasticities is thus slight, which implies that taking scale effects into consideration does not modify the conclusions reached for a given output level very much, when we are at the macro-economic level.

To be more precise, taking scale effects into consideration does not modify our results concerning the actual duration H^*, which is independent of the output level. Nor does it modify our results relative to a rise in fixed costs on employment: when Z rises, we have seen that conditional demand $\bar{N}$ for workers diminishes, and since scale effects do not affect the length H^* of the workweek, the rise in Z must indeed diminish the demand for workers. Conversely, scale effects might affect results concerning the signs of the impact of variations in variable costs Ω and x on employment. But for that, unconditional elasticity $\eta\frac{L}{W}$ would have to take values greater than unity. At the aggregate level, this eventuality is not in the least realistic.

Taking scale effects into consideration leads to a greater absolute value for elasticity of employment with respect to standard hours when $H^* > T$. This is because scale effects have a tendency to accentuate the impact of the rise in the cost of labor on employment. When the actual workweek is the same length as the standard one, $H^* = T$, the reduction in hours, which has a positive impact on employment for a given level of production, has a smaller impact, which can even become negative if the scale effect is large. Nevertheless, with a value of $\eta\frac{L}{W}$ equal to -0.5, the elasticity of employment with respect to standard hours amounts to -0.79. So it remains negative, which means that a reduction in standard hours always creates jobs. Overall, though, reducing standard hours tends to be more unfavorable for employment than it would be in a setting where production was given.

In concluding this discussion of the trade-off between workers and hours, it is important to emphasize that we have looked at the impact of variations in standard hours and the overtime premium, while taking the hourly wage as given. Now, there are good reasons to think that the hourly wage is influenced by these two variables, for with a constant real wage, a reduction in time worked entails a reduction in monthly earnings. We can well imagine that wage-earners would resist such a reduction in income by demanding higher wages. Conversely, a rise in the overtime premium brings them extra income, and that might lead to a reduction in the hourly wage. The empirical study of Trejo (1991), carried out using North American data, finds this type of effect. These problems will be tackled in chapter 6, where we study the setting of wages in the framework of collective bargaining models.

2 FROM THEORY TO ESTIMATES

Empirical studies based on the static theory of labor demand aim principally to estimate the different elasticities set out above. First we show how it is possible, on the basis of explicit functional forms, to utilize theoretical results in empirical investigations. We then summarize the main conclusions to be drawn from all the empirical work dedicated to labor demand.

2.1 SPECIFIC FUNCTIONAL FORMS FOR FACTOR DEMANDS

There are two methods for estimating the parameters of the factor demand functions. The first consists of postulating a particular production function on the basis of which it becomes possible to state explicitly the cost and profit functions; they in turn make it possible to arrive at the factor demands. The second is based directly on a cost function defined a priori, without specifying the associated production function.

2.1.1   The Choice of a Production Function

The solution of the problem of cost minimization allows us, with the help of a particular form of the production function, to obtain conditional demand functions in explicit form. The most commonly utilized production functions are the Cobb-Douglas type, and CES (for *constant elasticity of substitution*).

The Cobb-Douglas Function with Two Factors

When we take into consideration no more than two different factors of production, for example capital K and labor L, a Cobb-Douglas production function (Cobb and Douglas, 1928) has the following form:

$$Y = AK^{\theta(1-\alpha)}L^{\theta\alpha}, \qquad 0 < \alpha < 1, A > 0 \tag{40}$$

In this expression the parameter $\theta > 0$ designates the degree of homogeneity of the production function. It is easy to verify that the technical rate of substitution F_L/F_K is equal to $\alpha K/(1-\alpha)L$. Now, according to relation (5) from section 1.2.1, minimization of the total cost of production requires that this rate should coincide with the ratio of the cost of the factors. If W and R again designate respectively the unit costs of labor and capital, we get:

$$\frac{F_L}{F_K} = \frac{\alpha K}{(1-\alpha)L} = \frac{W}{R} \tag{41}$$

These equalities show that capital/labor ratio K/L is proportional to the ratio W/R. Since by definition—see (10)—the elasticity of substitution σ between capital and labor measures precisely the elasticity of the ratio K/L with respect to relative cost W/R, we will have $\sigma = 1$ here. Moreover, relation (41) implies that the share s of labor in the total cost is simply equal to parameter α. Equation (12) gives the value of the elasticities of conditional labor demand as functions of s and σ then takes the following form:

$$\bar{\eta}_W^L = -\bar{\eta}_R^L = -(1-\alpha)$$

Using a Cobb-Douglas production function thus imposes very restrictive conditions with regard to the possibilities of substitution between the inputs—since σ is always equal to 1—but it does allow a very simple estimation of the elasticities of labor demand.

The expressions of the conditional factor demands are deduced from relations (40) and (41). After several calculations, we get:

$$\bar{L} = \left[\frac{\alpha}{(1-\alpha)}\frac{R}{W}\right]^{1-\alpha}\left(\frac{Y}{A}\right)^{1/\theta} \qquad \text{and} \qquad \bar{K} = \left[\frac{(1-\alpha)}{\alpha}\frac{W}{R}\right]^{\alpha}\left(\frac{Y}{A}\right)^{1/\theta}$$

The cost function $C(W, R, Y)$, equal by definition to $W\bar{L} + R\bar{K}$, is then written:

$$C(W, R, Y) = \left(\frac{W}{\alpha}\right)^{\alpha} \left(\frac{R}{1-\alpha}\right)^{1-\alpha} \left(\frac{Y}{A}\right)^{1/\theta}$$

The Multifactor Cobb-Douglas Function

When there are $n > 2$ inputs, the Cobb-Douglas function is defined in the following manner:

$$Y = A \prod_{i=1}^{n} (X^i)^{\theta\alpha_i} \qquad \text{with} \qquad \sum_{i=1}^{n} \alpha_i = 1$$

In this expression, X_i represents the quantity of input i necessary for the production of output level Y. Calculations analogous to those made in the case of two inputs bring us to expressions of the conditional demands $\bar{X}^i$ and the cost function $C(W^1, \ldots, W^n, Y)$, with W^i again designating the unit cost of factor i. Here is the result:

$$\bar{X}^i = \left[\frac{\alpha_i}{W^i} \prod_{j=1}^{n} \left(\frac{W^j}{\alpha_j}\right)^{\alpha_j}\right] \left(\frac{Y}{A}\right)^{1/\theta}$$

$$C(W^1, \ldots, W^n, Y) = \left[\prod_{j=1}^{n} \left(\frac{W^j}{\alpha_j}\right)^{\alpha_j}\right] \left(\frac{Y}{A}\right)^{1/\theta}$$

Since, following (28), the partial elasticity of substitution σ_j^i between factors i and j is deduced from the cost function by the formula $\sigma_j^i = CC_{ij}/C_iC_j$, we easily find that $\sigma_j^i = 1$, $\forall(i, j)$, $i \neq j$. Finally, we verify that the direct elasticity $\bar{\eta}_i^i$ of the conditional demand for factor i, and the cross elasticity $\bar{\eta}_j^i$ with respect to the cost of factor $j \neq i$, are given by:

$$\bar{\eta}_i^i = -(1 - \alpha_i) \quad \forall i, \qquad \text{and} \qquad \bar{\eta}_j^i = \alpha_j \quad \forall i \neq j$$

By imposing an elasticity of substitution between two inputs always equal to 1, the Cobb-Douglas function often proves to be too restrictive. This difficulty can be got around by using a CES function.

The CES Function with Two Inputs

Let $\theta > 0$ continue to designate the degree of homogeneity; if we consider only two inputs K and L, the CES (*constant elasticity of substitution*) function proposed by Arrow et al. (1961) is expressed this way:

$$Y = [(a_L L)^{(\sigma-1)/\sigma} + (a_K K)^{(\sigma-1)/\sigma}]^{\theta\sigma/(\sigma-1)}, \qquad \sigma > 0, \, a_K > 0, \, a_L > 0 \tag{42}$$

If we equalize the technical rate of substitution with the ratio of the costs of inputs, we get:

$$\frac{K}{L} = \left(\frac{R}{W}\right)^{-\sigma} \left(\frac{a_K}{a_L}\right)^{\sigma-1} \tag{43}$$

We thus observe that parameter σ represents the elasticity of substitution between the two inputs. It must also be noted that equation (43), when put in logarithmic form, makes it possible to estimate this elasticity of substitution in linear form. Relations (42) and (43) supply the conditional demands of the two inputs. After several calculations, we find the following expressions:

$$a_L \bar{L} = \left(\frac{W}{a_L}\right)^{-\sigma} \left[\left(\frac{W}{a_L}\right)^{1-\sigma} + \left(\frac{R}{a_K}\right)^{1-\sigma}\right]^{-\sigma/(\sigma-1)} Y^{1/\theta}$$

$$a_K \bar{K} = \left(\frac{R}{a_K}\right)^{-\sigma} \left[\left(\frac{W}{a_L}\right)^{1-\sigma} + \left(\frac{R}{a_K}\right)^{1-\sigma}\right]^{-\sigma/(\sigma-1)} Y^{1/\theta}$$

With the help of these two equations, we deduce the cost function, which comes to:

$$C(W, R, Y) = \left[\left(\frac{W}{a_L}\right)^{1-\sigma} + \left(\frac{R}{a_K}\right)^{1-\sigma}\right]^{1/(1-\sigma)} Y^{1/\theta}$$

The Multifactor CES Function
With $n > 2$ inputs, the CES function takes the form:

$$Y = \left[\sum_{i=1}^{n}(a_i X^i)^{(\sigma-1)/\sigma}\right]^{\theta\sigma/(\sigma-1)}, \qquad \sigma > 0, \, a_i > 0$$

With W^i again designating the unit cost of factor i, minimization of the overall cost of production gives the conditional demands $\bar{X}^i$. They are written:

$$a_i \bar{X}^i = (W^i)^{-\sigma} \left[\sum_{j=1}^{n}(W^j)^{1-\sigma}\right]^{-\sigma/(\sigma-1)} Y^{1/\theta} \qquad \forall i = 1, \ldots, n$$

And the cost function has the expression:

$$C(W^1, \ldots, W^n, Y) = \left[\sum_{i=1}^{n}\left(\frac{W^i}{a_i}\right)^{1-\sigma}\right]^{1/(1-\sigma)} Y^{1/\theta}$$

Since $\sigma_j^i = CC_{ij}/C_i C_j$, this way of representing the cost function allows us to calculate the elasticity of substitution σ_j^i between the factors i and j. We thus get $\sigma_j^i = \sigma$, $\forall(i, j), i \neq j$.

The CES function imposes less restrictive hypotheses than the Cobb-Douglas function (which is, for that matter, a CES function in which we make σ tend to 1), but the elasticity of substitution takes a constant value, one that is moreover identical for all factor pairs. These characteristics are sometimes inappropriate when considering more than two inputs. We then have to imagine functions for which the elasticity of substitution is not a constant, or varies between the factor pairs. Such functions would lead to very complex expressions of the factor demands. That is the reason why certain empirical works adopt an alternative strategy, which consists of reasoning directly on the basis of the cost function, without postulating any particular form for the production function.

2.1.2   The Choice of a Cost Function

Empirical studies aiming to estimate a cost function directly postulate an analytic form satisfying the theoretical properties of such a function, i.e., concavity, homogeneity of degree 1 with respect to the costs of the factors, as well as being increasing with respect to the output level and the input quantities. Thanks to Shephard's lemma, the partial derivatives of the cost function give the conditional factor demands, which it thus becomes possible to estimate.

The Generalized Leontief Function (Diewert, 1971)

If we consider a production function homogeneous of degree $\theta > 0$ with n inputs, the generalized Leontief cost function is written:

$$C(W^1, \ldots, W^n, Y) = Y^{1/\theta} \sum_{i=1}^{n} \sum_{j=1}^{n} a_{ij} (W^i)^{1/2} (W^j)^{1/2}, \qquad a_{ij} = a_{ji}$$

Following Shephard's lemma (24), the conditional demand $\bar{X}^i$ for factor i is given by the partial derivative C_i of the cost function with respect to W^i. We thus get:

$$\bar{X}^i = Y^{1/\theta} \sum_{j=1}^{n} a_{ij} \left(\frac{W^i}{W^j} \right)^{-1/2}$$

This expression allows us to estimate the coefficients a_{ij} and then from that to deduce the elasticities of substitution σ_j^i between two factors i and j by the formula:

$$\sigma_j^i = \frac{a_{ij} (W^i W^j)^{1/2}}{2 s^i s^j} \qquad \forall (i, j), \ j \neq i$$

We see that the elasticity of substitution between two inputs is no longer a constant, for it depends on the costs of the factors as well as on the share of each input in the total cost. In this sense, it is less restrictive to utilize a generalized Leontief cost function than a CES production function in order to define and estimate the demand functions.

The Translog Cost Function (Christensen, Jorgenson, and Lau, 1973)

Assuming once more a production function homogeneous of degree $\theta > 0$ with n inputs, the "translog" (transcendental logarithmic) cost function is defined by:

$$\ln C = a_0 + \sum_{i=1}^{n} a_i \ln W^i + \frac{1}{2} \sum_{i=1}^{n} \sum_{j=1}^{n} a_{ij} \ln W^i \ln W^j + \frac{1}{\theta} \ln Y$$

In this expression, parameters a_i and a_{ij} must be such that $\sum_{i=1}^{n} a_i = 1$, $a_{ij} = a_{ji}$, $\sum_{j=1}^{n} a_{ij} = 0$, $\forall i = 1, \ldots, n$. For $a_i > 0$, and $a_{ij} = 0$, $i, j = 1, \ldots, n$, this function is of the Cobb-Douglas type. But in the general case ($a_{ij} \neq 0$), the conditional demand functions are not linear with respect to the parameters. With the help of Shephard's lemma, though, we can show that the shares s^i of each factor are linear functions of the coefficients of the cost function. Thus we have:

$$s^i = a_i + \sum_{j=1}^{n} a_{ij} \ln W^j$$

It then becomes possible to estimate the parameters of this equation and from that to deduce the elasticities of substitution. The resulting expression is:

$$\sigma_j^i = \frac{a_{ij} + s^i s^j}{s^i s^j}, \qquad \forall (i, j),\ i \neq j, \qquad \sigma_i^i = \frac{a_{ii} - s^i + (s^i)^2}{(s^i)^2}$$

Here again, the elasticities of substitution are not constant and can vary among the factors, taken two at a time. The cross and direct elasticities of the conditional demand functions are subsequently obtained using relation (29).

2.2   MAIN RESULTS

A large number of works have attempted to estimate the elasticities of labor demand and the possibilities of substitution; they are reviewed in Hamermesh (1993, chapter 3). From them it emerges, among other things, that the elasticity (conditional and unconditional) of labor demand with respect to the cost of this factor is negative. It has also been found that unskilled labor is more easily substitutable for capital than skilled labor.

2.2.1   Aggregate Labor Demand

The estimate most frequently made is that of the conditional elasticity $\bar{\eta}_W^L$ of aggregate labor demand. It is effected by positing that the labor factor L is a *homogeneous* quantity equal to the sum of hours worked, or the level of employment. The cost of labor W is most often assimilated to the total amount of wages divided by the number of workers, or by their hours. In reality, the definition of W raises numerous problems, for variations in the total amount of wages may correspond to deformations in the structure of employment arising, for example, from different levels of seniority or skill. We have also seen in the preceding section that the distinction between fixed costs and variable costs plays an important role when firms have to make a choice between the number of workers and the number of hours worked.

These difficulties notwithstanding, studies devoted to estimating $\bar{\eta}_W^L$ yield converging results, whatever the level (firm, sector, or nationwide) at which the data are collected. They show that the elasticity of conditional demand for labor with respect to the cost of this factor is *negative* and, in absolute value, *less than 1*. Hamermesh (1993), building on more than 70 different studies, takes the view that the most probable interval for $|\bar{\eta}_W^L|$ is [0.15–0.75]. If a single figure were to be chosen, 0.30 would surely be the best estimate. Knowledge of $\bar{\eta}_W^L$ allows us to deduce the value of the elasticity of substitution σ between capital and labor, since, according to (12), we know that these two quantities are linked by relation $\bar{\eta}_W^L = -(1 - s)\sigma$, where s represents the share of labor in total cost. Overall, s is close to 0.7. With $\bar{\eta}_W^L = -0.3$, we arrive at $\sigma = 1$. In other words, use of a global Cobb-Douglas production function, or $Y = K^{\theta(1-\alpha)} L^{\theta\alpha}$ with $\alpha = 0.7$, is not without empirical relevance when we are considering only two inputs.

Taking scale effects into account increases the absolute value of the elasticity of employment to its cost, which conforms to theoretical results. Works dedicated to estimating the elasticity η_W^L of the unconditional labor demand are less numerous and show wider divergence than those dedicated to estimating $\bar{\eta}_W^L$. Still, on the basis of macroeconomic data, η_W^L is negative, and Hamermersh estimates that its absolute value lies[8] on average at around 1. If we assign a value of 0.3 to $\bar{\eta}_W^L$, it becomes evident that the extent of the scale effect is far from being negligible.

2.2.2 Complementarity and Substitution Between Inputs

The degree to which one input is capable of replacing another in the production process has an important place in the assessment of the effects of economic policy. Several major results stand out.

If we take labor services into account with the help of a *sole* aggregate, the latter is, as a general rule, p-substitute with any other aggregate input. Hence, labor is p-substitute with capital, energy, and raw materials, which, as readers will recall, means that the *conditional* labor demand rises with the cost of these three inputs. This result is somewhat surprising if one thinks back, for example, to the effects of the hikes in the cost of oil in the 1970s on the level of employment. But it should be remembered that such hikes are accompanied by a scale effect, in other words by reduced production, which can lead in the end to reduced employment. In other words, labor and energy are p-substitutes, but probably are not gross substitutes.

Unskilled labor is easier to substitute for capital than skilled labor. There are even good reasons to think that at the overall level, or even at the level of one of the large sectors of the economy, skilled labor and capital are p-complements (for a far-reaching review of the literature, see Hamermesh, 1993, chapter 3). These results are confirmed by the fact that direct elasticity of the conditional labor demand, for a given category of manpower, diminishes in absolute value with the level of education in this category. Likewise, this elasticity diminishes, still in absolute value, with the level of skill. The results are evidently sensitive to the manner in which the breakdown between skilled and unskilled labor is carried out. In the United States, one breakdown views unskilled workers as those with a high school diploma at most, and skilled workers as all those with a higher qualification than that; the authors come to an estimate of the elasticity of substitution between skilled and unskilled labor lying between 1 and 2 (see Johnson, 1997, and Author et al., 1998, for whom this elasticity of substitution lies rather between 1.4 and 1.5). In his study of the Israeli labor market, Angrist (1996) finds that the elasticity of unskilled labor is equal to 3.

Results concerning the substitution between workers and hours do not yet display a real consensus. In large measure, the lack of precision comes from the difficulty of attributing different costs to workers and hours, i.e., of assessing what share to assign to variable costs and what share to fixed costs. According to Hamermesh (1993), the only property firmly established is that workers and hours are both p-substitutes for capital. With a reasonable degree of confidence, we may likewise assume that workers and hours are p-substitutes. For example, most studies show that the employment level rises unambiguously when the cost of overtime hours rises, a conclusion that also conforms to the theoretical analysis presented in section 1.5.3. We note further that Leslie and Wise (1980) and Hart and MacGregor (1988) give estimates of the elasticity of production with respect to hours of 0.64 and 0.87, respectively. Using French data, Gianella and Lagarde (1999) arrive at a figure equal to 0.9, whatever the size of the firm examined. As Hart and MacGregor (1988) emphasize, however, these results are fragile, and their summary of the empirical literature led them to conclude that the elasticity of production with respect to hours is close to (in fact not significantly different from) unity.

3 LABOR DEMAND AND ADJUSTMENT COSTS

The static theory of labor demand furnishes valuable indications about what determines elasticities, and about the possibilities of substitution over the long run between the different inputs. Regarding the manner in which the inputs reach their long-run values, however, and the length of time that these adjustments take, it gives no firm detail. Moreover, it does not take into account the fact that firms are faced with an ongoing process of reorganization arising from technological constraints, market fluctuations, and manpower mobility (the importance of which will be highlighted in chapter 9). In order to be able to assess these phenomena, we have to resort to the notion of adjustment cost, which focuses specifically on the losses generated whenever input quantities are changed. The functional form that serves to describe adjustment costs conditions the dynamics of labor demand and the properties of stationary solutions. That is why we look at different functional forms in this section: to take into account different types of adjustment cost. Additionally, we examine the dynamics of labor demand in a setting without uncertainty, then introduce stochastic elements into the models. The setting without uncertainty serves as a baseline and allows us to grasp the principal mechanisms at work. The models set in stochastic environments bring out the role of expectations in labor adjustment.

3.1 THE COSTS OF LABOR ADJUSTMENT

Adjusting the size of the workforce entails costs. Numerous studies show that the size of these costs is far from insignificant, and for that reason they play a large role in decisions to hire and fire. No real consensus has yet been reached regarding the analytical representation of these costs, but the quadratic symmetric form, historically the one most frequently utilized, is gradually being abandoned.

3.1.1 Definition and Size of Adjustment Costs

Adjustment costs are evaluated on the basis of several different sources. Some works give estimates of the difference between optimal employment, i.e., what the firm would choose if adjustment costs were absent, and the level of employment actually observed. Others supply indications of what the costs of hiring and firing workers amount to. Yet others attempt to assess the effects of employment protection, which play an important role in many OECD countries.

A Typology

Labor adjustment costs arise from variations in the number of hours worked and from the replacement of former employees with new ones. When the work process is reorganized, causing temporary loss of efficiency, we say that the firm is undergoing *internal adjustment costs*. Examples might be the adaptation of the workforce to new machinery, or the settling-in period for new workers. Costs like these are difficult to evaluate because they do not show up as distinct items in the firm's accounts. But when the reorganization is accompanied by costs that can be distinguished from variations in production, for example if a change in the work routine requires the advice of experts who charge a fee for their services, or severance pay for workers who are fired, we say that the firm is confronting *external adustment costs*. Note that the payment of a higher premium for overtime hours does not fall into the same category as adjustment costs, as long as the firm is choosing to make use of overtime in a systematic manner.

Changes in hours worked also come about through variations in the level of employment. In this case, it is both the costs of hiring and firing (which are external costs) and also the losses of efficiency arising from reorganization (which are internal, and eventually also external, costs) that give rise to adjustment costs. It is often helpful to distinguish *gross costs*, which are caused by gross changes in employment (the sum of all who join or leave the workforce), from *net costs*, which flow from net changes in employment (the difference between the joiners and the leavers). The existence of gross costs highlights the possibility of there being positive adjustment costs, even when the size of the firm's workforce remains constant. These costs are due to the operations of hiring and firing, to voluntary departures, and also to possible losses of efficiency caused by the time it takes less experienced workers to get up to speed. According to Hamermesh (1995), gross and net costs are equivalent in extent in the U.S. economy.

Evaluating Employment Surpluses

The size of the gap between observed levels of employment and those which firms would wish to have if there were no adjustment costs supplies an indication of how great the latter are. Fay and Medoff (1985) used a survey carried out in the manufacturing sector in the United States in order to evaluate surplus employment during the recession of 1980. They estimated that 8% of paid hours did not contribute directly to production, and that of this 8%, about half was used for maintenance, or for improving productivity in some way. These authors concluded that the manpower surplus was likely on the order of 4% during the recession of 1980. Fair (1985) confirmed these results using a different method. He calculated a trend on the assumption that surplus employment is null at the peaks of the economic cycle. Deviations from the trend were taken to correspond to manpower surpluses. He found that these represented from 4.5% to 8.5% of hours worked in the postwar period in the United States, with a figure of 4.5% for the recession of 1980.

Evaluating Hiring and Separation Costs
Studies carried out in the United States (reviewed by Hamermesh, 1993, p. 208) show that the extent of adjustment costs is far from negligible. In 1965–1966, the average cost of hiring in the New York region was on the order of $900 (expressed in terms of 1990 purchasing power). This cost rose with skill level, reaching $4660 for management personel. Another study carried out in the 1980s assessed the costs of hiring and training at $13,790 for management personel and $5110 for workers. Costs incurred when employees left the firm were clearly much lower, $1780 and $370, respectively. As a general rule, studies carried out on American data come to the conclusion that hiring costs are much greater than separation costs.

Studies based on French data also show that the adjustment costs of employment are substantial. Abowd and Kramarz (2003), utilizing a representative sample of French firms and their employees, found that in France, the costs of hiring are due solely to the hiring of skilled workers on long-term contracts, and are clearly less than the costs of separation. The average cost of a separation represents 56% of the annual cost of labor, whereas a hire (not including training costs) represents only 3.3% of the same cost. The cost of a separation itself depends heavily on the context. Rigorous employment protection means that to let an employee go for economic reasons brings a cost equivalent to 126% of the annual cost of labor. Goux et al. (2001) came to conclusions of the same order using longitudinal data on 1000 French firms followed from 1988 to 1992. They estimate that, for long-term contracts, the cost of hiring represents no more than 2.5% of the cost of separation.

What emerges from all these studies is that, in the United States, the costs of hiring are high and outstrip the costs of separation, while in countries where strong legal measures are in place to enhance job security (as is the case in many countries of continental Europe; see OECD, 1999, and chapter 12 of this book) the costs of separation far outstrip recruitment costs.

Employment Protection Measures
The usual view is that the higher the cost of a firing, the greater employment protection is. International comparisons try to rank job security norms by how strict they are (see OECD, 1999, and chapter 12). The wide range of criteria utilized shows us at a glance how complex this exercise is, and how difficult it is to evaluate precisely the effective cost of job protection. These criteria concern matters such as the possibility of using contracts of limited duration and the services of agencies supplying temporary labor; how long a period of trial employment can last; the administrative procedure to follow when terminating employment (notification, summons, authorization from a public agency); the amount of advance notice and severance pay applicable to different types of termination (firing for cause, firing for economic reasons, etc.); the definition of wrongful termination, and the possibility that a person wrongfully terminated can get his or her job back.

Most assessments conclude that employment protection is less strict in the United States, Canada, and the United Kingdom than in France, Germany, and the countries of southern Europe. Japan occupies an intermediate position (for more details, see chapter 12). In Europe, a large part of the cost of termination is regulatory in nature (period of advance notice, administrative procedure, etc.). The result, since the beginning of the 1980s, has been a massive recourse to short-term contracts precisely to avoid these administrative costs.

3.1.2 The Specification of Adjustment Costs

For ease of analysis, adjustment costs have most often been represented using a convex symmetric function (in general quadratic). But this way of specifying them does not allow us to explain asymmetric and discontinuous adjustments in employment. For this reason, it is now gradually being replaced by a piecewise linear representation that includes fixed costs.

Quadratic Costs

The first analyses of decisions made by a firm facing adjustment costs adopted a quadratic relation between the variations (gross or net) in employment and adjustment costs. This representation was introduced by Holt et al. (1960), who viewed net adjustment costs as equal to $b(\Delta L_t - a)^2$, $a, b > 0$, with $\Delta L_t = L_t - L_{t-1}$ or $\Delta L_t = \dot{L}_t$ according to whether time was represented discretely or continuously. This specification has the advantage of introducing an asymmetry between the cost of positive and negative variations in employment ($a > 0$). But this asymmetry is obtained at the cost of a strictly positive cost in the absence of any variation in employment. Eisner and Strotz (1963) got around this problem by assuming quadratic and symmetric adjustment costs ($a = 0$). A hypothesis of this kind allows us to obtain simple analytic results, which is why it was adopted in numerous studies. It proves vulnerable to criticism, however, on two points. First, it does not allow us to distinguish costs arising from recruitment from those arising from departure; however, the numerous studies referred to above show that these costs differ in amount and effect. Second, it implies that there is a *gradual* adjustment of employment since the marginal cost of adjustment rises with a change in the level of employment. This property gives firms an incentive not to vary their labor demand too much at each period, so as to minimize adjustment costs. So, the quadratic form does not allow us to explain the sudden adjustments in employment often observed in real life.

Asymmetric Convex Costs

For the reasons just mentioned, more recent studies postulate asymmetric adjustment costs. Pfann and Palm (1993) assume a relation of this form:

$$C(\Delta L) = -1 + \exp(a\Delta L) - a\Delta L + \frac{b}{2}(\Delta L)^2, \qquad a > 0, b > 0$$

This specification implies an asymmetry between positive and negative variations in employment. We return to the symmetric formulation with $a = 0$. Conversely, when $a > 0$ (or $a < 0$) the marginal cost of an increase in employment is greater (or less) than that of a reduction. The asymmetry may also originate in a function that is not continuously differentiable. For example, Chang and Stefanou (1988) and Jaramillo et al. (1993) adopt the following specification:

$$C(\Delta L) = c_h(\Delta L)^2 \quad \text{if } \Delta L \geq 0 \qquad \text{and} \qquad C(\Delta L) = c_f(\Delta L)^2 \quad \text{if } \Delta L \leq 0, \, c_h > 0, \, c_l > 0$$

Linear Costs

The specification of adjustment costs in the form of a piecewise linear function offers the advantage of achieving a more realistic representation of labor demand in which firms hire in some circumstances, let employees go in others, and sometimes leave their workforce unchanged (see below, section 3.2.2). The utilization of piecewise linear costs greatly expanded in the 1990s with the works of Bentolila and Bertola (1990), Bertola (1990), Bentolila and Saint-Paul (1994), and Bertola and Rogerson (1997), who examined linear adjustment costs of the form:

$$C(\Delta L) = c_h\Delta L \quad \text{if } \Delta L \geq 0 \qquad \text{and} \qquad C(\Delta L) = -c_f\Delta L \quad \text{if } \Delta L \leq 0, \, c_h > 0, \, c_l > 0$$

The coefficients c_h and c_f represent the respective unit costs of a hiring and a termination. The adjustment of employment is asymmetric, since $c_h \neq c_f$.

Lump-Sum Costs

In many circumstances, the adjustment costs of employment include a component that is fixed and therefore not directly linked to the size of the adjustment. For example, the costs of searching for certain categories of personnel or the administrative costs incurred in a mass termination are in large part independent of the number of individuals involved in these operations. Hamermesh (1993) adopted the hypothesis of a discontinuity in adjustment costs when he postulated that firms undergo a strictly positive fixed cost when $\Delta L \neq 0$, but that they are not subject to any cost if $\Delta L = 0$. Abowd and Kramarz (2003) considered different fixed costs for hirings and terminations. The existence of lump-sum costs allows us to explain why firms of a certain size sometimes have an interest in doing their hirings, and (in France especially) their terminations, in groups.

Empirical studies tried to discover which representation fits best. They made large strides in the 1990s (see section 3.4.2 for the main results). These studies are all the more necessary insofar as the analysis of the determinants of labor demand dynamics proves particularly sensitive to the specification of adjustment costs.

3.2 THE ADJUSTMENT OF EMPLOYMENT IN A DETERMINISTIC ENVIRONMENT

We will consider here a firm situated in a deterministic environment that incurs adjustment costs when it alters its workforce. To make things easier from a technical point of view, a large part of the literature has assumed that these costs were symmetric and could be represented by a quadratic function. We will begin by studying this case, which always serves as a baseline in this domain. But criticisms directed at the hypothesis of quadratic and symmetric costs, and outlined above, have led to the use of asymmetric functional forms, the linear one being chosen most often.

3.2.1   Quadratic and Symmetric Adjustment Costs

The use of quadratic costs has the advantage of leading to a very simple dynamic representation of the trajectory of employment in which employment gradually returns to its stationary value.

The Behavior of the Firm

We will work with a dynamic model in continuous time, in which, at each date $t \geq 0$, the adjustment cost concerns labor alone. When the firm utilizes a quantity L_t of this factor, it obtains a level of output $F(L_t)$ that is strictly increasing and concave with respect to L_t. Taking other inputs into account, such as capital, for example, greatly complicates the analysis without changing the import of the results that we want to highlight. Let $\dot{L}_t$ be the derivative with respect to t of the variable L_t. We will assume that variations in the level of employment are accompanied at every date t by an adjustment cost represented by the quadratic function $(b/2)\dot{L}_t^2$, $b \geq 0$.

To simplify the notations and calculations, from now on we will omit the index t and assume that at every date, the cost of labor and the interest rate are exogenous constants denoted respectively by W and r. At date $t = 0$, the discounted present value of profit, Π_0, is writtten:

$$\Pi_0 = \int_0^{+\infty} \left[F(L) - WL - \frac{b}{2}\dot{L}^2 \right] e^{-rt}\, dt$$

In this environment, free of random factors, the firm chooses its present and future levels of employment so as to maximize the discounted present value of profits Π_0. This is a classic problem of calculus of variations for which the first-order condition is given by the Euler equation[9]:

$$\frac{\partial J}{\partial L} = \frac{\partial}{\partial t}\left(\frac{\partial J}{\partial \dot{L}} \right) \quad \text{with} \quad J(L, \dot{L}, t) = \left[F(L) - WL - \frac{b}{2}\dot{L}^2 \right] e^{-rt} \tag{44}$$

After several simple calculations, we find that the employment path is described by a nonlinear second-order differential equation that takes the form:

$$b\ddot{L} - rb\dot{L} + F'(L) - W = 0 \tag{45}$$

The stationary value L^* of employment is obtained by making $\dot{L} = \ddot{L} = 0$ in this equation. It is thus defined by the usual equality between marginal productivity and wage, or $F'(L^*) = W$. In this simple model, the stationary level of employment does not depend on parameter b measuring the extent of adjustment costs, for $\dot{L} = 0$ in the stationary state, and there is no flow of hirings or terminations to give rise to costs of this type. This would no longer be the case if, for example, the stationary state were characterized by a permanent flow of hirings compensating for exogenous departures. On the other hand, the employment path described by differential equation (45) always depends on parameter b measuring the size of adjustment costs.

The Dynamics of Employment

It is possible to specify precisely the properties of the trajectory of employment in the neighborhood of the stationary state by taking the first-order approximation of $F'(L)$ around L^*. Replacing $F'(L)$ by $F'(L^*) + (L - L^*)F''(L^*)$ in equation (45), we arrive at:

$$b\ddot{L} - rb\dot{L} - aL = -aL^*, \qquad \text{with} \qquad a = -F''(L^*) > 0$$

Let A_1 and A_2 be two arbitrary constants. The general solution of this linear second-order differential equation is written[10]:

$$L = L^* + A_1 e^{\lambda_1 t} + A_2 e^{\lambda_2 t} \tag{46}$$

with:

$$\lambda_1 = \frac{1}{2}\left[r + \sqrt{r^2 + \frac{4a}{b}}\right] > 0 \qquad \text{and} \qquad \lambda_2 = \frac{1}{2}\left[r - \sqrt{r^2 + \frac{4a}{b}}\right] < 0 \tag{47}$$

The coefficient λ_1 being positive, it is necessary that A_1 be equal to zero in order to have a stable path. Let L_0 be the (given) level of employment at date $t = 0$. The value of A_2 is found by making $t = 0$ in (46), which gives $A_2 = L_0 - L^*$. The employment trajectory is thus completely defined by:

$$L = L^* + (L_0 - L^*)e^{\lambda_2 t} \tag{48}$$

This equality shows that employment *gradually* moves to its stationary value L^*. This property is the direct consequence of the utilization of a quadratic form to represent adjustment costs. With this specification, the firm has an interest in "smoothing out" the changes it makes to its workforce, for if the adjustment were to be made all at once at the initial date, the instantaneous cost of the hirings and terminations, or $b(L_0 - L^*)^2$, would exceed the total cost of an adjustment spread out over time.

Figure 4.3 gives an illustration of the adjustment trajectories, assuming a homogeneous production function $F(L) = L^{0.7}$, a labor cost $W = 0.7$, and an annual interest rate $r = 0.05$. We thus have $L^* = 1$. We assume that the initial level of employment is 10% greater than its stationary value. As well, we distinguish two kinds of job: skilled jobs (the broken line), for which the cost of adjustment is 80% of the annual labor cost, and unskilled jobs (the unbroken line), for which the cost of adjustment is 15% of the annual cost. These orders of magnitude correspond to the empirical results obtained by Bresson et al. (1996). We may note that the trajectory of unskilled jobs approaches the stationary value more rapidly than that of skilled jobs, for which the costs of adjustment are greater. In this regard, a graphic representation is particularly useful, since it allows us to visualize the amounts of time that adjustments take. But it is also useful to have a measure of the adjustment speed.

Median Lag and the Adjustment Speed

The time required for employment adjustment is conventionally measured by a *median lag*, which, by definition, indicates the time required for the level of employment to settle at a point equidistant from its initial value L_0 and its stationary value L^*. Consequently the median lag, denoted δ, is implicitly defined by the equality $L_\delta = (L_0 + L^*)/2$. Therefore, taking into account equation (48), which describes the employ-

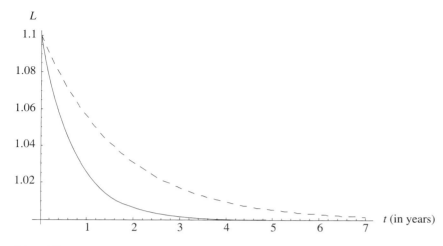

FIGURE 4.3

Employment adjustment in the model with quadratic adjustment costs. The broken line corresponds to an adjustment cost *b* equal to 80% of the annual labor cost and the unbroken line to a value of *b* equal to 15% of the same annual cost.

ment trajectory, the median lag is defined by the formula $\delta = -\ln 2/\lambda_2$. Given the expression of λ_2 that appears in relation (47), we see that the median lag increases with b. Hence a rise in adjustment costs prolongs the time that employment adjustment takes.

It is interesting to note that the existence of an adjustment lag allows us to understand why labor productivity follows the business cycle. We do indeed observe that in booms, production per hour of work is higher than it is in slumps. The adjustment costs of manpower contribute to explaining this phenomenon. Firms make little change to employment during booms, with the result that they have too few employees. Marginal productivity of labor is then high (higher than in the absence of adjustment costs). The same logic implies that the marginal productivity of labor is weaker during slumps.

Staying with a quadratic function means that employment adjustment takes place gradually, which on the one hand does not always correspond to observed facts, and on the other leads to an underestimate of the extent of adjustment costs in applied studies (see Hamermesh and Pfann, 1996). What is more, the hypothesis of symmetry prevents us from distinguishing between effects arising from the costs of terminating employment and those arising from the costs of hiring. In what follows, we examine the consequences of the asymmetry between these two types of cost with a linear adjustment costs function.

3.2.2 Linear and Asymmetric Adjustment Costs

It is possible to distinguish the costs of hiring and firing by adopting a piecewise linear specification. The hypothesis of linearity also brings out the fact that, contrary to the model with quadratic costs, employment adjustment can take place immediately.

The Demand for Workers

Let c_h and c_f be two positive constants, and let us assume from now on that the adjustment costs are represented by the function:

$$C(\dot{L}) = c\dot{L} \qquad \text{with} \qquad c = c_h \text{ if } \dot{L} > 0 \qquad \text{and} \qquad c = -c_f \text{ if } \dot{L} < 0 \qquad (49)$$

Parameters c_h and c_f allow us to distinguish hiring costs ($\dot{L} > 0$) from termination costs ($\dot{L} < 0$). The firm's problem consists of choosing, at date $t = 0$, levels of employment that maximize the discounted present value of profit Π_0. The latter is expressed thus:

$$\Pi_0 = \int_0^{+\infty} [F(L) - WL - C(\dot{L})]e^{-rt}\, dt$$

Once again, this is a problem of calculus of variations to which the Euler equation (44) applies when the quadratic function $-(b/2)\dot{L}^2$ is replaced by the linear function $C(\dot{L}) = c\dot{L}$. After several simple calculations, we find that the employment path is defined by the equation $F'(L) = W + rc$, which entails:

$$F'(L) = W + rc_h \quad \text{if } \dot{L} > 0, \qquad \text{and} \qquad F'(L) = W - rc_f \quad \text{if } \dot{L} < 0$$

These conditions signify that the firm hires when marginal productivity is sufficiently high to cover the wage W and the hiring cost rc_h. Conversely, the firm fires when productivity is so low that it just equals wage W less the provision rc_f for the termination cost. In all other cases, i.e., when productivity lies in the interval $[W - rc_f,\, W + rc_h]$, the firm has no interest in altering the size of its workforce, for the gains due to hiring and firing are less than the costs incurred by adjusting employment.

Labor adjustments take a particularly instructive form when the parameters W, r, c_h, and c_f are constants, which we have assumed. Let us define the employment levels L_h and L_f by the equalities:

$$F'(L_h) = W + rc_h \qquad \text{and} \qquad F'(L_f) = W - rc_f \qquad (50)$$

We see that the optimal values L_h and L_f do not depend on date t. That means that labor demand *immediately* (i.e., in $t = 0$) "jumps" to its stationary value. The firm adjusts its workforce to the value L_h (respectively L_f) if the latter is greater than (or less than) the initial value L_0 of employment. In the opposite case, i.e., if L_0 falls in the interval $[L_h, L_f]$, the optimal solution for the firm consists of making no change to the size of its workforce. In sum, labor demand is defined by:

$$L = \begin{cases} L_h & \text{if } L_0 \leq L_h \\ L_0 & \text{if } L_h \leq L_0 \leq L_f \\ L_f & \text{if } L_f \leq L_0 \end{cases} \qquad (51)$$

The result—that the level of employment immediately "jumps" to its stationary value—arises from our choice of a linear form to represent adjustment costs. In this case, it is not necessary to smooth out the trajectory so as to reduce costs. The firm always has an interest in reaching the stationary state as quickly as possible. Consequently the use of a linear form allows us to account for brutally rapid changes in the employment level.

The Effects of Hiring and Firing Costs

The choice of optimal employment is represented in figure 4.4. The upper part of the graph represents the marginal productivity of the initial level of employment $F'(L_0)$. The bold curve represents the relationship between the initial level and the optimal level of employment chosen by the firm. We see that if the marginal productivity of initial employment is greater than $W + rc_h$ the firm hires, whereas it fires if the marginal productivity of initial employment is less than $W - rc_f$. In all cases lying in between, the firm does not alter its employment level.

Figure 4.4 and relations (50) also show that the costs of hiring and firing have *opposing* effects on labor demand. If the size of the workforce is low at the outset ($L_0 \leq L_h$), then optimal employment is equal to L_h, and a rise in the hiring cost c_h

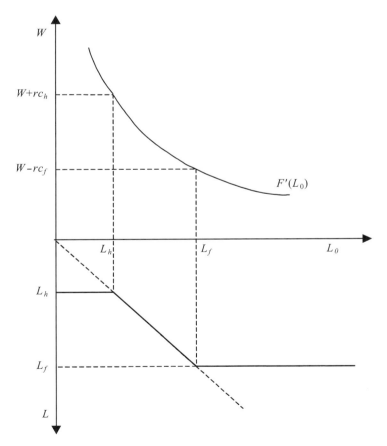

FIGURE 4.4
Labor demand in the model with linear adjustment costs of employment.

reduces employment. Conversely, if there is a large number of workers at the outset ($L_f \leq L_0$), the optimal level of employment takes the value L_f, and we clearly see that a *rise* in the termination cost c_f has the effect of *increasing* employment. We should not, however, conclude on the basis of this analysis that a rise in the termination cost (or a fall in the hiring cost) "augments" the firm's labor demand. In reality, since this demand immediately jumps to L_h or L_f (unless it simply remains at L_0), the level of employment is always equal to one of the three quantities L_h, L_f, or L_0. Let us suppose that the number of workers is L_f. A rise in the termination cost c_f will augment L_f up to a certain value L_f^+ and will thus have the effect of placing the *outset* level of the workforce (now equal to L_f) somewhere in the interval $[L_h, L_f^+]$. In this case, relation (51) describing labor demand shows that the firm then has an interest in remaining at L_f. In other words, a rise in the cost of terminating *hinders* the firm from going ahead with reductions in personnel, but gives it no incentive to hire. An analogous line of reasoning would show that a rise in the costs of hiring has the effect of *discouraging* further recruitment but does not lead to a reduction in employment. Conversely, a reduction in hiring costs always has a positive effect on employment to the extent that it increases the value L_h of optimal employment.

It emerges from this analysis that a rise in the termination cost of employment leads to a stabilization of labor demand when the latter is high ($L_t = L_f$) and that a fall in the hiring cost has the effect of increasing labor demand when it is low ($L_t = L_h$). Conclusions of this nature cannot be reached with a quadratic representation of adjustment costs. Moreover, the model just presented suggests that appropriate management of hiring and firing costs may play a stabilizing role vis-à-vis labor demand. This result must, however, be reexamined in an environment with uncertainty.

3.3 THE ADJUSTMENT OF LABOR DEMAND IN A STOCHASTIC ENVIRONMENT

In order to compare the results to follow with those already obtained in the absence of uncertainty, we shall take a stochastic environment, and shall examine the consequences of representing adjustment costs by a quadratic and symmetric function, and then by a linear asymmetric function.

3.3.1 Quadratic and Symmetric Adjustment Costs

The quadratic case serves as our baseline. Under the hypothesis of rational expectations, the dynamic path of employment is described by a linear equation with lag that fits estimates well. This representation extends to multiple inputs and allows us to define the notion of dynamic complementarity and substitution.

The Firm's Problem and the Euler Equation

Models in continuous time are not very well adapted to understanding the formation of expectation. For this reason we (provisionally) abandon the continuous representation of time in favor of a model in discrete time. The output of the firm is now written $F(A_t, L_t)$, where $A_t > 0$ is a random variable representing, for example, a shock to the selling price, or to productivity, that occurs at the beginning of period t. We assume that the realization of A_t is observed prior to the decisions to hire and fire made in period t. Production is always strictly increasing and concave with respect to employment L_t. In the course of period t, the firm supports adjustment costs arising from the hirings and firings represented by a quadratic and symmetric function that is expressed as $(b/2)(L_t - L_{t-1})^2$, $b > 0$. The firm's behavior is analyzed following the same procedure followed in the dynamic model with certainty. The problem of maximizing the expected profit yields optimality conditions that allow us to know the labor demand at each date. These conditions are generally equations in differences defining current employment, hirings, and firings as a function of past employment and expected future employment. At each date t, the expected discounted present value of profit is written:

$$\Pi_t = E_t \left\{ \sum_{i=0}^{+\infty} \left(\frac{1}{1+r} \right)^i \left[F(A_{t+i}, L_{t+i}) - W_{t+i}L_{t+i} - \frac{b}{2}(L_{t+i} - L_{t+i-1})^2 \right] \right\}$$

In this expression, E_t designates the expectation operator conditional upon all the information available to the employer at date t. The strict concavity of the production function and the convexity of the adjustment costs imply that the first-order condition defines a maximum. Differentiating the expression of expected discounted present value of profit with respect to L_t, we obtain the Euler equation:

$$F_L(A_t, L_t) = W_t + b(L_t - L_{t-1}) - \frac{b}{1+r} E_t(L_{t+1} - L_t), \qquad \forall t \geq 1 \tag{52}$$

The dynamics of employment is thus described by a second-order difference equation where current employment L_t depends both on past employment L_{t-1} and on expected employment $E_t L_{t+1}$.

The Formation of Expectations

At this point it is necessary to spell out the process by which expectations are formed. We will assume here that the producer is capable of making *rational* expectations. This signifies that the expectation formed at date t about the value X_{t+i} of a variable X at date $t + i$ is then equal to the mathematical expectation of X_{t+i} conditional upon all the information available at date t. This expectation is denoted $E_t X_{t+i}$ (for more detail on expectations in general, see chapter 8, section 3). Under the hypothesis of rational expectations, the "true" model of the economy is one of the available pieces of information. In particular, the employer knows that the future level of employment L_{t+1} is given by relation (52) applied to date $(t + 1)$. Step by step, we thus see that employment L_t will be a function of past employment L_{t-1} and of expectations made at date t about all future shocks A_{t+i}, $i \geq 1$. In order to obtain an explicit solution for labor demand, we will assume that the production function can be approximated by a linear quadratic function of the form $F(A_t, L_t) = A_t L_t - (B/2)L_t^2$, with $B > 0$. Equation (52) is then written:

$$a_0 E_t L_{t+1} - L_t + a_1 L_{t-1} + a_t = 0 \tag{53}$$

with:

$$a_0 = \frac{b}{(B+b)(1+r)+b}, \qquad a_1 = (1+r)a_0, \qquad \text{and} \qquad a_t = \frac{(A_t - W_t)a_1}{b}$$

The Dynamics of Employment

The solution of equation (53) can be obtained thanks to the "indeterminate coefficients" method (see Blanchard and Fischer, 1989, p. 261, and Sargent, 1986, chapter 14). It consists of postulating a particular form for the solution, then identifying the unknown parameters by writing that this particular form satisfies equation (53). Since L_t depends on its past value L_{t-1}, on the present realization of the random variable a_t, and on all the future expected values of the latter, we can seek a solution that is a linear form of these quantities. In this case, L_t is written:

$$L_t = \lambda L_{t-1} + \sum_{i=0}^{+\infty} \mu_i E_t a_{t+i} \tag{54}$$

In this expression, λ and μ_i $(i \geq 0)$ are unknown parameters that have to be determined. To do so, we begin by calculating the expectation at date t of L_{t+1} resulting from relation (54). We thus find that $E_t L_{t+1} = \lambda L_t + \sum_{i=0}^{+\infty} \mu_i E_t a_{t+i+1}$, and in substituting this expression of $E_t L_{t+1}$ in (53), we finally get:

$$L_t = \frac{1}{1 - \lambda a_0} \left(a_0 \sum_{i=0}^{+\infty} \mu_i E_t a_{t+i+1} + a_1 L_{t-1} + a_t \right) \tag{55}$$

It suffices now to identify the coefficients of L_{t-1} and of a_{t+i} $(\forall i \geq 0)$ in the expressions of L_t given by (54) and (55) in order to obtain the values of the coefficients λ and μ_i. These are:

$$\lambda = \frac{a_1}{1 - \lambda a_0}, \qquad \mu_0 = \frac{1}{1 - \lambda a_0}, \qquad \text{and} \qquad \mu_i = (a_0 \mu_0)^i \mu_0, \qquad \forall i \geq 1$$

Coefficient λ linked to lagged employment L_{t-1} is the root of the polynomial $a_0 \lambda^2 - \lambda + a_1$. We verify that this polynomial admits two real positive roots, one less than 1 and the other greater than 1. Only the value of λ less than 1 gives a stable non-explosive solution, and thus it is the only root that can be retained. Substituting the values of the coefficients calculated above in equation (54), we arrive at the definitive expression of the solution:

$$L_t = \lambda L_{t-1} + \mu_0 \sum_{i=0}^{+\infty} (a_0 \mu_0)^i E_t a_{t+i} \qquad \text{with} \qquad \lambda = \frac{1 - \sqrt{1 - 4a_0 a_1}}{2a_0} \tag{56}$$

It is easy to verify that the value of λ linked to lagged employment increases with parameter b, which measures the extent of the adjustment costs. The weight of past employment is thus more important the higher the adjustment costs are. In other words, fluctuations in labor demand are less marked when adjustment costs are large. Equations analogous in form to (56) have served as the foundation of numerous empirical estimates that attempt to measure the speed of employment adjustment. For that we have to postulate a particular form for the stochastic process governing the path of the random variables a_t and, if possible, to link the parameters of this process to certain observable variables (see section 3.4.1 below for an example).

Dynamic Substitution and Complementarity
Only adjustment costs linked to employment, assumed to be homogeneous, have been taken into consideration. But the firm incurs this type of cost for other inputs, notably capital. Lucas (1967) and Nadiri and Rosen (1973) have studied the case of quadratic adjustment costs with multiple inputs in a stationary environment. Messe (1980) has extended this study in a stochastic framework with rational expectations. The dynamics of employment is then described by an equation whose form is very close to (56). To be precise, if there are n inputs, of which the ith is utilized in quantity X_t^i at date t, the equation of the path of this input is written:

$$X_t^i = \sum_{j=1}^{n} \lambda_{ij} X_{t-1}^j + \sum_{k=0}^{+\infty} \gamma_i^k E_t x_{t+k}$$

In this expression, λ_{ij} are adjustment parameters, γ_i is a vector of parameters dependent on technology and adjustment costs, and x_t represents a vector relative to the price of the inputs. It is evident that the quantity of input i utilized at date t depends on the past quantities of all the inputs that give rise to adjustment costs. By extension, the definitions we gave in section 1.4.2 when looking at labor demand in the absence of adjustment cost, inputs i and j are called *dynamically substitutable* if $\lambda_{ij} < 0$ and *dynamically complementary* if $\lambda_{ij} > 0$. When two factors are dynamically substitutable (or complementary) the direction of their adjustments is identical (or inverted). We also see that the average time it takes to adjust an input is influenced by the adjustment costs of all the inputs. So the slowness with which employment is adjusted may be a consequence of the adjustment costs of capital if these two inputs are dynamically complementary.

3.3.2 Linear and Asymmetric Adjustment Costs
In a model set in a stochastic environment, the costs of hiring and firing *jointly* influence employment, for the firm, in making decisions in the present, takes into account possible future upturns or downturns in the health of the economy. Where adjustment costs are sizable, we should expect to observe low rates of employment turnover. However, the influence of adjustment costs on average employment is a priori indeterminate in sign.

A Model with Two States of Nature
We return to the model in continuous time of section 3.2.2, in which a firm faces linear adjustment costs described by the formula (49). We assume that instantaneous production is represented by the function $F(A, L)$, where A and L designate

respectively a parameter affecting productivity and the employment level (the indicator t is left out in order to simplify the notations). To bring out the contrast between the firm's behavior in booms and slumps, it is assumed that parameter A is a random variable following a Poisson process[11] with two states denoted by A_G and A_B, with $A_G > A_B$ and $F_{AL} > 0$. The realization A_G then represents the "good" state in which marginal productivity is highest for a given level of employment. The instantaneous transition probability from state A_G to state A_B is denoted by q_G, while the instantaneous transition probability from state A_B to state A_G is denoted by q_B. The ratio $1/q_G$ (respectively $1/q_B$) represents the average length of time the economy remains in state A_G (or A_B): it is a measure of the *persistence* of state A_G (or A_B).

The complete and rigorous solution of the optimization problem of a firm that finds itself in an environment of this type is possible, but encounters substantial technical difficulties (see Bentolila and Saint-Paul, 1994, and Dixit, 1997). For the sake of simplicity, we start by considering a stationary policy linking constant levels of employment L_G and L_B when the productivity variable takes the values A_G and A_B, respectively. We assume, moreover, that the different parameters of the model are such that $L_G > L_B$, which means that the firm hires when the economy passes from state A_B to state A_G, and that it fires when the economy passes from state A_G to state A_B (employment remains unaltered when productivity does not change).

The Decisions of the Firm

Let Π_G and Π_B be the stationary present discounted values of expected profit when the productivity variable is equal to A_G and A_B, respectively. Let W_G and W_B be the real wages linked to these states. Expected profits are then defined by the following trade-off equations:

$$r\Pi_G = F(A_G, L_G) - W_G L_G + q_G[-c_f(L_G - L_B) + \Pi_B - \Pi_G] \tag{57}$$

$$r\Pi_B = F(A_B, L_B) - W_B L_B + q_B[-c_h(L_G - L_B) + \Pi_G - \Pi_B] \tag{58}$$

We have met equations of this type in chapter 3, section 2, dedicated to the job search theory. We interpret them by reasoning as though there were multiple trade-off possibilities in the investment of an asset. In the present case, an asset worth Π_G brings in $r\Pi_G$ at every date if it is invested in the financial market. An asset corresponding to the same amount of money invested in the labor market brings in, at every date, instantaneous profit $F(A_G, L_G) - W_G L_G$, to which must be added the average gain linked to a change in the state of the economy. This eventuality comes about with a probability of q_G, in which case the firm lets $(L_G - L_B)$ individuals go, which costs it $c_f(L_G - L_B)$, and it then gets an expected profit equal to Π_B. Relation (58) defining Π_B is interpreted in analogous manner.

When the level of employment is, for example, equal to L_B, and state A_G comes about, the firm makes its hiring decisions in such as way as to maximize the value of its expected profit net of the costs of hiring. So it must solve the following problem:

$$\underset{L_G}{\text{Max}}[\Pi_G - c_h(L_G - L_B)] \quad \text{with } L_B \text{ given}$$

In symmetric fashion, if the number of workers equals L_G and state A_B comes about, it decides to terminate employment so as to maximize the value of its profit net of the termination costs. So it must solve the following problem:

$$\underset{L_B}{\text{Max}}[\Pi_B - c_f(L_G - L_B)] \qquad \text{with} \qquad L_G \text{ given}$$

The first-order conditions of these two problems come down to two equations, $(\partial\Pi_G/\partial L_G) = c_h$ and $(\partial\Pi_B/\partial L_B) = -c_f$. These two conditions are easy to grasp: the firm increases its workforce as long as the marginal profit of a hire surpasses its cost, and it terminates jobs to the point where the marginal loss due to a termination—equal to $-(\partial\Pi_B/\partial L_B)$—just covers the cost c_f of a termination.

Relations (57) and (58) allow us to find the partial derivatives of profits Π_G and Π_B with respect to employment levels:

$$\frac{\partial\Pi_G}{\partial L_G} = \left(\frac{1}{r+q_G}\right)\left[F_L(A_G, L_G) - W_G - q_G c_f + \frac{\partial\Pi_B}{\partial L_G}\right]$$

$$\frac{\partial\Pi_B}{\partial L_B} = \left(\frac{1}{r+q_B}\right)\left[F_L(A_B, L_B) - W_B + q_B c_h + \frac{\partial\Pi_G}{\partial L_B}\right]$$

Relations (57) and (58) also give $(\partial\Pi_B/\partial L_G) = q_B[-c_h + (\partial\Pi_G/\partial L_G)]$ and $(\partial\Pi_G/\partial L_B) = q_G[c_f + (\partial\Pi_B/\partial L_B)]$, which implies, with optimality conditions $(\partial\Pi_G/\partial L_G) = c_h$ and $(\partial\Pi_B/\partial L_B) = -c_f$, that $(\partial\Pi_B/\partial L_G) = (\partial\Pi_G/\partial L_B) = 0$. Consequently, the optimal levels L_G and L_B satisfy the following equations:

$$F_L(A_G, L_G) = W_G + q_G c_f + (r + q_G)c_h \tag{59}$$

$$F_L(A_B, L_B) = W_B - q_B c_h - (r + q_B)c_f \tag{60}$$

The values L_G and L_B correspond respectively to the levels of labor demand in states A_G and A_B if and only if these two equations imply $L_G > L_B$, which we assume. In this case, employment rises when the firm passes from a bad state to a good one, diminishes when it passes from a good state to a bad one, and remains constant in all other circumstances.

Fluctuations in Employment

We see that taking uncertainty into account through a two-state Poisson process considerably alters the results obtained from models in a stationary determinist environment. Hiring phases (which correspond to the good state of nature A_G) are linked to a level of employment L_G greater than the one L_B existing in firing phases (i.e., when the bad state A_B appears). Unlike the certain case, the level of employment does not settle definitively on value L_G or L_B; rather, it *alternates* from one value to the other according to the states of nature. Moreover, relations (59) and (60) indicate that labor demand depends, whatever the state of nature, on both turnover costs c_h and c_f. So it is that we see L_G *decrease* with c_h and c_f. The fact that recruitment is weaker when the cost c_h of a hire rises has nothing surprising about it; yet it appears that the same thing happens when it is the termination cost c_f that increases. This comes about simply because the entrepreneur foresees that in the future, he or she will have to deal with less favorable phases in the cycle, when terminations will have to be made. Hence, high costs of termination put a brake on hires in the upward phases of the cycle. Conversely, relation (60) shows that L_B *increases* with c_f and c_h. A rise in the termination cost c_f gives the firm an incentive to do less firing in the downward phases of the cycle, and a rise in the hiring cost c_h gives it incentive to act in the same way, since it foresees that it will have to set about recruiting personnel when the economic cycle turns up again. This analysis suggests that adjustment costs ought to have a stabilizing effect to the extent that a rise in these costs reduces hires when the economy turns up and puts a brake on firings when it turns down. In certain circumstances, it is even possible that adjustment costs may have a beneficial effect on average employment.

The Labor Turnover Rate

Let us suppose that the economy is composed of a continuum of identical firms and let us designate by ρ the proportion of these that, at a given date, find themselves in the good state of nature. The variable ρ then represents the proportion of firms for which $A = A_G$ holds. For the sake of simplicity, the measure of the continuum of firms is normalized to 1. At any date t, there are ρq_G firms that pass from state A_G to state A_B and that each fire $(L_G - L_B)$ workers. The destruction of jobs thus amounts to $\rho q_G(L_G - L_B)$. Conversely, there are $(1 - \rho)q_B$ firms whose state passes from A_B to A_G and which each hire $(L_G - L_B)$ workers. The creation of jobs thus amounts to $(1 - \rho)q_B(L_G - L_B)$. At stationary equilibrium of the economy, the number of jobs created is equal to the number of jobs destroyed, and parameter ρ is thus defined by the equality $\rho = q_B/(q_B + q_G)$. One interesting indicator often utilized to measure job flows is the *turnover rate*, equal, by definition, to the sum of all the jobs created and destroyed. In this model, the turnover rate, denoted by τ, is given by:

$$\tau = [(1 - \rho)q_B + \rho q_G](L_G - L_B) = 2\frac{q_G q_B}{q_B + q_G}(L_G - L_B)$$

Since, following (59) and (60), the employment levels L_G and L_B are functions, respectively decreasing and increasing, of adjustment costs, it results that the turnover rate falls when the "rigidity" of the labor market increases, i.e., when the costs of hiring c_h and firing c_f increase. Conversely, the turnover rate is a decreasing function of the wage differential $(W_G - W_B)$. All other things being equal, for that matter, an economy with rigid wages that vary little over the cycle will have a higher labor turnover rate than an economy with more flexible wages. This property may explain why labor turnover rates are just about the same in the United States and certain European countries such as France and Germany, although the employment market is far more flexible in the United States. According to Bertola and Rogerson (1997), higher wage rigidity in Europe might produce a reaction in the form of large job creations and destructions, so that in the end, the turnover rates in the United States and Europe turn out to be more or less the same (see also Bertola, 1999). This observation, which has to do with the labor market equilibrium and not just labor demand, will be more thoroughly documented in chapter 12, section 2, where wages are endogenous and so react to the adjustment costs of employment.

Average Employment

A "rigid" labor market will thus create and destroy fewer jobs than a "flexible" one, but we cannot a priori state anything about the *average* level of employment, which comes under pressure from two opposing directions. In certain circumstances, it is possible that the average employment level may be higher in a rigid economy than in a flexible one. To see why, let us suppose that the production function takes the quadratic form $F(A, L) = AL - (B/2)L^2$; the marginal productivities appearing on the left-hand side of relations (59) and (60) are then equal to $A_G - BL_G$ and $A_B - BL_B$, respectively. Let us denote average employment by $\bar{L} = \rho L_G + (1 - \rho)L_B$, average productivity by $\bar{A} = \rho A_G + (1 - \rho)A_B$, and the average wage by $\overline{W} = \rho W_G + (1 - \rho)W_B$. Since $\rho = q_B/(q_B + q_G)$, the addition of relations (59) and (60) defining L_G and L_B comes to:

$$\bar{A} - B\bar{L} = \overline{W} + \frac{r}{q_B + q_G}(q_B c_h - q_G c_f)$$

Consequently, under the hypothesis of a quadratic production function, average employment is an *increasing* function of termination costs and a *decreasing* function of hiring costs. This result, however, does not bear a general character: it depends on the specification of the production function and the nature of the shocks. With a homogeneous production function, the termination costs have ambiguous effects. Bertola (1999) has shown, with the help of numerical examples, that a rise in these costs likely has a positive impact, but one small in extent, on average employment. Using a discrete time model, Bentolila and Bertola (1990) have studied the case of a homogeneous production function with shocks that follow a random walk of the type $A_t = A_{t-1} + \varepsilon_t$, where ε_t is a white noise. The shocks have a permanent effect on the level of parameter A_t. These authors likewise conclude that there is a positive relationship between the firing costs and average employment. Nonetheless, for realistic values of the parameters, they show that the impact of firing costs on employment is small in extent. Conversely, Bentolila and Saint-Paul (1994) arrive at markedly different results by assuming that the shocks are independent and have a uniform distribution. They bring to light a nonmonotonic relationship between the firing costs and average employment. When these costs are low, the relationship is negative, but it becomes positive when they rise sufficiently high.

3.4 EMPIRICAL ASPECTS OF LABOR DEMAND IN THE PRESENCE OF ADJUSTMENT COSTS

To estimate the importance of employment adjustment costs has been the aim of many in-depth studies. Until recently, a quadratic and symmetric representation of these costs was always used. Today, however, studies using microeconomic data generally abandon this representation.

3.4.1   On Estimates

For convenience, numerous studies postulate that adjustment costs take quadratic and symmetric form. In a stochastic environment, and under the hypothesis of rational expectations, the level of present employment L_t is given by the difference equation (56), which brings in past employment L_{t-1} and expectations regarding shocks a_{t+i} ($i \geq 1$) affecting the firm's environment. When expectations are rational, the producer is capable, like the econometrician, of estimating the stochastic process of the a_{t+i}. For that, it is enough to substitute expectations of these variables at date t by the values predicted for them by the stochastic process estimated by the econometrician. For example, if the stochastic process generating the shocks is autoregressive of order one, or $a_\tau = \alpha a_{\tau-1} + \varepsilon_\tau$, $0 < \alpha < 1$, where ε_τ is a white noise, then $E_t a_{t+i} = \alpha^i a_t$ and equation (56) reads:

$$L_t = \lambda L_{t-1} + \frac{\mu_0}{1 - \alpha(a_0\mu_0)} a_t$$

All variables in this linear equation being observable at date t it can be estimated using, for example, the method of ordinary least squares. In this way we can deduce the median lag[12] δ. When the random variable a_t follows a more complex process, the hypothesis of rational expectations allows us to obtain an equation linking present employment to the (observable) values of shocks past and present. It then remains to estimate this equation with adequate methods.

The expression (56) of labor demand upon which the preceding method is based is obtained using precise hypotheses concerning the production function (linear quadratic) and adjustment costs (quadratic and symmetric). In order to get around having to postulate such restrictive hypotheses, another approach consists of estimating the Euler equations directly. These indicate—see, for example, (52)—that employment at date t depends on both past and expected future variables. The hypothesis of rational expectation allows us, in making our estimates, to replace expectation variables by their realizations, utilizing the technique of generalized moments or that of instrumental variables, with instruments belonging to the information set of the firm at date t (Hamilton, 1994, chapter 14).

3.4.2   Main Results

The results obtained from estimating dynamic equations of labor demand are given by Hamermesh (1993, chapters 7 and 8) and Hamermesh and Pfann (1996). From this it emerges, among other things, that the adjustment costs of employment cannot be validly represented by a simple quadratic and symmetric component.

On the Form of Adjustment Costs

Until the end of the 1980s, the great majority of empirical studies made use of quadratic and symmetric cost functions. Most often they found that adjustment costs were minor, on the order of 20% of the annual labor cost for the United States and United Kingdom. Since then, however, studies grounded in microeconomic data have developed notably, and all of them reach the same conclusion: the hypothesis that adjustment costs are symmetric and convex (like quadratic functions, for example) must be rejected. A good representation must, in all likelihood, be asymmetric, piecewise linear, and involve fixed costs (Hamermesh and Pfann, 1996).

The work of Abowd and Kramarz (2003), grounded in French individual data, confirms this judgment. They find that the costs of terminating employment are almost linear functions of terminations, with a very high lump-sum component, which can be explained by the existence in France of economically motivated procedures for mass termination. The fixed cost of a mass termination is 1138117 French francs (against an average annual labor cost of 171022 French francs). The marginal cost of terminating N workers is $(56299 - 31.2 \times N)$ French francs. The cost of terminating employment is thus concave with respect to the number of fired workers. Abowd and Kramarz also find that hiring costs are clearly lower, and are an increasing and concave function of the number of hires.

On the Extent of Adjustments

Many studies have tried to estimate the speed of adjustment of labor demand. They have adopted a quadratic and symmetric representation of labor turnover costs, and have not taken into account possible adjustment costs for other inputs. It appears that the speed of adjustment is relatively high, since according to Hamermesh (1993, p. 261), a reasonable estimate of the median lag is one to two quarters (1.4 quarters on the basis of quarterly data, and 1.2 quarters on the basis of monthly data). Estimating simultaneous adjustments of multiple inputs does not seem to change this conclusion. With a moderate degree of confidence, certain studies do show, however, that labor services would be dynamic substitutes with the rate of capital utilization. In other words, firms would adjust the utilization of their equipment all the more quickly, the greater the disequilibrium between desired employment and actual employment. It is worth noting that most of the estimates apply to the United States and Canada.

Firms adjust hours of work more rapidly than number of workers. This result points to the conclusion that adjustment costs are greater for workers than for hours, which also explains why workers are kept on during cyclical downturns. There exists no robust result, however, allowing us to assert that men and hours are dynamic substitutes, or complements.

Most international comparisons indicate that employment adjusts more rapidly in the United States than anywhere else. They also suggest that the adjustment takes place more rapidly in Europe than in Japan. The reasons for these divergences are not well established. Contrary to what one might think, the degree of unionization does not appear to be a significant variable. A greater or lesser rigor of legislation regarding the termination of employment might, however, be an explanation for this phenomenon. Abraham and Houseman (1993) compared labor adjustment practices in the United States and Germany. Lazear (1990) and Dertouzos and Karoly (1990) found that strengthened job security, i.e., an increased cost of terminating employment, has a negative impact, but Bertola (1990) estimates that these costs have practically no influence. We will return to this problem in detail in chapter 12, section 2.

4 SUMMARY AND CONCLUSION

- *Conditional* demands represent the quantities of each input which a firm desires to utilize to attain a *given* level of output. The cost function is the minimal value of the total cost of the inputs corresponding to this operation. *Unconditional* demands designate the quantities of each input that a firm desires to utilize to maximize its profit. The conditional and unconditional demands for an input always decrease with the cost of the input. The absolute value of the wage elasticity of unconditional labor demand decreases with the market power the firm. It increases with the elasticity of capital/labor substitution.

- Labor and capital are called *gross substitutes* when a rise in the price of a factor leads the firm to reduce the *unconditional* demand for this factor and increase that for another. When this rise implies a reduction in the unconditional demand for each factor, labor and capital are described as *gross complements*. Two factors are *p-substitutes* (or *p-complements*) if the *conditional* demand for one of them increases (or falls off) when the cost of the other factor rises. If the production function includes only two inputs, then they are necessarily p-substitutes.

- Cross elasticity of conditional demand for a factor i with respect to the price of a factor j increases in absolute value with the share of factor j in the total cost, and with the elasticity of substitution between these two factors.

- A reduction in standard hours has the same impact on employment as a rise in fixed costs. That is why, when a firm makes use of overtime hours, a reduction in standard hours increases the actual workweek by inflating the number of overtime hours used. The rise in fixed costs tends to hold back the level of production, and hence that of employment. Therefore, a reduction in standard hours may have deleterious effects on employment if it is not accompanied by a reduction in fixed costs.

- At the aggregate level, we may take it that the absolute value of the elasticity of conditional labor demand with respect to the cost of labor falls in the interval $[0.15, 0.75]$, with consensus settling on a figure of 0.30. Unskilled labor is more easily substitutable for capital than skilled labor is. Skilled labor and capital are p-complements. Workers and hours are p-substitutes with capital.

- The adjustment costs of labor are often sizable. In the United States, hiring costs are greater than termination costs. In France, termination costs clearly outrank other adjustment costs.

- When adjustment costs are quadratic, the firm gradually adjusts the size of its workforce. But it alters the size of the workforce instantaneously if adjustment costs are linear. Under this hypothesis, a rise in the costs of terminating employment allows the firm to stabilize labor demand when labor demand is high.

A decline in hiring costs has the effect of increasing labor demand when it is low. In a stochastic environment, a rise in hiring costs generally has a negative impact on average employment. But a rise in firing costs may have a positive impact on average employment.

- Studies grounded in microeconomic data reject the hypothesis of quadratic and convex adjustment costs. A good representation of these costs must be asymmetric, piecewise linear, and include a lump-sum component.

- The median lag needed for the adjustment of labor demand lies between one and two quarters in the United States. Firms adjust the volume of their hours more quickly than they do that of their workforce. Adjustment times are shorter for unskilled labor than for skilled labor.

- The fiction of a firm that lasts forever is no doubt inadequate to the task of characterizing fully the behavior of labor demand. We have to take into consideration firms that fail, and explain how new ones come into being. Empirically, job creation and destruction due to the closing down and starting up of firms may be as great as or greater than that caused by the expansion and contraction of existing firms. As Hamermesh (1993, chapter 4) points out, the problems posed by the creation and destruction of firms constitute one of the major challenges facing the traditional theory of labor demand and the empirical studies allied to it. These problems will be tackled in chapters 9 and 12, which deal with employment and unemployment from a macroeconomic perspective.

- The functioning of the firm is studied in abstraction from specific problems linked to the management of human resources. In reality, wages, working conditions, the scheduling of hours of work, and employment itself are all objects of formal or informal negotiation. As well, the efficiency of labor may be sensitive to the level and form of remuneration paid and to the hierarchical structure prevailing in the firm. These features of the wage relationship may affect labor demand. For example, the linkage between employment and wages may be affected by the bargaining power of the workers and their preferences. Such considerations are absent from the traditional theory of labor demand; they will be dealt with in chapters 6 and 7.

5   RELATED TOPICS IN THE BOOK

- Chapter 7, section 5: Bargaining over hours
- Chapter 9, section 3: Labor demand in the matching model
- Chapter 12, section 1: Labor market equilibrium with a minimum wage
- Chapter 12, section 2: Employment protection

6   FURTHER READINGS

Bertola, G. (1999), "Microeconomic perspectives on aggregate labor markets," in Ashenfelter, O., and Card, D. (eds.), *Handbook of Labor Economics*, vol. 3C, chap. 45, pp. 2985–3028, Amsterdam: Elsevier Science/North-Holland.

Hamermesh, D. (1993), *Labor Demand*, Princeton, N.J.: Princeton University Press.

Hamermesh, D., and Pfann, G. (1996), "Adjustment costs in factor demand," *Journal of Economic Literature*, 34, pp. 1264–1292.

7   APPENDICES

7.1   APPENDIX 1: THE CONVEXITY OF ISOQUANTS

In this appendix, we show that the isoquants of a production function with two inputs, denoted $F(K,L)$, are strictly convex when the production function is strictly increasing with respect to each of its arguments and strictly concave in (K,L). Readers will recall that a function $f : \mathbb{R}^n \to \mathbb{R}$ is strictly convex (or strictly concave) if and only if:

$$f[\lambda x + (1-\lambda)y] < (\text{resp. } >) \lambda f(x) + (1-\lambda)f(y), \qquad \forall(x,y) \in \mathbb{R}^n \times \mathbb{R}^n, \forall \lambda \in (0,1)$$

By definition, the isoquant corresponding to a given output level Y is a curve $K(L)$ defined by $F[K(L),L] \equiv Y$. This equality implies in particular:

$$F[K(\lambda L_1 + (1-\lambda)L_2), \lambda L_1 + (1-\lambda)L_2] = Y \qquad \forall(L_1,L_2), \forall \lambda \in [0,1] \tag{61}$$

The production function being strictly concave, for each quadruplet (K_1, K_2, L_1, L_2) we always have:

$$F[\lambda K_1 + (1-\lambda)K_2, \lambda L_1 + (1-\lambda)L_2] > \lambda F(K_1,L_1) + (1-\lambda)F(K_2,L_2), \qquad \forall \lambda \in (0,1) \tag{62}$$

Let us posit $K_1 = K(L_1)$ and $K_2 = K(L_2)$, which implies $F[K(L_1),L_1] = F[K(L_2),L_2] = Y$; the right-hand side of (62) is then equal to Y. Whatever the values of L_1 and L_2, and for all $\forall \lambda \in (0,1)$, relation (61) then gives:

$$F[\lambda K(L_1) + (1-\lambda)K(L_2), \lambda L_1 + (1-\lambda)L_2] > F[K(\lambda L_1 + (1-\lambda)L_2), \lambda L_1 + (1-\lambda)L_2] \tag{63}$$

The production function being taken as strictly increasing with respect to each of its arguments, inequality (63) allows us to write:

$$K[\lambda L_1 + (1-\lambda)L_2] < \lambda K(L_1) + (1-\lambda)K(L_2) \qquad \forall(L_1,L_2), \forall \lambda \in (0,1)$$

This last relation shows that the isoquant $K(L)$ is represented by a strictly convex curve in the plane (K,L).

7.2   APPENDIX 2: THE PROPERTIES OF COST FUNCTIONS

Let us consider a firm producing a unique good, whose technology can be represented by a production function with n arguments, denoted by $Y = F(X^1, \ldots, X^n)$. Let us designate the vector indicating the quantities of the inputs utilized in the production of a quantity Y of the good by $\mathbf{X} = (X^1, \ldots, X^n)$, and the vector indicating their respective price by $\mathbf{W} = (W^1, \ldots, W^n)$. Let $\mathcal{Y}$ be the set of the vectors $\mathbf{X}$ such that $F(\mathbf{X}) \geq Y$ for a given output level Y. The cost function of this firm, denoted by $C(\mathbf{W}, Y)$, is then defined by the following relation:

$$C(\mathbf{W}, Y) = \underset{\mathbf{X} \in \mathcal{Y}}{\mathrm{Min}} \sum_{i=1}^{n} W^i X^i \tag{64}$$

(i) $C(\mathbf{W}, Y)$ is increasing and homogeneous of degree 1 in $\mathbf{W}$

The cost function evidently increases with the price of each input, since, for a given vector $\mathbf{X}$ of inputs, the rise in price W^i of input i increases the total cost of production. In order to show that the cost function is homogeneous, it is enough to note that for any positive number λ we have:

$$\underset{\mathbf{X} \in \mathcal{Y}}{\mathrm{Min}} \sum_{i=1}^{n} (\lambda W^i) X^i = \lambda \underset{\mathbf{X} \in \mathcal{Y}}{\mathrm{Min}} \sum_{i=1}^{n} W^i X^i$$

Put another way:

$$C(\lambda \mathbf{W}, Y) = \lambda C(\mathbf{W}, Y), \qquad \forall \lambda \geq 0, \forall (\mathbf{W}, Y)$$

Consequently the cost function is homogeneous of degree 1 with respect to vector $\mathbf{W} = (W^1, \ldots, W^n)$ of the input costs.

(ii) $C(\mathbf{W}, Y)$ is concave in $\mathbf{W}$

Given two vectors $\mathbf{W} = (W^1, \ldots, W^n)$ and $\mathbf{V} = (V^1, \ldots, V^n)$ of the input costs, we always have:

$$C(\mathbf{W}, Y) \leq \sum_{i=1}^{n} W^i X^i \qquad \forall \mathbf{X} \in \mathcal{Y} \tag{65}$$

$$C(\mathbf{V}, Y) \leq \sum_{i=1}^{n} V^i X^i \qquad \forall \mathbf{X} \in \mathcal{Y} \tag{66}$$

Let us take a scalar $\lambda \in [0, 1]$ and let us multiply relations (65) and (66) respectively by λ and $(1 - \lambda)$. If we add the results obtained side by side, we get:

$$\lambda C(\mathbf{W}, Y) + (1 - \lambda)C(\mathbf{V}, Y) \leq \sum_{i} [\lambda W^i + (1 - \lambda)V^i] X^i, \qquad \forall \lambda \in [0, 1], \forall \mathbf{X} \in \mathcal{Y}$$

This inequality being satisfied for any vector of inputs $\mathbf{X}$ of the set $\mathcal{Y}$, it implies in particular:

$$\lambda C(\mathbf{W}, Y) + (1 - \lambda)C(\mathbf{V}, Y) \leq \underset{\mathbf{X} \in \mathcal{Y}}{\mathrm{Min}} \sum_{i} [\lambda W^i + (1 - \lambda)V^i] X^i, \qquad \forall \lambda \in [0, 1] \tag{67}$$

By the definition of the cost function, we also have:

$$C[\lambda \mathbf{W} + (1 - \lambda)\mathbf{V}, Y] \equiv \underset{\mathbf{X} \in \mathcal{Y}}{\text{Min}} \sum_{i=1}^{n} [\lambda W^i + (1 - \lambda)V^i]X^i \tag{68}$$

Comparison of relations (67) and (68) then shows that the cost function satisfies the following inequality:

$$C[\lambda \mathbf{W} + (1 - \lambda)\mathbf{V}, Y] \geq \lambda C(\mathbf{W}, Y) + (1 - \lambda)C(\mathbf{V}, Y) \qquad \forall \lambda \in [0, 1], \ \forall (\mathbf{W}, \mathbf{V}, Y)$$

This proves the concavity of function $C(\mathbf{W}, Y)$ with respect to $\mathbf{W}$.

(iii) Shephard's Lemma

Let $\bar{\mathbf{X}} = (\bar{X}^1, \ldots, \bar{X}^n)$ be a vector minimizing the total cost when the unit prices of inputs are given by the vector $\mathbf{W} = (W^1, \ldots, W^n)$. In other terms, $\bar{\mathbf{X}}$ is a solution of the problem described by relation (64). For given Y, $\mathbf{W}$ and so $\mathbf{X}$, let us consider the function with n arguments $\Phi = \Phi(\mathbf{V})$, with $\mathbf{V} = (V^1, \ldots, V^n)$, defined by:

$$\Phi(\mathbf{V}) \equiv C(\mathbf{V}, Y) - \sum_{i=1}^{n} V^i \bar{X}^i \tag{69}$$

Since, by construction, we have:

$$C(\mathbf{V}, Y) = \underset{\mathbf{X} \in \mathcal{Y}}{\text{Min}} \sum_{i=1}^{n} V^i X^i, \qquad \forall \mathbf{V}$$

Relation (69) implies $\Phi(\mathbf{V}) \leq 0$, $\forall \mathbf{V}$. Still by definition of the cost function, relation (69) likewise entails $\Phi(\mathbf{W}) = 0$. Vector $\mathbf{W}$ thus represents a maximum for function $\Phi(.)$. For all i, the partial derivative of the latter with respect to V^i is thus null at point $\mathbf{W}$. Differentiating the two members of relation (69) with respect to V^i, we get:

$$\bar{X}^i = C_i(\mathbf{W}, Y), \qquad \forall i = 1, \ldots, n. \tag{70}$$

where C_i designates the partial derivative of the cost function with respect to its ith argument. Relation (70) constitutes Shephard's lemma.

(iv) The Case of a Homogeneous Production Function

Let us henceforth assume that the production function is homogeneous of degree $\theta > 0$. By the definition of the cost function, we have:

$$C(\mathbf{W}, \lambda Y) = \underset{\mathbf{X}}{\text{Min}} \sum_{i=1}^{n} W^i X^i \text{ s.c. } F(\mathbf{X}) \geq Y \tag{71}$$

In this problem, let us make the change of variable $\mathbf{Z} = \lambda^{-1/\theta}\mathbf{X}$, i.e. $Z^i = \lambda^{-1/\theta}X^i$ for all $i = 1, \ldots, n$. Problem (71) is then written:

$$C(\mathbf{W}, \lambda Y) = \lambda^{1/\theta} \underset{\mathbf{Z}}{\text{Min}} \sum_{i=1}^{n} W^i Z^i \text{ s.c. } F(\mathbf{Z}) \geq Y$$

We can immediately deduce:

$$C(\mathbf{W}, \lambda Y) = \lambda^{1/\theta} C(\mathbf{W}, Y) \tag{72}$$

This last equation shows that the cost function is indeed homogeneous of degree $1/\theta$ in Y when the production function is homogeneous of degree θ. Making $\lambda = 1/Y$ in (72), we arrive at:

$$C(\mathbf{W}, Y) = C(\mathbf{W}, 1) Y^{1/\theta}, \qquad \forall (\mathbf{W}, Y)$$

Applying Shephard's lemma (70), we find:

$$\bar{X}^i = C_i(\mathbf{W}, Y) = C_i(\mathbf{W}, 1) Y^{1/\theta}$$

Consequently the conditional demands functions are equally homogeneous of degree $1/\theta$ with respect to Y.

(v) Production Function with Two Inputs

When the only arguments of the production function are capital and labor, or $Y = F(K, L)$, all the relations previously established of course remain satisfied. In particular, if W designates the labor cost and R the user cost of capital, Shephard's lemma is written with the evident notations:

$$\bar{L} = C_W(W, R, Y) \qquad \text{and} \qquad \bar{K} = C_R(W, R, Y) \tag{73}$$

In order to find a simple expression of the elasticity of substitution between capital and labor, we must first note that the homogeneity to degree 1 of the cost function with respect to (W, R) implies:

$$C(W, R, Y) = R C(W/R, 1, Y), \qquad \forall (W, R, Y)$$

Differentiating this relation with respect to W and R entails successively:

$$C_W(W, R, Y) = C_W(W/R, 1, Y) \tag{74}$$

$$C_R(W, R, Y) = C(W/R, 1, Y) - (W/R) C_W(W/R, 1, Y) \tag{75}$$

If we now, for example, derive (74) with respect to R, we get:

$$C_{WR}(W, R, Y) = -\frac{W}{R^2} C_{WW}(W/R, 1, Y) \tag{76}$$

The cost function being concave, C_{WW} is negative or null, and in consequence we will necessarily have $C_{WR} \geq 0$. In the case of two factors of production, the elasticity of substitution σ is defined by:

$$\sigma = \frac{W/R}{\bar{K}/\bar{L}} \frac{\partial(\bar{K}/\bar{L})}{\partial(W/R)}$$

With the help of Shephard's lemma (73) and relations (74) and (75), we can write:

$$\frac{\bar{K}}{\bar{L}} = \frac{C_R(W, R, Y)}{C_W(W, R, Y)} = \frac{C(W/R, 1, Y) - (W/R) C_W(W/R, 1, Y)}{C_W(W/R, 1, Y)}$$

Or again:

$$\frac{\bar{K}}{\bar{L}} = \frac{C(W/R, 1, Y)}{C_W(W/R, 1, Y)} - \frac{W}{R}$$

Differentiating this equation with respect to W/R, we arrive at:

$$\frac{\partial(\bar{K}/\bar{L})}{\partial(W/R)} = -\frac{C(W/R, 1, Y)C_{WW}(W/R, 1, Y)}{C_W^2(W/R, 1, Y)}$$

Using (76) and Shephard's lemma (73), we find after rearranging terms that the elasticity of substitution between capital and labor satisfies the relation:

$$\sigma = \frac{C(W, R, Y)C_{WR}(W, R, Y)}{C_W(W, R, Y)C_R(W, R, Y)}$$

7.3   APPENDIX 3: THE OPTIMAL VALUE OF HOURS WORKED

If the amount of hours desired is such that $H \leq T$, the following inequality is satisfied:

$$\frac{\Omega T + (1 + x)\Omega(H - T) + Z}{e(H)} \geq \frac{\Omega H + Z}{e(H)} \tag{77}$$

In this case, if the minimum of function $\varphi(H) \equiv (\Omega H + Z)/e(H)$ lies within interval $[0, T]$, it represents a *global* minimum for function W defined by (34). Differentiating $\varphi(H)$ with respect to H, we find after several calculations:

$$\varphi'(H) = \frac{1}{He(H)}[(1 - \eta_H^e)\Omega H - Z\eta_H^e] \tag{78}$$

From that we deduce that optimal number of hours worked is given by:

$$H^* = \frac{\eta_H^e}{1 - \eta_H^e}\frac{Z}{\Omega} \tag{79}$$

For this value of H to be smaller than T it is necessary and sufficient that the following inequality be satisfied:

$$\frac{Z}{\Omega T} \leq \frac{1 - \eta_H^e}{\eta_H^e}$$

Moreover, equations (78) and (79) show that at the optimum, we have:

$$\varphi''(H^*) = \frac{(1 - \eta_H^e)\Omega}{H^* e(H^*)}$$

And the second-order condition for a minimum, or $\varphi'' > 0$, then dictates $\eta_H^e < 1$. The first line of relation (35) is thus proved.

If the desired number of hours is such that $H \geq T$, the inequality (79) is inverted and the minimum of the function $\psi(H) \equiv [\Omega T + (1 + x)\Omega(H - T) + Z]/e(H)$ represents a global minimum for function W. Differentiating $\psi(H)$ with respect to H, we get:

$$\psi'(H) = \frac{1}{He(H)}[(1 - \eta_H^e)(1 + x)\Omega H - (Z - \Omega xT)\eta_H^e] \tag{80}$$

The optimum number of hours worked is then given by:

$$H = \frac{\eta_H^e}{1 - \eta_H^e} \frac{Z - \Omega x T}{(1 + x)\Omega} \tag{81}$$

This value of H is greater than T when:

$$\frac{Z}{\Omega T} \geq \frac{1 + x - \eta_H^e}{\eta_H^e}$$

Equations (80) and (81) again imply at the optimum:

$$\psi''(H) = \frac{(1 - \eta_H^e)(1 + x)\Omega}{He(H)}$$

And the second-order condition for a minimum always comes down to $\eta_H^e < 1$. The second line of relation (35) is thus established.

Finally, the optimum number of hours worked coincides with standard hours ($H = T$), when the minima of functions $\varphi(H)$ and $\psi(H)$ are not respectively in the intervals $[0, T]$ and $[T, +\infty]$. This configuration appears when the following inequalities are satisfied:

$$\frac{1 - \eta_H^e}{\eta_H^e} \leq \frac{Z}{\Omega T} \leq \frac{1 + x - \eta_H^e}{\eta_H^e}$$

Thus the third line of relation (35) is proved.

REFERENCES

Abowd, J., and Kramarz, F. (2003), ''The costs of hiring and separations,'' working paper #9543, CREST-INSEE, forthcoming in *Labour Economics*.

Abraham, K., and Houseman, S. (1993), *Job Security in America: Lessons from Germany*, Washington, D.C.: Brookings Institution.

Angrist, J. (1996), ''Short run demand for Palestinian labor,'' *Journal of Labor Economics*, 14, pp. 425–453.

Anxo, D., and O'Reilly, J. (2000), ''Working time regimes and transitions in comparative perspective,'' in O'Reilly, J. (ed.), *Working Time Changes: Social Integration Through Transitional Labour Market*, Edward Elgar.

Arrow, K., Chenery, H., Minhas, B., and Solow, R. (1961), ''Capital-labor substitution and economic efficiency,'' *Review of Economics and Statistics*, 43, pp. 225–250.

Author, D., Katz, L., and Krueger, A. (1998), ''Computing inequalities: Have computers changed the labor market?'' *Quarterly Journal of Economics*, 113, pp. 1169–1213.

Bentolila, S., and Bertola, G. (1990), ''Firing costs and labor demand: How bad is Eurosclerosis?'' *Review of Economic Studies*, 57, pp. 381–402.

Bentolila, S., and Saint-Paul, G. (1994), ''A model of labor demand with linear adjustment costs,'' *Labour Economics*, 1, pp. 303–326.

Bertola, G. (1990), "Job security, employment and wages," *European Economic Review*, 34, pp. 851–886.

Bertola, G. (1999), "Microeconomic perspectives on aggregate labor markets," in Ashenfelter, O., and Card, D. (eds.), *Handbook of Labor Economics*, vol. 3C, chap. 45, pp. 2985–3028, Amsterdam: Elsevier Science/North-Holland.

Bertola, G., and Rogerson, R. (1997), "Institutions and labor reallocation," *European Economic Review*, 41, pp. 1147–1171.

Blanchard, O., and Fischer, S. (1989), *Lectures on Macroeconomics*, Cambridge, Mass.: MIT Press.

Bresson, G., Sevestre, P., and Teurlai, J.-C. (1996), "The specification of labor adjustment costs: A microeconomic comparative study," Working Paper, ERUDITE, University of Paris 12.

Calmfors, L., and Hoel, M. (1988), "Work sharing and overtime," *Scandinavian Journal of Economics*, 90, pp. 45–62.

Chang, C., and Stefanou, S. (1988), "Specification and estimation of asymmetric adjustment rates for quasi fixed factors of production," *Journal of Economic Dynamics and Control*, 12, pp. 145–151.

Christensen, L., Jorgenson, D., and Lau, L. (1973), "Transcendental logarithmic production frontiers," *Review of Economics and Statistics*, 55, pp. 28–45.

Cobb, C., and Douglas, P. (1928), "A theory of production," *American Economic Review, Papers and Proceedings*, 18, pp. 139–165.

Dertouzos, J., and Karoly, L. (1990), "Labor market responses to employer liability," mimeo, Santa Monica, Calif.: Rand Corporation.

Diewert, W. (1971), "An application of the Shephard duality theorem, a generalized Leontief production function," *Journal of Political Economy*, 79, pp. 481–507.

Dixit, A. (1997), "Investment and employment dynamics in the short run and the long run," *Oxford Economic Papers*, 49, pp. 1–20.

Eisner, R., and Strotz, R. (1963), "Determinants of business investment," in *Impacts of Monetary Policy*, Part I, Commission on Money and Credit, Englewood Cliffs, N.J.: Prentice Hall, pp. 59–223.

Fair, R. (1985), "Excess labor and the business cycle," *American Economic Review*, 75, pp. 239–245.

Fay, J., and Medoff, J. (1985), "Labor and output over the business cycle," *American Economic Review*, 75, pp. 638–655.

Gianella, C., and Lagarde, P. (1999), "Productivity of hours in the aggregate production function: An evaluation on a panel of French firms from the manufacturing sector," Document de Travail G 9918, Direction des Etudes et Synthèses Economiques, INSEE.

Goux, D., Maurin, E., and Pauchet, M. (2001), "Fixed-term contracts and the dynamics of labour demand," *European Economic Review*, 45, pp. 533–552.

Hamermesh, D. (1993), *Labor Demand*, Princeton, N.J.: Princeton University Press.

Hamermesh, D. (1995), "Labour demand and the source of adjustment costs," *Economic Journal*, 105, pp. 620–634.

Hamermesh, D. (2001), "Overtime laws and the margins of work timing," mimeo, University of Texas, http://www.eco.utexas.edu/faculty/Hamermesh.

Hamermesh, D., and Pfann, G. (1996), "Adjustment costs in factor demand," *Journal of Economic Literature*, 34, pp. 1264–1292.

Hamermesh, D., and Trejo, S. (2000), "The demand for hours of labor: Direct evidence from California," *Review of Economics and Statistics*, 82, pp. 38–47.

Hamilton, J. (1994), *Time Series Analysis*, Princeton, N.J.: Princeton University Press.

Hart, R. (1987), *Working Time and Employment*, Boston: Allen and Unwin.

Hart, R., and MacGregor, P. (1988), "The returns to labour services in West German manufacturing industry," *European Economic Review*, 32, pp. 947–963.

Hicks, J. (1932), *The Theory of Wages*, New York: Macmillan.

Holt, C., Modigliani, F., Muth, J., and Simon, H. (1960), *Planning, Production, Inventories and Work Force*, Englewood Cliffs, N.J.: Prentice Hall.

Hunt, J. (1999), "Has work-sharing worked in Germany?" *Quarterly Journal of Economics*, 114, pp. 117–148.

Jaramillo, F., Schantarelli, F., and Sembenelli, A. (1993), "Are adjustement costs for labor asymmetric? An econometric test on panel data for Italy," *Review of Economics and Statistics*, 75, pp. 640–648.

Johnson, G. (1997), "Changing in earnings inequality: The role of demand shift," *Journal of Economic Perspectives*, 11(2), pp. 41–54.

Lazear, E. (1990), "Job security provision and employment," *Quarterly Journal of Economics*, 105, pp. 699–726.

Leslie, D., and Wise, J. (1980), "The productivity of hours in UK manufacturing and production industries," *Economic Journal*, 90, pp. 74–84.

Lucas, R. (1967), "Optimal investment policy and the flexible accelerator," *International Economic Review*, 8, pp. 78–85.

Marshall, A. (1920), *Principles of Economics*, New York: Macmillan.

Messe, R. (1980), "Dynamic factor demand schedules for labor and capital under rational expectations," *Journal of Econometrics*, 14, pp. 141–158.

Nadiri, M., and Rosen, S. (1973), *A Disequilibrium Model of Production*, New York: National Bureau of Economic Research.

OECD (1999), *Employment Outlook*, Paris: OECD.

Pfann, G., and Palm, F. (1993), "Asymmetric adjustment costs in non-linear labour demand models for the Netherlands and UK manufacturing sectors," *Review of Economic Studies*, 60, pp. 397–412.

Rosen, S. (1968), "Short run employment variation on class-1 railroads in the U.S., 1947–63," *Econometrica*, 36, pp. 511–529.

Sargent, T. (1986), *Macroeconomic Theory*, Boston: Academic Press.

Takayama, A. (1986), *Mathematical Economics*, and ed., Cambridge, U.K.: Cambridge University Press.

Trejo, S. (1991), "The effects of overtime pay regulation on worker compensation," *American Economic Review*, 81, pp. 719–740.

WAGE FORMATION

CHAPTER 5

COMPENSATING WAGE DIFFERENTIALS AND DISCRIMINATION

CONTENTS

In this chapter, we will:

- Understand why, in a situation of perfect competition, the hedonic theory predicts that wage differentials compensate for the laboriousness or danger of tasks

- See that the existence of social norms may hamper the efficiency of perfect competition

- Understand why obstacles to perfect competition, such as barriers to entry or imperfect information, may entail differences between wages and marginal productivity, as well as a level of employment falling below that achievable under perfect competition

- Understand why obstacles to perfect competition may give rise to situations of discrimination in which some persons obtain lower wages than others because of their membership in particular demographic groups

- Learn what "statistical discrimination" is and why it can lead to persistent inequalities among demographic groups

- See that empirical work indicates that the mechanisms of competition play an important role in the labor market, and that discrimination influences wage differences between certain demographic groups

INTRODUCTION

Why does John earn a lower wage than Jane? A number of possible reasons come to mind. Jane stayed in school longer, or obtained a more prestigious diploma. Jane's work is more demanding, with heavy responsibilities. Jane is older, or has been with her company longer. She is more highly motivated and efficient. John is the victim of discrimination against men. John works in a region where the average wage is lower, and so on.

One of the purposes of labor economics is to assess how relevant, and how significant, each of these reasons is. On the theoretical level, we must specify which hypotheses are being used to justify every explanation offered for wage differentials. For example, we must inquire into the extent to which discrimination against women (Jane is an exception) may exist and persist. The answers to questions of this type are not trivial, and without elaborating a simple yet rigorous conceptual framework to represent the different elements that influence wages, they cannot be given. The frame of reference adopted by economic analysis is the model of perfect competition. When applied to labor economics, it explains the formation of wages by assuming that they match all labor supply with all labor demand; the attendant hypotheses are that agents have no market power because there is free entry into the market and information is perfect. This frame of reference leads to positive conclusions about the setting of compensation for labor that empirical studies allow us to confirm or reject. If the conclusions are massively rejected, then we need to formulate theoretical frameworks in which competition is imperfect, and subject them in turn to the rigors of empirical testing.

In the first section of this chapter, we will see that the hypothesis of perfect competition yields a very rich theory about wage setting, with a number of implications. Since wages match labor supply and demand, they depend on both the characteristics of workers and the characteristics of jobs. Briefly, the model of perfect competition leads to the conclusion that each worker gets a wage equal to that job's marginal productivity. The productivity of a job depends on the abilities of the worker and the attributes of the job. This approach suggests that workers can always find a job if they are prepared to accept wages and working conditions compatible with their abilities, which in turn implies that the unemployed choose not to work because they judge the jobs on offer to be insufficiently attractive. In other words, perfect competition in labor markets leads to an *efficient allocation of resources* if the decisions of the agents do not entail externalities. In this connection, we will see that the existence of social norms may entail externalities, the consequence of which is that the equality between wages and marginal productivities does not ensure an optimal allocation of resources.

If the assumptions of perfect competition are not fulfilled, wage differentials reflect elements other than productivity differences. Sections 2 and 3 focus on what occurs when there are obstacles to perfect competitition. The first of these obstacles consists of barriers to free entry into the market, such as the presence of coalitions of workers—trade unions, for the most part—the behavior of which will be studied in chapter 7. Here we will merely highlight the consequences of market power by looking at the results of a monopsony, i.e., the presence of a single firm in a particular labor pool. More generally, monopsony power is a specific case of labor mobility costs, which in this case work to the benefit of employers. But we will see that other costs of this type, such as hiring and firing costs or training costs, may work to the advantage of wage-earners and may be accompanied by wage gaps that do not reflect productivity differences alone.

Another obstacle to perfect competition is the limited information available in the labor market. In chapter 3 we showed that imperfect information possessed by workers about the characteristics of the jobs on offer provoked search behavior on their part that entailed, in particular, a dispersion of wages resulting from the behavior of firms, which may have an interest in offering high wages so as to be able to attract and hire a large number of workers (see chapter 3, section 2.3). In this context, we noted that workers with greater seniority generally have higher wages, even if their productivity is exactly the same as that of co-workers with less experience. This kind of explanation for the rising relationship between age and wage earnings is very different from the one put forward by the competitive model of the labor market. Job search models therefore throw light on the consequences of the lack of information on the part of workers concerning the characteristics of *jobs*. This light is interesting but partial, inasmuch as employers too dispose of limited information about the characteristics of *workers*. Without perfect information, employers face selection problems that have repercussions on the way the labor market functions. Labor economics has identified three important problems linked to the recruitment strategies of employers. Firms in particular usually have incomplete information about the productive abilities of suppliers of labor and are thus faced with *selection* problems that affect their wage strategies. Conversely, workers may have an interest in "signaling" their abilities to employers by, for example, obtaining degrees from recognized educational institutions (see chapter 2, section 3). Finally, the limited transparency of labor markets may give rise to ongoing situations of discrimination. Whatever their origin, these deviations from perfect competition emerge in the form of wage differentials that do not compensate for any difference in working conditions or competence on the part of workers.

Empirical tests of the predictions of perfect competition and of the consequences of the obstacles to its application are often made jointly, and for that reason we have left our review of overall empirical results to the last section of this chapter.

1 PERFECT COMPETITION AND COMPENSATING WAGE DIFFERENTIALS

Economic analysis shows that perfect competition in the labor markets ought to lead to a wage heterogeneity that results purely from the fact that some jobs are harder to do than others, and some suppliers of labor are more competent than others. Differences arising from hard working conditions are explained by the *hedonic theory of wages*, the premises of which were sketched by Adam Smith at the end of the eighteenth century and have more recently been formalized by Rosen (1974). Wage differences linked to individual competence are explained by the *theory of human capital*, which rests on the idea that education leads individuals to become competent in ways that have value in the labor market. The foundations of this theory were laid by Becker (1964).

A wage-paying job entitles one to receive compensation. In exchange, the wage-earner must carry out a set of tasks that may be more or less harsh according to the speed at which he or she has to perform them, the work environment, the risk of accidents, and even the social prestige attached to that job. Adam Smith noted at the outset that workers with the same level of competence should be paid different wages if their working conditions are different. The hedonic theory of wages proposed by Rosen in 1974 accounts for wage heterogeneity arising from these "compensating differentials." It shows that the mechanism of perfect competition provides reimbursement for the workers who hold the hardest jobs. This mechanism also allows workers, whose preferences are by nature heterogeneous, to choose how hard a job they are willing to take in view of the wage differences created by competition. These mechanisms also ensure that the allocation of workers over a range of jobs is socially efficient.

To avoid any risk of confusion, we must distinguish clearly between the harsh conditions linked to a job, which vary from one job to another, and the disutility of work, which varies from one individual to another for the same job. To better grasp the implications of this distinction, let us first take the case in which all jobs are equally hard.

1.1 PERFECT COMPETITION WITH JOBS OF EQUAL DIFFICULTY

Let us recall that a market works according to the principles of perfect competition if it presents two characteristics. *Transparency:* agents are perfectly informed about the quality of the product and its price. *Free entry:* agents may enter and exit the market without cost. With these two hypotheses, perfectly competitive equilibrium is characterized by prices that match supply and demand. When all jobs are equally hard, supply is principally determined by the disutility of work, which varies from one individual to another.

Supply and Demand
Let us consider a market that has the two characteristics just outlined and in which it is possible to produce an exogenous quantity y of a good, thanks to a unit of labor,

which, for the sake of simplicity, is the sole input. There is a large number of workers, all of whom supply a unit of labor and receive a wage w (expressed in units of the good produced) if they are hired. The welfare of a worker is evaluated using a utility function $u(R, e, \theta)$ with three arguments. Income R is equal to wage w when the worker is employed, and equal to zero when he or she is not. Parameter e measures the effort (or the disagreeability) attached to each of the jobs. We assume that this disagreeability is identical for all jobs, and without any loss of generality, we will assume that parameter e is equal to 1 if there is a hire and equal to zero if not. The parameter $\theta \geq 0$ represents the disutility (or the opportunity cost) of labor for the individual considered. In this model, all the jobs thus have the *same* "intrinsic" difficulty e, but individuals react differently to the difficulty of the tasks confronting them. Those with a low θ accept it more easily than those with a high θ. The cumulative distribution function of parameter θ will be denoted by $G(.)$. Finally, in order to simplify, we will assume that an agent's utility function takes a linear form equal to the difference between the income and the opportunity cost of labor, or $u(R, e, \theta) = R - e\theta$.

Under the hypothesis of free entry, firms create jobs up to the point where no more opportunity for profit is left. Since firms make a profit equal to $y - w$ for every job, labor demand is infinite if $w < y$, lies between zero and infinity if $w = y$, and is zero if $w > y$. The labor demand that results from the condition of free entry is then written:

$$L^d = \begin{cases} +\infty & \text{if } w < y \\ [0, +\infty) & \text{if } w = y \\ 0 & \text{if } w > y \end{cases} \tag{1}$$

A worker with characteric θ attains a level of utility equal to $w - \theta$ if he or she is hired, and zero if he or she does not work. Consequently, only individuals whose opportunity cost θ is less than the wage decide to work. If we normalize the measure of the labor force to 1, then labor supply is equal to $G(w)$.

Equilibrium and Optimum

The functioning of the labor market is represented in figure 5.1, in which the quantity of labor is shown on the vertical axis and the wage on the horizontal axis. Labor demand is composed of two parts: a horizontal line with ordinate equal to zero if the wage is superior to individual production, and a vertical line with abscissa y. Labor supply, equal to $G(w)$, is represented by an increasing curve passing through the origin. At labor market equilibrium, supply is equal to demand. Figure 5.1 shows that labor supply and demand curves admit a sole intersection point, the coordinates of which are $(y, G(y))$. The equilibrium wage is thus necessarily equal to y, which entails zero profits. Employment and labor supply take the value $G(y)$, which signifies that only individuals for whom the disutility of work θ is less than the equilibrium wage y decide to work.

It is important to emphasize that the allocation of individuals between employment and nonparticipation is efficient, for every worker takes up the occupation at

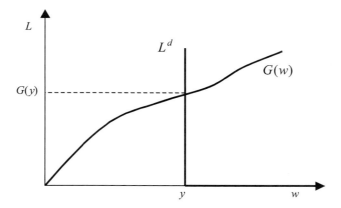

FIGURE 5.1
Market equilibrium with perfect competition.

which he or she is most productive. Workers whose opportunity cost θ is greater than productivity y remain outside the labor market, while all others enter it and find work. An omniscient planner with the task of assigning workers to employment or nonparticipation so as to maximize the sum of individual utilities would choose exactly the same allocation as the one that results from the competitive equilibrium, for such a planner must choose the threshold value of θ that maximizes the sum of individual utilities, equal to $\int_0^\theta (y - x)\, dG(x)$. The solution of this problem[1] gives $\theta = y$, which is the level of employment obtained at competitive equilibrium.

1.2 Compensating Wage Differentials and the Hedonic Theory of Wages

When the jobs on offer to workers vary with respect to how difficult they are to do, perfect competition ensures that these differences will be compensated for by wage differentials. Equilibrium is still identified as a social optimum, and any measures aimed at reducing the difficulty of jobs do not improve welfare.

Wages and the Difficulty of Jobs

Let us now introduce heterogeneity among jobs arising from the difficulty of the work to be done. To that end, we adapt the previous model by assuming that there exists a continuum of jobs, each requiring a different level of effort $e > 0$. This effort variable is a synthetic measure of the difficulty of jobs and so covers a number of dimensions such as accident risk, hours of work, environment, and the advantages, whether in kind or in status, that flow from holding a particular job. Strictly speaking, e should thus be a vector with as many coordinates as there are characteristics to any job, but for the sake of simplicity, we reduce heterogeneity to a single dimension. Various aspects of the actual content of jobs will be examined in greater detail in section 4.1 below, in which we present the relevant empirical work.

The productivity of every sort of job is an increasing and concave function of effort, or $y = f(e)$ with $f'(e) > 0$, $f''(e) < 0$, and $f(0) = 0$. Productivity y here corresponds to production *net* of any costs occasioned by employment. For example, if we interpret e as a measure of industrial accident risk, it is generally possible to reduce these risks by reducing the intensity of work, or by making expenditures that achieve the same result. In either case, jobs that offer lower risk have less productivity in our model. As previously, we assume that the utility function of an agent takes the linear form $u(R, e, \theta) = R - e\theta$, and that effort e is strictly positive when the worker is employed and amounts to zero when he or she is not participating.

The hypothesis of free entry here entails that, for every type of work, profits are zero and the wage equals productivity. If $w(e)$ denotes the equilibrium wage that applies to jobs that demand effort e, then we have $w(e) = f(e)$. A worker with information about all jobs at his or her disposal and who enjoys perfect mobility is able to "visit" different markets and choose the job that gives him or her the greatest satisfaction. If he or she chooses a job in which effort equals e, he or she will receive wage $f(e)$. Hence the problem for each worker consists of selecting a value of effort that maximizes his or her satisfaction $u[f(e), e, \theta]$ subject to participation constraint $u(w, e, \theta) \geq u(0, 0, \theta) = 0$. This constraint signifies that the worker accepts a waged job if in doing so his or her situation becomes preferable to nonparticipation (where $R = e = 0$). The first-order condition of this problem, necessary and sufficient as a consequence of the concavity of function f, gives:

$$\begin{cases} f'(e) = \theta \Leftrightarrow e = e(\theta) & \text{if } f[e(\theta)] - \theta e(\theta) \geq 0 \\ e = 0 & \text{otherwise} \end{cases} \tag{2}$$

The first line of this equation indicates that an agent chooses the job in which the marginal return to effort $f'(e)$ is equal to the disutility θ that it gives rise to. As $f'(e)$ is decreasing with e, optimal effort $e(\theta)$ diminishes with parameter θ measuring aversion to effort. The equilibrium wage received by a worker of type θ in equilibrium is $w[e(\theta)] = f[e(\theta)]$, the remuneration of tough jobs is a "compensating" wage differential, since wages increase with effort.

This point is illustrated graphically in figure 5.2, which represents the choice of two types of worker. Type θ^+ is characterized by a stronger aversion to effort than type $\theta^- < \theta^+$. The effort is on the horizontal axis and the wage is on the vertical axis. An indifference curve—which, let us recall, is the set of points (e, w) at which an individual obtains the same level of utility—is represented for both types of worker. The indifference curves are straight lines with slope θ. For a given θ, an upward shift of the indifference curve corresponds to increased satisfaction. Hence each worker chooses a level of effort e such that one of his or her indifference curves is tangent to $f(e)$. In consequence, individuals with a strong aversion to effort choose low-effort jobs with correspondingly low wages.

The second line of equation (2) indicates that individuals whose aversion to effort is too large, i.e., such that $\theta > f[e(\theta)]/e(\theta)$, decide not to work. In our model, scrutiny of figure 5.2 shows that all individuals of type $\theta > f'(0)$ prefer not to

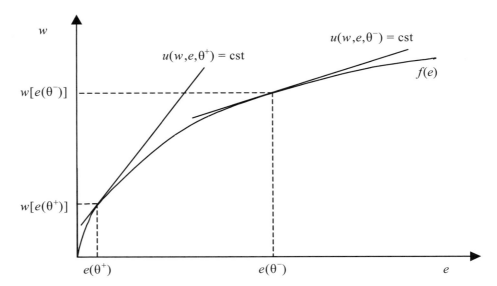

FIGURE 5.2
The hedonic theory of wages.

participate in the labor market, because they have indifference curves that are steeper at the origin than the slope of function $f(e)$.

Normative Implications of the Hedonic Theory of Wages
According to the hedonic theory of wages, the mechanisms of perfect competition allow workers to choose different working conditions, with wage differentials "compensating" for the greater difficulty of some jobs. Moreover, competitive equilibrium allocations are efficient, furnishing each worker with an income $w[e(\theta)] = f[e(\theta)]$ and inducing a level of employment $G'(\theta)$ on the job market of type θ. This means that each worker is engaged in the task for which the difference between what he or she produces and the disutility that he or she undergoes is greatest. This result emerges if we look at the problem of a planner assigning workers to different jobs in such a way as to maximize the sum of utilities. Such a planner would choose the effort of each individual and the threshold value of θ, denoted by θ^*, beyond which individuals no longer participate, in such a way as to resolve the following problem:

$$\max_{\{\theta^*, e(\theta)\}} \int_0^{\theta^*} \{f[e(\theta)] - \theta e(\theta)\}\, dG(\theta)$$

The first-order conditions of this problem give $f[e(\theta^*)] = \theta^* e(\theta^*)$ and $f'[e(\theta)] = \theta$, $\forall \theta \in [0, \theta^*]$. These last two equalities entail $f[e(\theta^*)]/e(\theta^*) = f'[e(\theta^*)]$. Function f being concave, this condition entails $e(\theta^*) = 0$, and so $\theta^* = f'(0)$. So we come back to the competitive equilibrium allocation, in which the return on effort and its marginal cost

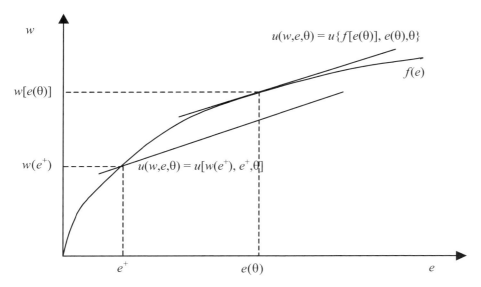

$u(w,e,\theta) = u\{f[e(\theta)], e(\theta),\theta\}$

$f(e)$

$w[e(\theta)]$

$w(e^+)$

$u(w,e,\theta) = u[w(e^+), e^+,\theta]$

e^+

$e(\theta)$

e

w

FIGURE 5.3
The impact of a legal constraint on accident risk.

are equal and in which only individuals of type $\theta \leq f'(0)$ participate in the labor market.

The efficiency of the competitive equilibrium has the corollary that steps taken by the public authorities to make jobs less demanding are undesirable if and only if markets function according to the principles of perfect competition. If there is no a priori restriction on the type of job supplied, the ones that are very difficult because, for example, they are highly dangerous are chosen and remunerated in full awareness of the pros and cons. In addition, any legal constraint that limits the difficulty of doing them results in a welfare loss. We can more clearly grasp the sense of this result if we ponder the impact of a policy aiming to reduce accident risk by putting security regulations in place. Let us assume that the variable of effort e simply equals accident risk and that public policy consists of imposing an upper limit e^+ to this risk. The introduction of this constraint entails a welfare loss for all individuals whose disutility of labor θ is such that effort $e(\theta)$, defined by equation (2), is greater than e^+. Figure 5.3 shows us how the situation of such an individual changes. This situation corresponds to an indifference curve associated with a lower level of utility in the presence of the constraint on accident risk. The individual in this case also receives a lower wage, equal to $f(e^+)$.

It is worthwhile to insist on the fact that the uselessness of public interventions when it comes to the difficulty or danger of working conditions has been established only when markets function in accordance with all the principles of perfect competition (perfect information, free entry). We will see in sections 2 and 3 that in a large number of cases, these conditions are not all met at the same time. Furthermore, as we will now proceed to demonstrate, the existence of externalities may constitute a source of inefficiency in the funtioning of the labor market, even if the hypotheses of free entry and perfect information are satisfied. Social norms provide an example of externalities of this kind.

1.3 Social Norms and the Inefficiency of Perfect Competition

Numerous empirical studies suggest that social norms such as equity or morality influence the formation of wages. For example, Bewley (1998) states, on the basis of a survey of 300 people involved in formulating wage policies (managers of companies, trade unionists, consultants, etc.): "My findings support none of the existing economic theories of wage rigidity, except those that emphasize the impact of pay cuts on morale" (Bewley, 1998, p. 460). Surveys of company managers by Blinder and Choi (1990) and Campbell and Kamlani (1997) found that managers gave the need for equity top priority. This need can be taken into account in our basic model by making the preferences of workers depend on the average wage that prevails in the economy.

1.3.1 Social Norms and Wage Formation

The idea that individuals are particularly attached to a feeling of *equity* is reinforced by work in psychology (Adams, 1963; Argyle, 1989) and organization theory (Lawler, 1994). When applied to labor relations within a firm, this idea signifies that an employee expects that his or her effort will be rewarded by remuneration regarded as fair. On the other side, the employer takes for granted that in exchange for the wage paid, his or her employee will also supply an effort regarded as fair. This concept is linked to the work of anthropologists in the tradition of Mauss (1923): it amounts to comparing a variety of exchange relationships, unfolding over a sufficiently extended period, to a sequence of *gifts* and *countergifts*. The article of Akerlof (1982) brought it back within the purview of economists. According to Akerlof, the employee's gift consists of exceeding prevailing work standards, in exchange for which the employer pays him or her a wage exceeding the so-called "reference" wage.

According to Akerlof (1982), the importance of fairness is enhanced by the fact, widely documented, that numerous employees do surpass prevailing work standards in their firms, yet at the same time those whose performance doesn't meet those standards are not systematically fired. Observations of this kind cannot be understood using the traditional neoclassical model. For Akerlof, the explanation has to be sought, in part, in the domain of sociology: an employee has a tendency to develop "feelings" for his or her firm, and for the smaller group consisting of his or her colleagues. In these circumstances, an employee derives satisfaction from making a "gift" of extra effort to the firm, a satisfaction analogous to that which he or she would feel when offering an unusually valuable present to a friend or relative. In this case, the employer clearly has no interest in raising work standards. Likewise, if an employee takes satisfaction from the well-being of the co-workers in his or her group, the firm does not necessarily have an interest in getting rid of those who are less productive, or even in checking on them more closely than on the rest. In their celebrated study of the behavior of American soldiers during the Second World War, Stouffer et al. (1949) observed that during training exercises, soldiers with greater physical capacities spontaneously helped out the weaker ones, without looking for any personal advantage. For those soldiers, it was probably a case of increasing their own satisfaction by raising that of the group as a whole.

1.3.2   An Illustrative Model

The consequences of equity for wage formation and employment can be illustrated by assuming, following Akerlof (1982), that the preferences of workers are influenced by social norms.

Effort and Equity

Let us consider a labor market with a continuum of identical workers, the measure of which is normalized to 1. Let ω be the average wage prevailing in the economy. The preferences of a worker are represented by a utility function $u(R, e, \omega) = R[1 + \beta(e/\omega)] - (e^2/2)$, with $\beta \geq 0$. In this expression, e represents the level of effort that will be chosen by a worker if he or she is hired (the value of e is zero for all those who do not participate in the labor market). The variable R designates income, equal to wage w if the worker is employed, and equal to the opportunity cost of labor, denoted by θ, otherwise. Parameter θ is characterized by a cumulative distribution function $G(.)$ defined for the set of nonnegative real numbers. When β is strictly positive, this specification of preferences expresses the hypothesis that an individual takes more satisfaction from his or her effort the higher his or her relative wage, w/ω, is. It fits well with the notion of fairness just discussed. Finally, we assume that individual production is simply equal to the level of effort e. The free entry condition entails zero profit, and thus a wage w equal to individual production.

If preferences are unaffected by considerations of fairness ($\beta = 0$), and if the labor market is perfectly competitive, the level of effort maximizes $e - (e^2/2)$, which entails $e = 1$. The utility of employed workers is equal to $\frac{1}{2}$. All individuals with a characteristic θ less than $\frac{1}{2}$ decide to work, and total employment amounts to $G\left(\frac{1}{2}\right)$.

If we now assume that $\beta > 0$, we are in a position to show that considerations of fairness can lead employers to offer relatively high wages in order to take advantage of the process of "gift exchange." Under this hypothesis, each worker takes ω as given and chooses his or her level of effort by solving the following problem:

$$\underset{e}{\text{Max}} \ e[1 + \beta(e/\omega)] - (e^2/2)$$

Optimal effort $e(\omega)$ is thus equal to $[1 - 2(\beta/\omega)]^{-1}$. Since each worker chooses his or her level of effort as a function of the average wage, the equilibrium is necessarily symmetric. We thus have $e = \omega$ at equilibrium, and so effort and wage are characterized by the equalities:

$$e = w = 1 + 2\beta$$

This relation shows that social norms influence productivity and effort at equilibrium. Workers are given an incentive to make an extra effort, and receive high wages in exchange. Employed workers obtain a utility equal to $\beta + \left(\frac{1}{2}\right)$, and employment rises to level $G\left[\beta + \left(\frac{1}{2}\right)\right]$, which is larger than that obtained in the absence of fairness considerations. Hence employment does also depend on social norms, and this dependence increases with the importance workers place on equity. This result is not, however, general; Akerlof (1982) and Akerlof and Yellen (1990) have presented examples of fairness actually increasing unemployment.

Nevertheless, this model does allow us to illustrate a very general result: the inefficiency of competitive equilibrium in the presence of social norms. For a given value of β, the optimal allocation is calculated by maximizing the sum of the utilities of workers present in the market in a symmetric situation in which each worker supplies the same level of effort, or $e = \omega$. That amounts to maximizing the utility of every worker with $e = \omega$. We then obtain $e = 1 + \beta$, which corresponds to a level of effort increasing with the degree of consideration for fairness, but inferior to that obtained at competitive equilibrium. The social norm is like an externality that compromises the efficiency of the competitive mechanism.

Fairness: A Vague Notion

The approach proposed by Akerlof makes the representation of preferences richer by integrating an explicitly social dimension. From this point of view it is of great interest and forms part of a larger movement attempting to take this dimension into account in different areas of economics (see Weiss and Fershtman, 1998, for a presentation of this current of thought). The drawback to this approach, however, is that it makes the core results depend on the choice of an a priori definition of the structure of individual preferences. Fundamentally, the theory of fairness amounts to postulating the existence of an externality in the utility function. The ad hoc aspect of this externality is not the weak point of this theory—theoretical work often proceeds in this way—but the absence of unanimous agreement about its nature is. At present there are too many elements that may enter into the concept of fairness for it to be capable of yielding a robust theory of wages. Economic analysis has simply not yet succeeded in formulating a concept of fairness strong enough to compel unanimity. Works based on experimental economics (see Fehr and Falk, 1999, for example) constitute an important source of information in this regard and may make it possible to achieve such a formulation in the future.

The hypotheses of perfect competition are very restrictive, and in practice their relevance is far from being universal. That being so, we cannot be certain that wage differences are the result of a socially efficient mechanism that rewards different levels of competence and different working conditions. In the next section, we begin by examining the consequences of barriers to entry into the markets, and then in section 3, the consequences of limited transparency of information.

2 OBSTACLES TO PERFECT COMPETITION (1): BARRIERS TO ENTRY

The presence of market power in numerous labor markets is manifested most commonly in the form of coalitions of employees and employers. These coalitions decide wages and working conditions jointly, through negotiation. We will study this question in chapter 7, dedicated to collective bargaining, but it is instructive to examine here the consequences of monopsony situations—those in which a single employer confronts a large number of suppliers of labor. We will see, on the basis of two examples, that a labor market dominated by a monopsony functions very differently from a market with perfect competition. In the first example, the introduction of a minimum wage in the presence of a monopsony may result in a rise in employment, something that cannot happen under perfect competition, where all workers whose productivity is inferior to the minimum wage see their jobs destroyed. In the second, the existence of a monopsony may give rise to a situation in which persons belonging to certain categories of the population—ethnic minorities, for example—receive lower wages than others although their productivity is identical. These categories undergo a discrimination that does not exist in a perfectly competitive market but that may persist in a monopsonistic one.

Fundamentally, monopsony is one of the textbook cases in which mobility costs work to the disadvantage of wage-earners. If these costs did not exist, the monopsony would be powerless vis-à-vis employees, who could quit their jobs at any time. But the converse is just as valid: the costs of hiring, firing, and training are obstacles to mobility of jobs that can be exploited by employees in such a way as to capture a share of the rent. No matter what their source, mobility costs and the rent-sharing that attends them generate wage differentials that are unrelated to productivity differentials and that hinder the efficiency of the competitive mechanism.

2.1 MONOPSONY

The existence of monopsony power is only conceivable in the presence of some kind of barrier that prevents others from gaining access to the labor market that it dominates. This form of imperfect competition allows the monopsonist firm to discriminate against certain categories of workers for long spells without being forced out of the market.

2.1.1 Wage, Employment, and Monopsony Power

A monopsony has a tendency to exert a negative effect on wages and employment. The existence of a monopsony presupposes limited mobility on the part of those who supply labor, and entry costs that bar other firms from coming in to compete.

The Basic Model

The monopsony faces a labor supply $L^s(w) = G(w)$, which is an increasing function of the wage w. We assume that each person employed is capable of producing an exogenous quantity y of goods. A monopsonist firm chooses the wage that allows it to maximize its profit, taking the labor supply function as a given. Formally, the problem of the monopsonist firm is written this way:

$$\text{Max}_{w} \; \pi(w) = L^s(w)(y - w)$$

The first-order condition of this problem is obtained by differentiating $\pi(w)$ with respect to w. Let $\eta_w^L(w)$ be the elasticity of the labor supply; the wage w^M of the monopsonist is defined by[2]:

$$w^M = \frac{\eta_w^L(w^M)}{1 + \eta_w^L(w^M)} \, y, \qquad \text{with} \qquad \eta_w^L(w) = \frac{wL^{s\prime}(w)}{L^s(w)} \geq 0 \tag{3}$$

The term $\eta_w^L/(1 + \eta_w^L)$ lying between 0 and 1, this relation shows that the wage chosen by the monopsonist is lower than the competitive wage y. These two wages coincide only if the elasticity of the labor supply becomes infinite, which corresponds exactly to the situation of perfect competition. Monopsony power enables the employer to obtain a strictly positive profit $\pi(w^M) = yL(w^M)/[1 + \eta_w^L(w^M)]$, whereas in a perfectly competitive market this profit is zero, since $\pi(w^M)$ tends to zero when η_w^L tends to infinity. Relation (3) also indicates that monopsony power, measured by the ratio y/w^M, decreases with the elasticity of the labor supply. A monopsonist trades off between lowered wages and falling employment. If the labor supply is highly elastic, any wage reduction leads to a steep fall in employment and profit, and this gives the employer an incentive to offer relatively high wages. Conversely, if the labor supply is little affected by wages, a monopsonist has the opportunity to cut back drastically on wages without suffering serious repercussions on employment and thereby on profit. This means that wage differentials unrelated to productivity differentials may exist. For given levels of competence and job specifications, workers unlucky enough to be in a market dominated by a monopsony receive a wage reduced in proportion to the weak labor supply elasticity proper to such a market.

The monopsony model is represented in figure 5.4. The equilibrium wage and employment are defined by the tangency point between the curve of isoprofit, the equation of which is $L(y - w) = \pi(w^M)$, and the labor supply curve $L^s(w) = G(w)$. Figure 5.4 shows that the monopsonist exerts negative pressure on both the wage and employment. The wage w^M is lower than the wage y that matches supply with demand under the hypothesis of perfect competition, and the level of employment $G(w^M)$ similarly lies below the level $G(y)$ reached under the same hypothesis.

From this perspective, the monopsony model sheds lights on the consequences of the minimum wage. Figure 5.4 does indeed indicate that if the minimum wage $\overline{w}$ lies somewhere between the wage w^M chosen by the monopsony and the competitive wage y, any rise in $\overline{w}$ allows the level $G(\overline{w})$ of employment to be increased. If, however, the minimum wage is greater than the competitive wage, the impact on employment is evidently negative, since no firm would consent to operate at wage levels that would bring it only losses. So the monopsony model suggests that the relationship between the minimum wage and employment is not monotonic but increasing for low

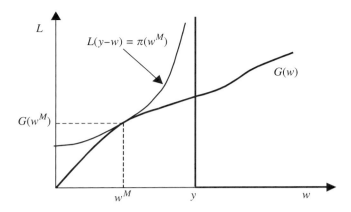

FIGURE 5.4
The monopsony model.

values of the minimum wage and decreasing for higher ones. The minimum wage may therefore affect employment positively in certain markets and negatively in others. We will return in greater detail to the effects of the minimum wage in chapter 12, which is dedicated to public policy.

The Sources of Monopsony Power

The monopsony model assumes, on the one hand, workers with limited mobility, and on the other, the existence of entry costs that allow the firm in place to escape competition. A number of factors might limit the mobility of those who supply labor. For example, the transportation costs affecting a particular labor pool might be significant (in a region poorly served by road and rail or remote from other labor pools). Monopsony power might also accrue to a firm dominating a profession requiring qualifications that cannot easily be used in other fields. For whatever reason, there must exist entry costs that impede one or more firms from stepping in to compete with a monopsonist for the same labor market, since the strictly positive profit $\pi(w^M)$ realized by the monopsonist ought to draw other employers to compete with it by offering higher wages. Only the costs of entering a labor market over which a monopsonist holds sway can explain this absence of competition.

A simple game model will enable us to show how a monopsonist firm may come into being when there exist costs attached to entering a market. The game unfolds in two stages. In stage 1, there is a waiting list made up of a large number N of firms that want to enter the market. All these firms know exactly what place they occupy on the list, and they can only enter the market one after the other. A firm that decides to enter pays a cost $c > 0$, which when paid allows it to hire as many workers as it wants. We assume that the technology is always such that each worker produces an exogenous quantity y of a good. In stage 2, the firms present on the market are involved in "Bertrand competition" (Bertrand, 1883), meaning that they each simultaneously offer a wage that maximizes their own profit, while taking the wages offered by the other firms as given. A game of this type is solved backward: we first determine the equilibrium in stage 2, then find the equilibrium in stage 1 under the assumption that the agents are capable of foreseeing what will occur in stage 2.

In stage 2, the value of wages depends on the number of firms present in the market. When there is just one, it is a monopsonist, and we have seen that its wage w^M is given by equation (3). Let us now assume that there are only $n > 1$ competitors present in the market. Firm i chooses its wage w_i so as to maximize its profit $\pi_i = L_i(y - w_i)$, taking as given the wages paid by the other firms. Employment L_i in firm i depends on all wages $(w_1, \dots, w_n)$ in the following manner:

$$L_i = \begin{cases} L^s(w_i) & \text{if } w_i > w_j, \forall j \neq i \\ (1/J)L^s(w_i) & \text{if } i \text{ sets the highest wage with } J-1 \text{ other firms, } 1 < J < n \\ 0 & \text{if there exists a firm } j \neq i \text{ which sets } w_j > w_i \end{cases}$$

The first line of this relation means that if the wage w_i of firm i is the highest of all the wages offered, firm i captures the entire supply of labor $L^s(w_i)$ corresponding to that wage level. Conversely, the third line indicates that if a firm comes forward with a wage strictly higher than that of firm i, no worker will accept employment with i (all agents prefer to work for wage w_j). Finally, the second line postulates that if the highest wage is jointly offered by J firms, they share the labor supply in equal parts.

Entry Costs and the Existence of a Monopsony
It can easily be shown that the situation in which every wage w_i is equal to productivity y is a Nash equilibrium, for when $w_i = y$ for all $i = 1, \dots, n$, each firm has zero profit and can improve its earnings neither by lowering its wage—the labor supply coming its way would be zero—nor by raising its wage, which would occasion losses. It can also be shown that no other Nash equilibrium exists with wages $w_i < y$. For that, it is sufficient to observe that the choice of a wage $w_i < y$ is not an equilibrium strategy. Under this hypothesis, the profit of firm i is strictly positive, and thus a competitor j would be in a position to offer a wage $w_j > w_i$ which would bring it an equally positive but smaller profit than that of firm i. In this case, firm j captures the entire labor supply at the expense of its competitor i. Hence, when workers are perfectly substitutable, competition over wages among a number n of employers *strictly* greater than 1 leads to a situation identical to that of perfect competition, in which workers are paid at their marginal productivity. This standard result of game theory is known as Bertrand's paradox (1883).

In stage 1, each firm makes its decision knowing that it will obtain zero profit in stage 2 if other firms are present in the market, and monopsony profit $\pi(w^M)$ if it is the only one to penetrate this market. The upshot is that once the firm at the top of the list has entered the market, no other firm has any interest in competing with it, since it is certain to make zero profit, while paying a supplementary cost $c > 0$ to get into the market. The firm at the top of the list foresees that its possible entry is going to dissuade the competitors waiting behind it from entering, and so decides to do so itself if $\pi(w^M) > c$. In sum, the presence of a cost of entry c entails the existence of a monopsony when $\pi(w^M) > c$. Conversely, if $\pi(w^M) \leq c$, no firm enters the market. The fact that an entry cost, however low, leads to the appearance of a monopsony is evidently an extreme result, which may be modified by assuming other types of competition in stage 2 of the game (see, for example, Mas-Colell et al., 1995, chapter 12). Such modifications are not, however, sufficient to alter the general import of this result, i.e., that the entry costs to labor markets may promote monopsony situations and so bring about wage gaps unrelated to any productivity differentials. The persistence of discrimination is an example of such a gap.

2.1.2 Monopsony and Discrimination

Discrimination is a situation in which individuals identical in regard to their productive ability are treated differently because of certain of their *non*productive characteristics. Becker (1957) pointed out that the preferences of employers and workers may constitute a source of discrimination.

There is employer discrimination when employers have an aversion to employing members of certain demographic groups. In this case, workers who belong to these groups must accept wages lower than those of other workers in order to compensate the employers for the dislike the latter feel for employing them. It must be emphasized that employer discrimination cannot exist under perfect competition with no productivity differences between workers. Employers with a preference for discrimination pay the discriminated workers at a rate below their marginal product. Free entry by color-blind firms that offer the potentially discriminated workers wages that equal their marginal product forces the discriminating firms out of the market.

Becker also discusses the case in which discrimination may arise out of the preferences of workers. In this situation, workers who belong to a majority group feel an aversion for working with members of a minority group, and employers must compensate the members of the majority group by paying them wages that exceed their productivity, financed by a levy on the wages of the minority workers, if they want the two types of workers to work together in the same firm. Clearly such a situation cannot arise under perfect competition, where the perfect mobility of workers must ensure that there is no firm employing members of both groups at the same time.

In sum, it is evident that employer and employee discrimination cannot occur in perfectly competitive markets, in which by definition all workers are paid according to their marginal productivity. Hence discrimination is necessarily linked to imperfect competition. Monopsony power may entail discrimination between groups with productive abilities that are a priori identical. The previous model has shown us that limitations on personal mobility (geographical, or between kinds of employment) permit firms to exercise monopsony power. Workers with identical productive abilities will thus have different wages if they reside in markets in which the conditions of mobility vary. This type of argument has been advanced to explain discrimination against women and certain ethnic minorities (see Gordon and Morton, 1974; Barth and Dale-Olsen, 1999). More generally, any employer enjoying some market power has, within limits, an opportunity to select workers according to his or her preferences.

Imperfect Competition and Employer Discrimination
Becker (1957) suggested that discrimination might arise from the fact that employers feel a disinclination to hire workers belonging to certain groups. He presented this hypothesis in formal terms by assuming that the gains these employers derive from a worker are equal to $y - w - u_i$, where y denotes productivity, w stands for the wage, and u_i is a positive term if the worker hired belongs to group i for which the employer feels an aversion, and zero if not. Under perfect competition, the condition of free entry results in aversion for certain groups having no incidence, since the entry into the market of employers endowed with "normal" preferences, i.e., who maximize their profit $y - w$ in all circumstances, allows workers who are potentially targets of discrimination to obtain a wage equal to their productivity y. Conversely, discrimination has a chance of persisting in a situation of imperfect competition: an employer enjoying monopsony power can discriminate against certain individuals *persistently* without being forced out of the market by competitive forces. Discrimination then leads to lower wages and levels of employment for those who are its victims. To demonstrate this, let us suppose that a monopsonist is present in a market composed of two groups, denoted A and B, of workers whose productive abilities and preferences are strictly identical to those we considered in arriving at figure 5.4. The labor supply of individuals of group i is thus equal to $L^s(w_i) = G(w_i)$, $i = A, B$, where G designates the cumulative distribution function of the reservation wages. If the entrepreneur feels a disinclination to employ workers of group A, his or her behavior is described by the following problem:

$$\underset{\{w_A, w_B\}}{\text{Max}} \ G(w_A)(y - w_A - u) + G(w_B)(y - w_B), \qquad 0 < u < y$$

In this problem, w_A and w_B designate the wages that apply respectively to the members of groups A and B. Parameter u measures the loss that the employer feels in the presence of persons of group A.

The Effects of Discrimination
Differentiating the criterion of the employer with respect to w_A and w_B, we find the values of the remunerations received by agents belonging to groups A and B. They are as follows:

$$w_i^M = \frac{\eta_w^L(w_i^M)}{1 + \eta_w^L(w_i^M)}(y - u_i), \qquad \text{with} \qquad \eta_w^L(w_i) = \frac{w_i G'(w_i)}{G(w_i)} \geq 0 \qquad \text{and}$$

$$u_i = \begin{cases} u \text{ if } i = A \\ 0 \text{ if } i = B \end{cases}$$

If the second-order condition is satisfied, we have $GG'' - 2(G')^2 < 0$, and we can verify that workers targeted for discrimination obtain a lower wage than that of the workers in group B. This result is easy to understand with the help of figure 5.4. Wage w_B^M obtained by workers in the group not targeted for discrimination corresponds to w^M, i.e., to a tangency point between an isoprofit curve for the jobs in group B and the graph of the labor supply of this group. The slope of the isoprofit curve for the jobs in group A is given by $dL/dw = L/(y - w - u)$. It is greater than the slope of the isoprofit curve for the jobs in group B for every pair (w, L). The tangency point between the isoprofit curve and the labor supply for group A is necessarily situated to the left of that for group B. Wages and employment are therefore both lower for group A.

The mechanisms brought to light in this simple monopsony model reappear in contexts in which the job search is costly. These search costs prevent workers from bringing the full weight of competition to bear on firms, and that confers some monopsony power on employers. With a job search model much like the one we developed in chapter 3, Black (1995) has shown that discrimination based on the preferences of employers can in fact persist if workers are faced with costly searches. Discrimination then takes the form of lower wages and longer periods of unemployment for the workers who are its victims.

2.2 SPECIFIC IRREVERSIBLE INVESTMENT AND RENT-SHARING

The monopsony model illustrates a situation in which a firm dominates a labor market composed of workers who, faced with substantial mobility costs, find it impossible to look for a job elsewhere. Conversely, there also exist mobility costs that allow employees to capture a part of the rents obtained by firms. Hiring and training costs may fall into this category. Being *irreversible*, they form significant obstacles to mobility and work in favor of employees already in place when it comes to the sharing out of rents.

2.2.1 Incomplete Contracts, Renegotiation, and Rents

To understand rent-sharing, we will take as our frame of reference the model of perfect competition from section 1.1. In this model, the condition of free entry entails zero profits and a wage w equal to individual productivity y. Let us suppose that an employer has made an innovation known to him or her alone, or protected by a patent, that allows him or her to produce a quantity $y^+ > y$ on condition that each worker hired is trained to make use of the new technology. Let us further assume that the cost of this training is a positive exogenous constant c; the firm can foresee putting this new technology (and the training that goes with it) into operation if $y^+ - c > y$. In what follows we will assume that this inequality is satisfied.

We will first take the case in which the firm is in a position to offer job-seekers a complete, nonrenegotiable contract setting out the wages to be paid throughout the period of the contract. This firm comes into the labor market offering wage $w = y$; this is accepted by the workers, who do not have an opportunity to obtain a higher wage with other firms, which (by assumption) do not have the benefit of the new technology. For each person hired, the "innovating" firm obtains a rent equal to $y^+ - c - y > 0$, while the employees, for their part, capture none of the rent due to the new technology as long as there exist complete, nonrenegotiable contracts. All of the rent flows back to the employer.

Now, let us suppose that the employee can renegotiate his or her contract *after* the employer has hired him or her and paid the cost of his or her training c. To determine the outcome of the renegotiation, it is necessary to define the gains the protagonists make if the labor relationship is maintained, or if it is broken off, as well as the rule for sharing out these gains. When the contract is renegotiated, the employer's profit is equal to $y^+ - w$, since the cost of the training has already been paid. Let $\overline{w}$ denote the wage of a new employee. If the labor relationship is broken off, the employer can hire a replacement and obtain a profit equal to $y^+ - c - \overline{w}$. His or her net gain from continuing to employ the former worker at wage w is thus equal to $c + \overline{w} - w$, which simply corresponds to the difference between the cost of a new worker and the cost of the present one. Through renegotiating, the employee already in place obtains a wage w; since he earns y in all the other firms, his or her net gain comes to $w - y$. By definition, the *surplus* (or, in other words, the rent), which we denote by S, generated by the continuation of the labor relationship is equal to the sum of the net gains of the employer and the employee, or $S = c + \overline{w} - y$. It should be noted that the surplus linked to jobs in the perfectly competitive sector is zero, since, for those jobs, we have $\overline{w} = y$ and $c = 0$. The surplus in the innovating firm can, on the other hand, be strictly positive, and in that case can become the object of a negotiation over how to share it out.

Let us assume that the worker has enough bargaining power to win for himself or herself fraction $\gamma \in [0, 1]$ of the surplus[3]; we will then have $w - y = \gamma S$. The wage w is then equal to $\gamma(\overline{w} + c) + (1 - \gamma)y$. Since the employer foresees that at equilibrium, he or she will have to pay a wage $\overline{w}$ satisfying the same relation, i.e., such that $\overline{w} = \gamma(\overline{w} + c) + (1 - \gamma)y$, he or she knows that wages w and $\overline{w}$ will be equal and, in consequence, defined by $w = \overline{w} = y + \gamma[c/(1 - \gamma)]$. The profit $y^+ - c - w$ of the innovating firm is therefore equal to $y^+ - y - [c/(1 - \gamma)]$. The new technology is in fact put into operation if this last quantity is positive. In the end, the negotiated wage satisfies:

$$w = \begin{cases} y + \gamma[c/(1 - \gamma)] & \text{if } y^+ > y + [c/(1 - \gamma)] \\ y & \text{otherwise} \end{cases}$$

Hence the opportunity to renegotiate contracts—which is a consequence of the absence of complete contracts—allows workers to capture a part of the surplus if there are costs attached to replacing manpower. In a sense, these costs protect wage-earners who already hold a job from the competition of other workers. The latter, often called *outsiders*, following the terminology introduced by Lindbeck and Snower (1988), cannot offer to take jobs for wages lower than those paid to the *insiders*, for such offers are not credible if it is impossible to sign complete, nonrenegotiable contracts.

2.2.2 The Holdup Problem

In the model just presented, the costs of replacing manpower originate from an investment in *specific human capital*, in the sense that the skill necessary to operate the innovative technology has no value in any other firm. When contracts are incomplete, a worker has no incentive to make this kind of investment, for he or she has no assurance that the employer will let him or her profit from the return to his or her investment. Conversely, if it is the employer who finances the investment in specific human capital, he or she is liable to a manpower replacement cost that may constrain him or her to allow the employee who has had the benefit of this investment to keep part of the surplus. This *holdup*, as it is called (Williamson, 1975; Grout, 1984; see also chapters 9 and 12), diminishes the returns on investments, or to be more precise, these returns decrease with the bargaining power of the party that does not invest. Sufficiently high bargaining power γ on the part of employees may even lead to negative profit—if $y^+ < y + [c/(1 - \gamma)]$ in our model—and thus the employment that would make a surplus available is not created.

This example shows that the coexistence of irreversible investments and incomplete contracts can give rise to wage gaps that do not reflect "compensating differentials." Moreover, in the presence of incomplete contracts, the labor market is not any more efficient: firms may underinvest in human capital. It should be noted that there are other costs linked to hiring that are sources of irreversible investment. In particular, we will see in chapter 9 that costs occasioned by the process of searching for and selecting workers play an important role in this respect.

3 OBSTACLES TO PERFECT COMPETITION (2): IMPERFECT INFORMATION

Within the framework of perfect competition, agents avail themselves of unlimited no-cost information about all the characteristics of the products exchanged and about the qualities of persons who offer their services. This hypothesis is clearly too simplistic to represent, in an accurate manner, the way many markets actually function.

In chapter 3 we showed that imperfect information possessed by workers about the characteristics of the jobs on offer provoked search behavior on their part that entailed, in particular, a dispersion of wages resulting from the behavior of firms, which may have an interest in offering high wages so as to be able to attract and hire a large number of workers (see chapter 3, section 2.3). Job search models therefore throw light on the consequences of the lack of information on the part of workers concerning the characteristics of *jobs*. This light is interesting but partial, inasmuch as employers, too, dispose of limited information about the characteristics of *workers*.

In the first place, the lack of information concerning the characteristics of workers obliges employers to opt for wage strategies that will attract the most productive people. These strategies can turn out to be very inefficient, and can have the paradoxical effect of eliminating the most productive workers from the market; this is the problem of *adverse selection*. In the second place, if employers conclude that membership in a given group yields an a priori estimate of individual productivity, a situation known as *statistical discrimination* between groups may become persistent. In all these textbook examples, market mechanisms lose their efficiency, and wage gaps no longer reflect compensating differentials.

3.1 Selection Problems

Ever since the fundamental work of Akerlof (1970), the selection problems agents face when they want to purchase a good the quality of which is known to them only imperfectly have been the focus of numerous studies (see, for example, Mas-Colell et al., 1995). These works have made their influence felt in labor economics, inasmuch as employers frequently encounter this type of problem during the hiring process. We will begin by presenting the phenomenon of adverse selection that emerges when employers' observation of the abilities of employees is imperfect, and then focus on the linkage between this phenomenon and unemployment.

3.1.1 Adverse Selection

When employers observe the abilities of workers imperfectly, the wage they pay loses its capacity to equal (unobservable) marginal productivity. This result emerges naturally from a simple model in which the opportunity cost of labor is the same for all agents.

A Model with Imperfect Information About the Abilities of Workers
We here consider a labor market made up of a continuum of individuals whose productive abilities are different. A worker with ability h can produce h units of a good. The distribution of productive abilities is given by a cumulative distribution function $G(h)$ defined on the interval $[h^-, h^+]$. The preferences of workers are represented by a utility function $u(R, d) = R + d$, where R designates income, equal to wage w if they are hired and zero otherwise, and d is an indicator function with a value of zero if the individual is hired and 1 if not. The function d thus represents the opportunity cost of labor; it includes earnings from outside the labor market and the value of leisure.

If we assume that there is free entry into the labor market and that firms observe the productive abilities of their employees *perfectly*, a line of reasoning identical to the one set out in section 1.1 of this chapter shows that perfect competition leads to zero profits, and wages that equal marginal productivities. For those who decide to participate in the labor market, we will thus have $w(h) = h$. Moreover, only those obtaining a remuneration that exceeds the opportunity cost of labor accept employment. Since this cost is here equal to 1, the wage must be greater than 1. If for simplicity's sake we normalize the size of the labor force to 1, equilibrium employment is equal to $\Pr\{h \geq 1\} = [1 - G(1)]$.

Let us now suppose that employers do not observe individual abilities h, but do know the cumulative distribution function $G(.)$. The wage cannot depend on abilities, since these are not observable. All workers thus necessarily get the same wage w.

The labor supply L^s, the graph of which is shown in figure 5.5, is equal to the labor force (normalized to unity) if the wage is greater than the opportunity cost of

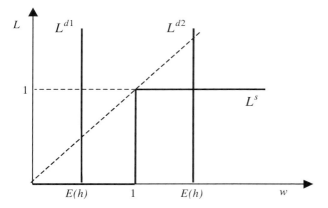

FIGURE 5.5
The adverse selection problem.

labor, i.e., if $w \geq 1$. It equals zero if $w < 1$, and takes any value lying between zero and 1 when $w = 1$. In consequence, if $w \geq 1$, the expected productivity of a job is simply equal to the average ability or $E(h) = \int_{h^-}^{h^+} \xi \, dG(\xi)$, and the profit expected from a job that is filled attains the value $E(h) - w$. The hypothesis of free entry entails that firms create jobs up to the point at which all profit opportunities disappear, with the result that labor demand is infinite if $w < E(h)$, comprised between zero and infinity if $w = E(h)$, and zero if $w > E(h)$, or:

$$L^d = \begin{cases} +\infty & \text{if } w < E(h) \\ [0, +\infty[& \text{if } w = E(h) \\ 0 & \text{if } w > E(h) \end{cases} \qquad (4)$$

Knowledge of labor supply and demand now allows us to determine labor market equilibrium.

Labor Market Equilibrium

At labor market equilibrium, the wage equates supply and demand. Figure 5.5 shows that two cases may exist.

In the first case, the average ability is less than the opportunity cost of working, or $E(h) \leq 1$. The intersection of the labor supply with the demand for this factor, denoted by L^{d1} in figure 5.5, corresponds to the interval $[E(h), 1]$ situated on the horizontal axis. Equilibrium employment is thus zero: firms have no interest in offering jobs for which expected productivity is less than the lowest wage that workers would accept. The unobservability of productive abilities prevents any transaction. To be more precise, the most efficient workers—those whose productive abilities are greater than the opportunity cost of labor ($h > 1$)—are forced out of the market, since firms cannot distinguish them from less productive individuals. It is because less efficient workers are attracted by a wage higher than the one they could get if employers did observe their ability that the average productivity of jobs is weak and employers have no interest in entering the market. Imperfect information thus creates a problem, known as *adverse selection*, that blocks the most profitable transactions from taking place (Akerlof, 1970). Adverse selection leads to unemployment, inasmuch as the most efficient workers do not find jobs that match their abilities, whereas they would have been hired if information had been perfect.

In the second case, $E(h) > 1$, the average ability is higher than the opportunity cost of labor. Labor demand, denoted by L^{d2} in figure 5.5, intersects with labor supply at the point of abscissa $E(h)$ and ordinate 1. There is thus full employment, and the equilibrium wage is equal to $E(h)$. Selection problems are now the source of overemployment, since the level of employment is equal to 1, whereas efficient employment, arrived at in the absence of information problems, comes to $[1 - G(1)]$. Moreover, all employees receive the same wage and thus are not being remunerated according to their abilities. Workers with low productivity are getting a remuneration greater than their productivity, while the most efficient workers are being underpaid. To be precise, persons whose productivity h is less than 1 come into the labor market, but they would be nonparticipants if information were perfect.

3.1.2   Adverse Selection and Efficiency Wage

In the preceding model, adverse selection problems prevented any transaction from taking place in a labor market in which the average ability of individuals was low. This was an extreme case; most often these problems lead to the exclusion of a *portion* of workers. It is possible to arrive at an equilibrium possessing this characteristic if we assume that the opportunity cost of labor is no longer independent of productive ability. We thus obtain a version of the so-called "efficiency wage" theories, a distinctive feature of which is that they make "excessively high" wages set by employers the cause of unemployment (see Akerlof and Yellen, 1986, for a panorama of efficiency wage theories).

An Efficiency Wage Model

We will assume from this point on that an increasing relationship exists between the opportunity costs of labor, d, and individual efficiency, h. Such a hypothesis seems natural, inasmuch as the most efficient individuals in the labor market generally have some way to make their competence pay off outside this market (or find the rewards of leisure meager). In these circumstances, Weiss (1980) has shown that firms have an interest in paying relatively high wages in order to attract good workers. Increasing the wage is thus a way to improve labor productivity.

Let $d(h)$, with $d'(h) > 0$, be the opportunity cost of labor for a person with characteristic h, and let us assume, in order to make the presentation simpler, that $d(h) < h$, $\forall h \in [h^-, h^+]$. The preferences of this worker are again represented by the utility function $u(R, d) = R + d$, where R designates income, equal to wage $w(h)$ if a hire occurs and zero if not, and d is an indicator function whose value is zero if the individual is hired and $d(h)$ if not. In other words, the utility of a person with the characteristic h is respectively equal to $w(h)$ if he or she is hired and to $d(h)$ if he or she does not participate in the labor market. When information is perfect, the hypothesis of free entry again entails $w(h) = h$. Moreover, as we have assumed that $d(h) < h$, the result is that $w(h) > d(h)$, $\forall h \in [h^-, h^+]$, with the consequence that all workers decide to participate in the labor market and find jobs that match their respective abilities.

Let us now take the case in which information on the qualities of workers is imperfect, with employers knowing only the distribution $G(.)$ of abilities. The wage cannot depend on individual abilities, which are not observable by the employer. The upshot is that workers all get the same wage w, and the labor supply is made up of all persons for whom the wage w exceeds the opportunity cost of labor $d(h)$, i.e., all those persons whose characteristic h is such that $d(h) \leq w$. The labor supply $L^s(w)$ is thus characterized by the equality $L^s(w) = G[d^{-1}(w)]$. The expected productivity of a job depends on the current wage, which is why we denote it by $E(h|w)$. It is defined by:

$$E(h|w) = \frac{\int_{h^-}^{\bar{h}} \xi \, dG(\xi)}{G(\bar{h})}, \qquad \text{with} \qquad d(\bar{h}) = w$$

This expression is to be understood as follows: when the current wage is equal to w, only persons having a characteristic $h \leq \bar{h} = d^{-1}(w)$ participate in the labor market. These persons produce an overall quantity $\int_{h^-}^{\bar{h}} \xi \, dG(\xi)$ of goods. The average output of an individual is found by dividing this quantity by the mass $G(\bar{h})$ of individuals present on the labor market. Under the hypothesis of free entry, firms create jobs up to the point at which expected profit $E(h|w) - w$ for a job is zero. As a result, labor demand is infinite if $w < E(h|w)$, comprised between zero and infinity if $w = E(h|w)$, and zero if $w > E(h|w)$, i.e.:

$$L^d = \begin{cases} +\infty & \text{if } w < E(h|w) \\ [0, +\infty[& \text{if } w = E(h|w) \\ 0 & \text{if } w > E(h|w) \end{cases} \tag{5}$$

Labor Market Equilibrium

A labor market equilibrium is a situation in which the demand matches the supply. It corresponds to a pair (w^*, h^*) satisfying the two equations $E(h|w^*) = \int_{h^-}^{h^*} \xi \, dG(\xi) = w^*$, and $d(h^*) = w^*$. This equilibrium is represented in figure 5.6, in the plane (w, h). The conditional expected productivity $E(h|w)$ varies between h^- and h^+. It is equal to h^- for $w = d(h^-)$ and it increases with the wage as long as $w < d(h^+)$ for in this case, any wage rise attracts workers whose efficiency is greater than that of individuals already present in the market. On the other hand, from the moment the wage reaches or exceeds the value $d(h^+)$, everyone participates in the labor market, and the expected productivity is equal to $\int_{h^-}^{h^+} \xi \, dG(\xi)$. In figure 5.6, we have assumed that the conditional expected productivity $E(h|w)$ intersects the 45° line just once, at abscissa point w^*. In this case, the equilibrium is unique—but there could be other configurations with multiple equilibria. Employment is equal to $G(w^*)$, since all the workers whose productivity h is less than w^* participate in the labor market.

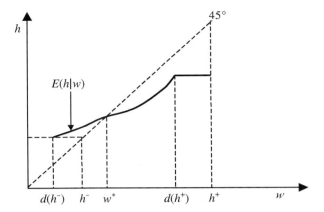

FIGURE 5.6
Adverse selection and efficiency wage.

In the equilibrium described by figure 5.6, the "good" workers—those whose productivity h lies to the right of the *efficiency wage* w^*—do not participate in the labor market, for the remuneration is too low to compensate for their opportunity cost of working. The equilibrium wage is too high, in the sense that it exceeds the productivity of a portion of the workers who are receiving it—those whose characteristic lies to the left of w^*. But the equilibrium wage remains too low to attract the whole set of workers. So once again we observe an adverse selection phenomenon that eliminates the best workers from the market. Adverse selection is also accompanied by under-employment, because labor market equilibrium with perfect information entails, for the same parameter values, full employment (see chapter 6 for another efficiency wage model that explains unemployment).

In a long-run perspective, the degree to which adverse selection problems affect the labor market must decline significantly. At that horizon, it is difficult to sustain the hypothesis that firms do not observe the productive characteristics of their employees. In countries where the procedures for terminating employment are not too costly, individuals who have shown that their ability is low will lose their jobs, and the problem of adverse selection will be remedied. But in countries where the legislation on termination of employment is more severe, what we find is that selection in hiring is strengthened through the use of contracts of limited duration or other forms of atypical employment (OECD, 1994), which has the effect of strongly reducing the chances of adverse selection.

3.2 SELECTION AND STATISTICAL DISCRIMINATION

Readers are reminded that, by definition, there is discrimination if individuals are treated differently because they belong to different demographic groups. We have seen that the presence of a monopsonist firm in the labor market might explain the persistence of a discrimination whose roots lie, as Becker (1957) suggested, in an aversion felt by the employer, clients, or other workers toward persons belonging to certain groups. Arrow (1973) and Phelps (1972) have shown that the unobservability of individual characteristics may also provoke discriminatory behavior on the part of firms. The latter generally dispose of limited information about individual characteristics. They possess pieces of information like age, experience, education, and performance on hiring tests that may have been administered, but these elements are only correlated with productivity, and so explain it only imperfectly. In order better to evaluate productivity, employers sometimes utilize supplementary information (or beliefs) on the *average* quality of one demographic group or another. A situation referred to as "statistical discrimination" may then arise. This expression signifies that individuals with identical abilities but belonging to different groups do not have equivalent career paths because of the average quality, real or imagined, of the group to which they belong. We will begin by showing how such a phenomenon may come about, and then focus on how statistical discrimination can become a source of *persistent inequality among groups* when the beliefs of employers influence the decisions agents make about education. These explanations of discrimination and inequalities throw valuable light on the consequences of quota policies of the kind that mandate, for example, the hiring of a given proportion of members of a certain group.

3.2.1 Statistical Discrimination as a Source of Individual Discrimination

Let us consider a labor market in which agents have zero opportunity cost of labor and two different levels of productivity: a low level, $h^- = 0$, and a high one, $h^+ > 0$. Employers evaluate the performance of workers by using hiring tests or trial periods, the cost of which we take to be zero for the sake of simplicity. The test makes it possible to detect efficient workers (the h^+ type) with a probability equal to 1. The inefficient ones, however, have a probability $p \in [0, 1]$ of passing the test and being wrongly taken for efficient. Moreover, employers estimate that the proportion of efficient workers in the demographic group considered is equal to $\pi \in [0, 1]$. In these conditions, passing the test does not guarantee that the person hired will be efficient (the h^+ type) since an inefficient one (the h^- type) has a probability p of passing the test. The employer's first task is to assess quantitatively the reliability of the test in selecting efficient persons. In other words, he or she must calculate the a posteriori probability, denoted by $\Pr\{h = h^+|\text{success}\}$, that a worker who passes the test will actually be of the h^+ type. By definition, this probability is given by the formula:

$$\Pr\{h = h^+|\text{success}\} = \frac{\Pr\{h = h^+ \text{ and success}\}}{\Pr\{\text{success}\}}$$

Since the test makes it possible to detect efficient workers infallibly, $\Pr\{h = h^+$ and success$\}$ is equal to $\Pr\{h = h^+\}$. So we have:

$$\Pr\{h = h^+|\text{success}\} = \frac{\Pr\{h = h^+\}}{\Pr\{\text{success}\}} = \frac{\pi}{\Pr\{\text{success}\}} \tag{6}$$

The problem thus comes down to calculating the total probability Pr{success} of passing the test. The outcome {success} breaks down into two separate outcomes according to the equality:

$$\{\text{success}\} = \{\text{success and } h = h^+\} + \{\text{success and } h = h^-\} \tag{7}$$

From what has gone before, we know that the probability of outcome {success and $h = h^+$} is equal to π; as for the probability of outcome {success and $h = h^-$} it is equal to the proportion $(1 - \pi)$ of inefficient workers times the probability p that one of them will pass the test. Taking the probabilities of both sides of relation (7) we find that Pr{success} is equal to $\pi + p(1 - \pi)$, and the equality (6) finally yields[4]:

$$\Pr\{h = h^+|\text{success}\} = \frac{\pi}{\pi + p(1 - \pi)}$$

For the employer, it turns out that the expected productivity of a person who passes the test is equal to $h^+\pi/[\pi + p(1 - \pi)]$. The condition of free entry then means that this quantity also represents the wage of a worker who has passed the test. This wage applies to all workers of the h^+ type, and to the proportion p of inefficient workers who pass the test (inefficient workers who fail it obtain a zero wage). It is increasing with the value π of the proportion of workers whom employers estimate to be efficient. This constitutes a source of statistical discrimination, for the wage paid to efficient individuals is reduced by their membership in groups believed by employers to contain a high proportion of inefficient workers. The degree of precision of the tests is another source of statistical discrimination, for we can see that an increased probability p of failing the test has a negative impact on the wage. In this connection, Lang (1986) has pointed out that specific cultural and linguistic attributes of ethnic minorities work to undermine the precision of their evaluation and for that reason constitute a source of statistical discrimination.

Statistical discrimination implies that individuals endowed with identical productive abilities may have different wages because they belong to different groups. Statistical discrimination does not, however, explain discrimination among groups. It does not allow us to understand why individuals belonging to different demographic groups *persistently* receive lower pay on average than their counterparts endowed with identical productive abilities. If individual performance is really independent of membership in a precise demographic group, repeated observation of this performance ought to cause employers to arrive sooner or later at an estimate of its true value, which is, by hypothesis, independent of membership in a group (Cain, 1986; Arrow, 1998).

3.2.2 Statistical Discrimination as a Source of Persistent Inequality Among Groups

Although statistical discrimination cannot persist, it is capable of creating inequalities, for the beliefs of employers and their capacity to make evaluations influence the behavior of workers. Let us assume that the efficiency of a worker depends in part on his or her investment in education. In a situation of statistical discrimination, the return to education is lower to the degree that employers believe that the proportion of inefficient workers in the group is substantial. This belief can act as an incentive for workers not to acquire education, and thus becomes a self-fulfilling prophecy: employers, anticipating that the proportion of efficient workers will be low, discourage efforts to acquire education and so do actually encounter fewer efficient workers (Lundberg and Startz, 1983; Coate and Loury, 1993; Loury, 2002).

A Model with Self-Fulfilling Prophecies

It is possible formally to illustrate this mechanism, in which beliefs lead to their own fulfillment, by slightly adapting the previous model. Let us now assume that workers can acquire education before starting their working lives. Their preferences are represented by a utility function $u(R, e) = R - e$, where R designates income, equal to wage w if they are employed, and zero otherwise. The variable e represents the cost of the effort to acquire education. This cost may be equal to 1, which makes it possible to achieve efficiency of $h^+ > 1$, or to zero, in which case the worker has a productivity h^-, assumed to amount to zero. We represent decisions about education using a two-stage game. In the first stage, workers decide on educational effort e. In the second stage, there is free entry into the labor market, and employers decide hires according to the process described in the previous model of statistical discrimination. At equilibrium, the beliefs of employers must be consistent, which means that their estimate of the proportion of efficient workers must be equal to the proportion actually observed.

We have shown that an educated worker obtains a wage $w^+ = h^+\pi/[\pi + p(1 - \pi)]$ in the second stage, whereas an uneducated worker has an expected gain given by $E(w^-) = pw^+$. An individual thus has an interest in acquiring education if $w^+ - 1 \geq E(w^-)$, which is equivalent to:

$$\pi \geq \frac{p}{(1 - p)(h^+ - 1)} \tag{8}$$

This condition indicates that workers decide to acquire education only if employers estimate that a sufficiently high proportion of the population is efficient. In this sense, the beliefs of employers are indeed capable of influencing the behavior of workers.

Multiple Equilibria and Persistent Inequalities

The term $p/[(1 - p)(h^+ - 1)]$ that appears in the right-hand side of (8) is greater than 1 if $p \geq (h^+ - 1)/h^+$. In this case, the inequality (8) is never satisfied, since the probability π must fall in the interval $[0, 1]$. The frequency p with which inefficient workers pass the test is so high with respect to the gains won through education that there is no interest in acquiring education, whatever employers believe. Labor market equilibrium then corresponds to a situation in which no worker acquires education and in which the beliefs of employers must be such that $\pi = 0$ in order to be consistent with their observations. So all workers obtain a zero wage. The imprecision of the method

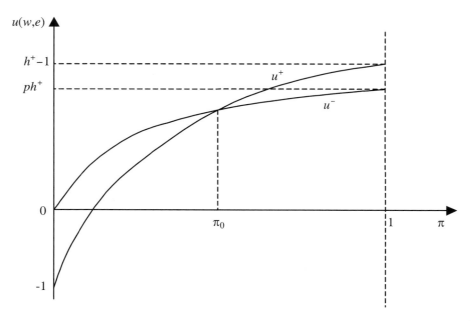

FIGURE 5.7
Statistical discrimination as a source of inequalities among groups.

of evaluation in this case represents an insurmountable source of statistical discrimination leading to deep inequalities, since the individuals who are victims of this discrimination decide not to acquire education.

If on the other hand $p \leq (h^+ - 1)/h^+$, there exist values of π capable of giving workers incentive to acquire education. Figure 5.7 shows that three equilibria, of which two are stable, are possible. In this figure, the curves u^+ and u^- represent the gains of workers in the plane (u, π). We see that for $\pi = 0$, workers prefer not to acquire education, since $u^- > u^+$. The value $\pi = 0$ thus represents an equilibrium at which no worker acquires education and where they all get a zero wage. But for $\pi = 1$, we necessarily have $u^+ > u^-$. The value $\pi = 1$ is then an equilibrium at which all workers get educated and thus obtain a wage equal to h^+. There also exists an equilibrium π_0 *strictly* comprised between 0 and 1. In this situation, workers are indifferent between acquiring education or remaining inefficient. But this equilibrium can be eliminated, for it is unstable: if a proportion $\pi_0 + \varepsilon$ (where ε is an arbitrarily small number) of workers get educated, all workers have an interest in getting educated for $\varepsilon > 0$ and none for $\varepsilon < 0$. A small deviation from equilibrium thus prevents a return to the initial position, which signifies that this equilibrium is unstable (the same line of reasoning will show that the other two equilibria are stable).

This very simple example shows that the influence of employers' beliefs may prevent groups from acquiring education and lead to persistent inequalities. If beliefs are unfavorable at the outset, $\pi < \pi_0$, it is possible that certain groups may be shackled to a low equilibrium ($\pi = 0$), while others, enjoying more favorable beliefs at the outset, $\pi > \pi_0$, may be coordinated at a high equilibrium ($\pi = 1$). In this respect, the weight of history becomes a significant source of discrimination, to the extent that beliefs are generally influenced by past experiences. Observation of poor performance by a group in the past is capable of influencing present beliefs and exerting a disincentive effect on the behavior of members of the group in question; the dynamic of self-fulfilling prophecies can engender persistent inequalities (Loury, 1998) that have to be combated through suitable programs. In order to illustrate this, the next subsection advances some considerations regarding affirmative action.

3.2.3   The Limits of Affirmative Action

Affirmative action forces employers to treat persons belonging to disadvantaged groups in the same way they treat those belonging to more favored ones. The imposition of quotas privileging the hiring of workers belonging to groups that are a priori disadvantaged by the functioning of the labor market forms part of the toolkit of affirmative action measures. Coate and Loury (1993) have pointed out that hiring quotas risk having a disincentive impact on the investments in education of persons belonging to groups that benefit from affirmative action, and thus turn out to be inefficient in the end. We can easily grasp this using the two-stage game set forth above and adding the assumption that the public authorities oblige employers to hire a minimum proportion π_g of workers at a minimum wage of $w^+ = h^+ \pi_g / [\pi_g + p(1 - \pi_g)]$. This wage corresponds to the equilibrium wage of efficient workers when these do in fact represent a part π_g of their group (if the hiring test is reliable enough for the inequality $p \leq (h^+ - 1)/h^+$ to be satisfied). In these circumstances, the government can implement affirmative action for the purpose of combating the perverse effects of statistical discrimination that lock the labor market into a suboptimal situation. Let us assume that the government is aware of the model developed just now, and is striving to reach the high equilibrium of figure 5.7 by imposing $\pi_g = 1$. Employers are thus obliged to hire all workers at wage h^+. The return to education becomes systematically negative, since an educated worker obtains $h^+ - 1$, while an uneducated one obtains h^+. The existence of the quota discourages education and leads ultimately to a highly inefficient situation in which firms make negative profits by being forced to hire workers who have no incentive to improve their productivity.

In order to combat the effects of statistical discrimination, Coate and Loury (1993) recommend instead the use of subsidies targeted so as to raise the returns on education. In figure 5.7, a subsidy equal to the cost of educational effort and financed by a lump-sum tax gives agents an incentive to get educated and leads to coordination at the good equilibrium by shifting the curve u^+ upward. Neumark (1999) and Altonji and Blank (1999) also suggest that giving employers incentive to improve the procedures they use to evaluate job applicants would constitute an effective means of combating statistical discrimination.

These considerations suggest that affirmative action can have detrimental consequences leading to efficiency losses. A review of empirical research carried out by Holzer and Neumark (2000a), however, indicates that these losses should be slight in comparison to the extent of the redistributive effects achieved.

4 WHAT EMPIRICAL STUDIES TELL US

Numerous empirical studies have been dedicated to wage-setting and the way the labor market functions. First we will present those studies that bear on the hedonic theory of wages. Wage discrimination and its connections with the theories set out above form the content of the second subsection. Finally, the theory of compensating differentials has been criticized on the basis of a purely empirical argument grounded in the fact that wage differentials persist between workers who are a priori endowed with identical abilities but who are employed in different industries. This is an established fact in many developed countries, and it suggests the systematic existence of rent sharing or monopsonies. We end with a review of works that try to account for these interindustry wage differences.

4.1 DOES THE HEDONIC THEORY OF WAGES REALLY APPLY?

The main prediction of the hedonic theory of wages is that wage differentials compensate for the conditions in which a job is performed. Tests of this prediction run up against methodological difficulties having to do, on the one hand, with unobserved individual characteristics, and on the other, with the heterogeneity of individual preferences about the attractive or unattractive features of doing any job. We will illustrate these difficulties by presenting the application of the hedonic theory of wages to the problem of evaluating the price of a human life.

4.1.1 Considerations of Method

The method used to test the predictions of the hedonic theory of wages consists of estimating the wage w received by an individual as a function of his or her personal characteristics, represented by a vector $\mathbf{x}$, and the non-wage characteristics of the job, represented by a vector $\mathbf{e}$. In general, the equation estimated is of the form:

$$\ln w = \mathbf{x}\boldsymbol{\beta} + \mathbf{e}\boldsymbol{a} + \varepsilon$$

In this expression, $\boldsymbol{a}$ and $\boldsymbol{\beta}$ are vectors of parameters to be estimated and ε is a disturbance term with zero mean that is assumed to be normally distributed. Vector $\mathbf{x}$ of personal characteristics generally includes age, sex, number of years of study or degree obtained, experience, seniority at work, ethnic origin, place of residence, family status, and trade union membership. Vector $\mathbf{e}$ of the non-wage characteristics of jobs incorporates variables like the duration and the flexibility of hours worked, the repetitive aspect of tasks, the risk of injury, the level of ambient noise, the physical strength required by the job, the risk of job loss, the cost of health insurance, the cost of saving for retirement, and so on.

The Impact of Unobserved Individual Characteristics

Taking the non-wage aspects of jobs into account poses two delicate problems. The first arises from *unobserved* individual characteristics. If some of these characteristics affect productivity positively, the results of the model have a good chance of underestimating the impact of non-wage characteristics on wages. Laborious tasks are likely to be inferior goods, the "consumption" of which diminishes as income rises. If the income effect is sufficiently strong,[5] then the most efficient individuals choose the less laborious jobs, which entails a negative relation between wages and the laboriousness of jobs. This point is illustrated in figure 5.8 which represents, in the plane (w, e), the choices of two individuals having different levels of efficiency. In this figure, parameter e is a unidimensional measure of the degree of laboriousness of tasks. In conformity with the theoretical elements developed in section 1.1, the choices of the efficient worker correspond to a tangency point between one of his or her indifference curves, denoted by u^+, and the frontier f^+ of possible combinations of wage and task laboriousness. The less efficient worker has lower productivity and finds himself or herself facing a set of trade-off possibilities between wages and task laboriousness of which the frontier f^- is situated beneath frontier f^+. Figure 5.8 represents a situation in which the wage obtained by the efficient worker is higher, but the degree to which his or her tasks are laborious is lower than that chosen by the less

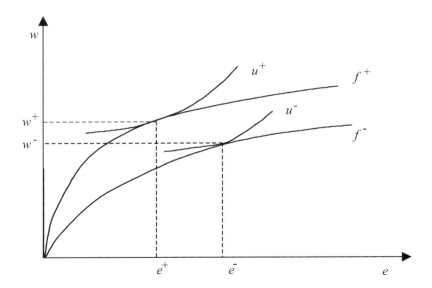

FIGURE 5.8
Compensating differentials and the unobserved characteristics of jobs.

efficient worker. So, what we have is a negative relation between wages and the degrees of laboriousness of jobs. If the difference between the frontiers f^+ and f^- is ignored by the econometrician, the negative correlation between wages and laboriousness of tasks will be underestimated. To escape this type of difficulty, it is preferable to make estimates using longitudinal data that allow us to follow individuals and thus get a better idea of their personal characteristics (Brown, 1980; Duncan and Holmlund, 1983). Nevertheless, Hwang et al. (1992) have shown that small errors in this domain can lead to very large biases.

The Importance of the Heterogeneity of Individual Preferences
The second problem encountered when estimating the impact of the non-wage elements of jobs on wages arises from the heterogeneity of individual preferences. There is not necessarily unanimous agreement that certain characteristics of jobs, like repetitiveness, use of physical strength, or flexible work schedules, are disagreeable, so the predictions of the hedonic theory of wages can only focus on certain elements that are clearly identifiable as drawbacks or advantages for all workers.

Empirical tests of the hedonic theory of wages give qualified results, which nevertheless, in many cases, highlight compensating wage differentials linked to the non-wage aspects of jobs. The first studies that focused on this area found that non-wage characteristics such as the repetitive content of jobs, bad working conditions, job security, freedom for persons to organize their own work, the opportunity for them to assist their fellow employees, the degree of supervision, the mortality rate, and the intensity of the work had a sign that conformed to theoretical predictions (see Brown, 1980). Nevertheless, Brown points out that numerous studies arrive at results that lack significance or even contradict theoretical predictions, and he suggests that these problems derive from the fact that all the studies conducted up to 1980 utilized cross-sectional data from which biases linked to the existence of unobserved variables might have arisen. His own work exploits longitudinal data and shows that correcting the biases does not significantly improve the results in a direction favorable to the theory. Other studies have highlighted other non-wage elements that influence wages, such as the degree of generosity of health insurance and retirement plans (Montgomery et al., 1992), but their conclusions remain fragile because of the weight of biases induced by excluded exogenous variables.

4.1.2 The Weight of Unobserved Characteristics: An Application to the Evaluation of the Price of a Human Life

The weight of unobserved variables renders estimates of wage equations fragile. In this regard, the contribution of Hwang et al. (1992) is particularly interesting. It shows that the biases depend on three variables: the heterogeneity in unobserved productivity, the percentage of earnings paid in non-wage form (advantages in kind, health insurance, retirement, etc.), and the dispersion of the preferences of workers when it comes to trading off between remuneration in the form of wages and in other forms. To show the importance of these variables, Hwang et al. (1992) take up the study

Table 5.1

Estimates of the price of a life saved.

Weekly wage (in levels)	Model 1 (Thaler and Rosen)	Model 2 (Hwang et al.)
Age	3.89 (0.80)	4.50
$(Age)^2$	−0.0479 (0.0092)	−0.0965
Education	3.40 (0.55)	4.87
Risk	0.0353 (0.0210)	0.3020
R^2	0.41	0.31
Price of a life saved (in years of average wage)	26.54	227.67

Values of variables (907 observations)	Average	Standard error
Age (years)	41.8	11.3
Education (years)	10.11	2.73
Weekly wage (1967 dollars)	132.65	50.80
Risk (probability $\times 10^5$)	109.8	67.6

Figures in parentheses are standard errors.

Source: Hwang et al. (1992).

carried out by Thaler and Rosen (1976) on the evaluation of the price of a human life, based on the impact of industrial accident risk on wages.

Thaler and Rosen estimated a weekly wage equation in which the explanatory variables were age, level of education, geographic location, amount of time worked, the presence of a trade union, and the risk of a fatal industrial accident per year multiplied by 10^5. The main results are presented in the first column of table 5.1. These figures lead Thaler and Rosen to calculate the value of a life saved in the following manner: "Suppose 1,000 men are employed on a job entailing an extra death risk of .001 per year. Then, on average, one man out of the 1,000 will die during the year. The regression indicates that each man would be willing to work for $176 per year less if the extra death probability were reduced from .001 to .0. Hence, they would together pay $176,000 to eliminate that death: the value of the life saved must be $176,000" (Thaler and Rosen, 1976, p. 292). If we divide this figure by the average value of annual wages (given by $132.65 \times 50 = \$6633.50$), we obtain the price of a human life expressed in years of wage. This price is given in the first column of table 5.1.

Hwang et al. (1992) correct the estimates of Thaler and Rosen by making hypotheses, supported by a number of empirical studies, about the values of unobserved variables capable of biasing the estimate. They show that the work of Thaler and Rosen probably leads to a considerable underevaluation of the price of a human life.

This point is illustrated in column 2 of table 5.1, which corresponds to a situation in which the heterogeneity of unobserved productivity (measured by the ratio of the variance of unobserved productivity to the variance of observed productivity) is equal to 0.395, the percentage of earnings paid in wage form is equal to 0.80, and the dispersion of wages due to the heterogeneity of preferences (measured by the ratio of the variance of wages conditional on observed productivity to the total variance of wages) is equal to 0.106. The "corrections" made by Hwang et al. lead to an evaluation of the price of a human life almost ten times higher than that obtained by Thaler and Rosen! So biases created by excluded exogenous variables are potentially very large, which ought to make us cautious in dealing with the results of studies of this type.

Our caution should be all the greater in that these results are grounded on the hypothesis of a perfectly competitive labor market. Now, both in theory and in practice, the problems of information, the costs of mobility, and the market power of individuals and firms influence the compensation mechanism between the wage and non-wage components of earnings. In this light, Hwang et al. (1998) have looked at what becomes of compensating wage differentials in an equilibrium job search model (analogous to the one we presented in chapter 3). They have shown that search costs influence the trade-off between the different components of overall remuneration. Empirical estimates of this trade-off therefore reflect not just the preferences of agents; they also echo constraints linked to the functioning of the labor market.

4.2   WAGE DISCRIMINATION

The assessment of wage discrimination poses methodological problems linked essentially to the insufficiency of information about individual characteristics. We will begin by laying out these problems before turning to an examination of empirical results.

4.2.1   Questions of Method

To gauge the magnitude of wage discrimination, an initial strategy consists of explaining wage differentials on the basis of a set of variables linked on the one hand to the characteristics of individuals and the jobs they hold, and on the other to their membership in particular groups. The portion explained by their membership in these groups is interpreted as a consequence of discrimination if the other factors account perfectly for all the other determinants of wage differentials. But the existence of unobserved variables blunts the precision of this strategy. For this reason, alternative methods that try to pinpoint discrimination directly with the help of experiments, or by comparing performances and remunerations, have been worked out.

Estimations of Wage Equations
The standard approach consists of estimating an equation in which the logarithm of income is explained by a set of factors such as the duration and quality of schooling, experience, region, and by dummy variables representing ethnic origin and sex (which are the principal sources of wage discrimination when it occurs). Let w_i be the income of individual i, $\mathbf{x}_i$ the vector of individual characteristics and of the job held,

and $\boldsymbol{\mu}_i$ a vector of dummy variables with a value of 1 if the individual belongs to groups potentially discriminated against and zero if not. The estimated equation is written:

$$\ln w_i = \mathbf{x}_i \boldsymbol{\beta} + \boldsymbol{\mu}_i \boldsymbol{\alpha} + \varepsilon_i \tag{9}$$

In this equation, $\boldsymbol{\alpha}$ and $\boldsymbol{\beta}$ are vectors of parameters to be estimated and the term ε_i represents a normally distributed disturbance term with zero mean. If the set of variables explaining the wage is sufficiently rich, a negative value for one of the components of vector $\boldsymbol{\alpha}$ indicates that there is discrimination against the corresponding group. More exactly, each component of estimated vector $\hat{\alpha}$ measures the average loss of income, evaluated in percentages, due to membership in the group to which this component relates. But this conclusion is highly questionable, for a negative value of a component of $\hat{\alpha}$ can be explained by unobservable individual characteristics that are independent of membership in such a group and that contribute to a lowering of income. A complementary approach aims to separate the contribution of observable characteristics from that of nonobservable characteristics (generally attributed to discrimination).

The Blinder-Oaxaca Decomposition
The so-called Blinder-Oaxaca decomposition (Blinder, 1974; Oaxaca, 1973) consists of estimating wage equations separately for a reference group and for the other groups to be compared to the reference group. Let w_{Ai} and $\mathbf{x}_{Ai}$ be respectively the wage and the vector of "objective" characteristics of an individual i belonging to the reference group A. The wage equation relative to this group takes the form:

$$\ln w_{Ai} = \mathbf{x}_{Ai} \boldsymbol{\beta}_A + \varepsilon_{Ai} \tag{10}$$

In this equation $\boldsymbol{\beta}_A$ designates the vector of parameters to be estimated and ε_{Ai} again represents a normally distributed disturbance term with zero mean. In the same manner, the wage equation relative to a group B is written:

$$\ln w_{Bj} = \mathbf{x}_{Bj} \boldsymbol{\beta}_B + \varepsilon_{Bj}$$

The last two equations allow us to calculate the difference between the *average* values of the wage logarithms. We get:

$$\ln w_A - \ln w_B = (\mathbf{x}_A - \mathbf{x}_B)\hat{\beta}_A + \mathbf{x}_B(\hat{\beta}_A - \hat{\beta}_B) \tag{11}$$

Here $\mathbf{x}_A$ and $\mathbf{x}_B$ designate the average values of the vectors of observed characteristics. The first term of the decomposition, $(\mathbf{x}_A - \mathbf{x}_B)\hat{\beta}_A$, represents the "explained" component of wage differences between groups. It regards elements such as education, experience, social milieu, and the nature of the jobs held. The second term, $\mathbf{x}_B(\hat{\beta}_A - \hat{\beta}_B)$, represents the "unexplained" component. It measures, for group B, the differences of return to characteristics due to membership in this group. For example, if k is an index number referring to professional experience, the term $x_{B_k}(\hat{\beta}_{A_k} - \hat{\beta}_{B_k})$ measures the difference in return to experience between groups A and B. The advantage of the Blinder-Oaxaca decomposition is that it does not demand that the coefficients linked to individual characteristics be identical. Nevertheless, the "unexplained" component always captures the effects of characteristics not observable by the econometrician, as well as any possible discrimination effects.

Clearly, though, the portion explained by discrimination using the Blinder-Oaxaca method depends on the reference group chosen. If B is the reference group instead of A, the explained part of the differences in average values of the wage logarithms is no longer $(\mathbf{x}_A - \mathbf{x}_B)\hat{\beta}_A$ but $(\mathbf{x}_A - \mathbf{x}_B)\hat{\beta}_B$. Since the difference in average values of the wage logarithms, $\ln w_A - \ln w_B$, is independent of the decomposition, the explained part of the portion of wage differences evidently depends on the reference group chosen. Hence if the returns to individual characteristics (education, experience, seniority, profession) of group A are higher, and if this group is also endowed with better characteristics on average, the explained part $(\mathbf{x}_A - \mathbf{x}_B)\hat{\beta}_A$ is greater than $(\mathbf{x}_A - \mathbf{x}_B)\hat{\beta}_B$, and the extent of discrimination against group B gauged by taking group A as a reference is weaker than in taking the other group.

Several studies have tried to solve this problem by proposing a more general form of the Blinder-Oaxaca decomposition. The idea is no longer to take any one group as reference but to assign each group an arbitrary weight. The decomposition is then written:

$$\ln w_A - \ln w_B = (\mathbf{x}_A - \mathbf{x}_B)\hat{\beta} + \mathbf{x}_A(\hat{\beta}_A - \hat{\beta}) + \mathbf{x}_B(\hat{\beta}_B - \hat{\beta}), \qquad \hat{\beta} = \lambda\hat{\beta}_A + (1 - \lambda)\hat{\beta}_B$$

In this equation, $\lambda \in [0, 1]$ designates the relative weight of group A in the definition of the reference group and $\hat{\beta}$ is interpreted as the vector of the returns on observable variables, such as education, professional experience, or seniority, in a competitive market. It is indeed possible that one group obtains, on average, returns greater than the competitive rate while another group obtains less than competitive returns. So parameter λ can be interpreted as the relative weight to be attributed to group A to reflect the returns of a competitive market. This weight is clearly very hard to define precisely, and a large area of arbitrariness always subsists (see Cotton, 1988; Oaxaca and Ransom, 1994; and the summary of Kunze, 2000).

In sum, the different methods of decomposing the wage gaps between demographic groups can give different results when applied to the same sample, so it is important to identify and clearly define the hypotheses of every empirical study in order to be able to interpret, and eventually compare, assessments of discrimination.

4.2.2 How to Estimate Changes in Discrimination

In the United States, wage inequalities between men and women tended to shrink during the 1980s and 1990s (Blau and Kahn, 1997; Fortin and Lemieux, 1998). This fact is surprising, for if one ponders the overall distribution of wages, inequalities mounted sharply over the same period. Less skilled workers in particular underwent relative losses of purchasing power. Why did the relative position of women improve, when on average they hold less skilled jobs than men? Is it the consequence of reduced discrimination or the result of an improvement in their relative productivity? On the other hand, wage gaps between black and white males tended to grow over the same period (Bound and Freeman, 1992). Why did the relative wages of black men decline while those of women rose?

In order to understand the dynamics of wage inequalities and the role of discrimination, several studies have utilized the decomposition of the evolution of wage differences introduced by Juhn et al. (1993). We begin by explaining the principles of this decomposition and then go on to emphasize the detrimental consequences of selection biases in this type of research.

The Decomposition of Juhn, Murphy, and Pierce

Juhn et al. (1993) begin by estimating the wage equation (10) for a demographic reference group A (men, for example) at date t. For an individual i of group A at date t, this equation takes the form:

$$\ln w_{Ait} = \mathbf{x}_{Ait}\boldsymbol{\beta}_{At} + \varepsilon_{Ait} \tag{12}$$

Juhn et al. (1993) decompose the statistical residual ε_{Ait} by positing $\varepsilon_{Ait} = \sigma_{At}\theta_{Ait}$, where $\sigma_{At} = \sqrt{\text{var}(\theta_{Ait})}$ is the standard error of the residuals of the distribution of wage logarithms at date t of the members of group A. The error term θ_{Ait} is interpreted as a standardized residual with zero mean and unitary variance. The estimation of equation (12) by ordinary least squares for the members of group A gives the estimated values $\hat{\beta}_{At}$, $\hat{\theta}_{Ait}$, and $\hat{\sigma}_{At}$. Let θ_{At} and $\mathbf{x}_{At}$ be respectively the average of the θ_{Ait} and of the $\mathbf{x}_{Ait}$; the average of the wage logarithms of group A, denoted by $\ln w_{At}$, is then defined by the equality:

$$\ln w_{At} = \mathbf{x}_{At}\hat{\beta}_{At} + \hat{\sigma}_{At}\hat{\theta}_{At}$$

Juhn et al. (1993) then assume that the coefficients $\hat{\beta}_{At}$ and the variance of the residuals $\hat{\sigma}_{At}$ are identical for the two groups, or $\hat{\beta}_{At} = \hat{\beta}_{Bt} = \hat{\beta}_t$ and $\hat{\sigma}_{At} = \hat{\sigma}_{Bt} = \hat{\sigma}_t$. Let us introduce the difference operator Δ, defined by $\Delta y_t = y_{At} - y_{Bt}$, $y = \mathbf{x}, \theta$. The difference of the average values of the wage logarithms between groups at date t is written thus:

$$D_t = \ln w_{At} - \ln w_{Bt} = \Delta \mathbf{x}_t \hat{\beta}_t + \hat{\sigma}_t \Delta \hat{\theta}_t \tag{13}$$

This equation indicates that the wage differential between the two groups includes a component arising from the differences of characteristics, $\Delta x_t \hat{\beta}_t$, and a component that results from the differences in the standardized residuals, $\Delta \hat{\theta}_t$, between the members of the two groups. The term $\hat{\sigma}_t \Delta \hat{\theta}_t$ is interpreted as the differences unexplained by the observable variables and which can therefore be attributed to discrimination. Equation (13) then gives the difference observed at dates t and s between the intergroup wage differentials. The result is:

$$D_t - D_s = (\Delta \mathbf{x}_t - \Delta \mathbf{x}_s)\hat{\beta}_t + \Delta \mathbf{x}_t(\hat{\beta}_t - \hat{\beta}_s) + (\Delta \hat{\theta}_t - \Delta \hat{\theta}_s)\hat{\sigma}_t + \Delta \hat{\theta}_t(\hat{\sigma}_t - \hat{\sigma}_s) \tag{14}$$

The first term of the right-hand side measures "the effect of changes in observed characteristics" and represents the contribution of changes in the averages of observable characteristics of the members of the two groups between dates s and t. The second term is "the observed price effect" and represents the contribution of differences in returns for characteristics observed at date t. The third term measures "the effect of changes in unobserved characteristics" and corresponds to the change in the average relative position of the members of the two groups in the distribution of wages that is not due to observed variables. Finally, the fourth term is an "unobserved price effect."

This method allows us to pinpoint the contributions of the different components of the changes in the gaps in average wage between demographic groups. Like all decompositions, it rests on arbitrary hypotheses of which we need to be aware in order to gauge its significance. First, as we have already pointed out in studying the Blinder-Oaxaca method, the distinction between observed characteristics and unobserved characteristics does not capture exclusively phenomena linked to discrimination. It also reflects, among other things, measurement errors, specification problems, and the existence of omitted variables. Moreover, the choice of reference group is as critical as in the Blinder-Oaxaca decomposition (Fortin and Lemieux, 1998). Finally, the hypothesis according to which the variation in residuals of the two demographic groups is identical (i.e., $\sigma_{At} = \sigma_{Bt} = \sigma_t$), which is indispensable in order to be able to distinguish the effect of changes in unobserved characteristics from the unobserved price effect, is highly debatable (see Suen, 1997, and the assessment of Blau and Kahn, 2001).

The Consequences of Selection Biases
Selection biases due to the fact that we only observe the wages of persons who work (see chapter 1, section 2) are an important source of error in the assessment of wage differentials between groups and in the evaluation of the components of these differentials. The average wage of all the members of a group should actually depend not just on the (observed) wages of workers who have a job, but also on the *potential* (and thus unobserved) wages of persons in this group who do not have a job. The distribution of observed wages therefore represents only a part of the distribution of the "offered wages," and it is necessary to know this last distribution in order to evaluate the wage differences between groups. The importance of this bias, to which Butler and Heckman (1977) drew attention, was illustrated by Brown (1984) and more recently by Chandra (2000) and Heckman et al. (2000) in the analysis of wage gaps between blacks and whites in the United States.

Figure 5.9 shows that the treatment of selection biases can profoundly alter our assessment of the movement of wage gaps between demographic groups. A calculation performed using data from the U.S. Decennial Census between 1940 and 1990 of average observed wages (i.e., without taking selection biases into account) suggests that the ratio of the average wage of black men to that of white men grew in stages between 1940 and 1990, falling back slightly during the 1980s. But this conclusion rests on arguments that neglect the fact that the participation rate of black men fell off more sharply than did that of white men over this period, and this contributed to reducing the weight of black men situated at the low end of the distribution of offered wages. To offset this bias, Brown (1984) calculated the average wage of each demographic group on the assumption that the wage offered to a nonparticipating individual came

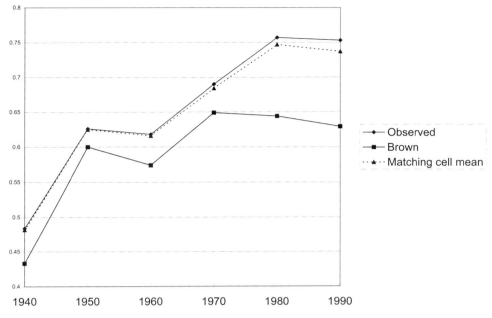

FIGURE 5.9

Ratios of weekly wages between black and white men (25–55 years) in the United States. Brown's decomposition identifies the unobserved wages (of nonparticipants) by a random draw in the distribution of observed wages lying below the median. The *matching cell mean* decomposition identifies unobserved wages by creating six age categories and seven educational levels and assigning to each nonparticipant the average wage of the category to which he or she belongs.

Source: Chandra (2000, table 3).

from a random draw below the median of the distribution of observed wages. On this basis, the movement of wage gaps turned out to be much less favorable to black men, for the members of this group situated at the low end of the wage distribution, who were excluded from the calculation of the average of observed wages, were then included, which contributed to bringing down the average wage of all black men. Figure 5.9 shows that the evaluation carried out according to Brown's method leads us to identify a diminution in the relative wage of black men since the beginning of the 1970s, whereas simple scrutiny of the observed data yields the very different conclusion that the gap in average observed wages shrank by 6% between 1970 and 1990. There are other ways of calculating average wage. The *matching cell mean* method brings in the unobserved wages by creating categories using age and educational criteria and assigning to each unemployed individual the average wage of the category to which he or she belongs. It portrays a movement of wage gaps close to that observed using the raw data. Finally, a more complete method consists of adjusting the distribution of wages offered by simultaneously estimating a wage equation and a participation equation, in conformity with the method of Heckman (1979).

4.2.3   Direct Assessment of Discrimination

Assessing the extent of discrimination by estimating wage equations poses problems that are difficult to overcome. The inevitable existence of omitted variables would point to the conclusion that the results obtained always *overestimate* discrimination. Another problem has to do with the influence of discrimination on explanatory variables. Our theoretical analysis in section 3.2 showed that discrimination may discourage education, and more generally any investment leading to increased incomes. In consequence, the observation of a lower level of education may be caused by discrimination. In this case, the results obtained through estimating wage equations *underestimate* discrimination. These limitations justify the use of alternative methods that aim to estimate discrimination directly. We will give the broad outlines of three of these approaches: audit studies, the experimental method, and a method based on the comparison of productivity differences and wage differences.

Audit Studies

Audit studies consist of setting up experiments in order to compare the performance in the labor market of individuals who are identical except for their membership in a clearly specified group. To that end, the investigator pairs off individuals who belong to different groups but who have the same individual characteristics in terms of education and social origin and who go about their job search in exactly the same way (for a summary presentation of the relevant works, see Darity and Mason, 1998; Altonji and Blank, 1999; and the critique of Heckman, 1998). In general, investigations carried out in the United States find that whites are more frequently given the opportunity to take hiring tests than blacks or Hispanics, and also receive more job offers. Moreover, whites have access to better jobs than blacks or Hispanics. The study by Goldin and Rouse (2000), which looks at the effects on hires of a change in recruitment policy by major symphony orchestras, follows a very similar approach. In order to guarantee the impartiality of the judging panels, the musicians audition behind an opaque screen. This type of audition was introduced by the Boston Symphony Orchestra in 1952 and has been adopted by many orchestras in the 1970s and 1980s. Goldin and Rouse find that the presence of the screen significantly increased the number of women hired, and that it explains almost one quarter of the increased presence of women in symphony orchestras in the 1970s and 1980s.

The Experimental Method

Another method, one little used at present, is based on setting up laboratory experiments. Fershtman and Gneezy (2001) have used it to study ethnic discrimination in Israel, bringing Ashkenazic students (descendants of European and American Jewish communities) and Oriental Jews (descendants of Jewish communities in Asia and Africa) together to participate in the *trust game* and in the *dictator game*.

The trust game is a game with two players in which player A holds a sum of money and must decide how much to hand over to player B. The experimenter triples the amount of the transfer and gives it to player B, who can decide to make a gift in return to player A. Within these rules, the efficient outcome—the one, that is, that gives both players the maximum of resources—dictates that player A should transfer the whole sum he holds to player B, so that B will receive the maximum from the experimenter. But on the assumption that both players are rational egoists, running the game in a noncooperative context makes it impossible to reach this efficient outcome. Player A, foreseeing that player B has no interest in returning anything at all to him or her in the final stage of the game, lacks any motive to give B a positive amount in the first stage. So the solution to this noncooperative game is a zero transfer, or in more technical terms, the zero transfer is the only subgame perfect equilibrium.[6] The experiments carried out by Fershtman and Gneezy (2001) reveal, however, that player A does give a positive amount, and that player B frequently gives back a greater amount. To be precise, Fershtman and Gneezy organize their experiment this way: the role of player A is assigned to students whose ethnic origin is not specified, and the role of player B to other students whose names sound either Ashkenazic or Oriental. Fershtman and Gneezy find that individuals with Oriental backgrounds receive lower transfers than others.

This result seems not to come from statistical discrimination, inasmuch as the behavior of players B during the running of the game is no different whether they are Ashkenazic or Oriental. Fershtman and Gneezy use the dictator game in order to show that their result does not come from a taste for discrimination either. In the dictator game, player A decides on a transfer to player B, who is unable to give anything back to player A. The amount of player A's gift is always tripled by the experimenter, which can only benefit player B, who has no strategic role in this game. On average, the experiment shows that those playing B obtain the same transfers whether they are Ashkenazic or Oriental. Hence it appears that the reduced gains of those of Oriental descent in the trust game do in fact result from a problem of trust on the part of player A, and not a taste for discrimination. Fershtman and Gneezy conclude that the discrimination springs from the existence of groundless stereotypes. What is more, when this experiment is run on a female population, women do not engage in discriminatory behavior; therefore they do not subscribe to the same stereotypes as men. The particular interest of this approach is that it sheds precise light on the origins of certain forms of discrimination.

Productivity Differences and Wage Differences

The third method consists of evaluating differences in productivity and comparing them to wage differences. Data available in the field of sports have made it possible to study wage discrimination between athletes of different ethnic origin (see Kahn, 1991 and 2000, for summaries). Discrimination of this kind against blacks was brought to light in the National Basketball Association in the 1980s. On the other hand, discrimination appears not to influence the salaries received by baseball players. Hellerstein et al. (1999) have tried to apply methods of this kind to industry by estimating the productivity differentials of workers belonging to different ethnic groups. They use surveys that match data about firms and individuals and compare them with estimated

Table 5.2

Coefficients relative to ethnic origin and sex in wage equations. The individual characteristics are education, experience, and region. The job characteristics are sector and status (full- or part-time).

Dependent variable: log hourly wage	Model 1	Model 2	Model 3
Blacks	−0.207 (0.012)	−0.119 (0.011)	−0.089 (0.011)
Hispanics	−0.379 (0.010)	−0.131 (0.010)	−0.102 (0.009)
Women	−0.279 (0.007)	−0.272 (0.006)	−0.221 (0.007)
Control			
Individual characteristics	No	Yes	Yes
Job characteristics	No	No	Yes

The figures in parentheses are standard errors.

Source: Altonji and Blank (1999).

wage differentials. The results they obtain tend to confirm assessments based on the estimation of wage equations: differences in income between ethnic groups generally correspond to differences in productivity, except for women, who on average receive wages lower than their productivity.

4.2.4 Main Results

As we have noted, the difficulty in estimating the impact of discrimination lies mainly in the assessment of the importance of omitted variables. Empirical results obtained through estimates of wage equations show that when the characteristics of individuals and the jobs available are controlled with sufficient care, the proportion of wage differences attributable to discrimination shrinks. It even tends to disappear for differences among ethnic groups in the United States.

The Importance of Omitted Variables

The size of the impact of unobserved variables is illustrated in tables 5.2 and 5.3, which present the results of estimates of hourly wage equations carried out by Altonji and Blank (1999) using the Current Population Survey panel in the United States in March 1996. Table 5.2 assesses the extent of discrimination following the method of dummy variables described by equation (9). The first column (Model 1) corresponds to estimates in which the only individual characteristics taken into account are membership in different groups (Hispanics, blacks, women). The figures reported in this column give the coefficients tied to the dummy variables. They are interpreted as the average loss of wage (in %) due to membership in the relevant group. According to these estimates, membership in these groups entails significant wage losses: around 21% for blacks, 38% for Hispanics, and 28% for women. The magnitude of these wage

Table 5.3

Decomposition of wage differences among ethnic groups and sexes.

Dependent variable: log hourly wage	Blacks/whites	Hispanics/whites	Women/men
Log hourly wage (difference)	−0.211	−0.305	−0.286
Amount due to:			
Characteristics	−0.114	−0.226	−0.076
Returns	−0.098	−0.079	−0.211
Differences due to characteristics:			
Education	−0.013	−0.024	−0.001
Experience	−0.048	−0.152	−0.003
Personal*	−0.020	0.008	−0.002
City and region	0.020	0.033	−0.001
Occupation	−0.058	−0.080	−0.012
Industry	0.006	−0.012	−0.036
Part-time and public sector	−0.000	0.001	−0.020
Differences due to returns:			
Education	0.082	0.012	−0.022
Experience	−0.197	−0.025	−0.023
Personal*	0.047	0.025	0.014
City and region	0.030	−0.032	−0.013
Occupation	−0.005	−0.058	−0.060
Industry	0.032	0.046	−0.004
Part-time and public sector	0.009	0.033	0.014

Source: Altonji and Blank (1999).

*Personal characteristics include gender and ethnic origin when necessary.

losses diminishes noticeably if we take into account individual characteristics like education, experience, and region (Model 2). It diminishes a little more if we add job characteristics, such as the industry in which the individual is working, and part-time work (Model 3). But these are steep losses nevertheless.

Table 5.3 pinpoints the wage differences among groups using the Blinder-Oaxaca decomposition. In this method, it is differences among objective characteristics that explain the largest part of wage differences among ethnic groups, whereas differences in the return to these characteristics explain the largest part of the wage differential between men and women. Hence, black and Hispanic ethnic minorities have lower levels of education and higher returns to schooling than whites. Conversely, these two groups have lower levels of, and lower returns to, professional experience than those of whites. Women have levels of education and experience very close to those of men, but the returns to these characteristics prove to be noticeably lower for them. The return to a given occupation likewise appears lower for women than for men.

Overall, tables 5.2 and 5.3 show that taking omitted variables into account can lead to substantial modifications of findings concerning the extent of wage discrimination.

Wage Differences and Gender

The bulk of empirical studies dedicated to estimating wage differentials between men and women conclude that a significant proportion of these differences remains unexplained by observable variables. Figure 5.10 gives values for the ratio between the average wage of women and men in 22 countries at the end of the 1980s and the beginning of the 1990s. Women's wages are shown to be systematically lower than those of men. The ratio of women's wages to men's varied between 87% in Slovenia and 42% in Japan. For all the reasons cited above, these gross ratios do not give us a measure of the degree of wage discrimination against women.

Nevertheless, estimations of wage equations do generally conclude that observed characteristics of jobs and individuals explain only a portion of the wage differentials between genders (see table 5.3). It is a phenomenon found in many countries. Blau and Kahn (2001) find that taking education and experience into account explains only a part of the wage difference observed between genders in the countries in figure 5.10. Alternative methods that rely on experiments or on the comparison of estimates of productivities and wages also throw light on the extent of discrimination. Thus, Hellerstein et al. (1999) found that women have a productivity around 15% lower than that of men in industry in the United States, but the wage they receive is around 30% lower. It should be noted, however, that the application of this method to French data leads to different results, since Crépon et al. (2001) found that wage differences between men and women exactly reflect differences in productivity. This study therefore suggests that the extent of discrimination against women is different from one country to another. The work of Blau and Kahn (2001) and the OECD (2002) confirms this general result. It shows that wage differences between men and women are significantly influenced by the overall distribution of wages in each country. In particular, the broader the area covered by collective negotiations—which generally leads to a reduction in the spread of wages—the less the difference between the wages of men and women.

The Movement of Women's Relative Wages

The study of the movement of the relative wages of women and men during the 1970s and 1980s in the United States has also drawn much attention. The wage gap between men and women remained stable between the Second World War and the end of the 1970s, but shrank noticeably during the 1980s, as figure 5.11 shows. This movement went along with an increase in inequalities assessed over the total distribution of wages. It may therefore seem surprising that the relative position of women, whose performance in the labor market is traditionally inferior to that of men, should have improved over this period.

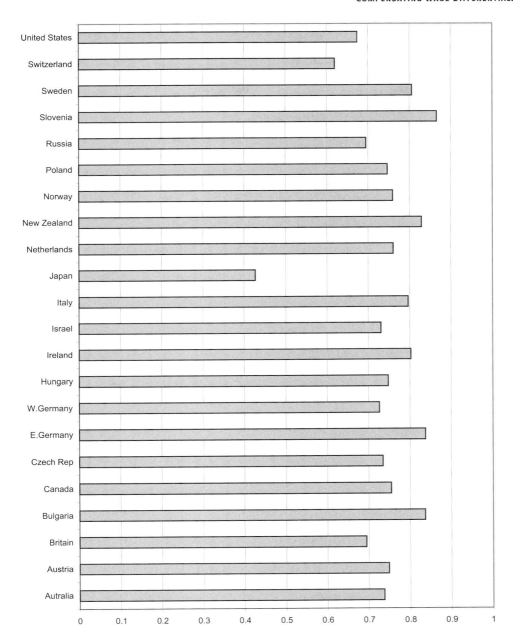

FIGURE 5.10
The ratio of women's wages to men's wages, adjusted for hours, in 22 countries at the end of the 1980s and beginning of the 1990s.

Source: Blau and Kahn (2001).

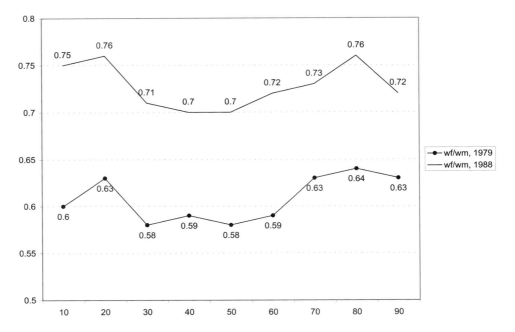

FIGURE 5.11
Ratio of hourly wages of women to those of men by decile in the United States.

Source: Blau and Kahn (1997, figure 1).

The decomposition of wage gaps during the decade of the 1980s suggests that the overall shift in a direction favoring women resulted from the combined working of opposing movements. Table 5.4 portrays the decomposition carried out by Blau and Kahn (1997) on the basis of equation (14). It shows that the reduction in the wage gap between men and women resulted from an improvement in the observed characteristics of women, like education, experience, types of jobs held, and the trend toward trade unionization, which was more favorable to women than men over this period. Nonetheless, the price effects observed have contributed to an *increase* in the wage gap between genders: women, who always hold less skilled jobs, the kind to which relative returns have fallen, have been disadvantaged by this phenomenon. The decomposition of terms corresponding to unobserved characteristics comes to the same type of conclusion. Unobserved price effects have contributed to increasing the wage gap, while changes in unobserved characteristics have pushed the wage gap the other way. Hence the combined trend in characteristics, observed and unobserved, of women, represented in the penultimate line of table 5.4, turns out to be favorable to women. In contrast, the total contribution of price effects, reported in the last line, has run counter to the reduction of wage gaps. Finally, the estimates of Blau and Kahn (1997) also show that the unobserved part of the wage gap between men and women has substantially declined—the decline is given by the sum of terms (3) and (4) in

Table 5.4

Decomposition of the movement in the wage gap, 1979–1988. Wage gaps D_t are defined as the gaps between the averages of the wage logarithms of men and women, hence: $D_t = \ln(w_{mt}) - \ln(w_{ft})$.

Change in differential ($D_{88} - D_{79}$)	−.1522
$(\Delta x_{88} - \Delta x_{79})\hat{\beta}_{88}$ (1)	−.1244
Education	−.0088
Experience	−.0529
Occupation	−.0458
Collective bargaining	−.175
Industry	−.0012
$\Delta x_{88}(\hat{\beta}_{88} - \hat{\beta}_{79})$ (2)	.0997
Education	.0013
Experience	.0219
Occupation	.0441
Collective bargaining	.0081
Industry	.0215
$(\Delta \hat{\theta}_{88} - \Delta \hat{\theta}_{79})\hat{\sigma}_{88}$ (3)	−.1420
$\Delta \hat{\theta}_{88}(\hat{\sigma}_{88} - \hat{\sigma}_{79})$ (4)	.0143
Sum gender-specific ((1) + (3))	−.2664
Sum wage structure ((2) + (4))	.1140

Source: Blau and Kahn (1997, table 2).

table 5.4—which points to the conclusion that either discrimination against women has declined or that their unobserved characteristics have moved closer to those of men.

Wage Differences Between Ethnic Groups

The results of certain studies—tables 5.2 and 5.3—which show that in the United States, a large part of the differences in income between ethnic groups could be explained by the differences between "objective" individual characteristics, have provoked numerous debates. These debates have been fueled by the work of Neal and Johnson (1996), who utilized the results of the Armed Forces Qualifying Test, education, and the type of job held by parents as supplementary individual characteristics. The unexplained component of the differences in income among groups then becomes not significantly different from zero (see also Altonji and Blank, 1999). These results have been confirmed by the study of Hellerstein et al. (1999), who directly compared estimates of wage differentials and productivities.

Other approaches, however, yield opposite conclusions. In particular, experiments carried out to compare the performances of workers through audit studies indicate that discrimination is present during the hiring process. On the other hand,

Eckstein and Wolpin (1999) have shown, utilizing a job search model, that discrimination in terms of *offered wages* at the time of hiring can lead to much weaker discrimination in terms of wages *accepted*. According to their estimates for high school graduates, the differences among ethnic groups in wages offered are three times greater than the differences in those accepted. These results suggest that it is not enough to focus on wages in order to detect the presence of discrimination in the labor market, and they also show the limits of estimations of wage equations in this area. It is necessary to take into account the histories of individuals, including their periods of unemployment, the manner in which they conduct job searches, and the kinds of jobs they wind up holding.

Studies on the movement of the inequalities between blacks and whites during the 1980s in the United States find that improvements in education and experience of blacks contributed to reducing the wage gap between whites and blacks. But observed and unobserved price effects—using the terminology of the decomposition of Juhn et al. (1993) presented above—have worked in the opposite direction and have prevailed, leading to an increase in the average wage gap between whites and blacks over this period (Juhn et al., 1993; Card and Lemieux, 1996). In sum, the relative wages of blacks have declined, for they were situated at the low end of a wage distribution that had a tendency to widen during a period in which inequalities generally increased. There is not, from this perspective, any indication of a marked shift in discrimination against blacks over this period.

Affirmative Action

We have pointed out that it is possible to combat discrimination by imposing constraints that compel firms to correct behaviors that create disadvantage for certain demographic groups. Affirmative action, in place in the United States since the beginning of the 1960s, is an example of this. It has led to a large number of decisions in the wake of Kennedy Executive Order 10925 in 1961, which requires that firms contracting with the government "take affirmative action to ensure that applicants are employed and employees are treated during employment without regard to their race, creed, color, or national origin." Following this decision, the policy of affirmative action underwent a number of developments. In 1965, Johnson Executive Order 11246 reiterated Kennedy Executive Order 10925. In 1967, Johnson Executive Order 11375 stated that Executive Order 11246 applied to women as well. In 1968, Department of Labor Regulations Governing Executive Orders 11266 and 11375 made it mandatory for firms contracting with the federal government and that had more than 50 employees or a contract worth more than $50,000 to establish the degree to which women and minorities were underrepresented in their workforce, then set out corrective goals and a timetable for achieving them. In 1979, in *United Steelworkers of America v Weber*, a case regarding a training program in which 50% of the places were reserved for blacks, the Supreme Court decided that the Civil Rights Act of 1964 "does not prohibit such race-conscious affirmative action plans." The judgment states clearly that such plans, which aim to remedy entrenched phenomena of segregation, are legitimate.

This series of decisions shows that demographic groups that are undergoing discrimination obtain the benefit of programs that give firms contracting with the government an incentive to hire them. Empirical studies dedicated to the consequences of affirmative action have sought, in the first place, to detect its impact on wages. The evidence is that it very probably favored blacks and women during the 1960s and 1970s, although to assess the extent of this effect with precision is a very tricky business (see Donohue and Heckman, 1991). Other studies focused on the distorting effects of these programs, attempting to discover whether they drove firms to recruit underperforming workers. In their overview of the literature, Holzer and Neumark (2000a, 2000b) emphasize that there is nothing to point to the conclusion that women who benefited from affirmative action had lower levels of education or experience than those of men in comparable types of jobs. Their performance in the labor market was likewise comparable. On the other hand, the levels of education and experience of ethnic minorities who benefited from affirmative action programs are frequently lower than those of their white colleagues. Their performance in the labor market is, however, very close to that of whites. Holzer and Neumark (2000b) show that this result arises from the fact that employers practicing affirmative action select members of ethnic minorities with greater rigor at the hiring stage. Overall, Holzer and Neumark (2000a) estimate that losses in productivity owing to affirmative action appear to be limited. The global effects of affirmative action remain little understood, however, and continue to be the focus of plentiful research.

4.3   INDUSTRY AND FIRM WAGE DIFFERENTIALS

In a perfectly competitive labor market, with given productive abilities and working conditions, the wage of any individual ought to be independent of the firm or industry in which he or she is employed. If one industry or firm pays better than others, perfect mobility of workers ought to lead to a flow of labor supply toward that firm or industry and a consequent drop in remuneration. But the existence of persistent wage differentials between industries and firms is a stark and abundantly documented fact. Slichter (1950) had already established that this was the case for American workers between 1923 and 1946.

4.3.1   The Traditional Approach

Let w_{it} be the hourly wage of an individual i at date t; let $\mathbf{x}_{it}$ be the vector of his or her personal characteristics and those of his or her job at the same date; and let γ_j be a fixed industry effect, where $j = J(i, t)$ is the industry of worker i in period t. Interindustry wage differences are generally highlighted by estimating an equation of the form:

$$\ln w_{it} = \mathbf{x}_{it}\boldsymbol{\beta} + \gamma_{J(i, t)} + \varepsilon_{it} \qquad (15)$$

In this equation, ε_{it} designates an independent, identically distributed statistic residual. The coordinates of vectors $\boldsymbol{\beta}$ and γ are parameters to be estimated. In particular, the coordinates of vector γ indicate the influence of the industries on wages. If these coefficients are null, the theory of compensating wage differentials is not

Table 5.5

Estimates of interindustry wage differences in France, 1990–1995.

Industry	Model without fixed individual effect	Model with fixed individual effect
Agriculture	−0.101 (0.07)	−0.017 (0.016)
Mining (coal)	0.139 (0.020)	0.058 (0.056)
Petroleum	0.210 (0.018)	0.049 (0.027)
Electricity	0.108 (0.007)	0.058 (0.019)
Chemical	0.163 (0.009)	0.016 (0.019)
Food retail	−0.112 (0.007)	−0.043 (0.014)
Hotels, bars, and restaurants	−0.175 (0.006)	−0.008 (0.012)

Figures in parentheses are standard errors.

Source: Goux and Maurin (1999).

Note: Aside from industry, the variables taken into account are experience in the labor market, job seniority, place of residence, education, nationality (French or foreign), and profession. How to read the table: according to the model without fixed individual effect, a wage-earner in agriculture receives, on average, a wage of 10.1.

invalidated. If they are significantly different from zero, we must conclude either that there are omitted variables or that the theory of compensating wage differentials is invalidated. Traditionally, the estimation of this type of equation gives coefficients for vector γ that are significantly different from 0. The first column of table 5.5 presents the results obtained by Goux and Maurin (1999) for France in 1990–1995, with a breakdown into 39 industries. According to these estimations, the standard gap due to industry is of the order of 8%–9%. We also observe that the industries that pay the least (agriculture, food retail, and hotel, bar, and restaurant) offered wages 15% lower on average than the rest of the economy. The industries that pay the most (petroleum, mining, chemicals) offered wages that were on average 15% above those in the rest of the economy. Goux and Maurin note as well that these wage differences persist over time.

4.3.2　The Importance of Unobserved Worker Ability Differences

The results presented in the first column of table 5.5 are similar to those obtained for France and the United States by Dickens and Katz (1987), Krueger and Summers (1988), Katz and Summers (1989), Abowd et al. (1999), and Abowd and Kramarz (1999). At first glance, these results suggest that the labor markets are far from being perfectly competitive. Their interpretation is a delicate matter, however. It is quite possible that wage differentials are caused by an unobserved heterogeneity of workers. If those with the greatest productive abilities (unobserved) are concentrated in the same industries, those industries must pay higher wages. In that case, the model explaining wages is described not by equation (15) but by:

$$\ln w_{it} = \mathbf{x}_{it}\boldsymbol{\beta} + \gamma_{J(i,t)} + \alpha_i + \varepsilon_{it} \tag{16}$$

where α_i designates the unobserved abilities of individual i. If data for several periods are available, it is possible to eliminate this term by estimating equation (16) in differences for workers who stay in the same industry. Such estimations, carried out on U.S. and French data and covering a sufficiently large number of industries (Murphy and Topel, 1987; Abowd et al., 1999; and Goux and Maurin, 1999), find that interindustry wage differentials are to a very large extent explained by the characteristics of workers. The second column of table 5.5, taken from Goux and Maurin (1999), gives a striking illustration of this. It shows that the contribution of industry to wage setting is much smaller, and often not significantly different from zero, at the threshold of 5%. Further, Goux and Maurin point out that there is a very weak correlation, less than 0.25, between the coefficients estimated by the models with and without fixed individual effect. Finally, they find that the wage variations undergone by an individual in changing industry do not exceed 2%–3%. These results point to the conclusion that interindustry wage differences are essentially explained by individual effects. They are very different from the results obtained by Krueger and Summers (1988) and Gibbons and Katz (1992), who, with a smaller number of industries (around 20, rather than around 40), found that industry makes a significant contribution to wage formation, after controlling for fixed individual effects. But by adopting a breakdown similar to that of Krueger and Summers (1988) and Gibbons and Katz (1992), Goux and Maurin (1999) arrived at conclusions close to theirs for French data. That being so, the results that tend to prove the importance of the industry component obtained by Krueger and Summers (1988) and Gibbons and Katz (1992) are most likely the result of an aggregation bias caused by using too few industries.

4.3.3 Industry Effect and Firm Effect

Although the impact of industry on wage formation appears very slight, all things considered, we should not jump to the conclusion that labor markets function in a perfectly competitive manner. It is quite possible that imperfect competition leads to heterogeneous wages among firms in the same industry. An approach like the one just described must be used to study this problem, but with identification of the firms, and not just the industries, in which individuals work. Studies that take this approach show unambiguously that the impact of the firm is greater than that of the industry (Abowd et al., 1999; Goux and Maurin, 1999). Goux and Maurin, for example, assess the average of the difference in wages paid to an identical worker employed at two different firms in France at 20%–30%, whereas it does not exceed 2%–3% for a change of industry. They show, moreover, that these differences are positively correlated with the size and the capital/labor ratio of firms. The correlations with productivity and profitability are much less significant. Once again, the interpretation of these results is a delicate matter. It is possible that wage differences among firms may be the result of unobserved differences linked to working conditions. The hedonic theory of wages postulates that a wage reflects not just productive ability, but also the content of the tasks an employee must carry out at his or her workplace: more dangerous, more unstable, and more laborious jobs are compensated for by higher wages. As these characteristics of jobs are generally poorly measured, it remains possible that the unobserved heterogeneity of jobs does explain wage differences among firms, according to a perfectly competitive logic.

5   SUMMARY AND CONCLUSION

- According to the model of perfect competition, workers receive wages equal to their marginal productivity. The hedonic theory of wages shows that the mechanism of perfect competition allows agents to choose different working conditions, and that wage differentials "compensate" for the laboriousness or danger of tasks. Testing the extent of such wage compensation runs into difficulties having to do, on the one hand, with unobserved individual characteristics, and on the other, with the heterogeneity of individual preferences when it comes to the advantageous or disagreeable aspects of the working conditions of a job. Empirical studies do, however, bring to light phenomena of wage compensation in many circumstances. But the orders of magnitude obtained must be interpreted with caution because of the weight of the omitted variables.

- Monopsony exerts a negative effect on wages and employment. Its existence presupposes limited mobility of workers and entry costs that hinder other firms from coming in to compete for the labor pool in question. This imperfection in competition allows the monopsony to discriminate against certain categories of workers for long periods without being forced out of the market.

- In the absence of complete contracts, hiring and training costs work in favor of insiders when it comes to rent sharing. Wage gaps then no longer reflect productivity differentials alone.

- Employers, who cannot observe the abilities of workers perfectly, are faced with a problem of adverse selection. This makes it impossible for a person's wage to match his or her (unobservable) marginal productivity, and labor market equilibrium ends by allocating resources inefficiently, with the most productive workers no longer participating in the labor market.

- The term "statistical discrimination" applies to a situation in which individuals with identical abilities but membership in different demographic groups have divergent career paths because of the average productivity, real or imagined, of agents belonging to their group. In this case, the beliefs of employers concerning the average quality of a demographic group can become "self-fulfilling prophecies" and provoke the appearance and persistence of productivity differences between groups, to the detriment of the ones discriminated against in the first place. A quota policy, providing for the hiring of a given proportion of members of a certain group, may turn out to be ineffective if it has the effect of discouraging efforts to acquire education.

- The difficulty of evaluating discrimination lies mainly in assessing the weight of unobserved individual characteristics. If we use sufficient care in controlling for the characteristics of individuals and those of jobs offered, the proportion of wage differences attributable to discrimination declines. The majority of studies, though, conclude that in the United States, women are the victims of significant wage discrimination. The extent of wage discrimination against women does vary from one country to another.

- Providing that the data are disaggregated to a sufficient degree, unobserved individual heterogeneity explains the core of interindustry wage differences. The share of wage differences explained by the heterogeneity of firms, on the other hand, remains large. In France, for example, the average of the differences in wage paid to an identical worker employed in two different firms lies in the 20%–30% range, but does not exceed the 2%–3% range from one industry to another.

6   RELATED TOPICS IN THE BOOK

- Chapter 3, section 2.1: Wages in the equilibrium search model

- Chapter 6, section 4.4: The efficiency wage model

- Chapter 7, section 3: Wage determination through collective bargaining

- Chapter 9, sections 3 and 6: The matching model and the efficiency of labor market equilibrium

- Chapter 9, section 4.2: Investment and the holdup problem

- Chapter 12, section 1: The effects of the minimum wage

7   FURTHER READINGS

Altonji, J., and Blank, R. (1999), "Race and gender in the labor market," in Ashenfelter, O., and Card, D. (eds.), *Handbook of Labor Economics*, vol. 3C, chap. 48, pp. 3143–3259, Amsterdam: Elsevier Science/North-Holland.

Arrow, K. (1998), "What has economics to say about racial discrimination?" *Journal of Economic Perspectives*, 12, pp. 91–100.

Becker, G. (1957), *The Economics of Discrimination*, Chicago: University of Chicago Press.

Rosen, S. (1986), "The theory of equalizing differences," in Ashenfelter, O., and Layard, R. (eds.), *Handbook of Labor Economics*, vol. 1, chap. 12, pp. 641–692, Amsterdam: Elsevier Science/North Holland.

REFERENCES

Abowd, J., and Kramarz, F. (1999), "Inter-industry and firm-size wage differentials in France and the United-States," mimeo, CREST-INSEE.

Abowd, J., Kramarz, F., and Margolis, D. (1999), "High wage workers and high wage firms," *Econometrica*, 67, pp. 251–335.

Adams, J. (1963), "Toward an understanding of inequity," *Journal of Abnormal and Social Psychology*, 67, pp. 442–436.

Akerlof, G. (1970), "The market for 'lemons': Qualitative uncertainty and the market mechanism," *Quarterly Journal of Economics*, 84, pp. 488–500.

Akerlof, G. (1982), "Labor contracts as partial gift exchange," *Quarterly Journal of Economics*, 87, pp. 543–569.

Akerlof, G., and Yellen, J. (1986), *Efficiency Wage Models of the Labor Market*, Cambridge, U.K.: Cambridge University Press.

Akerlof, G., and Yellen, J. (1990), "The fair wage-effort hypotheses and unemployment," *Quarterly Journal of Economics*, 105, pp. 255–283.

Altonji, J., and Blank, R. (1999), "Race and gender in the labor market," in Ashenfelter, O., and Card, D. (eds.), *Handbook of Labor Economics*, vol. 3C, chap. 48, pp. 3143–3259, Amsterdam: Elsevier Science/North-Holland.

Argyle, M. (1989), *The Social Psychology of Work*, 2nd ed., Harmondsworth, U.K.: Penguin.

Arrow, K. (1973), "The theory of discrimination," in Ashenfelter, O., and Rees, A. (eds.), *Discrimination in Labor Markets*, pp. 3–33, Princeton, N.J.: Princeton University Press.

Arrow, K. (1998), "What has economics to say about racial discrimination?" *Journal of Economic Perspectives*, 12, pp. 91–100.

Barth, E., and Dale-Olsen, H. (1999), "Monopsonistic discrimination and the gender-wage gap," NBER Working Paper W7197.

Becker, G. (1957), *The Economics of Discrimination*, Chicago: University of Chicago Press.

Becker, G. (1964), *Human Capital*, New York: National Bureau of Economic Research.

Bertrand, J. (1883), "Théorie mathématique de la richesse sociale," *Journal des Savants*, 67, pp. 499–508.

Bewley, T. (1998), "Why not cut pay," *European Economic Review*, 42, pp. 459–490.

Black, D. (1995), "Discrimination in an equilibrium search model," *Journal of Labor Economics*, 13, pp. 309–334.

Blau, F., and Kahn, L. (1996), "Wage structure and gender differentials: An international comparison," *Economica*, 63, suppl., pp. S29–S62.

Blau, F., and Kahn, L. (1997), "Swimming upstream: Trends in the gender wage differential in the 1980s," *Journal of Labor Economics*, 15, pp. 1–42.

Blau, F., and Kahn, L. (2001), "Understanding international differences in the gender pay gap," NBER Working Paper 8200.

Blinder, A. (1974), *Toward an Economic Theory of Income Distribution*, Cambridge, Mass.: MIT Press.

Blinder, A., and Choi, D. (1990), "A shred of evidence on theories of wage stickiness," *Quarterly Journal of Economics*, 105, pp. 1003–1015.

Bound, J., and Freeman, R. (1992), "What went wrong? The erosion of relative earnings and employment among young black men in the 1980s," *Quarterly Journal of Economics*, 107, pp. 201–232.

Brown, C. (1980), "Equalizing differences in the labor market," *Quarterly Journal of Economics*, 94, pp. 113–134.

Brown, C. (1984), "Black-white earnings ratios since the Civil Rights Act of 1964: The importance of labor market dropouts," *Quarterly Journal of Economics*, 99, pp. 31–44.

Butler, R., and Heckman, J. (1977), "The government's impact on the labor market status of black Americans: A critical review," in Farrell, B. (ed.), *Equal Rights and Industrial Relations*, pp. 235–281, Madison, Wis.: Industrial Relations Research Association.

Cain, G. (1986), "The economic analysis of labor market discrimination: A survey," in Ashenfelter, O., and Layard, R. (eds.), *Handbook of Labor Economics*, vol. 1, chap. 13, pp. 693–785, Amsterdam: Elsevier Science/North-Holland.

Campbell, C., and Kamlani, K. (1997), "The reasons for wage rigidity: Evidence from a survey of firms," *Quarterly Journal of Economics*, 112, pp. 759–789.

Card, D., and Lemieux, T. (1996), "Wage dispersion, returns to skill and black-white wage differentials," *Journal of Econometrics*, 74, pp. 319–361.

Chandra, A. (2000), "Labor market dropouts and the racial wage gap: 1960–1990," *American Economic Review*, 90, pp. 333–338.

Cho, K., and Kreps, K. (1987), "Signaling games and stable equilibria," *Quarterly Journal of Economics*, 102, pp. 179–221.

Coate, S., and Loury, G. (1993), "Will affirmative action eliminate negative stereotypes?" *American Economic Review*, 83, pp. 1220–1240.

Cotton, J. (1988), "On the decomposition of wage differentials," *Review of Economics and Statistics*, 70, pp. 236–243.

Crépon, B., Deniau, N., and Perez-Duarte, S. (2001), "Wages, productivity and worker characteristics: A French perspective," CREST-INSEE, http://www.ensae.fr.

Darity, W., and Mason, P. (1998), "Evidence on discrimination unemployment: Code of colors, codes of genders," *Journal of Economic Perspectives*, 12, pp. 63–90.

Dickens, W., and Katz, L. (1987), "Inter-industry wage differences and industry characteristics," in Lang, K., and Leonard, J. (eds.), *Unemployment and the Structure of Labor Markets*, Oxford, U.K.: Basil Blackwell.

Donohue, J., and Heckman, J. (1991), "Continuous versus episodic change: The impact of civil rights policy on the economic status of blacks," *Journal of Economic Literature*, 29, pp. 1603–1643.

Duncan, G., and Holmlund, B. (1983), "Was Adam Smith right after all? Another test of the theory of compensating wage differentials," *Journal of Labor Economics*, 1, pp. 366–379.

Eckstein, Z., and Wolpin, K. (1999), "Estimating the effect of racial discrimination on first job offers," *Review of Economics and Statistics*, 81, pp. 384–392.

Fehr, E., and Falk, A. (1999), "Wage rigidity in a competitive incomplete contract market," *Journal of Political Economy*, 107, pp. 1106–1134.

Fershtman, C., and Gneezy, U. (2001), "Discrimination in a segmented society: An experimental approach," *Quarterly Journal of Economics*, 116, pp. 351–377.

Fortin, N., and Lemieux, T. (1998), "Rank regressions, wage distributions and the gender gap," *Journal of Human Resources*, 33, pp. 610–643.

Gibbons, R., and Katz, L. (1992), "Does unmeasured ability explain inter-industry wage differentials?" *Review of Economic Studies*, 59, pp. 515–535.

Goldin, C., and Rouse, C. (2000), "Orchestrating impartiality: The impact of 'blind' auditions on female musicians," *American Economic Review*, 90, pp. 715–736.

Gordon, N., and Morton, T. (1974), "A low mobility model of wage discrimination with special reference to sex differential," *Journal of Economic Theory*, 7, pp. 241–253.

Goux, D., and Maurin, E. (1999), "Persistence of inter industry wage differentials: A reexamination using matched worker-firm panel data," *Journal of Labor Economics*, 17, pp. 492–533.

Grout, P. (1984), "Investment and wage in the absence of binding contracts: A Nash bargaining approach," *Econometrica*, 52, pp. 449–460.

Heckman, J. (1979), "Sample selection bias as a specification error," *Econometrica*, 47, pp. 153–162.

Heckman, J. (1998), "Detecting discrimination," *Journal of Economic Perspectives*, 12, pp. 101–116.

Heckman, J., Lyons, T., and Todd, P. (2000), "Understanding black-white wage differentials, 1960–1990," *American Economic Review, Papers and Proceedings*, 90, pp. 344–349.

Hellerstein, J., Neumark, D., and Troske, K. (1999), "Wages, productivity and workers characteristics: Evidence from plant-level production functions and wage equations," *Journal of Labor Economics*, 17, pp. 409–446.

Holzer, H., and Neumark, D. (2000a), "Assessing affirmative action," *Journal of Economic Literature*, 38(3), pp. 483–568.

Holzer, H., and Neumark, D. (2000b), "What does affirmative action do?" *Industrial and Labor Relations Review*, 53, pp. 240–271.

Hwang, H., Mortensen, D., and Reed, R. (1998), "Hedonic wages and labor market search," *Journal of Labor Economics*, 16, pp. 815–847.

Hwang, H., Reed, R., and Hubbard, C. (1992), "Compensating wage differentials and unobserved productivity," *Journal of Political Economy*, 100, pp. 835–858.

Juhn, C., Murphy, K., and Pierce, B. (1993), "Wage inequality and the rise in returns to skill," *Journal of Political Economy*, 101, pp. 410–442.

Kahn, L. (1991), "Discrimination in professional sports: A survey of the literature," *Industrial and Labor Relation Review*, 44, pp. 395–418.

Kahn, L. (2000), "The sports business as a labor market laboratory," *Journal of Economic Perspectives*, 14, pp. 75–94.

Katz, L., and Summers, L. (1989), "Industry rents: Evidence and implications," in *Brookings Papers on Economic Activity: Microeconomics*, pp. 209–275.

Krueger, A., and Summers, L. (1988), "Efficiency wages and the inter-industry wage structure," *Econometrica*, 56, pp. 259–293.

Kunze, A. (2000), "The determination of wages and the gender wage gap: A survey," IZA Discussion Paper No. 193, http://www.iza.org.

Lang, K. (1986), "A language theory of discrimination," *Quarterly Journal of Economics*, 10, pp. 363–382.

Lawler, E. (1994), *Motivation in Work Organizations*, San Francisco: Jossey-Bass.

Lindbeck, A., and Snower, D. (1988), "Cooperation, harassment and involuntary unemployment: An insider-outsider approach," *American Economic Review*, 78, pp. 167–188.

Loury, G. (1998), "Discrimination in the post-civil rights era: Beyond market interactions," *Journal of Economic Perspectives*, 12, pp. 117–126.

Loury, G. (2002), *The Anatomy of Racial Inequality*, Cambridge, Mass.: Harvard University Press.

Lundberg, S., and Startz, R. (1983), "Private discrimination and social intervention in competitive labor markets," *American Economic Review*, 73, pp. 340–347.

Mas-Colell, A., Whinston, M., and Green, J. (1995), *Microeconomic Theory*, New York: Oxford University Press.

Mauss, M. (1923), "Essai sur le don, forme et raison del'échange dans les sociétés archaïques," *Année Sociologiquej*, vol. 1, reprinted in Mauss, M., *Sociologie et Anthropologie*, PUF, collection Quadrige, 1983, Paris.

Mincer, J. (1974), *Schooling, Experience and Earnings*, New York: National Bureau of Economic Research.

Montgomery, E., Show, K., and Benedict, M.-H. (1992), "Pensions and wages: An hedonic price theory approach," *International Economic Review*, 33, pp. 111–128.

Murphy, K., and Topel, R. (1987), "Unemployment, risk and earnings," in Lang, K., and Leonard, J. (eds.), *Unemployment and the Structure of Labor Markets*, London: Basil Blackwell.

Neal, D., and Johnson, W. (1996), "The role of premarket factors in black-white wage differences," *Journal of Political Economy*, 104, pp. 869–895.

Neumark, D. (1999), "Wage differentials by race and sex. The roles of taste discrimination and labor market information," *Industrial Relations*, 38(3), pp. 414–445.

Oaxaca, R. (1973), "Male-female wage differentials in urban labormarkets," *International Economic Review*, 14, pp. 693–709.

Oaxaca, R., and Ransom, M. (1994), "On discrimination and the decomposition of wage differentials," *Journal of Econometrics*, 61, pp. 5–21.

OECD (1994), *The OECD Jobs Study: Evidence and Explanations*, Paris: OECD.

OECD (2002), "Women at work: Who are they and how are they faring?" in OECD, *Employment Outlook*, chap. 2, pp. 61–126, Paris: OECD.

Phelps, E. (1972), "The statistical theory of racism and sexism," *American Economic Review*, 62, pp. 639–651.

Rosen, S. (1974), "Hedonic prices and implicit markets," *Journal of Political Economy*, 82, pp. 34–55.

Rosen, S. (1986), "The theory of equalizing differences," in Ashenfelter, O., and Layard, R. (eds.), *Handbook of Labor Economics*, vol. 1, chap. 12, pp. 641–692, Amsterdam: Elsevier Science/North-Holland.

Slichter, G. (1950), "Notes on the structure of wages," *Review of Economics and Statistics*, 32, pp. 80–91.

Solon, G. (1999), "Intergenerational mobility in the labor market," in Ashenfelter, O., and Card, D. (eds.), *Handbook of Labor Economics*, vol. 3A, chap. 29, Amsterdam: Elsevier Science/North-Holland.

Stigler, G. (1946), "The economics of minimum wage legislation," *American Economic Review*, 36, pp. 358–365.

Stouffer, S., Suchman, E., de Vinney, L., Star, S., and Williams, R. (1949), *The American Soldier: Adjustment During Army Life*, vol. 1, Princeton, N.J.: Princeton University Press.

Suen, W. (1997), "Decomposing wage residuals," *Journal of Labor Economics*, 15, pp. 555–566.

Thaler, R., and Rosen, S. (1976), "The value of saving a life: Evidence from the labor market," in Terleckyj, N. (ed.), *Household Production and Consumption*, New York: Columbia University Press.

Weiss, A. (1980), "Job queues and layoffs in labor markets with flexible wages," *Journal of Political Economy*, 88, pp. 526–538.

Weiss, A. (1983), "A sorting-cum-learning model of education," *Journal of Political Economy*, 91, pp. 420–442.

Weiss, Y., and Fershtman, C. (1998), "Social status and economic performance: A survey," *European Economic Review*, 42, pp. 801–821.

Williamson, O. (1975), *Markets and Hierarchies*, New York: Free Press.

CHAPTER 6

CONTRACTS, RISK-SHARING, AND INCENTIVE

CONTENTS

In this chapter, we will see

- Why firms and workers engage in long-term relationships

- How the trade-off between insurance and incentive acts on the remuneration rule for labor

- Why firms make use of hierarchical promotions and internal markets

- The links between seniority, experience, and wages

- The efficiency wage theory

INTRODUCTION

Within firms, those who manage human resources have a toolkit of apparently quite varied measures at their disposal (Gibbons and Waldman, 1999b). The strategic variables currently used to optimize the return on labor include promotion, bonuses, profit-sharing, status distinctions, quality circles, investment in training, and dismissal. Such a toolkit leads us to ask, what form would an optimal remuneration rule for labor take? A priori, a remuneration rule ought to be based on the complete array of information available to both sides—primarily the results of the activity of the employees, and observation of the environment in which this activity takes place. The theory of contracts explains how technology and the preferences of actors both influence the choice of strategies for managing human resources (see Hart and Holmström, 1987; Salanié, 1997; Malcomson, 1999; and Prendergast, 1999, for complete presentations, and Milgrom and Roberts, 1992, for an excellent nontechnical one). To be more precise, this theory analyzes how contractual relations allow two different types of problem to be managed: the *uncertainty of the environment*, and the *private nature of certain information* concerning the activities and the performance of workers.

The wage relationship is generally a long-term one, which takes concrete form when a "labor contract" is signed. Curiously, this type of contract very often specifies only rights and duties of a purely *formal* nature, without always linking remuneration explicitly to performance. Simon (1951) had already noted this essential difference between an ordinary contract of sale and purchase, and a labor contract governing a hierarchical relationship. Above all, a labor contract betokens a relationship of *subordination*, meaning that an employer and an employee have agreed that the latter will exercise his or her profession under the authority of the former. It may also set out the length of time this agreement will last and the amount of remuneration to be paid. Such a remuneration very often depends on criteria, such as seniority, that do not, at first sight, appear to have much to do with individual performance. Doeringer and Piore (1971) have drawn attention to the fact that large firms set up "internal markets" that function according to a logic very different from that of a competitive market of the kind described in the previous chapter, where the remuneration of workers hinges on their productivity. A priori, though, it would seem to be more efficient to pay an employee according to the tasks that he or she effectively carries out, in other words to pay him or her a wage corresponding to his or her output—the system known as "piece rate." In reality the modes of remuneration vary widely. Freeman and Rogers (1999) estimate that around 45% of workers in the private sector in the United States in 1998 were receiving a remuneration that partly depended on their own performance, or that of their firm, through some type of collective profit-sharing or employee stock ownership plan. These authors highlight the fact that during the 1990s the way workers are paid in the United States tended to shift toward remuneration linked to performance. So the pay employees receive is made up of some combination (the weighting varies) of time wages, piece rate, stock ownership, and collective profit-sharing. Our aim in this chapter is to show that problems of incentive and risk-sharing play a determining role in how these components are weighted.

In section 1, key concepts relating to the labor contract are defined. Section 2 concentrates on contractual relationships when the actions of wage-earners are verifiable by an impartial judge and the economic environment is uncertain; in this situation, the labor contract proves useful as an efficient way to share risk. Section 3 analyzes the labor relationship when the actions of wage-earners are not verifiable, but the result of them is. This context permits us to understand incentive problems, and the linkage between a worker's pay and the results of his or her activity; in particular, it specifies how punishments, rewards, and the tailoring of individual remunerations come into play as means of incentive. Finally, section 4 deals with incentive problems in informational structures in which neither actions nor results are verifiable. Such is generally the case for workers performing complex tasks. In this setting, there is no point in making a contract that stipulates a remuneration based on performance, since the latter cannot be verified by a third party should a dispute arise. As we will see, the impossibility of verifying the actions and performances of agents explains two elements frequently encountered in systems of remuneration: wages that rise with seniority, and systems of internal promotion.

1 THE LABOR CONTRACT

The features of labor contracts depend, to a large extent, on whether or not the results of an employee's activity can be observed and taken into account. These results can only appear explicitly in the contract if they are verifiable. If they are not, the work relationship is governed by implicit and self-enforcing clauses.

1.1 EXPLICIT AND IMPLICIT CLAUSES

To set up a system of remuneration based on observed results is to presume that the latter can be established beyond dispute. This is why the terms used in drawing up the contractual document properly speaking are called *verifiable* elements. Under this heading are grouped all the parameters capable of being objectively assessed by an impartial court. For example, if the contract specifies the exact amount of wage to be paid, the task of checking to see whether this amount was indeed paid (by examining bank accounts, receipts, and so on) can actually be assigned to a third party. The notion of a verifiable clause contains the idea that, should a dispute arise, one of the parties would be able to supply *proof*, in the juridical sense of the term, sufficient to settle the matter.

As a general rule, there exist numerous parameters that cannot be assessed with sufficient precision by an impartial tribunal. The results of collective or individual activities usually fall into this category, because it is difficult to furnish real proof that what was accomplished fell short of what was intended. Hence parameters of this type will not appear in the contractual document. Note that the possibility of verifying the values of the parameters of a contract is not really tied to the possibility of observing these values. In fact the shared observation of parameters has only limited importance whenever no third party can certify what has been observed.

We can now state precisely the definition of *explicit* and *implicit* clause (Carmichael, 1989). Analysis of the *verifiable* character of the wording of a contract allows us, in theory, to place it in one or the other of these categories. All the clauses of an *explicit contract* being verifiable, they will appear in black and white in the text of the agreement, as will the penalties arising from their violation. For that matter, it is the existence of these penalties that ensures that in the great majority of cases, explicit contracts are respected. The case is different, however, with the clauses of an *implicit contract*. Since they are nonverifiable, there is no reason why they should appear in any written document at all—which amounts to saying that in this situation, there is no contract in the legal sense of the term.

1.2 COMPLETE AND INCOMPLETE CONTRACTS

The theoretical literature also adopts the terms *complete* and *incomplete* contract to distinguish between explicit and implicit contracts (Hart and Holmström, 1987). By definition, a contract is complete when it is possible, *at the moment of signing*, to foresee all the circumstances that could arise while it is in effect, and to set out *verifiable* clauses for each of them. A complete contract thus comes to the same thing as an explicit contract. Conversely, an incomplete contract does not take some of these circumstances into account. There are several reasons why it is curtailed in this way. First, the possible circumstances might simply be too numerous, and some of them highly improbable. The "production" costs of the contract (legal advice, preliminary study, the actual drafting, etc.) would outweigh the benefits to be derived. Second, certain circumstances cannot be verified, in which case there is no point in including them in the clauses of the contract. Finally, a contract that aimed to utilize all the available information in an optimal manner might lead to clauses or rules of application that would outstrip the cognitive capacity of one of the partners. It would then be necessary to adopt simplified rules, and in that case one might also take the view that the contract was incomplete. In sum, there is no real difference between the definition of an incomplete contract and that of an implicit contract. The notion of "unverifiable clause" encompasses all the reasons for which a contract may be incomplete (for recent work on the links between the incompleteness of contracts and the assumption of rational behavior, see Hart and Moore, 1999, and Maskin and Tirole, 1999).

The impossibility of having a third party verify individual performance has at least two important consequences when an employee and an employer wish to enter into a long-term relationship. In the first place, it becomes pointless to describe in minute detail the tasks the employee will be expected to carry out. In reality, the labor contract most often takes the form of a relationship of subordination that simply acknowledges the employer's authority and sets out a specified amount of remuneration. It is not generally possible to know in advance what services will be supplied in return for the wage. In the second place, if this relationship is extended, that means the two parties have a mutual interest and are no longer ruled by obligation. The contract is then said to be *self-enforcing*. As the celebrated expression (apparently coined by Okun, 1981) goes, an implicit contract then takes the form of an "invisible handshake."

Having set out the various possible categories of contract, our next step will be to highlight the main properties of optimal contracts. These will necessarily differ according to the explicit or implicit nature of the contract. In studying these problems, the so-called "agency" model supplies a framework both inclusive and rigorous, and has gradually come to dominate the literature.

1.3 THE AGENCY MODEL

The agency model—also called the principal–agent model—analyzes the problems arising from the working out of contracts between two actors, the principal and the agent. In labor economics, the principal is the employer, and the agent the employee. Confining the analysis to just two protagonists at this stage makes it possible to highlight a number of instructive traits, as the reader will see. More sophisticated models study the interactions among a larger number of actors (see Salanié, 1997).

The agency model assumes that the principal proposes a contract that the agent can either accept or refuse. This hypothesis allows the bargaining problem to be disposed of rapidly and lets us focus on analyzing the way the structure of information influences the characteristics of contracts (the theory of bargaining is set out in chapter 7). It is important to note that such an assumption makes no commitment as to whether labor market competition is perfect or imperfect. The only thing determined by the nature of labor market competition is the level of satisfaction the employer must offer the worker for the contract to be acceptable. For example, if the market is perfectly competitive, free entry entails zero profit, and the principal will necessarily have to offer a level of satisfaction that procures him or her zero profit, otherwise the worker will turn to another employer.

The information available to each party and the degree to which it can be verified influences the properties of contracts offered by the employer. Here we can set out two textbook cases. In the first, the employee's effort is observed by both parties and is verifiable. Though the effort made can be verified, the employee's output might be affected by contingencies unforeseen at the time the contract was signed. So both sides are faced with a problem of *risk-sharing*. The contract proposed by the employer then sets out the optimal division of risk and maximizes his or her expected profit. In the second case, the employee's effort is not verifiable, and the employer is faced with a problem of *moral hazard*. He or she must propose a contract that gives the worker an incentive to supply maximum effort at minimal cost.

As these observations show, the aim of labor contracts is to manage two types of problem: that of risk-sharing, and that of incentive.[1] We will study them in that order in the following sections.

2 RISK-SHARING

Risk-sharing between employers and workers has already been mentioned above to account for the rigidity of real wages. Empirical studies do in fact show that the real wage fluctuates less than production, employment, or hours worked, and is clearly procyclical (see Abraham and Haltiwanger, 1995, and chapter 8, this book).

These stylized facts do not fit well with a purely competitive determination of wages, in which the only contracts in existence are those made in a "spot market" that define the level of transactions in all foreseeable situations but include no provision for insurance. In the model of perfect competition laid out in chapter 5, section 1 (in which the labor market is represented as functioning solely on the basis of spot market contracts), variations in productivity lead to proportional variations in the wage. To grasp this, let us take the case of an agent entering such a market; this agent's preferences are represented by a quasi-concave utility function $U(C, L)$, where C and L designate respectively the agent's consumption of goods and his or her leisure. Here we shall assume that consumption of goods is identical to the agent's remuneration W, and that his or her leisure is equal to the difference between total endowment of time L_0, the duration of which is normalized to 1, and hours of work, denoted by h.

We will further assume that the production y of the agent depends on hours worked h and on a random variable ε according to function $f(h, \varepsilon)$ increasing in both its arguments, and such that, on the one hand, marginal productivity is decreasing ($f_{hh} \leq 0$) and, on the other, marginal productivity is strictly increasing with shock ε, which amounts to hypothesizing $f_{h\varepsilon} > 0$. Under these conditions, the profit Π of an employer is defined by the equality $\Pi = f(h, \varepsilon) - W$, and the zero profit condition then entails $W = f(h, \varepsilon)$.

The determination of work schedules and remuneration is represented in figure 6.1 for two values of ε, denoted ε_1 and $\varepsilon_2 > \varepsilon_1$, in the hours–wage plane. As we showed in chapter 5, section 1.1, each worker is able to force each employer to bid against the others, and therefore to choose a combination of work schedule and remuneration that maximizes his or her utility subject to the zero profit condition. In graphic terms, remuneration and work schedule are determined, in every state of nature, by the tangent point between curve $f(h, \varepsilon)$ and an indifference curve. In figure 6.1 we observe that variations in real wages are greater than variations in hours worked if the elasticity of

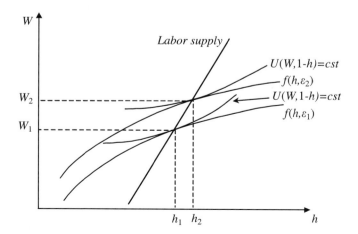

FIGURE 6.1
Wages and hours worked in a perfectly competitive spot market.

the labor supply is weak with respect to wages. Empirical studies have regularly found that the labor supply is weakly elastic with respect to the real wage (see chapter 1). So the model of a perfectly competitive spot market predicts that productivity shocks lead to greater variations in wage than in work schedules, something that empirical observation contradicts.

These limitations of the spot market model suggest that the demand for insurance may play a role in determining wages. The earliest models in this field came from Azariadis (1975), Baily (1974), and Gordon (1974). They are set in an environment in which the performance of workers is verifiable. These models explain, in a highly satisfactory manner, the rigidity of real wages, but prove to be of little use in understanding underemployment and unemployment. Subsequent work, which we will present later, has explored the consequences of the absence of verifiability of individual performance. Although this work has helped economists to understand certain characteristics of labor contracts, it has not allowed them to establish that the insurance motive constitutes an important source of persistent unemployment (for a simple presentation of the main results achieved regarding insurance contracts, see Azariadis and Stiglitz, 1983, and for more comprehensive overviews: Rosen, 1985, and Malcomson, 1999).

2.1 SYMMETRIC OR VERIFIABLE INFORMATION

The first studies of the consequences of the demand for insurance assumed that individual performance was verifiable, and showed how risk-sharing between an employer, who can diversify his or her assets on the financial markets, and an employee, whose access to such markets is limited, damps down the fluctuations in real wages. This approach also agrees with the most detailed empirical characteristics of wage formation: the well-established facts that the real wage of an employee is strongly correlated with the lowest rate of unemployment registered since the time he or she began his or her current job, and that it depends hardly at all on the current unemployment rate, or the rate that existed at the time he or she was hired (Beaudry and DiNardo, 1991). We will see how, by taking labor mobility and insurance mechanisms into account, we can explain facts of this kind.

2.1.1 An Individual Insurance Contract Model

In what follows, we will work with a model of an individual contract much like the models used by Green and Kahn (1983), Chari (1983), and Cooper (1983). It is a principal–agent model, in which the employer proposes a contract that the employee can only accept or reject.

Preferences and Technology

We retain the hypotheses adopted already in looking at a competitive spot market: the agent's preferences are represented by a quasi-concave utility function $U(C, L)$ where C and L designate respectively the agent's consumption of goods, and his or her leisure. Here we will assume that consumption of goods is identical to the agent's remuneration W, and that his or her leisure is equal to the difference between total endowment of time L_0, the duration of which is normalized to 1, and hours of work, denoted by h. The production y of the agent depends on hours worked h and on a random variable ε according to function $f(h, \varepsilon)$ increasing in both its arguments, and satisfying $f_{hh} \leq 0$ and $f_{h\varepsilon} > 0$. The random variable ε is a continuous variable defined over the interval $\mathscr{E} = [\varepsilon^-, \varepsilon^+]$ the density of which is denoted by $g(\varepsilon)$. The profit Π of the principal is defined by the equality $\Pi = f(h, \varepsilon) - W$. Finally, we do not a priori exclude the possibility that the principal may be risk-averse, and we will denote the utility function of the Von Neuman-Morgenstern type representing his or her preferences by $v(\Pi)$, with $v' > 0$ and $v'' \leq 0$.

In this subsection, the observation of the random variable ε will be assumed to be *verifiable*.[2] Under this assumption, the literature on contracts habitually speaks of *symmetric* information to signify that the principal and agent have access to the same information, and that neither one can manipulate it, because it is verifiable by a court. An insurance contract $\mathscr{A} = \{W(\varepsilon), h(\varepsilon)\}$ then specifies ex ante, in other words *before* knowing of the advent of the shock, the remuneration $W(\varepsilon)$ to be received by the agent and the hours of work $h(\varepsilon)$ that he or she must supply, whatever value of ε may be observed. An insurance contract is a *contingent* contract that takes into account all possible states of nature.

The Principal's Problem and the First-Order Conditions
The principal chooses a contract $\mathscr{A}$ that maximizes his or her expected utility and that offers the agent an earnings prospect at least equal to what he or she could obtain elsewhere. Let $\bar{U}$ be the expected utility corresponding to external opportunities, and $\Pi(\varepsilon)$ the profit $f[h(\varepsilon), \varepsilon] - W(\varepsilon)$ when the value of the shock is equal to ε. The optimal contract is the solution of the problem:

$$\text{Max}_{\mathscr{A}} \; Ev[\Pi(\varepsilon)] \tag{1}$$

subject to the *participation constraint*:

$$EU[W(\varepsilon), 1 - h(\varepsilon)] \geq \bar{U} \tag{2}$$

Let λ be the multiplier associated with this constraint; the Lagrangian of the principal's problem is written:

$$\mathscr{L} = Ev\{f[h(\varepsilon), \varepsilon] - W(\varepsilon)\} + \lambda\{EU[W(\varepsilon), 1 - h(\varepsilon)] - \bar{U}\}$$

The first-order conditions are obtained by setting the derivatives of this Lagrangian to zero with respect to $h(\varepsilon)$ and $W(\varepsilon)$ for all values of ε. Let U_C and U_L be the partial derivatives of function $U(C, L)$ and let f_h be the marginal productivity of hours worked; we thus have:

$$\frac{\partial \mathscr{L}}{\partial h(\varepsilon)} = g(\varepsilon)\{f_h[h(\varepsilon), \varepsilon]v'[\Pi(\varepsilon)] - \lambda U_L[W(\varepsilon), 1 - h(\varepsilon)]\} = 0, \qquad \forall \varepsilon \in \mathscr{E}$$

$$\frac{\partial \mathscr{L}}{\partial W(\varepsilon)} = g(\varepsilon)\{-v'[\Pi(\varepsilon)] + \lambda U_C[W(\varepsilon), 1 - h(\varepsilon)]\} = 0, \qquad \forall \varepsilon \in \mathscr{E}$$

If we eliminate the multiplier λ between these two equations, we see that the optimal contract is characterized by the following system:

$$\frac{U_L[W(\varepsilon), 1 - h(\varepsilon)]}{U_C[W(\varepsilon), 1 - h(\varepsilon)]} = f_h[h(\varepsilon), \varepsilon], \qquad \forall \varepsilon \in \mathscr{E} \tag{3}$$

$$\lambda U_C[W(\varepsilon), 1 - h(\varepsilon)] = v'[\Pi(\varepsilon)], \qquad \forall \varepsilon \in \mathscr{E} \tag{4}$$

Relation (3) shows that the marginal rate of substitution between consumption and leisure is equal to the marginal productivity of labor. So the insurance contract yields a *Pareto efficient* allocation, and can be described as a *first-best* contract. Relation (4) determines optimal risk-sharing; it entails:

$$\frac{U_C[W(\varepsilon), 1 - h(\varepsilon)]}{U_C[W(\theta), 1 - h(\theta)]} = \frac{v'[\Pi(\varepsilon)]}{v'[\Pi(\theta)]}, \qquad \forall (\varepsilon, \theta) \in \mathscr{E}^2$$

What we have here is the Arrow-Borch condition, well known in insurance theory (see, for example, Laffont, 1989), and according to which the sharing of risk is optimal when the marginal rate of substitution of a gain—measured by the marginal utility of consumption—in state ε for a gain in state θ is the same for the principal and for the agent.

2.1.2 The Properties of the Optimal Contract

Let us first take the most common case, in which the principal is supposedly risk-neutral ($v'' = 0$), because of his or her opportunity to diversify risk in a perfect financial market. As the reader can ascertain, differentiating the system (3) and (4) with respect to ε leads to the following comparative statics properties:

$$\left(\frac{U_{CL}^2 - U_{CC}U_{LL}}{U_C U_{CC}} - f_{hh}\right)\frac{dh}{d\varepsilon} = f_{h\varepsilon} \quad \text{and} \quad \frac{dW}{d\varepsilon} = \frac{U_{CL}}{U_{CC}}\frac{dh}{d\varepsilon} \tag{5}$$

It is evident as well that the first-best contract prescribes a wage independent of states of nature if the marginal utility of consumption is independent of hours worked ($U_{CL} = 0$). The functioning of a labor market with insurance contracts is thus very different from that of a spot market, in which the wage is highly sensitive to variations in productivity for empirically relevant values of labor supply elasticity. This was the result obtained by the early work of Azariadis (1975), Baily (1974), and Gordon (1974). It suggests that an employer who has low aversion to risk has a tendency to insure his or her employees by paying them a remuneration little dependent on the present state of the economy.

If we assume that the utility function is concave—which implies $U_{CC} < 0$ and $(U_{CL})^2 - U_{CC}U_{LL} < 0$—and that $f_{h\varepsilon} > 0$, it is clear that hours worked are an increasing function of the level ε of the random factor. This conclusion fits well with empirical observations, according to which hours worked rise when the economic trend turns up. However, Rosen (1985) and Malcomson (1999), among others, have pointed out that equations (3) and (4), which describe the optimal contract, also have some unconvincing implications: the direction in which remuneration W varies depends on the sign of U_{CL}, which is not a priori determined, so the model does not succeed in reproducing the procyclicity of wages unambiguously. It is easy to verify, moreover, that the utility of the agent diminishes with ε if leisure is a normal good. Since $dU = U_C\,dW - U_L\,dh$, we find with the help of relations (3) and (5) that the derivative $dU/d\varepsilon$ is of the sign of $(U_{CC}U_L - U_{CL}U_C)$. This quantity is negative if leisure is a normal good (see chapter 1, appendix 2). Hence, in adopting the usual hypothesis that leisure is a normal good, the model predicts that the agent's satisfaction *diminishes* when productivity increases (and even that his or her remuneration falls if $U_{CL} > 0$, which is also the prevalent hypothesis).

For the remuneration to be increasing unambiguously with ε, it would be necessary to adopt more restrictive hypotheses, for example, that the principal displays risk aversion ($v'' < 0$) and that hours worked take only two values, $h > 0$ and 0 (which amounts to supposing that the individual labor supply is inelastic). Under these hypotheses, differentiating the risk-sharing relation (4) implies $dW/d\varepsilon > 0$. But Malcomson (1999) points out that this relation also implies that remuneration and profit always vary in the same direction, something that is not verified for certain categories of workers. Finally, it should be noted that if the principal is risk-neutral ($v'' = 0$) and hours worked still take no more than two values, relation (4) implies a *constant* wage that does not depend on productivity ε. The principal insures the agent perfectly against fluctuations in his or her income, which does not fit well with the procyclicity of the real wage.

2.1.3   Insurance and Labor Mobility

According to the foregoing model, wages depend solely on conditions prevailing in the labor market at the time the contract is signed (conditions summed up by the parameter $\bar{U}$ representing the expected utility offered by external opportunities at that time). Real wages are not, therefore, correlated with the state of the labor market during the period covered by the contract, which clashes with the conclusions of Beaudry and DiNardo (1991, 1995), according to which the real wage is significantly correlated with the lowest rate of unemployment recorded from the time the contract began. Beaudry and DiNardo take the view that the model yields this bad prediction because of an implicit and quite groundless hypothesis: that the cost of mobility is prohibitive once a contract is signed. In what follows, we construct a model excluding this hypothesis, and as we will show, it really does match the stylized facts better. This model is a simple, stationary version of the models of Harris and Holmström (1982) and Beaudry and DiNardo (1991). Unlike these authors, we assume that the distribution of shocks is stationary, and that shocks are not autocorrelated.

A Model with Labor Mobility

We will illustrate the effect of taking labor mobility into account in a simplified model in which individuals, with lifetimes of infinite length, discount the future at the rate $\delta \in\,]0, 1[$. We assume that length of time worked h is a variable that can take only one value if agents decide to work. The instantaneous utility $U(W, 1 - h)$ of an employee is then denoted by $U(W)$ and, without any loss of generality, we assume that the agent's production per unit of time, $f(h, \varepsilon)$, is simply equal to ε. At the beginning of each unit of time, productivity ε takes a value obtained by a random draw from a distribution $G(\varepsilon)$ assumed to be stationary. For the sake of simplicity, the employer is assumed to be risk-neutral. In this context, we can verify that the previous model, with no labor mobility, entails a constant wage, independent of productivity ε. As we shall see, such is not the case when mobility is taken into account.

In order to introduce labor mobility simply, we will assume that, when the state of nature ε comes about, the agent has the opportunity to quit the firm he or she is with and work h hours externally, which in that period procures for him or her the gain $U[\overline{W}(\varepsilon)]$. In this expression, $\overline{W}(\varepsilon)$ designates the outside wage, which is assumed to be increasing with ε; this conveys the notion that an upturn in the economic trend makes itself felt throughout the economy. Opportunities outside the contract then offer the agent an expected discounted present value $\overline{V}(\varepsilon) = U[\overline{W}(\varepsilon)] + \delta E \overline{V}(\theta)$. In consequence, the expected discounted present value obtained in a firm offering a contract $\mathscr{A} = \{W(\varepsilon)\}$, amounts to $V(\varepsilon) = U[W(\varepsilon)] + \delta E \operatorname{Max}[V(\theta), \overline{V}(\theta)]$. Labor mobility forces the employer to offer a contract satisfying a *participation* constraint, which is written $V(\varepsilon) \overline{V}(\varepsilon)$, $\forall \varepsilon$. Let $\overline{U} = EU[\overline{W}(\varepsilon)]$; for any contract satisfying the participation constraints, the definitions of $\overline{V}(\varepsilon)$ and $V(\varepsilon)$ imply the equalities $EV(\varepsilon) = EU[W(\varepsilon)]/(1 - \delta)$ and $E\overline{V}(\varepsilon) = \overline{U}/(1 - \delta)$. In consequence, the participation constraints $V(\varepsilon) \overline{V}(\varepsilon)$ are writtten[3]:

$$U[W(\varepsilon)] + \frac{\delta}{1-\delta} EU[W(\theta)] \geq U[\overline{W}(\varepsilon)] + \frac{\delta}{1-\delta} \overline{U}, \qquad \forall \varepsilon \tag{6}$$

The left-hand side of this inequality represents the agent's expected utility if the state of nature ε occurs when the contract $\mathscr{A}$ applies, while the right-hand side represents the expected utility that he or she would get by quitting the firm where contract $\mathscr{A}$ is in force. If (6) is satisfied, the agent never has an interest in leaving his or her firm, whatever the state of nature that occurs may be. Taking the expectation of both sides of inequality (6), we observe that the "global" participation constraint, i.e., $EU[W(\theta)] \geq \overline{U}$, is satisfied if inequality (6) is satisfied for all ε.

The principal, henceforth assumed to be risk-neutral, chooses a contract that maximizes his or her expected gains, $E[\varepsilon - W(\varepsilon)]/(1 - \delta)$, taking into account participation constraints (6) for all possible values of ε. Let $\lambda(\varepsilon)$ be the multiplier associated with constraint (6) when state ε occurs. The Lagrangian of the principal's problem is defined by:

$$\mathscr{L} = \int \frac{[\varepsilon - W(\varepsilon)]}{1 - \delta} g(\varepsilon)\, d\varepsilon$$

$$+ \int \lambda(\varepsilon) \left\{ U[W(\varepsilon)] + \frac{\delta}{1-\delta} \int U[W(\theta)]g(\theta)\, d\theta - U[\overline{W}(\varepsilon)] - \frac{\delta}{1-\delta} \overline{U} \right\} g(\varepsilon)\, d\varepsilon$$

The first-order conditions are found by setting the derivatives of this Lagrangian to zero with respect to $W(\varepsilon)$. We thus get:

$$\frac{\partial \mathscr{L}}{\partial W(\varepsilon)} = g(\varepsilon) \left\{ -\frac{1}{1-\delta} + \lambda(\varepsilon) U'[W(\varepsilon)] + \frac{\delta}{1-\delta} U'[W(\varepsilon)] E\lambda(\theta) \right\} = 0$$

The optimal contract is thus characterized by the following equality:

$$[(1 - \delta)\lambda(\varepsilon) + \delta E\lambda(\theta)]U'[W(\varepsilon)] = 1 \qquad (7)$$

This equation differs from equation (4) describing risk-sharing in the model without mobility, which prescribed a constant wage with a risk-neutral principal and a production function $f(h, \varepsilon)$ additively separable with respect to h and ε. Here, wage $W(\varepsilon)$ depends on the state of nature ε through multiplier $\lambda(\varepsilon)$, which is not a priori a constant.

Properties of Contractual Wages

We can set out certain characteristics of contractual wages in detail by considering the set Λ^+ of states of nature for which the participation constraints are necessarily binding. Formally, this set is defined by $\Lambda^+ = \{\varepsilon|\lambda(\varepsilon) > 0\}$. Let us assume that this set is not empty, and consider two states ε_1 and ε_2 which belong to this set and are such that $\varepsilon_1 > \varepsilon_2$. For these values ε_1 and ε_2, the constraints (6) are equalities. If we subtract these equalities side by side, it becomes evident that $U[W(\varepsilon_1)] - U[W(\varepsilon_2)]$ is equal to $U[\overline{W}(\varepsilon_1)] - U[\overline{W}(\varepsilon_2)]$. Now the last expression is positive since $\varepsilon_1 > \varepsilon_2$ and outside wages $\overline{W}(\varepsilon)$ are increasing with ε. We can state, therefore, that optimal wages $W(\varepsilon)$ are likewise increasing with ε over the set Λ^+. Since the agent's risk aversion dictates $U'' < 0$, it results, following risk-sharing relation (7), that the multipliers $\lambda(\varepsilon)$ are likewise increasing with ε over the set Λ^+. Let ε_λ then be the smallest value of ε for which we have $\lambda(\varepsilon) > 0$. The previous line of reasoning proves that the set Λ^+ is also characterized by $\Lambda^+ = \{\varepsilon|\varepsilon \geq \varepsilon_\lambda\}$. Conversely, we can deduce that we have $\lambda(\varepsilon) = 0$ for all $\varepsilon < \varepsilon_\lambda$.

The first-order condition (7) then shows that the contractual wage is constant for all $\varepsilon < \varepsilon_\lambda$. Conversely, when $\varepsilon \geq \varepsilon_\lambda$, the participation constraint is binding and the contractual wage $W(\varepsilon)$ is defined by the equality:

$$U[W(\varepsilon)] = U[\overline{W}(\varepsilon)] - \frac{\delta}{1 - \delta}\{EU[W(\theta)] - \overline{U}\}$$

Since $EU[W(\theta)] \geq \overline{U}$, we observe that the contractual wage $W(\varepsilon)$ is less than the outside wage $\overline{W}(\varepsilon)$ for $\varepsilon \geq \varepsilon_\lambda$. To summarize, the participation constraints are binding in the "good" states of nature $(\varepsilon \geq \varepsilon_\lambda)$ with wages that are increasing, but less than outside wages, while in the "bad" states of nature $(\varepsilon < \varepsilon_\lambda)$ the wage is constant and the participation constraints are not necessarily binding. These properties[4] of contractual wages are shown in figure 6.2.

Under these same hypotheses, the model without mobility entailed a constant wage in all states of nature. This wage then ought to be correlated solely with the state of the economy at the moment the contract is signed, which contradicts the results of Beaudry and DiNardo (1991). On the other hand, if it is possible for the employees to leave their firms, the model shows that the contractual wage is no longer a constant, and that it rises when the economic trend turns up. This conclusion does agree with that of Beaudry and DiNardo, which brings out a positive correlation between the contractual wage and the weakest unemployment rate since the beginning of the con-

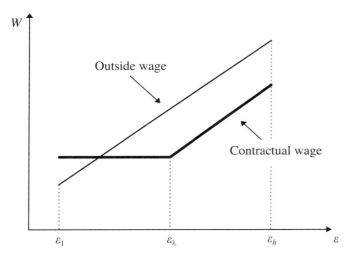

FIGURE 6.2
The wage contract with labor mobility.

tract. It should be noted that if we had assumed that the principal was also able to break the contract, the contractual wage would not have been completely rigid downward. There would have been "very bad" states of nature for which the principal's participation constraint would have been binding, which would have entailed a wage flexibility downward for these states; and this would have been a better fit with the fluctuations in the real wage over the cycle (see Thomas and Worral, 1988, for a model that takes this possibility into account). Finally, we must also note that in the model with labor mobility, fluctuations in the contractual wage are damped down in comparison to those in the outside wage (see figure 6.2). This result also agrees with the observed fluctuations in the real wage over the course of a cycle, which do appear to be damped in comparison to labor productivity (in our model, the outside wage can be likened to a competitive spot wage perfectly correlated with the marginal productivity of labor). Taking mobility into account in a model with symmetric information thus gives a better explanation of certain stylized facts. It now remains to examine the effects of information asymmetry.

2.2 ASYMMETRIC OR UNVERIFIABLE INFORMATION

We come back to the static model without labor mobility; the assumption will now be that the observed values of the random factor ε are not verifiable. The literature on insurance contracts most often employs the term *asymmetric* information to describe this situation. This means that one of the actors—for our purposes, the principal—observes the true values of the shocks. The main thing to remember, though, is that this is a situation in which it is impossible, or very costly, to have the actually occurring values of the random variable ε verified by an impartial third party. From this perspective, the terminology adopted by the literature using the agency model certainly has greater clarity. It uses the term *hidden* information to indicate that performances are unverifiable (see Salanié, 1997). With this hypothesis, a contract can no longer be simply a series of values of remuneration and effort indexed to future values of ε, for the principal will sometimes have an interest in claiming that the value of ε that applies is not the one that actually occurs. The "revelation principle" of Myerson (1979) makes it possible nonetheless to arrive at a characterization of optimal contracts.

2.2.1 The Revelation Principle

The revelation principle is of interest because it limits the search for optimal contracts to the set of contracts for which the principal does declare the true state of nature.

The Incentive-Compatible Contract

Let us imagine that the agent and the principal have agreed on a contract $\mathscr{A} = \{W(\varepsilon), h(\varepsilon)\}$; when the principal observes the value ε of the random shock, his interest is to declare that he has observed the state of nature $m(\varepsilon)$ which, given this contract $\mathscr{A}$, procures him the greatest possible profit. Formally, the state $m(\varepsilon)$ is defined by the equality:

$$m(\varepsilon) = \text{Arg Max}_{\theta}\{ f[h(\theta), \varepsilon] - W(\theta)\} \tag{8}$$

Let us now consider contract $\hat{\mathscr{A}} = \{\hat{W}(\varepsilon), \hat{h}(\varepsilon)\}$ where $\hat{W}(\varepsilon) = W[m(\varepsilon)]$ and $\hat{h}(\varepsilon) = h[m(\varepsilon)]$. Compared to contract $\mathscr{A}$, contract $\hat{\mathscr{A}}$ presents the advantage of being *incentive-compatible*; in other words, if it is in force, the principal always has an interest in revealing the *true* state of nature. To demonstrate this result, let us suppose that $\hat{\mathscr{A}}$ is in force and the principal declares that he or she has observed the state of nature θ, whereas the true state is ε. The profit attained by adopting this attitude is defined by the identity:

$$f[\hat{h}(\theta), \varepsilon] - \hat{W}(\theta) \equiv f\{h[m(\theta)], \varepsilon\} - W[m(\theta)] \tag{9}$$

Now, using definition (8) of signal $m(.)$, the right-hand side of this last equality satisfies:

$$f\{h[m(\theta)], \varepsilon\} - W[m(\theta)] \leq \text{Max}_{s}\{ f[h(s), \varepsilon] - W(s)\} \equiv f[\hat{h}(\varepsilon), \varepsilon] - \hat{W}(\varepsilon) \tag{10}$$

Finally, relations (9) and (10) entail:

$$f[\hat{h}(\theta), \varepsilon] - \hat{W}(\theta) \leq f[\hat{h}(\varepsilon), \varepsilon] - \hat{W}(\varepsilon)$$

This inequality signifies that the principal makes less profit by "lying," i.e., by announcing θ, than he or she does by revealing the true state ε of nature. So the principal does indeed have an interest in revealing the true state of nature when contract $\hat{\mathscr{A}}$ is in force.

This revelation principle also entails that contracts $\mathscr{A}$ and $\hat{\mathscr{A}}$ lead to the *same* allocation of resources. If ε comes about and contract $\mathscr{A}$ is in force, the principal declares that state $m(\varepsilon)$ has come about, which means that the agent must work

$h[m(\varepsilon)]$ in exchange for compensation $W[m(\varepsilon)]$. On the other hand, if it is contract $\hat{\mathscr{A}}$ that is in force, the principal announces the true state ε of nature since $\hat{\mathscr{A}}$ is incentive-compatible. The agent must then work $\hat{h}(\varepsilon) \equiv h[m(\varepsilon)]$ and receives wage $\hat{W}(\varepsilon) \equiv W[m(\varepsilon)]$, so the allocation of resources is identical under contracts $\mathscr{A}$ and $\hat{\mathscr{A}}$. Since it is possible to associate any contract with an incentive-compatible contract that leads to the same allocation of resources, the search for the optimal contract can be confined to the set of incentive-compatible contracts. In practice, the optimal contract is the solution of problem (1) of maximization of expected profit, given the participation constraint (2) and adding the *incentive-compatible constraints*, i.e.:

$$f[h(\varepsilon), \varepsilon] - W(\varepsilon) \geq f[h(\theta), \varepsilon] - W(\theta), \qquad \forall (\varepsilon, \theta) \tag{11}$$

The direct solution of this optimization problem is generally complex (see Rosen, 1985, and Salanié, 1997). But an astute observation made by Cooper (1983) gives us a very simple way to find out which incentive-compatible constraints will be binding.

A Method for Finding the Second-Best Contract

Let $\mathscr{A}_1 = \{W_1(\varepsilon), h_1(\varepsilon)\}$ be the first-best contract with symmetric information defined by the first-order conditions (3) and (4), and let us imagine that this contract is in force in a situation of *asymmetric* information. When state ε appears, the principal announces that it is state $m_1(\varepsilon)$, the solution of problem (8), that has occurred. It is not difficult to specify the properties of state $m_1(\varepsilon)$ according to the form of the utility function $U(C, L)$ of the agent. For that purpose, let $\Pi(\varepsilon, \theta)$ be the profit $f[h_1(\theta), \varepsilon] - W_1(\theta)$ that comes to the principal when, with the first-best contract $\mathscr{A}_1$ in force, he or she anounces that he or she has observed state θ whereas in reality it is state ε that has come about. Taking into account comparative statics relations (5) and risk-sharing condition (3) satisfied by the first-best contract, we find that the partial derivative Π_θ of profit $\Pi(\varepsilon, \theta)$ with respect to θ satisfies the equalities:

$$\Pi_\theta = h_1'(\theta) f_h[h_1(\theta), \varepsilon] - W_1'(\theta) = \left(\frac{U_L U_{CC} - U_{CL} U_C}{U_{CC}} \right)_{(h_1(\theta), W_1(\theta))} h_1'(\theta) \tag{12}$$

In the first place, this equation shows that $m_1(\varepsilon) = \varepsilon$ for all utility functions such that $U_L U_{CC} - U_{CL} U_C = 0$ at every point. Leisure demand is then independent of income (see chapter 1, appendix 2). This property is satisfied, for example, if the agent's utility function takes the form $U[W + \phi(1 - h)]$ with $U' > 0$, $U'' \leq 0$, $\phi' > 0$ and $\phi'' \leq 0$ (Azariadis, 1983). Under these hypotheses, the optimal contract with asymmetric information—also called the second-best contract—is no different from the first-rank contract. Moreover, it was established in chapter 1, appendix 2, that leisure is a normal good if and only if $U_{CL} U_C - U_L U_{CC} > 0$. If we accept this standard hypothesis, relation (12) shows that profit $\Pi(\varepsilon, \theta)$ is increasing with θ. The signal $m_1(\varepsilon)$ is thus equal to the upper bound ε^+ of the set of possible values of the random variable ε. Conversely, if $U_{CL} U_C - U_L U_{CC} < 0$, leisure is an inferior good, profit $\Pi(\varepsilon, \theta)$ becomes a decreasing function of θ, and state $m_1(\varepsilon)$ coincides with the lower bound ε^- of the possible values of ε. In conclusion, the results of this analysis are summed up in the following manner:

$$m_1(\varepsilon) = \begin{cases} \varepsilon & \text{if there is no income effect} \\ \varepsilon^+ & \text{if leisure is a normal good} \\ \varepsilon^- & \text{if leisure is an inferior good} \end{cases} \tag{13}$$

Thus, asymmetric information is not a source of any inefficiency when the demand for leisure is independent of income. Conversely, when the demand for leisure depends on income, the firm will most often have an interest in sending out misleading messages if the first-best contract applies. This contract is thus not incentive-compatible, and in the definition of the optimal second-best contract, incentive-compatible constraints (11) corresponding to states in which the principal would have lied if the first-rank contract had been in force will be binding.

2.2.2 An Example with Two States of Nature

We illustrate the revelation principle in a simple model with only two states of nature. Assuming that leisure is a normal good, the conclusions agree better with the stylized facts than the conclusions that issue from an equivalent model with symmetric information.

The Principal's Problem

With the help of response $m_1(\varepsilon)$ described by (13), it is possible to find out the properties of the second-best contract in a model with only two states of nature, ε^+ and ε^-, equiprobable and such that $\varepsilon^+ > \varepsilon^-$. To make the exposition simpler, we will assume as well that the principal is risk-neutral and that the production function takes the multiplicative form $f(h, \varepsilon) = \varepsilon h$. The optimal contract maximizes the principal's expected profit subject to the participation and incentive-compatible constraints; hence it is the solution of the problem:

$$\underset{(h^i, W^i)_{i=+, -}}{\text{Max}} \quad [\tfrac{1}{2}(\varepsilon^+ h^+ - W^+) + \tfrac{1}{2}(\varepsilon^- h^- - W^-)]$$

subject to constraints:

$$\tfrac{1}{2} U(W^+, 1 - h^+) + \tfrac{1}{2} U(W^-, 1 - h^-) \geq \overline{U} \tag{14}$$

$$\varepsilon^+ h^+ - W^+ \geq \varepsilon^+ h^- - W^- \tag{15}$$

$$\varepsilon^- h^- - W^- \geq \varepsilon^- h^+ - W^+ \tag{16}$$

Let $\lambda \geq 0$, $\mu_1 \geq 0$, and $\mu_2 \geq 0$ be the Kuhn and Tucker multipliers respectively associated with the participation constraint (14) and the incentive-compatible constraints (15) and (16); the first-order conditions of the principal's problem are found by setting the derivatives of the Lagrangian—which the reader may write out in full if he or she wishes—to zero with respect to variables W^i and h^i for $i = +, -$. The result is:

$$\frac{\partial \mathscr{L}}{\partial W^+} = -\frac{1}{2} + \frac{\lambda}{2} U_C(W^+, 1 - h^+) - \mu_1 + \mu_2 = 0 \tag{17}$$

$$\frac{\partial \mathscr{L}}{\partial W^-} = -\frac{1}{2} + \frac{\lambda}{2} U_C(W^-, 1 - h^-) + \mu_1 - \mu_2 = 0 \tag{18}$$

$$\frac{\partial \mathscr{L}}{\partial h^+} = \left(\frac{1}{2} + \mu_1\right)\varepsilon^+ - \frac{\lambda}{2} U_L(W^+, 1 - h^+) - \mu_2\varepsilon^- = 0 \tag{19}$$

$$\frac{\partial \mathscr{L}}{\partial h^-} = \left(\frac{1}{2} + \mu_2\right)\varepsilon^- - \frac{\lambda}{2} U_L(W^-, 1 - h^-) - \mu_1\varepsilon^+ = 0 \tag{20}$$

The Optimal Contract When Leisure Is a Normal Good

If we add up the equalities (17) and (18), we can easily verify that $\lambda > 0$; the participation constraint (14) is thus binding. Taking leisure to be a normal good, as usual, we know from rule (13) that the principal has an interest in overestimating the true state of nature when the first-best contract is in force. In other words, the principal would lie if it were the "bad" state of nature ε^- that came about. Consequently, constraint (15) is not binding, hence $\mu_1 = 0$, and constraint (16) is saturated, hence $\mu_2 \geq 0$. In addition, condition (19) entails:

$$\frac{\lambda}{2} U_L(W^+, 1 - h^+) = \frac{\varepsilon^+}{2} - \mu_2\varepsilon^- > \left(\frac{1}{2} - \mu_2\right)\varepsilon^+ \tag{21}$$

Noting once again that relation (17) gives $\lambda U_C(W^+, 1 - h^+) = 1 - 2\mu_2$, we arrive at the following inequality:

$$\frac{U_L(W^+, 1 - h^+)}{U_C(W^+, 1 - h^+)} > \varepsilon^+ \tag{22}$$

Since $\mu_1 = 0$, conditions (20) and (18) respectively entail $\lambda U_L(W^-, 1 - h^-) = (1 + 2\mu_2)\varepsilon^-$ and $\lambda U_C(W^-, 1 - h^-) = 1 + 2\mu_2$. Eliminating the positive quantity $1 + 2\mu_2$ between (21) and (22), we get:

$$\frac{U_L(W^-, 1 - h^-)}{U_C(W^-, 1 - h^-)} = \varepsilon^- \tag{23}$$

In the first place, we can show, using the incentive-compatible constraints, that wages and hours vary in the same direction. Thus, the binding constraint (16) entails $W^+ - W^- = \varepsilon^-(h^+ - h^-)$, whereas constraint (15), which is not binding, entails $\varepsilon^+(h^+ - h^-) \geq W^+ - W^-$. In consequence, we have $(\varepsilon^+ - \varepsilon^-)(h^+ - h^-) \geq 0$. Since $\varepsilon^+ > \varepsilon^-$, we deduce $h^+ > h^-$ and so $W^+ > W^-$. In contradistinction to the case in which information was symmetric, the wage now rises unambiguously when the economic trend turns up. This property is a direct consequence of the hypothesis of asymmetric information. The values of ε being unverifiable, the agent knows that the principal has no interest in declaring that the good state of nature ε^+ has appeared if such a declaration leads to a higher wage. Hart (1983) has shown in a much more general model that the principal has an incentive to reveal the true state of nature if a long work schedule is linked to a high wage.

Conditions (22) and (23) also indicate that the inefficiency due to asymmetric information only manifests itself in the good state of nature. In this state, the marginal rate of substitution between consumption and leisure surpasses marginal productivity, whereas these quantities must be equal—see (3)—in the first-best contract. With a few calculations, we can show that this inefficiency leads to higher remuneration and longer hours of work in the second-best contract when the good state of nature occurs. This result suggests that asymmetric information helps to increase employment. The absence of verifiability of workers' performance does not therefore help to explain underemployment. Malcomson (1999) notes that this result might, however, explain the fact that in many contracts the firm has the right to demand that its employees supply a certain volume of overtime hours. Overall, the model with asymmetric information, although a disappointment when it comes to explaining underemployment, does come to conclusions that fit better with the stylized facts than does the model in which information is assumed to be symmetric, i.e., verifiable.

Overall, taking risk-sharing between employers and employees into account fits well with certain empirical characteristics of wages and hours, such as the low variability of wages or the procyclicity of hours and compensation. We will now proceed to show that the labor contract also helps us to solve incentive problems when the employee's effort is not verifiable. This dimension of the wage relationship allows us to gain an understanding of a number of empirical elements concerning wage formation.

3 INCENTIVE IN THE PRESENCE OF VERIFIABLE RESULTS

To this point we have assumed that hours worked were perfectly verifiable and could therefore be written into the labor contract explicitly. But hours worked must not be confused with the "effort" made by an employee in carrying out his or her tasks. In practice, it is possible in most circumstances to check very easily that an employee is present at his or her place of work at the set times, but it is much harder to assess the intensity of his or her effort, although the latter determines the speed, precision, and quality with which tasks are carried out. For this reason, much thought has been devoted to the study of labor relations when workers' effort is not verifiable. The employer is faced with an incentive problem, that of working out a contract that will impel the worker to furnish the maximum of effort at the least cost.

In this section, we focus on situations in which effort is not verifiable, but the results of an agent's activity are. The case in which neither the effort *nor* the results are verifiable will be analyzed in the following section. We begin by showing, using the agency model with hidden action, how the absence of verifiability of effort keeps the employer from correctly insuring his or her employees against fluctuations in activity. The hunt for incentive mechanisms does, indeed, lead employers, in certain circumstances on which the theory of contracts sheds light, to offer remunerations tied to collective or individual results, when it would have been in his or her interest to offer constant remuneration, independent of results, if effort were verifiable. We will then see that the relationship between result and remuneration can take different forms, ranging from incentive pay to promotion based on hierarchical rules, the logic of which is closely similar to that governing sports tournaments.

3.1 THE PRINCIPAL–AGENT MODEL WITH HIDDEN ACTION

The situation analyzed by the agency model with hidden action is schematically comparable to that of a gold prospector or a salesman. When the owner of a gold property, or the manager of a firm, employs persons of this type, he or she anticipates remunerating them on the basis of their results, that is, on the basis of how much gold is found, or what volume of sales is achieved. In this context, a mediocre result does not necessarily reflect a feeble *effort* on the part of the gold prospector or the salesman. The fact is that in many circumstances the result in question also reflects general conditions, independent of the will of the actors, in which their activity takes place. The quality of the gold property worked over by the prospector, or the demand for the product sold by the salesman, fall into this category. There is generally an element of risk in the individual's activity, against which he or she wishes to be insured. But a complete insurance, providing remuneration independent of the result, and thus of the effort made, is highly likely to provide little incentive. The agency model shows how the rules of remuneration give rise to a trade-off between the need for insurance and incentive. Finally, in cases where the employer receives information from sources other than direct observation of individual performance (the performance of a team, for example, or reports made by supervisors), the question of what indicators to use in regulating remuneration arises, as does that of the efficiency of rules based solely on verifiable data.

In the agency model with hidden action, the principal—or the employer—is confronted with a problem of moral hazard, inasmuch as he or she does not know, a priori and with certainty, what actions the agent—or employee—has undertaken to achieve the observed results. In this context, the basic agency model shows that the remuneration rule chosen by the principal depends on the results of the agent's activity, and will arrive at a compromise between the motives of insurance and incentive.

The canonical agency model with hidden action focuses on the behavior of a principal and an agent whose decisions unfold in the following sequence: 1) the principal offers a contract; 2) the agent accepts the contract, or turns it down; 3) if the agent turns it down, the protagonists go their separate ways, but if the agent accepts it, he or she then supplies an effort; 4) a random event occurs that affects the result of the agent's effort; 5) the principal and the agent observe the result; 6) the principal remunerates the agent according to the terms of the contract. The optimal decisions can be found through backward induction, so we must first define the behavior of the agent who has accepted a contract, then determine the choice of the principal, who anticipates the agent's decisions.

The Agent's Behavior

In order to study the decisions of the two parties, we will consider a very simple static model. Thus, we assume that the utility function describing the agent's preferences takes the exponential form:

$$U[W - C(e)] = -\exp\{-a[W - C(e)]\} \tag{24}$$

In this expression, the variables W and e designate respectively the remuneration received by the agent, and the effort he or she has expended in the production process. The function $C(e)$ represents the cost linked to the supplying of effort e. To simplify the calculations, we will adopt the quadratic representation $C(e) = ce^2/2$, $c > 0$, but all the results of this section remain true on the assumption that the cost function is strictly convex. Finally, readers are reminded that the parameter $a > 0$ is the index of absolute risk aversion, equal to $-U''/U'$ (see, for example, Mas-Colell et al., 1995, chapter 6). The utility function chosen, which is of the CARA (constant absolute risk aversion) type, thus entails a constant index of absolute risk aversion. The choice of a hypothesis of this kind makes the exposition of the agency model a great deal simpler, while the conclusions reached extend, in essence, to more general environments (see Hart and Holmström, 1987; Salanié, 1997; and Macho-Stadler and Perez-Castrillo, 1997). When necessary, we will make clear which results flow specifically from this hypothesis.

When the agent supplies effort e, he or she allows the principal to reap the benefit of production $y = e + \varepsilon$, where ε is a normal random variable with zero mean and standard error σ. The presence of a random variable prevents an impartial third party from knowing exactly the effort e of the agent by observing his or her production y. The effort thus cannot be verified, but the production can. The principal is then in a position to contruct a remuneration rule based on observation of the production achieved. In order to simplify, we will assume that the principal adopts the linear rule $W = w + by$, where w represents a fixed wage independent of the performance of the agent and b is a piece rate on production y. (It can be shown that the optimal remuneration rule is indeed linear, with the hypotheses of constant index of absolute risk aversion and a normal random variable; see Holmström and Milgrom, 1987.) If we assume that the agent has to make his or her decisions before knowing the realization of the random variable ε, but with knowledge of the remuneration rule proposed by the principal, he or she chooses a level of effort that maximizes his or her expected utility. Since $W = w + b(e + \varepsilon)$, the definition (24) of the agent's preferences shows that this expected utility is then equal to $-\exp\{-a[w + be - C(e)]\}E[\exp(-ab\varepsilon)]$. And since the random variable ε follows a normal distribution with zero mean and standard variation σ, the random variable $\exp(-ab\varepsilon)$ follows a log-normal distribution, the mean of which[5] is equal to $\exp(a^2b^2\sigma^2/2)$. In sum, the utility expected by the agent is written:

$$EU = -\exp\left\{-a\left[w + be - C(e) - \frac{ab^2\sigma^2}{2}\right]\right\} \tag{25}$$

The maximization of expected utility implies that the level of effort e^* chosen by the agent is such that $C'(e^*) = b$, or $e^* = b/c$. This equality portrays the *incentive* properties of the remuneration rule. The agent's effort evidently does not depend on the fixed part w of this rule, but increases as the relationship between remuneration and performance, measured by the parameter b, rises in intensity.

The Principal's Behavior
In order to set the value of b, the principal reckons on level e^* of effort by the agent, since the contract is signed before the agent starts work. The relationship between the remuneration rule and the level of effort, $C'(e^*) = b$, is imposed on the principal, and is called the *incentive-compatible constraint*. The principal must also take into account the *participation constraint*, which indicates the conditions under which the agent accepts the contract. We shall assume that the agent can always attain an expected utility $\bar{U}$ outside the contractual relationship. Hence the participation constraint is written $EU \geq \bar{U}$ with $\bar{U} < 0$. The principal, assumed to be risk-neutral, chooses w and b in such a way as to maximize his or her expected profit, given this participation constraint and knowing that the agent's effort is equal to e^*. In these circumstances, the agent's production is given by $y = e^* + \varepsilon$ and his or her remuneration amounts to $W = w + b(e^* + \varepsilon)$. Since the random variable ε has zero mean, the profit expected by the principal, $E(y - W)$, is equal to $(1 - b)e^* - w$. In the end, the principal's problem comes down to the following optimization problem:

$$\underset{\{w, b\}}{\text{Max}}[(1 - b)e^* - w] \quad \text{subject to} \quad C'(e^*) = b \text{ and } EU \geq \bar{U} \tag{26}$$

Let us set $\bar{x} = -\ln(-\bar{U})/a$; taking the logarithms of the opposites of the two sides of the participation constraint $EU \geq \bar{U}$, we find that this constraint takes the form:

$$w + be - C(e) - \frac{ab^2\sigma^2}{2} \geq \bar{x} \tag{27}$$

The problem (26) can be simply solved by noting that the effort e^* defined by the incentive constraint is independent of the fixed part of the remuneration. Let us suppose that the principal has settled on the value of parameter b; it is clearly in his or her interest to select w in such a way as to bind the agents's participation constraint, since w does not affect e^*. Carrying the value of w thus obtained into the principal's problem, we observe that the optimal value of parameter b is the solution of the following problem:

$$\underset{b}{\text{Max}}\left[e^* - C(e^*) - \frac{ab^2\sigma^2}{2} - \bar{x}\right] \quad \text{subject to constraint} \quad C'(e^*) = b$$

The Optimal Remuneration Rule
The quadratic form $ce^2/2$ of the cost function allows us to define explicitly the optimal value of b, as follows:

$$b^* = \frac{1}{1 + ac\sigma^2} \tag{28}$$

This simple formula perfectly illustrates the trade-off between the motives of incentive and insurance. At the optimum, positive effort $e^* = b^*/c$ results from a positive value of b^*, since in this case the remuneration varies with the level of production. Note that parameter b^* goes to zero when the variance of ε is infinite. In this case, production is no longer linked to effort, and the incentive motive vanishes. We also see that b^* diminishes with the degree of absolute risk aversion a. In other words, the more risk-averse an agent is, the less marked the relationship between the result and the remuneration becomes. On the other hand, it is easy to verify that the fixed part of the remuneration grows in importance, the stronger risk aversion is. The optimal value w^* of the fixed part of the remuneration is found by bringing the value of b^* defined by (28) into the participation constraint (27) written in the form of an equality, or:

$$w^* = \bar{x} - \frac{1}{2c(1 + ac\sigma^2)} \tag{29}$$

We can also observe that parameter b^* decreases with measure c of the disutility of effort. Thus, an agent for whom the disagreeability of effort has less weight than it does for someone else will be more attracted to a compensation rule which privileges payment by results. When agents are heterogeneous according to characteristic c and when employers do not observe this characteristic, then employers may increase the relative importance of the variable part of the remuneration as compared to the fixed part in order to attract agents who are more tolerant of effort, or to put it another way, ones who are more efficient (see Lazear, 1986 and 2000, for models built around this mode of selection).

First-Best Optimum and Second-Best Optimum
It is important to point out that the nonverifiable character of effort and the variability of remuneration mean that the contract arrived at produces an allocation that is a *second-best optimum*. This means that it would have been possible to find a contract that improved the outcome for at least one of the partners, with no detriment to that of the other, if effort were verifiable. The fact is, given a contract prescribing variable remuneration, that any other contract which allotted the average of the remuneration prescribed by the earlier contract to the employee under all states of nature would provide the employer with the same expected profit. On the other hand, it would clearly improve the situation of the agent, since he or she is not risk-neutral. So the absence of complete insurance proves to be inefficient. When effort is unverifiable, the only possible incentive mechanisms necessarily link remuneration to production (the only verifiable variable) and so there cannot be total insurance.

In order better to grasp the consequences of this situation of moral hazard, let us suppose that effort e is verifiable, and that the contract stipulates a remuneration that always takes the form $W = w + by$. When effort is verifiable, it is as though the principal had the ability to decide how much effort the agent was making. The principal's problem then consists of maximizing his or her expected profit with respect to (b, w, e)

subject to the worker's participation constraint (27) only. The expected production and remuneration being respectively equal to e and $w + be$, the problem defining the so-called *first-best* contract is written:

$$\underset{\{w,b,e\}}{\text{Max}}\ [e - (w + be)] \quad \text{subject to} \quad w + be - C(e) - \frac{ab^2\sigma^2}{2} \geq \bar{x}$$

We see that the participation constraint is binding, and that the optimal values, denoted by (b^o, w^o, e^o), are defined by:

$$C'(e^o) = 1, \qquad b^o = 0, \qquad w^o = \bar{x} + C(e^o)$$

The first-best allocation corresponds to a pure insurance contract, in which the employer insures the worker totally against the hazards of production by giving him remuneration $w^o = \bar{x} + C(e^o)$, independent of production. We may also note that effort in the first-best contract, defined by $C'(e^o) = 1$, is greater than effort in the second-best contract, defined by equation (28), where $C'(e^*) = b^* < 1$, given that the employee is averse to risk. So the first-best contract entails a higher level of production.

It is worth noting that the level of effort e^o in the first-best contract is attained even if effort is unverifiable when the agent is risk-neutral ($a = 0$). In this case, equation (28) shows that the agent has no need to be insured, and the principal has an interest in offering a remuneration strongly linked to performance ($b^* = 1$). In this context, the first- and second-best allocations coincide. We see, then, that a value of a piece rate b strictly lower than unity, entailing a fall in production, is, in a sense, the price to pay for solving the problem of moral hazard facing a principal with a risk-averse agent.

An Empirical Illustration

Lazear (1986, 1999, 2000) studied the evolution of compensation schemes within a large autoglass installer in the United States; his observations clearly illustrate the main lessons of the basic agency model. Over the period covered by the available data, this firm moved gradually from a system of fixed hourly wages to a piece-rate system, following a change in management. Let us assume that in a fixed wage system all employees are more or less compelled to furnish a minimum verifiable effort. The agency model then predicts that moving to a piece-rate system ought to lead to a hike in individual productivity. Lazear does in fact estimate that the average productivity per worker rose by 22% in this case (see also the study of Paarsch and Shearer, 1999, on the compensation schemes of tree planters in British Columbia).

The agency model also predicts that changing the remuneration rule ought to lead to wide variation in individual performance. Lazear does indeed observe that the variance of individual production reached the level of 2.53 under the new system of performance pay, whereas it had been only 2.02 under the fixed wage system. Lazear also isolates a selection effect: the quit rate of the most productive workers shrank from 3.5% to 2.9% per month, while that of the other employees rose from 4.6% to 5.3%.

This study therefore suggests that financial incentives do influence the behavior and the performance of workers in the way predicted by the theory of incentive. Much empirical work confirms that this prediction is well-founded, especially by high-lighting the existence of a dilemma between incentive and insurance (see Chiappori and Salanié, 2003). It should nevertheless be pointed out that financial incentives can have counterproductive effects, something that psychologists have known for a long time (Kruglanski, 1978; Deci et al., 1999), and that economists have begun to focus on too. Indeed, experimental evidence confirms that explicit incentives sometimes result in worse compliance than incomplete labor contracts (Fehr and Falk, 1999; Fehr and Schmidt, 2000; Gneezy and Rustichini, 2000). This result is usually explained by the conflict between extrinsic motivation (contingent rewards) and intrinsic motivation (the individual's desire to perform the task for its own sake) (Kreps, 1997). In this perspective, Bénabou and Tirole (2003) provide a model that explains the counter-productive effect of financial incentives. They consider a framework in which the principal has private information about the abilities of agents, which means that agents do not know their own ability within the firm. In this context, the contract proposed by the principal sends the agent a signal about his or her own ability. A contract with a strong incentive component, in which remuneration is closely linked to performance, may send the agent a bad signal about his or her abilities, and so dis-courage him or her. The study of Bénabou and Tirole shows that the theory of con-tracts can be refined so as to account for phenomena that reveal the limited efficiency of purely incentive contracts. In the remainder of this chapter, we will concentrate on the case typically dealt with in the theory of contracts, in which the agent does have information about his or her own characteristics.

3.2 SHOULD REMUNERATION ALWAYS BE INDIVIDUALIZED?

To this point we have assumed that the principal could only make the remuneration of an agent depend on that person's individual production. But even in cases as sim-ple as that of the gold prospector or the salesman, there is no reason why the sharing rule need depend exclusively on individual production if there are other verifiable variables, the utilization of which would make it possible to work out more efficient contracts.

The Agency Model with Two Signals

In a very general way, we may suppose that the principal observes, not just individual production y, but a signal $\tilde{\varepsilon}$ independent of the agent's level of effort yet capable of being correlated with the random variable ε. Like production, the signal $\tilde{\varepsilon}$ is not only observable, but also verifiable. For example, meteorological conditions do not depend on how hard a farm worker exerts him- or herself, but they do very often affect the harvest, and are verifiable. More generally, signal $\tilde{\varepsilon}$ may concern macroeconomic vari-ables, or the observation of the production of other agents, or of the "team" to which the agent in question belongs. It is in the principal's interest to make use of this signal when the efforts of agents combine in more or less complex ways in the production process.

In this setting, the agent's compensation rule may depend on the observation of his or her individual production y and that of signal $\tilde{\varepsilon}$. A (linear) compensation rule thus takes the form $W = w + by - \tilde{b}\tilde{\varepsilon}$. The definition (24) of the agent's preferences shows that his or her expected utility is now equal to $-\exp\{-a[w + be - C(e)]\} \cdot E\{\exp[-a(b\varepsilon - \tilde{b}\tilde{\varepsilon})]\}$. Let us assume, in order to simplify, that the random variable $\tilde{\varepsilon}$ is normally distributed with zero mean and standard error σ, and let ρ be the correlation coefficient between the variables ε and $\tilde{\varepsilon}$. We thus have $cov(\varepsilon, \tilde{\varepsilon}) = \rho\sigma^2$. In these conditions the random variable $-a(b\varepsilon - \tilde{b}\tilde{\varepsilon})$ follows a normally distributed law with zero mean and variance $a^2\sigma^2(b^2 + \tilde{b}^2 - 2\rho b\tilde{b})$, and the random variable[6] $\exp[-a(b\varepsilon - \tilde{b}\tilde{\varepsilon})]$ has a log-normal distribution with mean $a^2\sigma^2(b^2 + \tilde{b}^2 - 2\rho b\tilde{b})/2$. The expected utility of the agent is now written:

$$EU = -\exp\left\{-a\left[w + be - C(e) - \frac{a\sigma^2}{2}(b^2 + \tilde{b}^2 - 2\rho b\tilde{b})\right]\right\}$$

We observe that optimal effort is always characterized by the equality $C'(e^*) = b$. The mean of the random variable $\tilde{\varepsilon}$ being zero, the principal's expected profit is again equal to $(1 - b)e^* - w$, and in consequence, the optimal compensation rule is again the solution of the problem (26). Taking the logarithms of the opposites of both sides of the participation constraint $EU \geq \bar{U}$, we find that the latter now takes the following form:

$$w + be - C(e) - \frac{a\sigma^2}{2}(b^2 + \tilde{b}^2 - 2\rho b\tilde{b}) \geq \bar{x} \tag{30}$$

The Optimal Compensation Rule
As before, the principal has an interest in choosing w in such a way as to bind the participation constraint. If we bring the value of w thus obtained into the principal's problem, we see that the optimal values of parameters b and $\tilde{b}$ solve:

$$\underset{\{b,\tilde{b}\}}{\text{Max}}\left[e^* - C(e^*) - \frac{a\sigma^2}{2}(b^2 + \tilde{b}^2 - 2\rho b\tilde{b}) - \bar{x}\right] \quad \text{subject to} \quad C'(e^*) = b$$

As $C(e) = ce^2/2$, we find, after simple calculations, that the optimal values b^* and $\tilde{b}^*$ are defined by:

$$b^* = \frac{1}{1 + ac\sigma^2(1 - \rho^2)} \qquad \text{and} \qquad \tilde{b}^* = \rho b^* \tag{31}$$

If variables ε and $\tilde{\varepsilon}$ are independent, the correlation coefficient ρ is equal to zero and the indexation coefficient $\tilde{b}^*$ is null. The observation of $\tilde{\varepsilon}$ then has no informative value. Conversely, if variables ε and $\tilde{\varepsilon}$ are not independent, the optimal remuneration rule takes into account all the information available. The optimal value of the fixed part of the remuneration is obtained by using the participation constraint (30) written in the form of an equality, and definitions (31) of b^* and $\tilde{b}^*$, or:

$$w^* = \bar{x} - \frac{1}{2c[1 + ac\sigma^2(1 - \rho)]} \tag{32}$$

We see that total remuneration, $W^* = w^* + b^* y - \tilde{b}^* \tilde{\varepsilon}$, *falls* when $\tilde{\varepsilon}$ increases for a given value of y. This result comes from the fact that the principal knows that a high value of production is less the consequence of a special effort on the part of the agent than it is of an exogenous rise in the random variable $\tilde{\varepsilon}$. An interesting case is that in which $\tilde{\varepsilon}$ becomes an indicator of the activity of others employed in the firm, or even of the activity in other firms taking place in an analogous environment. If the principal cannot "filter out" the contribution of other workers, or the general market trend, to the agent's production, then it is not optimal to make the remuneration of an individual depend solely on production. This justifies schemes in which a part of the remuneration depends on an indicator relative to the performance of others in the same firm, or the economic trend in a particular sector. For example, profit-sharing rules adopted in certain firms frequently seem to reflect thinking of this kind (Cahuc and Dormont, 1997). Along the same lines, Gibbons and Murphy (1990) have observed that there might be grounds for penalizing the managers of a firm when that firm's share price does not rise as fast as the average index of the stock market.

3.3 SOME REASONS WHY PERFORMANCE PAY MAY BE INEFFICIENT

Two major sources of inefficiency in compensation schemes based on verifiable observations are the multiplicity of the tasks that go to make up the content of the work done by any individual, and the fact that an agent's activities are generally observed by his or her supervisors, and their objectives do not necessarily overlap completely with those of the principal. That being the case, an employee may have an interest in focusing part of his or her effort on activities likely to catch the supervisor's approving eye.

3.3.1 Multitasking

In what has gone before, an employee's remuneration was based on the putatively verifiable observation of a *single* scalar deemed to represent the agent's production. This approach eliminates much of the difficulty arising from *multitasking*—the fact that the productive activities of most individuals have many dimensions. Given the reality of multitasking, the principal may be tempted to base an agent's remuneration on the only verifiable observations available. But in doing so, the principal actually gives the agent an incentive to put more effort into precisely the kind of actions that do give rise to verifiable observations but that may not necessarily bring the principal the most benefit. The history of the former USSR abounds in anecdotes about projects selected according to the number of nails used, or their weight (both verifiable quantities). Multitasking is one of the reasons firms usually adopt implicit contracts. Brown (1990), for example, shows that the frequency of implicit contracts rises, and that of piece-rate work diminishes, with an indicator of how many different tasks agents are assigned.

When possible, firms sometimes choose to index the remuneration of agents to *global* indicators strongly correlated with the objectives of the principal. Payment for managers in the form of stock options is a practice that is spreading precisely because it makes it possbile to align the interests of managers (i.e., agents) with those of share-holders (here considered as the principal). Likewise, all the players on a soccer team generally receive the same bonus when their team wins: if the center forward were paid for the number of goals he or she scored, he or she would probably have a tendency to try to score goals too often, instead of passing the ball to teammates in a better position to do so. (On questions of *multitasking*, see Holmström and Milgrom, 1991, and the summary of Prendergast, 1999.)

3.3.2 Supervision and Rent-Seeking

In firms above a certain size, it is not the principal who observes the performance of agents. This activity is delegated to supervisors whose precise role is to report what they observe to the principal. But supervisors are themselves agents, and their objectives do not necessarily overlap with those of the principal. For example, it is sometimes observed that in order to avoid friction with the people they have to work with every day, supervisors tend to write reports in which bad performances are made to look better than they are, thus minimizing the degree of difference among the employees they supervise (see, for example, Murphy and Cleveland, 1991).

Another, and surely more important problem, is known in the literature as *rent-seeking*. It is caused by the fact that agents may derive a comparative advantage from devoting a part of their efforts to actions that will "impress" supervisors so that the latter will write favorable reports about them, instead of devoting all their efforts to tasks that are the most beneficial to the principal (on this, see Milgrom, 1988, and Tirole, 1992). In France, for example, teachers are hired through competitions, and in some of these the members of the judging panel are well-known personalities. There is a tendency for the candidates to espouse the opinions of these personalities, or at any rate to demonstrate that they are acquainted with them (which bears a corresponding cost in time), so as to make a favorable impression. Prendergast (1993b, 1999) points out that rent-seeking most often makes its appearance in situations in which it would be extremely hard to find any objective yardstick by which to measure production, and our example of hiring competitions for teachers falls into this category to some extent. The same thing would be true for art critics or restaurant critics. Prendergast (1993b) shows that these situations breed "yes-men," whose purpose is simply to avoid standing out from the crowd.

A Model with Rent-Seeking

The inefficiency generated by rent-seeking comes to light naturally if we marginally change the basic agency model. Let us now suppose that the agent is able to exercise two types of effort. He or she can put effort e into activities that are directly productive, in which case his or her production y is again given by $y = e + \varepsilon$. But the agent can also put out effort α, which (for simplicity) has no productive value but allows him or her to impress the supervisor favorably. In doing so, the agent knows that the supervisor who observes y will write a report stating that the agent performed $y + \alpha$. Since the agent's remuneration depends only on the supervisor's report (the principal receives no other information), it can be written $W = w + b(y + \alpha)$. Let us assume that this agent's preferences can be described by the exponential function $U = -\exp\{-a[W - C(e) - K(\alpha)]\}$ in which the disutilities linked to efforts e and α are represented by the quadratic functions $C(e) = ce^2/2$ and $K(\alpha) = k\alpha^2/2$; reasoning identical to that followed in the basic agency model arrives at the following expression of expected utility:

$$EU = -\exp\left\{-a\left[w + b(e + \alpha) - C(e) - K(\alpha) - \frac{ab^2\sigma^2}{2}\right]\right\}$$

The reader will see that the levels of effort e^* and α^* chosen by the agent are such that $C'(e^*) = K'(\alpha^*) = b$. In this simple model, the agent equates the marginal costs of the two types of effort to the piece rate. Let $\bar{U}$ again be the reservation utility of the agent, and let us posit $\bar{x} = -\ln(-\bar{U})/a$; taking the logarithms of the opposites of the two sides of the participation constraint $EU \geq \bar{U}$, we find that the latter constraint comes down to the inequality:

$$w + b(e + \alpha) - C(e) - K(\alpha) - \frac{ab^2\sigma^2}{2} \geq \bar{x}$$

Since the agent's production is given by $y = e^* + \varepsilon$ and his or her remuneration amounts to $W = w + b(e^* + \alpha^* + \varepsilon)$, the principal's expected profit, or $E(y - W)$, is equal to $(1 - b)e^* - b\alpha^* - w$. The principal then decides on his or her remuneration rule by maximizing his or her expected profit subject to incentive and participation constraints, or:

$$\underset{\{w, b\}}{\text{Max}}[(1 - b)e^* - b\alpha^* - w] \quad \text{subject to} \quad C'(e^*) = K'(\alpha^*) = b \text{ and } EU \geq \bar{U}$$

Since the principal always has an interest in choosing the fixed part w of the compensation scheme in such a way as to bind the agent's participation constraint, we can carry the value of w thus obtained into the expected profit. We see then that the optimal value of parameter b solves:

$$\underset{b}{\text{Max}}\left[e^* - C(e^*) - K(\alpha^*) - \frac{ab^2\sigma^2}{2} - \bar{x}\right] \quad \text{subject to} \quad C'(e^*) = K'(\alpha^*) = b$$

The Inefficiency of Performance Pay
Given the quadratic cost functions, we easily find that the optimal remuneration rule b^* is characterized by:

$$b^* = \frac{1}{1 + \dfrac{c}{k} + ac\sigma^2} \quad \text{with} \quad e^* = \frac{b^*}{c} \text{ and } \alpha^* = \frac{b^*}{k}$$

These equalities show that the principal takes "rent-seeking" activity into account by reducing the piece rate b^*. The more profitable rent-seeking is to the agent, i.e., the weaker parameter k is, the less is paid for performance. In other words, rent-seeking weakens the variable part of total remuneration and strengthens the fixed part; this increases the inefficiency bred by the moral hazard problem. Hence the first-best optimum is not reached with risk-neutral agents ($a = 0$), since even in this case $b^* < 1$.

This model illustrates a more general result, which is that when an employee's performance is evaluated solely on the basis of *verifiable* data, there is a strong risk of provoking an inefficient allocation of that agent's efforts, because he or she will begin to focus his or her efforts exclusively on activities that will pay off, given the criterion being used to evaluate performance. In the preceding model, this criterion is simply performance *reported*—not observed—by supervisors; but the model actually applies to other situations too. For example, when it comes to the problem of multitasking, variable α can be interpreted as a particular effort intended to push up a specific indicator, upon which the agent's remuneration is in part based. Prendergast (1999) adduces a number of situations, from doctors paid on a fee basis to educational institutions rewarded for the number of degrees they grant, in which a system of "objective" compensation is a cause of inefficiency. As we shall see in the following section, one remedy for these detrimental outcomes, which surface when neither effort nor performance can be verified, lies in constructing systems of promotion based on the relative performance of agents, and/or grounding long-term relationships on implicit contracts; the latter are sometimes called "incomplete" contracts, or informal relationships.

4 INCENTIVE IN THE ABSENCE OF VERIFIABLE RESULTS

In this section we will assume that both the effort made *and* the results achieved by an agent are *unverifiable*. If we look again at the static agency model with this hypothesis, a double problem of moral hazard emerges, since the employee can no longer a priori trust his or her employer when the latter promises to pay a high wage in exchange for good performance: if remuneration increases with observed production, the employer always has an interest in declaring that he or she has observed the lowest level of production, so as to pay the lowest wage possible. This difficulty is sometimes got around by invoking the notion of *reputation*: a firm could not behave in this way, for its employees would inevitably quit, and would spread the news that the firm was behaving in this way; the firm would then have greater difficulty in recruiting new workers (the models of Bull, 1983, 1987, take up this idea). Another approach takes the view that when a relationship lasts for more than one period, that means the two parties have a mutual interest in it. The contract that binds them is thus *implicit* and *self-enforcing*.

We shall see that this last approach does allow us to understand several important features of wage relationships and the functioning of the labor market in the absence of verifiability of results (see Chiappori et al., 1994, for more details). In the first place, the occurrence of double moral hazard in this context explains the use of promotions, following a hierarchical logic that is very different from the logic that links remuneration directly to performance or productivity. The double moral hazard also accounts for the existence of compensation rules based on seniority, which are frequently observed in firms. Finally, the inefficiency induced by the double moral hazard may, in certain circumstances that the efficiency wage model of Shapiro and Stiglitz (1984) illustrates, be the source of involuntary unemployment.

4.1 PROMOTIONS AND TOURNAMENTS

Following the seminal work of Doeringer and Piore (1971), many studies have highlighted compensation rules specific to large firms and known as the *internal market*. Large firms appear to adopt rules that are apparently quite unconnected with the outside, and supposedly competitive, world. Among other things, these rules define the systems of promotion, the positions, and the wages that go with them. Wages seem to follow a hierarchical logic, largely independent of the productivity of labor. A wage raise generally goes along with a *promotion*, when the agent changes position in the hierarchy. In some large firms the salary of the CEO is more than three times higher than that of the vice-presidents. A gap that large would seem to indicate that the internal market of a firm is a structure that allows a solution to certain problems of incentive. "Tournament" theory makes it possible to explain some of the properties of internal markets by linking wages to the hierarchical grades at which agents arrive according to their relative performance.

4.1.1 A Tournament Model

Tournament theory starts with the idea that the principal creates competition among his or her agents by, on the one hand, promising them prizes specified *in advance*, and, on the other, making it clear to them that the awarding of these prizes will depend not on the *absolute* level of an individual's production but on the place that this level occupies *relative* to that of the other competitors. The model of reference is that of Lazear and Rosen (1981), but here we will make use of a slightly more general one, close to that of Malcomson (1984), which has the advantage of fitting better with the foregoing analyses of optimal remuneration rules.

The Rules of the Game

In analyzing the properties of a promotion system, one ought to use an explicitly dynamic model. But we prefer to avoid the excessive analytical complication to which that option leads and will therefore make do with a static model: a large firm in which a given number N of employees each produce a quantity $y = e + \varepsilon$ of goods, where ε is a normally distributed random variable with zero mean and standard error σ, proper to the individual in question. In order to simplify the notation, we do not index individuals, and we assume that random variables affecting individual production are independent. The N employees receive a given fixed wage w_0, and they all aspire to promotion, in which case they will receive wage $w_0 + b$, $b > 0$. The purpose of this simple formalization is to make it clear that the hierarchical structure of a firm rests on a given grid of remunerations in which wages change discontinuously, and only with promotion. The principal chooses the number L of those promoted and the value b of the "bonus" that comes with promotion. The tournament unfolds according to an extremely simple rule: the principal announces that he or she will offer a promotion to the L persons who have performed best. We will solve the principal's problem and show that there is no difference between choosing the number of those promoted L and the value of the bonus b, or the minimal level of production $\bar{y}$ that qualifies an agent for promotion and the bonus b.

On the Value of Promotions When Individual Effort Is Unverifiable

When an individual's production cannot be impartially assessed by a third party, the advantage of the tournament in comparison with other kinds of incentive is that it only contains *verifiable* clauses. The number L of those to be promoted and the wage $w_0 + b$ that each will receive are known before the competition begins, and an impartial tribunal can easily determine whether the prescribed promotions have in fact taken place, and whether every employee has been paid according to the agreed wage scale. Moreover, the firm has no a priori interest in lying about the possible finishing order, since in any case it pays the same wage bill $w_0 N + bL$, which is likewise known beforehand. At most, the firm's management might favor "pet" candidates, but it cannot change the number of promotions nor the value of the total wage bill. In this sense, promotions constitute a simple way for the employer to commit him- or herself to pay the bonuses he or she has promised, since the value of all the bonuses is verifiable.

So we see that promotions and internal markets in general allow the clauses of a contract to be made *explicit*. Just as in a tournament, the rules, the different stages of the game, and the rewards are made perfectly clear at the outset, and are verifiable. The wages corresponding to each grade in the hierarchy are totally uncoupled from the productivity of labor, and it is the number of promotions and the wage gap between the different rungs that, if correctly calibrated, constitute an optimal incentive scheme. In other words, your superior does not earn twice as much as you because he or she is twice as productive, but because that fact will give you reason to put plenty of effort into your current assignment, in the hope of climbing the rungs of the hierarchy.

The Behavior of the Agent

To simplify the analysis, and in order to concentrate solely on the characteristics of the internal market, we will suppose that all agents are risk-neutral. More precisely, the utility function of an agent is simply written $U = W - C(e)$, where the cost of effort is measured by the quadratic function $C(e) = ce^2/2$. Given the proposed compensation scheme, each agent knows that he or she will receive wage w_0 whatever his or her level of production may be, and that he or she will, in addition, be entitled to bonus b only if his or her production is greater than $\bar{y}$, or $\varepsilon \geq \bar{y} - e$. Let $\Phi(.)$ be the cumulative distribution function of the random variable ε; this event will happen with a probability equal to $[1 - \Phi(\bar{y} - e)]$, when an employee supplies effort e. His or her expected utility is then written:

$$EU = w_0 + b[1 - \Phi(\bar{y} - e)] - C(e) \tag{33}$$

Knowing b and $\bar{y}$, every agent chooses the level of effort e^* that maximizes his or her expected utility. Let $\phi = \Phi'$ be the probability density function of the disturbance ε; we then find that e^* is the solution to:

$$b\phi(\bar{y} - e^*) = C'(e^*) \tag{34}$$

It is easy to verify that with a normally distributed disturbance, relation (34) defines a unique value of effort $e^* = e^*(b, \bar{y})$ increasing with bonus b, but with a direction of variation which is ambiguous with $\bar{y}$ (this direction depends on the sign of $\bar{y} - e^*$). We can also verify that the second-order conditions dictate $b\phi' + C'' > 0$.

The Behavior of the Principal

If we assume, for the sake of simplicity, that the total production of the firm is the sum of individual productions, the expected profit per capita is:

$$E\pi = e^* - w_0 - b[1 - \Phi(\bar{y} - e^*)] \tag{35}$$

The principal determines b and $\bar{y}$ in such a way as to maximize this profit per capita, taking into account the incentive constraint (34) and the participation constraint $EU \geq \bar{U}$, where $\bar{U}$ again designates an exogenous level of utility accessible outside the firm. This problem is simple to solve if we limit ourselves at the outset to the values of variables b and $\bar{y}$ which make the participation constraint binding. In this case, relation (33) shows that b and $\bar{y}$ always verify:

$$w_0 + b[1 - \Phi(\bar{y} - e^*)] = \bar{U} + C(e^*) \tag{36}$$

If we carry this equality into definition (35) of expected profit per capita, we get $E\pi = e^* - C(e^*) - \bar{U}$. The maximization of this expression yields:

$$C'(e^*) = 1 \Leftrightarrow e^* = \frac{1}{c} \tag{37}$$

With the help of relations (34) and (36), we see that this level of effort can be attained by choosing a production norm $\bar{y}$ and a bonus b satisfying:

$$b\phi(\bar{y} - e^*) = 1 \tag{38}$$

$$w_0 + b[1 - \Phi(\bar{y} - e^*)] = \bar{U} + C(e^*) \tag{39}$$

Equations (38) and (39) define the optimal values of $\bar{y}$ and of b, given the value of e^* yielded by (37). Since all the workers whose individual production surpasses $\bar{y}$ are promoted, the number of promotions is defined by $L = N[1 - \Phi(\bar{y} - e^*)]$. It therefore makes no difference to the principal whether he or she proposes a contract stipulating the bonus and the minimal value of production that will trigger a promotion, or the bonus and the number of promotions that will be made.

Note that the system of promotions through the ranks of a pre-established hierarchy provides each competitor at the outset with an average gain equal to what he or she could achieve otherwise, i.e., $\bar{U}$. But in the aftermath, the winners of the tournament—those promoted—obtain a level of utility greater than that of the losers. If the latter remain with the firm, that is because they still have hope of being promoted in an upcoming tournament. This point could be taken into account in an explicitly dynamic model in which workers participate in a number of successive tournaments (see Meyer, 1992).

Increasing Risk

The system of relations (38) and (39) also furnishes some interesting details about the effects of increased uncertainty. This eventuality can be schematically likened to an increase in the complexity of the organization, which makes individual supervision more random. In this interpretation, the standard error σ must be an increasing function of the size N of the firm.

The consequence of increased uncertainty can be analyzed by approximating the solution defined by equations (38) and (39). Let us assume that the gap between $\bar{y}$ and e^* is not too large. Since $\Phi(0) = 1/2$, and since the probability density of a normal variable satisfies $\phi(0) = 1/\sigma\sqrt{2\Pi}$ and $\phi'(0) = 0$, a first-order expansion around the mean gives:

$$\phi(\bar{y} - e^*) \simeq \phi(0) = 1/\sigma\sqrt{2\Pi} \qquad \text{and} \qquad \Phi(\bar{y} - e^*) \simeq \tfrac{1}{2} + (\bar{y} - e^*)\phi(0)$$

Relations (38) and (39) then entail:

$$b \simeq \sigma\sqrt{2\Pi} \qquad \text{and} \qquad [1 - \Phi(\bar{y} - e^*)] \simeq \frac{C(e^*) + \bar{U} - w_0}{\sigma\sqrt{2\Pi}}$$

It can be seen that an increase in uncertainty, here deemed equivalent to a rise in σ, amplifies the wage gap and reduces the proportion $(1 - \Phi)$ of promotions. Hence, there ought to be few promotions in organizationally complex firms, in which the assessment of individual performances is imprecise, or in those in which "chance" plays a significant role—but the promotions that do occur ought to be accompanied by a strong increase in remuneration. To the extent that the standard error σ increases with the size N of the firm, this model also predicts that the level of compensation should increase with the number of individuals who aspire to a promotion. Note that these results have been reached on the assumption that agents are risk-neutral. Aversion to risk, on the other hand, would have the effect of reducing the gaps between the various grades of the hierarchy. Examination of wage policies and promotion rules in certain large firms confirms this prediction. But before presenting a few illustrations of these results, it will be instructive to reflect on the limitations of promotion based on performance.

Tournaments and Rent-Seeking

The tournament model formalizes and simplifies a system of promotions based on the respective performance of agents. But there exist many organizations, including certain large industrial firms, in which promotions are made essentially on the basis of seniority. It would seem that a hierarchy in which seniority is the preponderant factor must lead to an inefficient allocation of resources, since agents no longer have an incentive to make great effort. The seniority rule, like many other so-called "bureaucratic" rules, is partially explained by the fact that it makes it possible to avoid rent-seeking activity. The ground for this conclusion can easily be shown by crossing the rent-seeking model with the tournament model. To that end, let us suppose that each agent can put out respectively an effort α that does no more than impress the supervisor, and an effort e that only increases his or her individual production, still given by $y = e + \varepsilon$. Let us also assume that an agent's promotion depends only on the performance $y + \alpha$ reported by the supervisor. As before, the principal chooses the number L of those to be promoted and the value b of the bonus corresponding to the promotion. But now the principal announces that he or she will offer a promotion to the L persons who have the best performance as *reported* by the supervisors (since, by hypothesis, the principal delegates the observation of results to supervisors).

Let $\bar{r}$ be the level of reported performance that triggers a promotion, and let $K(\alpha) = k\alpha^2/2$ be the cost linked to rent-seeking activity. The expected utility of the agent, who is promoted if his or her performance is greater than $\bar{r}$, is now written:

$$EU = w_0 + b[1 - \Phi(\bar{r} - e - \alpha)] - C(e) - K(\alpha)$$

Knowing b and $\bar{r}$, the agent chooses levels of effort e^* and α^* which maximize his or her expected utility. We thus have:

$$b\phi(\bar{r} - e^* - \alpha^*) = C'(e^*) = K'(\alpha^*) \tag{40}$$

Relation (35) giving the expression of profit per capita here takes the form:

$$E\pi = e^* - w_0 - b[1 - \Phi(\bar{r} - e^* - \alpha^*)]$$

Likewise relation (36) giving the values of b and $\bar{r}$ which make the participation constraint binding is here written:

$$w_0 + b[1 - \Phi(\bar{r} - e^* - \alpha^*)] = \bar{U} + C(e^*) + K(\alpha^*) \tag{41}$$

Bringing this last equality into the expression of profit per capita, we find $E\pi = e^* - C(e^*) - K(e^*)$. The maximization of this expresssion leads to levels of effort e^* and α^* characterized by

$$e^* = \frac{1}{c\left(1 + \dfrac{c}{k}\right)} < \frac{1}{c} \quad \text{and} \quad \alpha^* = \frac{1}{c + k} > 0 \tag{42}$$

Finally, the performance norm $\bar{r}$ and the bonus b are found by substituting these values of e^* and α^* in equations (40) and (41). From that we can deduce the number of promotions proposed by the principal, which is given by $L = N[1 - \Phi(\bar{r} - \alpha^*)]$.

Relations (42) show that effort e^* (or α^*) increases (or decreases) with the cost k of rent-seeking. That means that rent-seeking reduces the effort dedicated to production. If k is small with respect to c, rent-seeking activity pays off handsomely for the agent, while the firm's interest in staging the tournament—that is, a system of promotions based on performance—is lessened, since productive effort falls off. In practice, above a threshold of minimum verifiable effort, it may be in the firm's interest to abandon the system of promotion based on performance for a system based on seniority, which does not elicit rent-seeking activity, and probably also makes it possible to save a portion of the supervision costs.

4.1.2 Empirical Illustrations

The predictions of the tournament model have often been tested in the realm of sport. As we would expect, studies show that golfers hit the ball more carefully, and racing drivers take greater risks, when the prizes offered are bigger (see Prendergast, 1999, who points out, however, that these studies are rather confirmations of the general principles of the theory of incentive than of the tournament model). In economics, the tournament model has relevance when applied to the properties of hierarchical structures, and the wages linked to each grade.

A Case Study

The study carried out by Baker et al. (1994a,b) on a large American firm in the service sector, for which the data available covered the period 1969–1988, sharpens and confirms certain predictions of the preceding models. In the first place, this study shows that the relative importance of each grade in the hierarchy remains very stable. Whereas the firm tripled in size over the period in question, the rates of promotion from one grade of the hierarchy to another hardly varied at all. Second, figure VI in Baker et al. (1994a), reproduced in figure 6.3, indicates that the average wage corresponding to each grade increases at an increasing rate as we move up the hierarchy. This property accords with the size effect highlighted in the tournament model, according to which compensation increases with the number of individuals aspiring to promotion. In the firm in question, the number of employees decreased very gradually from level 1 up through level 4 (the four lowest levels), and as we see, average wage growth is small in this part of the hierarchy. However, the relative size of each grade falls off very sharply between levels 5 and 8 (in 1980 there were 86 people in grade 5, 25 in grade 6, four in grade 7, and one in grade 8). As figure 6.3 shows, the more competitors there are in relation to the number of posts available in the next highest grade, the more steeply the average wage climbs.

Figure 6.3 also brings out the fact that the wage does not remain constant within each grade of the hierarchy. In other words, certain individuals (even the majority) see their wage rise without being promoted; this means that there are incentive mechanisms other than the tournament at work within each hierarchical grade.

The conclusions reached by Eriksson (1999) point in the same direction as those of Baker et al. (1994a,b). Using a sample group of 2600 managers taken from 210

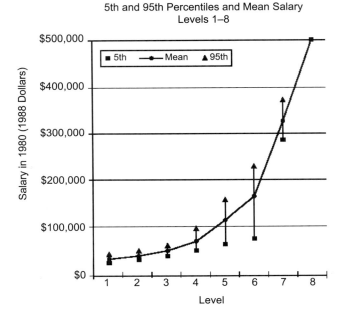

5th and 95th Percentiles and Mean Salary
Levels 1–8

FIGURE 6.3
Salary ranges by level of hierarchical grades. Salary levels are calculated in 1988 constant dollars. Level 8 had only one employee.

Source: Baker et al. (1994a).

Danish firms who were followed from 1992 to 1995, Eriksson estimates that hierarchical grade explains 60% of the variation in wages. He also confirms certain predictions of the tournament model, finding that the "prize" awarded (i.e., bonus b in the theoretical model) increases when the number of competitors rises. Further, he highlights a significant relationship between the variability of demand addressed to a sector and the dispersion of wages within that sector. This conclusion accords with the prediction of the theoretical model that bonus b increases with standard error σ characterizing the distribution of wages. Mention should be made as well of McCue (1996), a study of persons employed in the state of Michigan, which finds that *internal* mobility—that is, successive promotions within the same firm—explains around 15% of the wage rise for men over the life cycle.

More on Promotions
The models we have used in this part are very simple. They illuminate only a portion of the logic of promotions, and would need to be extended in various directions. Some works insist on the fact that promotions send a signal about the quality of employees, making it possible to assign them to the tasks best suited to their abilities (Waldman, 1984; Sattinger, 1993). This would explain the importance of the wage gains that gen-

erally go along with promotions. Higher pay with promotion keeps workers whose good qualities would be signaled to other employers by their promotion from quitting the firm. Promotions are also a way to give workers incentive to accumulate specific human capital (Carmichael, 1983; Prendergast, 1993a; Chang and Wang, 1996). Finally, promotions may also be explained by uncertainty about the efficiency of employees. Harris and Holmström (1982) consider a situation in which the quality of every employee is uncertain, and is gradually revealed by his or her performance. If the worker is risk-averse, a risk-neutral firm ought to have an interest in insuring him or her against this uncertainty by paying him or her a constant wage, dependent on his or her expected efficiency at the time of hiring. The most efficient workers, however, would then be given an incentive to look for other jobs, since other employers, observing their quality as revealed by their past performance, would be ready to offer them higher wages. In consequence, the firm has an interest in offering limited insurance, and in working out a system of promotion with a low starting wage and steep wage increases as justified by performance.

The model of Gibbons and Waldman (1999a) takes up the learning process of Harris and Holmström (1982) and adds the acquisition of human capital and the assignment of employees to tasks adapted to their abilities. This model, which integrates several dimensions of an individual's career within a firm, reproduces well the main results of empirical studies of the subject, such as significant wage increases accompanying promotion, or the existence of "fast tracks," in which an individual who has been rapidly promoted to one grade in the hierarchy is then promoted rapidly to the next one (on the subject of careers, see the comprehensive panorama of Gibbons and Waldman, 1999b).

4.2 The Role of Seniority

We will now take into explicit consideration the dynamic dimension of the wage relationship in a context where production is not verifiable; our purpose will be to illustrate the importance (which empirical observation confirms; see Lazear, 1979) of remuneration rules based on seniority. We can characterize optimal long-term contracts very simply using the so-called "shirking" model, which we begin by laying out. The grounds for remuneration by seniority are discussed subsequently.

4.2.1 The "Shirking" Model

The shirking model assumes two levels of effort: the first strictly positive and again denoted by e, which gives rise to a disutility $C > 0$ and allows the agent to realize production $y_t > 0$ at date t, and the second with a value of zero, the disutility and the production of which are both normalized to zero as well. Note that in this model it is *obligatory* for an agent furnishing level of effort e to achieve production y. So when the principal observes that production has taken the value zero, he or she can be sure that the employee has been shirking. If production were a verifiable magnitude, the principal could arrange this employee's remuneration as follows: the payment of a fixed wage w such that the participation constraint would be binding when the employee was not caught shirking, and a low wage (or even a penalty) w_1 when inspection found that he or she was not furnishing effort $e > 0$. But when individual production is not a verifiable magnitude, it becomes necessary to invent other remuneration rules.

The shirking model takes the dynamic dimension of the wage relationship into account, and assumes that the principal proposes a contract $\{w_t; t = 0, 1, \ldots, +\infty\}$ specifying the wage the employee will receive on each date. If the agent is caught shirking, i.e., is inspected and found to be furnishing a null effort, he or she is paid to the end of that period and is fired. Note that the shirker receives his or her wage for that period even if he or she has not supplied any effort during it. This is an offshoot of the unverifiable character of production, which prevents the employer from proposing a remuneration based on results. In what follows, we will use the exogenous constant parameter $p \leq 1$ to designate the probability that the principal will inspect the agent's activity in each period. This less-than-perfect supervision $(p \neq 1)$ is explained by the costs arising from checking up on the activities of employees—costs that are likely to be greater in a large firm. We will also assume that at each period the agent risks losing his or her job with an exogenous constant probability denoted by q.

The Behavior of the Principal
If $\delta \in [0, 1]$ designates the discount rate, the profit expected by the employer from the continuation of the contract after the tth period, or Π_t, is written:

$$\Pi_t = y_t - w_t + \delta[(1 - q) \operatorname{Max}(\Pi_{t+1}, \Pi_{t+1}^s) + q\bar{\Pi}_{t+1}] \tag{43}$$

In this expression, $\bar{\Pi}_{t+1}$ designates the profit expected when the contractual relationship winds up at the end of period t. This might, for example, be the profit expected in a "competitive" labor market, or the profit derived from leaving the position empty. We will assume that the employer considers this quantity to be a parameter dependent on general macroeconomic conditions and outside his or her control. The term Π_{t+1}^s represents the expected profit of the principal if he or she decides to "cheat," in other words to break the contract at the end of period t. Relation (43) is now easy to grasp. In the present period, the principal obtains an instantaneous profit equal to $y_t - w_t$, but at the end of this period the job is destroyed with a probability q, in which case the employer expects the gain $\bar{\Pi}_{t+1}$. If the job is not destroyed, which happens with probability $1 - q$, the principal decides to respect the implicit contract when this attitude procures for him or her a gain Π_{t+1} superior to the gain Π_{t+1}^s that he or she would achieve by not abiding by the contract.

If, at period t, the employer decides to fire his or her employee by wrongly claiming that the latter has not supplied the required effort, his or her expected profit amounts to:

$$\Pi_t^s = y_t - w_t + \delta\bar{\Pi}_{t+1} \tag{44}$$

At each date, the employer respects the contract if doing so permits him or her to expect a profit greater than the one he or she would obtain by breaking the contract. For that, it is necessary and sufficient that the *employer's incentive constraint* $\Pi_t \geq \Pi_t^s$, $\forall t \geq 0$ be satisfied. Now, relations (43) and (44) entail:

$$\Pi_t - \Pi_t^s = \delta(1-q)[\text{Max}(\Pi_{t+1}, \Pi_{t+1}^s) - \bar{\Pi}_{t+1}], \qquad \forall t \geq 0$$

We then easily verify that the incentive constraint $\Pi_t \geq \Pi_t^s$, $\forall t \geq 0$, is equivalent to condition $\Pi_{t+1} \geq \bar{\Pi}_{t+1}$, for all $t \geq 0$. Abiding by the contract also necessitates that the employer has no better alternative—a property that, as we have seen, characterizes the *participation constraint*. Since the gain expected by the principal at date t outside the contractual relationship amounts to $\bar{\Pi}_t$, the participation and incentive conditions finally come down to the inequalities $\Pi_t \geq \bar{\Pi}_t$, $\forall t \geq 0$.

The Behavior of the Agent

In order to focus our analysis more narrowly on the incentive problem, we will now assume that workers are risk-neutral. That being the case, if an agent supplies effort $e > 0$ during the tth period of the contract, he or she attains a level of utility equal to $w_t - C$ over the course of this period, and more generally, he or she expects an intertemporal level of utility V_t satisfying:

$$V_t = w_t - C + \delta[(1-q)\,\text{Max}(V_{t+1}, V_{t+1}^s) + q\bar{V}_{t+1}] \tag{45}$$

In this expression, V_{t+1}^s represents the expected utility of an agent who decides no longer to furnish effort e at period $t + 1$; it is defined by relation (46) below. The term $\bar{V}_{t+1}$ designates the utility expected when the contractual relationship comes to an end after t periods. This corresponds to the utility expected from searching for a job. Relation (45) signifies that, in the present period, the employee obtains instantaneous utility $w_t - C$, but that at the end of this period the probability is only $1 - q$ that the job will still be there. If it is, he or she decides to furnish effort $e > 0$ at date $t + 1$ if doing so procures for him or her a utility V_{t+1} greater than the utility V_{t+1}^s which he or she would get by not producing this effort. But if the job is destroyed, which happens with probability q, the employee then obtains a level of utility equal to $\bar{V}_{t+1}$.

When at the tth period of the contract an employee shirks, he or she receives wage w_t, but does not undergo the disutility C that comes with supplying effort e. As there is a probability p of being monitored, in which case he or she will be fired, his or her expected utility is written:

$$V_t^s = w_t + (1-p)\delta[(1-q)\,\text{Max}(V_{t+1}, V_{t+1}^s) + q\bar{V}_{t+1}] + p\delta\bar{V}_{t+1} \tag{46}$$

An employer who wishes the agent to supply effort e at each period must find a way to make the incentive constraint $V_t \geq V_t^s$ satisfy $\forall t \geq 0$. With the help of relations (45) and (46), we arrive at:

$$V_t - V_t^s = -C + p\delta[(1-q)\,\text{Max}(V_{t+1}, V_{t+1}^s) + q\bar{V}_{t+1}] - p\delta\bar{V}_{t+1}$$

We then easily verify that the incentive constraint $V_t \geq V_t^s$, $\forall t \geq 0$ is equivalent to condition:

$$V_{t+1} - \bar{V}_{t+1} \geq \frac{C}{p\delta(1-q)}, \qquad \forall t \geq 0 \tag{47}$$

Rent and the Set of Feasible Contracts

At this stage it will be helpful to bring the notion of *rent* associated with the labor contract into sharper focus. In a general way, this term designates the difference between the gains procured by the contract and those to be found in the best outside opportunity. In this case, for the agent the rent at date t is equal to $V_t - \bar{V}_t$, whereas for the principal it amounts to $\Pi_t - \bar{\Pi}_t$. The incentive constraint (47) signifies in particular that in order to give an employee incentive to put out effort *today*, he or she must expect a strictly positive rent from doing so *tomorrow*. In this model, the incentive mechanism is forward looking and the wage w_t exerts no influence on the effort of period t. The incentive to furnish strong effort during this period comes from the prospect of the *future* gains specified by the contract, in other words the series of wages starting from date $t + 1$. It is worth noting that, unlike future wages, the hiring wage plays no incentive role. The importance of this will become clear when we come to characterize the optimal contract.

Finally, in order for the employee to remain under contract at date t, it is also necessary that he or she not find any better alternative. This participation condition is given here by $V_t \geq \bar{V}_t$ for all $t \geq 0$. We immediately see that it is satisfied, *except* at $t = 0$, when the incentive constraint (47) is satisfied. The participation conditions thus dictate the only supplementary constraint $V_0 \geq \bar{V}_0$. In sum, the set P of levels of utility and profit attainable by using self-enforcing contracts is defined by:

$$P = \left\{ (\Pi_t, V_t) | \Pi_t \geq \bar{\Pi}_t, V_{t+1} - \bar{V}_{t+1} \geq \frac{C}{p\delta(1-q)}, V_0 \geq \bar{V}_0, \forall t \geq 0 \right\} \tag{48}$$

From now on we will simply refer to P as being the set of *feasible* contracts. The next step is to spell out the properties of optimal contracts. The characterization of optimal contracts is made a great deal easier by using the notion of surplus. We then see that the existence of a self-enforcing contract is equivalent to conditions that successive surpluses must satisfy, and that the optimal contract does not offer any rent to the agent at the time of hiring.

Surplus and the Existence of a Self-Enforcing Contract

By definition, an optimal contract satisfies the incentive and participation constraints of the worker and the employer and maximizes, at every date, the expected profit of the principal. A useful notion in this context is that of *global surplus* at date t. Let S_t be the global surplus. It is equal by definition to the sum of the rents that the contract procures. We thus have:

$$S_t \equiv V_t - \bar{V}_t + \Pi_t - \bar{\Pi}_t, \qquad \forall t \geq 0$$

Adding up relations (43) and (45), we get a difference equation that looks forward and that completely defines the series of surpluses. It is written:

$$S_t - \delta(1-q)S_{t+1} = y_t - C + \delta(\bar{\Pi}_{t+1} + \bar{V}_{t+1}) - (\bar{V}_t + \bar{\Pi}_t), \qquad \forall t \geq 0 \tag{49}$$

We observe that wages do not appear in this equation. In consequence, the value of the surplus does not depend on the level of wages. This property follows from the hypothesis that principal and agent are both risk-neutral, and would not be verified with individuals who did present risk aversion. It makes possible a simple answer to the question of the existence of self-enforcing contracts. The right-hand side of relation (49) contains only variables considered as *exogenous* parameters by the partners to the contract. Consequently the global surplus is also, at this stage, an exogenous parameter. Since, by definition, $\Pi_t - \bar{\Pi}_t = S_t - (V_t - \bar{V}_t)$ for all $t \geq 0$, the set P of feasible contracts described by relation (48) is also characterized in the following manner:

$$P = \left\{ V_t | S_{t+1} \geq V_{t+1} - \bar{V}_{t+1} \geq \frac{C}{p\delta(1-q)}, S_0 \geq V_0 - \bar{V}_0 \geq 0, \forall t \geq 0 \right\} \tag{50}$$

This way of presenting the set of feasible contracts allows us to deal with the question of the existence of self-enforcing contracts easily. The fact is that for a contract of this type to exist, it is necessary and sufficient that the set P not be empty. Relation (50) shows that this condition is satisfied when the series of surpluses has well-defined lower bounds. To be precise, we have:

$$P \neq \emptyset \Leftrightarrow S_0 \geq 0 \quad \text{and} \quad S_{t+1} \geq \frac{C}{p\delta(1-q)}, \quad \forall t \geq 0 \tag{51}$$

These inequalities show that an employer and a worker will agree on an implicit, self-enforcing contract when it offers them the opportunity to generate an overall nonnegative surplus over the *entire duration* of the contract, and strictly positive for every period $t \geq 1$. The initial period and the subsequent periods are different in kind because the incentive mechanism is forward looking. At the moment of hiring, it is sufficient that the surplus offered by the contract be simply positive, but at date $t \geq 1$, the surplus has to exceed quantity $C/p\delta(1-q)$, which is strictly positive, in order to give the agent incentive to supply effort e in all the periods subsequent to t.

In a world without moral hazard, a firm and a worker would have an interest in coming to terms when doing so allowed them to generate a non-zero surplus S_t at every date. So moral hazard has the effect of restricting the set of feasible contracts, since conditions (51) show that it becomes necessary for surplus S_t to be greater than $C/p\delta(1-q)$ for every $t \geq 1$. Taking moral hazard into account thus induces a form of Pareto inefficiency, inasmuch as exchanges such that $0 \leq S_t \leq C/p\delta(1-q)$ at a date $t \geq 1$ (mutually advantageous ones, that is), will not be realized. This inefficiency can lead to the exclusion of some workers with low productivity from long-term contractual relationships.

Rent and the Optimal Contract
We can easily find the expression of the optimal contract if we remember that it is equivalent to setting values for w_t or V_t. Relation (45) shows, in fact, that there is a bijection between the series of wages and the series of intertemporal utilities. Formally, then, we can view the employer's decision variables as the employee's utility levels rather than wages. The definition of the global surplus entails that the expected

profit be expressed in the form $\Pi_t = -V_t + (\bar{V}_t + \bar{\Pi}_t + S_t)$. Since the terms in parentheses in this equality are all exogenous parameters, the search for a self-enforcing contract maximizing profit Π_t at every date $t \geq 0$ is equivalent to minimizing intertemporal utility V_t over the set P of feasible contracts defined by (50). We then see that the optimal self-enforcing contract is characterized in the following manner:

(i) if $P \neq \varnothing$, then $V_0 = \bar{V}_0$ and $V_{t+1} = \bar{V}_{t+1} + C/p\delta(1-q)$, $\forall t \geq 0$

(ii) if $P = \varnothing$, no self-enforcing contract exists.

(52)

Thus, when the series of surpluses is such that the set P of feasible contracts is not empty, we have $V_0 = \bar{V}_0$ at date $t = 0$, which signifies that the optimal contract does not offer any rent to the worker at date $t = 0$. But at all subsequent periods, the agent obtains a gain V_{t+1} strictly greater than the external opportunity $\bar{V}_{t+1}$ of quantity $C/p\delta(1-q)$, which gives him or her an incentive, for one thing, so supply effort $e > 0$, and for another, not to voluntarily quit the firm in which he or she is working. It should also be noted that the principal captures the entire surplus of the contractual relationship ($\Pi_0 - \bar{\Pi}_0 = S_0$) and never has an interest in breaking the implicit contract that ties him or her to the employee, precisely because this contract procures him or her more than the outside opportunity if the set P is not empty: we in fact have $\Pi_t - \bar{\Pi}_t = S_t - C/p\delta(1-q)$ for all $t \geq 1$.

These properties of the optimal contract suggest that the wage at the time of hiring plays a special role. We shall now make this point clear by relating it to the role of seniority in the wage profile.

4.2.2   Seniority, Experience, and Wage

The wage profile over the course of careers is influenced by a number of factors. We can usefully distinguish *experience*—the cumulative duration of all periods of employment—from *seniority*—the duration of employment in the *same* firm.

The Reasons Why Wages Rise with Seniority

In the first place, the improvement in human capital that comes with the acquisition of knowledge and skill increases productivity, and this in itself is an explanation for the wage profile over the course of careers (Becker, 1975; Mincer, 1974; see chapter 2, this book). Specifically, the accumulation of *general* human capital of the sort that can be put to use in a large number of different firms ought to lead to an increasing relationship between *experience* and wages. Conversely, the accumulation of specific human capital of the sort that can only be put to use in one particular job may lead in certain circumstances to an increasing relationship between *seniority* and wages.

The existence of information problems may also explain an increasing relationship between experience or seniority and wages. In the equilibrium job search models laid out in chapter 3, workers knew the distribution of wages and had access to a limited number of job offers per unit of time. Within this framework, wages rise with experience, for the probability of having received a job offer from a firm proposing a high wage rises the longer an individual has been present in the labor market. Better knowledge of an employee's characteristics, which makes it possible to assign him or her to tasks at which he or she is most efficient, also constitutes a reason for wages to rise with seniority (Jovanovic, 1979; MacDonald, 1982). Finally, problems of incentive contribute to the existence of an increasing relationship between wages and seniority. In this connection, Lazear (1979, 1981) has put forward the proposition that a system of "deferred payment," in which workers get low pay at the outset of their careers but a promise of generous remuneration toward the end of them, constitutes a simple and particularly efficient incentive mechanism.

We will demonstrate that the mechanism of deferred payment and the role of human capital in wage-earning careers are well illustrated by the shirking model presented above. Further, we shall see that empirical investigation generally finds that experience and seniority do have a positive effect on wages, but do not actually pinpoint the causes of this increasing relationship.

The Optimal Wage Profile in the Shirking Model
Let us return to the shirking model in order to show how the mechanism of deferred payment emerges naturally as a solution to the incentive problem facing the firm. With some simple calculations, relations (45) and (52) that define the optimal contract allow us to express optimal wages in the following manner:

$$w_0 = \bar{V}_0 - \delta\bar{V}_1 + C - \frac{C}{p} \quad \text{and} \quad w_t = \bar{V}_t - \delta\bar{V}_{t+1} + C + \frac{C}{p}\left[\frac{1}{\delta(1-q)} - 1\right] \tag{53}$$

We see that the series of optimal wages is linked quite simply to the levels of utility associated with outside opportunities. In order to highlight this linkage more tellingly, let us assume that at each period t these outside opportunities procure an instantaneous level of satisfaction $\bar{w}_t - C$, where $\bar{w}_t$ represents the "outside" wage. Thus we have:

$$\bar{V}_t = \sum_{i=0}^{+\infty} \delta^i(\bar{w}_{t+i} - C), \qquad \forall t \geq 0 \tag{54}$$

If the human capital accumulated by an individual is of the *general* kind, he or she can expect ever larger external gains, and the series of $\bar{w}_t$ will be increasing (see, for example, Harris and Holmström, 1982). Conversely, if the human capital accumulated by an individual is of the *specific* kind, the effect on outside opportunities will be zero, and the series of $\bar{w}_t$ will not be increasing (Jovanovic, 1979, uses a model grounded on this hypothesis). It is possible to link the optimal wage profile to the series of outside wages $\bar{w}_t$. Relation (54) does in fact entail that $(\bar{V}_t - \delta\bar{V}_{t+1})$ is equal to $\bar{w}_t - C$. Equations (53) giving the optimal wages are then written:

$$w_0 = \bar{w}_0 - \frac{C}{p} \tag{55}$$

$$w_t = \bar{w}_t + \frac{C}{p}\left[\frac{1}{\delta(1-q)} - 1\right], \qquad \forall t \geq 1 \tag{56}$$

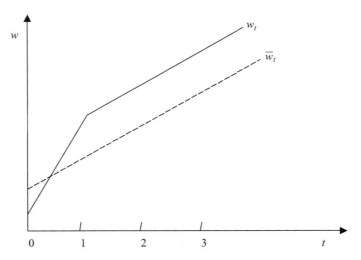

FIGURE 6.4
The profile of optimal wages with general human capital and deferred payments.

These last two relations show that the contractual wage is less than the outside wage ($w_0 < \overline{w}_0$) at career onset, but then overtakes it in the subsequent stages ($w_t > \overline{w}_t$). We also observe that starting from date $t = 1$, the wage increases (or diminishes) with the same frequency as outside opportunities. It is thus clear that only general human capital influences the observed wage, through its impact on outside opportunities. Specific human capital, on the other hand, which by definition has no influence on the outside wage, does not affect the observed wage. This result flows from the hypothesis that the worker has no bargaining power: the employer here unilaterally proposes a labor contract that binds the participation constraint of the worker. If the worker did have non-zero bargaining power, the participation constraint would not be binding, and specific human capital would exert a positive influence on the wage (see chapter 5, section 2.2, and chapter 9, section 4.2).

In figure 6.4 we have depicted the properties of a profile of optimal wages, on the hypothesis that levels of outside utility would be increasing. This figure brings out a particular form of the "deferred payment" mechanism, the theory of which was elaborated by Lazear (1979, 1981) in particular. In this mechanism, the workers with the most seniority in a firm would be paid at a rate that surpassed their marginal productivity, while the workers with less seniority would be paid at a rate falling short of their marginal productivity. This arrangement gives the workers hired most recently an incentive to furnish the efforts demanded of them in order to stay with the firm long enough to get the benefit of the wages reserved for "old hands." In our model, the mechanism of deferred payment takes an extreme form, since only the hiring wage w_0 is less than the competitive wage $\overline{w}_0$ which notionally reflects the agent's marginal productivity. Note that the discontinuity between the hiring wage and the subsequent wages would be attenuated if we were to take into account a certain heterogeneity in hires and in the amount of time needed for the firm to get a clear picture of the abilities of its workers. These elements would have the effect of spreading the deferred payment mechanism more evenly out over time, and so the wage profile would show a pattern of increase more like the empirical observations which we will look at later.

It is also evident that the incentive constraints impose a steep slope on the wage profile mainly at career *onset*, after which it is rather the participation constraints that influence this profile. Now, the levels of utility that an individual can expect outside his or her current job evolve with changes in his or her human capital. If this capital grows little or not at all over time, the wage profile ought to flatten out quickly; and the converse is true if the value of human capital increases over time. In other words, the positive effect of the incentive constraints on wage growth should be felt mainly at the onset of an individual's career, and that of the accumulation of human capital should be felt at a later stage.

4.3 EMPIRICAL ELEMENTS ON EXPERIENCE, SENIORITY, AND WAGES

Many empirical studies have examined the links between wages, experience, and seniority. They generally confirm the existence of a simultaneously increasing relationship between wages and experience and between wages and seniority. We begin by laying out the general principles that should govern the estimation of the returns on seniority and experience, and we give the essential results. As well, we have seen that the problems raised by moral hazard may lead firms to adopt a system of "deferred payment," which also entails an increasing relationship between wages and seniority. To complete this subsection, we refer to some studies that have tried to establish how large a part this system plays in compensation policies.

4.3.1 Estimating the Return to Seniority

The return to seniority is most often estimated by means of an equation in which the wage is the dependent variable and seniority is one of the explanatory variables.

The Basic Equation

Estimates of the returns to seniority and experience are governed by the same logic as that used in studying the return to education (see chapter 2, section 4). In practice, the returns to the three variables education (denoted by *ed*), experience (denoted by *ex*), and seniority (denoted by *te*) may be evaluated by estimating the following equation:

$$\ln w_{ijt} = \beta + \beta_{ed}ed_{ijt} + \beta_{ex}ex_{ijt} + \beta_{te}te_{ijt} + \varepsilon_{ijt} \qquad (57)$$

If we take the year as the unit of time, parameters β_k, $k = ed, ex, te$ represent the wage variations (expressed in percentage) that follow from an extra year of education, experience, or seniority. In order to fit the predictions of the theoretical models, it is possible to add quadratic terms for these three variables so as to take into account nonlinearity in the returns, but we omit this step in order to make the presentation easier. In equation (57), variable w_{ijt} designates the wage of an individual i in firm j at date t, and ε_{ijt} is an error term. Estimating this equation by ordinary least squares —including quadratic terms—on American data from the Panel Study of Income Dynamics (PSID) from the 1970s and 1980s produces a wage gain on the order of 27% for ten years of seniority and 34% for ten years of experience (see Altonji and Williams, 1997). These results suggest that the returns to experience and seniority are significant and likely do not differ much from each other. Nevertheless, two different problems are likely to generate biases.

For one thing, experience and seniority are *endogenous* variables in relation to wages. In the theory of labor supply, decisions to participate in the labor market, and consequently experience, depend on wages (see chapter 1). In equilibrium job search models, workers have a lower probability of quitting their firm the higher their wage is (see chapter 3). Seniority is thus an increasing function of wages. For another, the most efficient workers generally have more experience and seniority than others, and better matching between jobs and workers ought to increase seniority. To ignore this *unobserved heterogeneity* means that estimating equation (57) by ordinary least squares will overestimate the returns to seniority and experience, since a part of the positive correlation observed between wages and these two variables results from the fact that the most efficient workers also have more seniority, more experience, and higher wages, and from the fact that better matches also procure better wages and greater seniority. To solve these problems, several solutions have been proposed and tested on the PSID data.

Heterogeneity Biases
Abraham and Farber (1987) decompose the error term ε_{ijt} into an individual component η_i, a component linked to matching μ_{ij}, and a random term ζ_{ijt}, or:

$$\varepsilon_{ijt} = \eta_i + \mu_{ij} + \zeta_{ijt} \tag{58}$$

They distinguish seniority in the firm at date t (this is the variable te_{ijt}) from the *total* effective duration of the job of worker i in firm j (denoted by du_{ij} in what follows). For example, an individual hired in 1980 has two years of seniority in 1982 ($te_{ijt} = 2$), and if he or she quits firm j in 1990 the effective duration of his or her job in this firm will have been ten years ($du_{ij} = 10$). Abraham and Farber point out that the components specific to individuals η_i and to matchings μ_{ij} are in fact *indirectly* correlated with seniority but directly tied to the total duration of the job of worker i in firm j. Using data on the total durations of jobs, they modify equation (57) by including job duration as an explanatory variable of wages. Equation (57) thus becomes:

$$\ln w_{ijt} = \beta + \beta_{ed}ed_{ijt} + \beta_{ex}ex_{ijt} + \beta_{te}te_{ijt} + \beta_{du}du_{ij} + \varepsilon_{ijt}$$

The purpose of term du_{ij} is to eliminate the heterogeneity bias due to the influence of wages on the duration of jobs, and thereby on seniority. Estimating such an equation by ordinary least squares gives us a much smaller value of β_{te} than we get in the absence of the term du_{ij}. Altonji and Shakotko (1987) arrive at the same conclusion, and the same orders of magnitude, using a methodology close to that of Abraham and Farber (1987). They find that ten years of seniority leads to a 13% increment in wages, while ten years of experience leads to a wage increment of 34%. This work suggests, then, that the return to seniority is slight compared to the return to experience. But again, these estimates are not entirely satisfactory, since they do not control for the endogeneity of seniority with respect to wages.

Endogeneity Bias

The contribution of Topel (1991) focuses on the endogeneity of seniority. The results obtained differ greatly from those of Abraham and Farber (1987) and Altonji and Shakotko (1987) but approach those obtained by ordinary least squares applied to equation (57). Topel estimates that ten years of seniority leads to a wage increment of 25%, while ten years of experience makes possible an increment of 34%. Topel's method unfolds in two stages. The first is to estimate the following equation:

$$\ln w_{ijt} = b + b_{ed}ed_{ijt} + b_{ex}ex_{ij}^0 + b_{te}te_{ijt} + \varepsilon_{ijt}$$

The term ex_{ij}^0 designates the experience of individual i at the time he or she is hired for job j. Over duration te_{ijt} passed in firm j worker i has accumulated both experience and seniority. If we assume that the return to experience is the same before and after the hire in firm j, then parameter b_{te} represents the sum of the returns to seniority and experience. The return to seniority alone is thus equal to $b_{te} - b_{ex}$.

In order to eliminate the fixed individual effects represented by the components η_i and μ_{ij} in the decomposition (58) of the error term ε_{ijt}, Topel estimates this equation in differences, retaining only persons who do not change firms. Topel thus makes the hypothesis that the rate at which the wages of workers who do not change firms grows is a nonbiased estimator of the wages of all workers. Topel justifies this hypothesis by noting that all wages evolve according to a random walk[7] after removal of trend growth. Working with this hypothesis, Topel obtains a nonbiased estimator b_{te} denoted by $\hat{b}_{te}$. In the second stage, Topel fits the following equation:

$$\ln w_{ijt} - \hat{b}_{te}te_{ijt} = b + b_{ed}ed_{ijt} + b_{ex}ex_{ij}^0 + \varepsilon_{ijt} \tag{59}$$

Estimating this equation by ordinary least squares yields a nonbiased estimate of b_{ex} if the disturbances ε_{ijt} are not correlated with experience. We have seen that unobserved heterogeneity may be the source of a bias of this type, inasmuch as the most efficient individuals—those with the highest η_i in equation (58) of the decomposition of the error term—are also those with the most seniority. Ordinary least squares then overestimate b_{ex}, because a part of the correlation between wages and experience comes from unobserved individual effects. Although aware of this type of problem, Topel nonetheless estimates equation (59) by ordinary least squares, and finds an estimate $\hat{b}_{ex}$ with an upward bias. This estimate allows him to calculate a *lower* bound of the return to seniority, equal to $\hat{b}_{te} - \hat{b}_{ex}$. As this lower bound is very close to the value obtained by simply estimating (57) by ordinary least squares, Topel concludes that the returns to seniority are greater than those evaluated by Abraham and Farber (1987) and Altonji and Shakotko (1987).

Final Remarks on the Return to Seniority

Altonji and Williams (1997) have reviewed the problem of evaluating the returns to seniority and tried to pinpoint the reasons for the differences among the three studies just cited. They show in particular that Topel's results are sensitive to the method chosen for introducing a trend to generate stationary wages in the first stage of his estimates. Adopting Topel's method, but taking a different approach to generating stationarity in wages and to certain other related elements of estimation, Altonji and Williams (1997) obtain results close to those obtained by Abraham and Farber (1987) and Altonji and Shakotko (1987), the conclusion of which was that the return to seniority is very slight.

These works deal with problems of endogeneity and heterogeneity bias in a partial manner, focusing essentially on estimating seniority. The contribution of Buchinsky et al. (2001) stands farther back from the problem, since it examines the returns to experience and seniority while taking into account the endogenous nature of participation and mobility between jobs. Buchinsky et al. (2001) estimate a system of three equations, in which the dependent variables are wages, mobility between jobs, and participation, by a method of maximum likelihood much like the one presented in chapter 1, section 2.1.2. This approach makes it possible to limit the heterogeneity and endogeneity biases that occur when participation and mobility between jobs are assumed to be exogenous. Buchinsky et al. (2001) find that seniority has a very high return. For workers whose educational qualification falls in the range between a high school diploma at one end and college or university study (short of a graduate degree) at the other, ten years of seniority produces a wage increment of 40%, whereas ten years of experience produces a wage increment of 27%. In this context, the return to seniority is clearly greater than the return to experience.

The contribution of Parent (2000) looks at the effect of experience in a given *industry* on the return to seniority. Using data from the National Longitudinal Survey of Youth from 1979 to 1996, and the Panel Study of Income Dynamics from 1981 to 1991, he finds that the return to seniority is considerably reduced when experience in an industry is added as a control variable. For Parent, this result points to the conclusion that human capital specific to one industry has more weight than human capital specific to one firm in the increase in an individual's wage profile.

Aside from their divergences concerning orders of magnitude, these studies confirm that seniority and experience both increase wages. But they only partially explain this phenomenon, inasmuch as the increase in wages with seniority can be explained in a number of ways. The accumulation of specific human capital, selection processes, and problems of moral hazard may explain the increasing relationship between seniority and wages. We will now shift our attention to empirical works that have attempted to bring out the role of moral hazard. Empirical works devoted to specific human capital are summarized by Farber (1999) and are discussed in chapter 2.

4.3.2   On the Mechanism of Deferred Payment

Some empirical studies suggest that certain firms do in fact adopt wage policies based on the deferred payment mechanism. Lazear and Moore (1984), for example, compare the incomes of independent workers with the incomes of workers who are a priori identical but carry out similar functions within a firm of which they are employees. Since the independent worker has no need to give himself or herself incentive to make the necessary effort, his or her income profile ought to be identical to marginal productivity. Lazear and Moore find that the wage profile of employees is steeper than that of independent workers, which points to the conclusion that the mechanism of deferred payment is a way of giving employees incentive to make the desired efforts.

The work of Kotlikoff and Gokhale (1992) is even more convincing. Using data for the period 1969–1983 covering a sample of 300,000 employees of large North American firms specializing in sales, these authors achieve a reconstruction of the productivity profile of an employee from the time he or she enters a firm, based on the wage of new entrants. Their figures IV and III, reproduced here in figure 6.5, show respectively the wage profiles and productivity of a manager and a salesperson between ages 35 and 65, i.e., over a 30-year career with a firm.[8] The manager's wage profile conforms to the theory of deferred payment. It approximately lags marginal productivity over the course of the first 10 years, then overtakes productivity during the remaining 20 years. Conversely, the wage profile of a salesperson differs little from that of his or her productivity. This near overlap derives from the fact that the activity of a salesperson is *verifiable* (an impartial tribunal can determine an employee's sales volume by, for example, checking his or her sales records), and in consequence his or her wage can be largely based on the number of articles he or she has sold.

Another instructive feature of the shirking model—see relation (56)—is that, the hiring wage excepted, an employee's wage ought to increase when the frequency p of supervision declines. Now, this frequency is likely an increasing function of the ratio of the number of supervisors checking on the performance of employees to the number of employees. So, all other things being equal, the deferred payment mechanism suggests that firms paying high wages are also those in which the supervisor/employee ratio is lowest. The study of Groshen and Krueger (1990) on hospitals in the United States does in fact come to this conclusion.

4.4   EFFICIENCY WAGE AND INVOLUNTARY UNEMPLOYMENT

The optimal wage profile in the shirking model works like a bonding mechanism: workers accept being paid less than their productivity at the onset of their careers, and higher pay later on. In certain cases the hiring wage can even be negative. This means that workers accept that they are making a deposit with the employer, who will pay them back later on. Labor contracts do not generally stipulate this covenant. Hence it is useful to analyze the way the labor market functions when employers cannot manipulate wage profiles for incentive purposes as much as they wish. From this point of view, Shapiro and Stiglitz (1984) have built a celebrated "efficiency wage"

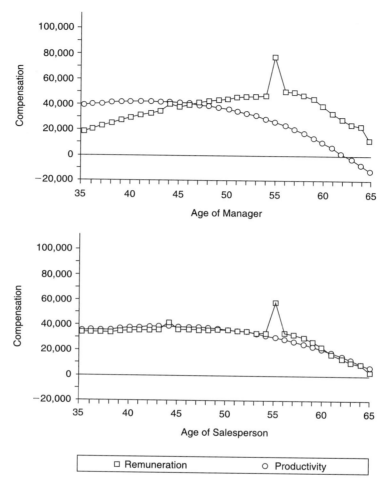

FIGURE 6.5
Profiles of remuneration and productivity.

Source: Kotlikoff and Gokhale (1992).

model, in which there exists *involuntary* unemployment at labor market equilibrium. This model illustrates how the labor market would function in a limit case in which employers had no choice in the matter of wage profiles, and on that account constitutes a very fragile explanation of unemployment.

4.4.1   The Model of Shapiro and Stiglitz (1984)

In order to suppress the bonding mechanism, Shapiro and Stiglitz (1984) adopt a stationary version of the shirking model in which firms are constrained to pay the same wage at all periods. The incentive mechanism is then based solely on the risk of unemployment.

A Bonding Mechanism

The optimal wage profile described by relations (55) and (56) is interpretable as an incentive mechanism in which there is a "bond" the agent is obliged to post at the time of hiring that will be gradually paid back to him or her. It is just as though the agent were to be paid a base wage equal to the outside wage $\bar{w}_t$ at every period $t \geq 0$, but had at the outset deposited a sum equal to C/p with the employer; this sum is gradually reimbursed starting at date $t \geq 1$ in the form of a bonus added to the base wage and amounting in each period to[9] $(C/p)\{[1/\delta(1 - q)] - 1\}$. Akerlof and Katz (1989) pointed out that when the shirking model is specified in this way, it is not possible to "smooth out" the profile of optimal wages, i.e., to narrow the gap between the hiring wage w_0 and the subsequent wages w_t. To grasp this point clearly, let us suppose that the agent receives a wage $w_m > w_0$ over the initial period of the contract. The employer cannot, at certain periods $t \geq 1$, pay a remuneration less than the optimal wage w_t characterized by (56), for in the periods that he or she did so, the employee's incentive constraint (47) would no longer be satisfied.

Accordingly, the shirking model displays a bonding mechanism that cannot be substituted for a regularly increasing wage profile. Such a mechanism is not at all realistic in practice, and in any case the payment of a deposit does not exist except in the rarest of cases in the labor market. One of the reasons used to explain this absence is the imperfection of the financial markets (Shapiro and Stiglitz, 1985): workers supposedly suffer from liquidity constraints that prevent them from collecting the sums necessary to put down the deposit. Shapiro and Stiglitz (1984) base their theory of the efficiency wage on the practical impossibility of making this deposit mechanism work, and show that it would lead to the emergence of involuntary unemployment.

A Particular Stationary Version of the Shirking Model

Shapiro and Stiglitz (1984) adopt a stationary version of the shirking model in which $\bar{V}_t = \bar{V}$, $\forall t \geq 0$. Moreover, this version radically suppresses the bonding mechanism by assuming that the principal pays the *same* wage w at every period. With this hypothesis, the agent is given incentive to furnish effort $e > 0$ throughout the duration of the contract if and only if the principal pays him or her the wage defined by the right-hand equality of relation (53), or:

$$w = (1 - \delta)\bar{V} + C + \frac{C}{p}\left[\frac{1}{\delta(1 - q)} - 1\right] \tag{60}$$

In this case, the utility V_t expected by the agent is the same at each period t and can be denoted simply by V. A consequence of the hypothesis of wage stationarity made by Shapiro and Stiglitz is that $V_0 = V$. In consequence, relation (52) shows that the agent benefits from a *rent* over the *whole* of the duration of the contract such that $V_0 - \bar{V} = C/p\delta(1 - q)$. If we take the view, as Shapiro and Stiglitz do, that $\bar{V}$ designates the expected utility of an unemployed person, the result is that accepting a job offer procures a gain V_0 *strictly* superior to the gain $\bar{V}$ of an unemployed person. Unemployment is thus *involuntary* in nature, since anyone looking for work prefers to accept a job at the current wage w (which offers him or her an expected utility V_0) rather than remain unemployed (which offers an expected utility equal to $\bar{V}$).

Let z be the gains of an unemployed person at every period, and let $s \in [0, 1]$ be the (endogenous) probability of returning to work at every period. In a stationary state, the intertemporal utility of an unemployed person $\bar{V}$ satisfies the following equation:

$$\bar{V} = z + \delta[sV + (1 - s)\bar{V}]$$

Since $V = \bar{V} + C/p\delta(1 - q)$, an unemployed person's expected utility is expressed as a function of the rate of return to work according to the formula:

$$(1 - \delta)\bar{V} = z + \frac{sC}{p(1 - q)}$$

If we carry this equality into the expression of the efficiency wage (60), we find a relationship between the wage paid to employees and the exit rate from unemployment, which takes the form:

$$w = z + C + \frac{C}{p}\left[\frac{1}{1-q}\left(s + \frac{1}{\delta}\right) - 1\right] \tag{61}$$

The exit rate from unemployment depends on the level L of overall employment. Relation (61) thus supplies a link between wages and employment that needs to be made explicit. To that end, let N be the (exogenous) size of the labor force; the level of unemployment is then equal to $N - L$. In a stationary state, the flow qL of entries into unemployment equals the flow of exits $s(N - L)$ out of it. Consequently we have $s = qL/(N - L)$, and in carrying this value into (61), we do indeed find a relationship between the wage level and the employment level, written:

$$w = z + C + \frac{C}{p}\left[\frac{1}{1-q}\left(\frac{qL}{N-L} + \frac{1}{\delta}\right) - 1\right] \tag{62}$$

This relation, which is often called the *incentive curve* (*IC*), is represented in figure 6.6. It is increasing and possesses a vertical asymptote at point $L = N$. This property signifies that there is never full employment at equilibrium. This is easy to see: in a situation where there is no risk of lasting unemployment, an employee knows that in case of job loss, he or she will immediately find another one. He or she then has an interest in shirking, since it no longer occasions any loss. In this model, the fear of unemployment plays an incentive role only if unemployment lasts a certain length of time, for it is during this period that the agent suffers losses.

Labor Market Equilibrium

To close this model, we must still specify the behavior of firms. Like MacLeod and Malcomson (1998) and Malcomson (1999), we can take the view that the profit linked to outside opportunities, equal to $\bar{\Pi}$ in the stationary state, designates the expected profit of vacant jobs. If y represents the constant exogenous production of a worker, the gain Π expected from a filled job is given by the equality:

$$\Pi = y - w + \delta[(1 - q)\Pi + q\bar{\Pi}] \tag{63}$$

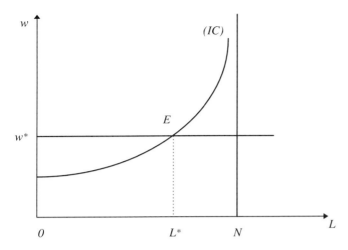

FIGURE 6.6
The equilibrium of the model of Shapiro and Stiglitz.

Let us also assume, for the sake of simplicity, that information is perfect in the labor market, which thus operates without friction. Let the situation be one in which $s < 1$, i.e., an equilibrium in which there are more unemployed persons than vacant jobs. Vacant jobs are then immediately filled by the unemployed, and so offer the same prospect of profit as jobs that are filled. With these hypotheses, we will have $\Pi = \bar{\Pi}$. Finally, let us assume that there is no barrier to entry into the labor market. Competition will then cause entrepreneurs to open up vacant jobs as long as the profit expected from such job creation surpasses the cost of installing new equipment. Let C_K be the exogenous, supposedly constant, value of this cost; entries into the market for goods will stop when the expected profit $\bar{\Pi}$ from a vacant job is exactly equal to C_K. At free entry equilibrium, we will thus have $\Pi = \bar{\Pi} = C_K$ and relation (63) defining the expected profit from a filled job entails that the equilibrium value w^* of the efficiency wage is given by $w^* = y - (1 - \delta)C_K$. Carrying this equality into equation (62), which characterizes the efficiency wage, we find ultimately that equilibrium employment L^* is given by:

$$w^* = y - (1 - \delta)C_K = z + C + \frac{C}{p}\left[\frac{1}{1-q}\left(\frac{qL^*}{N - L^*} + \frac{1}{\delta}\right) - 1\right]$$

Labor market equilibrium is thus situated at the intersection of the incentive curve (IC) and the horizontal line with ordinate $y - (1 - \delta)C_K$; it is represented by point E in figure 6.6.[10] This equilibrium is characterized by involuntary unemployment linked to a downward rigidity in the real wage. The $N - L^*$ unemployed persons would indeed all agree to work for a wage *less* than w^*, since the situation of an employed participant procures an expected utility superior to that of an unemployed one. But they would then have an interest in shirking, which dissuades employers from offering lower wages.

4.4.2   Final Remarks on Efficiency Wage Theory

The shirking model leads us to an equilibrium with involuntary underemployment, in which employees receive a rent that gives them incentive to supply an adequate level of effort. This model suffers, however, from a major theoretical weakness having to do with the fact the firms could think of other remuneration schemes more sophisticated than the payment of an unvarying wage (Yellen, 1994). These might include, for example, the payment of an award when an employee is found not to be shirking (MacLeod and Malcomson, 1989). More generally, we have shown that the shirking model with no restriction on individuals' strategies leads to a bonding mechanism that offers no rent to employees, so that there is no involuntary unemployment at labor market equilibrium (this objection to the efficiency wage theory is also known as the *bonding critique*; see Carmichael, 1985, 1989, and 1990). The result that there is no rent for the employee when the employer unilaterally decides on the clauses of the contract is not linked to the particular kinds of incentive mechanism that we have considered. Fundamentally, it illustrates a general principle of the theory of incentives, which is that a principal who has at his or her disposal a sufficiently wide range of strategies can always make the agent's participation constraint binding, and thus appropriate the entire surplus flowing from the contractual relationship (see, for example, Kreps, 1990, p. 604). The existence of a rent for the agent in a model with moral hazard is thus grounded on restrictions—that require explanation—on the strategic options of individuals.

The Financial Market and the Minimum Wage
Shapiro and Stiglitz (1985) made the objection that credit market imperfections rendered the bonding mechanism impracticable. It is not, however, certain that this argument carries the weight it may appear to at first sight, for it is grounded in an excessively strict interpretation of the shirking model. If we were to add certain hypotheses, such as the assumption that workers are heterogeneous and that it therefore takes time for each one's aptitudes to reveal themselves, the shirking model would produce a compensation policy resembling a wage profile increasing in normal fashion with seniority more than it would a bonding mechanism. In order to rescue the efficiency wage theory as a possible explanation of involuntary unemployment, we need to find reasons to explain why firms cannot reasonably offer an increasing wage profile that would bind the participation constraint of workers.

One reason might be the existence of a legal miminum wage w_m exceeding the hiring wage w_0. We have shown that in this case, firms pay wage w_m in the initial period, then wage w_t defined by (56) in the following periods. Each worker receives a rent equal to $w_m - w_0$, and unemployment becomes involuntary again. This situation is conceivable, but the reason for the rent, and thus involuntary unemployment, is not a necessity inherent in the incentive mechanism, in other words it is not a problem of moral hazard. On the contrary, the reason for the rent is the existence of a wage floor making remuneration downwardly rigid. A purely competitive model would have come to the same qualitative conclusions about unemployment. More precisely, moral hazard entails the existence of an abrupt step-up in the wage profile that would not have been necessary in a traditional supply-and-demand model. The equilibria are thus not a priori the same in the two types of model. But it is always a constraint on the downward flexibility of the real wage that enables us to explain the involuntary nature of unemployment.

Rent and Asymmetric Information

Beaudry (1994) and Arvan and Esfahani (1993) have advanced a justification for the existence of rents. It is based on the notion that workers who observe imperfectly the characteristics of the firm that hires them may doubt the credibility of undertakings given about remuneration profiles that will rise, or rewards that will be paid out. Let us suppose, for example, that there are two types of employers. With the "bad" ones, production y is low (independent of the efforts the workers make), and these employers have an interest in systematically discharging their employees after having promised them an increasing wage profile, or rewards. With the "good" employers, production y is high, and they can offer credible contracts. Within this framework, to offer remunerations that pay a rent constitutes a way for the "good" employers to signal their quality. The hypothesis of a double asymmetry of information grounded in moral hazard and adverse selection thus allows us to save the efficiency wage theory as the foundation of a form of involuntary unemployment. These models do not, however, explain why firms choose to signal their characteristics by offering high wages when they might, for example, spend more on advertising their products, which could turn out to cost less than letting rents go to their employees.

Wage Rigidity, Incentive, and Rent

The model of Shapiro and Stiglitz (1984) suggests that unemployed persons ought to offer their services at less than the current wage and that firms ought to refuse these offers. Some recent studies based on surveys of employers do in fact show that they are reluctant to lower wages, even in situations in which there is significant unemployment. According to Blinder and Choi (1990), Bewley (1995), and Campbell and Kamlani (1997), the company executives surveyed believed that wage reductions would be judged "unfair" by employees and would provoke increased turnover and reduced intensity of effort in response. Agell and Lundborg (1995) come to identical conclusions and also find that firms do not want to hire unemployed persons offering to work for less.

Fehr and Falk (1999) have studied the downward rigidity of wages within the framework of an experiment in which two groups, firms and workers, have the opportunity to agree on a wage contract through a mechanism of bilateral bidding. When the participants are forced to sign only *incomplete* contracts, in which the level of effort is not stipulated in advance, the experiment shows that firms refuse to bid wages down. On the other hand, when the actors have the opportunity to sign complete contracts, remunerations become markedly more flexible and approach their competitive values. These surveys and experiments reinforce the view that wage policies are, in the broad sense, driven by the need for incentive, but they give no particular indication as to the existence of *rents*. The downward rigidities highlighted by these empirical studies do not in the least contradict the general properties of self-enforcing contracts *without rent* developed in this section. For example, a deferred payment mechanism offering no rent over the whole course of the wage relationship is just as "rigid" as the unvarying wage in the model of Shapiro and Stiglitz (1984).

5   SUMMARY AND CONCLUSION

*   Labor contracts are used to deal with problems of risk sharing and incentive. The properties of wage contracts depend to a large extent on whether or not it is possible to take the observation of the results of a wage-earner's activity into account. All observations that can be objectively assessed by an impartial tribunal fall into the category of *verifiable* clauses. The labor relationship may be governed by implicit agreements that bear on nonverifiable clauses. Such agreements occur in the setting of long-term relationships, the existence of which depends only on the mutual interest the partners have in them. We then say that the agreement is *self-enforcing*.

*   The demand for insurance allows us to explain certain empirical characteristics of the movement of wages, in particular the fact that they are procyclical, fluctuating less than productivity, and the fact that they are not correlated with the current rate of unemployment.

*   The traditional agency model with hidden action analyzes the remuneration rule that a risk-neutral principal offers to a risk-averse agent when that agent's results are *verifiable*. The principal faces a problem of *moral hazard*, since he or she does not know with certainty what actions the agent took in order to achieve his or her observed results. The optimal remuneration rule exhibits a compromise between the demand for insurance and the need for incentive. It most often prescribes a remuneration that depends on performance. The optimal rule must take account of all the verifiable observations correlated with the effort of the agent.

*   Multitasking, only part of which is verifiable, constitutes a source of inefficiency that impels firms to adopt implicit contracts and/or overall indicators of performance. Another source of inefficiency is *rent-seeking*. Its cause is the comparative advantage that agents may derive from concentrating part of their efforts on actions that will impress the supervisors who are charged with informing the principal about observed performances.

*   The internal market in a firm, and more generally systems of hierarchical promotion, can be analyzed as *tournaments* in which the rules of promotion and the wages that go along with each promotion are specified in advance. A tournament offers the advantage of making the clauses of a contract explicit. The

tournament model also suggests that hierarchical levels ought in large measure to explain wage variation. It suggests further that the remuneration that comes with a grade in the hierarchy rises with the number of individuals who aspire to be promoted to that grade. These predictions match empirical results well. The rule of promotion by seniority is partially explained by the fact that it makes it possible to avoid rent-seeking activity.

- Empirical studies confirm the positive effect of seniority on wages. Still, this effect is probably less important than that of experience.

- The "shirking" model describes a long-term relationship between a principal and an agent in which the agent's effort *and* results are *unverifiable*. In this context, the optimal remuneration rule is a series of wages increasing with seniority but offering the agent no rent over the whole duration of the contract. Empirical studies confirm the existence of an increasing relationship between seniority and wages, as well as the influence of incentive mechanisms in this area. Moral hazard is a source of inefficiency, however, for employers cannot credibly enter into long-term engagements with agents who produce insufficient but positive surpluses. The exact wage profile depends on the combined effects of the acquisition of general human capital by the agent and the principal's wish to obtain an adequate level of effort.

6   RELATED TOPICS IN THE BOOK

- Chapter 1, section 1: The choice between consumption and leisure

- Chapter 2, section 4: The return to education

- Chapter 3, section 2.1: The wage profile in the equilibrium search model

- Chapter 5, section 1: Wage determination and perfect competition

- Chapter 5, section 2.2: The holdup problem

- Chapter 7, section 2: Wage determination and collective bargaining

- Chapter 9, section 4.2: More on the holdup problem

7   FURTHER READINGS

Gibbons, R., and Waldman, M. (1999b), "Careers in organizations: Theory and evidence," in Ashenfelter, O., and Card, D. (eds.), *Handbook of Labor Economics*, vol. 3, chap. 36, pp. 2373–2437, Amsterdam: Elsevier Science/North-Holland.

Lazear, E. (1999), "Personal economics: Past lessons and future directions," *Journal of Labor Economics*, 17, pp. 199–236.

Prendergast, C. (1999), "The provision of incentives in firms," *Journal of Economic Literature*, 37, pp. 7–63.

Rosen, S. (1985), "Implicit contracts: A survey," *Journal of Economic Literature*, 23, pp. 1144–1175.

Salanié, B. (1997), *The Economics of Contracts: A Primer*, Cambridge, Mass.: MIT Press.

REFERENCES

Abraham, K., and Farber, H. (1987), "Job duration seniority and earnings," *American Economic Review*, 77, pp. 278–297.

Abraham, K., and Haltiwanger, J. (1995), "Real wages and the business cycle," *Journal of Economic Literature*, 33(3), pp. 1275–1364.

Agell, J., and Lundborg, P. (1995), "Theories of pay and unemployment: Survey evidence from Swedish manufacturing firms," *Scandinavian Journal of Economics*, 97(2), pp. 295–307.

Akerlof, G., and Katz, L. (1989), "Workers trust funds and the logic of wage profiles," *Quarterly Journal of Economics*, 104, pp. 525–536.

Altonji, J., and Williams, N. (1997), "Do wages rise with job seniority? A reassessement," NBER Working Paper No. 6010, New York: National Bureau of Economic Research.

Altonji, J., and Shakotko, R. (1987), "Do wages rise with job seniority?" *Review of Economic Studies*, 54, pp. 437–459.

Arvan, L., and Esfahani, H. (1993), "A model of efficiency wages as a signal of firm value," *International Economic Review*, 34, pp. 503–524.

Azariadis, C. (1975), "Implicit contract and underemployment equilibria," *Journal of Political Economy*, 83(6), pp. 1183–1202.

Azariadis, C. (1983), "Employment with asymmetric information," *Quarterly Journal of Economics*, 98, Suppl., pp. 157–172.

Azariadis, C., and Stiglitz, J. (1983), "Implicit contracts and fixed price equilibria," *Quarterly Journal of Economics*, 98, Suppl., pp. 1–12.

Baily, M. (1974), "Wages and employment under uncertain demand," *Review of Economic Studies*, 41(1), pp. 37–50.

Baker, G., Gibbs, M., and Holmström, B. (1994a), "The internal economics of the firm: Evidence from personnel data," *Quarterly Journal of Economics*, 109, pp. 881–919.

Baker, G., Gibbs, M., and Holmström, B. (1994b), "The wage policy of a firm," *Quarterly Journal of Economics*, 109, pp. 921–955.

Beaudry, P. (1994), "Why an informed principal may leave rent to an agent?" *International Economic Review*, 35, pp. 821–833.

Beaudry, P., and DiNardo, J. (1991), "The effect of implicit contracts on the movement of wages over the business cycle: Evidence from microdata," *Journal of Political Economy*, 99, pp. 665–688.

Beaudry, P., and DiNardo, J. (1995), "Is the behavior of hours worked consistent with implicit contract theory?" *Quarterly Journal of Economics*, 110, pp. 743–768.

Becker, G. (1975), *Human Capital*, New York: Columbia University Press.

Bénabou, R., and Tirole, J. (2003), "Intrinsic and extrinsic motivation," *Review of Economic Studies*, 70, pp. 489–520.

Bewley, T. (1995), "A depressed labor market as explained by participants," *American Economic Review, Papers and Proceedings*, 85, pp. 250–254.

Blinder, A., and Choi, D. (1990), "A shred of evidence on theories of wage stickiness," *Quarterly Journal of Economics*, 105, pp. 1003–1015.

Brown, C. (1990), "Firms' choice of method of pay," *Industrial Labor Relation Review*, 43(3), pp. 165–182.

Bull, C. (1983), "Implicit contracts in the absence of enforcement and risk aversion," *American Economic Review*, 73, pp. 458–471.

Bull, C. (1987), "The existence of self-enforcing implicit contracts," *Quarterly Journal of Economics*, 102, pp. 147–159.

Buchinsky, M., Fougère, D., Kramarz, F., and Tchernis, R. (2001), "Interfirm mobility, wages, and the returns to seniority and experience in the U.S.," working paper, CREST-INSEE.

Cahuc, P., and Dormont, B. (1997), "Does profit-sharing increase productivity and employment? A theoretical model and empirical evidence on French micro data," *Labour Economics*, 4, pp. 293–319.

Campbell, C., and Kamlani, K. (1997), "The reasons for wage rigidity: Evidence from a survey of firms," *Quarterly Journal of Economics*, 112, pp. 759–789.

Carmichael, L. (1983), "Firm-specific human capital and promotion ladders," *Bell Journal of Economics*, 14, pp. 251–258.

Carmichael, L. (1985), "Can unemployment be involuntary? Comment," *American Economic Review*, 75(5), pp. 1213–1214.

Carmichael, L. (1989), "Self-enforcing contracts, shirking, and life cycle incentives," *Journal of Economic Perspectives*, 3, pp. 65–84.

Carmichael, L. (1990), "Efficiency wage models of unemployment: One view," *Economic Inquiry*, 28, pp. 269–295.

Chang, C., and Wang, Y. (1996), "Human capital investement under asymmetric information: The Pigouvian conjecture revisited," *Journal of Labor Economics*, 14, pp. 505–519.

Chari, V. (1983), "Involuntary unemployment and implicit contracts," *Quarterly Journal of Economics*, 98, Suppl., pp. 107–122.

Chiappori, P.-A., Macho, I., Rey, P., and Salanié, B. (1994), "Repeated moral hazard: The role of memory, commitment, and the access to credit market," *European Economic Review*, 38, pp. 1527–1555.

Chiappori, P.-A., and Salanié, B. (2003), "Testing contract theory: A survey of some recent work," in Dewatripont, M., Hansen, L., and Turnovsky, S. (eds), *Advances in Economics and Econometrics*, vol 1, New York: Cambridge University Press, pp. 115–149.

Cooper, R. (1983), ''A note on overemployment/underemployment in labor contracts under asymmetric information,'' *Economics Letters*, 12, pp. 81–87.

Deci, E., Koestner, R., and Ryan, R. (1999), ''A meta-analytic review of experiments: Examining the effects of extrinsic rewards on intrinsic motivation,'' *Psychological Bulletin*, 125, pp. 627–668.

Doeringer, P., and Piore, M. (1971), *Internal Labor Market and Manpower Analysis*, Lexington, Mass.: Heath.

Ehrenberg, R., and Smith, J. (1994), *Modern Labor Economics*, New York: HarperCollins.

Eriksson, T. (1999), ''Executive compensation and tournament theory: Empirical tests on danish data,'' *Journal of Labor Economics*, 17(2), pp. 262–280.

Farber, H. (1999), ''Mobility and stability: The dynamics of job change in labor markets,'' in Ashenfelter, O., and Card, D. (eds.), *Handbook of Labor Economics*, vol. 3, chap. 36, pp. 2373–2437, Amsterdam: Elsevier Science/North-Holland.

Fehr, E., and Falk, A. (1999), ''Wage rigidity in a competitive incomplete contract market,'' *Journal of Political Economy*, 107(1), pp. 106–134.

Fehr, E., and Schmidt, K. (2000), ''Fairness, incentives, and contractual choices,'' *European Economic Review*, 44, pp. 1057–1068.

Freeman, R., and Rogers, R. (1999), *What Workers Want*, New York: Russell Sage Foundation and Cornell University Press.

Gibbons, R., and Murphy, K. (1990), ''Relative performance evaluation for chief executive officers,'' *Industrial Labor Relation Review*, 43, pp. 30–52.

Gibbons, R., and Waldman, M. (1999a), ''A theory of wage and promotion dynamics inside firms,'' *Quarterly Journal of Economics*, 114, pp. 1321–1358.

Gibbons, R., and Waldman, M. (1999b), ''Careers in organizations: Theory and evidence,'' in Ashenfelter, O., and Card, D. (eds.), *Handbook of Labor Economics*, vol. 3, chap. 36, pp. 2373–2437, Amsterdam: Elsevier Science/North-Holland.

Gneezy, U., and Rustichini, A. (2000), ''Pay enough or don't pay at all,'' *Quarterly Journal of Economics*, 115, pp. 791–810.

Gordon, D. (1974), ''A neo-classical theory of Keynesian unemployment,'' *Economic Inquiry*, 12(4), pp. 431–459.

Green, J., and Khan, C. (1983), ''Wage employment contracts,'' *Quarterly Journal of Economics*, 98, Suppl., pp. 173–187.

Groshen, E., and Krueger, A. (1990), ''The structure of supervision and pay in hospitals,'' *Industrial and Labor Relation Review*, 43, pp. 134–147.

Harris, M., and Holmström, B. (1982), ''A theory of wage dynamics,'' *Review of Economic Studies*, 49, pp. 315–333.

Hart, O. (1983), ''Optimal labour contracts under asymmetric information: An introduction,'' *Review of Economic Studies*, 50, pp. 3–35.

Hart, O., and Holmström, B. (1987), ''The theory of contracts,'' in Bewley, R. (ed.), *Advances in Economic Theory*, pp. 71–156, Cambridge, U.K.: Cambridge University Press.

Hart, O., and Moore, J. (1999), "Foundations of incomplete contracts," *Review of Economic Studies*, 66, pp. 115–138.

Holmström, B., and Milgrom, P. (1987), "Aggregation and linearity in the provision of intertemporal incentives," *Econometrica*, 55, pp. 303–328.

Holmström, B., and Milgrom, P. (1991), "Multitask principal agent analyses, incentive contracts, asset ownership and job design," *Journal of Law, Economics and Organization*, 7, special issue, pp. 24–52.

Hutchens, R. (1989), "Seniority, wages and productivity: A turbulent decade," *Journal of Economic Perspectives*, 3, pp. 49–64.

Jovanovic, B. (1979), "Job matching and the theory of turnover," *Journal of Political Economy*, 69, pp. 972–990.

Kreps, D. (1990), *A Course in Microeconomic Theory*, Harvester Wheatsheaf.

Kreps, D. (1997), "Intrinsic motivation and extrinsic incentives," *American Economic Review*, 87(2), pp. 359–364.

Kruglanski, A. (1978), "Endogenous attribution and intrinsic motivation," in Greene, D., and Lepper, M. (eds.), *The Hidden Cost of Reward*, Hillsdale, N.J.: Erlbaum.

Kotlikoff, L., and Gokhale, J. (1992), "Estimating a firm's age–productivity profile using the present value of a worker's earnings," *Quarterly Journal of Economics*, 107, pp. 1215–1242.

Laffont, J.-J. (1989), *The Economics of Uncertainty and Information*, Cambridge, Mass.: MIT Press.

Lazear, E. (1979), "Why is there mandatory retirement?" *Journal of Political Economy*, 87, pp. 1261–1284.

Lazear, E. (1981), "Agency, earnings profiles, productivity and hours restrictions," *American Economic Review*, 71, pp. 606–620.

Lazear, E. (1986), "Salaries and piece rates," *Journal of Business*, 59, pp. 405–431.

Lazear, E. (1999), "Personal economics: Past lessons and future directions," *Journal of Labor Economics*, 17, pp. 199–236.

Lazear, E. (2000), "Performance, pay and productivity," *American Economic Review*, 90, pp. 1346–1361.

Lazear, E., and Moore, J. (1984), "Incentives, productivity and labor contracts," *Quarterly Journal of Economics*, 99(2), pp. 275–296.

Lazear, E., and Rosen, S. (1981), "Rank-order tournaments as optimum labor contracts," *Journal of Political Economy*, 89, pp. 841–864.

MacDonald, G. (1982), "A market equilibrium theory of job assignment and sequential accumulation of information," *American Economic Review*, 72, pp. 1038–1055.

Macho-Stadler, I., and Perez-Castrillo, D. (1997), *An Introduction to the Economics of Information: Incentives and Contracts*, Oxford, U.K.: Oxford University Press.

MacLeod, B., and Malcomson, J. (1989), "Implicit contracts, incentive compatibility and involuntary unemployment," *Econometrica*, 57, pp. 447–480.

MacLeod, B., and Malcomson, J. (1998), "Motivation and markets," *American Economic Review*, 88(3), pp. 388–411.

Malcomson, J. (1984), "Work incentives, hierarchy and internal labor market," *Journal of Political Economy*, 92, pp. 486–507.

Malcomson, J. (1999), "Individual employment contracts," in Ashenfelter, O., and Card, D. (eds.), *Handbook of Labor Economics*, vol. 3, chap. 35, pp. 2291–2372, Amsterdam: Elsevier Science/North-Holland.

Mas-Colell, A., Whinston, M., and Green, J. (1995), *Microeconomic Theory*, New York: Oxford University Press.

Maskin, E., and Tirole, J. (1999), "Unforeseen contingencies and incomplete contracts," *Review of Economic Studies*, 66, pp. 83–114.

McCue, K. (1996), "Promotions and wage growth," *Journal of Labor Economics*, 14(2), pp. 175–209.

Meyer, M. (1992), "Biased contests and moral hazard: Implication for career profiles," *Annales d'Economie et de Statistique*, 25/26, pp. 165–187.

Milgrom, P. (1988), "Employment contract, influence activity and efficient organization," *Journal of Political Economy*, 96, pp. 42–60.

Milgrom, P., and Roberts, J. (1992), *Economics, Organization and Management*, Englewood Cliffs, N.J.: Prentice-Hall.

Mincer, J. (1974), *Schooling, Experience and Earnings*, New York: Columbia University Press.

Murphy, K., and Cleveland, J. (1991), *Performance Appraisal: An Organizational Perspective*, Boston: Allyn and Bacon.

Myerson, R. (1979), "Incentive compatibility and the bargaining problem," *Econometrica*, 47, pp. 71–74.

Okun, A. (1981), *Prices and Quantities*, Washington, D.C.: Brookings Institution.

Paarsch, H., and Shearer, B. (1999), "The response of worker effort to piece rate: Evidence from the British Columbia tree planting industry," *Journal of Human Resources*, 33(4), pp. 643–667.

Parent, D. (2000), "Industry-specific capital and the wage profile: Evidence from the National Longitudinal Survey of Youth and the Panel Study of Income Dynamics," *Journal of Labor Economics*, 18(2), pp. 306–323.

Prendergast, C. (1993a), "The role of promotion in inducing specific human capital acquisition," *Quarterly Journal of Economics*, 108, pp. 523–534.

Prendergast, C. (1993b), "A theory of yes men," *American Economic Review*, 83(4), pp. 757–770.

Prendergast, C. (1999), "The provision of incentives in firms," *Journal of Economic Literature*, 37, pp. 7–63.

Rosen, S. (1985), "Implicit contracts: A survey," *Journal of Economic Literature*, 23, pp. 1144–1175.

Salanié, B. (1997), *The Economics of Contracts: A Primer*, Cambridge, Mass.: MIT Press.

Sattinger, M. (1993), "Assignment models of the distribution of earnings," *Journal of Economic Literature*, 31, pp. 831–880.

Shapiro, C., and Stiglitz, J. (1984), "Equilibrium unemployment as a worker discipline device," *American Economic Review*, 74, pp. 433–444.

Shapiro, C., and Stiglitz, J. (1985), "Can unemployment be involuntary? Reply," *American Economic Review*, 75(5), pp. 1215–1217.

Simon, H. (1951), "A formal theory of the employment relationship," *Econometrica*, 19, pp. 293–303.

Thomas, J., and Worral, T. (1988), "Self-enforcing wage contracts," *Review of Economic Studies*, 55, pp. 541–553.

Tirole, J. (1992), "Collusion and the theory of organizations," in J.-J. Laffont (ed.), *Advances in Economic Theory: Sixth World Congress*, vol. 2, Cambridge, U.K.: Cambridge University Press.

Topel, R. (1991), "Specific capital, mobility and wages: Wages rise with job seniority," *Journal of Political Economy*, 99, pp. 145–176.

Waldman, M. (1984), "Worker allocation, hierarchies and the wage distribution," *Review of Economic Studies*, 51, pp. 95–109.

Yellen, J. (1994), "Efficiency wage model of unemployment," *American Economic Review, Papers and Proceedings*, 74(2), pp. 200–205.

COLLECTIVE BARGAINING

CONTENTS

In this chapter, we will:

- See what the determinants of the behavior of unions are

- Learn how employees and employers arrive at an agreement on how to share the benefits from productive activities

- Study the different approaches to bargaining theory

- Review the standard models of collective bargaining over wages, employment, and hours

- Explore the consequences of the opposition between insiders and outsiders

- Assess empirically the impact of unions on wages, productivity, profits, employment, and working hours

INTRODUCTION

Bargaining over labor contracts can take place at the individual level, between each worker and his or her employer, or collectively, between organizations representing wage-earners and employers. The fact that wages are the upshot of bargaining between two partners indicates that both sides are looking for an agreement on how to *share* the outcome of the activity in which they are jointly involved, and that the resulting partition (or "share-out") depends on the bargaining *power* of each partner. In most major industrialized countries, a significant proportion of wages is regulated by *collective agreements* that codify the agreements reached through bargaining between unions representing employees and organizations representing employers. The purpose of this chapter is to study the course of events in a round of collective bargaining, and their consequences.

Collective bargaining presents two conceptual barriers to analysis. The first is how to represent the objectives of the partners to the bargaining. These actors are not economic "agents" in the ordinary sense of the term but *organizations* (most often unions). The objectives of these organizations arise, one way or another, out of those of their component members. As we will see, economic analysis of collective decisions can shed light on the connection between individual preferences and those of collective organizations. Once past this barrier, there remains a second difficulty: how to represent the bargaining process. Since the early 1980s, developments in noncooperative game theory—especially dynamic games—and the attendant concepts of equilibrium have made it possible to overcome this obstacle as well. Dynamic game theory allows us to understand fundamental aspects of the behavior of actors, i.e., of the strategies they pursue as bargaining unfolds, and the manner in which they agree to conclude it and share the future benefits.

The theory of collective bargaining furnishes a primarily *local* explanation of wage setting, in the sense that it compares the strategies of two clearly identified actors. It needs to be integrated into a general equilibrium model if we are to achieve an understanding of the *global* level of employment within an entire economy. In this chapter we remain at the stage of partial equilibrium, with two actors (an employees' union and an employer) controlling a labor pool. Only in chapter 12, section 4, do we integrate collective bargaining over wages into a general equilibrium model.

Section 1 gives a sketch of the importance of collective bargaining in the major industrialized countries. It also specifies the objectives of the different actors, and how to represent their respective choice criteria. Section 2 gives the essential concepts and results of game theory used to analyze the unfolding of the negotiations. They are applied in section 3, which lays out the basic models describing the consequences for wages and employment of bargaining between an employer and a union representing all the workers in a given labor pool. The last hypothesis is abandoned in section 4, where we assume that only employees in place (*insiders*) are able to make agreements with the management of the firm. Section 5 looks at the impact of collective bargaining on investment and the number of hours worked. And finally, section 6 offers a review of empirical findings on the consequences of collective bargaining.

1 UNIONS AND COLLECTIVE BARGAINING

Collective bargaining plays an important role in most industrialized countries. The collective bargaining coverage, the concrete manner in which it occurs, the degree to which it is coordinated, and the variables involved are all sources of diversity and can affect the performance of a nation. There have been numerous controversies over how best to represent the objectives and behavior of collective organizations, and choice theory has not succeeded in resolving them completely.

1.1 The Characteristics and Importance of Collective Agreements

A collective agreement is made up of a set of provisions negotiated between one or more employers and the representatives of their employees. Union density and the collective bargaining coverage of collective agreements are measures of their importance. The level at which they are negotiated and the aim of the agreements reached vary significantly in the different OECD countries.

1.1.1 Collective Bargaining Coverage and Union Density

Union density is to be distinguished from collective bargaining coverage. We present values for these two factors in 19 OECD countries before examining their development.

International Comparison

Figure 7.1 presents levels of union density and collective bargaining coverage in 19 OECD countries in 1994. Union density equals the proportion of wage-earners who are unionized, and collective bargaining coverage equals the proportion of wage-earners who are covered by collective agreements. The average collective bargaining coverage is high, equal to 68.3% for the set of 19 countries and 82.3% for the 12 European Union (EU) countries. On the other hand, the average union density proves to be significantly lower, amounting to 40% for the set of 19 countries and 44.3% for the 12 EU countries.

The gap between union density and collective bargaining coverage derives in large part from legal constraints and the institutional context. For example, in France and Spain collective agreements do not have the right to discriminate between union members and nonunionized workers. This prohibition may explain the large gap between the high collective bargaining coverage in these two countries and the remarkably low rate of union density. On the contrary, in Australia, New Zealand, the United States, and the United Kingdom, it is legal for collective agreements to discriminate between unionized and nonunionized workers, and this has certainly favored union membership. The upshot is that union density does not always provide a good measure of the power of unions. In France, although union density is low, unions play a preponderant role, for they are *legally* empowered to represent workers in collective bargaining—and collective bargaining is compulsory in firms with more than 50 employees. In the United States, on the other hand, where union density is higher,

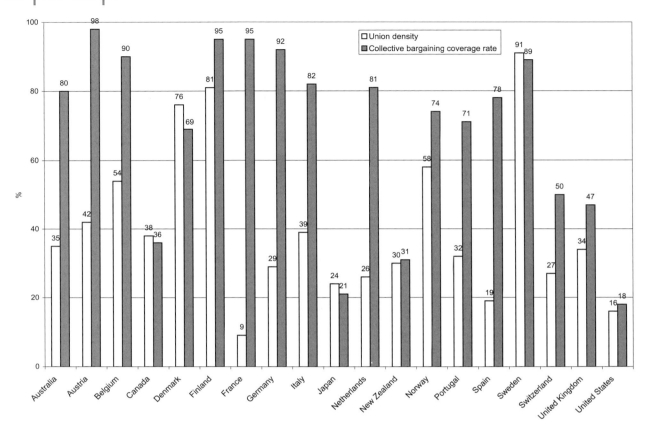

FIGURE 7.1
Union density and collective bargaining coverage in 1994.

Source: OECD (1997).

collective bargaining is mandated by law only if the majority of the employees in a plant vote in favor of union representation (Hartog and Theeuwes, 1993; Booth, 1995a, chapter 2). This no doubt explains the low collective bargaining coverage in the United States. Overall, collective bargaining coverage is surely a more reliable indicator of the power of unions than union density.

Recent Changes in Union Density and Collective Bargaining Coverage
Figure 7.2 depicts changes in union density between 1970 and 2000 (see Checchi and Lucifora, 2002, for a comprehensive study of the evolution of union density). Comparison shows that over this period there were gains in Denmark, Belgium, and Finland and major losses in, among others, Australia, Austria, the United States, France, Japan, Portugal, and the United Kingdom. Among the 18 countries included, three experienced an increase in union density and the other 15 experienced a decrease.

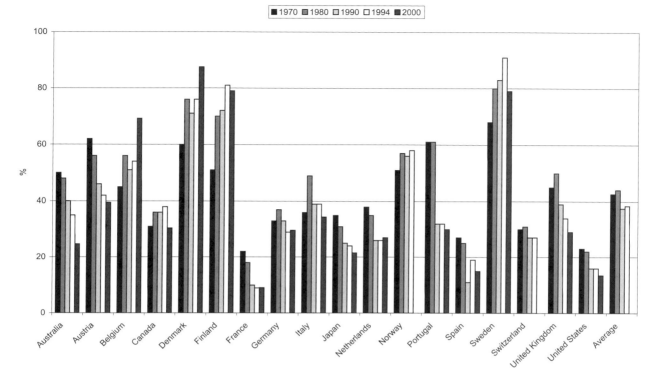

Figure 7.2

Changes in union density in 18 OECD countries, 1970–2000.

Source: OECD data.

Figure 7.2 also shows that union density rose in Germany and Italy between 1970 and 1980, but then fell off. In Sweden, union density rose between 1970 and 1994 and then fell sharply. Overall, we see very different movements in union density, and a significant drop in this indicator in many countries (see the histograms on the right in figure 7.2). The nonweighted average of union density has fallen off slightly since the beginning of the 1980s, after having risen slightly between 1970 and 1980.

Figure 7.3 depicts changes in collective bargaining coverage in 11 OECD countries between 1980 and 1994. The exent of coverage decreased in seven countries, held steady in Finland, and rose in France, the Netherlands, and Portugal. It was the United Kingdom that experienced the sharpest drop in the 1980s. This particular change was the result of refusals to extend collective agreements made at the beginning of the 1980s. Overall, we see that the nonweighted average of extent of coverage fell off very slightly between 1980 and 1990, but then turned up, also very slightly, between 1990 and 1994. Thus there is not a pervasive tendency for collective bargaining coverage to decline.

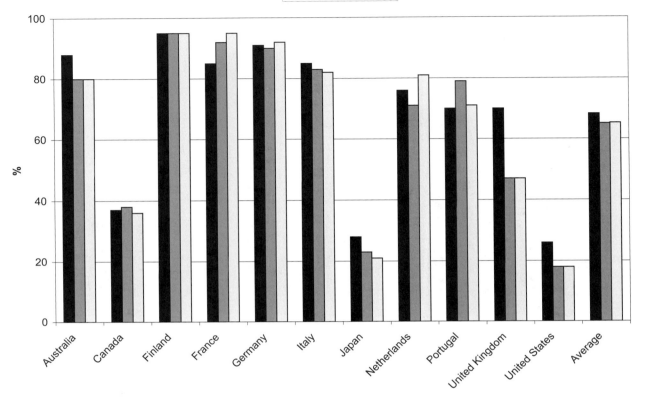

FIGURE 7.3
Changes in collective bargaining coverage in 11 OECD countries.

Source: OECD (1997).

1.1.2 The Level at Which Bargaining Takes Place

In order to represent the unfolding of collective bargaining, we have to know if it is taking place at the level of the firm, the industry, the region, or on a national scale. In reality, it is not always easy to classify countries by this criterion, for in most cases there is an overlap between negotiations taking place at several different levels. Table 7.1 bears witness to this diversity for 17 of the OECD countries already cited, and makes it clear that there is always some bargaining done at the firm level. Austria appears to be an exception to this rule, but although collective bargaining is indeed prohibited at the level of firms, a decentralizing trend has in practice enhanced the bargaining power of plant committees since the beginning of the 1990s (OECD, 1994, p. 191).

Table 7.1 also portrays the degree of coordination for the economy as a whole. In this regard, a distinction should be made between *explicit* and *implicit* coordination.

Table 7.1

Levels of collective bargaining and coordination, 1980–1994.

Country	Institutional level of collective bargaining	Privileged level of collective bargaining	Coordination at the level of the whole economy	
			As an objective	Achievability
Australia	1, 2, 3	2 → 3, 1	Explicit coordination	High
Austria	2, 3	2	Implicit coordination	High
Belgium	1, 2, 3	2	Explicit coordination	Limited
Canada	1, 2	1	Absence of coordination	Absent
Finland	1, 2, 3	3 → 2, 1	Explicit coordination	High
France	1, 2, 3	2	Explicit coordination	Limited
Germany	1, 2	2	Implicit coordination	High
Japan	1, 2	11	Implicit coordination	High
Netherlands	1, 2, 3	2	Explicit coordination	Limited
New Zealand	1, 2	2 → 1	Explicit coordination	Absent
Norway	1, 2, 3	2 → 3	Explicit coordination	High
Portugal	1, 2, 3	2 → 2, 3	Explicit coordination	Limited
Spain	1, 2, 3	2, 3 → 2	Explicit coordination	Limited
Sweden	1, 2, 3	3 → 2	Explicit coordination	Limited
Switzerland	1, 2	2	Absence of coordination	Limited
United Kingdom	1, 2	2 → 1	Absence of coordination	Absent
United States	1, 2	1	Absence of coordination	Absent

Source: OECD (1997).

Legend: 1 = firm; 2 = sector; 3 = central. The arrows indicate the direction of change. "Explicit coordination" means joint negotiations between workers' unions and employers' confederations, with perhaps participation by the state. "Implicit coordination" takes into account control by union federations, and the fact that certain leading sectors are models for others.

Explicit coordination means actual bargaining between trade union confederations and confederations of employers at the national level. Implicit coordination derives either from the control exercised by union confederations over their members or from the fact that agreements reached in certain industries serve as models for the rest. Note that the absence of centralized bargaining does not necessarily imply the absence of national coordination, for the latter may be implicit. Germany and Japan, for example, do not have collective bargaining at the national level, but there is a strong implicit coordination in both countries. In Japan, at the time of the "spring offensive" (*Shunto*), the unions announce the broad outlines of their wage demands vis-à-vis all the large firms in the country, and these guidelines are generally followed in individual cases. In Germany the logic of cohesion is different: it is agreements reached in the metalworking sector that traditionally serve as guidelines.

We will see in chapter 12, section 4, that the plurality of forms of coordination makes it very difficult to classify systems of industrial relations according to their degree of centralization. Institutional structures are not carved in stone, either. Certain countries like Sweden, the United Kingdom, and New Zealand are moving toward decentralization, while others, like Portugal, are moving toward a more centralized structure.

1.1.3   The Aim of Collective Bargaining

In the United States, collective agreements cover a particularly wide range of subjects, including wages, promotions, work schedules, holidays, retirement, seniority, training, handling, arbitration of grievances, and health insurance.[1] Collective agreements are in fact a way to compensate for the low level of involvement by the state in areas such as health and retirement. The state traditionally takes a larger role in these areas in other OECD countries, especially in Europe, with the result that collective agreements address a smaller number of issues in these countries. Still, bargaining there generally covers not only wages but other things as well, such as work schedules, working conditions, and professional training. The level of employment, however, is a topic that is seldom raised anywhere in the OECD (Hartog and Theeuwes, 1993).

1.2   THE BEHAVIOR OF UNIONS

The economic analysis of unions has long been highly controversial. The assumption that complex political institutions have rational objectives like those dealt with in the economic theory of individual choice appeared too simplistic to be relevant. Hicks (1932, p. 140) took the view that "to protect the customary standard of life (which may be conceived as a money wage or, in times of monetary disturbance, a real wage), to maintain fair wages, and to secure to the workers a share in exceptional profits, are the usual aims of the wage policy of trade unions." In other words, unions simply demanded a "fair wage" (or a "customary standard of living") determined by overall social conditions. Hicks saw no need to resort to choice theory in order to represent the behavior of a union.

Dunlop was the first to declare that "an economic theory of a trade union requires that the organization be assumed to maximize (or minimize) something" (Dunlop, 1944, p. 4). According to this author, the aim of a trade union is to maximize the total amount of wages received by its members. Ross (1948) reacted by insisting on the essentially political nature of unions; he criticized Dunlop's approach by emphasizing that unions are not made up of identical individuals, and that the content of their decisions reflects the struggle for power both within the membership and between members and leaders of unions. This objection highlights an important limitation of Dunlop's analysis by showing that the heterogeneity of a union's members affects its aims. The distribution of various individual characteristics, the way in which the leadership is selected, the organization of elections, the recruitment of members, and a number of given institutional factors are all capable of influencing a union's behavior. Ross's objection signifies, in other words, that it is insufficient to postulate a union objective independent of its members' preferences and its own institutional characteristics. So it becomes necessary to analyze the relationship between the union's preferences and those of its members. This has been the goal of the economic theory of unions for several decades; some empirical studies have helped to clarify the nature of union aims.

1.2.1 Union Preferences and Individual Preferences

The representation of the preferences of a union depends mainly on the homogeneity or heterogeneity of the individuals it comprises. To this dimension we sometimes have to add certain aims proper to the union leadership.

A Union with Identical Members
A union composed of identical members has, since the work of Drèze and Modigliani (1981), MacDonald and Solow (1981), and Oswald (1982), been the basis for representations of union preferences. The assumption is that the union defends the interests of N identical workers who form its "labor pool." Every union member supplies one unit of labor if the real wage w exceeds the reservation wage $\bar{w}$, equated to the income of an unemployed person. Individual preferences are represented by an indirect utility function of the Von Neumann and Morgenstern type, or $v(.)$, strictly increasing with respect to income. The labor demand addressed to the union is denoted by L. The (identical) workers each have the same probability $(1 - L/N)$ of being unemployed when $L < N$. If this inequality is satisfied, the probability of being employed amounts to L/N. Conversely, if labor demand is greater than or equal to the size of the labor pool, the probability of being hired is equal to 1, and a worker's expected utility is simply $v(w)$. We then assume that the objective of the union consists of maximizing the expected utility $\mathcal{V}_s$ of its members. This last quantity is defined by:

$$\mathcal{V}_s = \ell v(w) + (1 - \ell)v(\bar{w}), \qquad \ell = \text{Min}(1, L/N) \tag{1}$$

Given that the size N of the labor pool is exogenous, that comes to the same thing as assuming that the union maximizes the sum $N\mathcal{V}_s$ of the utility of its members. Such a union is then described as "utilitarian." If the workers have no aversion to risk—$v'(.)$ is then a constant—this specification is compatible with the hypothesis that the union maximizes the "union rent" (Rosen, 1970; De Menil, 1971), defined by the product $\ell(w - \bar{w})$. Dunlop's hypothesis that the union objective is to maximize the total wage bill further requires $\bar{w} = 0$.

The hypothesis that union members are identical allows us to lay precise microeconomic foundations for union preferences. This precision is however gained at the expense of realism. The heterogeneity of union members poses different problems according to how the union functions. If the organization is perfectly democratic, its preferences can be deduced from those of its members by analyzing the outcome of a vote. On the other hand, the objectives of union leaders play a determining role if they enjoy strong discretionary powers.

A Perfectly Democratic Union with Different Members

We learn from the analysis of collective decisions (Arrow, 1963) that the preferences expressed through the outcome of a vote by rational agents are themselves rational—, i.e., that they define a complete, reflexive, and transitive ordering—when a) majority rules; b) agents vote sincerely and do not try to shape the outcome by announcing their intentions beforehand; c) they are voting on a single question; and d) the utility function of each individual admits only one maximum with respect to the variable on which they are voting. If these conditions are satisfied, the decision taken expresses the preferences of the *median* voter.

These results show that when the heterogeneity of union members is introduced, the definition of a union's objective rests on highly restrictive hypotheses. In this regard, as Blair and Crawford (1984) point out, hypothesis c, that the vote can only address one question, proves extremely limiting. In practice, collective negotiations embrace a number of topics (see Hartog and Theeuwes, 1993). But to allow both heterogeneity of members and a number of variables to be negotiated becomes a perilous exercise, since the rationality of union decisions is no longer guaranteed (preferences are not necessarily transitive). For this reason, studies of the analysis of a union composed of diverse members make the assumption that the vote is exclusively about wages (Booth, 1984; Blair and Crawford, 1984; Carruth et al., 1986). Their main contribution is to show that the union has a slight preference for employment if the median voter has a slight probability of losing his or her job, as will be the case if layoffs are made by seniority (as in the United States), or if the median voter possesses specific human capital that gives him or her an advantage with respect to other workers hired more recently.

Conflicts Between Union Leadership and Membership

In many institutions, the leadership has discretionary power, and their objectives do not necessarily coincide with those of their membership. For example, the social prestige, the advantages in kind, and the remuneration of members of the leadership generally depend on the importance of the institution they represent. That being the case, it is most often assumed that their objective is to maximize the size of their organization (Ross, 1948; Atherton, 1973; Martin, 1980; Farber, 1986). Hence it is possible simply to study the consequences of the discretionary power of the leadership. If we assume (Farber, 1986) that the size of the union increases with the number of workers employed—a hypothesis justified by the observation that union density among the unemployed is much weaker than it is among workers who do have a job—union leaders in a position to fix the wage level unilaterally subject to the constraint of decreasing labor demand would set a wage equal to the reservation wage, so as to maximize the level of employment compatible with the participation constraint of workers. This conclusion, as Lewis (1963) points out, shows that a "boss-dominated union" keeps its members from profiting from its monopoly power, since this power is used exclusively for the benefit of the leadership; the latter attain their objectives in a situation of perfect competition.

This brief review of work dealing with the problems posed by the heterogeneity of union members reveals that the economic analysis of union behavior remains very crude. Nonetheless, a couple of things have been learned. For one thing, it is possible to represent the preferences of the union in terms of employment and wages on a precise microeconomic basis. For another, the goals of the union depend not just on the preferences of its members, but also on its institutional structure. The purely economic approach to trade unionism is, to a certain extent, relevant, since there do exist hypotheses permitting us to define union objectives on the basis of choice theory. But the highly restrictive nature of these hypotheses (identical members, validity conditions of the theorem of the median voter) leads to a neglect of institutional characteristics that may have important influence on employment and wages.

1.2.2 Union Goals According to Empirical Studies

Useful information about union goals comes from several sources. Freeman and Medoff (1984, chapter 14) have undertaken studies utilizing statements made by union members and leaders. They conclude that the American union movement functions very democratically, particularly at the local level. Work by labor sociologists is also instructive but is difficult to apply to the formal definition of the objective function of a union. For this reason, econometric studies based on individual data would appear to be best suited to this purpose. Their procedure is to estimate wage and employment functions on the assumption that remuneration is set by a union maximizing its objective function subject to the constraint of the labor demand. The estimation of the coefficients of the wage and employment equations thus obtained then allows us to characterize union preferences. For example, Dertouzos and Pencavel (1981) and Pencavel (1984) have tested a utility function of the Stone-Geary type, of the following form:

$$\mathcal{V}_s = (w - w^0)^\theta (L - L^0)^{1-\theta}, \qquad \theta \in [0, 1] \tag{2}$$

In this expression, w^0 and L^0 represent respectively the minimal wage and employment levels accepted by the union. Parameter θ measures the relative importance of wages. This formulation allows us to recover (as particular cases) the objective of the total wage bill ($\theta = 1/2, L^0 = w^0 = 0$) postulated by Dunlop (1944) and the objective of union rent ($\theta = 1/2, w^0 = \overline{w}, L^0 = 0$) put forward by Rosen (1970) and De Menil (1971).

Pencavel (1984) used data on six local unions of the International Typographical Union (United States) for the period 1946–1965. Each local union is assumed to maximize the objective just set out subject to the constraint of a linear labor demand function:

$$L = \alpha_0 + \alpha_1(w/r_1) + \alpha_2(r_2/r_1) + \alpha_3 X + \alpha_4 D \tag{3}$$

where r_1 is the price at which the product is sold, r_2 is an index of the cost of production, X is the number of lines of advertising sold annually, and D is a dummy variable. The first-order condition is written:

$$\frac{\theta}{\theta - 1} = \frac{\alpha_1(w - w^0)}{r_1(L - L^0)} \tag{4}$$

The estimation of these last two equations allows us to find the values of the parameters characterizing the utility function of unions. Three important lessons emerge from Pencavel's study. The first is that the estimates of each parameter are noticeably different for the six local unions. In particular, the values of w^0 and L^0 increase with the size of the local. The second is that the parameter θ is, on average, relatively weak, lying between 0.19 and 0.36 for four local unions, and reaching 0.61 and 0.88 for the other two. That means that the local unions studied weight the employment objective very strongly. Finally, the estimated values of the parameters reject the hypothesis of the maximization of the wage rent or of the total wage bill.

Farber (1978) and Carruth and Oswald (1985) have adopted an identical procedure, but with the assumption of different objective functions. Farber (1978) studies the behavior of the United Mine Workers (United States) over the period 1948–1973, on the assumption that this union maximizes the expected utility of a member with median seniority. He estimates that this member's relative degree of risk aversion—equal by definition to $-wv''(w)/v'(w)$, if $v(w)$ is the indirect utility function and w the individual's wage—is on the order of 3. Carruth and Oswald (1985) analyze the behavior of unions in the coal and steel industries in the United Kingdom over the period 1950–1980. They too assume that the union maximizes the sum of the utilities of its members, and they find a relative degree of risk aversion on the order of 0.8. Such results lead us to reject the objective of total wage bill or union rent, based on the risk neutrality of workers.

All of these results must, however, be interpreted with caution, for union preferences are not being estimated directly. The estimates actually bear on both the functional form of the union objective and the mode of wage formation. The equations tested all assume that the union determines the wages of its members unilaterally. In reality, wages are the object of bargaining, and this can perceptibly modify the form of the equation estimated.

2   BARGAINING THEORY

Bargaining theory studies situations in which it is possible for rational agents to come to an agreement over how to share a quantity of (any) goods. Since Edgeworth (1881), a number of authors have sought to define the rational principles that preside over such a partition. Only recently has the work of Nash (1950, 1953), Stahl (1972), and Rubinstein (1982) systematically solved the bargaining problem. Nash launched the *axiomatic* approach, while Stahl and Rubinstein have developed the *strategic* approach. These two approaches make it possible to represent bargaining through simple models, which cast light on the notion of bargaining power and on the origins of conflict such as strikes.

2.1 THE PRECURSORS

The earliest analyses of bargaining ran into the problem of the indeterminacy of the solution. Edgeworth (1881) had noted that this solution should be Pareto optimal, since rational individuals would not accept a partition knowing that there existed other, more advantageous ones for at least one of the partners. But this criterion is not, in general, sufficient to define a unique solution. It simply indicates that agents exploit as far as possible the mutual benefits of cooperation. It is also necessary to explain *how* these benefits are shared. Zeuthen (1930) and Hicks (1932) were the first to propose solutions to the problem raised by Edgeworth.

The model of Hicks (1932) describes bargaining between a workers' union and the management of a firm, on the hypothesis that each player possesses a *bargaining power* arising from his or her potential to hold out in case of conflict. This model can be presented graphically, with the duration of the strike on the horizontal axis and the wage on the vertical axis (see figure 7.4). The firm's "concession" schedule is denoted by the symbol (C). It is increasing, for the longer the strike lasts, the readier the employer is to accept high wages. Symmetrically, (R) designates the "resistance" schedule of the union. It is decreasing, for it seems natural to assume that the union will accept lower wages if the strike drags on. The wage settled on, denoted by w^*, is determined by the intersection of curves (C) and (R). Assuming that the capacity of both sides to hold out is "common knowledge," Hicks deduces that strikes are only *potential*, since the firm and the union are perfectly capable of foreseeing the duration of the strike and the wage to which the bargaining will eventually lead.

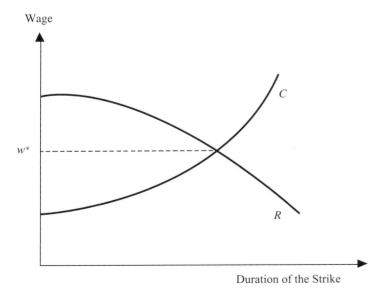

FIGURE 7.4
The model of Hicks.

The solution proposed by Hicks has the advantage of simplicity. Its drawback is that it remains very vague about the elements that determine the capacity of the players to hold out. Does it come from their risk aversion, their preference for the present, gains while the strike lasts, or alternative wages? It is indispensable for the theory of bargaining to state precisely the part played by these different factors. The model of Zeuthen (1930) adopts this perspective, since it represents the behavior of the players during the unfolding of negotiations. Today, however, the hypotheses adopted by this author to represent the strategic behavior of the players appear ad hoc, i.e., incompatible with the postulate of rationality (see the presentation of Friedman, 1986, p. 159). In this field, the contribution of game theory has been to clarify precisely how rational individuals behave during the unfolding of negotiations.

It was the work of Nash (1950, 1953), Stahl (1972), and Rubinstein (1982) that made it possible to solve the problem of bargaining in a systematic fashion. Nash (1953) approached the question from two different angles, which in practice turn out to be complementary. The first is the *axiomatic* approach, the aim of which is to define a priori the properties that it would seem natural for the solution to possess. The second is the *strategic* approach, in which the bargaining process is explicitly formalized, but without prejudging the final properties of the solution. In this section, we examine the problem of a negotiation between two players (the extension to a larger number of participants raises no special difficulties; see, for example, Osborne and Rubinstein, 1990). We will look first at the axiomatic approach, then at the strategic one, and finally analyze the linkage between these two ways of dealing with the bargaining problem.

2.2   THE AXIOMATIC APPROACH

The works of Nash (1950, 1953) marked a decisive step in the analysis of bargaining between two agents. The aim of the axiomatic approach is to define the solution to the bargaining problem on the basis of a set of properties that it must "naturally" satisfy. Nash (1950, 1953) advances four such properties. To be precise, let G be the set of vectors of utility $u = (u_1, u_2)$ that players 1 and 2 can attain at the conclusion of the bargaining, and let $d = (d_1, d_2)$ be the vector of the utility obtained in a situation of status quo, in other words the failure of bargaining. It is assumed that G is compact and convex, and that if $u \in G$, $u \geq d$. A set of solutions is then a function f linking every pair (G, d) to a vector $u^N = (u_1^N, u_2^N) \in G$ that satisfies the following four axioms:

(i) *Pareto optimality.* $u \in G$ and $u \geq u^N \Rightarrow u = u^N$

(ii) *Invariance to positive linear utility transformations.* $\forall (a_1, a_2, b_1, b_2) \in R_{*+}^2 \times R^2$. Let us define the linear function T which links every vector (u_1, u_2) to vector (u_1', u_2') such that $u_i' = a_i u_i + b_i$ for $i = 1, 2$; then $f[T(G), T(d)] = T[f(G, d)]$.

(iii) *Independence of irrelevant alternatives.* $B \subset G$, and $f(G, d) \in B \Rightarrow f(B, d) = f(G, d)$.

(iv) *Symmetry.* If $d_1 = d_2$ and if $(u_1, u_2) \in G \Rightarrow (u_2, u_1) \in G$, then $u_1^N = u_2^N$.

The first two axioms signify respectively that the players exploit all mutual benefits and that the solution must not depend on a particular representation of their preferences. The fourth axiom postulates that the players are "interchangeable" in the following sense: when player 1 takes the place of player 2, he obtains the same gain as the latter. This property supposes that the players have an identical "bargaining power." Axiom (iii) posits that if the players come to an agreement belonging to a subset B of the set G of all possible agreements, they will not change their attitudes if they confine themselves *straightaway* to taking into account only the possibilities offered by the subset B.

It is then possible to show that there exists a unique solution u^N satisfying properties (i) to (iv). It is defined by (see Nash, 1950, and Osborne and Rubinstein, 1990, p. 13):

$$u^N = \operatorname*{Arg\,Max}_{u \in G}(u_1 - d_1)(u_2 - d_2)$$

This so-called Nash solution thus corresponds simply to the maximization of the product of the net gains of the players. If we suppress the symmetry axiom (iv), we arrive at solution u^G, called the generalized Nash solution. It is defined by:

$$u^G = \operatorname*{Arg\,Max}_{u \in G}(u_1 - d_1)^{\gamma}(u_2 - d_2)^{1-\gamma}, \qquad \gamma \in [0, 1]$$

In this expression, γ represents the bargaining power of player 1. Within the framework of the axiomatic approach, this concept lacks precision. We will see below that the strategic approach allows us to establish a link between the preferences of players, the unfolding of the negotiation, and this notion of bargaining power.

It also needs to be emphasized that the properties stipulated by Nash have sometimes been criticized, and that it is possible to imagine others (see, for example, Kalai and Smorodinsky, 1975, who discuss the independence axiom (iii)). As well, it can be difficult to define precisely the situation of status quo that corresponds to the gains d. During wage bargaining, are these gains the ones obtained if a strike occurs, or do they correspond to outside opportunities, i.e., to gains obtained should the protagonists go their separate ways? To answer these questions, it is necessary to define the bargaining process completely. That is precisely the aim of the strategic approach.

2.3 THE STRATEGIC APPROACH

Stahl (1972) and Rubinstein (1982) worked out the first models of bargaining to use the theory of noncooperative games in a dynamic setting describing a process of offers and counteroffers. We describe the game that serves as a point of reference for all theories of collective bargaining first, then we look at the solutions.

2.3.1 A Noncooperative Bargaining Game

In dynamic noncooperative games, the relevant concept of equilibrium is that of "subgame perfect equilibrium." With this concept, it becomes possible to eliminate noncredible threats.

Rubinstein's Model

We present here a simplified version of the model of Rubinstein (1982). It is a game between two persons whose life span is infinite, and unfolds in a discrete sequence of periods; in each of these, it is possible for the two players to share a good, the size of which is normalized to unity. In other words, in each period the two players have before them a "pie" of a given size, which they can share if they can reach an agreement about how much each will get. If they cannot agree, the pie is forfeited for that period and they must content themselves with their reservation utility. To be more precise: we assume that on even dates, player 1 proposes a partition $(x_t, 1 - x_t)$ which player 2 accepts or refuses. According to this partition, player 1 gets x_t and player 2 gets $(1 - x_t)$. On odd dates, player 2 proposes a partition $(y_t, 1 - y_t)$ which player 1 accepts or refuses. The agents have an infinite life span, and at every date their preferences are represented by strictly increasing and strictly concave utility functions denoted by $u_1(x)$ and $u_2(1 - x)$. Parameters $\delta_1 \in (0, 1)$ and $\delta_2 \in (0, 1)$ will designate the discount factors. We assume that each player is able to attain an instantaneous level of utility $\bar{u}_i = u_i(0)$, $i = 1, 2$, at every date during the unfolding of the bargaining. These levels of utility are exogenous and correspond to what each agent can obtain as long as no agreement is reached. Bargaining ceases when an agreement is reached between the players. This agreement then applies to all the subsequent periods. In other words, at the date an agreement stipulating partition $(z, 1 - z)$ is accepted, the gains of players 1 and 2 are respectively defined by:

$$U_1 = \sum_{t=0}^{\infty} \delta_1^t u_1(z) = \frac{u_1(z)}{1 - \delta_1} \quad \text{and} \quad U_2 = \sum_{t=0}^{\infty} \delta_2^t u_2(1 - z) = \frac{u_2(1 - z)}{1 - \delta_2}$$

In this dynamic game, each agent adopts a *strategy* that specifies the offers that he or she makes, and his or her reactions to the offers made by the other player. A strategy pair—one for each player—forms a Nash equilibrium if the strategy of one player is the best response to the strategy of the other. Hence, at Nash equilibrium, neither player has an interest in modifying his or her plan of action unilaterally *at the outset* of the bargaining.

Subgame Perfect Equilibrium

In dynamic games, however, the notion of Nash equilibrium thus defined is not completely satisfactory, since it offers no way to eliminate equilibria resting on non-credible threats. The example of the ultimatum game illustrates this point. Let us imagine a game unfolding over a single period (for example, date $t = 0$), and let us suppose that the strategy of player 1 consists simply of putting forward a partition offer $(x, 1 - x)$. Player 2's only options are to accept or reject it. If player 2 accepts the offer, he or she receives $(1 - x)$ and player 1 receives x, at which point the game ends. If player 2 refuses, each player must be satisfied with his or her reservation utility $\bar{u}_i$, $i = 1, 2$, and the game also ends. Let us now assume that player 2 adopts the following strategy: accept every offer $x \leq 1/2$ and refuse every offer $x > 1/2$. The outcome is a

Nash equilibrium characterized by the partition $(1/2, 1/2)$, for at this point, each player obtains the highest possible gains given the strategy of the other player. For if player 2 undertakes to refuse every offer $x > 1/2$, player 1's best option is to offer $1/2$. In that situation, player 2 does indeed have an interest in undertaking to refuse any offer $x > 1/2$. More generally, every partition $(x, 1 - x)$, $x \in [0, 1]$, corresponds to a Nash equilibrium. But this type of equilibrium implies that player 2's strategy rests on a *noncredible* threat, for when player 1 has put forward an offer x, player 2 has an interest in accepting every partition such that $u_2(1 - x) \geq \bar{u}_2 \equiv u_2(0)$, which is equivalent to $x \leq 1$. To undertake to refuse an offer $x \leq 1$ is thus not a credible threat.

For this reason, the general practice is to adopt a concept of equilibrium that eliminates noncredible threats. The idea is to search for each agent's optimal strategy *at every date* (and no longer just at the outset of the game), given all the other actions, past and present, chosen by the other agent. A pair of strategies respecting this condition is a Nash equilibrium for every *subgame*, i.e., for every date t at which a player acts and not just for the initial game that begins at date $t = 0$. The consequence of this definition is that no agent individually has an interest in deviating from strategies that form a subgame perfect equilibrium, since each individual chooses his or her best strategy *at every instant*. In other words, the players do not prepare plans of action which, the moment they were put into operation, it would be in their interest to renounce.

In the example just given of the ultimatum game, there is just one subgame perfect equilibrium. As we saw, player 2 accepts all $x \leq 1$, the moment he or she has to respond to the offer of player 1. Player 1 knows this, and so proposes the ultimatum $x = 1$. The only perfect subgame equilibrium of the bargaining game, at a period beginning with an offer from player 1, thus ends in a partition $(1, 0)$.

Let us now look at how the concept of subgame perfect equilibrium makes it possible to determine solutions to a bargaining process. Clearly the properties of solutions will be quite different according to whether the horizon of the bargaining process is finite or infinite.

2.3.2 Bargaining with a Finite Horizon (Stahl, 1972)

Subgame perfect equilibria are obtained by backward induction. We will show that it is in the interest of both players to agree *at the outset of the game* on a well-defined partition. For that purpose, let us suppose that the final date of the game, denoted by n, is even. If no agreement has been reached by that time, player 1 would make the final offer, and player 2 would necessarily accept any value $x \leq 1$. So on the final date, player 1 would offer $x_n = 1$. Knowing that, player 2 could, at date $n - 1$, make an offer acceptable to player 1 that took advantage of player 1's preference for the present: player 2 would offer partition $(y, 1 - y)$ at date $(n - 1)$, knowing that player 1 will obtain $\bar{u}_1 + \sum_{t=1}^{\infty} \delta_1^t u_1(1)$ by refusing and $\sum_{t=0}^{\infty} \delta_1^t u_1(y)$ by accepting. If we calculate the difference between these two quantities, we see that player 1 accepts all offers y

such that:

$$u_1(y) - \bar{u}_1 \geq \delta_1[u_1(1) - \bar{u}_1]$$

Since player 2 obtains no more than his or her reservation utility if player 1 refuses the offer, at date $(n-1)$ he or she makes an offer acceptable to player 1 which is the most advantageous for him- or herself. This partition, $(y_{n-1}, 1 - y_{n-1})$, is defined by:

$$u_1(y_{n-1}) - \bar{u}_1 = \delta_1[u_1(1) - \bar{u}_1]$$

The reader can verify that $y_{n-1} < 1$ when $\delta_1 < 1$ and that $y_{n-1} = 1$ if $\delta_1 = 1$. This result means that wasting time is "costly" when an agent has a certain preference for the present ($\delta_1 < 1$). The line of reasoning now proceeds backward. Let us place ourselves at an even date $t \leq n - 2$; player 1 makes an offer $(x_t, 1 - x_t)$ knowing that at date $(t+1)$ player 2 will make an acceptable offer $(y_{t+1}, 1 - y_{t+1})$. Should player 1's offer be refused, player 2 attains the level of utility $\bar{u}_2 + \sum_{\tau=1}^{\infty} \delta_2^{\tau} u_2(1 - y_{t+1})$ and if it is accepted, he or she obtains $\sum_{\tau=0}^{\infty} \delta_2^{\tau} u_2(1 - x_t)$. For player 1, it is optimal that these last two quantities be equal and x_t is thus defined by relation:

$$u_2(1 - x_t) - \bar{u}_2 = \delta_2[u_2(1 - y_{t+1}) - \bar{u}_2] \tag{5}$$

Likewise, at odd date $(t-1)$ player 2 makes an offer $(y_{t-1}, 1 - y_{t-1})$ knowing that player 1 will make an acceptable offer $(x_t, 1 - x_t)$ at date t. By refusing player 2's offer, player 1 obtains $\bar{u}_1 + \sum_{\tau=1}^{\infty} \delta_1^{\tau} u_1(x_t)$ while he or she attains a level of utility $\sum_{\tau=0}^{\infty} \delta_1^{\tau} u_1(y_{t-1})$ by accepting. For player 2, it is optimal that these last two quantities be equal, and y_{t-1} is thus defined by:

$$u_1(y_{t-1}) - \bar{u}_1 = \delta_1[u_1(x_t) - \bar{u}_1] \tag{6}$$

Relations (5) and (6) form a system of difference equations describing the offers that one of the players makes at a given date in the knowledge that the other player will make an acceptable offer on the following date. Step by step, it appears that optimal strategies in subgame perfect equilibrium depend on both the *initial date* and the *final date* of the game. If the game begins at $t = 0$, it is player 1 who makes the first offer and the equilibrium corresponds to the partition $(x_0, 1 - x_0)$ where x_0 is the value of x_t deduced from the system of equations (5) and (6) at $t = 0$, with $x_n = 1$. Conversely, if the game begins at $t = 1$, it is player 2 who makes the first offer, and the equilibrium corresponds to partition $(y_1, 1 - y_1)$ where y_1 is the value of y_t deduced from the system of equations (5) and (6) at $t = 1$, with $x_n = 1$. As intuition suggests, preference for the present causes the players to have an interest in coming to terms right at the start of the game.

The hypothesis of a finite horizon lets us define a simple solution to the bargaining. It is seldom adopted, however, since it gives the terminal date of the game such essential importance. Bargaining over wages, for example, is not generally set in such a framework. For this reason, it is no doubt more relevant to take the view that the horizon is a priori infinite, since the date at which a bargaining process will come to an end is rarely spelled out.

2.3.3 Bargaining with an Infinite Horizon (Rubinstein, 1982)

With an infinite horizon, it becomes possible to analyze the stationary strategies of the agents directly. A precise description of the bargaining process will better enable us to grasp the notion of bargaining power.

The Outcome of the Bargaining

When the game horizon is infinite, all subgames beginning on even dates are identical, and the same holds true for all subgames beginning on odd dates. Since the players are rational, offers made on a date t will be the same as the ones that would have been made on date $(t + 2)$. Hence we can characterize a subgame perfect equilibrium based solely on stationary strategies. Let us assume that the strategy of agent 1 consists, on the one hand, of accepting any offer $y \geq y^*$ and refusing any offer $y < y^*$ on odd dates, and on the other of offering x^* on even dates; and let us further assume that the strategy of agent 2 consists of accepting every offer $x \leq x^*$ and refusing every offer $x > x^*$ on even dates, and offering y^* on odd dates. For these two strategies to constitute a subgame perfect equilibrium, x^* must be the highest value that player 2 (who then receives $1 - x^*$) is prepared to accept at every date, given y^*, and y^* must be the smallest value that player 1 (who then receives y^*) is ready to accept, at every date, given x^*.

If, on any odd date, player 1 accepts offer y^*, he or she attains a level of utility $\sum_{t=0}^{\infty} \delta_1^t u_1(y^*)$, while by refusing, he or she obtains $\bar{u}_1 + \sum_{t=1}^{\infty} \delta_1^t u_1(x^*)$. The smallest value y^* that player 1 is prepared to accept at every odd date, given x^*, is then defined by:

$$u_1(y^*) - \bar{u}_1 = \delta_1[u_1(x^*) - \bar{u}_1] \tag{7}$$

Symmetrically, the highest value x^* that player 2 is prepared to accept at every even date, given y^*, is defined by:

$$u_2(1 - x^*) - \bar{u}_2 = \delta_2[u_2(1 - y^*) - \bar{u}_2] \tag{8}$$

In appendix 1 to this chapter, we show that these two equations define a unique solution. The reader may note that relations (7) and (8) could have been obtained by making t go to infinity in equations (5) and (6) describing the solutions of the finite horizon game. As before, it is preference for the present that gives players an incentive to accept an offer. If the game begins on date $t = 0$, player 1 makes the first offer, and the solution to the bargaining is defined by partition $(x^*, 1 - x^*)$, for player 2 is indifferent between accepting this solution now or offering y^* at $t = 1$. Conversely, if the game begins on date $t = 1$, the solution to the bargaining is partition $(y^*, 1 - y^*)$.

Hence the bargaining process is only *virtual* in this model, for the players have no interest in wasting valuable time in bargaining when they know what the unique solution to the bargaining process is. So this model does not explain why bargaining should not be concluded immediately, nor (consequently) why it should be interrupted by strikes. We will see below how conflicts may emerge in such a setting.

Bargaining Power

Although bargaining is taking place virtually, preference for the present plays a very large role. Each player's share decreases with preference for the present, which means that impatience reduces bargaining power. This general result can be illustrated with the help of utility functions $u_1(x) = x$ and $u_2(1 - x) = 1 - x$, from which we get $x^* = (1 - \delta_2)/(1 - \delta_1\delta_2)$ and $y^* = \delta_1(1 - \delta_2)/(1 - \delta_1\delta_2)$. Player 1's share increases with δ_1 and decreases with δ_2. Moreover, scrutiny of this solution shows that there is an advantage in making the first offer, since $x^* > y^*$.

The models of bargaining just laid out are of interest because they describe a process that ends with a unique, noncooperative solution. They show that it is necessary to know with precision the structure of the game, i.e., the whole set of possible actions and the characteristics of the players, in order to define the solution. Note, however, that there exist other noncooperative games capable of representing a bargaining process. Binmore et al. (1986) built a model very close to the one set forth here, in which, for one thing, bargaining can be interrupted at every instant with a positive probability, and for another, it is risk aversion that gives players an incentive to accept a sharing arrangement immediately (see Osborne and Rubinstein, 1990, and chapter 9, section 3.4, this book). Finally, it must be emphasized that, thanks to the precise description of the bargaining process, we now have a better grasp of the notion of bargaining power. In the models we have studied, this notion is linked to a preference for the present. An "impatient" player has less bargaining power than a more patient one. In the model of Binmore et al. (1986), it is risk aversion that determines the power of each player. An agent with low risk aversion will have more bargaining power than an agent more hesitant to face the same risks. In the axiomatic approach, there was no suitable way to get at this idea of bargaining power. Nevertheless, there are linkages between the strategic and axiomatic approaches, which we will now clarify.

2.3.4   The Relationship Between the Axiomatic and the Strategic Approaches

Nash's axiomatic solutions can also be obtained as limit solutions to a noncooperative game in which the interval between two offers has been rendered arbitrarily small. Comparison of these two approaches clarifies the manner in which the status quo points are conceived.

Convergence on Nash's Axiomatic Solution

Binmore et al. (1986) showed that if the interval between successive offers in Rubinstein's game, described above, tends to zero, then the solution converges on the *axiomatic* solution of Nash (1953). When the elapsed time between two successive offers goes to zero, the two players are in the end going to make identical offers. More precisely, we show in appendix 2 to this chapter that if the two players have the same discount rates, the solution to Rubinstein's game goes toward x^N defined by:

$$x^N = \operatorname*{Arg\,Max}_{x}[u_1(x) - \bar{u}_1][u_2(1 - x) - \bar{u}_2]$$

Thus we come back to the axiomatic solution of Nash from section 2.1 above, on the condition that we identify the gains made in a status quo situation with payoffs obtained by the players during the unfolding of the negotiation.

Binmore et al. (1986) and Osborne and Rubinstein (1990) have shown that, starting with the same Rubinstein's bargaining game, we arrive at the generalized Nash solution if we assume that agents have different discount factors or different response times. For example, when the two players have different discount rates, $r_i > 0$, the discount factor of player i takes the expression $\delta_i = e^{-r_i \Delta}$, where Δ represents the interval between two successive offers. When this interval tends to zero, the solution of the Rubinstein bargaining game converges on the following generalized Nash solution (see appendix 2 of this chapter):

$$x^G = \operatorname*{Arg\,Max}_{x}[u_1(x) - \bar{u}_1]^{\gamma}[u_2(1 - x) - \bar{u}_2]^{1-\gamma}, \qquad \gamma = \frac{r_2}{r_1 + r_2} \tag{9}$$

The most impatient player, i.e., the one for whom the discount rate r_i is the highest, has the weakest bargaining power.

The Status Quo Situation

The correspondence between the generalized Nash solution and that of the noncooperative Rubinstein's game thus allows us to define both the status quo situation and the bargaining power of the players with precision. If the game that allows us to obtain the Nash solution is the one proposed by Rubinstein (1982), the payments in a status quo situation are different from those the players would obtain *outside* the relationship. In fact, they coincide with the gains they obtain *during the negotiation*. In the case of wage bargaining between a union and a firm, that means that the status quo payments should not be defined by outside wages for the workers, or by the profits that could have been realized with other wage-earners for the firm. These payments should correspond to what the agents obtain if there is a strike, i.e., what they can receive during the unfolding of the bargaining without resorting to outside opportunities. The latter should therefore appear in the form of *constraints* in the bargaining problem, since each player must, at the conclusion of the bargaining, attain a utility greater than that which outside opportunies offer him or her. More generally, interpretations of the Nash solution are contingent on the noncooperative game that underlies them. Hence, the axiomatic Nash solution can be obtained as the limit solution of a noncooperative game in which the bargaining could be interrupted at any moment with a positive probability. In this case, it is risk aversion and the probability of the negotiation breaking off that determine both the power of each player and the status quo point (see Binmore et al., 1986, and Osborne and Rubinstein, 1990).

The Limits of Rationality

Bargaining theory yields simple models that define the solution of bargaining between rational individuals. The attraction of formal consistency must not, however, hide a certain fragility. A number of experiments—see, for example Ochs and Roth (1989) and the discussion in Kreps (1990)—have in fact sought to test the validity of the theory. They show that the choices of players are frequently different from what the rationality hypothesis and reasoning by backward induction, the foundations of the logic of subgame perfect equilibrium, would predict. For example, we have seen that if one of the players is able to announce an ultimatum in a credible manner, the subgame perfect equilibrium outcome leaves the other player nothing. Numerous experiments show that players rarely adopt such strategies. When placed in these conditions, it appears that the player who is able to announce an ultimatum will rather have a tendency to propose a "fair" partition, leaving a not insignificant part of the pie to the other player. Symmetrically, the other player will tend to refuse a partition that procures him or her a level of utility which he or she views as unfair. Finally, it is worth noting that backward induction in certain circumstances requires chains of reasoning too complex to be systematically followed through by the players.

Despite these limitations, the overwhelming majority of collective bargaining models follow the Rubinstein approach and adopt the generalized Nash solution—a model with simple and precisely defined microeconomic foundations, which can subsequently be enriched by abandoning, or adding, supplementary hypotheses.

2.4 LABOR CONFLICT: STRIKES AND ARBITRATION

The bargaining models presented above do not allow us to investigate labor conflict. Labor conflict is a phenomenon that most often takes the form of strikes (where they are permitted), or, as in the public sector in the United States, arbitration procedures.

2.4.1 Strikes

In the strategic models presented above, strikes are no more than threats which are never carried out, for the players are able to anticipate the consequences of offers and counteroffers perfectly, without having to experience them. There are, however, two ways of accounting for strikes in this context.

First, it is possible to alter the Rubinstein (1982) bargaining model marginally by supposing that the players have a choice between striking or "holding out"— continuing to work under an out-of-date contract during the unfolding of the negotiation. Solutions to the bargaining game then exhibit an array of subgame perfect equilibria, some with a strike and others without (Fernandez and Glazer, 1991). This approach is of interest because it shows that strikes can emerge from a bargaining process in which the actors can choose among a number of strategies in case of disagreement. Its limitation is the lack of a clear criterion for selecting a particular equilibrium from among the various possible equilibria. The predictive power of this strike model is thus very low.

Another course is to assume that the players know each other's characteristics imperfectly. The delays in the bargaining then become a means to force the revelation of the information each agent disposes of. For example, to withstand a strike may be the only action that allows an employer to prove that he or she is incapable of paying a high wage (see the summary of Kennan and Wilson, 1993). The frequency of strikes ought then to rise with the degree of uncertainty about the profitability of firms. Tracy

(1986) tested this prediction using the volatility of the return on shares as a measure of uncertainty about profitability. He does indeed find a positive correlation between strikes and uncertainty. These models with asymmetric information have been enhanced by introducing a choice between striking or holding out. Cramton and Tracy (1992), in their data on labor conflict in the United States over the period 1970–1989, emphasize that holding out is five times more common than striking. This means that it is important to take this characteristic of wage bargaining into account. The model of Cramton and Tracy (1992) predicts that strikes will be more frequent to the extent that past real wages covered by current contracts have shrunk due to inflation, for in this case holding out is more costly for workers. Their empirical results do indeed highlight a positive correlation between frequency of strikes and shrinkage of past wages. The gains to be made by striking or holding out evidently depend on the labor legislation in force. In particular, if the employer is permitted to hire replacement workers during strikes, that reduces the harm a strike can do, and thus ought to exert downward pressure on the wage negotiated. Cramton et al. (1999) studied the effects of legislation allowing the hiring of temporary workers in strike situations, using Canadian data from 1967 to 1993. They estimate that wages are 4% lower, and that the average duration of strikes is two weeks shorter, when such legislation is on the books.

2.4.2 Arbitration

In the United States, arbitration is frequently used in the public sector when strikes are forbidden. The arbitrators are generally experts picked by the employers and unions, following a procedure set out by the government. For example, in selecting an arbitrator for police and firefighters in New Jersey, the New Jersey Public Employment Relations Commission must present a list of seven candidates to representatives of the employers and employees; each side has a right of veto over three of the names, and must rank its preferences among those who remain. Usually arbitration procedures fall into two categories. In *conventional* arbitration, the arbitrator is free to impose a settlement as he or she sees fit. In *final-offer arbitration*, the two sides each make a final offer, and the arbitrator must select one of them.

It is possible to study the effects of arbitration procedures using strategic bargaining models, as long as the objectives of the arbitrator are specified. For example, Farber and Bazerman (1986) assume that the arbitrator attempts to minimize the sum of square deviations between his proposals and the allocations preferred by the parties to the dispute (which permits him or her to maximize his or her chances of being nominated again in the future, according to Faber and Bazerman). Let us consider a conventional arbitration procedure in the bargaining game from section 2.3.1 above, where two players are trying to split up a pie of size 1. When the arbitrator allots share x to player 1, player 2 obtains a complementary share of $1 - x$. If we assume that the players are risk-neutral and that each player wants to obtain the whole pie, the arbitrator's problem can be written as follows:

$$\operatorname*{Min}_{x} \ \alpha(x - 1)^2 + (1 - \alpha)x^2, \qquad 0 < \alpha < 1$$

In this expression, α is a parameter representing the relative weight of player 1 in the arbitrator's goal and the term $(x-1)^2$ (or x^2) designates the square deviation between the share allotted to player 1 (or 2), and his or her preferred allocation. The solution of this problem corresponds to the partition x_a chosen by the arbitrator. It is defined by:

$$x_a = \alpha$$

Let us assume that the players know the arbitrator's preference α imperfectly and that they anticipate values α_1 and α_2, which may turn out to be different. If going to arbitration has a cost denoted by c_i, $i = 1, 2$, (the cost of waiting for the arbitrator's decision, for example), player 1 anticipates that with this procedure, his or her net gain will be equal to $\alpha_1 - c_1$, while player 2 anticipates a net gain amounting to $1 - \alpha_2 - c_2$. Consequently, the players have no interest in going to arbitration if they can agree on a partition x satisfying the two inequalities $x \geq \alpha_1 - c_1$ and $1 - x \geq 1 - \alpha_2 - c_2$. Partitions negotiated without mediation thus fall in the interval $[\alpha_1 - c_1, \alpha_2 + c_2]$. This interval is not empty when $\alpha_1 - c_1 \leq \alpha_2 + c_2$. In the opposite case, which corresponds to inequality $\alpha_1 - \alpha_2 > c_2 + c_1$, the players will resort to arbitration. This model shows that the probability of using the arbitrator diminishes with the sum $(c_2 + c_1)$ of the costs and increases with the relative optimism $(\alpha_1 - \alpha_2)$ of each side.

For the purpose of illustrating this example in a simple context, let us assume that the players know the true value of α, and that the bargaining process is represented by the Rubinstein model from section 2.3.3 above, in which there exists an exogenous probability that the outcome of the negotiation will be settled by conventional arbitration between each offer and counteroffer. More precisely, let us suppose that the probability that the bargaining will break off during the interval of time Δ following a refusal by player i is equal to $e^{\Delta p_i}$. That being so, the bargaining is represented by problem (9) from section 2.3.4 with $\bar{u}_1 = \alpha - c_1$, $\bar{u}_2 = 1 - \alpha - c_2$ and $\gamma = p_2/(p_1 + p_2)$. We then get the solution[2] $x = \gamma(\alpha - c_2) + (1 - \gamma)(\alpha - c_1)$. We see that the outcome of bargaining in the presence of a conventional arbitration procedure depends on the probability of the arbitrator intervening, on the arbitrator's preferences, and on the cost of arbitration. The bargaining model in the presence of a final-offer arbitration procedure comes to the same qualitative conclusions (Farber and Bazerman, 1986; Ashenfelter et al., 1992).

This model shows that decisions assigned to arbitrators play a determining role. They influence not just the occurrence of arbitration procedures, but also the wages settled by bargaining, even without the effective intervention of an arbitrator. Empirical work suggests that arbitrators all have approximately the same criteria, depending on the observable characteristics of employers and employees. In other words, the "interchangeability hypothesis" concerning arbitrators, based on the assumption that arbitrators maximize their probability of being nominated again in the future, which we did assume in the model above, is not generally rejected (Farber and Bazerman, 1986; Ashenfelter, 1987). This model is also compatible with the fact that recourse to an arbitrator is less common when the costs of going to arbitration are higher (Ashenfelter et al., 1992). Moreover, comparing the wages of police officers in states with a system of arbitration and in ones without between 1969 and 1998 in the United States, Ashenfelter and Hyslop (2001) estimate that the presence of a system of arbitration has no significant effect on the average wage, and appears to reduce the dispersion of wages only slightly. Finally, all empirical work suggests that the two arbitration procedures, conventional and final-offer, have similar effects on the frequency of conflicts and on wages.

We have been studying the bargaining process in a very general framework, which might as easily have comprised individual negotiations as collective ones. This has allowed us to present simple models that clarify the factors that influence the partition of surpluses between two protagonists. In what comes next, we will direct our attention to collective bargaining between workers' representatives and employers.

3 STANDARD MODELS OF COLLECTIVE BARGAINING

Models of collective bargaining generally consider an environment with a firm that is able to make positive profits and a union that negotiates wages for all employees. The first model to represent collective bargaining between a firm and a union was the "monopoly union" model of Dunlop (1944), in which the union sets the wage unilaterally, knowing the labor demand of the firm. The "right-to-manage" model (Nickell and Andrews, 1983) generalizes this case by assuming that wages are bargained over, with the employer retaining the prerogative to hire and fire. This hypothesis is actually highly questionable, inasmuch as unions and employers may have an interest in negotiating over variables other than wages. On that basis, two models have arisen: the model of weakly efficient bargaining over wages and employment, and the model of strongly efficient bargaining, in which the protagonists can negotiate about as many variables as they judge necessary.

3.1 THE RIGHT-TO-MANAGE MODEL

The right-to-manage model is a generalization of the union monopoly model, with the assumption that the firm always decides its own labor demand, but that wages are bargained over.

3.1.1 The Negotiated Wage and the Employment Level

Here we consider a union composed of N identical workers. The union's objective is to maximize the expected utility of each of its members, knowing that if the firm's labor demand is less than the number of union members, the employer chooses whom to hire at random. When the wage paid by the firm is equal to w, an individual who is hired attains a level of utility equal to $v(w)$, and one who is not—an unemployed person—obtains $v(\overline{w})$. In this expression, $\overline{w}$ is an exogenous parameter designating the reservation wage, taken to be equivalent to a unemployed person's income. We can assume that a person looking for work can always be hired in a perfectly competitive labor market offering wage $\overline{w}$ to every employee. Unless the opposite is explicitly stated, we will assume that the members of the union are risk-averse ($v'' < 0$). Let L be employment. The union's objective is then written:

$$\mathcal{V}_s = \ell v(w) + (1 - \ell)v(\overline{w}) \qquad \text{with} \qquad \ell \equiv \text{Min}(1, L/N)$$

The union is facing a firm that has a competitive advantage that allows it to make strictly positive profits: its market is protected by entry costs (see chapter 5, section 2.2). When wage w is fixed, the firm's profit takes the form $\Pi = R(L) - wL$, where $R(L)$ designates the revenue function (this function is such that $R' > 0$ and $R'' < 0$). Profit maximization gives the labor demand of the firm: it is defined by $L^d(w) \equiv R'^{-1}(w)$.

In the unfolding of the bargaining process, we will follow the standard practice in the literature and assume that the members of the union get the level of utility of an unemployed person and the employer gets zero profit in case of disagreement. If γ designates the power of the union then the negotiated wage solves the following problem:

$$\text{Max}_{w}[\Pi(w)]^{1-\gamma}[v(w) - v(\overline{w})]^{\gamma}[L^d(w)]^{\gamma} \qquad \text{with} \qquad \Pi(w) \equiv R[L^d(w)] - wL^d(w)$$

subject to:

$$L^d(w) \leq N \qquad \text{and} \qquad w \geq \overline{w}$$

For an interior solution, the maximization of the logarithm of the generalized Nash criterion gives the first-order condition:

$$\frac{\gamma}{L^d(w)}\frac{dL^d(w)}{dw} + \frac{\gamma w v'(w)}{v(w) - v(\overline{w})} + \frac{(1 - \gamma)}{\Pi(w)}\frac{d\Pi(w)}{dw} = 0$$

Let $\eta_w^L = -(w/L)(dL/dw)$ and $\eta_w^\pi = -(w/\Pi)(d\Pi/dw)$ be respectively the absolute values of the elasticity of employment and profit with respect to wages. In general, these quantities depend on the wage w. In order to study their influence on the latter, it proves useful to assume that they are increasing functions of parameters z_L and z_π. In other words, we can posit $\eta_w^L = \eta_w^L(w, z_L)$ and $\eta_w^\pi = \eta_w^\pi(w, z_\pi)$ with $\partial\eta_w^L/\partial z_L > 0$ and $\partial\eta_w^\pi/\partial z_\pi > 0$ by definition. The first-order condition is then written:

$$\Phi(w, \overline{w}, z_L, z_\pi, \gamma) \equiv -\gamma\eta_w^L - (1 - \gamma)\eta_w^\pi + \frac{\gamma w v'(w)}{v(w) - v(\overline{w})} = 0$$

The second-order condition is satisfied when $\Phi_w < 0$. Furthermore, for every parameter x, we have $\partial w/\partial x = -\Phi_x/\Phi_w$. In consequence, $\partial w/\partial x$ is of the sign of Φ_x. Hence, as:

$$\Phi_\gamma = -\eta_w^L + \eta_w^\pi + \frac{w v'(w)}{v(w) - v(\overline{w})} = \frac{\eta_w^\pi}{\gamma} > 0$$

we see that the wage is an *increasing* function of the bargaining power γ of the union. The marginal productivity of labor being equal to this wage, employment decreases with parameter γ. The same reasoning shows that the wage is an increasing function of the income $\overline{w}$ of a jobless person. The reader will also be able to verify that function Φ depends negatively on parameters z_L and z_π. That means that any increase in the absolute value of the wage elasticity of labor demand or profit entails a reduction in the wage.

3.1.2 Markup and Union Power

The first-order condition also allows us to express the difference between the gains made by a worker who is hired and those of a jobless person. Thus we have:

$$\frac{v(w) - v(\overline{w})}{wv'(w)} = \frac{\gamma}{\gamma\eta_w^L + (1-\gamma)\eta_w^\pi} \equiv \mu_s \tag{10}$$

This equation shows that those who are hired have a utility greater than that of the jobless, given that $\gamma > 0$. To be precise, variable μ_s is interpreted as a *markup* indicating the gap between the utility of a worker with a job and that of a jobless person. At the optimum of the bargaining problem, this markup increases with union power γ and decreases with the absolute values of the wage elasticity of labor demand and profit. In the limit case in which the union has all the bargaining power—the "monopoly union" model—the gap between the utility of an employee and that of a jobless person depends only on the wage elasticity of labor demand. When the union's bargaining power is null, workers hired and the jobless have the same gains. Such a situation is generally described as *competitive*, inasmuch as employees get no "rent" with respect to the jobless. The negotiated wage then equals the reservation wage $\overline{w}$.

If the revenue function of the firm is homogeneous of degree $\alpha \in (0,1)$, then we have $\eta_w^L = 1/(1-\alpha)$, $\eta_w^\pi = \alpha/(1-\alpha)$, and $\mu_s = \gamma(1-\alpha)/(\gamma(1-\alpha) + \alpha)$. In this case, shocks to productivity or the firm's selling price do not affect the wage and lead only to employment adjustments. According to Bruno and Sachs (1985), this property makes it possible to explain the rigidity of real wages observed on aggregate data in the OECD countries at the end of the 1970s and beginning of the 1980s (see also chapter 8).

In figure 7.5 we represent the solution of the right-to-manage model. Note that an indifference curve for the union, defined by the equation $L[v(w) - v(\overline{w})] = cst$, has a negative slope in the plane (L, w) when $L \leq N$. Differentiating this equation, one gets:

$$\frac{dw}{dL}\bigg|_{\mathcal{V}_s = cst} = \frac{-[v(w) - v(\overline{w})]}{Lv'(w)} \leq 0$$

$$\frac{d^2w}{dL^2}\bigg|_{\mathcal{V}_s = cst} = \frac{[v(w) - v(\overline{w})]}{L^2[v'(w)]^2}\left\{2v'(w) - \frac{v''(w)[v(w) - v(\overline{w})]}{v'(w)}\right\} \geq 0$$

The indifference curves are thus decreasing and convex. Moreover, they have a horizontal asymptote at the point $w = \overline{w}$ in the plane (w, L). We can also show that an

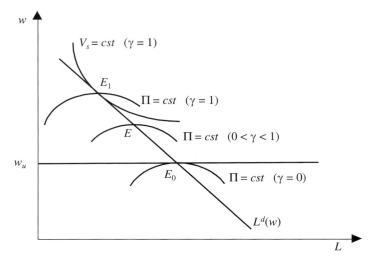

Figure 7.5
The right-to-manage model.

isoprofit curve, defined by the equation $R(L) - wL = cst$, reaches a maximum on the labor demand curve. Differentiating this equation, we get:

$$\frac{dw}{dL}\bigg|_{\Pi=cst} = \frac{R'(L) - w}{L}$$

$$\frac{d^2w}{dL^2}\bigg|_{\Pi=cst} = \frac{LR''(L) - 2[R'(L) - w]}{L^2}$$

The first equation implies that the isoprofit curves have a horizontal tangent on the labor demand curve, where $R'(L) = w$. Moreover, the second equation implies, together with the concavity of $R(L)$, that the isoprofit curves are concave at the point where they cross the labor demand curve, which means that the isoprofit curves reach a maximum on the labor demand curve.

In the right-to-manage model, the solutions lie on the labor demand. If the union's bargaining power is zero, the wage is equal to $\bar{w}$ and the isoprofit curve is tangential to the union's indifference curve at point E_0 (the first-order conditions of profit maximization entail that the isoprofit curves have a zero slope when they cross labor demand). In the other extreme situation, in which the union disposes of all the bargaining power, the solution lies at point E_1, where the indifference curve of the union is tangential to the labor demand. In all cases lying in between $(0 < \gamma < 1)$ the solution lies at point E on the portion of the labor demand delimited by points E_0 and E_1.

The monopoly union model, and more generally the right-to-manage model, come to the conclusion that the bargaining power of unions lowers employment. They are not, however, totally satisfactory, because the union and the employer agree, when

$\gamma > 0$, on a Pareto-inefficient contract. At every point $E \neq E_0$, figure 7.5 shows that the indifference curves and the isoprofit curves are not tangent. Starting from point E, the employer and the union could thus agree on an employment–wage pairing that would raise the level of satisfaction of at least one of them. In this regard, Leontief (1946) pointed out that it was possible to reach Pareto-efficient allocations by bargaining over wages and employment.

3.2 EFFICIENT CONTRACTS

The outcome of collective bargaining is not usually a mere agreement about wage. The number of hours to be worked, working conditions, employment, and union representation are also privileged as objects of negotiation. The right-to-manage model is thus seen to lie relatively far from reality. In this subsection, we will study the properties of collective bargaining over a number of variables. It will be instructive to begin by examining the case in which the bargaining is about just two variables, wages and employment, then extend the analysis to larger numbers of variables. We will see that assuming that bargaining does not concern wages alone leads to very different predictions from those arrived at with the right-to-manage model. In particular, increases in union power are not necessarily bad for employment if a sufficient number of topics are bargained over. Moreover, this approach is useful in overcoming certain limitations of the simple models developed hitherto, which assumed a homogeneous labor force, while in reality unions are generally composed of members with different productivities. Considering unions composed of heterogeneous workers, which bargain over many variables, allows us to show that collective bargaining has a tendency to reduce wage dispersion among workers with different productivities.

3.2.1 Weakly Efficient Contracts

If bargaining is not solely about wages, the other variables to be agreed on must, directly or indirectly, have an influence on the level of employment. For this reason, MacDonald and Solow (1981) proposed to represent collective bargaining by a negotiation over employment and wages at the same time. In this case, the bargaining problem is written:

$$\underset{\{w,L\}}{\text{Max}}[R(L) - wL]^{1-\gamma}[v(w) - v(\overline{w})]^{\gamma} L^{\gamma}$$

subject to:

$$0 \leq L \leq N \qquad \text{and} \qquad w \geq \overline{w}$$

For the interior solutions, differentiating the Nash criterion with respect to L and w, the first-order conditions imply:

$$(1 - \gamma)\frac{R'(L) - w}{R(L) - wL} + \frac{\gamma}{L} = 0$$

$$-(1 - \gamma)\frac{L}{R(L) - wL} + \gamma\frac{v'(w)}{v(w) - v(\overline{w})} = 0$$

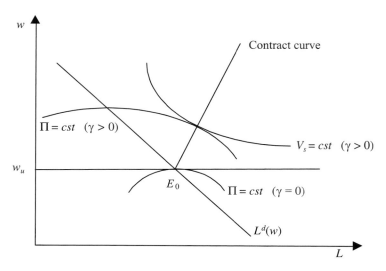

FIGURE 7.6
The model of bargaining over wages and employment.

Eliminating parameter γ between these two relations, we find the equation of the *contract curve*. It is written:

$$w - R'(L) = \frac{v(w) - v(\overline{w})}{v'(w)}$$

This curve represents the locus of the tangency points between the curves of isoprofit and isoutility. Hence, bargaining over wages and employment arrives at a Pareto-optimal contract. Differentiating the equation of the contracts curve gives:

$$\frac{dw}{dL} = \frac{R''(L)}{v''(w)[w - R'(L)]}$$

We see that the contract curve has a positive slope if workers are risk averse $(v'' < 0)$. This situation is represented in figure 7.6, where we see that wages *and* employment increase with the union's bargaining power, since the union utilizes its room for maneuver both to protect workers against the risk of unemployment and to increase their remuneration. When $\gamma = 0$, the negotiated wage is equal to the reservation wage, and employment reaches its "competitive" value as defined by the equality between marginal revenue and $\overline{w}$ (this equality is often called the *productive efficiency* condition). This solution corresponds to point E_0 in figure 7.6. The presence of the union thus entails a level of employment *higher* than that which would prevail in a competitive situation. If workers are risk-neutral $(v'' = 0)$, the contracts curve is a vertical line in plane (L, w), having the competitive level of employment as its abscissa. Employment decreases with the bargaining power of the union only if workers are risk lovers.

The model with bargaining over wages and employment entails a level of employment that equalizes the marginal revenue and the reservation wage $\overline{w}$ only when workers are risk neutral. If workers are risk-averse, this type of bargaining yields overemployment, since the marginal revenue is less than the reservation wage. In other words, bargaining over wages and employment generally does not entail productive efficiency. For this reason, bargaining over employment and wages is frequently described as "weakly efficient."

3.2.2 Strongly Efficient Contracts

A priori, nothing prevents the union and the firm from coming to an agreement over certain variables other than employment and wages, if they have a mutual interest in doing so. Hence we will assume that bargaining also extends to unemployment insurance benefits. We then see that the solution to the bargaining always arrives at an equalization of the marginal revenue from labor and the reservation wage.

The Indifference Principle

Let b be the unemployment benefit paid to each unemployed union member. Assuming that a jobless person can receive income $\overline{w}$ under all circumstances, he or she then attains a level of utility equal to $v(\overline{w} + b)$. In this static framework, such an unemployment benefit can also be interpreted as a severance payment given to workers forced to leave the firm. In this case, the number N of workers bargaining with the firm is equal to the number of employees present in the firm at the beginning of the period taken into consideration (see Booth, 1995b, for example). Let us consider the situation in which bargaining extends directly to wages w and unemployment benefit b, with the firm preserving the "right to manage." Let $\mathscr{C} = (w, b)$, $w \geq \overline{w} + b$ be a contract of this type. We will show that, if workers are risk-averse ($v'' < 0$), this contract is Pareto dominated by a contract $\hat{\mathscr{C}} = (\hat{w}, \hat{b})$ giving the same utility to the jobless and to employees, whatever the level L of employment. To that end, let us define the components of $\hat{\mathscr{C}}$ in the following manner:

$$\hat{w} = \ell w + (1 - \ell)(\overline{w} + b) \qquad \text{with} \qquad \ell = \text{Min}(L/N, 1) \text{ and } \hat{b} = \hat{w} - \overline{w}$$

By construction, contract $\hat{\mathscr{C}}$ satisfies $v(\hat{w}) = v(\hat{b} + \overline{w})$. Moreover, risk aversion entails:

$$v(\hat{w}) = v[\ell w + (1 - \ell)(\overline{w} + b)] \geq \ell v(w) + (1 - \ell)v(\overline{w} + b)$$

Let $\mathscr{V}_s$ and $\hat{\mathscr{V}_s}$ be the expected utility of a union member with contract $\mathscr{C}$ and contract $\hat{\mathscr{C}}$, respectively. We then have:

$$\hat{\mathscr{V}_s} = \ell v(\hat{w}) + (1 - \ell)v(\overline{w} + \hat{b}) = v(\hat{w}) \geq \mathscr{V}_s$$

Thus the union always prefers contract $\hat{\mathscr{C}}$ to contract $\mathscr{C}$. As well, it is easy to verify that the firm is indifferent. Employment L being the same in both types of contract, revenue $R(L)$ is thus identical. A simple calculation shows that the total wage bill does not change either. It is given by:

$$\hat{w}L + \hat{b}(N - L) = \hat{w}L + (\hat{w} - \overline{w})(N - L) = \hat{w}L - \overline{w}(N - L)$$
$$= [Lw + (N - L)(w - \overline{w})] - \overline{w}(N - L) = wL + b(N - L)$$

The passage from contract $\mathscr{C}$ to contract $\hat{\mathscr{C}}$ thus involves an improvement in the Pareto sense. In consequence, optimal contracts will respect the "indifference principle" $v(w) = v(\overline{w} + b)$. Workers are then perfectly insured against the risks of unemployment, without that affecting the value of the firm's profit. Note that this conclusion does not depend on the employer's attitude to risk, since revenues and total wage bills are strictly identical for the two types of contract $\mathscr{C}$ and $\hat{\mathscr{C}}$.

The Optimal Contract

On the basis of the foregoing, when unemployment benefits are included in the negotiated variables, it is enough to study contracts of the form $\mathscr{C} = (b + \overline{w}, b)$. Profit is then written:

$$\Pi = R(L) - \overline{w}L - bN$$

We see that, from the point of view of the firm, it is as if it were paying wage b to all members of the union, and compensating those who were actually working by offering them a supplement $\overline{w}$. Profit maximization thus defines a labor demand L^* independent of the unemployment benefit b. The firm simply makes marginal revenue equal to the reservation wage: $\overline{w} = R'(L^*)$. In sum, the negotiation will only concern the unemployment benefits b. We will assume that in case of disagreement the firm does not pay these benefits. Moreover, its profit is zero in this case, because it is assumed that nobody is working. The utility of each worker then being equal to $v(\overline{w})$, the contribution $\mathscr{V}_s - v(\overline{w})$ of the union to the Nash problem is equal to $v(b + \overline{w}) - v(\overline{w})$. The reader will note that the union's objective is independent of the level of employment, since all workers are insured against the risk of unemployment. If we assume $L^* < N$, the bargaining problem takes the form:

$$\underset{b}{\text{Max}}[R(L^*) - \overline{w}L^* - bN]^{1-\gamma}[v(\overline{w} + b) - v(\overline{w})]^{\gamma}$$

The optimal level of unemployment benefits is then defined by:

$$\frac{v(\overline{w} + b) - v(\overline{w})}{v'(\overline{w} + b)} = \frac{\gamma}{1 - \gamma} \frac{[R(L^*) - \overline{w}L^* - bN]}{N} \quad \text{with} \quad w = \overline{w} + b \text{ and } R'(L^*) = \overline{w}$$

The possibility of bargaining over the amount of the unemployment benefits as well thus has the effect of making the level of employment equal to its *competitive* value. The union members obtain a portion of the firm's profit, which increases with their bargaining power, without that causing reduced production or employment. In this context, the contract curve, which is the locus of the tangency points between the union's isoutility curves and the firm's isoprofit curves, is a vertical line defined by the relation $R'(L) = \overline{w}$. For an optimal contract, the utility function of the union

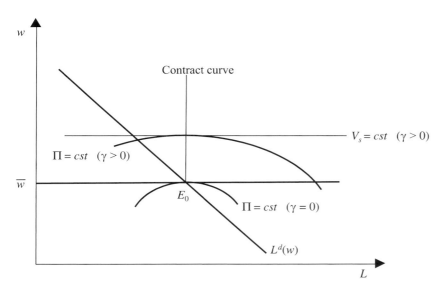

FIGURE 7.7
The strongly efficient bargaining model.

is written $V_s = v(w)$, and the expression of the firm's profit is $\Pi = R(L) - \overline{w}L - (w - \overline{w})N$. We thus get:

$$\left. \frac{dw}{dL} \right|_{V_s = cst} = 0 \quad \text{and} \quad \left. \frac{dw}{dL} \right|_{\Pi = cst} = \frac{R'(L) - \overline{w}}{N}$$

The graphic representation of the strongly efficient bargaining model is given in figure 7.7. In this model the opportunity to bargain over unemployment benefits makes it possible to insure workers against the risk of unemployment. Bargaining of this kind, which reconciles productive efficiency and Pareto efficiency between the union and the firm, is called strongly efficient, in order to distinguish it from bargaining limited to employment and wages, in which it is impossible to arrive at productive efficiency when workers are risk-averse.

3.2.3 Collective Bargaining and Wage Dispersion

Collective bargaining generally covers workers whose productive characteristics are heterogeneous. Very frequently, workers with different skill levels are represented by the same union. We will show that collective bargaining models suggest a tendency to reduce the spread of wages, as compared to a situation in which workers are remunerated at their marginal productivity. This result is confirmed by empirical studies (see section 6.1.2).

Let us consider a firm with two types of workers indexed by $i = 1, 2$, whose revenue is given by $R(L_1, L_2)$, where L_i designates the number of employed workers of type i, and R is a concave function increasing with respect to each of its arguments. Workers of type 1 have higher productivity than workers of type 2, which leads to a higher reservation wage for workers of type 1. By hypothesis, we thus have $\overline{w}_1 > \overline{w}_2$. Assuming that the firm's employment pool comprises N_i workers of type i, a utilitarian union representing all the workers has as its objective:

$$\mathcal{V}_s = \sum_{i=1}^{2} L_i v(w_i) + (N_i - L_i)v(\overline{w}_i + b_i), \qquad L_i \le N_i$$

In this expression, b_i designates the amount of unemployment benefits paid to a worker of type i by the firm. We assume that the bargaining is strongly efficient. That means that it covers unemployment benefits as well as employment and wages. As in the preceding model with a homogeneous workforce, employees' risk aversion always entails the indifference principle. Thus, the optimal contract necessarily satisfies $w_i = \overline{w}_i + b_i$, $i = 1, 2$. The Nash problem is then written:

$$\underset{\{b_1, b_2, L_1, L_2\}}{\text{Max}} \left[R(L_1, L_2) - \sum_{i=1}^{2} (\overline{w}_i L_i + b_i N_i) \right]^{1-\gamma} \left[\sum_{i=1}^{2} N_i [v(\overline{w}_i + b_i) - v(\overline{w}_i)] \right]^{\gamma}$$

subject to:

$$0 \le L_i \le N_i, \qquad i = 1, 2$$

The first-order conditions are found by setting to zero the derivatives with respect to L_i and b_i of the logarithm of the Nash criterion. For the interior solutions, we thus get:

$$\frac{\partial R(L_1, L_2)}{\partial L_i} = \overline{w}_i, \qquad i = 1, 2 \tag{11}$$

$$v'(\overline{w}_i + b_i) = \frac{(1-\gamma)[\sum_{i=1}^{2} N_i [v(\overline{w}_i + b_i) - v(\overline{w}_i)]]}{\gamma [R(L_1, L_2) - \sum_{i=1}^{2} (\overline{w}_i L_i + b_i N_i)]}, \qquad i = 1, 2 \tag{12}$$

Equality (11) is a consequence of the hypothesis of strongly efficient bargaining. It indicates that the marginal productivity of each type of worker is equal to his or her reservation wage: the condition of productive efficiency is thus satisfied for each skill category. The right-hand side of equation (12) is a quantity independent of index i, so the wages $w_i = \overline{w}_i + b_i$ of the two types of worker are identical. Collective bargaining thus leads to the same wage level for the two types of worker, even though their productivities are different. This result is due to the properties of the utilitarian criterion of the union. All the workers being identical in terms of preference, and all having the same weight in the union's objective, the concavity of function $v(.)$ entails that the union always prefers a contract offering identical wages. Formally, this property can be proved with inequality:

$$\frac{N_1}{N_1 + N_2} v(w_1) + \frac{N_2}{N_1 + N_2} v(w_2) \le v \left[\frac{N_1}{N_1 + N_2} w_1 + \frac{N_2}{N_1 + N_2} w_2 \right]$$

According to this inequality, given a contract offering wage w_i to N_i workers of type i, the union's contribution to the Nash criterion will always be greater with a contract offering the same wage, equal to $[(N_1/(N_1 + N_2))w_1 + (N_2/(N_1 + N_2))w_2]$, to all the workers. Collective bargaining thus reduces wage dispersion with respect to a competitive situation in which each worker would receive his or her reservation wage $\overline{w}_i$. It should be noted that the equalization of the wages of different types of worker is obtained under very restrictive hypotheses. In particular, the union has to attribute the same importance to the different categories of worker, and the bargaining must be strongly or weakly efficient (it can be verified that bargaining over employment and wages also ends in equalized wages). Conversely, bargaining over wages alone generally arrives at a different result, since the wage of each manpower category depends on the labor demand elasticity of that particular category. This model nevertheless illustrates the fact that collective bargaining potentially has the effect of reducing the spread of wages.

3.3   IS BARGAINING EFFICIENT?

We have just seen that collective bargaining leads to efficient contracts if unions and firms do actually bargain over wages, employment, and perhaps other variables like unemployment insurance benefits or severance payments. Manning (1987), Espinosa and Rhee (1989), and Strand (1989) have suggested that a contract covering employment and wages is more difficult to negotiate than a contract simply covering wages, inasmuch as an efficient choice of the level of employment of each type of manpower requires a thorough knowledge of the firm and must prescribe contingent contracts when the environment is uncertain, as the analysis developed in chapter 6 shows. On the other hand, bargaining over unemployment benefits or severance payments raises incentive problems that may prevent the achievement of efficient contracts.

3.3.1   Negotiations over Employment

The model of Manning (1987) starts with the principle that the power of the union varies according to which variables are being bargained over. It nonetheless adopts the same sequence of decisions as that of the right-to-manage model, i.e., the firm and the union agree at the outset on the amount w of wages. Knowing that, they launch a bargaining process over the level of employment, the outcome of which corresponds to the solution of the following Nash problem:

$$\text{Max}_{L}[R(L) - wL]^{1-\gamma_L}[v(w) - v(\overline{w})]^{\gamma_L}L^{\gamma_L}$$

subject to:

$$0 \leq L \leq N$$

Parameter $\gamma_L \in [0, 1]$ designates the power of the union during the bargaining over *employment*. The solution of this problem defines labor demand, or $L = \hat{L}(\gamma_L, \overline{w}, w)$, a function of wage w negotiated beforehand, bargaining power γ_L, and reservation wage $\overline{w}$. Bargaining over wages takes this labor demand $\hat{L}$ into account and is represented by another Nash problem:

$$\underset{w}{\text{Max}}[R(L) - wL]^{1-\gamma}[v(w) - v(\overline{w})]^{\gamma}(L)^{\gamma}$$

subject to:

$$L = \hat{L}(\gamma_L, \overline{w}, w) \qquad \text{and} \qquad w \geq \overline{w}$$

Parameter $\gamma \in [0, 1]$ designates the power of the union during the bargaining over *wages*. The two-stage solution of this bargaining process corresponds to that of the right-to-manage model if $\gamma_L = 0$, and to that of the weakly efficient contract model when $\gamma_L = \gamma$. In all other cases, the solution is not found either on labor demand or the contract curve.

Manning (1987) justifies this description of the unfolding of negotiations by arguing that wages, in general, are determined before employment is, but that that does not mean that unions never play a part in determining the level of employment. He also points out that bargaining over wages takes place at a more centralized level than bargaining over employment. The latter is often informal in nature and takes place primarily at the level of the firm or the plant. These two reasons can indeed justify a representation of bargaining by a two-stage process, as well as different bargaining powers according to whether the bargaining is taking place over wages or employment. The model of Manning (1987) offers the advantage of showing that bargaining over employment and wages does not necessarily conclude with an efficient contract. It is not, however, completely satisfying, for the two-stage representation, strictly separating bargaining over employment from bargaining over wages, has no precise theoretical foundation. It is, moreover, difficult to interpret the difference between bargaining power over employment and bargaining power over wages, on the basis of a noncooperative game.

Espinosa and Rhee (1989) and Strand (1989), starting from a different perspective, arrive at a conclusion close to that of Manning (1987). They consider a repeated game with an infinite horizon, in which a union and a firm bargain over wages at predetermined dates. In this framework, the decision to bargain over employment corresponds to a cooperative strategy within a strategic structure of the prisoner's dilemma type. The firm has an interest in bargaining over employment, and in hiring workers whose marginal productivity is lower than their wage, only if the union agrees to lower wages. But once wage concessions have been extracted, the firm has an interest in renouncing its implicit undertaking regarding employment by equalizing the marginal productivity of labor to wages. Espinosa and Rhee (1989) and Strand (1989) exploit the properties of repeated games in order to show that bargaining will only implicitly cover employment if the firm has a sufficiently weak preference for the present. They further prove the existence of values of the firm's discount rate for which the solution of the bargaining lies between the labor demand curve and the contract curve.

These contributions suggest, overall, that the right-to-manage model, and the model of bargaining over wages and employment represent limit cases of the same model.

3.3.2   Negotiations over Unemployment Benefits or Severance Payments

Negotiations over unemployment benefits or severance payments raise incentive problems that may constitute a barrier to obtaining efficient contracts. The strongly efficient bargaining model just presented does indeed come to the conclusion that the jobless, or workers who are fired, have a level of welfare *identical* to that of workers who are employed. The majority of empirical studies (see, for example, Atkinson and Micklewright, 1991, and Clark and Oswald, 1994) find that unemployment benefits are far from offering perfect insurance. The situation of those who do have a job is preferable to that of the jobless. Imperfect unemployment insurance may come from a moral hazard problem (see chapter 6). Kiander (1993) shows that it may be optimal to insure workers partially if excessively high unemployment benefits reduce the job search effort of the unemployed, and if checking on this effort proves too costly. Kiander's analysis applies to a representative union in a position to set unemployment benefits at a centralized level, as in Sweden, for example. The moral hazard problem is even clearer at the local level. It lets us understand why unions do not generally negotiate supplementary unemployment insurance at the level of firms in their labor pool. Benefits of this kind would risk attracting a large number of unemployed persons, which would cut back the profits of firms and the wages of workers in that labor pool. Layard et al. (1991, p. 95) have in fact observed that, with very few exceptions, collective agreements signed at the level of the firm do not make provision for unemployment benefits.

To this point we have assumed that the union represented all the workers in the labor pool of the firm in question. At bargaining time, however, workers do not all have the same status. Some are unemployed, while others have a job. Actually, the unemployed are generally excluded from the bargaining process. They are "outsiders," with no power to influence the decisions of firms. Conversely, the "insiders"—the employees—can defend their interests and exploit position advantages without having to worry about the effects on the outsiders. Does this exclusion of outsiders from the bargaining explain their exclusion from employment? This is the question the following section will try to answer.

4   INSIDERS AND OUTSIDERS

Numerous contributions have explored the consequences of the opposition between insiders and outsiders (see the survey of Lindbeck and Snower, 2001). Following Blanchard and Summers (1986), Gottfries and Horn (1987), and Lindbeck and Snower (1987), we will assume that the insiders bargain over their remuneration collectively.

These authors, to whom must be added Layard et al. (1991), have maintained that the opposition between insiders and outsiders might constitute an important source of unemployment, and might also explain its persistence. This result is not, however, confirmed by empirical observation, and on top of that, it is arrived at by arbitrarily limiting the set of variables covered by the bargaining. If we abandon these restrictions, we see that the opposition between insiders and outsiders gives us an explanation for the *segmentation* of the labor market rather than for the persistence of unemployment.

4.1 INSIDERS AND THE PERSISTENCE OF UNEMPLOYMENT

The specific human capital of insiders and the costs of hiring and firing entail that insiders have the chance to exploit a position advantage, for they can obtain a wage higher than the wage for which the outsiders would be willing to work, with no danger to their jobs, as long as the cost of replacing them is sufficiently high. The opposition between insiders and outsiders should thus make it possible to explain why firms refuse to hire persons willing to work for wages lower than those being paid to the insiders.

4.1.1 The Wage–Employment Relationship

We will work with a model close to that of Lindbeck and Snower (1987, 1988) in which the firm cannot hire an outsider unless it keeps all its insiders. It is then possible to show that there is a decreasing relationship between the negotiated wage and the initial stock of insiders.

A Simple Model

In the insiders–outsiders model, it is important to pinpoint how, and after how long, a person just hired—an "entrant"—accedes to the status of insider. We will sidestep the complications linked to this aspect of the problem by taking the view that the firm and the insiders negotiate in a timeframe limited to a single period. That being so, the future of entrants plays no part in the choice criteria of the insiders, since at the end of this period entrants do not become insiders. More precisely, we will assume that the firm disposes of a stock L_0 of insiders and that it must decide on the number $L_I \leq L_0$ that it wants to retain, as well as the number $L_E \geq 0$ of outsiders that it wants to hire. To simplify, we take it that insiders and entrants are perfectly substitutable in production. The firm's revenue is then written $R(L_I + L_E)$. Nonetheless, we will assume that it is impossible to replace insiders with outsiders, an impossibility explained by, among other things, hiring and firing costs (which for simplicity do not appear in the model; see Lindbeck and Snower, 1988, for a more complete analysis). We could also take into account the productivity differential between insiders and outsiders by, for example, adopting the representation $R(L_I + aL_E)$ with $a < 1$. This formulation would measurably increase the complexity of the exposition without changing the general import of the results (see also Lindbeck and Snower, 1988). We assume, too, that all employees receive the same wage w.

The setting for the analysis is the right-to-manage hypothesis. The insiders then bargain over wages with the employer, who subsequently adjusts employment so as to maximize his or her revenue. The firm's profit is written:

$$\Pi = R(L_I + L_E) - w(L_I + L_E)$$

Labor demand is broken down into L_I insiders and L_E entrants. It is found by maximizing profit subject to constraints $L_I \leq L_0$ and $L_E \geq 0$. Let us define wage w_0 by $R'(L_0) \equiv w_0$ and let $\tilde{L}$ be the level of employment such that the marginal revenue equals the current wage, or $R'(\tilde{L}) \equiv w$. Labor demand then takes the following form:

$$L_I = \tilde{L} \quad \text{and} \quad L_E = 0 \quad \text{if } w \geq w_0 \tag{13}$$

$$L_I = L_0 \quad \text{and} \quad L_E = \tilde{L} - L_0 \quad \text{if } w \leq w_0 \tag{14}$$

The marginal revenue being decreasing, relation (13) entails that, if $w > w_0$, the insiders do not keep all their jobs, for we then have $L_I = \tilde{L} < L_0$.

The Negotiated Wage

The expected utility of an insider is written:

$$\mathscr{V}_I = \ell v(w) + (1 - \ell)v(\overline{w}), \qquad \ell \equiv \text{Min}(1, \tilde{L}/L_0)$$

In this expression, revenue $\overline{w}$ again designates the reservation wage. It corresponds to what each employee gets in case no agreement is reached. During the bargaining, the insiders give no consideration to the outsiders and their contribution $\mathscr{V}_I - v(\overline{w})$ to the Nash problem is then equal to $\ell[v(w) - v(\overline{w})]$. Let $\gamma \in (0, 1)$ be the bargaining power of the insiders; the wage is the solution of the problem:

$$\underset{w}{\text{Max}}[\Pi(w)]^{1-\gamma}\{\ell[v(w) - v(\overline{w})]\}^{\gamma} \quad \text{with} \quad \Pi(w) \equiv R(\tilde{L}) - w\tilde{L} \tag{15}$$

Let w_1 be the solution of this problem when $\ell = \tilde{L}/L_0$. The negotiated wage is then the same as with a "standard" union having L_0 members; it is defined by equation (10). Let w_2 be the wage when $\ell = 1$; this wage is given by an equation identical to (10) with $\eta_w^L = 0$, since the insiders are indifferent to employment. Thus, we get:

$$\frac{v(w_2) - v(\overline{w})}{w_2 v'(w_2)} = \frac{\gamma}{(1 - \gamma)\eta_w^{\pi}}$$

Wage w negotiated between the insiders and the firm then takes three different values according to the initial number of insiders L_0, and thus according to the wage $w_0 \equiv R'(L_0)$:

(i) If $w_1 \geq w_0$, then $w = w_1$ and $L_I = L_1$, $L_E = 0$ with $R'(L_1) = w_1$

(ii) If $w_2 \leq w_0$, then $w = w_2$ and $L_I = L_0$, $L_I + L_E = L_2$ with $R'(L_2) = w_2$

(iii) If $w_1 \leq w_0 \leq w_2$, then $w = w_0$ and $L_I = L_0$, $L_E = 0$

In figure 7.8 we portray the relationship between the initial stock L_0 of insiders, the negotiated wage w, and the optimal levels of employment L_I and $L = L_I + L_E$. We see that wage w is a *decreasing* function of L_0 whereas L_I and L increase with L_0.

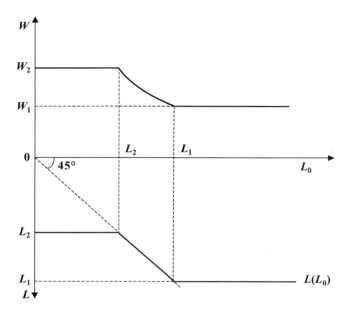

FIGURE 7.8
Wage and employment in the insiders/outsiders model.

In case (i), the initial stock of insiders is in a sense too large ($L_0 \geq L_1$) and a certain number of them are fired. Conversely, in case (ii), this stock proves too small ($L_0 \leq L_2$) and the firm has to hire outsiders, but since the wage is higher than it is in (i), total employment is less. Finally, in the intermediate case (iii), total employment is simply equal to the initial stock L_0 of insiders. The employer has no interest in getting rid of a portion of his or her insiders, for if they were fewer they would receive a higher wage. Neither does he or she have an interest in hiring outsiders whose marginal revenue would be less than their wage.

4.1.2   An Explanation for the Persistence of Unemployment

In many respects, the decreasing relationship between the negotiated wage and the initial stock of insiders, as shown in figure 7.8, constitutes the main characteristic of theories of unemployment based on the power of insiders. According to Blanchard and Summers (1986), Lindbeck and Snower (1987), and Gottfries and Horn (1987), this relationship yields an explanation for the *persistence* of unemployment. If, at a given moment, the number of insiders is diminished, the wage negotiated for the following period will indeed remain constant or increase, and employment will on average have a tendency to fall. In other words, when the insiders are few—with consequent high levels of unemployment and temporary employment—those insiders get no benefit from negotiating low wages, for they do not risk losing their jobs. Low wages would diminish their satisfaction and would make it possible to hire outsiders, some of whom would later become insiders—and this would have the effect of bringing down the future wages of those holding a job in the present. Accordingly, unemployment does not lower wages when the power to bargain over remuneration belongs solely to insiders.

Empirical work that tries to estimate a relationship between wages and lagged employment generally rejects the predictions of the insiders–outsiders model (Lever, 1995). Admittedly, Nickell and Wadhwani (1990) have highlighted the existence of such an effect, albeit slight, using data from firms in the United Kingdom, but Layard et al. (1991, p. 202) point out that this result is not robust for other samples of firms. Holmund and Zetterberg (1991) have estimated wage equations on sectoral data for Sweden, Norway, Finland, Germany, and the United States, with lagged employment included. This variable is significant only in Germany, but with a positive sign, which is the reverse of the sign predicted by the model just set out.

This divergence between facts and theory might derive from a circumscribed representation of bargaining. The explanation for the persistence of unemployment assumes in particular that insiders do not negotiate either a severance payment or a specific wage for possible entrants. We will show that if we permit the protagonists to sign contracts more complex than the one considered in the basic model, the consequences of the opposition between insiders and outsiders change.

4.2 INSIDERS AND LABOR MARKET SEGMENTATION

If bargaining over unemployment benefits is rare, bargaining over severance payments, on the contrary, proves to be frequent (see Layard et al., 1991, p. 95, and Hartog and Theeuwes, 1993). Hence it is important to take this item of bargaining into account in models in which insiders are explicitly distinguished from outsiders. Moreover, we shall reconsider the hypothesis that the wages of outsiders are identical to those of insiders. In fact, firms often use temporary workers, whose status is much less favored than that of insiders.

4.2.1 Bargaining Leading to a Competitive Level of Employment

In order to take these characteristics of the wage relationship into account, we will assume that the insiders negotiate their own wage w, severance payments b_L and a wage w_E for entrants. An insider who is fired thus obtains a utility equal to $v(\overline{w} + b_L)$. Severance payments constitute a means of insuring workers against the risk of losing their jobs, and, just as in the case where bargaining covered unemployment insurance premiums (see section 3.2.3), the indifference principle applies. In other words, contracts that insure insiders perfectly against the risk of losing their jobs are dominant according to the Pareto criterion. For given (L_E, L_I, w_E) and for every contract $\mathscr{C}_L = (w, b_L)$, it is indeed possible to associate a contract $\hat{\mathscr{C}}_L = (\hat{w}, \hat{b}_L)$ defined by:

$$\hat{w} = \ell w + (1 - \ell)(\overline{w} + b_L) \quad \text{with} \quad \hat{b}_L = \hat{w} - \overline{w} \quad \text{and} \quad \ell = \text{Min}(L_I/L_0, 1)$$

When insiders are risk-averse, the same proof as the one in section 3.2.3 would show that contract $\hat{\mathscr{C}}_L$ is strictly preferred to contract $\mathscr{C}_L$ by the insiders, while the firm is indifferent between these two contracts. This result leads us to consider only contracts for which $w = \overline{w} + b_L$; the insiders are then perfectly insured against the risk of job loss. As in the case of a strike, they attain a level of utility $v(\overline{w})$, and their contribution $\mathscr{V}_I - v(\overline{w})$ to the Nash problem is equal to $v(\overline{w} + b_L) - v(\overline{w})$. Symmetrically, the contribution of the employer to the Nash problem is equal to his or her profit:

$$\Pi = R(L_I + L_E) - w_E L_E - \overline{w} L_I - b_L L_0 \tag{16}$$

Since the wage w_E of the entrants has a negative effect on the firm's profit, and has no weight in the objective of the insiders, maximization of the Nash criterion dictates that this wage be set at the lowest possible level; so we will always have $w_E = \overline{w}$. When the firm retains the right to manage, the expression (16) of profit shows that labor demand necessarily satisfies:

$$R'(L_I + L_E) = \overline{w} \tag{17}$$

In other words, total employment is equal to its *competitive* value. All the firm does is decide on its composition (hires of outsiders or fires of employees in place) according to the value of the initial stock L_0 of insiders. More precisely, if L_u designates the competitive level of employment, defined by $R'(L_u) \equiv \overline{w}$, the firm's labor demand takes the following form:

$$L_I = L_u \quad \text{and} \quad L_E = 0 \quad \text{if } L_u \leq L_0$$

$$L_I = L_0 \quad \text{and} \quad L_E = L_u - L_0 \quad \text{if } L_u \geq L_0$$

Bargaining between the insiders and the firm now covers only the amount b_L of the severance payment. The optimal value of the latter corresponds to the solution of the Nash problem:

$$\underset{b_L}{\text{Max}}[\Pi(b_L)]^{1-\gamma}[v(\overline{w} + b_L) - v(\overline{w})]^{\gamma} \quad \text{with} \quad \Pi(b_L) \equiv R(L_u) - \overline{w} L_u - b_L L_0$$

4.2.2   Discrimination or Unemployment?

This model leads to conclusions very different from those of the simple model of section 4.1.1, in which the wages of insiders and outsiders were taken to be identical. Here, employment is always equal to its competitive level, whatever the initial number of insiders taking part in the bargaining. Being perfectly insured against the risk of job loss, they use their bargaining power to obtain the highest possible wage $(\overline{w} + b_L)$. It is easy to verify that the optimal level of b_L is increasing with γ. Moreover, insiders who are few in number have an interest in seeing the firm hire workers at the reservation wage in order to increase profit, and thus indirectly their wages. In this sense, the insiders exploit the entrants, profiting from their bargaining power to extract a portion of the profits realized through the labor of the entrants. In other words, the insiders have no interest in opposing the hiring of outsiders as long as that is profitable for the firm, since what is profitable for the firm is profitable for them as well. These observations show that the opposition between insiders and outsiders, as Fehr (1990) points out, induces *discrimination* rather than unemployment. Certain workers capture a portion of the rent thanks to the acquisition of specific human capital, for example, or the existence of firing costs, or the costs of looking for manpower. These workers have an interest in exploiting this situation by tilting the partition of the value added to their own advantage.

Evidently this description of the segmentation of manpower is relevant only if the insiders are able to keep the entrants in a situation less favorable than their own over the long run. Legal constraints that impede recourse to temporary labor and subcontracting, and the power that entrants may gradually acquire, might set limits to the discrimination imposed by the insiders. Formally, we could incorporate a limit on the possibility of discrimination by supposing that the firm is constrained to pay the same wage to all its employees. We then return to a model in which the set of possible contracts has been voluntarily curtailed, and the conclusions lie in the vicinity of those obtained when we assumed that all workers received the same wage: the power of insiders has a negative effect on the level of employment, and unemployment can stubbornly persist.

The models developed to this point leave out the existence of capital and the opportunity to trade off among different values of the number of hours worked. These topics are examined in the next section.

5   INVESTMENT AND HOURS

In this section, we will enrich our collective bargaining models in two ways. First we will focus on the interaction between wage bargaining and investment decisions, which can entail inefficiencies caused by the *irreversibility* of investments. We will see that if the union is able to *renegotiate* agreements already reached, the level of investment is generally suboptimal. Second, in examining labor supply and demand in chapters 1 and 3, we saw that work schedules constitute an important element in the labor relationship. Work schedules can be negotiated collectively, just as wages and employment can.

5.1   NEGOTIATIONS AND INVESTMENT

The traditional models of labor demand presented in chapter 4 suggested that unions have an ambiguous effect on investment. By raising wages, the union tends to favor the substitution of capital for labor, which increases investment. But upward pressure on wages also exerts scale effects that work in the opposite direction. Bargaining influences investment in yet other ways related to the incompleteness of contracts. The fact is that, once installed, equipment generally cannot be modified without cost, and if it is not utilized, the firm risks suffering substantial losses. This characteristic of equipment means that firms have an incentive to invest less if bargaining over wages can be begun at any time, for once the investment has been made, employees are tempted to demand a new round of bargaining in order to benefit from the improved productivity induced by the increase in capital stock. Conversely, if renegotiation is impossible, firms do invest more, and all agents benefit from the extra investment (Grout, 1984). This is the "holdup" problem already encountered in chapter 4, and which we will return to in chapter 9. It crops up when collective agreements lead to incomplete contracts that can be renegotiated.

5.1.1 Contracts Without Renegotiation

In order to highlight the holdup problem, we consider a firm whose revenue function $R(K, L)$ is strictly concave and strictly increasing with capital K and employment L. In order to concentrate on the choice of level of investment, we will assume that employment is given. This hypothesis is no doubt restrictive, but the results derived do not differ in substance from those obtained with a labor demand dependent on wages (see Anderson and Devereux, 1988). We will assume as well that the firm chooses its capital stock unilaterally. In consequence, only wages w are negotiated. If r designates the user cost of capital, the firm's profit is written:

$$\Pi = R(K, L) - wL - rK \tag{18}$$

Employment L being fixed, we need not consider the possibility of bargaining over unemployment insurance or severance payments. Hence an employee obtains a level of utility $v(w)$ if he or she works and $v(\overline{w})$ in case of disagreement. Since L is a constant, we can neglect this variable in the union's contribution to the Nash problem, which is thus simply equal to $v(w) - v(\overline{w})$. The firm's contribution to the Nash problem depends on the possibility of wages being renegotiated. If the union can undertake in a credible manner not to demand new wage negotiations once the investment has been made, the firm takes wages as *given* in making its decisions about equipment. Formally that amounts to supposing that investment decisions are made *after* wage bargaining. Conversely, if it is not possible for the union to commit itself in a credible manner to the wage, then we can regard investment decisions as being made *before* wage bargaining. Wages then become a function of the capital stock, and the firm takes this linkage into account when the time comes to choose its volume of equipment (see Grout, 1984; van der Ploeg, 1987; Anderson and Devereux, 1988; Devereux and Lockwood, 1991).

If the union can undertake credibly not to reopen wage negotiations, the firm does not run the risk of making an investment that could be immobilized by a strike, leading to losses. Under those conditions, its losses are zero, and its contribution to the Nash problem is identical to the profit given by relation (18). The optimal level of capital K^* is then obtained by maximizing profit at a given wage; it is defined by equation:

$$R_K(K^*, L) = r \tag{19}$$

The level of employment L being fixed, we observe that K^* does not depend on the value of the negotiated wage. Overall, the bargaining problem is written:

$$\underset{w}{\text{Max}}[v(w) - v(\overline{w})]^\gamma [R(K^*, L) - wL - rK^*]^{1-\gamma}$$

If w^* designates the solution of this problem, the pair (w^*, K^*) represents a Pareto optimum for the firm and the union. K^* being independent of wages, the pair (w^*, K^*) does in fact correspond to the solution of the following Nash problem too:

$$\underset{\{w, K\}}{\text{Max}} [v(w) - v(\overline{w})]^\gamma [R(K, L) - wL - rK]^{1-\gamma}$$

The pair (w^*, K^*) is thus indeed a Pareto optimum.

5.1.2 Contracts with Renegotiation

Let us now suppose that wages can be renegotiated after the employer has installed new equipment. If an investment K is made before wage bargaining and if the union cannot credibly undertake to stick to the negotiated wage, the firm will suffer a loss equal to $-rK$ if there is a strike. For given K the bargaining problem is then written as follows:

$$\underset{w}{\text{Max}} [v(w) - v(\overline{w})]^\gamma [R(K, L) - wL]^{1-\gamma} \tag{20}$$

Let $w(K)$ be the solution of this problem; the firm takes this relation into account in deciding its investment. The optimal level $\hat{K}$ of capital is then found by maximizing the firm's profit, which now takes the form:

$$\Pi = R(K, L) - w(K)L - rK$$

Settting the first derivative of this expression to zero with respect to K, we get:

$$R_K(\hat{K}, L) = w'(\hat{K})L + r \tag{21}$$

Scrutiny of relations (19) and (21) indicates that comparison of levels of investment K^* and $\hat{K}$ depends on the sign of the derivative of function $w(K)$. This sign may be found easily with the help of the Nash criterion that comes into problem (20). It is written in logarithmic form:

$$\Phi(w, K) = \gamma \ln[v(w) - v(\overline{w})] + (1 - \gamma) \ln[R(K, L) - wL] \tag{22}$$

Function $w(K)$ is defined by the first-order condition:

$$\Phi_w[w(K), K] = 0 \tag{23}$$

The second-order condition dictates $\Phi_{ww} < 0$. Now the derivation of equation (23) with respect to K gives $w'(K) = -\Phi_{wK}/\Phi_{ww}$, so $w'(K)$ is of the sign of Φ_{wK}. With (22), we find after several simple calculations:

$$\Phi_{wK} = \frac{(1 - \gamma)LR_K(K, L)}{[R(K, L) - wL]^2} > 0$$

The negotiated wage $w(K)$ is thus an *increasing* function of the level of capital. Derivative $w'(K)$ being positive, relations (19) and (21) then entail $\hat{K} < K^*$.

In sum, the irreversible character of investment gives the firm an incentive to underinvest when the union cannot make a credible commitment not to renegotiate wages once the equipment has been installed. In this situation, the union knows that every strike costs the firm rK, whereas the strike has a cost of zero if it is impossible to renegotiate wages. The union can thus demand a larger share of the profits in the first case, which provokes a reduction in investment. Although we have taken labor demand as fixed, the consequences of underinvestment in terms of employment can be imagined on the basis of its impact on the marginal productivity of labor. If capital and labor are *gross substitutes*, which means that the demand for one factor increases when the cost of the other factor rises (see chapter 4 on labor demand for more detail), underinvestment ought to be favorable to employment, to the extent that any fall in the level of capital will be compensated for by an increase in employment. Conversely, when capital and labor are *gross complements*, which means that the demand for one factor declines when the cost of the other factor rises (see chapter 4), underinvestment ought to be unfavorable for employment. Because capital and low-skilled labor are generally highly substitutable, the underinvestment that would result from the possibility of wage renegotiations probably does not yield a satisfactory explanation of the massive underemployment of low-skilled workers in continental Europe in the 1990s.

5.2 BARGAINING OVER HOURS

Introducing hours of work into the collective bargaining model makes it necessary to represent the impact of this factor on individual preferences and on technology. It then becomes possible to shed light on the response of wages and employment when the *standard* workweek is modified, as well as the determinants of the *negotiated* duration of work.

5.2.1 A Model of Bargaining over Work Schedules

Bargaining models offer a highly intuitive explanation of the foregoing observations (see Booth and Ravaillon, 1993, and Contensou and Vranceanu, 2000). They show that bargaining over hours does not allow jobs to be shared out among all the workers if, on the one hand, wage-earners have a strong preference for purchasing power as compared to leisure, and, on the other, the gains from the reduction of work schedules in terms of productivity are low. In order to show this result, we have to take into account the disutility of labor in the union's choice criterion and the impact of hours worked on production. Hence we will assume that the preferences of workers are represented by a utility function $v(\Omega, T - H)$, where Ω, T, and H designate respectively income, the time allocation, and actual hours worked. If w represents the hourly wage, then we have $\Omega = wH$. The production of the firm depends on the number L of workers hired and the hours of work H. We assume that the productivity $e(H)$ of each employee is an increasing function of H. For the sake of simplicity, we will assume that the revenue of the firm is described by an isoelastic function taking the form $R[e(H)L] = [e(H)L]^{\alpha}/\alpha$, with $\alpha \in (0, 1)$. Let $\eta_H^e \equiv He'(H)/e(H) > 0$ be the elasticity of the productivity of an employee with respect to hours worked. The *hourly* productivity of labor—i.e., $e(H)/H$—increases with the number of hours worked if $\eta_H^e > 1$. Conversely, if $\eta_H^e < 1$, hourly productivity decreases with H. Consequently, reducing the hours worked increases hourly efficiency if and only if $\eta_H^e < 1$ (see chapter 4, section 1.5).

We will assume that bargaining concerns only the hourly wage and the hours to be worked. Unemployment insurance benefits are thus not negotiated (we mentioned at the end of section 3 that this can be justified by moral hazard problems). We will assume further that a legal constraint imposes an upper limit, denoted by $\bar{H}$, on the number of hours worked. In reality, the standard duration should be distinguished from the upper limit, for the hours worked above the standard duration are remunerated at a higher rate. In France, with only a few exceptions, the upper limit cannot exceed the standard duration by a volume of more than 130 hours in every year. To simplify the exposition, we will neglect the distinction between the standard duration and the upper limit.

The union's objective is always to maximize the expected utility of each of its members. In case of failure to conclude an agreement between the union and the firm, each member of the union attains a level of utility $v(\bar{w}, T)$ and the union's contribution to the Nash problem is written:

$$\mathscr{V}_s - v_u = \ell[v(\Omega, T - H) - v(\bar{w}, T)], \qquad \ell = \mathrm{Min}(1, L/N)$$

In this expression, N again designates the (exogenous) size of the union. When employment is equal to L and each employee supplies H hours, the firm's profit takes the following form:

$$\Pi = \frac{1}{\alpha}[e(H)L]^\alpha - \Omega L \tag{24}$$

We will again assume that the firm retains the right to manage; here, this hypothesis signifies that the employer decides on the size of his or her workforce after bargaining over the hourly wage w and the number H of hours to be worked has been completed. In these conditions, labor demand, denoted by $L(\Omega, H)$, is found by maximizing profit, with w and H taken as given. Setting the derivative of (24) to zero with respect to L, we get:

$$L(\Omega, H) = [e(H)]^{\alpha/(1-\alpha)}\Omega^{1/(\alpha-1)} \tag{25}$$

When this value of labor demand does not exceed the size N of the union, the profit of the firm is expressed thus:

$$\Pi(\Omega, H) = \left(\frac{1-\alpha}{\alpha}\right)\left[\frac{e(H)}{\Omega}\right]^{\alpha/(1-\alpha)}$$

Assuming that if there is failure to reach agreement the firm obtains zero profit, the bargaining problem takes the following form:

$$\underset{\{\Omega, H\}}{\mathrm{Max}}\left[\frac{L(\Omega, H)}{N}\right]^\gamma [v(\Omega, T - H) - v(\bar{w}, T)]^\gamma [\Pi(\Omega, H)]^{1-\gamma}$$

subject to:

$$L(\Omega, H) \leq N \quad \text{and} \quad H \leq \bar{H}$$

5.2.2 The Optimal Number of Hours Worked

For an interior solution, the derivatives of the logarithm of the Nash criterion with respect to Ω and H yield the first-order conditions. They are written:

$$\frac{\gamma v_1(\Omega, T - H)}{v(\Omega, T - H) - v(\overline{w}, T)} = \frac{\alpha(1 - \gamma) + \gamma}{(1 - \alpha)\Omega} \tag{26}$$

$$\frac{\gamma v_2(\Omega, T - H)}{v(\Omega, T - H) - v(\overline{w}, T)} = \frac{\alpha}{1 - \alpha} \frac{e'(H)}{e(H)} \tag{27}$$

Dividing these last two relations member to member, we get:

$$\frac{v_1(\Omega, T - H)}{v_2(\Omega, T - H)} = \frac{H}{\Omega} \frac{\alpha(1 - \gamma) + \gamma}{\alpha \eta_H^e} \tag{28}$$

This equation defines the marginal rate of substitution between income and leisure as a function of the wage $w = \Omega/H$ and the elasticity η_H^e of individual productivity with respect to hours. The general study of the system formed by equations (26) and (27) is possible, but we will arrive at the main results more rapidly by assuming that the utility of each member of the union is a function of the Cobb-Douglas type $v(\Omega, T - H) = (\Omega)^\mu (T - H)^{1-\mu}$, with $\mu \in (0, 1)$, and assuming that elasticity η_H^e is a constant. In particular, equation (28) then immediately gives us the number of hours worked:

$$H^* = \frac{\eta_H^e \mu \alpha}{(1 - \mu)[\gamma + \alpha(1 - \gamma)] + \eta_H^e \mu \alpha} T \tag{29}$$

The parameter μ is interpreted as a measure of the importance of income with respect to leisure for each worker. Equation (29) shows that the optimal number of hours worked is an increasing function of this parameter, and of elasticity η_H^e. In consequence, constraint $H^* \leq \overline{H}$ is less likely to be binding if this elasticity is weaker, or if workers attach less importance to income than they do to leisure. The number of hours worked also decreases with the bargaining power of the union. An increase in bargaining power leads workers to opt to increase both their wage and their leisure time. We shall see below that empirical studies generally confirm this prediction.

In other words, bargaining over hours worked makes the hourly constraint binding ($H^* = \overline{H}$) even in the presence of underemployment if a diminution in the number of hours worked entails a strong diminution in the efficiency of labor (high η_H^e), if workers are strongly averse to a reduction in their income, or if their bargaining power is weak. This result can explain why, despite the rise in unemployment, the number of hours worked does not undergo a downward adjustment. The least skilled workers are the ones most directly affected by changes in the number of hours worked: having relatively low incomes, they probably have strong reluctance to see them decline even further. Moreover, in developed countries, the number of hours worked is at present sufficiently small that a further reduction does not necessarily entail an improvement in hourly productivity. Overall, these results allows us to understand why, at the conclusion of collective bargaining, the tendency is for employment to be adjusted rather than hours. Hence it legitimizes, in many cases, the use of bargaining models that neglect the adjustment of hours in order to focus on the determination of employment.

5.2.3   The Consequences of a Reduction in Working Time on Wage and Employment

Bargaining models explain why employees are likely have an interest in not sharing employment by working fewer hours individually. So we may ask whether it is possible to force workers and employers to share employment more widely by imposing a maximum number of hours to be worked. This idea inspires employment policy in parts of Europe, especially France, where the workweek was reduced from 40 to 39 hours in 1982, and from 39 to 35 hours in 2000, with the avowed aim of increasing employment. In chapter 4, section 1.5, we pointed out that the impact of reductions in the standard workweek on employment is conditioned by the response of wages. In this regard, the model of bargaining over the number of hours worked is particularly interesting, since it allows us to analyze the reaction of wages.

We assume that there is a compulsory number of hours, $\bar{H}$, lower than the number arrived at through bargaining, defined by equation (29). The negotiated wage is then given by equation (26) with $H = \bar{H}$. Assuming, as above, that preferences are of the Cobb-Douglas type, this equation implicitly defines the negotiated wage as follows:

$$\Omega^{\mu}(T - \bar{H})^{1-\mu} = \frac{\gamma(1 - \alpha) + \alpha}{\gamma(1 - \mu)(1 - \alpha) + \alpha} v(\overline{w}, T)$$

Since the right-hand side of this equation does not depend on hours, we deduce from it the elasticity $\eta_{\bar{H}}^{\Omega}$ of the weekly wage with respect to hours $\bar{H}$. We thus arrive at $\eta_{\bar{H}}^{\Omega} = \bar{H}(1 - \mu)/\mu(T - \bar{H})$. This elasticity is positive; hence a reduction in the weekly number of hours worked induces a reduction in the weekly wage. Moreover, this elasticity increases with $\bar{H}$, which signifies that the reduction in the weekly wage entailed by the reduction in the number of hours worked is greater if the number of hours worked is high to begin with. This expression of wage elasticity with respect to hours allows us to determine the impact of a reduction in hours on employment, using equation (25) defining labor demand. To find this impact, we calculate the elasticity of employment with respect to hours, taking wage variations into account. We get:

$$\eta_{\Omega}^{L}\eta_{H}^{\Omega} + \eta_{H}^{L} < 0 \Leftrightarrow \bar{H} > \hat{H} \qquad \text{with} \qquad \hat{H} \equiv \frac{\eta_{H}^{e}\mu\alpha}{(1 - \mu) + \eta_{H}^{e}\mu\alpha} T \tag{30}$$

The term $\eta_{\Omega}^{L}\eta_{H}^{\Omega} + \eta_{H}^{L}$ corresponds to the elasticity of labor demand with respect to hours when wage variations are taken into consideration. Condition (30) indicates that a reduction in hours worked is favorable to employment if and only if the number of hours worked is superior to the threshold value $\hat{H}$. Comparison of equations (29) and (30) indicates that the threshold value $\hat{H}$ is equal to the number of hours negotiated H^{*} when the union disposes of all the bargaining power ($\gamma = 1$). In this case, it

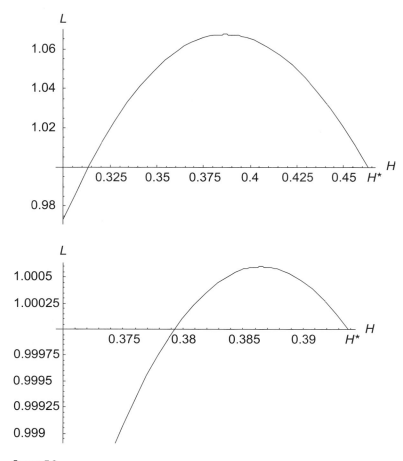

FIGURE 7.9
The impact of a reduction in the number of hours worked. The graph on the top corresponds to a value $\gamma = 0.1$ of bargaining power and the one on the bottom to $\gamma = 0.9$. The number of hours worked is given on the horizontal axis and stops at the negotiated number, H^*, which has a value of 0.463 (on the top) and 0.394 (on the bottom), knowing that the time allocation $T = 1$. The ratio between actual employment and its value for H^* is given on the vertical axis.

is impossible to increase employment by reducing the number of hours worked, since any reduction in $\bar{H}$ for values of $\hat{H} = H^*$ then induces a fall in employment. Conversely, since the optimal number of hours worked decreases with the bargaining power of workers, it is possible to increase employment by reducing hours worked $\bar{H}$ to the threshold $\hat{H} < H^*$ when the power of workers is limited ($\gamma < 1$). Nonetheless, any reduction in hours worked beyond that threshold is unfavorable to employment. These properties are illustrated in figure 7.9, which presents employment as a function of hours worked on the assumption that $T = 1$, $\eta_H^e = 0.9$, $\mu = 0.5$, and $\alpha = 0.7$. We observe that a reduction in hours worked beyond the negotiated level may be significantly favorable to employment when the power of the union is slight (left-hand graph, where $\gamma = 0.1$), since employment can rise by about 6%. Conversely, the impact on employment is insignificant when union power is strong (right-hand graph, where $\gamma = 0.9$).

In sum, models of bargaining over the number of hours to be worked show that union power should exert downward pressure on these hours. Moreover, it is evident that forcible reductions in the number of hours worked have a more favorable impact on employment when union bargaining power is slight.

6   EMPIRICAL EVIDENCE REGARDING THE CONSEQUENCES OF COLLECTIVE BARGAINING

In all the models of partial equilibrium looked at to this point, an increase in union power affects the sharing of income to the advantage of wage-earners. As for its effects on employment, they are a priori ambiguous. A number of contributions have assessed the impact of collective bargaining on wages, and certain general lessons emerge. The impact of unions on productivity, profits, and the number of hours worked is also well documented. Studies on employment are less numerous, and knowledge of the effects of unions on employment remains very fragmentary.

6.1   WAGES

The great majority of studies on collective bargaining deal with the United States, and focus on its effects on wages. These studies bring out a wage differential between unionized workers and others. A further finding is that unions exert an influence on wage inequalities.

6.1.1   The Union/Nonunion Wage Differential

Empirical studies generally attempt to estimate the wage differential between unionized and nonunionized workers, known as the union wage gap. Let W_u and W_n be respectively the wage of a unionized and a nonunionized worker. This gap is defined by[3]:

$$\Delta = \frac{W_u - W_n}{W_n} \approx \ln W_u - \ln W_n$$

In order to interpret this wage gap, it is useful to distinguish two types of effect. First, there is a direct effect, which corresponds to the influence of the union on the wages it negotiates. There is also an indirect effect deriving from the fact that the union exerts influence on wages not covered by collective bargaining. So an increase in union-negotiated wages may show up as a contraction of production in the unionized sector, and thus an increase in the demand for goods and labor, from which the nonunionized sector profits. In this case, wages in the nonunionized sector should rise with union power. Conversely, if wage rises due to union power entail a reduction in labor demand in the unionized sector, a worker who fails to find a job in that sector may move into the nonunionized sector. That ought to exert downward pressure on the wages of workers not covered by collective agreements. These observations suggest that wages as a whole are influenced by collective bargaining, and that the gap between wages in the unionized sector and those in the nonunionized sector reflects a combination of interactions, the result of which is ambiguous in sign.

Estimation of the Union Wage Gap by Ordinary Least Squares
To estimate the impact of unions on wages, the earliest work utilized aggregate data at the industry level. It concluded that the rate of unionization had a positive impact on wages (Lewis, 1963). The results of these studies are very difficult to interpret, however, for it is very difficult to assess differences in the characteristics of manpower between "unionized" sectors, i.e., sectors where collective agreements prevail, and "nonunionized" sectors. The most recent work estimates the impact of collective bargaining utilizing individual data.

Studies carried out, beginning in the mid-1970s, on individual data generally estimate two separate wage equations for the unionized and nonunionized sectors, in order to take account of possible differences of return to individual characteristics between these two sectors. These two equations are written respectively:

$$w_{ui} = \sum_j a_{uj} x_{ij} + \varepsilon_{ui} \quad \text{and} \quad w_{nk} = \sum_j a_{nj} x_{kj} + \varepsilon_{nk} \tag{31}$$

In these equations, index u locates an individual i belonging to the unionized sector, and index n an individual k from the nonunionized sector. The dependent variable w_{ui} is thus the wage (expressed as a logarithm) of individual i from the unionized sector. The exogenous variables x_{ij} represent the characteristics of individual i (age, sex, region, education, experience, etc.) and ε_{ui} is a random disturbance term. Likewise w_{nk} designates the logarithm of the wage of an individual k located in the nonunionized sector, and variables x_{kj} measure his or her characteristics. The term ε_{nk} again represents a random disturbance.

The estimation of equations (31) by ordinary least squares allows us to calculate, for each individual, the wage differential due to the existence of a union. Let $\hat{a}_{uj}$ and $\hat{a}_{nj}$ be the estimates of the coefficients appearing in equations (31); the gain of an individual i belonging to the unionized sector is measured by the difference:

$$\hat{w}_{ui} - \hat{w}_{ni} = \sum_j (\hat{a}_{uj} - \hat{a}_{nj}) x_{ij}$$

In summing up 143 different studies covering the period 1967–1979 in the United States, Lewis (1986) found that the average markup $(w_u - w_n)/w_n$, where w_u and w_n represent respectively the average of the estimates of the w_{ui} and the w_{ni}, was on the order of 15%. For the United Kingdom, the summary of Booth (1995a) arrives at a lower average, on the order of 8%. Dell'Aringa and Lucifora (1994) estimate that the wage differential is 4.4% for unskilled workers and 7.4% for skilled workers in mechanical industry in Italy. Studies of the impact of collective bargaining on wages, based on individual data from various countries, conclude that the impact is greatest in the United States, followed at a distance by the United Kingdom. Blanchflower and Freeman (1992) found that the union markup for the period 1985–1987 was 20% in the United States, 10% in the United Kingdom, and between 4% and 8% in Australia, Austria, Switzerland, and Germany. These results are confirmed and complemented by Blanchflower and Bryson (2002), who estimate the impact of trade unions in 17 countries. The markup from the 17 countries averages out at 12%. Unions do not have the same impact on wages in all countries. Blanchflower and Bryson (2002) find that the union differential in the United States is higher on average than that found in the United Kingdom, 18% compared with 10%. Unions in other countries, such as Australia, Austria, Brazil, Canada, Chile, Denmark, Japan, New Zealand, Norway, Portugal, and Spain, also raise wages by significant amounts. In France, Germany, Italy, the Netherlands, and Sweden, where union wage settlements spill over into the nonunion sector, Blanchflower and Bryson find no significant union wage differentials. Blanchflower and Bryson also analyze the changes over time in union-relative wage effect in the United States and the United Kingdom. It turns out that the union wage premium was untrended from the beginning of the 1980s to the mid-1990s in both countries. However, the wage premium fell between 1994 and 2001 in both countries. It went from 14% to 4% in the United Kingdom and from 18% to 13.5% in the United States between these two dates.

The Limits of Ordinary Least Squares

Overall, the results given above point to the conclusion that unions exert a positive impact on wages. These results must nevertheless be interpreted with care, for the method of estimating the wage differential runs up against several difficulties.

In the first place, unionized workers can have unobserved characteristics different from those of nonunionized ones, which induces selection bias. We emphasized that collective bargaining reduces the wage gaps between workers with different productivity. If that is the case, the most efficient workers prefer to be employed in the nonunionized sector, and the unionized sector is composed of less productive workers. This type of selection bias, resulting from workers' choices, is known as the "worker choice model" (Lee, 1978). The study of Farber and Saks (1980) finds that the probability of a worker wishing to have a union in his or her workplace decreases with his or her position in the distribution of wages in that workplace. It thus confirms the relevance of the hypothesis of the worker choice model. It is also possible that the presence of a union gives firms an incentive to select a better quality workforce—an adaptation to the high wages of less qualified workers. That assumes that all workers who wish to be employed in the unionized sector do not necessarily find such employment. This description of worker allocation resulting from the joint choice of workers and firms is known as the "queuing model" (Abowd and Farber, 1982; Farber,

1983). In this context, workers with lower performance are excluded from the union- ized sector. The choices of workers and firms thus ought to lead to an allocation of the best-performing workers (who refuse to be unionized) and the worst-performing workers (who are turned down by firms in the unionized sector) to the nonunionized sector. The unionized sector is then composed of workers with an intermediate level of productivity (Abowd and Farber, 1982; Farber, 1983).

In the second place, ordinary least squares estimates are not biased if the rate of unionization is an exogenous variable. But the wage hikes that a union may obtain because of high productivity in a firm or sector, for example, may in return increase the rate of unionization (Duncan and Stafford, 1980; Checchi and Lucifora, 2002), which must then be considered an endogenous variable.

These two observations lead to the conclusion that ordinary least squares pro- duces a biased estimator of the wage differential. Numerous contributions have tried to overcome selection and endogeneity biases by estimating systems of simultaneous equations and utilizing longitudinal data that make it possible to observe the wage variations of workers whose unionized status changes (see Hirsch and Addison, 1986; Robinson, 1989; and the surveys of Booth, 1995a, and Blanchflower, 1996). The esti- mation of simultaneous equations, by the method of instrumental variables or by the two-stage estimation procedures of Heckman (1979), arrives at results that lack robustness and are divergent, being very sensitive to the method of estimation, hypotheses concerning the error terms, and the inclusion of supplementary variables.

Longitudinal data supply information about movement between unionized and nonunionized jobs and make it possible to suppress biases due to fixed individual effects not observed by the econometrician (this question was discussed in chapter 5, section 4.1). Nevertheless, longitudinal data are very sensitive to measurement errors, for small measurement errors concerning the status of workers lead to major biases if there is low mobility between unionized and nonunionized jobs. From this per- spective, Card (1996) studied the impact of unions on wages with the help of longitu- dinal data, taking into account classification errors regarding the status of workers, as well as potential correlations between productivity and unionization. Card estimates a model with simultaneous equations for workers belonging to five different skill levels, utilizing data from the Current Population Survey (United States) for 1987–1988. His results suggest that the positive effect of unions on wages is greater, the less skilled the workers are. Moreover, he finds that selection biases differ from one group to another. Among the least skilled workers, the most efficient ones are in the unionized sector on average (in conformity with the queuing model), while the opposite is true for the most highly skilled workers (in conformity with the worker choice model). Lemieux (1998) obtains qualitatively similar results on longitudinal data from Canada.

Despite the problems of interpretation of wage differentials and the problems of estimation, the generally accepted conclusion is that unions do in fact have a positive impact on the wages they negotiate, and that they reduce the returns to observable and unobservable characteristics of workers.

6.1.2 The Impact of Unions on Wage Dispersion

We have just stated that workers covered by collective agreements obtain higher wages. This effect ought to tend to increase the dispersion of wages throughout the economy as a whole. We have also stated, however, that workplaces covered by collective agreements have more compressed wage structures than others. These observations suggest that the impact of collective agreements on wage dispersion is a priori ambiguous.

This impact may be grasped by decomposing the variance v of the logarithm of wages in the economy as a whole, as a function of the proportion α of unionized workers (or ones covered by a collective agreement), the variances v_u and v_n of the logarithms of wages in the unionized and nonunionized sectors, and the averages of the logarithms of wages w_u and w_n in these two sectors. The result is[4] (Freeman, 1980; Fortin and Lemieux, 1997):

$$v = \alpha(1 - \alpha)(w_u - w_n)^2 + \alpha v_u + (1 - \alpha)v_n \tag{32}$$

This relation shows that the variance may be decomposed as the sum of a between-group variance and a within-group variance. The between-group variance, $\alpha(1 - \alpha)(w_u - w_n)^2$, shows that the wage differential between the unionized and nonunionized sectors accentuates the inequalities. But unions also exert an influence that may work in the opposite direction, to the extent that they alter the dispersion of the wages they negotiate. This effect is represented by the last two terms, which take into account the variances of the two sectors weighted by their respective size. Empirical studies generally show that wage variance is weaker in the unionized sector, and conclude that this second effect tends to play a dominant role, so that the total impact of unions on inequalities as a whole is negative (Freeman and Medoff, 1984; Blau and Kahn, 1999).

The experience of each country when it comes to inequality depends on its institutions, in particular the union density, the coverage of collective agreements, and the degree to which bargaining is coordinated. The studies of Rowthorn (1992), Blau and Kahn (1996), and Kahn (1998, 2000), carried out on data from OECD countries, find negative correlations between the union density (or the coverage of collective agreements) and wage inequalities. They also obtain significant negative correlations between the degree to which collective bargaining is centralized and wage inequalities. The study of Kahn (2000) in particular, which uses individual data for 15 OECD countries for the period 1985–1994, shows that an increase in the collective bargaining coverage of collective wage bargaining leads to relatively higher wages for low-skilled workers.

These results suggest that as institutions change, changes in wage inequalities may follow. Figures 7.2 and 7.3 show that union density and collective bargaining coverage fell sharply between the end of the 1970s and the beginning of the 1990s in certain OECD countries, in particular the United States and the United Kingdom. It is tempting to make a connection between these changes and the increased inequality of wages observed in these two countries (see chapter 10). In this respect, DiNardo et al.

(1996) estimate that the fall in the union density contributed to 10% of the increase in the differential of (the logarithms of) wages between the first and last decile and one-third of the increase between the first and the fifth decile in the United States in the 1980s. Card (2001) finds that the decline in unionization explains between 15% and 20% of the growth in wage inequalities (measured by the variance of wage logarithms). For women, on the other hand, wage inequalities are not affected by the change in the global rate of unionization. This may be a result of the constancy of the rate of unionization for women over the period considered.

6.2 PROFITABILITY

The rise in wages achieved by unions ought to entail a fall in profits if the presence of unions has no other effect on the organization of work, in particular if it does not improve productivity. This point is the focus of numerous debates, which empirical studies have not yet succeeded in resolving.

6.2.1 Productivity and Profits

In theory, unions and collective agreements have an ambiguous impact on productivity. For some economists, unions reduce productivity by limiting the powers of employers (Robinson, 1989). For others, unions improve productivity by improving the circulation of information among workers and their motivation. Following the work of Hirschman (1970), Freeman and Medoff (1984) maintain that this second characteristic of unions plays an essential role in the United States, in combination with the exercise of their monopoly power. They assert that unions, by giving workers a voice, profoundly change social relations within the firm. Without them, workers adopt a strategy of defection or "exit"; i.e., they disengage from the relationship established with a person or an organization when that relationship proves unsatisfactory. The efficiency of the union lies in the fact that it favors the choice of a strategy of "voice," by transmitting complaints, grievances, and demands, with the aim of correcting and improving the relationship. Freeman and Medoff (1984) estimate that the reduction in the turnover rate due to unions allows American firms, on average, to reduce their labor costs by around 2%. They show as well that the productivity of labor is often higher in unionized firms. Examination of the upshot of collective agreements in France leads to results of the same type (Cahuc and Kramarz, 1997).

These results are, however, subject to the same biases as the ones encountered in the estimation of wage differentials. Productivity gaps and turnover of manpower may result from unobserved characteristics of workers and may influence behavior when it comes to unionization or the bargaining of collective agreements. The importance of the problems raised by these biases leads to an absence of consensus as to the effects of unions on productivity, inasmuch as many studies also highlight a negative effect on productivity (see Hirsch and Addison, 1986, pp. 192–208; Booth, 1995a, chapter 7).

The impact of unions on profits is less subject to debate. Studies of the process of setting up a procedure for collective bargaining (through a majority vote of the workers in the United States), or of the effect of the announcement of a renegotiation, show that the share price of firms falls (Ruback and Zimmerman, 1984, and Abowd, 1989). Freeman and Medoff (1984) examine the link between unionization and the rate of return on capital coming to similar conclusions. Van Reenen (1996) studied the movement of wages in firms which had introduced innovations in manufacturing industry in the United Kingdom. These firms had also signed collective agreements with unions. Van Reenen shows that the innovations had a positive impact on wages over at least seven years. This result indicates that workers covered by collective agreements obtain a share of the profit of their firms.

6.2.2 Investment

We have stated that the capacity to renegotiate wages may lead to a reduced level of investment, and that this effect is greater, the more bargaining power the wage-earners have. To verify this prediction, empirical studies estimate a relation of the type:

$$\ln I_{it} = \mathbf{x}_{it}\beta + \delta u_{it} + \varepsilon_{it}$$

In this equation, I_{it} and $\mathbf{x}_{it}$ designate respectively the level of investment and a vector of the characteristics of the firm or sector i at date t which influence investment. The term u_{it} is an indicator of the union presence (such as the rate of unionization and the number of days lost through strikes), ε_{it} is a random disturbance term, and β and δ are coefficients to be estimated.

The results obtained by this method indicate that unions exert a negative effect on investment in physical capital in the United States (Connolly et al., 1986; Hirsch, 1992; Bronars et al., 1994), in Canada (Odgers and Betts, 1997), and in the United Kingdom (Denny and Nickell, 1992). The loss of investment attributed to unions is generally of significant size. Hirsch finds figures on the order of 20% for the United States, while Denny and Nickell obtain, for the United Kingdom, a reduction lying between 3% and 16% according to the firm in question. Moreover, the estimates show that the effects are not linear. The marginal impact of an increase in union presence on investment in a sector is greater when the union density is slight (Hirsch, 1992; Odgers and Betts, 1997). This phenomenon can be explained by the effect of the spread of incipient unionization in a sector, to which nonunionized firms respond by increasing wages in order to make unionization harder in their plants.

These studies deal with the accumulation of physical capital in firms. Tan et al. (1992) suggest that the presence of a union is favorable to investment in the human capital of firms, since it is generally associated with outlays on training on the part of employers; such investment is higher in the United States, the United Kingdom, and Australia.

6.3 EMPLOYMENT

Models of wage bargaining have shown that the effect of collective agreements on employment depends strongly on the hypotheses made about the sequence of decisions and about the set of variables submitted to bargaining. It is helpful to distinguish assessments of the impact of collective bargaining on employment according to whether they adopt the efficient contract model or the right-to-manage model.

6.3.1   Tests of Efficient Contract Models

Two different approaches have been used to test the efficiency of collective agreements. Ashenfelter and Brown (1986) have estimated the properties of the relationship between employment and wages, while Abowd (1989) worked directly on the payoff functions of firms and unions.

(i) Ashenfelter and Brown (1986) used data concerning a particular union (the International Typographical Union in the United States). The employment–wage relationship corresponds to the equation of the contract curve of the model of bargaining over wages and employment described in section 3.2 above. Applied to workplace i, this equation is written in log-linear form:

$$\ln L_{it} = a_0 + a_1 z_{it} + a_2 \ln w_{it} + a_3 \ln w_{ait} + u_{it} \tag{33}$$

In this relation, L_{it} designates employment or the number of hours worked, z_{it} represents a vector of nonwage variables comprising lagged employment, fixed effects for localization, and productivity indicators, w_{it} is the (minimum) hourly negotiated wage, w_{ait} is the outside wage (including, according to specifications, the average wage in manufacturing industry and unemployment insurance benefits), and finally u_{it} represents a random error term.

Whatever the value of the negotiated wage, the equation of the contract curve described in section 3.2 shows that the outside wage (denoted by $\overline{w}$ in section 3.2) generally has an impact on employment. Conversely, if the solution of the bargaining is situated on labor demand—which is the case in the right-to-manage model—employment becomes independent of the outside wage, since labor demand, deduced from profit maximization behavior, does not depend on this parameter.

The negotiated wage being an endogenous variable, equation (33) is estimated by the method of instrumental variables. The instruments chosen are the lagged wage and the levels, actual and lagged, of the consumer price index. It is most often found that the values of coefficients a_2 and a_3 are very sensitive to the specification of the variables and have little significance. Thus Ashenfelter and Brown (1986) reject the hypothesis that the outside wage has a significant impact on employment, but do not go so far as to exclude the hypothesis of the absence of influence of the negotiated wage. These results would thus indicate that the contracts negotiated (by the International Typographical Union) are not optimal. It is best, though, to remain cautious, for as Pencavel (1991) points out, the absence of a relationship between the level of employment and that of the outside wage does not necessarily signify that the contract is not optimal. For example, if the utility function of the union takes the form $\mathscr{V}_s(w, L) = h(L)(w/\overline{w})^{\zeta}$; $\zeta > 0$, $g'(L) > 0$, the contract curve is independent of $\overline{w}$. It is easy to verify that its expression is $R'(L) = w - (g'(L)/g(L))/(w/\zeta)$. In addition, the difficulties inherent in the definition of the outside wage and the sensitivity of results to the specification chosen render any conclusion about the role of this variable fragile.

(ii) Card (1986, 1990) has also studied the impact of the outside wage in employment equations of the type (33). He shows, relying on data for the aeronautical industry in the United States (Card, 1986) and the manufacturing industry in Canada (Card, 1990), that the correlations observed between employment and the outside wage are not consistent with the predictions of efficient contract models. Abowd and Kramarz (1993) come to a similar conclusion. They find, for French data on 1097 firms in the period 1978–1987, that estimates of labor demand equations incorporating solely the outside wage (specified as the minimum wage multiplied by an index of the average wage of the decile below the category of manpower under consideration) are much less good than estimates that take only the negotiated wage into account.

(iii) Abowd (1989) adopts a strategy that makes it possible to overcome the difficulty linked to the specification of the outside wage. He assumes that the union maximizes the rent of its members, defined as employment multiplied by the difference between the negotiated wage and the outside wage: $\mathcal{V}_s = L(w - \overline{w})$. In this case, it is easy to verify that the contract curve is a vertical line, the equation of which is $R'(L) = \overline{w}$. The total revenue $R(L)$ then becomes independent of bargaining power (which is not the case if the solution of bargaining is found on labor demand or on the contract curve, which is not a vertical). In consequence, the sum of profit $\Pi = R(L) - wL$ and union rent $\mathcal{V}_s$ amounts to $R(L) - \overline{w}L$ which depends *only* on wage $\overline{w}$. Any variation in union bargaining power will then entail $\Delta\Pi = -\Delta\mathcal{V}_s$. In other words, any increase in the wealth $\Delta\Pi$ of shareholders should entail a reduction in union rent by the same amount when the power of the union diminishes. For 2228 private sector contracts, excluding construction, in the United States for the period 1976–1982, Abowd estimates relation:

$$\Delta\Pi = a_1 + a_2\Delta\mathcal{V}_s + u \tag{34}$$

In this equality, u represents a random error term. Variations in profit are measured using the difference in the price of shares three months before the date a collective agreement is signed, and the price observed on that date. A similar approach is used to find variations in the union rent. Abowd calculates the value of the rent $L[w - R'(L)]$ at every date and from that deduces its variations. The estimation of this equation does not allow us to reject the hypothesis $a_1 = 0$ and $a_2 = -1$. In consequence, we cannot exclude the possibility that collective bargaining may arrive at efficient contracts.

Attempts to assess the efficiency of contracts have not achieved clear conclusions. The estimation of an employment–wage relationship leads to rejection of the hypothesis that the alternative wage plays a determining role. This makes it possible to exclude only the model with a vertical contracts curve. But the study of Abowd (1989) ends by accepting this very model, i.e., the opposite result.

6.3.2   Tests of the Right-to-Manage Model

Tests of the right-to-manage model try to verify whether the solution of the bargaining lies on labor demand. MaCurdy and Pencavel (1986) use the result that, in the right-to-manage model, the marginal productivity of labor is equal to its cost. With the same data as Ashenfelter and Brown (1986), they first estimate production functions, in order to find the marginal productivity of labor. They then show that variations in the latter are explained by the current wage, but also by other variables, like the outside wage or the level of employment which the union incorporates into its objective. They conclude that the solution of bargaining is not situated on labor demand. The validity of this approach rests on the quality of the estimate of marginal productivity. Now, variables modifying the utility of the union can have an impact on the behavior of individuals, which affects their productivity and shifts labor demand. In light of this, the results of MaCurdy and Pencavel (1986) are very fragile.

Nickell and Wadhwani (1990) test the sequential model of Manning (1987), in which bargaining power regarding employment differs from bargaining power regarding wages. Using data relative to 219 firms in the manufacturing industry in the United Kingdom between 1972 and 1982, they estimate the labor demand function resulting from bargaining over employment, with an exogenous wage. We have seen in section 3.2 that this function depends on, among other things, the outside wage and bargaining power regarding employment (captured in this study by the rate of unionization). It appears that neither of these two variables has a significant impact on employment. This result may point to the conclusion that firms are on their labor demand. Nickell and Wadhwani emphasize, however, that their results are fragile, since the reservation wage is very poorly defined, and the rate of unionization is not a good measure of bargaining power regarding employment.

6.3.3 Direct Estimations

Boal and Pencavel (1994) tried to estimate the effects of bargaining on wages and employment directly. Their study utilizes data relative to labor in the coal mines of Virginia between 1897 and 1938. These data are available for 35 different counties. At each date, there are counties in which the unions actually play a part in the bargaining process, and other counties where there are no unions. The authors assume that employment and wages are determined competitively in these counties. This division of the counties into two groups makes it possible to estimate the wage gap between the "unionized" counties and the "competitive" counties. Assuming that firms preserve the right to manage, an estimate of the gap in terms of employment is then deduced. It emerges that, starting in 1921, the wage gap differs significantly from zero. It reaches 18% over the period 1921–1930 and 23% between 1931 and 1938. On the other hand, differences in terms of employment are never significantly diffferent from zero, although the number of days worked is, on average, 17% lower in the counties where unions exist. Hence, the study of Boal and Pencavel shows that a large wage differential does not necessarily have a negative effect on employment. It is possible that the presence of a union leads to a change in internal relationships in firms that, in return, alters the linkage between employment and wages.

Changes in legislation influencing union power constitute interesting experiments for the assessment of the impact of unions on employment: they are like exogenous shocks, the consequences of which the econometrician can identify. The reforms introduced by the Thatcher government in the United Kingdom in the 1980s fit this category, since they limited union power, notably by abolishing the "closed shop" (the obligation for all workers in a firm with a collective agreement to belong to the union). The effect of these reforms was to diminish the rate of unionization and the collective bargaining coverage of collective agreements, and studies find that the response of wages and employment to variations in demand rose following these changes. The reforms did not, however, appear to have had an impact on unemployment, or on the chances of exiting from unemployment (Blanchflower and Freeman, 1994). The study of Maloney (1994), which looks at reforms introduced in New Zealand in 1991 that substantially reduced union power, comes to different conclusions. Maloney finds that the strong reduction in the rate of unionization had a positive impact on employment. The contribution of Kahn (2000), on 15 OECD countries for the period 1985–1994, brings out a negative correlation between the degree of union coverage and the relative employment rate of low-skilled workers. Kahn also shows that unions allow these workers to obtain higher relative wages, which suggests that unions contribute to the compression of the wage structure at the expense of the employment of less skilled workers.

All in all, empirical studies arrive at very heterogeneous results, so it is impossible, on the basis of these works, to satisfactorily assess the impact of collective bargaining on employment. Empirical studies appear to converge on only two points. For one thing, the hypothesis that the marginal productivity of labor is equal to the outside wage must be rejected, and for another, there are grounds for positing a negative correlation between employment and negotiated wages (Hamermesh, 1993). It should be noted that the conclusions of the right-to-manage model (see section 3.1) and those of the insiders–outsiders model with no discrimination against entrants (see section 4.1) do not contradict these two stylized facts.

7   SUMMARY AND CONCLUSION

- In Europe, the area of the economy covered on average by collective bargaining lay in the neighborhood of 80% in the middle of the 1990s. It was clearly less in the United States and Japan, where the values were respectively 18% and 21%.

- Unions, or more generally institutions representing wage-earners, have as their objective to obtain the highest wage and employment levels possible. Trading off between employment and wages depends on the internal organization of the union and the preferences of workers. Hence, a union made up solely of insiders is indifferent to the level of employment as long as it is sufficiently high for all the insiders to remain in employment. Conversely, a boss-dominated union seeking to maximize the size of the organization will have as its objective an increase in employment at the expense of wages.

- Models of bargaining, derived from the theory of noncooperative games, allow us to pinpoint the elements that determine the partition of gains between protagonists taking part in a bargaining process. This partition depends on the preference for the present and the risk aversion of the agents, and on the gains they obtain during the unfolding of the negotiation, or when negotiations break off.

- All analyses of wage bargaining agree on the conclusion that the bargaining power of unions increases wages. Their effect on employment, however, is ambiguous. Employment decreases with the bargaining power of workers if the bargaining is exclusively over wages, but employment may rise if it also concerns hires. If bargaining covers wages and unemployment benefits or severance payments, the bargaining is strongly efficient, and employment always reaches its competitive level.

- The opposition between insiders and outsiders excluded from the bargaining does not necessarily entail the exclusion of outsiders from employment. Rather, it should lead to a discrimination between insiders possessing bargaining power, who can on that account obtain good jobs, and workers lacking this power, who are pushed into badly paid jobs.

- Workers' bargaining power has a negative effect on investment if it is impossible to negotiate long-term commitments concerning wages. Once an investment has been made, workers are tempted to push for new wage negotiations in order to benefit from the improved productivity flowing from the increase in capital stock. Without a long-term commitment, the chance that wages will be renegotiated diminishes the return on investment. But the effect on employment of lowered investment is ambiguous: it is positive if labor and capital are gross substitutes and negative if they are gross complements.

- A priori, bargaining over hours worked could allow employers and employees to share jobs, and so solve the unemployment problem. The increase in unemployment in Europe has not, though, led to a significant diminution in the number of hours worked in these countries. Analysis of bargaining shows that unions and firms negotiate a reduction in the number of hours to be worked if the marginal utility of income is low for workers, if the productivity gains induced are strong, and if the bargaining power of unions is high. Moreover, it appears that a compulsory reduction (by legal fiat, for example) in the number of hours worked increases employment only if the bargaining power of unions and the marginal utility of income are sufficiently low.

- Empirical studies suggest that collective bargaining has a positive impact on wages while reducing their dispersion. Collective bargaining probably has a positive effect on productivity and a negative effect on profits, the number of hours worked, and investment in physical capital. The effect of collective bargaining on employment proves to be ambiguous.

8 RELATED TOPICS IN THE BOOK

- Chapter 4, section 1.1: The substitution between capital and labor

- Chapter 4, section 1.5: The substitution between men and hours

- Chapter 5, section 2.2: The holdup problem

- Chapter 6, section 2: Risk-sharing and efficient contracts

- Chapter 9, section 3.4: Individual bargaining in the matching model

- Chapter 9, section 4.2: More on the holdup problem

- Chapter 10, section 2.5: Unions and wage inequality

- Chapter 12, section 4: The wage bargaining level and the labor market equilibrium

9 FURTHER READINGS

Booth, A. (1995a), *The Economics of the Trade Union*, Cambridge, U.K.: Cambridge University Press.

Farber, H. (1986), ''The analysis of union behavior,'' in Ashenfelter, O., and Layard, R. (eds.), *Handbook of Labor Economics*, vol. 2, pp. 1139–1189, Amsterdam: Elsevier Science/North-Holland.

Freeman, R., and Medoff, J. (1984), *What Do Unions Do?* New York: Basic Books.

Lindbeck, A., and Snower, D. (2001), ''Insiders versus outsiders,'' *Journal of Economic Perspectives*, 15, pp. 165–188.

Osborne, M., and Rubinstein, A. (1990), *Bargaining and Markets*, San Diego: Academic Press.

Pencavel, J. (1991), *Labor Market Under Trade Unionism: Employment, Wages and Hours*, Cambridge, Mass.: Blackwell.

10 APPENDICES

10.1 APPENDIX 1: UNICITY OF SOLUTION ($x*, y*$)

Consider the system of equations:

$$u_1(y) - \bar{u}_1 = \delta_1[u_1(x) - \bar{u}_1] \tag{35}$$

$$u_2(1-x) - \bar{u}_2 = \delta_2[u_2(1-y) - \bar{u}_2] \tag{36}$$

Relation (35) defines y as a function of x, i.e. $y = y(x) \equiv u_1^{-1}[\delta_1(u_1(x) - \bar{u}_1) + \bar{u}_1]$. Let us now define function $H(x)$ by:

$$H(x) = u_2(1-x) - \bar{u}_2 - \delta_2[u_2(1-y(x)) - \bar{u}_2] \tag{37}$$

Since $u_2(0) = \bar{u}_2$, we have $H(1) < 0$ when $x > 0$. Likewise, since (35) shows that $y(0) = 0$, (37) entails $H(0) = (1 - \delta_2)[u_2(1) - \bar{u}_2] > 0$. Moreover, differentiating (37), we get:

$$H'(x) = u_2'(1 - y(x)) \left[\frac{\delta_1 \delta_2 u_1'(x)}{u_1'(y(x))} - \frac{u_2'(1 - x)}{u_2'(1 - y(x))} \right]$$

Since $y(x) < x$, for $x > 0$ (see (36)), the concavity of the utility function entails $u_1'(x)/u_1'(y(x)) < 1$ and $u_2'(1 - x)/u_2'(1 - y(x)) > 1$. The derivative $H'(x)$ is thus strictly negative for $x > 0$. Therefore, there exists a unique value x^* such that $H(x^*) = 0$. There is thus a unique solution (x^*, y^*), with $y^* = y(x^*)$, for the system of equations (35) and (36).

10.2   APPENDIX 2: THE CORRESPONDENCE BETWEEN THE NASH AXIOMATIC SOLUTION AND THE SUBGAME PERFECT EQUILIBRIUM OF RUBINSTEIN'S MODEL

We take up Rubinstein's game, presented in section 2.3.1, with the assumption that the players have different preferences for the present. Let Δ be the interval between successive offers. The discount factor of the agents is denoted by $\delta_i = e^{-r_i \Delta}$; $r_i > 0$, $i = 1, 2$; where r_i is the discount rate of player i. We will show that the solution of the bargaining in Rubinstein's game approaches the Nash axiomatic solution when Δ goes to zero.

The solution of the bargaining $(x(\Delta), y(\Delta))$ in Rubinstein's game is defined by the system of equations:

$$u_1[y(\Delta)] - \bar{u}_1 = e^{-r_1 \Delta}[u_1(x(\Delta)) - \bar{u}_1]$$

$$u_2[1 - x(\Delta)] - \bar{u}_2 = e^{-r_2 \Delta}[u_2(1 - y(\Delta)) - \bar{u}_2]$$

In the neighborhood of $\Delta = 0$, we have $e^{-r_i \Delta} \simeq 1 - r_i \Delta$, and these two equations then entail:

$$[u_1(y(\Delta)) - u_1(x(\Delta))] \simeq r_1 \Delta[u_1(x(\Delta)) - \bar{u}_1] \tag{38}$$

$$[u_2(1 - x(\Delta)) - u_2(1 - y(\Delta))] \simeq r_2 \Delta[u_2(1 - y(\Delta)) - \bar{u}_2] \tag{39}$$

These relations show that $y(\Delta)$ and $x(\Delta)$ converge toward the same value, $\tilde{x}$, when Δ goes to zero. They then entail:

$$u_1'(\tilde{x}) = \operatorname*{Lim}_{\Delta \to 0} \frac{u_1[y(\Delta)] - u_1[x(\Delta)]}{y(\Delta) - x(\Delta)}$$

$$u_2'(1 - \tilde{x}) = \operatorname*{Lim}_{\Delta \to 0} \frac{u_2[1 - x(\Delta)] - u_2[1 - y(\Delta)]}{y(\Delta) - x(\Delta)}$$

Using these last two relations and taking the ratio between equations (38) and (39) for $\Delta \to 0$, we get:

$$\frac{u_1'(\tilde{x})}{u_2'(1 - \tilde{x})} = \frac{r_1}{r_2} \frac{[u_1(\tilde{x}) - \bar{u}_1]}{[u_2(1 - \tilde{x}) - \bar{u}_2]} \tag{40}$$

The axiomatic solution of the generalized Nash negotiation, or x^G, is defined by:

$$x^G = \operatorname*{Arg\,Max}_{x}[u_1(x) - d_1]^\gamma [u_2(1 - x) - d_2]^{1-\gamma}$$

The first-order condition then entails:

$$\frac{u_1'(x^G)}{u_2'(1 - x^G)} = \frac{(1 - \gamma)}{\gamma} \frac{u_1(x^G) - d_1}{u_2(1 - x^G) - d_2} \tag{41}$$

Comparison of equations (40) and (41) then shows that $x^G = \tilde{x}$ if, and only if, $d_i = \bar{u}_i$, $i = 1, 2$; and $\gamma = r_2/(r_1 + r_2)$.

REFERENCES

Abowd, J. (1989), "The effect of wage bargaining on the stock market value of the firm," *American Economic Review*, 79, pp. 774–800.

Abowd, J., and Farber, H. (1982), "Job queues and the union status of workers," *Industrial and Labor Relation Review*, 36, pp. 354–367.

Abowd, J., and Kramarz, F. (1993), "A test of negotiation and incentive compensation models using longitudinal French enterprise data," in van Ours, J., Pfann, G., and Ridder, G. (eds.), *Labour Demand and Equilibrium Wage Formation*, Amsterdam: Elsevier Science.

Anderson, S., and Devereux, M. (1988), "Trade unions and the choice of capital stock," *Scandinavian Journal of Economics*, 90(1), pp. 27–44.

Arrow, K. (1963), *Social Choice and Individual Values*, New Haven, Conn.: Yale University Press.

Ashenfelter, O. (1987), "Arbitration and the negotiation process," *American Economic Review, Papers and Proceedings*, 77, pp. 342–346.

Ashenfelter, O., and Brown, J. (1986), "Testing the efficiency of employment contracts," *Journal of Political Economy*, 94, pp. 40–87.

Ashenfelter, O., Currie, J., Farber, H., and Spiegel, M. (1992), "An experimental comparison of dispute rates in alternative arbitration systems," *Econometrica*, 60, pp. 1407–1433.

Ashenfelter, O., and Hyslop, D. (2001), "Measuring the effect of arbitration on wage levels: The case of police officers," *Industrial and Labor Relations Review*, 54, pp. 316–328.

Atherton, W. (1973), *Theory of Union Bargaining Goals*, Princeton, N.J.: Princeton University Press.

Atkinson, A., and Micklewright, J. (1991), "Unemployment compensation and labor market transitions: A critical review," *Journal of Economic Literature*, 39, pp. 1679–1727.

Binmore, K., Rubinstein, A., and Wolinsky, A. (1986), "The Nash solution in economic modelling," *Rand Journal of Economics*, 17(2), pp. 176–188.

Blair, D., and Crawford, D. (1984), "Labor unions' objectives and collective bargaining," *Quarterly Journal of Economics*, 99, pp. 547–566.

Blanchard, O., and Summers, L. (1986), "Hysteresis and the European unemployment problem," in Fischer, S. (ed.), *NBER Macroeconomics Annual*, 1, pp. 15–78.

Blanchflower, D. (1996), "The role and influence of trade unions in the OECD," Dartmouth College, mimeo, www.dartmouth.edu/~blnchflr/Projects/html.

Blanchflower, D., and Bryson, A. (2002), "Changes over time in union relative wage effects in the UK and the US revisited," NBER Working Paper No. 9395.

Blanchflower, D., and Freeman, R. (1992), "Unionism in the U.S. and in other advanced O.E.C.D. countries," *Industrial Relations*, 31, pp. 56–79.

Blanchflower, D., and Freeman, R. (1994), "Did the Thatcher reforms change British labour performance?" in Barell, R. (ed.), *The UK Labour Market: Comparative Aspects and Institutional Developments*, pp. 51–72. Cambridge, U.K.: Cambridge University Press.

Blau, F., and Kahn, L. (1996), "International differences in male wage inequality: Institution versus market forces," *Journal of Political Economy*, 104, pp. 791–837.

Blau, F., and Kahn, L. (1999), "Institutions and laws in the labor market," in Ashenfelter, O., and Card, D. (eds.), *Handbook of Labor Economics*, vol. 3A, chap. 25, pp. 1399–1461. Amsterdam: Elsevier Science/North-Holland.

Boal, W., and Pencavel, J. (1994), "The effects of labor unions on employment, wages and day of operation: Coal mining in West Virginia," *Quarterly Journal of Economics*, 109, pp. 267–298.

Booth, A. (1984), "A public choice model of trade union behaviour and membership," *Economic Journal*, 94, pp. 883–898.

Booth, A. (1995a), *The Economics of the Trade Union*, Cambridge, U.K.: Cambridge University Press.

Booth, A. (1995b), "Layoffs with payoffs: A bargaining model of union wage and severance pay determination," *Economica*, 62, pp. 551–564.

Booth, A., and Ravaillon, M. (1993), "Employment and the length of the working week in a unionized economy in which hours of work influence productivity," *Economic Record*, 69, pp. 428–436.

Bronars, S., Deere, D., and Tracy, J. (1994), "The effects of unions on firm behavior: An empirical analysis using firm-level data," *Industrial Relations*, 33, pp. 426–451.

Bruno, M., and Sachs, J. (1985), *Economics of Worldwide Stagflation*, Oxford, U.K.: Basil Blackwell.

Cahuc, P., and Kramarz, F. (1997), "Voice and loyalty as a delegation of authority: A model and a test on a panel of French firms," *Journal of Labor Economics*, 15(4), pp. 658–688.

Card, D. (1986), "Efficient contracts with costly adjustment: Short run employment determination for airline mechanics," *American Economic Review*, 76, pp. 1045–1071.

Card, D. (1990), "Unexpected inflation, real wages, and employment determination in union contracts," *American Economic Review*, 80, pp. 669–688.

Card, D. (1996), "The effect of unions on the structure of wages: A longitudinal analysis," *Econometrica*, 64, pp. 957–979.

Card, D. (2001), "The effect of unions on wage inequality in the U.S. labor market," *Industrial and Labor Relations Review*, 54, pp. 296–315.

Carruth, A., and Oswald, A. (1985), "Miners' wages in post-war Britain: An application of a model of trade union behaviour," *Economic Journal*, 95, pp. 1003–1020.

Carruth, A., Oswald, A., and Findlay, L. (1986), "A test of a model of trade union behaviour: The coal and steel industry in Britain," *Oxford Bulletin of Economics and Statistics*, 48, pp. 1–18.

Checchi, D., and Lucifora, C. (2002), "Unions and labour market institutions in Europe," *Economic Policy*, 35, pp. 363–408.

Clark, A., and Oswald, A. (1994), "Unhappiness and unemployment," *Economic Journal*, 104, pp. 648–669.

Connolly, R., Hirsch, B., and Hirschey, M. (1986), "Union rent seeking, tangible capital and market value of the firm," *Review of Economics and Statistics*, 68, pp. 567–577.

Contensou, F., and Vranceanu, R. (2000), *Working Time: Theory and Policy Implications*, Edward Elgar.

Cramton, P., Gunderson, M., and Tracy, J. (1999), "The effect of collective bargaining legislation on strikes and wages," *Review of Economics and Statistics*, 81, pp. 475–487.

Cramton, P., and Tracy, J. (1992), "Strikes and holdouts in wage bargaining: Theory and data," *American Economic Review*, 82, pp. 1200–1210.

De Menil, G. (1971), *Bargaining: Monopoly Power Versus Union Power*, Cambridge, Mass.: MIT Press.

Dell'Aringa, C., and Lucifora, C. (1994), "Wage dispersion and unionism: Do unions protect low pay?" *International Journal of Manpower*, 15, pp. 150–169.

Denny, K., and Nickell, S. (1992), "Unions and investment in British industry," *Economic Journal*, 102, pp. 874–887.

Dertouzos, J., and Pencavel, J. (1981), "Wage and employment determination under trade unionism: The case of the International Typographical Union," *Journal of Political Economy*, 89, pp. 1162–1181.

Devereux, M., and Lockwood, B. (1991), "Trade unions, nonbinding wage agreements, and capital accumulation," *European Economic Review*, 35, pp. 1411–1426.

DiNardo, J., Fortin, N., and Lemieux, T. (1996), "Labor market institutions and the distribution of wages, 1973–1992: A semi-parametric approach," *Econometrica*, 64, pp. 1001–1044.

Drèze, J., and Modigliani, F. (1981), "The trade-off between real wage and employment in an open economy," *European Economic Review*, 15, pp. 1–40.

Duncan, G., and Stafford, F. (1980), "Do union members receive compensating wage differential?" *American Economic Review*, 70, pp. 355–371.

Dunlop, J. (1944), *Wage Determination Under Trade Unions*, New York: Macmillan.

Edgeworth, F. (1881), *Mathematical Psychics*, London: Kegan Paul.

Espinosa, P., and Rhee, C. (1989), "Efficient wage bargaining as a repeated game," *Quarterly Journal of Economics*, 104, pp. 565–588.

Farber, H. (1978), "Individual preferences and union wage determination: The case of the United Mine Workers," *Journal of Political Economy*, 86, pp. 923–942.

Farber, H. (1983), "The determination of the union status of workers," *Econometrica*, 51, pp. 1417–1438.

Farber, H. (1986), "The analysis of union behavior," in Ashenfelter, O., and Layard, R. (eds.), *Handbook of Labor Economics*, vol. 2, pp. 1139–1189, Amsterdam: Elsevier Science/North-Holland.

Farber, H., and Bazerman, M. (1986), "The general basis of arbitrator behavior: An empirical analysis of conventional and final-offer arbitration," *Econometrica*, 54, pp. 1503–1528.

Farber, H., and Saks, D. (1980), "Why workers want unions: The role of relative wages and job characteristics," *Journal of Political Economy*, 88, pp. 349–369.

Fehr, E. (1990), "Cooperation, harassment and involuntary unemployment: Comment," *American Economic Review*, 80, pp. 624–630.

Fernandez, R., and Glazer, J. (1991), "Striking for a bargain between two completely informed agents," *American Economic Review*, 81, pp. 240–252.

Fortin, N., and Lemieux, T. (1997), "Institutional changes and rising wage inequality: Is there a linkage?" *Journal of Economic Perspectives*, 11, pp. 75–96.

Freeman, R. (1980), "Unionism and the dispersion of wages," *Industrial and Labor Relations Review*, 34, pp. 3–23.

Freeman, R., and Medoff, J. (1984), *What Do Unions Do?* New York: Basic Books. French translation: *Pourquoi les syndicats? Une réponse américaine*, Paris: Economica, 1987.

Friedman, J. (1986), *Game Theory with Applications to Economics*, Oxford, U.K.: Oxford University Press.

Gottfries, N., and Horn, H. (1987), "Wage formation and the persistence of unemployment," *Economic Journal*, 97, pp. 877–886.

Grout, P. (1984), "Investment and wages in the absence of binding contracts," *Econometrica*, 52, pp. 449–460.

Hamermesh, D. (1993), *Labor Demand*, Princeton, N.J.: Princeton University Press.

Hartog, J., and Theeuwes, J. (eds.) (1993), *Labour Market Contracts and Institutions: A Cross National Comparison*, Amsterdam: Elsevier Science/North-Holland.

Heckman, J. (1979), "Sample selection bias as a specification error," *Econometrica*, 47, pp. 153–161.

Hicks, J. (1932/1963), *The Theory of Wages*, 2nd ed., New York: Macmillan.

Hirsch, B. (1992), "Firm investment behavior and collective strategy," *Industrial Relations*, 31, pp. 95–121.

Hirsch, B., and Addison, J. (1986), *The Economic Analysis of Unions: New Approaches and Evidence*, Boston: Allen and Unwin.

Hirschman, A. (1970), *Exit, Voice and Loyalty*, Cambridge, Mass.: Harvard University Press.

Holmund, B., and Zetterberg, J. (1991), "Insiders' effects in wage determination: Evidence from five countries," *European Economic Review*, 35, pp. 1009–1034.

Kahn, L. (1998), "Collective bargaining and the interindustry wage structure," *Economica*, 65, pp. 507–534.

Kahn, L. (2000), "Wage inequality, collective bargaining and relative employment from 1985 to 1994: Evidence from fifteen OECD countries," *Review of Economics and Statistics*, 82, pp. 564–579.

Kalai, E., and Smorodinsky, M. (1975), "Other solutions to Nash's bargaining problem," *Econometrica*, 43, pp. 513–518.

Kennan, J., and Wilson, R. (1993), "Bargaining with private information," *Journal of Economic Literature*, 31, pp. 45–104.

Kiander, J. (1993), "Endogenous unemployment insurance in a monopoly union model when job search matters," *Journal of Public Economics*, 52, pp. 101–115.

Kreps, D. (1990), *A Course in Microeconomics Theory*, Harvester Wheatsheaf.

Layard, R., Nickell, S., and Jackman, R. (1991), *Unemployment*, Oxford, U.K.: Oxford University Press.

Lee, L. (1978), "Unionism and wage rates: A simultaneous equations model with qualitative and limited dependent variables," *International Economic Review*, 19, pp. 415–434.

Lemieux, T. (1998), "Estimating the effect of unions on wage inequality in a panel data model with comparative advantage and nonrandom selection," *Journal of Labor Economics*, 16, pp. 261–291.

Leontief, W. (1946), "The pure theory of the guaranteed annual wage contract," *Journal of Political Economy*, 54, pp. 76–79.

Lever, M. (1995), "Insiders-outsiders effects in wage formation: An empirical survey," *Bulletin of Economic Research*, 47, pp. 257–274.

Lewis, H. (1963), *Unionism and Relative Wages in the United States: An Empirical Inquiry*, Chicago: University of Chicago Press.

Lewis, H. (1986), "Union relative wage effects," in Ashenfelter, O., and Layard, R. (eds.), *Handbook of Labor Economics*, vol. 2, Amsterdam: Elsevier Science/North-Holland.

Lindbeck, A., and Snower, D. (1987), "Union activity, unemployment persistence and wage employment ratchets," *European Economic Review*, 31, pp. 157–167.

Lindbeck, A., and Snower, D. (1988), "Cooperation, harassment and involuntary unemployment: An insider-outsider approach," *American Economic Review*, 78, pp. 167–188.

Lindbeck, A., and Snower, D. (2001), "Insiders versus outsiders," *Journal of Economic Perspectives*, 15, pp. 165–188.

MacDonald, I., and Solow, R. (1981), "Wage bargaining and employment," *American Economic Review*, 71(5), pp. 896–908.

MaCurdy, T., and Pencavel, J. (1986), "Testing between competing models of wage and employment determination in unionised markets," *Journal of Political Economy*, 94, suppl., pp. 513–539.

Maloney, T. (1994), "Estimating the effects of the employment contracts act on employment and wages in New Zealand," *Australian Bulletin of Labour*, 20, pp. 320–343.

Manning, A. (1987), "An integration of trade union models in a sequential bargaining framework," *Economic Journal*, 97, pp. 121–139.

Martin, D. (1980), *An Ownership Theory of the Trade Union*, Berkeley and Los Angeles: University of California Press.

Nash, J. (1950), "The bargaining problem," *Econometrica*, 18, pp. 155–162.

Nash, J. (1953), "Two-person cooperative game," *Econometrica*, 21(1), pp. 128–140.

Nickell, S., and Andrews, M. (1983), "Unions, real wage and employment in Britain 1951–79," *Oxford Economic Papers*, 35, suppl., pp. 183–206.

Nickell, S., and Wadhwani, S. (1990), "Insider forces and wage determination," *Economic Journal*, 100, pp. 496–509.

Ochs, J., and Roth, A. (1989), "An experimental study of sequential bargaining," *American Economic Review*, 79, pp. 355–384.

Odgers, C., and Betts, J. (1997), "Do unions reduce investment?" *Industrial and Labor Relations Review*, 51, pp. 18–36.

OECD (1994), *Employment Outlook*, Paris: OECD.

OECD (1997), *Employment Outlook*, Paris: OECD.

Osborne, M., and Rubinstein, A. (1990), *Bargaining and Markets*, San Diego, Calif.: Academic Press.

Oswald, A. (1982), "The microeconomic theory of the trade union," *Economic Journal*, 92, pp. 576–595.

Pencavel, J. (1984), "The empirical performance of a model of trade union behavior," in Rosa, J.-J. (ed.), *The Economics of Trade Unions: New Directions*, Boston: Kluwer-Nijhoff.

Pencavel, J. (1991), *Labor Market Under Trade Unionism: Employment, Wages and Hours*, Cambridge, Mass.: Blackwell.

Robinson, C. (1989), "The joint determination of union status and union wage effects: Some tests of alternative models," *Journal of Political Economy*, 97, pp. 639–667.

Rosen, S. (1970), "Unionism and the occupational wage structure in the United States," *International Economic Review*, 11, pp. 269–286.

Ross, A. (1948), *Trade Union Wage Policy*, Berkeley and Los Angeles: University of California Press.

Rowthorn, R. (1992), "Centralisation, employment and wage dispersion," *Economic Journal*, 102, pp. 506–523.

Ruback, S., and Zimmerman, M. (1984), "Unionization and profitability: Evidence from the capital market," *Journal of Political Economy*, 92, pp. 1134–1157.

Rubinstein, A. (1982), "Perfect equilibrium in a bargaining model," *Econometrica*, 50, pp. 97–109.

Stahl, I. (1972), *Bargaining Theory*, Stockholm: Economic Research Institute, Stockholm School of Economics.

Strand, J. (1989), "Monopoly unions versus efficient bargaining: A repeated game approach," *European Journal of Political Economy*, 5, pp. 473–486.

Tan, H., Chapman, B., Peterson, C., and Booth, A. (1992), "Youth training in the United States, Britain and Australia," *Research in Labor Economics*, 13, pp. 63–99.

Tracy, J. (1986), ''An investigation into the determinants of U.S. strike activity,'' *American Economic Review*, 76, pp. 423–36.

van der Ploeg, R. (1987), ''Trade unions, investment and employment: A noncooperative approach,'' *European Economic Review*, 31, pp. 1465–1492.

Van Reenen, J. (1996), ''The creation and capture of economic rents: Wages and innovations in UK manufacturing plants,'' *Quarterly Journal of Economics*, 111, pp. 195–226.

Zeuthen, F. (1930), *Problems of Monopoly and Economics*, London, U.K.: G. Routledge.

PART THREE

UNEMPLOYMENT AND INEQUALITY

CHAPTER **8**

UNEMPLOYMENT AND INFLATION

CONTENTS

In this chapter, we will:

- Survey the evolution of aggregate unemployment in the major industrialized countries during the last 30 years

- Compare the classical theory and the Keynesian theory of unemployment

- Discover the Phillips curve, the NAIRU, and some of their estimates

- Study the inflation–unemployment trade-off and the dynamics of unemployment

- Learn what the hysteresis effect is and why unemployment may be persistent

INTRODUCTION

The goal of macroeconomic analysis is to explain changes occurring over time in the main aggregates that characterize the economic activity of a nation. For labor economics, the essential ones are the aggregate values of employment and wages. The theory of wages examined in chapters 5, 6, and 7 assign a central role to the behavior of agents, who take a direct part in the setting of wages through the bargaining process or through putting incentive mechanisms in place. We will see in this chapter that recent developments in macroeconomics have been influenced by these advances in wage theory.

The model of perfect competition has also played a very important role in the development of macroeconomics, however. According to the classical economists, who adopted the model of perfect competition as the best way to represent the functioning of the economy, real wages achieve *ongoing* equilibrium between supply and demand in the labor market. Keynesians, on the other hand, take the view that markets, in particular labor markets, can find themselves stuck in situations of disequilibrium for long periods. Keynesianism certainly allows that in the long run, real wages do align supply and demand, but it insists that in the short and medium run this variable displays a certain rigidity that hinders permanent adjustment in the labor market. From this standpoint, the process of wage setting is no longer represented by a competitive model but rather by a "Phillips curve"—the expression of a decreasing relation between the unemployment rate and the growth rate of the average wage.

This conceptual difference leads to divergent views about how to assess the efficiency of policies for managing aggregate demand. For Keynesian economists, prolonged disequilibria in different markets lead to periods of more or less durable underemployment, which should be countered by stabilization policies that affect the volume of aggregate demand. Conversely, classical economists see business cycles as movements of a state of equilibrium subjected to shocks. From this standpoint, stabilization policies that aim at stabilizing aggregate demand are not necessary, for the equilibrium level of aggregate output is determined by real variables, over which such policies have no influence.

The theory of fixed price equilibria (presented in Bénassy, 1993) supplied a rigorous framework, enabling a better understanding of the different possible causes of unemployment. These analyses do not fall within our purview here, as they are too peripheral to the subject of this book and deal only with a very short-run perspective, in which prices as a whole remain totally rigid. Instead, our horizon will be the short to medium run, over which it is generally taken for granted that markets for goods reach equilibrium through price and that the labor market alone is liable to experience durable disequilibria. It appears that stabilization of aggregate demand is effective only if wages display some *nominal* rigidity, i.e., a certain delay in the reaction of nominal wages to variations in the general level of prices. When such nominal rigidity is absent, stabilization policies are ineffective and influence only the inflation rate.

Unemployment is the result, then, of rigidity in real wages. On that basis, supply side policies should be adopted in order to influence unemployment.

The aim of this chapter is to present standard macroeconomic analysis of unemployment. For this purpose, it is important to keep in mind stylized facts regarding unemployment, employment, and wages, in different OECD countries (section 1). These facts clearly show that countries that faced a high unemployment rate during the 1980s and 1990s did so because of low job creation compared with countries with low rates of unemployment, and not because of a large increase in the labor supply. Standard macroeconomics explains these stylized facts on the basis of a Keynesian model, presented in section 2. This type of model has been used for several decades, by a number of institutions engaged in economic forecasting, for the purpose of assessing the impact of macroeconomic policies. In this regard a number of critiques, particularly concerning the process of wage formation, have been directed at it. Section 3 lays out the ones that bear on the origins of nominal rigidities, while section 4 is devoted to the examination of real rigidities. Finally, section 5 presents empirical estimates that enable us to assess the relevance of the different explanations for unemployment proffered by standard macroeconomics.

1 SOME FACTS

During the last 30 years, the industrialized countries have evolved in very different directions with respect to unemployment. In contradistinction to the United States or Japan, most countries of continental Europe have not succeeded in creating enough jobs, and at the turn of the millennium, they showed a high proportion of long-term unemployed.

1.1 THE DIFFERENT UNEMPLOYMENT EXPERIENCES

Table 8.1 shows rates of unemployment, labor market participation, and employment in 19 OECD countries for the year 2001. We see that unemployment is a phenomenon that touches all OECD countries, but in very different proportions. Some countries, such as the United States, Japan, Norway, Luxembourg, the Netherlands, Switzerland, and Portugal, have an unemployment rate below 5%. But other countries, such as France, Italy, and Spain, display an unemployment rate higher than 10%. For the European Union as a whole, the average unemployment rate is in the neighborhood of 10%.

The third column of table 8.1 reports the employment rates, i.e., the ratio of the number of persons employed to the number of persons in the population who are of working age (from 15 to 64 years old). This indicator is a useful complement to the data on unemployment, given that the definition of unemployment is necessarily subjective (see chapter 1). All the figures given in this table correspond to the standardized OECD definition of unemployment, but national specifics are important

Table 8.1

Rates of unemployment, participation, and employment in 19 OECD countries in 2001.

Country	Unemployment rate (%)	Participation rate (%)	Employment rate (%)
Australia	6.7	73.8	68.9
Austria	4.0	70.7	67.8
Belgium	6.2	63.6	59.7
Canada	7.3	76.5	70.9
Denmark	4.2	79.2	75.9
Finland	9.2	74.6	67.7
France	8.8	68.0	62.0
Germany	8.0	71.6	65.9
Italy	9.6	60.7	54.9
Japan	5.2	72.6	68.8
Luxembourg	1.9	64.2	63.0
Netherlands	2.1	75.7	74.1
Norway	3.5	80.3	77.5
Portugal	4.3	71.8	68.7
Spain	10.5	65.8	58.8
Sweden	5.1	79.3	75.3
Switzerland	2.5	81.2	79.1
United Kingdom	4.8	74.9	71.3
United States	4.8	76.8	73.1
European Union	7.4	69.2	64.1
Total OECD	6.4	69.8	65.3

Source: OECD data.

sources of heterogeneity. For example, generous unemployment benefits may impel individuals to look for a job, or claim to be doing so, in order to gain access to unemployment benefits. In this case, unemployment is in part the result of a high level of labor market participation, not of an insufficient number of jobs.

Scrutiny of table 8.1 and figure 8.1 indicates, however, that the countries with a high unemployment rate are also the ones with low rates of employment. In particular, figure 8.1 shows that there exists a decreasing relation between the unemployment rate and the rate of employment, and that the dispersion of the cluster of points around the regression line is relatively weak. The unemployment rate is thus a relevant indicator of the abundance of jobs in a country. The second column of table 8.1 also shows that participation rates are highly dispersed, since they vary from 60.7% in Italy to 81.2% in Switzerland (readers will recall that the participation rate equals the ratio of the labor force to the working-age population). Moreover, countries that face a

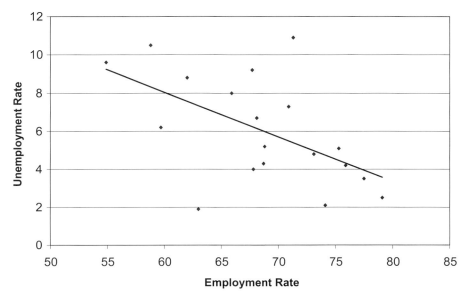

FIGURE 8.1

The relationship between the unemployment rate and the employment rate in 19 OECD countries in 2001.

Source: OECD data.

high unemployment rate generally have a relatively weak rate of participation. This observation is illustrated in figure 8.2, which reveals a decreasing relation between participation rates and unemployment rates. Thus, high unemployment does not result from an excessively high participation rate.

This rapid overview of unemployment, employment, and labor market participation as experienced in different OECD countries suggests that certain countries face a relatively high unemployment rate because of insufficient job creation, not abnormally high participation rates. Examination of *changes over time* since the beginning of the 1960s in employment, unemployment, and the labor force in the United States, Japan, and three continental European countries—Germany, France, and Italy—that have experienced high unemployment will throw further light on the origins of underemployment.

1.2 CHANGES IN EMPLOYMENT, UNEMPLOYMENT, AND LABOR FORCE

Figure 8.3 shows that the unemployment rate has evolved very differently in Japan, the continental European countries of Germany, France, and Italy, and the United States. Between 1960 and 1994, Japan was characterized by great stability in this indicator, so much so that the two oil shocks of 1974 and 1979 seem not to have had much impact. But between 1994 and 2001, the unemployment rate rose steadily in this country. Conversely, the American unemployment rate has fluctuated significantly. The

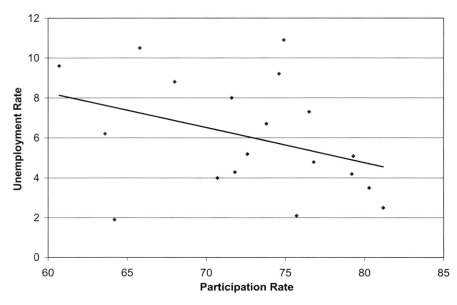

Figure 8.2

The relationship between the unemployment rate and the participation rate in 19 OECD countries in 2001.

Source: OECD data.

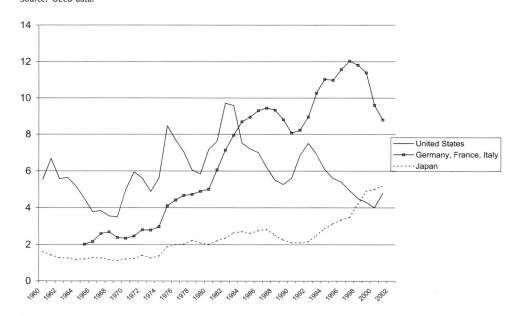

Figure 8.3

Change in the unemployment rate in the United States, Japan, and continental Europe (Germany, France, Italy), 1960–2001.

Source: OECD data.

unemployment rate in the continental European countries stayed relatively low until the 1970s, but rose steadily until 1997; from then to the end of the period considered, it diminished.

The Relation Among Unemployment, Employment, and the Labor Force
We can assess change in the unemployment rate with the help of the following accounting equality:

$$N_t \tau_t = L_t + U_t$$

In this relation N_t, L_t, U_t, and τ_t designate respectively the population of working age, the level of employment, the number of unemployed, and the participation rate at period t. The unemployment rate being defined by $u_t \equiv U_t/(L_t + U_t)$, we have:

$$N_t \tau_t = \frac{L_t}{1 - u_t}$$

Using this equation in logarithms at dates t and $t - 1$, and using the approximation $\text{Lim}_{x \to 1} \ln x = x - 1$, we get ($\Delta$ is the difference operator, $\Delta N_t = N_t - N_{t-1}$):

$$\frac{\Delta N_t}{N_{t-1}} + \frac{\Delta \tau_t}{\tau_{t-1}} = \frac{\Delta L_t}{L_{t-1}} + \frac{\Delta u_t}{1 - u_{t-1}}$$

With the assumption that u is a small number, which is the case in reality, this relation allows us to express the variations in the unemployment rate as a function of the growth rates of the working-age population, employment, and participation:

$$\Delta u_t \simeq \frac{\Delta N_t}{N_{t-1}} + \frac{\Delta \tau_t}{\tau_{t-1}} - \frac{\Delta L_t}{L_{t-1}}$$

This decomposition shows that variations in the unemployment rate come from variations in the employment rate, the size of the working-age population, and changes in the participation rate. The relationship between the unemployment rate and employment is thus not a simple one. It is entirely possible for the unemployment rate to fall without employment rising if, for example, the labor force shrinks. Figure 8.4 shows that the growth of unemployment in Europe is not the outcome of this scenario, for Germany, France, and Italy, where the unemployment rates rose steeply until 1997, experienced relatively slow rates of expansion of the labor force compared with the United States or even Japan (the sudden jump in the labor force in Europe in 1990 came from German reunification).

The Chronic Weakness of Job Creation in Continental Europe
We observe that, without exception, the expansion of the labor force is weaker in the continental European countries than in the United States and Japan. The relatively strong expansion of the labor force in the United States and Japan is the result of a rise in the rates of participation and a more sustained growth in the size of the working-age population. It is interesting to note that the rate of participation has risen considerably in the United States, and even in Japan (since 1975), whereas it reached the

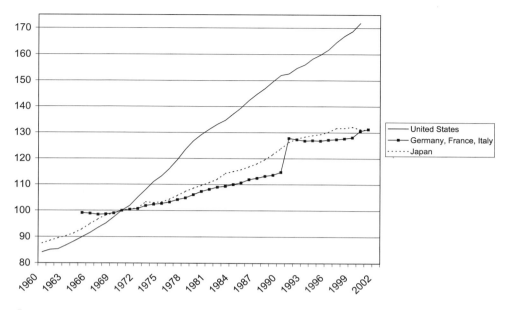

FIGURE 8.4

Changes in the labor force in the United States, Japan, and continental Europe (Germany, France, Italy), 1960–2001, base 100, 1970.

Source: OECD data.

same level in Germany, France, and Italy (figure 8.5) in 1965 and 1997, and then began to rise in 1997 in these three countries, when the unemployment rate began to decrease. The good performances of the United States and Japan when it comes to unemployment are thus not due to less growth of the labor force. We observe further that participation rates are higher in the countries where unemployment has not risen over the period as a whole.

All these elements suggest that the United States and Japan clearly have a greater capacity to create jobs than do Germany, France, and Italy. This conclusion emerges sharply in figure 8.6, showing that the increase in employment in the United States and Japan has been much greater than in the European countries on which we have focused (the sudden jump that appears in continental Europe is an effect of German reunification, which brought a purely mechanical increase in employment).

Figure 8.7 tells us that the European countries' poor performance in job creation leads to low employment rates. Since 1975, in Germany, France, and Italy, the employment rate (which equals the ratio of the number of jobs to the size of the working-age population) has continually been lower than that of the United States and Japan. Moreover, the employment rate has risen constantly in the two latter countries since 1975. So it is that at the beginning of the third millennium, the difference in employment rates between the continental European countries, on the one hand, and the

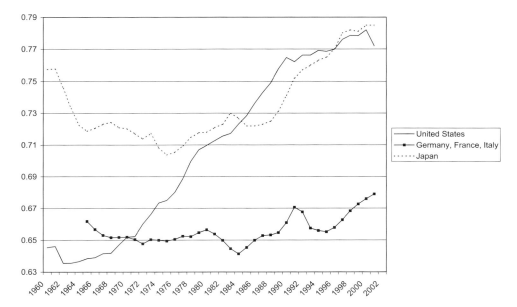

FIGURE 8.5
Changes in the rates of participation in the United States, Japan, and continental Europe (Germany, France, Italy), 1960–2001.

Source: OECD data.

United States and Japan, on the other, is considerable, and clearly larger than the difference in unemployment rates.

In sum, the picture is particularly negative for Germany, France, Italy, and other European countries, such as Belgium and Spain. It reveals a structural incapacity to create enough jobs for more than 30 years. During the 1960s, this lack was offset by a significant fall in the overall participation rate. But since 1970 the latter variable has remained more or less stable, and the weakness of job creation has been fully reflected in unemployment.

1.3 LONG-TERM UNEMPLOYMENT

A very high proportion of long-term unemployed persons—those who have been looking for a job for more than a year—clearly distinguishes many countries of continental Europe from certain other industrialized countries. Figure 8.8 shows that the long-term unemployed represent a major share of overall unemployment in Belgium, France, Germany, Italy, the Netherlands, and Spain. The corresponding share in the United States and Japan is very small. Long-term unemployment is a phenomenon proper to certain countries of continental Europe. It is capable of having dire effects on the "employability" of suppliers of labor, and constitutes an important source of degradation in the overall functioning of the labor market (see section 4.1 below). The

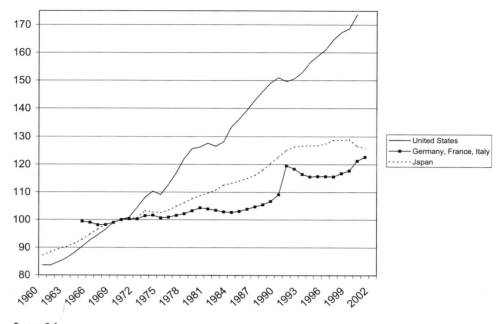

FIGURE 8.6

Changes in employment in the United States, Japan, and continental Europe (Germany, France, Italy), 1960–2001. 1970 = 100.

Source: OECD data.

overall level of unemployment is intimately tied to the level of long-term unemployment. As we see in figure 8.9, the countries where the unemployment rate is high are also the ones with a strong percentage of long-term unemployed.

1.4 FLUCTUATIONS IN REAL WAGES AND EMPLOYMENT

Fluctuations in real wages and employment share common features in all OECD countries. In order to spotlight the cyclical properties of a variable, we calculate the relative variations of this variable with respect to its trend. The latter is generally found using a moving average. The method most frequently employed by economists to calculate a moving average is to use the Hodrick and Prescott filter (1997). This filter yields the trend x_t of a series y_t, defined at dates $t = 1, \ldots, T$, by minimizing the sum of the variance of y_t around x_t and a term that increases with the second differences of the trend x_t. The "filtered" series defining trend x_t is thus the solution of the following problem:

$$\underset{\{x_t\}}{\text{Min}} \sum_{t=1}^{T} (y_t - x_t)^2 + \lambda \sum_{t=2}^{T-1} [(x_{t+1} - x_t) - (x_t - x_{t-1})]^2$$

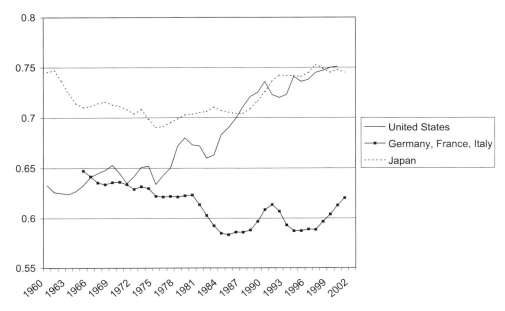

FIGURE 8.7

Changes in the employment rate in the United States, Japan, and continental Europe (Germany, France, Italy), 1960–2001.

Source: OECD data.

In this problem, $\lambda > 0$ is a parameter making it possible to control the variability of the trend. The greater this parameter, the weaker the variability of the trend. If $\lambda \to 0$, the trend merges with the series x_t and it becomes linear with $\lambda \to \infty$.

Figures 8.10 and 8.11 present the relative deviations of the productivity of labor, real wages, and employment with respect to their trend (calculated on annual data with the Hodrick and Prescott filter for $\lambda = 100$) in the United States and France over the period 1970–1998. We observe a positive correlation between the productivity of labor and employment. A rise in the productivity of labor has a tendency to increase hires, and thus to increase aggregate production. Moreover, real wages are also positively affected by an increase in the productivity of labor. These three variables, which are in addition positively correlated with the GDP, are therefore procyclical. It is interesting to note that the volatility of these three variables taken together is greater in the United States. The standard deviation of the wage (relative to its trend) is equal to 0.0099 in France and 0.0111 in the United States, whereas the standard deviation of employment (relative to its trend) takes the values 0.0138 in the United States and 0.0078 in France. The cycle is thus much less pronounced in France, and more generally in a number of European countries, than in the United States.

We have highlighted three "stylized facts," which can be summed up as follows: 1) high unemployment in Europe is not caused by growth in the labor force more

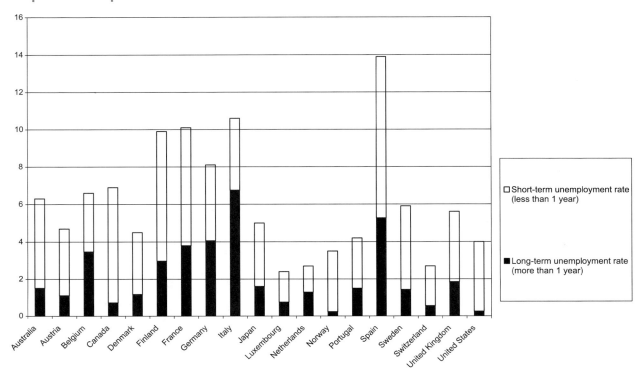

FIGURE 8.8

Rates of short- and long-term unemployment in 19 OECD countries in 2000.

Source: OECD data.

rapid than that of the United States or Japan; it is caused by less job creation; 2) many EU countries are distinguished by a high proportion of long-term unemployed; 3) employment and real wages are two procyclical variables that are positively correlated with labor productivity.

2   FROM THE CLASSICAL MODEL TO THE KEYNESIAN VIEW

The classical model, in which wages perpetually bring about equilibrium between labor supply and demand, constitutes the model of reference for macroeconomic analysis and the point of departure for all subsequent developments. It does not, however, supply a totally convincing theory of fluctuations in aggregate quantities.

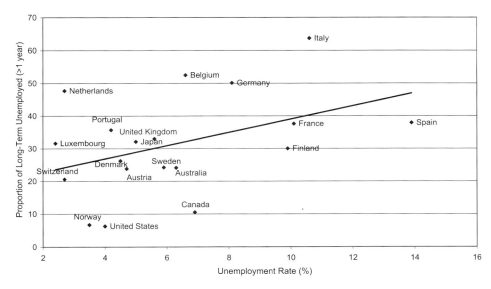

FIGURE 8.9

The relationship between the unemployment rate and the proportion of long-term unemployed in 19 OECD countries in 2000.

Source: OECD data.

Nor does it grant that changes in aggregate demand have any influence on real variables, even in the short run, and it proves to be incapable of explaining involuntary unemployment. These limitations have led to alternative explanations. In the Keynesian approach, nominal wages are characterized by a short-run rigidity. More precisely, the progressive adjustment of wages involves a relationship between nominal wage changes and the unemployment rate, known as the *Phillips curve*. It exhibits a short run trade-off between inflation and unemployment, and thus endorses the effectiveness of policies aimed at stimulating global demand in order to combat unemployment in the short run. In the long run, however, macroeconomic policies aimed at stimulating demand have no influence on the level of unemployment, which depends on the structural features of the economy.

2.1 THE CLASSICAL THEORY

The hypothesis of the perfect flexibility of prices in the classical theory entails that changes in aggregate demand can have no effect, even in the short run. This prediction is not verified. Moreover, for the classical model to agree with observed correlations between employment and productivity, the elasticity of the aggregate labor supply would have to be much greater than it is in reality.

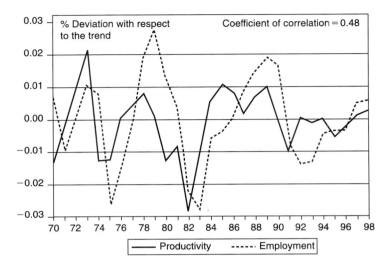

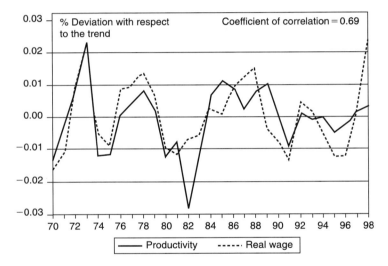

FIGURE 8.10

Fluctuations in the productivity of labor, real wages, and employment in the United States, 1970–1998 (annual data). Real wages are equal to the average wage deflated by the consumer price index.

Source: OECD data.

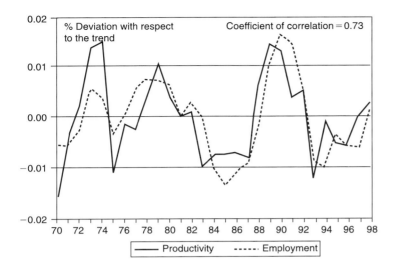

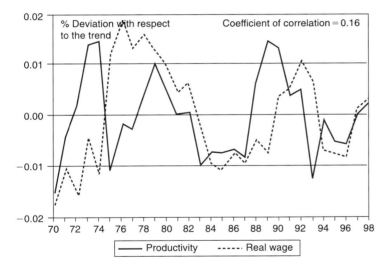

FIGURE 8.11

Fluctuations in the apparent productivity of labor, real wages, and employment in France, 1970–1998 (annual data).

Real wages are equal to the average wage deflated by the consumer price index.

A Simple Model

The microeconomic foundations of the model we will work with are laid out in detail in appendix 1 to this chapter. The economy will comprise three goods: labor, offered by households and utilized by firms in production; a good, representing all the goods and services produced by firms and consumed by households; and money, the numeraire, which is storable and created by the state to serve as a medium of exchange.

Let y_t be the logarithm of the aggregate output, let m_t be the logarithm of the money supply, and let p_t be the logarithm of the price index. We show in appendix 1 that the equality of supply and demand in the market for goods and services entails:

$$y_t = m_t - p_t \tag{1}$$

Firms produce with a constant-return-to-scale technology which is represented by the following production function:

$$y_t = a_t + \ell_t \tag{2}$$

where ℓ_t designates the logarithm of employment and a_t is a strictly positive productivity parameter. The price p_t is set by firms, which are assumed to have some market power. It is obtained by multiplying the marginal cost by a markup. Denoting by w_t the logarithm of the nominal wage, one gets:

$$p_t = w_t - a_t + \chi \tag{3}$$

Appendix 1 to this chapter presents a simple model showing that parameter χ increases with the market power of firms. This appendix also explains that in a richer model, parameter χ must increase with the cost of capital (or energy) and the payroll tax.

The logarithm of the labor supply of households, denoted by ℓ_t^s, is an increasing function of real wages:

$$\ell_t^s = \bar{\ell} + \eta(w_t - p_t) \tag{4}$$

In this expression, $\bar{\ell}$ and η are constant parameters. These last four equations have five unknowns, $\ell_t, \ell_t^s, y_t, p_t,$ and w_t. Therefore, one equation needed to determine the equilibrium values of the unknowns is missing.

The Labor Market Equilibrium

The classical theory rests on the idea that the real wage maintains the labor market equilibrium. The equation allowing us to close the model is therefore written $\ell_t = \ell_t^s$ for all t. The price rule (3) and the labor supply (4) then make it possible to find the equilibrium level ℓ_t^* of employment:

$$\ell_t^* = \bar{\ell} + \eta(a_t - \chi) \tag{5}$$

For this value of employment, equilibrium in the market for goods determines the price p_t^*. Equalizing demand (1) with supply (2) thus entails $p_t^* = m_t - \ell_t^* - a_t$. This equilibrium is represented by points E and E' in figure 8.12. In this figure, line D_t

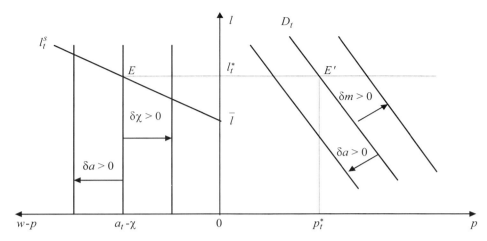

FIGURE 8.12
Classical equilibrium.

represents aggregate demand as a function of employment, or $p_t = m_t - \ell_t - a_t$. It illustrates the classical dichotomy: the *real* fundamentals of the economy—the tastes of consumers and the characteristics of production, summarized here by parameters $a_t, \chi, \bar{\ell}$, and η—determine real equilibrium E *independently* of the quantity of money m_t. The latter simply gives the equilibrium value of the price (it is the abscissa of point E' in figure 8.12).

In relation (1), a rise in m_t (denoted by $\delta m > 0$ in figure 8.12) is interpreted as a positive demand shock. We see that the only effect it has is to increase the price. A policy increasing transfers to households, financed by money creation (precisely represented in this model by a rise in m_t), thus has no real effect, either in the short run or the long one. So money is neutral. But a positive productivity shock ($\delta a > 0$) increases real wages and employment by reducing the price. In this regard, it is interesting to note that money neutrality requires only that prices equilibrate markets. This result holds whether the competition is perfect ($\chi = 0$) or imperfect ($\chi > 0$). The nature of competition does, however, alter the allocation of resources: the market power of firms decreases output and employment.

The Limits of the Classical Model
The classical model has been the target of numerous critiques. In the first place, it does not permit us to explain *involuntary* unemployment. More exactly, there are no unemployed persons in this model, only *nonparticipants* who choose not to work at the current wage. In the second place, we saw in chapter 1, section 2, that for most countries, particularly in Europe, the elasticity of aggregate labor supply is small. That means that the line ℓ_t^s in figure 8.12 is almost horizontal. Scrutiny of this figure shows that a productivity shock makes real wages change significantly but has a negligible

effect on employment. This prediction contradicts the stylized facts set forth in section 1.4 of this chapter, which indicate on the contrary that employment is strongly correlated with labor productivity: the coefficient of correlation takes the value 0.73 in France and 0.48 in the United States. Generally speaking, the classical model predicts too much volatility in real wages. It could be maintained that movements in the level of employment are caused by changes in labor supply (in figure 8.12, that corresponds to shifts of the whole line ℓ_t^s). But we would then observe a total absence of volatility in real wages, or, assuming that short-run labor demand decreases with wages—since, for a given stock of capital, the marginal productivity of labor is decreasing, and labor demand must decrease with wages (see chapter 4)—countercyclical movements in real wages, which would have a tendency to fall off when production rose. Such a prediction conflicts with the stylized facts presented in the previous section.

Finally, according to the classical model, changes in aggregate demand have no real effect, even in the very short run. Thus, in figure 8.12, we see that $\delta m > 0$ increases the price without changing employment. This conclusion does not fit well with empirical observations, which reveal that changes in aggregate demand do have effects, however transitory (see the survey of Christiano et al., 1999).

2.2 THE INFLATION–UNEMPLOYMENT TRADE-OFF

In the Keynesian approach, the *nominal* wage is rigid in the short run, and there is not necessarily equilibrium between labor supply and demand at every instant. The process of wage adjustment is represented by the Phillips relation.

2.2.1 The Phillips Curve

To describe the functioning of the labor market, the earliest Keynesian works adopted a process of wage formation that depicted a negative relation between the rate of growth of the nominal wage and the unemployment rate. This relation is known as the Phillips curve, in reference to the work of Phillips (1958), who was the first to empirically establish the existence of such a negative correlation, using British data for the period 1861–1957. The simplest interpretation of this curve is to consider that unemployment exerts downward pressure on nominal wages. So, when there are few unemployed, workers are in a position to obtain higher wage increases than they are in situations of high unemployment, because competition among employers to attract workers is intensified by low unemployment.

For the sake of simplicity, we will assume that labor supply is inelastic. If we set $\eta = 0$ in relation (4), labor supply is equal to the constant $\bar{\ell}$. We will likewise assume that a part of this supply is not satisfied at the current wage, whereas firms are all on their labor demand curve. Formally, this hypothesis is set out in the inequality $\ell_t < \bar{\ell}$. Let u_t be the unemployment rate; assuming that it is sufficiently close to zero, then we have $u_t \equiv (\bar{L} - L_t)/\bar{L} \simeq \mathrm{Log}(\bar{L}/L_t)$, and consequently:

$$u_t = \bar{\ell} - \ell_t > 0 \tag{6}$$

In the Keynesian models based on the Phillips curve, unemployment comes from the fact that nominal wages do not immediately react in such a way as to close the gap between supply and demand in the labor market. Yet nominal wages are not totally rigid, because the Phillips curve stipulates a negative relationship between the growth rate of this variable and the unemployment rate. The unemployment rate is not the only variable capable of guiding the movement of nominal wages. In many countries, increases in nominal wages are de facto indexed to inflation. We will take this characteristic into account by adding the inflation rate to the Phillips curve, or, with Δ denoting the difference operator, $\Delta p_t \equiv p_t - p_{t-1}$. We then speak of an "augmented" Phillips curve. The initial formulation has been enriched by other explanatory variables for the purpose of obtaining the best econometric results. In particular, the growth rate Δa_t of productivity is frequently included (for more detail on the possible specifications, see OECD, 1994, 1997, and Richardson et al., 2000). Limiting ourselves to a linear form, the equation of the Phillips curve takes the following form:

$$\Delta w_t = \lambda_0 + (1 - \lambda_1)\Delta p_t + \lambda_1 \Delta p_{t-1} - \lambda_2 u_t + \lambda_3 \Delta a_t \tag{7}$$

This equation makes it possible to clarify the notions of nominal and real rigidity.

The notion of *nominal rigidity* refers to the degree to which nominal wages are sensitive to movements in the price. Among the causes of this rigidity, we may include the money illusion of suppliers of labor, and the costs linked to the negotiation of wage contracts, which prevent wages from being perfectly indexed to prices. In equation (7), parameter λ_1, representing the average length of time wage adjustments take, supplies a measure of the degree of nominal rigidity. If it is close to unity, the degree of nominal rigidity is high, in the sense that an increase in the current inflation rate only entails a slight adjustment of nominal wages in the period. Conversely, if this parameter is close to zero, there is little nominal rigidity, for current inflation is transmitted almost entirely through an increase in nominal wages in the period. In practice, the degree of nominal ridigity is evaluated by estimating a distribution of lags over past inflation rates, not just the inflation rate in the preceding period. Equation (7) thus represents a simplified form of the Phillips relation used in empirical work. The coefficient of the long run indexation of wages to prices is equal to the sum of the coefficients of Δp_t and of Δp_{t-1}. It is thus equal to 1 in the formulation we have adopted. A number of studies have in fact shown that this coefficient was not significantly different from unity, at least for G5 countries (United States, Japan, Germany, France, and the United Kingdom) and from the beginning of the 1960s (see Coe, 1985; Chan-Lee et al., 1987; Gordon, 1997; OECD, 1994, 1997).

In order to grasp the notion of real ridigity, it is helpful to rewrite equation (7) in the following form:

$$\Delta(w_t - p_t) = \lambda_0 - \lambda_1(\Delta p_t - \Delta p_{t-1}) - \lambda_2 u_t + \lambda_3 \Delta a_t \tag{8}$$

Real rigidity portrays the reaction of the real wages growth rate to the level of unemployment. We observe that the influence of the unemployment rate on wage variations increases with λ_2, which is why we consider that $1/\lambda_2$ gives a measure of the degree of real rigidity. Finally, parameter λ_3, generally lying between 0 and 1, represents the degree to which real wages are indexed to productivity gains.

2.2.2 The NAIRU

The Keynesian model comprises five unknowns, $\ell_t, u_t, y_t, w_t,$ and $p_t,$ of which the equilibrium values are the solutions of the system of five equations (1), (2), (3), (6), and (7). The price-setting rule (3) and the Phillips curve (7) make it possible to define a relationship between the unemployment rate and inflation. In the first place, the difference operator applied to equation (3) entails $\Delta p_t = \Delta w_t - \Delta a_t$. This equality signifies that firms immediately pass on increases in nominal wages when they set the selling price of their products. In a more complete model, we could conceive of a certain lag between wage rises and price rises. Substituting the expression of wage growth rate defined by the Phillips curve (7) in this equality, we arrive at a relationship between the *variation* in the inflation rate and the unemployment rate which we shall continue, for simplicity, to describe as the Phillips relation. It is written:

$$\lambda_1(\Delta p_t - \Delta p_{t-1}) = \lambda_0 - \lambda_2 u_t - (1 - \lambda_3)\Delta a_t \tag{9}$$

This equation allows us to define the unemployment rate $\bar{u}_t$ compatible with a constant inflation rate $(\Delta p_t - \Delta p_{t-1} = 0)$. This unemployment rate is commonly called the NAIRU (nonaccelerating inflation rate of unemployment). The NAIRU is sometimes referred to as the "natural" unemployment rate, or the equilibrium unemployment rate, since it also represents, as we will demonstrate below, the long-run equilibrium value of the unemployment rate. Setting $\Delta p_t = \Delta p_{t-1}$ in (9), we immediately get:

$$\bar{u}_t = \frac{\lambda_0 - (1 - \lambda_3)\Delta a_t}{\lambda_2} \tag{10}$$

In particular, when productivity grows at a constant rate $(\Delta a_t = \Delta a, \forall t)$, the NAIRU takes a stationary value $\bar{u}$ defined by:

$$\bar{u} = \frac{\lambda_0 - (1 - \lambda_3)\Delta a}{\lambda_2} \tag{11}$$

It appears that the NAIRU increases with the degree of real rigidity $(1/\lambda_2)$ and that it depends on the rate of growth—not the level—of productivity. If nominal wages are not perfectly indexed to productivity gains $(0 \leq \lambda_3 < 1)$, a slowing of productivity growth (a diminution of Δa_t) will entail a rise in the NAIRU. Bringing the value (10) of the latter into the equation of the Phillips curve (9), we obtain a new form of this equation linking the current unemployment rate, the NAIRU, and the acceleration of inflation. It is written:

$$u_t = \bar{u}_t - \frac{\lambda_1}{\lambda_2}(\Delta p_t - \Delta p_{t-1}) \tag{12}$$

In the absence of nominal rigidity $(\lambda_1 = 0)$, the current unemployment rate is always equal to the NAIRU. Conversely, when $\lambda_1 > 0$, the current unemployment rate is inferior to the NAIRU if and only if inflation increases $(\Delta p_t > \Delta p_{t-1})$.

Equation (12) shows that the unemployment rate can only be lowered by an increase in the inflation rate. Conversely, it is evident that a reduction in the inflation rate must necessarily lead to a transitory increase in unemployment. From this perspective, the ratio λ_1/λ_2, commonly called the *sacrifice ratio*, measures the increase in the unemployment rate necesssary to reduce the inflation rate by one percentage point. The stronger nominal and real rigidities are, the greater this ratio is.

2.3 THE CONSEQUENCES OF MACROECONOMIC POLICY

Macroeconomic policies that act on aggregate demand ought, in principle, to have little effect on long-run employment, but they are liable to have a positive impact in the short run. Conversely, policies that act on the supply side have structural effects that alter the long-run equilibrium of the labor market.

2.3.1 Demand Side Policies

In order to analyze the consequences of changes in aggregate demand, we will begin by studying the properties of long-run equilibria and contrasting them with those of short-run equilibria. We will then concentrate on studying the dynamics of unemployment and inflation when the money supply increases.

Short-Run Equilibrium and Long-Run Equilibrium

To facilitate our study of the relationship between short-run and long-run equilibria, we will assume that productivity and the money supply grow at a constant rate ($\Delta a_t = \Delta a$ and $\Delta m_t = \Delta m$ for all t). This hypothesis entails that the NAIRU remains constant and attains the level $\bar{u}$ given by (11). The analysis of equilibrium and the passage from the short run to the long run prove to be particularly instructive when reasoning in the inflation–unemployment plane. The new form (12) of the Phillips relation yields a first relationship between the inflation rate and the unemployment rate. Using relations (1) and (2), we find an equation defining employment as a function of aggregate demand, or $\ell_t = m_t - a_t - p_t$. Applying the difference operator to this last equality, we get $\Delta p_t = \pi - \Delta \ell_t$, where $\pi \equiv \Delta m - \Delta a$ designates the stationary value of the inflation rate. Assuming that the labor force is constant, relation (6) between the unemployment rate and employment entails $\Delta u_t = -\Delta \ell_t$. In sum, we get a new version of the aggregate demand function that directly ties the inflation rate to the unemployment rate. It is written:

$$\Delta p_t = \pi + u_t - u_{t-1} \qquad \text{with} \qquad \pi = \Delta m - \Delta a \qquad \text{(13)}$$

At date t, the variables inherited from the past, i.e., u_{t-1} and Δp_{t-1}, are known, and the *short-run* equilibrium values of the unemployment rate and inflation correspond to the intersection of two curves defined by relations (12) and (13) for given u_{t-1} and Δp_{t-1}. The Phillips curve, described by (12), reflects the mode of wage formation. It has become customary to designate this type of curve by the abbreviation WS (for "wage schedule"). Relation (13), for its part, portrays the mechanism of price formation. It is often identified by the abbreviation PS (for "price schedule"). For given u_{t-1} and Δp_{t-1}, we thus obtain the curves $(WS)_t$ and $(PS)_t$ which we have represented in figure 8.13. The short-run equilibrium, E_t, lies at the intersection of these two curves.

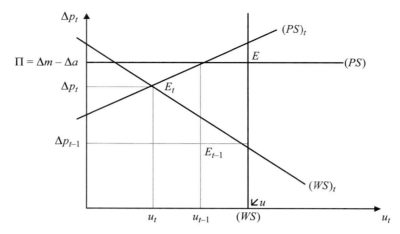

FIGURE 8.13
Short-run equilibrium and long-run equilibrium.

The long-term equilibrium values of the unemployment rate and the inflation rate, u and Δp, are identified with the stationary values of these variables. Setting $u_t = u_{t-1} = u$ and $\Delta p_t = \Delta p_{t-1} = \Delta p$ in relations (12) and (13), we immediately find $u = \bar{u}$ and $\Delta p = \pi \equiv \Delta m - \Delta a$. It should be noted that these last two expressions are also the respective equations of the long-term curves $(WS)_t$ and $(PS)_t$. The first is the vertical line (WS) and the second the horizontal line (PS) of figure 8.13. Point E, representing the long-term equilibrium of the economy, lies at the intersection of these two lines (its position with respect to the short-term equilibrium point has been chosen arbitrarily). We observe that in the long term, the unemployment rate is equal to the NAIRU, which explains why the latter is sometimes described as "natural." Line (WS) represents the long-term Phillips curve. The fact that it is vertical signifies that there is no longer a dilemma between increasing inflation and lowering unemployment at that horizon.

The Short-Term Effects of a Permanent Increase in the Growth Rate
of the Money Supply

Increasing aggregate demand is ineffective in the long run, since the equilibrium unemployment rate, here equal to the NAIRU, depends exclusively on the structural components of the economy. But what about the short run? By way of illustration, it is easy to assess the impact of a change in the growth rate of the money supply in the first period in which the change takes place. Let us suppose that the economy initially (at date zero) is in a steady state corresponding to a growth rate Δm in the money supply, which implies an inflation rate $\pi = \Delta m - \Delta a$. Let us then imagine that the government decides, starting at date 1, to permanently increase the growth rate of the money supply from Δm to $\infty \Delta m' > \Delta m$. Equations (12) and (13) then allow us to calculate the new values of the inflation rate and the unemployment rate at date 1, respectively denoted by Δp_1 and u_1. Setting $\pi' = \Delta m' - \Delta a$, we get:

$$\Delta p_1 = \frac{\pi + \dfrac{\lambda_2}{\lambda_1}\pi'}{1 + \dfrac{\lambda_2}{\lambda_1}} > \pi \qquad \text{and} \qquad u_1 = \bar{u} + \frac{\Delta m - \Delta m'}{1 + \dfrac{\lambda_2}{\lambda_1}} < \bar{u} \tag{14}$$

We see that the increase in the growth rate of the money supply has a greater impact on the inflation rate Δp_1 in the first period, to the degree that nominal rigidity is weak. At the limit, if $\lambda_1 \to 0$ (i.e., no nominal rigidity), the inflation rate of the first period is equal to π', i.e., the new stationary value of the inflation rate. Monetary policy does, on the contrary, have a significant impact on the unemployment rate when there is strong nominal rigidity. We observe as well that the unemployment rate declines following an increase in the growth rate of the money supply.

Inflation and Unemployment Dynamics
In order to determine the consequences of demand side policies over time, it is necessary to study the dynamics of the model. This we can do without too much difficulty, by noting that equations (12) and (13) are equivalent to a linear first-order system taking the following form:

$$\begin{bmatrix} \Delta p_t - \pi \\ u_t - \bar{u} \end{bmatrix} = \mathcal{A} \begin{bmatrix} \Delta p_{t-1} - \pi \\ u_{t-1} - \bar{u} \end{bmatrix} \qquad \text{with} \qquad \mathcal{A} = \frac{1}{1 + (\lambda_2/\lambda_1)} \begin{bmatrix} 1 & -\dfrac{\lambda_2}{\lambda_1} \\ 1 & 1 \end{bmatrix} \tag{15}$$

The general principles of the resolution of systems of difference equations are set out in the mathematical appendix at the end of this book. In particular, we show there that the stability conditions depend on the eigenvalues of the matrix $\mathcal{A}$. In the present case, we can easily verify that the discriminant of the characteristic equation, equal to $-4\lambda_1\lambda_2/(\lambda_1 + \lambda_2)^2$, is negative, and that the determinant of the matrix $\mathcal{A}$, equal to $\lambda_1/(\lambda_1 + \lambda_2)$, lies between 0 and 1. The eigenvalues are thus two complex conjugate numbers, with modulus inferior to unity. This property is a necessary and sufficient condition for the system to converge to its stationary state, showing increasingly damped oscillations. It should be noted that the existence of oscillations arises from hypotheses particular to our model, in particular the ones relative to constant returns to scale. It is possible to obtain a stable monotonic dynamics in a closed economy if the returns to scale are decreasing, which amounts to replacing equation (2) by $y_t = a_t + \alpha \ell_t, 0 < \alpha < 1$; the price-setting rule becomes:

$$p_t = w_t - (a_t/\alpha) + (1 - \alpha) y_t/\alpha + \chi - \ln \alpha$$

The phase diagram presented in figure 8.14 allows us to visualize the dynamics of the system (15). This diagram indicates how the economy shifts from one short-run equilibrium to another short-run equilibrium (the method of its construction is likewise explained in the mathematical appendix at the end of this book). Here it is easily found if we note that equations (12) and (13) are written:

$$\Delta p_t - \Delta p_{t-1} = \frac{\lambda_2}{\lambda_1}(\bar{u} - u_t) \qquad \text{and} \qquad \Delta u_t = \Delta p_t - \pi \tag{16}$$

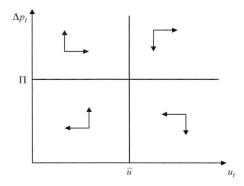

FIGURE 8.14
The phase diagram.

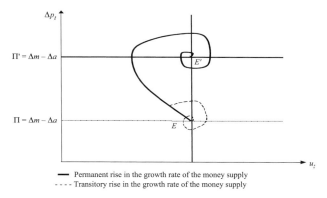

— Permanent rise in the growth rate of the money supply
- - - - Transitory rise in the growth rate of the money supply

FIGURE 8.15
Inflation and unemployment dynamics.

We see that we will have, on the one hand, $\Delta p_t > \Delta p_{t-1}$ when the short-run equilibrium lies to the left of line (WS), defined by $u = \bar{u}$, and, on the other hand, $\Delta u_t > 0$ when this equilibrium lies above line (PS), defined by $\Delta p = \pi$.

Figure 8.15 illustrates the effects of an expansionary demand side policy when the economy is initially in a stationary state E corresponding to a growth rate Δm of the money supply. Let us now imagine that the government decides to increase this growth rate *permanently* from Δm to $\Delta m' > \Delta m$. The new long-run equilibrium is characterized by the same value $\bar{u}$ of the unemployment rate, but by an inflation rate $\pi' = \Delta m' - \Delta a$ higher than $\pi = \Delta m - \Delta a$. It is represented by point E' in figure 8.15. With the help of the phase diagram, it is possible to visualize the passage from E to E'. It can be seen that the monetary policy is effective in the short run—from point E on, unemployment starts to fall—but the economy progressively reverts to the stationary state E', and the long-run unemployment rate always remains equal to the natural rate $\bar{u}$.

The government can take this short-run trade-off into account, for purposes of *stabilization* only, by speeding up or slowing down inflation, according to circumstances; but policies for managing aggregate demand have no influence on the long-run equilibrium value of the unemployment rate. Finally, it should be noted that these policies have real effects in the short run because of nominal rigidities. When the latter do not exist ($\lambda_1 = 0$), the unemployment rate is permanently equal to the natural rate. In other words, the short-run efficiency of demand side policies comes from nominal rigidities ($\lambda_1 \neq 0$). When there are no longer such rigidities in the long run—the long-run coefficient of indexation, corresponding to the sum of the coefficients of Δp_t and Δp_{t-1} in the Phillips equation (7), is equal to unity—demand side policies are ineffective. This result proves on the contrary that this type of measure would be effective in the long run if there existed nominal rigidities at this horizon, i.e., if the sum of the coefficients of Δp_t and of Δp_{t-1} were less than 1. Denoting this sum by $\gamma < 1$, we can easily verify that the long-run unemployment rate, u, is given by the following expression:

$$u = \bar{u} - \frac{(1-\gamma)(\Delta m - \Delta a)}{\lambda_2}$$

For $\gamma < 1$, it is possible to trade off in the long run between unemployment and accelerated inflation. An increase in public expenditure shows up as a rise in the long-run inflation rate and a fall in unemployment. Recall, however, that for a majority of countries, the hypothesis that $\gamma = 1$ is not rejected.

The Effects of a Transitory Increase in the Money Supply
We can also inquire into the effects of a *transitory* increase in the money supply. Let us imagine that the economy is at stationary equilibrium E in figure 8.15, and that the government decides to raise the growth rate of the money supply from Δm to $\Delta m'$ during a single period. Equation (14) describes the equilibrium of period 1 following an increase in the growth rate of the money supply. But when this increase is transitory, the economy returns to its long-run equilibrium E following a trajectory oscillating around this point, rather than converging toward point E' (this trajectory is represented in figure 8.15). A *transitory* demand side policy thus has real effects in the short run.

2.3.2 The Phillips Curve in the United States and France

In Keynesian models, demand side policies are effective in the short run, but are neutral or even detrimental in the long run. Clearly it is important to know exactly what the short run represents. This question can be answered in part by estimating the Phillips curve (7) and by using the preceding model to study the dynamic behavior of the unemployment rate and the inflation rate when the economy is hit by demand or supply shocks. By way of illustration, table 8.2 presents estimates of Phillips curves for France and the United States using annual data for the period 1970–1998, by ordinary least squares.[1] It shows that the degree of real rigidity $1/\lambda_2$ of wages is of the same order of magnitude in the United States and France, but that nominal rigidities

Table 8.2

Estimates of the Phillips relation (annual data, 1970–1998).

Country	λ_0	λ_1	λ_2	λ_3	$\bar{R}^2$	DW
United States	0.03** (2.28)	0.46*** (2.81)	0.34** (2.11)	0.38** (2.36)	0.81	1.31
France	0.05*** (9.67)	0.18* (1.83)	0.34*** (6.27)	N.S.	0.97	1.17

Source: OECD data.

Note: Figures in parentheses designate the *t*-statistics. DW stands for Durbin-Watson. The wage is the annual wage in the private sector. Asterisks indicate the threshold of significance of the coefficients, respectively, 1%, 5%, and 10% for 3, 2, and 1 asterisks.

(identified by the extent of parameter λ_1) are greater in the United States. More thorough econometric analyses find qualitatively similar results (see section 5 below).

Figure 8.16 describes the consequences for the American economy if the growth rate of the money supply moves from 3% to 4%, on the assumption that growth rate of productivity is equal to 1%, which corresponds to the average of this variable since the beginning of the 1970s. We observe that the unemployment rate fluctuates around the NAIRU, here equal to 7%. The adjustment lag of the unemployment rate is relatively rapid, since the unemployment rate begins to grow in the second year, after having fallen by 0.6%. The effects of monetary policy gradually fade out, becoming very weak from the eighth year on. The consequences for the French economy of an expansionary policy are represented in figure 8.17 (the growth rate of labor productivity is 2%). It should be noted that, according to our estimates, the NAIRU, amounting to 8.8%, is higher in France than it is in the United States. Moreover, the adjustment lag for wages is shorter. This result, frequently obtained, suggests that

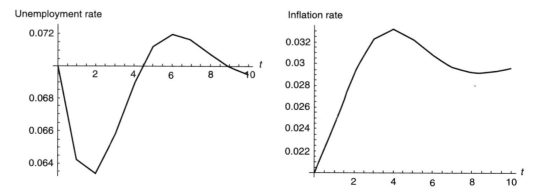

FIGURE 8.16

The impact of an increase in the growth rate (from 3% to 4%) of the money supply on the American economy.

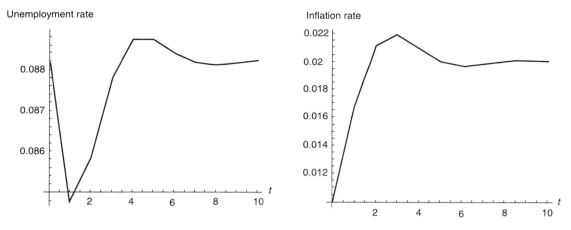

FIGURE 8.17
The impact of an increase in the growth rate (from 3% to 4%) of the money supply on the French economy.

expansionary policies are less effective in France than in the United States, for the purpose of combating unemployment. An increase of 1% in the growth rate of the money supply leads to a maximum reduction in the unemployment rate of 0.3 percentage points (this variable falls from 8.8% to 8.5%), and the impact of expansionary policy is practically null from the seventh year on.

2.3.3 Supply Side Policies and Supply Shocks

We have just seen that only the inflationary effects of expansionary policies are durable, since the NAIRU is not affected by policies of this type. On the other hand, shocks or policies affecting supply can have an influence on the NAIRU. In particular, the reduction of the growth rate of labor productivity at the beginning of the 1970s exerted upward pressure on the natural unemployment rate. This pressure was probably greater in Europe than in the United States. From this point of view, the Keynesian model throws an interesting light on the consequences of certain supply shocks.

The Slowdown in Labor Productivity Growth
Figures 8.18 and 8.19 depict the impact of a fall in the growth rate of labor productivity on the American and French economies. The annual growth rate of labor productivity passed from around 2% between 1960 and 1973 to 1% between 1974 and 1998 in the United States. According to our model, this change in the economic environment entails a durable but relatively moderate increase in the American unemployment rate, since the NAIRU passes from 5.2% to 7.0%. During the same periods, the French economy—and more generally, the European economy—was confronted by a greater productivity shock, since the growth rate of labor productivity fell from 4% to 2%. The consequences of this shock are illustrated in figure 8.19. The NAIRU rose considerably, from 2.9% to 8.8%. The French economy is thus clearly more sensitive

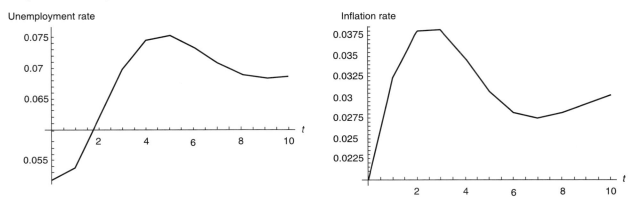

FIGURE 8.18
The impact of a fall in the growth rate (from 2% to 1%) of labor productivity on the American economy.

to variations in productivity than the American one. This difference arises from the fact that wages are not indexed to productivity in France, leading to a coefficient λ_3 not significantly different from zero when the Phillips equations are estimated (see table 8.2). The rise in inflation—the annual growth rate of the money supply is assumed to be constant at 4%—is due to the falling off in productivity growth, since the long-run inflation rate takes the value $\Delta m - \Delta a$.

A simple model based on the Phillips equation thus makes it possible to take account of the rise in unemployment consequent upon a fall in the growth rate of labor productivity. It suggests that differences in performance between the United States and France as regards unemployment could be explained by differences in wage setting and the size of the productivity shock.

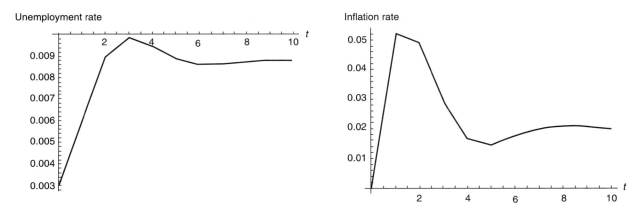

FIGURE 8.19
The impact of a fall in the growth rate (from 4% to 2%) of labor productivity on the French economy.

The Limitations of the Phillips Curve in Analyzing Supply Side Policies

Governments have limited room to maneuver when it comes to the growth rate of labor productivity, which depends mainly on the development of technology. On the other hand, they can affect supply by influencing the profitability of firms, or altering the way the labor market functions.

In the Keynesian model, the behaviors of firms as regards supply are represented by the price equation (3). A reduction of the markup χ between prices and wages is liable to diminish the unemployment rate in the short run, but not the NAIRU, which is independent of this parameter. Readers will recall that the markup χ increases with the monopoly power of firms over the goods market, the user cost of capital, and the pressure of payroll deductions on the revenue from labor. An increase in one of these three variables ought to lead to a temporary increase in the unemployment rate, which subsequently reverts, in oscillating fashion, to its long-run equilibrium value. These three parameters thus have no impact on the NAIRU. We shall see below that this property of Keynesian models probably results from an incomplete specification of the wage formation equation, and makes them vulnerable to criticism on that account.

Another way to intervene would be to reduce the degree of real rigidity of wages, in order to reduce the natural unemployment rate. The Phillips curve, however, is an ad hoc relation, the foundation of which in terms of behaviors is not generally spelled out. Hence it is not possible to interpret the sources of wage ridigity using this relation. Policies aimed at altering the functioning of the labor market cannot, therefore, be elaborated on the basis of this type of model.

Models representing wage formation by a Phillips curve thus appear ill-suited to examining the consequences of supply side policies. We will now see that consideration of the origin of nominal rigidities has also led to a critique of the relevance of Keynesian models for assessing the consequences of demand side policies.

3 NOMINAL RIGIDITIES: THE CRITIQUES OF FRIEDMAN AND LUCAS

Friedman (1968) and Lucas (1972) sought to establish that the Phillips curve was compatible with the competitive functioning of a labor market in which agents observe prices imperfectly. That being the case, wage-earners are incapable of correctly assessing their real wage, and there can be a lag in the adjustment of nominal wages when prices change. The essential contribution of this approach was to show that the impact of demand side policies is conditioned by the *expectations* of agents. Assuming that agents have *adaptive* expectations about the inflation rate, Friedman (1968) emphasized that the real wage ought to be perfectly indexed to the general level of prices in the long run. That makes it possible to account for the inefficiency of macroeconomic policies at that horizon. Friedman's message was stated more radically by Lucas (1972): adopting the hypothesis of *rational* expectations, he showed that demand side policies, when systematically applied—and thus "foreseen" by agents—have no real effect, even in the short run. Only *unexpected* demand side policies can have real effects in the short run.

3.1 THE FRIEDMAN VERSION

Friedman's work has emphasized that the formation of expectations does much to determine the properties of macroeconomic equilibrium. In particular, it allows us to provide foundations for the Phillips curve.

A New Form of Labor Supply

Friedman (1968) and Lucas (1972) put forward the hypothesis that the real wages intervening respectively in the decisions of firms and those of suppliers of labor were not identical. Friedman and Lucas assume that each worker observes his or her own nominal wage w_t perfectly, but is incapable of knowing the price level p_t with the same perfection. Let p_t^a be the expected price for period t. Households then decide on the volume of labor they will supply on the basis of a real wage $w_t - p_t^a$ which is expected. Relation (4), describing labor supply, should thus be altered as follows:

$$\ell_t^s = \bar{\ell} + \eta(w_t - p_t^a) \tag{17}$$

Firms, unlike households, do not have the problem of acquiring information about prices. The price level does not actually come into their decisions about labor demand. As equation (3) shows, each firm simply sets the price of its product, which equals the nominal wage paid to employees multiplied by a markup. The functioning of the market for goods and the behavior of firms is thus always represented by equations (1), (2), and (3). In order to simplify, we will assume that labor productivity is constant, with $a_t = 0$, $\forall t$.

It is possible to determine global equilibrium on the assumption that the nominal wage equalizes labor supply—defined by equation (17)—to labor demand, $\ell_t^s = \ell_t$, $\forall t$. Using (17) and the price-setting rule $p_t = w_t + \chi$, we thus get the following relation:

$$\ell_t^s = \bar{\ell} + \eta(p_t - p_t^a) - \chi\eta \tag{18}$$

In the literature, this relation is often called the Lucas supply function, in reference to the work of Lucas (1972, 1975). Because the labor market is assumed to be always in equilibrium ($\ell_t = \ell_t^s$, $\forall t$), this relation shows that the demand side policies that have an impact on employment are the ones that affect expectation errors.

Adaptative Expectations

Friedman assumes that agents form their expectations about the inflation rate in an *adaptative* manner. Let $\pi_t^a \equiv p_t^a - p_{t-1}$ be the inflation rate expected for date t. This hypothesis leads to relation:

$$\pi_t^a - \pi_{t-1}^a = (1 - \lambda)(\Delta p_{t-1} - \pi_{t-1}^a), \qquad \lambda \in [0, 1) \tag{19}$$

This formula signifies that agents revise their expectations upward if the inflation rate in $t - 1$ exceeds the rate expected for that date, and downward if the contrary occurs.

Parameter λ measures the inertia of the expectation revision process. The greater λ is, the less past expectation errors provoke revisions of current expectations. Proceeding by iteration and noting that $\text{Lim}_{t \to \infty} \lambda^t \pi_0^a = 0$, relation (19) entails:

$$\pi_t^a = (1 - \lambda) \sum_{\tau=1}^{+\infty} \lambda^{\tau-1} \Delta p_{t-\tau}$$

In this form, it turns out that adaptive expectations are also *extrapolative* expectations, i.e., that the expected inflation rate is a weighted average of past rates of inflation, to which is applied a coefficient that diminishes as they recede into the past. In order to make the calculations simpler, we will assume that this extrapolative process concerns only the most recent period, which amounts to supposing that the speed with which expectations are revised is maximal ($\lambda = 0$). That immediately entails, on the basis of equation (19), $\pi_t^a = \Delta p_{t-1}$, or again, using this relation and equation (3):

$$p_t^a \equiv p_{t-1} + \Delta p_{t-1} = w_{t-1} + \chi + \Delta p_{t-1} \tag{20}$$

The Phillips Curve
If we substitute the value of the price expectation defined by equation (20) in relation (17), we get, with $\ell_t^s = \ell_t$:

$$\Delta w_t = \chi + \Delta p_{t-1} - \frac{1}{\eta}(\bar{\ell} - \ell_t) \tag{21}$$

This equation defines a positive relationship between the wage growth rate and employment. If we take the view, in a Keynesian perspective, that unemployment varies inversely with employment, it can be interpreted as a Phillips curve close to the initial formulation described by relation (7). The adaptive character of expectations and the hypotheses about the information available to agents entail a nominal wage rigid in the short run, since its contemporaneous variations depend only on the past inflation rate; this corresponds to the case $\lambda_1 = 1$ in equation (7). The degree of real rigidity, measured by quantity $1/\lambda_2$ in equation (7), is here equal to the inverse of the elasticity of the labor supply function.

The dynamics of employment and real wages in Friedman's model is thus a particular case of the model studied in the previous section. It suffices to set $\lambda_0 = \chi$, $\lambda_1 = 1$, $\lambda_2 = 1/\eta$, and $\Delta a_t = 0$ in equation (7). Equation (18) shows that in the long run, employment converges on its stationary level equal to $\bar{\ell} - \chi\eta$. Demand side policies have the same effects as in the preceding model. An increase in the level, or the growth rate, of the money supply has real effects in the short run, which are progressively damped.

The approach laid out by Friedman makes it possible to deduce a Phillips curve on the basis of clearly specified microeconomic behavior. It should be noted, nonetheless, that the labor market is always in equilibrium, since labor supply, defined by equation (17), is always equal to demand. Conversely, in a Keynesian model the rigidity of nominal wages prevents the realization of equality between labor supply and labor demand.

The work of Friedman, which makes the short-run efficiency of demand side policies depend on expectation errors by agents, has led to the "revival" of the classical school, with its grounding in the notion of rational expectation.

3.2 RATIONAL EXPECTATIONS AND THE "NEW CLASSICAL MACROECONOMICS"

Rational agents ought gradually to learn how the economic system works, and, after a certain period of time, no longer make *systematic* forecasting mistakes. This idea underpins what, at the end of the 1970s, was called the "new classical macroeconomics" (see Lucas, 1981, and Blanchard and Fischer, 1989, chapter 2). It maintains that, in general, publicly announced demand side policies are ineffective, *even in the short run*, if agents are capable of forming *rational expectations*.

Employment in Short-Run Equilibrium

In order to clarify the notion of rational expectation already encountered in chapter 4, we keep the model proposed by Friedman, but henceforth assume that the money supply m_t is a random variable, the realization of which is not observed by agents in the current period t. The hypothesis of rational expectation signifies that agents do not make systematic mistakes in their forecasts, given the information set I_t at their disposal. If $E(.)$ designates the mathematical expectation operator we will thus have $p_t^a = E(p_t | I_t)$. Since by definition $E(p_t | I_t) = p_{t-1} + E(\Delta p_t | I_t)$, if we substitute this expression of expected price in labor supply (17) and use equation (3) of price formation, we get a new relationship between the growth rate of nominal wages and employment:

$$\Delta w_t = \chi + E(\Delta p_t | I_t) - \frac{1}{\eta}(\bar{\ell} - \ell_t)$$

What we have is an expression similar to relation (21) in the Friedman model, which assumed adaptive expectations. The difference results from the indexation of the growth rate of wages to the expectation of *current* inflation. This new formulation of the Phillips curve entails that the growth rate of wages adjusts instantaneously to the conditional expectation of the inflation rate. Let us assume that the information set I_t available to agents comprises the model describing the economy, the probability distribution of the random variable m_t, all the exogenous variables present and past, except for the current price level and the current nominal average wage. This last variable is unknown because every agent observes his or her own nominal wage but has no way of knowing instantaneously all the wages in the whole economy. Agents are capable of calculating the expected current price from this information set. In the first place, equations (1) and (2) make it possible to write the expected demand in the form $E(m_t | I_t) - E(p_t | I_t) = E(\ell_t | I_t)$. Further, under the hypothesis of rational expectations, the Lucas supply function (18) entails $E(\ell_t^s | I_t) = \bar{\ell} - \eta\chi$. Equalizing the expected supply and the expected demand, we get the expected equilibrium price:

$$E(p_t | I_t) = p_t^a = E(m_t) + \eta\chi - \bar{\ell} \tag{22}$$

The value of the equilibrium price depends on the realization of m_t; it is found by equalizing the labor supply defined by the Lucas supply equation (18), where p_t^a is given by (22), with demand, which may be written $\ell_t = m_t - p_t$. We obtain:

$$p_t = \frac{1}{1+\eta}[m_t - \bar{\ell} + \eta(E(p_t \mid I_t) + \chi)] \tag{23}$$

Equations (22) and (23) then entail:

$$p_t - p_t^a = \frac{1}{1+\eta}[m_t - E(m_t)]$$

Substituting this value of the expectation error in the Lucas supply function (18), we get the equilibrium level of employment in the short run:

$$\ell_t^* = \bar{\ell} + \frac{\eta}{1+\eta}[m_t - E(m_t)] - \eta\chi \tag{24}$$

This solution is very close to that of the standard classical model, without uncertainty, given by equation (5). It differs only in the term $(\eta/(1+\eta))[m_t - E(m_t)]$, which expresses the effects of economic policy.

Expected and Unexpected Components of Demand Side Policies

The model of the new classical macroeconomics thus proposes a conception of fluctuations in the level of employment based on "surprise." The *systematic* (or expected) component of the money supply, $E(m_t)$, is taken into account by agents when forming expectations and has no influence on employment. Equation (24) entails that $E(\ell_t^* \mid I_t) = \bar{\ell} - \eta\chi$, which corresponds to the equilibrium employment level in the classical model when $a_t = 0$, $\forall t$—see equation (5). Only the *unexpected* component of the money supply, $[m_t - E(m_t)]$, can affect this level. This vision of the cycle excludes any persistence effect. If a shock was permanent, or if shocks were correlated, these systematic components would be taken into account by expectations, and, as in the model set out here, only unexpected components could have any short-run effect (for a more general model, see Blanchard and Fischer, 1989, chapter 11).

It should be noted that it is not the hypothesis of rational expectation *in itself* that makes any expected monetary policy ineffective. In order to arrive at that conclusion, it is also necessary that prices and wages should be able permanently to equilibrate supplies and demands in the markets, which assumes a total absence of nominal rigidity. Now in reality, many contracts stipulate wages in nominal terms. Because of the costs of renegotiation, contracts of this type are not instantaneously revised when the economic environment turns out to be different from what had initially been expected. Hence it can happen that nominal wages do not instantaneously equalize labor supply and demand, even if the agents have rational expectations and know the working of the economy perfectly. That being so, demand side policies that are expected can have real effects (Fischer, 1977; Taylor, 1979, 1980; and Chari et al., 2000, have studied the dynamics of the economy in such a setting. For a clear and detailed presentation, see Blanchard and Fischer, 1989, chapter 8, and Taylor, 1999).

The result that policy measures which are expected have no effect rests as well on very bold hypotheses concerning the information available to agents. It assumes in particular that the information set contains the true model of the economy, so that agents are able to know the true relationship between variations in the money supply and the price level. It is no doubt more relevant to assume that knowledge of the economic environment is the result of a learning process (see the survey of Evans and Honkapohja, 1999). The result that demand side policies that are expected are totally without effect is thus a textbook case, grounded in extreme hypotheses. What we should learn from the new classical macroeconomics is that the efficiency of demand side policies is limited. Such policies are especially inefficient in increasing labor market participation *durably*, for it is impossible in the long run to systematically deceive the expectations of agents by systematically increasing aggregate demand. Agents do in the end figure out, at least to some extent, the relationship between prices and increased demand, and so do expect the consequences of expansionary policies. In sum, in the long run, expansionary demand side policies will have only a very limited effect on employment, and will essentially lead to an increase in inflation.

4   REAL RIGIDITIES: HYSTERESIS AND THE WAGE CURVE

The foregoing analyses are based on a very cursory representation of real wage rigidity. The Phillips curve integrates the idea of real rigidity without spelling out its theoretical underpinning, while the approach of Friedman and Lucas, centered on the study of nominal rigidities, neglects the analysis of real rigidities. More fundamentally, we may question the necessity of postulating a relationship between the growth rate of the nominal wage and the unemployment rate. Much thought has been devoted to this question, and has made it possible to spell out the linkage between wage setting and the unemployment rate. Two currents stand out at the present time. The first explores the consequences of the heterogeneity of the unemployed for wage formation, and highlights phenomena of hysteresis. The second calls into question the relevance of the relationship between the *growth rate* of wages and the unemployment rate, concentrating instead on a relationship between the wage *level* and the unemployment rate. These two currents have made possible much richer explanations of unemployment persistence.

4.1   THE HYSTERESIS OF UNEMPLOYMENT

The models of unemployment examined to this point rest on a stark distinction between a long-run equilibrium, on which demand side policies have no effect, and a short-run equilibrium, which can, on the contrary, be influenced by such policies. Such a conception has the merit of explaining both why demand side policies have only transitory effects and how the economy moves toward its long-run equilibrium. It neglects, however, certain dynamic effects induced by transitory changes in unemployment. It is possible that an increase in current unemployment alters the long-run equilibrium unemployment rate. For example, certain unemployed persons may be excluded persistently from the labor market because their productivity is too low to make it profitable to hire them, even at a much lower wage than the current one. If there is no regulating mechanism that can reintegrate these unemployed, any increase in their number has a durable effect on the unemployment rate. When this phenomenon is included in the wage-setting process, then what comes to light is a dynamics in which the long-run unemployment rate depends on the current equilibrium unemployment rate. This property is called the *hysteresis effect*.

4.1.1 The Sources of Persistent Unemployment

Three mechanisms have been put forward to explain the irreversibility of certain rises in unemployment. The first is built around the bargaining power of insiders, who are supposedly able to impede the process of competitive wage adjustment. The other two focus on the low employability of some categories of workers.

The Bargaining Power of Insiders

The opposition between insiders, who already have a job, and outsiders, who don't, can lead to irreversible rises in unemployment (Blanchard and Summers, 1986; Lindbeck and Snower, 1988; see also chapter 7, section 4). Let us assume that a transitory negative shock to labor demand leads to job losses. When the effects of the shock are over, firms are prepared to rehire workers if the wage remains constant. But the insiders, fewer now than they were before the shock, have an interest in demanding pay raises, up to the point at which their pay equals their marginal productivity. If the insiders have the wherewithal to make their demand stick (because of the high cost of labor turnover, for example), they succeed in durably excluding the laid-off workers, who could have been rehired if wages had not gone up. In this context, after a transitory negative shock to labor demand, an improvement in the economic climate leads to a wage increase for the insiders at the expense of hiring.

The Depreciation of Specific Human Capital

Another source of persistent unemployment comes from the fact that certain layoffs have irreversible effects when the workers who lose their jobs have an obsolete skill, or find it impossible to make the specific human capital they have accumulated to that point pay off. Topel (1990) suggests that this phenomenon was significant in the United States in the 1970s and 1980s. After losing a job, workers suffer, on average, a wage reduction of between 15% and 40% when they do find a new one. These results mean that the forfeit of specific human capital when a job is lost is significant. Jacobson et al. (1993) obtain similar results, again using American data, in their study of the career paths of wage-earners who are laid off after they have attained six years or more of seniority. They show that the laid-off workers suffer significant and durable wage reductions, since five years out from the time of their job loss, their wages are still 25% less than those of workers who do not lose their jobs.

Ruhm (1991) and Farber (1993) confirm this observation, pointing out that the probability of still being unemployed is much higher for workers who have lost a job recently. Ruhm (1991) estimates, using American data for 1971–1975, that the unemployment rate for workers who have lost a job within the last year is 17% higher than it is for other wage-earners in the year subsequent to the job loss. Four years after the job loss, the differential in the unemployment rate remains noticeable, and earnings are 15% less than those of comparable workers who have not lost a job. Thus, although the average duration of unemployment was short in the United States in 1971–1975, on the order of several weeks, the loss of a job left its mark on workers for a number of years. This effect of exclusion is heightened by the evolution of the probability of being hired during the period of unemployment. The same type of result is obtained from French data by Margolis (1999), who shows that laid-off workers who find a job after a year of unemployment have a wage 25% less, on average, than the wage of persons who have kept their job.

The Low Employability of the Long-Term Unemployed

A number of empirical studies suggest that the employability of jobless persons deteriorates as their joblessness persists. This phenomenon can be grasped by assessing the influence of the duration of unemployment on the rate of return to employment. The probability of exiting from unemployment $s(t)$ is generally estimated as a function of the duration t of unemployment, using the Weilbull model (see chapter 3, section 3.2), which adopts the following functional form: $s(t) = \beta^\alpha \alpha^{1-\alpha} \Gamma(1/\alpha) t^{\alpha-1}$ where $\Gamma(\cdot)$ designates the gamma function,[2] β corresponds to the average duration of unemployment, and α measures the duration dependence. If $\alpha = 1$, there is no duration dependence, and the exit rate from unemployment depends solely on β. If $\alpha < 1$, the probability of exiting from unemployment decreases with the duration of unemployment; there is then a negative duration dependence. Table 8.3 presents the results of estimates of the Weilbull model carried out by Machin and Manning (1999). These estimates confirm the existence of a duration dependence in the set of countries studied. They also suggest that this phenomenon did not become more acute between the 1960s–1970s and the 1980s–1990s, even though the duration of unemployment rose over this span of time. Results of this type are obtained by other empirical studies carried out in this area (see Machin and Manning, 1999).

It might be objected that the negative correlation between the duration of unemployment and the rate of exit from unemployment is determined by the intrinsic characteristics of workers, less efficient persons having a weaker probability of finding employment and thus a longer duration of unemployment. However, the contributions of van den Berg and van Ours (1994, 1996), dealing with France, the United Kingdom, the Netherlands, and the United States, show that the negative relationship between unemployment duration and the probability of being rehired appears to persist when the problems of selection bias linked to the heterogeneity of workers are

Table 8.3

The structure of unemployment and duration dependence.

Country	Average duration of unemployment (in months)		Duration dependence (a)	
	1960s–1970s	1980s–1990s	1960s–1970s	1980s–1990s
Belgium	6.2 (0.07)	15.1 (0.06)	0.39 (0.002)	0.58 (0.002)
France	3.6 (0.01)	12.7 (0.01)	0.54 (0.001)	0.93 (0.001)
Germany	4.2 (0.01)	5.3 (0.01)	0.86 (0.001)	0.58 (0.001)
Netherlands	2.4 (0.01)	13.7 (0.04)	0.68 (0.002)	0.66 (0.002)
Spain	2.3 (0.37)	17.7 (0.17)	0.58 (0.06)	0.91 (0.01)
United Kingdom	0.8 (0.14)	6.5 (0.36)	0.35 (0.02)	0.57 (0.02)
Australia	1.2 (0.22)	6.5 (0.56)	0.72 (0.10)	0.79 (0.10)
United States	1.1 (0.04)	1.2 (0.03)	0.61 (0.01)	0.52 (0.01)

Standard errors are in parentheses.

Source: Machin and Manning (1999, table 4).

taken into consideration. The depreciation of human capital, the demotivation of the unemployed, and the fact that a long spell of unemployment may be interpreted as a signal of a worker's quality at hiring time could all explain the bad performance of the long-term unemployed.

The dependency between unemployment duration and employability constitutes a potential source of the persistence of unemployment. Each transitory shock that increases unemployment does in fact increase the average duration of unemployment, and thus can durably reduce the average probability of re-employment. Job destruction, and temporary increases in unemployment can thus have irreversible effects by excluding workers from the labor market. The extent of this phenomenon is not yet well known empirically, however.

4.1.2 The Heterogeneity of the Unemployed and the Hysteresis Effect

There is a simple way to take phenomena of exclusion from the labor market into account when considering the process of wage setting: to distinguish the pressure exerted on wages by the short-term unemployed from that exerted by the long-term unemployed. The Phillips curve then takes account of variations in the unemployment rate, and the dynamics of the model exhibits a hysteresis effect.

A New Phillips Curve

If the long-term unemployed become "unemployable," it is the same as if they were no longer participating in the labor market, and only the number of short-term unemployed will have an influence on wage variation. We can grasp this distinction within the population in search of a job if we assume that a rise or a fall in wages depends both on the level of and the *variation* in the unemployment rate. The latter constitutes a simple indicator of short-term unemployment. The Phillips curve (7) then takes the following form:

$$\Delta w_t = \lambda_0 + (1 - \lambda_1)\Delta p_t + \lambda_1 \Delta p_{t-1} - \lambda_2 u_t - \lambda_2' \Delta u_t + \lambda_3 \Delta a_t \tag{25}$$

Since, following (3), we always have $\Delta p_t = \Delta w_t - \Delta a_t$, we get:

$$\lambda_1(\Delta p_t - \Delta p_{t-1}) = \lambda_2(\bar{u}_t - u_t) - \lambda_2' \Delta u_t \tag{26}$$

In this relation, $\bar{u}_t = [\lambda_0 - (1 - \lambda_3)\Delta a_t]/\lambda_2$, always designates the NAIRU defined by (10). The view is sometimes taken that this variant (26) of the Phillips curve, taken in isolation, defines a NAIRU, denoted by $\hat{u}_t$, called short-run or instantaneous, which has the property of not increasing inflation in the current period. Setting $\Delta p_t = \Delta p_{t-1}$ in (26), we find:

$$\hat{u}_t = \frac{\lambda_2}{\lambda_2 + \lambda_2'}\,\bar{u}_t + \frac{\lambda_2'}{\lambda_2 + \lambda_2'}\,u_{t-1} \tag{27}$$

We observe that the short-run NAIRU at date t is an average of the effective unemployment rate at date $(t - 1)$ and of the long-run equilibrium NAIRU $\bar{u}_t$. That being the case, a temporary increase in unemployment, due for example to a negative shock to aggregate demand, entails an increase in the instantaneous NAIRU. Conversely, there is no impact on the long-run NAIRU, which is always equal to $\bar{u}_t$, if $\lambda_2 \neq 0$. Appendix 2 at the end of this chapter offers an analysis of the dynamics of this model, on the assumption that the growth rates of the money supply Δm and productivity Δa are constants. The economy then converges toward its long-run equilibrium, if $\lambda_2 \neq 0$. This long-run equilibrium is again characterized by an inflation rate $\pi = \Delta m - \Delta a$—see equation (13)—and an unemployment rate equal to the natural unemployment rate $\bar{u}$ defined by (11).

Dynamics with Hysteresis

In the limit case in which the growth rate of nominal wages depends *solely* on the variation in the unemployment rate ($\lambda_2 = 0, \lambda_2' > 0$), the economy does not converge to a stationary equilibrium independent of the initial conditions; it then displays a *hysteresis effect*. In order to show this, we first note that the Phillips curve (26) is now written:

$$\lambda_1(\Delta p_t - \Delta p_{t-1}) = \lambda_0 - (1 - \lambda_3)\Delta a - \lambda_2' \Delta u_t \tag{28}$$

Writing the aggregate demand (13) in differences, we get $\Delta p_t = \pi + \Delta u_t$, which implies that $\Delta p_t - \Delta p_{t-1} = \Delta u_t - \Delta u_{t-1}$. Substituting this value of the acceleration of prices in (28), we arrive at a difference equation that reads:

$$\Delta u_t = \frac{\lambda_1}{\lambda_1 + \lambda_2'} \Delta u_{t-1} + \frac{\lambda_0 - (1 - \lambda_3)\Delta a}{\lambda_1 + \lambda_2'} \tag{29}$$

Since $\lambda_1/(\lambda_1 + \lambda_2')$ is comprised between 0 and 1, it turns out that the *variation* in the unemployment rate goes to a stationary value, which is found by setting $\Delta u_t = \Delta u$, $\forall t$, in (29):

$$\Delta u = \frac{\lambda_0 - (1 - \lambda_3)\Delta a}{\lambda_2'}$$

In sum, the series of unemployment rates does not necessarily converge to a finite value, but in the *long run* it does nevertheless reach a *stationary path*, described by the difference equation:

$$u_t^* = u_{t-1}^* + \frac{\lambda_0 - (1 - \lambda_3)\Delta a}{\lambda_2'}, \qquad u_t^* \in (0, 1) \; \forall t \geq 1$$

This relation describes a *hysteresis* phenomenon. By definition, this term signifies that the *long-run* equilibrium unemployment rate depends on past levels of unemployment. The fact that this definition applies to the long-run equilibrium is essential, for the short-run equilibrium always depends on the past values of the equilibria actually realized.

The Permanent Effects of Transitory Shocks

A corollary of the notion of hysteresis is the idea that a *transitory* shock has *permanent* effects. Such is indeed the case here, for the long-run equilibrium unemployment rate depends on initial conditions. This emerges clearly if we assume that $\lambda_0 = 0$, and $\lambda_3 = 1$. That being so, the stationary value of the variation in unemployment Δu is null, which means that in the long run the system goes to stationary states in which the unemployment rate is constant. Let us suppose that the economy is in one of these states, and let u_{-1} be the value of the unemployment rate. Let us suppose that a shock occurs at date $t = 0$, so that the unemployment rate reaches the level $u_0 \neq u_{-1}$. The time path of this variable from this date forward is given by equation (29), which entails in particular:

$$\Delta u_t = \left(\frac{\lambda_1}{\lambda_1 + \lambda_2'} \right)^t \Delta u_0, \qquad \Delta u_0 \equiv u_0 - u_{-1}$$

By iterating from the initial date, this relation entails:

$$u_t = u_{-1} + \Delta u_0 \sum_{\tau=0}^{t} \left(\frac{\lambda_1}{\lambda_1 + \lambda_2'} \right)^{\tau}$$

And the economy goes to a new stationary state u^* defined by:

$$u^* = u_{-1} + \Delta u_0 \frac{\lambda_1 + \lambda_2'}{\lambda_2'}$$

The long-run unemployment rate is thus dependent on initial conditions. In this sense, the transitory shocks that modify the current unemployment rate have permanent effects. Thus, if there is hysteresis, demand side policies have effects on employment in the *long run*. This conception is opposed to that of the new classical macroeconomics, which assumes that the economy always converges to a natural unemployment rate, independent of the current values of employment.

In empirical studies, a value of the coefficient λ_2' significantly different from zero is often described as a hysteresis effect, whatever the value of λ_2. There is no harm in adopting this usage, as long as we remember that in theory we should only speak of hysteresis when $\lambda_2 = 0$. In reality, a nonnegligible coefficient λ_2' is often associated with a small coefficient λ_2; this is a sign that adjustments take place very slowly, in other words, a phenomenon of *persistence*. From the point of view of applied studies, the difference between persistence and hysteresis is probably not highly relevant, for a lengthy period of adjustment is surely equivalent to the infinity of theoretical models.

4.2 The Relationship Between the Level of Wages and the Unemployment Rate

The Phillips curve is also called into question by the observation that theoretical models explaining wage formation arrive at a relationship between the *level* of wages and the unemployment rate, rather than the relationship between the *wage growth rate* and the unemployment rate postulated by the Phillips curve. Blanchflower and Oswald (1995) have indeed pointed out that efficiency wage and bargaining models (set out in chapters 6 and 7, respectively) show that wages are determined by a markup on the reservation wage, which itself depends on the exit rate from unemployment, and thus on the unemployment rate. Thus an increase in the unemployment rate must exert downward pressure on the wage *level*. These considerations naturally lead us to estimate wage equations that take into account a relationship between the wage level and the unemployment rate, and to study the consequences of this specification on the determinants of unemployment (see Blanchard and Katz, 1997, 1999).

4.2.1 A Reexamination of the Wage Equation

The models of wage setting presented in chapters 6 and 7 indicate that the wage depends on characteristics proper to the job held and the outside options of the worker concerned. Let b_t be the logarithm of the real value of the reservation wage. A very general rule of wage setting can then be written as follows:

$$w_t - p_t = \lambda_0 + b_t \tag{30}$$

This relation stipulates that the real wage resulting from the bargaining process, or $w_t - p_t$, is found by applying a markup to the real value b_t of the reservation wage. The reservation wage depends on the prospect of gains in case of job loss; it increases with the instantaneous gains of unemployed persons and with the probability of exiting from unemployment. The expression of the reservation wage is found by making the two following hypotheses. The first is that the instantaneous gains of unemployed persons depend on unemployment benefits, the value of which is partly indexed to past values of prices and wages, and on the current level of productivity. The second is that the probability of exiting from unemployment decreases with the current unemployment rate. We then arrive at:

$$b_t = \lambda_3 a_t + (1 - \lambda_3)(w_{t-1} - p_{t-1}) - \lambda_2 u_t, \qquad \lambda_3 \in [0, 1], \lambda_2 \geq 0 \tag{31}$$

Relations (30) and (31) then give, after several calculations:

$$\Delta w_t - \Delta p_t = \lambda_0 - \lambda_2 u_t + \lambda_3 \Delta a_t - \lambda_3 (w_{t-1} - p_{t-1} - a_{t-1}) \tag{32}$$

The right-hand side of this equation represents the value of the real wage growth rate in the absence of any nominal rigidity. It is possible to introduce such rigidities by assuming, as in the framework of the Phillips curve (7), that the adjustment lag of the growth rate of nominal wages to variations in the inflation rate is equal to λ_1. Denoting by $\Delta \omega_t$ the right-hand side of equation (32), one gets: $\Delta w_t - \Delta p_t = \Delta \omega_t - \lambda_1 (\Delta p_t - \Delta p_{t-1})$, which entails:

$$\Delta w_t = \lambda_0 + (1 - \lambda_1)\Delta p_t + \lambda_1 \Delta p_{t-1} - \lambda_2 u_t + \lambda_3 \Delta a_t - \lambda_3 (w_{t-1} - p_{t-1} - a_{t-1}) \tag{33}$$

This equation shows that models of wage formation with microeconomic foundations yield a relationship between the growth rate of wages and the unemployment rate identical to that of the Phillips equation (7) only when $\lambda_3 = 0$. For that, the reservation wage must be indexed only to the past value of the negotiated wage, and not labor productivity. Equation (33) then corresponds to a Phillips curve in which the degree of indexation of wages to productivity is null. In all other cases, wage formation defines a relationship different from the one postulated by the Phillips curve. It turns out, then, that the nominal wage growth rate is influenced not only by expected inflation and the unemployment rate, but also by an *error correction* term representing the difference between real wages and productivity in the past period. We will see further that in many countries, estimations of wage equations frequently end by rejecting the hypothesis $\lambda_3 = 0$, according to which the error correction term has no effect. Hence the consequences of the presence of the error correction term in the wage equation must be looked at closely.

4.2.2 The Phillips Curve and the Error Correction Term

Taking the microeconomic foundations of wage formation into account may change the determinants of the NAIRU that have been exhibited previously.

New Determinants of the NAIRU

With the help of the price rule (3), relation (33) is rewritten as follows:

$$\lambda_1(\Delta p_t - \Delta p_{t-1}) = \lambda_0 + \lambda_3 \chi - \lambda_2 u_t - (1 - \lambda_3)\Delta a_t \tag{34}$$

The dynamics of the unemployment rate and the inflation rate is then defined by the system of equations (13) and (34). We observe that it is analogous to the system (9) and (13) defining the evolution of these two variables in the model based on the Phillips equation. It thus possesses the same property of convergence with damped oscillations. Conversely, the determinants of the NAIRU are different in the two models.

Placing $\Delta p_t = \Delta p_{t-1}$ in equation (34) and assuming that the growth rate of productivity is a constant equal to Δa, it turns out that the NAIRU now reads:

$$\bar{u} = \frac{\lambda_0 + \lambda_3 \chi - (1 - \lambda_3)\Delta a}{\lambda_2} \tag{35}$$

The NAIRU depends on parameter χ representing the markup of prices on wage. This parameter did not come into the definition (10) of the NAIRU based on the Phillips curve. Since the markup depends on the market power of firms, the rate of compulsory payroll deductions from wages, and the costs of capital and energy, a number of supply side macroeconomic policies, which have no long-run effect in the Keynesian model of the Phillips curve, are now capable of acting durably on unemployment.

The Wage Curve
It is also interesting to note that relation (35) defining the NAIRU dictates, if $\lambda_3 \neq 0$, a negative linkage in the long run between the *level* of the real wage and the unemployment rate. Since the price rule (3) is identical to equality $\chi = a_t + p_t - w_t$, at stationary equilibrium we get:

$$\lambda_3(w_t - p_t - a_t) = \lambda_0 - \lambda_2 \bar{u} + (1 - \lambda_3)\Delta a \tag{36}$$

In the literature, this type of relation between the real wage level and the unemployment rate is known as the *wage curve*. It has been the subject of numerous empirical tests (see Blanchflower and Oswald, 1995, and section 5.1 below).

An Empirical Assessment
According to Blanchard and Katz (1999), a potential explanation of the different performances of Europe and the United States when it comes to unemployment lies in the fact that the wage level does not come into the wage equation in the United States, whereas it plays an important role in Europe. We can illustrate this argument by estimating the wage equation (33). We find that this equation gives bad results for the United States, in any case ones clearly less good than those obtained by estimating a simple Phillips equation. Moreover, λ_3 is not significantly different from zero. The growth rate of nominal wages would thus not be influenced by the error correction term in the United States, and the Phillips equation would, all in all, give a "good" representation of wage setting there. On the other hand, the results obtained from annual French data for the period 1970–1998 are noticeably better. Noting that $\Delta a_t + a_{t-1} = a_t$, the estimation of equation (33) gives[3]:

$$\Delta w_t - \Delta p_t = \underset{(5.54)}{0.46} - \underset{(4.21)}{0.30}(\Delta p_t - \Delta p_{t-1}) - \underset{(9.95)}{0.51}u_t - \underset{(5.00)}{0.18}(w_{t-1} - p_{t-1} - a_t),$$

$$\bar{R}^2 = 0.98, \text{DW} = 1.54$$

This equation indicates that the growth rate of nominal wages in France depends on the error correction term, with a relatively slow adjustment speed. That being so, changes in the markup do indeed have a long-run impact on the unemployment rate, as Blanchard and Katz emphasize. The expression (35) of the NAIRU indicates that the derivative of the latter with respect to logarithm χ of the markup v is equal to λ_3/λ_2. The value of this ratio is 0.35 in the present case. This result makes it possible to grasp the effect of the interest rate on the long-run unemployment rate. Assuming a Cobb-Douglas production function of the form $K^{\alpha}(AL)^{1-\alpha}$, if firms have no market power, profit maximization, which has the value $PK^{\alpha}(AL)^{1-\alpha} - WL - (r+\delta)PK$, entails $P = [(r+\delta)/\alpha]^{\alpha/(1-\alpha)} W/[(1-\alpha)A]$, where r and δ designate respectively the interest rate and the rate of depreciation of capital. The markup v can thus be written $cst \cdot (r+\delta)^{\alpha/(1-\alpha)}$ and the elasticity of the markup with respect to the user cost of capital takes the value $\alpha/(1-\alpha)$, which entails:

$$d\bar{u} = \frac{\alpha}{(1-\alpha)} \frac{\lambda_3}{\lambda_2} \frac{d(r+\delta)}{(r+\delta)}$$

Taking the value 1/3 for α, which corresponds to the share of capital in the total factors cost, and utilizing the result of the estimation of the wage equation, we get $d\bar{u} = [0.175/(r+\delta)] dr$. By way of illustration, let us suppose that the interest rate r takes the value of 5% and the depreciation rate of capital δ takes a value of 10%. We find in the end that the NAIRU increases by 1.2 percentage points ($d\bar{u} = 0.012$) when the interest rate climbs by one percentage point ($dr = 0.01$ with $d\delta = 0$). This model thus predicts that the French NAIRU increases with the interest rate, but only slightly. It suggests that the real interest rate, which grew by around five points between the 1970s and the beginning of the 1980s, may have contributed, to a limited extent, to the climb in unemployment (Fitoussi and Phelps, 1988). We will see in chapter 9, section 3.5, that models of unemployment endowed with more explicit microeconomic foundations arrive at similar conclusions.

5   ESTIMATES OF THE NAIRU AND WAGE EQUATIONS

The foregoing sections set out several forms of wage equation that can be estimated. They also allow us to arrive at a measure of the NAIRU that plays an important role in the decisions of the monetary authorities.

5.1   ESTIMATES OF WAGE EQUATIONS

We have reviewed different forms of wage equations that express the growth rate of nominal wages as a function of different explanatory variables, including the unemployment rate in level and difference, present and past inflation rates, the rate of productivity growth, and an error correction term. The practice consists of estimating a general form of wage equation, including the set of all the potential explanatory variables (see, for example OECD, 1997, and Blanchard and Katz, 1997). Table 8.4 presents, by way of illustration, the results of estimates of wage equations including the different variables mentioned in this chapter for the United States, Japan, France, Germany, Italy, and the United Kingdom. These estimates suggest that the same wage equation does not apply to all countries. National specifics lead to different modes of

Table 8.4

Estimation of the wage equation for six OECD countries (annual data for the period 1970–1998).

$\Delta w_t - \Delta p_t$	Germany	U.S.	France	Italy	Japan	U.K.
Constant	0.94*** (6.41)	0.03** (2.29)	0.47*** (5.54)	1.11* (1.82)	0.04*** (2.90)	0.10*** (3.91)
$\Delta p_t - \Delta p_{t-1}$		−0.46*** (−2.81)	−0.30*** (−4.21)	−0.19 (−1.12)	−0.14 (−1.60)	
u_t	−0.52*** (−4.29)	−0.34** (−2.11)	−0.51*** (−9.95)	−0.52*** (−4.52)	−1.46*** (−3.19)	−0.15 (−1.16)
Δa_t		0.38** (2.35)			0.69*** (4.91)	
Δu_t				−0.89* (−1.83)		
$w_{t-1} - p_{t-1} - a_t$	−0.58*** (−6.20)		−0.18*** (−5.00)	−0.13* (−1.73)		−0.27*** (−2.68)
$\bar{R}^2$	0.75	0.81	0.98	0.95	0.95	0.89
DW	1.41	1.31	1.54	1.71	1.62	1.86

Note: The dependent variable is the growth rate of real wages. The data are taken from the database of the OECD. Wage is the earnings per worker in the private sector. Price is the price index of private consumption. Unemployment rate is the standardized rate of unemployment. Productivity of labor is equal to the ratio of GDP to employment. Method of estimation: ordinary least squares. t-statistics are given in parentheses. 3, 2, and 1 stars means that the coefficient is significant at 1%, 5%, and 10%, respectively.

wage formation. The most robust results of a number of studies dedicated to the estimation of wage equations are summed up in what follows.

(i) *On Long-Run Indexation.* In table 8.4, the coefficient of indexation of nominal wages to prices is taken to be equal to unity. Many empirical studies corroborate this hypothesis. Only Italy and the United Kingdom may be exceptions to this rule, but that conclusion is contested by the study of Chan-Lee et al. (1987), who found a coefficient close to unity for these two countries.

(ii) *On Nominal Rigidities.* Our estimates suggest that there are few nominal rigidities, since the adjustment lag of real wage growth rate to variations in inflation is not significantly different from zero (at the 10% threshold, for annual data) in Germany, Japan, and the United Kingdom. The United States, and to a lesser extent France, present the greatest degree of nominal rigidity. More generally, the extent of nominal rigidities is measured using an average adjustment interval of nominal wages to prices. For that purpose, we estimate a Phillips equation slightly different from the one presented in equations (7) or (25). To be precise, we replace the term $(1 - \lambda_1)\Delta p_t + \lambda_1 \Delta p_{t-1}$ by a distributed lag of past rates of inflation, which reads $\sum_{i=0}^{\infty} v_i \Delta p_{t-i}$. The mean lag is then equal to $\sum_{i=0}^{\infty} i v_i / \sum_{i=0}^{\infty} v_i$ (see, for example, Hendry, 1995). The mean lag of nominal wages obtained using this method on quarterly data is generally short: on the order of one quarter in Japan, France, and Germany and two quarters in the United Kingdom. On the other hand, it lies between two and one-half and three quarters in the United States according to estimates (see Bruno and Sachs, 1985; Drèze and Bean, 1990; and Turner and Seghezza, 1999). This high degree of nominal ridigity in the United States is generally explained by the existence of collective agreements lasting three years and including only partial indexation clauses. This result can also be explained by the fact that in the United States, the rate of coverage of collective agreements is much less (18% in 1990) than it is in Europe (close to 80%). In sum, it is safe to say that the United States and Canada exhibited greater nominal rigidity than other OECD countries from the beginning of the 1970s to the end of the 1990s.

(iii) *On Real Rigidities*. We observe that the unemployment rate exerts significant downward pressure on wage growth in all countries except the United Kingdom. The degree of real rigidity is of comparable size in the United States and Europe: an increase of one point in the unemployment rate reduces the real wage growth rate on the order of 0.5%. Japan, on the other hand, is characterized by a degree of real rigidity clearly much smaller than in the other countries. A rise of one point in the unemployment rate reduces the real wage growth rate by 1.5% there—three times more than in continental Europe or the United States. We should no doubt see here one of the reasons for Japan's good results in terms of employment over this period. The estimates of Bean et al. (1986), Alogoskoufis and Manning (1988), Elmeskov and MacFarlan (1993), OECD (1997), and Turner and Seghezza (1999) come to essentially the same conclusions.

(iv) *On Hysteresis Effects*. Variations in the unemployment rate influence wages in Italy alone. Nevertheless, because the unemployment rate also exerts a significant influence on wages, there is no pure hysteresis mechanism causing the NAIRU to depend solely on the current unemployment rate in this country (see section 4.1.2 above). OECD (1997) comes to a similar result. Hence the short-run NAIRU is distinct from the long-run NAIRU in Italy, whereas there is no way to establish such a distinction in the other countries, according to our results. Yet estimates carried out on quarterly data generally bring to light an influence of variation in the unemployment rate on the growth rate of wages in Germany. Elmeskov and MacFarlan (1993) find for their part that this effect also exists in the United States. Conversely, France and Japan present no significant hysteresis effect. That means that, for these countries, variations in the instantaneous NAIRU are due to variations in the long-run NAIRU. Overall, these results suggest that hysteresis effects exist, but that their size is too small to entail pure hysteresis phenomena, implying a NAIRU equal to the current unemployment rate.

(v) *On Productivity and the Error Correction Term*. The error correction term is not significant in the United States and Japan, whereas it does influence wages in the other countries. Thus the Phillips equation, which expresses a relationship between the unemployment rate and the growth rate of wages, proves inappropriate to represent the setting of wages in the United States and Japan. Conversely, in the other countries on which our results bear, the relevant wage equation contains an error correction term. Readers will recall that this error correction term appears if the wage depends on labor productivity and if unemployment benefits depend little on past wages. Such characteristics reveal labor markets functioning in such a way that employees have a bargaining power that allows them to obtain a share of the surplus, and in which the welfare state is relatively generous, leading to gains in case of unemployment little dependent on the past incomes of workers. It is thus not surprising that the error correction term should be significant in the European countries, in which labor law and the welfare state possess these characteristics (see chapter 12, this book). On the whole, these results are compatible with other empirical work, which systematically finds that the error correction term is not significant in the United States, but that it does have a certain importance in European countries (Blanchard and Katz, 1997, 1999; OECD, 1997). The growth rate of labor productivity influences the growth rate of wages when wage formation is represented by a Phillips relation, as in Japan and the United States. From this point of view, the results of table 8.4 conform to those usually obtained. The coefficient of indexation is higher in Japan, where it is generally on the order of 60%, while it lies at around 30% in the United States.

(vi) *On Wage Curves.* When coefficient λ_3 is not null, we have seen that there exists a long-run negative linkage between the real wage level and the unemployment rate described by the wage curve (36). All empirical studies dedicated to the estimation of a linkage of this type confirm its existence. The results concerning five OECD countries assembled in table 8.5 show, however, that the elasticity of the real wage with respect to the unemployment rate is small, on the order of -0.1 in most countries. In other words, the unemployment rate must rise by 10% for real wages to fall by

Table 8.5

The relationship between the wage level and the unemployment rate.

Country	Period	η_u^w
United States	1963–1990	-0.10 ($t > 25$)
United Kingdom	1973–1990	-0.08 ($t = 6.23$)
Italy	1986–1989	-0.10 ($t = 0.63$)
Netherlands	1988–1991	-0.17 ($t = 2.35$)
Germany	1986–1991	-0.13 ($t = 1.75$)

Source: Blanchflower and Oswald (1995, p. 363).

Note: The logarithm of wage level is explained by a set of variable including the logarithm of the local unemployment rate. The parameter estimated is the elasticity of real wages with respect to the unemployment rate. The variable t designates the t-statistics.

1% (see Bils, 1985; Solon et al., 1994; and the survey of Card, 1995, and Blanchflower and Oswald, 1995).

5.2 Estimates of the NAIRU

Estimating the NAIRU is a matter of great importance, because the unemployment rate is considered a leading indicator of inflation. For that reason, it is an important guideline in monetary policy. A unemployment rate inferior to the NAIRU indicates inflationary pressures that should lead the monetary authorities to tighten their controls on the growth of the money supply. Thus, in the United States, the concomitant reductions in the inflation rate and the unemployment rate at the end of the 1990s suggest that the NAIRU has a tendency to diminish over this period (see the study of Richardson et al., 2000). The unemployment rate has indeed fallen below the 5% barrier without inducing inflationary pressure. It is important to know how far unemployment can fall without triggering this type of pressure. The NAIRU can be grasped very simply using form (34) of the Phillips equation. A first approximation of the NAIRU is obtained by using a figure that places the acceleration of inflation on the horizontal axis and the unemployment rate on the vertical axis. To that end, it is sufficient to trace the curve linking the actual unemployment rate u_t at a determined date and the acceleration of prices $(\Delta p_t - \Delta p_{t-1})$ at that same date. Figure 8.20 depicts the curves for France, the United States, Japan, and Germany for the period 1970–1998. Since the difference between the current unemployment rate u_t and the NAIRU $\bar{u}_t$ is always given by the term $(-\lambda_1/\lambda_2)(\Delta p_t - \Delta p_{t-1})$—see equation (12), which always applies when the wage equation contains an unemployment rate term in differences, or an error correction term—the observation of $(\Delta p_t - \Delta p_{t-1})$ and knowledge of the sacrifice ratio (λ_1/λ_2), given by table 8.4, makes it possible to easily assess the NAIRU.

Table 8.4 indicates that the ratio (λ_1/λ_2) takes the respective values 0.59, 1.35, 0.10, and 0, for France, the United States, Japan, and Germany. Because variations in the inflation rate $(\Delta p_t - \Delta p_{t-1})$ are relatively weak since the end of the 1970s, it turns out that the observed unemployment rate is always very close to the NAIRU over this period. The value of the NAIRU is then always given approximately, for each country, by the intersection of the curve linking the different points with the vertical line with abscissa zero in the graphs in figure 8.20. As we see, the NAIRU increases in Germany, France, and to a lesser extent in Japan. On the other hand, it fluctuates around a value lying between 6% and 7% in the United States. The regression lines indicate that there does indeed exist a negative relation between the acceleration of inflation and the unemployment rate. Moreover, they bring out the variability of the NAIRU over certain subperiods. We see that the points corresponding to the 1990s lie above the regression line for Germany, Japan, and France, which suggests that the NAIRU is above its average value, calculated for the period 1970–1998, in the 1990s. Since the wage equations of France and Germany contain an error correction term, Blanchard and Katz (1999) explain this phenomenon by variations in the variable χ, representing the markup between prices and wages. For the United States, on the contrary, we see

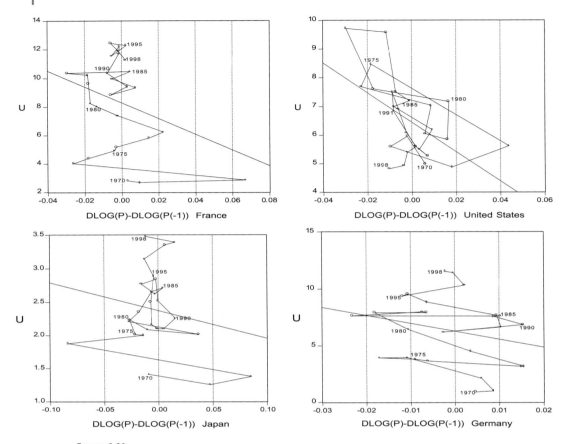

FIGURE 8.20
The relationship between increases in the inflation rate and the unemployment rate in four OECD countries.

that the points for the 1990s are situated beneath the regression line (see Katz and Krueger, 1999, for a similar observation regarding the United States).

The graphs in figure 8.20 allow us to visualize the time path of the NAIRU, but it is also possible to estimate it. Assuming that the adjustment interval for wages can take any value, the NAIRU $\bar{u}$ is deduced from an equation of the following form (Staiger et al., 1997):

$$\Delta^2 p_t = \beta_1(u_{t-1} - \bar{u}) + \beta_2(u_{t-2} - \bar{u}) + \beta_3 X_t$$

In this equality, X_t designates a vector of variables including past inflation rates and measurements of supply shocks, for example the difference between labor productivity and its trend, or the growth rate of the prices of imports relative to the producer price index. This equation can also be written in the following manner:

$$\Delta^2 p_t = \beta_0 + \beta_1 u_{t-1} + \beta_2 u_{t-2} + \beta_3 X_t$$

The coefficients β_i can then be estimated by ordinary least squares, and the NAIRU $\bar{u}$ is simply equal to $-\beta_0/(\beta_1 + \beta_2)$. This method of estimation, which is applied in many studies, leads to an estimate of the NAIRU for the United States of around 6% for the period 1960–1995 (see the synthesis of Staiger et al., 1997). The application of this method to subperiods on quarterly data suggests that the NAIRU was effectively falling in the United States in the beginning of the 1990s (Gordon, 1997; Staiger et al., 1997; Brayton et al., 1999; see also the studies of Fair, 2000, and Richardson et al., 2000, who develop methods complementary to this approach in order to assess the dynamics of the NAIRU).

6 SUMMARY AND CONCLUSION

- The high degree of unemployment in Europe does not come from a more rapid growth in the labor force than in the United States or Japan; it is the upshot of particularly weak job creation. Continental Europe is distinguished by a high proportion of long-term unemployed. The real wage and employment are two procyclical variables positively correlated with labor productivity. The business cycle is more damped in Europe than in the United States.

- In the classical model, the real fundamentals of the economy determine the equilibrium levels of the real variables, and the quantity of money acts only on nominal variables. When the elasticity of aggregate labor supply is low, the classical model predicts that fluctuations in the real wage will always be accompanied by much smaller fluctuations in employment. This is contrary to the stylized facts.

- The Phillips curve links the growth rate of nominal wages to the inflation rate (present and past) and the unemployment rate. It makes it possible to define the NAIRU—the nonaccelerating inflation rate of unemployment. The Phillips curve portrays a trade-off in which a fall in the unemployment rate can be achieved, in the short run, by an acceleration of inflation. In the long run, the equilibrium unemployment rate is equal to the NAIRU, and this trade-off disappears.

- In a Keynesian perspective, the short-run efficiency of demand side policies arises from the existence of nominal rigidities. In the long run, these rigidities do not exist. Empirical work shows that the degree of nominal rigidity of wages is relatively low, but is greater in the United States than in France. In consequence, demand side policies have a significant impact over a short span of time, on the order of two to five years.

- The growth rate of labor productivity is one of the determinants of the NAIRU. Simulations carried out using the Phillips curve model suggest that the slowdown in labor productivity growth that occurred between the 1960s and the 1980s caused a hike in the American NAIRU of around 1.8 percentage points.

On the other hand, the slowing of productivity is thought to have raised the French NAIRU by almost six percentage points. The reason for this difference is the absence of indexation of wages to productivity in France. But it should be stressed that models based on a Phillips curve are ill-suited to the analysis of supply side policies that change the rules of wage formation. This curve takes such rules into account in an ad hoc manner, and therefore does not rest on any definite hypothesis regarding the behavior of agents.

- Friedman (1968) and Lucas (1972) gave a "classical" interpretation of the Phillips curve by assuming that the labor market is always in equilibrium. According to these authors, the expectation errors of agents condition the impact of demand side policies in the short run. For those who subscribe to the "new classical macroeconomics," the short-run efficiency of systematic demand side policies vanishes if agents are capable of forming *rational expectations*. Under this hypothesis, only the *unexpected* component of demand side policies has an effect in the short run.

- An economy displays *hysteresis* effects if the long-run equilibrium unemployment rate depends on past levels of the current unemployment rate. Related to this is the idea that a *transitory* shock has permanent effects. This will be the case if variations in nominal wages depend solely on the short-term unemployment, and not on the total stock of the unemployed. Demand side policies then have a permanent impact on the unemployment rate.

- In certain continental European countries, the time path of nominal wages depends significantly on the difference between past real wages and past productivities. This is an error correction mechanism which entails that the NAIRU depends on the interest rate, payroll taxes, and the market power of firms.

- In the long run, the indexation coefficient of the nominal wage to inflation is not significantly different from unity in most countries. The median adjustment lag of nominal wages to prices is generally shorter in Europe and Japan. It is clearly longer in the United States.

- The unemployment rate exerts significant downward pressure on wage growth, except in the United Kindom. The degree of real rigidity is of the same order of magnitude in the United States and Europe, but clearly lower in Japan. In the European countries, the wage growth rate is influenced by the gap between wage levels and productivity. The NAIRU then depends on the markup of firms, and the rise in unemployment in the 1980s and 1990s in Germany, France, and Italy might be explained by changes in the elements that influence the markup. Thus the increase in payroll taxes, and to a lesser extent the high interest rates that prevailed in the 1980s, are potential causes for the rise in the NAIRU observed in these countries.

- In the majority of countries, it has been estimated that the elasticity of the real wage *level* with respect to the unemployment rate is of the order of -0.1.

- The theories set forth in this chapter do not, however, allow a precise diagnosis of the reasons for changes in the NAIRU. Recent analyses of the functioning of the labor market, which are based on the behavior of agents, have enriched and focused the conclusions of the (standard) macroeconomic approach. These analyses are presented in the following chapters.

7   RELATED TOPICS IN THE BOOK

- Chapter 1, section 2.2: The elasticity of labor supply

- Chapter 3, section 3.2: The duration of unemployment

- Chapter 7, section 4: Insiders, outsiders, and persistent unemployment

- Chapter 9, section 3.1: Job creation and job destruction

- Chapter 9, section 3.2: Labor market equilibrium

- Chapter 11, section 2: Active labor market policies

- Chapter 12, section 5: Macroeconomic assessments of institutions

8   FURTHER READINGS

Bean, C. (1994), "European unemployment: A survey," *Journal of Economic Literature*, 32, pp. 573–619.

Blanchard, O., and Katz, L. (1997), "What we know and do not know about the natural unemployment rate," *Journal of Economic Perspectives*, 11, pp. 51–72.

Blanchflower, D., and Oswald, A. (1995), *The Wage Curve*, Cambridge, Mass.: MIT Press.

Friedman, M. (1968), "The role of economic policy," *American Economic Review*, 58(1), pp. 1–17.

Lucas, R. (1981), *Studies in Business Cycle Theory*, Cambridge, Mass.: MIT Press.

Machin, S., and Manning, A. (1999), "The causes and consequences of long-term unemployment in Europe," in Ashenfelter, O., and Card, D. (eds.), *Handbook of Labor Economics*, vol. 3C, chap. 47, Amsterdam: Elsevier Science/North-Holland.

9   APPENDICES

9.1   APPENDIX 1: THE MICROECONOMIC FOUNDATIONS OF THE LINEAR MODEL

Models in which firms producing differentiated products engage in price competition are now widely used in macroeconomics. By making the way in which the prices of goods are set completely explicit, they supply a coherent framework for the study of a great many issues (see Weitzman, 1985, and Blanchard and Kiyotaki, 1987, for the basic models, and Bénassy, 1991, for a complete review of monopolistic competition). Here we consider an economy with a large number n of firms, each producing a different consumer good. The same index $i = 1, \ldots, n$ designates either a good or the firm that makes it. Production makes use of labor supplied by households as the sole input. There are many identical households. We further assume that this economy has a specific good—money—that serves as the numeraire, i.e., the unit of account and store of value. Time is represented by an infinite succession of discrete periods. In each period, a two-stage game unfolds. In the first stage, firms set the prices of their products simultaneously and without prior consultation. In the second stage, a fixed price equilibrium defining the quantities exchanged is achieved. This game is solved backward, by first determining the quantities exchanged at fixed prices in the second stage, and then seeking the prices chosen by the firms in the first stage, in the knowledge that firms are able to calculate the quantities exchanged in the second stage as a function of the vector of prices. We begin by describing the mechanism of exchanges proper to one period.

The Demands for Goods and Aggregate Output
In order to obtain explicit demand functions for goods, we will assume that in each period an individual h makes his or her choices on the basis of the following utility function:

$$U = \left(\frac{C_h^i}{\theta}\right)^{\theta} \left(\frac{M_h}{(1-\theta)P}\right)^{1-\theta} - \left(\frac{d}{\varepsilon}\right) L_h^{\varepsilon}, \qquad \theta \in (0,1), \, \varepsilon \geq 1, \, d > 0 \tag{37}$$

with:

$$C_h = n^{1/(1-\sigma)} \left[\sum_{i=1}^{n} C_{ih}^{(\sigma-1)/\sigma}\right]^{\sigma/(\sigma-1)}, \qquad \sigma > 1$$

In these relations, C_{ih} and M_h designate respectively the consumption of goods i and the money held by individual h at the end of the period. Variable P represents the price index in the current period, and L_h designates the quantity of labor supplied by the household. We see that the utility function of agents is of the Cobb-Douglas form as regards the trade-off between global consumption C_h and money holdings M_h, and of the CES form as regards the choice between consumption C_{ih} of different goods. When the price of good i is P_i, Dixit and Stiglitz (1977) have shown that the price index P linked to a utility function of this type takes the form:

$$P = \left(\frac{1}{n}\sum_{i=1}^{n} P_i^{1-\sigma}\right)^{1/(1-\sigma)} \tag{38}$$

Parameter σ represents the elasticity of substitution among the n consumer goods. Let R_h be the wealth of individual h. His or her budget constraint is written:

$$\sum_{i=1}^{n} P_i C_{ih} + M_h = R_h \tag{39}$$

The maximization of utility (37) subject to constraint (39) gives the demands for goods C_{ih} and the demand for money M_h of individual h. After several calculations, we arrive at:

$$C_{ih} = \frac{\theta R_h}{nP} \left(\frac{P_i}{P}\right)^{-\sigma} \quad \text{and} \quad M_h = (1-\theta)R_h$$

By substituting these values for consumption and demand for money in the utility function defined by equation (37), it is possible to calculate the indirect utility of household h as a function of its wealth and the quantity of labor. We obtain: $U_h = R_h/P - (d/\varepsilon)L_h^\varepsilon$. Let W be the nominal wage in the period. Since the wealth of an agent is equal to the sum of his or her initial money holdings M_{0h}, his or her share Π_h of profits, and his or her income from wages WL_h, we arrive at:

$$U_h = \left(\frac{WL_h + M_{0h} + \Pi_h}{P}\right) - \left(\frac{d}{\varepsilon}\right)L^\varepsilon$$

Maximization of U_h with respect to L_h defines the labor supplied by household h:

$$L_h^s = \left(\frac{W}{dP}\right)^{1/(\varepsilon-1)} \tag{40}$$

Designating the global wealth of agents by $R = \sum_h R_h$, the total consumption of goods i, $C_i = \sum_h C_{ih}$, is written:

$$C_i = \frac{\theta R}{nP} \left(\frac{P_i}{P}\right)^{-\sigma} \tag{41}$$

Let us define the index Y of aggregate output by $PY \equiv \sum_i P_i C_i$. Relations (38) and (41) then entail:

$$Y = \theta R/P \tag{42}$$

And the demand for good i, or $Y_i = C_i$, takes the following form:

$$Y_i = \frac{Y}{n} \left(\frac{P_i}{P}\right)^{-\sigma} \tag{43}$$

Assuming that all profits are redistributed to households, their global wealth R corresponds to the total value PY of the output plus the stock $M_0 = \sum_h M_{0h}$, of initial money holdings, $R = PY + M_0$. Using (42), we then get a particularly simple expression of aggregate output. It is written:

$$Y = \frac{\theta}{(1-\theta)} \frac{M_0}{P}$$

This expression of aggregate output is reminiscent of that of aggregate demand issuing from an IS-LM model. We observe, in particular, that if the price index remains constant, the multiplier associated with an increase in the money supply in the form of transfers to households takes the value $\theta/(1 - \theta)$. Parameter θ is thus equivalent to the marginal propensity to consume.

The Price-Setting Rule

For the sake of simplicity, and with no prejudice to the generality of our results, we will assume that the production function of each firm i is linear, or $Y_i = AL_i$, where Y_i and L_i designate respectively output and employment in firm i. A represents a productivity parameter common to all firms. We will assume that each production unit decides its own variables (Y_i, L_i, P_i) considering that its decision has no influence on the aggregate quantities Y and P. Since the latter do in fact depend on decisions taken by all firms, this hypothesis signifies that each production unit takes the actions of its competitors as given. Equilibrium is thus noncooperative; it is also called Nash equilibrium. The problem of firm i is written:

$$\underset{\{P_i, L_i, Y_i\}}{\text{Max}} (P_i Y_i - WL_i) \quad \text{s.c.} \quad Y_i = \frac{\theta M_0}{(1 - \theta)n} \left(\frac{P_i}{P}\right)^{-\sigma} \quad \text{and} \quad Y_i = AL_i$$

After several calculations, we find the optimal price level P_i of good i:

$$P_i = v\frac{W}{A} \quad \text{with} \quad v = \frac{\sigma}{\sigma - 1} > 1$$

It turns out that each producer sets his or her price by applying a markup v to the nominal wage W deflated by the productivity term A. Parameter v measures the monopoly power exerted by each firm. If $v = 1$, all goods are perfectly substitutable, and we are back in a situation of perfect competition. Readers can verify that, for a given wage level, the price of consumer goods increases with the monopoly power of producers.

A Linear Version of the Model

The nominal wage being the same for all firms, the prices of consumer goods all settle on the same value vW/A. That being the case, the price index P will also be equal to this common value. Relation (43) then shows that we have $Y_i = Y/n$, and aggregate labor demand attains the level $nL_i = nY_i/A = Y/A$. Let H be the number of households; equation (40) makes it possible to define the aggregate labor supply:

$$L^s = \sum_{h=1}^{H} L_h^s = Hd^{1/(1-\varepsilon)}(W/P)^\eta \quad \text{with} \quad \eta = 1/(\varepsilon - 1)$$

Eventually, we have four equations with five unknown variables (P, W, Y, L^s, L). They are written:

$$P = v\frac{W}{A}, \qquad Y = AL, \qquad Y = \frac{\theta}{1 - \theta}\left(\frac{M_0}{P}\right), \qquad \text{and} \qquad L^s = Hd^{1/(1-\varepsilon)}\left(\frac{W}{P}\right)^\eta \tag{44}$$

Let us assume that time is represented by a succession of discrete periods, and that at the beginning of period t—or the end of period $(t - 1)$—the stock of money is equal to M_t. Denoting by a lowercase letter the logarithm of the corresponding variable (for example, $p = \mathrm{Log}\, P$), the system (44) can be written in a linear form as follows:

$$y_t = m_t - p_t$$

$$y_t = \ell_t + a_t$$

$$p_t = w_t - a_t + \chi, \qquad \chi = \ln v$$

$$\ell_t^s = \bar{\ell} + \eta(w_t - p_t), \qquad \bar{\ell} = \ln Hd^{1/(1-\varepsilon)}$$

In this system, the parameters with no time index are taken to be constant over time. These four equations correspond to the relations from (1) to (4) in the text. If Δ represents the difference operator, by definition we have $\Delta m_t = m_t - m_{t-1} = \ln(M_t/M_{t-1})$. Assuming that the increase in the money supply is small with respect to the stock of money, we also have $\ln(M_t/M_{t-1}) \simeq (M_t - M_{t-1})/M_{t-1}$, and consequently $(M_t - M_{t-1})/M_{t-1} \simeq \Delta m_t$. The variable Δm_t is thus approximately equal to the growth rate of the money supply between dates t and $(t-1)$.

Interest Rate and Markup
In the foregoing, the markup v does not depend on the interest rate. That changes if we cause capital to appear explicitly. So let us assume that each firm i is endowed with a production function $F(K_i, AL_i)$ with constant returns, using labor in quantity L_i and capital in quantity K_i. Let τ and ρ be respectively the rate of payroll tax and the (nominal) user cost of capital. The problem of firm i is now written:

$$\underset{\{P_i, L_i, K_i\}}{\mathrm{Max}}\ P_i Y_i - W(1+\tau)L_i - \rho K_i \qquad \mathrm{s.c.} \qquad Y_i = F(K_i, AL_i) = \frac{Y}{n}\left(\frac{P_i}{P}\right)^{-\sigma}$$

The reader can verify that the solution of this problem comes to the usual conclusion that capital intensity $k_i = K_i/AL_i$ is an increasing function of the relative cost $W(1+\tau)/\rho$ of labor with respect to capital. Let k^* be the optimal capital intensity common to all firms, and let F_2 be the partial derivative of function F with respect to its second argument. It is easy to establish that the price-setting rule is now written:

$$P_i = \mu\frac{W}{A} \qquad \text{with} \qquad \mu = \frac{\sigma}{\sigma-1}\frac{1+\tau}{F_2(k^*, 1)}$$

Since $F_2(k^*, 1)$ is increasing with k^* (see chapter 4), the markup μ diminishes with the relative cost of labor with respect to capital. Inasmuch as the user cost ρ is positively linked with the interest rate r, the markup becomes an increasing function of the interest rate. Finally, it is possible to show further that the markup increases with the rate τ of payroll taxes.

9.2   APPENDIX 2: THE DYNAMICS OF AN ECONOMY WHERE THE UNEMPLOYED ARE HETEROGENEOUS

The dynamics of unemployment and inflation is defined by equations (13) and (26). We assume that the growth rates of the money supply and productivity are constants, defined respectively by Δm and Δa. The stationary values of unemployment and inflation are then equal to $\bar{u}$ and $\pi = \Delta m - \Delta a$. After rearranging terms, relations (13) and (26) allow us to arrive at the following linear system:

$$\begin{bmatrix} \Delta p_t - \pi \\ u_t - \bar{u} \end{bmatrix} = \mathscr{A} \begin{bmatrix} \Delta p_{t-1} - \pi \\ u_{t-1} - \bar{u} \end{bmatrix}$$

where $\mathscr{A}$ is a matrix which has the expression:

$$\mathscr{A} = \frac{1}{\lambda_1 + \lambda_2 + \lambda_2'} \begin{bmatrix} \lambda_1 & -\lambda_2 \\ \lambda_1 & \lambda_1 + \lambda_2 \end{bmatrix}$$

The trace and the determinant of this matrix take the values:

$$T = \frac{2\lambda_1 + \lambda_2'}{\lambda_1 + \lambda_2 + \lambda_2'} > 0 \qquad \text{and} \qquad D = \frac{\lambda_1}{\lambda_1 + \lambda_2 + \lambda_2'} \in [0, 1]$$

The discriminant of the characteristic equation of matrix $\mathscr{A}$ is written:

$$\delta_{\mathscr{A}} = \frac{(\lambda_2')^2 - 4\lambda_1\lambda_2}{(\lambda_1 + \lambda_2 + \lambda_2')^2}$$

It turns out that two cases must be distinguished:

1. $\lambda_2' < 2\sqrt{\lambda_1\lambda_2}$. The eigenvalues of $\mathscr{A}$ are two complex conjugate numbers. Because the determinant falls in the interval between 0 and 1, that means that the modulus of these eigenvalues is smaller than unity. The system is thus stable, and converges to its stationary state, presenting oscillations that are more or less damped (see conditions (64) and (65) in mathematical appendix D at the end of this book).

2. $\lambda_2' > 2\sqrt{\lambda_1\lambda_2}$. The eigenvalues of $\mathscr{A}$ are now two real numbers. We then verify that D and T are such that $1 > D > |T| - 1$. Following relation (65) in mathematical appendix D, this last condition ensures that the system is stable.

REFERENCES

Alogoskoufis, C., and Manning, A. (1988), "On the persistence of unemployment," *Economic Policy*, 5, pp. 2–43.

Bean, C., Layard, R., and Nickell, S. (1986), "The rise in unemployment: A multi-country study," *Economica*, 53, Suppl., pp. 1–22.

Bénassy, J.-P. (1991), "Monopolistic competition," in Hildenbrand, W., and Sonnen-schein, H. (eds.), *Handbook of Mathematical Economics*, vol. 4, ch. 37, pp. 1997–2045, Amsterdam, North-Holland.

Bénassy, J.-P. (1993), "Nonclearing markets: Microeconomic concepts and macro-economic applications," *Journal of Economic Literature*, 31, pp. 732–761.

Bils, M. (1985), "Real wages over the business cycle: Evidence from panel data," *Journal of Political Economy*, 93, pp. 666–689.

Blanchard, O., and Fischer, S. (1989), *Lectures on Macroeconomics*, Cambridge, Mass.: MIT Press.

Blanchard, O., and Katz, L. (1997), "What we know and do not know about the natural unemployment rate," *Journal of Economic Perspectives*, 11, pp. 51–72.

Blanchard, O., and Katz, L. (1999), "Wage dynamics: Reconciling theory and evidence," *American Economic Review, Papers and Proceedings*, 89, pp. 69–74.

Blanchard, O., and Kiyotaki, N. (1987), "Monopolistic competition and the effects of aggregate demand," *American Economic Review*, 77, pp. 647–666.

Blanchard, O., and Summers, L. (1986), "Hysteresis and the European unemployment problem," *NBER Macroeconomic Annual*, 1, pp. 15–78.

Blanchflower, D., and Oswald, A. (1995), *The Wage Curve*, Cambridge, Mass.: MIT Press.

Brayton, F., Roberts, J., and Williams, J. (1999), "What's happened to the Phillips curve?" Finance and Economics Discussion Series 1999–49. Washington: Board of Governors of the Federal Reserve System.

Bruno, M., and Sachs, J. (1985), *Economics of Worldwide Stagflation*, Oxford, U.K.: Basil Blackwell.

Card, D. (1995), "The wage curve: A review," *Journal of Economic Literature*, 33, pp. 785–799.

Chan-Lee, J., Coe, D., and Prywes, M. (1987), "Microeconomic changes and macroeconomic wage disinflation in the 1980s," *OECD Economic Studies*, 8, pp. 122–157.

Chari, V., Kehoe, P., and McGrattan, E. (2000), "Sticky price models of the business cycle: Can the contract multiplier solve the persistence problem?" *Econometrica*, 68, pp. 1151–1179.

Christiano, L., Eichenbaum, M., and Evans, C. (1999), "Monetary policy shocks: What have we learned and to what end?" in Woodford, M., and Taylor, J. (eds.), *Handbook of Macroeconomics*, vol. 1A, chap. 2, Amsterdam: Elsevier Science.

Coe, D. (1985), "Nominal wages, the NAIRU and wage flexibility," *OECD Economic Studies*, Autum, pp. 87–126.

Devine, T., and Kiefer, N. (1991), *Empirical Labor Economics: The Search Approach*, Oxford, U.K.: Oxford University Press.

Dixit, A., and Stiglitz, J. (1977), "Monopolistic competition and optimum product diversity," *American Economic Review*, 67, pp. 297–308.

Drèze, J., and Bean, C. (1990), "European unemployment: Some lessons from an econometric multi-country study," *Scandinavian Journal of Economics*, 92(2), pp. 135–165.

Elmeskov, J., and MacFarlan, M. (1993), "Unemployment persistence," *OECD Economic Review*, 21, pp. 63–94.

Evans, G., and Honkapohja, S. (1999), "Learning dynamics," in Woodford, M., and Taylor, J. (eds.), *Handbook of Macroeconomics*, vol. 1A, chap. 7, Amsterdam: Elsevier Science.

Fair, R. (2000), "Testing the NAIRU model for the United States," *Review of Economics and Statistics*, 82, pp. 64–71.

Farber, H. (1993), "The incidence and costs of job loss: 1982–91," *Brookings Papers on Economic Activity*, vol. 1, pp. 73–119.

Fischer, S. (1977), "Long run contracts, rational expectations and the optimal money supply rule," *Journal of Political Economy*, 85, pp. 163–190.

Fitoussi, J.-P., and Phelps, E. (1988), *The Slump in Europe*, Oxford, U.K.: Basil Blackwell.

Friedman, M. (1968), "The role of economic policy," *American Economic Review*, 58(1), pp. 1–17.

Gordon, R. (1997), "The time-varying NAIRU and its implications for economic policy," *Journal of Economic Perspectives*, 11(1), pp. 11–32.

Hendry, D. (1995), *Dynamic Econometrics*, Advanced Texts in Econometrics, Oxford, U.K.: Oxford University Press.

Hodrick, R., and Prescott, E. (1997), "Postwar U.S. business cycles: An empirical investigation," *Journal of Money, Credit, and Banking*, 29, pp. 1–16.

Jacobson, L., Lalonde, R., and Sullivan, D. (1993), "Earnings losses of displaced workers," *American Economic Review*, 83, pp. 685–709.

Katz, L., and Krueger, A. (1999), "The high pressure U.S. labor market of the 1990s," *Brookings Papers on Economic Activity*, 1, pp. 1–87.

Lindbeck, A., and Snower, D. (1988), *The Insider–Outsider Theory of Employment and Unemployment*, Cambridge, Mass.: MIT Press.

Lucas, R. (1972), "Expectations and the neutrality of money," *Journal of Economic Theory*, 4, pp. 103–124.

Lucas, R. (1975), "An equilibrium model of the business cycle," *Journal of Political Economy*, 83(6), pp. 1113–1144.

Lucas, R. (1981), *Studies in Business Cycle Theory*, Cambridge, Mass.: MIT Press.

Machin, S., and Manning, A. (1999), "The causes and consequences of long-term unemployment in Europe," in Ashenfelter, O., and Card, D. (eds.), *Handbook of Labor Economics*, vol. 3C, chap. 47, Amsterdam: Elsevier Science/North-Holland.

Margolis, D. (1999), "Part-year employment, slow reemployment and earnings losses: The case of worker displacement in France," in Haltiwanger, J., Lane, J., Spletzer, J., Theeuves, J. and Troske, K. (eds) *The Creation and Analysis of Employer–Employee Matched Data*, Amsterdam: North-Holland.

OECD (1994), *The OECD Jobs Study*, 2 vols., Paris: OECD.

OECD (1997), *Employment Outlook*, Paris: OECD.

Phillips, A. (1958), "The relation between unemployment and the rate of change of money wage in the United Kingdom, 1861–1957," *Economica*, 25, pp. 283–299.

Richardson, P., Boone, L., Giorno, C., Meacci, M., Rae, D., and Turner, D. (2000), "The concept, policy use and measurement of structural unemployment: Estimating a time-varying NAIRU across 21 OECD countries," OECD Economics Department Working Paper No. 250, http://www.oecd.org/eco/eco.

Ruhm, C. (1991), "Are workers permanently scarred by job displacemenets?" *American Economic Review*, 81, pp. 319–324.

Solon, G., Barsky, R., and Parker, J. (1994), "Measuring the cyclicality of real wages: How important is composition bias?" *Quarterly Journal of Economics*, 109, pp. 1–26.

Staiger, D., Stock, J., and Watson, M. (1997), "The NAIRU, unemployment and monetary policy," *Journal of Economic Perspectives*, 11, pp. 33–49.

Taylor, J. (1979), "Staggered price setting in a macro model," *American Economic Review*, 69, pp. 108–113.

Taylor, J. (1980), "Aggregate dynamics and staggered contracts," *Journal of Political Economy*, 88, pp. 1–24.

Taylor, J. (1999), "Staggered price and wage setting in macroeconomics," in Taylor, J. B., and Woodford, M. (eds.), *Handbook of Macroeconomics*, vol. 1B, chap. 15, Amsterdam: Elsevier Science/North-Holland.

Topel, R. (1990), "Specific capital and unemployement: Measuring the costs and consequences of job loss," *Carnegie-Rochester Conference Series on Public Policy*, 33, pp. 181–214.

Turner, D., and Seghezza, E. (1999), "Testing for a common OECD Phillips curve," OECD Economics Department Working Paper No. 219, Paris: OECD.

van den Berg, G., and van Ours, J. (1994), "Unemployment dynamics and duration dependence in France, the Netherlands and the United Kingdom," *Economic Journal*, 104, pp. 432–443.

van den Berg, G., and van Ours, J. (1996), "Unemployment dynamics and duration dependence," *Journal of Labor Economics*, 14, pp. 100–125.

Weitzman, M. (1985), "The simple macroeconomics of profit-sharing," *American Economic Review*, 75(5), pp. 937–953.

JOB REALLOCATION AND UNEMPLOYMENT

CONTENTS

In this chapter, we will:

- Observe the magnitude of job creation, job destruction, and worker flows

- Discover the meaning and the importance of the Beveridge curve

- Analyze the functioning of the labor market as a matching process between employers and employees

- Understand the difference between an aggregate shock and a reallocation shock

- Think about the efficiency of a labor market with trading externalities

INTRODUCTION

In all the OECD countries, workers' mobility among the different possible states in the labor market (from one job to another, from a job to unemployment, from unemployment to nonparticipation, etc.) is a phenomenon of major dimensions. For example, in firms with more than ten employees in the United States in 1987, for every 100 jobs there were on average 26 hires and 27 quits (Burda and Wyplosz, 1994). The duration of the transition periods between all possible states results mainly from imperfections inherent in the functioning of the labor market. For a worker, the search for a job that fits his or her requirements and skills is a process that often takes a lot of time. Likewise, when a firm wants to recruit new workers, it often chooses to devote substantial resources (with a corresponding cost in time) to the selection of suitable individuals. These imperfections in the information available in the labor market entail the simultaneous presence of unemployed persons and vacant jobs. This is the origin of *frictional* unemployment.

The intensity of the processes of job destruction and creation has an effect on the level of frictional unemployment. When the economy is restructured, job rotation increases workers' mobility, and thus pushes up frictional unemployment. But the latter also depends on more institutional factors, like the amount of unemployment benefits, for example, which determines how long the unemployed can wait, or the level of hiring and firing costs, which influences the behavior of firms. The first dynamic analyses of the labor market date from the 1960s. They were based principally on the job search behavior of workers, and explained frictional unemployment by the fact that the unemployed reject job offers that pay wages they consider too low, in the hope of subsequently receiving more attractive offers. We have seen in chapter 3 that the main determinants of unemployment duration are the unemployment benefits, the arrival rate of job offers, and the characteristics of the distribution of possible wages.

This chapter is devoted to the study of a complementary approach, which brings in the behavior of firms when faced with a costly hiring process. This approach envisages the hiring process as phenomenon of *matches* between employers and workers. In this framework, the probability for every unemployed person of receiving a job offer suited to his or her abilities depends on the *tightness* prevailing in the labor market, i.e., the ratio of the number of vacant jobs to the number of unemployed persons. If this ratio is high, every unemployed person has a high probability of finding a job. Symmetrically, the probability of filling a vacant job has to decrease when this ratio increases. This representation of the process of matching up jobs and workers, especially those developed by Hall (1979), Bowden (1980), and Pissarides (1979, 2000), makes it possible to analyze the determinants of unemployment in a framework that takes into explicit consideration the transaction costs linked to labor mobility and the imperfection of information in the labor market. In particular, it makes it possible to grasp the determinants of unemployment in a dynamic environment where jobs are created and destroyed continually, and in which there are transaction costs attached to reallocating employment.

The first section lays out the main characteristics of manpower mobility and the processes of job creation and destruction as they emerge from empirical studies. Section 2 develops the competitive model with perfect information and highlights its limitations. Section 3 presents the basic matching model. This model takes the flow of jobs into consideration and is grounded in an imperfectly competitive mode of wage formation. Section 4 introduces capital explicitly, in order to focus on the relationship among investment, the interest rate, and unemployment. Section 5 is devoted to analyzing the dynamics of unemployment. Finally, the problem of the inefficiency of market equilibrium is dealt with in section 6.

1 JOB FLOWS AND WORKER FLOWS

Two kinds of data allow us to understand the dynamics of the labor market better. The first pertains to the processes of job creation and destruction and the second to worker flows. Examination of these data reveals that the labor market is characterized by intense reallocation of jobs and workers. This reallocation is revealed by, among other things, the coexistence of vacant jobs and persons looking for work.

1.1 JOB CREATION AND DESTRUCTION

Table 9.1 gives an idea of the magnitude of job creation and destruction in several OECD countries. In this table, job creation represents the sum of job gains due to the opening of new production units (either firms or plants, according to the studies) and the expansion of jobs within existing workplaces. Job destruction represents the sum of job losses resulting from the closing of production units and contractions in the number of jobs in units that stay open. The net employment growth is equal to the difference between job creation and job destruction, whereas job reallocation corresponds to the sum of these two quantities.

It is evident, in the first place, that for all countries, net employment growth is always much smaller than job creation or destruction. In the United States, for example, 10.4% of jobs are destroyed every year, while the proportion of jobs created with

Table 9.1

Job creation and destruction. Annual average rate as a percentage of total employment.

Country	Job creation	Job destruction	Net employment growth	Job reallocation
France (84–91)	12.7	11.8	0.9	24.5
Germany (83–90)	9.0	7.5	1.5	16.5
Netherlands (84–91)	8.2	7.2	1.0	15.4
United Kingdom (85–91)	8.7	6.6	2.1	15.3
United States (84–91)	13.0	10.4	2.6	23.4

Source: OECD (1996, table 5.1, p. 176).

respect to the stock of existing jobs is equal to 13.0%. In the second place, we observe that job reallocation belongs to a different order of magnitude than net employment growth, being about ten times higher in Germany, the United States, the United Kingdom, and the Netherlands, and practically 30 times higher in France. That means that the *excess job reallocation*, which equals the difference between job reallocation and the net employment growth, is considerable. In the United States, it would have sufficed to reallocate 2.6% of jobs in order to transform production units, but a reallocation of 23.4% would have been needed, or an excess job reallocation of 20.8%, in order for these reallocations actually to take place.

It should be noted that the job creation and destruction presented in Table 9.1 do not include job reallocations that take place within individual firms or plants. For example, a firm that gets rid of a worker's job in order to create a managerial job is recorded as having job creation and destruction equal to zero. Studies that have attempted to assess job reallocations within workplaces suggest that this factor is not negligible. Hamermesh et al. (1996) use a survey which indicates whether hires correspond to newly created jobs in the Netherlands. They find that reorganizations within firms explain 11% of overall job reallocations. Using data on the structure of job creation and destruction in relation to skill within firms in France, Lagarde et al. (1995) estimate that job reallocations within firms are much greater than that, representing almost half of all job reallocations.

1.1.1 The Extent of Within-Sector Reallocation

Contrary to what is sometimes stated as obvious fact, job movements most frequently take place within the *same* sector, not between *different* sectors. It is possible to assess the extent of within-sector reallocation by comparing two indicators (see Davis and Haltiwanger, 1992). If S designates the number of sectors, we look at the net employment growth in a given sector s (V_n^s) and the net employment growth in the economy as a whole (V_n). An initial indicator assesses the extent of job reallocations due to between-sector movements. It is defined by:

$$R_E = \sum_{s=1}^{S} |V_n^s| - |V_n|$$

Let T_s be the job reallocation in sector s; the second indicator corresponds to the sum of excess job reallocations within each sector. It is defined by:

$$R_I = \sum_{s=1}^{S} (T_s - |V_n^s|)$$

The fraction of job reallocations due to between-sector shifts is then measured by the ratio $R_E/(R_I + R_E)$. Table 9.2 shows that job movements are to a large extent within sectors.

It turns out that between-sector reallocations are never more than a small component of overall job reallocations, even when sectors are broken down finely. Since

Table 9.2

Fraction of job reallocation accounted for by employment shifts between sectors.

Country	Period	Number of sectors	$R_E/(R_I + R_E)$
Germany	83–90	24	0.03
United States	72–88	980	0.14
France	84–88	15	0.06
France	84–91	600	0.17
Italy	86–91	28	0.02
Sweden	85–91	28	0.03

Source: Davis and Haltiwanger (1999a, table 5).

Table 9.3

The persistence of job creation and destruction.

Country	United States		France		Netherlands	
Period	1973–1988		1985–1991		1979–1993	
Horizon	1 year	2 years	1 year	2 years	1 year	2 years
Creations	70.2	54.4	73.4	61.5	77.9	58.8
Destructions	82.3	73.6	82.1	68.2	92.5	87.3

Source: Davis and Haltiwanger (1999a, table 6).

the beginning of the 1980s, the process of job creation and destruction has thus been essentially within sectors.

1.1.2 The Persistence of Job Creation and Destruction

Job creation and destruction can be temporary or relatively persistent. In order to assess the impact of job creation and destruction in a dynamic perspective, Davis and Haltiwanger (1999a) define the indicator of persistence of n periods of job creation as the percentage of jobs created in period t that are still in existence at the end of period $t + n$. An indicator of the persistence of job destruction is similarly defined as the percentage of jobs destroyed during period t that have not reappeared at date $t + n$.

Table 9.3 shows that job creation and destruction have major persistent effects, since more than 70% of jobs created in one year have not been destroyed in the following year in the three countries considered. This result means that business units that expand in one year have a high probability of expanding in the following year as well. In reality, we observe that job destruction and creation are clustered in a relatively small segment of business units that are expanding or contracting. Such units generally make large adjustments, often amounting to more than 20% of their total workforce. Studies on U.S., Canadian, Danish, and Israeli data (see Davis and Haltiwanger, 1999a) find that more than two thirds of job destruction is carried out by firms that adjust their workforces by more than 20%. Table 9.3 indicates that these adjustments have effects on employment for a number of years.

The extent of gross job creation and destruction relative to net variations, and the preponderance of within-sector reallocation, are characteristics shared by G5 countries. But a comparison of movements in employment related to the business cycle brings out certain disparities.

1.1.3 Movements in Employment and Business Cycles

For the United States, Davis et al. (1996) highlight three distinguishing features of the dynamics of job creation and destruction. In the first place, job destruction is highly countercyclical, hence more frequent in periods of recession. In the second place, job creation is weakly procyclical, or even acyclical. Finally, destruction varies much more widely than creation does. So cycles are marked by weak variations in the number of jobs created and strong variations in the number of jobs destroyed. These three properties entail that in the United States the rate of job reallocation is countercyclical: there is more job reallocation in phases of recession. This result is not observed in all OECD countries, where job destruction is generally countercyclical and job creation procyclical; but job destruction does not always vary to a significantly greater degree than job creation (see OECD, 1996, chapter 5).

1.2 WORKER REALLOCATION

Worker reallocation can be identified by observing the flow of entries into and exits from employment and unemployment. The Beveridge curve depicts the extent of these movements.

1.2.1 Employment Inflows and Outflows

Worker flows are different from job flows, for in addition to entries and exits linked to the creation and destruction of jobs, they also include rotations on the same job. A number of workers can in fact succeed one another in the same job. With data on French firms for 1987–1990, Abowd et al. (1999) estimate that over the course of a year, the creation of one job corresponds to the hiring of three persons and the separation of two. As a general rule, workers' reallocations are clearly greater than those of jobs. They are assessed by observing, for a given period—most often a month or a year—the flow of entries into and exits from unemployment, on the one hand, and the flow of entries into and exits from employment, on the other. An entry into employment corresponds to a hire, and an exit from employment corresponds to a separation. An exit from employment leads to unemployment, nonparticipation, or a new hire. An exit from unemployment occurs when someone either finds a job or decides not to participate any longer. Table 9.4 portrays the flow of entries into and exits from employment for the G5 countries during the year 1987.

Table 9.4

Annual employment inflows and outflows, in percentages, for the year 1987.

Country	Entry rate	Exit rate
United States	26	27
France	29	31
Japan	9	9
United Kingdom	11	11
Germany	22	21

Source: Burda and Wyplosz (1994, p. 1288).

The rates of entry and exit are equal respectively to the number of entries into and exits from employment with respect to the average stock of jobs.

Table 9.4 highlights the magnitude of entries into and exits from employment with respect to the stock of jobs. Worker flows are seen to be systematically greater in size than job flows. Thus, the exit rate from employment in table 9.4 is, for most countries except the United Kingdom, almost three times greater than the rate of job destruction given in the second column of table 9.1. Likewise, except for the United Kingdom, the rate of entry into employment is between two and three times greater than the rate of job creation set out in the first column of table 9.1. We observe too that worker mobility differs from country to country. The rates of entry into and exit from employment are relatively high in Germany, the United States, and France, while they are between two and three times lower in the United Kingdom and Japan. These two countries are thus characterized by low worker rotation.

1.2.2 On Displacements

Exits from employment comprise quits, the ending of short-term contracts, retirements, firings for cause, and job loss through no fault of the employee. By definition, in what follows we will refer to the latter simply as displacement. It comes to the same thing as the permanent separation, at the employer's initiative, of an employee. It is interesting to compare figures for overall workers' movements with those for displacements alone. Tables 9.5 and 9.6 reproduce the values of the displacement rate for different industrialized countries. Regrettably, for reasons that have to do with the comparison and availability of data, the definitions of a displacement are noticeably different in the two tables. In table 9.5, all displacements are recorded: individual displacements, mass layoffs, and displacements due to the closing of a business unit. In table 9.6, however, only displacements of workers caused by the closing of business units are reported. In the two tables, the displacement rate is equal to the annual number of displacements (according to the definition proper to each table) divided by the number of persons employed during the course of the same year.

In fact, the figures in table 9.6 are not very far from the ones in table 9.5, since, for one thing, workers with high seniority have lower displacement rates, and for

Table 9.5

Annual displacement rate (total).

Country	Period	Population	Annual rate
United States	1993–1995	Age 20–64	4.9
Netherlands	1993–1995	Under 60	4.1
Canada	1995	Age 15 and over	4.9
United Kingdom	1990–1996	More than 18	4.7
Australia	1995	Employed worker	5.2*

Source: Kuhn (2002, table 17).

*Men only.

Table 9.6

Annual displacement rate (plant closing only).

Country	Period	Population	Annual rate
France	1984–1990	25–50†	0.5*
Germany	1984–1990	25–50†	1.1*
Belgium	1983	All tenures	2.1
Denmark	1988	All tenures	1.6

Source: Kuhn (2002, table 17).

*Men only.

†Tenure at least 4 years.

another, Kuhn and Sweetman (1999) have estimated that in the United States, around one third of displacements come from the closure of business units. In these circumstances, the data in table 9.6 are compatible with global displacement rates of between 4% and 5%. Displacement rates are thus quite clearly lower than the exit rates from employment. For example, table 9.4 indicates that the exit rates amount respectively to 31% and 27% for France and the United States. Hence the great majority of exits from employment are not due to displacements. It is also worth noting the great similarity of displacement rates in all the industrialized countries.

1.2.3 Unemployment Inflows and Outflows

Table 9.7 sets out the rate of entry into and exit from unemployment for several large industrialized countries. The strong heterogeneity of these rates is striking. The United States stands out from the other countries. We see that in the United States in 1993, more than 2% of employees enter into unemployment every month, while in France or Japan the figures are less than 0.4%. Likewise, more than 37% of the unem-

Table 9.7

Monthly unemployment inflows and outflows, in percentage, for 1993.

Country	Entry rate	Exit rate
United States	2.06	37.4
France	0.34	3.4
Japan	0.38	17.1
United Kingdom	0.67	9.3
Germany	0.57	9.0

Source: OECD (1995, pp. 28–29).

The entry rate is the ratio between monthly entries into unemployment and the total number of employed persons during the month in question; the exit rate is the ratio between monthly exits from unemployment and the total number of unemployed persons during the month in question.

ployed exit from unemployment every month in the United States. The corresponding figure for Japan is 17%, and in France, only 3.4%. So in 1993, the probability of exiting from unemployment was around ten times higher in the United States than in France.

Comparison of tables 9.4 and 9.7 allows us to specify the differences between the United States and most of the other OECD countries. We see that the United States is much less different from other countries if we look at employment entries and exits than it is if we look at entries into and exits from unemployment. That means that an exit from employment is most often followed by an entry into unemployment in the United States, while elsewhere, particularly in continental Europe, it is mobility *from one job to another* that predominates. Hence certain European labor markets—France is a good example—are well described by dividing them into workers shut out from employment, whose probability of exiting from unemployment is low, and workers who, in addition to having a job, also have the possibility of exchanging it for another.

1.2.4 Worker Reallocation and the Business Cycle

Entries into and exits from employment are procyclical in the United States (Anderson and Meyer, 1994; Davis et al., 1996) and in European countries (Burda and Wyplosz, 1994). These observations conform to intuition as regards entries: we should expect hires to rise in periods of economic upturn and fall during recessions. On the other hand, the result that exits from employment also move up and down with the business cycle is more surprising. Since flows between employment and unemployment are countercyclical, that means that movements between jobs are highly procyclical. Thus, upturns in the business cycle are marked by an intensification of the reallocation of workers among jobs.

Entries into and exits from unemployment appear to be equally countercyclical (Burda and Wyplosz, 1994). These results may also cause surprise: since there are fewer hires during periods of recession, there ought to be fewer exits from unemployment. The fact is that exits from unemployment into employment rise during periods of recession, even though the number of hires falls, because the reduction in movements between jobs is even more pronounced than the reduction in hires. Hence recessions are characterized by weak reallocation of workers among jobs and more numerous hires of the unemployed—probably into temporary positions.

1.2.5   The Beveridge Curve

The English economist William Beveridge in 1944 proposed using the relationship between vacant jobs and the level of unemployment to assess the extent of workers' reallocation. Problems of reallocation ought indeed to be greater, the higher the number of jobs vacant for a given number of unemployed. The "Beveridge curve" illustrates this linkage between the unemployment rate u and the vacancy rate v (the ratio of the number of vacant jobs to the labor force). It is shown in figure 9.1. When economic activity slows, firms open up few vacant jobs, and there are many unemployed. During the recovery phase, the point representing equilibrium in the economic system shifts along the Beveridge curve, as the number of jobs vacant grows and the number of unemployed persons falls.

The very existence of a Beveridge curve signifies the simultaneous presence of unemployed persons and vacant jobs. This simultaneity originates from mobility costs associated with location and with skill, and from imperfect information. One of the purposes of labor markets is to allow the best possible match-up between the skills required by firms and the skills existing in the labor force. The search activity required costs time and resources, but it is indispensable, given that the information necessary to both sides constitutes a rare resource.

The greater or lesser efficiency of the adjustment process is shown by the position of the Beveridge curve with respect to the origin of the axes in figure 9.1. The closer this curve lies to the origin of the axes, the more efficient the process of reallocating manpower is, for in these circumstances every vacant job will quickly be filled

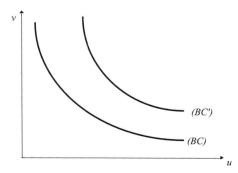

FIGURE 9.1
The Beveridge curve.

by an unemployed person. For example, in figure 9.1, curve (BC) reflects a more efficient process of allocating manpower resources than does curve (BC'). In a labor market described by (BC), for the *same* number of vacant jobs, there will be fewer unemployed persons than there will in the labor market described by (BC').

Figure 9.2 gives examples of empirical relationships between the unemployment rate and the vacancy rate over the period 1960–1999 for the United Kingdom, the United States, France, and Germany. It appears that the efficiency of the matching process fell off in the United Kingdom, France, and Germany over the entire period considered. In the United States, the efficiency of the matching process decreased during the sixties and the seventies and then improved during the eighties and the nineties. Moreover, we see that the relationship between the unemployment rate and the vacancy rate describes counterclockwise loops—a phenomenon which, as we will see, the study of labor market dynamics makes it possible to explain.

This presentation of the functioning of the labor market reveals intense activity as jobs and workers are reallocated. This is why models that explictly integrate labor

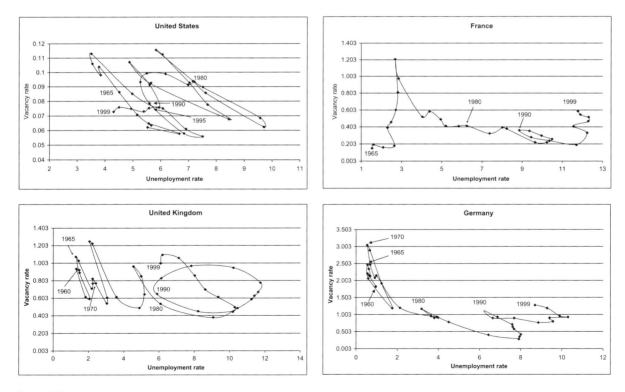

FIGURE 9.2

The Beveridge curves in the United Kingdom, the United States, France, and Germany.

Source: OECD data.

market flows have gradually come to the fore. They are known in the literature as *matching models*. The main question these models have to answer is, what is the relation between unemployment and this reallocation activity? But before examing what they have to tell us, we will do well to review the principal lessons to be learned from the traditional approach to the labor market, based on the competitive model. This review follows.

2 THE COMPETITIVE MODEL WITH JOB REALLOCATION

The competitive model, already discussed in chapters 5 and 8, is a benchmark representation of the labor market that makes it possible to analyze the influence of the turnover of jobs and workers. Here we extend this representation by taking into account the adjustment costs linked to turnover.

2.1 JOB REALLOCATION AND LABOR MARKET EQUILIBRIUM

In the competitive model, labor supply and demand result from decisions taken by agents who have no power over the setting of prices. Hence wages equalize labor supply and demand. Let us assume that the labor force is composed of a large number N of individuals having different reservation wages z, the distribution of which is given by the cumulative distribution function $H(.)$. Readers will recall that in labor supply theory, the reservation wage represents the remuneration threshold at which an individual will accept to work (see chapter 1). It can also be interpreted as the domestic production achievable by this person outside the labor market. If we assume that every individual offers a unit of labor when the current wage w is superior to his or her reservation wage z, then labor supply is equal to $NH(w)$. It is an increasing function of wages, the graph of which is identified by the symbol (LS) in figure 9.3.

In chapter 4, we saw that labor demand could be deduced from profit maximization in the presence of employment adjustment costs. Let us assume, in order to simplify, that the production function of a representative firm has constant returns to scale and that each worker is capable of producing an exogenous quantity y of goods. Let L be the level of employment, and let us suppose that an exogenous proportion q of jobs is destroyed at every instant. As in chapter 4, we represent adjustment costs by a function $C(\Lambda)$ where Λ designates net variations in the level of employment. Function $C(.)$ is assumed to be increasing and convex; consequently $C' > 0$ and $C'' > 0$. In a stationary state, the stock of jobs L is constant, and the firm thus hires qL workers per unit of time. Instantaneous profit is then written:

$$\Pi = Ly - [wL + C(qL)]$$

Instantaneous profit maximization[1] with respect to employment entails:

$$y = qC'(qL) + w \qquad \text{(1)}$$

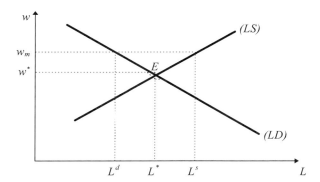

FIGURE 9.3
The competitive equilibrium.

This equality shows that at the firm's optimum, the marginal productivity y of labor is equal to the marginal adjustment cost $qC' + w$ of a job. Equation (1) defines labor demand. Adjustment cost $C(.)$ being a convex function, labor demand is decreasing with respect to wages. Its graph is identified by the symbol (LD) in figure 9.3. It should be noted that a rise in the rate q of job destruction increases marginal adjustment costs $C'(qL)$ and thus increases the total marginal cost of a job. In these circumstances, the firm reduces employment. In figure 9.3, an increase in q leads to a downward shift of curve (LD). An exogenous rise in adjustment costs $C(.)$ has the same effect. Conversely, an increase in marginal productivity y shifts curve (LD) upward.

The competitive equilibrium lies at the intersection of curves (LS) and (LD). As labor supply is simply equal to $NH(w)$, wages w^* and equilibrium employment L^* are defined by the following system of equations:

$$y = qC'[qNH(w^*)] + w^*, \qquad L^* = NH(w^*) \tag{2}$$

The hypotheses made about functions $H(.)$ and $C(.)$ entail that there is a unique competitive equilibrium. Figure 9.3 also indicates that an increase in the rate q of job destruction leads to a fall in employment and the equilibrium wage. An improvement in individual productivity y has the opposite effect.

It is worth noting that although certain individuals are not employed, there is no unemployment in this model, since every person who wants to work at the current wage can do so. Individuals who are not employed simply prefer to remain outside the labor market and do not look for a job. In sum, the competitive model makes it possible to understand certain determinants of employment. It shows that the process of job destruction is capable of having a negative impact on employment if adjustments in this variable are costly. However, it does not help us in understanding unemployment.

2.2   THE EFFICIENCY OF THE COMPETITIVE EQUILIBRIUM

As a general rule, a competitive market arrives at an efficient allocation of resources. Within the framework of the model just presented, this result is easily established by considering the problem of a benevolent social planner seeking to maximize collective welfare. For simplicity, we will assume, on the one hand, that individuals are risk-neutral—the indirect utility function is linear—and, on the other, that the planner has no preference for the present. In these conditions, his or her objective is to maximize the sum of instantaneous productions realized inside and outside the market minus the labor turnover costs, since these represent a loss for the economy.

If we assume that the productivity z of an individual outside the market is again a random variable with cumulative distribution function $H(.)$, the question of the optimal allocation of resources boils down to the search for a threshold $\bar{z}$ of productivity—and thus a proportion $H(\bar{z})$ of the individuals that must be employed in the labor market—that makes it possible to maximize net aggregate production. The planner's problem is written as follows:

$$\underset{z}{\text{Max}}\left\{ yNH(z) - C[qNH(z)] + N \int_{z}^{+\infty} x \, dH(x) \right\}$$

In this expression, the term in which the integral appears represents total production outside the market, whereas the product $yNH(z)$ designates the production of goods achieved by the market. In the market, the costs due to employment adjustments amount to $C[qNH(z)]$. The first-order condition entails that the threshold $\bar{z}$ is the solution of equation:

$$y = qC'[qNH(\bar{z})] + \bar{z}$$

This equality defines an optimal value for the productivity threshold identical to the equilibrium wage w^* given by equation (2). The competitive equilibrium is thus indeed a social optimum. The planner actually decides to allocate workers to the technology used in the market as long as the marginal productivity, net of turnover costs, of one more individual is greater than what he or she is able to achieve outside the market. This result shows that at the competitive equilibrium, the level of employment is socially optimal, even if some individuals are not employed. It should also be noted that the process of job destruction exerts a negative effect on the stock of jobs in the presence of labor turnover costs, but that this process entails *no inefficiency* in the allocation of resources.

2.3   THE LIMITATIONS OF THE COMPETITIVE MODEL

The competitive model displays significant limitations that make it ill-adapted to the study of problems linked to unemployment and the determinants of employment.

(i) Most empirical studies show that productivity shocks have much more effect on employment than on wages (Hall, 1999). Now, the competitive model summed up in figure 9.3 arrives at predictions that contradict this. With a labor supply close to the vertical (which agrees with the small wage elasticity of labor supply found by empirical studies; see chapter 1), a productivity shock affecting labor demand leads to strong variation in wage and weak variation in employment. Many strategies have been proposed to elaborate competitive models predicting small variations in the wage when the economy undergoes productivity shocks. The dynamic model of labor supply presented in chapter 1 belongs in this category. However, the various attempts have not yet led to a convincing rehabilitation of the competitive model as a representation of the labor market (see Hall, 1999).

(ii) The hypothesis of perfect competition does not allow us to explain inefficiencies arising from the functioning of the labor market. The allocation of resources is optimal in this model, which particularly entails the absence of unemployment. As we have seen in section 1.2.4, the existence of the Beveridge curve illustrates the simultaneous presence of unemployed persons and vacant jobs. This stems from the imperfect information and the mobility costs prevailing in the labor market. Within this framework, unemployed workers adopt job search strategies, and firms adopt recruitment strategies, that may give rise to externalities that are themselves sources of inefficiency in the allocation of resources.

(iii) The hypothesis of perfect competition also postulates a mode of wage formation that ignores the institutional characteristics of labor markets. In chapters 7 and 6 we emphasized that wage bargaining and manpower management policies have a preponderant influence on levels of remuneration. Here again, the strategic dimensions of behavior can have consequences very different from those we find in the competitive model, in which wages are determined by an abstract process that is assumed to equalize supply and demand.

Thus, in the presence of imperfect information, and when wages do not clear markets, it is highly likely that the labor market will operate inefficiently. That makes it important to have at our disposal an analytical tool that does not postulate the absence of inefficiency a priori, a tool enabling us to identify, understand, and if necessary define remedies for these inefficiencies. To furnish a representation of the labor market possessing these qualities has been the aim of a number of studies. Of these, the matching model proposed and developed by Pissarides (2000) (see also Mortensen and Pissarides, 1999) is, at the present time, the analytical framework most often used.

3 THE MATCHING MODEL

In this section, we develop a simple model of the labor market in which transaction costs explain the simultaneous existence of vacant jobs and unemployed persons. Wage formation is here described by a bargaining process between employers and workers; in other words, the hypothesis of competitive wages is dropped. The model is structured around the concept of a *matching function*, which sums up, at the aggregate level, the outcomes of encounters between persons in search of a job and firms with positions vacant.

3.1 TRANSACTION COSTS IN THE LABOR MARKET

At every instant, the number of hires depends on the interface between vacant jobs and workers looking for a job. For given levels of supply and demand, and when workers are perfectly suited to the jobs offered and there is no imperfection in the available information, the number of hires is equal to the minimum of job-seekers and job vacancies, and the labor market functions efficiently. But in reality jobs and workers are heterogeneous, and information never circulates perfectly. Hence some workers risk not finding work at the same time that some firms have positions vacant. The existence of these transaction costs in the labor market is usually represented by a matching function that determines the number of hires on the basis of the quantity of labor being supplied and demanded. This matching function and the equilibrium conditions of flows in the labor market make it possible to give an analytical foundation for the Beveridge curve.

3.1.1 The Matching Function

In practice, job search procedures are characterized by a large number of "frictions." The most important of these concern the mismatch between certain vacant jobs and the skills of workers, as well as ignorance of the whereabouts and/or the actual characteristics of the jobs available. Faced with these frictions, employers and job seekers adopt search strategies which include reading newspapers, applying to government employment offices, using personal networks, sending letters of application, and so on. All these actions take time and often have high costs. But at every instant they produce a certain number of "successes," which can be measured by the number of hires at the date in question. The *matching function* goes straight to an *aggregate* level (for example, a country, region, or industry) and does not take into account the diversity of individual actions. It summarizes the entire search process in a single relation giving the flow M of hires achieved over a given interval of time as a function of the stock of vacant jobs V and persons in search of work D. The matching function is analogous in nature to other aggregate functions utilized by macroeconomists, like the aggregate production function. For it to be a useful instrument, we have to be able to give it extremely precise properties that rest, if possible, on microeconomic foundations, and above all, we need to verify that the empirical estimates of such a function are coherent with these properties.

On the Microeconomic Foundations

A simple but not truly realistic way of obtaining an aggregate matching function consists of comparing vacant jobs to "urns," and job applications to "balls" tossed at the urns by job-seekers (Pissarides, 1979; Blanchard and Diamond, 1994). A match occurs when a ball goes into an urn. The inefficiency of the job search process is reflected in the greater or lesser precision with which the balls are tossed in the direction of the urns. We will omit the time index for simplicity, and D and V will again denote respectively the number of job-seekers and the number of vacant jobs at a given date. Let us assume that job-seekers know the locations of all vacant jobs, and that a particular job-seeker, whom we shall call Mr. i, simultaneously sends e_i applications out randomly among the V jobs vacant. Parameter $e_i \leq V$ is an indicator of the effort that Mr. i puts into his job search. When more than one application is received for the same vacant job, a random draw determines who will get it, and the other applications go into the wastepaper basket. Let us further suppose that there is no coordination among the job-seekers. That being so, it is possible that one vacant job will receive a heap of applications while another will not receive any. More precisely, the probability that a given vacant job will receive the application of Mr. i is equal to e_i/V. Conversely, the probability that this job will not receive an application from Mr. i amounts to $1 - (e_i/V)$. It results that the probability of a vacant job receiving no applications takes the value $\prod_{i=1}^{i=D}[1 - (e_i/V)]$. In consequence, the probability of a vacant job receiving at least one application is equal to $1 - \prod_{i=1}^{i=D}[1 - (e_i/V)]$. As we have assumed that, for each vacant job, the firms draw the successful applicant at random from among the applications received, the number of hires M is given by relation:

$$M = V\left[1 - \prod_{i=1}^{i=D}\left(1 - \frac{e_i}{V}\right)\right]$$

If V is large with respect to e_i (which is a reasonable hypothesis), it is possible to approximate $1 - (e_i/V)$ by $\exp[-(e_i/V)]$. Let $\bar{e}$ be the average of the e_i; the matching function is finally written:

$$M = M(V, \bar{e}D) = V\left\{1 - \exp\left[-\left(\frac{\bar{e}D}{V}\right)\right]\right\}$$

It can be verified that this function is increasing in V and D, and that it is homogeneous of degree 1 with respect to its two arguments. The value $\bar{e}$ of the average search intensity also appears among the arguments of the matching function. That justifies the inclusion, in the estimates of the matching function, of all the variables that may affect job search effort, such as the characteristics of the unemployment insurance system, the demographic profile of job-seekers, indicators of the ease of geographic mobility, and so on. Note further that, the total number of applications being equal to $\bar{e}D$, the probability of Mr. i finding a job is written $e_i M(V, \bar{e}D)/\bar{e}D$. He thus has a better chance, the greater his level of relative effort $e_i/\bar{e}$.

Simple urns-and-balls models thus give us the foundations of the aggregate matching function. But they leave too much up to chance; strategic, nonrandom elements play a role in the job search, on the part of both workers and firms. Other models attempt to incorporate these aspects.

Ranking models, like that of Blanchard and Diamond (1994), start from the hypothesis that firms have preferences among the applications they receive. They will, for example, prefer skilled employees to unskilled ones, or short-term unemployed persons to long-term ones. That being the case, the matching function depends, directly or indirectly, on the preferences of employers and the characteristics of job-seekers. So, if firms give priority to the short-term unemployed, it can be shown that the average probability of finding a job diminishes with the incidence of long-term unemployment. This result has been confirmed by the work of Mumford and Smith (1999) for Australia, and that of Burgess (1993) for the United Kingdom. Petrongolo and Pissarides (2001) do point out, though, that a result of this type does not necessarily reinforce the hypothesis that applicants are ranked. It might also be caused by reduced search effort on the part of the long-term unemployed.

Stock-flow matching models begin with the idea that the existence of stocks of vacant jobs and unemployed persons reflects, to some degree at least, an inadequate fit between the characteristics of vacant jobs and those of job-seekers that is already perfectly well *known* and does not need to be discovered. From that it follows that the job search process, on the part of both firms and workers, will privilege new inflows of applications over stocks already examined. Coles and Smith (1998) construct a model of this type, which they estimate using British data for 1987–1995. The empirical results partially corroborate their hypotheses. They find that only new flows of vacant jobs significantly increase the hazard rates of the long-term unemployed, while the hazard rates for the short-term unemployed are positively affected both by stocks of vacant jobs and by new flows.

Some Empirical Elements

The matching function can be estimated on the basis of macroeconomic data. If we postulate a Cobb-Douglas form for the function $M(V, \bar{e}D)$, the equation to be estimated is linear in logarithms. The dependent variable is represented by the flows of hires, and the explanatory variables are the stocks of unemployed persons and vacant jobs. (On the problems arising from the measurement of these variables, and the methods of estimating the matching function, see the comprehensive survey of Petrongolo and Pissarides, 2001, which also supplies references to a broad range of works in this field.) With a few notable exceptions, such as Blanchard and Diamond (1990) on data from the manufacturing sector in the United States and Yashiv (2000) on Israeli data, most empirical studies based on macroeconomic data accept the hypothesis of constant returns. If the flows of hires are all hires of the unemployed, the elasticity of the matching function with respect to the stock U of unemployed persons lies in the range $[0.5, 0.7]$. But if the dependent variable comprises all hires (which includes persons who move from one job to another, and hires of nonparticipants), this elasticity lies in the range $[0.3, 0.4]$.

Analysis of the microeconomic foundations of the aggregate matching function also suggests that all the elements that might have an influence on the job search effort ought to be included among the explanatory variables. Empirical studies do indeed add variables of this type to the list of exogenous factors. It turns out that the incidence of long-term unemployment, the geographic dispersion of vacant jobs and unemployed persons, and the demographic structure of the labor force all exert significant influence on the matching process. On the other hand, unemployment benefits do not really appear to have an influence on this process. But, according to Petrongolo and Pissarides (2001), that result might spring from the difficulty of constructing relevant macroeconomic indicators for unemployment benefits. We note in conclusion that studies using microeconomic data arrive at very heterogeneous results, certain of which do tend to confirm the conclusions of studies carried out on macroeconomic data (see, for example, Coles and Smith, 1996, and Petrongolo, 2001).

The Properties of the Matching Function

With no loss of generality, we will simply denote the aggregate matching function by $M(V, D)$. In a model in continuous time such as the one we will use throughout the rest of this book, $M(V, D)$ represents the *instantaneous* flow of hires at a given date. In other words, if V_t and D_t designate respectively the stock of vacant jobs and the stock of persons looking for work at date t, the number of hires over interval $[t, t + dt]$ is equal to $M(V_t, D_t) \, dt$. In order to simplify the notation, we will generally omit the time index. Function $M(V, D)$ will be assumed to be strictly increasing with respect to each of its arguments and such that $M(V, 0) = M(0, D) = 0$. These hypotheses signify, on one hand, that hires increase when the number of job applicants, or the number of vacant jobs, increases, and, on the other, that no hire can occur without at least one vacant job and one job applicant. A frequently used formulation of the matching function adds two supplementary hypotheses (Pissarides, 2000). First, only unemployed persons are assumed to be job applicants. If U designates the number of unemployed persons, then we will have $U = D$. This hypothesis amounts to setting aside the job search activities of wage-earners who are already employed (see Mortensen, 1994, and Pissarides, 2000, who present models that include this possibility). Finally, we will assume that the matching function has constant returns to scale. The probability of filling a vacant job per unit of time is then expressed as follows:

$$\frac{M(V, U)}{V} = M(1, U/V) \equiv m(\theta), \qquad \theta \equiv V/U \tag{3}$$

Parameter θ, which equals the ratio of the number of vacant jobs to the number of unemployed persons, is an indicator of the "tightness" prevailing in the labor market. Differentiating the expression (3) with respect to U, we get:

$$m'(\theta) = -\frac{U^2}{V^2} M'_U(1, U/V) < 0$$

Hence vacant jobs are filled at a rate that diminishes with the labor market tightness. The reason for this is as follows: for a given number U of unemployed persons, each firm has greater difficulty in filling its vacant positions when the total number of vacant jobs rises. For an unemployed person, the exit rate from unemployment—also called the *hazard rate* (see chapter 3, section 3.1.1)—also depends on the labor market tightness. It is defined by:

$$\frac{M(V, U)}{U} = \frac{V}{U} \frac{M(V, U)}{V} = \theta m(\theta) \tag{4}$$

Differentiating this relation with respect to V, we find:

$$[\theta m(\theta)]' \equiv m(\theta) + \theta m'(\theta) = M_V(V, U) > 0$$

In consequence, the exit rate from unemployment is an increasing function of the labor market tightness. That means that for a given number of unemployed persons, each of them has a greater chance of finding a job when the number of vacant jobs increases. It can also be verified that the absolute value of the elasticity of function $m(\theta)$, $\eta(\theta) = -\theta m'(\theta)/m(\theta)$, is less than 1. Scrutiny of the exit rate from unemployment and employment shows that there are *trading externalities*. The increase in the number of vacant jobs diminishes the rate at which vacant jobs are filled and increases the exit rate from unemployment. So it is in the interest of unemployed persons for firms to create jobs, but in the interest of each firm for the number of vacancies to be as low as possible, so as to have the benefit of numerous applications for the jobs it needs to fill. It is also in the interest of each unemployed individual for other job-seekers to withdraw from the labor market, so as to reduce the competition. *Between-group* externalities are positive, therefore, but *within-group* externalities are negative, corresponding to congestion effects.

3.1.2 Equilibrium of Flows and the Beveridge Curve

Labor market tightness and the rate of job destruction, along with the matching technology, condition the dynamics of flows of jobs and workers. To show this, we designate the stock of unemployed persons by U, employment by L, and the size of the labor force at a given date by N. At every instant, the labor force grows by quantity $\dot{N}$. Assuming that all the new entrants into the labor force begin by looking for a job, the number of unemployed persons is increased by the total of these new entrants, to whom must be added the qL workers who have just lost their jobs. Unemployment thus increases by $\dot{N} + qL$. Conversely, at every instant there are $\theta m(\theta)U$ unemployed persons who find a job. The variation $\dot{U}$ in the stock of unemployed persons is then written:

$$\dot{U} = \dot{N} + qL - \theta m(\theta)U \tag{5}$$

Let $n = \dot{N}/N$ be the rate of growth of the labor force and $u = U/N$ the rate of unemployment. As we have $N = L + U$ and also $\dot{U} = \dot{u}N + u\dot{N}$, the law of motion of the rate of unemployment is found by dividing the two sides of relation (5) by N. The result is:

$$\dot{u} = q + n - [q + n + \theta m(\theta)]u \tag{6}$$

The stationary value of the unemployment rate, the only thing that interests us here, corresponds to $\dot{u} = 0$. It is thus given by:

$$u = \frac{q + n}{q + n + \theta m(\theta)} \tag{7}$$

If we define the vacancy rate by $v = V/N$, the labor market tightness θ is also equal to the ratio v/u. Equation (7) then describes a relationship between the unemployment rate u and the vacancy rate v. This linkage expresses the equilibrium of worker flows between employment and unemployment, given the properties of the matching function. In the plane (v, u), this relationship yields the Beveridge curve. It is possible to show, using the hypotheses made about the matching function, that the Beveridge curve is decreasing and convex. In figures 9.1 and 9.5, it is identified by (BC). Moreover, the position of the Beveridge curve reflects the efficiency of the matching technology, for this curve lies farther out from the origin, the more inefficient this technology is.

In what follows, we will develop a model of labor market equilibrium based on the matching process just described, and will confine ourselves to the stationary state (the dynamics is presented in section 5.1). We begin by studying the behaviors that firms and workers adopt when faced with the matching process.

3.2 THE BEHAVIOR OF FIRMS

There are only two goods in the economy: a good produced by the firms and consumed by all individuals, and labor, assumed to be homogeneous, which is the sole factor of production. The good produced by the firms is the numeraire. Each firm has one job that can be either vacant or filled; when this job is filled, it makes possible the production of an exogenous quantity y of the good per unit of time. Section 4.2 reverts to the traditional representation of the firm using a production function, and brings in capital as another input. This more general model does not produce very different conclusions, but it does supply the foundations of the simplified model we use here, and allows us to specify the impact of variations in the cost of capital on investment and employment. We begin by defining the expected profit from a job in order to determine the labor demand of firms.

3.2.1 Expected Profits

At every instant, a job can either be filled or vacant. When it is filled, it yields an expected profit Π_e which is different from the profit expected Π_v when the job falls vacant.

The Profit Expected from a Filled Job

In each small interval of time dt, a filled job is liable to fall vacant with an exogenous probability $q\,dt$. This probability covers all exits from employment, whether their cause is layoffs, or the destruction of jobs, or whatever. It must be remembered, though, that letting an employee go or destroying a job are by nature endogenous decisions, made on the basis of an analysis of the present and future prospects of the firm. So to choose an exogenous probability q to describe these phenomena is not a satisfactory solution. Chapters 10 and 12 will show how it is possible to make this probability endogenous (see also Mortensen and Pissarides, 1994, and Pissarides, 2000). A large number of results (but not all) still stand with the hypothesis of an exogenous probability of exiting from employment.

We will also assume that the real interest rate r is exogenous. Implicitly, then, we place ourselves in the framework of a small open economy with perfect mobility of financial assets. The existence of a financial market entails that a dollar invested at date t brings in $1 + r\,dt$ dollars in $t + dt$, or, in other words, that the discounted value of a dollar at date t that will be available at date $t + dt$ is $1/(1 + r\,dt)$. So the term $1/(1 + r\,dt)$ represents the discount factor for each small interval of time dt. In the stationary state, if we denote by w the real wage received at every instant by an employee, the profit expected from a filled job takes this form:

$$\Pi_e = \frac{1}{1 + r\,dt}[(y - w)\,dt + q\,dt\Pi_v + (1 - q\,dt)\Pi_e] \qquad (8)$$

This relation indicates that the expected profit from a job is equal to the discounted sum of the flow of instantaneous profit $(y - w)\,dt$ in the interval of time dt and of the discounted expected future profits. With a probability $q\,dt$, these future profits coincide with the expected profit Π_v from a vacant job, and with the complementary probability $(1 - q\,dt)$ they coincide with the expected profit Π_e from a filled job. It is particularly interesting to note that relation (8) can be rewritten in simpler form:

$$r\Pi_e = y - w + q(\Pi_v - \Pi_e) \qquad (9)$$

It is worth noting that this equation portrays the equality of the returns of different assets in a perfect financial market. In the present case, an asset worth Π_e invested in the financial market brings in $r\Pi_e$ at every instant. This same asset, invested in the labor market, offers an instantaneous profit $(y - w)$ to which is added the average gain $q(\Pi_v - \Pi_e)$ associated with the job possibly changing state. For a filled job, this gain is in fact a loss resulting from the employee's leaving. Several times before—see chapters 3 and 4 in particular—we have encountered formulas analogous to relation (9). Mathematical appendix D at the end of the book supplies a rigorous proof of these formulas, showing that they do indeed correspond to the stationary state of a model in which a particular event (here, the destruction of jobs) follows a Poisson process.

The Profit Expected from a Vacant Job

The costs of a vacant job per unit of time are denoted by h. These costs represent the expenses incurred in holding the position open and looking for an employee with the right skills to fill it (advertising, agency fees, the services of a consultant, etc.). Since vacant jobs are filled at rate $m(\theta)$, the profit expected from a vacant job is written:

$$\Pi_v = \frac{1}{1 + r\,dt}\{-h\,dt + m(\theta)\,dt\Pi_e + [1 - m(\theta)\,dt]\Pi_v\}$$

Or again, rearranging the terms of this relation:

$$r\Pi_v = -h + m(\theta)(\Pi_e - \Pi_v) \qquad (10)$$

This relation equates the instantaneous return $r\Pi_v$ of the "unfilled job" asset in the financial market to its return in the labor market. Its return in the labor market comprises the instantaneous cost $-h$ and the average gain $m(\theta)(\Pi_e - \Pi_v)$ associated with a change of state (in this case, the passage from the vacant state to the filled state).

3.2.2 Labor Demand

As long as the profit expected from a vacant job remains strictly positive, new entrepreneurs enter the market to create jobs. This inflow ends when the profit expected from a vacant job goes to zero. We thus have the *free entry* condition; it is written simply $\Pi_v = 0$. When this condition is satisfied, relation (10) then entails $\Pi_e = h/m(\theta)$. On the other hand, equation (9) defining the profit expected from a filled job also gives $\Pi_e = (y - w)/(r + q)$. Equalizing these two values of Π_e we arrive at the following equation:

$$\frac{h}{m(\theta)} = \frac{y - w}{r + q} \tag{11}$$

The left-hand side of this equation represents the average cost of a vacant job. At every instant a vacant job brings an expense equal to h and is filled at rate $m(\theta)$. We know² that, on average, this vacant job remains unfilled for an interval of time $1/m(\theta)$. So the average cost of a vacant job is indeed equal to quantity $h/m(\theta)$. If we recall that the right-hand side of relation (11) is equated to the profit expected from a filled job, the interpretation of this relation becomes very simple: at free entry equilibrium, the average cost of a vacant job must be equal to the profit expected from a filled job.

Since the rate $m(\theta)$ at which vacant jobs are filled decreases with the labor market tightness θ, equation (11) defines a decreasing relation between the wage and the labor market tightness. This negative relation is analogous to *labor demand* in the neoclassical theory of the firm (see chapter 4). It reveals the fact that an increase in wage w degrades the profit outlook of a filled job. Since at free entry equilibrium the expected profit of a filled job equals the average cost of a vacant job, entrepreneurs react to a decrease in the expected profit of filled jobs by creating fewer vacant jobs, which lowers the expected duration and then the expected cost of vacant jobs.

Since we have shown that the unemployment rate can be deduced from labor market tightness using the Beveridge curve (7), it is possible to define the equilibrium values of the unemployment rate u and of labor market tightness θ using the system of equations (7) and (11) when wages are exogenous. Readers are invited to perform this exercise for themselves.

In matching models, wages are usually bargained over between each employer and each employee. This is a very natural approach, for as relation (11) shows, the fact that there is a cost attached to creating jobs induces a strictly positive profit for employers with filled jobs. A strictly positive profit from filled jobs is indeed required, if employers are to have an interest in posting vacant slots. In these circumstances, part of the profit will flow to the employees if they have bargaining power. In order to grasp the way a labor market with transaction costs functions, it is therefore important to represent the process of sharing the gains produced by filled jobs, and analyze its influence. For that, it is necessary in the first place to specify the way in which workers derive benefit from being employees, and from being unemployed.

3.3 The Behavior of Workers

The labor force is composed of N individuals, whose life span is infinite. Any worker can be either employed, with an expected utility V_e, or unemployed, with an expected utility $V_u \leq V_e$. When a worker is employed, he or she produces a quantity y and gets a real wage w per unit of time. He or she also risks losing his or her job at rate q. Assuming that workers are risk-neutral (which amounts to assuming that the indirect instantaneous utility function is linear), the expected utility of an employee at stationary equilibrium is found by repeating the procedure used to calculate the value of a job, so that:

$$rV_e = w + q(V_u - V_e) \tag{12}$$

An unemployed worker is always in search of a job. At each instant, this search procures him or her a net gain denoted by z. We have seen in chapter 3, in studying the theory of the job search, that this net gain comprises benefits linked to being unemployed (unemployment insurance, social welfare transfers, and also whatever utility comes from not having to work) minus the various costs attached to searching for a job (transportation, postage, perhaps extra training, etc.). Since the exit rate from unemployment is $\theta m(\theta)$, the expected utility of an unemployed person satisfies:

$$rV_u = z + \theta m(\theta)(V_e - V_u) \tag{13}$$

3.4 Wage Bargaining

When a worker and a vacant job come together, the employer and the potential employee bargain over the wage. Theory suggests that this bargaining yields a wage that increases with labor market tightness. Empirical studies confirm the existence of a relation of this type.

3.4.1 Surplus Sharing

Under suitable assumptions, the wage bargaining outcome is a simple surplus sharing rule, i.e., a rule for the sharing of the surplus yielded by a filled job between employer and employee. Moreover, it turns out that very simple noncooperative games make it possible to explain this sharing rule.

Surplus and the Nash Criterion

In dealing with the problem of bargaining, it is often helpful to work with the *surplus* S that derives from the match between an employee and an employer. This surplus is defined by the sum of the *rents* that a filled job paying negotiated wage w procures. Rent represents the difference between what individuals obtain through the contractual relationship and what the best opportunity outside the contract would bring them (see chapters 5 and 6). In the present context, for the employee the rent amounts to $(V_e - V_u)$, while for the employer it is equal to $(\Pi_e - \Pi_v)$. The surplus is thus defined by:

$$S = V_e - V_u + \Pi_e - \Pi_v \tag{14}$$

Bargaining gives each participant a share of the surplus proportional to his or her relative power. Let $\gamma \in [0, 1]$ be the relative power of the worker; the result of the negotiation is written:

$$V_e - V_u = \gamma S \qquad \text{and} \qquad \Pi_e - \Pi_v = (1 - \gamma)S \tag{15}$$

There are several ways of explaining such a division of the surplus. In chapter 7, we learned that the outcome of bargaining between two players could, under certain conditions, equal the maximum of the generalized Nash criterion. In this case, the value of the wage negotiated at each date is the solution of the following problem:

$$\underset{w}{\text{Max}}(V_e - V_u)^{\gamma}(\Pi_e - \Pi_v)^{1-\gamma} \tag{16}$$

Using equations (9) and (12), which define respectively the expected gain of an employee and an entrepreneur, we can easily verify that the first-order condition of this problem gives the sharing rule (15).

A Bargaining Game

We can also explain the surplus sharing rule (15) with the help of a noncooperative bargaining game. Let us assume, for example, that the bargaining unfolds, at each instant, as a two-stage game with the following characteristics:

Stage 1: The two players propose a contract that stipulates a wage to be paid in the future small interval of time *dt*.

Stage 2: If one of the two players has refused to sign the contract proposed in stage 1, the worker makes a new, take-it-or-leave-it offer with probability γ, and the employer in turn makes an offer of the same kind, with the complementary probability $(1 - \gamma)$. If there is again no agreement, the job is destroyed.

It is not hard to show that the surplus sharing rule (15) emerges as the subgame perfect equilibrium in this bargaining game (see chapter 7 for a definition of this equilibrium). If it is the worker who makes the offer in stage 2, the employer obtains a gain of Π_v, and the worker takes the whole surplus, which means that his or her expected utility amounts to $(S + V_u)$. If, on the other hand, it is the employer who makes the second-stage offer, the worker obtains V_u, the employer takes the whole surplus, and his or her expected profit amounts to $(S + \Pi_v)$. So in the first stage, the worker knows that at the outcome of stage 2, his or her expected utility will amount to $(1 - \gamma)V_u + \gamma(S + V_u)$, which is equal to $V_u + \gamma S$. Symmetrically, the employer knows that his or her expected profit will be equal to $(1 - \gamma)(S + \Pi_v) + \gamma\Pi_v$, which amounts to $\Pi_v + (1 - \gamma)S$. In consequence, it makes no difference to either player whether they sign a contract at stage 1 stipulating an expected utility V_e equal to $V_u + \gamma S$ for the employee, and an expected profit Π_e equal to $\Pi_v + (1 - \gamma)S$, for the employer, or wait until stage 2 to make the offers already defined. In the first stage, then, to sign a contract conforming to sharing rule (15) constitutes a subgame perfect equilibrium of the bargaining game. If we assume that there is a cost attached to going to stage 2, even a small cost, the bargaining game possesses a single equilibrium, corresponding to the immediate agreement of a surplus sharing contract as described by condition (15).

To this point, we have set out a very simple and excessively artificial game that leads to the surplus sharing rule usually adopted in matching models. Actually, it is possible to construct a large number of bargaining games that all lead to this sharing rule. These different games yield different interpretations of parameter γ, which can, in particular, depend on the preference of the players for the present, and their degree of risk aversion (see chapter 7 for a fuller exposition of this type of problem, and the work of Osborne and Rubinstein, 1990). At present, we will concentrate on the consequences of the surplus sharing rule.

The Negotiated Wage

In the first place, we get a simple expression of the surplus by adding up relations (9) and (12), which define respectively the expected utility and profit associated with a filled job for which the wage negotiated amounts to w. We thus have:

$$S = \frac{y - r(V_u + \Pi_v)}{r + q} \tag{17}$$

Moreover, definitions (9) and (12) of the profit and utility expected from a filled job can be written as follows:

$$V_e - V_u = \frac{w - rV_u}{r + q} \quad \text{and} \quad \Pi_e - \Pi_v = \frac{y - w - r\Pi_v}{r + q} \tag{18}$$

Combining the two first equalities of relations (15) and (18) with the expression (17) of the surplus taken at free entry equilibrium, where $\Pi_v = 0$, we arrive at a formula characterizing the negotiated wage. It is written:

$$w = rV_u + \gamma(y - rV_u) \tag{19}$$

This expression has a very intuitive interpretation. When the employee has all the bargaining power ($\gamma = 1$), then he or she garners all of production y at every date. If, on the contrary, it is the employer who possesses all the bargaining power ($\gamma = 0$), the wage w is then equal to rV_u and relation (18) shows that $V_e = V_u$; the employee then obtains no rent. In the intermediate cases, ($0 < \gamma < 1$), the wage negotiated is a linear combination of the value y of the production and of the reservation wage, rV_u, weighted by the respective power of the employee and the employer.

3.4.2   The Wage Curve

The wage curve synthesizes the linkages between the wage and the labor market tightness, as they emerge out of the bargaining process. Estimates of numerous wage equations allow us to specify the properties of this curve.

Wage Curve and Labor Supply

It is possible to obtain a relationship between the wage w and the tightness θ of the labor market using equation (19), which gives us the value of the negotiated wage. To that end, it is enough to note that definition (13) of V_u and surplus sharing rule (15) entail $rV_u = z + \gamma\theta m(\theta)S$, and, taking into account form (17) of the value of surplus S at free entry equilibrium, we arrive at:

$$rV_u = \frac{z(r+q) + \gamma y\theta m(\theta)}{r + q + \gamma\theta m(\theta)}$$

Substituting this expression of rV_u in wage equation (19), we get:

$$w = z + (y - z)\Gamma(\theta) \qquad \text{with} \qquad \Gamma(\theta) = \frac{\gamma[r + q + \theta m(\theta)]}{r + q + \gamma\theta m(\theta)} \qquad \text{(20)}$$

Since the exit rate $\theta m(\theta)$ from unemployment increases with labor market tightness θ, function $\Gamma(\theta)$ likewise increases with θ. This function represents the *actual* weight of the employee in the bargaining. Hence, the balance of power shifts in favor of the employee when θ increases, for in this case the probability of exiting from unemployment, and thus the value V_u of the outside opportunity, climb in tandem. The employee then fears the prospect of unemployment less, which pushes the negotiated wage up. A similar line of reasoning will show us why function $\Gamma(\theta)$ is decreasing with the exit rate q from employment. Of course, this function increases with the intrinsic weight γ of the employee in the bargaining. In sum, if $y > z$, equation (20) defines a rising monotone curve between the negotiated wage w and the labor market tightness θ. In the literature, it has become habitual to use the abbreviation (*WC*), for *wage curve*, to denote the curve that precisely encapsulates the outcome of this bargaining. It is worth noting that the wage curve replaces the labor supply curve from the competitive model. For a given number of vacant jobs, it defines a decreasing relation between wages and the stock of unemployed persons, which is equivalent to a rising relation between wages and employment. Now, this property also characterizes the labor supply function in certain circumstances. But this formal analogy should not conceal the profound differences that distinguish the wage curve from the labor supply curve when workers have bargaining power greater than zero. The wage curve is the upshot of a bargaining process over wages and takes into account characteristics of the labor market such as the job destruction rate q and the form $m(.)$ of the matching function. All these parameters are absent in the standard labor supply function, which is the upshot of a limit case in which workers have no bargaining power. In that situation, the gains of unemployed persons z are interpreted as the reservation wage (see chapter 1 for a definition of this notion) below which workers turn down jobs offered to them. That makes the wage offered by employers independent of labor market tightness.

Empirical Elements Relating to Bargaining Power
Much empirical work has been devoted to estimating wage equations similar in form to the one given by relation (20) (see Blanchflower and Oswald, 1995, and chapter 8, section 5). Some of these works aim to estimate the bargaining power of workers by trying to establish that they do in fact obtain a portion of the rent of firms. Abowd and

Lemieux (1993) have shown that wages are higher in Canadian firms with little exposure to international competition. They estimate that workers capture 30% of the rent obtained by firms protected from competition. Van Reenen (1996) has, for his part, studied the partition of rents created by innovation, using British data for the period 1945–1983. He obtains a result similar to that of Abowd and Lemieux, since he estimates that 29% of rent is captured by employees. Blanchflower et al. (1996) carried out the same sort of exercise, attempting to estimate the relationship between wages and profit per capita in the United States for the period 1964–1985. The elasticity of wages with respect to profit per capita amounts to 8%. On the whole, these results suggest that workers do in fact capture a portion of the rent of jobs. The representation of the mode of wage formation as a process of rent-sharing is therefore not invalidated empirically.

3.5 Labor Market Equilibrium

In the matching model, three relations make it possible to characterize completely the equilibrium values of the unemployment rate, wages, and labor market tightness. They are labor demand, the wage curve, and the Beveridge curve.

3.5.1 The Determination of Wages, Tightness, and the Unemployment Rate

In the competitive model, summed up by figure 9.3, the intersection of the labor supply and demand curves determines the equilibrium values of wages and employment. In the matching model, the wage curve takes the place of the supply curve. Hence, in plane (θ, w), the equilibrium values θ^* and w^* of the labor market tightness and the wage correspond to the coordinates of the intersection of the wage curve with labor demand respectively defined by relations (20) and (11). In figure 9.4, we have identified the labor demand curve and the wage curve by the abbreviations (LD) and (WC), respectively.

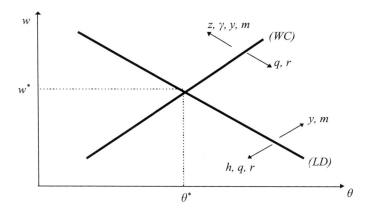

Figure 9.4
The negotiated wage and labor market tightness.

For some of what follows, it will be useful to have a relation that completely defines the equilibrium value of labor market tightness. We obtain this relation by eliminating the wage w between equations (11) and (20). Taking into account the definition of function $\Gamma(\theta)$—see (20) again—we finally get:

$$\frac{(1-\gamma)(y-z)}{r+q+\gamma\theta m(\theta)} = \frac{h}{m(\theta)} \tag{21}$$

Most often the impact of exogenous parameters on labor market equilibrium can easily be deduced by looking at the shifts of the (WC) and (LD) curves which they cause. But certain ambiguities sometimes persist, and it is then useful to refer to relation (21). It is interesting to note that the left-hand side of this relation represents the value of the profit expected from a filled job when the value of the negotiated wage is taken into account; it is a decreasing function of θ. Readers are reminded that the right-hand side represents the average cost of a vacant job; it is an increasing function of θ.

We can easily deduce the equilibrium unemployment rate from that of labor market tightness, taking into account entries into and exits from unemployment. More generally, figure 9.5 represents labor market equilibrium in the plane (v, u). Knowing the equilibrium value θ^* of labor market tightness, the equilibrium value u^* of the unemployment rate is equal to the abscissa of the intersection of the Beveridge curve, labeled BC, and the line that starts from the origin with slope θ^*. This line is usually labeled VS, for supply of job vacancies. It shows the supply of jobs that maximizes profits when wages and employment are in equilibrium.

3.5.2 Comparative Statics

The comparative statics properties of labor market equilibrium can be deduced by examining figures 9.4 and 9.5, and using equation (21), which defines the equilibrium value of the labor market tightness, in case of ambiguity. Table 9.8 assembles the

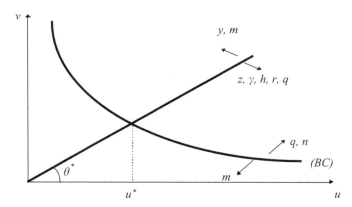

FIGURE 9.5
Vacant jobs and unemployment.

Table 9.8

Comparative statics of stationary equilibrium.

	z	γ	h	m	y	q	r	n
w	+	+	−	+	+	−	−	0
θ	−	−	−	+	+	−	−	0
u	+	+	+	−	−	+	+	+

results obtained. We limit ourselves here to presenting succinctly the impact of each parameter, in order to illustrate the functioning of the model. The empirical dimension will be addressed in detail later.

The Growth of the Labor Force

The size N of the labor force has no influence on the equilibrium of the model. On the other hand, a rise in the *growth rate n* of the labor force shifts the Beveridge curve upward without changing the (WC) and (LD) curves. The wage remains constant, but unemployment mounts. This result is an offshoot of the hypothesis that all new entrants into the labor market are unemployed. For the same number of vacant jobs, each person in search of work sees his or her probability of being hired diminish if the number of new entrants is increased, which is equivalent to a deterioration of the matching process.

Bargaining Power

Parameter γ measuring the bargaining power of the employee appears only in expression (20) of the wage curve. For a given value of θ, an increase in the employee's power pushes the negotiated wage upward. Since labor demand is unchanged, figure 9.4 shows that the rise in γ involves a shift upward of the wage curve, which in the end provokes a rise in the negotiated wage. This wage rise lowers the profit expected from a filled job, which at free entry equilibrium ought to be equal to the average cost of a vacant job. There will thus be a fall in the number of vacant jobs, which is equivalent to a diminution of θ. The Beveridge curve being independent of γ, unemployment is, in sum, going to increase.

Unemployment Insurance Benefits

The effect of an increase in unemployment insurance benefits z is exactly the same as that of an increase in the bargaining power γ of the employee. By improving the expected utility of an unemployed person, it increases wage pressure. In figure 9.4, we see that the wage curve shifts toward the NE, which pushes the wage up. In total, unemployment increases. Yet, as we saw in chapter 3, section 1.2.1, unemployment benefits are also attended by an *eligibility effect* that runs counter to the effects at work in this simple model. We will return to this aspect of employment policy in chapter 11.

Productivity

Figure 9.4 shows that a rise in individual productivity y increases the negotiated wage, but has an effect that is a priori ambiguous on the equilibrium value of labor market tightness θ. This ambiguity arises from two effects that have the same origin but work in opposite directions. A rise in y mechanically increases the "size of the pie" that the worker and the entrepreneur have to divide up. Consequently, with bargaining power held constant, the two protagonists obtain more wages for the one and more profit for the other. The first movement drives firms to diminish the number of vacant jobs, the second gives them an opposing incentive to increase it. This ambiguity as regards the final outcome is illustrated by a simultaneous shift upward of the (WC) and (LD) curves in figure 9.4. Nonetheless, this ambiguity disappears if we go back to equation (21), characterizing the equilibrium value of θ. It then becomes evident that an increase in y has a positive effect on θ overall, and reduces the unemployment rate. This result is due to the fact that the profit expected from a filled job, taking account of the negotiated value of the wage—which corresponds to the left-hand side of equation (21)—always increases with labor productivity.

It is important to note that these individual productivity effects depend strongly on the hypotheses that the gains of unemployed persons z and recruitment costs h do not hinge on labor productivity. Now, there are good reasons to think that these two parameters are not independent of productivity in the long run: unemployment benefits are most often defined as a fraction of past wages—which is the same as linking them to labor productivity—and search costs certainly rise with the cost of labor. If z and h were perfectly indexed to wages (i.e., $z = z'w$ and $h = h'w$, where z' and h' are constants), it is easy to verify, by referring to the main equations, that the level of productivity would no longer have any influence on labor market equilibrium. This result signifies that the unemployment rate is likely affected by the *level* of productivity in the short to medium run, but is independent of it in the very long term. As we will see in chapter 10, however, the *rate of growth* of productivity affects the unemployment rate even when the gains of unemployed persons and the costs of vacant jobs are perfectly indexed to productivity.

The Efficiency of the Matching Process

Formally, improved efficiency in the matching process comes to the same thing as multiplying the matching function $m(.)$ by a positive coefficient greater than unity. In figures 9.4 and 9.5, we have identified this operation by the letter m. Improved efficiency in the matching process increases the probability of individuals returning to work. The expected utility of an unemployed person increases, which likewise increases the actual power $\Gamma(\theta)$ of workers in wage bargaining. Upward pressure on wages follows; it is revealed in figure 9.4 by an upward shift of the wage curve. In parallel fashion, greater efficiency in the matching process increases the probability of filling vacant jobs, which lowers their average cost. For a given wage, then, firms offer more vacant jobs and θ increases. In figure 9.4, the (LD) curve shifts to the right. In total, wages rise, but the effect on θ is ambiguous, since, on the one hand, this wage rise reduces the number of vacant jobs that are opened up, but, on the other, the reduction in the average cost of vacant jobs provides an opposing incentive to open up more of them. Relation (21), defining the equilibrium value of the labor market tightness, allows us to solve this indeterminacy. We verify that θ increases when the matching process improves. Once again, therefore, the effect on labor demand (LD) proves to be dominant. Finally, figure 9.5 indicates that the unemployment rate falls, since improved efficiency in matching shifts the Beveridge curve downward.

The Job Destruction Rate
Figures 9.4 and 9.5 describing labor market equilibrium show that a rise in the job destruction rate q is strictly equivalent to lowering the efficiency of the matching process m. This is indeed a perfectly logical result, for in this simple model the job destruction rate q and the rate at which vacant jobs are filled, identified by m, represent two facets of the same phenomenon: the reallocation of jobs and workers. The variable m reflects the "job creation" facet, while parameter q reflects, by hypothesis, the "job destruction" facet. Chapters 10 and 12 will focus on making the job destruction rate endogenous. This enrichment of the basic model will shed valuable light on the consequences of job protection and technological innovation.

The Interest Rate
A rise in the interest rate decreases the surplus of filled jobs (as shown by equation (21)). Relation (21) indicates that a rise in the interest rate, by depreciating the discounted value of future profits, reduces the incentive to post vacant jobs, and in consequence increases the unemployment rate. It is important to point out that the interest rate can also affect employment by altering capital investment and thus labor productivity. This problem will be dealt with in section 4.1.

3.5.3 Some Quantitative Elements
The results obtained to this point have enabled us to highlight the elements that influence unemployment in purely qualitative terms. The next step will be to quantify the respective weight of each element.

Calibrating the Model
An approach frequently taken is to "calibrate" the model, i.e., to assign plausible orders of magnitude to the parameters in order to find out what it quantitatively predicts (Mortensen, 1994; Merz, 1995; Andolfatto, 1996; Millard and Mortensen, 1997; Mortensen and Pissarides, 1999). The results of these exercises must obviously be interpreted with caution, inasmuch as they can be highly sensitive to the values selected for the parameters and the functional forms chosen. Nevertheless, certain results prove to be robust for broad ranges of the parameters. Moreover, these calibration exercises have useful things to teach us about the properties of the models we utilize.

Parameter values are presented in table 9.9. The unit of time corresponds to one year. Annual production y has been normalized to 1. In line with the vast majority of

Table 9.9

Parameter values for the matching model.

γ	h	q	r	n
0.5	0.3	0.15	0.05	0.01

studies, we assume that the matching process is represented by a Cobb-Douglas function, written $M(V, U) = V^{0.5} U^{0.5}$. The job destruction rate is slightly higher than the annual rate of gross job losses reported in table 9.1 so as to take into account the fact that these gross losses neglect internal job movements within firms or plants (see the comments on table 9.1). The annual interest rate of 5% corresponds on average to the real interest rates recorded in the 1990s.

We do not have at our disposal a reliable order of magnitude for the parameters representing the bargaining power of workers γ and the cost h of vacant jobs. The usual procedure is to assume that γ is equal to the elasticity of the matching function with respect to the unemployment rate. We will see in section 6 that this hypothesis ensures the efficiency of decentralized equilibrium. Finallly, the value of h is chosen in such a way as to obtain unemployment rates compatible with the data.

Strengths and Weaknesses of the Basic Model

The graph situated in the NE quadrant of figure 9.6 represents the effect of a variation in the replacement ratio $b = z/w$, taken to be exogenous, on the unemployment rate. The three other graphs in figure 9.6 trace the impact on this variable of a reduction in productivity y, of a hike in the interest rate r, and of a rise in the growth rate n of the labor force. For these three graphs, we have considered two values of the replacement ratio. The first, $b = 0.1$, illustrates the U.S. and Canadian case, and the second, $b = 0.4$, characterizes the countries of western Europe, where the replacement ratio is clearly greater than it is in Canada and the United States (according to OECD, 1996). This exercise allows us to show in a very crude way how the basic matching model could highlight the impact of macroeconomic shocks on Canada and the United States, and European labor markets over the 1980s and the beginning of the 1990s.

To begin, the graph in the NE quadrant of figure 9.6 shows that the difference between the levels of the replacement ratio in Canada and the United States and continental Europe entails a differential of less than two points in the unemployment rate, clearly below that observable in the data for the period considered here (see chapter 8). The three other graphs in figure 9.6 show that shocks have impacts of the same size for the two levels of replacement ratio considered. Moreover, variations in the interest rate and in the growth rate of the labor force affect the unemployment rate only slightly. An increase of eight points in the interest rate increases the unemployment rate by less than 0.5 points, and a rise of one percentage point in the growth rate of the labor force exerts a downward pressure of 0.5 points on the unemployment rate. Thus our simple calibration of the basic matching model does not succeed in reproducing

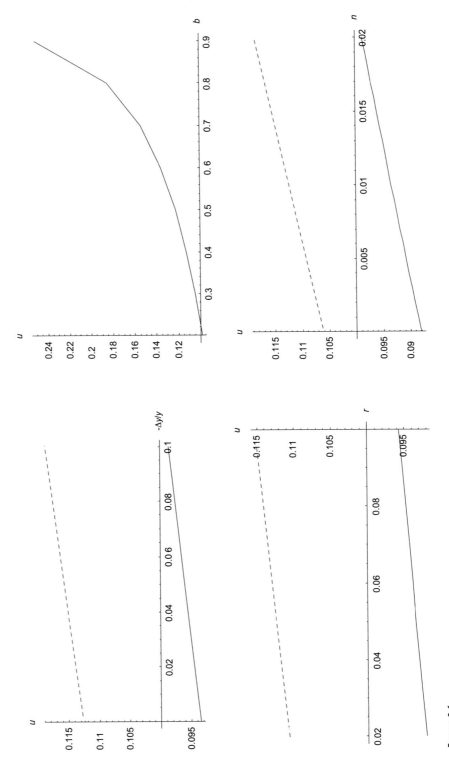

FIGURE 9.6

Simulations on the basis of the matching model.

Solid line: $b = 0.1$; dashed line: $b = 0.4$.

quantitatively the upswing of European unemployment on the basis of variations in the interest rate, productivity, or the growth rate of the labor force. The unemployment differential between continental Europe and the United States cannot be attributed solely to the gap between the replacement ratios. Other factors, which will be examined in chapters 10, 11, and 12, are affecting unemployment.

4   INVESTMENT AND EMPLOYMENT

In the preceding section, the problem of choosing capital, and the consequences of this for employment, were set aside completely. This is an important limitation of the model, inasmuch as labor productivity, which influences employment, is itself conditioned by capital. We will see that it is possible to represent investment decisions quite simply in the matching model (Pissarides, 2000, and Cahuc and Wasmer, 2001). Doing so will make it possible to analyze the impact of interest rate variations on employment in a more satisfactory manner, and will lead us to emphasize that the way wage bargaining is conducted influences investment choices in many circumstances.

4.1   INTEREST RATE, INVESTMENT, AND UNEMPLOYMENT

We study the determinants of investment within the traditional framework, in which the technology of firms is represented by a production function with two substitutable factors, labor and capital. This approach allows us to specify the impact of interest rates on employment by taking into account their influence on capital.

4.1.1   The Investment Decision

We henceforth assume that the production sector of the economy is composed of a large number of identical firms bearing the index i. At every instant, firm i utilizes quantities K_i of capital and L_i of labor to produce a quantity $F(K_i, L_i)$ of the numeraire good. This last expression represents the production function of firm i; it is taken to be strictly increasing with respect to each of its arguments, strictly concave, and with constant returns to scale. The behavior of workers is identical to the one described in the basic model; in particular, all individuals are assumed to be risk-neutral. It should be kept in mind that all the variables in the model depend on time, but in what follows we omit the time index for the sake of simplicity.

The Problem of the Firm
In every firm, at every instant, decisions unfold in the following order:

1.   The firm decides on its hires. The employers therefore preserve the ''right to manage,'' the principal consequences of which were discussed in chapter 7.

2.   The employer negotiates over wages with each worker, one to one, so there is no collective bargaining between the employer and a union representing the interests of the employees. Capital is chosen simultaneously with the wage

bargaining. This hypothesis signifies that the employer cannot commit him- or herself to a stock of capital in order to manipulate the wage being negotiated, which depends on productivity. We assume that there exists a capital market in which the firm can buy and sell without delay (see Cahuc and Wasmer, 2001).

Hence, at every date, firm i opens up V_i vacant jobs, each of which is filled at rate $m(\theta)$. The number of hires per unit of time is then equal to $m(\theta)V_i$. It should be noted that the rate $m(\theta)$ is given for the firm: because labor market tightness is a macroeconomic variable (formally, θ is not indexed by i). Let I_i be the instantaneous investment of firm i, and δ the rate of depreciation of capital. If w_i designates the prevailing wage in firm i, then the problem of this firm is written:

$$\underset{V_i, I_i}{\text{Max}}\ \Pi_i = \int_0^{+\infty} [F(K_i, L_i) - w_i L_i - h V_i - I_i] e^{-rt}\, dt \tag{22}$$

subject to:

$$\dot{L}_i = m(\theta) V_i - q L_i \tag{23}$$

$$\dot{K}_i = I_i - \delta K_i \tag{24}$$

In these expressions, h, q, and r are exogenous parameters representing, as in the basic model, the cost of a vacant job, the exit rate from employment, and the real interest rate. Constraint (24) expresses the law of motion of capital, and constraint (23) signifies that in firm i the variation of employment $\dot{L}_i$ is equal to hires $m(\theta)V_i$ minus quits qL_i.

The Optimal Solutions

Problem (22), the maximization of the firm's intertemporal profit, is a dynamic optimization problem in which the state variables are employment L_i and capital K_i. The solution of this type of problem is explained in detail in mathematical appendix B at the end of the book. Let μ and λ be the multipliers associated respectively with constraints (23) and (24). The Hamiltonian of this problem is written:

$$H = [F(K_i, L_i) - w_i L_i - h V_i - I_i] e^{-rt} + \mu[m(\theta) V_i - q L_i] + \lambda(I_i - \delta K_i) \tag{25}$$

The first-order conditions read:

$$\frac{\partial H}{\partial I_i} = 0 \quad \text{and} \quad \frac{\partial H}{\partial K_i} = -\dot{\lambda} \tag{26}$$

$$\frac{\partial H}{\partial V_i} = 0 \quad \text{and} \quad \frac{\partial H}{\partial L_i} = -\dot{\mu} \tag{27}$$

To these equations must be added the transversality conditions:

$$\underset{t \to \infty}{\text{Lim}}\ \mu L_i = 0 \quad \text{and} \quad \underset{t \to \infty}{\text{Lim}}\ \lambda K_i = 0 \tag{28}$$

Equalities (26) entail $e^{-rt} = \lambda$ and $\lambda \delta - F_K(K_i, L_i) e^{-rt} = \dot{\lambda}$. The first equation entails that $\dot{\lambda} = -r\lambda$. Substituting this expression of $\dot{\lambda}$ into the second equation, we arrive at:

$$F_K(K_i, L_i) = r + \delta \tag{29}$$

Relation (29) expresses the usual equality between the marginal productivity of capital and its user cost $(r + \delta)$. Conditions (27) in turn entail $he^{-rt} = \mu m(\theta)$ and $q\mu - [F_L(K_i, L_i) - w_i]e^{-rt} = \dot{\mu}$. At stationary equilibrium, where $\dot{\theta} = 0$, after several simple calculations we get:

$$F_L(K_i, L_i) = w_i + \frac{h(r+q)}{m(\theta)} \tag{30}$$

Relation (30) conveys that the marginal productivity of labor must be equal to the wage plus the employment adjustment costs at the optimum. Relations (29) and (30) show that capital and employment depend on parameters such as wages and job destruction rates that are, in principle, specific to each firm, but also on macroeconomic variables such as the labor market tightness and the interest rate.

4.1.2 Wage Bargaining

If we follow the decision sequence set out at the beginning of this section, in stage 2 each employee bargains over his or her wage individually with the employer. Accordingly, bargaining concerns the *marginal* surplus created by each job—i.e., by definition, the expected supplementary gains produced by this job. The value of a marginal job is easily defined in a stationary situation. The marginal job brings in a flow of gains $F_L(K_i, L_i) - w_i$; as well, it is destroyed with a probability q per unit of time. Since every job destroyed brings in zero profit, the value π_i of a marginal job in firm i is written as follows:

$$\pi_i = \left(\frac{1}{1+r\,dt}\right)\{[F_L(K_i, L_i) - w_i]\,dt + [1 - q\,dt]\pi_i\} \Leftrightarrow \pi_i = \frac{F_L(K_i, L_i) - w_i}{r + q}$$

This definition of the value of the marginal job is identical to that giving the value of a filled job in the basic model—see (8)—on condition of having $\Pi_v = 0$ and identifying individual production y with marginal productivity $F_L(K_i, L_i)$.

From this point of view, it is important to note that the hypothesis of constant returns to scale entails that the marginal productivity of labor does not depend on employment when capital reaches its optimal level. Let us set $k_i = K_i/L_i$ and $f(k_i) = F(K_i, L_i)/L_i$; differentiating this last equation with respect to K_i and L_i we find the marginal productivities of capital and labor, i.e., $F_K(K_i, L_i) = f'(k_i)$ and $F_L(K_i, L_i) = f(k_i) - k_i f'(k_i)$. Equality (29) between the marginal productivity of capital and its user cost shows that the capital–labor ratio k_i is the same in all firms; we simply denote it by k. In this case, the negotiated wage is also the same in all firms; we denote it by w. More precisely, the first-order conditions (29) and (30) entail:

$$f'(k) = r + \delta \tag{31}$$

$$f(k) - kf'(k) = w + \frac{h(r+q)}{m(\theta)} \tag{32}$$

As the capital–labor ratio k is completely defined by the user cost of capital $(r + \delta)$, the marginal productivity of labor $f(k) - kf'(k)$ is also completely determined by knowledge of r and δ. This result allows us to justify the hypothesis of constant individual production y in the basic model, since in reality it represents the marginal productivity of labor, which, with the hypotheses of constant returns of the production function and an exogenous interest rate, does not depend on employment. It should be noted that this marginal productivity is a decreasing function of the interest rate. With this new definition of y, equation (32) is identical to relation (11) defining labor demand in the basic model.

A further task is to verify the transversality conditions (28). When computing the first-order conditions, we saw that multipliers λ and μ were proportional to e^{-rt} at stationary equilibrium. Since $K_i = kL_i$ and since, in the stationary state, L_i grows at rate n in all firms, we observe that the transversality conditions are satisfied if and only if $r > n$.

Finally, the Beveridge curve derives directly from condition (23) describing the evolution of employment in the representative firm. Since, by definition, $L = N + U$ with $\dot{N}/N = n$, we come back exactly to equation (7) characterizing the Beveridge curve. In sum, this analysis of the matching model with large firms both justifies and clarifies the use of the simplified model in section 3. In particular, it enables us to study the impact of variations in the interest rate on unemployment in greater depth.

4.1.3 The Impact of the Interest Rate on Unemployment

Table 9.10 traces the real interest rates in a handful of OECD countries from the 1960s to the 1990s. In the period from 1981 to 1993, interest rates rose sharply, and this period was also marked by a strong rise in the unemployment rate in certain countries. The explanation most often put forward is that the large size of budget deficits from the end of the 1970s, and restrictive monetary policies in the decade that followed, pushed interest rates upward and were in large part responsible for the climb in unemployment (Fitoussi and Phelps, 1988). This explanation is not, however, completely convincing, for several reasons.

Table 9.10

Long-term interest rates.

Country	1956–1973	1974–1980	1981–1993
United States	1.1	−0.3	5.6
Japan	0.3	0.5	4.4
Germany	3.0	3.0	4.5
France	1.0	0.4	5.7
United Kingdom	1.8	−3.3	4.5

Source: Rowthorn (1995, table 3, p. 36).

In the first place, the matching model suggests that the interest rate has only a limited impact on the unemployment rate. Figure 9.7 gives the results of a simulation of the large firm model, with the parameter values given in table 9.9, and assumes as well a Cobb-Douglas production function $Y = AK^{0.3}L^{0.7}$. The value of A has been chosen in such a way as to obtain a labor productivity y equal to 1 when the interest rate is 5%. The replacement ratio, $b = 0.4$, corresponds to that found on average in continental Europe, and the rate of capital depreciation is fixed at 5%. We observe that the interest rate differentials among the G5 countries, which rarely exceed 1%, can only explain small differences among the unemployment rates in these countries, since a ten-point increase in the interest rate induces a rise on the order of only three points in the unemployment rate.

Moreover, the climb in interest rates that occurred at the beginning of the 1980s does not give us any insight into either the rise in unemployment at the beginning of

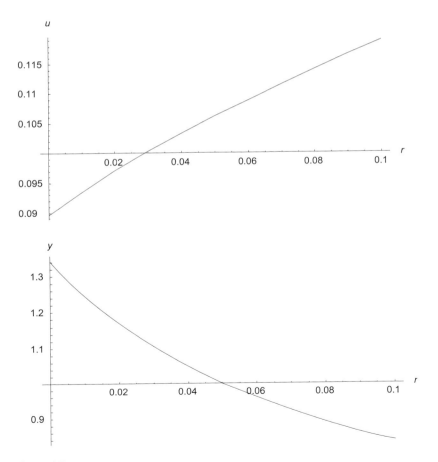

FIGURE 9.7
The impact of the interest rate on unemployment.

the 1970s or national differences in this regard. The fact is that the rise in unemployment preceded the rise in interest rates, and international capital mobility entails that in the long run, real interest rates follow approximately the same path in the various national markets.

So it is likely that the rise in the real interest rate did contribute to increased unemployment in certain countries, but interest rate differentials can account for only a very limited portion of the differences among rates of unemployment.

4.2 INVESTMENT IN SPECIFIC CAPITAL, "HOLDUP," AND UNEMPLOYMENT

The investment decisions analyzed to this point in the present chapter concern *general* capital, which the firm can utilize in any job at all and resell at will. Becker (1964) pointed out, though, that certain investments go into *specific* capital, committing the firm to irreversible expenditures that only have value in the context of the relationship between the employer and the employee, who share the benefits of this investment. Training costs for highly specialized tasks, which endow the employee with a skill that can only be applied in the firm in which he or she works, are a typical example of investment in specific capital. Actually, every investment is to some degree specific. As Williamson (1975) and Grout (1984) emphasized, the incentives to invest in specific capital may be drastically reduced when contracts are incomplete, i.e., when they do not specify, in advance and irreversibly, all the possible situations that may arise and the corresponding wage in each case. In order to grasp this problem, let us suppose that one of the two parties—the employer, for example—decides to invest in a specific capital that improves the productivity of a worker. The latter then has an interest in declaring to the employer that he or she will not demand a wage rise when his or her productivity will have been raised because of the investment. But after the investment has been made and his or her productivity actually has risen, the employee then has an interest in going back on his or her word and trying to renegotiate the wage so as to capture a share of the productivity gains. This configuration is known in the literature as the "holdup" problem. The absence of a contract specifying the path of future wages and blocking any possibility of renegotiation leads to underinvestment on the part of the employer, which may be detrimental to both parties to the contract. This problem may be illustrated formally with the help of our basic model from section 3 above. Let us suppose that the individual productivity of a worker depends on an investment in training, the entire cost of which, denoted by i, is paid by the employer at the time of hiring. Formally, production per capita is an increasing and concave function, denoted by $y(i)$, of the initial investment in training. It is interesting to note that the "large firm" model also arrives at this description; all we have to do is represent the production function by $F[K, e(i)L]$, where individual productivity $e(i)$ is an increasing, concave function of the investment in training. Let $k = K/e(i)L$ be capital per unit of efficient work; it is easy to verify that profit maximization with respect to capital K and employment L entails that relation (31) is always satisfied and that equation (32) now takes the form:

$$[f(k) - kf'(k)]e(i) = w + \frac{h(r + q)}{m(\theta)}$$

This equality shows that the basic model is equivalent to the "large firm" model on condition that we set $y(i) = [f(k) - kf'(k)]e(i)$. The holdup problem can be analyzed by distinguishing two situations. The first corresponds to the case in which the protagonists sign a contract stipulating a nonrenegotiable wage. We then have a complete contract defining the wage for as long as the employer–employee relationship lasts. In the second, long-term commitments are impossible, which means that contracts are renegotiable and the holdup problem arises.

4.2.1   Investment with a Complete Contract

The situation in which renegotiation is excluded is represented by a two-stage game. In the first stage, bargaining determines a wage for the whole duration of the employer–employee relationship. In the second stage, the employer decides how much to invest. The solution of this game is obtained by backward induction, in order to ensure that all decisions are optimal at the instant they are taken. In the second stage, the employer maximizes his or her expected profit, taking the wage negotiated $w(i)$ as given, which makes it a function of investment i. Utilizing the definition of expected profit (8), the employer's optimization problem is written:

$$\text{Max}_i (\Pi_e - i) = \text{Max}_i \frac{y(i) - w(i) + q\Pi_v}{r + q} - i \Rightarrow y'(i) - w'(i) = r + q \qquad \textbf{(33)}$$

Thus the employer selects an investment that equalizes marginal return and marginal cost. In the first stage, the employer and the employee bargain over the wage. Note that the employer obtains $(\Pi_e - i)$, and so the surplus, net of the investment cost, denoted by $S_n(i)$, now takes the form:

$$S_n(i) = V_e - V_u + \Pi_e - i - \Pi_v = S(i) - i$$

where $S(i)$ corresponds to the definition (17) of the surplus, so that here:

$$S(i) = \frac{y(i) - r(\Pi_v + V_u)}{r + q}$$

Since the bargaining always gives a share $(1 - \gamma)$ of the net surplus to the employer, we have:

$$\Pi_e - i - \Pi_v = (1 - \gamma)S_n(i)$$

Utilizing expressions (18) and (17), the negotiated wage is written, with $\Pi_v = 0$:

$$w(i) = \gamma[y(i) - (r + q)i] + (1 - \gamma)rV_u \qquad \textbf{(34)}$$

This equality entails $w'(i) = \gamma[y'(i) - (r + q)]$, and the first-order condition (33) then allows us to characterize completely the investment chosen by the employer. We thus have:

$$y'(i^*) = r + q \tag{35}$$

Note that the investment defined by this last relation maximizes the net surplus $S_n(i)$. In this sense, a complete, nonrenegotiable contract ensures efficient investment in specific capital.

4.2.2   Investment with an Incomplete Contract

The situation in which a complete contract is impossible can also be represented by a two-stage game in which the employer decides on the investment in the first stage, knowing that the wage will be negotiated afterward. As before, this game is solved by backward induction. In the second stage, the wage is bargained over. The employer's gains amount to $(\Pi_e - i)$ if the bargaining is successful and to $(\Pi_v - i)$ if it fails. His or her net gains are thus $(\Pi_e - \Pi_v)$, and the definition of the surplus corresponds to that given by equation (14). So the bargaining arrives at a wage analogous to that defined by relation (19), which we will write in the following manner:

$$\overline{w}(i) = \gamma y(i) + (1 - \gamma) r V_u \tag{36}$$

It is interesting to note that, for the same productivity level $y(i)$, the renegotiated wage is higher than the wage set by a complete nonrenegotiable contract. This difference is due to the fact that renegotiation allows the employee to appropriate a share of the return on the investment made by the employer. In the first stage of the game, the employer decides on the amount $\bar{i}$ of investment knowing the renegotiated wage. His or her problem is then written:

$$\underset{i}{\text{Max}}(\Pi_e - i) = \underset{i}{\text{Max}} \frac{y(i) - \overline{w}(i)}{r + q} - i \Rightarrow y'(\bar{i}) = \frac{r + q}{1 - \gamma} \tag{37}$$

As function $y(i)$ is increasing and concave, equations (35) and (37) entail that the possibility of renegotiating contracts leads to an investment in specific capital inferior to the efficient level i^*. The inefficiency induced by the incompleteness of the labor contract increases with γ, the bargaining power of workers. The effect on equilibrium employment is immediate. When the contract is incomplete, productivity is lower and firms have a lower level of profit for given productivity. In consequence, expected profit is smaller when labor contracts are incomplete, and free entry equilibrium entails that the equilibrium labor tightness is lower, which in the end means a higher level of unemployment. To the extent that the parties to a contract are able to define clauses that protect them against the consequences of the holdup, it is not certain that the incompleteness of labor contracts necessarily leads to underinvestment in specific capital. Agents may decide to allocate property rights before investing (Williamson, 1975; Grossman and Hart, 1986; Hart and Moore, 1990). For example, giving the employer the right to determine wages unilaterally, in exchange for a payment to the worker at the outset, makes it possible to ensure that the employer will be the residual claimant of his or her investment and will thus be given an incentive to invest efficiently. Another means of solving the holdup problem is to make provision for transfers should the contract be broken (MacLeod and Malcomson, 1993), which makes it possible to avoid renegotiation. Only through close analysis of labor contracts is it possible to assess the extent of the holdup problem. There does not, to our knowledge, exist any empirical study allowing us to assess the real extent of this problem within the framework of the employer–employee relationship.

5 OUT-OF-STATIONARY-STATE DYNAMICS

To this point, we have limited ourselves to the study of stationary equilibrium. The study of out-of-stationary-state dynamics allows us to exhibit a significant contrast between the movement over time of vacant jobs and that of unemployment. Dynamic analysis also sheds light on the propagation mechanisms of shocks affecting the economy.

5.1 BARGAINING AND THE DYNAMICS OF THE SURPLUS

Analysis of the dynamics of the basic model requires that we reconsider the equations defining the expected utilities and profits. Hence, when the economy moves away from its stationary state, relations (12) and (13), defining the expected utility of an employee and an unemployed person, respectively, are now written[3]:

$$rV_e = w + q(V_u - V_e) + \dot{V}_e \tag{38}$$

$$rV_u = z + \theta m(\theta)(V_e - V_u) + \dot{V}_u \tag{39}$$

The terms $\dot{V}_e$ and $\dot{V}_u$, which represent the time derivatives of V_e and V_u, are interpreted as expected capital gains from changes in the valuation of the assets V_e and V_u. As there is no source of regular growth in the basic model, these terms are null at stationary equilibrium. Symmetrically, profits expected from a filled job and a vacant one, defined by equations (9) and (10), now take the form:

$$r\Pi_e = y - w + q(\Pi_v - \Pi_e) + \dot{\Pi}_e \tag{40}$$

$$r\Pi_v = -h + m(\theta)(\Pi_e - \Pi_v) + \dot{\Pi}_v \tag{41}$$

The matching of an unemployed person to a vacant job occasions a surplus S, the time derivative of which is denoted by $\dot{S}$. By definition, we will thus have:

$$S = V_e - V_u + \Pi_e - \Pi_v \quad \text{and} \quad \dot{S} = \dot{V}_e - \dot{V}_u + \dot{\Pi}_e - \dot{\Pi}_v \tag{42}$$

Just as in the basic model, we assume that the free entry condition $\Pi_v = 0$ is satisfied at every date, so it likewise comes to $\dot{\Pi}_v = 0$. With the help of definitions (42), adding up equations (38) and (40), which characterize respectively an employee's expected utility and the profit expected from a filled job, entails:

$$(r + q)S = \dot{S} + y + \dot{V}_u - rV_u \tag{43}$$

This differential equation describes the time path of the surplus. The surplus is independent of the wage. Accordingly, just as in the basic model, the wage bargaining outcome is similar to a surplus sharing rule conditioned by the respective powers of the participants. So we will again have:

$$V_e - V_u = \gamma S \quad \text{and} \quad \Pi_e - \Pi_v = (1 - \gamma)S \tag{44}$$

The Dynamics of Vacancies and Unemployment

The free entry condition ($\Pi_v = \dot{\Pi}_v = 0$) and definition (41) of the profit expected from a vacant job yield the usual equality between expected profit and average cost $\Pi_e = h/m(\theta)$. The second of the sharing rules (44) then entails:

$$S = \frac{h}{(1 - \gamma)m(\theta)} \Rightarrow \dot{S} = -\frac{hm'(\theta)}{(1 - \gamma)m^2(\theta)} \dot{\theta} \tag{45}$$

This equation, relation (39) characterizing the expected utility of an unemployed person, and the first of the sharing rules (44) again entail:

$$rV_u - \dot{V}_u = z + \theta m(\theta)\gamma S = z + \frac{\gamma \theta h}{1 - \gamma} \tag{46}$$

Bringing the values of S, $\dot{S}$, and $(rV_u - \dot{V}_u)$ given by relations (45) and (46) into differential equation (43) describing the time path of the surplus, and rearranging terms, we arrive at:

$$\frac{hm'(\theta)}{(1 - \gamma)m^2(\theta)} \dot{\theta} + \frac{h[r + q + \gamma \theta m(\theta)]}{(1 - \gamma)m(\theta)} - y + z = 0 \tag{47}$$

This differential equation completely characterizes the path of labor market tightness. In the stationary state ($\dot{\theta} = 0$), this equation is of course identical to relation (21) giving the stationary value θ^* of labor market tightness. Equation (47) is a first-order, nonlinear differential equation of the form $\varphi(\dot{\theta}, \theta) = 0$. The convergence of θ in the neighborhood of stationary equilibrium can nevertheless be studied very easily by linearizing function φ around point ($\dot{\theta} = 0, \theta = \theta^*$). After several calculations, we arrive at the following linear differential equation:

$$\dot{\theta} + a\theta = a\theta^* \quad \text{with} \quad a = \gamma \frac{m^2(\theta^*)}{m'(\theta^*)} - (r + q) < 0$$

The general solution of this equation is of the form $\theta = Be^{-at} + \theta^*$, where B is a constant. Parameter a being negative, the unique stable path of θ corresponds to $B = 0$. We then have, at every instant, $\theta = \theta^*$. This result signifies that variable θ immediately "jumps" to the stationary value. It arises from the fact that opening up a vacant job is a "forward-looking" decision that takes into account only expectations of *future* profit and contains no inertia factor. The number of vacant jobs can thus adapt immediately to any change in the environment. More generally, all decisions of agents are directed toward the future, so it is easy to verify that the wage negotiated is also a variable that jumps instantaneously to its stationary value.

When labor market tightness has reached its stationary value θ^*, the differential equation (6) describing the evolution of the unemployment rate takes the following form:

$$\dot{u} + [q + n + \theta^* m(\theta^*)]u = q + n$$

This is a first-order linear differential equation in which the coefficient of u is positive. The unemployment rate thus exhibits a monotonic convergence to its stationary value given by relation (7). Note that the unemployment rate is thus not a purely forward-looking variable. The average duration of a job search being a positive quantity, there exists at every instant a stock of unemployed persons who represent an element of inertia for the dynamics of the economy. Following a shock, the unemployment rate only gradually reaches its new stationary value.

5.2   AGGREGATE SHOCK AND REALLOCATION SHOCK

An important and ever controversial question is that of the origin of the perturbations that affect movements in employment. Empirical analysis most often strives to distinguish between the effects of an *aggregate* shock and those of a *reallocation* shock. An aggregate shock refers to a change in aggregate demand or supply of goods, and would not shift the Beveridge curve. In our basic model, it can be likened to a change in the levels of individual production y, the interest rate r, unemployment benefits z, or the balance of power γ. A reallocation shock, on the other hand, refers to a restructuring of production units, which would shift the Beveridge curve without noticeably affecting the components of aggregate supply or demand. In our model, a reallocation shock is akin to changes in the matching function $m(.)$ or in the job destruction rate q. It is important to diagnose the origin of shocks with precision, for the remedies adopted to reduce underemployment will vary with this diagnosis. An aggregate shock may in certain circumstances require policies to support aggregate demand, while a reallocation shock is an incentive to undertake structural reforms. The dynamic elements set out immediately above, combined with the comparative statics results set out in section 3.5.2, allow us to pinpoint the origin of shocks.

Figure 9.8 illustrates the effects of an aggregate shock, identified with a permanent hike in the interest rate r (a fall in production y would be equivalent). Points E^* and E' represent respectively the stationary equilibria before and after the time at which the aggregate shock occurred. From E^*, the labor market tightness "jumps" instantaneously from its initial level θ^* to its final level θ'. This movement is accompanied by a jump in the vacancy rate, which goes from v^* to v_1, while the unemployment rate stays at its initial value u^*. Then, starting at point E_1, the economy gradually attains its final state E' by moving along the segment $E_1 E'$. Figure 9.9 illustrates the impact of a reallocation shock, identified with a permanent hike in the job destruction rate q. The Beveridge curve now shifts, and the new stationary equilibrium E' lies on the (CB') curve. From point E^* on, the dynamics of the economy is analogous to what we described in relation to an aggregate shock and does not need to be repeated.

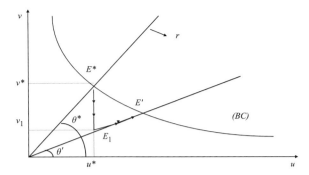

FIGURE 9.8
Aggregate shock.

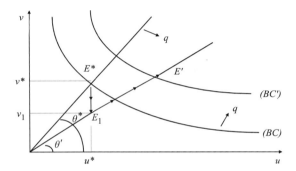

FIGURE 9.9
Reallocation shock.

Readers can observe, in figures 9.8 and 9.9, that the relationship between the unemployment rate and the vacancy rate describes counterclockwise loops. This characteristic is also to be seen in figure 9.2, which represents the Beveridge curves for the United Kingdom, the United States, France, and Germany; more generally, it is to be found in all the OECD countries. Its source is the strong volatility of the vacancy rate with respect to the unemployment rate.

5.2.1   Diagnosing the Nature of Shocks

Scrutiny of figures 9.8 and 9.9 tells us that, if we look only at long-run stationary equilibria, aggregate shocks are characterized by *opposite* movements in unemployment and vacancies, but reallocation shocks are, on the contrary, marked by movements of these two variables in the *same* direction. These observations change somewhat if we take the transitory dynamics into account: figure 9.8 shows that path E_1E' also displays movements in the same direction as unemployment and vacant jobs following an aggregate shock. This result is caused by the absence of inertia in the adjustment of vacant jobs and has little chance of being verified in practice. Blanchard

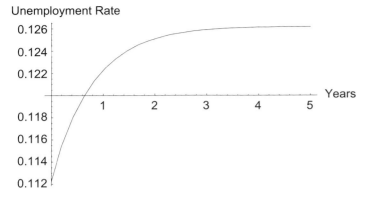

FIGURE 9.10
The impact of a permanent increase in the annual growth rate of the labor force from 0% to 2%.

and Diamond (1989, 1992) have remarked that taking adjustment costs for vacant jobs into account would attenuate the initial leap, and that an aggregate shock ought rather to be characterized by opposite movements of unemployment and vacant jobs. On the other hand, figure 9.9 suggests, if we look at both path E_1E' and the shifts in long-run equilibrium from E^* to E', that a reallocation shock should be marked rather by movements of unemployment and vacant jobs in the same direction.

Most empirical studies rely on this contrast in trying to assess the nature of the shocks affecting the economy. For the United States, Abraham and Katz (1986) and Blanchard and Diamond (1989) attribute the major portion of fluctuations in the unemployment rate over the cycle to aggregate shocks. Over the long run, though, the impact of aggregate shocks dwindles away, whereas the consequences of reallocation shocks persist. The most recent work of Davis and Haltiwanger (1999b) on American data for the period 1940–1990 comes to a more nuanced conclusion. They find that the effects of reallocation shocks on cyclical movements of employment are very sensitive to the hypotheses adopted in treating the data. The study of Jackman et al. (1991) on the United Kingdom suggests a preponderant influence of reallocation shocks, both over the cycle and in the long run.

5.2.2   The Propagation of Shocks

Analysis of the out-of-stationary-state dynamics allows us to shed some fresh light on the adjustment lag that follows a shock. Since all adjustment lags are provoked solely by the time necessary to effect hires, the law of motion of the unemployment rate entirely determines the dynamics of employment. Figure 9.10 represents the impact of an increase of 2% in the rate of growth of the labor force on the dynamics of the unemployment rate in the basic model, for the parameter values set out in table 9.9 and a replacement ratio b equal to 0.4. The stationary unemployment rate goes from 10.9% to 12.2%. We see that adjustment takes place very swiftly, since the unemployment rate rises from 10.9% to 11.7% in one year.

This rapidity likely underestimates the adjustment lags of the rates of unemployment and employment, because in the basic model that serves as the support for our analysis, the only mechanism through which shocks are propagated is the delay necessary to effect hires. The contributions of Merz (1995) and Andolfatto (1996) bear witness to this insufficiency. Their results suggest that such a model, even in a general equilibrium framework with an endogenous interest rate, does not make it possible to reproduce satisfactorily the movement of employment over time on American data. That makes it necessary to bring in other mechanisms by which shocks are propagated in order to represent the dynamics of employment satisfactorily. Den Haan et al. (2000) have constructed a matching model that takes the adjustment costs of capital into account and renders decisions about job destruction explicit (a subject studied in detail in chapter 12, section 2). Their model exhibits persistence effects that clearly fit better with reality. Hence it would seem important to take into account the interactions among job destruction decisions and the delays necessary to effect hires, and to adjust capital to its desired value, in order to represent the dynamics of employment more adequately. Hall (1995, 1999) nevertheless maintains that such mechanisms are still quite clearly insufficient. He suggests that the fragility of newly created jobs constitutes a potentially important source of propagation of shocks to unemployment and employment (see also Cole and Rogerson, 1999). Hall (1995) does indeed point out that negative shocks to employment are followed by an increase in the exit rate from employment for several years. A possible interpretation of this phenomenon is that the creation of durable jobs is the upshot of a long process of trial and error, during which numerous jobs are created and destroyed, since employers and workers are unable correctly to assess the return on jobs until periods of variable length have passed. Stochastic matching models (Jovanovic, 1979; Pissarides, 2000; and chapter 11, section 4.3, this book) in which the expected productivity of jobs is random, but a priori identical for all matches, allow us to formalize this type of phenomenon, and to include another source of unemployment inertia (for a critical appraisal of the capacity of the matching model to generate the observed business cycle, see Shimer, 2003).

6   THE EFFICIENCY OF MARKET EQUILIBRIUM

The matching process guiding the allocation of labor resources in the market is characterized by the presence of positive between-group externalities, and negative within-group congestion effects. An efficient state of the economy will combine these two types of externalities in an adequate fashion.

6.1   TRADING EXTERNALITIES

If the number of vacant jobs rises, each vacant job has a smaller probability of being matched with a worker, but each unemployed person has a higher probability of finding a job. Firms prefer to have as few vacant jobs as possible, so that they will be filled as rapidly as possible, but unemployed persons prefer the inverse: that there should be many vacant jobs, so as to increase their likelihood of being hired. Symmetrically, if the number of unemployed persons rises, each of them has fewer chances of finding a job, while firms see their chances of being able to fill their vacant positions increase. To put it in summary fashion: every unemployed person would like to be the only member of that category, and would like the category of vacant jobs facing him or her to be as full as possible, while every employer would like to be the only one with positions vacant, and to be facing a broad array of job-seekers. There are *congestion effects* within each category and *positive externalities* between the categories.

An omniscient planner who wished to maximize efficiency would internalize these externalities and would arrive at a social optimum in which the congestion effects and the positive externalities would be "blended" in the manner that best met his or her choice criterion. Now, wage negotiations taking place *after* the match-up between a vacant job and an unemployed person has occurred will not internalize these externalities, and the decentralized equilibrium of the labor market is not required a priori to correspond to a social optimum. Still, given that the partners to wage bargaining evidently have opposing interests, it is possible that in certain circumstances the optimal "blend" of positive externalities and congestion effects may occur at labor market equilibrium.

In what follows, to simplify the calculations, we will proceed within the framework of the basic model, but our conclusions would be exactly the same in the model with large firms (see Pissarides, 2000, chapter 7, and Hosios, 1990, for an exhaustive analysis of the effects of the job search process on global efficiency).

6.2 THE SOCIAL OPTIMUM

We begin by defining the social optimum when agents have no preference for the present (the interest rate r goes to zero). That allows us to characterize efficient allocation simply, setting aside the problem of dynamic optimization. The general case is addressed subsequently.

6.2.1 A Useful Particular Case

Assuming that individuals are risk-neutral, the planner's criterion corresponds to the discounted value of production per capita, since the marginal utility of a unit of output is independent of the level of income, and so is identical for employers, employees, and the unemployed. Reverting to the notations already utilized, total instantaneous production, denoted by Ω, is defined in the following manner:

$$\Omega = yL + zU - hV$$

Note that in this definition of aggregate production, search costs hV linked to the existence of vacant jobs are counted negatively, as they correspond to a loss. Note further that, strictly speaking, the gain z of an unemployed person does not include any transfers like unemployment benefits. In this formulation, z represents an indicator of the return on leisure or of domestic production. Finally, aggregate production evidently takes positive account of production yL of employees. Dividing by the size N of the labor force and recalling that, by definition, $v = \theta u$, we arrive at the expression of ouput per capita:

$$\omega = y(1 - u) + zu - h\theta u \tag{48}$$

With a constant labor force ($n = 0$), it is possible to characterize the properties of the social optimum very simply when the interest rate r goes to zero. In this case, the planner attempts to maximize output per capita, given the equilibrium of flows in the labor market described by equation (7) of the Beveridge curve. The planner's problem is then written:

$$\underset{\{\theta, u\}}{\text{Max}} \ \omega = y(1 - u) + zu - h\theta u$$

subject to constraint:

$$u = \frac{q}{q + \theta m(\theta)}$$

Substituting the value of u given by the Beveridge curve equation in ω, the planner's problem takes the form:

$$\underset{\theta}{\text{Max}} \left[y + \frac{q(z - h\theta - y)}{q + \theta m(\theta)} \right]$$

The first-order condition of this problem yields an equation implicitly defining the optimal value of labor market tightness:

$$\frac{[1 - \eta(\theta)](y - z)}{q + \theta m(\theta)\eta(\theta)} = \frac{h}{m(\theta)}, \qquad \eta(\theta) = -\frac{\theta m'(\theta)}{m(\theta)} \tag{49}$$

This equation highlights the elasticity $\eta(\theta)$ of the matching function with respect to the unemployment rate—readers will easily verify that $\eta(\theta) = U M_U(V, U)/M(V, U)$—although this quantity played no role in decentralized equilibrium. It acquires great importance here, for it is the sensitivity of the matching function that defines the blend of congestion effects and positive externalities in the matching process. When $r = 0$, comparison of relation (49) with equation (21) giving the value of tightness at decentralized labor market equilibrium shows that this equilibrium coincides with the social optimum if and only if $\gamma = \eta(\theta)$. This condition, known as the "Hosios condition," indicates that only a value of employee bargaining power equal to the elasticity of the matching function with respect to the unemployment rate gives the right blend of congestion effects and positive externalities. As a general rule, there is no reason for this equality to be satisfied, so market equilibrium is inefficient when wages are negotiated in a decentralized fashion. The following, more strictly technical, subsection shows that the Hosios condition remains true with a strictly positive interest rate.

6.2.2   The General Case

When the interest rate r is greater than zero, welfare analysis no longer comes down to the maximization of the criterion ω in the *stationary* state of the economy, for the social planner must now take into account the losses tied to the inertia present in the evolution of certain variables—here, the evolution of the unemployment rate described by equation (6). Again assuming that the labor force remains constant $(n = 0)$, the planner's problem takes the following form[4]:

$$\underset{\theta}{\text{Max}} \int_0^{+\infty} \omega e^{-rt}\, dt \tag{50}$$

subject to constraint:

$$\dot{u} = q(1 - u) - \theta m(\theta)u$$

Let μ be the multiplier associated with this constraint. The Hamiltonian of the planner's problem is written:

$$H = [y(1 - u) + zu - h\theta u]e^{-rt} + \mu[q(1 - u) - \theta m(\theta)u]$$

The first-order conditions are given by equations:

$$\frac{\partial H}{\partial \theta} = 0 \quad \text{and} \quad \frac{\partial H}{\partial u} = -\dot{\mu} \tag{51}$$

Differentiating the Hamiltonian with respect to θ, the first of conditions (51) entail, after rearranging terms:

$$he^{-rt} = -\mu m(\theta)[1 - \eta(\theta)] \tag{52}$$

And the transversality condition is written:

$$\underset{t \to \infty}{\text{Lim}}\ \mu \cdot u = 0$$

If we now derive the Hamiltonian with respect to u, the second of the first-order conditions (51) yields:

$$(z - y - h\theta)e^{-rt} - \mu[q + \theta m(\theta)] = -\dot{\mu} \tag{53}$$

From this point on we only consider the stationary equilibrium $(\dot{\theta} = 0)$, and derivation of relation (52) with respect to t entails $\dot{\mu} = -r\mu$. Substituting this value of $\dot{\mu}$ in (53) and taking into account the expression of μ extracted from the first-order condition (52), it is possible after several rearrangements to write the equation giving the optimal value of labor market tightness in the following form:

$$\frac{[1 - \eta(\theta)](y - z)}{r + q + \theta m(\theta)\eta(\theta)} = \frac{h}{m(\theta)} \tag{54}$$

Comparison of this relation with equation (21) giving the value of labor market tightness at decentralized labor market equilibrium shows that this equilibrium coincides with the social optimum if and only if $\gamma = \eta(\theta)$. So, with a strictly positive interest rate, we again find ourselves at the Hosios condition.

6.3 Is Labor Market Equilibrium Necessarily Inefficient?

In the matching model utilized to this point, the inefficiency of decentralized equilibrium comes from the absence of mechanisms giving agents an incentive to take the externalities linked to their decisions into account. However, in a great many situations, these mechanisms do exist, thanks to wage-setting rules or wage contracts more elaborate than those encompassed by our basic model.

A Model with Wage Posting

In the basic model wages are bargained over in such a way as to share the rent deriving from job–worker matches. But there exist other modes of wage setting. Employers often announce the remunerations attached to their vacant jobs, for example. In order to show that a mode of wage setting different from that of the basic model is capable of restoring efficiency to decentralized equilibrium, we will consider a model close to that proposed by Moene (1997). He assumes that wages are no longer bargained over but are fixed by employers at the time they open up vacant jobs.

The economy comprises a large number of labor pools or "islands" indexed by i. The mobility of workers between labor pools is perfect, and a vacant job can be created in any labor pool whatsoever. At every instant, the number of hires in each labor pool is determined by a matching function identical to the one considered hitherto. In consequence, if there are U_i unemployed persons and V_i vacant jobs, the exit rate from unemployment and the rate at which vacancies are filled in labor pool i are respectively equal to $\theta_i m(\theta_i)$ and $m(\theta_i)$. In each labor pool, the employers with vacant jobs decide to announce a hiring wage, denoted by w_i. We shall assume that all employers offer the same wage in each labor pool.[5] This wage is not renegotiable, and applies throughout the employer–employee relationship.

The hypothesis of workers' perfect mobility implies that the expected utility of an unemployed person is the same in all the labor pools, so it will simply be denoted by V_u. Assuming further that the job destruction rate q is identical in each labor pool, the expected utility V_{ei} of a person employed in labor pool i satisfies:

$$rV_{ei} = w_i + q(V_u - V_{ei}) \tag{55}$$

If the instantaneous gain z of an unemployed person is the same everywhere, the expected utility V_u of a person in search of work satisfies:

$$rV_u = z + \theta_i m(\theta_i)(V_{ei} - V_u) \quad \forall i \tag{56}$$

Eliminating V_{ei} between these last two equations, we get, for given V_u, a decreasing relation between w_i and θ_i taking the form:

$$\theta_i m(\theta_i) = (r + q)\frac{(rV_u - z)}{w_i - rV_u} \tag{57}$$

This last equation reveals the implications of the competition among entrepreneurs to attract workers into their respective labor pools. Each entrepreneur must offer the same expected utility V_u to those in search of work, but this objective may be attained in several different ways. An entrepreneur may open up few jobs, which entails a low exit rate from unemployment $\theta_i m(\theta_i)$, balanced against a high wage. Or he or she might open up many jobs, which entails a high exit rate from unemployment, balanced against a low wage. Mobility of the unemployed among the different labor pools thus entails that each entrepreneur must trade off between opening up a large number of jobs and offering high wages in order to attract enough workers.

The Efficiency of Decentralized Equilibrium

For a given number U_i of unemployed persons in pool i, the optimal strategy for the entrepreneurs present in this pool consists of offering a wage w_i so as to maximize the expected gain from vacant jobs, subject to constraint (57). Now the expected gain Π_{vi} from an unfilled job, and the expected profit Π_{ei} from a filled one in pool i, are defined by:

$$r\Pi_{vi} = -h + m(\theta_i)(\Pi_{ei} - \Pi_{vi}) \tag{58}$$

$$r\Pi_{ei} = y - w_i + q(\Pi_{vi} - \Pi_{ei}) \tag{59}$$

Eliminating Π_{ei} between these last two equations, we get the expression of the profit expected from a vacant job as a function of the wage w_i and the labor market tightness θ_i:

$$\Pi_{vi} = \frac{-h(r+q) + m(\theta_i)(y - w_i)}{r + q + m(\theta_i)} \tag{60}$$

We can consider that relation (57) defines θ_i as a function of w_i; setting to zero the derivative of Π_{vi} with respect to w_i then gives us the first-order condition of the entrepreneurs' problem in labor pool i. It comes to:

$$\left[(y - w_i)m'(\theta_i)\frac{\partial \theta_i}{\partial w_i} - m(\theta_i) \right] [r + q + m(\theta_i)]$$

$$-m'(\theta_i)\frac{\partial \theta_i}{\partial w_i}[m(\theta_i)(y - w_i) - h(r+q)] = 0 \tag{61}$$

with, following (57):

$$\frac{\partial \theta_i}{\partial w_i} = \frac{-\theta_i}{[1 - \eta(\theta_i)](w_i - rV_u)}, \qquad \eta(\theta_i) \equiv -\frac{\theta_i m'(\theta_i)}{m(\theta_i)} \tag{62}$$

The free entry condition entails that the entrepreneurs open up jobs as long as the opportunities for profit linked to the opening up of a vacant job are positive. This comes to a stop when $\Pi_{vi} = 0$. The definition (60) of the profit expected from a vacant job entails, then, that at equilibrium the last term between brackets in the first-order condition (61) is null. Substituting the value of $\partial \theta_i / \partial w_i$ specified by (62) in (61) and rearranging terms, we arrive at:

$$w_i = rV_u + \eta(\theta_i)(y - rV_u)$$

Comparison of this equation with equality (19), which characterizes the negotiated wage in the basic model, shows that the mode of wage setting we have just set out arrives systematically at the Hosios condition $\gamma = \eta(\theta_i)$ and so ensures the efficiency of decentralized equilibrium. This example suggests that competition among firms to attract workers is capable of restoring the efficiency of market equilibrium. It is worth noting, however, that this result arises from the hypothesis that labor contracts are not renegotiated, since they specify a fixed wage. Actually, if $\gamma \neq \eta(\theta_i)$, either party has an interest in proposing a new round of wage bargaining once the hires have been made. So the equilibrium efficiency of the market rests on the hypothesis that employers can make very firm commitments—and this is not necessarily satisfied.

When Union Power Leads to Efficient Allocation

It is interesting to note that other ways of organizing the labor market also make it possible to arrive at an efficient allocation. In particular, a union setting wages for the economy as a whole chooses an efficient allocation if its objective is to maximize the expected utility of the unemployed. This is easily seen if we note that the expected utility V_u of an unemployed person, eliminating V_e from equations (12) and (13), is written:

$$rV_u = \frac{z(r + q) + w\theta m(\theta)}{r + q + \theta m(\theta)}$$

Maximization of V_u subject to the labor demand constraint (11) gives the solution (54) corresponding to the social optimum.

Efficiency and the Incompleteness of Markets

In the presence of externalities, the inefficiency of decentralized equilibrium is caused by the fact that the economy does not comprise enough markets capable of giving individuals the incentive to take all the consequences of their decisions into account. But in that situation, there are incentives to create supplementary markets, and thus the possibility of offering mutually advantageous contracts. In the matching model, as in every configuration, it is necessary to specify the origin of the incompleteness of markets. From this standpoint, Greenwald and Stiglitz (1988) and Mortensen and Pissarides (1999) have proposed models in which intermediaries intervene in the labor market, offering contracts to both unemployed persons and employers with vacancies, in which the wages that will apply to future hires are specified as a function of the amount of time that passes before the hires take place. In that setting, competition among the intermediaries leads to a social optimum.

These examples show that it is possible to imagine institutions compatible with the efficiency of decentralized equilibrium. But it is far from certain that the *actual* functioning of the different labor markets comes close to these theoretical constructions. At the present time, the efficiency of decentralized equilibrium remains an open question.

7 SUMMARY AND CONCLUSION

- In most industrialized countries, job creation and destruction are large-scale phenomena. The combined total of these two flows amounts to between 15% and 30% of total employment every year. Movements in employment most often take place within the same sector. There is no tendency for the between-sector reallocation of jobs to increase.

- Workers' reallocation is just as intense in the United States as it is in Europe. But in Europe, job-to-job mobility predominates, while in the United States (and Japan), it is much more common to pass through unemployment. The result is that in Europe, the exit rate from unemployment is much weaker than it is in the United States.

- In the presence of transaction costs, reallocation of jobs and workers can lead to the simultaneous existence of unfilled jobs and unemployed persons. The process through which unemployed persons and vacant jobs are brought together is usually represented by a *matching function*, indicating the number of hires as a function of the number of vacant jobs and unemployed persons. This function is characterized by positive between-group externalities (the unemployed have an interest in job creation by firms) and congestion effects (each job-seeker has an interest in the number of job-seekers being as low as possible). The matching process and the equilibrium of workers' flows entail a Beveridge curve that links the unemployment rate to the vacancy rate.

- The simultaneous presence of labor reallocation and transaction costs gives a competitive advantage to those who hold jobs. Empirical work suggests that rents are shared between employers and wage-earners. This rent sharing takes concrete form in wage bargaining, and entails a negative relationship between the unemployment rate and the wage negotiated. The "wage curve" that results takes the place of the labor supply function found in models of perfect competition. Empirical studies estimate that the elasticity of the real wage with respect to the unemployment rate is slight, on the order of -0.1.

- The wage curve, together with labor demand, determines wages and the equilibrium unemployment rate. The matching model allows us to specify the impact of different parameters, such as the gains of the unemployed, the interest rate, the growth rate of the labor force, labor productivity, and the job destruction rate, on labor market equilibrium. Simulations based on the calibration of a simple matching model suggest that the unemployment differential between continental Europe and the United States cannot be attributed solely to the gap between replacement ratios. They also indicate that, in this model, the effects of interest rates, labor productivity, and labor force growth on the unemployment rate are too slight to explain the large differences in unemployment rates across these countries in the 1980s and the 1990s.

- Study of the out-of-stationary-state dynamics of the matching model makes it possible to distinguish between the effects of an *aggregate* shock (one affecting aggregate supply or aggregate demand) and those of a reallocation shock (one relating to the restructuring of production units). It turns out that we can attribute a shift along the Beveridge curve to an aggregate shock, whereas a reallocation shock is characterized by a shift of this curve as a whole. In the first case, there is an inverse relationship between the unemployment rate and the vacancy rate; in the second case, they vary in the same direction.

- Transaction costs in the labor market lie at the source of exchange externalities which entail that decentralized equilibrium is generally inefficient when wages are bargained over between employers and workers. There do, nevertheless, exist modes of wage determination such as, for example, competition among entrepreneurs who post wages to attract workers that make it possible to restore the efficiency of decentralized equilibrium. Overall, the inefficiency of decentralized equilibrium is an open question.

8 RELATED TOPICS IN THE BOOK

- Chapter 3, section 1: Job search theory

- Chapter 3, section 2.1: Equilibrium search model

- Chapter 4, section 3: Labor demand and adjustment costs

- Chapter 5, section 2.2: Specific irreversible investment and rent sharing

- Chapter 7, section 2: Bargaining theory

- Chapter 10, section 1: The capitalization effect versus creative destruction

- Chapter 11, section 2: Active labor market policies

- Chapter 12, section 2: The effects of employment protection

- Chapter 12, section 3: Taxes and labor market equilibrium

9 FURTHER READINGS

Davis, S., and Haltiwanger, J. (1999), ''Gross job flows,'' in Ashenfelter, O., and Card, D. (eds.), *Handbook of Labor Economics*, vol. 3B, Amsterdam: Elsevier Science/North-Holland.

Davis, S., Haltiwanger, J., and Schuh, S. (1996), *Job Creation and Destruction*, Cambridge, Mass.: MIT Press.

Kuhn, P. (ed.) (2002), *Losing Work, Moving On: International Perspectives on Worker Displacement*, Kalamazoo, Michigan: Upjohn Institute for Employment Research.

Mortensen, D., and Pissarides, C. (1999), "Job reallocation, employment fluctuations and unemployment," in Woodford, M., and Taylor, J. (eds.), *Handbook of Macroeconomics*, vol. 1B, chap. 18, pp. 1171–1228, Amsterdam: Elsevier Science/North-Holland.

Petrongolo, B., and Pissarides, C. (2001), "Looking into the black box: A survey of the matching function," *Journal of Economic Literature*, 39, pp. 390–431.

Pissarides, C. (2000), *Equilibrium Unemployment Theory*, 2nd ed., Cambridge, Mass.: MIT Press.

REFERENCES

Abowd, J., Corbel, P., and Kramarz, F. (1999), "The entry and exit of workers and the growth of employment: An analysis of French establishments," *Review of Economics and Statistics*, 81(2), pp. 170–187.

Abowd, J., and Lemieux, T. (1993), "The effect of product market competition on collective bargaining agreements: The case of foreign competition in Canada," *Quarterly Journal of Economics*, 108, pp. 983–1004.

Abraham, K., and Katz, L. (1986), "Cyclical unemployment: Sectoral shifts or aggregate disturbances?" *Journal of Political Economy*, 94, pp. 507–522.

Anderson, P., and Meyer, D. (1994), "The extent and consequences of job turnover," *Brookings Papers on Economic Activity, Microeconomics*, pp. 177–236.

Andolfatto, D. (1996), "Business cycle and labor-market search," *American Economic Review*, 86, pp. 112–132.

Becker, G. (1964), *Human Capital: A Theoretical and Empirical Analysis with Special Reference to Education*, New York: Columbia University Press.

Beveridge, W. (1944), *Full Employment in a Free Society*, London: Allen and Unwin.

Blanchard, O., and Diamond, P. (1989), "The Beveridge curve," *Brookings Papers on Economic Activity*, 1, pp. 1–76.

Blanchard, O., and Diamond, P. (1990), "The aggregate matching function," in Diamond, P. (ed.), *Growth, Productivity and Unemployment*, Cambridge, Mass.: MIT Press.

Blanchard, O., and Diamond, P. (1992), "The flow approach to labor market," *American Economic Review*, 82, pp. 354–359.

Blanchard, O., and Diamond, P. (1994), "Ranking, unemployment duration and wages," *Review of Economic Studies*, 61, pp. 417–434.

Blanchflower, D., and Oswald, A. (1995), *The Wage Curve*, Cambridge, Mass.: MIT Press.

Blanchflower, D., Oswald, A., and Sanfrey, P. (1996), "Wages, profits and rent sharing," *Quarterly Journal of Economics*, 111(1), pp. 227–251.

Bowden, R. (1980), "On the existence and secular stability of a u-v loci," *Economica*, 47, pp. 35–50.

Burda, M., and Wyplosz, C. (1994), "Gross worker and job flows in Europe," *European Economic Review*, 38, pp. 1287–1315.

Burgess, S. (1993), "A model of competition between unemployed and employed job-searchers: An application to the unemployment outflow in Britain," *Economic Journal*, 103, pp. 1190–1204.

Cahuc, P., and Wasmer, E. (2001), "Does intrafirm bargaining matter in the large firm's matching model?" *Macroeconomic Dynamics*, 5, pp. 742–747.

Cole, H., and Rogerson, R. (1999), "Can the Mortensen-Pissarides matching model match the business cycle facts?" *International Economic Review*, 40(4), pp. 933–959.

Coles, M., and Smith, E. (1996), "Cross-section estimation of the matching function: Evidence from England and Wales," *Economica*, 63, pp. 589–598.

Coles, M., and Smith, E. (1998), "Marketplaces and matching," *International Economic Review*, 39, pp. 239–254.

Davis, S., and Haltiwanger, J. (1992), "Gross job creation, gross job destruction, and employment reallocation," *Quarterly Journal of Economics*, 107, pp. 819–863.

Davis, S., and Haltiwanger, J. (1999a), "Gross job flows," in Ashenfelter, O., and Card, D. (eds.), *Handbook of Labor Economics*, vol. 3B, Amsterdam: Elsevier Science/North-Holland.

Davis, S., and Haltiwanger, J. (1999b), "On the driving forces behind cyclical movements in employment and job reallocation," *American Economic Review*, 89(5), pp. 1234–1258.

Davis, S., Haltiwanger, J., and Schuh, S. (1996), *Job Creation and Destruction*, Cambridge, Mass.: MIT Press.

Den Haan, W., Ramey, G., and Watson, J. (2000), "Job destruction and propagation of shocks," *American Economic Review*, 90(3), pp. 482–498.

Fitoussi, J.-P., and Phelps, E. (1988), *The Slump in Europe*, London: Basil Blackwell.

Greenwald, B., and Stiglitz, J. (1988), "Pareto inefficiency of market economies: Search and efficiency wage models," *American Economic Review, Papers and Proceedings*, 78, pp. 351–355.

Grossman, S., and Hart, O. (1986), "The costs and benefits of ownership: A theory of vertical and lateral integration," *Journal of Political Economy*, 94, pp. 691–719.

Grout, P. (1984), "Investment and wage in the absence of binding contracts: A Nash bargaining approach," *Econometrica*, 52, pp. 449–460.

Hall, R. (1979), "A theory of the natural unemployment rate and the duration of employment," *Journal of Monetary Economics*, 5, pp. 153–169.

Hall, R. (1995), "Lost jobs," *Brookings Papers on Economic Activity*, 1, pp. 221–273.

Hall, R. (1999), "Labor-market frictions and employment fluctuations," in Woodford, M., and Taylor, J. (eds.), *Handbook of Macroeconomics*, vol. 1B, chap. 17, pp. 1137–1170, Amsterdam: Elsevier Science/North-Holland.

Hamermesh, D., Hassink, W., and van Ours, J. (1996), "Job turnover and labor turnover: A taxonomy of employment dynamics," *Annales d'Economie et de Statistique*, 34, pp. 1264–1292.

Hart, O., and Moore, J. (1990), "Property rights and the nature of the firms," *Journal of Political Economy*, 98, pp. 1119–1158.

Hosios, D. (1990), "On the efficiency of matching and related models of search and unemployment," *Review of Economic Studies*, 57, pp. 279–298.

Jackman, R., Layard, R., and Savouri, S. (1991), "Mismatch: A framework for thought," in Padoa Schioppa, F. (ed.), *Mismatch and Labour Mobility*, Cambridge, U.K.: CEPR, Cambridge University Press.

Jovanovic, B. (1979), "Firm specific capital and turnover," *Journal of Political Economy*, 87, pp. 1246–1260.

Kuhn, P. (2002), "Summary and synthesis," in Kuhn, P. (ed.), *Losing Work, Moving On: International Perspective on Worker Displacement*, chap. 1, Kalamazoo, Michigan: Upjohn Institute for Employment Research.

Kuhn, P., and Sweetman, A. (1999), "Vulnerable seniors: Unions, tenure and wages following permanent job loss," *Journal of Labor Economics*, 17, pp. 671–693.

Lagarde, S., Maurin, E., and Torelli, C. (1995), "Flows of workers and job reallocation," mimeo, Insee: Direction des Statistiques Démographiques et Sociales.

MacLeod, B., and Malcomson, J. (1993), "Investment, holdup and the form of market contracts," *American Economic Review*, 83, pp. 811–837.

Merz, M. (1995), "Search in the labor market and the real business cycle," *Journal of Monetary Economics*, 36, pp. 269–300.

Millard, S., and Mortensen, D. (1997), "The unemployment and welfare effects of labour market policy: A comparison of the U.S. and U.K., in Snower, D., and de la Dehesa, G. (eds.), *Unemployment Policy: Government Options for the Labour Market*, Cambridge, U.K.: Cambridge University Press.

Moene, E. (1997), "Competitive search equilibrium," *Journal of Political Economy*, 105, pp. 385–411.

Mortensen, D. (1994), "The cyclical behavior of job and worker flows," *Journal of Economic Dynamic and Control*, 18, pp. 1121–1142.

Mortensen, D., and Pissarides, C. (1994), "Job creation and job destruction in the theory of unemployment," *Review of Economic Studies*, 61, pp. 397–415.

Mortensen, D., and Pissarides, C. (1999), "Job reallocation, employment fluctuations and unemployment," in Woodford, M., and Taylor, J. (eds.), *Handbook of Macroeconomics*, vol. 1B, chap. 18, pp. 1171–1228, Amsterdam: Elsevier Science/North-Holland.

Mumford, K., and Smith, P. (1999), "The hiring function reconsidered: On closing the circle," *Oxford Bulletin of Economics and Statistics*, 61, pp. 343–364.

OECD (1995), *Employment Outlook*, Paris: OECD.

OECD (1996), *Employment Outlook*, Paris: OECD.

Osborne, M., and Rubinstein, A. (1990), *Bargaining and Markets*, San Diego: Academic Press.

Petrongolo, B. (2001), "Re-employment probabilities and returns to matching," *Journal of Labor Economics*, 19, pp. 716–741.

Petrongolo, B., and Pissarides, C. (2001), "Looking into the black box: A survey of the matching function," *Journal of Economic Literature*, 39, pp. 390–431.

Pissarides, C. (1979), "Job matching with state employment agencies and random search," *Economic Journal*, 89, pp. 818–833.

Pissarides, C. (2000), *Equilibrium Unemployment Theory*, 2nd ed., Cambridge, Mass.: MIT Press.

Rowthorn, R. (1995), "Capital formation and unemployment," *Oxford Review of Economic Policy*, 11(1), pp. 26–39.

Shimer, R. (2003), "The cyclical behavior of equilibrium unemployment and vacancies: Evidence and theory," NBER Working Paper No. w9536.

Van Reenen, J. (1996), "The creation and capture of economic rents: Wages and innovations in a panel of UK companies," *Quarterly Journal of Economics*, 111(1), pp. 195–226.

Williamson, O. (1975), *Markets and Hierarchies*, New York: Free Press.

Yashiv, E. (2000), "The determinants of equilibrium unemployment," *American Economic Review*, 90(5), pp. 1297–1322.

TECHNOLOGICAL PROGRESS, GLOBALIZATION, AND INEQUALITIES

CONTENTS

In this chapter, we will:

- Observe the impact of technological progress on job creation and job destruction

- Analyze the effects of globalization and biased technological progress on wage inequality and unemployment

- Learn what the economic consequences of immigration are

- Compare the American and European experience with respect to wage inequality and unemployment

INTRODUCTION

Are inequality and unemployment the consequences of technological progress and globalization? This question has provoked many disputes, which the media have blown up, with the most far-fetched answers often getting the greatest attention. The specter of machines devouring jobs is repeatedly conjured up whenever technological innovation makes it possible to replace men with mechanical equipment for the accomplishment of certain tasks. Multinational firms wiping out jobs in rich countries in order to exploit workers in poor countries is another image frequently invoked to explain the rising tide of unemployment, or increasing inequality.

The notion that technological progress destroys jobs, taken to the limit, gives rise to the most fantastic predictions. At the beginning of the nineteenth century, Sismondi foresaw a world "where the King sits alone on his island, endlessly turning cranks to produce, with automatons, all that England now manufactures" (Sismondi, 1991, p. 563). More recently, in a book that quickly became a worldwide bestseller and was greeted by reviewers as a prophecy, J. Rifkin predicted the "end of work" as the West moves toward an information economy practically devoid of workers (Rifkin, 1995, p. 93). Fortunately a number of economists have criticized this view. In particular O. J. Blanchard, a macroeconomist and currently a member of the faculty at MIT, took strong exception to Rifkin's work, noting in an interview with the French magazine *Capital* that there has not been a robust statistical relationship between growth due to technological progress and unemployment for more than a century.

Rifkin's mode of argument is to cite examples and situations—numerous, but always one-sided—which, taken together, can give the impression that technological progress actually does destroy jobs and push up unemployment. The fact is that we need to take into account *all* reallocations of jobs and manpower. On average more than 10% of jobs are destroyed every year in the rich countries, but this phenomenon is largely offset by job creation, and we observe no systematic rise in unemployment over the long term (see chapters 8 and 9). So, in order to assess the impact of technological progress on employment, we have to use a conceptual framework that combines the interactions among technological progress, job destruction, *and* job creation. Conclusions based on accumulated examples neglect the fact that technological progress sets off the process of *creative destruction* highlighted by Schumpeter (1934), the impact of which on unemployment is a priori ambiguous, since it both favors job creation and engenders job destruction. Analysis, both theoretical and empirical, of the impact of technological progress on the level of employment has to be carried out on the macroeconomic scale, not that of particular firms or sectors.

This chapter is devoted to the relationships among what happens in the labor market, technological progress, and the creation and destruction of jobs. Technological progress is an important component of growth and contributes to the endless restructuring of production units. As we shall see, it has opposing effects on employment, which it favors by creating opportunities for profit, but which it also destroys through restructuring. Empirical research confirms these theoretical results, suggesting that technological progress has an ambiguous effect on employment. In section 2, we study the effects of technological progress and international competition on wage inequalities among workers with different skill levels. In this regard, the experience of the industrialized countries of the OECD over the last two decades of the twentieth century is particularly interesting. These countries have indeed faced rising wage inequality, or increased risk of unemployment among those with the fewest skills. With the help of this documented experience, we will show how technological progress, international trade, international migration, changes in labor market institutions, and organizational change all affect wages and job opportunities according to skill level. For this purpose it is instructive, as we will see, to contrast a "European" model, characterized by significant compression of wages, thanks to a minimum wage and higher minimum social standards, and an "Anglo-Saxon" model in which the state intervenes in the labor market to a much less marked extent.

1 DOES TECHNOLOGICAL PROGRESS DESTROY MORE JOBS THAN IT CREATES?

Technological progress contributes significantly to output growth, but its effect on employment is a priori ambiguous. On the one hand, by improving labor productivity, it increases profits and stimulates more job creation. But on the other, it destroys jobs the technology of which is too outdated to be profitable. Hence technological progress drives a process of job creation and destruction, the outcome of which no one knows beforehand.

1.1 TECHNOLOGICAL PROGRESS AND PRODUCTIVITY

Technological progress is not applied in identical fashion to all the inputs, but whatever form it takes, it allows us to explain a large part of productivity growth.

1.1.1 Different Forms of Technological Progress

Technological progress improves inputs efficiency. Thus, in the seventeenth and eighteenth centuries, the introduction of new crops and the abandonment of the practice of fallowing land led to a strong increase in agricultural production per hectare and per worker. In the nineteenth and twentieth centuries, mastery of the powers of steam, electricity, and internal combustion made it possible greatly to increase the ratio of industrial production to the quantities of inputs used. At the end of the twentieth century, innovations in the areas of computerization and telecommunications improved productivity in the service sector. Over a span of centuries, history has been marked by technological innnovations that have strongly increased the efficiency of the inputs in the rich countries.

Technological progress does not alter the efficiency of the different inputs uniformly. It generally arrives as an abrupt change in the way the factors are combined, and even the disappearance of some of them. The internal combustion engine, for example, rendered the horse superfluous as a provider of traction. Still, at the aggregate level the number of inputs is necessarily limited, and it is reasonable to think that technological progress is constantly altering their proportions. In the simplest case, we identify only two inputs, capital K and labor L; the quantity Y produced is then defined by relation $Y = F(K, L, t)$, where F designates the production function and t represents the time index. It is this last argument that allows us to take into account the reshaping of the production function due to technological progress, of which three different forms are normally distinguished.

Let us suppose that the production function is homogeneous of degree 1 with respect to K and L. If technological progress increases the efficiency of each input in strictly proportional fashion, the production function can be written $F(K, L, t) = A(t)F(K, L)$, where $A(t)$ designates an indicator of the state of technology. This form of technological progress has been described as neutral by Hicks, since for a given capital–labor ratio, it leaves the ratio of marginal productivities unchanged. Another term often used for this type of technological progress is "nonbiased." When technological progress increases the productivities of the inputs in nonproportional fashion, then we describe it as "biased" in favor of labor or capital, as the case may be. If innovations make it possible to obtain the same production with less labor, we say they are *labor saving* or (since they increase the efficiency of this factor) *labor augmenting*. We then write $F(K, L, t) = F[K, A_L(t)L]$, where $A_L(t)$ is an indicator of labor efficiency. Finally, if technological progress is *capital saving* (i.e., spares capital, or increases its efficiency), then the formal notation is $F(K, L, t) = F[A_K(t)K, L]$, where $A_K(t)$ is an indicator of capital efficiency. Note that, whatever its form, technological progress increases overall production for given quantities of the inputs.

In attempting to assess the contribution of each input to rising production, we need to remember that three kinds of technological progress are liable to appear simultaneously.

1.1.2 Technological Progress and Growth

In order to take the different aspects of technological progress into account, we write the aggregate production function as $Y = AF(A_K K, A_L L)$, leaving out the time index for simplicity. Technological progress is represented by an increase in the coefficients A, A_K, or A_L. Let Δ be the difference operator (for example, at date t, $\Delta K_t = K_t - K_{t-1}$), and $F_i(A_K K, A_L L)$, $i = 1, 2$, the partial derivative of function F with respect to its ith argument. An expansion of this function limited to the first order gives:

$$\Delta Y = (\Delta A)F + [(\Delta K)A_K + (\Delta A_K)K]AF_1 + [(\Delta L)A_L + (\Delta A_L)L]AF_2 \tag{1}$$

In competitive markets, profit maximization entails that the marginal productivity of each input, $AA_K F_1$ and $AA_L F_2$, equals the costs of these inputs. Let $\alpha = L(AA_L F_2)/Y$ be the share of labor in total income. Assuming constant returns to scale, the share of capital is then equal to $(1 - \alpha)$. Let us further agree to denote the growth rate of a variable x by g_x. Dividing both members of equation (1) by Y, we arrive at the celebrated decomposition of Solow (1957):

$$g_Y = g_A + (1 - \alpha)(g_K + g_{A_K}) + \alpha(g_L + g_{A_L}) \tag{2}$$

According to this decomposition, output growth comes from three different sources: technological progress (which can itself take three distinct forms), capital accumulation, and the growth of the labor force (most often measured by the number of hours worked); the contribution of these last two sources is proportional to their share of total income. Using series that describe the time path of the inputs and their respective share in GDP, formula (2) allows us to estimate the term $g_A + (1 - \alpha)g_{A_K} + \alpha g_{A_L}$ linked to technological progress and commonly called the "Solow residual." In all the research carried out using this approach, the significance of the technological progress term is invariably emphasized.

Much effort has been expended on explaining the determinants of the Solow residual. Denison (1967) and Jorgenson (1980) attempted to take into account improvement in the *quality* of inputs. In particular, the prolongation of schooling and better human health both help to raise the quality of labor, independently of technological progress. In order to take improvement in the quality of labor into account, Denison (1967) and Jorgenson (1980) measure aggregate labor L as follows:

$$\Delta \ln L = \sum_{i=1}^{q} Q_i \Delta \ln L_i, \qquad \text{where } Q_i = \left(\frac{w_i L_i}{\sum_{j=1}^{q} w_j L_j} \right)$$

In this expression, L_i and w_i designate respectively the number of hours and the hourly wage of labor of quality $i = 1, \ldots, q$, and Δ represents the difference operator. This formulation entails that as the proportion of workers receiving high wages increases, aggregate labor grows more quickly. Application of this method shows that improvement in the quality of labor is an important source of growth: in the United States between 1948 and 1968, according to Jorgenson (1980), the labor factor grew by 1.73% per annum, of which 0.72% was assignable to the quality of labor and 1.01% to hours worked. The same study shows that educational level plays an essential role, explaining about half the growth in the quality of labor.

Assessing the evolution of the quality of capital also poses specific problems. Growth may arise from the improved quality of new, more efficient equipment as it replaces older installations. Hence we make a distinction between *embodied* technological progress, which increases the productivity of new equipment only, and *disembodied* progress, which increases the productivity of capital as a whole. This distinction is important in pinpointing the sources of growth, since disembodied technological progress affects growth independently of capital accumulation, whereas investment must take place in order for embodied technological progress to have an effect on production (Solow, 1960; Jorgenson, 1966). Moreover, taking the embodied character of technological progress into account affects our assessment of the stock of capital. This is easy to grasp once we note that it is possible to represent embodied technological progress by assuming that the efficiency of investment varies over the course of time. In the economy with two goods (labor, and a good consumed and invested) envisaged by the simplest models of growth, this idea is formalized by assuming that one unit of investment at date t produces q_t units of capital. The variable q_t thus represents the productivity of new equipment, which can evolve over time. From this perspective, the capital stock at date t depends on the past values of

q_t. Denoting the rate of capital depreciation by $\delta \in [0, 1]$ and investment by I_t, the law of motion of capital is written $K_t = (1 - \delta)K_{t-1} + q_{t-1}I_{t-1}$, and by successive iterations we get:

$$K_t = (1 - \delta)^T K_{t-T} + \sum_{i=1}^{T}(1 - \delta)^{i-1} q_{t-i}I_{t-i}$$

This expression demonstrates that the evolution of the efficiency of investment has to be taken into account in order correctly to assess the stock of capital. Some of the work in this domain suggests that this problem is significant. For example, Greenwood et al. (1997) estimate that technological progress embodied in capital explains 60% of the growth of production per hour worked in the United States in the period 1954−1990 (see the survey of Hercowitz, 1998, and Scarpetta et al., 2000).

Table 10.1 shows that the Solow residual (denoted by r_S) contributed a very significant portion of GDP per capita growth in the G7 countries during the last three decades of the twentieth century. This result signifies that technological progress profoundly influences growth in the industrialized countries.

On this basis, the absence of significant increase in the Solow residual in the 1980s in the United States (see columns 2 and 4 of table 10.1), and its low value there in comparison to that in other countries, has raised a number of questions, because new information technologies were spreading throughout this period, especially in this country. In the celebrated phrase of Robert Solow, during the 1980s computers were everywhere except in the statistics. There are probably several reasons for this apparent paradox, ranging from the effect of the oil shocks on investment to the time it took for the new technology to spread, as new jobs that were not highly sensitive to technological progress developed in the services sector. The good performance of the

Table 10.1

Growth rates (in percentage) of GDP per capita (g_y) and total factor productivity in the private sector (r_S) between 1970 and 1998.

Country	1970–1980		1980–1990		1990–1998	
	g_y	r_S	g_y	r_S	g_y	r_S
Germany	2.6	1.2	2.0	1.1	1.0	1.0
United States	2.1	0.7	2.3	0.8	2.0	1.1
France	2.7	1.5	1.8	1.5	0.9	0.9
Japan	3.3	1.6	3.4	1.6	1.1	0.8
Italy	3.1	1.4	2.2	1.2	1.2	1.2
Canada	2.8	0.6	1.6	0.3	1.1	0.7
United Kingdom	1.8	1.7	2.5	2.0	1.7	1.2

Source: Scarpetta et al. (2000, tables 1 and 6).

U.S. economy in the 1990s and the higher value of the Solow residual for this period suggest that the effect of the new technologies did in the end show up in the statistics, following a period of adaptation during which productivity gains were slight (Aghion, 2002). The conjunction of a relatively high Solow residual with a low unemployment rate in the United States during the 1990s might suggest that technological progress is favorable to employment.

Economic analysis does not come to such a stark conclusion. It prefers to isolate certain mechanisms that allow us to explain why the growth in overall factor productivity leads either to a fall in unemployment or to a rise, as the case may be.

1.2 THE CAPITALIZATION EFFECT

Technological progress improves labor productivity and therefore increases the profit due to job creation. This so-called *capitalization* effect changes the behavior of agents and influences labor market equilibrium. The basic model from chapter 9, slightly modified, allows us to study the consequences of the capitalization effect. Technological progress can easily be brought into the basic model by assuming that an individual employee's (exogenous) production y grows at a constant rate denoted by g. We may note that there exists a relationship between the components of the Solow residual and the growth rate of labor productivity. Individual production $y \equiv Y/L$ grows at rate $g = g_Y - g_L$, and if we denote the Solow residual by $r_S = g_A + (1 - \alpha)g_K + \alpha g_{A_L}$, equation (2) entails $g = r_S + (1 - \alpha)(g_K - g_L)$. Individual productivity growth rate is equal to the Solow residual if the capital–labor ratio, K/L, and the share α of labor in total income remain constant. On the other hand, a reduction in the growth rate of the capital stock, which might for example occur as certain firms relocate to low-wage countries, leads to a reduction in the growth rate of labor productivity.

1.2.1   The Discount Rate and the Capitalization Effect

It turns out that productivity growth changes act like changes in the discount rate and thus play a part in intertemporal choices.

The "Effective" Discount Rate and Growth

If production grows at rate g, the incomes of agents increase at this rate as well along a balanced growth path (which we can also refer to as stationary equilibrium; in what follows we will use both expressions indifferently). Consequently we need to modify the expressions of expected profit and utility, returning to chapter 9, section 3.2, and considering a short interval of time lying between dates t and $t + dt$. If Π_e designates the profit expected from a job occupied at date t, at stationary equilibrium this profit will have increased by $g\,dt$ % between dates t and $t + dt$. Let w be the real wage and let Π_v be the profit expected from a vacant job at date t. Relation (8) from chapter 9, giving the value of the profit expected from a filled job in the stationary state, will now be written:

$$\Pi_e = \frac{1}{1 + r\,dt}[(y - w)\,dt + q\,dt(1 + g\,dt)\Pi_v + (1 - q\,dt)(1 + g\,dt)\Pi_e] \tag{3}$$

This equation indicates that the discounted expected profit from a job is equal to the discounted sum of the flow of instantaneous profit $(y - w)\,dt$ over interval of time dt and of the discounted expected future profits. With a probability $q\,dt$ these future profits will coincide with the expected profit $(1 + g\,dt)\Pi_v$ from a vacant job, and with the complementary probability $(1 - q\,dt)$ they will equal the expected profit $(1 + g\,dt)\Pi_e$ from a filled job. After several rearrangements of terms, relation (3) takes this form:

$$(r - g)\Pi_e = (y - w) + q(1 + g\,dt)(\Pi_v - \Pi_e)$$

Making dt go to zero, one gets:

$$(r - g)\Pi_e = y - w + q(\Pi_v - \Pi_e) \tag{4}$$

This equation[1] expresses the equality of the returns of different assets on a perfect financial market. An asset worth Π_e at date t "invested" in the labor market procures an instantaneous profit of $(y - w)$, to which is added the average gain $q(\Pi_v - \Pi_e)$ resulting from a possible change of state (a filled job can fall vacant at rate q). During this same interval of time, the value of this asset has risen by $g\Pi_e\,dt$. In other words, the possessor of the asset can make a capital gain of $g\Pi_e\,dt$ by selling his or her good at date $t + dt$. Let us now suppose that this same asset is "invested" in a financial market offering a fixed interest rate r between dates t and $t + dt$. It then earns $r\Pi_e\,dt$ for its possessor. It turns out that there is an *opportunity cost*, precisely equal to $g\Pi_e\,dt$, when the asset is invested in a financial market offering a fixed interest rate r in an environment characterized by regular growth at rate g. The *effective* return on the investment in the financial market is thus equal to $(r - g)\Pi_e\,dt$. In sum, in an economy growing regularly at rate g, the effective rate of interest—i.e., the discount rate actually used by agents to calculate the present discounted value of their income—is equal to $(r - g)$. So the growth of the economy is simply accompanied by a capitalization effect equivalent to a reduction in the interest rate by an amount equal to the growth rate of productivity.

Labor Demand

On a balanced growth path, the exogenous parameters of the model all have to increase at the same rate. With no loss of generality, we may take the view that the costs arising from a vacant job are indexed to production y and can thus be written hy, where h is a constant exogenous parameter. The expected profit from a vacant job is then written:

$$(r - g)\Pi_v = -hy + m(\theta)(\Pi_e - \Pi_v)$$

When the free entry condition $\Pi_v = 0$ is satisfied, the expected profit from a filled job Π_e should be equal to the average cost of a vacant job $hy/m(\theta)$, and relation (4) then gives labor demand:

$$\frac{y - w}{r - g + q} = \frac{hy}{m(\theta)} \tag{5}$$

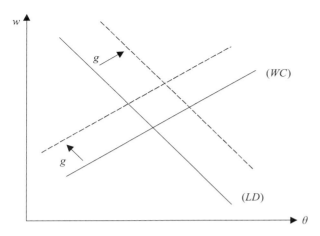

FIGURE 10.1
The effect of an increase in productivity.

For given wage w, the expected profit from an occupied job, represented by the left-hand side of (5), increases with g. Since the latter must exactly cover the average cost of an unfilled job, the average duration of a job remaining unfilled $1/m(\theta)$ increases, and consequently the labor market tightness θ rises too. In other words, for a given stock of unemployed persons and a given wage, firms open up more vacant jobs when g increases. Thanks to the capitalization effect, the growth in productivity exerts a *positive* effect on labor demand. In the (θ, w) plane, a rise in g shows up as a shift upward of the (LD) curve. This shift is shown in figure 10.1.

1.2.2 When Technological Progress Reduces Unemployment

The capitalization effect alters the negotiated wage and through this channel influences the properties of the wage curve exhibited in the basic matching model (chapter 9, section 3.4).

Bargaining and the Wage Curve
With a line of reasoning analogous to that which brought us to condition (4) describing the expected profit of an occupied job, we find that the expected utility V_e of an employee receiving wage w satisfies:

$$(r - g)V_e = w + q(V_u - V_e) \tag{6}$$

In this relation, V_e and V_u designate respectively the expected utility of an employee and an unemployed person at date t. The existence of a balanced growth path entails that the gains of unemployed persons also increase at rate g. With no loss of generality, we will assume that these gains are indexed to individual productivity and will denote them by zy, where $z \in [0, 1)$ is a constant exogenous parameter. The expected utility V_u of an unemployed person then solves:

$$(r - g)V_u = zy + \theta m(\theta)(V_e - V_u) \tag{7}$$

As regards wage bargaining, we note that this model is identical to the basic model of chapter 9, provided we simply change z to zy and r to $(r - g)$. If we make these substitutions in relation (20) from chapter 9, we get the equation of the wage curve describing the bargaining outcome in an economy growing regularly at rate g:

$$w = y[z + (1 - z)\Gamma(\theta)] \quad \text{with} \quad \Gamma(\theta) = \frac{\gamma[r - g + q + \theta m(\theta)]}{r - g + q + \gamma\theta m(\theta)} \tag{8}$$

We see that the capitalization effect entails that the strength Γ of an employee in bargaining increases with g. The reason for this result is that a rise in g corresponds to a reduction in the effective interest rate, which reduces the "capital" losses that ensue when a job is destroyed. So the employee has less fear of the prospect of unemployment, his or her bargaining position is strengthened, and in figure 10.1 the wage curve, denoted by (WC), shifts upward. All other things being equal, productivity growth thus has a tendency to increase the negotiated wage.

Labor Market Equilibrium

The equilibrium values of θ and w correspond to the coordinates of the intersection of the (WC) and (LD) curves in figure 10.1. Knowing θ, the unemployment rate u on a balanced growth path can be deduced with the help of the relationship between θ and u compatible with equilibrium of flows in the labor market, expressed by the Beveridge curve: $u = (q + n)/[q + n + \theta m(\theta)]$, where n designates the growth rate of the labor force (see chapter 9, section 3.1). Note that the growth rate g of productivity does not come into the equation of this curve.

Figure 10.1 shows, first of all, that a rise in g has a positive effect on the equilibrium real wage. This result signifies that stronger productivity growth raises the *level* of the real wage. On the other hand, the effect of g on the equilibrium value of the labor market tightness θ turns out to be ambiguous a priori. By combining relations (5) and (8), which define the (LD) and (WC) curves, however, we get an implicit equation that brings in θ alone:

$$\frac{(1 - \gamma)(1 - z)}{r - g + q + \gamma\theta m(\theta)} = \frac{h}{m(\theta)} \tag{9}$$

It is easy to verify that θ rises with g. Hence, stronger productivity growth increases the exit rate from unemployment $\theta m(\theta)$. The Beveridge curve being independent of g, we can deduce that stronger growth also reduces the unemployment rate. This conclusion springs from the fact that the profit from a filled job taking account of the negotiated wage—this profit is represented by the left-hand side of equation (9)—rises with g.

This model describes a linkage between growth and unemployment. It has (at least) one major drawback, though: the source of job destruction is exogenous. Yet one of the strong tenets of the theory of growth is that technological innovations favor the creation, temporarily at least, of jobs that incorporate the most recent innovations and render certain existing jobs obsolete. This is the process of *creative destruction* described by Schumpeter (1934) and formalized by Aghion and Howitt (1992, 1998) and Mortensen and Pissarides (1998). Let us suppose that stronger productivity growth accelerates the destruction of jobs; we will then have $q = q(g)$ with $q'(g) > 0$. Relation (9) then shows that it is far from certain that the expected profit from a filled job increases with g. The acceleration of job destruction runs counter to the capitalization effect, and it is possible that a rise in unemployment will occur. The model developed in the next subsection throws light on these chains of causality and suggests that productivity growth could be positively linked to the level of unemployment.

1.3   CREATIVE DESTRUCTION

In the previous model, the productivity of any job whatsoever increased regularly at rate g. To some extent, this hypothesis means that all jobs benefit uniformly, and at no cost, from the latest technological innovations. But in reality it is not, as a general rule, possible to apply the latest innovations to existing jobs without significant expense. For example, the study carried out by Foster et al. (2001) on the automobile repair sector in the United States between 1987 and 1992 estimates that the contribution of new firms to the growth of labor productivity in this sector was greater than the total growth of this variable. This result means that the "older" firms still in business contribute *negatively* to the growth of labor productivity in that sector. In many areas, individual jobs continue to use more or less the same technology they began with, for as long as they last, and are finally destroyed precisely when the evolution of technology makes it unprofitable to keep them going. They are then "replaced," but not necessarily in the same firm, by a new job that incorporates the most recent technological innovations. In this process, the life span of each job, and thus the job destruction rate, are *endogenous* variables determined by, among other things, the rate of innovations.

1.3.1   A Model with Endogenous Job Destruction

In an economy that is growing regularly and that suffers no exogenous shocks, jobs disappear when the technology they employ no longer yields a positive surplus. This condition allows us to characterize the life span of a job, and therefore the rate at which jobs are destroyed.

The Life Span of a Job

In order to give the simplest possible notion of the mechanism of job destruction and creation, we will assume that the productivity of each *new* job increases at a constant exogenous rate g, but that all jobs keep their original productivity over the whole span of their existence. In other words, if y designates the productivity of a job created at date $t = 0$, that job keeps its productivity y permanently, whereas a job created at date $t \geq 0$ is assigned a productivity of $y(t) = ye^{gt}$ over its life span. In this model, the definition of job creation needs to be specified. By definition, a job is created when an unemployed person and a vacant job are matched up. We will assume that the productivity of a job incorporates the most recent innovations available when it is created, and not at the moment a vacant job is opened up.

In order better to contrast the lessons of this model with those of the preceding models, we will assume further that there is no exogenous source of job destruction. A job disappears when the cost of keeping it going is greater than what it brings in, so the life span T of a job is an endogenous variable. The rate of job destruction, which we shall again denote by q, is thus also an endogenous variable, the stationary value of which is easily deduced from knowledge of T. If θ and U designate respectively the stationary values of the labor market tightness and the stock of unemployed persons present at every instant in the labor market, the number of jobs created per unit of time is equal to $\theta m(\theta)U$. Because every job has a life span T, there are $L = \theta m(\theta)UT$ jobs occupied at every instant. If we assume, for simplicity, that the growth rate of the population is null, then at stationary equilibrium we have $qL = \theta m(\theta)U$, and so $q = 1/T$.

Expected Utilities and Profits

Let us consider a job created at date x the life span of which is equal to T, and let us denote by $w(x, s, T)$ the wage attached to this job after it has lasted for a period $s \in [0, T]$. Let us denote by $V_e(x, s, T)$ the expected utility of a worker at date $x + s$ who occupies a job created at date x with a life span equal to T. We can then define $V_e(x, 0, T)$ as follows:

$$V_e(x, 0, T) = \int_0^T w(x, s, T)e^{-rs}\, ds + e^{-rT}V_u(x + T) \tag{10}$$

where $V_u(x + T)$ designates the expected utility of an unemployed person whose job is destroyed at date $(x + T)$. The existence of a balanced growth path dictates that the gains of unemployed persons increase at rate g. For simplicity, we will assume that these gains are indexed to productivity, and we will denote them by $zy(t)$, where $z \in [0, 1)$ is an exogenous parameter. In these conditions, the equation describing the time path of the expected utility of an unemployed person on a balanced growth path takes the form:

$$(r - g)V_u(t) = zy(t) + \theta m(\theta)[V_e(t, 0, T) - V_u(t)] \tag{11}$$

In order to lighten the notations from this point forward, we will reason on the basis of a match-up occurring at date $x = 0$. Because there is no exogenous source of job destruction and because the level of productivity is always equal to y, the expected profit at a date $t \in [0, T]$ thanks to a hire made at date 0, i.e., $\Pi_e(0, t, T)$, is written as follows:

$$\Pi_e(0, t, T) = \int_t^T [y - w(0, s, T)]e^{-r(s-t)}\, ds + e^{-r(T-t)}\Pi_v(T) \tag{12}$$

where $\Pi_v(t)$ designates the expected profit from a job that falls vacant at date t. Symmetrically, a person employed in a job created at date 0 attains at date $t \in [0, T]$ an expected utility $V_e(0, t, T)$ given by:

$$V_e(0, t, T) = \int_t^T w(0, s, T)e^{-r(s-t)}\, ds + e^{-r(T-t)}V_u(T) \tag{13}$$

The Surplus
By definition, the surplus $S(0, t, T)$ yielded at date $t \in [0, T]$ by a match at date 0 is equal to:

$$S(0, t, T) = V_e(0, t, T) - V_u(t) + \Pi_e(0, t, T) - \Pi_v(t)$$

When the free entry condition $\Pi_v(t) = 0$ is satisfied at every date t, relations (12) and (13) allow us to write the surplus $S(0, t, T)$ in the following form:

$$S(0, t, T) = y \int_t^T e^{-r(s-t)}\, dt + e^{-r(T-t)}V_u(T) - V_u(t), \qquad \forall t \in [0, T] \tag{14}$$

Recalling that at stationary equilibrium $V_u(T) = V_u(t)e^{g(T-t)}$, after several simple calculations, we get:

$$S(0, t, T) = \frac{1 - e^{-r(T-t)}}{r}\, y - [1 - e^{-(r-g)(T-t)}]V_u(t) \tag{15}$$

The Optimal Life Span of a Job
Let $\gamma \in [0, 1]$ again be the relative bargaining power of an employee. At each date $t \in [0, T]$ the outcome of bargaining corresponds to a share-out of the surplus $S(0, t, T)$ according to the usual formulas:

$$V_e(0, t, T) - V_u(t) = \gamma S(0, t, T) \qquad \text{and}$$

$$\Pi_e(0, t, T) - \Pi_v(t) = (1 - \gamma)S(0, t, T), \quad \forall t \in [0, T] \tag{16}$$

This sharing rule shows that the employer and the employee both have an interest in staying together as long as the job yields a positive surplus. In other words, the job should be destroyed on the date the marginal surplus yielded by extending its life span becomes negative. Let $S_3(0, t, T)$ be the partial derivative of the surplus with respect to its third argument; the optimal life span of a job must then satisfy conditions $S_3(0, T, T) = 0$, and $S_{33}(0, T, T) < 0$. Using definition (15) of the surplus, we arrive at $S_3(0, T, T) = y - (r - g)V_u(T)$. In consequence, the optimal life span of jobs is defined by the equality[2]:

$$y = (r - g)V_u(T) \tag{17}$$

This condition simply means that the employer and his or her employee have an interest in ending their relationship from the date at which, by looking for a new job, the worker will obtain a flow of gain $(r - g)V_u(T)$ greater than the flow of production y generated by the current job. Individual production y being an exogenous constant, and $V_u(T)$ being equal to $e^{gT}V_u(0)$, there exists a single value of T satisfying equation (17). Moreover, for this value of T, we find after several calculations that $S_{33}(0, T, T) = -gy < 0$. The marginal surplus due to an increase in the life span of the job at date T is thus indeed negative when this limit is extended.

1.3.2 The Balanced Growth Path

It is possible to determine the equilibrium values of labor market tightness θ and the life span T of a job with the help of two relations that portray the conditions of job creation and job destruction.

Job Creation

The job creation equation results from free entry equilibrium, which indicates that the expected cost of a vacant job is equal to the expected gain of a filled one. Let us assume that the search costs arising from a vacant job increase at rate g, taking the form $hy(t)$ where h is a positive exogenous constant. At date t, the value $\Pi_v(t)$ of a vacant job will then be expressed as:

$$(r - g)\Pi_v(t) = hy(t) + m(\theta)[\Pi_e(t, 0, T) - \Pi_v(t)]$$

We obtain a relationship between T and θ, noting that in the context proper to this model, the free entry condition at $t = 0$, $\Pi_v(0) = 0$, entails that the expected profit $\Pi_e(0, 0, T)$ from a job created at date 0 must exactly cover the average cost $hy/m(\theta)$ of a vacant job posted at the same date $t = 0$. With the help of sharing rule (16), we will thus have $(1 - \gamma)S(0, 0, T) = hy/m(\theta)$. If we consider relation (15) at $t = 0$, and note that condition (17) characterizing the optimal life span of a job entails $V_u(0) = ye^{-gT}/(r - g)$, we arrive, after rearranging terms, at the following relation:

$$\frac{h}{m(\theta)} = \frac{(1 - \gamma)}{r}\left[1 + \frac{ge^{-rT} - re^{-gT}}{r - g}\right] \tag{18}$$

When $r > g$, it is easy to verify that the expected profit from a job at the time of its creation, represented by the right-hand side of equation (18), rises with the life span of this job. As the average unit cost $h/m(\theta)$ is an increasing function of θ, equation (18) in sum defines an increasing relation between labor market tightness θ and the life span T of a job which we can assimilate to a labor demand. We have identified it by the abbreviation (C) in figure 10.2. We can also verify that, for a given life span T, the expected profit from a new job increases with the rate of growth of productivity.[3] In figure 10.2, a rise in g shifts the (C) curve to the right.

For given T, i.e., for a given job destruction rate $q = 1/T$, relation (18) is in fact analogous to relation (9) defining the equilibrium value of the labor market tightness θ in the previous model, where the rate of destruction q was exogenous. In the latter case, the capitalization effect entails that the profit expected from a filled job increases with g, and it is thus not surprising to find that θ rises with g for given T. In this model, however, the life span of jobs is an endogenous variable that, as we will prove below, *diminishes* with the growth rate g of productivity. In consequence, accelerated

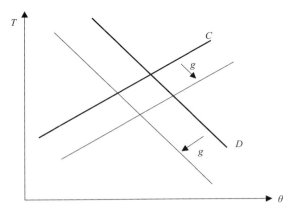

FIGURE 10.2
The equilibrium values of T and θ.

growth increases the destruction of jobs, running counter to the capitalization effect. The direction in which θ varies with g becomes a priori ambiguous. In order to get rid of this ambiguity, we have to define the relationship between T and θ that corresponds to decisions to destroy jobs.

Job Destruction
We obtain a second relationship between θ and T using relation (11), which defines the expected utility of an unemployed person at instant $t = 0$, and applying the sharing rules (16). We thus get:

$$(r - g)V_u(0) = zy + \theta m(\theta)\frac{\gamma}{1 - \gamma}\Pi_e(0, 0, T)$$

Following (17), $(r - g)V_u(0) = ye^{-gT}$, and since the expected profit $\Pi_e(0, 0, T)$ is equal to the average cost $h/m(\theta)$, we finally get:

$$e^{-gT} = z + \frac{\gamma h\theta}{1 - \gamma} \tag{19}$$

This equation defines a decreasing relation between labor market tigthness θ and the life span of a job T. It is represented by the (D) curve in figure 10.2. Relation (19) indicates that high labor market tightness entails a strong exit rate from unemployment and a high expected utility for unemployed persons, which entails a weak surplus and consequently a shorter life span for jobs. We also see that an increase of g shifts this curve downward.

Equilibrium
Figure 10.2 shows that the life span of a job diminishes when growth accelerates. But the effect on θ is a priori ambiguous. In the appendix at the end of this chapter,

however, we show that θ diminishes with the growth rate g of productivity, so an increase in g here lowers the exit rate $\theta m(\theta)$ from unemployment. When the labor force is constant, the unemployment rate is given by the formula:

$$u = \frac{q}{q + \theta m(\theta)} \qquad \text{with} \qquad q = 1/T \tag{20}$$

Since an increase in g lowers the exit rate from unemployment and increases the rate q of job destruction, a stronger rise in productivity unambiguously increases unemployment.

In sum, technological progress increases the unemployment rate in this model with endogenous job destruction. But it must be understood that this result is not general. It follows from the fact that older jobs derive no benefit from technological progress and must necessarily be destroyed when they reach a certain age. This case is directly opposed to the one envisaged in the previous model, with exogenous destruction, in which all jobs benefit from technological progress independently of the date at which they were created. Clearly an intermediate model incorporating the two forms of technological progress would show that technological progress is favorable to employment if and only if a sufficiently large share of technological progress is automatically incorporated into all jobs. The capitalization effect would then dominate the job destruction effect. From this perspective, Mortensen and Pissarides (1998) have built a model in which firms can overhaul jobs when their surplus becomes negative, at a certain cost. They then show that technological progress is favorable to employment if the costs of overhaul are slight, and unfavorable if they are not. Aghion and Howitt (1998, p. 129) present a model, similarly inspired, that yields similar results.

These analyses indicate that the impact of technological progress depends on the form it takes and the opportunities to reorganize available to firms. In this respect, it is important to know whether the market mechanisms at work in the previous model lead to an optimal reallocation of jobs.

1.3.3 The Efficiency of Creative Destruction

In what circumstances is the restructuring caused by technological progress too rapid, or, on the contrary, too slow? In a perfectly competitive economy, the answer to this question is evident: since the free play of competition leads to efficient allocations, the pace of technological progress is necessarily efficient too. In the presence of transaction costs in the labor market, the problem becomes thornier. Job destruction gives rise to reallocation unemployment, which may be thought to be socially inefficient. In order to answer this question, which has been studied by Caballero and Hammour (1996), it is necessary to characterize the social optimum, i.e., the values of labor market tightness, the unemployment rate, and the job destruction rate, which maximize discounted aggregate production. For the sake of simplicity, we will proceed as we did in chapter 9, leaving out preference for the present. In this model with growth, this hypothesis amounts to setting $r = g$. Moreover, we will consider only stationary states.

The Planner's Problem

At date t, total output is equal to the sum of all the production achieved by all the jobs created between dates $t - T$ and t. As there are $\theta m(\theta)u$ jobs created at each date, and since a job created at date x produces $y(x) = ye^{gx}$, total production at date t is equal to $\int_{t-T}^{t} yu\theta m(\theta)e^{gx}\,dx$. At this same date, unemployed persons produce $uzy(t) = uzye^{gt}$, and the cost of vacant jobs comes to $\theta uhy(t) = \theta uhye^{gt}$. Noting that $\int_{t-T}^{t} e^{gx}\,dx = [e^{gT} - e^{g(t-T)}]/g$, aggregate production $\omega(t)$ at date t, equal by definition to the sum of all production minus the cost of vacant jobs, is therefore expressed as:

$$\omega(t) = ye^{gT}u\left[\theta m(\theta)\frac{1 - e^{-gT}}{g} + z - h\theta\right]$$

Following definition (20) of the stationary unemployment rate, we have $u = 1/[1 + T\theta m(\theta)]$, and the planner's problem can be written as:

$$\underset{(\theta,\,T)}{\text{Max}}\ \frac{1}{1 + T\theta m(\theta)}\left[\theta m(\theta)\frac{1 - e^{-gT}}{g} + z - h\theta\right]$$

Let us again denote by $\eta(\theta) = -\theta m'(\theta)/m(\theta)$ the elasticity of the matching function with respect to the unemployment rate. After several calculations, we verify that the optimal values of labor market tightness, θ^*, and of the life span of jobs, T^*, are defined by the two following equations:

$$\frac{h}{m(\theta^*)} = [1 - \eta(\theta^*)]\left[\frac{1 - e^{-gT^*}}{g} - T^*e^{-gT^*}\right] \tag{21}$$

$$e^{-gT^*} = z + \frac{\eta(\theta^*)\theta^*h}{1 - \eta(\theta^*)} \tag{22}$$

We can compare the optimal values of labor market tightness and life span of jobs with those obtained at decentralized equilibrium by making r go to g in equation (18). In this configuration of the parameters, equation (18) is written[4]:

$$\frac{h}{m(\theta)} = (1 - \gamma)\left[\frac{1 - e^{-gT}}{g} - Te^{-gT}\right] \tag{23}$$

Comparison of the two systems of equations (19)–(23), on the one hand, and (21)–(22), on the other, respectively defining decentralized equilibrium and the social optimum, shows that these two states coincide if and only if the Hosios condition $\gamma = \eta(\theta^*)$ is satisfied (see chapter 9, section 6, for more detail on this condition). Differentiating equations (19) and (23), we easily verify that the labor market tightness at decentralized equilibrium decreases with the bargaining power of workers, γ, and that the life span T of jobs reaches a minimum when $\gamma = \eta(\theta^*)$. The linkage between the life span of jobs and bargaining power is represented in figure 10.3.

Inefficiency and the Hosios Condition

We see that labor market tightness lies below its efficient level if and only if workers have bargaining power greater than $\eta(\theta^*)$. On the other hand, labor market equilibrium is always characterized by an *insufficient* reallocation of jobs when the Hosios

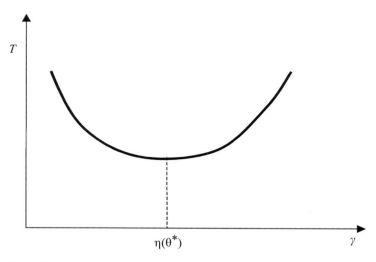

FIGURE 10.3
The relation between the life span of jobs and the bargaining power of workers.

condition is not met. This result, obtained by Caballero and Hammour (1996), suggests that the market imperfections resulting from an inefficient sharing of rents lead systematically to sclerosis of the process of job reorganization. We can understand this by going back to relation (17), which defines the optimal life span of jobs as a function of the expected utility of unemployed persons. As in the basic model of chapter 9, it is easy to verify here that the expected utility of unemployed persons reaches a maximum when the Hosios condition is satisfied. Relation (17) does indeed entail $(r - g)V_u(t) = e^{-g(T-t)}y$ on a balanced growth path, and since T reaches a minimum when $\gamma = \eta(\theta^*)$, the expected utility of unemployed persons is indeed maximal for $\gamma = \eta(\theta^*)$. Now, the greater the expected utility of unemployed persons is, the less surplus a job generates (see relation (14)), and therefore the higher the gains of unemployed persons are, the shorter the life spans of jobs. In sum, the insufficient reallocation of jobs in decentralized markets results from a very simple logic: when the labor market is inefficient, the gains from searching for a job are relatively slight, which tends to increase the rent of individuals holding jobs and thus gives them an incentive to keep their jobs as long as possible. In other words, labor market efficiency ensures a maximal return to job search and produces a maximum of incentive to reorganize production units.

These results are obviously pertinent to economic policy. They suggest that measures to protect employment are ill-suited to countering the effects of technological progress on unemployment. The model with endogenous job destruction, as we have studied it in this section, represents a situation where technological progress is embodied only in new jobs and indicates that more rapid growth increases unemployment. It also allows us to show that this source of unemployment ought not to be

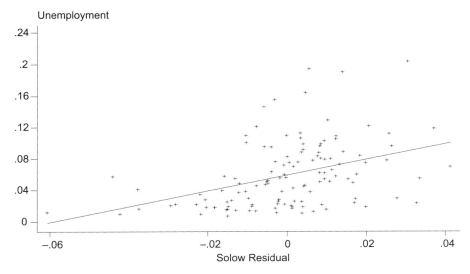

FIGURE 10.4

The relationship between the Solow residual and the unemployment rate in 17 OECD countries over the period 1960–1999. The 17 countries are Australia, Austria, Belgium, Canada, Denmark, Finland, France, Germany, Ireland, Italy, Japan, Netherlands, Norway, Spain, Sweden, the United Kingdom, and the United States.

Source: OECD and Blanchard and Wolfers, 2000.

combated by putting in place measures to protect jobs. Caballero and Hammour (1996) suggest instead using subsidies to create employment. With this type of measure, market equilibrium can indeed be made to coincide with the social optimum. In our model, the values of labor market tightness and the job destruction rate defined by the systems (19)–(23) and (21)–(22) are identical if entrepreneurs receive a subsidy amounting to $h[\gamma - \eta(\theta^*)]/[1 - \eta(\theta^*)]$ per unit of time for each vacant job. The subsidy is thus positive if the bargaining power of workers is greater than the elasticity of the matching function with respect to the unemployment rate, and negative if not.

1.4   EMPIRICAL ILLUSTRATIONS

There are a limited number of empirical studies dedicated to the relationship between the unemployment rate and the growth rate of productivity. They generally conclude that there is not a systematic and robust correlation between the different measures of the growth rate of productivity and the unemployment rate (see Bean and Pissarides, 1993, and Caballero, 1993, for example). In order to illustrate these results we have looked at the correlation between the Solow residual and the unemployment rate over the period 1960–1999 for 17 OECD countries. These two variables are presented as five-year averages (1960–64, 1965–69 ...) for each country. Figure 10.4 brings out a positive linkage between the unemployment rate and technological progress measured by the Solow residual, the coefficient of determination being equal to 1.02 with a standard error of 0.21. But this correlation is deceptive and has no causal significance, because technological progress and unemployment are influenced by common variables. This emerges clearly if we regress the unemployment rate onto the Solow residual by introducing fixed effects for each country and for each period. We then obtain a negative coefficient of determination, equal to -0.24 with a standard error of 0.18, which entails that this coefficient is not significantly different from zero (at the 10% threshold). At the aggregate level, technological progress does not seem to exert any effect of well-determined sign on unemployment. It is necessary to resort to a finer-grained analysis, taking special notice of the characteristics of the innovations that give rise to technological progress (see Acemoglu, 2002; Aghion, 2002) and labor market institutions (see chapter 12, this book) in order better to understand the impact of technological progress on unemployment.

2   GLOBALIZATION, INEQUALITY, AND UNEMPLOYMENT

Changes in the economic environment, such as technological progress, international competition, the organization of production, and labor market institutions, do not just affect the rate of global unemployment and the average wage. They also influence the distribution of employment opportunities offered to different types of individual. So, technological progress alters the return on certain kinds of educational investment. Competition with low-wage countries producing goods highly substitutable for those made by low-skilled workers in industrialized countries may prove unfavorable to the latter. We can discover the determinants of the evolution of wage inequalities and employment opportunities among workers of different skill levels by studying the evolution of the supply and demand for each category of worker. An increase in the demand for a given type of labor is favorable to the opportunities of individuals who can supply this type of labor, while an increase in supply is unfavorable to them. The supply and the demand for each type of labor are themselves influenced by technological progress, international competition, demographic phenomena, and labor market institutions as a whole.

The last two decades of the twentieth century constitute a particularly interesting period for the analysis of inequality. Over this period the situation of skilled workers as compared to that of persons with few skills changed a great deal in the industrialized countries of the OECD. In different cases, this change led to a widened spread of earnings, or a widened spread of unemployment rates across categories. This trend was caused by the conjunction of interdependent elements. Technological progress and competition from low-wage countries contributed, in varying and much-debated degrees, to this increase of inequality. International migration, the evolution of labor market institutions, and certain organizational changes have also played a role, although probably a more marginal one.

We will first lay out the salient facts regarding the evolution of inequality during the last two decades of the twentieth century, then present the main explanations for them. We will see in particular that shifts in the structure of labor demand induced by biased technological progress and competition from low-wage countries have undoubtedly played a major role. The different OECD countries have reacted in sharply different ways to this alteration in the structure of labor demand. Certain countries of continental Europe have preserved rigid wage structures that have had the effect of increasing the unemployment of less skilled workers, while other countries, such as the United States, have opted for wage flexibility. The conclusion of this section examines the upshot of these choices for income and welfare inequality.

2.1   THE FACTS

The 1980s and 1990s were marked by an increase in the inequalities between workers of different skills in the industrialized countries of the OECD, a phenomenon that took different forms in different countries. In some countries it was mainly wage inequality that deepened, while in others it was inequality of access to employment. Before presenting the evolution of these inequalities, we must emphasize that there is no single measure of inequality. In empirical studies, inequality is generally assessed by indicators such as the standard deviation, or interdecile or intercentile differentials. Each measure describes one characteristic of the dispersion of the indicator under study. It is generally necessary to use several measures in order to describe the evolution of inequality (for more information, see Gottschalk and Smeeding, 1997; Katz and Autor, 1999; Bertola et al., 2001; and Card and DiNardo, 2002).

The Increase in Wage Inequality in the United States at the End
of the Twentieth Century
The increase in wage inequality in the United States in the 1980s and 1990s has been widely documented. According to Katz and Autor (1999) and Card and DiNardo (2002), its main characteristics are as follows:

*   The time path of wage inequality can be divided into three subperiods. This point is illustrated by figure 10.5, which reproduces the time path of several different measures of U.S. aggregate wage inequality between 1967 and 2000. Between 1967 and 1980, aggregate wage inequality is virtually constant. Aggregate wage inequality then rises strongly during the 1980s, especially between 1980 and 1985. The available data suggest that this phenomenon bulks even larger if we consider not just wages but also the other elements of wage remuneration like retirement, and various aspects of social security (Pierce, 2001). From the end of the 1980s until 2000, aggregate wage inequality holds steady.

*   Wage differences among different levels of education and experience, and different professions, have grown.

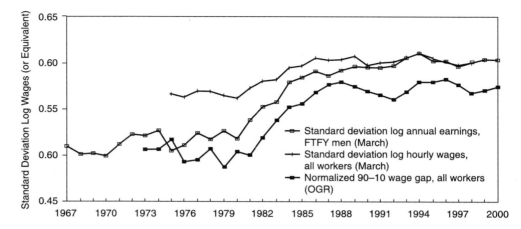

Figure 10.5

Alternative measures of aggregate wage inequality in the United States.

Legend: FTFY = full-time, full-year. OGR data come from the CPS. They refer to individuals in the "outgoing rotation group" of every monthly CPS. The normalized 90–10 wage gap is the log of the ratio of the 90th percentile of wages to the 10th percentile. For convenience, this ratio is divided by 2.56.

Source: Card and DiNardo (2002, figure 2).

- The spread of wages within the same levels of education and experience, and the same professions, has also grown.

- Increasing inequality led to significant shrinkage of the real wage of workers situated at the low end of the wage distribution. As figure 10.6 shows, the real weekly wage of white men in the tenth percentile of the distribution was weaker (by around 10%) at the end of the 1990s than at the beginning of the 1960s.

The Evolution of Inequality in Other OECD Countries

Wage inequality did not increase in the OECD countries as a whole during the last two decades of the twentieth century. It did increase in the United States and the United Kingdom especially (Gosling and Lemieux, 2001, show that between 1979 and 1998, the British labor market underwent reforms that caused it to converge with its American counterpart). Wage inequality remained stable in France, Italy, and Germany, and grew to a lesser degree in Australia, Canada, Japan, and Sweden (see Katz and Autor, 1999).

Table 10.2 portrays the evolution of the D5/D1 ratio for wages between the end of the 1970s and the middle of the 1990s in several large OECD countries. Let us recall that the distribution of wages is ranked by deciles in ascending order, and that the term D5 refers to the average of the fifth decile, while D1 refers to the average of the first decile. So the D5/D1 ratio is a measure of the extent of inequality in the bottom half of the wage distribution. The data in table 10.2 indicate, in the first place, that the spread of wages is noticeably more compressed in Europe and Japan than in

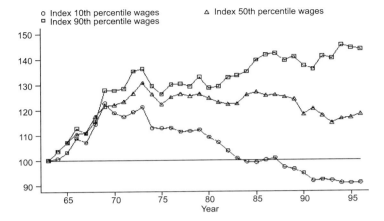

FIGURE 10.6

The evolution of the weekly wages of white men in the United States over the period 1963–1997 (base 100 in 1963).

Source: Acemoglu (2002, figure 2).

Table 10.2

Evolution of the D5/D1 ratio among men in the 1980s and 1990s.

Country	1975–79	1995–96	1975–79 to 1995–96
Australia	1.57	1.68	0.11
Canada*	2.07	2.22	0.15
France	1.68	1.60	−0.08
Germany†	1.52	1.46	−0.06
Japan	1.58	1.60	0.02
Sweden	1.32	1.40	0.08
United Kingdom	1.58	1.80	0.22
United States	1.93	2.20	0.27

Source: Bertola et al. (2001, table 3).

*Periods 1980–1984 and 1990–1994.

† The first period is 1980–1984.

Table 10.3

Evolution of unemployment rates per skill level between 1981 and 1996.

Country	u_ℓ			u_h			
	1981	1996	Δu_ℓ	1981	1996	Δu_h	$\Delta u_\ell - \Delta u_h$
Canada	7.3	13.4	6.1	2.0	6.6	4.6	1.5
France	5.4	13.0	7.6	3.0	5.9	2.9	4.7
Sweden	3.0	10.5	7.5	0.6	5.4	4.8	2.7
United Kingdom	13.7	15.1	1.4	2.7	4.1	1.4	0
United States	10.3	11.0	0.7	2.2	2.6	0.4	0.3

Source: OECD data and personal calculations.

Note: u_ℓ designates the unemployment rate of individuals with low educational levels (secondary school education not completed). u_h designates the unemployment rate of individuals with high educational levels (college or university training). Δ designates the difference between 1996 and 1981.

Canada and the United States. They also show that wage inequalities grew significantly between the end of the 1970s and the middle of the 1990s in the United Kingdom and the United States, and to a lesser extent in Canada, Australia, and Sweden. Conversely, the D5/D1 ratio shrank in France and Germany over this period, and remained practically stable in Japan. These observations have to be set alongside the evolution of unemployment in relation to skill level.

The Evolution of Unemployment in Relation to Skill Level

The evolution of unemployment rates in relation to education (which largely follows that of skill level) reveals a worsening of the situation of workers with low levels of education in many countries. Table 10.3 shows that their unemployment rate, denoted by u_ℓ, rose significantly during the 1980s and 1990s. This table also indicates that the unemployment rate of workers with high levels of education, denoted by u_h, advanced considerably, although remaining lower than that of less skilled workers. These parallel evolutions in unemployment rates signify that the 1980s were probably marked by a negative shock to the *entire* labor force.

Were some workers more affected than others? Table 10.3 indicates that the unemployment rate of low-skilled men rose much more than that of skilled men in France, Sweden, and to a lesser extent in Canada. Conversely, the movements in the unemployment rate for these two manpower categories are similar in the United States and the United Kingdom. Table 10.4 shows that employment rates for men (i.e., the ratio of the number of jobs to the size of the working-age population) fell more for low-skilled men than for skilled ones. These differences in the movement of employment rates are less marked in the United States than in continental Europe.

This descriptive account suggests that the majority of industrialized countries were faced with the same changes to their environment during the 1980s (and in what

Table 10.4

The evolution of employment rates per skill level between 1981 and 1996.

Country	e_ℓ			e_h			
	1981	1996	Δe_ℓ	1981	1996	Δe_h	$\Delta e_\ell - \Delta e_h$
Canada	79.6	64.3	−15.3	74.6	84.7	−9.9	−5.4
France	80.3	67.2	−12.8	92.5	87.4	−5.1	−7.7
Sweden	85.3	73.5	−12.2	95.2	93.1	−2.1	−10.1
United Kingdom	71.7	61.7	−10	91.3	88.8	−2.5	−7.5
United States	69.8	66.1	−3.7	91.8	90.5	−1.3	−2.4

Source: OECD data and personal calculations.

Note: e_ℓ designates the employment rate of individuals with low educational levels (secondary school education not completed). e_h designates the employment rate of individuals with high educational levels (college or university training). Δ designates the difference between 1996 and 1981.

follows we examine the reasons for this), but took different steps in response. Some countries, such as France and Italy, succeeded in maintaining stable pay scales, at the cost of a rise in the relative unemployment rate for less-skilled workers. And it would be tempting to contrast this with an "Anglo-Saxon" model, in which the relative employment situation of the less skilled was upheld, at the cost of a steep rise in wage inequality. The description we have given here is clearly no more than illustrative, inasmuch as the relationship between employment and wages is influenced by many factors, such as economic policy, the macroeconomic environment, and the demographic profile of the population. Nevertheless, econometric research on the evolution of unemployment and wage inequality does confirm this line of interpretation (see Bertola et al., 2001).

To sum up, the 1980s and 1990s probably underwent a labor demand shift that favored skilled workers, and the consequence of this has been an apparent trade-off between keeping wages up, with rising unemployment among the low-skilled, or keeping employment among the low-skilled up, to the detriment of their remuneration. It will now be our task to understand the reasons for this shift, and the mechanisms that have led to such different responses to it in different countries.

2.2 BIASED TECHNOLOGICAL PROGRESS

What is the impact of technological progress on wage inequality and employment opportunity? The new computer-based information technologies have probably favored the most highly skilled workers at the expense of those with the fewest skills. So technological progress may be said to have been *biased* in favor of those with skills. This explanation of the evolution of wage inequality provided the impetus for a large body of research in the 1990s, summarized especially in Katz and Autor (1999), Card and DiNardo (2002), Aghion (2002), and Acemoglu (2002), from which the following synthesis derives at many points. We will start by showing how technological progress influences wage inequality between workers with different skill levels. We will then see how empirical work suggests that technological progress played an important part in the development of inequality in the main OECD countries during the last two decades of the twentieth century. And finally, we will highlight the fact that the form taken by technological progress is not independent of the incentives within which agents act over time, and that it might in part be determined by the composition of the labor force.

2.2.1 Exogenous Technological Progress

The effects of technological progress on demand for skilled and unskilled labor are not difficult to analyze: we consider an aggregate production function that defines aggregate production Y as a function of employment and technology, i.e., $Y = F(A_h L_h, A_\ell L_\ell)$. In this expression, the production function F has constant return to scale. The variables L_h and L_ℓ designate respectively skilled and unskilled labor. The coefficients A_i, $i = h, \ell$ are parameters representing technological progress that improve the efficiency of the two types of labor. Technological progress is said to be *biased* if it alters the *relative* productivity of the inputs, i.e., if it changes the A_h/A_ℓ ratio. It is *neutral* (or unbiased) when this ratio remains unchanged. Many technological innovations lead to non-neutral technological progress. Robotization, for example, could have a tendency to increase the productivity of the least-skilled and middle-skilled workers. Computerization could increase the productivity of certain categories of employee occupying the middle portion of the skill spectrum (consensus has not yet been achieved about the effects of the use of computers; see Card and DiNardo, 2002).

This aggregate production function can be interpreted in several ways (see Acemoglu, 2002).

- It might represent a situation in which there is a final good, produced by a representative firm using skilled and unskilled labor.

- Alternatively, we may assume that the economy produces quantity Y of a final good, using a technology represented by the production function $F(Y_h, Y_\ell)$, where Y_h and Y_ℓ are two intermediate goods, respectively produced by skilled and unskilled labor using a technology with constant returns: $Y_i = A_i L_i$, $i = h, \ell$.

- It is also possible to assume that the economy comprises two consumption goods, Y_i, $i = h, \ell$, with a representative consumer whose preferences are represented by a utility function, $U(Y_h, Y_\ell)$, homogeneous of degree 1, and that each good is produced by a technology with constant returns: $Y_i = A_i L_i$, $i = h, \ell$. In this setting the utility index $U(Y_h, Y_\ell) = Y$ is a measure of the aggregate production of the economy.

These different interpretations prove to be useful for analyzing a wide range of problems within a unified analytical context.

An Economy with Two Categories of Worker

If w_i designates the real wage of a worker of type i and if the exogenous parameter Y represents the desired level of production, the cost minimization problem of the firm is written:

$$\underset{(L_h, L_\ell)}{\text{Min}} \ w_h L_h + w_\ell L_\ell \tag{24}$$

subject to constraint:

$$F(A_h L_h, A_\ell L_\ell) \geq Y$$

This way of representing the behavior of the firm differs from that set out in chapter 4, which focused on the theory of labor demand, because we now include parameters of technological progress, A_h and A_ℓ. Formally, we can return to the standard problem of total cost minimization, if we consider the "intensive" quantities of labor, $\tilde{L}_h = A_h L_h$ and $\tilde{L}_\ell = A_\ell L_\ell$, to which the wages $\tilde{w}_h = w_h/A_h$ and $\tilde{w}_\ell = w_\ell/A_\ell$ respectively apply. Having adopted these conventions, the elasticity of substitution between $\tilde{L}_h$ and $\tilde{L}_\ell$ defined by equation (10) in chapter 4 reads $\sigma = d \ln(\tilde{L}_h/\tilde{L}_\ell)/d \ln(\tilde{w}_\ell/\tilde{w}_h)$. Let us denote by $\omega = w_h/w_\ell$ the relative wage of skilled workers, by $\alpha = A_h/A_\ell$ the ratio between the technological progress parameters, and by $\lambda = L_h/L_\ell$ the labor demand ratio. We then get $\sigma = d \ln(\alpha\lambda)/d \ln(\alpha/\omega)$. This last equality can also be written[5]:

$$\frac{d\lambda}{\lambda} = (\sigma - 1)\frac{d\alpha}{\alpha} - \sigma\frac{d\omega}{\omega} \tag{25}$$

This equation shows that, for a given wage structure, i.e., when the ratio $\omega = w_h/w_\ell$ remains constant, the proportion of skilled labor increases in two cases:

1. If $\alpha = A_h/A_\ell$ increases and the two types of labor are sufficiently substitutable ($\sigma > 1$). The increased relative productivity of skilled labor gives firms an incentive to substitute this input for unskilled labor.

2. If $\alpha = A_h/A_\ell$ decreases and the two types of labor are weakly substitutable ($\sigma < 1$). Now it is the relative productivity of unskilled workers that increases, but firms have an incentive to economize on this type of personnel because of the low substitutability between these two inputs.

Note that in the case of a Cobb-Douglas technology, the elasticity of substitution σ is equal to 1 and technological progress has no effect on relative input demand. Note as well that the effects of technological progress on the structures of labor demand and/or wages depend on the degree of substitutability between these inputs. The belief that mechanization and robotization, by greatly increasing the productivity of the least skilled persons, also destroy their jobs has to be put in perspective. Robotization or mechanization reshape the structure of labor demand to the profit of the unskilled if the elasticity of substitution between skilled and unskilled labor is greater than unity. In that case, firms have an interest in substantially reorganizing their production process by shifting demand onto the factor whose efficiency rises the most. On the other hand, if the elasticity of substitution is less than unity, the available technology makes it hard to substitute between these two kinds of manpower. Firms then have an interest in economizing on the factor whose efficiency has risen, without profoundly reorganizing production, and this in the end entails a reduction in the proportion of unskilled workers. Note as well that everything we have said to this point concerns exclusively the *substitution* effect, i.e., the proportion of skilled employees to unskilled ones for a given level of production. Technological progress, with bias or without, may also have a *scale* effect capable of increasing the employment of all categories of workers (see chapter 4, on labor demand, for more on these notions).

Technological Progress and Wage Inequality: First Steps Toward an Assessment
The foregoing line of reasoning considers the effects of technological progress while taking wages as given. But from a macroeconomic perspective, it is important to explain how wages react. To assess this reaction, let us suppose that the labor markets are perfectly competitive. If the composition of the labor force is a given, technological progress changes the wage structure only, since the economy is always at full employment. Let N_h be the supply of skilled labor, and N_ℓ the supply of unskilled labor; ratio λ between the labor demands is then equal to the ratio, assumed to be given, $v = N_h/N_\ell$. Then, equation (25), which implies that $d\omega/\omega = [(\sigma - 1)/\sigma]\, d\alpha/\alpha$, shows that the forms of biased technological progress, which have a tendency to alter labor demand at the expense of the unskilled when wages are given, have the effect of cutting back their relative earnings when wages are endogenous and relative labor supply is exogenous. In other words, wage adjustments can absorb the impact of the changes to the structure of labor demand caused by technological progress. This result, which has been obtained from a very rudimentary model, nonetheless suggests that there is a trade-off between employment and wage for the unskilled when the evolution of technological progress is unfavorable to them.

2.2.2 What Empirical Research Tells Us

A number of studies have attempted to estimate the technological progress bias. They suggest that there has been a bias in favor of skilled workers in the industrialized countries throughout the second half of the twentieth century.

Estimating the Technological Progress Bias
On the assumption that the production function is of the CES type and is expressed as:

$$F(A_h L_h, A_\ell L_\ell) = [(A_h L_h)^{(\sigma-1)/\sigma} + (A_\ell L_\ell)^{(\sigma-1)/\sigma}]^{\sigma/(\sigma-1)} \tag{26}$$

one line of research estimates the evolution of the technological progress bias using the relation which defines the ratio of the demands for labor. With this CES production function, it is easy to verify that the relative demand λ for skilled labor is given by the formula:

$$\lambda = \omega^{-\sigma}\alpha^{\sigma-1} \tag{27}$$

This simple relationship between the relative demand for skilled labor, the wage differential, and the technological progress bias has been exploited using two different methods.

The first consists simply of estimating equation (27), written in logarithm, using aggregate data on a national scale (Freeman, 1995) or longitudinal data by region (Topel, 1993). The dependent variable is the relative wage ω of skilled workers. Parameter λ is equal to the relative supply of skilled workers, $N_h/N_\ell = v$, since equality of labor supply and demand entails, assuming a competitive labor market, $L_h/L_\ell = N_h/N_\ell$. More precisely, the following equation is estimated:

$$\ln \omega = \frac{1}{\sigma} \ln v + \frac{\sigma-1}{\sigma} \ln \alpha \tag{28}$$

With data for v and for ω at our disposal, we can then estimate the elasticity of substitution σ and the technological progress bias α. Katz and Murphy (1992) estimate such a relation for the United States over the period 1963–1987. The dependent variable ω represents the ratio between the average wage of workers with, at minimum, a college degree (at least 16 years of schooling) and that of high school graduates (12 years of schooling). They obtain the following result:

$$\ln \omega = \underset{(0.150)}{-0.709} \ln v + \underset{(0.007)}{0.33} \, t + c, \qquad R^2 = 0.52$$

In this equation, t designates a trend, c is a constant, R^2 is the coefficient of determination, and the figures in parentheses designate the standard errors of the coefficients. These results allow us, first of all, to give an estimate of the elasticity of substitution, $\sigma = 1/0.709 \simeq 1.4$, which is greater than unity. The positive coefficient associated with the trend signifies, moreover, that there exists a technological bias which increases the relative wage of the most highly skilled workers. Since the elasticity of substitution between the two categories of worker considered is greater than one, this bias can be interpreted, in line with equation (28), as an increase in the relative productivity of skilled workers ($\alpha = A_h/A_\ell$). A number of studies carried out on various OECD countries using similar methodology obtain results closely similar, with an elasticity of substitution lying between 1 and 3 (see Katz and Autor, 1999, p. 1551). This appproach yields precious insight, but it should be treated with caution, inasmuch as the estimate of the elasticity of substitution relies on the hypothesis that the relative labor supply is exogenous.

A second method consists of using equation (27) and external information giving the value of the elasticity of substitution σ directly. If Δ designates the difference operator, we can write equation (27) in the form:

$$\frac{\Delta\alpha}{\alpha} = \frac{\sigma}{\sigma-1}\frac{\Delta\omega}{\omega} + \frac{1}{\sigma-1}\frac{\Delta v}{v} \tag{29}$$

Table 10.5

Evolution of the technological bias in the United States (annual variation, in percent).

Period	$\Delta\omega/\omega$	$\Delta v/v$	$\Delta a/a$
1940–1950	−1.3	2.6	1.3
1950–1963	0.6	2.4	6.6
1963–1970	0.8	2.3	7.0
1970–1979	−0.7	4.8	7.5
1979–1989	1.3	2.7	9.3
1989–1993	1.1	3.3	9.9

Source: Johnson (1997, table 2, p. 43).

Once a plausible a priori value for elasticity of substitution σ has been set, the estimation strategy consists of inferring the variation $\Delta\alpha/\alpha$ of the technological bias from the variations $\Delta\omega/\omega$ and $\Delta v/v$ of the relative wage and relative employment of skilled workers. For example, Johnson (1997) considers that v is represented by the ratio of college graduates to high school graduates. Most of the studies on American data that adopt this split (with similar, but not always exactly the same, definitions) opt for a value of σ lying between 1 and 2 (Bound and Johnson, 1992; according to Johnson, 1997, and Autor et al., 1998, the value of σ to be used in the calibrations ought to lie between 1.4 and 1.5). The average wages of these two categories are likewise known, so it is possible as well to quantify ratio ω. The first two columns of table 10.5 trace the movement of v and of ω in the United States between 1940 and 1993. Setting $\sigma = 1.5$, we calculate the variations in the technological bias with the help of formula (29). The latter appear in the last column of table 10.5. We observe an acceleration of technological progress in favor of those with skills since 1980. This period is exactly the one that saw the strongest rise in wage inequality. Autor et al. (1998) have carried out the same type of exercise, and obtain similar results, for the 1980s, though they do observe a slowdown in biased technological progress between 1990 and 1996. This divergence appears to be due essentially to differences in the definition of the two categories of worker. That underlines the fact that the results are highly sensitive to the type of split adopted.

It is worth noting that the relative supply of skilled workers, represented by the variable v, has also risen strongly since 1980 (around 3% annually). But since the relative wages of skilled workers have nevertheless risen, we obviously must conclude that the increase in the relative supply of skilled labor was not enough to offset the bias of technological progress in favor of skilled labor. With the data in table 10.5, we can calculate that, for the period 1979–1989, the relative supply of skilled labor would have had to increase at an annual rate of 4.6% instead of 2.7% for the ratio of skilled to unskilled wages to remain stable.

All these elements point to the conclusion that technological bias has played an important role in reshaping the demand for labor from workers with different skill levels. They also suggest that the bias of technological progress accelerated during the 1980s and the 1990s. According to Card and DiNardo (2002), this acceleration was greater during the 1990s. Yet wage inequalities leveled off during this period (see figure 10.5). Card and DiNardo conclude from this that the bias of technological progress was not the main cause of the rise in inequality in the United States during the 1980s. The decline in the real value of the minimum wage during this period likely played a large part, a subject to which we will return in section 2.5.1 below.

From another point of view, it is important to note that technological bias in favor of the most skilled workers obviously depends on the type of innovation that underlies technological progress, and that the intensity of the bias of technological progress during the 1980s was not, in all probability, greater than at certain periods in the more distant past. Goldin and Katz (1998) show that in the United States, the adoption of electrical energy during the years 1910–1930 profoundly altered production processes and led to a reshaping of labor demand in favor of those with skills at least as powerful as that of the contemporary period. Conversely, the trend to mechanization in the nineteenth century, which entailed the replacement of handicraft production (employing skilled labor intensively) by mechanized mass production (employing low-skilled labor intensively) was likely biased in favor of low-skilled labor (Goldin and Katz, 1998).

Sectoral Studies

Sectoral studies shed further, and more qualitative, light on the nature of technological bias. They show that it is linked to the utilization of new technologies and more capital-intensive means of production, which spread throughout the whole economy.

Research on U.S. data generally finds that the introduction of new technologies (investment in computerization, expenditures in research and development, changes to the capital–labor ratio, employment of scientists and engineers . . .) is accompanied by alterations to the structure of employment at the expense of unskilled manpower. For example, Berman et al. (1994) estimate, on sectoral U.S. data, that the relative growth of skilled labor is positively correlated with investment in computer equipment and research and development. Autor et al. (1998) show that, in every sector, the bias of technological progress is linked to the utilization of computers. This relationship turns up in the principal industrialized countries of the OECD (Machin and Van Reenen, 1998). This research emphasizes, in addition, that the reshaping of labor demand has spread through all sectors of the American economy. According to Berman et al. (1994), intrasectoral reallocation explains 70% of the rise in the proportion of nonmanual workers in manufacturing jobs. No more than 30% of this rise is attributed to between-sector reallocation.

The spread of computer technology has spurred much research. Krueger (1993) observes that more intensive use of computer technology goes hand in hand with rising earnings inequality. He claims that the increasing use of computers in the 1980s was essentially restricted to more skilled workers, and contributed to widening the wage gap in their favor. The wage bonus associated with the use of computers is thought to be on the order of 20% in 1989. Research by Entorf and Kramarz (1997) and

Entorf et al. (1999) on French data indicate, however, that too much may be read into estimates of this type. These authors emphasize the possibility of a selection bias: firms may have chosen the most productive employees to work with the new equipment. For that matter, their estimates suggest that this selection bias explains the largest part of the wage bonus. When this selection bias is corrected for, it turns out that the wage bonus linked to the use of the computer amounts to only 2%. This result is confirmed by a study on German data by DiNardo and Pischke (1997), which shows that pens, pencils, and even the sitting position exert positive effects on wages similar to those induced by computers. Users of computers, pens, and pencils, or even persons who work in a sitting position, likely possess unobservable characteristics that favor high productivity. Therefore, individuals receiving relatively high wages would have been the first to be provided with computers. Whatever the reasons for the influence of computers on wage inequality may be, all the research suggests that computerization changes the way firms function by reshaping labor demand to the advantage of workers whose relative productivity is high.

2.2.3 Technological Progress and Labor Supply

To this point, technological progress has been considered as exogenous. But the fact is that the form an innovation takes is not independent of the capacities of those who will be assigned to make use of it. It is likely that a relative abundance of manpower with low skills will spur the invention of technologies that complement this input. This seems to have been the case at the end of the eighteenth century and early in the nineteenth century, when the rural exodus of low-skilled manpower was accompanied by new kinds of machinery that workers of that sort could operate to carry out repetitive manufacturing tasks (see Acemoglu, 2002). So it is entirely possible, on that basis, that the increase in the supply of skilled labor in the second half of the twentieth century (shown in table 10.5) spurred innovations of the kind that complement skilled labor.

Endogenous Technological Progress

We can illustrate the determinants of technological progress by assuming that firms choose not only quantities of skilled and unskilled labor, but also technology, represented by parameters A_h and A_ℓ in the model with two categories of workers utilized to this point. Let us consider a simplified limit case, in which one unit of output is required to produce one unit of technological factor h or ℓ. The problem of the representative firm is then written:

$$\underset{(A_h, L_h, A_\ell, L_\ell)}{\text{Max}} \quad G(A_h L_h, A_\ell L_\ell) - w_h L_h - w_\ell L_\ell - A_h - A_\ell$$

The production function $G(A_h L_h, A_\ell L_\ell)$ has to have constant returns to scale with respect to all inputs, A_h, L_h, A_ℓ, and L_ℓ. Assuming, for the sake of simplicity, that the production function is of the CES type, it reads:

$$G(A_h L_h, A_\ell L_\ell) = [(A_h L_h)^{(\sigma-1)/\sigma} + (A_\ell L_\ell)^{(\sigma-1)/\sigma}]^{\sigma/2(\sigma-1)}$$

It can easily be verified that the first-order conditions entail that the relative demand for skilled labor satisfies equation (27), and that the choices of technological factors must satisfy:

$$\alpha = \lambda^{\sigma-1} \tag{30}$$

If we assume competitive labor markets, the relative employment of skilled workers is equal to the relative supply of skilled labor, i.e., $\lambda = v$. Equation (30) then shows that the relative productivity $\alpha = A_h/A_\ell$ of skilled workers increases with the supply of skilled workers if and only if the elasticity of substitution is greater than unity. We can also eliminate the technological bias α from equations (27) and (30) to find a relationship between the structure of the labor supply and the wage structure; what we get is:

$$\omega = v^{((1-\sigma)^2-1)/\sigma} \tag{31}$$

This relation shows that the increase in the relative supply of skilled labor, v, leads to a reduction in the relative wage of skilled workers if $\sigma < 2$, and to an increase if not. So the endogenous response of technological progress can lead to an increasing relation between the relative supply of skilled labor and the relative wage of skilled workers, for a sufficiently high value of the elasticity of substitution; and such a value is plausible according to the empirical studies presented above. This rising relation, which does not exist when technological progress is exogenous, arises from the choice by firms of technologies complementary to skilled labor when the quantity of this input grows. Note, however, that the model presented here is very simple, and leaves out the dynamic aspects of the adoption of new technologies. In reality, the installation of new technology is generally accompanied by adjustment costs that can reduce the incomes of the individuals least adaptable to change (on the dynamics of inequality and its links with technological progress, see Aghion, 2002, and Caselli, 1999).

This rudimentary model does nevertheless allow us to understand why an increase in the proportion of highly skilled workers may, on its own, support technological bias and steep wage inequalities. It also highlights the potential ambiguity of the impact of government aid for education on inequality: the general rise in educational level achieved by prolonging compulsory schooling does not always lead to a reduction in inequality. The response of innovators affects the direction of technical progress, and may on the contrary help to increase the inequality between those who succeed in accumulating enough knowledge and know-how to master the new technologies, and the rest. In these circumstances, a rise in supply of skilled labor may increase inequality and have the opposite effect to the one intended.

Overall, theoretical and empirical studies suggest that technological bias has contributed significantly to deepening the inequality between workers with different skill levels. These studies also suggest that the interactions between education and inequality are complex: in order to reduce wage inequality, it is not enough just to increase the proportion of skilled workers, for the direction of technological progress itself depends on the economic environment. But on this point, empirical knowledge is still very slight.

2.3 INTERNATIONAL TRADE

For several decades now, international trade has been on the rise, and the poor countries with a large volume of low-skilled labor ready to accept low pay are playing a larger part. The theory of international trade teaches us that this expanded participation by low-wage countries can lead, in certain circumstances illustrated by the Stolper and Samuelson theorem (1947), to a fall in the demand for low-skilled labor in the rich countries. This result does not, however, hold true in all circumstances. There are situations where we may plausibly argue that stronger competition from low-wage countries benefits low-skilled workers in the rich countries. Empirical research reveals that competition from low-wage countries does have a negative impact, but probably a limited one, on the demand for low-skilled labor.

2.3.1 The Facts

The integration of the world economy, designated by the term "globalization," advanced at some periods and retreated at others during the twentieth century (see Temin, 1999). During recent years, however, the volume of trade between the industrialized countries and the emerging economies has risen, both in terms of exports and imports. The gap in the cost of low-skilled manpower between the rich and the poor countries suggests that the latter have an advantage in the export of goods produced by this type of labor.

The Evolution of Trade Between Industrialized Countries and Developing Countries
Since the end of the 1970s, the fall in demand for unskilled labor in the developed countries has gone along with a strong advance in international trade, and in particular, commercial exchange between rich countries and poor ones. Figure 10.7 presents the openness rate (calculated as the average share of GDP of imports plus exports of goods and services) of several OECD countries. It shows that on average these rates have grown since 1970, notably for the United States, where the openness rate has gone from 10.3% in 1970 to 26.7% in 1999.

Over the same period, the importation of manufactured goods coming from emerging economies has regularly risen. It came to 0.3% of GDP in the OECD zone in 1967, and reached 1.7% in 1998. But this advance has differed noticeably from one country to another. In 1998, the European Union and Canada imported respectively 7.8% and 8.7% of their manufactured products from emerging economies, while imports from this source represented respectively about 25% and 36% of the total imports of manufactured goods for the United States and Japan. Table 10.6 shows that the developing countries have a very modest share of imports into the EU countries at the beginning of the millennium. The share held by the United States is larger, but that country does the largest part of its trading with the industrialized countries of the OECD, and has a lower trade openness than the EU countries.

The growth in imports by rich countries has been more than offset by the growth in their exports. Except for the end of the 1980s, the OECD zone has remained a net exporter of goods and services to emerging economies. Here again, the global data

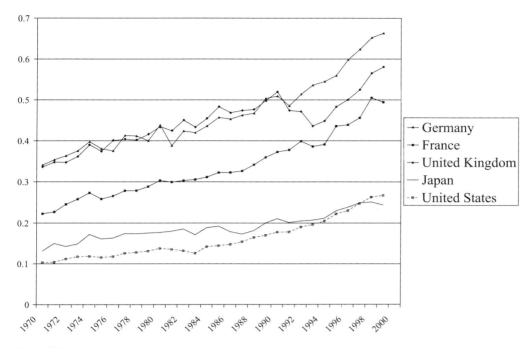

FIGURE 10.7

The openness rate of several OECD countries from 1970 to 2000. The openness rate is defined by (exports + imports)/ GDP.

Source: OECD data.

Table 10.6

The imports of the European Union countries and the United States in 2001.

European Union (15)		United States	
European Union (15)	60.9	European Union (15)	19.2
USA	7.4	Canada	18.7
Japan	2.9	Mexico	11.3
China	2.9	Japan	11.0
Switzerland	2.3	China	9.3
Russian Fed.	1.5	Korea, Rep. of	3.1
Poland	1.0	Taipei, Chinese	2.9
Czech Rep.	1.0	Malaysia	2.0
Hungary	0.9	Venezuela	1.4
Taipei, Chinese	0.9	Thailand	1.3

Source: World Trade Organization, http://www.wto.org.

Legend: Eleven percent of the goods and services imported into the United States come from Japan.

mask important disparities. Since the end of the 1980s, Canada and the United States have been net importers (net imports from emerging economies represented about 1% of the GDP of each of these countries in 1998). Japan, on the other hand, has been a net exporter for more than 30 years (with 2% of its GDP going to developing countries in 1998). Except for the end of the 1980s, the EU is in the same situation as Japan. In 1998, the net exports of the 15 EU countries to emerging economies came to approximately 0.2% of their GDP (the Netherlands, the United Kingdom, and Norway are exceptions to this rule).

The Skills and the Costs of Labor in the Developing Countries
If we examine the structure of employment in the developing countries, we find that they do indeed have large resources of unskilled labor. Skilled labor, in contrast, is relatively rare there. The level of education is much lower in the emerging economies than in the industrialized countries. At the end of the 1980s, almost half the population had no education, and the proportion of individuals with secondary or postsecondary schooling was less than 20%, whereas it was close to 60% in the OECD zone. Of the latter, more than 18% had postsecondary training, whereas the comparable figure in the emerging economies was only around 4% (OECD, 1994, vol. 1, p. 102).

Table 10.7 compares the cost per hour per blue-collar worker in industry in the United States with that of certain developing countries in 1980 and 2000. We see that the differences are considerable. The cost of labor is about three times lower in Hong Kong and Taiwan, and 50 times lower in Sri Lanka. Note, however, that cost differences expressed in dollars do not reflect purchasing power differences. In reality, the currencies of developing countries are generally undervalued. Since workers in poor countries primarily consume products produced locally, the differences in purchasing power are less than the differences in cost. Still, even if the developing countries have a technological lag in many areas, the size of the cost difference for low-skilled labor gives them an advantage in the production of goods requiring intensive utilization of this type of labor.

Table 10.7

Cost of labor of blue-collar workers in the manufacturing industry, in U.S. dollars (100 = United States).

Country	1980	2000
Mexico	22	12
Hong Kong	15	28
Korea	10	41
Sri Lanka	2	2
Taiwan	10	30

Source: Bureau of Labor Statistics, http://www.bls.gov/fls/.

2.3.2   An Illustration of the Stolper and Samuelson Theorem

In international trade theory, each country should export goods the production of which demands the relatively intensive use of the factors of which it has a relatively abundant supply (see Obstfeld and Rogoff, 1996). So increased participation by poor countries in international trade should entail an increased supply of the kind of goods that use unskilled labor intensively and a fall in the price of those goods. International trade theory also establishes that movements in the price of the traded goods have an impact on the price of the inputs needed to produce these goods. The Stolper and Samuelson theorem (1947) establishes that, in every country, trade liberalization entails that the real remuneration of the scarce factor is liable to decline, and that of the abundant factor to rise. So, according to this theorem the wages of the unskilled should decline in the developed countries and rise in the poor countries, whereas the wages of the skilled should rise in the rich countries and decline in the less developed ones. Yet, after reviewing the Stolper and Samuelson theorem, we shall see that it only holds good in particular circumstances. We shall also see that empirical work suggests that these circumstances may not actually come about.

The Closed Economy

In order to examine the impact of international competition on the price of the inputs, let us begin by considering a closed economy, and then open its borders. Three goods are produced: a final good, consumed by agents, and two intermediate ones used in making the final one. The final good is the numeraire, and the price of a unit of intermediate good of type i is denoted by p_i, $i = h, \ell$. Intermediate good h is produced using skilled labor alone, whereas intermediate good ℓ is produced using unskilled labor alone. One unit of labor is needed to produce one unit of intermediate good in every sector. The supply of each kind of labor, denoted by N_i, $i = h, \ell$, is assumed to be given. Production of the final good is represented by a concave function with constant returns $F(A_h Y_h, A_\ell Y_\ell)$, where Y_h and Y_ℓ designate the quantities of intermediate goods produced respectively by the skilled and the unskilled workers. Parameters A_h and A_ℓ are measures of technological progress that increases the efficiency of, respectively, skilled and unskilled labor.

Assuming that the market for the final good is perfectly competitive, the demands for the intermediate goods are found using the maximization problem of the representative firm in this sector:

$$\underset{\{Y_h, Y_\ell\}}{\text{Max}} \ F(A_h Y_h, A_\ell Y_\ell) - p_h Y_h - p_\ell Y_\ell \tag{32}$$

The solutions to this problem are:

$$p_i = A_i F_i(A_h Y_h, A_\ell Y_\ell), \qquad i = h, \ell \tag{33}$$

In this expression, F_i, $i = h, \ell$, designates respectively the partial derivative of function F with respect to its first and second arguments. Assuming that the markets are perfectly competitive, we have $Y_i = N_i$, for $i = h, \ell$, and in every sector, the wage

w_i equals the price p_i. Using the equilibrium conditions, $Y_i = N_i$ and $w_i = p_i$, together with the homogeneity of degree zero of the partial derivatives of function F, we arrive, with the help of (33), at:

$$w_i = p_i = A_i F_i(\alpha v, 1), \quad i = h, \ell \quad \text{with} \quad \alpha = A_h/A_\ell \text{ and } v = N_h/N_\ell \tag{34}$$

This relation entails that any increase in the relative supply of skilled labor v reduces the price p_h and the wage w_h in the skilled sector, and has an effect of the opposite sign in the other sector.[6] The result is that the relative price p_h/p_ℓ of the good produced by the skilled workers and the relative wage of these workers diminish with the relative supply of skilled labor. So in countries richly endowed with skilled labor, skilled workers should get a lower relative wage than in countries poorly endowed with this type of labor.

The Open Economy

Let us now open up the economy, and assume that the rest of the world produces the same goods with the same technologies and is endowed with skilled and unskilled labor in quantities $\tilde{N}_h$ and $\tilde{N}_\ell$. Since all the technologies yield constant returns, production of the final good and the demand for the intermediate goods can always be obtained from the behavior of a representative firm as formalized by the optimization problem (32). Relation (33) thus continues to hold. But equilibrium in each labor market entails that the total supply of intermediate good i now equals $\tilde{N}_i + N_i$. The equilibrium conditions in the markets for goods are thus written $Y_i = \tilde{N}_i + N_i$, which, with the help of relation (33), gives us the equilibrium values of wages, $\bar{w}_i$, and prices, $\bar{p}_i$:

$$\bar{w}_i = \bar{p}_i = A_i F_i(\alpha \bar{v}, 1), \quad i = h, \ell \quad \text{with} \quad \bar{v} = (N_h + \tilde{N}_h)/(N_\ell + \tilde{N}_\ell) \tag{35}$$

Comparison of $\bar{p}_i$, and p_i tells us that the price of good h is higher after the opening of the economy if $\bar{v} < v$, i.e., if the rest of the world is less intensively endowed with skilled labor. The relative price of good h does indeed rise with the ratio of unskilled to skilled labor. If the relative supply of skilled labor in the world market is inferior to that in the closed economy, then opening it up leads to an increase in the relative price of the good produced using skilled labor. Relation (35) illustrates the Stolper and Samuelson theorem (1947). It indicates that the increase in trade reduces the remuneration of the factors that are scarce (relative to other countries) and increases that of the factors that are abundant. According to this theorem, liberalizing trade with low-wage countries ought to increase the wage of skilled workers and reduce that of low-skilled workers in the rich countries that are well endowed with skilled labor.

The Limitations of the Stolper and Samuelson Theorem

The validity of the Stolper and Samuelson theorem is grounded in quite specific assumptions. This theorem assumes that all goods are traded, that the markets are perfectly competitive, and that countries have access to the same technologies. If these hypotheses are not fulfilled, the results may turn out differently. To confirm this, let us assume that countries do not use the same technologies to produce the final good: for example, let the rest of the world make use of a production function $F(\tilde{A}_h \tilde{Y}_h, \tilde{A}_\ell \tilde{Y}_\ell)$. In that case, the same line of reasoning as the one followed above entails that the equilibrium values of the price and the wage are now defined by:

$$\overline{w}_i = \overline{p}_i = A_i F_i \left(\frac{A_h N_h + \tilde{A}_h \tilde{N}_h}{A_\ell N_\ell + \tilde{A}_\ell \tilde{N}_\ell}, 1 \right), \qquad i = h, \ell \tag{36}$$

As we see, the wage of skilled workers (which decreases with respect to the first argument of function F_h) no longer depends exclusively on the relative proportions of skilled and unskilled workers, but also on the technologies of the two countries. If the rest of the world has a relative abundance of low-skilled labor ($\tilde{v} < v$), but if this labor is relatively less efficient than in the domestic economy ($A_\ell/A_h > \tilde{A}_\ell/\tilde{A}_h$), then it is possible to arrive at situations in which liberalization of trade with countries that abound in low-skilled manpower will lead to a rise in the wages of low-skilled workers in the domestic economy and a fall in the wages of skilled ones (if $\alpha v < \tilde{\alpha}\tilde{v}$). This example illustrates a situation in which the developed countries complement low-skilled labor with technologies more capital-intensive than the ones used in the developing countries. In this case, trade liberalization may be favorable to low-skilled workers in the industrialized countries and may help to reduce wage inequality in these countries.

These points suggest that the impact of international trade on the welfare of unskilled workers is strongly dependent on the structure of the economies in which they live and work. So it is not an ascertained fact that the shift in labor demand at the expense of workers with fewer skills observed in the industrialized countries is the consequence of increased participation by low-wage countries in international trade. To find out more, we must turn our attention to empirical research.

2.3.3 Empirical Results

Four different methods are used to assess the impact of competition from low-wage countries on employment. The first, launched by Leontief (1953), is pure accounting. It consists of assessing the employment content of exports and imports, and then, with reference to the country's balance of trade, calculating the gains (or losses) in employment connected with international trade. The second method tries to quantify the effect of imports from developing countries on the price of products intensive in low-skilled labor. The third method assesses the impact of imports from low-wage countries on the evolution of employment, using longitudinal country data. The last method focuses on the impact of imports on the structure of employment in different sectors of the same economy.

Assessing the Employment Content of Exports and Imports
The assessment of the employment content of exports and imports is based on simple principles, which it is, however, a delicate matter to apply. We calculate the content of type j employment in one dollar of exports and one dollar of imports in sector i,

denoted by e_i^j and m_i^j respectively. Let EXP_i be the exports and let IM_i be the imports of good i, both expressed in dollars; the balance B_j of type j jobs is then defined by:

$$B_j = \sum_i (e_i^j EXP_i - m_i^j IM_i)$$

The problems posed by the calculation of this balance arise from the assessment of the coefficients m_i^j. The statistics that let us obtain such coefficients for low-wage countries are often of doubtful quality. Moreover, the goods imported are often different from the goods that would be produced locally, and even if they were identical, they could be produced locally with different technologies, generally ones more intensive in skilled labor.

We may distinguish two methods of calculating coefficients m_i^j. First, it is possible to take the view that the employment content of one dollar of imports in sector i is equal to the employment content of one dollar of exports in the same sector. If that is so, it suffices to estimate e_i^j, and to set $m_i^j = e_i^j$ (method 1 in table 10.8). Another way to proceed is to assume that the job losses arising from imports should be calculated on the basis of the coefficients of the developing countries, to the extent that imported goods are not identical to the goods produced in the developed countries. It would then be necessary to correct these coefficients in order to take into account the higher cost of unskilled labor in the developed countries, which should give firms an incentive to utilize technologies more intensive in skilled labor. It is also important to take into account the fact that products would cost more if they were not imported, and so would be purchased in smaller quantities (method 2 in table 10.8).

These two kinds of calculation can yield very different results when the technologies in the countries considered are themselves different. Poor countries use technologies that are much more intensive in unskilled labor than ones used in developed countries. Table 10.8 shows that the balances in employment vary considerably according to the kind of calculation chosen.

Table 10.8

The employment balance of trade in manufactured products in 1990.

Employment	Method 1	Method 2
Total	−5.7	−10.8
Skilled	−4.3	0.3
Unskilled	−6.2	−21.8

Source: Wood (1995, p. 66).

Legend: Methods 1 and 2 are defined in the text. Method 1 applies to the United States and method 2 to the OECD countries. The figures for method 1 come from Sachs and Schatz (1994), and those for method 2 come from Wood (1994). According to method 1, the employment balance of trade in manufactured products with the emerging countries is in deficit by 5.7% with respect to a scenario with no international trade.

Although the data presented in table 10.8 do not concern exactly the same countries, they do highlight the fact that these assessments are highly sensitive to the choice of the coefficients defining the employment content of imported goods. The figure obtained by Wood (1994) for the industrialized countries as a whole is three times greater than that obtained by Sachs and Shatz (1994) for the United States. Method 1 probably underestimates the losses of unskilled jobs, inasmuch as competition from low-wage countries entails the disappearance of technologies intensive in unskilled labor in the developed countries, and studies that adopt this method do generally conclude that trade with low-wage countries has a low incidence, reducing the demand for unskilled industrial labor by around 2% in the United States and Europe (Freeman, 1995). Conversely, method 2, the one used by Wood (1994), might overestimate job losses, for it assumes that the developed countries would utilize the same technology as that used in the low-wage countries if they were to produce the goods themselves instead of importing them. But we may suppose that technology in the developed countries is more efficient than it is in developing ones, and given that, the job losses would be smaller than the ones calculated by Wood (see OECD, 1997, chapter 4, and Borjas et al., 1997, for more detail).

The assessment of the employment content of exports and imports supplies a first evaluation of the effect of international trade on employment. But it leaves out many factors. In particular, Wood (1994, 1998) maintains that globalization stimulates ''defensive'' innovations in the developed countries that let employers economize on low-skilled labor. This type of argument highlights the fact that technological bias and international competition are interdependent factors. Models with endogenous technological progress allow us to study these phenomena (Acemoglu, 1999; Thoenig and Verdier, 1999).

Wood estimates, on the basis of very simple methods that need to be refined, that these effects, which are left out of the strict analysis of employment content, are significant, and explain around 10% of the shift of labor demand in favor of those with skills. More generally, globalization exerts pressure on the economy as a whole. It alters the price system and provokes chain reactions that have to be comprehended within a general equilibrium framework explaining price formation. Nevertheless, Krugman (1995) shows, within such a framework, that the method of employment content does give good approximations as long as the share of imports from the low-wage countries in the GDP remains slight.

Changes in Relative Price
International trade theory teaches us that the effect of competition from low-wage countries should be estimated by observing the fall in the price of goods intensive in low-skilled labor. In the two-sector model presented above, the fall in the price of goods intensive in unskilled labor can lead to a strong decline in unskilled employment when the purchasing power of unskilled workers in the developed countries is downwardly rigid. Conversely, if wages are perfectly flexible, the fall in the price of the good intensive in unskilled labor has no effect on employment as long as the

Table 10.9

Evolution of import and export prices between 1980 and 1990 (in %).

Country	Import prices	Export prices
France	20.9	38.0
Germany	20.2	40.4
United States	0.7	30.3
OECD average	18.0	29.5

Source: OECD (1997, chapter 4, table 4.6, p. 120).

Legend: The prices of imports rose by an average of 18% in OECD countries between 1980 and 1990. Import prices are the average unit prices of imports in sectors exposed to competition from foreign products. Export prices are average unit prices in the exporting sectors.

supply of unskilled labor remains constant. Then it is the wage of the unskilled that falls.

So the first thing we must do is to verify that the prices of internationally traded products that are highly intensive in low-skilled labor have actually fallen *with respect* to other prices. This does indeed appear to have been the case according to the data in table 10.9. Between 1980 and 1990, the import prices of products in sectors exposed to foreign competition rose by an unweighted average of 18% over the whole OECD zone (the rise was less than 1% in the United States). But at the same time the export prices of products in exporting sectors saw a much stronger rise, on the order of 30% both in the United States and in the OECD countries as a whole. Consequently the fall in the *relative price* of goods exposed to foreign competition was significant in practically all the industrialized countries (this fall was on the order of 12% for the whole OECD zone).

It is possible, using (among other things) estimates of the elasticities of labor supply and demand, to quantify the impact of movements in the relative price of products exposed to competition from emerging economies on employment in the industrialized countries. The results are not all uniform, but at the time of writing the prevalent conclusion is that trade with the developing countries has played a small part in worsening the situation of low-skilled workers. For example the OECD study (1997, chapter 4) finds that the fall in the relative price of exposed goods explains less than 10% of the increase in the wage gaps observed in the United Kingdom and the United States. Similarly, this fall explains no more than a small part, between 1% and 7% according to the country examined, of the relative deterioration in the employment of low-skilled workers.

What Longitudinal Country Data Tell Us

Another way to grasp the impact of competition from low-wage countries is to see whether the countries most exposed to this competition are the ones where employment has fallen off the most, all other things being equal. The econometric studies carried out by Wood (1994), Saeger (1997), and Rowthorn and Ramaswamy (1998) show that there exists a relationship between increased imports from low-wage countries and the decline in industrial employment. The results of these estimates are sensitive to the specifications chosen, but these three studies obtain significant results which point to the conclusion that international trade does have an effect. Rowthorn and Ramaswamy estimate that the emergence of the poor countries explains 20% of the fall in industrial employment between 1970 and 1994, while for Saeger this figure amounts to 25%–30%, and Wood puts it as high as 70%. This last figure is clearly larger because it takes into account the defensive innovations induced by the competition from low-wage countries.

On the whole, research suggests that competition from low-wage countries has helped to alter the structure of labor demand at the expense of low-skilled workers in the rich countries. Nevertheless, the growth of international trade probably explains no more than a limited portion of the change that labor demand has undergone.

2.4 MIGRATIONS

The immigration of workers with few skills is sometimes denounced as a factor in both the decline of wages and the rise of unemployment for this category of worker. The putative consequence is a diminution in the well-being of native workers with few skills and an increase in inequality. Scrutiny of migratory flows does reveal that the rich countries do have immigrant populations less skilled, on average, than natives. We will nevertheless see that the immigration of low-skilled workers has, in theory, an ambiguous impact on inequality. Empirical research confirms this point of view, suggesting that the immigration of low-skilled workers has little effect on earnings and employment among the least skilled native workers.

2.4.1 The Characteristics of Migrations

As table 10.10 bears witness, the foreign-born represent widely varying percentages of the populations of the different OECD countries. Among the 15 countries present in table 10.10, in 1998, Australia leads with 21.1% and Spain brings up the rear with 1.5%. The United States occupies a middle position. These differences reflect different degrees of attractiveness, as well as differences in immigration policy, which itself varies over time in each country. The characteristics of migration have evolved markedly for the last several decades in the OECD countries. Historically the United States is an important destination, and receives the largest number of immigrants of all the OECD countries. It took in 650,000 persons in 1998, but the rate of immigration there at present is two or three times lower than it was in the middle of the nineteenth century and the early part of the twentieth century. Thus, in 1998 there were two arrivals for every thousand inhabitants (see Coppel et al., 2001). On the other hand, many European countries have gone from being sending countries to receiving countries. This emerges from figure 10.8, which shows that the net flow of migrants became largely positive in the European countries after the 1980s, and reached a peak at the beginning of the 1990s in the wake of the collapse of the Soviet bloc.

Table 10.10

Immigrants as a percentage of the total population.

Country	1981	1991	1998
Australia	20.6	22.7	21.1
Austria	3.9	6.6	9.1
Belgium	9.0	9.2	8.7
Canada	16.1	15.6	17.4
Denmark	2.0	3.3	4.8
Finland	0.3	0.7	1.6
France	6.8	6.3	6.3
Germany	7.5	8.2	8.9
Italy	0.6	1.5	2.1
Netherlands	3.8	4.8	4.4
Norway	2.1	3.5	3.7
Spain	0.5	0.9	1.5
Sweden	5.0	5.7	5.6
United Kingdom	2.8	3.1	3.8
United States	6.2	7.9	9.8

Source: OECD.

Legend: Immigrants are defined as persons of foreign nationality in the European countries, and persons born abroad in Australia, Canada, and the United States.

   Global orders of magnitude aside, it is important to emphasize that the migrants arriving in the rich countries of the OECD have socioeconomic characteristics that generally differ from those of natives. The migrants are younger, the proportion of men is larger, they are concentrated in the major cities, their educational level is lower, they hold less skilled jobs for comparable levels of education and experience, and they are more frequently unemployed. These average differences may conceal differences among nationalities, inasmuch as socioeconomic characteristics are strongly influenced by the country of origin. What is more, differences between the performance of migrants and that of natives appear to dwindle, the longer immigrants are present in the receiving country. Chiswick (1978) initially identified this phenomenon in the United States from U.S. census data for 1970. He shows that immigrants arriving in the United States earn, on average, an income 17% lower than that of natives with comparable characteristics (educational level, experience, sex, region). This difference dwindles by around 1% per year. The earnings of migrants who arrived more than 15 years ago even overtake those of natives. This phenomenon, which also seems to be discernible in other OECD countries, has drawn much attention. It might result from the progressive integration of immigrants into the receiving economy, which would explain the shrinkage of the gap in relative earnings between migrants and natives, but not the fact that the migrants end up with higher earnings than

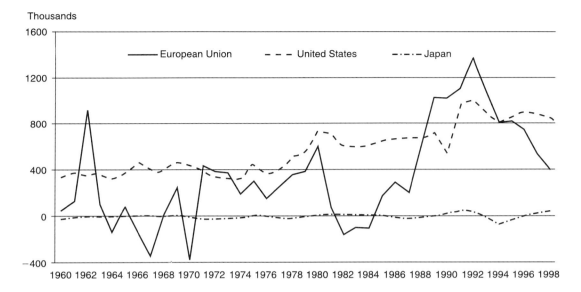

Thousands

FIGURE 10.8
Net migration in three regions of the OECD.
Legend: Net migration is measured as the difference between the total population on January 1 and December 31 for a given calendar year, minus the difference between births and deaths.

Source: Coppel et al. (2001, figure 2). Original data from OECD Labour Force Statistics; Eurostat (1999), Demographic Statistics.

natives. Selection biases might be at the origin of this finding: migrants whose unobservable characteristics (appetite for work, efficiency,…) are above average should end up with higher average earnings once the integration phase is over. Finally, it is not out of the question that the cross-section estimate of Chiswick (1978) is sensitive to a cohort effect if the average quality of migrants falls off over time. If this is the case, the observation of an improvement in the relative earnings of immigrants with time passed in the United States may simply result from the fact that the migrants who have been there longest belong to cohorts the average quality of which was higher. In sum, it does seem that the relative earnings of migrants are influenced by how long they have been in the receiving country, but it is still very difficult to identify the exact influence that length of residence, age, cohort, and selection biases have on the earnings profile of migrants (see the survey of Borjas, 1999).

This rapid review of the facts suggests that immigration may potentially increase inequality in the rich countries of the OECD, since these take in workers whose performance in the labor market is on average less good than that of natives. Let us now examine what theory has to tell us on this point.

2.4.2   Theory

The impact of migrations on the labor market is usually studied using an elementary model of labor demand. The procedure is to analyze the consequences of migration for wages, which are assumed to be determined in perfectly competitive markets. Labor supply is equal to the size of the labor force, including natives and immigrants, and it is the properties of labor demand that play a determining role (see Borjas, 1999).

What the Elementary Model of Short-Run Labor Demand Tells Us

Let us begin by considering an economy in which labor is a homogeneous factor. Production is described using a function with constant returns $F(K, L)$, of which the two arguments are the quantity of labor L and the quantity of capital K. Let us assume that the labor market is competitive, and let N be the size of the labor force. The wage w is then given by the marginal productivity of labor at full employment, i.e., $w = F_L(K, N)$. In the short run, the stock of capital does not vary, and an increase in the labor force (through a wave of immigration, for example) necessarily leads to a wage reduction due to the decrease in the marginal productivity of labor. This reasoning shows that the immigration of a population whose productive characteristics are identical to those of the residents entails a reduction in all wages in the short run, and an increase in the remuneration of capital, $r = F_K(K, N)$, inasmuch as capital is less quickly adjustable than employment. It is possible to assess the wage reduction from knowledge of wage elasticity with respect to employment, η_L^w, which is equal to the inverse of the wage elasticity of labor demand, $\eta_w^L = F_L/LF_{LL}$. For a given stock of capital,[7] we can estimate that η_w^L takes the approximate value -3. An immigration corresponding to 1% of the labor force then reduces the wage by $(1/3)\% \simeq 0.3\%$. So the short-run effects are potentially slight.

Despite the wage reduction, immigration entails an overall gain for the natives as a whole if they are owners of capital. This we can show by calculating the variations in their wages and the variations in the remuneration of capital due to immigration. Figure 10.9 represents the impact of immigration when the labor force comprises N natives and M migrants, and the labor market is assumed to be perfectly competitive. Let w_0 be the wage in the absence of immigration; in this hypothesis, we have $w_0 = F_L(K, N)$ and the GDP, equal to $F(K, N)$, is represented by the surface of the quadrilateral $OABE$.[8] With the presence of immigrants, the GDP is higher, since it corresponds to the surface of the quadrilateral $OACG$, of which an amount Mw_1 is obtained by the immigrants in the form of labor remuneration. Immigration thus produces a surplus to the profit of natives equal to the surface of the triangle BCD. This surplus represents the sum of the variations in the labor and capital earnings. We can approximate it by the term $(M/2)(w_0 - w_1)$. Since $w_1 - w_0 = F_L(K, N + M) - F_L(K, N)$, assuming that M is small with respect to N, a first-order expansion gives $w_1 - w_0 = MF_{LL}(K, N)$, and the surplus S is equal to $-(M^2/2)F_{LL}(K, N)$. In practice, it is more instructive to focus on the relationship between the surplus and production Y. Since the wage elasticity of labor demand is $\eta_w^L = F_L/LF_{LL}$, we get:

$$\frac{S}{Y} = -\frac{1}{2}\left(\frac{M}{N}\right)^2 \frac{NF_{LL}}{F_L}\frac{F_L N}{Y} = -\frac{m^2 s^L}{2\eta_w^L}$$

In this expression, $s^L = wN/Y$ designates the share of labor earnings in the GDP and $m = M/N$ represents the ratio of the number of migrants to the number of natives.

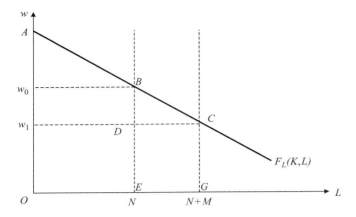

FIGURE 10.9
The consequences of immigration in a model with homogeneous labor and fixed capital.

This expression of the surplus allows us to make quantitative evaluations, inasmuch as the labor share in the GDP is of the order of 2/3, and the wage elasticity of labor demand takes the value, in the framework chosen with fixed capital, of around -3. With these orders of magnitude, for $m = 10\%$, we get $S/Y = 0.1\%$. A population of immigrants representing 10% of the native population thus gives the natives a surplus of around 0.1% of GDP (evaluated before immigration).

This line of reasoning, pursued with the hypothesis of homogeneous labor, clarifies only one part of the impact of immigration on the remuneration of labor and capital earnings. If we distinguish between skilled and unskilled labor, using a function of the type $F(K, L_h, L_\ell)$, it turns out that the immigration of a population less qualified on average than the native population leads to a reduction in wages for the unskilled—since $w_\ell = F_\ell(K, L_h, L_\ell)$ and $F_{\ell\ell} < 0$—and to an increase in the remuneration of capital. The impact on the wages of skilled workers is a priori ambiguous, for skilled labor is complementary to capital, itself substitutable for low-skilled labor (see chapter 4 on this point). Simulations carried out for reasonable values of the elasticities of the factor demands show that the wages of skilled workers are reduced by the immigration of workers with few skills, but in a smaller proportion than is the case with the unskilled. In the short run, the immigration of workers with few skills thus entails an increase in inequality, since it increases the remuneration of capital and reduces wages, with the latter effect being more pronounced for those earning low wages.

What the Elementary Model of Labor Demand Tells Us in the Long Run
Let us come back to the case of homogeneous labor. In the long run, the marginal productivity of capital equals the interest rate, i.e., $r = F_K(K, N)$. This condition determines the capital–labor ratio, $k = K/N$, which satisfies $r = F_K(k, 1)$, and entails, with

labor demand, that wages are finally independent of the size of the labor force, since $w = F_L(k, 1)$. Variations in the stock of capital, financed by domestic or foreign savings, ensure that in the long run, wages and population size are independent of each other. In figure 10.9, the graph of the labor demand function becomes a horizontal line $w = F_L(k, 1)$.

Obviously, if labor is heterogeneous, the composition of the population affects the relative incomes from different types of labor. To illustrate this phenomenon, let us return to the labor demand model used in the previous section, leaving capital aside (the mechanisms are generalizable to the case with capital; see Borjas, 1999). In a closed economy, the wage level of each category of labor is given by relation (34), i.e., $w_i = A_i F_i(\alpha v, 1)$, $i = h, \ell$, with $\alpha = A_h/A_\ell$ and $v = N_h/N_\ell$. It turns out that immigration has an impact on the structure of wages if and only if it alters the proportion of skilled workers. On the contrary, if the immigrants have, on average, levels of skill identical to those of the natives, immigration has the effect of increasing production while leaving wage inequality untouched. When the immigrants are less skilled than the natives, immigration helps to reduce the relative number of skilled workers, v, which increases their wage and reduces that of the unskilled. So the immigration of low-skilled workers does have the effect of deepening the inequality between the skilled and the unskilled.

Overall, the picture painted by the labor demand model indicates that the immigration of low-skilled workers increases inequality. This prediction is not, however, ironclad.

The Influence of Technological Progress and International Trade
A number of arguments undermine the generality of the notion that the immigration of low-skilled workers increases inequality. These include the endogeneity of the technological bias, the influence of international trade, and access to social assistance.

The very simple model of labor demand used to study the impact of immigration on factor remuneration leaves out the response of technological progress to changes in labor supply. We have pointed out, applying relation (31), that the interactions between technological progress and labor demand might lead to an increasing relation between the relative supply of skilled labor and the relative wage of this type of labor. It is indeed possible for firms to promote innovation using techniques that complement the type of labor that is most abundant. In consequence, an increase in the relative supply of low-skilled labor may bend the technological bias in their favor, and entail, in the end, if strong enough, an increase in their relative wage.

Another limitation of the labor demand model lies in its failure to take international trade into account. Actually, it turns out that in an open economy, immigration may have no impact on inequality whatever its composition (Johnson and Stafford, 1999). If we go back to the model from the preceding section, the wage level of each category of labor is given by relation (35), or $\bar{w}_i = A_i F_i(\alpha \bar{v}, 1)$, $i = h, \ell$, with $\bar{v} = (N_h + \tilde{N}_h)/(N_\ell + \tilde{N}_\ell)$. In an economy facing international competition in the goods market, wages depend on the *global* structure of labor supply, independently of where it is located. By equalizing the prices of inputs, international trade has the effect of neutralizing the impact of migrations on wages. Here again, this textbook case illustrates a very stylized situation, in which the only source of heterogeneity among countries lies in their factor endowments. If we take a situation in which countries utilize different technologies, equation (36) shows that equilibrium wages depend on the ratio $(A_h N_h + \tilde{A}_h \tilde{N}_h)/(A_\ell N_\ell + \tilde{A}_\ell \tilde{N}_\ell)$, and are thus influenced by where the inputs are located. For example, if low-skilled migrants are less productive than in their country of origin, immigration leads to a reduction in the global productivity of low-skilled labor—represented by quantity $(A_\ell N_\ell + \tilde{A}_\ell \tilde{N}_\ell)$—and thus an increase in ratio $(A_h N_h + \tilde{A}_h \tilde{N}_h)/(A_\ell N_\ell + \tilde{A}_\ell \tilde{N}_\ell)$, which entails a wage reduction for all low-skilled workers (see equation (36)). It should be noted that immigrants may be attracted to a country where they are less productive than they are in their countries of origin because of differences between, for example, collective goods or amenities.

Finally, immigrants, because they are generally unskilled, resort more frequently to social assistance and unemployment insurance than natives (see Borjas and Hilton, 1996, for the United States and Brücker et al., 2001, for Europe). From this perspective, if the fiscal system is progressive, immigration, by increasing the amount of payroll deductions, may compress the magnitude of take-home pay and so reduce inequality. The corollary of this reduction in inequality is evidently a transfer from natives to immigrants, which reduces the surplus the natives derive from immigration. If these transfers are large, this surplus can even become negative.

These different lines of reasoning show that the immigration of low-skilled workers has, in theory, ambiguous effects on inequality. Empirical research has much to tell us about this matter.

2.4.3   Empirical Results

In essence, three methods are used to study the impact of migration on the labor market. The first consists of carrying out simulations using the elementary model of labor demand presented above. The second analyzes correlations between spatial movements of workers and earnings. Finally, the third method relies on natural experiments. The results of empirical research converge to suggest that migrations have a very feeble impact on inequality.

The Simulations

The elementary model of labor demand allows us to calculate the impact of variations in the quantities of the different inputs on their prices from our knowledge of the elasticities of substitution and of the shares of the factor remunerations in the total cost (see chapter 4). Borjas (1999) presents the results of simulations for the American economy, using a production function comprising three arguments: capital K, skilled labor L_h, and unskilled labor L_ℓ. In the United States in 1995, if we take a high school diploma as marking the boundary between the unskilled and the skilled, the skilled represented 91% of the labor force but only 68% of the migrant population. Assuming that this proportion continued to hold, Borjas studies the impact of a 10% increase in

Table 10.11

Impact of an inflow of immigrants equal to 10% of the labor force.

Variation (%)	Capital (fixed)	Price of capital (fixed)
Earnings of capital	6.49	–
Earnings of skilled workers	−2.29	0.46
Earnings of unskilled workers	−3.72	−4.27
Dollar gain to natives over GDP	0.27	0.14

Source: Simulations made by Borjas (see Borjas, 1999, table 1).

Note: In the first column, the stock of capital is fixed. In the second column, the price of capital is fixed. The boundary between the unskilled and the skilled corresponds to a high school diploma.

the labor force as a result of immigration. He considers several plausible values of the elasticities of labor demand and capital demand. Table 10.11 presents the results for intermediate values of these elasticities. Overall, the simulations carried out point to the conclusion that immigration has a limited impact on wages. These orders of magnitude imply that immigration explains no more than a very small part of the evolution of wage inequality in the United States.

The Spatial Correlations

The elementary model of labor demand concludes that wages, or the probability of employment, for workers who are highly substitutable by immigrants ought to be reduced by immigration. The method of spatial correlations aims to test this type of prediction, and assess the influence of immigration on the opportunities of natives. It consists of estimating the effect of variation in the number of migrants Δm_{ijt} of skill level i, in region j between dates $t-1$ and t, on the variations in the employment opportunities (wages or probability of employment), Δy_{ijt}, of similarly skilled native workers present in region j at dates t and $t-1$. Let $\mathbf{x}_{it}$ be a vector of the characteristics of the natives and of the labor market of type i at date t (age, sex, size of the market,...) and ε_{ijt} a disturbance term; we then seek to estimate an equation of this form:

$$\Delta y_{ijt} = a_t \Delta m_{ijt} + \mathbf{x}_{it} b_t + \varepsilon_{ijt} \tag{37}$$

Estimation of parameter a_t by ordinary least squares generally leads to results not significantly different from zero, with average values that change erratically according to periods (see Borjas et al., 1997; Borjas, 1999; and Friedberg and Hunt, 1995). This approach raises delicate problems, however. The first arises from the endogeneity of the number of new migrants, inasmuch as the latter are attracted by regions where wages are rising. That being so, the observation of a positive correlation between employment opportunities and variations in the number of migrants may simply reflect migrants' choice of where to settle. It is possible to solve this problem by using the instrumental variables method: attempts to do so assume that the immigrants are attracted by the presence of compatriots, and take the foreign-born proportion of the labor force at $t-1$ as an instrument for the variation in the number of migrants between dates $t-1$ and t. The results obtained using these methods still pose the same problems as those obtained by ordinary least squares, inasmuch as they are not generally significantly different from zero, with average values that change erratically according to periods. The second problem arises from the mobility of natives, who may themselves leave regions that receive an inflow of immigrants. Quite clearly, if every immigrant drives out a native, it is not surprising to find that immigration has no impact on wages, in the model of spatial correlation represented by equation (37). Card and DiNardo (2000) suggest, however, that this problem is not statistically significant in the United States.

Natural Experiments

In order to solve the difficulties encountered by research based on spatial correlations, other studies have looked at certain exceptional flows of migration—most often due to political events, such as the Cuban immigration to Miami in May 1980 (Card, 1990), or immigration to France in the wake of Algerian independence in 1962 (Hunt, 1992)—as "natural experiments."

The study of Card (1990) deals with the Cuban immigration, which swelled the labor force of Miami by around 7% between May and September 1980, following the opening of Cuba's borders. Card's strategy was to compare the evolution of unemployment rates and wages in Miami with those of cities presenting characteristics taken to be similar for this purpose. Examination of the evolution of these variables before 1980 led Card to select Atlanta, Los Angeles, Houston, and Tampa–St. Petersburg, cities which, like Miami, have large black and Hispanic populations. The impact of the immigration was assessed with the help of a difference-in-differences estimator, which consists of comparing the changes in the variables pertaining to the group studied in Miami and those pertaining to the "control" group in the other cities between 1979 and subsequent years (see chapter 11 for a more detailed presentation of this approach). More precisely: let Δu_m be the variation in Miami's unemployment rate between 1979 and a subsequent year (1981, for example), and let Δu_c be the average variation in the unemployment rate in the other cities over the same span of time. The estimated impact of the immigration on the unemployment rate is simply equal to $\Delta u_m - \Delta u_c$. Table 10.12 shows that the immigration had no significant impact on the differences in the evolution of unemployment rates of black workers between 1979 and 1981, since the difference-in-differences estimator takes a value of -1 (meaning that the unemployment rate rose less in Miami than in the other cities during this period), with a standard error of 2.8. The results for wages are of the same order.

The study by Hunt (1992), which deals with a flow of migration that swelled the labor force in France by 1.6% in 1962 in the wake of Algerian independence, also finds that migration had a very small, even insignificant, impact on unemployment and wages. Overall, research dedicated to immigration suggests that it has little impact on inequality as regards wages and access to employment.

Table 10.12

Difference-in-differences estimates of the impact of immigration on the unemployment rate in Miami in 1980.

Unemployment rate (%)	1979	1981	1981–1979
Miami	8.3 (1.7)	9.6 (1.8)	1.3 (2.5)
Other cities	10.3 (0.8)	12.6 (0.9)	2.3 (1.2)
Miami–other cities	−2 (1.9)	−3 (2.0)	−1.0 (2.8)

Figures in parentheses are standard deviations.

Source: Angrist and Krueger (1999, table 4).

2.5 Reorganizations, Institutional Changes, and Inequality

Changes in labor market institutions and the organization of the production process can also affect wage inequality and the employment opportunities of the various types of workers. Atkinson (2001) highlighted the fact that the steep rise in the wage gap within the top decile contributed significantly to the overall increase in the spread of wages in the United States during the 1980s. According to Atkinson, it is possible that a modification of "social norms" came about during the 1980s, with a shift from a redistributive pay norm to one where market forces dominate. Institutional change would thus explain a portion of the increase in inequality in the United States during the 1980s. In this section, we examine certain aspects of institutional change, beginning with a brief discussion of the impact of unionization and the minimum wage, then focusing on the role played by reorganizations.

2.5.1 Unions and the Minimum Wage

We saw in chapter 7 that the decline in the unionization rate has helped to increase wage inequality in certain OECD countries. In particular, DiNardo et al. (1996) estimate that the decline in the unionization rate contributed to 10% of the increase in the differential of the (logarithms of) wages between the first and last deciles of the distribution, and to one-third of the increase between the first and the fifth decile in the United States in the 1980s. Card (2001) finds that the decline of unionization explains between 15% and 20% of wage inequality (measured by the variance of the wage logarithms) for the same period.

We will also see, in chapter 12, that the evolution of the minimum wage profoundly influences wage inequality, especially at the low end of the distribution. In the United States, the nominal hourly minimum wage remained constant at $3.35 throughout the 1980s. This constant nominal wage led to a strong reduction in the real wage and an increased bulk at the bottom of the wage distribution. Figure 10.10 shows that the real value of the minimum wage fell sharply during the 1980s, but then

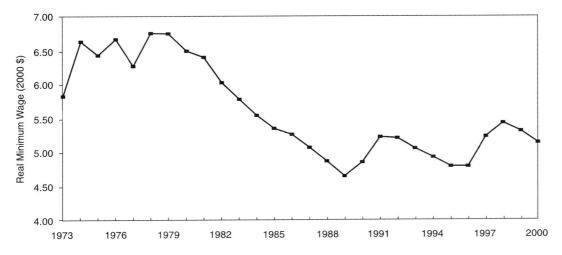

FIGURE 10.10

The real minimum wage in the U.S., 1973–2000.

Source: Card and DiNardo (2002, fig. 22).

leveled off and climbed slightly during the 1990s. The shrinkage of the real minimum wage went along with the increase in inequality observed during this period.

DiNardo et al. (1996) and Lee (1999) estimate that the essential part of the increase in the difference between the first and fifth deciles of the distribution of the wage logarithm is explainable by the decline in the real value of the minimum wage between 1979 and 1988 in the United States. These results contrast with those observed in other OECD countries, such as France, Luxembourg, and Japan, where the ratio between the minimum wage and the average wage remained approximately constant and where wage inequality did not increase significantly over the same period.

Overall, these works suggest that de-unionization and the minimum wage reduction played an essential role in the development of inequality below the median wage in the United States. Although their impact on inequality above the median wage is much less clear, the fact remains that changes to labor market institutions significantly influence wage inequality. That makes it important to understand the evolution of institutions and the choices countries make, if we are to grasp the dynamics of inequality clearly. But this domain remains largely unexplored by economics, inasmuch as the determinants of de-unionization and minimum wages are ill-understood. For this reason, the contribution of Acemoglu et al. (2001) is particularly interesting. They maintain that de-unionization may be the consequence of technological bias if it induces an increase in the relative productivity of skilled workers that defeats the compression of wages exerted by unions. In this context, the technological bias gives the most skilled workers an incentive to go it alone, and breaks off the cooperation with those less skilled that led to the founding of trade unions in the first place.

2.5.2 Organizational and Institutional Changes

Technological change generally goes along with profound change in the organization of production. The first industrial revolution, based on the exploitation of thermal energy, marked the passage from handicraft production to manufacturing. The second industrial revolution, based on mastery of electric power and the combustion engine, led to mass production. It favored the emergence of Taylorism in the factory, with workers being assigned precisely described and scheduled tasks. More recently, information technology and the production of differentiated goods in small batches appear to have favored the development of more flexible work methods. Since the middle of the 1970s products have had shorter life spans, and the niches to be exploited have been smaller and less stable; organizational change has tried to increase the adaptability and the reaction time of the production process through decentralized decision-making and the development of teamwork (Osterman, 1994; Ichinovsky et al., 1997; OECD, 1999). These organizational changes have had the effect of modifying the hiring practices of firms, which today have a tendency to be more selective, particularly those employing new technologies and requiring workers endowed with significant ability to adapt (Murnane and Levy, 1996). Such phenomena are not without effect on inequality. In particular, the new forms of organization have a tendency to accentuate segmentation among workers with different skill levels, which tends to increase inequality. Kremer (1993) gives a good illustration of these chains of cause and effect. He starts with the observation that the explosion of the space shuttle Challenger was caused by the failure of an O-ring costing 25 cents, which was incapable of withstanding high temperatures. Kremer goes on to suggest that the quality of many products, especially ones with high technology content, depends on that of all their components. A product may fail if just one of its components proves defective. The most efficient workers risk seeing their efforts wasted on account of mistakes made by workers less able than they are. Efforts at innovation may then become focused on reducing the interdependence of the tasks performed by workers of different skill levels, which will favor the segmentation of labor.

It is possible to illustrate this phenomenon by considering an economy with a final good produced using two different technologies. The "old" technology employs both skilled and unskilled workers. It is represented by a production function $F(L_h, L_\ell)$ with constant returns, necessarily satisfying[9] $F_{h\ell} > 0$. The "new" technology employs only skilled workers and is represented by the linear function $A_h L_h$. In this framework, an innovation or a technological bias in favor of those with skills corresponds to an increase in productivity in the sector with the new technology, i.e., an increase in A_h.

The wage of skilled workers, whose mobility between the two sectors is assumed to be perfect, necessarily satisfies $w_h = F_h(\lambda, 1) = A_h$ with $\lambda = L_h/L_\ell$. The wage of low-skilled workers is equal to marginal productivity in the sector utilizing the old technology, i.e., $w_\ell = F_\ell(\lambda, 1)$. Since equality $F_h(\lambda, 1) = A_h$ entails that λ decreases with A_h (differentiating with respect to λ and A_h, we get $d\lambda/dA_h = 1/F_{hh}(\lambda, 1) < 0$), relation $w_\ell = F_\ell(\lambda, 1)$ then entails that the wage of low-skilled workers falls when A_h increases (differentiating with respect to λ and w_ℓ, we get $dw_\ell/d\lambda = F_{\ell h}(\lambda, 1) > 0$). In this model, the new technologies attract the most efficient workers into the sector where productivity is rising. Less skilled workers then lose part of the benefit of interacting with more skilled workers, which reduces their productivity and thus their wage. This example shows that labor market segmentation, and the reorganization of the production process that is an inherent part of it, may have a tendency to increase the impact of technological progress on wage inequality. It may even lead to a fall in the lowest wages, which corresponds to the situation in which the United States found itself between the middle of the 1970s and the end of the 1990s, as figure 10.6 shows.

It is important to note that labor market segmentation illustrates just one dimension of the relationship between new technology, reorganization, and inequality. Two other dimensions, highlighted by Thesmar and Thoenig (2000) and by Saint-Paul (2001), deserve mention. Thesmar and Thoenig (2000) studied the impact of the instability of product markets on organizational choices and wage inequality. They show that the reduced life span of products caused by the increased pace of innovation impels firms to choose more flexible modes of production, which are linked to greater wage inequality. Saint-Paul (2001) analyzes the consequences of the increased communication capacity that comes with the new technologies. More precisely, Saint-Paul distinguishes two types of labor input: ideas, which are goods reproducible at low or zero marginal cost, and the physical effort of labor. He shows that the increased dimensions of communications networks have ambiguous effects on wage inequality between the producers of ideas and the producers of physical effort. The increased size of networks benefits not just the producers of ideas, who can make their discoveries pay off more easily, but also the producers of physical effort, who benefit from ideas. Saint-Paul's contribution is particularly interesting because it undermines the often-heard notion that progress in communications technology leads to a society in which a few "superstars" capture most of the productivity gains linked to the new technologies (see Frank and Cook, 1995).

These works throw precious light on the ways that technological progress spreads and the macroeconomic effects it has, emphasizing that technological innovations are accompanied by organizational changes that we must take into consideration if we are to understand the relationship between technological progress and inequality. But in the present state of knowledge they are still very fragmentary.

2.6 THE ANGLO-SAXON MODEL VERSUS THE EUROPEAN MODEL

We have already suggested that the fall in demand for low-skilled labor during the last two decades of the twentieth century led to an increase in wage inequality in the Anglo-Saxon economies and to a heightened incidence of unemployment in continental Europe. To simplify somewhat, we can distinguish two types of behavior in response to the reshaping of labor demand. On the one hand there is the "Anglo-Saxon" model, characterized by wage flexibility and resulting in an increase in wage inequality. Katz and Autor (1999, p. 1502) emphasize that the increase in the wage spread between workers with different skill levels in the 1980s was indeed greatest in the United States and the United Kingdom. On the other hand, the "European" model (especially in Germany, France, Italy, and to a lesser extent Sweden), marked by refusal to accept increasing wage inequality, saw heightened disparity in the incidence of unemployment. In order to understand the impact of the reshaping of labor demand on unemployment and wage inequality, we will introduce two types of skill into the basic matching model from chapter 9. It then becomes possible to assess the evolution of a global inequality index—discounted average gains—for the two types of workers in the Anglo-Saxon and European models. It will be shown that controlling the spread of remunerations by means of a minimum wage can lead, in the end, to an increase in inequality in terms of discounted average gains.

2.6.1   A Matching Model with Two Types of Workers

In the presence of more than one category of worker, labor market equilibrium depends on the possibilities of substitution between the different types of labor. This substitution depends principally on the technology specific to each firm, usually represented by a production function. In reality, the replacement of one employee by another with different skills is imperfectly described by the usual properties of production functions with several substitutable factors. For example, in certain sectors, skilled workers are capable of performing tasks ordinarily assigned to unskilled ones, while the converse does not hold. If there is unemployment, skilled workers can accept performing the tasks of unskilled workers rather than staying unemployed. In these circumstances, skilled labor offsets unskilled labor (Albrecht and Vroman, 2002). We will exclude this possibility for the sake of simplicity.

The Characteristics of the Economy

We will thus assume that there are two labor markets, perfectly sealed off from each other, and corresponding to skilled labor ($i = h$) and unskilled labor ($i = \ell$). In each of these labor markets, there is a matching function $M_i(V_i, U_i)$ where V_i and U_i designate respectively vacant jobs and unemployed persons belonging to category i.

The productive sector of the economy is identical to that considered above in section 2.3. This sector produces three goods: a final good, consumed by agents, and two intermediate goods that serve to produce the final good. The final good is the numeraire, and the price of a unit of intermediate good of type i is denoted by p_h, $i = h, \ell$. Intermediate good h is produced using skilled labor alone, while intermediate good ℓ is produced using unskilled labor alone. Each employee is capable of making one unit of intermediate good per unit of time. Production of the final good is represented by a function with constant returns $F(A_h L_h, A_\ell L_\ell)$, where L_h and L_ℓ can designate either the quantities of intermediate goods produced by the skilled and the unskilled respectively, or the number of skilled and unskilled jobs respectively. Parameters A_h and A_ℓ then measure technological progress that increases the efficiency of skilled and unskilled labor.

The Demands for Intermediate Goods

Assuming that the market for the final good is perfectly competitive, the demands for the intermediate goods are found using the first-order conditions (33) of the maximization problem (32). The result is:

$$p_i = A_i F_i(A_h L_h, A_\ell L_\ell) \qquad \text{and so} \qquad \frac{p_h}{p_\ell} = \frac{A_h F_h(A_h L_h, A_\ell L_\ell)}{A_\ell F_\ell(A_h L_h, A_\ell L_\ell)} \tag{38}$$

At equilibrium, the ratio of the prices of the intermediate goods will thus depend on technological progress and the number of jobs in each of the two worker categories.

The Labor Demands

Let w_i ($i = h, \ell$) be the real wage applying to an employee of type i. In the stationary state, the expected marginal profit Π_i of a job filled by an employee of type i satisfies:

$$r\Pi_i = p_i - w_i + q_i(\Pi_{vi} - \Pi_i) \tag{39}$$

In this relation, the exogenous parameter q_i designates the rate at which jobs of type i are destroyed, and Π_{vi} represents the expected profit from a vacant job reserved for a worker of category i. Let $h_i, \theta_i \equiv V_i/U_i$, and $m_i(\theta_i) \equiv M_i(V_i, U_i)/V_i$ be respectively search costs, the labor market tightness, and the rate at which vacant jobs are filled in the labor market for type i workers. Then Π_{vi} solves:

$$r\Pi_{vi} = -h_i + m_i(\theta_i)(\Pi_i - \Pi_{vi}) \tag{40}$$

When the free entry condition $\Pi_{vi} = 0$ is satisfied, we can eliminate Π_i between relations (39) and (40), in order to obtain the demand for type i labor. It has the expression:

$$\frac{h_i}{m_i(\theta_i)} = \frac{p_i - w_i}{r + q_i} \tag{41}$$

Wage Negotiations

Let z_i again be the instantaneous gain of a type i unemployed person; the expected utilities V_{ei} and V_{ui} of, respectively, an employed worker and an unemployed one of type i are given by the same relations as those in the basic model of chapter 9, i.e.:

$$rV_{ei} = w_i + q_i(V_{ui} - V_{ei}) \qquad \text{and} \qquad rV_{ui} = z_i + \theta_i m(\theta_i)(V_{ei} - V_{ui})$$

Formally, we come back exactly to the simple matching model applied to each labor market separately. In consequence, the wage negotiated is given by equation (20) from chapter 9 defining the wage curve. Let γ_i be the bargaining power of a supplier of type i labor. We will thus have:

$$w_i = z_i + (p_i - z_i)\Gamma_i(\theta_i) \qquad \text{with} \qquad \Gamma_i(\theta_i) = \frac{\gamma_i[r + q_i + \theta_i m(\theta_i)]}{r + q_i + \gamma_i \theta_i m(\theta_i)}; \quad i = h, \ell \tag{42}$$

The effects of the technological bias emerge with particular sharpness if we assume that unemployment benefits are written $z_i = b_i w_i$, where the replacement ratio

b_i is an exogenous parameter, and also that search costs h_i are directly proportional to the sale price of good p_i, i.e., $h_i = hp_i$, where h is an exogenous parameter (it would be equivalent to assume that search costs are proportional to the wage for each category of worker). With these hypotheses, relation (42) shows that the wage is directly proportional to the selling price in the sector. The equation of the wage curve is then written $w_i = p_i \Phi(\theta_i)$ where Φ_i is a function defined from Γ_i by the equality $\Phi_i = \Gamma_i/(1 - b_i + b_i \Gamma_i)$. In consequence, at equilibrium in the labor markets the wage of each category of worker takes the form:

$$w_i = p_i \Phi_i(\theta_i), \qquad i = 1, 2 \tag{43}$$

2.6.2 An "Anglo-Saxon" Labor Market

The Anglo-Saxon model is characterized by flexible wages, freely negotiated at the level of the firm. This flexibility ensures, within the framework of our hypotheses, the independence of unemployment rates with respect to the reshaping of labor demand, but entails the corollary that wage inequalities increase.

Unemployment and the Technological Bias
When wages are freely bargained over in each labor market, the equilibrium value of labor market tightness θ_i is found by setting $w_i = p_i \Phi(\theta_i)$ in equality (41) defining labor demand. It is thus implicitly determined by the equation:

$$\frac{h}{m_i(\theta_i)} = \frac{1 - \Phi_i(\theta_i)}{r + q_i} \tag{44}$$

In consequence, at equilibrium, labor market tightness is independent of the sale prices of the intermediate goods, and so does not depend on the technological bias either. Thus, knowing the equilibrium value of θ_i, the unemployment rate u_i for suppliers of type i labor is found with the help of the Beveridge curve described by relation (7) in chapter 9. Denoting by n_i the labor force growth rate of type i, we get:

$$u_i = \frac{q_i + n_i}{q_i + n_i + \gamma_i m_i(\theta_i)} \tag{45}$$

The equilibrium unemployment rate thus does not depend on the technological bias either. Conversely, relation (43) indicates that the relative wage w_h/w_ℓ is proportional to the ratio of relative prices p_h/p_ℓ, and so does depend on the technological bias.

The Ratio of Wages
In order to make the results more explicit, we will assume that the production function of the final good is of the CES type, defined by equation (26), but in reality our results do not depend on a particular form of the production function. Equation (38) then entails that the ratio p_h/p_ℓ is written:

$$\frac{p_h}{p_\ell} = \left(\frac{A_h}{A_\ell}\right)^{(\sigma-1)/\sigma} \left(\frac{L_h}{L_\ell}\right)^{-1/\sigma} \tag{46}$$

where $\sigma > 0$ designates the elasticity of substitution between skilled and unskilled labor. If N_i represents the (exogenous) size of the labor force of category i, we have $L_i = N_i(1 - u_i)$ and equation (43) gives the relative wage of a skilled person, or:

$$\frac{w_1}{w_\ell} = \left(\frac{A_h}{A_\ell}\right)^{(\sigma-1)/\sigma} \left[\frac{N_h(1 - u_h)}{N_\ell(1 - u_\ell)}\right]^{-1/\sigma} \frac{\Phi_h(\theta_h)}{\Phi_\ell(\theta_\ell)} \tag{47}$$

This model well reproduces the characteristics of the American and British labor markets mentioned in section 2.1 above. The technological bias, represented by the ratio A_h/A_ℓ, does not affect the equilibrium levels of unemployment (see relations (44) and (45)). In particular, the *relative* unemployment rate of the unskilled u_ℓ/u_h remains unvaried when technological evolution is unfavorable to them. But equation (47) shows that wage inequalities will then increase. In this equation, the values of θ_i and of u_i do not depend on the ratio A_h/A_ℓ, and the ratio w_h/w_ℓ increases in both configurations, corresponding to a reshaping of technological progress in favor of skilled workers, i.e., an increase in A_h/A_ℓ when the two types of manpower are highly substitutable ($\sigma > 1$) or a fall in A_h/A_ℓ when the two categories of personnel have low substitutability ($\sigma < 1$). Note that an aggregate shock common to all labor markets would change the equilibrium level of the rates of unemployment in all those markets without necessarily modifying the relative unemployment rate.

The result that the relative unemployment rate does not depend on the technological bias arises principally from the indexation of unemployment benefits and the cost of vacant jobs to individual productivity. Each labor market is thus isolated from the shocks affecting the other one, and the wage for a given category of worker adjusts only in reaction to a specific shock to that category. Any element likely to rupture the hermetic seal between the different labor markets would make the relative unemployment rate dependent on the evolution of the technological bias and would bring us closer to the European model which we are contrasting to the Anglo-Saxon model. There are a number of ways in which the hermetic seal between the different labor markets could be broken, and our model does not take them into account. For example, in many European countries the system of social transfers entails that the gain z_ℓ of the least skilled job-seekers is linked to the evolution of the average wage, or to that of the total factor productivity. The existence of a minimum wage, the variations of which follow those of the average wage, constitutes another potential channel through which the reshaping of technological progress could be transmitted. We will now focus on this eventuality, which well illustrates the situation of the labor markets of continental Europe.

2.6.3   A "European" Labor Market

When the wage of unskilled workers is no longer bargained over, the technological bias affects unemployment for this category of worker. Let us suppose that unskilled workers are paid the minimum wage, and that the minimum wage is indexed to the wage of skilled personnel. With the help of wage equation (43), we will thus have $w_\ell = \mu w_h = \mu p_h \Phi_h(\theta_h)$, where μ is an exogenous parameter lying between zero and 1.

Taking into account the value of ratio p_h/p_ℓ given by relation (46) and again making use of identity $L_i = N_i(1 - u_i)$, equation (41) of demand for unskilled labor takes the form:

$$\frac{h(r + q_\ell)}{m_\ell(\theta_\ell)} = 1 - \mu \left(\frac{A_h}{A_\ell}\right)^{(\sigma-1)/\sigma} \left[\frac{N_h(1 - u_h)}{N_\ell(1 - u_\ell)}\right]^{-1/\sigma} \Phi_h(\theta_h) \tag{48}$$

In this new form of the demand for unskilled labor, θ_h and u_h are determined by equations (44) and (45) for $i = h$. In consequence, they do not depend on the technological bias. Since by definition $\theta_\ell = v_\ell/u_\ell$, equation (48) defines a relation between the vacancy rate v_ℓ and the unemployment rate u_ℓ of unskilled workers. Function $m_\ell(\theta_\ell)$ being decreasing with θ_ℓ, it is easy to verify that this relation between v_ℓ and u_ℓ is increasing. In figure 10.11, it is identified by the symbol $(LD)_\ell$. Labor market equilibrium for unskilled labor lies at the intersection of this curve $(LD)_\ell$ and the Beveridge curve $(CB)_\ell$ proper to this category, the equation of which is given by equality (45) with $i = \ell$.

A technological bias unfavorable to unskilled workers (for example in figure 10.11 we have considered a rise of $x = A_h/A_\ell$ with $\sigma > 1$, but a fall of x with $\sigma < 1$ would have the same effect) shifts the $(LD)_\ell$ curve downward without changing the Beveridge curve. The unemployment rate of unskilled labor increases, and in consequence the relative unemployment rate u_ℓ/u_h likewise increases. This model well describes the situation of a country like France, where the minimum wage is de facto indexed to the average wage. If wages could be adjusted through bargaining, the technological bias would actually lead to an adjustment of remunerations without changing the unemployment rate. But the indexation of the minimum wage to the wage of skilled workers prevents these adjustments from taking place, and in sum, the technological bias entails a rise in unemployment among the unskilled.

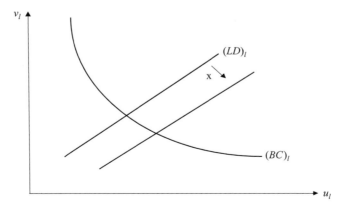

FIGURE 10.11
The unskilled labor market equilibrium.

2.6.4   Does the Minimum Wage Help to Make the European Model More Egalitarian Than the Anglo-Saxon Model?

One of the purposes of the minimum wage is to reduce inequality of income. However, in the preceding model, the minimum wage increases inequality of exposure to the risk of unemployment when the economy is affected by a reshaping of labor demand. So the minimum wage has an ambiguous effect on the *average* gains of unskilled workers. This effect must be grasped through an equilibrium model, taking into account the interactions between the productivities and the wages of the different types of worker. The matching model developed immediately above possesses these characteristics and so allows us to compare the evolution of the inequality of average gains provoked by a reshaping of labor demand in the "European" and "Anglo-Saxon" labor markets. The average gains of a type i, $i = h, \ell$, worker, denoted by G_i, are defined by:

$$G_i = u_i V_{ui} + (1 - u_i) V_{ei}$$

The model is calibrated by choosing parameter values similar to those from chapter 9, section 3.5.3. They are presented in table 10.13. The matching function continues to be expressed as $M(V, U) = V^{1/2} U^{1/2}$. For the sake of simplicity, the labor markets of the two categories of worker are assumed to be identical, except for the replacement ratio, which is higher for the low-skilled workers. Moreover, and again for simplicity, the size of the labor force of each type of worker is assumed to be identical, and has a zero growth rate. For elasticity of substitution, we retain the value $\sigma = 1.5$ chosen by Johnson (1997). The value of A_ℓ is arbitrarily normalized to unity.

Figure 10.12 reproduces the effects of an increase in the labor productivity of skilled workers (A_h rises from 1.5 to 2). In an Anglo-Saxon labor market, the gains of skilled workers improve with an increase in their relative productivity, as their wage rises. Unskilled workers also benefit from the improvement in the productivity of skilled workers, but to a lesser extent, which entails that inequality, measured by the ratio G_h/G_ℓ, increases. The unemployment rates of the two manpower categories remain unchanged, taking the values $u_h = 5.8\%$, and $u_\ell = 7.6\%$).

For a labor market of the European type, we assume that the wage of the unskilled is indexed to the wage of the skilled in such a way as to preserve a constant ratio between the wages, identical to that obtained when $A_h = 1.5$. We observe that technological bias always increases the average gains of skilled workers, but less

Table 10.13
Calibration of the matching model with two categories of worker.

γ_i	h_i	q_i	r	σ	b_h	b_ℓ	A_ℓ
0.5	0.1	0.15	0.05	1.5	0.3	0.6	1

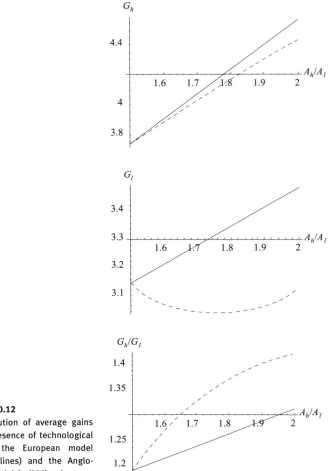

FIGURE 10.12
The evolution of average gains in the presence of technological bias in the European model (dashed lines) and the Anglo-Saxon model (solid lines).

markedly, for increased unemployment among the unskilled diminishes the marginal productivity of skilled labor. On the other hand, it turns out that the average gains of unskilled workers diminish globally. This result is the upshot of the increased unemployment of this category of worker, and of the relatively high value of the elasticity of substitution between the two types of labor. When this elasticity is less (between 1 and 1.2), the gains of the unskilled mount, but always more weakly than they do in the Anglo-Saxon model.

This simulation also shows that the European model induces *greater inequality in terms of average gains* than the Anglo-Saxon model. It is worth noting that Flinn (2002) has shown that comparison of the Italian with the U.S. experience provides an illustration of this type of result. Using a job search model and individual-level data for Italy and the United States, he shows that while the cross-sectional wage distributions of young Italian males are much more compressed than are the comparable distributions for young white U.S. males, it turns out that the distribution of lifetime welfare is no more dispersed in the United States than in Italy.

Overall, these results suggests that the minimum wage may be a very poor instrument for the redistribution of income. We will see in chapter 12 that fiscal measures are probably a better way to neutralize the effects of the reshaping of labor demand, but that certain categories of the population may be opposed to using the fiscal system as an instrument of income redistribution.

3   SUMMARY AND CONCLUSION

- Growth in labor productivity improves the profit outlook. This *capitalization effect* is favorable to employment.

- As a general rule, technological progress does not apply to all jobs in a uniform manner. Jobs based on obsolete technologies are destroyed, and only those capable of integrating the latest innovations survive. This process of *creative destruction* can be unfavorable to employment.

- Empirical studies suggest that, overall, technological progress has an ambiguous effect on employment. The impact of technological progress on employment depends on the type of innovation that underpins it, and on labor market institutions.

- During the last two decades of the twentieth century, most industrialized countries were faced with increased competition from low-wage countries, and technological bias that altered labor demand in favor of skilled workers. In certain countries the scale of wages remained more or less stable while the relative unemployment rate of the unskilled rose (the "European" model). Conversely, in other countries the relative employment situation of the low-skilled did not change, but wage inequality grew much steeper (the "Anglo-Saxon" model). Empirical work tends to favor the bias of technological progress as the factor that explains the shift in relative labor demand; the part played by trade with low-wage countries in this shift is likely limited.

- Examination of migratory flows shows that the rich countries do indeed have an immigrant population less well qualified, on average, than natives. From a theoretical standpoint, the immigration of low-skilled workers has an ambiguous effect on inequality. Empirical work confirms this conclusion, suggesting that the immigration of low-skilled workers has little effect on wages and employment among workers with the fewest skills.

- The Anglo-Saxon model is characterized by high wage flexibility. Conversely, in the European model wages are most often downwardly rigid, and a large portion of adjustment occurs through variation in employment. The existence of a high minimum wage is a major element in this type of regulation. Simulations based on a calibration of the matching model show that more severe technological bias may entail more inequality in terms of *average gains* (that is, over the whole of the life cycle) in the presence of a minimum wage.

4   RELATED TOPICS IN THE BOOK

*   Chapter 4, section 1: Labor demand with (at least) two inputs
*   Chapter 7, section 6.1: Unionization and wage inequality
*   Chapter 9, section 3: The matching model
*   Chapter 12, section 1: The effects of the minimum wage
*   Chapter 12, section 5: Institutions and unemployment

5   FURTHER READINGS

Acemoglu, D. (2002), "Technical change, inequality, and the labor market," *Journal of Economic Literature*, 40(1), pp. 7–72.

Borjas, G. (1999), "The economic analysis of immigration," in Ashenfelter, O., and Card, D. (eds.), *Handbook of Labor Economics*, vol. 3A, chap. 28, pp. 1697–1660, Amsterdam: Elsevier Science/North-Holland.

Card, D., and DiNardo, J. (2002), "Skill biased technological change and rising wage inequality: Some problems and puzzles," NBER Working Paper No. 8769, http://www.nber.org/papers/w8769.

Johnson, G., and Stafford, F. (1999), "The labor market implications of international trade," in Ashenfelter, O., and Card, D. (eds.), *Handbook of Labor Economics*, vol. 3B, chap. 34, pp. 2216–2288, Amsterdam: Elsevier Science/North-Holland.

Katz, L., and Autor, D. (1999), "Changes in the wage structure and earnings inequality," in Ashenfelter, O., and Card, D. (eds.), *Handbook of Labor Economics*, vol. 3A, chap. 26, pp. 1463–1559, Amsterdam: Elsevier Science/North-Holland.

6   APPENDIX

Differentiating the two sides of relation (19) defining the wage curve comes to:

$$\frac{\partial T}{\partial g} = -\left(T + \frac{\gamma h e^{gT}}{1-\gamma} \frac{\partial \theta}{\partial g} \right) \Big/ g \tag{49}$$

Equation (18) defining labor demand can be written in the following manner:

$$\frac{h}{m(\theta)} = \frac{1-\gamma}{r} H(g, T) \qquad \text{with} \qquad H(g, T) = 1 + \frac{g e^{-rT} - r e^{-gT}}{r - g}$$

Differentiating this equation with respect to g, we get:

$$-\frac{hm'(\theta)}{m^2(\theta)}\frac{\partial\theta}{\partial g} = \frac{1-\gamma}{r}\left(H_g + H_T\frac{\partial T}{\partial g}\right)$$

Bringing the value of $\partial T/\partial g$ that issues from (49) into this last inequality, we find:

$$\left[\frac{\gamma hH_t e^{gT}}{rg} - \frac{hm'(\theta)}{m^2(\theta)}\right]\frac{\partial\theta}{\partial g} = \frac{1-\gamma}{r}\left(H_g - \frac{TH_T}{g}\right) \tag{50}$$

with:

$$H_T = \frac{rg}{r-g}\left(e^{-gT} - e^{-rT}\right) > 0$$

$$H_g = \frac{1}{(r-g)^2}\left[(r-g)(e^{-rT} + rTe^{-gT}) + ge^{-rT} - re^{-gT}\right]$$

After several rearrangements, we see that $H_g - TH_T/g$ is of the same sign as $e^{-rT} - e^{-gT} + T(r-g)e^{-rT}$, and a second-order expansion of $e^{-rT} - e^{-gT}$ then shows that this expression is negative. Equation (50) then entails $\partial\theta/\partial g < 0$.

REFERENCES

Acemoglu, D. (1999), "Patterns of skill premia," NBER Working Paper No. 7018, forthcoming in *Review of Economic Studies*.

Acemoglu, D. (2002), "Technical change, inequality, and the labor market," *Journal of Economic Literature*, 40(1), pp. 7–72.

Acemoglu, D., Aghion, P., and Violante, G. (2001), "Technical change, deunionization and inequality," Carnegie-Rochester Conference Series on Public Policy, 55, pp. 229–264.

Aghion, P. (2002), "Schumpeterian growth theory and the dynamics of income inequality," *Econometrica*, 70, pp. 855–882.

Aghion, P., and Howitt, P. (1992), "A model of growth through creative destruction," *Econometrica*, 60, pp. 323–351.

Aghion, P., and Howitt, P. (1998), *Endogenous Growth Theory*, Cambridge, Mass: Harvard University Press.

Albrecht, J., and Vroman, S. (2002), "A matching model with endogenous skills requirement," *International Economic Review*, 43, pp. 283–305.

Angrist, J., and Krueger, A. (1999), "Empirical strategies in labor economics," in Ashenfelter, O., and Card, D. (eds.), *Handbook of Labor Economics*, vol. 3, chap. 23, Amsterdam: Elsevier Science/North-Holland.

Atkinson, A. (2001), "A critique of the transatlantic consensus on rising income inequality," *World Economy*, May.

Autor, D., Katz, L., and Krueger, A. (1998), "Computing inequalities: Have computers changed the labor market?" *Quarterly Journal of Economics*, 113, pp. 1169–1213.

Bean, C., and Pissarides, C. (1993), "Unemployment, consumption and growth," *European Economic Review*, 37, pp. 837–854.

Berman, A., Bound, J., and Griliches, Z. (1994), "Changes in the demand for skilled labor within U.S. manufacturing: Evidence from the Annual Survey of Manufacturers," *Quarterly Journal of Economics*, 109, pp. 367–397.

Berman, E., Bound, J., and Machin, S. (1998), "Implications of skill-biased technological change: International evidence," *Quarterly Journal of Economics*, 113, pp. 1245–1279.

Bertola, G., Blau, F., and Kahn, L. (2001), "Comparative analysis of labor market outcomes: Lessons for the US from international long-run evidence," in Krueger, A., and Solow, R. (eds.), *The Roaring Nineties: Can Full Employment Be Sustained?* New York: Russell Sage and Century Foundations.

Blanchard, O., and Wolfers, J. (2000), "The role of shocks and institutions in the rise of European unemployment," *Economic Journal*, 110, suppl., pp. 1–33.

Borjas, G. (1999), "The economic analysis of immigration," in Ashenfelter, O., and Card, D. (eds.), *Handbook of Labor Economics*, vol. 3A, chap. 28, pp. 1697–1760, Amsterdam: Elsevier Science/North-Holland.

Borjas, G., Freeman, R., and Katz, L. (1997), "How much do immigration and trade affect labor market forces?" *Brookings Papers on Economic Activity*, 1, pp. 1–85.

Borjas, G., and Hilton, L. (1996), "Immigration and the welfare state: Immigrant participation in means-tested entitlement programs," *Quarterly Journal of Economics*, 111, pp. 575–604.

Bound, J., and Johnson, G. (1992), "Changes in the structure of wages in the 1980's: An evaluation of alternative explanations," *American Economic Review*, 82, pp. 371–392.

Brücker, H., Epstein, G., McCormick, B., Saint-Paul, G., Venturini, A., and Zimmerman, K. (2001), *Managing Migration in the European Welfare State*, mimeo, Berlin: DIW.

Caballero, R. (1993), "Comment on the Bean and Pissarides paper," *European Economic Review*, 37, pp. 855–859.

Caballero, R., and Hammour, M. (1996), "On the timing and efficiency of creative destruction," *Quarterly Journal of Economics*, 111, pp. 805–852.

Card, D. (1990), "The impact of the Mariel boatlift on the Miami labor market," *Industrial and Labor Relations Review*, 43, pp. 245–257.

Card, D. (2001), "The effect of unions on wage inequality in the U.S. labor market," *Industrial and Labor Relations Review*, 54, pp. 296–315.

Card, D., and DiNardo, J. (2000), "Do immigrant inflows lead to native outflows?" *American Economic Review, Papers and Proceedings*, 90, pp. 361–367.

Card, D., and DiNardo, J. (2002), "Skill biased technological change and rising wage inequality: Some problems and puzzles," NBER Working Paper No. 8769, http://www.nber.org/papers/w8769.

Caselli, F. (1999), "Technological revolutions," *American Economic Review*, 87, pp. 78–102.

Chiswick, B. (1978), "The effect of Americanization on the earnings of foreign-born men," *Journal of Political Economy*, 86, pp. 897–921.

Coppel, J., Dumont, J.-C., and Visco, I. (2001), "Trends in immigration and economic consequences," OECD working paper, Ecowp(2001)10, http://www.oecd.org/eco/eco.

Denison, E. (1967), *Why Growth Rates Differ*, Washington, D.C.: Brookings Institution.

DiNardo, J., Fortin, N., and Lemieux, T. (1996), "Labor market institutions and the distribution of wages, 1973–1992: A semi-parametric approach," *Econometrica*, 64, pp. 1001–1044.

DiNardo, J., and Pischke, J. (1997), "The returns to computer use revisited: Have pencils changed the wage structure too?" *Quarterly Journal of Economics*, 114, pp. 291–303.

Entorf, H., and Kramarz, F. (1997), "Does unmeasure ability explain the higher wages of new technology workers?" *European Economic Review*, 41, pp. 1489–1509.

Entorf, H., Gollac, M., and Kramarz, F. (1999), "New technologies, wages, and worker selection," *Journal of Labor Economics*, 17, pp. 464–491.

Flinn, C. (2002), "Labor market structure and inequality: A comparison of Italy and the U.S.," *Review of Economic Studies*, 69, pp. 611–645.

Foster, L., Haltiwanger, J., and Krizan, C. (2001), "Aggregate Productivity Growth: Lessons from Microeconomic Evidence," in *New Directions in Productivity Analysis* (eds. Edward Dean, Michael Harper and Charles Hulten), Chicago: University of Chicago Press.

Frank, R., and Cook, P. (1995), *The winner-Takes-All Society*, New York: Free Press.

Freeman, R. (1995), "Are your wages set in Beijing?" *Journal of Economic Perspectives*, 9, pp. 15–32.

Friedberg, R., and Hunt, J. (1995), "The impact of immigrants on host country wages, employment and growth," *Journal of Economic Perspectives*, 9, pp. 23–34.

Goldin, C., and Katz, L. (1998), "The origin of technology-skill complementarity," *Quarterly Journal of Economics*, 113, pp. 693–732.

Gosling, A., and Lemieux, T. (2001), "Labour market reforms and changes in wage inequality in the United Kingdom and the United States," NBER Working Paper No. 8413, http://www.nber.org/papers/w8413.

Gottschalk, P., and Smeeding, T. (1997), "Cross-national comparisons of earnings and income inequality," *Journal of Economic Literature*, 35, pp. 633–687.

Greenwood, J., Hercowitz, Z., and Krusell, P. (1997), "Long-run implications of investment-specific technological change," *American Economic Review*, 87, pp. 342–362.

Hercowitz, Z. (1998), "The 'embodiment' controversy: A review essay," *Journal of Monetary Economics*, 41, pp. 217–224.

Hunt, J. (1992), "The Impact of the 1962 repatriates from Algeria on the French labor market," *Industrial and Labor Relations Review*, 43, pp. 245–257.

Ichinovsky, C., Shaw, K., and Prennushi, G. (1997), "The effects of human resource management practices on productivity: A study of steel finishing lines," *American Economic Review*, 87, pp. 291–313.

Johnson, G. (1997), "Changing in earnings inequality: The role of demand shifts," *Journal of Economics Perspectives*, 11(2), pp. 41–54.

Johnson, G., and Stafford, F. (1999), "The labor market implications of international trade," in Ashenfelter, O., and Card, D. (eds.), *Handbook of Labor Economics*, vol. 3B, chap. 34, pp. 2216–2288, Amsterdam: Elsevier Science/North-Holland.

Jorgenson, D. (1966), "The embodiment hypothesis," *Journal of Political Economy*, 74, pp. 1–17.

Jorgenson, D. (1980), "The contribution of education to U.S. economic growth, 1948–73," in Brunner, K., and Meltzer, A. (eds.), *The Problem of Inflation*, Amsterdam: North-Holland.

Katz, L., and Autor, D. (1999), "Changes in the wage structure and earnings inequality," in Ashenfelter, O., and Card, D. (eds.), *Handbook of Labor Economics*, vol. 3A, chap. 26, pp. 1463–1559, Amsterdam: Elsevier Science/North-Holland.

Katz, L., and Murphy, K. (1992), "Changes in relative wages, 1963–1987," *Quarterly Journal of Economics*, 107, pp. 357–358.

Kremer, M. (1993), "The O-ring theory of economic development," *Quarterly Journal of Economics*, 108, pp. 551–575.

Krueger, A. (1993), "How computers have changed the wage structure: Evidence from microdata 1984–89," *Quarterly Journal of Economics*, 108, pp. 33–60.

Krugman, P. (1995), "Technology, trade and factor prices," NBER Working Paper No. 5356. Cambridge, Mass.: National Bureau of Economic Research.

Lee, D. (1999), "Wage inequality in the United States during the 1980s: Rising dispersion or falling minimum wage?" *Quarterly Journal of Economics*, 114, pp. 977–1023.

Leontief, W. (1953), "Domestic production and foreign trade: The American position reexamined," reprint in Bhagwati, S. (1969), *International Trade: Selected Readings*, Baltimore: Penguin.

Machin, S., and Van Reenen, J. (1998), "Technology and changes in skill structure: Evidence from seven OECD countries," *Quarterly Journal of Economics*, 113, pp. 1215–1244.

Mortensen, D., and Pissarides, C. (1998), "Technological progress, job creation, and job destruction," *Review of Economic Dynamics*, 1, pp. 733–753.

Murnane, R., and Levy, F. (1996), *Teaching the Basic New Skills*, New York: Free Press.

Obstfeld, M., and Rogoff, K. (1996), *Foundations of International Macroeconomics*, Cambridge, Mass.: MIT Press.

OECD (1994), *Employment Outlook*, Paris: OECD.

OECD (1997), *Employment Outlook*, Paris: OECD.

OECD (1999), *Employment Outlook*, Paris: OECD.

Osterman, P. (1994), "How common is workplace transformation and who adopts it?" *Industrial and Labor Relations Review*, 47, pp. 173–188.

Pierce, B. (2001), "Compensation inequality," *Quarterly Journal of Economics*, 116(4), pp. 1493–1525.

Rifkin, J. (1995), *The End of Work: The Decline of the Global Labor Force and the Dawn of the Post-Market Era*, New York: Tarcher and Putnam's Sons.

Rowthorn, R., and Ramaswamy, R. (1998), "Growth trade and deindustrialisation," IMF working paper, WP/98/60, Research Department, International Monetary Fund.

Sachs, J., and Schatz, H. (1994), "Trade and jobs in U.S. manufacturing," *Brookings Papers on Economic Activity*, 1, pp. 1–81.

Saeger, S. (1997), "Globalisation and deindustrialisation: Myth and reality in the OECD," *Weltwirtschaftliches Archiv*, 133(4), pp. 579–608.

Saint-Paul, G. (2001), "On the distribution of income and workers assignment under intrafirm spillovers, with an application to ideas and networks," *Journal of Political Economy*, 110, pp. 1–37.

Scarpetta, S., Bassani, A., Pilat, D., and Schreyer, P. (2000), "Economic growth in the OECD Area: Recent trends at the aggregate and sectoral level," OECD Working Paper No. 248, http://www.oecd.org/eco.

Schumpeter, J. (1934), *The Theory of Economic Development*, Cambridge, Mass: Harvard University Press.

Sismondi, J. (1991), *New Principles of Political Economy*, Transactions Publishers.

Solow, R. (1957), "Technical change and the aggregate production function," *Review of Economics and Statistics*, 39, pp. 312–320.

Solow, R. (1960), "Investment and technological progress," in Arrow, K., Karlin, S., and Suppes, P. (eds.), *Mathematical Methods in the Social Sciences*, pp. 89–104, Stanford, Calif.: Stanford University Press.

Stolper, W., and Samuelson, P. (1947), "Protection and real wages," *Review of Economic Studies*, 9, pp. 58–73.

Temin, P. (1999), "Globalization," *Review of Economic Policy*, 15, pp. 76–89.

Thesmar, D., and Thoenig, M. (2000), "Creative destruction and firm organization choice," *Quarterly Journal of Economics*, 115, pp. 1209–1238.

Thoenig, M., and Verdier, T. (1999), "Trade induced technical bias and wage inequalities: A theory of defensive innovations," mimeo, Paris: DELTA.

Topel, R. (1993), "Regional labor markets and the determinants of wage inequality," *American Economic Review*, 83, pp. 110–115.

Wood, A. (1994), *North-South Trade, Employment and Inequality: Changing Fortunes in a Skill-Driven World*, Oxford, U.K.: Clarendon Press.

Wood, A. (1995), "How trade hurts unskilled workers," *Journal of Economic Perspectives*, 9, pp. 57–80.

Wood, A. (1998), "Globalisation and the rise in labour market inequalities," *Economic Journal*, 108, pp. 1463–1482.

INSTITUTIONS AND ECONOMIC POLICY

LABOR MARKET POLICIES

CONTENTS

In this chapter, we will:

- Survey the variety of labor market policies that have been tried in the OECD countries

- Consider the efficiency of active labor market policies in an equilibrium framework

- Learn the methodological principles that guide the evaluation of labor market policies

- Find out what assessments of labor market policies reveal

- Learn what the macroeconomic effects of unemployment benefits are

INTRODUCTION

Intervention by the state in the labor market is generally viewed as taking two forms: active policies and passive policies. The goal of active policies is to increase employment and wages among persons who find insertion into the labor market difficult. Job search assistance, upgrades to professional training, employment subsidies, and even public sector job creation are the commonest forms. Passive policies aim rather to increase the material welfare of disadvantaged populations without a priori attempting to improve their labor market performance. Unemployment insurance and provisions for early retirement fall under this heading.

Naively, it might be thought that putting in place active policies to improve labor market performances was enough, and that the role of passive policies ought to be limited, so as not to create too many disincentives to taking a job. In reality, active policies, while they are generally justified by the many sources of inefficiency in the functioning of the labor markets, do not make it possible systematically to improve the performances of these markets. Theoretical study and empirical evaluation both show that they can even turn out to be counterproductive. For example, the creation of temporary public sector jobs intended to facilitate the entry of youth into the labor market can, because of cost and low efficiency, lead to a decline in the total number of jobs held by this category of the population. Similarly, subsidies to promote certain types of employment run the risk of displacing workers whose jobs do not benefit from these subsidies. So-called passive policies can, moreover, have beneficial effects on labor market performance in certain circumstances. For instance, we will see that an increase in unemployment insurance benefits is capable of reducing the numbers of the unemployed when not all workers are eligible for them. Financial compensation for unemployment, by helping the recipients bear the cost of looking for work, allows them to choose jobs with greater care, which improves the quality of the resulting matches and may increase overall production in the economy. These observations show that it is misleading to prejudge the effect of public interventions without engaging in closer scrutiny and evaluating all of their effects quantitatively. The purpose of this chapter is to set forth the state of theoretical and empirical knowledge in this area.

The first section supplies the main facts regarding employment policies in the OECD countries, highlighting the fact that different countries have had different experiences in this regard. Section 2 is dedicated to theoretical analysis of active labor market policies, and makes abundant use of the matching model set out in chapter 9. Section 3 presents the methods of evaluation and the main empirical results that have been obtained in the domain of active policy. Finally, the last section looks at the consequences of unemployment insurance on labor market equilibrium.

1 LABOR MARKET POLICIES: AN INTERNATIONAL PERSPECTIVE

We see great diversity in the policies adopted and the amount of financing channeled into them from one country to another. Active labor market policies aim to improve the situation, in terms of employment and wages, of the unemployed, and of disadvantaged populations generally. They are to be distinguished from passive policies, which aim to increase the well-being of these groups without automatically pursuing a particular outcome in terms of placement in the labor market. They are also to be distinguished from more general policies like those intended to protect employment or guarantee a minimum wage, for the latter affect all the labor force, not just narrowly targeted groups.

1.1   WHAT ARE LABOR MARKET POLICIES?

The OECD employs a typology of labor market policies, distinguishing active measures from passive ones. This typology has the advantage of being universally adopted, and thus allowing us to make international comparisons.

1.1.1   The OECD Classification

In the OECD's nomenclature, active employment policy embraces the five following categories:

1.   Public employment services

2.   Labor market training
     a.   Training for unemployed adults and workers threatened with job loss
     b.   Training for employed adults

3.   Youth employment and training measures
     a.   For the unemployed and the disadvantaged
     b.   Aid for apprenticeship and other general kinds of youth training

4.   Subsidized employment
     a.   Subsidies for private sector employment
     b.   Help for unemployed persons in launching new enterprises
     c.   Direct job creation in the public sector or in nonprofit organizations

5.   Employment programs for the disabled
     a.   Professional rehabilitation
     b.   Jobs specifically for the disabled

The OECD includes just two items under the heading of passive policy:

6.   Unemployment insurance

7.   Early retirement for reasons connected to the labor market

1.1.2   The Purposes of Active Labor Market Policies

Active labor market policies may affect employment in different ways. Public employment services have the goal of reducing job search costs. Training programs, and many of the measures in favor of youth, aim to increase the ''employability'' of the persons concerned, and ought to lead to a rise in individual productivity. Other policies have the objective of reducing the cost of labor or creating public sector jobs directly. Unemployment insurance is viewed as a passive policy when it is regarded as pure insurance against risk, and is quantified as all the transfers that go to eligible unemployed persons. However, we must carefully distinguish between this strictly financial aspect of the unemployment insurance system and the other things it does, such as checking on search effort and sanctioning those who search half-heartedly; these ought instead to be considered as belonging to active policy. Analysis of the macroeconomic effects of unemployment insurance is reserved for section 4 below. In what follows, we merely set out the specific purposes of the various active policies.

Public Employment Services

One of the aims of public employment services is to promote matches between firms with vacant jobs and persons looking for work. In all industrialized countries, specialized public agencies like the U.S. Employment Service or the Agence Nationale Pour l'Emploi in France supply services of this kind. But certain countries, such as Japan, the United Kingdom, and the United States, have authorized private organizations to compete with the public agencies in the job placement "market" (see section 2.1 below for a theoretical analysis). Among the activities of these public agencies or private organizations, it is *job search assistance* (JSA) that falls into the category of active labor market policy. This assistance takes various forms according to cases. Sometimes it simply comes down to offering a certain number of free telephone calls for jobs listed by the agency. But unemployed persons may also be given help in drafting their résumés, in defining personalized search strategies and then putting them into operation, or in finding appropriate training. Checking on the effort being made by the unemployed, and applying sanctions if necessary, are also part of the role of public employment services (see OECD, 2001, for a complete description of this role).

Labor Market Training

In many countries—Denmark and Germany, for example—labor market training represents the bulk of active policy. It is often endorsed by politicians as the best weapon against unemployment. The prevalent form of labor market training is *classroom training* (CT). It takes place not in firms but in courses or temporary placements created by specialized establishments. The duration is generally brief, on the order of three or four weeks in Denmark, and three months on average in the United States. The training may be general, or specific to an industry or a firm. It may serve to make up for a gap in the basic education of some individuals (those, for example, who failed to finish, or even to start, secondary school), or to bring the knowledge of skilled employees up to date.

Youth Employment and Training Measures

Apprenticeship represents a large part of training measures aimed specifically at the young in most countries. Apprenticeship typically includes classroom instruction and on-the-job training. There are also programs to help disadvantaged or unemployed youth addressed primarily to young people who leave school with no job to go to, and those who drop out of high school prematurely. The *Job Corps* program in the United States is an example. It is aimed at young people from difficult urban neighborhoods who must take training that gets them out of their normal environment. Many programs to help youth are not so precisely targeted, and there is little that really distinguishes them from general training programs. Some other training measures are not, for the most part, aimed specifically at the young. Rather, they represent an alternative to traditional classroom instruction. The goal of such *on-the-job training* (OJT) programs is to give employers an incentive, by means of a subsidy, to give training to disadvantaged categories of workers. An on-the-job training placement generally lasts from three to 12 months, and at the end of that period the employer has the opportunity to hire the trainee on a permanent basis. According to Heckman et al. (1999), in the United States these programs make it possible primarily to insert, or reinsert, certain persons into a work environment, and there may be no real distinction between them and programs that simply subsidize hiring.

Subsidized Employment

Subsidized employment covers a wide gamut of measures. Subsidies for employment in the private sector generally take the form of transfers to firms that hire members of particular groups. The transfer may be temporary or permanent, such as the reduced payroll taxes for low-wage jobs in France, for example. *Public service employment* as an active policy measure is addressed in principle to the young and to the long-term unemployed. The purpose is to allow persons who find themselves in this situation to hold a temporary job in the public sector so that they can acquire minimal skills or seniority as a step toward finding a regular job (or simply to make them eligible for unemployment insurance). Programs of this kind form a large part of the spectrum of active policy measures in Europe but are practically nonexistent in the United States (see Brodsky, 2000, for a comparative study of several OECD countries). It is important, however, to distinguish *temporary* public jobs created as part of an active labor market policy from general public sector policy, which consists of creating *permanent* civil service jobs. The overall breadth of employment in the public sector is an "institution" specific to each country. The creation of temporary jobs in the public sector or in nonprofit organizations is intended to give a semblance of training and work habits to persons with little or no work experience and belonging to economically disadvantaged groups. Finally, unemployed persons are given help in launching new enterprises in a number of countries (including the United States). Most often this involves using unemployment benefits to subsidize unemployed persons willing to have a go at becoming self-employed. Observation tells us that in general, this measure applies only to a limited number of unemployed persons.

Another thing to point out is that the same individual may benefit from several of these measures at the same time, for public policy is often structured around programs with several facets. For example, the Job Corps program in the United States combines job search assistance, classroom training, and apprenticeship. Many programs are similar, which makes it more difficult to assess the effects specific to each measure. We also need to be aware that the distinction between active and passive measures is useful for analysis, but that in practice the line between them is not always easy to draw. In the Netherlands, for example, the proportion of those benefiting from employment programs for the disabled is much higher than in most other countries. In this specific case what we really have is more a disguised form of assistance for certain categories of the unemployed, or preretirement support, than a measure specifically intended to get disabled people back into the labor force, and the costs, at least in part, ought to fall under the rubric of passive policy. (The same phenomenon is not unknown in the United States: Autor and Duggan, 2001, estimate that if access to disability insurance had not been made easier there in the middle of the 1980s, the current unemployment rate would be two thirds of a percentage point higher.) Similarly, certain youth training placements serve only to "park" the participants without really improving their productive capacities.

1.2 DIFFERENCES BETWEEN COUNTRIES

Public employment policies vary widely both as regards the amount of money earmarked for them, and the way that money is divided up among the various policy options.

1.2.1 The Amount of Public Expenditure on Labor Market Policy

The amount of public funding for labor market policy varies widely from one country to another. Table 11.1 gives an overview of this diversity. Japan and the United States are the countries that spend the least in this area (respectively 0.42% and 0.61% of GDP). The other Anglo-Saxon countries (Australia, Canada, the United Kingdom) spend a larger share of their resources (between 1% and 2% of GDP). In contrast, other countries—mainly northern European ones—spend much more. In Denmark, for example, total public expenditure on labor market policy represents almost 5% of GDP; in the Netherlands, this figure comes to around 4.61%, and in Sweden, 3.56%. Norway stands out among the Nordic countries on account of its relatively low outlay on labor market policy: the order of magnitude is the same as in the United Kingdom. Germany and France occupy an intermediate position, spending a little more than 3% of GDP. The last column of table 11.1 gives the ratios of passive to active expenditure. As a general rule, the amount spent on passive policies clearly outstrips that spent on active ones. The Swedish and Norwegian exceptions deserve notice. In Sweden, expenditure on labor market policy is divided in approximately equal parts between active measures and passive ones. Norway spends twice as much on active policy measures as it does on passive ones.

1.2.2 How Public Expenditure on Active Employment Policy Is Divided Up

Table 11.2 breaks down expenditure on active policy according to the five OECD headings mentioned at the start of this section for the 11 countries listed above. Independent

Table 11.1

Public expenditure on labor market policy in some OECD countries as a percentage of GDP.

Country	Year	Total expenditure	Passive expenditure	Active expenditure	Passive/ Active
Australia	2000–01	1.43	0.98	0.46	2.13
Canada	2000–01	1.13	0.72	0.41	1.76
Denmark	2000	4.56	3.00	1.56	1.92
France	2000	2.96	1.65	1.31	1.37
Germany	2001	3.13	1.92	1.20	1.60
Japan	2000–01	0.86	0.55	0.31	1.77
Netherlands	2001	3.44	1.86	1.58	1.18
Norway	2001	1.23	0.44	0.79	0.56
Sweden	2001	2.28	1.19	1.09	1.09
United Kingdom	1999–2000	0.92	0.56	0.36	1.56
United States	2000–01	0.45	0.30	0.15	2.00

Source: OECD data.

Note: The last column gives the ratio of passive expenditures to active ones.

Table 11.2

Breakdown of expenditures on active measures as percentages of total expenditure on active policy.

Country	Year	Public employment services	Labor market training	Youth employment and training measures	Subsidized employment	Employment programs for the disabled
Australia	2000–01	44.4	4.4	15.5	24.4	11.1
Canada	2000–01	41.5	41.5	4.9	7.3	4.9
Denmark	2000	7.6	54.1	6.4	10.8	21.0
France	2000	13.7	19.1	32.1	28.2	6.9
Germany	2000	19.2	28.3	7.5	20.8	24.2
Japan	2000–01	62.5	9.4	—	25.0	3.1
Netherlands	2001	16.5	19.7	2.5	24.2	36.9
Norway	2001	15.2	7.6	1.3	1.3	74.7
Sweden	2001	20.9	27.3	1.8	21.8	28.2
United Kingdom	1999–2000	36.1	13.9	41.7	2.8	5.5
United States	2000–01	26.7	26.7	20.0	6.7	20.0

Source: OECD data.

of the volume spent on active employment policy, we note the wide range of choices about how to allocate it. Denmark, for example, dedicates more than 55% of its active policy expenditure to training, whereas the figures for Australia and Norway are 10% and 6% respectively for this item. The other countries fall in between, spending from 20% to 30%. France and Germany are distinguished by large outlays on subsidized employment—a particularly small item in the United States, the United Kingdom, Norway, and even Denmark. Expenditure on the disabled is very high in Sweden and the Netherlands, where it represents almost 30% of overall expenditure on active policies. This item comes to almost 72% in Norway! The large size of these sums indicates that they really represent disguised forms of unemployment insurance, and ought to be counted as passive policy measures. Finally, it is interesting to note that the countries that, in global terms, spend little on active employment policy (Japan and the Anglo-Saxon countries) are also the ones that devote proportionally the most resources to public employment services. In these countries, between 30% and 40% of the money spent on active policies is dedicated exclusively to job-searching assistance.

As for passive policy measures, the largest item of expenditure is unemployment insurance. Expenditures on early retirement for reasons connected with the labor market bulk particularly large in France and Denmark, where they come respectively to 20% and 40% of all money spent on passive policy.

1.2.3 Examples of Active Policy in Several Countries

By way of illustration, we compare the American case with that of two European countries, Sweden and the United Kingdom. The United States and the United Kingdom display a degree of convergence, while the rise in unemployment during the 1990s brought a palpable change of direction to Swedish policy.

The United States

In the United States, active employment policy targets economically disadvantaged groups, and the beneficiaries are often defined with reference to a poverty threshold.

The public job creation programs born in the 1970s, especially under the umbrella of the *Comprehensive Employment and Training Act* (CETA) of 1973, were gradually restricted to persons in difficulty before being abolished in 1983 by the government of Ronald Reagan. The *new jobs tax credit*, set up in 1977, was a very large-scale program of nontargeted subsidies for employment in the private sector. It was replaced at the beginning of the 1980s by the more limited *targeted jobs tax credit*, which, as its title indicates, was intended for economically disadvantaged groups.

Programs of this kind, which aim to increase labor demand, are the exception in the United States. Most of the active policy measures that have followed one another since the beginning of the 1960s in this country are "supply-side" measures that aim to increase the human capital of the recipients. This approach is shared by the *Manpower Development and Training Act* (MDTA, 1962), the *Comprehensive Employment and Training Act* (CETA, 1973), and the *Job Training and Partnership Act* (JPTA, 1983). So, the JPTA seeks to promote on-the-job training, classroom training, and work experience. This emphasis on education was maintained throughout the Clinton presidency. Another major item of active policy expenditure in the United States is job search assistance: table 11.2 indicates that 35.3% of active policy expenditure goes to public employment services and 23.5% to labor market training. The *Worker Profiling and Reemployment Services System*, set up in 1993, obliges all recipients of unemployment insurance to draw up an individual list of their skills. In exchange, they gain access to many services to help them improve their job search strategy.

Sweden

The "Swedish model" created after the Second World War long combined a macroeconomic policy privileging competitivity in international trade with a wage policy indexed to productivity growth in the sector exposed to international competition, and an active employment policy favoring mobility of labor from declining industries toward growing ones. But after the first oil shock, combating unemployment became a new objective of employment policy. The creation of temporary jobs in the public and private sectors, and subsidies for hires, then became prominent. The crisis of the 1990s, which saw the unemployment rate exceed 8% in 1996 (it had been less than 3% before 1990), caused doubts, and even accusations, to be leveled at active employment policy (Calmfors, 1994; Calmfors and Lang, 1995). Since then, active policy has privileged labor market training and subsidized employment, especially for young people and the long-term unemployed.

The United Kingdom

The Thatcher government progressively abandoned all the measures put in place by Labour governments to support demand, in favor of "supply-side" policies. So, the *Job Start Allowance* set up in 1986 offers a lump-sum bonus to long-term unemployed persons who agree to take low-wage jobs. But, in general, active employment policy in the United Kingdom focuses on unskilled youth. The *Youth Training Scheme*, set up in 1983 and continued in the 1990s as *Youth Training*, provides periods of training, financed by the public authorities, for this category. Training policies addressed to broader categories of workers are in place as well, such as the *Training Enterprise Councils*, set up in 1991, which are decentralized organizations charged with creating professional training programs under the auspices of large local firms. With the creation of *Job Centers* in 1987, emphasis was also placed on measures to enhance job searching (table 11.2 confirms this picture). This policy direction has been continued under the Labour government headed by Tony Blair, with the *New Deal for Young People*, set up in 1998, which targets all unemployed benefit recipients between 18 and 24 years old who have been unemployed for at least six months. It is compulsory and begins with a period, lasting no longer than four months, of intensive job-search assistance and small basic skills courses. If the unemployed person does not find a job during this phase, the program provides several options, including the possibility of offering a subsidy to potential employers, or enrollment in a full-time training course (see Blundel et al., 2003, for a detailed description of this program).

2   ACTIVE POLICIES: THEORETICAL ANALYSIS

If we are to form an idea of how efficient active labor market policies are, it is important to work from an equilibrium model that takes into account the combined reactions of labor demand and wages, as well as possible inefficiencies arising from the functioning of the labor market. In this regard, the matching model used to this point proves particularly useful, allowing us to represent a labor market that functions inefficiently for reasons that have to do with the process of job destruction and creation, and the mode of wage formation. Within this framework, a positive study of employment policy is possible. It is important to note that we will be studying the consequences of active employment policies without reference to how they are financed, so throughout this section there is an implicit assumption that active policies are paid for by a lump-sum tax, i.e., one independent of income. This hypothesis is evidently unrealistic. Its only purpose is to highlight the consequences of public expenditure on employment and earnings independently of any distortions that may arise from how it is financed.

2.1   Manpower Placement Services

Manpower placement agencies, whether public or private, have a double mission. On the one hand, they are charged with registering the unemployed and verifying that they are indeed looking for work, so that if necessary they can receive unemployment insurance. On the other, these agencies assemble offers of, and demands for, employment, and help the unemployed search for a job more effectively. The existence of such agencies is justified if, in their absence, individual decisions result in an insufficient allocation of the resources devoted to job searching. By reducing individual search costs, placement agencies can improve labor market efficiency, collecting all available information and putting it at the disposal of workers. From another point of view, the justification of the *public* character of some of these agencies must lie in imperfections inherent in the functioning of the "market" for job placements, as, for example, when it requires very large networks to be set up. Fixed costs for these are very high, and congestion effects may occur. That being so, the decentralized functioning of the placement market leads to an inefficient allocation of resources. Table 11.3 shows that public agencies predominate when it comes to managing job offers; they share this role with private firms in some countries, such as the United States and the United Kingdom, but monopolize it in others, such as France, Germany, and Sweden.

   If we are to analyze placement agencies, private or public, we need to adapt our basic model so as to include placement activity. It will then be possible to characterize efficient outcomes and compare them with market equilibria.

2.1.1   A Matching Model with Placement Agencies

Yavas (1994) set out a formal framework for analyzing the efficiency of a labor market with placement agencies. The essential hypothesis is that an agency can ensure a

Table 11.3

The activity of public placement agencies in the beginning of the nineties.

Country	Regulation	Registration rate (%)
Germany	M	27
Belgium	M	25
Spain	M	19
United States	C	9
France	M	28
Japan	M	73
Sweden	M	36
United Kingdom	C	33

Source: Walwei (1996, p. 413).

Note: The registration rate equals the ratio of the job vacancies handled by the public agencies to the total number of job vacancies. M signifies a public monopoly, and C signifies the coexistence of public and private agencies.

better match-up between unemployed persons and vacant jobs than individual job searches can. This improvement in the contacting process comes at the cost of an extra drain on the resources of society (the first column of table 11.2 gives an order of magnitude for the amount of this cost). Fundamentally, then, to set up a placement agency is to create a different kind of matching technology as an alternative to the one spontaneously available to all workers and employers. We will assume that this alternative technology has increasing returns, since placement agencies generally make large outlays in order to set up a network of connections that will enable them to fill jobs at low marginal cost.

Let us assume, for simplicity, that the labor force is of constant size, normalized to 1, and let $x \in [0, 1]$ be the number of unemployed persons resorting to the services of placement agencies. There is also a continuum of these agencies, indexed by $i \in [0, a]$. The agencies are assumed to be uniformly distributed, such that the mass[1] of agencies is equal to a. Let us also assume, again for simplicity, that these agencies are *instantaneously* capable of locating an entrepreneur ready to hire anyone looking for a job (which indubitably represents an improvement in the matching process). Under these conditions, we can simply denote by $c(x_i)$ the cost attached to the placement of x_i individuals by agency i. It is composed of a fixed cost $c_0(a)$ and a variable cost $c_v(x_i)$, that is, $c(x_i) = c_0(a) + c_v(x_i)$. The fixed cost $c_0(a)$ is assumed to rise with the number of agencies, and satisfies $c_0(0) \geq 0$, $c_0''(a) > 0$ as well. The hypothesis that the fixed cost rises with the number of agencies gives us a simple way of taking into account the congestion effects that occur in job placement. Job placement consists of creating networks so as to bring employers and workers into contact with one another, and this occasions fixed costs that probably increase when more agencies are involved. The variable cost is increasing, convex, and satisfies $c_v(0) = 0$.

Since an individual who resorts to the services of an agency finds a job immediately, only persons who undertake to look for a job on their own are described as unemployed. We will designate the number of unemployed persons by $u \in [0, 1]$, and will assume that the number of matches per unit of time is defined by a matching function $M(u, v)$ with the usual properties. In this expression, v again designates the number of vacant jobs, so the exit rate from unemployment is equal to $\theta m(\theta)$ with $\theta = v/u$. Let q be the exogenous job destruction rate. At stationary equilibrium the number of persons who have lost their jobs, $q(1 - u)$, must be equal to the number of persons who have found a job, $x + \theta m(\theta)u$. Hence, the mass, $x = \int_0^a x_i \, di$, of individuals resorting to the services of placement agencies is defined as a function of u and θ by the equality:

$$x = q(1 - u) - \theta m(\theta)u \tag{1}$$

We should point out that this last equation also characterizes the Beveridge curve adapted to the matching model with placement agencies.

2.1.2 The Social Optimum in the Presence of Placement Agencies

In chapter 9, section 4.4.2, we saw that the social optimum is characterized very simply when the interest rate r goes to 0. Let us again place ourselves in this situation; the planner's problem then amounts to the maximization of *instantaneous* aggregate production subject to the constraint of the Beveridge curve. If, at every date, an employed individual is capable of producing an exogenous quantity y of goods, whereas an unemployed person can only make a quantity $z < y$ of these same goods "at home," instantaneous aggregate production is equal to total production $(1 - u)y + uz$, from which we must deduct the total costs $hu\theta + \int_0^a c(x_i) \, di$ corresponding to the "natural" process of matching and to the placements made by agencies. We thus have:

$$\omega = (1 - u)y + uz - hu\theta - \int_0^a c(x_i) \, di \tag{2}$$

Equation (1) of the Beveridge curve allows us to eliminate the unemployment rate u from the definition (2) of instantaneous production, which then takes the form:

$$\omega = -\int_0^a [c_0(a) + c_v(x_i)] \, di + y - \frac{(q - \int_0^a x_i \, di)(y - z + h\theta)}{q + \theta m(\theta)} \tag{3}$$

The planner's problem consists simply of maximizing ω with respect to x_i, a, and θ. Scrutiny of the expresssion (3) of aggregate production ω shows that this problem is *dichotomic*. For all values of a and x_i, the optimal value of the labor market tightness is the solution of the problem:

$$\underset{\theta}{\text{Max}} \; \frac{y - z + h\theta}{q + \theta m(\theta)}$$

We thus come back to the planner's problem described in chapter 9, section 4.4.2. In other words, the presence of placement agencies has no influence on the optimal value of the labor market tightness. This value is thus always given by equation (49) from chapter 9, i.e.:

$$\frac{(y - z)[1 - \eta(\theta)]}{q + \eta(\theta)\theta m(\theta)} = \frac{h}{m(\theta)} \quad \text{with} \quad \eta(\theta) = -\frac{\theta m'(\theta)}{m(\theta)} \tag{4}$$

For this optimal value of θ, assuming that there exists a unique interior solution[2] such that $a > 0$ and $x_i \in (0, 1)$, maximization with respect to x_i and a of criterion (3) immediately yields:

$$c_v'(x_i) = \frac{y - z + h\theta}{q + \theta m(\theta)} = \frac{h}{[1 - \eta(\theta)]m(\theta)}, \quad \forall i \in [0, a] \tag{5}$$

$$ac_0'(a) + c_0(a) + c_v(x_a) = x_a \frac{y - z + h\theta}{q + \theta m(\theta)} \tag{6}$$

Equation (5) indicates that it is optimal to use the services of placement agencies up to the point where the marginal cost of a placement is equal to its marginal gain. This equation thus determines the volume of placements by each agency. Equation (6) defines the number of agencies a. The left-hand side of (6) corresponds to the marginal cost of a supplementary agency, while the right-hand side represents its marginal gain. At the optimum, the two sides must be equal. The number of agencies is smaller, the higher the fixed cost $c_0(\cdot)$, and rises strongly with a, i.e., with the introduction of new agencies.

2.1.3 Decentralized Equilibrium with Private Placement Agencies

From now on we assume that there are private placement agencies, charging for their services at price p_v for firms and price p_u for unemployed workers. So a firm can instantly fill one of its vacant jobs by paying price p_v, and an unemployed worker can instantly find a job by paying price p_u. That being the case, if a firm decides to turn to a placement agency for one of its vacant positions, it receives an expected gain equal to $\Pi_e - p_v$, where Π_e designates the expected profit from a filled job. At equilibrium, the free entry condition entails that the value Π_v of a vacant job is null, and equality $\Pi_e = p_v$ will thus always be satisfied. Symmetrically, at equilibrium, the tariff of the placement agencies will be such that the expected utility V_u of an unemployed person who does not make use of an agency's services will equal the expected utility $V_e - p_u$ of a person who has found a job immediately thanks to these services (V_e designates the expected gain from a filled job). We will thus have $p_u = V_e - V_u$. Let us assume that wage bargaining takes place in decentralized fashion, in such a way that an employee obtains fraction $\gamma \in [0, 1]$ of the global surplus $S = \Pi_e - \Pi_v + V_e - V_u$. Bearing in mind that the condition of free entry likewise dictates that the profit expected Π_e from a filled job is equal to the average cost $h/m(\theta)$ of a vacant job, and that the sharing of the surplus entails $(1 - \gamma)(V_e - V_u) = \gamma \Pi_e$, we have:

$$p_v = \frac{1 - \gamma}{\gamma} p_u = \frac{h}{m(\theta)} \tag{7}$$

When placement agencies are in a perfectly competitive market, they do not take into account the linkage (7) between the labor market tightness—which depends on the mass x of individuals who have resorted to placement agencies, through the medium of the Beveridge curve (1)—and the prices p_u and p_v. In other words, each agency considers these prices as given and determines the volume x_i of its placements in such a way as to maximize its profit $(p_u + p_v)x_i - c(x_i)$. Since relation (7) defining prices p_u and p_v entails $p_u + p_v = h/(1 - \gamma)m(\theta)$, this maximization arrives at a relation between x_i and θ taking the form:

$$c_v'(x_i) = \frac{h}{(1 - \gamma)m(\theta)}, \qquad \forall i \in [0, a] \tag{8}$$

Moreover, free entry into the market for placement services entails that firms are created as long as profit opportunities exist. Since the fixed cost rises with the number of agencies, at equilibrium the zero-profit condition in this market determines the number of firms a:

$$(p_u + p_v)x_i - [c_0(a) + c_v(x_i)] = 0 \Leftrightarrow c_0(a) + c_v(x_i) = x_i c_v'(x_i) \tag{9}$$

Since, for given θ, the presence of placement agencies does not change the wage setting on each job, the model yields a wage curve identical to the one obtained in the basic model of chapter 9. In particular, the equilibrium value of the labor market tightness is given by equation (21) in chapter 9, i.e.:

$$\frac{(1 - \gamma)(y - z)}{r + q + \gamma\theta m(\theta)} = \frac{h}{m(\theta)} \tag{10}$$

Setting $r = 0$ in relations (4) to (6) characterizing the social optimum, and comparing them to equations (7) to (10), we see that decentralized equilibrium is not efficient, even if the Hosios condition $\gamma = \eta(\theta)$ is satisfied. This result arises from the existence of congestion effects among the placement agencies. In this economy, there is no mechanism giving placement agencies entering the market an incentive to take account of the losses they inflict on agencies already present. The upshot is that decentralized equilibrium leads to an excessive number of agencies and an overproduction of placements when the Hosios condition is satisfied. This result is easily verified by comparing equations (6) and (9). The notion that free competition in the placement agencies market leads to a situation of overproduction should nevertheless be put into perspective. Inasmuch as the size of the fixed costs attached to this type of business limits the number of firms present in this market, it is likely that monopolistic behavior in the form of restricted supply will appear.

The existence of congestion effects and the size of the fixed costs attached to the job placement business suggest that decentralized equilibrium probably leads to an inefficient allocation characterized by states of under- or overproduction. This inefficiency, and the need to check on the search effort being made by those receiving unemployment benefits, generally justify state intervention in the job placement market.

But this intervention must itself be efficient. The empirical research on this problem is presented in section 3.2 below.

2.2   WHY PROMOTE TRAINING?

A large portion of the money spent on labor market policy goes to promote training. Leaving aside the question of how they are financed, these measures have the capacity to increase employment by raising labor productivity. Nonetheless, public intervention is justified only if individual decisions lead to levels of training inadequate with respect to what would be socially desirable. We saw in chapter 2 that in a perfectly competitive economy, where it is possible to sign complete contracts, individual training decisions are socially efficient. It would be difficult to justify the need for public intervention in such a setting.

Individual decisions about training are no longer necessarily efficient, though, when competition is imperfect. Imperfection in competition may arise from many sources, which create distortions and give private agents an incentive to take inefficient decisions. We have already pointed out, in chapter 2, that the unobservability of the characteristics of employees drives them, in certain circumstances, to over-educate themselves in order to signal their quality to employers. In many cases, imperfect competition is also revealed by too low a level of investment in education. For example, the imperfection of the credit market may block access to training that would pay off, both individually and socially, and so impede individuals with few resources from acquiring some kinds of training (see Becker, 1964).

In this section, we will concentrate on the consequences of imperfections in the labor market as regards education. In particular, we will demonstrate, on the basis of the work of Acemoglu (1997), Acemoglu and Pischke (1998, 1999a, 1999b), and Stevens (1994), that the existence of *transaction costs* in the labor market generally leads to *underinvestment* in training when state intervention plays no part. Such underinvestment reduces productivity and proves harmful to employment.

In order to examine decisions about training, it is best to adopt the distinction introduced by Becker (1964) between *general training*, which enhances the productivity of the individual concerned for all types of jobs, and *specific training*, which enhances his or her productivity only for one particular type of job. This distinction is clearly theoretical, to the extent that all training has a certain degree of specificity, but it is analytically useful. General training is fundamentally associated with the worker, who can apply it in different types of jobs and so bring employers to compete for his or her services. The structure of competition between employers is thus capable of affecting decisions about training that potentially concern a multitude of individuals. Specific training, on the other hand, is associated with a match between a particular worker and a particular employer, and the payoff it brings depends only on the relations between these two persons.

We will begin by studying the problems linked to *general training*, showing that the length of time matching takes, and the costs it incurs, are sources of underinvestment. We will then study specific training, emphasizing that the difficulty of signing complete contracts is the source of underinvestment for this type of training.

2.2.1 Acquiring General Training

Decisions about general training in a perfectly competitive economy were presented in chapter 2. According to the standard analysis of Becker (1964), in that context investment in general training is entirely financed by workers. Moreover, the level of investment chosen corresponds to a social optimum. The costs of achieving matches and the monopsony power of employers, however, entail an underinvestment in general training with respect to the socially desirable situation (Stevens, 1994; Acemoglu, 1997; Acemoglu and Pischke, 1998, 1999a, 1999b). This we will demonstrate, beginning by integrating investment in general training into the matching model of chapter 9, then going on to characterize the social optimum of this economy and compare it with decentralized equilibrium.

The Labor Market with Matching Costs and Investment in General Training
In order to represent decisions to invest in general training in the presence of matching costs without too much difficulty, we will assume that a person entering the labor market possesses no training of this kind at the outset. At the time he or she finds his or her *first* employer, he or she decides to invest an amount i in general training. For simplicity, the duration of training is assumed to be null. Once trained, each worker is capable of producing quantity $y(i)$ of goods at every future instant. In other words, workers never need to be retrained. As workers are always assumed to have infinite lifetimes, this property obliges us to consider that the labor force is always growing, for if it were not, everyone would have acquired the necessary general training at the end of some greater or less period of time, and at the stationary state, the optimal level of investment would be zero. Thus, we assume that the labor force increases at the constant exogenous rate $n > 0$, and that all the new entrants into the labor market are unemployed persons, who by hypothesis have no general training. They find themselves in competition with older unemployed persons, who have the general training they got when they were first hired.

As in the preceding sections and in chapter 9, the imperfection of the process by which firms and workers match up is summarized by a matching function possessing the usual properties. The exit rate from unemployment is then equal to $\theta m(\theta)$, where the labor market tightness θ represents the ratio V/U between the stock of vacant jobs and the stock of unemployed persons. In what follows, we omit, with no risk of confusion, the time index, and we denote by U_f, U_n, and N the number of trained unemployed persons, the number of unemployed persons with no training, and the size of the labor force at any date. We then have $U = U_f + U_n$. The unemployed, trained or not, have the same probability of exiting from unemployment, for employers are incapable of telling them apart a priori, before meeting them. We will use $u_f \equiv U_f/N$ and $u_n \equiv U_n/N$ to designate the number of unemployed in each of these categories with respect to the labor force, and $u \equiv U/N$ to designate the unemployment rate. At every instant, the stock of unemployed persons without training increases by nN units, but loses $\theta m(\theta)U_n$ individuals who find jobs. The instantaneous variation $\dot{U}_n$ in the number of untrained unemployed is thus defined by the equality $\dot{U}_n = nN - \theta m(\theta)U_n$. Since $\dot{U}_n \equiv nNu_n + N\dot{u}_n$, the law of motion of u_n is:

$$\dot{u}_n = n - [n + \theta m(\theta)]u_n \tag{11}$$

From that we deduce the stationary level of unemployed persons for this category:

$$u_n = \frac{n}{n + \theta m(\theta)} \tag{12}$$

Let us further assume that the job destruction rate q is an exogenous constant; the instantaneous variation $\dot{U}$ in the total stock of unemployed persons is equal to the difference between the number of persons who at every instant become unemployed, i.e., $qN(1 - u) + nN$, and the number $\theta m(\theta)U$ of persons who find a job. Since $\dot{U} \equiv nNu + N\dot{u}$, the time path of the unemployment rate is given by:

$$\dot{u} = q + n - [q + n + \theta m(\theta)]u \tag{13}$$

The stationary unemployment rate is then written:

$$u = \frac{q + n}{q + n + \theta m(\theta)} \tag{14}$$

We are back to the equation of the Beveridge curve, which defines a decreasing relation between the unemployment rate and the rate of vacant jobs.

The Social Optimum

In chapter 9, section 6.2, we saw that if we assume that all agents are risk-neutral, the social optimum is found by maximizing the present discounted value of net aggregate output, taking into account the dynamics of the variables that enter into this discounted value. With the notations employed to this point, net instantaneous aggregate output Ω is defined as follows:

$$\Omega = N(1 - u)y + zU - hV - \theta m(\theta)U_n i \tag{15}$$

In this formulation, the variable y represents the average production per employed worker, which must formally be distinguished from the production $y(i)$ realized by a person who has benefited from an investment i at the current date, precisely because the production of employed workers depends exclusively on investments in general training made in the past. It should also be noted that the training costs $\theta m(\theta)U_n i$ of the untrained unemployed who find a job form part of Ω. Let $Y = N(1 - u)y$ be the instantaneous gross production of employees. This variable increases at each instant by the production $\theta m(\theta)U_f y$ of trained unemployed persons who find a job, and the production $\theta m(\theta)U_n y(i)$ of unemployed persons trained at the current date, because they have just found their first job. Taking into account the losses due to the destruction of jobs, the instantaneous variation in gross aggregate output is defined by $\dot{Y} = \theta m(\theta)[U_f y + U_n y(i)] - qY$. Since by definition $\dot{Y} \equiv (1 - u) \cdot$

$(ny + N\dot{y}) - N\dot{u}y$ and $u \equiv u_n + u_f$, relation (13) allows us, after several easy calculations, to arrive at an equation describing the law of motion of average production per employed person. It comes to:

$$\dot{y} = \frac{\theta m(\theta)u_n}{1 - u}[y(i) - y] \tag{16}$$

At any instant t, the size N of the labor force is equal to $N_0 e^{nt}$, where N_0 designates the exogenous size of this population at date $t = 0$. With the help of expression (15) of instantaneous net aggregate output, the planner's problem takes the following form:

$$\underset{\theta, i}{\text{Max}} \int_0^{+\infty} [(1 - u)y + (z - \theta h)u - \theta m(\theta)u_n i]e^{-(r-n)t} \, dt$$

subject to constraints (16), (13), and (11).

Socially Efficient Investment

Let λ, μ, and ν be the multipliers respectively linked to constraints (16), (13), and (11). The Hamiltonian of the planner's problem is written[3]:

$$H = [(1 - u)y + (z - \theta h)u - \theta m(\theta)u_n i]e^{-(r-n)t} \, dt + \lambda \dot{y} + \mu \dot{u} + \nu \dot{u}_n$$

The first-order conditions are given by the equations:

$$\frac{\partial H}{\partial i} = 0, \quad \frac{\partial H}{\partial \theta} = 0 \quad \text{and} \quad \frac{\partial H}{\partial y} = -\dot{\lambda}, \quad \frac{\partial H}{\partial u} = -\dot{\mu}, \quad \frac{\partial H}{\partial u_n} = -\dot{\nu} \tag{17}$$

Differentiating the Hamiltonian with respect to i, the first of the conditions (17) immediately entails:

$$\lambda = \frac{(1 - u)e^{-(r-n)t}}{y'(i)} \tag{18}$$

Differentiating the Hamiltonian now with respect to y, condition $\partial H / \partial y = -\dot{\lambda}$ brings us to:

$$(1 - u)e^{-(r-n)t} - \lambda \frac{\theta m(\theta)u_n}{1 - u} = -\dot{\lambda} \tag{19}$$

Henceforth we are at stationary equilibrium where $\dot{\theta} = \dot{u} = 0$; differentiating relation (18) with respect to t gives $\dot{\lambda} = -(r - n)\lambda$. Bringing this value of $\dot{\lambda}$ into (19), we deduce the value of the multiplier λ. Equation (18) then yields $y'(i)$ as a function of u, u_n, and θ. Utilizing definitions (12) and (14) of the unemployment rates at stationary equilibrium, we can express $y'(i)$ as a function of the variable θ alone. It comes to:

$$y'(i^*) = r + \frac{nq}{n + \theta m(\theta)} \tag{20}$$

This equation completely characterizes the level of efficient investment i^* for any value of the labor market tightness θ. For given θ, integrating differential equations (11) and (13) does indeed allow us to express the unemployment rates u_f and u_n as a function of the variable θ alone. There is then no more need to take constraints (11) and (13) into account in the planner's problem. Since relation (20) was only obtained on the basis of conditions $\partial H/\partial i = 0$ and $\partial H/\partial y = -\dot{\lambda}$, it is thus indeed satisfied for any given value of θ. Note that we find the level corresponding to perfect competition, i.e., $y'(i) = r$, when $\theta m(\theta)$ goes to $+\infty$, i.e. when it is possible for a person who has lost his or her job to be rehired immediately.

Decentralized Equilibrium

We will now establish that decentralized equilibrium is characterized by under-investment in general training even if firms and workers are capable of entering into complete contracts (this result was obtained by Acemoglu, 1997). It is assumed that a complete contract is negotiated when a match occurs and is not renegotiable later. In chapter 9, section 4.2.1, we showed that investment decisions in the presence of complete contracts lead to the maximization of the surplus net of investment costs. The level of the wage negotiated depends on the share of the surplus obtained by each party and the amounts they respectively invest.

By definition, the surplus from a match that takes place with a worker who has not yet acquired any general training is equal to the sum of the expected profit $\Pi_e(i)$ and the expected utility $V_e(i)$, reduced by the value Π_v of a vacant job, and of the expected gains V_u of an untrained unemployed person, where i designates the level of investment made in the job in question. When an untrained worker is hired, the optimal investment maximizes the net surplus. When the free entry condition $\Pi_v = 0$ is satisfied, the net surplus reads:

$$S_n(i) = V_e(i) - V_u + \Pi_e(i) - i \tag{21}$$

Let us denote respectively by i_e and i_f, with $i_e + i_f = i$, the amount of investment made by the employee and the firm, and let us assume that a part γ of the net surplus goes to the worker; the negotiated wage is implicitly determined by the surplus-sharing rules:

$$V_e(i) - i_e - V_u = \gamma S_n(i) \qquad \text{and} \qquad \Pi_e(i) - i_f = (1 - \gamma)S_n(i)$$

These equations indicate that the wage of workers without initial training depends not just on the amount of total investment i but also on their personal contribution to this investment. For a given amount of investment i, the wage negotiated is evidently lower, the smaller the worker's contribution is. We will simply denote this wage by w.

It is important to point out that the expected utility of a trained worker, should he or she lose his or her current job, depends on his or her training, since in negotiating with potential employers, he or she can make his or her productive abilities, equal to $y(i)$, pay off. Consequently we will denote by $V_u(i)$ the gains expected by an unemployed person who has had the benefit of an investment in general training amounting to i. The expected gains are then defined by the usual equations:

$$rV_e(i) = w + q[V_u(i) - V_e(i)] \tag{22}$$

$$r\Pi_e(i) = y(i) - w + q[\Pi_v - \Pi_e(i)] \tag{23}$$

Let $\overline{V}_e(i)$ and $\overline{w}(i)$ be respectively the expected utility and the wage of an employee hired when he or she was already trained (for whom the investment i in general training was thus made on a previous job); we then have:

$$rV_u(i) = z + \theta m(\theta)[\overline{V}_e(i) - V_u(i)] \quad \text{and} \quad r\overline{V}_e(i) = \overline{w}(i) + q[V_u(i) - \overline{V}_e(i)] \tag{24}$$

For trained workers, bargaining covers only the wage level $\overline{w}(i)$, since it is no longer necessary to invest in their general training. At this stage, the model becomes identical to the basic model of chapter 9 and the outcome of the negotiation is described by equation (20) from that chapter, i.e.:

$$\overline{w}(i) = z + [y(i) - z]\Gamma(\theta) \quad \text{with} \quad \Gamma(\theta) = \frac{\gamma[r + q + \theta m(\theta)]}{r + q + \gamma\theta m(\theta)}$$

Relations (24) then allow us to express $V_u(i)$ as a function of i and θ; it comes to:

$$rV_u(i) = z + [y(i) - z]\frac{\gamma\theta m(\theta)}{r + q + \gamma\theta m(\theta)} \tag{25}$$

This formula indicates how the investment i in general training made today increases the expectation of future gain of a worker in search of a job. It should be taken into account at the time of choosing the amount of optimal investment. Taking relations (22) and (23) into account, when the free entry condition $\Pi_v = 0$ is satisfied, the surplus net of investment costs (21) is written:

$$S_n(i) = \frac{y(i) + qV_u(i)}{r + q} - i - V_u \tag{26}$$

With the help of definition (25) of $V_u(i)$, the maximization of the net surplus gives an investment i_m defined by:

$$y'(i_m) = r + \frac{rq}{r + \gamma\theta m(\theta)} \tag{27}$$

Setting aside the case of perfect competition (which is obtained by making $\theta m(\theta)$ go to $+\infty$), comparison of this relation with equation (20) characterizing the socially efficient level of investment i^* shows that if $r > n$ then $y'(i_m) > y'(i^*)$ for all values of θ. The concavity of function $y(.)$ then entails $i^* > i_m$. In an imperfectly competitive labor market, there is thus a tendency to underinvest in general training even if agents can sign complete contracts.[4] That comes from the fact that a part of the investment decided by a worker and an employer will necessarily benefit future employers, who are not parties to the investment decision.

Underinvestment and Incomplete Markets
We have just seen that agents underinvest in general training because it is not possible for them to negotiate with *future* employers. The latter will benefit from the investment made today, for in a imperfectly competitive market they will capture a part of

the surplus produced by workers. This positive externality is not taken into account by the market, and this in turn justifies state intervention in the area of general training (on these questions, see Acemoglu, 1997, and Acemoglu and Pischke, 1998, 1999a, 1999b). We note that if decentralized equilibrium with complete contracts is inefficient, it is so a fortiori with incomplete contracts.

There are many other sources of externality associated with training decisions. Most often the acquisition of human capital by an agent represents a positive externality for his or her immediate circle without these benefits being acknowledged through any remuneration. The transmission of know-how through simple discussions, or by observation, are classic examples of such externalities. Individual training has social consequences that the market does not necessarily place a value on. Many sociological studies carried out in the 1960s have shown that the performance of students is influenced by the average level of performance of the students with whom they go to school (Coleman et al., 1966). These externalities play a very important role in models of endogenous growth (Lucas, 1988; Benabou, 1996; Aghion and Howitt, 1998).

Formally, these direct externalities can be taken into account in the model developed above by taking the view that a worker's productivity is an increasing function of his or her own investment i and of the average level of investment $\bar{i}$ of all workers. Individual production is then represented by the concave function $y(i, \bar{i})$. If we go back to the model with this formulation, the possibility arises of a multiplicity of market equilibria when a rise in average investment improves the marginal return on individual investment (that is, if the second derivative y_{12} is positive). In the terminology of Cooper and John (1988), the decisions of agents are then characterized by "strategic complementarities" capable of causing coordination failures and holding the market at a low level of investment.

Complex contracts obliging possible future employers to pay a transfer to the initial employer or to pay a wage supplement to previously trained workers, would in theory allow the social optimum to be reached (Acemoglu, 1997). But this contractual structure is not realistic, because for it to be put into practice there would have to be commitments binding *all* employers, something very hard to envisage. Snower (1995), Ulph (1995), and Acemoglu (1997) have also shown that firms might be given an incentive to choose technologies using mainly low-skilled manpower, if workers have little training. Such behavior by firms would accentuate underinvestment in general training, since the incentive for workers to invest in this type of training increases with the demand for skilled labor.

The imperfection of the financial markets is another barrier to investment in general training. When wage-earners are obliged to borrow in order to get training, the difficulties of access to credit do indeed lead to an insufficient level of training. The imperfection of financial markets most often arises from an asymmetry of information between the organizations granting credit and the investors. Uncertainty about the capacities of individuals applying for credit, and the chance that they might use the money for purposes other than training, constitute sources of inefficiency in the credit market that must lead to rationing. Becker (1964) emphasizes that this type of problem ought to be solved by public intervention in the credit market instead of by regulating the general training of workers. Thus underinvestment in training does not always necessitate subsidies or action by the state in this area.

The imperfect information of employers about the characteristics of workers is another potential source of underinvestment in general training. If employers observe the amount invested in human capital, and the return on it, imperfectly, then workers do indeed risk not being able to make their training pay off fully, which leads them to invest less. So employers have an interest in completing general training after hiring (Katz and Ziderman, 1990; Chang and Wang, 1996). In that case, investment by firms will be optimal if it is possible to sign complete, nonrenegotiable contracts.

2.2.2 Acquiring Specific Training

Unlike general training, specific training demands a new investment every time a worker changes firms. In that context, the incompleteness of the labor contract becomes the principal source of inefficiency in decentralized decisions. We will prove this point, beginning with a definition of the social optimum in the presence of transaction costs in the labor market, and costs of specific training. We will then show that decentralized equilibrium coincides with the social optimum when there are complete contracts. This result is thus different from that obtained within the framework of general training, where the costs of matching constitute a source of inefficiency in decentralized decisions. Conversely, when labor contracts are incomplete, decentralized decisions entail underinvestment with respect to the socially desirable level.

The Social Optimum with Specific Training

With no risk of confusion, we shall again denote by i the investment in specific training from which a worker benefits at each new hire. Once this investment is made, the employee is capable of producing a quantity $y(i)$ of goods *solely* in the firm he or she has just joined. The function $y(i)$ possesses the same properties as before: it is increasing, concave, and such that $y(0) > z$. Formally, the analysis of the social optimum with specific training is deduced from that with general training, with these addenda: an unemployed person never possesses specific training, and an investment i must be made in every unemployed person when he or she finds a job. In other words, from now on we have $u_f \equiv 0$ and $u_n \equiv u$. Relations (13) and (14) describing the law of motion of the unemployment rate u and the stationary value of this variable apply here as well. On the other hand, we must replace u_n by u in equation (16) characterizing the evolution of average production y per employed person. Thus we will now have:

$$\dot{y} = \frac{\theta m(\theta) u}{1 - u}[y(i) - y] \tag{28}$$

The planner's problem is then written as follows:

$$\underset{\theta, i}{\text{Max}} \int_0^{+\infty} [(1 - u)y + (z - \theta h)u - \theta m(\theta)ui]e^{-(r-n)t}\,dt \qquad \text{s.c. (13) and (28)}$$

Let λ and μ again denote the multipliers respectively associated with constraints (28) and (13); the Hamiltonian of the planner's problem takes the form[5]:

$$H = [(1 - u)y + (z - \theta h)u - \theta m(\theta)ui]e^{-(r-n)t} dt + \lambda \dot{y} + \mu \dot{u}$$

The first-order conditions are given by equations:

$$\frac{\partial H}{\partial i} = 0, \quad \frac{\partial H}{\partial \theta} = 0 \quad \text{and} \quad \frac{\partial H}{\partial y} = -\dot{\lambda}, \quad \frac{\partial H}{\partial u} = -\dot{\mu} \tag{29}$$

Differentiating the Hamiltonian with respect to i, the first of conditions (29) again brings us to the equality (18) giving the value of the multiplier λ as a function of u and of i. If we now derive the Hamiltonian with respect to y, condition $\partial H/\partial y = -\dot{\lambda}$ entails:

$$(1 - u)e^{-(r-n)t} - \lambda \frac{\theta m(\theta)u}{1 - u} = -\dot{\lambda} \tag{30}$$

At stationary equilibrium where $\dot{\theta} = \dot{u} = 0$, the derivation of relation (18) with respect to t gives $\dot{\lambda} = -(r - n)\lambda$. Bringing this value of $\dot{\lambda}$ into (30), we deduce from that the value of the multiplier λ. Equation (18) then yields $y'(i)$ as a function of u and θ. Using definition (14) of the unemployment rate at stationary equilibrium, we can then express $y'(i)$ as a function of θ alone. The socially optimal level of investment in specific training, again denoted by i^*, thus satisfies:

$$y'(i^*) = r + q \tag{31}$$

It should be pointed out that efficient investment in specific training depends neither on the matching process nor on labor market tightness θ. These properties are highly intuitive, for the investment in specific training is only made after the match-up between a worker and a firm, and this investment has to be made again at each new match-up. The time spent searching for a job thus plays no part in the decision to invest in specific training.

Equilibrium with Complete Contracts and Specific Training

Contrary to the result we reached in the case of general training, here we will show that decentralized equilibrium selects a socially optimal amount of investment in specific training when firms and workers are capable of committing themselves to complete contracts. Formally, the only difference from the case of general training lies in the independence of the expected utility of any unemployed person when an investment in specific training is made. Specifically, it is enough to set $V_u(i) = V_u$ in the decentralized market model with general training in order to find equilibrium with specific training. Therefore, setting $V'_u(i) = 0$ in the expression (26) of the surplus from a filled job, we see that the equilibrium value, again denoted by i_m, of the global investment in specific training satisfies the equality $y'(i_m) = r + q$. In a decentralized equilibrium, the investment in specific training is thus socially optimal. The absence of externalities arising from specific training ensures that the privately chosen investment is socially efficient. Note that to arrive at this result, it is not necessary to specify the exact form of V_u, nor to refer to the matching process that takes place in the labor market. The efficiency of decentralized equilibrium when it comes to investment in specific training is thus a property that is satisfied with and without labor market frictions. The reason for this is the same as the one adduced for the determination of efficient investment i^*: the time spent searching for a job plays no part in the decision to invest in specific training.

The hypothesis that there is commitment to complete contracts renders the participation of agents in financing the investment inconsequential. As in the case of general training, to the extent that there are binding commitments, the parties agree to compensate changes in workers' share of investment in training by changes in the wage. In what follows, we show that this compensation does not operate if contracts are incomplete.

Equilibrium with Incomplete Contracts and Specific Training
A necessary condition (but not always a sufficient one; see the case of general training) of the efficiency of investment decisions is that it must be possible to sign long-term, nonrenegotiable contracts in such a way as to avoid the holdup problem. But it is impossible under many circumstances to have the clauses of a contract verified by a third party (see chapter 6), and this leads to the adoption of incomplete contracts— ones that are vulnerable to renegotiation. That being so, there is a risk of underinvestment. This situation is illustrated for physical capital in chapter 7, section 5.1.2, and investment in training is no different.

This will emerge clearly if we go back to the previous model: but now we assume that each party decides, at the time of hiring, how much to contribute to the investment in specific training, knowing that the wage might be renegotiated at any time. It is easiest to represent this situation by a two-stage game. In the first stage, the employer and the worker choose, simultaneously and without cooperation, their respective specific investments i_f and i_e. Total investment $(i_f + i_e)$ is always denoted by i. In the second stage, the wage is negotiated in such a way as to share the surplus in accordance with the bargaining power of each of the agents. The outcome of this game is found by backward induction.

The expected utility of an employee and the expected profit from a filled job are again given by relations (22) and (23) on condition that we replace $V_u(i)$ by V_u in (22). In the second stage of the game, the gains of the employer and the worker are respectively equal to $[\Pi_e(i) - i_f]$ and $[V_e(i) - i_e]$ if the bargaining is successful. But if the bargaining fails, the respective gains amount to $(\Pi_v - i_f)$ and $(V_u - i_e)$ since at this stage the investment has already been made. So the surplus released by a match is equal to:

$$S(i) = V_e(i) - V_u + \Pi_e(i) - \Pi_v = \frac{y(i) - rV_u}{r + q} \tag{32}$$

The wage bargaining that takes place at this stage shares out the surplus in accordance with the bargaining power of each of the agents. Since V_u does not depend on i, relations (22), (23), and (32) defining the gains of agents and the surplus show that this stage of the game is formally identical to wage bargaining in the basic model from chapter 9. We thus have:

$$w = \gamma y(i) + (1 - \gamma)rV_u \tag{33}$$

In the first stage of the game, the employer determines the amount i_f of his or her investment by maximizing his or her net profit $\Pi_e(i) - i_f$. He or she then knows the reaction of the negotiated wage described by equality (33) and considers the investment i_e of the employee as given. So with the help of the definition of $\Pi_e(i)$ given by (23), we arrive at:

$$(1 - \gamma)y'(i) = r + q \tag{34}$$

Symmetrically, the worker knows the reaction of the wage, and decides his or her investment i_e by maximizing his or her net gain $V_e(i) - i_e$ with given i_f. The definition of $V_e(i)$ given by (22) then entails:

$$\gamma y'(i) = r + q \tag{35}$$

Relation (34) describing the best response from the employer indicates that he or she announces a *global* amount of desired investment, denoted by $\tilde{i}$, and defined by the equality $(1 - \gamma)y'(\tilde{i}) = r + q$. Relation (35) likewise shows that the employee desires a global amount of investment, denoted by $\hat{i}$, such that $\gamma y'(\hat{i}) = r + q$. In a noncooperative equilibrium, it is the agent with the highest level of desired investment who will assume the entire cost of the investment. Consequently, if $\gamma > 1/2$, $\hat{i}$ is superior to $\tilde{i}$ and only the worker invests in his or her own specific training. At market equilibrium, this investment amounts to $\hat{i}$. Relation (31) giving the value i^* of the socially efficient investment then shows that $\hat{i} \leq i^*$, with $\hat{i} = i^*$ if $\gamma = 1$. On the other hand, if $\gamma < \frac{1}{2}$, the employer assumes the entire burden of the investment, which then comes to $\tilde{i}$. Relation (31) again shows that we have $\tilde{i} \leq i^*$, with $\tilde{i} = i^*$ if $\gamma = 0$. If $\gamma = \frac{1}{2}$, there is a range of equilibria, all of them inefficient. Hence, market equilibrium leads to underinvestment in specific training except when one of the agents has all the bargaining power. In that situation, the fact that no commitment can be made no longer matters, for the agent with all the power is also the only one to benefit from the payback on the investment; this explains why he or she invests in an efficient fashion.

We have just shown that transaction costs in the labor market constitute sources of underinvestment in training, both specific and general. This justifies state intervention in this area, in order to upgrade all levels of training. The intervention itself has to be adequately efficient as well. Many empirical studies have been dedicated to this problem, and the results are brought together in section 3.2 below.

2.3 EMPLOYMENT SUBSIDIES

When the matching process is imperfect, social efficiency requires strictly positive unemployment, so that vacant jobs can be filled. To try to get rid of unemployment by creating a great many vacant jobs would be a waste of resources. Nevertheless, there are a number of reasons why an excessively high unemployment rate may occur at market equilibrium. When that happens, employment subsidies are a means to reduce

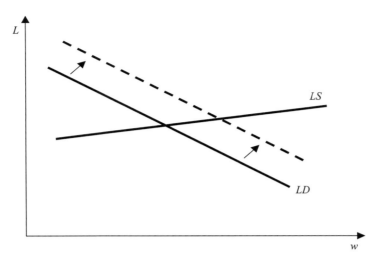

FIGURE 11.1
The effect of employment subsidies in the competitive model.

the unemployment rate while improving overall welfare. The main limitation on the efficiency of employment subsidies lies in the upward pressure they exert on wages, which has a tendency to bid up the cost of labor and reduce labor demand. This phenomenon emerges clearly in the case of a perfectly competitive labor market as represented in figure 11.1. An increase in labor demand on account of a fall in the cost of labor increases wages. These increases are greater, the less the wage elasticity of labor supply. At the limit, if the wage elasticity of the labor supply is null (a case not very remote from many empirical estimates, see chapter 1), the shift in labor demand leads solely to a wage rise, with no impact on employment. The matching model associated with noncompetitive wage setting allows us to clarify these results.

2.3.1 Who Benefits from Employment Subsidies?

The simple matching model from chapter 9 allows us to see clearly that a subsidy (or a tax) does not necessarily benefit the direct recipient. It turns out that a subsidy granted to a firm only benefits the firm to some degree (and perhaps not at all, in certain circumstances), and that the worker derives benefit from it as well. The sharing of the gains induced by subsidies is part of the wider problem of the fiscal incidence of taxes and transfers by the state.

The Matching Model with Employment Subsidies
We consider an economy in which filled jobs are subsidized. If the negotiated wage amounts to w, the employer receives a subsidy equal to sw, and the cost of labor thus comes to $w(1-s)$. For the rest, we restore all the components of the basic model from chapter 9. The expected profit Π_e and Π_v respectively associated with a filled job and

a vacant one thus satisfy:

$$r\Pi_e = y - (1-s)w + q(\Pi_v - \Pi_e) \qquad \text{and} \qquad r\Pi_v = -h + m(\theta)(\Pi_e - \Pi_v) \tag{36}$$

When the free entry condition $\Pi_v = 0$ is satisfied, we get $\Pi_e = h/m(\theta)$ and the labor demand equation takes the following form:

$$\frac{h}{m(\theta)} = \frac{y - (1-s)w}{r+q} \tag{37}$$

The expected utilities V_e and V_u of an employee and an unemployed person are still defined by:

$$rV_e = w + q(V_u - V_e) \qquad \text{and} \qquad rV_u = z + \theta m(\theta)(V_e - V_u) \tag{38}$$

We further assume that the wage on which the worker and the employer agree corresponds to the solution of the Nash problem described in chapter 9, section 3.4.1. Let γ again be the relative power of the worker in the bargaining process; the negotiated wage is found by maximizing the Nash criterion $(V_e - V_u)^\gamma (\Pi_e - \Pi_v)^{1-\gamma}$ with respect to w. Relations (36) and (38) give the contributions of the players to this criterion. They are:

$$\Pi_e - \Pi_v = \frac{y - (1-s)w - r\Pi_v}{r+q} \qquad \text{and} \qquad V_e - V_u = \frac{w - rV_u}{r+q}$$

It is easy to deduce that if the free entry condition $\Pi_v = 0$ is satisfied, the negotiated wage is given by:

$$w = \gamma \frac{y}{1-s} + (1-\gamma)rV_u \tag{39}$$

If we compare this equation with relation (19) giving the negotiated wage in the basic model from chapter 9, it turns out that, from the point of view of the employer, the grant of a subsidy is formally equal to an increase in individual production for the same wage w paid to his or her employee. But for the latter, the subsidy paid to the employer proves formally equivalent to a wage rise for the same level of productivity. So we have to specify exactly how the subsidy received by the firm is finally shared out.

An Illustration of the Problem of Fiscal Incidence
In order to arrive at the expression of the wage curve encapsulating the outcome of the wage bargaining, it suffices to replace y by $y/(1-s)$ in formula (20) from chapter 9, which gives precisely the equation of the wage curve. We thus find:

$$w = z + \Gamma(\theta)\left[\frac{y}{1-s} - z\right] \qquad \text{with} \qquad \Gamma(\theta) = \frac{\gamma[r + q + \theta m(\theta)]}{r + q + \gamma\theta m(\theta)} \tag{40}$$

This relation shows that for given θ, i.e., at the partial equilibrium of a decentralized wage negotiation, the payment of a subsidy to the employer leads to a rise in the wage received by the employee. To subsidize firms in this way amounts to increasing the global surplus generated by filled jobs. During wage bargaining, the worker captures a portion of this additional surplus in the form of a wage rise. The result would be identical if the employee were to benefit from a direct subsidy in his or her favor, for example, the right to hold on to certain social transfers while working for pay; in that case it would be the employer who, during wage bargaining, would capture a portion of the additional surplus.

We have seen, especially in chapters 1 and 9, that unemployment benefits are most often indexed, partly at least, to wages. This property is summed up by the equality $z = bw + z_0$ where b and z_0 are exogenous constants. That being so, the wage curve takes the form:

$$w(1 - s) = \frac{\Gamma(\theta)y + z_0[1 - \Gamma(\theta)](1 - s)}{1 - b[1 - \Gamma(\theta)]} \tag{41}$$

This equation highlights the fundamental role played by the degree of indexation of unemployment benefits to wages (Pissarides, 1998, insists particularly on this point). When unemployment benefits are perfectly indexed to wages ($z_0 = 0$), the effect of a wage subsidy takes a particularly distinct form. Relation (41) shows that, for given θ, the cost of labor for the employer, i.e., $w(1 - s)$, does not depend on the amount of the subsidy. In other words, wage bargaining entails that the employee captures the totality of the subsidy initially paid to the employer. This result spectacularly illustrates the question of *fiscal incidence*: the application of a fiscal measure to a specific agent (here, the employer) does not necessarily make this individual the ultimate beneficiary or victim of the measure. The hypotheses of risk neutrality and the indexation of unemployment benefits make the employee the real beneficiary of the subsidy. When unemployment benefits are partially indexed to wages, the cost of labor does effectively diminish with the subsidy. But there is always an additional surplus-sharing mechanism generated by the subsidy that pushes the negotiated wage upward.

The Impact of Subsidized Hiring on Labor Market Equilibrium
Equilibrium values of the wage and the labor market tightness lie at the intersection of the wage curve and the labor demand curve respectively defined by relations (41) and (37). Wages come into these relations through the cost of labor, i.e., $w(1 - s)$. Hence we can eliminate this variable in order to obtain an equation implicitly defining the equilibrium value θ^* of labor market tightness; the equilibrium value w^* of the negotiated wage can immediately be deduced thanks to (41) and comes to:

$$\frac{h}{m(\theta^*)} = \frac{y(1 - b) - z_0(1 - s)}{(r + q)} \Phi(\theta^*) \quad \text{with} \quad \Phi(\theta) \equiv \frac{1 - \Gamma(\theta)}{1 - b[1 - \Gamma(\theta)]} \tag{42}$$

Finally, the equilibrium value of the unemployment rate is found by examining, in the (v, u) plane, the intersection of the Beveridge curve with the line issuing from the origin with slope θ^* (see chapter 9, fig. 4.7). As the Beveridge curve is not affected by employment subsidies, their impact on the unemployment rate is immediately deducible from the variation in labor market tightness.

Equation (42) shows that labor market tightness is not affected by subsidies if the gains of unemployed persons are perfectly indexed to wages ($z_0 = 0$). When that is so, employment subsidies induce only a redistribution from firms, whose profits fall, to workers, here both the employed and the unemployed, *with no effect on employment*. When the gains of the unemployed are not perfectly indexed to wages, employment subsidies increase labor market tightness and so reduce the unemployment rate. It should be noted that these conclusions no longer hold when the worker is paid at the minimum wage. In that case, w is given and equation (37) of labor demand completely determines the equilibrium value of the labor market tightness. Then an employment subsidy always reduces unemployment, for the cost of labor falls without the income w of the employee rising.

The points made here highlight the complementarities between different employment policies (emphasized by Coe and Snower, 1997, and Pissarides, 1998). The efficiency of employment subsidies depends in part on the attribution rules of unemployment benefits. These subsidies may have no more than a very slight effect on employment, if the gains of the unemployed are perfectly indexed to wages.

2.3.2 Quantifying the Effect of Employment Subsidies

It is possible to assess the impact of employment subsidies quantitatively by using the estimates of the elasticity η_u^w of wages with respect to the unemployment rate made by Blanchflower and Oswald (1995). These authors find that in most countries this quantity lies close to -0.1. In order to bring out this linkage between the unemployment rate and wages, we will write the level of employment in the form $N[1 - u(w)]$ where N represents the size, assumed to be exogenous, of the labor force. Labor demand, for its part, depends in a very general way—see, for example, relation (37)—on the global cost of labor. Hence it can be denoted by $L^d[w(1 - s)]$, and labor market equilibrium is conveyed by the equality:

$$L^d[w(1 - s)] = N[1 - u(w)]$$

Let η^d be the elasticity of labor demand with respect to the cost of this factor; differentiating this equality with respect to s it becomes possible, after several simple calculations, to express the elasticity η_s^w of wages with respect to the rate of the subsidy in the following manner:

$$\eta_s^w = \frac{(1 - u)\eta^d}{(1 - u)\eta^d + \dfrac{u}{\eta_u^w}} \tag{43}$$

A relevant order of magnitude for η^d is -0.5 (see chapter 4, section 2.2 on empirical estimates of the labor demand elasticity). For an unemployment rate equal to 10% and with $\eta_u^w = -0.1$, we then have $\eta_s^w \simeq 0.31$. This result signifies that a subsidy reducing the cost of labor by 1% provokes a wage rise on the order of 0.3%. Thus the reduction in the labor cost is on the order of 0.7%, so labor demand and employment increase by $0.7 \cdot 0.5\% = 0.35\%$ for subsidies amounting to 1% of the labor cost. It is worth noting that this elasticity entails that job creation by means of this type of subsidy has a relatively high cost. An increase in the subsidy of Δs costs $w\Delta s$ per job subsidized, and makes it possible to create $0.35\Delta s$ jobs. The cost of each job created is thus equal to $w/0.35$, i.e., around three times the average cost of a job. The gain for society corresponds to the extra production achieved by creating the extra job, and the savings made thanks to the hiring of an unemployed person. Assuming that an unemployed person costs society around half the production of a job, the net collective gain from the creation of an extra job is *negative*, since it is worth y (the production of the job created), minus $3w$ (the cost of the job created), plus $0.5y$ (the savings made thanks to the decrease in unemployment), which gives a total gain, assuming that the average wage is equal to $(2/3)y$, of $-0.5y$.

This calculation assumes that all jobs are subsidized. There are, however, reasons to think that employment subsidies are more efficient when they are targeted to low-skilled workers. Two arguments support this case. For one thing, equation (43) indicates that the elasticity η_s^w depends on the unemployment rate. Now, the least skilled workers are also the ones for whom this variable takes the highest value. For another, demand for low-skilled labor is probably more elastic to wages (see chapter 4 and Hamermesh, 1993), on the order of -1, for workers whose wage is close to the minimum wage. If we make the same calculation as before with an unemployment rate equal to 15%, we can show that a subsidy reducing the cost of low-skilled labor by 1% increases employment by 0.64%. The cost of one job created comes to approximately 1.6 times the average cost of an unskilled job. This figure is about half the one we arrived at when all jobs are subsidized, and suggests that it is possible to increase global employment using employment subsidies for the low-skilled (relatively sensitive to lightened labor cost) financed by taxes on skilled employment (relatively insensitive to increased labor cost). Concretely, these measures, which have been proposed by Drèze and Malinvaud (1994) and Drèze and Sneessens (1997) in particular, could be put into effect by recalibrating payroll taxes to make them less onerous for low wages and more onerous for higher wages.

2.4 THE CREATION OF PUBLIC SECTOR JOBS

In comparison to employment subsidies, the creation of public sector jobs presents the advantage of making it possible actually to create jobs within a short time frame. For this reason they are often adopted either as a remedy for unemployment or as a springboard to regular jobs for persons who have difficulty entering the labor force. The creation of public sector jobs is liable to crowd out private sector ones, however, through the same mechanism as employment subsidies: the increase in labor demand provokes a wage rise that may, over time, completely cancel out the impact of the public sector jobs created, if the labor supply is insensitive to wages (Calmfors, 1994; Calmfors and Lang, 1995; Algan et al., 2002). We will begin by looking at the crowding-out effect induced by the creation of public sector employment in the matching model, before proceeding to a quantitative assessment of the extent of this effect.

2.4.1 The Crowding-out Effects of Public Sector Jobs

It is possible to represent the impact of the creation of public sector jobs schematically, using the matching model and assuming that these jobs have the same characteristics as those in the private sector (less rudimentary models will be found in Holmlund and Linden, 1993; Calmfors and Lang, 1995; and Algan et al., 2002).

The Beveridge Curve with Public Sector Jobs

By hypothesis, workers in the private and public sectors receive the same wage w and face the same probability q of losing their jobs. The assumption is that the state aligns civil service wages with those negotiated in the private sector. For the sake of simplicity, the size of the labor force is assumed to be constant, equal to 1; we denote public sector employment by L_g. If L designates employment in the private sector, the unemployment rate u is defined by the equality:

$$u = 1 - L_g - L$$

We assume that the matching process in the public sector is perfectly efficient. The state recruits its employees by a random draw from among all the unemployed. Let g be the rate at which an unemployed person is hired in the public sector. At stationary equilibrium, the volume of jobs destroyed per unit of time in this sector, qL_g, must equal the volume gu of jobs created. Hence rate g depends on the unemployment rate, the job destruction rate, and the volume of public sector jobs, according to the formula:

$$g = \frac{qL_g}{u} \tag{44}$$

Assuming that the usual matching process goes on in the private sector, at every instant there are respectively $[g + \theta m(\theta)]u$ jobs created and $q(1 - u)$ jobs destroyed in the economy as a whole. At stationary equilibrium, these two quantities are equal, and using definition (44) of g, the unemployment rate is expressed as follows:

$$u = \frac{q(1 - L_g)}{q + \theta m(\theta)} \tag{45}$$

This equation defines the Beveridge curve in the presence of a public sector of size L_g. It turns out that the creation of public sector jobs reduces the unemployment rate when the vacancy rate in the private sector is given. But the number of vacancies is an endogenous variable, determined by the profit outlook of firms, so we must focus on the determinants of labor demand and negotiated wages to understand the consequences of public employment on unemployment.

Labor Market Equilibrium

Wages and the job destruction rate being identical in both sectors, an employee has the same expected utility V_e everywhere. Since an unemployed person finds a job in the public and private sectors at respective rates g and $\theta m(\theta)$, his or her expected utility V_u satisfies the relation:

$$rV_u = z + [g + \theta m(\theta)](V_e - V_u) \tag{46}$$

Comparing this relation with the definition of V_u in the basic matching model of chapter 9, it turns out that this matching model with public-sector employment is formally equivalent to the basic model, on condition that we replace the probability $\theta m(\theta)$ of returning to employment by the sum $g + \theta m(\theta)$. Consequently, the negotiated wage is written as follows:

$$w = z + \Gamma(\theta, g)(y - z) \qquad \text{with} \qquad \Gamma(\theta, g) = \frac{\gamma[r + q + g + \theta m(\theta)]}{r + q + \gamma[g + \theta m(\theta)]} \tag{47}$$

It is, moreover, possible to eliminate the unemployment rate u between relations (44) and (45), which allows us to write g as a function of L_g and θ. We thus get $g = L_g[q + \theta m(\theta)]/(1 - L_g)$. Bringing this value of g into the wage equation (47), we find the remuneration of an employee as a function of the labor market tightness θ and the level L_g of public sector employment, i.e.:

$$w = z + \hat{\Gamma}(\theta, L_g)(y - z) \qquad \text{with} \qquad \hat{\Gamma}(\theta, L_g) = \frac{\gamma[r(1 - L_g) + q + \theta m(\theta)]}{r + q + \gamma \theta m(\theta) - L_g[r + q(1 - \gamma)]} \tag{48}$$

In the (θ, w) plane, labor market equilibrium lies at the intersection of the wage curve (WC), represented by equation (48), with labor demand. The latter arises from the equality between the average cost $h/m(\theta)$ of a vacant job and the expected profit $(y - w)/(r + q)$ from a filled job, so it does not depend on the size L_g of the public sector. On the other hand, it is easy to verify that, for given θ, the negotiated wage rises with L_g. In the (θ, w) plane, the wage curve shifts to the right. Labor market equilibrium is represented in figure 11.2. It turns out that public sector employment,

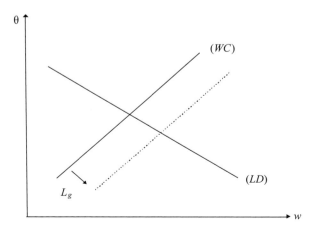

Figure 11.2
The effects of public sector jobs on wages.

by increasing the exit rate from unemployment, exerts upward pressure on the nego-tiated wage and thus proves liable to crowd out private employment.

The equilibrium unemployment rate is obtained by focusing on the intersection of the Beveridge curve (*BC*) defined by equation (45) with the line issuing from the origin with slope θ. Figure 11.3 sums up this situation. An increase in public sector employment also leads to a downward shift of the Beveridge curve, so it is equivalent to greater efficiency in the matching process. This improved efficiency runs counter to the crowding-out effect on private sector jobs, and, to sum up, the variations in the unemployment rate are ambiguous. The calibration exercise that follows allows us to specify the orders of magnitude of these contradictory effects.

2.4.2 Quantifying the Impact of Public Sector Job Creation

It is possible to assess the impact of public sector job creation by a method analogous to that adopted for employment subsidies. Let $L^d(w)$ be labor demand in the private sector, and let us consider a measure that consists of creating $(p-1)L^d(w)$ public sector jobs. Labor market equilibrium is then written:

$$(p-1)L^d(w) + L^d(w) = pL^d(w) = N[1 - u(w)]$$

Differentiating this relation with respect to p, we find the expression of the elasticity η_p^L of total employment with respect to the rate of public sector job creation. After several simple calculations, it comes to:

$$\eta_p^L = \frac{u}{u + (1-u)\eta^d\eta_u^w}$$

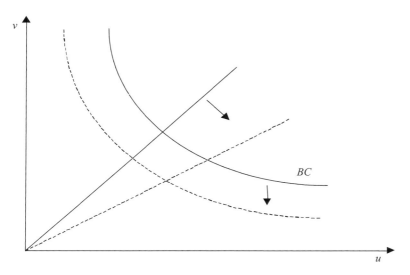

FIGURE 11.3
Labor market equilibrium with public sector job creation.

This relation gives the variation in total employment following an increase in public sector employment corresponding to 1% of private sector employment. If we adopt the same calibration as that used to analyze employment subsidies, i.e., $u = 0.1$, $\eta^d = -0.5$, and $\eta_u^w = -0.1$, we find $\eta_p^L \simeq 0.7$. The creation of a public sector job therefore destroys around 0.3 private sector jobs.

In order to compare the efficiency of public sector job creation with that of employment subsidies, we must first point out that a public sector job does not necessarily have the same productivity as a private sector one. Let y_p be the production of a public sector job; the net gains from the creation of a public sector job are equal to production y_p minus wage w and production loss in the private sector, or $0.3y$. We must add the gains that flow from the hiring of an unemployed person, which we take to be equal to $0.5y$. The total net gain for the collectivity is thus equal to $y_p - w + 0.2y$, and depends on the productivity of public sector jobs and their remuneration. It is not necessarily positive.

These orders of magnitude are evidently no more than indicative. They suggest that the systematic subsidization of private sector jobs, or the creation of public sector ones, are very costly measures that should only be used marginally to combat unemployment.

3   THE EVALUATION OF ACTIVE LABOR MARKET POLICIES

In order to judge labor market policies, we need to be able to assess their impact both on the agent who benefits from them and on the collective welfare. We will see that, in practice, this assessment most often halts at the individual agent, largely because of the difficulties of modeling global effects in comparison to the simplicity of the so-called Roy-Rubin model used to make individual estimates. Although the expenditures devoted to active employment policies in the United States are smaller than elsewhere, the great majority of assessments concern programs put in place there. We begin by describing the methodological principles that should guide the evaluation of labor market policies, then give the main results of the abundant research in this area, distinguishing American studies from European ones.

3.1   THE METHOD

The evaluation of labor market policies is grounded in the notion of potential gain, which represents the difference in the levels taken by a given indicator (wages, for example) in the presence and in the absence of the policy measure being examined. In practice, potential gain is pinpointed with the help of several standard estimators, of which the calculation and the validity depend on the available data. Data of this kind generally come from surveys, so we speak of observational or nonexperimental data. Selection bias is the main weakness of assessments made on this type of data, and in response, the "social experiment" approach has undergone considerable development in recent years. Such experiments aim to reproduce the experimental techniques that exist in sciences like agronomy, biology, and medicine, in the field of economics.

3.1.1 The Roy-Rubin Model of Potential Outcome

Most empirical research tries to judge the value of labor market policies by comparing the observed impact of a policy measure on the agent who benefits (for example, the number of hires by a firm receiving subsidies) with what would have been the outcome if the measure in question had not been applied to that agent. The difficulty of this exercise lies in the fact that the latter result is not observed. The solution to the problem of missing data is to assume that available data on the behavior of *other* agents can, under certain conditions, take its place. The impact of a policy measure on a particular agent should only be the first step in the assessment. In line with the theoretical structures presented in this chapter, we must pursue the analysis with the help of an equilibrium model of the whole labor market. As we will see, empirical research conforming to this prescription is still rare.

The Evaluation Problem

Every labor market policy has a precise goal: for example, a training placement is intended to increase the human capital of an individual. The success of such policies will be judged on the basis of a tangible result, which, in this example, might be a higher wage or a higher probability of employment. In the literature on labor market policy, this result is often referred to as the individual's *response*. The observer generally knows the gross impact of a policy on the beneficiary, for example the wage received after a training placement. But in order to assess the efficiency of this policy, the observer must also know what wage the same person would be receiving if he or she had not had the benefit of the placement. This is the nub of the problem, since the latter wage is not observed. Hence the essential question facing any evaluation of a policy measure is this: how would a person or a firm who has benefited from a measure—a *"treated"* person or firm—have responded if they had not benefited from that measure?

This approach to the evaluation problem is therefore based on the notion of "potential outcome," attributed to, among others, Fisher (1935), Roy (1951), Quandt (1972), and Rubin (1974). The literature on the subject generally refers to the Roy-Rubin model. In this literature, time is represented by a series of discrete periods (or dates). Let t_P be the period, assumed to be unique, over which the "treatment" is applied. In the simplest version, the Roy-Rubin model attributes two potential responses to each individual, which we will designate by Y_{it}^T and Y_{it}^C. The variable Y_{it}^T represents the response of agent i that would be observed at date t if he were treated, while the variable Y_{it}^C represents the response of agent i that would be observed at date t if he were not treated. Readers should note that date t can be posterior or anterior to the period t_P of the treatment, and should pay close attention to the terminology used. Before the treatment, a person referred to as treated has not yet undergone the treatment, but will definitely do so during period t_P. Conversely, after the treatment a person referred to as treated has in fact undergone the treatment. Results Y_{it}^T and Y_{it}^C are described as *potential*, for "to be treated" and "not to be treated" are two mutually exclusive states: it is not possible to observe the responses of the *same* individual at the *same* date in these two states.

In order to distinguish potential outcomes from *actual* ones, it is best to work with a dummy variable D_i, which takes a value of 1 if agent i has actually benefited from the measure, and 0 if not. The difficulty of the evaluation problem comes from the fact that the econometrician observes the realizations of the variable $Y_{it} = D_i Y_{it}^T + (1 - D_i) Y_{it}^C$, but never observes *simultaneously* the realizations of variables Y_{it}^T and Y_{it}^C for the same individual. In particular, he or she never observes the realizations of the gain of the treatment defined by $\Delta_{it} = Y_{it}^T - Y_{it}^C$. The unobserved result is called the "counterfactual outcome." For a treated person i, the counterfactual outcomes correspond to realizations of Y_{it}^C, whereas for an untreated agent j, the counterfactual outcomes correspond to realizations of Y_{jt}^T. Formally, the evaluation problem is a missing data problem.

Contrast Variables and Identifying Hypotheses
If we limit ourselves to direct effects, the efficiency of a measure is generally assessed with the help of a *contrast variable*; the one most commonly adopted is the *average treatment effect on the treated*, defined by (omitting indices i and t for simplicity):

$$E(\Delta \,|\, D = 1) = E(Y^T \,|\, D = 1) - E(Y^C \,|\, D = 1) \tag{49}$$

In principle, the data allow us to know $E(Y^T \,|\, D = 1)$ and $E(Y^C \,|\, D = 0)$, which represent respectively the average response of a treated person and an untreated one, but they do not allow us to determine $E(Y^C \,|\, D = 1)$, which represents what would, on average, have been the response of that person if he or she had not undergone the treatment that in reality he or she did undergo.[6] In order to assess the average gain from treatment defined by (49), the econometrician is thus obliged to make a so-called *identifying* hypothesis, which gives him or her the means to estimate the expected value of the counterfactual outcome $E(Y^C \,|\, D = 1)$ using the available data. Whatever the type of data (experimental or observational), the general principle is to specify a "control group" that has not undergone the treatment and is as nearly identical to the treated group as possible, then make an identifying hypothesis that lets the econometrician link the *unobserved* responses of the treated group to the *observed* responses of the members of the control group. The identifying hypothesis depends on the data available and influences the estimation procedure.

Policy measures can also be judged with the help of other contrast variables, like $\Pr(\Delta > 0 \,|\, D = 1)$, for example, which represents the proportion of participants for whom the program was beneficial. For simplicity, we will take the view that the only contrast variable is the average gain from the treatment, but what follows can easily be applied to any contrast variable. In general, the assessment of the "success" of the treatment is achieved by comparing this average gain to an indicator of the cost of the treatment.

Indirect Effects: From Partial Equilibrium to General Equilibrium

Most of the studies aiming to evaluate labor market policies choose the framework of the Roy-Rubin model, which is, by hypothesis, one of partial equilibrium. It tries to assess the behavior of an agent reacting to a precise measure, without taking into account the effect this measure might have on the decisions of other agents—which might in turn change the environment within which the agent responds to the measure under consideration. If we want to assess these "indirect" effects, to use the terminology of Lewis (1963), then we have to work with an equilibrium model of the entire labor market. Our theoretical exposition in this chapter follows this procedure, which was initiated by Layard and Nickell (1986) and taken further by Calmfors (1994), who established the following typology of the principal indirect effects that the Roy-Rubin model leaves out.

1. Displacement or crowding-out effects: the jobs created by a measure destroy other jobs to which the measure does not apply. This happens when, for example, firms employing subsidized workers increase their production and their market share at the expense of firms that are unable to use that category of worker, and so reduce their workforce.

2. Windfall effects: the impact of a measure differs hardly at all from what would have been the case if it had not been applied. This will occur if, for example, a firm receiving a subsidy to hire a worker would have done so anyway. The subsidy represents a "windfall" for the firm.

3. Substitution effects: the jobs created flow to the beneficiaries of a particular measure at the expense of those who are not targeted. For example, a firm hires a "young" subsidized worker instead of an "old" one who does not have access to this subsidy.

4. Tax effects: the taxes needed to finance a measure affect the decisions of all agents.

From the empirical point of view, the great majority of studies have looked only at the direct effects of labor market policies, neglecting their effects on the general equilibrium of the economy. Aside from the fact that it is clearly harder to make a global assessment anyway, the emphasis on direct effects arises from the predominance of U.S. research in this area. In the United States, the amounts budgeted for employment policy are relatively small, so it seems reasonable to assume that their macroeconomic effects are negligible. Heckman et al. (1999) do, however, argue that the global effects ought to be given more prominence in the assessment since, apart from the costs, a policy measure affects the behavior of both the beneficiaries and the nonbeneficiaries. In recent years there has been an increasing number of empirical studies that do evaluate the effects of labor market policy using a model of labor market equilibrium. We may cite Davidson and Woodbury (1993), who analyze the consequences of unemployment benefits, and Heckman et al. (1998), who study the effects of subsidies for college enrollment in the United States, using a general equilibrium model with overlapping generations. These works show that there can sometimes be a considerable gap between microeconomic estimates and the estimates that issue from such general equilibrium models. The future ought to see an expansion of this type of model, which brings the impact of labor market policy within a wider purview.

3.1.2 Observational Data and Experimental Data

Social experiments study the responses of two groups, randomly chosen so that on average the characteristics of the individuals who go to make them up are identical. Observational data generally do not satisfy this requirement, so there is no guarantee that selection biases do not arise in their interpretation.

Selection Bias with Observational Data

The econometrician wishing to assess a policy measure generally disposes of data resulting from surveys that give the responses of individuals who have had the benefit of the measure—the treated group—and those of untreated individuals—the control group. These data do not in themselves make it possible to distinguish the specific impact of the measure (which is what the econometrician wants to know) from the impact of differences that may exist between the *characteristics* of the two groups (which is what the econometrician wants to eliminate). In the real world, an individual decides to take part in a program or benefit from a policy measure according to his or her characteristics and personal desires. It is in addition possible that only a portion of the individuals who wish to benefit from a measure are chosen by the agency in charge. Therefore, estimates based on data from surveys are subject to *selection biases*, which the econometrician strives to minimize through appropriate methods. The most common of these methods is "matching," which consists of extracting, from the control group, a subset of individuals *similar* to the ones in the treatment group on the basis of characteristics that existed before the treatment. Let X be the vector of these characteristics. The econometrician's task is then to estimate the average gain from the treatment for individuals characterized by X, i.e., $E(\Delta|X, D = 1)$. This method takes for granted, among other things, that there is sufficient detailed information about the control group—which is not always the case with observational data—to construct a subset of individuals who have all the characteristics used to define the treated group. The aim of the matching method is to eliminate, or reduce as much as possible, selection biases that depend only on the *observable* characteristics of individuals; hence it assumes that agents' decisions to take part in a program, and their responses, depend mainly on the observable characteristics of individuals. Without further assumptions, it does not solve problems arising from nonobserved heterogeneity.

Social Experiments

Data from social experiments escape this selection bias, in principle. Let us suppose that we wanted to assess the benefits of a training program. A social experiment consists of dividing the individuals eligible for the program, and who agree to take part in the experiment, into two randomly chosen groups: a treatment group, which does in fact benefit from the program, and a control group, which does not. This random division of the participants is called "randomization." If the two groups are large enough, randomization entails that on average, observed and unobserved characteristics are identical in the two groups. That being so, the differences in the average results observed between these two groups depend only on the program, and selection bias is eliminated.[7]

In practice, this conclusion depends on several explicit or implicit hypotheses, and the impact of these on each particular experiment must be assessed. In the first place, it must be remembered that a social experiment aims to gain knowledge about a specific measure, so that it may eventually be applied in a "normal," i.e., a nonexperimental, context. In other words, it is assumed that the average gain from a measure, as evaluated through a social experiment, is equal or nearly equal to the average gain that will flow from the same measure in a "normal" setting. For that to be true, it is necessary in particular that the mere existence of a random draw does not change the composition of the population agreeing to participate in the experiment.[8] In the second place, we often observe that a significant proportion of the treatment group drops out of the experimental protocol along the way, and that an equally significant proportion of the control group is benefiting from services more or less similar to those offered in the program being tested but originating elsewhere. These biases of *attrition* and *substitution* do not disqualify the experimental data, since they also exist in nonexperimental data. The assessment of the effects of a measure must simply take them into account appropriately (see Heckman et al., 1999, pp. 1907–1914).

3.1.3 The Main Estimators

In what follows, we present the main estimators used, specifying their conditions of validity. It emerges from this analysis that the estimator chosen to evaluate the efficiency of a measure depends on the identifying hypothesis made on the available data.

The "Before-After" Estimator

Let us assume that we wish to assess the effects of a training program on persons having the observed characteristics represented by the vector X. If we have longitudinal data, or repeated cross-sectional data on the same population, the first idea that springs to mind is to compare the average response of the persons treated *before* and *after* their participation in the program. Let us generically denote by B and A the dates that respectively precede (B stands for *before*) and follow (A stands for *after*) the period of participation in the program. With longitudinal data, the econometrician knows the realization of the response Y_A^T of a representative person taking part in the program after having been treated, but does not observe the realization of the potential response Y_A^C of this person if he or she had not undergone the treatment that he or she did in fact undergo. So, without a supplementary hypothesis, the econometrician cannot infer the average gain from the treatment, which is here defined by the quantity

$E(Y_A^T - Y_A^C \mid X, D = 1)$. With longitudinal data, however, the realizations of the response Y_B^T of a representative participant before the application of the program are known. Then a possible identifying hypothesis is:

$$E(Y_A^C - Y_B^C \mid X, D = 1) = 0 \tag{50}$$

This hypothesis means that *for a person having taken part in the program* ($D = 1$), the responses if he or she had not benefited from the program would have been the same, on average, before and after the period when the program was applied. *For the participants in the program*, let $\overline{Y}_A^T$ and $\overline{Y}_B^T$ be the empirical average responses after and before the period when the program was applied; the "before-after" estimator of the average gain from the treatment, denoted by $\tilde{\Delta}_{BA}$, is then written:

$$\tilde{\Delta}_{BA} = \overline{Y}_A^T - \overline{Y}_B^T \tag{51}$$

This estimator offers the advantage of making it possible to do without data on nonparticipants, which is clearly helpful when these data are not available. If hypothesis (50) is satisfied, the estimator $\tilde{\Delta}_{BA}$ is unbiased. But there are a number of circumstances in which this hypothesis must be rejected.

In the first place, hypothesis (50) excludes any influence from unobserved heterogeneity. Suppose, for example, that there are two classes of workers, the "good" ones and the "bad" ones, such that the productivity of the "good" ones rises between dates A and B independently of their participation in the program (because labor demand shifts in their favor, for example), whereas the productivity of the "bad" ones rises only if they take part in the program. If the fact of being "good" or "bad" is not observed, and if there is at least one "good" worker who takes part in the program, hypothesis (50) is not satisfied.

Another reason to reject hypothesis (50) is that the global state of the economy and/or the situation of an individual taking part in the program are liable to undergo change between dates B and A. In that case, the estimator will credit the program for successes or failures that are in fact due to macroeconomic and/or life-cycle factors.

Ashenfelter's "dip" is another example in which hypothesis (50) is not satisfied. Ashenfelter (1978) observed that the wages of (future) participants in a training program had a tendency to fall off in the period before they entered the program. Many subsequent studies have confirmed this observation, both in the United States and in certain European countries (see, for example, Heckman and Smith, 1998, and Regnér, 1997). If Ashenfelter's dip describes a permanent tendency of the wages of individuals drawn into training programs, the average gain of this type of program is in fact estimated without bias by the "before-after" estimator defined by relation (51). But if Ashenfelter's dip is no more than a transitory phenomenon due, for example, to the existence of the program itself, then the "before-after" estimator overestimates the effect of the training program.

The Difference-in-Differences Estimator

The identifying hypothesis (50) signifies that the gain from nontreatment is null for the participants. It says nothing about the value of this gain for nonparticipants. But if we have data for the latter, it is possible to find the average gain from nontreatment for the group of nonparticipants. We can then postulate that this average gain is the same as that for the group of participants. This identifying hypothesis is written thus:

$$E(Y_A^C - Y_B^C | X, D = 1) = E(Y_A^C - Y_B^C | X, D = 0) \tag{52}$$

This equality clearly shows that the (observed) average gain $E(Y_A^C - Y_B^C | D = 0)$ from nontreatment for the nonparticipants is equal to the (unobserved) average gain $E(Y_A^C - Y_B^C | D = 1)$ of nontreatment for the participants. *For the nonparticipants in the program*, let $\bar{Y}_A^C$ and $\bar{Y}_B^C$ be respectively the average responses after and before the period in which the program is applied; the difference-in-differences estimator, denoted by $\tilde{\Delta}_{DD}$, is defined by:

$$\tilde{\Delta}_{DD} = (\bar{Y}_A^T - \bar{Y}_B^T) - (\bar{Y}_A^C - \bar{Y}_B^C)$$

Thus the difference-in-differences estimator is equal to the difference between the before-after estimator of the treated group and the before-after estimator of the control group. It can easily be verified that this is an unbiased estimator of the average gain from the program, $E(Y_A^T - Y_A^C | X, D = 1)$, since the identifying hypothesis (52) is satisfied. The difference-in-differences estimator has the advantage of being insensitive to changes in the global state of the economy. On the other hand, its use assumes that the "common-trend assumption" (the terminology of Blundell and MaCurdy, 1999) is valid, i.e., that the trends that may affect the results of participants *and* nonparticipants are identical. Note that with this hypothesis, the difference-in-differences estimator eliminates the biases due to observed *and* unobserved heterogeneity. For example, the difference-in-differences estimator is actually without bias if Ashenfelter's dip also exists in the wage profile of the *non*-participants in the experiment. The studies cited above show that this is not always the case, so the difference-in-differences estimator overestimates the impact of the program. We may also note that this hypothesis is not satisfied in the example of the "good" and "bad" workers imagined above if the composition of the group of participants and the group of nonparticipants is not symmetrical.

The Cross-Section Estimator

If we have cross-sectional data describing the responses of treated and untreated persons at one or more dates A following the treatment period—which clearly we do with social experiments—another possibility consists simply of comparing the average result of the treated and untreated persons at dates A following the treatment. In these conditions, we have to make the following identifying hypothesis:

$$E(Y_A^C | X, D = 1) = E(Y_A^C | X, D = 0) \tag{53}$$

This equality signifies that the average effect of nontreatment is the same for a participant in the experiment and a nonparticipant. The cross-section estimator of the average gain from the program, denoted by $\tilde{\Delta}_{CS}$, is then defined by relation:

$$\tilde{\Delta}_{CS} = \bar{Y}_A^T - \bar{Y}_A^C$$

When the identifying hypothesis (53) is accepted, the estimator $\tilde{\Delta}_{CS}$ is an unbiased estimator of the average gain $E(Y_A^T - Y_A^C | X, D = 1)$. Since the cross-section estimator only takes account of data subsequent to the date of the treatment, it is not subject to the same criticism as the two previous estimators. In particular, it does not require us to make the "common-trend assumption" and it is not sensitive to the existence of Ashenfelter's dip. The identifying hypothesis (53), however, risks not being satisfied if the selection of individuals for participation in the program, or as beneficiaries of a measure, does not respect the randomization condition. In other words, the composition of the treated group and the control group must be identical. If we have only nonexperimental, observational data, this prerequisite has little chance of being respected. The protocol of social experiments, however, exists precisely to satisfy this condition. That is why the cross-section estimator is the one most commonly used on data gathered from social experiments.

3.2 THE MAIN EMPIRICAL RESULTS

In the United States, the evaluation of labor market policies focuses primarily on the impact on wages, whereas in Europe, where the level of unemployment was higher in the 1980s and 1990s, employment has drawn more attention. Expenditure on labor market policy is also very different there. For these reasons, it is preferable to present the results for these two geographic areas separately. In judging the social efficiency of a measure or program, the results concerning wages and employment are most often set in the balance against the real costs of the program, including the cost of running it, the income that the participants could have earned if they had not been engaged in the program, and the direct costs they have to pay, such as transportation and child care. As we have already pointed out, social efficiency is rarely assessed using a general equilibrium model, and the comprehensive evaluation of the gains and costs of large-scale measures remains a challenge for economists.

3.2.1 What American Studies Tell Us

Studies carried out on observational data or through social experiments come to similar conclusions. They find that active employment policies have a positive effect on the wages of economically disadvantaged adult women. It does not, however, appear to be the case that these policies significantly improve the situation of economically disadvantaged youth.

What Social Experiments Tell Us

Table 11.4 reproduces the results of some social experiments carried out in the United States on groups of economically disadvantaged women; the programs involved were ones offering job search assistance, temporary work experience in the public or nonprofit sectors, and training programs. Referring to the OECD typology of labor market policies set out at the beginning of this chapter, readers will see that these three types of program correspond to active policies. Job search assistance falls under "public employment services," temporary work experience falls under "subsidized employ-

Table 11.4

The results of some social experiments in the United States, on economically disadvantaged women.

Measure	Cost[1]	Δ Employment[2]	Δ Wages[3]
JSA			
Arkansas WORK	244	6.2*	487*
Louisville (WIN-1)	206	5.3*	643*
JSA + WE			
Virginia ES	631	4.6*	387*
Baltimore	1407	0.4	764*
WE + Training			
NSW	8614	7.1	1062
NJS (JTPA)	1028	—	441*

Source: Heckman et al. (1999, table 22, pp. 2057–2059).

Notes: JSA = Job search assistance; WE = work experience; JPTA = Job Training Partnership Act; NJS = National JTPA Study; NSW = National Supported Work demonstration. *A significant effect at the 10% threshold. [1] Marginal cost of treatment for one person for one year in 1997 dollars. [2] Difference in employment rates between the treated group and the control group in the last quarter of the year subsequent to the experiment. [3] Difference in annual average wages between the treated group and the control group in the third, fourth, or fifth years subsequent to the experiment, in 1997 dollars.

ment," since its aim is to open up access to employment for disadvantaged groups, and training programs fall under "labor market training."

Table 11.4, which sums up the overall trend of other social experiments carried out on this population, shows that the wage gains are relatively modest, although not negligible. They are, moreover, persistent. Still, aside from job search assistance programs, the costs of running these experiments are high in comparison to the resulting wage gains. Experiments carried out on groups of economically disadvantaged men (which are less numerous than those on women) also show that the wages of those who were treated rose, but mainly for training programs. For this population, the effects of temporary work experience (WE) and job search assistance (JSA) are often negligible, or even negative.

Table 11.5 illustrates, with several examples, the conclusions of social experiments regarding training programs carried out in the United States on groups of economically disadvantaged youth (men and women). It turns out that the programs tested have high costs, and do not really improve the situation of these young people, in terms of either employment or wages, except to a very modest degree for women. Social experiments carried out in the United States also find that it is the least skilled individuals who derive the least advantage from training programs. Temporary job creation (WE) seems to benefit them, however. One possible interpretation of this

Table 11.5

The results of some social experiments in the United States, on economically disadvantaged youth.

Measure	Cost[1]	Δ Employment[2]	Δ Wages[3]
NSW	9314	0.3	−79
JOBSTART	6403	−0.9	−721
NJS (JTPA)			
Women	1116	—	133
Men	1731	—	−553

Source: Heckman et al. (1999, table 22, p. 2058).

Notes: The programs tested are ones combining training and subsidy. JPTA = Job Training Partnership Act; NJS = National JTPA Study; NSW = National Supported Work demonstration. [1] Marginal cost of treatment for one person for one year in 1997 dollars. [2] Difference in employment rates between the treated group and the control group in the last quarter of the year subsequent to the experiment. [3] Difference in annual average wages between the treated group and the control group in the first or second year subsequent to the experiment, in 1997 dollars.

result is that this type of measure gives persons in this category the chance to acquire work habits that more skilled categories already possess.

Results from Nonexperimental Data

Table 11.6 contains several illustrations that sum up the conclusions that emerge from research based on nonexperimental American data. The measures assessed mainly concern training for economically disadvantaged populations. In the first place, readers will note the great divergence that may exist between studies utilizing identical data. For example, estimates of the annual gains for male participants in the Comprehensive Employment and Training Act (CETA) program in 1976 range from $−1553 to $+1638. For the women in the same cohort, the estimates of average gains are positive, but they nevertheless range from $24 to $2038. According to Heckman et al. (1999), these wide spreads come from the difficulty of constructing a control group in a coherent manner using the matching method, which, as we noted above, does not automatically take unobserved heterogeneity into account. Still, if we set aside the studies most affected by this type of bias, the results obtained from nonexperimental data are very close to those obtained from experimental data. One highly general point is that training programs focusing on disadvantaged populations benefit adult women especially. Conversely, the effects of these programs on the wages of adult men are not always positive, and when they are, the extent of the effect is less than it is with women. The figures in the lower part of table 11.6 confirm what nonexperimental studies tell us about the impact of training programs on economically disadvantaged youth—an impact that often proves to be negative for young white males (it is sometimes slightly positive for young males from ethnic minorities), and at best slightly positive for young females.

Table 11.6

Nonexperimental estimates of the effects of federal government programs in the United States.

Study	Program[1]	Δ Wage M[2]	Δ Wage W[3]
Economically disadvantaged adults			
Cooley et al. (1979)	1969–1971 MDTA	1395	2038
Dickinson et al. (1986)	1976 CETA	−1553	24
Geraci (1984)	1976 CETA	0	2026
Ashenfelter and Card (1985)	1976 CETA	1638	2220
Economically disadvantaged youth			
Gay and Borus (1980)	1969–1972 Job Corps	−261	−1555
Dickinson et al. (1986)	1976 CETA	−1347	449
Bassi et al. (1984)	1977 CETA	−1225	97

Source: Heckman et al. (1999, table 24, p. 2065).

Notes: [1] MDTA refers to programs set up under the Manpower Development and Training Act of 1962; CETA refers to programs set up under the Comprehensive Employment and Training Act of 1973. [2,3] Annual wage increase after the program for white men (M) and white women (W), expressed in 1997 dollars.

The Unimpressive Balance Sheet of Training Programs

Overall, the evaluations of training programs in the United States that we have summed up briefly here do not produce an impressive balance sheet when it comes to their efficiency. Only the group of economically disadvantaged adult women appears to derive a real benefit for an acceptable cost from these programs. Conversely, the effects on other categories of the population, in particular young people, are most often very modest, and sometimes even negative. Upon reflection, these conclusions are not at all surprising, for as we saw in chapter 2, a year of extra education raises income by between 6% and 10%. It would have been astonishing if the gains from training programs, which are generally of short duration and cost much less than a year of education in school or college, were to exceed these figures.

These evaluations, however, were made in a partial equilibrium framework, and thus register only a part of the impact of training programs. The existence of positive externalities linked to training points to the conclusion that these studies likely underestimate the gains from these programs. Yet on the other hand, we cannot rule out the possibility of negative effects being induced when the program demands large investments and concerns a high proportion of the population. The study of Heckman et al. (1998) suggests that these effects are not negligible, analyzing the consequences of an extra subsidy of $500 to those who enroll in college in the United States, financed by a proportional tax on income. The estimates show that college enrollments increase by 5.3% at *partial* equilibrium, i.e., on the assumption that the structure of wages is not affected by the increase in the subsidy, and leaving aside the effects of taxes. But when this policy is assessed at *general* equilibrium, the estimated effect falls to 0.46% on account of the decline in the wage of a college graduate with respect to that of a high school graduate, a decline itself due to the rise in the number of those enrolled in colleges.

In sum, empirical studies on American data produce only slight evidence in favor of public policies to promote training, despite the many theoretical arguments showing the inefficiency of market mechanisms when it comes to the accumulation of human capital. The reason for this might be the fact that state intervention is also subject to disfunctionalities which may undermine its efficiency. Given the existence of information asymmetries between the private sector and the public authorities, problems arise regarding the verifiability of investments in training which limit the efficiency of subsidies paid to firms and workers. Public institutions can obviously take the place of the private sector in training workers directly. This will be general training only, for the know-how specific to a firm can only be gained "on the job." In this sense, the training supplied by public institutions, since it is not closely related to production, is often less efficient than that gained within firms (Acemoglu and Pischke, 1999a, 1999b). Moreover, the quality of the production of public institutions providing training itself proves difficult to verify.

All the studies cited so far were carried out on training programs aimed at adults or young people entering the labor market. Other studies, though, have assessed programs intended for younger and more precisely targeted populations, and their conclusions are markedly more optimistic.

Assistance Targeting Children from Disadvantaged Backgrounds
Heckman (2000) and Carneiro and Heckman (2003) have brought together the results of a number of studies on the effectiveness of primary and secondary schooling in the United States; they find that expenditure per student and class size have a weakly significant impact on the probability that students will stay in school longer, and on their future earnings. The return on assistance programs proves to be higher when they are aimed at young children. Heckman estimates, however, that the net return on this type of imprecisely targeted investment is negative at all levels of primary and secondary schooling in the United States, even though the quality of the teaching there is often criticized. These results do not mean that the quality of teaching has no influence on individual performance. Rather, they indicate that assistance spread thinly over the whole of primary and secondary education is not socially efficient (not in the United States, at any rate). Conversely, a number of studies have emphasized that public assistance in the training of children from disadvantaged backgrounds is highly effective (see Carneiro and Heckman, 2003).

These studies evaluate the returns on assistance by comparing their costs to their benefits. The high-quality preschool program set up in the state of Michigan in 1962 is a benchmark in this field (Parks, 2000). It consists of a controlled experiment, on an initial population of 123 African-American children aged 3 and 4 from disadvantaged backgrounds and with low IQs (between 70 and 85). Out of these 123

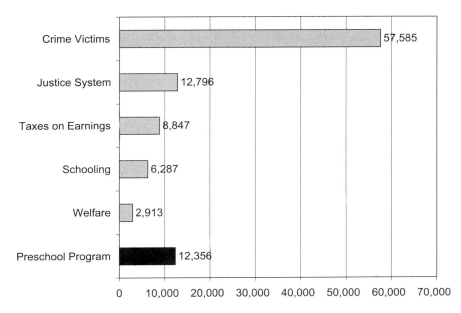

FIGURE 11.4
Costs (in black) and benefits (in gray) of the high-quality preschool program in 1992 dollars.

Source: http://www.highscope.com.

children, 58 had the benefit of special classes with low teacher–pupil ratios (1/6) for two and one-half hours per day, Monday to Friday, over two years. During this period the teachers also had weekly interviews, lasting an hour and a half, with the parents. The performance of the children from the test group down to adulthood is compared with that of the control group (the ones who did not attend the special classes) in figure 11.4. We see that the special classes made a considerable difference to their social integration and wage earnings. Cost–benefit analysis of this type of intervention shows that each dollar invested brings the state a total return of $7.20, in the form of savings on social assistance ($.30) and future educational assistance ($.50) and reduced expenditure on the legal and penitentiary systems and harm to victims ($5.70), as well as the higher tax returns that flow from the bettter wages of the beneficiaries ($.70). So, in addition to its positive impact on the well-being of the beneficiaries and the reduction in social inequality, the money expended on the high-quality preschool program made a substantial positive contribution to the state's budget.

Taken as a whole, studies in this area carried out in the United States confirm the results achieved by the high-quality preschool program. Overall, the programs studied give substantial help to very young children in difficulty, increasing their rate of social integration and their performance in the labor market. Note, however, that these positive effects result much more from improvements in socialization and motivation than from any enhancement of cognitive capacity as measured by IQ. Programs focused on older children, like Big Brothers/Big Sisters of America, which consists of providing mentorship for children aged 10 to 16 from single-parent families, confirm these results: public investment that helps children from disadvantaged backgrounds to stay in school longer is socially effective (see Tierney et al., 2000).

What Can We Learn from Evaluations of Training Policies?
Training policies can have widely differing effects according to the populations concerned. Figure 11.5, taken from Heckman (2000), sums up the main lessons to be learned from studies in this field. It displays net returns to education as a function of age for two types of individual. A battery of criteria (social background, IQ test score, etc.) makes it possible to distinguish persons with high innate capacities for learning and socialization from those with low ones. Figure 11.5 shows, first of all, that the returns to education diminish with age for all categories of the general population, as retirement draws nearer. It also shows that the net return to education is greater for very young children with low capacities than for very young children with high ones. Conversely, this return falls off more rapidly for those with low capacities, since the boost given by special education in terms of intellectual development and socialization declines quickly as individuals grow older.

Figure 11.5 suggests that educational assistance should be specifically targeted at young children from socially disadvantaged backgrounds and/or ones whose capacities for social integration are low. Expenditure of this type brings a much higher return than educational assistance to adults. This does not mean that nothing should be done to help the most disadvantaged adults. The conclusion to be drawn is rather that education is not the most suitable way to assist such persons: the return to society is inadequate, and the boost to the earning power of the beneficiaries insignificant.

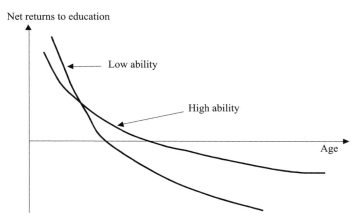

FIGURE 11.5
The relationship between age and net returns to education for two types of individual.

Source: Heckman (2002).

Hence Heckman (2000) suggests that it is preferable to help them by subsidizing their jobs through lower payroll taxes or reductions in income tax.

3.2.2   What European Research Tells Us

Assessments of employment policy began to be made in Europe later than they did in the United States and are still very rare, although in recent years there has been a significant increase in their number. In Europe, social experiments are generally less accepted than they are in the United States for "ethical" reasons: they introduce arbitrary inequalities of treatment, and the cost of this arbitrariness is judged to be greater than the value of the information produced by social experiments. Some countries, such as the United Kingdom, Sweden, and the Netherlands, are exceptions to this rule. In addition, European assessments focus more on employment, and even more particularly on youth employment, than American ones, which look mainly at the wages of economically disadvantaged persons, whatever their age.

Job Search Assistance

Table 11.7 gives some partial indications of the effect of active labor market policies in Europe. The study of Björklund and Regnér (1996) looks at a social experiment in which the services delivered to the unemployed in 1975 in a small city in central Sweden were intensified. For three months the 216 unemployed persons in the treated

Table 11.7

Estimated effects of labor market policies in Europe.

Studies	Country	Type	Responses	Impact[1]
Social experiments				
Björklund and Regnér (1996)	Sweden	JSA	Employment rate	13*
			Monthly wage	6
Dolton and O'Neill (1996)	United Kingdom	JSA	Employment rate	4
Torp et al. (1993)	Norway	Training	Employment rate	3
Observational data				
Westergard-Nielsen (1993)	Denmark	Training	Male hourly wage	1
Dolton et al. (1994)	United Kingdom	Training	Male hourly wage	26
			Female hourly wage	−8*
Main and Shelly (1990)	United Kingdom	Training	Youth employment rate	11*
			Wage	32
Björklund (1994)	Sweden	Training	Youth employment rate	8*
			Wage	10*

Source: Heckman et al. (1999, table 25, pp. 2070–2075).

Notes: [1]Estimated variations of consecutive responses to the program expressed in percentages for rates of employment. *Result significant at threshold of 5%.

group received intensive job search assistance of 7.5 hours per week, while the 194 in the control group received normal assistance of around 1.5 hours per week. Nine months after the experiment, the percentage of persons belonging to the treated group who had found a job was higher by 13 points than that of persons belonging to the control group.

Dolton and O'Neill (1996) studied the impact of the Restart placement program in the United Kingdom in 1989. This program had been introduced in 1987 with the purpose of helping the long-term unemployed. Individuals unemployed for six months are contacted and given six monthly interviews, each lasting about 15–25 minutes, with a counselor who attempts to improve their job search strategies and who can initiate contacts with possible employers. Persons who refuse this program lose their unemployment benefits. Dolton and O'Neill have experimental data, for in 1989 the authorities set up a random sample of individuals summoned to the interviews. Individuals not summoned form the control group, but they can ask to take part in these interviews. The method adopted by Dolton and O'Neill is to compare the performance of the beneficiaries of the Restart program with that of individuals belonging to the control group. After one year, the beneficiaries had an average employment rate 4% higher than that of the nonbeneficiaries.

Fougère et al. (1999) have studied the impact of public placement services in France in the period 1986–1988, using a job search model with endogenous search effort. In the theoretical model, the placement agency exerts an ambiguous effect on search effort and on the exit rate from unemployment, since the intensity with which personal searches are carried out declines when the agency plays a larger part. Nonetheless, econometric estimates suggest that public placement services have a positive impact on the exit rates from unemployment of disadvantaged individuals, in other words poorly trained youth and women.

Studies evaluating job search assistance programs and the activity of placement agencies are now becoming numerous (see Meyer, 1995, and chapter 3, section 3.2). They encounter difficulty, however, in distinguishing the impact of incentive measures (for example, sanctions when search effort is judged inadequate) from that of the help given to unemployed persons by these agencies in approaching potential employers. Dolton and O'Neill (1996) have insisted on the fact that the threat of being cut off from unemployment benefits, and the checking up on the search effort of the unemployed that forms part of the Restart program, significantly influence the exit rates of the beneficiaries from unemployment. Black et al. (2002) arrive at a similar conclusion on the basis of a social experiment on job search assistance carried out in the state of Kentucky. This problem crops up in all experiments, even when those who refuse to participate are not cut off, inasmuch as individuals who benefit from placement services are likely to search with a different intensity from what they would have chosen if they were not beneficiaries of these services. These studies nevertheless suggest that the specific activity of counseling the unemployed exerts a positive effect on the employment rate, and, more weakly, on the hiring wages, of those who benefit from it.

Training Programs

In general, European studies find that training programs have a significant positive effect on the employment rate of the beneficiaries. With observational data, Main and Shelly (1990) and Björklund (1994) arrive at high figures, whereas the study of Torp et al. (1993), which reports on a social experiment carried out in Norway in 1991, with training periods of around five months, finds that this training had no more than a very slight effect on the probability of being employed 12 months later. Too much weight should not be placed on these orders of magnitude, which were obtained by different methods and apply to different programs; the important thing to note is that these figures are, in the majority of studies, significantly positive. But the costs of some of these programs points to the conclusion that the indirect effects of these measures, which we mentioned above, might be large, and might even, from the macroeconomic perspective, reverse the direction of the results that this research, based on partial equilibrium, yields.

The effect on wages appears more ambiguous. For example, Björklund (1994) finds that the active labor market policies of the late 1970s in Sweden were the cause of a very strong rise in wages. With English data, Dolton et al. (1994) estimate a very large positive effect on the wages of men, but a negative one on the wages of women. The research of Westergard-Nielsen (1993) reports on a sample of more than 30,000 observations covering a period of eight years. The aim here was to assess the effects of a "vocational classroom training" program applied for two to four weeks. The authors found an increase of around 1% in the wages of men.

The wide spread of these estimates should make us cautious in drawing conclusions about the effect of training policies on wages. Selection biases might lead to overestimates of this effect. It is quite possible that it is the most efficient individuals who apply for and are admitted to these training programs. If that is the case, we will observe that the individuals who get the training have better results than others, even if the programs themselves did nothing to improve the efficiency of the enrollees. The case of "*formation continue*" in France is a good example of this. In order to obviate the risk of underinvestment in training (highlighted by the theoretical analysis above), France set up a system in 1971 that obliges firms to spend a figure currently set at 1.5% of their total payroll on ongoing training for employees. Using a survey of training and skills upgrading, Goux and Maurin (2000) show that ongoing training within firms does not have a large effect on the wages of those who receive it, but that it does increase the length of time these same recipients remain with the firm. To be precise, they show that the apparent wage premium of employees enrolled in ongoing training (on the order of 5% for a week of training!) comes solely from unobserved characteristics. In other words, it is likely the "best" employees in the eyes of the firm who benefit from extra training and higher wages. This study also notes that firms predominantly finance *specific* training only, which accounts for the extended careers of the recipients with the same firms and the observed absence of further wage premiums for those who change firms after having been trained (and who are, as it happens, very few in number).

Table 11.8

Lessons from the evaluation literature.

Program	Appears to help	Appears not to help	General observations on effectiveness
Formal classroom training	Women re-entrants	Prime-age men and older workers with low initial education	Important that courses have strong labor market relevance, or signal "high" quality to employers. Should lead to a qualification that is recognized and valued by employers. Keep programs relatively small in scale.
On-the-job training	Women re-entrants single mothers	Prime-age men (?)	Must directly meet labor market needs. Hence, need to establish strong links with local employers, but this increases the risk of displacement.
Job-search assistance (job clubs, individual counseling, etc.)	Most unemployed but in particular, women and sole parents		Must be combined with increased monitoring of the job-search behavior of the unemployed and enforcement of work tests.
Of which: re-employment bonuses	Most adult unemployed		Requires careful monitoring and controls on both recipients and their former employers.
Special youth measures (training, employment subsidies, direct job creation measures)		Disadvantaged youths	Effective programs need to combine an appropriate and integrated mix of education, occupational skills, work-based learning and supportive services to young people and their families. Early and sustained interventions are likely to be most effective. Need to deal with inappropriate attitudes to work on the part of youths. Adult mentors can help.
Subsidies to employment	Long-term unemployed; women re-entrants		Requires careful targeting and adequate controls to maximize net employment gains, but there is a trade-off with employer take-up.
Of which: Aid to unemployed starting enterprises	Men (below 40, relatively better educated)		Only works for a small subset of the population.
Direct job creation		Most adult and youth unemployed	Typically provides few long-run benefits and principle of additionality usually implies low marginal-product jobs.

Source: Grubb and Martin (2001, table 2, p. 14)

3.2.3   A Provisional Summary

Grubb and Martin (2001) have drawn up a comprehensive balance sheet of what we can learn from empirical studies of active employment policy in the OECD counties. Table 11.8 sums up their results.

Direct temporary job creation in the public sector has not yielded much success. Unemployed persons who have benefited have generally experienced a great deal of difficulty in finding a job subsequently. Similarly, public training programs have not demonstrated their effectiveness. Aside from some encouraging results with adult women in the United States, the effects have been feeble in light of the high cost of setting them up.

On the contrary, job search assistance is the least costly of the active policies, and social experiments carried out in a number of countries (Sweden, Canada, the United Kingdom, and the United States) yield convincing results. However, it remains an open question whether checking up on job search effort or helping the unemployed while they look (or what combination of these two) is the most important factor. Of all the measures aimed at young people, only employer wage subsidies give much reason for satisfaction. Finally, it is worth recalling that measures aimed at the very young— early childhood, including the preschool period—have also demonstrated their effectiveness (see section 3.2.1 above).

4   THE MACROECONOMIC EFFECTS OF UNEMPLOYMENT BENEFITS

Public unemployment insurance systems were created in many European countries at the beginning of the twentieth century. In this area, state intervention is intended to insure workers against the risk of unemployment. It proved to be necessary because imperfect information represents an obstacle to the creation of private insurance systems (Chiu and Karni, 1998). The state also intervenes to provide social assistance, redistributing income in favor of the most disadvantaged workers, the ones who are generally faced with more frequent and lengthier spells of unemployment than other workers.

The criticism directed at unemployment benefits is of long standing and well known. Essentially, they are said to reduce the incentive to look for a job, to increase the reservation wage (see chapter 1), and to exert upward pressure on wages (see chapter 9). These effects reinforce one another to increase the duration of unemployment. Overall, then, we ought to expect that generous unemployment benefits have a positive impact on the unemployment rate and lead to a reduction in aggregate output. But this expectation needs to be put in context, and clarified. In the first place, unemployment benefits give the unemployed the means to better select the jobs that are offered to them. From this standpoint, they constitute a "subsidy" to the job search, and an increase in the level of the benefit payments can improve the average quality of jobs and increase global production. Moreover, unemployment benefits have multiple dimensions: the level of the payments, the duration over which they are payable, and the eligibility conditions. The level of the benefit payment may decrease the longer the spell of unemployment lasts, and may depend on past wages and on how long the worker has been contributing to the insurance fund. We will see that it is important to take into account these various characteristics of unemployment benefits, in order to be in a position to assess their impact on the labor market.

We will begin by giving an overview of the unemployment benefits of several OECD countries, then look at the consequences of unemployment benefits for the efficiency of the labor market and the unemployment rate. In conformity with the OECD classification, we focus here on the "passive" aspect only of unemployment benefits, i.e., the effect of the level of benefit payments on labor market equilibrium. We will not return to elements already analyzed in chapter 3, section 2.2: the incentive effect that the temporal profile of the benefit payments may have, and the systems of control and sanction that certain countries have adopted (the main empirical results in this connection are given in chapter 3, section 3.2.2).

4.1 An Overview of Unemployment Insurance Systems

In chapter 1 we pointed out the difficulties of measuring the income of persons who are looking for work (see Atkinson and Mickelwright, 1991, for a complete account of this subject). This income most often derives both from an insurance system and a social security system. Insurance systems generally pay benefits for a limited period, from several months to several years, to persons who have already been employed and paid in to the fund (Grubb, 2001). Their level is often linked to the wage earned in the most recent job. Payments made by the social security system, on the other hand, are means-tested, are generally of unlimited duration, and are independent of past earnings. To social security payments made specifically to the unemployed we must add the various allowances (family allowance, housing allowance, single parent allowance, etc.) that may be paid to any member of the labor force when he or she meets certain means criteria.

4.1.1 The Replacement Ratio

The OECD has constructed a synthetic indicator for unemployment benefits: an average of the entitlements of single unemployed persons and married ones, whose spell of unemployment has lasted from zero to six years. This indicator is a *gross* replacement ratio, equal to the ratio of gross benefit payments to gross wages; hence, it differs from a *net* replacement ratio, which takes into account payroll deductions, taxes, and transfers. Figure 11.6 gives an overview of the evolution of the replacement ratios in several OECD countries. We see that the replacement ratio exhibits an increasing trend on average. Still, this average trend masks strong disparities. In Japan and the United States replacement ratios are low and remained most stable over the last three decades of the twentieth century. Conversely, Denmark, France, and Sweden, begin-

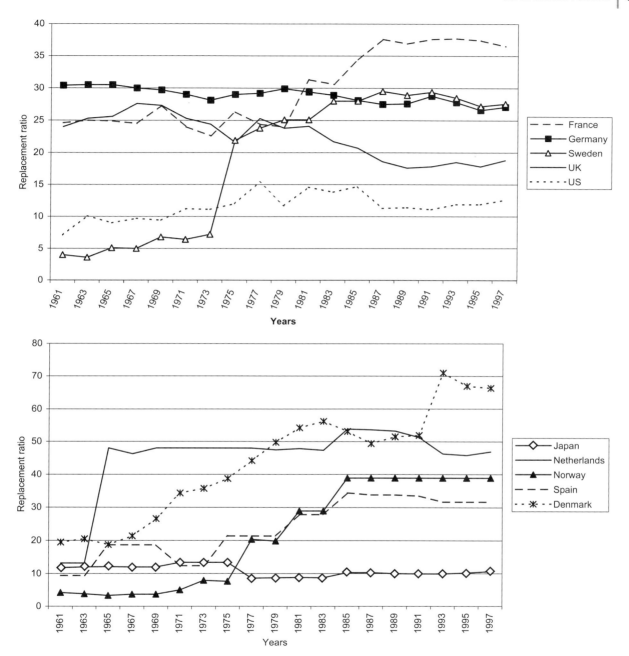

FIGURE 11.6

The synthetic indicator of entitlement to unemployment benefits (gross replacement ratio in %).

Source: OECD data.

Table 11.9

Replacement ratios as a function of the duration of unemployment for a single person in 1994–1995 (in %).

Country	First year	Second and third years	Fourth and fifth years	General average
Denmark	79	79	79	79
France	79	63	61	65.5
Germany	66	63	63	63.5
Japan	78	41	41	48.5
Sweden	81	76	65	72.5
United Kingdom	64	64	64	64
United States	34	9	9	14

Source: Martin (1996, table 2).

ning in the 1980s, have higher replacement ratios, which leveled off in the 1990s. Germany remains stable at a high level, which decreases slightly, while the United Kingdom saw a significant decline in the synthetic indicator of entitlements over the whole period.

Net replacement ratios are significantly higher than gross ones. The cause of this is the progressivity of taxes and income redistribution policies. The average net replacement ratio is around two-thirds higher than the average gross ratio for the OECD countries as a whole. Table 11.8 shows that it is Denmark that has the highest ratio, and the United States the lowest. No data are available to compare net replacement ratios over the long run. Nonetheless, given the strong correlation between net ratios and gross ratios, it is likely that the average net ratio has risen since the beginning of the 1960s in the OECD countries.

The synthetic indicator masks the linkage between the duration of unemployment and the level of the benefit payments. In many countries, unemployment benefits decline as the unemployment spell lengthens. Table 11.9 shows that benefits fall off very steeply in the United States, and that the replacement ratio is relatively high in Japan for the first year, but then falls off sharply at the beginning of the second year of unemployment. This decline in replacement ratios generally reflects a shift from unemployment insurance to social security.

The synthetic indicator also masks factors having to do with the conditions under which unemployment benefits are paid. These conditions concern the reasons for the job loss, and many systems provide for sanctions when a person quits voluntarily, or is fired for cause. Table 11.10 gives an overview of the extent of such sanctions in some OECD countries. The eligibility conditions for unemployment benefits also concern the job search, with many systems specifying that beneficiaries must furnish proof that they are actively looking for work, must not actually be working,

Table 11.10

Sanctions applicable when an employee quits voluntarily for the first time, or is fired for cause, at the end of the 1990s.

Country	Sanction period	% of applicants sanctioned
Finland	3 months	3.44
France	4 months	Unknown
Germany	3 months	3.62
Norway	2 months	10.55
Spain	Exclusion	Unknown
United Kingdom	1–26 weeks	4.32
Belgium	8–52 weeks	4.70

Source: Grubb (2001, tables 1 and 2).

Table 11.11

Annual sanctions as percentages of the average volume of applications for unemployment insurance benefits at the end of the 1990s.

Country	Refusal of employment	Refusal of an ALMP	Proof of a job search
Belgium	0.02	0.76	Unknown
Denmark	0.57	1.55	Unknown
Germany	0.64	0.50	Unknown
Norway	5.01	2.31	Unknown
United Kingdom	1.23	2.21	2.08
United States	1.90	Unknown	33.46

Source: Grubb (2001, table 2).

Note: ALMP = Active Labor Market Program.

and must accept the jobs offered them when these are judged to meet the criteria defined by the unemployment insurance system (see Grubb, 2001, for more details). Table 11.11 shows the incidences of refusal of benefits for these reasons in some OECD countries.

4.1.2 A High Proportion of Uninsured Unemployed Persons

The OECD synthetic indicator is often used in international comparisons of unemployment benefits, but it is important to point out that it conceals their great heterogeneity. In particular, a large number of persons who are looking for work do not receive unemployment insurance benefits because the insurance system does not

Table 11.12

Percentages of unemployed persons qualifying for unemployment insurance benefits in 1995.

Austria	66
Belgium	81
Denmark	66
Finland	73
France	45
Germany	70
Greece	9
Ireland	67
Italy	7
Netherlands	50
Portugal	27
Spain	24
Sweden	70

Source: Manning (1998, table 1, p. 144).

apply to them; they may, however, receive transfers from the social security system. Table 11.12 gives an idea of the extent of this phenomenon.

Essentially, persons who do not benefit from unemployment insurance are entrants into the labor market, or have not paid in to an unemployment insurance fund for a long time, or have exhausted their entitlement to benefits after a long spell of unemployment. Scrutiny of table 11.12 reveals that very few of those looking for work receive unemployment benefits in the countries of southern Europe. In France, 45% of the unemployed do not receive them. The figure is high even in the northern European countries, since around 30% of the unemployed fall into this category in Denmark or Sweden. These data give us reason to go back to the basic model from chapter 9 in order to introduce into it a difference between unemployed persons who are receiving unemployment insurance benefits and those who are not.

4.2 ELIGIBILITY AND UNEMPLOYMENT

We have seen that there are a number of arguments to justify a rising relationship between the generosity of the benefits received while looking for work, and unemployment. In reality this does not always hold true. We will see that the relationship between the level of benefits and unemployment is influenced by the eligibility conditions.

In the basic model from chapter 9, unemployment benefits always have an unfavorable effect on unemployment, since they push up the wages that employees can win through wage bargaining. This result flows largely from the hypothesis that persons looking for work form a homogeneous population receiving the same benefit payment, denoted by z at every instant. But as we pointed out above, the payment of benefits is subject to precise conditions, particularly that the worker should have held a job and so paid in to the unemployment insurance fund for a specified time (see chapter 3 as well). When all these conditions are met, the person in question becomes *eligible* to receive unemployment insurance benefits. Now, table 11.12 shows that a large number of unemployed persons receive no such benefits. For them, to find a job, or find another job, which they will hold for a sufficient period of time, contains the promise that they will *in the future* be able to benefit from unemployment insurance. We saw in chapter 3 that the *reservation* wage of this category of the unemployed was thus a *decreasing* function of unemployment benefits—a property that must also apply to the wage *negotiated* by a worker not eligible for unemployment benefits. For that worker, the higher the benefits paid by unemployment insurance, the worse his or her position in wage bargaining is, for if he or she breaks off the bargaining process, he or she will be back in the position of receiving no benefits. So the wage negotiated between an employer and an ineligible worker should *fall* when unemployment benefits rise.

From a somewhat different perspective, Atkinson (1995) has shown that unemployment benefits can have a negative effect on wages. He utilizes an efficiency wage model in which workers caught shirking, and so fired for cause, receive no benefits. Within that framework, a rise in benefits represents a greater potential loss for workers who do decide to shirk, since they then lose the right to receive benefits. Hence higher benefits enable employers to achieve incentive constraints with lower wages. When all wages are subject to bargaining, what follows below will show that the level of unemployment benefits and the wage of an ineligible person are also linked by a decreasing relationship. This property may lead, in certain circumstances, to the level of benefits having a positive impact on employment.

A Model with Ineligible and Eligible Workers
In order to study the consequences of the eligibility effect, we take up the basic model from chapter 9, and postulate simply that new entrants into the labor market receive, at every instant, a payment z_n strictly inferior to the level z_e of benefit received by those who have already held a job. The payment z_n depends on the *social security* system, while the payment z_e falls under the unemployment insurance system. We assume, then, that the labor force grows at rate $n > 0$ and that persons looking for work only receive a benefit payment if they have already worked in the past. This hypothesis clearly oversimplifies: its purpose is merely to describe the impact of eligibility conditions. To bring it closer to the real world, we would have to assume that these conditions depend on the duration of unemployment and on how long the worker had been paying in to the insurance fund. But to bring in these factors would burden the model considerably, without changing the sense of the results.

The Behavior of Agents
We assume that all wages are bargained over, and (for simplicity) that the hiring wage cannot be renegotiated. Since eligible and ineligible workers have different gains

should the bargaining break off, the wage w_n negotiated with an ineligible worker will differ from the wage w_e negotiated with an eligible one. In consequence, the profit Π_n expected by an employer from hiring a new entrant into the labor market will not be the same as the profit Π_e expected from matching up with a "veteran." If we assume (again for simplicity) that all workers have the same productivity y and that the rate of job destruction is always equal to q whatever the category of worker, the expected profit from a match-up is written:

$$r\Pi_i = y - w_i + q[\text{Max}(\Pi_{ve}, \Pi_{vn}) - \Pi_i], \qquad i = e, n \tag{54}$$

In this expression, $\Pi_{vi}, i = e, n$, designates the value of a vacant job respectively offered to eligible workers and ineligible ones. Hence, we assume that there exist two labor markets: one for young people with no experience, and one for experienced workers. In addition, employers are able to offer their vacant jobs either to new entrants or to experienced workers (hypotheses adopted, yet again, for simplicity).

If V_i and U_i designate respectively the stock of vacant jobs and the stock of unemployed persons of category i, we will assume that at every instant the number of hires for this category is given by the matching function with constant returns $M(V_i, U_i)$. We can then define a labor market tightness $\theta_i = V_i/U_i$ proper to each type of worker, and the instantaneous probability of filling a vacant job with a person of type i is equal to $M(V_i, U_i)/V_i = M(1, U_i/V_i) = m(\theta_i)$. The expected profit from a vacant job will then take the following form:

$$r\Pi_{vi} = -h + m(\theta_i)[\Pi_i - \text{Max}(\Pi_{ve}, \Pi_{vn})], \qquad i = e, n \tag{55}$$

For each category of worker, when the free entry condition $\Pi_{vi} = 0$ for $i = e, n$ is satisfied, the equality between the average cost of a vacant job (55) and the expected profit (55) from a filled one leads to a decreasing relation between labor market tightness θ_i and the wage w_i. We have indicated in chapter 9, section 3, that this relation is similar to a labor demand curve; here it reads:

$$\frac{h}{m(\theta_i)} = \frac{y - w_i}{r + q}, \qquad i = e, n \tag{56}$$

The behavior of workers eligible for unemployment benefits is analogous to that of the basic model from chapter 9. The expected utility V_e for an eligible employee is thus written:

$$rV_e = w_e + q(V_{ue} - V_e) \tag{57}$$

In this expression, V_{ue} thus designates the expected utility of a person in search of a job and receiving unemployment benefits. A new entrant into the labor market becomes eligible for unemployment benefits from the time he or she succeeds in being hired. The expected utility V_n of a newly hired entrant employed at wage w_n (recall that the labor contract is assumed to be nonrenegotiable) thus takes the expression:

$$rV_n = w_n + q(V_{ue} - V_n) \tag{58}$$

In this last relation, readers should note the presence of the term V_{ue} which conveys precisely the hypothesis that a person who has found a job becomes eligible for unemployment benefits. Conversely, a new entrant into the labor market receives no benefits before finding his or her first job. Using obvious notations, the expected utilities of workers looking for a job are written thus:

$$rV_{ui} = z_i + \theta_i m(\theta_i)(V_i - V_{ui}), \qquad i = e, n \tag{59}$$

Wage Negotiations and Eligibility Effect

For eligible workers, the model developed here is strictly identical to the basic model from chapter 9. The bargaining outcome is described by a wage curve corresponding to equation (20) from chapter 9 on condition that we replace w and z respectively by w_e and z_e. The equilibrium value θ_e^* of the labor market tightness applying to eligible workers is again given by equation (21), where we substitute z_e for z. At this stage, the equilibrium value of an eligible worker's expected utility, denoted by V_{ue}^*, is thus perfectly determined. For what follows, it is important to point out that this expected utility does not depend on payments z_n, but does rise with the level z_e of unemployment benefits.[9]

When a new entrant into the labor market matches up with an employer, he or she negotiates a wage the amount of which is given by maximizing the generalized Nash criterion:

$$\underset{w_n}{\text{Max}}(V_n - V_{un})^{\gamma}[\Pi_n - \text{Max}(\Pi_{ve}, \Pi_{vn})]^{1-\gamma} \tag{60}$$

In this criterion, it is the expected utility V_{un} of an ineligible job seeker which comes into the employee's contribution—and not the expected utility V_{ue} of an eligible unemployed person—since a new entrant who broke off the bargaining over his or her hiring contract would never receive unemployment benefits. The contributions of the employee and the employer to the Nash problem (60) are found using relations (58) and (54). We thus have:

$$V_n - V_{un} = \frac{w_n + q(V_{ue}^* - V_{un}) - rV_{un}}{r + q} \tag{61}$$

and

$$\Pi_n - \text{Max}(\Pi_{ve}, \Pi_{vn}) = \frac{y - w_n - \text{Max}(\Pi_{ve}, \Pi_{vn})}{r + q}$$

At free entry equilibrium, where $\Pi_{vi} = 0$ for $i = e, n$, the solution of the generalized Nash problem (60) yields:

$$w_n = \gamma y + (1 - \gamma)rV_{un} - (1 - \gamma)q(V_{ue}^* - V_{un}) \tag{62}$$

The first of equalities (61) shows that, from the point of view of a new participant in the labor market, becoming eligible for unemployment benefits can be interpreted as a form of subsidy, the amount of which equals the average additional gain $q(V_{ue}^* - V_{un})$ resulting precisely from the payment of unemployment benefits in case of

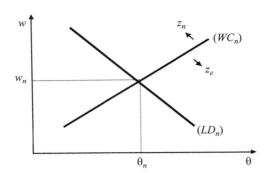

FIGURE 11.7
Wage and labor market tightness for new entrants.

job loss. A subsidy to one partner in the bargaining process entails a rise in the global surplus which, wholly or in part, will flow to the other bargaining partner. Relation (62) portrays this phenomenon exactly: considering V_{un} as given, i.e., at the partial equilibrium of decentralized bargaining between a worker and an employer, the latter "takes" from the wage the fraction of the additional gain $q(V_{ue}^* - V_{un})$, corresponding to his or her power $(1 - \gamma)$. The instantaneous remuneration of the employee declines, but (61) then shows that his or her expected utility rises by fraction γ of this additional gain. This mechanism for sharing the increase in the surplus generated by the eligibility effect causes (all other things being equal) the wage negotiated by a new entrant into the labor market to *diminish* with the expected utility V_{ue}^* of an eligible unemployed person. This property reveals the downward pressure on wages exerted by the prospect of being able to take advantage in the future of unemployment benefits. Using relations (59) and (58), it is then possible to arrive, after several calculations, at a relationship between the wage w_n and labor market tightness θ_n which is the equation of the wage curve that applies to new entrants into the labor market:

$$w_n = \frac{\gamma y[r + \theta_n m(\theta_n)] + (1 - \gamma)[(r + q)z_n - qrV_{ue}^*]}{r + \gamma \theta_n m(\theta_n)} \tag{63}$$

The equilibrium values of the wage and the labor market tightness for the new entrants are defined by the labor demand curve (LD_n) and the wage curve (WC_n) respectively defined by equations (56) and (63). Figure 11.7 illustrates this situation.

The Effects of Unemployment Benefits
Equation (63) shows that the (WC_n) curve shifts upward when payment z_n rises. Conversely, it also indicates that this curve shifts downward when unemployment benefits z_e increase, the equilibrium wage of new entrants into the labor market diminishes, and the labor market tightness θ_n rises. Thus the prospect of being able in the future to get unemployment benefits exerts a downward pressure on the wage of those who are not eligible today, and increases their probability $\theta_n m(\theta_n)$ of exiting from unemployment.

Knowing the equilibrium levels of labor market tightness θ_i, $i = e, n$, it is easy to obtain the values of the unemployment rate for each category of worker. Let U_i be the stock of unemployed persons of category $i = e, n$, and let N again be the size of the labor force. Since the latter grows at every instant by quantity $\dot{N}$, the volume U_n of ineligible unemployed persons grows by this same quantity. On the other hand, at every instant $\theta_n m(\theta_n) U_n$ individuals from this category find a job. The number U_n of these unemployed persons diminishes by that amount. As for the eligible workers, at every instant $q(N - U_n - U_e)$ of them lose their jobs, and $\theta_e m(\theta_e) U_e$ of them find new jobs. In sum, the law of motion of unemployment is described by the two following relations:

$$\dot{U}_n = \dot{N} - \theta_n m(\theta_n) U_n \qquad \text{and} \qquad \dot{U}_e = q(N - U_n - U_e) - \theta_e m(\theta_e) U_e \qquad \text{(64)}$$

Let n again be the growth rate (assumed to be constant) of the labor force ($\dot{N}/N = n$), and let us define the unemployment rates[10] $u_i = U_i/N$, for $i = e, n$. Differentiating this equality with respect to time, we immediately get $\dot{U}_i = \dot{u}_i + u_i N$; and bringing this last equality for $i = e, n$ into relations (64) and dividing by N, we find the laws of motion of the unemployment rates. They are written:

$$\dot{u}_n = n - [n + \theta_n m(\theta_n)]u_n \qquad \text{and} \qquad \dot{u}_e = q(1 - u_n) - [n + q + \theta_e m(\theta_e)]$$

The stationary unemployment rates correspond to $\dot{u}_i = 0$, $i = e, n$, so they are given by:

$$u_n = \frac{n}{n + \theta_n m(\theta_n)} \qquad \text{and} \qquad u_e = \frac{q(1 - u_n)}{n + q + \theta_e m(\theta_e)} \qquad \text{(65)}$$

Finally, the global unemployment rate u which is equal to $u_n + u_e$ is defined by:

$$u = \frac{q + [n + \theta_e m(\theta_e)]u_n}{n + q + \theta_e m(\theta_e)} \qquad \text{(66)}$$

The effect of a rise in payments z_n is equivalent to that of a rise in unemployment benefits z in the basic model where all the unemployed were identical. It stimulates an increase in the unemployment rate u_n of new entrants into the labor market and a rise in the global unemployment rate u. The consequences of a rise in the unemployment benefits z_e paid to workers who have already held a job show greater contrast. This rise reduces the unemployment rate u_n of those who do not receive these benefits—this is the eligibility effect—but it increases the unemployment rate u_e of those who are already eligible. The expression of u_e in relations (65) shows that this last rise results, on the one hand, from upward pressure on wage w_e leading to a fall in the exit rate from unemployment $\theta_e m(\theta_e)$—these are the sequences of cause and effect at work in the basic model of chapter 9, section 3—and on the other, from a reduction in the number of ineligible unemployed persons. In sum, relation (66) indicates that the global unemployment rate, equal to the sum $u_e + u_n$ of the unemployment rates in the two categories, varies in an ambiguous manner when unemployment benefits are increased.

4.3 Improvement of Productivity

High unemployment benefits permit workers to be more selective about the quality of the jobs they accept. That being the case, Diamond (1981), and more recently Marimon and Zilibotti (1999), and Acemoglu and Shimer (1999) have put the case that higher benefits can increase the average productivity of a job, but at the cost of reducing the number of jobs created: although unemployment increases, society can have more goods to distribute among its members. Hence a rise in unemployment benefits may lead to a rise in aggregate output and collective welfare, even if unemployment increases. In order properly to investigate this matter, we must first adapt the basic matching model from chapter 9 to an environment in which jobs are heterogeneous.

A Stochastic Job Matching Model

We will utilize a "stochastic job matching" model, close to the one in Pissarides (2000, chapter 6). In this model, employers and employees discover the productivity of jobs at the moment they match up with one another, so an employer does not know what the productivity of a vacant job will be when he or she posts it. This hypothesis is a simple way of conveying the idea that the productivity depends on many different characteristics of the job held, and the worker who holds it. This productivity cannot be known in advanced, but is revealed by experience. In this setting, high unemployment benefits give workers an incentive to turn down low-productivity jobs, and this helps to increase the *average productivity* of a job. This does not mean that a rise in unemployment benefits will systematically cause aggregate output to grow, for the basic matching model presented in chapter 9 taught us that (all other things being equal) an increase in the gains of unemployed persons pushes wages up and job creation down, which reduces aggregate output. A priori, therefore, unemployment benefits have opposite effects on aggregate output, tending both to reduce job creation and increase average productivity.

In order to assess the respective extents of these two effects, we shall consider a stationary version of the basic matching model identical to the one from chapter 9, section 3, with one exception: the instantaneous production of each job, still denoted by y, is a random variable, the realization of which is only discovered after the match-up between the employer and the job-seeker. This random variable is endowed with a cumulative distribution function, denoted by $G(.)$ and common to all jobs. When an employer and a job-seeker match up, they observe the value y of productivity and then negotiate a wage $w(y)$. Let Π_v again be the value of a vacant job, and let us assume that jobs are destroyed at the constant exogenous rate q. The expected profit from a filled job in which productivity is equal to y, denoted by $\Pi_e(y)$, satisfies:

$$r\Pi_e(y) = y - w(y) + q[\Pi_v - \Pi_e(y)] \tag{67}$$

The profit Π_v expected from a vacant job does not depend on a particular realization y of productivity, since the latter is unknown at the time a vacant job is posted. On the other hand, this profit does depend on the *average* productivity of a filled job. Let h be the cost of a vacant job per unit of time, and $m(\theta)$ the rate at which vacant jobs are filled; the profit expected from a vacant job is then written:

$$r\Pi_v = -h + m(\theta) \int_{-\infty}^{+\infty} \text{Max}[\Pi_e(y) - \Pi_v, 0]\, dG(y) \tag{68}$$

This relation simply conveys the fact that a job remains vacant as long as potential match-ups yield values y of productivity such that $\Pi_e(y) \leq \Pi_v$, and is only filled when $\Pi_e(y) > \Pi_v$. The expected utility of a worker filling a job where the productivity is equal to y, denoted by $V_e(y)$, and the expected utility of an unemployed person, again denoted by V_u, are found by analogous reasoning. Let us assume, for simplicity, that workers are risk-neutral, and that the unemployed obtain an income made up of two elements: gains from outside the market, denoted by z, and unemployment benefits, denoted by b. These benefits are financed by a lump-sum payroll deduction amounting to τ from the gains of every employee; balanced budgeting then dictates (denoting the unemployment rate by u and normalizing the size of the labor force to 1): $bu = (1 - u)\tau$. The exit rate from unemployment always being equal to $\theta m(\theta)$, the expected utilities of an unemployed person and an employee satisfy:

$$rV_u = z + b + \theta m(\theta) \int_{-\infty}^{+\infty} \text{Max}[V_e(y) - V_u, 0]\, dG(y) \tag{69}$$

$$rV_e(y) = w(y) - \tau + q[V_u - V_e(y)] \tag{70}$$

Labor Market Equilibrium
As in the basic model from chapter 9, we assume that wage bargaining allows the worker to obtain a share γ of the surplus $S(y)$. Using equations (67) and (70) we get:

$$S(y) = V_e(y) - V_u + \Pi_e(y) - \Pi_v = \frac{y - \tau - r(V_u + \Pi_v)}{r + q} \tag{71}$$

Since the solution of the bargaining entails $V_e(y) - V_u = \gamma S(y)$ and $\Pi_e(y) - \Pi_v = (1 - \gamma)S(y)$, workers and employers have a common interest in creating jobs the productivity of which yields a positive surplus $S(y)$. All matches in which productivity y exceeds the reservation productivity $y_r = r(V_u + \Pi_v) + \tau$ (given by equation (71)) result in the creation of a job. For what follows, it will be useful to note that the surplus is written in the following form:

$$S(y) = \frac{y - y_r}{r + q} \tag{72}$$

When the free entry condition $\Pi_v = 0$ is satisfied, relation (68) defining the expected profit of a vacant job entails:

$$\int_{y_r}^{+\infty} \Pi_e(y)\, dG(y) = \frac{h}{m(\theta)} \tag{73}$$

To grasp the sense of this equality, note that a vacant job is filled when an unemployed person applies for it, which happens with probability $m(\theta)$, *and* when

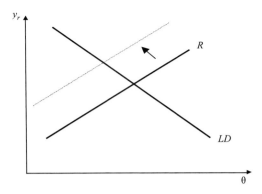

FIGURE 11.8
The impact of an increase in unemployment benefits on labor market tightness and the reservation productivity.

the observed productivity exceeds the threshold y_r, which happens with probability $[1 - G(y_r)]$. Hence the average vacancy of a job lasts $1/m(\theta)[1 - G(y_r)]$ and its average cost amounts to $h/m(\theta)[1 - G(y_r)]$. On the other hand the average profit from a filled job is equal to $[\int_{y_r}^{+\infty} \Pi_e(y)\,dG(y)]/[1 - G(y_r)]$. Equation (73) thus signifies that, at free entry equilibrium, the average profit of a filled job must equal the average cost of a vacant one. The solution of the bargaining, which is written $\Pi_e(y) = (1 - \gamma)S(y)$, and expression (72) of the surplus then yields a relationship between labor market tightness and reservation productivity:

$$\frac{1 - \gamma}{r + q} \int_{y_r}^{+\infty} (y - y_r)\,dG(y) = \frac{h}{m(\theta)} \tag{74}$$

The bargaining outcome also satisfies $V_e(y) - V_u = \gamma \Pi_e(y)/(1 - \gamma)$. Definition (69) of the expected utility V_u of an unemployed person and relation (73) then entail:

$$rV_u = z + b + \theta m(\theta) \int_{y_r}^{+\infty} \frac{\gamma}{1 - \gamma} \Pi_e(y)\,dG(y) = z + b + \frac{\gamma \theta h}{1 - \gamma} \tag{75}$$

Finally, in accord with definition (71) of the surplus, the reservation productivity verifies $y_r = rV_u + \tau$, and equation (75) entails:

$$y_r = z + b + \tau + \frac{\gamma \theta h}{1 - \gamma} \tag{76}$$

Equations (74) and (76) define the equilibrium values of labor market tightness and the productivity threshold for given values of b and τ. Equation (74), represented by the (LD) curve in figure 11.8, is interpreted as a labor demand. In the (θ, y_r) plane, it defines a decreasing relation between reservation productivity and labor market tightness, explainable as follows: firms open up fewer vacant jobs when the productivity threshold, which conditions the average duration of job vacancy, equal to $1/m(\theta)[1 - G(y_r)]$, is high. Equation (76) defines an increasing curve, denoted by (R) in figure 11.8. It conveys the notion that the expected utility of an unemployed person (which, readers will recall, satisfies $y_r = rV_u + \tau$) is greater, the higher labor market tightness is.

At stationary equilibrium, the expression of the unemployment rate u is found by equalizing the flow of entries into and exits from unemployment. At every moment an unemployed person finds a vacant job with probability $\theta m(\theta)$ and is hired if the productivity exceeds the threshold value y_r. Hence the exit rate from unemployment is equal to $\theta m(\theta)[1 - G(y_r)]$ and the number of unemployed persons finding a job amounts to $u\theta m(\theta)[1 - G(y_r)]$. Since there are, at every instant, $q(1 - u)$ job destructions, equilibrium of flows entails:

$$u = \frac{q}{q + \theta m(\theta)[1 - G(y_r)]} \tag{77}$$

Figure 11.8 shows that, at given τ, an increase in unemployment benefits b entails a fall in labor market tightness and an increase in the reservation productivity. Equation (77) then indicates that, at given τ, the unemployment rate increases with unemployment benefits. This phenomenon is accentuated if we take into account the mechanism that finances these benefits, for the increase in unemployment benefits entails an upward adjustment of the tax τ needed to ensure a balanced budget, which is written $bu = \tau(1 - u)$. As we see in figure 11.8, this rise in payroll deductions provokes a decline in labor market tightness and an increase in reservation productivity—which reinforces the rise in unemployment. In sum, the increase in unemployment benefits leads to a rise in unemployment. Nonetheless, aggregate output can rise, if the increase in the average productivity of a job is high enough to offset the rise in unemployment. Thus the collective welfare, taken as a whole, might also improve. It will be instructive to find out what the circumstances are in which this might actually come about.

Unemployment Benefits and the Social Optimum
The social optimum is characterized the same way as in the basic model (see chapter 9, section 6.2). With risk-neutral agents, the collective welfare criterion corresponds to the present discounted value of per capita output net of the cost of vacant jobs. Let $\hat{y}$ be the average productivity of a filled job; net instantaneous output per capita, denoted by ω, is then equal to $\hat{y}(1 - u) + zu - h\theta u$. For simplicity, we limit ourselves to looking at the limit case, in which $r = 0$. We have already seen, in chapter 9, section 6.2, that the planner's problem consists simply of maximizing the instantaneous net output per capita. Since average productivity per job $\hat{y}$ takes the expression $[\int_{y_r}^{+\infty} y \, dG(y)]/[1 - G(y_r)]$, instantaneous net output per capita is written:

$$\omega = \frac{1 - u}{1 - G(y_r)} \int_{y_r}^{+\infty} y \, dG(y) + uz - hu\theta$$

If we replace the unemployment rate u by its value as given by relation (77), we get an expression of instantaneous net output per capita depending only on y_r and θ.

Table 11.13

Values of the parameters in the stochastic job matching model.

q	r	z	η	h
0.15	0.05	0.1	0.5	0.05

It comes to:

$$\omega = \frac{1}{q + \theta m(\theta)[1 - G(y_r)]} \left[\theta m(\theta) \int_{y_r}^{+\infty} y \, dG(y) + q(z - h\theta) \right]$$

Setting to zero the partial derivatives of ω with respect to y_r and θ gives, after several (tiresome) calculations and rearrangements of terms:

$$\frac{1 - \eta(\theta)}{q} \int_{y_r}^{+\infty} (y - y_r) \, dG(y) = \frac{h}{m(\theta)} \qquad \text{with} \qquad \eta(\theta) = -\frac{\theta m'(\theta)}{m(\theta)} \tag{78}$$

$$y_r = z + \frac{\eta(\theta)\theta h}{1 - \eta(\theta)} \tag{79}$$

Comparison of the optimal values of θ and y_r, respectively defined by equations (78) and (74) with those resulting from decentralized equilibrium for $r = 0$, shows immediately that these values are identical if and only if the Hosios condition $\gamma = \eta(\theta)$ is satisfied (see chapter 9, section 6.2). Relations (76) and (79) indicate that $b = \tau = 0$ is likewise necessary. In other words, unemployment benefits can only degrade the efficiency of the labor market when the Hosios condition is satisfied. Conversely, when it is not, unemployment benefits may increase not just the average productivity of a job, but the global efficiency of the labor market too.

In order to illustrate this result, let us undertake a simulation exercise based on a calibration of the matching model for plausible values of the parameters; it is summed up in table 11.13. The matching function is of the form $M(u, v) = u^\eta v^{1-\eta}$, where v designates the vacancy rate. The probability distribution of productivity is taken to be uniform over the interval $[0, 1]$. The consequences of variations in unemployment benefits for two different values of bargaining power γ are represented in figure 11.9. In conformity to the foregoing theoretical analysis, an increase in benefits increases the unemployment rate and the reservation productivity in all cases. On the other hand, increased benefits improve aggregate output when bargaining power γ is less than the elasticity η of the matching function with respect to the unemployment rate; but they necessarily reduce it if the Hosios condition ($\gamma = \eta = 0.5$) is satisfied. Aggregate net output attains a maximum for a value of b equal to 0.2; the average wage then takes the value 0.83.

This calibration exercise shows that unemployment benefits can actually improve collective welfare by increasing the productivity of jobs for a wide range of plausible values of the parameters. Acemoglu and Shimer (1999, 2000) have obtained similar results in a context where investment by firms amplifies the impact of un-

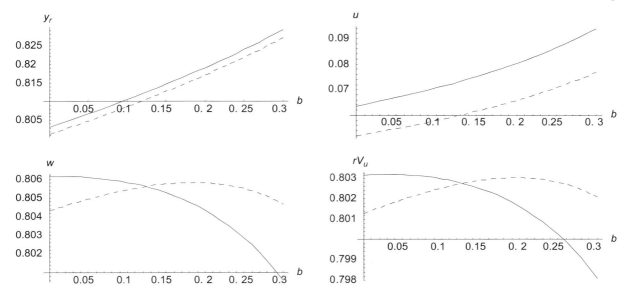

FIGURE 11.9
The impact of an increase in unemployment benefits for $\gamma = 0.5$ (straight line) and $\gamma = 0.4$ (dashed line).

employment benefits. They introduce capital into a matching model, and assume that firms invest at the moment they create new vacant jobs. This investment is irreversible. In this setting, the investment is a decreasing function of the duration of a job vacancy. Consequently an increase in unemployment benefits, by increasing the unemployment rate and bringing labor market tightness down, may increase investment and the average productivity of jobs.

4.4   A REVIEW OF EMPIRICAL STUDIES

We have already given a review of empirical studies based on microeconomic data relative to labor market participation and the job search in chapters 1 and 3. Here we present only the results of macroeconomic studies. From this standpoint, published work falls into two categories. The first focuses on the impact of unemployment benefits on the unemployment rate, while the second examines the consequences of benefits for production and welfare.

Unemployment Benefits and the Unemployment Rate
In general, studies attempting to assess the impact in this regard of the unemployment insurance system compare economies in which the system is structured differently. It is equally possible to exploit time series relative to a single country (a summary will be found in Holmlund, 1998).

Using cross-sectional data for 20 OECD countries, Layard et al. (1991) find that a 10% rise in the replacement ratio would increase the unemployment rate by 1.7%.

This order of magnitude is confirmed by more recent studies. Using richer data for the period 1983–1993, Scarpetta (1996) arrives at a figure of 1.3, and the study of Nickell (1997) on 20 OECD countries finds a coefficient of 1.1. Blanchard and Wolfers (2000) arrive at comparable orders of magnitude. Thus a rise in unemployment benefits would tend to increase unemployment, but this rise is a modest one. Single-country studies based on time series arrive at similar results, but the possibility of a reverse causality should not be discarded (Holmlund, 1998), for the extended duration of unemployment in a certain number of countries may indeed be the source of the increase in the benefits paid to unemployed persons so as to preserve their living conditions, or keep them from degrading too much.

More generally, the model developed above suggests that unemployed persons respond differently to changes in the unemployment insurance system according to their present or future situation in the labor market. This wide heterogeneity of possible responses probably explains in part the modest effects of unemployment benefits on the *global* unemployment rate. But it is possible that some particular segments of the labor force (youth, the long-term unemployed, etc.) are particularly sensitive to variations in the unemployment insurance system.

Unemployment Benefits, Global Production, and Welfare
We have emphasized that unemployment benefits can increase aggregate output and welfare thanks to their influence on the quality of match-ups. The very simple stochastic job matching model that we presented suggests that an economy with a positive level of unemployment benefits can achieve higher aggregate output than one without such benefits, for plausible values of these parameters. Acemoglu and Shimer (2000) have taken this analysis much farther, using a matching model in which risk-averse workers are able to save. This model is calibrated to represent the labor market of high school graduates in the United States. Acemoglu and Shimer estimate that an increase in unemployment benefits beyond that prevailing in the 1990s would have a positive impact on the unemployment rate, but would increase production and improve welfare (evaluated with a utilitarian criterion). These results run counter to conclusions derived from partial equilibrium job search models, which emphasize the disincentive effects of unemployment benefits.

5 CONCLUSION AND SUMMARY

- In considering public expenditures on labor market policies, a distinction is made between *active policy* measures, which aim to improve the functioning of the labor market, and *passive policy* measures, which seek instead to improve the living conditions of workers. As a general rule, the amount spent on passive measures exceeds that spent on active ones.

- Public agencies occupy an important place in the array of institutions that manage job offers in many countries. From the standpoint of the social optimum, placement agencies (public or private) are justified only if they guarantee a better matching of unemployed persons to vacant jobs than the "natural" process would, and if running them does not incur excessively high fixed costs. Decentralized equilibrium with private agencies is likely inefficient, on account of congestion effects and the potentially oligopolistic structure of the placement market. Empirical studies suggest that public employment services have a significant effect, at a reasonable cost, on the exit rate from unemployment of the individuals concerned.

- General training improves the productivity of an individual for all jobs, while specific training increases only his or her productivity for a particular job. In a perfectly competitive economy, the investment in general training would be entirely financed by workers, since they would benefit exclusively from the investment. Individual choices would then be socially optimal. The same does not hold true if the matching process governing the labor market is imperfect. In this context, decentralized equilibrium is characterized by underinvestment in general training, even if firms and workers can commit themselves to complete contracts, since it is impossible for agents to bargain over the amount of this type of training with *future* employers—who will benefit tomorrow from the investment made today.

- When it comes to specific training, decentralized equilibrium is socially efficient when the employer and the worker can commit themselves to complete contracts. This result is independent of any possible imperfection in the matching process, since the amount of time spent looking for work does not play a part in decisions regarding investment in specific training. But as we know (see chapter 2), agents most often cannot sign complete contracts. In the presence of incomplete contracts, decentralized equilibrium leads to underinvestment in this type of training.

- Employment subsidies in the form of reduced labor costs for the employer generate upward pressure on the negotiated wages. When unemployment benefits are perfectly indexed to wages, the employee captures the *whole* subsidy initially granted to the firm in the form of a wage rise, and at equilibrium subsidies have no effect on employment. Conversely, when unemployment benefits are imperfectly indexed or wages are rigid, employment subsidies reduce the unemployment rate.

- The creation of public sector jobs, by exerting upward pressure on wages, can crowd out private sector jobs. Its effect on unemployment is thus a priori ambiguous. Empirical assessments suggest that nontargeted employment subsidies, or the creation of public sector jobs, are costly measures that should only find marginal application.

- To evaluate the impact of employment policies, we must compare the performances of the individuals who benefit from measures with those of individuals who do not. This kind of assessment poses problems, since the characteristics of the individuals who do benefit from employment policies are generally particular, which creates a potential selection bias. It is possible to deal with this problem, on the basis of observational data gathered from surveys, by assessing the performance of policies for groups of individuals possessing identical characteristics (the matching method). The existence of unobserved characteristics nevertheless constitutes an unavoidable limitation on this type of approach. Social experiments, which consist of choosing the beneficiaries of employment policies at random within the guidelines of a precisely defined protocol and comparing their performances with those of nonbeneficiaries, make it possible to deal with this problem.

- The appraisal of active employment policies yields very mixed results. Studies carried out in the United States conclude that only adult, economically disadvantaged women appear to derive any real benefit, for an acceptable cost, from measures to promote training. In Europe, the highly divergent results and the assortment of methods adopted do not make it possible to draw a firm conclusion about the impact of such programs. Job search assistance appears to have positive effects on the exit rate from unemployment and wages, and the overall benefits exceed the costs in the United States and Europe. Still, the studies that arrive at these conclusions generally do not allow us to distinguish between the impact of aid to the unemployed and the impact of the sanctions applied against half-hearted job searches. Finally, all empirical research dedicated to assessing employment policies generally neglects their macroeconomic effects, which may be great.

- The *gross* replacement ratio is equal to the ratio of gross unemployment benefits to gross wages. It differs from the *net* replacement ratio, which takes taxes and transfers into account. For all the OECD countries, the average net ratio is about two-thirds higher than the average gross ratio. Everywhere there is a large percentage of unemployed persons receiving no unemployment benefits. In 1995, 30% were in this situation in Denmark and Sweden, 45% in France, and 70% in Germany.

- The simplest models conclude that an increase in unemployment benefits leads to a fall in employment and output. This claim is questionable for two reasons. First, in order to receive benefits from an unemployment insurance fund, an individual has to have held a job and paid in to that fund for a well-defined period. If not, he or she is not *eligible*, and the higher the benefits are, the weaker his or her bargaining position will be. In the end, the wage negotiated with an ineligible worker will tend to diminish with the unemployment insurance benefits level. Hence a rise in benefits should bring down unemployment among ineligible persons, but since it increases unemployment among the eligible ones, its effect on the *global* unemployment rate is ambiguous. Second, benefits give the unemployed the opportunity to choose better quality jobs. Empirical research carried out on the industrialized countries suggests that benefits have weak but slightly positive effects on the unemployment rate. Studies carried out in the United States for the 1990s conclude that a rise in the level of unemployment benefits may increase global output and the welfare of high school graduates.

6 RELATED TOPICS IN THE BOOK

- Chapter 2, section 2: Investment in human capital, general and specific training

- Chapter 3, section 3.2: Unemployment benefits and the determinants of unemployment duration

- Chapter 4, section 2.2: Main results on labor demand elasticity

- Chapter 7, section 5.1: Negotiation and investment, the holdup problem

- Chapter 9, section 3: The matching model

- Chapter 9, section 6: The efficiency of labor market equilibrium

7 FURTHER READINGS

Acemoglu, D., and Pischke, J.-S. (1999), "Beyond Becker: Training in imperfect labour markets," *Economic Journal*, 112, pp. 112–142.

Björklund, A., and Regnér, H. (1996), "Experimental evaluation of European labour market policy," in Schmid, G., O'Reilly, J., and Schömann, K. (eds.), *International Handbook of Labour Market and Evaluation*, pp. 89–114, Adelshot, U.K.: Edward Elgar.

Grubb, D., and Martin, J. (2001), "What works and for whom: A review of OECD countries' experiences with active labour market policies," *Swedish Economic Policy Review*, 8, pp. 9–56.

Heckman, J., Lalonde, R., and Smith, J. (1999), "The economics and econometrics of active labor market programs," in Ashenfelter, O., and Card, D. (eds.), *Handbook of Labor Economics*, vol. 3a, chap. 31, pp. 1865–2097, Amsterdam: Elsevier Science/North-Holland.

REFERENCES

Acemoglu, D. (1997), "Training and innovation in an imperfect labour market," *Review of Economic Studies*, 64, pp. 445–467.

Acemoglu, D. (2001), "Good jobs versus bad jobs: Theory and some evidence," *Journal of Labor Economics*, 19, pp. 1–22.

Acemoglu, D., and Pischke, J.-S. (1998), "Why do firms train? Theory and evidence," *Quarterly Journal of Economics*, 113, pp. 79–119.

Acemoglu, D., and Pischke, J.-S. (1999a), "The structure of wages and investment in general training," *Journal of Political Economy*, 107, pp. 539–572.

Acemoglu, D., and Pischke, J.-S. (1999b), "Beyond Becker: Training in imperfect labour markets," *Economic Journal*, 112, pp. 112–142.

Acemoglu, D., and Shimer, R. (1999), "Efficient unemployment insurance," *Journal of Political Economy*, 107, pp. 893–928.

Acemoglu, D., and Shimer, R. (2000), "Productivity gains from unemployment insurance," *European Economic Review*, 44, pp. 1115–1125.

Aghion, P., and Howitt, P. (1998), *Endogenous Growth Theory*, Cambridge, Mass.: MIT Press.

Algan, Y., Cahuc, P., and Zylberberg, A. (2002), "Public employment and labour market performances," *Economic Policy*, 34, pp. 9–64.

Ashenfelter, O. (1978), "Estimating the impact of training programs on earnings," *Review of Economics and Statistics*, 6(1), pp. 47–57.

Ashenfelter, O., and Card, D. (1978), "Using the longitudinal structure of earnings to estimate the effects of training programs," *Review of Economics and Statistics*, 6(3), pp. 648–660.

Ashenfelter, O., and Card, D. (1985), "Using the longitudinal structure of earnings to estimate the effect of training programs," *Review of Economics and Statistics*, 67, pp. 648–660.

Atkinson, A. (1995), *Incomes and the Welfare State*, Cambridge, U.K.: Cambridge University Press.

Atkinson, A., and Mickelwright, J. (1991), "Unemployment compensation and labor market transitions: A critical review," *Journal of Economic Literature*, 29, pp. 1679–1727.

Autor, D., and Duggan, M. (2001), "The rise in disability and the decline in unemployment," NBER Working Paper No. 8336, Cambridge, Mass.: National Bureau of Economic Research.

Bassi, L., Simms, M., Burnbridge, L., and Betsey, C. (1984), "Measuring the effect of CETA on youth and the economically disadvantaged," Report for the U.S. Department of Labor, 20-11-82-19, Washington, D.C.: Urban Institute.

Becker, G. (1964), *Human Capital*, Chicago: University of Chicago Press.

Benabou, R. (1996), "Heterogeneity, stratification, and growth," *American Economic Review*, 86, pp. 584–609.

Björklund, A. (1994), "Evolutions of Swedish labor market policy," *International Journal of Manpower*, 15(5), pp. 16–31.

Björklund, A., and Regnér, H. (1996), "Experimental evaluation of European labour market policy," in Schmid, G., O'Reilly, J., and Schömann, K. (eds.), *International Handbook of Labour Market and Evaluation*, pp. 89–114, Adelshot, U.K.: Edward Elgar.

Black, D., Smith, J., Berger, M., and Noel, B. (2002), "Is the threat of reemployment services more effective than the service themselves? Experimental evidence from the UI system," NBER Working Paper No. 8825, forthcoming *American Economic Review*.

Blanchard, O., and Wolfers, J. (2000), ''The role of shocks and institutions in the rise of European unemployment: The aggregate evidence,'' *Economic Journal*, 110, suppl., pp. 1–33.

Blanchflower, D., and Oswald, A. (1995), *The Wage Curve*, Cambridge, Mass.: MIT Press.

Blundell, R., and MaCurdy, T. (1999), ''Labor supply: A review of alternative approaches,'' in Ashenfelter, O., and Card, D. (eds.), *Handbook of Labor Economics*, vol. 3A, chap. 27, Amsterdam: Elsevier Science/North-Holland.

Blundell, R., Costa Dias, M., Meghir, C., and Van Reenen, J. (2003), ''Evaluating the employment impact of a mandatory job search assistance program,'' IFS Working Paper W01/20.

Brodsky, M. (2000), ''Public-service employment programs in selected OECD countries,'' *Monthly Labor Review*, October, pp. 31–41.

Calmfors, L. (1994), ''Active labour market policy and unemployment: A framework for the analysis of crucial design features,'' *OECD Economic Studies*, 22, pp. 7–47.

Calmfors, L., and Lang, H. (1995), ''Macroeconomic effects of active labor market programs in a union wage-setting model,'' *Economic Journal*, 105, pp. 601–619.

Carneiro, P., and Heckman, J. (2003), ''Human capital policy,'' NBER Working Paper No. 9495, forthcoming in Heckman, J., and Krueger, A. (eds), *Inequality in America: What Role for Human Capital Policy?*, Cambridge, Mass.: MIT Press.

Chang, C., and Wang, Y. (1996), ''Human capital investment under asymmetric information: The Pigovian conjecture revisited,'' *Journal of Labor Economics*, 14, pp. 505–519.

Chiu, H., and Karni, E. (1998), ''Endogenous adverse selection and unemployment insurance,'' *Journal of Political Economy*, 106, pp. 806–827.

Coe, D., and Snower, D. (1997), ''Policy complementarities: The case for fundamental labor market reform,'' *IMF Staff Papers*, 44(1), pp. 1–35.

Coleman, J., Campbell, E., Hobson, C., McPartland, J., Mood, A., Weinfelde, F., and York, R. (1966), *Equality of Educational Opportunity*, Washington, D.C.: U.S. Government Printing Office.

Cooley, T., McGuire, T., and Prescott, E. (1979), ''Earnings and employment dynamics of manpower trainees: An exploratory econometric analysis,'' in Ehrenberg, R. (ed.), *Research in Labor Economics*, vol. 4, Suppl. 2, pp. 119–147, Greenwich, Conn.: JAI Press.

Cooper, R., and John, A. (1988), ''Coordinating coordination failures in Keynesian models,'' *Quarterly Journal of Economics*, 103, pp. 441–465.

Davidson, C., and Woodbury, S. (1993), ''The displacement effect of reemployment and training programs,'' *Journal of Labor Economics*, 11(4), pp. 575–605.

Diamond, P. (1981), ''Mobility costs, frictional unemployment, and efficiency,'' *Journal of Political Economy*, 89, pp. 798–812.

Dickinson, K., Johnson, T., and West, R. (1986), ''An analysis of the impact of CETA on participant's earnings,'' *Journal of Human Ressources*, 21, pp. 64–91.

Dolton, P., Makepeace, G., and Treble, J. (1994), ''The wage effect of YTS: Evidence from YCS,'' *Scottish Journal of Political Economy*, 41(4), pp. 444–453.

Dolton, P., and O'Neill, D. (1996), "Unemployment duration and the restart effect: Some experimental evidence," *Economic Journal*, 106, pp. 387–400.

Drèze, J., and Malinvaud, E. (1994), "Growth and employment: The scope of a European initiative," *European Economic Review*, 38, pp. 489–504.

Drèze, J., and Sneessens, H. (1997), "Technological development, competition from low-wage economies and low-skilled unemployment," in Snower, D., and de la Dehesa, G. (eds.), *Unemployment Policy: Government Options for the Labour Market*, Cambridge, U.K.: Cambridge University Press.

Fisher, R. (1935), *Design of Experiments*, New York: Hafner.

Fougère, D., Pradel, J., and Roger, M. (1999), "The influence of the state employment service on the search effort and on the probability of leaving unemployment," CREST-INSEE Working Paper No. 9904.

Gay, R., and Borus, M. (1980), "Validating performance indicators for employment and training programs," *Journal of Human Resources*, 15, pp. 29–48.

Geraci, V. (1984), "Short-term indicators of job training program effects on long-term participant earnings," Report for the U.S. Department of Labor, 20-48-82-16, Washington, D.C.: Urban Institute.

Goux, D., and Maurin, E. (2000), "Returns to firm-provided training: evidence from French worker-firm matched data," *Labour Economics*, 7(1), pp. 1–20.

Grubb, D. (2001), "Eligibility criteria for unemployment benefits," in *Labour Market Policies and the Public Employment Service*, pp. 205–237, Paris: OECD.

Grubb, D., and Martin, J. (2001), "What works and for whom: A review of OECD countries' experiences with active labour market policies," *Swedish Economic Policy Review*, 8, pp. 9–56.

Hamermesh, D. (1993), *Labor Demand*, Princeton, N.J.: Princeton University Press.

Heckman, J. (2000), "Policies to foster human capital," *Research in Economics*, 54, pp. 3–56.

Heckman, J., Lalonde, R., and Smith, J. (1999), "The economics and econometrics of active labor market programs," in Ashenfelter, O., and Card, D. (eds.), *Handbook of Labor Economics*, vol. 3a, chap. 31, pp. 1865–2097, Amsterdam: Elsevier Science/North-Holland.

Heckman, J., Lochner, L., and Taber, C. (1998), "General equilibrium treatment effects: A study of tuition policy," *American Economic Review*, 88, pp. 381–386.

Heckman, J., and Smith, J. (1998), "The sensitivity of experimental impact estimates: Evidence from the national JTPA study," in Freeman, R., and Katz, L. (eds.), *Youth Employment and Unemployment in the OECD Countries*, Chicago: University of Chicago Press.

Holmlund, B. (1998), "Unemployment insurance in theory and practice," *Scandinavian Journal of Economics*, 100(1), pp. 113–141.

Holmlund, B., and Linden, J. (1993), "Job matching, temporary public employment, and equilibrium unemployment," *Journal of Public Economics*, 51, pp. 329–343.

Katz, E., and Ziderman, A. (1990), "Investment in general training: The role of information and labour mobility," *Economic Journal*, 100, pp. 1147–1158.

Layard, R., and Nickell, S. (1986), "Unemployment in Britain," *Economica*, 53, pp. 121–169.

Layard, R., Nickell, S., and Jackman, R. (1991), *Unemployment*, London: Oxford University Press.

Lewis, H.-G. (1963), *Unionism and Relative Wages*, Chicago: University of Chicago Press.

Lucas, R. (1988), "On the mechanics of economic development," *Journal of Monetary Economics*, 22(1), pp. 3–42.

Main, B., and Shelly, M. (1990), "The effectiveness of the Youth Training Scheme as a manpower policy," *Economica*, 57(228), pp. 495–514.

Manning, A. (1998), "Comment on B. Holmlund: 'Unemployment insurance in theory and practice,'" *Scandinavian Journal of Economics*, 100(1), pp. 143–145.

Marimon, R., and Zilibotti, F. (1999), "Unemployment vs. mismatch of talents: Reconsidering unemployment benefits," *Economic Journal*, 109, pp. 266–291.

Martin, A. (1996), "Measures of replacement rates for the purposes of international comparisons: A note," *OECD Economic Studies*, 26, pp. 99–116.

Meyer, B. (1995), "Lessons from the U.S. unemployment insurance experiments," *Journal of Economic Literature*, 33, pp. 91–131.

Nickell, S. (1997), "Unemployment and labor market rigidities: Europe versus North America," *Journal of Economic Perspectives*, 3, pp. 55–74.

OECD (2001), *Labour Market Policies and the Public Employment Service*, Paris: OECD.

Parks, G. (2000), "The High Scope Perry Preschool Project," *Juvenile Justice Bulletin*, U.S. Department of Justice, http://www.ncjrs.org/pdffiles1/ojjdp/181725.pdf.

Pissarides, C. (1998), "The impact of employment tax cuts on unemployment and wages: The role of unemployment benefits and tax structure," *European Economic Review*, 42, pp. 155–183.

Pissarides, C. (2000), *Equilibrium Unemployment Theory*, 2nd ed., Cambridge, Mass.: MIT Press.

Quandt, R. (1972), "Methods for estimating switching regressions," *Journal of the American Statistical Association*, 67(338), pp. 306–310.

Regnér, H. (1997), *Training at the Job and Training for a New Job: Two Swedish Studies*, Stockholm, Sweden: Swedish Institute for Social Research.

Roy, A. (1951), "Some thoughts on the distribution of earnings," *Oxford Economic Papers*, 3, pp. 135–146.

Rubin, D. (1974), "Estimating the causal effects of treatments in randomized and non-randomized studies," *Journal of Educational Psychology*, 66, pp. 688–701.

Scarpetta, S. (1996), "Assessing the role of labour market policies and institutional settings on unemployment: A cross-country study," *OECD Economic Studies*, 26, pp. 43–98.

Snower, D. (1995), "The low-skill, bad-job trap," in Booth, A., and Snower, D. (eds.), *Acquiring Skills*, chap. 6, Cambridge, U.K.: CEPR-Cambridge University Press.

Stevens, M. (1994), "A theoretical model of on-the-job training with imperfect competition," *Oxford Economic Papers*, 46, pp. 537–562.

Tierney, P., Grossman, J.-B., and Resch, N. (2000), "Making a difference: An impact study of Big Brother Big Sisters," Public Private Ventures, http://www.ppv.org/content/reports/makingadiff.html.

Torp, H., Raaum, O., Heraes, E., and Goldstein, H. (1993), "The first Norwegian experiment," in Jensen, K., and Masden, P. (eds.), *Measuring Labour Market Measures*, pp. 97–140, Copenhagen: Ministry of Labour.

Ulph, D. (1995), "Dynamic competition for market share and the failure of the market for skilled workers," in Booth, A., and Snower, D. (eds.), *Acquiring Skills*, chap. 5, Cambridge, U.K.: CEPR-Cambridge University Press.

Walwei, U. (1996), "Improving job-matching through placement services," in Schmid, G., O'Reilly, J., and Schömann, K. (eds.), *International Handbook of Labour Market Policy and Evaluation*, chap. 13, pp. 402–430.

Westergard-Nielsen, N. (1993), "The effects of training: A fixed effect model," in Jensen, K., and Masden, P. (eds.), *Measuring Labour Market Measures*, pp. 167–200, Copenhagen: Ministry of Labour.

Yavas, A. (1994), "Middlemen in bilateral search markets," *Journal of Labor Economics*, 12, pp. 406–429.

CHAPTER 12

INSTITUTIONS AND LABOR MARKET PERFORMANCE

CONTENTS

In this chapter, we will:

- Understand why a minimum wage has positive and negative effects on labor market outcomes

- See that the effects of employment protection depend on the mode of wage formation

- Learn what the tax wedge is, and see that changes in the marginal and average tax rates have different consequences

- Understand the importance of the level (centralized, intermediate, or local) at which bargaining takes place

- Discover what empirical research tells us about the interactions between shocks and institutions

INTRODUCTION

Comparison of the employment performance of the OECD countries and the various approaches they take to regulating their labor markets has attracted a great deal of attention. It is widely believed that the "rigidity" of these markets is responsible for unemployment. Labor markets subjected to stringent state regulation through high minimum wages, strict employment protection measures, high mandatory contributions, and powerful unions are seen as constituting unfavorable terrain for employment, which is negatively affected by the increased cost of labor and the reduced incentives to work.

The aim of this chapter is to gain an understanding of the linkages that exist between public policy, institutions, and labor market performance. From that standpoint, the terms "rigidity" and "flexibility" appear much too broad; our task will be to pinpoint the specific effects of each type of state intervention. We will therefore begin by analyzing the consequences of the factors that are generally taken to constitute the main sources of labor market rigidity: minimum wages, employment protection, and mandatory contributions. The matching model set out in chapter 9 again proves particularly useful: it represents the dynamic functioning of an imperfectly competitive labor market, and describes behaviors with enough precision to allow us to study the impact of these sources of rigidity in the labor market on unemployment and employment. Using this model, much recent theoretical work has succeeded in undermining a range of received ideas. For example, we will see that increases in the minimum wage can have opposite effects on employment, according to circumstances. The same thing is true for job protection. Moreover, institutions interact one with another. For example, the effects of employment protection and taxes on unemployment and the distribution of income are influenced by the presence of a minimum wage.

The difficulty of identifying a systematic relationship between the elements that make up labor market "rigidity," on the one hand, and bad employment performance on the other, has led certain economists to suggest that what really creates unemployment is failure of coordination among employers and employees who are competing to share income. High unemployment is seen as the upshot of badly coordinated wage bargaining, taking place at the wrong level (centralized, intermediate, or local). Research, theoretical and empirical, does indeed allow us to show linkages between the level at which bargaining takes place and labor market performance. But these linkages are complex and highly dependent on other institutions, making it impossible to specify a preferred bargaining level under all circumstances.

We will then proceed to examine the consequences of the minimum wage, employment protection, taxes, and the diverse modes of wage setting. This chapter will end by presenting the results of the empirical research that has attempted to establish relationships among the various kinds of regulation and labor market performances in the OECD, on the basis of aggregate data. This research is valuable for the light it casts on the interdependence among certain institutional features, and does succeed—on occasion—in pinpointing the combinations most favorable to employment.

1 THE MINIMUM WAGE

Minimum wage legislation exists in 22 OECD countries. Such legislation has generally been framed with the intent to compress wage inequality. But the effectiveness of the minimum wage as an income redistribution tool is often criticized, since by raising the cost of labor it can have negative effects on output and employment. Economic analysis suggests that the effects of the minimum wage on employment actually depend on the initial level of the minimum wage. When it is set relatively low to start with, subsequent increases are not necessarily unfavorable to employment. But if the minimum wage is set relatively high to start with, subsequent increases do likely exert a negative impact on hiring. These results are confirmed to some extent by empirical studies.

1.1 A CONSTRAINT OF VARYING STRENGTH FROM COUNTRY TO COUNTRY

Minimum wage legislation, and its incidence, vary greatly from country to country, but a minimum wage covers populations that are much alike everywhere.

1.1.1 Legal Aspects and Importance of the Minimum Wage

Minimum wages exist in all European Union countries and a large number of OECD ones. The legislation governing them, however, varies widely. The minimum wage may be regional (the United States, Canada, Japan) or national (France, the Netherlands, the United Kingdom since April 1999). It can also vary according to industry (Germany, Ireland, Portugal) and professional qualification (Luxembourg). Very often the age of the beneficiary makes a difference; for example, a minimum wage set at a reduced rate for young people exists in Belgium, the Netherlands, and New Zealand. The minimum wage can be set on an hourly, daily, or monthly basis. Everywhere the public authorities govern the mode of its calculation, but it can also be bargained over between employers and employees. From one country to another, the minimum wage may be reset according to inflation (Belgium) or the evolution of the average wage (France, Japan, Spain), and sometimes even according to criteria thought to reflect the impact of the minimum wage itself on employment (the Netherlands, Spain). In the United States, minimal hourly wages are set by law at the federal and state levels, and there is no automatic indexation to inflation or the average wage.

In order to make international comparison possible, the relative size of the minimum wage is often measured by the Kaitz index. The Kaitz index (Kaitz, 1970) is a coverage-weighted minimum wage relative to the average wage. It is defined as $\sum_i f_i(w_m/\overline{w}_i)s_i$, where f_i denotes the fraction of teenage employment in industry i, w_m is the minimum wage, $\overline{w}_i$ is the average hourly wage in industry i, and s_i is the proportion of workers covered by the minimum wage in industry i. Table 12.1 gives the value of this index for four OECD countries and indicates the percentage of workers receiving minimum wage.

Table 12.1

The relative size of the minimum wage.

Country (year)	Kaitz index	Percentage of employees paid at minimum wage
Denmark (1994)	0.54	6
France (1994)	0.50	11
Netherlands (1993)	0.55	3.2
United States (1993)	0.39	4

Source: Dolado et al. (1996, table 1, p. 322).

According to the Kaitz index, minimum wage levels are clearly set higher in Europe than in the United States. The incidence of the minimum wage is particularly striking in France, where 11% of workers are compensated at that level.

The evolution of the minimum wage has varied greatly from one country to another; in figures 12.1a and 12.1b it is shown for several OECD countries over the period 1960–2000. Figure 12.1a shows that Luxembourg, France, and Japan have seen the real value of their minimum wage rise constantly from 1960 (1975 for Japan) to 2000. In France, the purchasing power of the minimum wage has been multiplied by 3 between 1960 and 2000. As shown by figure 12.1b, in the Netherlands, Canada, and the United States, however, the real value of the minimum wage has not stopped declining since the start of the 1980s. For instance, in the United States, the purchasing power of the hourly minimum wage was 10% *less* in 2000 than it was in 1960, although it had been rising until 1968.

1.1.2 The Populations Concerned

The populations employed at minimum wage possess particular characteristics which recur in all countries. Table 12.2 sets out some of these characteristics for France and the United States. In 1996 the proportion of workers being paid minimum wage was approximately twice as high in France as it was in the United States, but the composition of the two populations was much alike. These are mainly persons without a secondary-school diploma or university degree, and the majority are women and youth. Almost 32% of those 25 and under in France are paid at minimum wage, which highlights its importance there. Workers paid at minimum wage are likewise overrepresented in the commercial field (especially the hotel and restaurant trades) and in part-time jobs.

1.2 Economic Analysis of the Minimum Wage

The effects of the minimum wage depend on the characteristics of the labor market to which it applies. The model of the perfectly competitive labor market, and the version of the basic matching model presented in chapter 9, highlight the negative aspects of

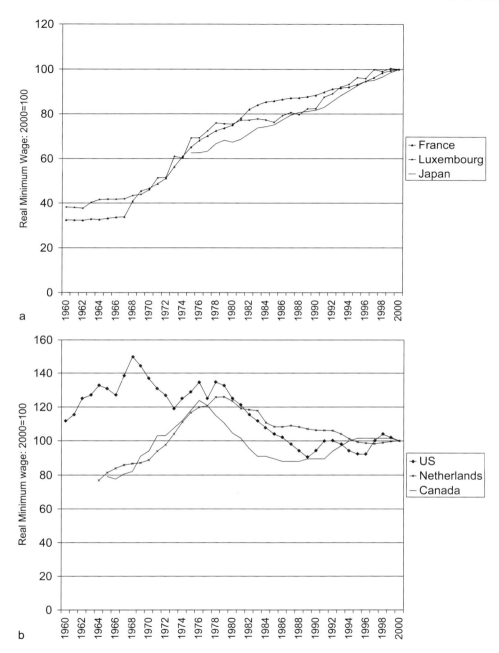

a

b

FIGURE 12.1

The minimum wage in several OECD countries.

Source: OECD data.

Table 12.2
Minimum wage jobs as a function of different labor force characteristics in 1996 (in %).

Country	Total	Men	Women	<25 years	Commerce
France	11.0	7.5	16.5	31.6	15.3
United States	5.1	3.8	6.5	13.7	10.6

Source: OECD (1998, table 2.4, p. 43).

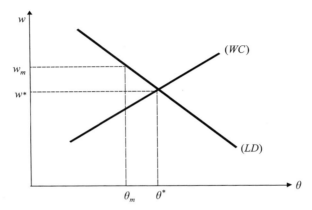

FIGURE 12.2
The effect of the minimum wage.

the minimum wage for employment. However, other theoretical frameworks, like the monopsony model or the matching model with endogenous labor market participation or job search effort, highlight situations in which a rise in the minimum wage leads to an increase in hiring.

1.2.1 Negative Effects on Employment

It is easiest to begin by analyzing the effects of the minimum wage within the model of the perfectly competitive labor market, set out in chapter 9, section 2. If we assume that the minimum wage exceeds the competitive wage (i.e., the wage that allows supply to equal demand), classical unemployment arises and can only be reabsorbed by lowering the minimum wage. This result flows directly from chapter 9, figure 9.3, if we identify wage w_m as the minimum wage. As for the conclusions to be drawn from the matching model of chapter 9, they conform entirely to those of the perfectly competitive equilibrium model. This can be seen in figure 12.2, which summarizes the effects of the minimum wage in the matching model from chapter 9, section 3.

In the matching model, if the minimum wage w_m is greater than the wage w^* that results from the bargaining process between the employee and the employer, the equilibrium value θ_m of labor market tightness is given by labor demand (LD). We see immediately that this value lies below the equilibrium value θ^* in the absence of a minimum wage, which means that the exit rate from unemployment falls off, and that in the end the unemployment rate rises, since the Beveridge curve is not affected by the minimum wage. The difference between the competitive equilibrium model and the matching model arises mainly from the wage to which the minimum wage is being compared. In the first case, it is the wage that clears the market; in the second, it is the negotiated wage. But in both models a constraining minimum wage leads to a higher level of unemployment than the equilibrium level in the absence of the minimum wage. These conclusions are not, though, verified in all circumstances: they depend on the way the labor market functions.

1.2.2 What the Monopsony Model Tells Us

A monopsony over a particular segment of the labor market is defined by the presence of a single ''buyer'' of labor services in that segment (see chapter 5). Knowing the labor supply that he or she faces, this buyer affects the equilibrium wage directly by deciding on his or her volume of hires. If the labor supply grows as wages rise, the monopsony is given an incentive to restrict its hires so as to get the benefit of low wages. Stigler (1946) had already noted that, in this context, there is a theoretical possibility that a wage rise is accompanied by a rise in employment.

The Monopsony Model

A monopsonist firm chooses the lowest wage that lets it attract a number of workers sufficient to reach the desired output at minimal cost. The simplest model has a firm employing a number L of workers and using a technology represented by an increasing and concave production function $F(L)$. Labor supply, denoted by $L^s(w)$, is taken to increase with respect to the wage w. In these conditions, when the firm decides to pay wage w, it knows that its level of employment will be $L^s(w)$; its profit is then written:

$$\Pi(w) = F[L^s(w)] - wL^s(w)$$

The equilibrium values w° and L° of the wage and employment are found by differentiating this expression of profit with respect to w. We get:

$$F'(L^\circ) = w^\circ(1 + \eta_L^w) \qquad \text{and} \qquad L^\circ = L^s(w^\circ) \tag{1}$$

In this relation, the positive quantity $\eta_L^w = L^s(w)/wL^{s\prime}(w)$ designates the inverse of the wage elasticity of labor supply. Equation (1) conveys the usual equality between the marginal productivity of labor and the marginal cost of this factor. In a monopsony situation, this marginal cost is higher than the wage, because the elasticity of the labor suppy with respect to this variable is positive. A monopsony pays the marginal employee at a level beneath his or her productivity; that is how the monopsony's gain comes about. This result also means that in the (L, w) plane, the curve with equation $F'(L) = w(1 + \eta_L^w)$ is situated below the labor demand curve $L^d(w)$ defined by $F'(L) = w$. Since employment is determined by the labor supply, the wage paid by

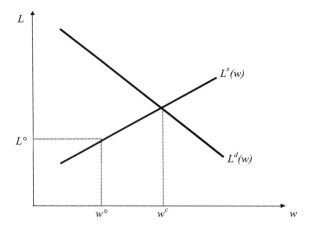

FIGURE 12.3
Minimum wage and monopsony.

the monopsony is below the competitive wage w^c that would equalize labor supply $L^s(w)$ with the labor demand $L^d(w)$ issuing from firms in a competitive market. We depict this situation in figure 12.3.

Scrutiny of figure 12.3 reveals that if the minimum wage lies between w° and w^c, a rise in its level entails an increase in employment. As long as the minimum wage is less than the competitive wage w^c, the marginal productivity of labor does indeed lie above the wage, and the monopsony has an interest in staying on the labor supply. In this case, employment is determined by labor supply, which is an increasing function of the wage. Conversely, if the minimum wage climbs higher than w^c, the monopsony no longer has an interest in staying on the labor supply curve, where wages now exceed the marginal productivity of this input. Thus the most advantageous situation for it is one that equalizes the wage with marginal productivity, which is precisely the case on the $L^d(w)$ curve representing the competitive labor demand. In this configuration, the relationship between the minimum wage and employment is decreasing.

The Positive Effects of the Minimum Wage on Employment

Thus the monopsony model brings out the possibility of a nonmonotonic relationship between the minimum wage and employment. The importance of this possibility should, however, be set in perspective, for at least three reasons. In the first place, pure monopsony situations such as the one that has just been considered are very uncommon; they occur principally in specific geographic areas where mobility is low and the number of firms small. In the second place, the minimum wage acts positively on employment only when it lies *below* the competitive wage, in other words, for wage levels probably a lot lower than those that exist in many European countries. Finally, the impact on employment of a rise in the minimum wage is all the stronger, the greater the wage elasticity of the labor supply. But as we saw in chapter 1, labor supply has little elasticity on average.

A number of studies have enriched the monopsony model by giving different foundations to the labor supply function. If manpower is mobile, for example, and information costly, workers sometimes have an interest in refusing job offers when the wage is too low, since they may hope to obtain other and better offers. The firm must then choose a wage level that allows it to attract a sufficient number of workers, in order to minimize hiring and firing costs. The work of Burdett and Mortensen (1998) and Masters (1999) has developed this idea. Drazen (1986) and Rebitzer and Taylor (1995) have proposed variants of the monopsony model grounded in the theory of efficiency wage. They focus respectively on problems linked to the quality of workers, and verification. Starting with the efficiency wage model of Shapiro and Stiglitz (1984), Rebitzer and Taylor (1995) assume that the probability of checking up on what an employee is accomplishing diminishes as the size of the workforce in the firm grows. This hypothesis entails an increasing relation between employment and wages, for the latter rise when the probability of effective supervision falls (see chapter 6). Employers then have an incentive to limit employment, in order to keep wage costs down. In this setting, the minimum wage may have a positive impact on employment. Manning (1995) offers a systematic analysis of different efficiency wage models and shows that there are many cases in which the minimum wage exerts a positive effect on employment.

In the matching model developed in chapter 9, firms also have some monopsony power, since the employees are paid below their marginal productivity. From this perspective, it is not surprising that simple enrichments of the basic matching model can explain a positive linkage between the minimum wage and employment.

1.2.3　Minimum Wage, Labor Market Participation, and Job Search Effort

In the basic version of the matching model, a rise in minimum wage leads necessarily to a reduction in equilibrium employment. But this result overlooks the influence of wages on labor market *participation* and on the *job search effort* made by the unemployed. Taking these two elements into account may substantially change the conclusion derived from the basic model.

The Influence of the Minimum Wage on Labor Market Participation

In the matching model presented in chapter 9, we deduce labor demand from the free entry condition. There is a negative relation between labor market tightness θ and wage w. This relation is described by equation (11) from chapter 9, reproduced here:

$$\frac{h}{m(\theta)} = \frac{y - w}{r + q} \tag{2}$$

Let us recall that h designates the instantaneous cost of a vacant job, $m(\theta)$ the rate at which job applications arrive, y productivity, r the interest rate, and q the rate of job destruction. This equation simply indicates that at free entry equilibrium, where the expected profit from vacancies is zero, the average cost of a vacancy, $h/m(\theta)$, is equal to the expected profit of a filled job $(y - w)/(r + q)$. That being so, an increase in the wage w reduces labor market tightness and necessarily provokes an increase in the unemployment rate u defined by equality $u = q/[q + \theta m(\theta)]$. Still, the expected utility of unemployed persons is not a monotonic function of wages. As chapter 9, section 6.3, shows, maximization of the expected utility of an unemployed person with respect to wages, subject to the labor demand (2) constraint, gives a wage identical to that obtained at the outcome of decentralized wage bargaining for which the bargaining power of workers, measured by the share γ of the surplus they get, is equal to the elasticity $\eta(\theta)$ of the matching function with respect to the unemployment rate. In other words, the wage that emerges from decentralized equilibrium gives unemployed persons a maximal expected utility only if the Hosios condition $(\gamma = \eta(\theta))$ is satisfied. In consequence, when the bargaining power of workers is too low to satisfy the Hosios condition $(\gamma < \eta(\theta))$, an increase in the minimum wage w_m, with w_m lower than the equilibrium wage w^* in figure 12.2, improves the welfare of the unemployed. As the welfare of the unemployed reaches a maximum when the Hosios condition is fulfilled, this remark implies that minimum wage hikes can improve labor market efficiency (Flinn, 2003, reaches the same conclusion in the stochastic job-matching model, presented in chapter 11, section 4.3, estimated for young labor market participants in the U.S. economy).

If we assume that decisions to participate in the labor market result from a trade-off between being an unemployed job-seeker and not participating at all, any improvement in the welfare of the unemployed leads to an increase in participation. Let H be the cumulative distribution function of the expected utilities outside the labor market of the entire working-age population. All the individuals whose expected utility outside the labor market is less than the expected utility of an unemployed person V_u decide to participate in the labor market, which entails that the participation rate is equal to $H(V_u)$. As H is necessarily an increasing function, the participation rate increases with the expected utility of unemployed persons. In this model, the employment rate is equal to $H(V_u)(1 - u)$. If $w_m < w^*$, we see that any increase in the minimum wage increases participation *and* the unemployment rate, and has an ambiguous impact a priori on employment. On the other hand, if $w_m \geq w^*$, any increase in the minimum wage entails a decline in labor market participation and an increase in unemployment, which necessarily leads to a fall in employment.

Hence, taking participation into account in a matching model allows us to understand how increases in the minimum wage may be favorable to employment for low values of the minimum wage, and become unfavorable to employment when the minimum wage is high. Nonetheless, this model does suggest that the unemployment rate necessarily grows with the minimum wage. As we shall see, such is not always the case.

The Influence of the Minimum Wage on Job Search Effort
A revision of the minimum wage upward increases the gap between the expected gains of employed and unemployed persons. Thus it may provide an incentive for the

latter to search harder for work, increase the exit rate from unemployment, and so help to lower unemployment. Obviously the minimum wage also exerts a negative effect on employment because it raises the cost of labor. Taking job search effort into account suggests that, overall, the minimum wage has effects on unemployment that run counter to one another. The matching model allows us to shed light on the impact of the minimum wage in this context.

Taking job search effort into account noticeably alters the formulation of the matching function. At every instant the number of hires depends on the number of unemployed *and* the search effort that each of them puts into looking for work. Let $\bar{e}$ be the average effort; if U always designates the number of unemployed persons, the product $\bar{e}U$ representing the global job search effort gives us an indicator of the "effective" stock of unemployed persons. Let V again be the number of jobs vacant; the number of hires per unit of time is then equal to $M(V, \bar{e}U)$, where M is a matching function analogous to the one utilized in the basic model of chapter 9. In particular, it is increasing with each of its arguments and has constant returns to scale.

The labor market tightness, denoted by $\bar{\theta}$, is then defined as the ratio of the number V of vacancies to the number $\bar{e}U$ of "effective" unemployed persons, i.e., $\bar{\theta} = V/\bar{e}U$. The rate at which vacant jobs are filled is equal to $M(V, \bar{e}U)/V$. Taking into account the degree-one homogeneity of function M, this rate is written simply $M(1, 1/\bar{\theta}) \equiv m(\bar{\theta})$. For an unemployed person, each unit of effort yields an exit rate $M(V, \bar{e}U)/\bar{e}U = \bar{\theta}m(\bar{\theta})$ from unemployment. If he or she decides to make an effort e, his or her exit rate from unemployment is equal to $e\bar{\theta}m(\bar{\theta})$.

Labor Demand

The behavior of an employer who is paying his or her employees the minimum wage w is identical to what it is in the basic model. We continue to employ the usual notation; the profits Π_e and Π_v respectively expected from a filled job and a vacant one are written:

$$r\Pi_e = y - w + q(\Pi_v - \Pi_e) \qquad \text{and} \qquad r\Pi_v = -h + m(\bar{\theta})(\Pi_e - \Pi_v)$$

When the free entry condition $\Pi_v = 0$ is satisfied, these two equalities give a relationship between w and $\bar{\theta}$ which is interpretable as a labor demand. Thus we have:

$$\frac{h}{m(\bar{\theta})} = \frac{y - w}{r + q} \tag{3}$$

For a given level of the minimum wage, this equation completely determines the equilibrium value of the labor market tightness $\bar{\theta}$. In figure 12.4, this value is represented by the horizontal line (LD). Thus we also verify that the labor market tightness $\bar{\theta}$ is a decreasing function of the minimum wage w.

Optimal Search Effort

At every instant, an individual chooses his or her effort by trading off between the expected gains from looking harder for work and the disutility that this gives rise to. It

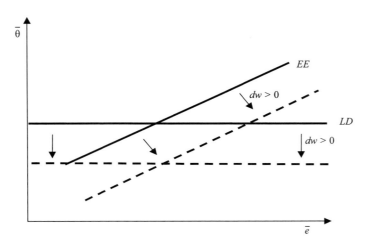

FIGURE 12.4
The impact of an increase in the minimum wage on job search effort and labor market tightness.

will be useful to assume that an effort e leads to a cost $c(e)$, where $c(.)$ is a function strictly increasing, convex, and equal to zero at the origin ($c' > 0$, $c'' > 0$ and $c(0) = 0$). If z again designates the instantaneous gain of an unemployed person, then his or her instantaneous utility is simply equal to $z - c(e)$. Let us suppose that between instants t and $t + dt$ the labor market tightness is equal to $\bar{\theta}$. When an unemployed person decides to put forth an effort e_t, his or her expected utility $V_u(t)$ at date t is written as follows:

$$V_u(t) = \left(\frac{1}{1 + r\,dt}\right)\{[z - c(e_t)]\,dt + e_t\bar{\theta}_t m(\bar{\theta}_t)\,dt V_e(t + dt) + [1 - e_t\bar{\theta}_t m(\bar{\theta}_t)\,dt]V_u(t + dt)\}$$

The terms $V_e(t + dt)$ and $V_u(t + dt)$ of the right-hand side of this equation designate respectively the expected utilities of an employed person and an unemployed one at date $t + dt$. Thus they do not depend on the search effort e_t put forth over the interval $[t, t + dt]$. Bearing this in mind, the optimal effort is found by setting the derivative of $V_u(t)$ to zero with respect to e_t. It comes to[1]:

$$-c'(e_t)\,dt + \bar{\theta}_t m(\bar{\theta}_t)\,dt[V_e(t + dt) - V_u(t + dt)] = 0$$

At stationary equilibrium, the values of the different variables do not depend on the date on which they were realized, so we will simply denote them by $\bar{\theta}, e, V_e$, and V_u. At stationary equilibrium the effort e, the labor market tightness $\bar{\theta}$ and the rent $(V_e - V_u)$ of an employed person are thus bound together by the equality:

$$c'(e) = \bar{\theta} m(\bar{\theta})(V_e - V_u) \tag{4}$$

This relation signifies that an unemployed person chooses his or her effort in such a way that the marginal cost of a unit of extra effort $c'(e)$ equals the gain expected from this same unit of extra effort. This expected gain is equal to the rent $(V_e - V_u)$ of an employee multiplied by the exit rate $\bar{\theta}m(\bar{\theta})$ from unemployment associated with a unit of effort.

Labor Market Equilibrium

At stationary equilibrium, the expected utilities V_e and V_u representing respectively the expected utilities of an employee and an unemployed person are defined by the usual equations, i.e.:

$$rV_e = w + q(V_u - V_e) \qquad \text{and} \qquad rV_u = z - c(e) + e\bar{\theta}m(\bar{\theta})(V_e - V_u)$$

These two equalities allow us to express the rent of an employee as a function of the minimum wage w and the labor market tightness $\bar{\theta}$:

$$V_e - V_u = \frac{w - z + c(e)}{r + q + e\bar{\theta}m(\bar{\theta})}$$

Bringing this value of $(V_e - V_u)$ into relation (4), we arrive at an implicit equation between the equilibrium value of effort, denoted by $\bar{e}$, and that of the labor market tightness $\bar{\theta}$. It is written:

$$\bar{\theta}m(\bar{\theta}) = \frac{(r + q)c'(\bar{e})}{w - z + c(\bar{e}) - \bar{e}c'(\bar{e})} \tag{5}$$

The left-hand side of this equality is an increasing function of $\bar{\theta}$, and we can verify that the right-hand side is an increasing function of $\bar{e}$ under the hypothesis of the convexity of function $c(.)$. Equation (5) thus defines a unique value of job search effort $\bar{e}$ increasing with labor market tightness. This equation has a natural interpretation: a rise in labor market tightness increases the return on search effort, and that gives unemployed persons an incentive to look harder for work. This relationship is represented by the (EE) curve in figure 12.4. It is interesting to note that, for given $\bar{\theta}$, equation (5) shows that job search effort depends in a positive manner on the difference $(w - z)$. It is, in other words, not the absolute level of the minimum wage that produces the incentive, but the gap between this level and the income that a person is capable of obtaining by remaining unemployed.

Equations (3) and (5), characterizing labor demand and optimal search effort respectively as functions of labor market tightness, determine the equilibrium values of $\bar{e}$ and of $\bar{\theta}$. Figure 12.4 illustrates the impact of a rise in the minimum wage in the $(\bar{e}, \bar{\theta})$ plane. The rise in the minimum wage shifts labor demand (LD) and the graph (EE) of the optimal job search effort function downward. As we see, a hike in the minimum wage has an ambiguous impact on search effort. A higher minimum wage increases the rent obtainable from every job, which gives the unemployed an incentive to strive harder to find work. But at the same time the hike in the minimum wage has a negative effect on labor demand. The number of vacant jobs shrinks, so the unemployed have greater difficulty in finding employment. The gain from searching declines, and that impels the unemployed to reduce the intensity of their job search.

At stationary equilibrium, the unemployment rate u is found by equalizing the flow of entries into and exits from unemployment. Assuming that the labor force is of constant size normalized to 1, the number of jobs destroyed per unit of time is equal to $(1 - u)q$. The exit rate from unemployment being equal here to $\bar{e}\bar{\theta}m(\bar{\theta})$, the number of jobs created per unit of time takes the value $u\bar{e}\bar{\theta}m(\bar{\theta})$. Equalization of the flows of entry into and exit from unemployment then yields the stationary value of the unemployment rate u as a function of the equilibrium values of $\bar{e}$ and $\bar{\theta}$:

$$u = \frac{q}{q + \bar{e}\bar{\theta}m(\bar{\theta})} \tag{6}$$

For given $\bar{e}$, this equation defines a Beveridge curve in the (v, u) plane. We see that a hike in the minimum wage has an ambiguous effect on employment, for on one hand it reduces equilibrium tightness $\bar{\theta}$, which increases unemployment, but on the other it can have a positive effect on job search effort, which would have a tendency to push up the exit rate from unemployment and—overall—to push unemployment down (the Beveridge curve approaches the origin). For a hike in the minimum wage to be favorable to employment, it is necessary that the elasticity of job search effort with respect to the expected wage be high, and that the elasticity of labor market tightness with respect to the wage be low.

An Assessment of the Effects of the Minimum Wage

A calibration of the preceding model will allow us to arrive at a quantitative assessment of the effects of the minimum wage. To that end, we revert to the values of certain parameters presented in chapter 9, section 3.5.3, table 9.9: $q = 0.15$, $h = 0.3$, and $r = 0.05$. Individual production y continues to be normalized to 1, and we assume that the replacement ratio z/w is a constant equal to 0.4. There is a Cobb-Douglas matching function: $M(V, U) = V^{1/2}U^{1/2}$. The disutility associated with job search effort is represented by the quadratic function $c(e) = e^2/2$. We saw in chapter 9 that when there is no constraint on the level of compensation, the equilibrium wage is an increasing function of parameter γ representing the bargaining power of workers. We can verify that the equilibrium wage does indeed vary from 0 to 1 when γ itself varies from 0 to 1 for the selected values of the parameters.

Figure 12.5 presents the impact of an increase in the minimum wage. It shows that the reactions of agents in terms of job search effort play an important role in determining labor market equilibrium. When search effort is exogenous, the unemployment rate increases with the minimum wage (to make this clear, the value of job search effort has been set at its equilibrium value of 0.75 when the minimum wages equals 0.5). On the other hand, if search effort is endogenous, the unemployment rate decreases with the minimum wage when the latter is low. In that circumstance, a moderate hike in the minimum wage intensifies search effort, and so favors exits from unemployment. This positive effect overrides the fall in the number of vacant jobs offered by firms because of the increased cost of labor. If, however, the minimum wage is high at the outset, the negative effect on labor demand is the overriding one.

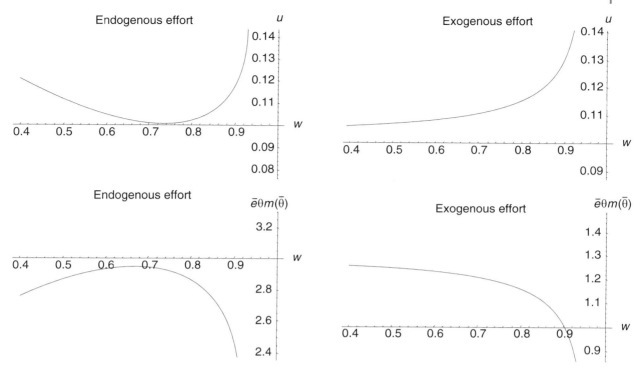

FIGURE 12.5
The effects of the minimum wage in the matching model with endogenous job search effort (graphs on the left) and exogenous job search effort (graphs on the right).

1.2.4 The Quality of Jobs and the Distribution of Incomes

The minimum wage affects not just employment but also the kinds of jobs offered. From this perspective, it may improve the allocation of resources by favoring the creation of more productive jobs. To point out that the minimum wage has positive effects of this kind does not, however, fully justify the use of this measure, since there may be more efficient tools available, like taxation, to improve resource allocation and redistribute income. Still, research focusing on this question arrives at results that are not systematically favorable to exclusive reliance on taxation either.

Improved Job Allocation
The monopsony model and the matching model with endogenous job search effort both reveal the complex effects of the minimum wage. They also reveal the idiosyncrasy of the competitive equilibrium model, with its conclusion that the minimum wage has a systematically negative impact on employment. Models built on different premises confirm this view. Jones (1987) looked at the impact of the minimum wage on a labor market in which "good" jobs requiring the accomplishment of

complex tasks coexist with "bad" jobs, the results of which are perfectly verifiable. The workers with the good jobs, whose effort at work can only be observed imperfectly, receive an efficiency wage, while the ones with the bad jobs are paid at a lower rate, equal to their reservation wage. When a minimum wage lying somewhere between the reservation wage and the efficiency wage is introduced into this model, it reduces the efficiency wage and increases the number of good jobs opened up. In some circumstances, the increase in the number of good jobs even exceeds the decline in the number of bad ones, and that makes for an overall reduction in unemployment.

Substitution effects among different skill levels may also help to bring about a rising relation between the minimum wage and employment when compensations lying above minimum wage are bargained over. From this perspective, Cahuc et al. (2001) consider a model with skilled workers who bargain over their wage collectively, and unskilled workers paid at the minimum wage. The impact of the minimum wage on the employment of the unskilled workers then depends on the elasticity of substitution between the two categories of worker. It results that an increase in the minimum wage can lead to increased global employment, including increased employment among the unskilled, for plausible values of the parameters of the model.

The minimum wage can improve global efficiency in other settings. Drazen (1986) assumes that workers and employers know the productivity of jobs imperfectly before hiring takes place. He also assumes that there is a positive linkage between the productivity of a worker and the compensation that he or she can obtain outside the labor market. In consequence, the payment of high wages makes it possible to attract good workers. If it is not possible for workers to look for a job while simultaneously receiving compensation outside the labor market, then an individual decides to take part in the labor market only if he or she will receive an expected gain that exceeds the compensation available outside the market. Obviously this expected gain increases with the average wage observed in the labor market. In this setting, the equilibrium is suboptimal, for single employers have no market power and therefore no capacity to affect the average wage: each has an individual interest in offering low wages. That being so, the introduction of a minimum wage makes it possible to attract high-productivity workers into the market and improve efficiency.

The effect of the minimum wage on the structure of employment has also been analyzed by Acemoglu (2001) in a matching model with good and bad jobs. The good jobs have higher productivity, and cost more to create, than the bad ones. Wages, which firms and employees bargain over, are therefore higher for the good jobs. Acemoglu shows that decentralized equilibrium systematically leads to too few good jobs, and that introducing a minimum wage slightly higher than the lower limit of the distribution of wages makes it possible to improve welfare, thanks to an increase in the number of good jobs. Cahuc and Michel (1996) obtain the same type of result in a model of endogenous growth in which the introduction of the minimum wage improves welfare by giving individuals an incentive to accumulate human capital, which favors growth.

Is the Minimum Wage an Efficient Way to Redistribute Income?

The fact that the minimum wage can have beneficial effects does not constitute a sufficient reason to justify its utilization, for there may be other, more efficient ways to achieve the desired goals. In particular, it is possible to act on inequality, the structure of employment, and the accumulation of human capital, by fiscal adjustments. In theory, when market equilibrium is inefficient, it is possible to design an "optimal" taxation system that conduces to a socially efficient allocation. In practice, though, information asymmetries limit the possibilities of redistribution. This problem in particular was highlighted by the seminal article of Mirrlees (1971), which examines what could be done through taxation in an environment where workers have different levels of productivity and can work varying volumes of hours. Each individual's income is equal to his or her hourly productivity y multiplied by the number of hours worked, ℓ. The government observes individual incomes but is incapable of distinguishing hours from productivity, so taxes can only depend on income, not on individual hours or productivity. In this setting, taxes exert disincentive effects that the government controls imperfectly, and the minimum wage may play a virtuous part. Guesnerie and Roberts (1987) have shown that the minimum wage could redistribute income efficiently in the presence of linear taxes, in a model where a wage of this type entails underemployment (in the form of reduced hours), but not unemployment. On the other hand, Allen (1987) has shown that the minimum wage becomes an inefficient redistribution tool if it is possible to manipulate marginal rates. Marceau and Boadway (1994) obtain conclusions opposite to Allen's in a model where the minimum wage entails unemployment rather than underemployment. Finally, Boadway and Cuff (2001) show that the combination of unemployment benefits and the minimum wage can be an efficient tool of redistribution, making it possible to improve welfare even in the presence of nonlinear taxes. These debates suggest that the minimum wage is capable of redistributing income efficiently in certain circumstances.

1.3 THE IMPACT OF THE MINIMUM WAGE IN LIGHT OF EMPIRICAL RESEARCH

Three different approaches are used to assess the impact of the minimum wage on employment. In general, empirical research highlights a negative effect on youth employment, and a tendency for exits from employment to rise.

1.3.1 Correlations Between Employment and the Minimum Wage

The large majority of empirical studies adopt a methodology that consists of bringing out possible correlations between variations in employment and the minimum wage, while controlling for the other factors that might affect employment. These studies make use of the temporal evolution of the minimum wage, as well as differences in its level as between industries and/or geographic regions. They generally conclude that the minimum wage has a negligible impact on employment, except perhaps for youth employment. For example, the OECD study (1998, chapter 2) of nine countries (Belgium, Canada, France, Greece, Japan, the Netherlands, Portugal, Spain, and the United

States) for the period 1975–1996 finds that a rise of 10% in the minimum wage entails a fall of between 2% and 4% in employment among *those less than 20 years old*. The impact proves to be just as negative for those 20–24 years old, but lies close to zero. On the other hand, the minimum wage is shown to have no effect on the employment of workers 25 years of age and older. Dolado et al. (1996) come to the same type of conclusion for the European Union countries, suggesting that the minimum wage reduces youth employment but increases total employment, while pointing out that the dimensions of this effect are slight. It is clear, however, that too many variables are left out in this type of approach for the conclusions reached to be sound.

1.3.2   Studies Based on "Natural Experiments"

In chapter 1, section 2.2.2, and chapter 11, section 4, we saw that the method of natural experiments consists of exploiting exogenous changes in the economic environment of certain agents in order to compare their reactions to those of other (a priori identical) agents who have not undergone these changes. In this sense, Card and Krueger (1994, 1995) studied the impact of increases in the minimum wage in New Jersey in 1992 and California in 1988; Pennsylvania, where the minimum wage did not change, constitutes the control group. They use a difference-in-differences estimator, and find that after the minimum wage was raised from $4.25 to $5.05, the level of employment in fast-food establishments in New Jersey rose faster than it did in Pennsylvania. In California, their data do not allow them to isolate significant effects. They conclude that an increase in the minimum wage can lead to an increase in employment when this wage was low to start with, as it was in New Jersey.

A debate arose in the wake of the study of Card and Krueger (1995). Kennan (1995) and Dolado et al. (1996) have emphasized that the interpretation of the results demands caution, inasmuch as consumers of fast food are not necessarily representative of the population as a whole. It is in fact probable that persons earning minimum wage patronize fast-food restaurants more frequently than those earning higher wages, and so, on the assumption that hamburgers, cheeseburgers, and carbonated soft drinks are normal goods, a higher minimum wage will increase the purchasing power of those who regularly consume them—and this in turn will entail a rise in production and employment in fast-food places, despite the increase in the cost of labor. Neumark and Wascher (2000) critique the data of Card and Krueger (1994), which comes from telephone interviews. Neumark and Wascher carry out the same exercise as Card and Krueger, but utilize administrative payroll records for the same fast-food restaurants in the same states. Contrary to Card and Krueger, they find that the minimum wage reduced employment in New Jersey. Nonetheless, Card and Krueger (2000), this time using a larger sample of administrative payroll records than that of Neumark and Wascher, obtain results that confirm their earlier work.

1.3.3   Following up Individual Histories

Individual longitudinal data make it possible to follow the labor market histories of persons whose wages are at or close to minimum wage with greater precision, and have the advantage of assessing the impact of changes to the minimum wage on the populations actually affected by this level of compensation. Recent studies exploiting this type of data find that changes to the minimum wage have a significant effect on employment among this class.

The Impact of the Minimum Wage on the Transition Probabilities into and out of Employment

Studies grounded in individual longitudinal data have made it possible to assess the effects of minimum wage with greater precision. The comparative study of Abowd et al. (1999) of France and the United States is an illustration of this. It exploits the fact that during the 1980s, the minimum wage advanced in real terms in France, while it receded in the United States. For France, the authors analyze the histories of individuals whose current wage lay *below* the minimum wage in the interval between one increase in the minimum wage and the next. They show that such persons had a higher probability of losing their jobs than those whose wage was not overtaken by the minimum wage. For example, young people 21–25 years old whose wage was marginally higher than the latest value of the minimum wage (i.e., lying between minimum wage and 1.15 times minimum wage) had a probability of losing their jobs equal to 10%, whereas this probability rose to 16% for young people whose wage lay between the previous value of the minimum wage and the latest one. For the United States, this study looked at the outcomes of persons whose wage became *higher* than the minimum wage, as the latter gradually declined. They show that these individuals had a higher probability of keeping their jobs. To sum up, this study suggests that in France, an increase of 1% in the minimum wage reduces the probability, among men receiving minimum wage, of keeping their jobs by 1.3%, while for women the figure is 1%. In the United States a reduction of 1% in the minimum wage increases the probability that workers paid at this level will keep their jobs by 0.4% for men and 1.6% for women.

The study of the French case by Kramarz and Philippon (2001) supplies further interesting results. It uses the same methodology but takes the *cost* of labor as the pertinent variable in trying to assess the impact of the minimum wage on employment. It estimates that an increase of 1% in the cost of jobs compensated at minimum wage entails a rise of 3% in the probability of job loss for workers who are being paid minimum wage.

Portugal and Cardoso (2001) find different results using the same type of methodology. They exploit changes made in 1987 to Portuguese legislation regarding the minimum wage of young people 19 and under. The minimum wage was raised by 50% for youths of 17, and 33% for youths of 18 and 19. Portugal and Cardoso find that these minimum wage hikes had a depressant effect on the hiring of this category of workers. But they also highlight a "supply effect," which was that after the reform of 1987, young people 19 and under had a greater tendency to keep their jobs. Portugal and Cardoso observed fewer separations, which ran counter to the fall in hires. This result, coherent with the prediction of the monopsony model, probably reveals a greater attachment of youth to their jobs when wages improve.

Overall, this research shows that the minimum wage can have significant effects on the probabilities of being hired and of losing a job. However, it does not invariably exert a positive effect on the probability of job loss among the populations whose livelihoods are directly dependent on this level of compensation.

The Impact of the Minimum Wage on the Nonemployment of Women in France
Every year the French statistical agency (INSEE) carries out a survey of 70,000 households (called the Enquête Emploi) which reveals the labor market situation of all the individuals sampled, as well as their compensation. Laroque and Salanié (1999) use the survey carried out in March 1997 to estimate an equation giving the wage of a woman living with a partner as a function of her personal characteristics (education, experience, etc.). Their model also includes a participation equation based on comparison of the potential income of a household when the woman works and when she does not.

The wage equation makes it possible to construct the distribution of income that would have resulted in the absence of the minimum wage. Laroque and Salanié use this potential wage distribution and the participation equation to decompose nonemployment in France into three categories. *Voluntary nonemployment* represents persons who do not want to take a job; *classical nonemployment* includes all the individuals who would like to work but who would only be able to find work at a wage below the minimum wage; and *other nonemployment* embraces all those wanting to work, and who have skills that would earn them a compensation superior to minimum wage, but who fail to find a job (a combination, so to speak, of those suffering from Keynesian and frictional unemployment). Table 12.3 illustrates this distribution for the subpopulation of women living with a partner. It shows that classical

Table 12.3

Breakdown of nonemployment among women living with a partner, France, 1997.

Category	Voluntary	Classical	Other
All	42.8	8.6	5.8
Graduate	17.6	0.4	29.9
Undergraduate	26.2	2.0	12.1
High school	35.4	5.4	5.4
Basic technical training	42.3	8.2	2.3
Junior high school	45.6	8.0	3.0
No diploma	54.3	13.7	3.8

Source: Laroque and Salanié (1999, table 5).

Note: 13.7% of nonemployment among women living with a partner and with no educational qualification is of the classic type.

nonemployment rises as the educational level falls; the same thing holds for voluntary nonemployment. The minimum wage has a particularly strong incidence in the case of women with no diploma who are living with a partner, where it is assigned responsibility for almost 14% of total nonemployment in this category of the population (8.6% for the entire sample, and only 0.4% for college graduates). It is instructive to note in passing that more than 40% of the subpopulation in question are voluntarily nonemployed. What is more, simulations carried out by Laroque and Salanié quantify the rise in employment that would follow the complete abolition of the minimum wage at 8.4% of the total employment of women living with a partner. These results, obtained in a competitive equilibrium model in which workers are compensated at the level of their productivity, suggest that the minimum wage may have a significant impact on employment in certain categories of the population.

1.3.4   The Minimum Wage and Inequality

A rise in the minimum wage has opposite effects on income inequality; the latter is generally measured by the standard deviation of the logarithm of incomes, or by the ratios between the average values of different deciles of the overall income distribution. On the one hand, the minimum wage allows some people to receive a higher wage, and this favors the reduction of inequality. But on the other, it can also destroy jobs, which leads to reduced incomes for those who would have been able to find a job in the absence of the minimum wage.

Empirical research generally concludes that the minimum wage makes it possible to reduce wage inequality (Brown, 1999). The contributions of DiNardo et al. (1996) and Lee (1999) suggest that the fall in the real value of the minimum wage contributed strongly to increasing wage inequality in the United States in the 1980s. DiNardo et al. (1996) look at the evolution of the distribution of men's and women's wages between 1979 and 1988, finding that the fall in the minimum wage explains one-quarter of the rise in the standard deviation of the distribution of men's wages and 30% of that for women. Lee (1999), for his part, estimates that the shrinking minimum wage over this period explains 70% of the increase in the ratio of average fifth-decile wages to average first-decile wages. So, changes in the minimum wage have had a significant impact on wage inequality in the United States.

In theory, increases in minimum wage have an ambiguous impact on the poverty rate, which is measured by the proportion of individuals whose *income* is less than a threshold value; this value is defined in absolute terms in most U.S. studies and in relative terms, generally half the median income, in most European studies. Moving from the distribution of wages to the distribution of income of households is complicated because some families have several wage-earners and others have few or no labor earnings. A poor individual employed at minimum wage sees his or her income rise if his or her job is not destroyed, and this will tend to bring the poverty rate down if this individual belongs to a family with few or no labor earnings. But if the increase in minimum wage destroys jobs, some individuals will see their incomes diminish, and this will tend to push the poverty rate up, especially if these individuals belong to households with few labor earnings (see Brown, 1999). The study of Addison and Blackburn (1999) suggests that the rises in minimum wage that occurred in the United States in the 1990s contributed to reducing the poverty rate among youth 24 and under, and among those over 24 who left school early.

Empirical research generally tries to describe the distribution of instantaneous wages and incomes (Flinn, 2002, 2003, is an exception, as we noticed in chapter 10, section 2.6.4). This static approach gives a very limited idea of the impact of the minimum wage on incomes. In fact, the minimum wage affects transitions between employment and unemployment. As we saw in chapter 10, section 2.4, a reduction in the dispersion of *instantaneous* incomes goes along with an increase in the dispersion of *discounted* lifetime incomes, when increases in the minimum wage lead to longer spells of unemployment. Such phenomena are as yet very poorly understood empirically.

2   EMPLOYMENT PROTECTION

Employment protection legislation is a set of mandatory restrictions governing the dismissals of employees. Their stated purpose is to increase the volume and stability of employment. Despite that, there is intense debate about their actual effects. Firing costs do indeed reduce job destruction, but they also exert a negative effect on job creation, so the effect on employment is ambiguous. Furthermore, firing costs may increase the stability of the jobs directly shielded by these costs, but they can also heighten the instability of the unshielded ones, such as temporary work, for example. Much theoretical and empirical endeavor has been expended on examining the effects of employment protection measures in a dynamic setting. These analyses do indeed suggest that employment protection has large-scale effects on workers and job flows, but whether these effects push unemployment up or down remains ambiguous. It depends especially on the wage-setting process. In addition, the mandatory rules that apply when a hiring or a firing takes place turn out to vary widely from one country to another. This variety makes it possible to obtain valuable information by comparing the record of different countries. Empirical studies that do so tend to confirm the conclusions resulting from theoretical analysis.

2.1   WHAT IS EMPLOYMENT PROTECTION?

Measures to protect employment comprise a set of instruments such as severance payments, administrative firing taxes, advance notice of dismissal, administrative authorization, and prior negotiation with trade unions. The way contracts of variable length are phrased (for example, in many European countries, the move from a temporary job to an open-ended job situation subject to protection measures) is also covered by employment protection. What follows is a list of the principal rules utilized to protect jobs (OECD, 1994, part 2, chapter 6, and OECD, 1999, chapter 2):

- The obligation to notify the employee concerned in advance that he or she is to be fired, or to notify him or her in writing of the reasons for the dismissal, and the obligation to inform a third party (union, public employment service, etc.) as well.

- The obligation to obtain authorization from a third party in order to carry out the firing, or the obligation to try to find another position for that employee before firing him or her.

- The obligation either to give the employee several months' notice, or else give him or her a severance payment (except when the employee is at fault).

- Appeal procedures for wrongful dismissal, which may lead to the payment of damages and interest or to reinstatement of the fired worker if he or she was indeed wrongly dismissed.

- Obligations incurred by the employer vis-à-vis personnel supplied by subcontractors or temporary help agencies.

Employment protection gives rise to costs of two kinds: severance payments, which are transfers from the employer to the employee, and administrative costs to the firm with no transfer to the employee. It is worth noting that some rules include both kinds of costs. For instance, the advance notice of dismissal and the obligation to try to find another position are both administrative costs and transfers to the employee. Nevertheless, we will see below that it is useful to distinguish these two kinds of costs, for they affect labor market equilibrium differently.

Many studies have tried to establish indicators of the ''strictness'' of employment protection by weighting (with greater or less justification) and combining the regulatory measures just listed (see, for example, Bertola, 1990, and Grubb and Wells, 1993). The OECD has constructed a synthetic index based on all these studies, and it is the one most often used in international comparisons. The second column of table 12.4 ranks 21 OECD countries by this index for the end of the 1990s, in order of increasing strictness. By way of illustration, the next two columns give information about two of the criteria that enter into the calculation of this index: severance payments, and the length of advance notice.

According to the OECD index, the United States, Canada, and the United Kingdom appear more ''flexible'' than France, Germany, and the countries of southern Europe, such as Italy, Spain, and Portugal. It is also worth noting that the Scandinavian countries are not the most ''rigid'' ones. Sweden and France, for example, resemble one another in their strictness, whereas the Netherlands, Finland, and Denmark are among the countries where employment protection is noticeably less stringent than in many other parts of the world.

The impact of employment protection on unemployment and labor mobility has attracted a great deal of research. Models of labor market equilibrium generally show that firing costs have an ambiguous impact on unemployment and reduce manpower

Table 12.4

The strictness (ranked in ascending order) of employment protection at the end of the 1990s.

Country	Rank	Severance payments*	Length of advance notice[†]
United States	1	0	0
United Kingdom	2	2.4	2.8
New Zealand	3	5.0	0.5
Canada	4	1.3	0.5
Ireland	5	1.5	2.0
Australia	6	2.2	1.2
Switzerland	7	2.0	3.0
Denmark	8	1.5	4.3
Finland	9	0	6.0
Netherlands	10	0	3.0
Japan	11	4.0	1.0
Austria	12	9.0	2.5
Belgium	13	0	9.0
Sweden	14	0	6.0
Norway	15	0	5.0
Germany	16	0	7.0
France	17	2.7	2.0
Spain	18	12.0	1.0
Italy	19	18.0	2.2
Greece	20	5.8	8.0
Portugal	21	20.0	2.0

Source: OECD (1999, table 2.2, pp. 57–58).

*Expressed in monthly wage after 20 years of seniority.

[†] Expressed in months, after 20 years of seniority.

mobility, since they reduce both job creation and job destruction (see Millard and Mortensen, 1997; Garibaldi, 1998; and Mortensen and Pissarides, 1999). Models of partial equilibrium representing the behavior of firms when confronted with the costs of adjusting their workforce come to analogous conclusions (see Bentolila and Bertola, 1990; Bertola, 1990, 1999; and chapter 4 of this book). The results of calibration exercises often confirm that the impact of firing costs on unemployment is weak with an ambiguous sign, and that their impact on job creation and destruction, and on manpower mobility, is significant and negative.

We will now proceed to analyze the consequences of employment protection, starting with a consideration of the simplest case, that in which wages are exogenous.

Analysis of the consequences of employment protection when wages are endogenous will follow.

2.2 The Effects of Employment Protection When Wages Are Exogenous

The effects of employment protection are easy to analyze using a matching model close to the one presented in chapter 9. In the versions of this model which we have used to this point, the exit rate from employment q was most often considered as an exogenous parameter—a hypothesis clearly ill-suited to studying the effects of employment protection, which are intended to make the destruction of jobs, and the firing of employees, less frequent. It is necessary, therefore, to make decisions to destroy jobs endogenous. We can achieve that by adopting a model analogous to the one of Mortensen and Pissarides (1994, 1999), and within that framework we will start by assuming that wages are exogenous. This hypothesis makes it possible to present decisions to destroy jobs, and the impact of employment protection on unemployment and labor market flows, in a very simple fashion. Moreover, it clearly illustrates how the labor market functions in the presence of a minimum wage.

2.2.1 The Matching Model with Endogenous Job Destruction

In what follows, the firing of an employee occurs following a negative productivity shock of such magnitude that it costs the firm more to keep him or her on than it does to fire him or her. The basic matching model as formalized in chapter 9 will have to be altered somewhat in order to represent this scenario.

The Threshold of Job Destruction

We will assume that the production of an individual, which has hitherto been a constant parameter denoted by y, is now a random variable ε with support[2] $]-\infty, \varepsilon_u]$. The cumulative distribution function of this random variable is designated by $G(\cdot)$. Another important element of the analysis is the *degree of persistence* of shocks, i.e., the length of the period during which individual productivity keeps the same value. In order to grasp this notion, we assume that this productivity varies according to a Poisson process with parameter λ. Let us recall that this means that productivity changes with a probability $\lambda \, dt$ over every small interval of time dt. When a shock supervenes, the new value of productivity is found by a random draw from the distribution $G(.)$. Finally, individual productivities are independent of one another. Shocks are thus *idiosyncratic*: they affect every job independently.[3]

The strictness of employment protection is identified by a single parameter, denoted by f, which represents all the costs to the firm of firing an employee: the severance payments made to the fired employee, and the administrative costs listed above. It is thus a global measure of the rigor of employment protection, analogous to the synthetic OECD index by which countries are ranked in table 12.4. Severance payments and administrative costs actually have exactly the same impact on employment when wages are exogenous. But as we will see, the case is different when wages are bargained over.

Let w be the wage. When current productivity takes the value ε, the expected profit $\Pi_e(\varepsilon)$ from a filled job at stationary equilibrium is written:

$$r\Pi_e(\varepsilon) = \varepsilon - w + \lambda[\Pi_\lambda - \Pi_e(\varepsilon)] \tag{7}$$

In this equality Π_λ designates the expected profit when a productivity change occurs; we will give its exact expression below. Equation (7) is interpreted the same way as all the equations defining expected profits and utilities encountered thus far. For a given level ε of current productivity, the instantaneous profit is equal to $(\varepsilon - w)$, and the term $\lambda[\Pi_\lambda - \Pi_e(\varepsilon)]$ corresponds to the average gain linked to a possible change of state of the job. The only change of state envisaged here is a change in the level of individual productivity. This event comes about with probability $\lambda\, dt$ over every small interval of time dt.

When the employer fires a worker, he or she incurs fixed costs amounting to f, and is left with a vacant job offering an expected profit equal to Π_V. In total, the expected profit following from the separation of an employee amounts to $-f + \Pi_V$. In consequence, the employer fires the employee when the discounted profit $\Pi_e(\varepsilon)$ from a filled job falls below the gain he or she gets by firing. This situation comes about when the inequality $\Pi_e(\varepsilon) < -f + \Pi_V$ is satisfied. Now, relation (7) shows that profit $\Pi_e(\varepsilon)$ increases with individual productivity ε. In these conditions, the employer will fire the employee if $\varepsilon \leq \varepsilon_d$, where the *reservation productivity* ε_d is defined by the equality $\Pi_e(\varepsilon_d) = -f + \Pi_V$. Using equation (7), we immediately find that when the free entry condition $\Pi_V = 0$ is satisfied, the reservation productivity is given by:

$$\varepsilon_d = w - (r + \lambda)f - \lambda\Pi_\lambda \tag{8}$$

The Job Destruction Rate

In relation (8), Π_λ is endogenous. This variable must be known in order to describe labor market equilibrium completely. For that purpose, it will be helpful to note at the outset that the definition (7) of expected profit from a filled job entails $(r + \lambda)[\Pi_e(\varepsilon) - \Pi_e(\varepsilon_d)] = \varepsilon - \varepsilon_d$. Now, when the free entry condition $\Pi_V = 0$ is satisfied, we have $\Pi_e(\varepsilon_d) = -f$, and the expression of the expected profit from a filled job takes the following form:

$$\Pi_e(\varepsilon) = \frac{\varepsilon - \varepsilon_d}{r + \lambda} - f \tag{9}$$

When a shock alters productivity, two eventualities may ensue: if the new value of productivity is below the threshold ε_d, the employee is fired and the employer assumes the costs f arising from this firing; conversely, if productivity takes a new value ε above the threshold ε_d, the employer keeps the worker on, and his or her expected profit amounts to $\Pi_e(\varepsilon)$. Using relation (9), the average profit Π_λ in the wake of a productivity shock is written thus:

$$\Pi_\lambda = \int_{-\infty}^{\varepsilon_d} -f \, dG(\varepsilon) + \int_{\varepsilon_d}^{\varepsilon_u} \Pi_e(\varepsilon) \, dG(\varepsilon) = -f + \frac{1}{r+\lambda} \int_{\varepsilon_d}^{\varepsilon_u} (\varepsilon - \varepsilon_d) \, dG(\varepsilon) \tag{10}$$

If we bring this expression of Π_λ into definition (8) of the threshold value ε_d, it becomes:

$$\varepsilon_d = w - rf - \frac{\lambda}{r+\lambda} \int_{\varepsilon_d}^{\varepsilon_u} (\varepsilon - \varepsilon_d) \, dG(\varepsilon) \tag{11}$$

This equation defines ε_d as a function of the parameters of the model. It shows that the reservation productivity ε_d is *inferior* to the wage w. In other words, for values of productivity lying close to the destruction threshold ε_d, the employer may suffer a loss in the current period. If he or she does not fire the employee when $\varepsilon < w$, it is because, for one thing, he or she must immediately pay costs f, and for another, he or she expects to be able, in the future, to make up for this loss through positive profits deriving from higher productivity. This possibility of future gain is represented by the term $\lambda\Pi_\lambda$ in equation (8), the equivalent of an "option value" of a filled job. The inequality $\varepsilon_d < w$ portrays a phenomenon of *labor hoarding*: the costs of firing give the firm an incentive to keep its workers in downturns because it anticipates future profits when the cycle turns back up.

The job destruction rate, which we will again denote by q, is easy to find if the value of the reservation productivity ε_d is known. For a job to be destroyed, the value of current productivity has to change—which happens at rate λ—and the new value of productivity has to lie below ε_d—which comes about with probability $G(\varepsilon_d)$. Hence, at every date, a filled job is destroyed at rate $\lambda G(\varepsilon_d)$. Therefore, if there is a large number of firms, the job destruction rate amounts to $q = \lambda G(\varepsilon_d)$. Differentiating equation (11) defining ε_d with respect to f and λ, we easily arrive at:

$$\frac{\partial \varepsilon_d}{\partial f} < 0, \quad \frac{\partial q}{\partial f} < 0 \quad \text{and} \quad \frac{\partial \varepsilon_d}{\partial \lambda} < 0$$

Hence an increase in firing costs lowers the reservation productivity ε_d and consequently lowers the rate of job destruction. This result is highly intuitive and corresponds to the stated goal of firing costs, which is precisely to increase the rate of labor hoarding when unfavorable shocks occur. We see as well that a reduction in the degree of persistence of shocks (i.e., an increase in λ) will also tend to increase labor hoarding, so the effect on the job destruction rate is ambiguous.

2.2.2 The Impact of Firing Costs on Labor Market Equilibrium

To complete our description of the equilibrium that comes about in the labor market, we still have to specify the value of the labor market tightness θ that occurs in the expression $\theta m(\theta)$ of the exit rate from unemployment. To accomplish that, we will assume that the life span of a filled job always starts at the maximal value ε_u of productivity. This hypothesis is not at all essential in this context. It is made for the sake of simplicity, and it is justified when we introduce productivity growth (see chapter

10). It serves to convey the idea that newly created jobs most often have the benefit of the latest technological innovations and thus are the most productive. If h designates, as it did above, the costs arising from the search for an employee, then the value of a vacant job is written:

$$r\Pi_v = -h + m(\theta)[\Pi_e(\varepsilon_u) - \Pi_v]$$

When the free entry condition $\Pi_v = 0$ is satisfied, this last relation entails $\Pi_e(\varepsilon_u) = h/m(\theta)$. We are back at the result that, at free entry equilibrium, the average cost $h/m(\theta)$ of a vacant job is equal to the expected profit $\Pi_e(\varepsilon_u)$ of a job that has just been filled. Making $\varepsilon = \varepsilon_u$ in (9) we get the expression of $\Pi_e(\varepsilon_u)$ as a function of ε_d, and if we make this expression equal to the average cost of a vacant job, we arrive at:

$$\frac{h}{m(\theta)} = \frac{\varepsilon_u - \varepsilon_d - (r + \lambda)f}{r + \lambda} \tag{12}$$

Knowing ε_d given by (11), this equation completely defines the labor market tightness θ. It is analogous to the "labor demand" equations that we obtained from different versions of the matching model when we assumed that the job destruction rate was an exogenous parameter. With the help of relation (11) giving the equilibrium value of the threshold ε_d, it is easy to verify that the expected profit $\Pi_e(\varepsilon_u)$ from a new job—which corresponds to the right-hand side of equality (12)—is reduced when firing costs increase. Firms then open up fewer vacant jobs (or, if one prefers, the period $1/m(\theta)$ during which a job remains vacant diminishes), and the labor market tightness θ and the exit rate from unemployment $\theta m(\theta)$ fall off. In sum, after several calculations we arrive at the following results:

$$\frac{\partial \theta}{\partial \lambda} < 0, \qquad \frac{\partial \theta}{\partial f} < 0 \qquad \text{and} \qquad \frac{\partial \theta m(\theta)}{\partial \lambda} < 0, \qquad \frac{\partial \theta m(\theta)}{\partial f} < 0$$

Given that the job destruction rate q is here equal to $\lambda G(\varepsilon_d)$, relation (16) from chapter 9 giving the expression of the stationary unemployment rate u is now written:

$$u = \frac{q + n}{\theta m(\theta) + q + n} = \frac{\lambda G(\varepsilon_d) + n}{\theta m(\theta) + \lambda G(\varepsilon_d) + n} \tag{13}$$

Firing costs f thus have an *ambiguous* impact on the unemployment rate, since they combine two effects that work against one another. First, they favor labor hoarding and so reduce the job destruction rate, but at the same time they reduce job creation (the exit rate from unemployment falls) because higher firing costs have the effect of degrading the profit outlook of every new hire. From the standpoint of labor market equilibrium, these results confirm the ones already reached in chapter 4, where adjustment costs were introduced into models of labor demand. It is interesting to note that the degree to which shocks persist conditions the impact of firing costs on job destruction and so on unemployment (see Cabrales and Hopenhayn, 1998). By way of example, let us imagine that after a shock, productivity falls irreversibly to zero. In that circumstance, the job destruction rate is necessarily equal to λ, so it is independent of firing costs. The result is that firing costs have the effect of decreasing labor market tightness without altering the job destruction rate, which entails a positive impact on unemployment.

All these results were obtained on the assumption that the wage was exogenous. But it is intuitive that wages are influenced by the rules in place regarding employment protection, and will thus in turn affect labor market equilibrium. These sequences of cause and effect we will now proceed to examine.

2.3 EMPLOYMENT PROTECTION AND WAGE BARGAINING

The model just developed well illustrates the functioning of a labor market in the presence of a compulsory minimum wage. But if wages are open to bargaining, firing costs affect the level of compensation, and so, indirectly, employment. Thus, when wages are bargained over, it is easy to show that severance payments (i.e., transfers from employer to employee) have no impact on the exit rate from unemployment and the job destruction rate, for they simply make themselves felt in the form of a reduction in wages. Likewise, it will be evident that a portion of the administrative costs are in fact borne by the workers at the time of hiring, which has the effect of limiting their impact on job creation. In order to take these possibilities into account, we shall explicitly distinguish two components of firing costs by setting $f = f_a + f_e$. Parameter f_a designates the costs arising from various administrative hurdles (advance notice, prior obligations, possible legal proceedings, etc.), whereas parameter f_e represents an effective transfer from the firm to the employee. The two parameters f_a and f_e are here always taken to be exogenous (in the framework of the matching model, Pissarides, 2001, endogenizes severance payments f_e by assuming that employees are risk-averse and so wish to be insured against fluctuations in their future income). We will see that calibration exercises carried out on the model confirm the importance of the reaction of wages to employment protection. They suggest that firing costs may be favorable to employment when wages are flexible, but that they may destroy a significant volume of jobs in the presence of a minimum wage.

2.3.1 Bargaining in the Presence of Firing Costs

We return to the previous model, but now we assume that wages are bargained over at the time of hiring, and every time a shock affects productivity. The existence of firing costs requires that we distinguish between wage bargaining at the start of the job, when these costs are still virtual, no contract having yet been signed, and wage renegotiations, which lead to firing costs if they fail.

The Surplus
We must also distinguish between the expected profit Π_0 from a new job, and the expected profit $\Pi_e(\varepsilon)$ from a filled job with current productivity ε. We thus have:

$$r\Pi_0 = \varepsilon_u - w_0 + \lambda(\Pi_\lambda - \Pi_0) \tag{14}$$

$$r\Pi_e(\varepsilon) = \varepsilon - w(\varepsilon) + \lambda[\Pi_\lambda - \Pi_e(\varepsilon)] \tag{15}$$

In these relations, w_0 and $w(\varepsilon)$ designate respectively the wage negotiated at hiring, and the wage renegotiated when productivity takes the value ε. The term Π_λ is always defined by equation (10). In similar fashion, the expected utility V_0 of a worker who has just been hired, and the expected utility $V_e(\varepsilon)$ of a worker who holds a job with current productivity ε, are defined by the formulas:

$$rV_0 = w_0 + \lambda(V_\lambda - V_0) \tag{16}$$

$$rV_e(\varepsilon) = w(\varepsilon) + \lambda[V_\lambda - V_e(\varepsilon)] \tag{17}$$

The term V_λ designates the expected utility of a worker when his or her job is affected by a productivity shock. With the reservation productivity (which, as we will demonstrate below, is unique) again denoted by ε_d, this expected gain has the expression:

$$V_\lambda = \int_{-\infty}^{\varepsilon_d} (f_e + V_u) \, dG(\varepsilon) + \int_{\varepsilon_d}^{\varepsilon_u} V_e(\varepsilon) \, dG(\varepsilon) \tag{18}$$

where V_u is the expected utility of an unemployed person, defined by:

$$rV_u = z + \theta m(\theta)(V_0 - V_u) \tag{19}$$

These equations allow us to define the surplus S_0 of a new job, and the surplus $S(\varepsilon)$ of a continuing job already hit by a shock with current productivity ε. It comes to:

$$S_0 = \Pi_0 - \Pi_v + V_0 - V_u, \qquad S(\varepsilon) = \Pi_e(\varepsilon) - (\Pi_v - f_a) + V_e(\varepsilon) - V_u \tag{20}$$

These definitions are easily understood. At the time of hiring, breaking off the bargaining entails neither the payment of a severance, nor administrative costs. But during renegotiation, the various costs and transfers take effect if the bargaining fails, and the fallback profit of the firm amounts to $(\Pi_v - f_a - f_e)$, while the fallback utility of the worker takes the value $(V_u + f_e)$ since it is he or she who benefits from transfer f_e. The result is that the severance payments f_e do not come into the definition of the surplus. Moreover, for the same productivity, the surplus of a continuing job is greater than the one released by a new job. Noting that equations (14), (15), (16), and (17) entail $\Pi_0 + V_0 = \Pi_e(\varepsilon_u) + V_e(\varepsilon_u)$, the definitions (20) of the surpluses entail:

$$S_0 = S(\varepsilon_u) - f_a \tag{21}$$

The Impact of Firing Costs on Wages

As in the basic model of chapter 9, we assume that bargaining leads to a surplus-sharing rule dependent on the bargaining power of each of the agents. Let γ again be the relative power of a worker. For a new job this rule is written:

$$V_0 - V_u = \gamma S_0, \qquad \Pi_0 - \Pi_v = (1 - \gamma)S_0 \tag{22}$$

On the other hand, since renegotiation gives rise to a severance payment in case of disagreement, the surplus-sharing rule determining the renegotiated wage takes the form:

$$V_e(\varepsilon) - (V_u + f_e) = \gamma S(\varepsilon), \qquad \Pi_e(\varepsilon) - (\Pi_v - f) = (1 - \gamma)S(\varepsilon) \tag{23}$$

Assuming that the free entry condition $\Pi_v = 0$ is satisfied, this rule entails that jobs are destroyed when the value of the surplus $S(\varepsilon)$ becomes negative. We see that the employer and the worker have an interest in separating for the *same* values of productivity, since equations (20) and (23) entail:

$$S(\varepsilon) < 0 \Leftrightarrow \Pi_e(\varepsilon) < -f \Leftrightarrow V_e(\varepsilon) < V_u + f_e$$

In other words, jobs are destroyed by common consent when they release a negative surplus. This result comes from the fact that the firm and the worker are capable of finding a mutually advantageous contract, one preferable to separation, if and only if the surplus obtained by keeping the job going is positive. It can be shown that there exists a unique threshold value of productivity, beneath which jobs are destroyed. Using relations (15), (17), and (20), the surplus $S(\varepsilon)$ is written as follows:

$$S(\varepsilon) = \frac{\varepsilon + \lambda(V_\lambda + \Pi_\lambda)}{(r + \lambda)} - (V_u - f)$$

As V_λ and Π_λ are independent of current productivity ε, this expression of the surplus entails $S'(\varepsilon) = 1/(r + \lambda) > 0$. The surplus is thus an increasing function of productivity. Consequently there exists a single value of ε, denoted by ε_d, such that $S(\varepsilon_d) = 0$ and below which jobs are destroyed. Using relations (10) and (18) defining Π_λ and V_λ, we arrive at:

$$(r + \lambda)S(\varepsilon) = \varepsilon - rV_u + rf_a + \lambda \int_{\varepsilon_d}^{\varepsilon_u} S(x)\, dG(x) \tag{24}$$

With sharing rule (23), definition (15) of profit, and equation (10), this definition of the surplus allows us to write the renegotiated wage in the following manner:

$$w(\varepsilon) = rV_u + \gamma(\varepsilon - rV_u) + r(f_e + \gamma f_a) \tag{25}$$

And the wage negotiated at hiring, obtained from (14), (21), (22), and (24), takes the form:

$$w_0 = rV_u + \gamma(\varepsilon_u - rV_u) - \lambda(f_e + \gamma f_a) \tag{26}$$

These expressions of the hiring wage and the renegotiated wage well illustrate the effects of firing costs at the partial equilibrium of a decentralized negotiation (i.e., for given V_u). The hiring wage diminishes with firing costs, since firms anticipate that they will have to endure them in the future. The renegotiated wage, however, rises with firing costs, since the latter enhance the gains of workers if they do separate from their employer.

Labor Market Equilibrium

The equilibrium values of the reservation productivity ε_d and of the labor market tightness θ are found, as they were when the wage was exogenous, using a job creation equation and a job destruction equation. The expected profit Π_v from a vacant job satisfies:

$$r\Pi_v = -h + m(\theta)(\Pi_0 - \Pi_v)$$

When the free entry condition $\Pi_v = 0$ is satisfied, we find the usual equality between the expected profit Π_0 of a job newly filled and the average cost $h/m(\theta)$ of a vacant job. The sharing rule (22) thus entails $(1 - \gamma)S_0 = h/m(\theta)$. On the other hand, the definition (24) of the surplus allows us to write the latter as a function of the threshold ε_d in the form $S(\varepsilon) = (\varepsilon - \varepsilon_d)/(r + \lambda)$. Utilizing (21), it comes to:

$$\frac{h}{m(\theta)} = (1 - \gamma)\left[\frac{\varepsilon_u - \varepsilon_d}{r + \lambda} - f_a\right] \tag{27}$$

This job creation equation defines a decreasing relation between labor market tightness and the reservation productivity. We can account for this result by noting that the average life span of a job, i.e., $1/\lambda G(\varepsilon_d)$, decreases with the reservation productivity ε_d. Consequently, when the reservation productivity rises, expected profit falls, and firms open up fewer vacant jobs.

Since $\Pi_0 = h/m(\theta)$, the job destruction equation is found by first noting that the expected utility (19) of an unemployed person is written, using sharing rule (22):

$$rV_u = z + \theta m(\theta)\gamma S_0 = z + \frac{\gamma h\theta}{1 - \gamma} \tag{28}$$

If we substitute this value of rV_u in (24), the job destruction condition, $S(\varepsilon_d) = 0$, finally yields:

$$\varepsilon_d = z + \frac{\theta\gamma h}{1 - \gamma} - rf_a - \frac{\lambda}{r + \lambda}\int_{\varepsilon_d}^{\varepsilon_u}(\varepsilon - \varepsilon_d)\,dG(\varepsilon) \tag{29}$$

The job destruction equation defines an increasing relation between labor market tightness and the reservation productivity, for high tightness corresponds to a strong exit rate from unemployment, and thus to high expected gains on the part of unemployed persons. Since the surplus diminishes with the expected utility of unemployed persons, a high value of labor market tightness signifies a small surplus, and that entails a high job destruction rate.

The equilibrium values of labor market tightness θ and the reservation productivity ε_d are defined by the system of equations (27) and (29). These values are independent of the severance payment f_e, which thus has the sole effect of altering the wage profile. Administrative costs, on the other hand, act simultaneously on the equations of job creation and job destruction. The impact of an increase in administrative costs is represented in figure 12.6. The curve of job creation shifts downward, because an increase in these costs exerts downward pressure on job creation, and that has the effect of lowering the reservation productivity and labor market tightness. The job destruction curve shifts to the left, because fewer jobs are destroyed when hiring costs are greater. Equilibrium thus moves from point A to point B. The threshold ε_d, and so the job destruction rate $\lambda G(\varepsilon_d)$, both decrease. The effect on the labor market tightness is a priori ambiguous. It is possible to show, using equations (27) and (29), however, that labor market tightness falls with firing costs. The effect on the unemployment rate is thus indeterminate, since the new equilibrium is characterized by a lower exit rate from unemployment $\theta m(\theta)$ and a lower job destruction rate $\lambda G(\varepsilon_d)$.

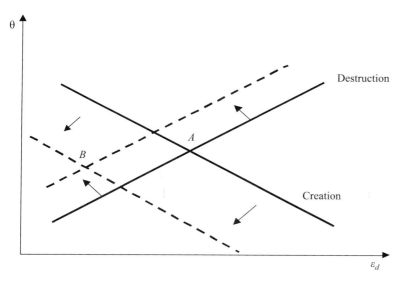

FIGURE 12.6
The impact of an increase in administrative firing costs.

2.3.2   The Importance of Wage Setting

Whether the wage is exogenous or negotiated, strengthened employment protection reduces manpower flows and has an ambiguous impact on unemployment. Negotiated wages, however, react to this strengthening. At equilibrium the hiring wage in particular falls. This result is established by substituting the expression (28) of rV_u in (26), which yields:

$$w_0 = (1 - \gamma)z + \gamma(\theta h + \varepsilon_u - \lambda f_a) - \lambda f_e \tag{30}$$

Since firing costs have a negative impact on labor market tightness θ, relation (30) shows that they also exert a downward pressure on hiring wages. The decline in the hiring wage thus makes it possible to lessen the negative effects of firing costs on profits, and thus on job creation. And on the contrary, a mandatory minimum wage, by preventing wages from declining, must amplify the impact of firing costs on job creation. The calibration exercises that follow confirm these intuitions.

Flexible Wages

As regards the common parameters, the models in this section have been calibrated by taking values identical to those selected in chapter 9, section 3, in our study of the model with exogenous job destruction (see table 12.5). The matching function likewise has the expression $M(v, u) = v^{1/2}u^{1/2}$. For the new parameters, we have assumed that the cumulative distribution function $G(\cdot)$ is uniform over the interval $[0, 1]$ and that the productivity shocks follow a Poisson process with parameter λ equal to 0.15 (for calibrations of the matching model using functional forms and similar numerical

Table 12.5

Parameters value of the model with endogenous job destruction.

γ	h	λ	r	n
0.5	0.3	0.15	0.05	0.01

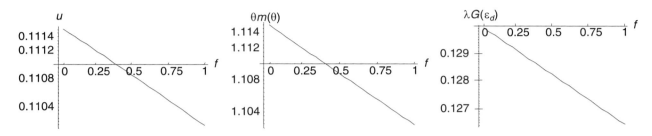

FIGURE 12.7

The impact of firing costs on the unemployment rate u, the exit rate from unemployment $\theta m(\theta)$, and the job destruction rate $\lambda G(\varepsilon_d)$ with negotiated wages and $z = 0.5$. f is expressed as a fraction of average quarterly production.

values, see Millard and Mortensen, 1997, and Mortensen and Pissarides, 1999). These values give plausible rates of job destruction lying between 10% and 15% per annum.

Figure 12.7 presents the impact of an increase in the administrative firing costs on the unemployment rate u, the exit rate from unemployment $\theta m(\theta)$ and the job destruction rate $\lambda G(\varepsilon_d)$, when wages are negotiated. We see that employment protection has little influence on the unemployment rate. An increase in firing costs by an amount equal to the average quarterly production of a worker provokes a fall in the unemployment rate of around 0.1% when wages are negotiated. It should also be noted that the exit rate from unemployment and the job destruction rate do not show much sensitivity either to this rise in the administrative firing costs. It is important to emphasize that the negative relationship between the firing costs and the unemployment rate is not robust to changes in the values of the parameters. The degree to which shocks persist does play an important part in this domain. Figure 12.8 shows, on the other hand, that firing costs exert a positive effect on unemployment if the gains of unemployed persons are relatively high (the average wage is respectively equal to 0.955 and 0.932 when the gains of unemployed persons diminish from 0.75 to 0.5). The extent of this effect is always very slight, however.

Other studies analyze the effects of firing costs by resorting to calibrated versions of matching models close to that of Mortensen and Pissarides (1994) on the constant assumption that wages are flexible. Thus Mortensen and Pissarides (1999) find that the rise in firing costs reduces both labor market flows and the unemployment rate. Garibaldi (1998) arrives at an analogous result when the values taken by firing costs are not too high. On Spanish data, Cabrales and Hopenhayn (1997) estimate that higher

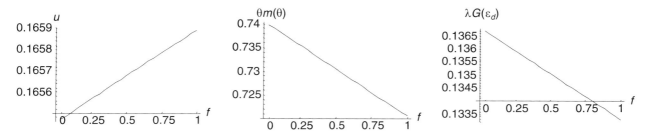

FIGURE 12.8
The impact of firing costs on the unemployment rate u, the exit rate from unemployment $\theta m(\theta)$, and the job destruction rate $\lambda G(\varepsilon_d)$ with negotiated wages and $z=0.75$. f is expressed as a fraction of average quarterly production.

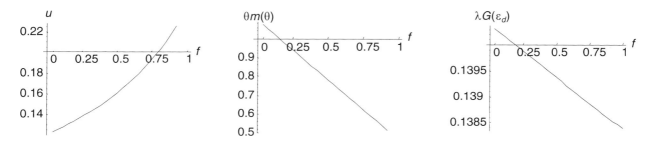

FIGURE 12.9
The impact of firing costs on the unemployment rate u, the exit rate from unemployment $\theta m(\theta)$, and the job destruction rate $\lambda G(\varepsilon_d)$ with exogenous wages. f is expressed as a fraction of average quarterly production.

firing costs are responsible for the reduced job turnover rate, but that they explain no more than a small part of the equilibrium unemployment rate. Blanchard and Portugal (2001) develop a matching model in which the wage is negotiated once and for all at the outset of the match-up between employer and employee. A simulation of this model then shows that the unemployment rate is an increasing, then a decreasing, function of firing costs. This result indicates that two countries—in this case the United States and Portugal, in the study of Blanchard and Portugal—may display identical unemployment rates while having very different legislation about employment protection (on the scale of strictness in employment protection reproduced in table 12.4, the United States is the least strict country and Portugal the most strict one). The simulations of Blanchard and Portugal do show, however, that the average duration of unemployment rises rapidly, and to a significant degree, when employment protection is strengthened.

Rigid Wages
The results are quite different when wages are rigid. Figure 12.9 represents the impact of administrative firing costs on the assumption that there is a constant mandatory minimum wage, and a corresponding unemployment rate of 12.5% in the absence of

employment protection. In this situation, an increase in firing costs has a very marked impact on the unemployment rate. The latter rises by more than ten points when firing costs increase by an amount corresponding to the average quarterly production of a worker. The exit rate from unemployment plummets, while job destruction is little changed. These results highlight the degree of interaction between the various institutions of the labor market. Employment protection has very different results according to the nature of the other institutions that regulate the labor market. To be precise, the results obtained suggest that firing costs are probably unfavorable to the employment of low-skilled workers in certain European countries, where a high proportion of them are paid at minimum wage. High firing costs would, however, have only negligible effects on employment if they were accompanied by high wage flexibility (Blanchard and Portugal, 2001).

It should be noted that the minimum wage and employment protection act on the job destruction rate in directly opposite ways. Equation (11), which defines the reservation productivity when the wage is exogenous, shows that the minimum wage increases the job destruction rate, while firing costs reduce it. Bertola and Rogerson (1997) have pointed out that this type of effect might explain the similar rates of job destruction observed in different OECD countries with very different kinds of employment protection. For example, in chapter 9, table 9.1, we saw that the United States and France have job destruction rates of the same order of magnitude, 10.4% for the United States and 11.8% for France—surprising figures at first sight, given that the United States has very liberal legislation about firing, while France has adopted stringent measures to protect employment. In France, the high minimum wage increases the job destruction rate, which helps in part to explain the fact that rates of job destruction are similar in these two countries.

Also worthy of note is the fact that the effects of minimum wage and employment protection on the exit rate from unemployment have a tendency mutually to reinforce one another (see figure 12.9). The conjunction of a high minimum wage and rigorous employment protection ought thus to lead to relatively low exit rates from unemployment, and consequently to a high proportion of long-term unemployed. Here again, comparison of worker flows in France and the United States well illustrates this kind of effect, showing that the exit rate from unemployment is ten times higher in the United States (see chapter 9, table 9.7).

2.4 WHAT EMPIRICAL STUDIES SHOW

Many studies try to assess the impact of employment protection by regressing the unemployment rate, or indicators of workers and job mobility, onto a set of explanatory variables, among them an index of the strictness of employment protection. The theoretical analysis set out above suggests that mobility between the situation of having a job and the situation of being unemployed ought to be greater in countries where employment protection legislation is lax, and empirical studies generally confirm this prediction.

The Effect of Firing Costs on Employment and Unemployment

Lazear (1990) looked at the effect of severance payments, using data from 22 OECD countries for the period 1956–1984. He finds that in several European countries the evolution of firing costs is largely responsible for the rise in unemployment. In France, for example, 59% of the rise in unemployment may be attributed to changes in the rules about firing, while in Portugal the figure is 71% and in Belgium 8%. The relevance of these results is not entirely clear, though, since the only explanatory variables are severance payments and the length of advance notice, to which is added a time trend.

Studies based on other explanatory variables arrive at divergent results. In a study carried out on 20 OECD countries for the period 1983–1994, Nickell (1997) finds that employment protection (measured by the OECD synthetic index) has a tendency to reduce unemployment slightly. Elmeskov et al. (1998) arrive at opposite results, since they obtain an increasing relation between the OECD synthetic index and the unemployment rate. Using the same indicator, however, Bertola (1990) and Garibaldi et al. (1997) find no significant relationship with the unemployment rate. The very detailed study by the OECD (1999) confirms this result (see also Addison and Teixeira, 2003). So the correlation between the unemployment rate and employment protection proves fragile, and extremely sensitive to the specification of the equations estimated and the econometric methods adopted. In essence, empirical studies confirm the conclusions of theoretical analysis: firing costs have an ambiguous impact on the unemployment rate that is slight in extent.

Firing costs do, however, appear to impact employment rates[4] and the composition of unemployment in a more systematic fashion. Scarpetta (1996), Nickell (1997), and OECD (1999) bring to light a negative impact of these costs on employment rates. This correlation can be understood in light of the theoretical model developed above, which shows that firing costs reduce the expected utility V_u of an unemployed person. Equation (28) does indeed indicate that V_u increases with labor market tightness, which is itself a decreasing function of firing costs. If we consider labor market participation to be the result of a comparison between V_u and the expected utility to be found outside the labor market, distributed according to a distribution function $H(\cdot)$, the participation rate is equal to $H(V_u)$ because individuals decide to enter the labor market only if doing so brings them expected utilities superior to the ones they get by remaining nonparticipants (see chapter 1). So employment protection, by exerting downward pressure on the exit rate from unemployment and the expected utility of the unemployed, reduces participation rates. Theoretical analysis also suggests that firing costs ought to have a more systematically negative impact on the employment of workers whose productivity is weak, who are often paid minimum wage, and who benefit from a relatively high replacement ratio. Empirical results do indeed highlight a more marked effect of firing costs on young people (Scarpetta, 1996, and OECD, 1999) and so indirectly confirm this conclusion.

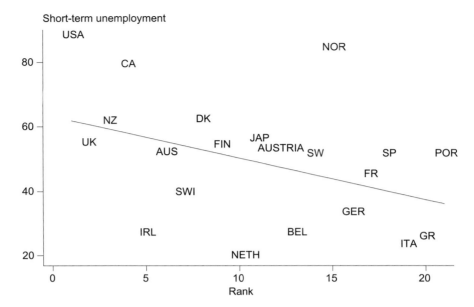

FIGURE 12.10

Employment protection and short-term unemployment (as a proportion of total unemployment) in 1999.

The Effect of Firing Costs on Workers' Mobility

Many studies bring out a positive relationship between the strictness of employment protection and the duration of unemployment (Bertola and Rogerson, 1997; Blanchard and Portugal, 2001; Boeri, 1999; OECD, 1999). Consequently, the long-term unemployment rate ought to be higher when firing costs are high, and symmetrically the frequency of short-term unemployment ought to be higher where employment protection is lax. In order to illustrate these results simply, we represent, in figures 12.10 and 12.11, respectively, the correspondence between the frequency of short-term unemployment (less than six months spent looking for work), the frequency of long-term unemployment (more than a year spent looking for work), and the OECD synthetic index (found in the "rank" column of table 12.4).

Figure 12.10 clearly brings out a negative linkage between the strictness of employment protection and the frequency of short-term unemployment. In other words, countries with lax employment protection will mainly have short-term unemployment. Inasmuch as the frequency of short-term unemployment is evidently positively linked to exits from employment, the lessons of the theoretical model are confirmed. In figure 12.11, we represent the proportion of long-term unemployed and the synthetic index. What we see with stark clarity is an increasing linkage between long-term unemployment and the strength of employment protection. Long-term unemployment being strongly correlated with the exit rate from unemployment, figure 12.11 also confirms the lessons of the theoretical model.

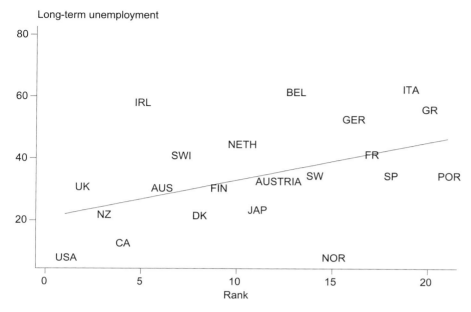

FIGURE 12.11
Employment protection and long-term unemployment (more than a year) as a proportion of total unemployment in 1999.

3 TAXATION

Taxes on labor income create a gap between the cost of labor borne by the employer and the purchasing power of the wage paid to the employee. Taxes are often progressive, which means that the marginal gain is more heavily taxed than the average gain. The pressure of mandatory contributions is frequently denounced as an obstacle to job creation. From that standpoint, strong income redistribution through mandatory contributions is seen as incompatible with good performance by the economy. Close scrutiny will reveal that this judgment must be considerably qualified. It is worth noting that the issue of taxation has been encountered in chapter 11, section 2.3, in the analysis of employment subsidies. There we studied how proportional taxes on wages affected employment and compensation. In this section we adopt a wider perspective: we present the main features of taxes in some OECD countries and pay close attention, theoretical and empirical, to the incidence of progressivity of taxes. It will emerge that variations in marginal and average tax rates have very different consequences on labor market outcomes.

3.1 THE MAIN FEATURES OF TAXES IN SOME OECD COUNTRIES

The structure of mandatory contributions and the extent of redistribution differ noticeably from country to country. The "tax wedge" is a synthetic indicator that proves useful in assessing the extent of fiscal pressure in many circumstances. It is a notion that needs to be complemented by measures of the degree to which taxes are progressive, if we are to have an adequate overview of the characteristics of the fiscal system.

3.1.1 Mandatory Contributions

Mandatory contributions are all payments made by all actors to public authorities with no direct compensation in return. They comprise taxes in the strict sense, and social security contributions. Taxes are collected by the government and by local public authorities. Social security contributions are collected by the government, or by dedicated organizations, for the purpose of insuring persons against certain contingencies like illness. Among mandatory contributions, a distinction is normally made between contributions paid by the employer and ones paid by the employee. In reality this distinction has little meaning, because in either case, mandatory contributions are entirely deducted from the value added that production creates. For employees and employers, the relevant magnitude is the difference between the value added and the *total* amount of contributions. Out of this difference they must compensate themselves, and pay their remaining taxes. Table 12.6 gives an idea of the system of mandatory contributions in several OECD countries.

The first line of this table shows the values of personal income tax in 1998, assessed on income from labor and capital. There is not a deep divide between the countries of continental Europe and the Anglo-Saxon ones. Personal income tax is high in Sweden but lower in France, Germany, the United Kingdom, and the United States. Social security contributions, on the other hand, constitute a fault line between what we may schematically see as two blocs. In the first, comprising France, Germany, and Sweden, social security contributions come to around 15% of GDP, while in the second, comprising Australia, the United Kingdom, the United States, and Japan, social security contributions are less than 10% of GDP. Other taxes (this means prin-

Table 12.6

Tax revenues expressed as a percentage of GDP at market prices in 1998.

	Australia	France	Germany	Japan	Sweden	United Kingdom	United States
Personal income taxes	13	8	9	5	18	10	12
Social security contributions, employee + employer	0	15	14	10	15	6	7
All other taxes	17	22	14	13	19	21	10
Total tax revenue	30	45	37	28	52	37	29

Source: OECD (2001, table II.A, p. 346).

cipally indirect taxes) are not insignificant either, running from 10% in the United States to more than 20% in France and the United Kingdom. The last line of table 12.6, in which the three lines above are added up, gives total tax revenue. This total, expressed as a percentage of GDP, is also called the "rate of mandatory contributions." By this criterion, it turns out that European countries have high tax pressure.

Table 12.6 suggests a distinction between an Anglo-Saxon model and a European one. This distinction, which is often mentioned in the literature, has to be set in perspective by taking into account the extent of social security *benefits*. These benefits for the most part assume the profile of an insurance system. To get them, one has to have paid in for a defined period. Unemployment insurance, retirement pensions, and allowances for days lost to illness enter into this category. There are also allowances providing social assistance on a means-tested basis that do not require prior payments into a specific fund. In France, family allowance, housing allowance, and minimum guaranteed income (*revenu minimum d'insertion*) fall into this category. In the United States the Medicare and Medicaid programs, which cover the health care costs of the elderly and the most disadvantaged, are examples (see OECD, 1996, for a description of the minimal levels of social assistance in the industrialized countries). In general, the European countries deliver measurably higher social security benefits (although the level of social assistance is comparable), which means that the *net* rates of mandatory contributions to social security present less divergence between European countries and Anglo-Saxon countries than the gross rates (see Bourguignon, 2001). In other words, a large part of the gap in the rates of mandatory contributions in the two models is explained by the *different coverage* provided by the various social insurance systems. The respective roles of the *public* sector and the *private* sector are not constant from one country to another.

3.1.2 The Tax Wedge

The gap between the cost of labor and the purchasing power of wages is usually gauged by the *tax wedge*. Let W and P_f respectively be the nominal wage received by an employee and the producer price index. If we denote by t_f the average rate of mandatory deductions from wages borne by firms, the real labor cost for the employer is written:

$$w_f = \frac{W(1 + t_f)}{P_f}$$

Let us again denote by t_c and t_e respectively the average rate of indirect taxes on consumption and the average rate at which earned income is taxed—approximate indicators of these two magnitudes appear in the third and first lines respectively of table 12.6—and let P_c represent the consumer price index exclusive of consumption taxes. The *purchasing power* of an employee takes the form:

$$w_e = \frac{W(1 - t_e)}{P_c(1 + t_c)}$$

Table 12.7

Income tax plus employees' and employers' contributions (as percentages of labor cost for single persons without children) in some OECD countries.

Country	1979	1989	1999
Germany	40.8	45.5	51.9
United States	31.9	31.5	31.1
Japan	16.7	20.4	24.0
United Kingdom	36.1	34.2	30.8
Sweden	50.7	52.7	50.5
Netherlands	48.0	47.0	44.3
Spain	36.4	35.9	37.5

Source: OECD (2001, table 1.4, p. 341).

Eliminating the nominal wage W between the expressions of w_e and w_f, we get:

$$w_f = \rho w_e \qquad \text{with} \qquad \rho = \frac{(1+t_c)(1+t_f)}{(1-t_e)}\left(\frac{P_c}{P_f}\right)$$

The term ρ defines the *wedge*; it measures the gap between the cost of labor borne by the employer and the purchasing power of wages. The wedge has two components. First is the ratio (P_c/P_f), which is influenced by the price of imports, because P_c comprises imports prices whereas the producer price index only comprises prices of domestic goods. The ratio (P_c/P_f) is a relatively volatile component of the wedge, especially because of variations in the exchange rates. Second is the *tax wedge*, which hinges on the tax rates t_c, t_e, and t_f. Henceforth we will focus only on the tax wedge by setting the ratio (P_c/P_f) equal to 1.

Table 12.7 gives the value of the direct contributions paid by employers and employees for certain OECD countries between 1979 and 1999, that is to say, during a period of mounting unemployment in Europe. We see that direct contributions represent a high proportion of the labor cost. The countries of continental Europe have contribution rates superior to those of Japan, the United States, and the United Kingdom at the close of the period (which corroborates the picture painted by table 12.6). Moreover, this indicator followed diverging paths. It shrank in the United Kingdom and the Netherlands, remained stable in the United States, Spain, and Sweden, and grew in Germany.

3.1.3 The Progressivity of Taxes

When dealing with taxation, it is important to distinguish the *average* tax rate from the *marginal* tax rate. The average rate is an indicator of the global volume of taxation, while the marginal rate, which measures the increase in taxation on each extra unit of income or expenditure, is an indicator of the *progressivity* of taxes. Most systems of mandatory contribution show a certain progressivity, in which case the marginal rate exceeds the average rate.

Marginal Rates and Average Rates

In order to study the consequences of progressivity, we must first define a system of mandatory contributions that will allow us to distinguish marginal rates from average ones. We will designate by w the real gross wage received by the worker and will assume, in order to simplify the exposition, that contributions are indexed to it. The purchasing power w_e of wages and the labor cost w_f for the firm can then be written in the following manner:

$$w_e = w - T_e(w) \quad \text{and} \quad w_f = w + T_f(w) \tag{31}$$

Function T_e represents the sum of the direct and indirect taxes on earned income paid by the worker, and function T_f stands for all the payroll taxes paid by the employer. In reality, these two functions depend on many parameters characterizing taxation in each country, including different tax brackets and the marginal tax rates that apply to each of them, thresholds that trigger tax relief, and ceilings on certain contributions (see Malcomson and Sator, 1987). In order to simplify the notation, we have not included these parameters in writing the functions T_e and T_f. It is the extent of the variation in the contributions T_e and T_f when income rises that allows us to pinpoint how progressive a system of mandatory contributions is. This is why the respective elasticities η_e and η_f of w_e and w_f with respect to w play an essential part in measuring this progressivity. Differentiating relations (31), we find that they can be written:

$$\eta_e = \frac{1 - T'_e}{1 - (T_e/w)} \quad \text{and} \quad \eta_f = \frac{1 + T'_f}{1 + (T_f/w)} \tag{32}$$

In these relations, T'_e and T'_f designate respectively the derivatives of functions T_e and T_f with respect to w. These quantities represent the *marginal rates* of taxation of the employee and the firm, while the quantities (T_e/w) and (T_f/w) represent the *average rates*. The gap between the average rates and the marginal rates characterizes the degree to which taxation is progressive or regressive. These notions can be understood clearly by focusing on the elasticities η_e and η_f (for more detail on this subject, see Musgrave and Musgrave, 1989):

- If $\eta_e < 1$, a rise of 1% in the wage corresponds to a rise of *less* than 1% in the purchasing power of this wage. This property tells us that the income tax (or the consumption tax) is progressive. When this is the case, the marginal rate T'_e is higher than the average rate (T_e/w). Elasticity η_e is often called the "coefficient of residual income progression."

- If $\eta_f > 1$, a rise of 1% in the real wage leads to a rise of *more* than 1% in the cost of labor for the firm. This property tells us that the payroll tax borne by firms is progressive. When this is the case, the marginal rate T'_f is higher than the average rate (T_f/w). When η_f is less than unity, this system is *regressive*.

Table 12.8

Average rates and marginal rates for a single person with an income equivalent to 167% of that of an average worker in 1999.

Country	Average rate	Marginal rate	η_e
Denmark	51.6	63.3	0.76
France	31.0	35.4	0.93
Germany	47.5	58.5	0.79
Japan	19.3	30.8	0.85
Netherlands	39.1	50.0	0.82
Sweden	40.3	50.6	0.83
United Kingdom	26.6	33.0	0.91
United States	31.9	42.9	0.84

Source: OECD (2001, tables 3 and 6, pp. 44 and 47).

Note: These rates include income tax and the social security contributions deducted from wages.

- If $\eta_e = 1$, the income tax system is said to be *proportional*. The marginal rate T'_e is then equal to the average rate (T_e/w). Likewise, if $\eta_f = 1$, the payroll tax borne by firms is said to be *proportional*. The marginal rate T'_f is then equal to the average rate (T_f/w).

Progressivity in Some OECD Countries

Table 12.8 gives the values of the average rate, the marginal rate, and the coefficient η_e of residual income progression as they apply to taxation on the income of a single person with an income equivalent to 167% of that of an average worker in 1999 in some OECD countries. We see that tax progressivity is prevalent in these countries. The countries of northern Europe are distinguished by high marginal rates; the situation in Germany is analogous to that in the United States. France and the United Kingdom have marginal rates clearly lower than those of the other countries (Japan excepted), and the gap between the average rate and the marginal rate is also relatively narrow there, which is a sign that they are less progressive.

3.2   THE EFFECT OF TAXES ON THE LABOR MARKET

Mandatory contributions act on the behavior of agents and the allocation of resources in a number of ways. We must therefore work within a coherent analytical framework, one that describes both wage setting, labor supply, and labor demand. The matching model presented above in chapter 9 fits this prescription, as long as we introduce hours worked into it, because hours worked are influenced by taxes (as shown in chapter 1). In such a context, it is evidently very important to distinguish between the impact of the average tax rate and the progressivity of taxation.

3.2.1 The Matching Model with Hours Worked

We will suppose that at every date an individual disposes of a unit of time, which he or she divides between ℓ hours of work and $(1 - \ell)$ hours of leisure. If s designates the hourly wage rate, the total wage received by a worker who has supplied ℓ hours of work amounts to $w = s\ell$. The purchasing power w_e of a worker and the cost w_f of this worker to the employer are defined by:

$$w_e = s\ell - T_e(s\ell) \qquad \text{and} \qquad w_f = s\ell + T_f(s\ell) \tag{33}$$

We will suppose that the instantaneous utility of a worker is now written $w_e\phi(1 - \ell)$. In this expression, $\phi(.)$ is a function measuring the disutility of labor, such that $\phi' > 0$ and $\phi'' \leq 0$. (Pissarides, 2000, chapter 7, uses a similar formulation.) This specification of preferences entails, in particular, that the optimal duration of work chosen by the employee is independent of the hourly wage rate s and the average tax rate when taxes are proportional ($\eta_e = 1$). That being so, the substitution effect and income effect that underlie decisions to supply labor balance out exactly when the wage rate and taxes vary (see chapter 1). We emphasized in chapter 1 that the wage elasticity of the labor supply is slight, and in broad terms this hypothesis holds good. But in the present context, we must also note that increased progressivity leads to a reduction in hours worked, for a given hourly wage rate. To show this, let $\eta_e(s\ell, x)$ be the coefficient of residual income progression, where x is a parameter influencing the progressivity of the taxes paid by workers. Hence we will assume, by convention, that an increase in x corresponds to steeper progressivity, i.e., $\partial\eta_e/\partial x < 0$. Maximizing instantaneous utility $[s\ell - T_e(s\ell, x)]\phi(1 - \ell)$ with respect to ℓ, we arrive at the first-order condition, which may be written as follows:

$$F(s, x, \ell) \equiv \frac{\eta_e(s\ell, x)}{\ell} - \frac{\phi'(1 - \ell)}{\phi(1 - \ell)} = 0$$

Since the second-order condition dictates $\partial F/\partial\ell < 0$, differentiating this equation with respect to x entails $\partial\ell/\partial x = -(\partial F/\partial x)/(\partial F/\partial\ell) < 0$. Thus, an increase in the progressivity of taxes entails a reduction of the labor supply, for a given hourly wage rate. We have come to the usual conclusion yielded by labor supply models, i.e., that more steeply progressive taxes lead to fewer hours being worked. Still, the logic of this result depends on the hourly wage being given. Now, the hourly wage is influenced by taxation, so we must adjust the framework of analysis to make the wage an endogenous variable, in order to assess the impact of taxation on hours and employment.

Labor Demand

Once again, we use the model from chapter 9, and introduce the following new specification of preferences: assuming that an unemployed person does not work, i.e., $\ell = 0$, and receives a flow of income z, his or her instantaneous utility is written $z\phi(1)$. To lighten the notation, we will adopt the normalization $\phi(1) = 1$. With these hypotheses, the expected utilities V_e and V_u of a person respectively employed and looking for work satisfy:

$$rV_e = w_e\phi(1 - \ell) + q(V_u - V_e) \tag{34}$$

$$rV_u = z + \theta m(\theta)(V_e - V_u) \tag{35}$$

In these equations, q and $\theta m(\theta)$ still designate respectively the job destruction rate and the exit rate from unemployment. If $f(\ell)$, with $f'(\ell) > 0$ and $f''(\ell) < 0$, now represents individual production, which is assumed to rise as more hours are worked, the expected profit Π_e from a filled job is written:

$$r\Pi_e = f(\ell) - w_f + q(\Pi_v - \Pi_e) \tag{36}$$

while the expected profit from a vacant job always satisfies the equality:

$$r\Pi_v = -h + m(\theta)(\Pi_e - \Pi_v) \tag{37}$$

When the free entry condition $\Pi_v = 0$ is satisfied, expression (37) of the expected profit from a vacant job again gives $\Pi_e = h/m(\theta)$. Bringing this equality into definition (36) of the profit from a filled job, we arrive at a relationship between w, ℓ and θ which is the "labor demand" curve. It is written:

$$\frac{h}{m(\theta)} = \frac{f(\ell) - w_f}{r + q} \tag{38}$$

As we have pointed out more than once, the left-hand side of this equality represents the average cost of a vacant job, while the right-hand side designates the expected profit from a filled one. At free entry equilibrium, these two quantities must be equal to one another.

Bargaining

We will assume that bargaining covers simultaneously the hourly wage s and hours worked ℓ. The outcome of the bargaining corresponds to the solution of the generalized Nash problem described in chapter 9, section 3.4.1. It is written:

$$\underset{(s, \ell)}{\text{Max}} \; \gamma \ln(V_e - V_u) + (1 - \gamma) \ln(\Pi_e - \Pi_v) \tag{39}$$

Let us recall that $\gamma \in [0, 1]$ is a parameter representing the bargaining power of the worker. Relations (36) and (34) let us find the contributions of the players to the Nash problem. They are written:

$$\Pi_e - \Pi_v = \frac{f(\ell) - w_f - r\Pi_v}{r + q} \quad \text{and} \quad V_e - V_u = \frac{w_e\phi(1 - \ell) - rV_u}{r + q} \tag{40}$$

The first-order conditions of the problem (39) are found by setting to zero the derivatives with respect to s and ℓ of the Nash criterion. The calculations will become a little easier, however, if we derive this criterion with respect to variables $w = s\ell$ and ℓ instead. After some rearrangements of terms, we deduce that at free entry equilibrium where $\Pi_v = 0$, the first-order conditions of problem (39) take the following form:

$$\Omega^w(w,\ell) \equiv \gamma \frac{\eta_e w_e \phi(1-\ell)}{w_e \phi(1-\ell) - rV_u} - (1-\gamma) \frac{\eta_f w_f}{f(\ell) - w_f} = 0 \tag{41}$$

$$\Omega^\ell(w,\ell) \equiv -\gamma \frac{w_e \phi'(1-\ell)}{w_e \phi(1-\ell) - rV_u} + (1-\gamma) \frac{f'(\ell)}{f(\ell) - w_f} = 0 \tag{42}$$

where w_e and w_f are always defined by equations (31). Eliminating the term $\gamma/(1-\gamma)$ from these two first-order conditions, we arrive at the equation of the "contracts curve":

$$f'(\ell) \frac{\phi(1-\ell)}{\phi'(1-\ell)} = \Psi w_f \qquad \text{with} \qquad \Psi = \frac{\eta_f}{\eta_e} \tag{43}$$

In this expression, there appears the coefficient $\Psi = \eta_f/\eta_e$, which is an indicator of the global progressivity of taxes. A rise in Ψ corresponds to a system becoming globally more progressive, as for example when the progressivity of income tax is made steeper (η_e falls) and/or the progressivity of payroll taxes is made steeper (η_f rises). In what follows, we will assume that coefficient Ψ is an exogenous parameter controlled by the government. That signifies that the government can, for example, keep average rates constant while raising marginal rates. Equation (43) is that of the "contracts curve," which corresponds to the Pareto optima between the employee and the employer.

The pair (ℓ, w), the solution of the bargaining, can be found from equations (42) and (43) using definitions (31) of wage and the labor cost. Figure 12.12 represents the solution of the bargaining in the (ℓ, w) plane. The contract curve, denoted by CC, is decreasing, and the graph of equation (42), denoted by BB, is increasing.[5] This figure

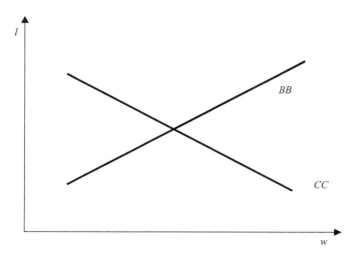

FIGURE 12.12
Bargaining over wages and hours.

is useful in analyzing the impact of taxes on the wage w and number of hours worked that are negotiated, given the reservation wage rV_u.

Increased progressivity with no change to average rates leads to a shift downward of the contract curve (since the left-hand side of equation (43) decreases with ℓ) without affecting the BB curve. Thus, more progressive taxes entail a reduction in wage w and hours worked. The reduction in hours worked is a consequence of the fall in the marginal return on labor, which gives workers an incentive to substitute leisure for consumption. The reduction of wage w results from two effects. For one thing, the reduction in hours worked brings it down, since wage w is equal to hourly wage s multiplied by the number of hours worked ℓ. And for another, as progressivity becomes steeper, any wage rise procures a smaller marginal utility for workers and entails a higher marginal cost for the firm. For this reason progressivity exerts a downward pressure on the negotiated wage, making any wage rise less attractive to workers and more costly for the firm (Lockwood and Manning, 1993). To sum up, steeper progressivity tends to limit the wage of, and reduce the number of hours worked by, individuals.

Let us now turn our attention to proportional taxes, such that $\eta^e = \eta^f = \Psi = 1$. An increase in proportional taxes paid by workers has no effect on the CC curve and shifts the BB curve downward[6] in figure 12.12. Hours worked decline and the gross wage increases, pushing the cost of labor up, for the decline in the surplus induced by the tax increase does not entail a proportional decline in wages. Workers accept a reduction in their purchasing power, but it is less than the amount of taxes deducted, thanks to their bargaining power. An increase in the taxes paid by employers has a similar impact. To sum up, an increase in average rates reduces hours worked, reduces workers' purchasing power, and increases the labor cost.

These results have been derived from a very partial framework, by considering an employer and a worker whose reservation wage, rV_u, is independent of taxes. The matching model lets us assess the impact of taxes on labor market equilibrium, by taking into account the reactions of wages, labor supply, and demand.

3.2.2 The Contrasting Effects of the Average and the Marginal Tax Rates

It is possible to represent labor market equilibrium using a wage curve depicting the outcome of bargaining, and a labor demand curve representing labor demand.

The Wage Curve

The first-order condition (41) obtained by differentiating the Nash criterion (39) with respect to the gross wage $s\ell$ is similar to a wage curve (see chapter 9, section 3.4.2). We can arrive at a more user-friendly expression of it if we first note that equations (34) and (35) defining the expected utilities of a worker and an unemployed person entail:

$$V_e - V_u = \frac{w_e\phi(1-\ell) - z}{r + q + \theta m(\theta)} \tag{44}$$

Bringing this expression of $(V_e - V_u)$ into the first-order condition (41) and assuming that unemployment benefits are indexed to the purchasing power of workers—i.e., $z = bw_e$—where the net replacement ratio b is an exogenous constant, the equation of the wage curve becomes:

$$\frac{f(\ell) - w_f}{r + q} = \frac{1 - \gamma}{\gamma} \frac{\Psi w_f}{\phi(1 - \ell)} \frac{\phi(1 - \ell) - b}{r + q + \theta m(\theta)} \tag{45}$$

Labor demand, the contracts curve, and the wage curve form a system of three equations, (38), (43), and (45), with three unknowns, w_f, ℓ, and θ. It is possible to arrive at a system with just two unknowns by means of several substitutions. The contract curve will let us express the cost of labor w_f as a function of hours worked, i.e., $w_f = f'\phi/\Psi\phi'$, and bringing this expression of w_f into the labor demand (38), we find a relationship between ℓ and θ which we will continue to refer to as labor demand and which is written:

$$\frac{h}{m(\theta)} = \frac{f'(\ell)}{r + q} \left[\ell - \frac{1}{\Psi} \frac{\phi(1 - \ell)}{\phi'(1 - \ell)} \right] \tag{46}$$

Furthermore, (38) shows that the left-hand side of equation (45) of the wage curve is equal to the average cost $h/m(\theta)$ of a vacant job. Using the new equality $w_f = y\phi/\Psi\phi'$ in the right-hand side of equation (45), we arrive at a second equation, which we will continue to refer to as the wage curve, and which takes the following form:

$$\frac{r + q + \theta m(\theta)}{m(\theta)} = \frac{(1 - \gamma) f'(\ell)}{\gamma h} \frac{\phi(1 - \ell) - b}{\phi'(1 - \ell)} \tag{47}$$

This form of the wage curve presents the advantage of not depending on parameter Ψ.

Labor Market Equilibrium with Unemployment Benefits Indexed to Wages

The two equations (46) and (47) form a system with two unknowns θ and ℓ which it is possible to represent graphically by the curves denoted (*LD*), for labor demand, and (*WC*), for wage curve, in figure 12.13. In the (θ, ℓ) plane, the (*LD*) and (*WC*) curves are respectively increasing and decreasing. Inasmuch as the contracts curve (43) indicates that the number of hours worked ℓ is negatively linked to the cost of labor w_f, and thus to gross wages $w = s\ell$, the representation of labor market equilibrium in figure 12.13 is analogous to the representations of this equilibrium that we have presented to this point in the (w, θ) plane.

We see that making progressivity steeper leaves the wage curve (*WC*) unchanged but shifts labor demand (*LD*) downward. The result is a reduction in hours worked ℓ and a rise in the labor market tightness θ. As the unemployment rate u continues to be given by the Beveridge curve of equation $u = q/[q + \theta m(\theta)]$, steeper progressivity proves beneficial in terms of employment. This result comes from the fact that steeper progressivity tends to put a damper on the negotiated wages and the cost of labor per

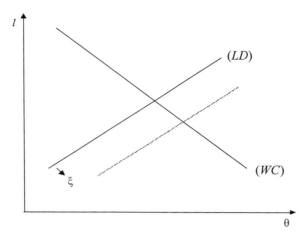

FIGURE 12.13
The effect of steeper progressivity.

employee, which increases the number of persons employed (Hansen, 1999, and Fuest and Huber, 2000, come to an analogous conclusion with collective bargaining models). The reduction in the hours worked by individuals comes from the decline in the net marginal gain per hour worked. The upshot is that the *total volume* of hours worked, equal to the number of persons employed multiplied by individual hours worked, reacts ambiguously to steeper progressivity. As regards variations in wages, equation (38), which defines labor demand, entails that the cost w_f of this factor falls when coefficient Ψ rises. On the other hand, it is impossible to deduce from it the behavior of the purchasing power w_e of the wage received by the employee without a supplementary hypothesis. If, however, we assume that average tax rates do not vary, a rise in Ψ also leads to a fall in w_e. Thus steeper progressivity ought to go along with a reduction in the cost of labor and the purchasing power of the wage received. In summary, steeper progressivity reduces hours worked and lowers the unemployment rate, the cost of labor, and the purchasing power of wages received by workers.

It is interesting to note that if taxes are proportional, then $\Psi = 1$, and equations (46) and (47) show that hours worked, labor market tightness, and thus the unemployment rate are totally independent of the level of taxes. Equation (43) of the contract curve indicates that the labor cost w_f is iself then independent of taxes, too. In other words, bargaining entails that the employee bears the *full* tax burden. Essentially, under these conditions, an increase in proportional contributions diminishes the purchasing power of the negotiated wage, which reduces the gains of unemployed persons and the reservation wage, and in turn reinforces the downward pressure on the negotiated wage. In the end, this process leads to a reduction in wages equal to the amount of the taxes. This is an illustration of the problem of fiscal incidence: a new tax applying to a specific individual does not necessarily decrease his or her net income. It can be the case that variations in incomes induced by the tax leave his or her net income unchanged (this problem has already been encountered in chapter 11, section 2.3). Here, the indexation of unemployment benefits to wages makes the person who has a job the one who, in the final analysis, pays all of the mandatory contributions. This result suggests that taxes on labor do not necessarily have a negative effect on employment when the net wage is capable of absorbing a large part of any increase in mandatory contributions.

Labor Market Equilibrium Without Unemployment Benefits Indexed to Wages
In the setting just discussed, taxes acted on labor market equilibrium exclusively through parameter Ψ measuring the global progressivity of mandatory contributions. In particular, the amount of these contributions had no effect in itself. This result points to the conclusion that the progressivity or regressivity of contributions is more important than their sheer amount. But that has to be set in perspective, because it flows mainly from the hypothesis that unemployment benefits are indexed. This will be clear if we assume, as we now shall, that the gain z of the unemployed is an exogenous constant. The labor demand (LD) continues to be defined by (46). To obtain the wage curve (WC), we may first bring the expression (44) of $V_e - V_u$ into the first-order condition (42). It comes to:

$$\frac{f(\ell) - w_f}{r + q} \frac{1}{r + q + \theta m(\theta)} = \frac{1 - \gamma}{\gamma} \frac{w_e \phi(1 - \ell) - z}{w_e \phi'(1 - \ell)} \tag{48}$$

Now, following relation (38), which defines labor demand, the term $[f(\ell) - w_f]/(r + q)$ appearing in the left-hand side of equation (48) is equal to $h/m(\theta)$. Let ρ again be the tax wedge; following equation (43) of the contract curve, we have $w_e = w_f/\rho = f'(\ell)\phi/\rho\phi'\Psi$. Equation (48) then becomes, after several rearrangements:

$$\frac{r + q + \theta m(\theta)}{m(\theta)} = \frac{1 - \gamma}{\gamma h} \left[\frac{\phi(1 - \ell)}{\phi'(1 - \ell)} - \frac{\rho z \Psi}{f'(\ell)\phi(1 - \ell)} \right] \tag{49}$$

Labor market equilibrium is now described by the system of two equations (46) and (49). We can easily verify that steeper progressivity always entails a reduction in hours worked and an increase in labor market tightness. The amount of taxation now has an impact too, which it did not in the setting where the gains of the unemployed were proportional to the net wage w_e. The wage curve described by (49) now depends on the tax wedge ρ. To make this clear, let us assume that the coefficient Ψ that measures global progressivity is now held constant (by supposing, for example, that taxes are proportional and thus that $\Psi = 1$), and that the tax wedge ρ is made larger. The new labor market equilibrium is represented in figure 12.14. The (LD) curve, which is independent of ρ, does not move, while the (WC) curve shifts downward. An increase in the tax wedge reduces the equilibrium value of the labor market tightness, and so pushes unemployment up. It also entails a decline in individual hours worked, and the result of that is a fall in the total volume of hours worked. The effect on the labor cost and the purchasing power of wages proves ambiguous.

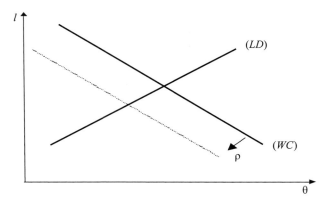

Figure 12.14
The effect of an increase in the tax wedge.

The theoretical models suggest that more progressive taxes reduce unemployment and hours worked, whereas a greater tax wedge increases unemployment and reduces hours when the gains of the unemployed are not perfectly indexed to net wages. It is important to note that these results have been obtained by taking the participation rate as given. But taxes influence labor market participation. In particular, any increase in the amount of mandatory contributions, which reduces gains in the labor market, tends to discourage participation and amplifies the effects that have just been illustrated.

3.3 What Empirical Studies Tell Us

We first present results concerning the impact of the tax wedge on labor market performance, then turn our attention to the (less numerous) studies that have focused their analysis on the role of progressivity.

3.3.1 The Incidence of the Tax Wedge

The preceding analyses show that the effects of mandatory contributions on employment depend a great deal on how the labor cost reacts. Empirical research in this area does indeed suggest that a rise in the taxes weighing on labor becomes detrimental to employment when it leads to a rise in the cost of this factor. From this standpoint, the study of Daveri and Tabellini (2000), which builds on the work of Summers et al. (1993) and Alesina and Perroti (1997), throws a particularly interesting light on the relationship between taxes, wages, and unemployment.

Daveri and Tabellini (2000) have estimated the effect of the taxes weighing on labor using data from 14 OECD countries for the period 1965–1995. One of the original features of their work is that they begin by grouping these 14 countries according to the rate of unionization, the extent of coverage of collective bargaining, and an indicator of the degree to which bargaining is centralized. Three groups emerge. The

Table 12.9

Labor tax and unemployment.

	Labor tax ANGLO	Labor tax EUCON	Labor tax NORDIC	Unemployment benefit	Employment protection
Unemployment rate	0.25** (0.107)	0.54** (0.062)	0.11 (0.162)	0.14** (0.051)	−1.00* (0.571)

Source: Daveri and Tabellini (2000, table 9, column 1, p. 75).

Notes: ** significant at the threshold of 1%; * significant at the threshold of 10%. Standard errors in parentheses.

"Anglo-Saxon" countries (henceforth ANGLO), i.e., Canada, Japan, the United States and the United Kingdom, are characterized by labor markets in which wage setting is highly decentralized. The "continental European" countries (henceforth EUCON) are characterized by strong unions and relatively decentralized bargaining; they are Australia, Belgium, France, Germany, Italy, the Netherlands, and Spain. Finally, the "Nordic" countries (henceforth NORDIC) are distinguished by strong unions and highly centralized bargaining.[7]

The Effect of Taxes on Unemployment

Daveri and Tabellini estimate the impact of taxes on unemployment from the following equation:

$$u_{it} = \beta_E \tau_{it}^E + \beta_A \tau_{it}^A + \beta_N \tau_{it}^N + \beta_x \mathbf{x}_{it} + \varepsilon_{it}^u \tag{50}$$

In this expression, the dependent variable u_{it} is the unemployment rate of country i at date t and $\mathbf{x}_{it}$ is a vector of characteristics that, according to how they are specified, relate to institutions or lagged variables. The explanatory variables τ_{it}^j, $j = E, A, N$, represent the rates of tax on earned income (calculated by the ratio of all the taxes on labor to the wage used to calculate these taxes) of country i at date t when it belongs to group $j = E$ (EUCON), A (ANGLO), N (NORDIC). Finally, the error term ε_{it}^u contains a fixed effect per country. All variables correspond to five-year averages in order to even out fluctuations.

Table 12.9 gives the results of an estimation of equation (50) by ordinary least squares (the fixed effects are not reported). We see that taxes weighing on wages have a high and significant positive impact in the EUCON countries. The effect is similar but more damped in the ANGLO countries. In the NORDIC ones, however, this effect is close to zero, and is insignificant. This result is compatible with the models of decentralized wage setting that have been presented above, since these models predict that a greater tax burden entails an increase in the unemployment rate. On the other hand, when bargaining is centralized (see section 4 below for a model of centralized bargaining) taxes exert less pressure on wages, because individuals take into account the fact that they serve to redistribute resources (see Summers et al., 1993).

Other econometric studies highlight a positive, but limited, linkage between mandatory contributions and the global level of unemployment. For example, Coe (1990) finds that payroll taxes may have increased the natural rate of unemployment in Canada in the 1970s, but he also estimates that income tax and indirect taxes played no part. Layard and Nickell (1999) come to the same conclusion for the United Kingdom. According to them, a decline of 10% in all mandatory contributions would on average reduce the unemployment rate by around 25%. It should be kept in mind that a reduction of 10% in mandatory contributions would be a considerable one; reductions on the order of 1% are more conceivable. On the other hand, Nickell (1997) estimates that changes to the structure of the tax wedge (for example, lowering social security contributions and increasing value-added taxes) have no long-term effect on employment. The long-term equilibrium value of the cost of labor does not, in his view, depend on the *composition* of mandatory contributions, and the right indicator to look at would be the overall size of the tax wedge, not the value of one or another of its component parts.

The Effect of Taxes on the Cost of Labor

The study of Daveri and Tabellini (2000) also examines how taxes on earned income affect gross wages. To that end, they estimate an equation analogous to (50), but in which the dependent variable is the growth rate of gross real wages. The explanatory variables are the increases in the rates of taxation taken into account in (50), as well as the growth rate of the GDP per capita. The results of the estimation by ordinary least squares is given in table 12.10. We see that a hike in taxes increases gross wages in the EUCON group, but not in the ANGLO group, where, on the contrary, they have a tendency to decrease. The coefficient for the NORDIC group is very slightly positive, but not significant. The variables pinpointing the effects of unemployment insurance benefits and employment protection are not significant (but they varied very little over the period studied). Finally, the growth rate of productivity is strongly significant, in the expected direction. To sum up what tables 12.9 and 12.10, taken together, have to tell us: they suggest that the effect of taxes on employment is transmitted in the form of an increase in the cost of labor. In the EUCON countries, increased taxes on labor led to a

Table 12.10

Real wages and labor taxes.

	Labor tax ANGLO	Labor tax EUCON	Labor tax NORDIC	Unemployment benefit	Employment protection	Growth rate of GDP per capita
Wage growth	−0.18 (0.291)	0.34* (0.159)	0.07 (0.205)	−0.050 (0.071)	−1.22 (0.728)	1.92* (0.436)

Source: Daveri and Tabellini (2000, table 11, column 1, p. 83).

Notes: *Significant at the threshold of 1%. Standard errors in parentheses.

rise in the cost of this factor and an aggravation of unemployment. Conversely, in the ANGLO countries, increased taxes did not provoke a rise in gross real wages, which entails a fall in net wages. The effect on employment was also less in these countries. In the NORDIC countries, the tax rate has little influence on gross wages and employment (coordinated wage bargaining might account for this result; see section 4 below). Overall, these results are confirmed by the studies of Tyrvaïnen (1995) and Alesina and Perroti (1997).

3.3.2 The Incidence of Progressivity

The complexity of the various systems of mandatory contributions makes it very difficult to assess degrees of progressivity (see OECD, 2001, for the OECD countries). Yet certain studies do suggest that progressivity plays an important part, for example Lockwood and Manning (1993) for the United Kingdom. On data covering the period 1954–1987, they estimate an equation in which the dependent variable is the logarithm of the ratio of the net wage of an employee to the net gain of an unemployed person, for a married worker with two children (which corresponds to the w_e/z in our theoretical model). Table 12.11 gives the main results of this estimate. In this table, the explanatory variables appear in the first line. To designate the components of the taxes we again use the notations from our theoretical model. The other explanatory variables are the unemployment rate u, the rate of unionization den and the rate of indirect tax vat. In the first place, we see that indirect taxes do not have a significant effect, and that the coefficients of the unemployment rate and the rate of unionization are significant, in the expected direction. This regression also shows that a rise in the marginal rate of tax on earned income reduces the purchasing power of this income, whereas a rise in the average rate has a tendency to increase it. These results conform to the theoretical model developed above, which shows that wages depend on the coefficient $\Psi = \eta_f/\eta_e$, which measures the global progressivity of taxes. In this context, equation (32) shows that a rise in the marginal rate and the average rate ought to have opposing effects on wages. We also see that a rise in the marginal rate of payroll taxes leads to a rise in the purchasing power of wages, and that a rise in the average rate of payroll taxes has the opposite effect. These conclusions do not entirely corroborate

Table 12.11

Real consumer wage and the tax system.

	$\ln u$	$\ln den$	$\ln(1 - T_e')$	$\ln[1 - (T_e/w)]$	$\ln(1 + T_f')$	$\ln[1 + (T_f/w)]$	vat
Real consumer wage	−0.09 (1.70)	0.60 (1.67)	0.95 (1.54)	−0.66 (0.56)	2.87 (1.45)	−4.10 (1.71)	0.71 (0.13)

Source: Lockwood and Manning (1993, table 3, column 4, p. 19).

Notes: t-statistics in parentheses, constant omitted. u = unemployment rate, den = union density, vat = indirect tax rate.

our theoretical model; they might be explained, according to Lockwood and Manning (1993), by the weak variation in the rates affecting payroll taxes over the period.

These conclusions have been partially confirmed by the work of Padoa-Schioppa (1990) for Italy, and by that of Hansen et al. (2000) for Denmark. Padoa-Schioppa has shown that the wages received by workers fall when the degree of progressivity rises. On Danish data covering the period 1970–1992, Hansen et al. (2000) have estimated wage equations analogous to that of Lockwood and Manning (1993). They show that the gross wage of "blue-collar workers" decreases with the marginal rate of taxation, while the wage of "white-collar workers" varies the other way (but the relation is not significant). None of these studies has looked at the effects of progressivity on employment.

4 THE LEVEL AT WHICH WAGE BARGAINING TAKES PLACE

To this point, we have assumed that wage bargaining takes place in a decentralized manner in each firm. But in reality, this bargaining take place at very different levels from one country to the next (see chapter 7, table 7.1). In the Scandinavian countries and Austria, bargaining is done at the national level; in the United States and the United Kingdom the firm is the preferred setting; and in France and Germany, bargaining is done at the industry level. Since the beginning of the 1980s, many studies, both empirical and theoretical, have tried to assess the relative efficiency of the different levels at which bargaining occurs by assessing their impact on global employment. The earlier ones—McCallum (1983), Tarantelli (1983), and Bruno and Sachs (1985)—came to the conclusion that countries where bargaining was decentralized had higher unemployment rates, probably because of excessive real wages. Calmfors and Driffill (1988) have questioned these results, showing that countries where collective bargaining takes place at the level of the industry display worse performances in terms of unemployment.

They obtain a hump-shaped relation between the degree of centralization of bargaining and the unemployment rate; it is presented in figure 12.15. Either the absence of coordination or complete coordination is seen as being preferable to the partial coordination of the parties at the industry level.

The matching model, properly adapted, will allow us to understand why bargaining at the industry level ought to be less efficient than bargaining taking place at the other levels. Different arguments, and scrutiny of the empirical research, will, however, give us reason to qualify this conclusion strongly.

4.1 EFFICIENCY AND UNEMPLOYMENT

We will begin by introducing a model that represents an economy made up of a number of industries, producing different goods, and will then show how negotiations

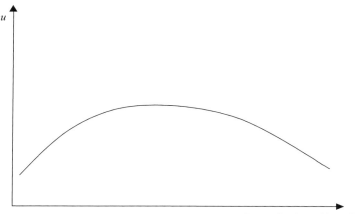

FIGURE 12.15
The relation between the degree of centralization of bargaining and the unemployment rate according to Calmfors and Driffill (1998).

taking place at the level of the firm, the industry, or the whole country may be represented. This will allow us, finally, to compare the implications of bargaining at these different levels.

4.1.1 An Economy Composed of Several Industries

Like Calmfors and Driffill (1988), we will take into account different levels of wage bargaining by assuming that the economy is made up of J industries (indexed by $j = 1, \ldots, J$). Each industry produces a different good in quantity y_j, and there are a great many firms in perfect competition. In order to get explicit demand functions, we make use of the representation of agents' preferences already set out in chapter 8, appendix 1. The main hypothesis is that the aggregate consumption of each agent is a CES type function of the consumption of various goods j, consumed in quantities c_{jk}. More precisely, every consumer k consumes all the goods produced, and the utility he or she derives from the consumption of these goods is defined by:

$$u_k = J^{1/(1-\sigma)} \left[\sum_{j=1}^{J} c_{jk}^{(\sigma-1)/\sigma} \right]^{\sigma/(\sigma-1)}, \qquad \sigma > 1 \tag{51}$$

In this expression, u_k represents a "composite" good dependent on the quantity of all goods, and σ is the elasticity of substitution among goods. This composite good is the numeraire. If p_j designates the relative price of good j, then chapter 8, appendix 1, shows that the demand for good j reads:

$$y_j = \frac{Y}{J} p_j^{-\sigma} \quad \text{with} \quad Y \equiv \sum_{j=1}^{J} p_j y_j \tag{52}$$

We will also assume that there is no labor mobility between industries, and that in each industry the size of the labor force is normalized to 1. In industry j, the process of matching unemployed persons to vacant jobs is described by a function $M(v_j, u_j)$ representing hires per unit of time, with v_j representing the number of vacant jobs and u_j the number of unemployed persons. The function M has the usual properties. It is homogeneous of degree 1, increasing with respect to each of its arguments, and satisfies $M(0, u_j) = M(v_j, 0) = 0$. Let us recall that, with $\theta_j = v_j/u_j$ denoting the labor market tightness in industry j, vacancies are filled at rate $M(v_j, u_j)/v_j = m(\theta_j)$, while the exit rate from unemployment amounts to $\theta m(\theta)$. Assuming further that the job destruction rate q is an exogenous constant, in the stationary state the flow $u_j \theta_j m(\theta_j)$ of exits from unemployment equals the flow $q(1 - u_j)$ entries into unemployment. The unemployment rate u_j is thus defined as a function of labor market tightness θ_j by the Beveridge curve:

$$u_j = \frac{q}{q + \theta_j m(\theta_j)} \tag{53}$$

Let us assume, for simplicity, that an employee produces a unit of good per unit of time, and is paid a wage w_j; the respective values Π_{vj} and Π_{ej} of a vacant job and a filled one in industry j satisfy the following relations:

$$r\Pi_{vj} = -h + m(\theta_j)(\Pi_{ej} - \Pi_{vj}) \qquad \text{and} \qquad r\Pi_{ej} = p_j - w_j + q(\Pi_{vj} - \Pi_{ej}) \tag{54}$$

If we again designate the instantaneous gain of an unemployed person by $z < 1$, the expected utilities V_{ej} and V_{uj} of, respectively, an employed person and an unemployed one satisfy the following equations:

$$rV_{ej} = w_j + q(V_{uj} - V_{ej}) \qquad \text{and} \qquad rV_{uj} = z + \theta_j m(\theta_j)(V_{ej} - V_{uj}) \tag{55}$$

Taking into account equations (54), which define the expected profit of an employer, the free entry condition $\Pi_{vj} = 0$ allows us to obtain a relation between wages, prices, and the labor market tightness proper to a given industry, which has a form analogous to labor demand in the basic model, being written:

$$w_j = p_j - \frac{(r + q)h}{m(\theta_j)} \tag{56}$$

4.1.2   Labor Market Equilibrium

We distinguish three levels of wage bargaining. Bargaining is described as decentralized when it involves a single employer and a single worker. This is the type of bargaining we have focused on to this point. In industry bargaining, the coordination between agents covers a complete sector of industry; and finally, in centralized bargaining, the coordination extends to the entire economy.

Decentralized Bargaining

When bargaining is decentralized, there is no coalition whose actions might be able to affect the price of goods directly. In other words, the relative prices p_j are considered as given by agents. We can therefore go right back to the basic model of chapter 9, where bargaining does satisfy this assumption, in order to find solutions to the problem we are considering here. In particular, the labor market tightness in industry j is still defined by equation (21) from chapter 9, as long as we replace individual production y by p_j, and note that at symmetric equilibrium, the relative prices p_j are all equal to 1. If γ designates the fraction of the surplus that goes to the worker through bargaining, the equilibrium value θ^d of labor market tightness (identical in all industries) satisfies:

$$\frac{(1-\gamma)(1-z)}{r+q+\gamma\theta^d m(\theta^d)} = \frac{h}{m(\theta^d)} \tag{57}$$

The unemployment rate is then deducible from θ^d with the help of the Beveridge curve (53).

Bargaining at the Industry Level

We will assume that those who take part in bargaining at the industry level are capable of coordinating their actions in order to achieve *efficient* contracts that maximize the net discounted output of the industry, and redistribute this output among the agents belonging to that industry (see chapter 7, section 3, for a discussion of efficient contracts). Moreover, and for the sake of simplicity, we will also assume that agents have no preference for the present (formally we have $r = 0$). In this setting, as we saw in chapter 9, section 6.2.1, it suffices to consider the stationary value of net instantaneous output, which, for industry j, is found by subtracting the costs $h\theta_j u_j$ of vacant jobs from the real value of aggregate output, i.e.[8]:

$$\omega_j = p_j(1-u_j) + zu_j - h\theta_j u_j$$

All the agents in industry j engage in coordination so as to maximize net output ω_j, taking the actions of the agents in the other industries as given. So we have a Nash equilibrium between these coalitions. As they engage in coordination, the agents in industry j are cognizant of the effects of their decisions on the price p_j of the good produced in their industry. The production of good j being equal to $1 - u_j$, and the demand for this good being defined by (52), we have $1 - u_j = (Y/J)p_j^{-\sigma}$, which entails $p_j(1-u_j) = (Y/J)^{1/\sigma}(1-u_j)^{(\sigma-1)/\sigma}$. As the Beveridge curve (53) allows us to express the unemployment rate u_j as a function of labor market tightness θ_j, the problem of the coalition present in industry j comes down to:

$$\underset{\theta_j}{\text{Max}}\ \omega_j = \left(\frac{Y}{J}\right)^{1/\sigma}\left[\frac{\theta_j m(\theta_j)}{q+\theta_j m(\theta_j)}\right]^{(\sigma-1)/\sigma} + \frac{q(z-h\theta_j)}{q+\theta_j m(\theta_j)}$$

Differentiating this expression with respect to θ_j, and noting that at symmetric equilibrium we have $p_j = 1$ and $Y = J(1-u_j)$, we get an equation implicitly defining the equilibrium value θ^b of labor market tightness (identical in all industries). It comes to[9]:

$$\frac{[1-\eta(\theta^b)]\left[\left(\dfrac{\sigma-1}{\sigma}\right)-z\right]}{q+\theta^b m(\theta^b)\eta(\theta^b)} = \frac{h}{m(\theta^b)} \tag{58}$$

Knowing θ^b, we can deduce the unemployment rate from the Beveridge curve (53), while the equilibrium wage follows from labor demand (56) with $p_j = 1$. Evidently this wage does not depend on the bargaining power of the workers. This property derives from the hypothesis that bargaining is efficient, which amounts to supposing that the agents dispose of an array of redistribution tools (lump-sum transfers, for example) that make it possible to attain the socially efficient level of production in their industry.

Assuming that $\eta(\cdot)$ is constant—which amounts to assuming that the matching function is of the Cobb-Douglas type, or $M(v, u) = v^{1-\eta}u^{\eta}$—equation (58) defining labor market tightness shows that this variable increases with the elasticity σ of demand for the good, and the consequence of that is a fall in the unemployment rate. The coalition in each industry j actually has an interest in producing less to increase its relative price p_j, all the more so when demand is weakly elastic to price. Hence employment is pushed higher when the elasticity of demand is strong.

Centralized Bargaining

In order to compare the different equilibria in a coherent manner, it is necessary to assume that centralized bargaining is characterized by a coordination of all agents in all industries with the goal of maximizing aggregate net output. Limiting ourselves to a symmetric solution we can proceed directly to set $p_j = 1$, for $j = 1, \ldots, J$. All industries being identical, the problem of the centralized coalition is written:

$$\underset{u_j, \theta_j}{\mathrm{Max}}(1 - u_j) + zu_j - h\theta_j u_j \qquad \text{with} \qquad u_j = \frac{q}{q + \theta_j m(\theta_j)}$$

We find ourselves back with the problem of the social optimum from the basic model studied in chapter 9, section 4.4.2. The equilibrium value of labor market tightness θ^c (the same in every industry) is thus defined by the following relation:

$$\frac{[1 - \eta(\theta^c)](1 - z)}{q + \theta^c m(\theta^c)\eta(\theta^c)} = \frac{h}{m(\theta^c)} \tag{59}$$

As before, the unemployment rate can be deduced from this condition and the Beveridge curve (53).

4.1.3   The Effects of the Bargaining Level

Comparison of equations (57), (58), and (59), with $r = 0$, indicates that the three levels of bargaining generally lead to different equilibria. Yet if the decentralized level is efficient, i.e., if it satisfies the Hosios condition $\gamma = \eta(\theta^c)$, both decentralized and centralized bargaining arrive at the *same* allocation of resources, i.e., at the same labor market tightness and the same unemployment rate. On the other hand, since $(\sigma - 1)/\sigma < 1$ equation (58) indicates that labor market tightness is weaker, and so unemployment is greater, when bargaining takes place at the industry level. We come back to the hump-shaped curve of Calmfors and Driffill (1988), illustrated in figure 12.15. The reason is that bargaining within industries gives the agents in each industry an incentive to exploit their market power by limiting their production, in order to benefit from an increase in the relative price of the good they are selling. Since the agents in all industries do the same thing, industry-level bargaining leads to a level of employment inferior to that obtained with centralized or decentralized bargaining, where agents do not manipulate relative prices in this way.

These results must be interpreted with caution, however, for they rely on very particular hypotheses. Thus, when the Hosios condition is not satisfied, decentralized bargaining leads to an inefficient outcome. In particular, if $\gamma > \eta(\theta^c)$, we have $\theta^c > \theta^d$, and the unemployment rate is higher in decentralized than in centralized bargaining. Moreover, if the degree of substitutability among goods is sufficiently great, it is possible to obtain $\theta^b > \theta^d$, in which case industry-level bargaining leads to a lower unemployment rate than the decentralized kind. We would then have a *decreasing* monotonic relationship between the degree of centralization of bargaining and the unemployment rate.

From another point of view, the hypothesis of the efficiency of centralized bargaining is debatable. At that level, transaction costs are likely to be important and to cause inefficiency. The instability of union coalitions, strikes, and lobbying all bear witness to the importance of these transaction costs. For example, at the national level it is possible that union representatives, distanced from their own memberships, would give more weight to the interests of "insiders" and neglect those of the unemployed. Were that to occur, union preferences would be biased in favor of the wages of those with a job, and would not meet the criterion of the social welfare. Unemployment would be higher than it would if bargaining were decentralized.

All these considerations suggest that there probably is no "ideal" level for wage bargaining (see Beaudry et al., 2000). Examination of empirical research confirms this point of view.

4.2 FRAGILE EMPIRICAL RESULTS

On the empirical level, the debate has gradually shifted from the supposed virtues of "corporatism" to attempts to highlight a stable linkage between the degree of coordination of bargaining and the economic performance of a country.

4.2.1 On the Efficiency of Corporatism

The first empirical research attempted to demonstrate the existence of an increasing relation between the "degree of corporatism" and macroeconomic performance, measured principally by unemployment rates, inflation, and GDP growth. Bruno and Sachs (1985) proposed a measure of corporatism that has often been used subsequently. It relies on an index indicating the influence of centralized unions of workers on wage setting, the degree of coordination among employers, the power of unions in firms, and the presence of work councils. The purpose of this last variable is to take account of the "degree of consensus" between employers and workers. Thus the level at which bargaining takes place does not constitute the sole factor enabling us to define a degree of corporatism; the existence of a social consensus is also taken into account. Bruno and Sachs (1985) then showed that countries characterized by a high degree of corporatism also have the best macroeconomic performance. These results were backed up by estimates of wage equations or Phillips curves. McCallum (1983) and Bruno and Sachs (1985) found that the degree of corporatism had a negative influence on inflation. According to Bean et al. (1986), real wages are more sensitive to variations in unemployment in the most corporatist countries, which entails a lower unemployment rate in the long run (see chapter 8).

Calmfors and Driffill (1988), however, insisted that the term "corporatism" was imprecise. On this question, it is illuminating to compare the rankings found in various studies of the subject; they are set out in the first four columns of table 12.12. We see that some countries occupy very different places in the different rankings. Japan is considered the least corporatist country by Cameron (1984), while Blyth (1987) and Bruno and Sachs (1985) place it somewhere in the middle. France has a lower degree of corporatism than the United States and Canada, according to Schmitter (1981) and Cameron, but Blyth and Bruno and Sachs take precisely the opposite view. Since these international comparisons are limited to a small number of countries,

Table 12.12

Various rankings of countries by their degree of corporatism, in decreasing order (first four columns) or by the degree to which wage bargaining is centralized (last column).

	Schmitter	Cameron	Blyth	Bruno-Sachs	Calmfors-Driffill
1	Austria	Sweden	Austria	Austria	Austria
2	Norway	Norway	Norway	Germany	Norway
3	Sweden	Austria	Sweden	Netherlands	Sweden
4	Denmark	Belgium	Denmark	Norway	Denmark
5	Finland	Finland	Finland	Switzerland	Finland
6	Netherlands	Denmark	New Zealand	Sweden	Germany
7	Belgium	Netherlands	Australia	Denmark	Netherlands
8	Germany	Germany	Germany	Finland	Belgium
9	Switzerland	United Kingdom	Belgium	Belgium	New Zealand
10	United States	Australia	Netherlands	Japan	Australia
11	Canada	Switzerland	Japan	New Zealand	France
12	France	Italy	France	United Kingdom	United Kingdom
13	United Kingdom	Canada	United Kingdom	France	Italy
14	Italy	United States	Italy	Italy	Japan
15	—	France	United States	Australia	Switzerland
16	—	Japan	Canada	Canada	United States
17	—	—	—	United States	Canada

Source: Calmfors and Driffill (1988).

any change in the ranking will generally have a significant impact on estimates of the relationship between the degree of corporatism and macroeconomic performance.

For this reason, Calmfors and Driffill (1988) have proposed abandoning the use of a hypothetical degree of corporatism and replacing it with a measure of the centralization of wage bargaining, which ought in principle to be easier to define. The ranking they propose is based on a system of weightings linked to two criteria: the level of coordination within organizations of workers and employers (3 for the national level, 2 for the industry level, 1 for the firm, and 0 when there is no coordination), and the number of confederations of workers or employers coordinating their decisions at the national level (3 for a country with just one confederation of this type, 2 when there are between two and five of them, and 1 for more than that). This ranking is shown in the last column of table 12.12.

Using data for the period 1963–1985, Calmfors and Driffill categorize countries into three groups: the centralized countries, which are (in decreasing order) Austria, Norway, Sweden, Denmark, and Finland; the intermediate countries, Germany, the Netherlands, Belgium, New Zealand, and Australia; and the decentralized ones, France, the United Kingdom, Italy, Japan, Switzerland, the United States, and Canada. Calmfors and Driffill then show that the relationship between the degree to which bargaining is centralized and certain indicators of macroeconomic performance over the period 1963–1985, like the unemployment rate, or the unemployment rate plus the inflation rate, or the unemployment rate plus the balance of payments deficit expressed as a percentage of GDP, is close to a hump-shaped curve like the one represented in figure 12.15.

4.2.2   On the Inefficiency of Wage Bargaining at the Industry Level

At least three reasons point to the conclusion that the relative inefficiency of wage bargaining at the industry level is a fragile result.

(i) If we adopt the same ranking as Calmfors and Driffill (1988), we see that the relationship between the degree to which bargaining is centralized and the unemployment rate changes after 1990. Table 12.13, for example, shows that in 1993 there was an increasing monotonic relation between the unemployment rate and the degree

Table 12.13

Average unemployment rates.

	1974–1985	1986–1996	1993
Centralized economies	4.0	6.6	9.3
Intermediate economies	6.1	8.3	8.7
Decentralized economies	5.8	6.6	8.1

Source: Calmfors and Driffill (1988) and OECD (1999).

to which wage bargaining was centralized. But on average, over the period 1986–1996, the relationship is always hump-shaped. The poor employment performance of Sweden, and especially Finland, at the end of the 1980s and the beginning of the 1990s qualifies the notion that economies with centralized bargaining are more efficient than others in all cases. During this period the positive relationship between centralization and macroeconomic performance that had emerged from the earlier research on corporatism was inverted.

(ii) The measure of the degree of centralization which Calmfors and Driffill propose is not exempt from criticism either. Soskice (1990) pointed out that for one thing, the criteria chosen by these authors only concern the formal structure of workers' and employers' organizations, but do not allow us to take account of the way bargaining really unfolds. For example, Soskice estimates that in reality, Japan and Switzerland have very strongly coordinated bargaining, and so ought to be ranked among the centralized economies. In Switzerland, wage formation is strongly influenced by arbitration committees, which decide cases when the parties themselves cannot agree. In Japan, the "spring offensive," in which the major firms announce their intentions with regard to wages, has a preponderant impact on all wage bargaining. If we follow Soskice and assume that Japan and Switzerland belong with the centralized economies, then there is a *decreasing* relationship between the unemployment rate and the degree of centralization for the same period as that studied by Calmfors and Driffill.

The relevance of Soskice's critique is confirmed, partially at least, by the research published by the OECD (1994), in which a distinction is made between *explicit* and *implicit* coordination. In the former, there is actual collaboration between the employers' confederation and that of the workers during wage bargaining. In the latter, these confederations may merely sway their members, or agreements made in the principal sectors of the economy may serve as guidelines for the rest. According to the OECD survey, Japan is indeed characterized by strong implicit coordination at the national level. The situation in Switzerland, though, is harder to grasp. The OECD estimates that the extent of coordination there is limited, whereas Soskice sees it as significant enough to assign Switzerland a degree of centralization comparable to that of Norway and superior to that of Sweden. This indeterminacy proves that the degree of centralization of bargaining is actually just as hard to define as the degree of corporatism.

(iii) The coexistence of more than one level of bargaining (see chapter 7, table 7.1) has great impact on wage formation. Table 12.14 gives an indication of the "wage drift," in other words the gap between the agreements reached at the national level and their application at the level of individual firms, in the Scandinavian countries. The extent of this drift is very large, for it rarely represents less than 30% of growth in hourly wages, and sometimes reaches 70%. These figures can be interpreted in different ways. It is possible that the centralization of wage bargaining is no more than illusory, and that decentralized bargaining, or even a simple competitive market, are better models of the way wages are really set. It is equally possible that these wage

Table 12.14

Wage drift in the private sector as a percentage of the increase in the hourly wage rate.

	1971–75	1976–80	1981–85	1971–85
Denmark				
Overall	41	47	37	42
Finland				
Overall	30	28	33	30
Workers	34	18	26	26
Executives	18	22	18	19
Norway				
Overall	50	62	69	60
Sweden				
Workers	45	42	43	43
Executives	20	20	46	29

Source: Flanagan (1990, p. 398).

drifts are more or less anticipated, and so implictly woven into the national agreements. The few monographic studies of this subject (see the ones mentioned in Calmfors, 1990) do not make it possible to decide. But the idea that the Scandinavian countries have a totally centralized system for setting wages must surely be qualified (see Flanagan, 1990, as well).

5 MACROECONOMIC ASSESSMENTS OF INSTITUTIONS

Analysis of the institutions proper to each country has shown that their impact on labor market performance is generally not without ambiguity, and varies with the context in which they apply. The effect of the minimum wage on employment depends, for example, on the relative level of the minimum. Moreover, institutions interact and may cancel each other out. Hence it is important to assess the impact of public policies within a macroeconomic framework that takes their interactions into account. A number of studies, using very similar methodology and OECD data, have undertaken such an assessment (Scarpetta, 1996; Nickell, 1997; Layard and Nickell, 1999; Blanchard and Wolfers, 2000; Belot and van Ours, 2000).

5.1 THE IMPACT OF INSTITUTIONS

Our discussion relies mainly on the study of Blanchard and Wolfers (2000), which is one of the most comprehensive in this area. It makes use of data from 20 OECD countries[10] for the period 1960–1996 and tries to pinpoint the impact of macroeconomic shocks, on the one hand, and the influence of public policy and institutions, on the other, on the unemployment rate. Blanchard and Wolfers suggest that the *interaction* between economic shocks that were *common* to all of the 20 OECD countries, and their *different* institutions, makes it possible to explain a large amount of the diversity of their performance when it comes to unemployment.

Blanchard and Wolfers identify three kinds of macroeconomic shocks capable of having pushed unemployment in Europe up: the decline in the growth rate of the total factor productivity,[11] which underwent a continuous slide from 5% at the beginning of the 1960s to around 2% at the beginning of the 1990s; the increase in real interest rates since the end of the 1970s, which went from around 2% in 1980 to 5% at the beginning of the 1990s; and a decline in labor demand leading to a reduction of the labor share in GDP. After having risen in the 1970s, the labor share in GDP began to fall at the beginning of the 1980s, and has reached a value 10% lower than that of 1960. Let us recall that the labor share in GDP depends on technological factors and the functioning of markets. For example, if technology is of the Cobb-Douglas type, production Y being a function $Y = K^{1-\alpha}L^{\alpha}$ of capital K and labor L, with $\alpha \in (0,1)$, labor demand can be written $\alpha Y/L = \mu w$, where w designates the real wage and μ the markup measuring the market power of firms. The labor share in GDP is thus equal to α/μ. It might be reduced on account of a change in the technology or an increase in the market power of firms.

The institutions taken into account are the replacement ratio of unemployment benefits, their duration, active employment policies, employment protection, the tax wedge, the extent of coverage of collective bargaining, the rate of unionization, and the degree of coordination of collective bargaining. The equation estimated is of the form:

$$u_{it} = c_i + d_t \left(1 + \sum_j X_{ij}b_j\right) + e_{it} \tag{60}$$

In this equation, the indexes i, t, and j refer respectively to the country, the period (each period lasts five years), and the public policy or institution. Parameter c_i designates a country fixed effect, while d_t represents the time effect for period t. The independent variable X_{ij} measures the value of public policy or institution j for country i, and b_j is an estimated coefficient capturing the impact of characteristic j on the unemployment rate of all the countries considered. Finally, e_{it} is a random error term. In this specification, the macroeconomic shocks, assumed to be common to all countries, are simply represented by the variable d_t, which is the time effect for period t.

The results of the estimation of equation (60) are presented in table 12.15. We see that the equation explains almost 87% of the variance in unemployment rates. In addition, all the coefficients are statistically significant, with the expected sign. The exception is the coefficient of union coverage, the effect of which is not significantly different from zero. We see that the temporal effect increases the unemployment rate

Table 12.15

Institutions and unemployment in 20 OECD countries (1960–1995).

	(1) Coefficients	(2) Range of independent variable	(3) Implied range of effect of shock (mean 1)
Time effect	7.3%		
Replacement ratio	0.017 (5.1)	[−46.3, 32.6]	[0.21, 1.55]
Benefit length	0.206 (4.9)	[−2.0, 1.6]	[0.60, 1.33]
Active labor policies	0.017 (3.0)	[−47.2, 9.5]	[0.20, 1.16]
Employment protection	0.045 (3.1)	[−9.5, 9.5]	[0.58, 1.42]
Tax wedge	0.018 (3.2)	[−17.8, 22.2]	[0.68, 1.40]
Union coverage	0.098 (0.6)	[−1.7, 0.3]	[0.83, 1.03]
Union density	0.009 (2.1)	[−30.4, 39.6]	[0.73, 1.36]
Coordination	0.304 (5.1)	[−2.0, 2.0]	[0.40, 1.60]
$\bar{R}^2$	0.863		

Source: Blanchard and Wolfers (2000, table 1).

Note: t-statistics in parentheses in column 1.

by 7.3 percentage points[12] over the period. In other words, a country where the value of public policies and institutions was equal to the average of the OECD countries would have seen an increase of 7.3 points in its unemployment rate.

The purpose of columns (2) and (3) in table 12.15 is to illuminate the manner in which different public policies and institutions influence the response of the unemployment rate to the shocks affecting the economy. Column (2) gives the range for each institutional measure in terms of deviations from the cross-country mean. Column (3) takes as its point of reference a "representative" country where the public policies and institutions are equal to the mean of the 20 OECD countries included in the study. By hypothesis, we consider a shock that increases the unemployment rate by 1 percentage point in this country. The first line of column (3) then indicates that the increase in the unemployment rate in a country that underwent the same shock, and in which the only difference with respect to the representative country was that it had the lowest replacement ratio, would be 0.21 points. Conversely, the unemployment rate would have risen by 1.55 points if it had the highest replacement ratio. Scrutiny of column (3) shows that the differences in the response of the unemployment rate for each measure are not very great. Thus it is not possible to isolate a particular variable that might explain the essential differences in unemployment performance. It is likely a complex of characteristics of the policies and institutions affecting the labor market that is the source of differences in performance in this area.

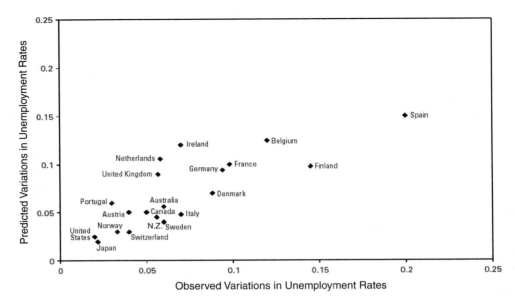

FIGURE 12.16
Actual and predicted change in unemployment rates, 1995–1996, with respect to 1965–1969.

Blanchard and Wolfers suggest that the set of characteristics taken into account by them correctly explains the differences in the evolution of unemployment rates in the countries considered. Figure 12.16 represents the relationship between variations in the unemployment rate as observed and as predicted by the estimate of equation (60) between the periods 1995–1996 and 1965–1969. It shows that interactions among particular institutional characteristics and common macroeconomic shocks make it possible to explain satisfactorily the relative performance of most of the 20 countries observed. The second part of the study of Blanchard and Wolfers, which is dedicated to the robustness of these results and the exploration of alternative models, suggests that the very simple specification of equation (60) yields very good results. In particular, it appears that introducing macroeconomic shocks particular to each country, represented by the evolutions of the factor productivity, the real rate of interest, and the determinants of the labor share in GDP, does not arrive at better econometric results.

Overall, the study of Blanchard and Wolfers (2000) comes to, and in many respects completes, the conclusions of Nickell (1997), Layard and Nickell (1999), Elmeskov et al. (1998), and Nickell et al. (2002). Bad employment performance is generally associated with the presence of *a number* of characteristics of public policy and institutions. For example, Nickell (1997) concludes that these characteristics are the following: (1) unemployment benefits have a high replacement ratio and long duration; (2) the rate of unionization is high and there is little coordination between employers and/or employees during bargaining; (3) taxes on earned income are high, or there is both a high tax wedge and a high minimum wage; (4) the system of training for the least educated performs poorly. *A contrario*, these results suggest that the battle against unemployment has to be waged on a number of fronts at once.

5.2 INTERACTIONS AND COMPLEMENTARITIES OF POLICIES AND INSTITUTIONS

Beyond assessing the impact proper to each of the characteristics of institutions and public policies, macroeconomic studies also indicate that the interactions among these characteristics play an important part.

The result is that a country may have certain institutions a priori unfavorable to employment that have no significant effect on unemployment when they are coupled with other policies and institutions. Portugal, for example, has very strict employment protection measures that apparently have little effect on unemployment because of the way wages are set (Blanchard and Portugal, 2001). More generally, it seems, according to Elmeskov et al. (1998), that employment protection pushes unemployment up to a greater extent, the weaker the coordination of employers and workers during bargaining is. These authors also find that higher unemployment insurance benefits are more unfavorable to employment in countries that spend large amounts on active labor market policies. Active policies may produce few results if at the same time passive policy is too "generous," i.e., if there is little incentive for an unemployed person to look for a job or get training. In this regard, Nickell (1997) notes that many of the characteristics of labor markets that are frequently taken to constitute rigidities unfavorable to employment are not found more often in countries with high unemployment than they are in countries with low unemployment. These characteristics include high tax rates, stringent employment protection, high union densities, and high unemployment benefits. These conclusions are easy to explain. Tax rates, unionization, and employment protection will have a significant impact on employment only if the coordination of employers and workers during wage bargaining is weak. High unemployment benefits have a significant effect on unemployment only when they are paid out for a very long period.

Interactions between different institutions naturally lead to attempts to identify the synergies or complementaries that will favor employment. The study of Belot and van Ours (2000) attempts to detect the interactions among labor market institutions using data from 18 OECD countries for the period 1960–1995. Belot and van Ours estimate equations in which the unemployment rate is explained by variables measuring institutions. Let $X_{i,j,t}$ be the value of institution j in country i at date t; the unemployment rate of country i at date t, $u_{i,t}$, is explained by the terms $X_{i,j,t}$, by variation in the inflation rate $\Delta^2 p$, but also by the multiplicative terms $X_{i,j,t} \cdot X_{i,j',t}$ (where j' designates an institution different from j), the role of which is precisely to take interactions among institutions into account. In comparing estimates obtained with and without multiplicative terms, Belot and van Ours show, first, that taking interactions into account makes it possible to improve econometric results significantly. Their results, presented in table 12.16, suggest that complementarities play a leading role.

Table 12.16

Unemployment and the interaction of labor market institutions.

	Dependent variable: standardized rate of unemployment								
$\Delta^2 p$	τ	b	f	ds	cs	co	$\tau \cdot b$	$\tau \cdot f$	$\tau \cdot ds$
−0.19 (0.03)	0.29 (0.02)	0.00 (0.02)	0.00 (0.02)	0.16 (0.03)	−0.22 (0.03)	0.00 (0.00)	0.66 (0.11)	−0.51 (0.08)	−0.32 (0.11)
$\tau \cdot cs$	$\tau \cdot co$	$b \cdot ds$	$b \cdot cs$	$f \cdot ds$	$f \cdot cs$	$f \cdot co$	$ds \cdot cs$	$cs \cdot co$	R^2
0.64 (0.09)	0.09 (0.03)	0.17 (0.08)	−0.40 (0.09)	0.46 (0.07)	0.21 (0.07)	−0.04 (0.02)	−0.42 (0.10)	−0.11 (0.02)	0.78

Source: Belot and van Ours (2000, table 6).

Notes: $\Delta^2 p$ = variation in inflation. $\tau \in [0, 1]$ = tax rate. $b \in [0, 1]$ = replacement ratio. $f \in [0, 1]$ employment protection. $ds \in [0, 1]$ = density of unionization. $cs \in [0, 1]$ = coverage of collective bargaining. co (1/2/3) = index of the coordination in collective bargaining. Standard deviations are in parentheses.

We see that the replacement ratio b, employment protection f, and union coordination co have no direct influence on unemployment. But these variables do exert an impact through their interaction with other institutions. Thus the combination of a high replacement ratio and high taxes proves unfavorable to employment. The combination of strong employment protection and strong union power is also unfavorable to employment.

The mechanisms of complementarity among the various policies and institutions are still poorly understood in theory (see, however, the work of Bertola and Rogerson, 1997; Coe and Snower, 1997; and Orszag and Snower, 1998). Moreover, we must point out that all the research exploiting panel data on OECD nations yields valuable indications about the potential origins of unemployment, but comes to very fragile results. For this there are two important reasons. The first has to do with the nature of the data utilized. Institutional variables such as the degree of employment protection or the generosity of unemployment benefits actually sum up many different aspects of these institutions in a single figure, and the choices made by each researcher working in this field can affect the results profoundly. The problem is made worse by the fact that estimates are based on a restricted number of observations. This is the second important reason why the results may be fragile.

Reflection on the economic performance of labor markets suggests that institutions do exert a significant impact on employment, unemployment, and the distribution of income. They also suggest that there are no institutions that are "good" or "bad" in all circumstances. Neither, in all likelihood, is there is a miraculous combination that would fit every situation (Freeman, 2000). The technology used by the economies, the nature of competition in other markets, their degree of openness, their demographic characteristics—all these are parameters that must be taken into account in attempting to judge the efficiency of existing institutions. And from this standpoint, the knowledge acquired to date in this area is still highly inadequate.

6 SUMMARY AND CONCLUSION

- The level of the minimum wage is clearly higher in Europe (where it exceeds 50% of the average wage) than it is in the United States (where it barely reaches 40% of the average wage). In France in 1996, 32% of workers 25 years of age and under were paid at minimum wage, as opposed to 14% in the United States.

- In the monopsony model, a rise in minimum wage from a low initial value leads to an increase in employment. In the matching model, the same situation arises when labor market participation or job search effort are endogenous. Revising the minimum wage upward exerts a negative effect on labor demand, but may in certain circumstances give unemployed persons an incentive to intensify their search effort. The latter effect will have a tendency to increase returns to employment, and so bring down the unemployment rate. A reasonable calibration of the matching model with endogenous job search tells us that a moderate increase in minimum wage, if the initial value is low, does indeed have a positive effect on employment.

- Macroeconomic studies that attempt to establish correlations between employment and minimum wage generally conclude that the effect of this instrument is negligible, except perhaps when it comes to youth employment. Recent research, based on individual longitudinal data, shows that the level of minimum wage has a significant positive effect on the probability of job loss, and more generally on nonemployment among the populations affected by this level of remuneration.

- Employment protection legislation is a set of mandatory restrictions governing the dismissal of employees. According to the synthetic index of the strictness of employment protection established by the OECD, the United States and the United Kingdom are the most "flexible" countries. Germany, France, and southern Europe are among the least "flexible" areas.

- A priori, firing costs have an ambiguous effect on unemployment, and reduce manpower mobility by reducing both job creation and job destruction at the same time. When wages are bargained over, an increase in firing costs entails lower wages, and this attenuates the negative effects on job creation. On the other hand, if wages are exogenous (as they are, for example, in the case of workers being paid minimum wage), this attenuating mechanism vanishes. Calibration exercises confirm that, if wages are bargained over, employment protection measures have little influence on job creation, job destruction, and the unemployment rate. If wages are rigid, the job destruction rate shows little sensitivity to firing costs, but exit rates from unemployment fall off sharply, and the unemployment rate soars.

- At the macroeconomic level, the correlation between the unemployment rate and employment protection measures proves to be fragile, and highly sensitive to the specification of the estimated equations. Essentially, empirical research confirms that firing costs have an impact the sign of which is ambiguous, and the extent of which on global unemployment is slight. It does, however, highlight a negative impact of these costs on manpower flows. Countries with little employment protection experience mainly short-term unemployment, while countries with strong unemployment protection have more long-term unemployment than others.

- Mandatory contributions comprise taxes and social security contributions. In continental Europe, the rate of mandatory contributions is at least ten points higher than it is in the Anglo-Saxon countries. A large portion of this gap can be accounted for by the divergent nature—public for the former, private for the latter—of the social insurance system.

- The gap between the cost of labor and the purchasing power of wages is measured by the *wedge*. The contribution of taxes to the wedge is referred to as the *tax wedge*.

- Theory shows that variations in marginal and average tax rates have very different consequences on labor market outcomes. More progressive taxes reduce unemployment and hours worked, whereas a greater tax wedge increases unemployment and reduces hours when the gains of the unemployed are not perfectly indexed to net wages. Empirical research confirms, to a certain extent, these predictions.

- If agents are capable of coordination among themselves to achieve efficient contracts, the unemployment rate ought to rise when bargaining takes place at the industry level, rather than being decentralized to the level of individual firms, or centralized to a level embracing the whole economy. But this conclusion proves fragile on the empirical level, and no longer holds from the early 1990s.

- Macroeconomic research conducted with the aim of pinpointing the influence of public policy and institutions does not succeed in isolating one particular variable capable of explaining the core of unemployment. It does suggest that the *interaction* between macroeconomic shocks common to all 20 OECD countries, and different institutions will allow us to explain a large part of the diversity in their performance when it comes to unemployment. Bad employment performance must be linked to *a number* of characteristics of public policy and institutions. It is, in all likelihood, the *interactions* among these characteristics, on the one hand, and macroeconomic shocks, on the other, that play a dominant part.

7   RELATED TOPICS IN THE BOOK

- Chapter 1, section 2.2: Main results on the elasticity of labor supply
- Chapter 4, section 3: Labor demand and adjustment costs

- Chapter 5, section 2.1: Wage, employment, and monopsony power

- Chapter 7, section 1.1: The level at which bargaining takes place

- Chapter 7, section 3: The right-to-manage model and efficient contracts

- Chapter 9, section 3: The matching model

- Chapter 10, section 2.6: The minimum wage and inequalities

- Chapter 11, section 2.3: Employment subsidies

- Chapter 11, section 3: The evaluation of active labor market policies

8 FURTHER READINGS

Blanchard, O., and Wolfers, J. (2000), ''The role of shocks and institutions in the rise of European unemployment: The aggregate evidence,'' *Economic Journal*, 110, suppl., pp. 1–33.

Brown, C. (1999), ''Minimum wages, employment, and the distribution of income,'' in Ashenfelter, O., and Card, D. (eds.), *Handbook of Labor Economics*, vol. 3B, chap. 32, pp. 2101–2163, Amsterdam: Elsevier Science/North-Holland.

Calmfors, L., and Driffill, J. (1988), ''Bargaining structure, corporatism and macroeconomic performance,'' *Economic Policy*, 6, pp. 16–61.

Dolado, J., Kramarz, F., Machin, S., Manning, A., Margolis, D., and Teulings, C. (1996), ''The economic impact of minimum wages in Europe,'' *Economic Policy*, October, pp. 319–372.

Layard, R., and Nickell, S. (1999), ''Labor market institutions and economic performances,'' in Ashenfelter, O., and Card, D. (eds.), *Handbook of Labor Economics*, vol. 3C, chap. 46, Amsterdam: Elsevier Science/North-Holland.

REFERENCES

Abowd, J., Kramarz, F., Lemieux, T., and Margolis, D. (1999), ''Minimum wages and youth employment in France and the United States,'' in Blanchflower, D., and Freeman, R. (eds.), *Youth Employment and the Labor Market*, Chicago: University of Chicago Press.

Acemoglu, D. (2001), ''Good jobs versus bad jobs,'' *Journal of Labor Economics*, 19, pp. 1–22.

Addison, J., and Blackburn, M. (1999), ''Minimum wages and poverty,'' *Industrial and Labor Relations Review*, 52(3), pp. 393–409.

Addison, J., and Teixeira, P. (2003), ''The economics of employment protection,'' *Journal of Labor Research*, 24(1), pp. 85–129.

Alesina, A., and Perroti, R. (1997), ''The welfare state and competitiveness,'' *American Economic Review*, 87, pp. 921–939.

Allen, S. (1987), "Taxes, redistribution and the minimum wage: A theoretical analysis," *Quarterly Journal of Economics*, 101, pp. 477–489.

Bean, C., Layard, R., and Nickell, S. (1986), "The rise in unemployment: A multi-country study," *Economica*, 53, S1–S22.

Beaudry, P., Cahuc, P., and Kempf, H. (2000), "Is it harmful to allow partial cooperation?" *Scandinavian Journal of Economics*, 102, pp. 7–21.

Belot, M., and van Ours, J. (2000), "Does the recent success of some OECD countries in lowering their unemployment rates lie in the clever design of their labour market reforms?" Working Paper No. 147, IZA, http://www.iza.org.

Bentolila, S., and Bertola, G. (1990), "Firing costs and labour demand: How bad is Eurosclerosis?" *Review of Economic Studies*, 57, pp. 381–402.

Bertola, G. (1990), "Job security, employment and wages," *European Economic Review*, 34, pp. 851–886.

Bertola, G. (1999), "Microeconomic perspectives on aggregate labor market," in Ashenfelter, O., and Card, D. (eds.), *Handbook of Labor Economics*, vol. 3C, chap. 45, pp. 2985–3028, Amsterdam: Elsevier Science/North-Holland.

Bertola, G., and Rogerson, R. (1997), "Institutions and labor reallocation," *European Economic Review*, 41, pp. 1147–1171.

Blanchard, O., and Portugal, P. (2001), "What hides behind an unemployment rate: Comparing Portuguese and US labor markets," *American Economic Review*, 90(1), pp. 187–207.

Blanchard, O., and Wolfers, J. (2000), "The role of shocks and institutions in the rise of European unemployment: The aggregate evidence," *Economic Journal*, 110, suppl., pp. 1–33.

Blyth, C. (1987), "The interaction between collective bargaining and government policies in selected member countries," in *Collective Bargaining and Government Policies*, Paris: OECD.

Boadway, R., and Cuff, K. (2001), "A minimum wage can be welfare improving and employment-enhancing," *European Economic Review*, 45, pp. 553–576.

Boeri, T. (1999), "Enforcement of employment security regulations: On-the-job search and unemployment duration," *European Economic Review*, 43, pp. 65–89.

Bourguignon, F. (2001), "Redistribution and labor-supply incentives," in Buti, M., Sestito, P., and Wijkander, H. (eds.), *Taxation, Welfare and the Crisis of Unemployment in Europe*, pp. 23–51, Northampton: Edward Elgar.

Brown, C. (1999), "Minimum wages, employment, and the distribution of income," in Ashenfelter, O., and Card, D. (eds.), *Handbook of Labor Economics*, vol. 3B, chap. 32, pp. 2101–2163, Amsterdam: Elsevier Science/North-Holland.

Bruno, M., and Sachs, J. (1985), *The Economics of Worldwide Stagflation*, Oxford, U.K.: Basil Blackwell.

Burdett, K., and Mortensen, D. (1998), "Wage differentials, employer size and unemployment," *International Economic Review*, 39, pp. 257–273.

Cabrales, A., and Hopenhayn, H. (1997), "Labor market flexibility and aggregate employment volatility," *Carnegie-Rochester Conference Series on Public Policy*, No. 46, pp. 189–228.

Cabrales, A., and Hopenhayn, H. (1998), "Job dynamics, correlated shocks and wage profiles," working paper UPF 501, Universitat Pompeu Fabra.

Cahuc, P., and Michel, P. (1996), "Minimum wage, unemployment and growth," *European Economic Review*, 40, pp. 1463–1482.

Cahuc, P., Saint-Martin, A., and Zylberberg, A. (2001), "The consequences of the minimum wage when other wages are bargained over," *European Economic Review*, 45, pp. 337–352.

Calmfors, L. (ed.) (1990), *Wage Formation and Macroeconomic Policy in the Nordic Countries*, Oxford, U.K.: Oxford University Press.

Calmfors, L., and Driffill, J. (1988), "Bargaining structure, corporatism and macroeconomic performance," *Economic Policy*, 6, pp. 16–61.

Cameron, D. (1984), "Social democracy, corporatism, labour quiescence and the representation of economic interest in advanced capitalist society," in Goldthorpe, J. (ed.), *Order and Conflict in Contemporary Capitalism*, Oxford, U.K.: Clarendon.

Card, D., and Krueger, A. (1994), "Minimum wages and employment: A case study of the fast-food industry in New Jersey and Pennsylvania," *American Economic Review*, 84, pp. 772–793.

Card, D., and Krueger, A. (1995), *Myth and Measurement: The New Economics of Minimum Wage*, Princeton, N.J.: Princeton University Press.

Card, D., and Krueger, A. (2000), "Minimum wages and employment: A case study of the fast-food industry in New Jersey and Pennsylvania: Reply," *American Economic Review*, 90, pp. 1397–1420.

Coe, D. (1990), "Structural determinants of the natural rate in Canada," *IMF Staff Papers*, 37(1), pp. 94–115.

Coe, D., and Snower, D. (1997), "Policy complementarities: The case for fundamental labor market reform," *IMF Staff Papers*, 44(1), pp. 1–35.

Daveri, F., and Tabellini, G. (2000), "Unemployment, growth and taxation in industrial countries," *Economic Policy*, April, pp. 49–104.

DiNardo, J., Fortin, N., and Lemieux, T. (1996), "Labor market institutions and the distribution of wages, 1973–1992: A semi-parametric approach," *Econometrica*, 64, pp. 1001–1044.

Dolado, J., Kramarz, F., Machin, S., Manning, A., Margolis, D., and Teulings, C. (1996), "The economic impact of minimum wages in Europe," *Economic Policy*, October, pp. 319–372.

Drazen, A. (1986), "Optimal minimum wage legislation," *Economic Journal*, 96, pp. 774–784.

Elmeskov, J., Martin, J., and Scarpetta, S. (1998), "Key lessons for labour market reforms: Evidence from OECD countries' experiences," *Swedish Economic Policy Review*, 5, pp. 205–253.

Flanagan, R. (1990), "Centralized and decentralized pay formation in Nordic countries," in Calmfors, L. (ed.), *Wage Formation and Macroeconomic Policy in the Nordic Countries*, Oxford, U.K.: Oxford University Press.

Flinn, C. (2002), "Labor market structure and inequality: A comparison of Italy and the U.S.," *Review of Economic Studies*, 69, pp. 611–645.

Flinn, C. (2003), "Minimum wage effects on labor market outcomes under search with bargaining," working paper, Department of Economics, New York University, New York.

Freeman, R. (2000), "Single peaked vs diversified capitalism: The relation between economic institutions and outcome," NBER Working Paper No. 7546, http://www.nber.org/papers/w7556.

Fuest, C., and Huber, B. (2000), "Is tax progression really good for employment? A model with endogenous hours of work," *Labour Economics*, 7(1), pp. 79–93.

Garibaldi, P. (1998), "Job flow dynamics and firing restrictions," *European Economic Review*, 42, pp. 245–275.

Garibaldi, P., Konings, J., and Pissarides, C. (1997), "Gross job reallocation and labour market policy," in Snower, D., and de la Dehesa, G. (eds.), *Unemployment Policy: Government Options for the Labour Market*, Cambridge, U.K.: Cambridge University Press.

Grubb, D., and Wells, W. (1993), "Employment regulation and pattern of work in EC countries," *OECD Economic Studies*, 21, pp. 7–59.

Guesnerie, R., and Roberts, R. (1987), "Minimum wage legislation as a second-best policy," *European Economic Review*, 31, pp. 490–498.

Hansen, C. (1999), "Lower tax progression, longer hours and higher wages," *Scandinavian Journal of Economics*, 101(1), pp. 49–65.

Hansen, C., Pedersen, L., and Slok, T. (2000), "Ambiguous effects of tax progressivity: Theory and Danish evidence," *Labour Economics*, 7(3), pp. 335–347.

Jones, S. (1987), "Minimum wage legislation in a dual labor market," *European Economic Review*, 33, pp. 1229–1246.

Kaitz, H. (1970), "Experience of the past: The national minimum wage," in *Youth Unemployment and Minimum Wages*, U.S. Department of Labor, Bureau of Labor Statistics, Bulletin 1657, pp. 30–54.

Kennan, J. (1995), "The elusive effects of minimum wage," *Journal of Economic Literature*, 33, pp. 1949–1965.

Kramarz, F., and Philippon, T. (2001), "The impact of differential payroll tax subsidies on minimum wage employment," *Journal of Public Economics*, 82, pp. 115–146.

Laroque, G., and Salanié, B. (1999), "Breaking down married female non-employment in France," CEPR Discussion Paper No. 2239.

Layard, R., and Nickell, S. (1999), "Labor market institutions and economic performances," in Ashenfelter, O., and Card, D. (eds.), *Handbook of Labor Economics*, vol. 3C, chap. 46, Amsterdam: Elsevier Science/North-Holland.

Lazear, E. (1990), "Job security provisions and employment," *Quarterly Journal of Economics*, 105, pp. 699–725.

Lee, D. (1999), "Wage inequality in the United States during the 1980s: Rising dispersion or falling minimum wage?" *Quarterly Journal of Economics*, 114, pp. 977–1023.

Lockwood, B., and Manning, A. (1993), "Wage setting and the tax system: Theory and evidence for the United Kingdom," *Journal of Public Economics*, 52, pp. 1–29.

Malcomson, J., and Sator, N. (1987), "Tax push inflation in a unionized labour market," *European Economic Review*, 31, pp. 1581–1596.

Manning, A. (1995), "How do we know that real wages are too high?" *Quarterly Journal of Economics*, 110, pp. 1111–1125.

Marceau, N., and Boadway, R. (1994), "Minimum wage legislation and unemployment insurance," *Scandinavian Journal of Economics*, 96, pp. 67–81.

Masters, A. (1999), "Wage posting in two-sided search and the minimum wage," *International Economic Review*, 40, pp. 809–826.

McCallum, J. (1983), "Inflation and social consensus in the seventies," *Economic Journal*, 93, pp. 784–805.

Millard, S., and Mortensen, D. (1997), "The unemployment and welfare effects of labour market policy: A comparison of the USA and the UK," in Snower, D., and de la Dehesa, G. (eds.), *Unemployment Policy: Government Options for the Labour Market*, CEPR, Cambridge, U.K.: Cambridge University Press.

Mirrlees, J. (1971), "An exploration in the theory of optimum income taxation," *Review of Economic Studies*, 38, pp. 175–208.

Mortensen, D., and Pissarides, C. (1994), "Job creation and job destruction in the theory of unemployment," *Review of Economic Studies*, 61, pp. 397–415.

Mortensen, D., and Pissarides, C. (1999), "Unemployment responses to 'skill-biased' technology shocks: The role of labour market policy," *Economic Journal*, 109, pp. 242–265.

Musgrave, R., and Musgrave, P. (1989), *Public Finance in Theory and Practice*, 5th ed., New York: McGraw-Hill.

Neumark, D., and Wascher, W. (2000), "Minimum wages and employment: A case study of the fast-food industry in New Jersey and Pennsylvania: Comment," *American Economic Review*, 90, pp. 1362–1396.

Nickell, S. (1997), "Unemployment and labor market rigidities: Europe versus North America," *Journal of Economic Perspectives*, 3, pp. 55–74.

Nickell, S., Nunziata, L., Ochel, W., and Quintini, G. (2002), "The Beveridge curve, unemployment and wages in the OECD from the 1960s to the 1990s," Discussion Paper No. 502, Center for Economic Performance, London School of Economics, London.

OECD (1994), *The OECD Jobs Study*, Paris: OECD.

OECD (1996), *Employment Outlook*, Paris: OECD.

OECD (1998), "Making the most of the minimum: Statutory minimum wages, employment and poverty," in *Employment Outlook*, chap. 2, pp. 31–77, Paris: OECD.

OECD (1999), "Employment protection and labor market performance," in *Employment Outlook*, chap. 2, Paris: OECD.

OECD (2001), *Taxing Wages: Income Tax, Social Security Contributions and Cash Family Benefits, 1999–2000*, Paris: OECD.

Orszag, M., and Snower, D. (1998), "Anatomy of policy complementarities," *Swedish Economic Policy Review*, 5(2), pp. 303–345.

Padoa-Schioppa, F. (1990), "Union wage setting and taxation," *Oxford Bulletin of Economics and Statistics*, 52, pp. 143–167.

Pissarides, C. (2000), *Equilibrium Unemployment Theory*, 2nd ed., Cambridge, Mass.: MIT Press.

Pissarides, C. (2001), "Employment protection," *Labour Economics*, 8, pp. 131–159.

Portugal, P., and Cardoso, A.-R. (2001), "Disentangling the minimum wage puzzle: An analysis of job accessions and separations from a longitudinal matched employer-employee data set," CEPR Discussion Paper No. 2844.

Rebitzer, J., and Taylor, L. (1995), "The consequences of minimum wage laws: Some new theoretical ideas," *Journal of Public Economics*, 56, pp. 245–255.

Scarpetta, S. (1996), "Assessing the role of labour market policies and institutionnal settings on unemployment: A cross-country study," *OECD Economic Studies*, 26, pp. 43–98.

Schmitter, P. (1981), "Interest intermediation and regime governability in contemporary Western Europe and North America," in Berger, S. (ed.), *Organizing Interest in Western Europe*, Cambridge, U.K.: Cambridge University Press.

Shapiro, C., and Stiglitz, J. (1984), "Equilibrium unemployment as a worker discipline device," *American Economic Review*, 74, pp. 433–444.

Soskice, D. (1990), "Wage determination: The changing role of institutions in advanced industrialized countries," *Oxford Review of Economic Policy*, 6, pp. 36–61.

Stigler, G. (1946), "The economics of minimum wage legislation," *American Economic Review*, 36, pp. 535–543.

Summers, L., Gruber, J., and Vergara, R. (1993), "Taxation and the structure of labor markets: The case of corporatism," *Quarterly Journal of Economics*, 108(2), pp. 385–411.

Tarantelli, E. (1983), "The regulation of inflation in Western countries and the degree of neocorporatism," *Economica*, 7, pp. 67–83.

Tyrväinen, T. (1995), "Real wage resistance and unemployment: Multivariate analysis of cointegrating relationship in 10 OECD countries," *The OECD Jobs Study Working Paper Series*, No. 10, Paris: OECD.

Mathematical Appendices

The purpose of these appendices is to set out in detail the main mathematical materials the reader needs in order to be able to follow the technical reasoning in certain chapters of this book. They deal with static and dynamic optimization, random variables, Poisson processes, and linear dynamic systems.

1 APPENDIX A: STATIC OPTIMIZATION

In this appendix, we establish heuristically the results that must be known in order to solve a problem of static optimization. For a more complete and rigorous exposition, readers are advised to consult works such as Takayama (1986), Hoy et al. (2001), and Carter (2001).

1.1 Unconstrained and Constrained Maximum

In economics, many optimization problems occur in the form:

$$\underset{(C_1,\ldots,C_n)}{\text{Max}}\ U(C_1,\ldots,C_n) \tag{1}$$

subject to constraint

$$\Phi(C_1,\ldots,C_n) \leq R \tag{2}$$

In this problem, U and Φ are twice continuously differentiable functions of R^n in R. Criterion U, for example, represents the utility of a consumer, and the variables $(C_1,\ldots,C_n)$ are then his or her consumption of different goods. In this interpretation, parameter R designates the income of the consumer, and the inequality (2) is identified as his or her budget constraint.

In a first phase, let us set the constraint (2) to one side and consider simply the unconstrained maximum of the problem (1). Its solutions, denoted by C_i^* for $i = 1,\ldots,n$, satisfy equations:

$$\frac{\partial U}{\partial C_i} = 0 \qquad \text{for } i = 1, \ldots, n \tag{3}$$

For vector $(C_1^*, \ldots, C_n^*)$ to be a solution of problem (1) subject to the budget constraint (2), it is necessary that $\Phi(C_1^*, \ldots, C_n^*) \leq R$. If this inequality is not satisfied, it is certain that the constraint (2) will be binding at the optimum of problem (1) and so will be written $\Phi(C_1, \ldots, C_n) = R$. Let us assume that, using this last equality, we can express variable C_1 as a function of the vector $(C_2, \ldots, C_n)$, i.e., $C_1 = \Psi(C_2, \ldots, C_n)$. Problem (1) thus becomes:

$$\underset{(C_2, \ldots, C_n)}{\text{Max}} \ U[\Psi(C_2, \ldots, C_n), C_2, \ldots, C_n]$$

The solutions $(\bar{C}_2, \ldots, \bar{C}_n)$ of this problem are then implicitly defined by the equations:

$$\frac{\partial \Psi}{\partial C_i} \frac{\partial U}{\partial C_1} + \frac{\partial U}{\partial C_i} = 0 \qquad \text{for } i = 2, \ldots, n \tag{4}$$

with:

$$\bar{C}_1 \equiv \Psi(\bar{C}_2, \ldots, \bar{C}_n) \Leftrightarrow \Phi[\Psi(\bar{C}_2, \ldots, \bar{C}_n), \bar{C}_2, \ldots, \bar{C}_n] \equiv R \tag{5}$$

The derivation of the second equality appearing in (5) gives $\partial \Psi/\partial C_i = -(\partial \Phi/\partial C_i)/(\partial \Phi/\partial C_1)$, and if we bring this last relation into (4) we find that the vector $(\bar{C}_1, \ldots, \bar{C}_n)$ is characterized by:

$$\frac{\partial U}{\partial C_i} \Big/ \frac{\partial U}{\partial C_1} = \frac{\partial \Phi}{\partial C_i} \Big/ \frac{\partial \Phi}{\partial C_1} \quad \forall i = 1, \ldots, n, \qquad \text{with} \qquad \Phi(\bar{C}_1, \ldots, \bar{C}_n) = R \tag{6}$$

Relations (3) and (4) are called the *first-order conditions* of the maximization problem (1) subject to constraint (2). These are the *necessary* conditions *for vector* $(C_1^*, \ldots, C_n^*)$ or vector $(\bar{C}_1, \ldots, \bar{C}_n)$ actually to be a local maximum of problem (1). They become sufficient when functions U and Φ are concave.

1.2 THE TECHNIQUE OF THE LAGRANGIAN

The *Lagrangian L* relative to problem (1) subject to constraint (2) is defined by:

$$L(C_1, \ldots, C_n, \lambda) = U(C_1, \ldots, C_n) + \lambda[R - \Phi(C_1, \ldots, C_n)]$$

Variable λ is called the Lagrange (or Kuhn and Tucker) *multiplier* associated with constraint (2). We will show that we return to the first-order conditions (3) and (4) if we set the partial derivatives of the Lagrangian to zero with respect to variables C_i, i.e., $(\partial L/\partial C_i) = 0$ for all $i = 1, \ldots, n$, and take into account the so-called *complementary-slackness* condition:

$$\lambda[R - \Phi(C_1, \ldots, C_n)] = 0 \qquad \text{with} \qquad \lambda \geq 0 \tag{7}$$

We thus have:

$$\frac{\partial L}{\partial C_i} = 0 \Leftrightarrow \frac{\partial U}{\partial C_i} = \lambda \frac{\partial \Phi}{\partial C_i} \qquad \forall i = 1, \ldots, n \tag{8}$$

If the budget constraint is not binding, we have $R > \Phi(C_1, \ldots, C_n)$ and the complementary-slackness condition (7) then dictates $\lambda = 0$. That being so, equation (8) is identical to the first-order condition (3) for an "unconstrained" maximum of problem (1). Conversely, if constraint (2) is binding, we have $R = \Phi(C_1, \ldots, C_n)$ and (8) entails $(\partial U/\partial C_1) = \lambda(\partial \Phi/\partial C_1)$. Eliminating the multiplier λ between this last equality and relation (8) for $i \neq 1$, we come back to the first-order conditions (6) for a constrained optimum.

1.3 THE INTERPRETATION OF THE LAGRANGE MULTIPLIERS

Multiplier λ is very easy to interpret by considering the variations in the optimal value of criterion $U(C_1, \ldots, C_n)$ when parameter R changes. Let us assume that the budget constraint (2) is binding; we then have:

$$\sum_{i=1}^{n} \frac{\partial \Phi}{\partial C_i} \frac{\partial C_i}{\partial R} = 1$$

Using this last equality and the first-order conditions (8), we get:

$$\frac{\partial U}{\partial R} = \sum_{i=1}^{n} \frac{\partial U}{\partial C_i} \frac{\partial C_i}{\partial R} = \sum_{i=1}^{n} \lambda \frac{\partial \Phi}{\partial C_i} \frac{\partial C_i}{\partial R} = \lambda$$

The Lagrange multiplier λ thus represents the increase in the criterion $U(C_1, \ldots, C_n)$ when constraint (2) is "relaxed" by one unit. In a sense, it measures the "weight" of this constraint, which is why it is also called the *shadow price* or the *shadow value* of budget constraint (2). If the latter is not binding, its shadow value is null, since the complementary-slackness condition (7) dictates $\lambda = 0$.

1.4 SUMMARY AND PRACTICAL GUIDE TO STATIC OPTIMIZATION

When faced with a problem of the form:

$$\underset{(C_1, \ldots, C_n)}{\text{Max}} \quad U(C_1, \ldots, C_n) \tag{9}$$

subject to constraints:

$$\Phi_j(C_1, \ldots, C_n) \leq R_j, \qquad j = 1, \ldots, m \tag{10}$$

these are the steps to follow:

1. Attribute a multiplier λ_j to every constraint (10) and write the Lagrangian:

$$L = U(C_1, \ldots, C_n) + \sum_{i=1}^{n} \lambda_j[R_j - \Phi_j(C_1, \ldots, C_n)]$$

2. Set the derivatives of the Lagrangian to zero with respect to choice variables C_i:

$$\frac{\partial L}{\partial C_i} = \frac{\partial U}{\partial C_i} - \sum_{j=1}^{m} \lambda_j \frac{\partial \Phi_j}{\partial C_i} = 0 \qquad \text{for } i = 1, \ldots, n \tag{11}$$

3. Write the complementary-slackness condition:

$$\lambda_j[R_j - \Phi_j(C_1, \ldots, C_n)] = 0 \qquad \text{with} \qquad \lambda_j \geq 0, \quad \forall j = 1, \ldots, m \qquad (12)$$

4. The first-order conditions of problem (1) are found by eliminating the Lagrange multipliers λ_j between relations (11) and (12).

5. Relations (11) and (12) are *necessary* conditions of optimality. The solution must also satisfy the *second-order conditions* in order to be a maximum. The second-order conditions are satisfied if functions $U(C_1, \ldots, C_n)$ and $\Phi_j(C_1, \ldots, C_n)$ are concave. More detail about second-order conditions will be found in Takayama (1986), Hoy et al. (2001), and Carter (2001).

2 APPENDIX B: DYNAMIC OPTIMIZATION

As with the preceding appendix, we will not give an exhaustive account of this matter here. We present, in an intuitive manner, the results and techniques with which one must be familiar in order to work through a problem of dynamic optimization. For a more rigorous approach, readers may turn to Takayama (1986), Gandolfo (1997), and Hoy et al. (2001).

2.1 THE OPTIMAL CONTROL PROBLEM

In economics, problems of dynamic optimization in continuous time most often occur in the form:

$$\underset{C(t)}{\text{Max}} \int_0^T U[K(t), C(t), t] \, dt \qquad (13)$$

subject to constraints:

$$\dot{K}(t) = G[K(t), C(t), t] \qquad (14)$$

$$K(0) = K_0 \text{ given} \qquad (15)$$

$$K(T) \geq 0 \qquad (16)$$

Parameter T represents the terminal date, which may be infinite. Variable $K(t)$ is the *state variable*, serving to describe the evolution of the system under scrutiny. Variable $C(t)$ is the *control variable*, and in the majority of problems it is identified with the decisions taken by an agent. The instantaneous criterion U is generally a function describing the utility of a consumer, or the profit of a firm, or a social welfare function. Since program (13) consists of finding control variables that maximize a well-specified intertemporal objective, this program is also called the *optimal control* problem. Equation (14) describes the interactions between the control variables and the state variables, and is known as the *transition equation* or the equation of motion. It may, for example, describe the accumulation of capital within a firm. Equality (15) specifies the *initial condition*, declaring that the value $K(0)$ of the state variable at the initial date $t = 0$ is a known datum K_0. Finally, inequality (16) is a *terminal condition* which dictates that the final value $K(T)$ of the state variable is either positive or null. It means, for example, that an agent does not have the right to leave his or her debts to his or her descendants.

2.2 THE FIRST-ORDER CONDITIONS

We will establish, in a manner more intuitive than rigorous, the first-order conditions of problem (13). For that, we will rely on the technique of Lagrange multipliers developed in appendix A on static optimization. Let us, at every date t, associate a multiplier $\lambda(t)$ to the transition equation (14). Let us also associate a multiplier μ to the terminal condition (16). In this context, $\lambda(t)$ is called a *dynamic multiplier* or *costate variable*. The Lagrangian of problem (13) is then written as follows:

$$L = \int_0^T U[K(t), C(t), t]\, dt + \int_0^T \lambda(t)\{G[K(t), C(t), t] - \dot{K}(t)\}\, dt + \mu K(T)$$

This expression is distinguished from a "static" Lagrangian by the appearance of the derivative $\dot{K}(t)$ of the state variable. It is possible to eliminate this derivative by integrating by parts[1] the term in which $\dot{K}(t)$ is found. We thus have:

$$\int_0^T \lambda(t)\dot{K}(t)\, dt = [\lambda(t)K(t)]_0^T - \int_0^T K(t)\dot{\lambda}(t)\, dt$$

After regrouping terms, the Lagrangian takes the form:

$$L = \int_0^T \{U[K(t), C(t), t] + \lambda(t)G[K(t), C(t), t]\}\, dt + \int_0^T K(t)\dot{\lambda}(t)\, dt + \lambda(0)K_0 - [\lambda(T) - \mu]K(T)$$

Function $H = U + \lambda G$ appearing in the first integral of the Lagrangian is called the *Hamiltonian* of problem (13). By analogy with the static problem studied in appendix A, the first-order conditions are found by setting the derivatives of the Lagrangian L to zero with respect to variables $C(t)$ and $K(t)$ for all t comprised between 0 and T. Thus we have:

$$\frac{\partial L}{\partial C(t)} = 0 \Leftrightarrow \frac{\partial H}{\partial C(t)} = 0 \tag{17}$$

$$\frac{\partial L}{\partial K(t)} = 0 \Leftrightarrow \frac{\partial H}{\partial K(t)} + \dot{\lambda}(t) = 0 \tag{18}$$

$$\frac{\partial L}{\partial K(T)} = 0 \Leftrightarrow \frac{\partial H}{\partial K(T)} + \dot{\lambda}(T) + \lambda(T) - \mu = 0 \tag{19}$$

Condition (17) is called the *Maximum Principle*. It indicates that, at the optimum, the derivative of the Hamiltonian with respect to the control variable must be null for all t. The set formed by transition equations (14) and condition (18) is known as the *Euler equations*. Finally, equality (19) expresses the terminal condition of the optimization problem. Now, as we saw in appendix A, the optimal solutions must satisfy the complementary-slackness conditions (7). These conditions here dictate $\mu K(T) = 0$ in particular. By continuity, relation (18) is true in $t = T$. Using (19), we thus obtain the *transversality condition*:

$$\lambda(T)K(T) = 0 \tag{20}$$

By analogy with the static case, the multiplier $\lambda(t)$ is interpreted as the shadow price, assessed at date $t = 0$, of an extra unit of the state variable at date t. The transversality condition (20) thus means that if the terminal date $K(T)$ is strictly positive, its shadow price is necessarily null. Conversely, if $\lambda(T) > 0$, the final stock $K(T)$ is equal to zero.

2.3 INFINITE HORIZON

We move from problem (13), where the horizon is finite, to one with an infinite horizon by making the terminal date T tend to infinity. The transition equation (14) and the initial condition (15) remain unchanged, but the terminal condition (16) is now written:

$$\lim_{t \to +\infty} K(t) \geq 0$$

The first-order conditions (17) and (18) remain unchanged, but we make $T \to +\infty$ in (20), so the transversality condition now takes the form:

$$\lim_{t \to +\infty} [\lambda(t)K(t)] = 0 \tag{21}$$

If, for example, $K(t)$ represents a stock of capital increasing at constant rate g, relation (21) entails that the costate variable—i.e., the shadow price of capital—must tend to zero at a rate greater than g. In fact, notwithstanding the intuitive nature of this result, Michel (1982) has shown that the solutions of the dynamic optimization problem with an infinite horizon are not obliged to satisfy equality (21). The "real" transversality condition would be $\lim_{t \to +\infty} H(t) = 0$, equation (21) being a sufficient condition, however. In the majority of problems dealt with in economics, it is quite easy to ensure that condition (21) is satisfied.

2.4 CALCULUS OF VARIATIONS AND THE EULER EQUATION

We sometimes encounter problems of dynamic optimization having the particular form:

$$\underset{K(t)}{\text{Max}} \int_0^T U[K(t), \dot{K}(t), t]\, dt \tag{22}$$

Here the only constraints are the initial and terminal conditions (15) and (16). This might be a case, as in chapter 3, for example, of intertemporal profit maximization in a firm bearing adjustment costs linked to variations $\dot{K}(t)$ in the state variable. Program (22) is often referred to as a problem of "calculus of variations." Formally, we move from the optimal control problem (13) to the calculus of variations problem (22) by taking the transition equation (14) as being simply written $\dot{K}(t) = C(t)$. That being so, the Hamiltonian of problem (13) is given by $H = U + \lambda C$, and the Maximum Principle (17) entails:

$$\frac{\partial H}{\partial C(t)} = \frac{\partial U}{\partial C(t)} + \lambda(t) = 0 \tag{23}$$

The Euler equation (18) is here written:

$$\frac{\partial H}{\partial K(t)} + \dot{\lambda}(t) = \frac{\partial U}{\partial K(t)} + \dot{\lambda}(t) = 0$$

Deriving relation (23) with respect to t and bearing in mind that $C(t) = \dot{K}(t)$, we get:

$$\frac{d}{dt}\left[\frac{\partial U}{\partial \dot{K}(t)}\right] + \dot{\lambda}(t) = 0$$

Eliminating $\dot{\lambda}(t)$ between the last two equations, in the end we find:

$$\frac{\partial U}{\partial K(t)} = \frac{d}{dt}\left[\frac{\partial U}{\partial \dot{K}(t)}\right] \tag{24}$$

This condition, which is likewise known as the *Euler equation*, yields a differential equation characterizing the optimal trajectory of the variable $K(t)$. The transversality conditions (20) and (21) remain valid.

2.5 SUMMARY AND PRACTICAL GUIDE TO OPTIMAL CONTROL

Let us consider the dynamic optimization problem with n control variables $C_1(t), \ldots, C_n(t)$, and m state variables $K_1(t), \ldots, K_m(t)$, and with the form:

$$\max_{\{C_1(t),\ldots,C_n(t)\}} \int_0^T U[K_1(t),\ldots,K_m(t); C_1(t),\ldots,C_n(t), t]\, dt \qquad \text{with} \qquad T \leq +\infty$$

subject to constraints:

$$\dot{K}_j(t) = G_j[K_1(t),\ldots,K_m(t); C_1(t),\ldots,C_n(t), t] \qquad \forall j = 1,\ldots,m \tag{25}$$

$$K_j(0) = K_{j0} \text{ given } \forall j = 1,\ldots,m$$

$$K_j(T) \geq 0 \qquad \text{or} \qquad \lim_{t \to +\infty} K_j(t) \geq 0 \qquad \forall j = 1,\ldots,m$$

Readers are advised to follow these steps (the index t is most often omitted in order to simplify the notation):

1. Attribute a costate variable $\lambda_j(t)$ to each transition equation (25) and write the Hamiltonian:

$$H = U(K_1,\ldots,K_m; C_1,\ldots,C_n, t) + \sum_{j=1}^{m} \lambda_j G_j(K_1,\ldots,K_m; C_1,\ldots,C_n, t)$$

2. Apply the Maximum Principle, which amounts to setting the partial derivatives of the Hamiltonian to zero with respect to the control variables, i.e.:

$$\frac{\partial H}{\partial C_i} = 0 \qquad \forall i = 1, \ldots, n \tag{26}$$

3. Write the Euler equations:

$$\frac{\partial H}{\partial K_j} = -\dot{\lambda}_j \qquad \text{with} \qquad \dot{K}_j = G_j(K_1, \ldots, K_m; C_1, \ldots, C_n, t), \quad \forall j = 1, \ldots, m \tag{27}$$

4. Relations (26) and (27) make it possible to arrive at a system of differential equations in λ_j and K_j. The resolution of this system gives the optimal trajectories of the state variables K_j.

5. Do not forget to verify the transversality conditions, which, according to whether the horizon is finite or infinite, are written:

$$\lambda_j(T)K_j(T) = 0 \qquad \text{or} \qquad \lim_{t \to +\infty} \lambda_j(t)K_j(t) = 0, \quad \forall j = 1, \ldots, m$$

6. The Maximum Principle (26) and the Euler equations (27) are necessary conditions of optimality. They become sufficient if functions U and G_j are concave.

3 APPENDIX C: BASIC NOTIONS CONCERNING RANDOM VARIABLES

For appendices C and D, supplementary information can be found in Ross (2000).

3.1 RANDOM VARIABLES AND PROBABILITY DENSITIES

A *discrete* random variable (henceforth r.v.) X is characterized by the set of all its possible realizations $(x_1, \ldots, x_i, \ldots, x_n)$, n being able to equal infinity, and the probabilities $(p_1, \ldots, p_i, \ldots, p_n)$ linked to its realizations. These probabilities are evidently such that $\sum_{i=1}^{n} p_i = 1$. The *mathematical expectation* (or the *mean*), denoted by $E(X)$, of this r.v. is defined by:

$$E(X) = \sum_{i=1}^{n} p_i x_i$$

The *variance* $V(X)$ and the *standard deviation* $\sigma(X)$ are rudimentary indicators of the dispersion of the values of r.v. X around its average. They are given by the formulas:

$$V(X) = \sum_{i=1}^{n} p_i [x_i - E(X)]^2 = \left(\sum_{i=1}^{n} p_i x_i^2 \right) - E^2(X) \qquad \text{and} \qquad \sigma(X) \equiv \sqrt{V(X)}$$

A *continuous* r.v., still denoted by X, is defined over an interval $[a, b]$ of the set of real numbers; bounds a and b can be infinite. A continuous r.v. is characterized by its *probability density*, denoted by $f(x)$, which is a function greater than or equal to zero defined over $[a, b]$. Let us consider a small interval $[x, x + dx]$ belonging to segment $[a, b]$; intuitively, quantity $f(x)\, dx$ is equivalent to probability p_i for a discrete variable; it represents the probability that the realizations of the continuous r.v. X lie in the interval $[x, x + dx]$. The probability density is such that $\int_a^b f(x)\, dx = 1$ and the mathematical expectation is defined by the formula:

$$E(X) = \int_a^b x f(x)\, dx$$

The *cumulative distribution function*, denoted by $F(x)$, measures the probability of event $\{X \leq x\}$ for a given value of x. We thus have:

$$F(x) = \Pr\{X \leq x\} = \int_a^x f(\xi)\, d\xi \Leftrightarrow F'(x) = f(x)$$

Finally, the variance $V(X)$ and the standard deviation $\sigma(X)$ of a continuous r.v. are again defined by:

$$V(X) = \sigma^2(X) = E[X - E(X)]^2 = E(X^2) - E^2(X)$$

3.2 INDEPENDENCE AND CORRELATION

Let us consider two discrete r.v., with probability distributions respectively denoted by $\{x_i; i = 1, \ldots, n\}$, $\{y_j; j = 1, \ldots, m\}$ and $\{p_i; i = 1, \ldots, n\}$, $\{q_j; j = 1, \ldots, m\}$. Intuitively, these r.v. are *independent* if the observation of the realization of one of them gives no indication about the realization of the other. More formally, this means that events $\{X = x_i\}$ and $\{Y = y_j\}$ are disjunct $\forall(i, j)$. That being the case, we can write:

$$\Pr\{X = x_i \text{ and } y = y_j\} = \Pr\{X = x_i\} \cdot \Pr\{y = y_j\}, \qquad \forall(i, j) \tag{28}$$

By definition, the expectation of product XY is given by:

$$E(XY) = \sum_{i, j} x_i y_j \Pr\{X = x_i \text{ and } y = y_j\}$$

Taking account of (28), we get:

$$E(XY) = \sum_{i, j} x_i y_j \Pr\{X = x_i\} \cdot \Pr\{y = y_j\} = \left(\sum_i x_i \Pr\{X = x_i\}\right)$$

$$\left(\sum_j y_j \Pr\{Y = y_j\}\right) = E(X)E(Y) \tag{29}$$

Hence, when two discrete r.v. are independent, the expectation $E(XY)$ of the product is equal to the product $E(X)E(Y)$ of the expectations. This property holds true for continuous r.v. Conversely, when two r.v. are not independent, the properties (28) and (29) are no longer verified. The *covariance* $\text{Cov}(X, Y)$ and the *correlation coefficient* $\rho(X, Y)$ allow us to assess the direction and degree of the dependence between two r.v.; they are defined by:

$$\text{Cov}(X, Y) = E(XY) - E(X)E(Y) \quad \text{and} \quad \rho(X, Y) = \frac{\text{Cov}(X, Y)}{\sigma(X)\sigma(Y)}$$

Note that if $\text{Cov}(X, Y) = 0$, the random variables are not necessarily independent (except if they are normal variables). Coefficient $\rho(X, Y)$ takes its values over the interval $[-1, +1]$.

Given two r.v., X and Y, and parameters a, b and c, the expectation and variance operators satisfy the following properties:

$$E(aX + bY + c) = aE(X) + bE(Y) + c$$

$$V(aX + bY + c) = a^2 V(X) + b^2 V(Y) + 2ab \, \text{Cov}(X, Y)$$

3.3   THE PROBABILITY DISTRIBUTIONS UTILIZED IN THIS BOOK

• *Uniform Distribution*

The probability density and the cumulative distribution function of a uniform r.v. X defined over the interval $[a, b]$, are given by:

$$f(x) = \frac{1}{b - a} \quad \text{and} \quad F(x) = \frac{x - a}{b - a}$$

We can then easily calculate:

$$E(X) = \frac{a + b}{2} \quad \text{and} \quad V(X) = \frac{(b - a)^2}{12}$$

• *Exponential Distribution*

We say that a r.v. X follows an exponential distribution with parameter $\lambda > 0$ over the interval $[0, +\infty[$, when it has the probability density:

$$f(x) = \lambda e^{-\lambda x}$$

Its cumulative distribution function is then given by:

$$F(x) = \int_0^x \lambda e^{-\lambda \xi} \, d\xi = 1 - e^{-\lambda x}$$

with:

$$E(X) = \frac{1}{\lambda} \quad \text{and} \quad V(X) = \frac{1}{\lambda^2}$$

The exponential distribution comes into the definition of the Poisson process in particular (see appendix D below).

• *Normal Distribution*

A r.v. X follows a normal distribution with mean μ and standard deviation σ; we utilize the notation $X \rightsquigarrow \mathcal{N}(\mu, \sigma)$ when its probability density is defined over $(-\infty, +\infty)$

by the function:

$$f(x) = \frac{1}{\sigma\sqrt{2\Pi}} \exp\left[-\frac{1}{2}\left(\frac{x-\mu}{\sigma}\right)^2\right] \tag{30}$$

Readers may, as an exercise, verify for themselves that the average and the standard deviation of a r.v. having the function (30) for its density are effectively equal to μ and σ.

• *Log-Normal Distribution*

The r.v. X follows a log-normal distribution with parameters (x_0, μ, σ) over the interval $[x_0, +\infty]$ if the r.v. $\ln(X - x_0)$ follows the normal distribution $\mathcal{N}(\mu, \sigma)$. In other words, if $Z \rightsquigarrow \mathcal{N}(\mu, \sigma)$, X is also defined by the equality $X = x_0 + e^Z$. Its probability density is then given by:

$$f(x) = \frac{1}{\sigma(x-x_0)\sqrt{2\Pi}} \exp\left[-\frac{1}{2}\left(\frac{\ln(x-x_0)-\mu}{\sigma}\right)^2\right], \qquad \forall x \geq x_0$$

We can then calculate the expectation and the standard deviation; they come to:

$$E(X) = x_0 + \exp\left(\mu + \frac{\sigma^2}{2}\right) \qquad \text{and} \qquad \sigma(X) = \sqrt{1 - \exp(-\sigma^2)} \exp\left(\mu + \frac{\sigma^2}{2}\right)$$

4   APPENDIX D: THE POISSON PROCESS AND THE VALUE OF AN ASSET

4.1   THE POISSON PROCESS

In models in continuous time, we often assume that certain random events follow a Poisson process. With this hypothesis, the probability of these events occurring (or lasting) depends on a set of parameters having a precise economic significance. Moreover, it turns out that the equation describing the evolution of the value of an asset whose states change according to a Poisson process takes a simple analytical form.

Given a series of parameters $\lambda(t) \geq 0$, defined for $t \in [0, +\infty]$, we say that an event X (for example, the occurrence of a productivity shock) follows a Poisson process with parameters $\{\lambda(t)\}$ if the duration $T(t)$ it is necessary to wait, starting from date t, for X to occur is a random variable having an exponential cumulative distribution function defined by:

$$F_t(y) \equiv \Pr\{T(t) \leq y\} = 1 - e^{-\int_t^{t+y} \lambda(\xi)\, d\xi}$$

The probability density of the random variable $T(t)$ then takes the form:

$$f_t(y) = F_t'(y) = \lambda(t+y) e^{-\int_t^{t+y} \lambda(\xi)\, d\xi} \tag{31}$$

Making y go to 0 in this relation, we see that parameter $\lambda(t)$ is interpreted as the *instantaneous* probability of the realization of event X at date t. When the parameters take the same value at every date, which amounts to setting $\lambda(t) = \lambda$ for all $t \geq 0$, the r.v. $T(t)$ no longer depends on date t. The Poisson process is "stationary"; the cumulative distribution function and the probability density are then written simply:

$$F(y) = 1 - e^{-\lambda y} \quad \text{and} \quad f(y) = \lambda e^{-\lambda y}$$

The unconditional expectation $E[T(t)]$ of the r.v. $T(t)$ is identifiable as the *average* duration it is necessary to wait, starting from date t, for event X to occur. This expression takes a particularly interesting form when the parameter of the Poisson process is constant. With this hypothesis, let T simply be the r.v. $T(t)$; it comes to:

$$E(T) = \int_0^\infty y \lambda e^{-\lambda y} \, dy = \frac{1}{\lambda}$$

The ratio $(1/\lambda)$ thus represents the average duration of the event studied. If, for example, λ represents the instantaneous probability (assumed constant) that an unemployed person finds a job every week, the ratio $(1/\lambda)$ represents the average duration of unemployment, measured in weeks.

4.2 EVOLUTION OF THE VALUE OF AN ASSET

We will determine the value of an asset (for example, a filled job) that, at every x, can bring in an instantaneous income $\omega(x)$ or change state (become vacant for example). This change of state is a random event which follows a Poisson process with parameters $\{\lambda(t)\}$. The duration $T(t)$ it is necessary to wait, starting at date t, for this change of state to occur, is thus a r.v. the probability density of which is the function $f_t(.)$ defined by relation (31). We will assume further that if the asset changes state at instant $(t + y)$, its present discounted value at that date is a known quantity denoted by $\bar{\Pi}(t + y)$. Assuming that the interest rate is an exogenous constant r, the present discounted value at date t of the asset, $\Pi(t)$, is written:

$$\Pi(t) = E\left\{ \int_t^{t+T(t)} \omega(x) e^{-r(x-t)} \, dx + e^{-rT(t)} \bar{\Pi}[t + T(t)] \right\}$$

In this equality, the symbol E designates the mathematical expectation operator. As the sole r.v. that comes into the term between braces is the duration $T(t)$ of the probability density $f_t(.)$, we get:

$$\Pi(t) = \int_0^\infty \left\{ \left[\int_t^{t+y} \omega(x) e^{-r(x-t)} \, dx + e^{-ry} \bar{\Pi}(t + y) \right] \lambda(t + y) e^{-\int_t^{t+y} \lambda(\xi) \, d\xi} \right\} dy \tag{32}$$

This expression of $\Pi(t)$ can be simplified using the integration by parts formula, i.e., $\int u \, dv = uv - \int v \, du$. Let us set $u = \int_t^{t+y} \omega(x) e^{-r(x-t)} \, dx$ and $dv = \lambda(t + y) e^{-\int_t^{t+y} \lambda(\xi) \, d\xi} \, dy$; we then have $du = \omega(t + y) e^{-ry} \, dy$ and $v = -e^{-\int_t^{t+y} \lambda(\xi) \, d\xi}$, and so:

$$\int_0^\infty \left[\int_t^{t+y} \omega(x) e^{-r(x-t)} \, dx \right] \lambda(t + y) e^{-\int_t^{t+y} \lambda(\xi) \, d\xi} \, dy = \left[-e^{-\int_t^{t+y} \lambda(\xi) \, d\xi} \int_t^{t+y} \omega(x) e^{-r(x-t)} \, dx \right]_0^\infty$$

$$+ \int_0^\infty \omega(t + y) e^{-ry} e^{-\int_t^{t+y} \lambda(\xi) \, d\xi} \, dy$$

Assuming that the discounted value of incomes $\int_t^{t+y} \omega(x)e^{-r(x-t)}\,dx$ is bounded when y tends to infinity, the term between square brackets is null, and equation (32) is rewritten as follows:

$$\Pi(t) = \int_0^\infty [\omega(t+y) + \lambda(t+y)\bar{\Pi}(t+y)]e^{-\int_t^{t+y}[r+\lambda(\xi)]\,d\xi}\,dy$$

With the change of variable $x = t + y$, we then have:

$$\Pi(t) = \int_t^\infty [\omega(x) + \lambda(x)\bar{\Pi}(x)]e^{-\int_t^x[r+\lambda(\xi)]\,d\xi}\,dx \qquad (33)$$

Deriving this last equation with respect to t, we get:

$$\dot{\Pi}(t) = -[\omega(t) + \lambda(t)\bar{\Pi}(t)] + [r+\lambda(t)]\int_t^\infty [\omega(x) + \lambda(x)\bar{\Pi}(x)]e^{-\int_t^x[r+\lambda(\xi)]\,d\xi}\,dx$$

where $\dot{\Pi}(t)$ designates the time derivative of $\Pi(t)$. In the last part of the right-hand side of this equality, we recognize the expression of the discounted value of the asset $\Pi(t)$ given by relation (33). Finally, the evolution of the value of the asset is completely described by the following equation:

$$r\Pi(t) = \omega(t) + \lambda(t)[\bar{\Pi}(t) - \Pi(t)] + \dot{\Pi}(t) \qquad (34)$$

Thus we obtain the the asset-value functions or the arbitrage equations used throughout this book.

4.3 AN ALTERNATIVE PROOF

It is possible to arrive at formula (34) in an intuitive manner, proceeding by approximation. Assuming that the asset brings in a flow of income $\omega(t)\,dt$ over a small interval of time dt, and that this asset may be destroyed over this small interval of time dt with a probability $\lambda(t)\,dt$, the value of the asset is written:

$$\Pi(t) = \frac{1}{1 + r\,dt}\{\omega(t)\,dt + \lambda(t)\,dt\bar{\Pi}(t+dt) + [1 - \lambda(t)\,dt]\Pi(t+dt)\}$$

Rearranging the terms of this equality, we get:

$$r\Pi(t) = \omega(t) + \lambda(t)[\bar{\Pi}(t+dt) - \Pi(t+dt)] + \frac{\Pi(t+dt) - \Pi(t)}{dt}$$

We have arrived exactly at relation (34) by making dt go to 0.

5 APPENDIX E: SYSTEMS OF LINEAR DIFFERENCE EQUATIONS

We offer here a simple analysis of two-dimensional systems of linear equations. To follow the subject further, the reader may consult, Azariadis (1993), Gandolfo (1997), and Hoy et al. (2001). We study dynamic systems defined by a system of linear equations taking the following form:

$$z_{t+1} = \mathscr{A} z_t + b \tag{35}$$

In this relation, $\mathscr{A}$ and b represent respectively a (2×2) matrix and a (2×1) vector the coefficients of which are exogenous parameters independent of time. Vector z_t, of dimension (2×1), has the endogenous variables of the model at date t for its elements. In this appendix, we give the details of the study of system (35), but readers who wish only to find a user guide may go directly to section 5.6.

5.1 A PARTICULAR SOLUTION

In explicit fashion, equation (35) is written:

$$\begin{bmatrix} x_{t+1} \\ y_{t+1} \end{bmatrix} = \begin{bmatrix} a_{11} & a_{12} \\ a_{21} & a_{22} \end{bmatrix} \begin{bmatrix} x_t \\ y_t \end{bmatrix} + \begin{bmatrix} b_1 \\ b_2 \end{bmatrix} \tag{36}$$

Let I be the identity matrix; we will assume that matrix $I - \mathscr{A}$ is not singular. That being the case, system (36) admits a sole steady state $\bar{z} = b(I - \mathscr{A})^{-1}$. This vector is also a *particular solution* of system (36) the components of which read:

$$\bar{x} = \frac{a_{12}b_2 + b_1(1 - a_{22})}{\mathrm{Det}(I - \mathscr{A})} \tag{37}$$

$$\bar{y} = \frac{a_{21}b_1 + b_2(1 - a_{11})}{\mathrm{Det}(I - \mathscr{A})} \tag{38}$$

with $\mathrm{Det}(I - \mathscr{A}) = (1 - a_{11})(1 - a_{22}) - a_{12}a_{21}$.

System (35) can be written in a so-called "homogeneous" form, the variables of which are deviations from the steady state $\bar{z}$, i.e.:

$$(z_{t+1} - \bar{z}) = \mathscr{A}(z_t - \bar{z}) \tag{39}$$

System (36) then takes the following form:

$$\begin{bmatrix} x_{t+1} - \bar{x} \\ y_{t+1} - \bar{y} \end{bmatrix} = \begin{bmatrix} a_{11} & a_{12} \\ a_{21} & a_{22} \end{bmatrix} \begin{bmatrix} x_t - \bar{x} \\ y_t - \bar{y} \end{bmatrix} \tag{40}$$

5.2 THE GENERAL SOLUTION

The *general solution* of the homogeneous system is easily found when the matrix $\mathscr{A}$ is diagonalizable, which we will assume to be the case. There then exists a matrix H, allowing us to write the system (39) in the form:

$$\hat{z}_{t+1} - \hat{z} = \Lambda(\hat{z}_t - \hat{z}), \quad \Lambda \equiv \begin{bmatrix} \lambda_1 & 0 \\ 0 & \lambda_2 \end{bmatrix} \quad \text{with} \quad z_t = H\hat{z}_t \text{ and } z = H\hat{z} \tag{41}$$

The elements of matrix H are expressed as a function of the scalars λ_i and the elements of the matrix $\mathscr{A}$. Since $\hat{z}_{t+1} - \hat{z} = H^{-1}(z_{t+1} - \bar{z})$ and $\hat{z}_{t+1} - \hat{z} = \Lambda(\hat{z}_t - \hat{z}) = \Lambda H^{-1}(z_t - \bar{z})$, we have $z_{t+1} - \bar{z} = H\Lambda H^{-1}(z_t - \bar{z})$. Equation (39) then entails $\mathscr{A}H =$

$H\Lambda$. This last equality can also be written:

$$\mathscr{A} h_i = \lambda_i h_i, \qquad h_i = \begin{pmatrix} h_{i1} \\ h_{i2} \end{pmatrix}, \qquad i = 1, 2 \tag{42}$$

In this expression, h_{ij} designates the element situated at the intersection of the ith line and of the jth column of matrix H. Vector h_i represents *the eigenvector associated to the eigenvalue* λ_i. Relation (42) allows us to express the coordinates of each eigenvector as a function of the elements of matrix $\mathscr{A}$ and the associated eigenvalue. Since these coordinates are defined to within a multiplicative constant, it is possible to use the normalization $h_{12} = 1$ and $h_{22} = 1$. We thus get:

$$h_{i1} = \frac{\lambda_i - a_{22}}{a_{21}}, \qquad h_{i2} = 1, \qquad i = 1, 2 \tag{43}$$

Let us consider the vector $\hat{z}_t - \hat{z} = H^{-1}(z_t - \bar{z})$ and denote its elements by $\hat{x}_t - \hat{x}$ and $\hat{y}_t - \hat{y}$; we see that equation (41) is written simply:

$$\begin{bmatrix} \hat{x}_{t+1} - \hat{x} \\ \hat{y}_{t+1} - \hat{y} \end{bmatrix} = \begin{bmatrix} \lambda_1 & 0 \\ 0 & \lambda_2 \end{bmatrix} \begin{bmatrix} \hat{x}_t - \hat{x} \\ \hat{y}_t - \hat{y} \end{bmatrix}$$

This system breaks down into two independent equations $\hat{x}_{t+1} - \hat{x} = \lambda_1(\hat{x}_t - \hat{x})$ and $\hat{y}_{t+1} - \hat{y} = \lambda_2(\hat{y}_t - \hat{y})$, which have the respective solutions:

$$\hat{x}_t - \hat{x} = c_1 \lambda_1^t \qquad \text{and} \qquad \hat{y}_t - \hat{y} = c_2 \lambda_2^t \tag{44}$$

In these two equalities, c_1 and c_2 are constants determined by the particular values of x_t and of y_t. These last are most often the initial conditions x_0 and y_0. That being so, (44) entails $c_1 = x_0 - \hat{x}$ and $c_2 = y_0 - \hat{y}$. Since $z_t - \bar{z} = H(\hat{z}_t - \hat{z})$, system (44) can be writtten:

$$\begin{bmatrix} x_t - \bar{x} \\ y_t - \bar{y} \end{bmatrix} = \begin{bmatrix} h_{11} & h_{12} \\ h_{21} & h_{22} \end{bmatrix} \begin{bmatrix} c_1 \lambda_1^t \\ c_2 \lambda_2^t \end{bmatrix} \tag{45}$$

The *general solution* of system (35) then takes the following form:

$$\begin{cases} x_t = \bar{x} + c_1 h_{11} \lambda_1^t + c_2 h_{12} \lambda_2^t \\ y_t = \bar{y} + c_1 h_{21} \lambda_1^t + c_2 h_{22} \lambda_2^t \end{cases} \tag{46}$$

where the values of the h_{ij} are defined by relations (43).

A *particular solution* is obtained with the initial values x_0 and y_0. Equation (44) entails $c_1 = \hat{x}_0 - \hat{x}$, $c_2 = \hat{y}_0 - \hat{y}$, and since $x_0 - \bar{x} = H(\hat{x}_0 - \hat{x})$, $y_0 - \bar{y} = H(\hat{y}_0 - \hat{y})$, c_1 and c_2 satisfy the system:

$$\begin{pmatrix} x_0 - \bar{x} \\ y_0 - \bar{y} \end{pmatrix} = H \begin{pmatrix} c_1 \\ c_2 \end{pmatrix}$$

Or again, solving this system:

$$c_1 = \frac{h_{22}(x_0 - \bar{x}) - h_{12}(y_0 - \bar{y})}{h_{11}h_{22} - h_{12}h_{21}}, \qquad c_2 = \frac{-h_{21}(x_0 - \bar{x}) + h_{11}(y_0 - \bar{y})}{h_{11}h_{22} - h_{12}h_{21}}$$

5.3 STABILITY

System (46) is *stable* if the endogenous variables x_t and y_t converge to their stationary value $\bar{x}$ and $\bar{y}$ when t tends to infinity. Relations (46) show that the stability of the system depends on the magnitude of the eigenvalues. Let us recall that the latter are the solutions of the *characteristic equation* defined by:

$$\det(\mathscr{A} - \lambda I) = \begin{bmatrix} a_{11} - \lambda & a_{12} \\ a_{21} & a_{22} - \lambda \end{bmatrix} = 0 \qquad (47)$$

This equation can also be written:

$$\lambda^2 - \lambda T + D = 0 \qquad (48)$$

where $T = a_{11} + a_{22}$ and $D = a_{11}a_{22} - a_{12}a_{21}$ represent respectively the trace and the determinant of matrix $\mathscr{A}$. The eigenvalues will be two real numbers if the discriminant $\delta_{\mathscr{A}} = T^2 - 4D$ is positive, and they will be two conjugate complex numbers if this discriminant is negative. In order to study stability, we must therefore envisage these two eventualities separately.

(i) The eigenvalues of $\mathscr{A}$ are complex numbers.

In order to make the reasoning easier to follow, we will adopt the trigonometric representation of complex numbers. Since the eigenvalues are conjugate, we have:

$$\lambda_1 = re^{i\theta} = r(\cos \theta + \sin \theta) \qquad (49)$$

$$\lambda_2 = re^{-i\theta} = r(\cos \theta - \sin \theta) \qquad (50)$$

with $i^2 = -1$. In these last two equations, $r > 0$ designates the common modulus of the eigenvalues and θ represents the argument of λ_1, the other eigenvalue having the argument $(-\theta)$. Relations (46) then give the general solutions of the system. They are written:

$$\begin{cases} x_t = \bar{x} + r^t(c_1 h_{11} e^{i\theta t} + c_2 h_{12} e^{i\theta t}) \\ y_t = \bar{y} + r^t(c_1 h_{21} e^{i\theta t} + c_2 h_{22} e^{i\theta t}) \end{cases} \qquad (51)$$

The terms between parentheses being bounded quantities, the stability of the system requires simply $r < 1$. That being the case, the trajectories converge to the steady state with increasingly damped oscillations. If, on the contrary, r is greater than 1, the system diverges in an explosive manner. In the particular case where $r = 1$, the system does not converge to $\bar{z}$, but it oscillates around this point without exploding. The eigenvalues being conjugate complex numbers, we also have $r^2 = \lambda_1 \lambda_2 = D$. This point gives us a way to know if the system is stable without calculating the eigenvalues. When $\delta_{\mathscr{A}}$ is negative, it is enough to verify that the determinant of the matrix $\mathscr{A}$ is less than to 1.

(ii) The eigenvalues of $\mathscr{A}$ are real numbers.

The system is stable if and only if the two eigenvalues are, in absolute value, less than 1, i.e., $|\lambda_1| < 1$ and $|\lambda_2| < 1$. If the two eigenvalues are, in absolute value, greater than 1, the system is unstable. If only one of the eigenvalues, for example λ_1, is, in absolute value, greater than 1, the system is unstable, except for one trajectory. Equations (46) show that this latter corresponds to initial conditions such that the coefficient c_1 is equal to zero. A system having this configuration of the eigenvalues has a *saddle point* and is said to be saddle-path stable.

5.4 A USEFUL FORM FOR THE STABILITY CONDITIONS

More generally, we will now prove that the stability properties of a linear dynamic system can always be obtained from knowledge of the trace and the determinant of the matrix $\mathscr{A}$, with no need to calculate its eigenvalues. These last being solutions of the characteristic equation (48), we have:

$$P(\lambda) \equiv \lambda^2 - \lambda T + D = (\lambda - \lambda_1)(\lambda - \lambda_2) \qquad \text{(52)}$$

This entails:

$$P(1) = 1 - T + D = (1 - \lambda_1)(1 - \lambda_2) \quad \text{and} \quad P(-1) = 1 + T + D = (1 + \lambda_1)(1 + \lambda_2) \qquad \text{(53)}$$

In what follows, we will consider that the eigenvalues are real numbers, and that λ_1 always designates the largest among them. Relation (53) then entails the following equivalences:

$$P(1) > 0 \Leftrightarrow (\lambda_1 < 1 \text{ and } \lambda_2 < 1) \qquad \text{or} \qquad (\lambda_1 > 1 \text{ and } \lambda_2 > 1) \qquad \text{(54)}$$

$$P(1) < 0 \Leftrightarrow \lambda_1 > 1 \qquad \text{and} \qquad \lambda_2 < 1 \qquad \text{(55)}$$

$$P(-1) > 0 \Leftrightarrow (\lambda_1 < -1 \text{ and } \lambda_2 < -1) \qquad \text{or} \qquad (\lambda_1 > -1 \text{ and } \lambda_2 > -1) \qquad \text{(56)}$$

$$P(-1) < 0 \Leftrightarrow \lambda_1 > -1 \qquad \text{and} \qquad \lambda_2 < -1 \qquad \text{(57)}$$

We then verify the property:

$$(|\lambda_1| < 1 \text{ and } |\lambda_2| < 1) \Leftrightarrow (P(1) > 0, P(-1) > 0 \text{ and } |D| < 1) \qquad \text{(58)}$$

This equivalence is easy to prove: the direct implication ($\Rightarrow$) is evident, and the reciprocal implication ($\Leftarrow$) makes it necessary to set aside the values of λ_1 and λ_2 verifying $P(1) > 0$ and $P(-1) > 0$ of which the modulus is greater than 1. This condition is realized by imposing that the determinant $D = \lambda_1 \lambda_2$ is, in absolute value, less than 1.

In the same way, we define the conditions needed for the system to possess a saddle point. Thus we can easily verify that the following equivalence is satisfied:

$$(|\lambda_1| > 1 \text{ and } |\lambda_2| < 1) \Leftrightarrow (P(1) < 0 \text{ and } P(-1) > 0) \qquad \text{or} \qquad (P(-1) < 0 \text{ and } P(1) > 0) \qquad \text{(59)}$$

Finally, it is possible to express the conditions needed for the system to be unstable. They are:

$$(|\lambda_1| > 1 \text{ and } |\lambda_2| > 1) \Leftrightarrow (P(1) > 0, P(-1) > 0 \text{ and } |D| > 1) \qquad \text{(60)}$$

Relation (53) allows us to express the conditions (58), (59), and (60) with the help of the trace T and the determinant D of matrix $\mathscr{A}$. After several calculations, we arrive at:

$$(|\lambda_1| < 1 \text{ and } |\lambda_2| < 1) \Leftrightarrow 1 > D > |T| - 1 \tag{61}$$

$$(|\lambda_1| > 1 \text{ and } |\lambda_2| < 1) \Leftrightarrow |T| - 1 > D > -|T| - 1 \tag{62}$$

$$(|\lambda_1| > 1 \text{ and } |\lambda_2| > 1) \Leftrightarrow D > \text{Max}(1, |T| - 1) \tag{63}$$

We can now recapitulate the set of results concerning the stability of the system (CV signifies convergence and DIV signifies divergence):

$$\underset{\text{Complex eigenvalues}}{T^2 - 4D} < 0 \quad \text{and} \quad \begin{cases} D < 1 & \text{CV with oscillations} \\ D > 1 & \text{DIV in a spiral} \end{cases} \tag{64}$$

$$\underset{\text{Real eigenvalues}}{T^2 - 4D} > 0 \quad \text{and} \quad \begin{cases} 1 > D > |T| - 1 & \text{CV} \\ |T| - 1 > D > -|T| - 1 & \text{Saddle point} \\ D > \text{Max}(1, |T| - 1) & \text{DIV} \end{cases} \tag{65}$$

5.5 THE PHASE DIAGRAM

The purpose of the phase diagram is to visualize the trajectories of the system in the plane (x_t, y_t). It is found by writing equations (36) in the following manner:

$$\begin{bmatrix} x_{t+1} - x_t \\ y_{t+1} - y_t \end{bmatrix} = \begin{bmatrix} a_{11} - 1 & a_{12} \\ a_{21} & a_{22} - 1 \end{bmatrix} \begin{bmatrix} x_t \\ y_t \end{bmatrix} + \begin{bmatrix} b_1 \\ b_2 \end{bmatrix} \tag{66}$$

Using the difference operator Δ defined by $\Delta x_t \equiv x_t - x_{t-1}$, we get:

$$\Delta x_{t+1} = (a_{11} - 1)x_t + a_{12}y_t + b_1 \tag{67}$$

$$\Delta y_{t+1} = a_{21}x_t + (a_{22} - 1)y_t + b_2 \tag{68}$$

Making $\Delta x_{t+1} = \Delta y_{t+1} = 0$ in these two relations, we define two straight lines of the plane (x_t, y_t) which have as their equations respectively:

$$\Delta x_{t+1} = 0 \Leftrightarrow y_t = \frac{1 - a_{11}}{a_{12}}x_t - \frac{b_1}{a_{12}} \tag{69}$$

$$\Delta y_{t+1} = 0 \Leftrightarrow y_t = \frac{a_{21}}{1 - a_{22}}x_t + \frac{b_2}{1 - a_{22}} \tag{70}$$

The straight line whose equation is given by (69) separates the plane into two regions where, according to the values of coefficients a and b, we have $\Delta x_{t+1} > 0$ or $\Delta x_{t+1} < 0$. The straight line whose equation is given by (70) for its part allows us to separate the plane into two zones such that $\Delta y_{t+1} > 0$ or $\Delta y_{t+1} < 0$. We can also separate the plane (x_t, y_t) into four regions, with the straight lines of equations (69) and (70). The phase diagram represented in figure A.1 consists of visualizing, with the help of horizontal and vertical arrows, the movements of a point E the coordinates of which are (x_t, y_t). For example, in figure A.1, the straight lines with equations $\Delta x_{t+1} = 0$ and $\Delta y_{t+1} = 0$ have slopes such that, starting from point E, we have $\Delta y_{t+1} > 0$ and $\Delta x_{t+1} < 0$. The trajectory, represented by a portion of the curve issuing from E, moves toward the vertical axis. We follow the same procedure for the four regions delimited

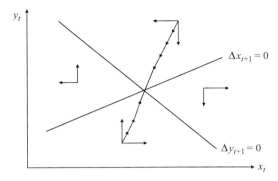

FIGURE A.1
The phase diagram.

by the straight lines of equations (69) and (70). The example chosen in designing figure A.1 suggests that the system is saddle-path stable.

5.6 USER GUIDE FOR THE STUDY OF TWO-DIMENSIONAL LINEAR SYSTEMS

In order to study the properties of a dynamic system of the form:

$$\begin{bmatrix} x_{t+1} \\ y_{t+1} \end{bmatrix} = \mathscr{A} \begin{bmatrix} x_t \\ y_t \end{bmatrix} + \begin{bmatrix} b_1 \\ b_2 \end{bmatrix} \quad \text{with} \quad \mathscr{A} = \begin{bmatrix} a_{11} & a_{12} \\ a_{21} & a_{22} \end{bmatrix}$$

it is advisable to follow this procedure:

1. Find the steady state $(\bar{x}, \bar{y})$ using equations (37) and (38).

2. Calculate the trace $T = a_{11} + a_{22}$ and the determinant $D = a_{11}a_{22} - a_{12}a_{21}$ of the matrix $\mathscr{A}$.

3. Use conditions (64) and (65) giving the properties of the trajectories as a function of the values of the determinant and the trace of $\mathscr{A}$.

4. If a graphic representation is desired, construct a phase diagram according to the method set out in section 5.5.

REFERENCES

Azariadis, C. (1993), *Intertemporal Macroeconomics*, London: Basil Blackwell.

Carter, M. (2001), *Foundations of Mathematical Economics*, Cambridge, Mass.: MIT Press.

Gandolfo, G. (1997), *Economic Dynamics*, New York: Springer-Verlag.

Hoy, M., Livernois, J., McKenna, C., Rees, R., and Stengos, T. (2001), *Mathematics for Economics*, Cambridge, Mass.: MIT Press.

Michel, P. (1982), "On the transversality condition in infinite horizon optimal problems," *Econometrica*, 50(4), pp. 975–985.

Ross, S. (2000), *Introduction to Probability Models*, 7th ed., New York: Academic Press.

Takayama, M. (1986), *Mathematical Economics*, 2nd ed., Cambridge, U.K.: Cambridge University Press.

Notes

Chapter 1

1. Appendix A at the end of this work summarizes what is necessary to know to solve a static optimization problem.

2. In deriving (3) with respect to R, we find that dw_A/dR has the same sign as $(U_{LC}U_C - U_{CC}U_L)$. In appendix 2, we show that this expression is positive if and only if leisure is a normal good.

3. A "public good" consumed by the household (children are usually given as the example) is generally added to the arguments of the utility function. It is also possible to integrate the possibility of home productions into this framework.

4. The interpretation of the Lagrange multipliers is presented in appendix A3 at the end of this book.

5. In this program, the terminal age $T \geq T_m$ must be interpreted as an indicator of anticipated length of life.

Chapter 2

1. The mechanisms of perfect competition are presented in detail in chapter 5, section 1.

2. The time derivative of $h(t)$ is denoted by $\dot{h}(t)$.

3. Let us recall that if $g(x) = \int_{a(x)}^{b(x)} f(x, i)\, di$, where $f, a,$ and b are continuously differentiable functions, then $g'(x) = b'(x)f(x, b(x)) - a'(x)f(x, a(x)) + \int_{a(x)}^{b(x)} ((\partial f(x, i))/\partial x)\, di$.

4. See mathematical appendix B on dynamic optimization at the end of this book.

5. See chapters 7 and 12.

6. These problems are brought into sharper focus in chapter 10, on inequality.

Chapter 3

1. Mathematical appendix D at the end of the book supplies a rigorous proof of formulas analogous to equation (2) and shows that they effectively correspond to the stationary state of a model where a particular event (here, the loss of work) follows a Poisson process.

2. Mathematical appendix D at the end of the book shows that if a random variable follows a Poisson process of parameter a, then the mathematical expectation of this variable is equal to $1/a$.

3. The reader who is not yet sufficiently familiar with this type of equation will benefit from working with a small interval of time $[t, t + dt]$. In the stationary state, we thus have:

$$(1 + r\,dt)V_e(w) = w\,dt + q\,dtV_u + (1 - q\,dt)$$

$$\left[\lambda_1\,dt \int_w^{+\infty} V_e(\xi)\,dH(\xi) + \lambda_1\,dtV_e(w)H(w) + (1 - \lambda_1\,dt)V_e(w) \right]$$

By rearranging a few terms and making $dt \to 0$ in this formula, we come back to equation (16).

4. This formula reads $\int u\,dv = uv - \int v\,du$, where u and v are two functions. Here, we posit: $u = V_e(\xi) - V_u$, $du = V_e'(\xi)\,d\xi$, $dv = H(\xi)\,d\xi$, and $v = -\bar{H}(\xi)$.

5. One can check as well that the second derivative with respect to s of the term between brackets is negative when this equality is satisfied. So what we have is indeed a maximum.

6. By way of illustration, the interested reader can characterize the reservation wages associated with a system of unemployment insurance benefit such that $z(t) = z_0$ for $0 \le t \le T$, and $z(t) = z < z_0$ for $t > T$, where z, z_0, and T are constant exogenous parameters. A reduction in the length of time over which benefits are paid is similar to a lowering of T.

7. Recall that the general solution of a linear differential equation is obtained by adding a particular solution to the general solution of the *homogeneous* equation. The latter is written $H'(w)/H(w) = -1/2(y - w)$; it is integrated exactly like equation (28), which gives us $H(w) = A\sqrt{y - w}$, where A is an arbitrary constant. We get a particular solution of equation (31). By making $H' = 0$ in this equation, we immediately find $H(w) = (q + \lambda_e)/\lambda_e$, and from that the general solution of equation (31).

8. In the literature on equilibrium search models, a distinction is often made between the global distribution of wages $H(w) = \Pr\{\xi \le w\}$ and the distribution $G(w)$ of the wages that *employed* persons face. By definition, $G(w)$ represents the probability that an individual *with a job* is earning less than w. Function $G(w)$ is such that $L(w) = (1 - u)G(w)$. Using the different equilibrium relations in the model, the reader can verify that:

$$G(w) = \frac{qH(w)}{q + \lambda_e \bar{H}(w)} = \frac{\lambda_e}{q}\left[1 - \sqrt{\frac{y - w}{y - x}}\right]$$

9. The dynamics and the construction of the phase diagram are presented in mathematical appendix E at the end of the book. This appendix considers only models in discrete time, but the results are not qualitatively different for models in continuous time. For a presentation of these models, the reader may consult the references given in appendix E, in particular Gandolfo (1997).

10. For the sake of simplicity, we will not prove formally that stationary equilibrium is a saddle point. This proof can be accomplished by adapting the procedure given in appendix E to continuous time.

11. Good introductions to the econometrics of duration models can be found in Kiefer (1988), van den Berg (2001), and Bonnal et al. (1999).

12. Given two events A and B, this definition is written:

$$\Pr\{A|B\} = \frac{\Pr\{A \cap B\}}{\Pr\{B\}}$$

With $A = \{t \le T < t + dt\}$ and $B = \{T \ge t\}$, we find the formula given in the text.

13. This expression of the likelihood function assumes that the censoring mechanism is independent of the duration T_i of unemployment.

14. The estimated variance is given by:

$$\hat{V} = -\left(\frac{\partial^2 L}{\partial \gamma^2}\right)^{-1}_{\gamma = \hat{\gamma}} = \frac{(\hat{\gamma})^2}{\sum_{i=1}^{n} c_i} = \frac{\sum_{i=1}^{n} c_i}{\left(\sum_{i=1}^{n} t_i\right)^2}$$

15. The sample comes from the Employment Survey of INSEE (the body that gathers statistics in France), which makes it possible to follow the trajectory on the labor market of around 20,000 households month by month for three years.

16. This hypothesis amounts to assuming that the cumulative distribution function of the random variable T takes the expression $F(t) = 1 - e^{-\rho(x, \theta_x) \int_0^t \varphi_0(\tau, \theta_0)\, d\tau}$.

17. Recall that the elasticity of function $f(x) : \mathbb{R}^n \to \mathbb{R}$, with respect to x_i is $(x_i/f(x))(\partial f(x)/\partial x_i) = \partial \ln(f(x))/\partial \ln(x_i)$.

18. To see this clearly, consider an example in which there is a fraction p of the population which has a constant hazard function γ_1 and a fraction $(1 - p)$ which has a constant hazard function γ_2. The hazard function of the whole sample is equal to:

$$\varphi(t) = \frac{p\gamma_1 e^{-\gamma_1 t} + (1 - p)\gamma_2 e^{-\gamma_2 t}}{p e^{-\gamma_1 t} + (1 - p)e^{-\gamma_2 t}}$$

It is easy to verify that $\varphi'(t) < 0$. Consequently, the omission of unobserved heterogeneity can falsely introduce a negative duration dependence, since in reality the individual probability of finding a job is independent of the amount of time spent unemployed.

19. The same type of indicator is also frequently calculated for gross incomes.

20. These are averages of estimates for Lynch (1983) and Holzer (1986). The study by van den Berg (1990) estimates the value of reservation wage elasticity at the onset of a period of unemployment in relation to the future income of an unemployed person.

Chapter 4

1. The second derivative of the profit is written $\Pi''(L) = (1 + \eta_Y^P)(F'^2 P' + F'' P)$. Since $P' < 0$ and $F'' < 0$, the second-order condition $\Pi''(L) < 0$ dictates that we have $(1 + \eta_Y^P) > 0$.

2. See as well relation (76) in appendix 2.

3. It is possible to obtain an expression of the elasticity of substitution depending only on the partial derivatives of the production function using optimality condition (5). We then find:

$$\sigma = \frac{F_K F_L (K F_K + L F_L)}{KL(2 F_{KL} F_K F_L - F_{KK} F_L^2 - F_{LL} F_K^2)}$$

When the production function is homogeneous of degree 1, the elasticity of substitution takes a particularly simple form:

$$\sigma = \frac{F_K F_L}{Y F_{KL}}$$

4. Deriving profit (14) with respect to Y gives:

$$\Pi_Y(W, R, Y) = P(Y)(1 + \eta_Y^P) - C_Y(W, R, Y)$$

The first equation of (7) implies that the marginal cost C_Y is linked to the average cost C/Y by the identity $C_Y \equiv (C/Y)/\theta$. To find the value of the second derivative of the profit at a point satisfying the first-order condition (15), we replace C_Y by $C/\theta Y$ in the expression of Π_Y and we differentiate with respect to Y. Taking into account (15), the result, after several calculations, is:

$$\Pi_{YY}(W, R, Y) = (1 + \eta_Y^P) \frac{P(Y)}{\theta Y} (\theta \eta_Y^P - 1 + \theta) = \frac{P(Y)}{\theta Y} \frac{\theta - v}{v^2}$$

The second-order condition is thus satisfied, since $v > \theta$.

5. With the help of expression (14) of the firm's profit, we can verify that the second-order condition implies $[P'(Y) - v C_{YY}] < 0$. Differentiating equation (15) with respect to W, we find that $\partial Y / \partial W$ is of opposite sign to C_{WY}.

6. A line of reasoning analogous to the one that allowed us to establish the direction of the scale effects in relation (19) would show that $\bar{\eta}_Y^L \eta_R^Y$ has a sign opposite

that of $C_{WY}C_{RY}$. Now, following Shephard's lemma (6), the latter quantity is equal to the product $(\partial \bar{L}/\partial Y)/(\partial \bar{K}/\partial Y)$. We have seen in section 1.2.2 that the conditional demands for factors rise with the level of output when the production function is homogeneous. In all other cases, the sign is ambiguous.

7. Rigorously speaking, the term $\bar{\eta}_W^L$ means something measurably different from what it represented before: the elasticity of the labor demand, expressed in terms of hours or number of employees, with respect to its cost. Now, L refers to a number of units of efficient labor. But the function linking the demand for labor to its cost is, by construction, identical to that linking the demand for efficient labor to the cost of efficient labor. The elasticity $\bar{\eta}_W^L$ is thus the same in the two configurations. Relation (12) indicates that $\bar{\eta}_W^L = -(1-s)\sigma$, where s designates the share of labor cost in total cost and σ the elasticity of substitution between capital and labor. We will see later that the majority of empirical studies suggest that σ is smaller than 1, and even close to 1 on the basis of macroeconomic data. The absolute value of $\bar{\eta}_W^L$ is thus likely smaller than 1.

8. More precisely, in this case we estimate $\eta_{\frac{L}{W}}$ defined by relation (20).

9. See Takayama (1986, chapter 5) and the mathematical appendix B at the end of this book. The Euler condition is also sufficient if function J is concave in L and $\dot{L}$, which is the case here.

10. Readers are reminded that the solution of a linear second-order differential equation $af''(t) + bf'(t) + cf(t) = d$, where a, b, c, d are given constants, is found by first calculating the solution of the homogeneous equation $af'' + bf' + cf = 0$. This solution is of the form $f(t) = A_1 e^{\lambda_1 t} + A_2 e^{\lambda_2 t}$, where A_1 and A_2 are arbitrary constants and λ_1 and λ_2 are the roots of the "characteristic" equation $a\lambda^2 + b\lambda + c = 0$. We then calculate the solution of the nonhomogeneous equation, which is equal to the sum of the solution of the homogeneous equation and a particular solution of the nonhomogeneous equation. Here a particular solution is d/c. So the general solution is of the form $f(t) = A_1 e^{\lambda_1 t} + A_2 e^{\lambda_2 t} + (d/c)$. In the end we get a particular solution on the basis of a known value (generally the initial or teminal value of $f(t)$. The constants A_1 and A_2 are determined by the initial conditions and the stability conditions.

11. The properties of a Poisson process are set out in mathematical appendix D at the end of this book.

12. In a discrete time model, the median lag is equal to $-\ln 2/\ln \lambda$.

Chapter 5

1. Readers will recall that in order to differentiate the expression $f(x) = \int_{a(x)}^{b(x)} g(x, t)\, dt$, where a, b, and g are three continuously differentiable functions, it is necessary to apply the formula $f'(x) = b'(x)g[x, b(x)] - a'(x)g[x, a(x)] + \int_{a(x)}^{b(x)} ((\partial g(x, t))/\partial x)\, dt$.

2. The second-order condition is satisfied if $L^s L^{s\prime\prime} - 2(L^{s\prime})^2 < 0$.

3. Bargaining theory is presented in chapters 7 and 9.

4. It would have been possible to obtain this equality directly by applying Bayes' formula:

$$\Pr\{h = h^+ | \text{success}\}$$

$$= \frac{\Pr\{\text{success}|h = h^+\} \cdot \Pr\{h = h^+\}}{\Pr\{\text{success}|h = h^+\} \cdot \Pr\{h = h^+\} + \Pr\{\text{success}|h = h^-\} \cdot \Pr\{h = h^-\}}$$

5. The utility function $w - \theta e$ which we have used in presenting the hedonic theory of wages does not incorporate any income effect (see chapter 1).

6. See chapter 7, section 2.3.1 for a definition of this concept.

Chapter 6

1. Firms and their wage-earners sometimes enter into contracts the purpose of which is to protect, or to make possible, certain investments, for example investments in training. These contracts pose specific problems having to do with the fact that one of the parties could capture a part of the benefits from the investment without necessarily having to bear the costs. This question, known as the holdup problem, is dealt with in chapters 6, 8, and 9 from different angles.

2. Note that this hypothesis is satisfied if we assume that function f, hours h, and performance y are verifiable, since $y = f(h, \varepsilon)$.

3. For the contract to be self-enforcing, it would also have to include the possibility that the principal could break it in certain states of nature. We examine the consequences of this eventuality below.

4. The horizontal part of the profile of contractual wages necessarily intersects with the curve representing the outside wage, otherwise the contract would offer a gain inferior to outside opportunities.

5. At this point the reader may wish to refer to mathematical appendix C, section 3.3, at the end of the book, which establishes the main properties of normal and log-normal distributions. Here we simply note that the probability density of a random variable X following the normal distribution $\mathcal{N}(m, \sigma)$ is given by $f(x) = (1/(\sigma\sqrt{2\pi})) \exp[-(x - m)^2/2\sigma^2]$. The random variable $\exp(X)$ then follows a log-normal distribution with the mean $\exp[m + (\sigma^2/2)]$.

6. Mathematical appendix C, section 3.3, points out that if $X \sim \mathcal{N}(0, \sigma_X)$, then $\exp(X)$ has a log-normal distribution with mean $\exp(\sigma_X^2/2)$.

7. Readers will recall that a variable x_t is a random walk if it satisfies $x_t = x_{t-1} + \varepsilon_t$, where ε_t is a random variable with zero mean, the distribution of which is identical at every date t.

8. The peaks at around 55 years of age correspond to the payout of "retirement capital."

9. It is easy to verify that the deposit C/p is equal to the present value, discounted at rate $\delta(1 - q)$, of the sum of the bonuses.

10. The existence of this equilibrium assumes, for one thing, that the exit rate from unemployment, equal to $qL^*/(N - L^*)$, is inferior to unity, and for another, that the horizontal line with ordinate w^* intersects the curve (IC); this occurs when the following condition is satisfied:

$$y - (1 - \delta)C_K > z + C + \frac{C}{p}\left[\frac{1}{\delta(1 - q)} - 1\right]$$

Chapter 7

1. Plentiful information is available at the site Compensation and Working Conditions Online of the Bureau of Labor Statistics: http://www.bls.gov/opub/cwc/cwchome.htm.

2. This result can, as an exercise, be demonstrated simply by using appendix 2, with the hypothesis that the players have no preference for the present and that gains are zero during the unfolding of the negotiation.

3. Since $\ln x \approx x - 1$ when x is close to 1, we can accept the approximation $\Delta \approx \ln W_u - \ln W_n$ for wages that differ little.

4. Let N and w respectively be the size of the sample and the average of the logarithms of the wages. We thus have:

$$v = \left(\frac{1}{N}\sum_{i=1}^{i=N} w_i^2\right) - w^2 \quad \text{with} \quad w = \frac{1}{N}\sum_{i=1}^{i=N} w_i = \alpha w_u + (1 - \alpha)w_n$$

Let $\mathscr{U}$ (respectively $\mathscr{N}$) be the set of unionized (resp. nonunionized) workers. The variances v_u and v_n satisfy the following equalities:

$$\frac{1}{N}\sum_{i=1}^{i=N} w_i^2 = \frac{1}{N}\sum_{i \in \mathscr{U}} w_i^2 + \frac{1}{N}\sum_{i \in \mathscr{N}} w_i^2 = \alpha(v_u + w_u^2) + (1 - \alpha)(v_n + w_n^2)$$

Substituting this expression into relation (32), we have:

$$v = \alpha(v_u + w_u^2) + (1 - \alpha)(v_n + w_n^2) - [\alpha w_u + (1 - \alpha)w_n]^2$$

Developing and rearranging terms, we find formula (33).

Chapter 8

1. This method does not correct biases arising from the endogeneity of the inflation rate and the unemployment rate, because econometric work carried out in this area generally shows that these biases are small (OECD, 1997).

2. The gamma function takes the expression $\Gamma(x) = \int_0^\infty z^{x-1} e^{-z}\, dz$. For every whole positive n, $\Gamma(n) = (n-1)!$ The gamma function can thus be interpreted as a generalization of the factorial function.

3. The figures in parentheses are the t-statistics. The estimates were made using OECD data.

Chapter 9

1. We leave out problems related to discounting by implictly assuming, in order to simplify, that the interest rate is null. We return to these problems again in section 4 of this chapter.

2. If a variable can change state at rate p, it will, on average, remain in the state it is in at the present moment for an interval of time equal to $1/p$ (see mathematical appendix D at the end of this book, which is dedicated to the properties of Poisson processes).

3. See mathematical appendix D at the end of this book.

4. This is a problem of dynamic optimization that is studied in mathematical appendix B at the end of the book.

5. Moene (1997) considers a more general case, where the entrepreneurs in the same labor pool can offer different wages but, at equilibrium, offer the same wage.

Chapter 10

1. Mathematical appendix D at the end of this book includes a rigorous proof of this type of formula, based on the assumption that certain well-specified random events follow Poisson processes.

2. We could, in like manner, have taken the view that the optimal life span of a job maximizes the surplus $S(0, t, T)$ for all $t \in [0, T]$. That would again give us relation (17).

3. Deriving equation (18), we note that $\partial\theta/\partial g$ is of the sign of $(r - g)rTe^{-gT} + r(e^{-rT} - e^{-gT})$. For given T, this expression amonts to zero if $r = g$. Moreover, the derivative of this expression with respect to g is equal to $-(r - g)T^2 e^{-gT} < 0$ for $r > g$. In consequence $\partial\theta/\partial g$ is positive.

4. Formula (23) is found by noting first that $ge^{-rT} - re^{-gT} = e^{-gT}[ge^{-(r-g)T} - r]$. In the neighborhood of 0, $e^{-(r-g)T}$ is equivalent to $1 - (r - g)T$ and thus $ge^{-rT} - re^{-gT}$ is equivalent to $-(r - g)(1 + gT)e^{-gT}$. When r tends to g, the bracketed expression in (18) is thus equal to $1 - e^{-gT} - gTe^{-gT}$.

5. Since $\ln(ab) = \ln a + \ln b$, this relation is equivalent to $\sigma(d \ln \alpha - d \ln \omega) = d \ln \alpha + d \ln \lambda$, which yields equation (25).

6. The concavity of F entails $F_{ii} < 0$, and deriving equation (34), we get $dw_h/dv = \alpha A_h F_{hh}(\alpha v, 1) < 0$ and $dw_\ell/dv = \alpha A_\ell F_{\ell h}(\alpha v, 1) = -A_h(1/\alpha v)^2 F_{\ell\ell}(1, 1/\alpha v) > 0$.

7. Readers will recall that the elasticity of substitution between capital and labor can be written $\sigma = F_K F_L/Y F_{KL}$ when the production function is homogeneous of degree 1 (see chapter 4). Moreover, homogeneity of degree 1 of F entails $LF_{LL} = -KF_{KL}$. Since $w = F_L$, the wage elasticity of labor demand is $\eta_w^L = F_L/LF_{LL} = -\sigma/(1 - s^L)$ with $s^L = wL/Y = 1 - (KF_K/Y)$. Assuming that $\sigma = 1$ and that $s^L = 0.7$, we get $\eta_w^L = -1/0.3 \simeq -3$. One can remark that η_w^L stands here for the elasticity of the unconditional demand for a given capital stock, that is different from the elasticity of the conditional demand, denoted by $\bar{\eta}_w^L = (1 - s^L)\sigma$ (see chapter 4, sections 1.2.2 and 1.3.1).

8. Since $F(N) = \int_0^N F_L(\xi)\, d\xi$.

9. Following the Euler theorem, we have $F = L_\ell F_\ell + L_h F_h$. Deriving this equality with respect to L_ℓ, we get $L_\ell F_{\ell\ell} + L_h F_{\ell h} = 0$. Since the concavity of F entails $F_{\ell\ell} < 0$, we will necessarily have $F_{\ell h} > 0$.

Chapter 11

1. In what follows, we will refer indifferently to the mass or the number of agencies.

2. Let us recall that if $g(x) = \int_{a(x)}^{b(x)} f(x, i)\, di$, where f, a, and b are continuously derivable functions, then $g'(x) = b'(x)f[x, b(x)] - a'(x)f[x, a(x)] + \int_{a(x)}^{b(x)} (\partial f(x, i)/\partial x)\, di$.

3. The principles of dynamic optimization are set out in mathematical appendix B at the end of the book.

4. It is easy to verify that employers have no interest in reinvesting in workers who are already trained. If they did, they would maximize a net surplus defined by $((y(i) + qV_u(i))/(r + q)) - i - V_u(i)$, which necessarily gives a level of investment inferior to i_m, since $V_u'(i) > 0$.

5. The technique of dynamic optimization is set out in mathematical appendix B at the end of the book.

6. Evidently it is not possible either to determine $E(Y^T|D = 0)$, which represents the response without treatment of a person treated.

7. "Social experiments" must not be confused with "natural experiments." The latter term applies to studies that use an exogenous change in a policy measure, such as a rise in the minimum wage or a tax reduction, to estimate the effects of this measure on a given population. The treated group is then the set of persons belonging to the population who benefit from this change, and the control group is the set, or a subset, of the persons in the same population to whom it does not apply. The data produced by natural experiments do not, therefore, automatically respect the conditions imposed by randomization, and must be considered as *non*experimental data. Chapter 1, section 2.2.2, gives more detail about the way certain properties of the labor supply are estimated using natural experiments.

8. In fact, this hypothesis is sufficient but not really necessary. Heckman et al. (1999, p. 1901) supply two hypotheses, measurably less stringent, for which the experimental data make it possible to obtain unbiased estimators of the average gain from the treatment.

9. This last property is easily established from the equations describing labor market equilibrium in the basic model.

10. Variables u_i are not unemployment rates per category; for that we would have to relate the number of unemployed of type i to the size of the labor force i concerned.

Chapter 12

1. The convexity of function $c(.)$ ensures that we do indeed have a maximum of $V_u(t)$.

2. The fact that the support has the upper limit ε_u is not essential. We follow the presentation of Mortensen and Pissarides (1994) here, which makes the exposition somewhat easier.

3. For more on random variables and Poisson processes, see mathematical appendices C and D, respectively, at the end of the book.

4. Let us recall that the employment rate equals the ratio of the number of jobs to the working-age population (see chapter 8, section 1).

5. To determine the slope of this curve, we use the second-order conditions, which entail that $\partial \Omega^\ell(w, \ell)/\partial \ell < 0$.

6. Here again we use the second-order conditions to get this result.

7. The United Kingdom belonged to the EUCON group until 1980, then to the ANGLO group subsequently, with the passage from Labour to Conservative governments.

8. Using (56) and (53), it is possible to show that, if $r = 0$, ω_j is also equal to $w_j(1 - u_j) + u_j z$, which corresponds to the sum of the incomes of the workers present in sector j. This quantity is also the criterion of a "utilitarian" union representing all workers in the sector.

9. If we want to introduce preference for the present, we must solve an explicitly dynamic program (see chapter 8, section 6.2.2). Apart from the calculations

involved, this resolution presents no particular difficulty, and readers are therefore invited to perform it for themselves. They will find that equation (58) always defines the equilibrium value of the labor market tightness, provided that q is replaced by $r + q$.

10. The 20 include 15 European countries: Austria, Belgium, Denmark, Finland, France, Germany, Ireland, Italy, the Netherlands, Norway, Portugal, Spain, Sweden, Switzerland, and the United Kingdom, and five non-European ones: Australia, Canada, Japan, New Zealand, and the United States.

11. This notion is defined precisely in chapter 10.

12. This means that, for example, the estimated average unemployment rate rose from 3% to 10.3%.

Mathematical Appendices

1. Readers are reminded that the integration by parts formula is:

$$\int_a^b u\,dv = [uv]_a^b - \int_a^b v\,du$$

NAME INDEX

SUBJECT INDEX